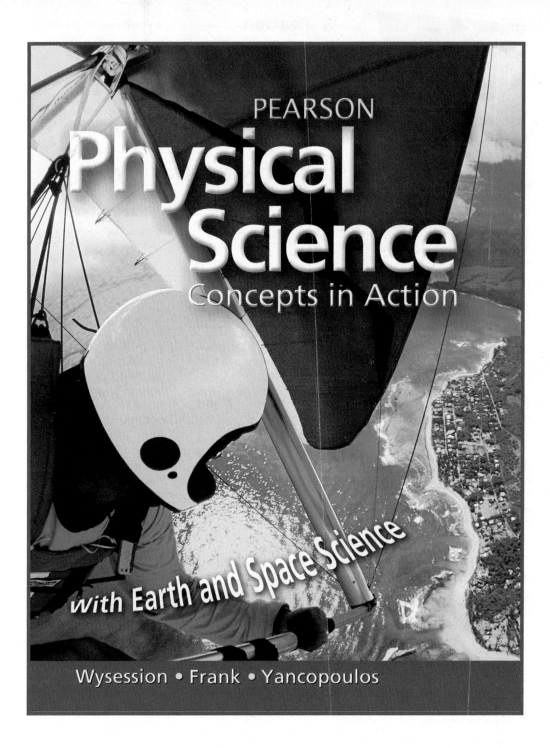

PEARSON

Physical Science
Concepts in Action

with Earth and Space Science

Wysession • Frank • Yancopoulos

PEARSON

Boston, Massachusetts
Chandler, Arizona
Glenview, Illinois
Upper Saddle River, New Jersey

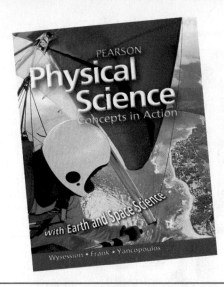

Pearson

Physical Science

Concepts in Action

With Earth and Space Science

The cover photograph of a hang glider shows chemistry, physics, and Earth science concepts in action.

Print Components
Student Edition
Progress Monitoring Assessments
Teacher's Edition
Easy Planner
Laboratory Manual
Laboratory Manual, Teacher's Edition
Reading and Study Workbook, Levels A and B
Reading and Study Workbook, Levels A and B,
    Teacher's Editions
Chapter and Unit Tests
Transparencies
Test-Taking Tips With Transparencies
Test Preparation Blackline Masters
Standardized Test Preparation Workbook
Math Skills and Problem Solving Workbook
Virtual Physical Science Lab Record Sheets Workbook

Technology
Interactive Textbook Online
StudentEXPRESS CD-ROM
PresentationEXPRESS CD-ROM
Probeware Lab Manual With CD-ROM
Virtual Physical Science CD-ROM
ExamView® Computer Test Bank CD-ROM
TeacherEXPRESS CD-ROM
Web site at PHSchool.com

Spanish Resources
Spanish Reading and Study Workbook
Spanish Chapter and Unit Tests
Spanish Section Summaries on Audio CD

ISBN-13: 978-0-13-317211-9
ISBN-10:   0-13-317211-2

5 6 7 8 9 10 V057 16 15

About the Authors

Michael Wysession

Michael Wysession received his Ph.D. in geophysics from Northwestern University in 1991. He is an Associate Professor in Earth and Planetary Sciences at Washington University in St. Louis, Missouri. His area of specialization is using seismic waves to explore Earth's interior. Dr. Wysession is an author on more than 50 scientific publications. For his research, he was awarded a Packard Foundation Fellowship, and in 1996 was awarded a Presidential Faculty Fellowship at the White House. He also has created educational simulations to accurately show how seismic waves propagate. He currently chairs the Education & Outreach program for the Incorporated Research Institutions for Seismology (IRIS).

David Frank

David Frank completed his Ph.D. at Purdue University. For the last ten years he has been the head of the Physical Sciences Department at Ferris State University in Big Rapids, Michigan. He has taught general chemistry courses for science majors and for allied health students. With the assistance of his colleagues, he helped develop a new B.A. program in biochemistry. He has taught students in the university's Math/Science/Technology program, which enrolls gifted high school students. Recently he has worked with Michigan's "Connecting With the Learner" group, which produced a toolkit to help elementary and secondary teachers address diversity issues in the classroom.

Sophia Yancopoulos

Sophia Yancopoulos received her Ph.D. in physics from Columbia University. She has done postdoctoral research in astronomy at Yale University and in biophysics at the Mount Sinai School of Medicine. She considers teaching to be a vital and exciting part of her experience, having taught at Barnard College, Vassar College, the Stevens Institute of Technology, and Columbia University, as well as at Bronx High School of Science. She has worked on a neutrino oscillations experiment at Fermi National Laboratory, conducted experiments on acoustic modeling, and analyzed data on the extreme astrophysics of neutron stars. Currently she does research in genome evolution. She works with a team of scientists at the Feinstein Institute for Medical Research, trying to find a cure for a form of leukemia.

Contributing Writers

Steve Miller
Science Writer
State College,
Pennsylvania

Polly Weissman
Science Writer
New York, New York

Dr. Carolyn Sumners
Houston Museum of
  Natural Science
Houston, Texas

T. Griffith Jones
P.K. Yonge Developmental
  Research School
College of Education—
University of Florida
Gainesville, Florida

Contributing Writers for DK

Robert Dinwiddie
M.A. M.Sc.
Science Writer
London, England

Susan Watt
M.A. M.Sc.
Science Writer
London, England

Reading Consultant

Bonnie Armbruster, Ph.D.
Department of Curriculum
  and Instruction
University of Illinois
Champaign, Illinois

Laboratory Activity Writers

Robert W. Arts
Associate Professor of
  Physics
Pikeville College
Pikeville, Kentucky

Hasan Fakhrudin
Physics Instructor
Indiana Academy for
  Science, Mathematics,
  and Humanities
Muncie, Indiana

Yvonne Favaro
Science Teacher (retired)
Englewood Cliffs,
New Jersey

JoAnne Mowczko, Ed.D.
Science Writer
Gaithersburg, Maryland

Brian Rohrig
Science Teacher
Columbus Public Schools
Columbus, Ohio

Safety Consultant

Dr. Kenneth R. Roy
Director, Science and
  Safety
Glastonbury Public
  Schools
Glastonbury, Connecticut

Content Reviewers

Contents

Earth and Space Science 654

Warm wishes from the tropics!

Skills and Reference Handbook   866

Labs and Activities

xii

Quick Lab

Introduce and reinforce key lesson content using simple materials.

Probe or sensor versions are available in the Probeware Lab Manual.

Go Online
PHSchool.com   Share data with students from across the country at phschool.com

Features

CONCEPTS in Action

Explore science in depth with practical applications.

DK HOW It Works

Understand technology with exciting visual essays.

Science Skills

21st Century Learning

Information and Media Literacy

How does curiosity lead to scientific discoveries?

Science begins with curiosity and often ends with discovery. Go online and search for articles about a scientific discovery that you have previously read about or heard about. Identify the types of questions that drove and guided the scientists' investigation. Create a timeline or flowchart that summarizes the progress of the investigation, and present it to your class.

How do science concepts apply to your world? Here are some questions you'll be able to answer after you read this chapter.

- **How do scientists plan to study Mars in the future?** *(Section 1.1)*

- **Which keeps you drier in the rain, walking or running?** *(Section 1.2)*

- **How do police investigators use scientific methods to solve a crime?** *(page 12)*

- **How many stars are there in the Milky Way galaxy?** *(Section 1.3)*

- **What is Earth's crust made of?** *(Section 1.4)*

A technician tends a reactor that contains bacteria. The bacteria produce proteins that will be used in medicines.

Chapter Preview

Inquiry > Activity

How Do Scientists Use Their Observations?

Procedure

1. Observe the liquid that your teacher gives you. Record your observations. **CAUTION** *Do not touch or drink the liquid.*

2. Use scissors and a metric ruler to cut a 5-cm square of aluminum foil. Loosely crumple the foil and drop it into the liquid.

3. Use a stirring rod to push the foil below the surface of the liquid. Observe and record any changes that occur in the liquid and foil.

Think About It

1. **Posing Questions** Write three questions about the materials or the changes that you observed.

2. **Designing Experiments** What could you do with the same or other materials to discover an answer to one of your questions?

3. **Communicating Results** Share your proposed experiments with your classmates. What results would you expect to observe?

1.1 What Is Science?

Reading Focus

Key Concepts

- How does the process of science start and end?
- What is the relationship between science and technology?
- What are the branches of natural science?

Vocabulary

- science
- technology
- chemistry
- physics
- geology
- astronomy
- biology

Reading Strategy

Previewing Skim the section to find out what the main branches of natural science are. Copy the concept map below. As you read, complete the concept map based on what you have learned.

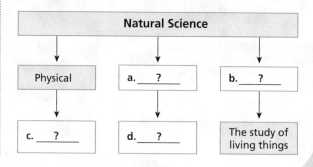

Figure 1 In July 1997, the six-wheeled Sojourner rover became the first robot to explore planet Mars. The next generation of Mars rovers will help scientists further study the planet's geology, geography, and climate.

Suppose you could send a robot to another planet. What kinds of experiments would you program the robot to carry out? Before you programmed the robot, you would need to figure out what information you wanted it to gather. Scientists are currently developing robots, like the one in Figure 1, that they plan to send to Mars. These robots are being designed to examine the atmosphere, rocks, gravity, and magnetic fields of the planet.

Science involves asking questions about nature and then finding ways to answer them. This process doesn't happen by itself—it is driven by the curiosity of scientists.

Science From Curiosity

Throughout history, human beings have had a strong sense of curiosity. Human curiosity led to the use of fire, the building of tools, and the development of languages. Have you ever checked what was living at the bottom of a pond? Taken off the cover of a baseball to see what was inside? Tried putting more chocolate or less in your milk to find out how much would give the best flavor? These are all examples of curiosity, and curiosity is the basis of science.

Science is a system of knowledge and the methods you use to find that knowledge. Part of the excitement of science is that you never know what you will find. For instance, when you flip over a rock, will you see crawling insects, a snake, or nothing at all? You won't know until you look. **Science begins with curiosity and often ends with discovery.**

Curiosity provides questions but is seldom enough to achieve scientific results. Methods such as observing and measuring provide ways to find the answers. In some experiments, observations are qualitative, or descriptive. In others, they are quantitative, or numerical. Some experiments are impossible to do, such as observing what happened at the start of the universe. Scientists cannot go back in time to observe the creation of the universe. However, they can use the evidence of the universe around them to envision how this event occurred.

✓ **Reading Checkpoint** *What is science?*

Science and Technology

As scientific knowledge is discovered, it can be applied in ways that improve the lives of people. **Technology** is the use of knowledge to solve practical problems. While the goal of science is to expand knowledge, the goal of technology is to apply that knowledge. Imagine living in the late 1700s, when there were no televisions, cars, antibiotics, or electricity. In a relatively small amount of time, people's lives changed dramatically. Perhaps your grandparents were born at a time when there were no televisions, and your parents were born at a time when there were no personal computers. Technology will have also changed your world dramatically by the time the generation following yours comes along.

Figure 2 illustrates the rapid evolution of the telephone, a technology invented in 1876. Within two years, the first telephone operators were connecting calls by hand. The first coin-operated phones appeared in 1889. By 1927, it was possible to make a phone call from New York to London. World War II saw the development of the first mobile telephones, which paved the way for modern cellular phones. Today, you can communicate by telephone between almost any two places in the world.

Science and technology are interdependent. Advances in one lead to advances in the other. For example, advances in the study of physics led to the invention of the transistor. The use of transistors, in turn, led to advances in various other scientific fields, such as computer science and space science.

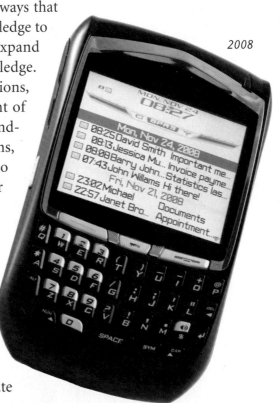

1876
1914
1955
2008

Figure 2 Telephones have quickly evolved from cumbersome, expensive machines to practical, cheap tools for communicating. **Classifying** *How is a telephone an example of both science and technology?*

Figure 3 Natural science covers a very broad range of knowledge.
Interpreting Diagrams *How could you change this diagram to show how the branches of science can overlap?*

Branches of Science

The study of science is divided into social science and natural science. **Natural science is generally divided into three branches: physical science, Earth and space science, and life science.** Each of these branches can be further divided, as shown in Figure 3.

Physical science covers a broad range of study that focuses on non-living things. The two main areas of physical science are chemistry and physics. **Chemistry** is the study of the composition, structure, properties, and reactions of matter. **Physics** is the study of matter and energy and the interactions between the two through forces and motion.

The application of physics and chemistry to the study of Earth is called Earth science. The foundation of Earth science is **geology,** the study of the origin, history, and structure of Earth. Geology has traditionally focused on the study of Earth's rocks. However, modern Earth science also involves the study of systems that may include living organisms. The foundation of space science is **astronomy,** the study of the universe beyond Earth, including the sun, moon, planets, and stars.

The study of living things is known as **biology,** or life science. Biology is not only the physics and chemistry of living things, but the study of the origin and behavior of living things. Biologists study the different ways that organisms grow, survive, and reproduce.

The problem with subdividing science into different areas is that there is often overlap between them. The boundary around each area of science is not always clear. For instance, much of biology is also chemistry, while much of chemistry is also physics. And a rapidly growing area of physics is biophysics, the application of physics to biology.

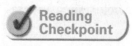 **Reading Checkpoint** *What is physical science?*

The Big Ideas of Physical Science

What are the basic rules of nature? You can read this book to find out. As a sneak preview, some of these rules are summarized here. You can think of them as the big ideas of physical science. Keep in mind that there are also unknown rules of nature that are waiting to be discovered. In fact, you can take part in the search for these unknown laws if you become a scientist. Even though scientists have already discovered a great deal about the universe, there is still much to learn.

Space and Time The universe is both very old and very big. The age of the universe is about 13,700,000,000 (13.7 billion) years. The observable universe is about 700,000,000,000,000,000,000,000,000 (700 million billion billion) meters in diameter. The diameter of Earth is "only" 12,700,000 meters. To get an idea of how big this distance is, the diameter of a giant beach ball is about 1 meter.

Matter and Change A very small amount of the universe is matter. Matter has volume and mass, and on Earth usually takes the form of a solid, liquid, or gas. All matter that you are familiar with, from plants to stars to animals to humans, is made up of building blocks called atoms. Atoms consist of even smaller building blocks called electrons, protons, and neutrons.

Forces and Motion If you push on something that is sitting still, it starts to move. If you push on something that is already moving, you will change its motion. Forces cause changes in motion. As Figure 4 shows, your world is filled with motion and forces. Calculating these forces can sometimes be very challenging. For example, on a NASA mission to Mars, the Mars Exploration Rover must blast off from Earth on a rocket with enough speed to escape Earth's gravity. The rover must then travel a great distance through space on the rocket and land delicately on a planet that is moving very rapidly around the Sun. The laws of physics allow these movements to be calculated exactly so that the NASA robots get to where scientists want them to go.

Go Online
NSTA SciLINKS

For: Links on motion
Visit: www.SciLinks.org
Web Code: ccn-0011

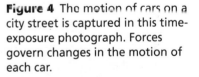

Figure 4 The motion of cars on a city street is captured in this time-exposure photograph. Forces govern changes in the motion of each car.

Figure 5 Panels on a solar car convert energy from the sun into the mechanical energy of its moving parts.

Energy Energy exists in many forms. Moving objects have a kind of energy called kinetic energy. Objects moved against a force have another kind of energy called potential energy. Energy also exists in matter itself. When one form of matter changes into another form, energy is either absorbed or released. Matter itself can also be changed into energy.

Energy can be transferred from one form or object to another, but it can never be destroyed. If you push on a door and it swings open, you transfer energy from yourself to the door. Your cells are using the chemical energy stored in the food you have eaten to supply energy to your muscles, which then transfer energy to the door.

Science and Your Perspective

As you read this book, remember that science is both a process and a body of knowledge. The information in this book represents the best up-to-date models of how the universe works. However, like all models, some of these models will be rejected and replaced in the future. For instance, more moons revolving around Jupiter and Saturn will most likely be discovered as telescopes get better. It is therefore possible that by the time you read this book Saturn will be known to have more than the 62 moons currently identified. Be skeptical. Ask questions. Be aware that the scientific facts of today might change tomorrow. However, believe in the scientific process that has discovered them. And believe that you may be the one who makes the discoveries that will change scientific facts in the future.

Section 1.1 Assessment

Reviewing Concepts

1. How does the scientific process start and end?

2. How are science and technology related?

3. What are the branches of natural science?

4. Explain the advantages and disadvantages of subdividing science into many different areas.

5. Why do scientists seek to discover new laws of the universe?

Critical Thinking

6. **Evaluating** Why does the progress of science require both curiosity and methodology? Explain the role of each in scientific investigations.

7. **Making Judgments** Advances in science do not always immediately lead to advances in technology. Why are such scientific advances still valuable?

8. **Classifying** Is the study of the muscle movements in the human body an example of biology or of physics? Explain.

Writing in Science

Compare and Contrast Paragraph Write a paragraph comparing two branches of science. (*Hint:* Use an example that shows how these branches can overlap.)

1.2 Using a Scientific Approach

Key Concepts

- What is the goal of a scientific method?
- How does a scientific law differ from a scientific theory?
- Why are scientific models useful?

Vocabulary

- scientific method
- observation
- hypothesis
- manipulated variable
- responding variable
- controlled experiment
- scientific theory
- scientific law
- model

Reading Strategy

Using Prior Knowledge Before you read, copy the web diagram below. Add to the web diagram what you already know about scientific methods. After you read, revise the diagram based on what you have learned.

If you've ever been caught in the rain without an umbrella, your first instinct was probably to start running. After all, the less time you spend in the rain, the less water there is falling down on you. So you might think that running in the rain keeps you drier than walking in the rain over a given distance. However, by running in the rain you run into more raindrops than by walking, thereby wetting more of your face, chest, and legs. Have your instincts been getting you wetter instead of keeping you drier?

You now have a question that you can try to answer with a scientific approach. Which keeps you drier in the rain—walking or running?

Scientific Methods

In order to answer questions about the world around them, scientists need to gather information. An organized plan for gathering, organizing, and communicating information is called a **scientific method.** Despite the name, a scientific method can be used by anyone, including yourself. All you need is a reason to use it. **The goal of any scientific method is to solve a problem or to better understand an observed event.**

Figure 6 To run, or not to run: that is the question. **Designing Experiments** *How can you test if running in the rain keeps you drier than walking in the rain over the same distance?*

Figure 7 A scientific method provides a useful strategy for solving problems.
*Inferring **Is an observation required in order for you to arrive at a question? What does this tell you about the strictness of the scientific method?***

Figure 7 outlines an example of a scientific method. Each step in the method shown involves specific skills, some of which you will be learning as you read this book. It is important to note that scientific methods can vary from case to case. For example, one scientist might follow the steps shown in Figure 7 in a different order, or another might choose to skip one or more steps.

Making Observations Scientific investigations often begin with observations. An **observation** is information that you obtain through your senses. Repeatable observations are known as facts. For example, when you walk or run in the rain, you get wet. Standing in the rain leaves you much wetter than walking or running in the rain. You might combine these observations into a question: How does your speed affect how wet you get when you are caught in the rain?

Forming a Hypothesis A **hypothesis** is a proposed answer to a question. To answer the question raised by your observations about traveling in the rain, you might guess that the faster your speed, the drier you will stay in the rain. What can you do with your hypothesis? For a hypothesis to be useful, it must be testable.

 What is a hypothesis?

Testing a Hypothesis Scientists perform experiments to test their hypotheses. In an experiment, any factor that can change is called a variable. Suppose you do an experiment to test if speed affects how wet you get in the rain. The variables will include your speed, your size, the rate of rainfall, and the amount of water that hits you.

Your hypothesis states that one variable, speed, causes a change in another variable, the amount of water that hits you. The speed with which you walk or run is the **manipulated variable,** or the variable that causes a change in another. The amount of water that you accumulate is the **responding variable,** or the variable that changes in response to the manipulated variable. To examine the relationship between a manipulated variable and a responding variable, scientists use controlled experiments. A **controlled experiment** is an experiment in which only one variable, the manipulated variable, is deliberately changed at a time. While the responding variable is observed for changes, all other variables are kept constant, or controlled.

In 1997, two meteorologists conducted a controlled experiment to determine if moving faster keeps you drier in the rain. In the experiment, both scientists traveled 100 yards by foot in the rain. One of them walked; the other ran. By measuring the mass of their clothes before and after traveling in the rain, the scientists were able to measure how much water each had accumulated. One of the controlled variables was size—the two scientists were about the same height and build. Another was the rate of rainfall—the scientists began traveling at the same time during the same rainstorm on the same path. A third was the ability to absorb water—the scientists wore identical sets of clothes.

For: Articles on the nature of science
Visit: PHSchool.com
Web Code: cce-0011

Drawing Conclusions The scientists' rainy-day experiment produced some convincing data. The clothes of the walking scientist accumulated 217 grams of water, while the clothes of the running scientists accumulated 130 grams of water. Based on their data, the scientists concluded that running in the rain keeps you drier than walking—about 40 percent drier, in fact. Now you have scientific evidence to support the hypothesis stated earlier.

What happens if the data do not support the hypothesis? In such a case, a scientist can revise the hypothesis or propose a new one, based on the data from the experiment. A new experiment must then be designed to test the revised or new hypothesis.

Developing a Theory Once a hypothesis has been supported in repeated experiments, scientists can begin to develop a theory. A **scientific theory** is a well-tested explanation for a set of observations or experimental results. For example, according to the kinetic theory of matter, all particles of matter are in constant motion. Kinetic theory explains a wide range of observations, such as ice melting or the pressure of a gas.

Theories are never proved. Instead, they become stronger if the facts continue to support them. However, if an existing theory fails to explain new facts and discoveries, the theory may be revised or a new theory may replace it.

Scientific Laws

After repeated observations or experiments, scientists may arrive at a scientific law. A **scientific law** is a statement that summarizes a pattern found in nature. For example, Newton's law of gravity describes how two objects attract each other by means of a gravitational force. This law has been verified over and over. However, scientists have yet to agree on a theory that explains how gravity works. **A scientific law describes an observed pattern in nature without attempting to explain it. The explanation of such a pattern is provided by a scientific theory.**

Figure 8 An environmental scientist collects a sample for a water pollution study. After analyzing the sample, the scientist can draw conclusions about how the water became polluted.

Figure 9 Two engineers discuss a computer-aided design, or CAD, of an aircraft component.

Scientific Models

If you have ever been lost in a city, you know that a street map can help you find your location. A street map is a type of **model,** or representation, of an object or event. ⬤ **Scientific models make it easier to understand things that might be too difficult to observe directly.** For example, to understand how Earth rotates on its axis, you could look at a globe, which is a small-scale model of Earth. The computer model in Figure 9 represents the interior of an airplane. Other models help you visualize things that are too small to see, such as atoms. As long as a model lets you mentally picture what is supposed to be represented, then the model has done its job.

An example of a mental, rather than physical, model might be that comets are like giant snowballs, primarily made of ice. Scientists tested this model with observations and experiments. In 2006, a space probe collected samples from a comet. Tests on the samples confirmed that comets are made of ice, but the tests also showed that comets contain rocky material that is formed near the sun. So, a modified model of comets was adopted.

If new data show that a model is wrong, then it must either be changed or be replaced by a new model. If scientists never challenged old models, then nothing new would be learned, and we would still believe what we believed hundreds of years ago. Science works by making mistakes. The fact that newer models are continually replacing old models is a sign that new discoveries are continually occurring. As the knowledge that makes up science keeps changing, scientists develop a better and better understanding of the universe.

 Reading Checkpoint **What is a model?**

Working Safely in Science

Scientists working in the field, or in a laboratory, like those in Figure 10, are trained to use safe procedures when carrying out investigations. Laboratory work may involve flames or hot plates, electricity, chemicals, hot liquids, sharp instruments, and breakable glassware.

Whenever you work in your science laboratory, it's important for you to follow safety precautions at all times. Before performing any activity in this course, study the rules in the Science Safety section of the Skills Handbook. Before you start any activity, read all the steps. Make sure that you understand the entire procedure, especially any safety precautions that must be followed.

The single most important rule for your safety is simple: Always follow your teacher's instructions and the textbook directions exactly. If you are in doubt about any step in an activity, always ask your teacher for an explanation. Because you may be in contact with chemicals you cannot see, it is essential that you wash your hands thoroughly after every scientific activity. Remember, you share responsibility for your own safety and that of your teacher and classmates.

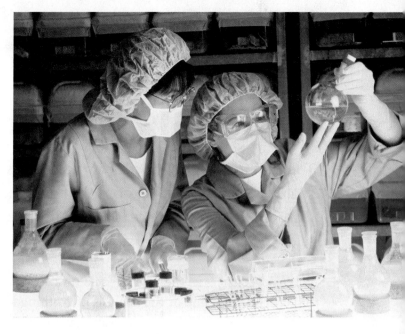

Figure 10 Safety plays an important role in science. **Interpreting Photos** *What safety measures are these scientists taking in their laboratory work?*

Section 1.2 Assessment

Reviewing Concepts

1. What is the goal of scientific methods?
2. How does a scientific law differ from a scientific theory?
3. Why are scientific models useful?
4. What are three types of variables in a controlled experiment?
5. Does every scientific method begin with an observation? Explain.

Critical Thinking

6. **Classifying** The scientists who tested the hypothesis on running in the rain performed only one controlled experiment that supported their hypothesis. Can their supported hypothesis be called a theory? Explain.

7. **Designing Experiments** Suppose you wanted to find out how running affects your pulse rate. What would your hypothesis be? Explain how you could test your hypothesis.

8. **Using Models** A scientific model can take the form of a physical object or a concept. List one example of each type of model. How does each one resemble what it is supposed to model?

Writing in Science

Descriptive Paragraph Write a paragraph describing two examples of pseudoscience. Use your examples to explain why pseudoscience is not actual science.

Forensic Science

The first job of police officers at a crime scene is to seal off the area so that potential evidence is not disturbed. Such evidence will be sent to a forensic science laboratory for examination.

Forensic science is the use of scientific methods, such as fingerprint matching or the analysis of clothing fibers, to solve crimes. As techniques in analytical chemistry have become more advanced, the amount of information that can be gleaned from tiny crime-scene samples has grown. Forensic science is becoming ever more powerful as a crime-solving tool.

Criminal investigators need to use several scientific techniques. They include making observations, establishing the problem to be solved, collecting evidence and gathering information, forming hypotheses, analyzing evidence, testing hypotheses, and drawing conclusions.

The crime scene
At the scene, the investigators make observations that may shed light on the nature of the crime. The investigators establish the problem to be solved—in this case, who committed the murder?

DNA evidence can be obtained from blood stains.

Collecting evidence and forming a hypothesis
Forensic scientists take photographs and collect materials from the crime scene. Investigators use all of the information gathered to formulate hypotheses about how and why the crime took place.

Analyzing the evidence

Much of the physical evidence must be analyzed in a laboratory. With a blood sample, for example, DNA is extracted and analyzed and the blood type is established.

Forensic blood sampling *Articles from a crime scene, such as the blood-stained clothing and the hatchet shown here, may match DNA to a suspect.*

Displaced objects can help determine a sequence of events.

Testing hypotheses against the evidence

Investigators now test hypotheses on who committed the crime—looking for matches in DNA, fingerprints, or clothing fibers, for example. In some cases, this testing excludes a suspect. In other cases it strengthens the case against a particular person.

Drawing conclusions

To build a convincing case against a suspect, various pieces and types of evidence may be needed. Evidence might include a fingerprint match, a piece of clothing left at the crime scene, or a connection to the murder weapon.

Documents may provide evidence for a motive.

Going Further

■ Describe how criminal investigators use scientific methods to solve their cases. (*Hint:* start by creating a flowchart of a scientific method. Then identify how criminal investigators carry out each step.)

Fibers can link a suspect to a crime scene.

1.3 Measurement

Reading Focus

Key Concepts

- Why is scientific notation useful?
- What units do scientists use for their measurements?
- How does the precision of measurements affect the precision of scientific calculations?

Vocabulary

- scientific notation
- length
- mass
- volume
- density
- conversion factor
- precision
- significant figures
- accuracy
- thermometer

Reading Strategy

Previewing Make a table like the one below. Before you read the section, rewrite the green and blue topic headings as questions. As you read, write answers to the questions.

Measurement		
Why is scientific notation useful?		
a.	?	
b.	?	

Figure 11 Scientists estimate that there are more than 200 billion stars in the Milky Way galaxy. **Applying Concepts** *What is this number in scientific notation?*

How old are you? How tall are you? The answers to these questions are measurements. Measurements are important in both science and everyday life. Hardly a day passes without the need for you to measure amounts of money or the passage of time. It would be difficult to imagine doing science without any measurements.

Using Scientific Notation

How many stars do you see in Figure 11? There are too many to count. Scientists often work with very large or very small numbers. For example, the speed of light is about 300,000,000 meters per second. On the other hand, an average snail has been clocked at a speed of only 0.00086 meter per second.

Instead of having to write out all the zeroes in these numbers, you can use a shortcut called scientific notation. **Scientific notation** is a way of expressing a value as the product of a number between 1 and 10 and a power of 10. For example, the number 300,000,000 written in scientific notation is 3.0×10^8. The exponent, 8, tells you that the decimal point is really 8 places to the right of the 3.

For numbers less than 1 that are written in scientific notation, the exponent is negative. For example, the number 0.00086 written in scientific notation is 8.6×10^{-4}. The negative exponent tells you how many decimals places there are to the *left* of the 8.6. **Scientific notation makes very large or very small numbers easier to work with.**

When multiplying numbers written in scientific notation, you multiply the numbers that appear before the multiplication signs and *add* the exponents. For example, to calculate how far light travels in 500 seconds, you multiply the speed of light by the number of seconds.

$$(3.0 \times 10^8 \text{ m/s}) \times (5.0 \times 10^2 \text{ s}) = 15 \times 10^{10} \text{ m} = 1.5 \times 10^{11} \text{ m}$$

This distance is about how far the sun is from Earth.

When dividing numbers written in scientific notation, you divide the numbers that appear before the exponential terms and *subtract* the exponents. For example, to calculate how long it takes for light from the sun to reach Earth, you would perform a division.

$$\frac{1.5 \times 10^{11} \text{ m}}{3.0 \times 10^8 \text{ m/s}} = \frac{1.5}{3.0} \times 10^{11-8} \text{ s} = 0.50 \times 10^3 \text{ s} = 5.0 \times 10^2 \text{ s}$$

For: Links on universal measurements

Visit: PHSchool.com

Web Code: ccc-0013

 Math Skills

Using Scientific Notation

A rectangular parking lot has a length of 1.1×10^3 meters and a width of 2.4×10^3 meters. What is the area of the parking lot?

1 Read and Understand

What information are you given?

Length (l) = 1.1×10^3 m

Width (w) = 2.4×10^3 m

 Plan and Solve

What unknown are you trying to calculate?

Area (A) = ?

What formula contains the given quantities and the unknown?

$A = l \times w$

Replace each variable with its known value.

$$A = l \times w = (1.1 \times 10^3 \text{ m})(2.4 \times 10^3 \text{ m})$$
$$= (1.1 \times 2.4)(10^{3+3})(\text{m} \times \text{m})$$
$$= 2.6 \times 10^6 \text{ m}^2$$

 Look Back and Check

Is your answer reasonable?

Yes, the number calculated is the product of the numbers given, and the units (m^2) indicate area.

Math Practice

1. Perform the following calculations. Express your answers in scientific notation.

   a. $(7.6 \times 10^{-4} \text{ m}) \times (1.5 \times 10^7 \text{ m})$

   b. $0.00053 \div 29$

2. Calculate how far light travels in 8.64×10^4 seconds. (*Hint:* The speed of light is about 3.0×10^8 m/s.)

SI Units of Measurement

For a measurement to make sense, it requires both a number and a unit. For example, if you told one of your friends that you had finished a homework assignment "in five," what would your friend think? Would it be five minutes or five hours? Maybe it was a long assignment, and you actually meant five days. Or maybe you meant that you wrote five pages. You should always express measurements in numbers and units so that their meaning is clear. In Figure 12, students are measuring temperature in degrees Celsius.

Many of the units you are familiar with, such as inches, feet, and degrees Fahrenheit, are not units that are used in science. **Scientists use a set of measuring units called SI, or the International System of Units.** The abbreviation stands for the French name *Système International d'Unités*. SI is a revised version of the metric system, which was originally developed in France in 1791. By adhering to one system of units, scientists can readily interpret one another's measurements.

Base Units and Derived Units SI is built upon seven metric units, known as base units, which are listed in Figure 13. In SI, the base unit for **length,** or the straight-line distance between two points, is the meter (m). The base unit for **mass,** or the quantity of matter in an object or sample, is the kilogram (kg).

Additional SI units, called derived units, are made from combinations of base units. Figure 14 lists some common derived units. For example, **volume** is the amount of space taken up by an object. The volume of a rectangular box equals its length times its width times its height. Each of these dimensions can be measured in meters, so you can derive the SI unit for volume by multiplying meters by meters by meters, which gives you cubic meters (m^3).

Figure 12 A measurement consists of a number and a unit. One of the units used to measure temperature is the degree Celsius.

SI Base Units		
Quantity	Unit	Symbol
Length	meter	m
Mass	kilogram	kg
Temperature	kelvin	K
Time	second	s
Amount of substance	mole	mol
Electric current	ampere	A
Luminous intensity	candela	cd

Figure 13 Seven metric base units make up the foundation of SI.

Derived Units		
Quantity	Unit	Symbol
Area	square meter	m^2
Volume	cubic meter	m^3
Density	kilograms per cubic meter	kg/m^3
Pressure	pascal ($kg/m \cdot s^2$)	Pa
Energy	joule ($kg \cdot m^2/s^2$)	J
Frequency	hertz ($1/s$)	Hz
Electric charge	coulomb ($A \cdot s$)	C

Figure 14 Specific combinations of SI base units yield derived units.

SI Prefixes			
Prefix	Symbol	Meaning	Multiply Unit by
giga-	G	billion (10^9)	1,000,000,000
mega-	M	million (10^6)	1,000,000
kilo-	k	thousand (10^3)	1000
deci-	d	tenth (10^{-1})	0.1
centi-	c	hundredth (10^{-2})	0.01
milli-	m	thousandth (10^{-3})	0.001
micro-	μ	millionth (10^{-6})	0.000001
nano-	n	billionth (10^{-9})	0.000000001

Figure 15 Metric prefixes allow for more convenient ways to express SI base and derived units.

Another quantity that requires a derived unit is density. **Density** is the ratio of an object's mass to its volume.

$$\text{Density} = \frac{\text{Mass}}{\text{Volume}}$$

To derive the SI unit for density, you can divide the base unit for mass by the derived unit for volume. Dividing kilograms by cubic meters yields the SI unit for density, kilograms per cubic meter (kg/m^3).

 Reading Checkpoint *What is the SI derived unit for density?*

Metric Prefixes The metric unit for a given quantity is not always a convenient one to use. For example, the time it takes for a computer hard drive to read or write data—also known as the seek time—is in the range of thousandths of a second. A typical seek time might be 0.009 second. This can be written in a more compact way by using a metric prefix. A metric prefix indicates how many times a unit should be multiplied or divided by 10. Figure 15 shows some common metric prefixes. Using the prefix *milli-* (m), you can write 0.009 second as 9 milliseconds, or 9 ms.

$$9 \text{ ms} = \frac{9}{1000} \text{ s} = 0.009 \text{ s}$$

Note that dividing by 1000 is the same as multiplying by 0.001.

Metric prefixes can also make a unit larger. For example, a distance of 12,000 meters can also be written as 12 kilometers.

$$12 \text{ km} = 12 \times 1000 \text{ m} = 12,000 \text{ m}$$

Metric prefixes turn up in non-metric units as well. If you have used a digital camera, you may know that a megapixel is 1,000,000 pixels. A kiloton is a unit of explosive force equal to 1,000 tons of TNT.

Figure 16 A bar of gold has more mass per unit volume than a feather. **Inferring** *Which takes up more space—one kilogram of gold or one kilogram of feathers?*

Nutrition Facts

Serving Size 1 oz (28g/about 18 chips)
Servings Per Container 7

Amount Per Serving

Calories 150	Calories from Fat 80

% Daily Value*

Total Fat 9g	**14%**
Saturated Fat 1g	**5%**
Polyunsaturated Fat 1g	
Monounsaturated Fat 7g	
Cholesterol 0mg	**0%**
Sodium 160mg	**7%**

Figure 17 Nutrition labels often have some measurements listed in grams and milligrams.
Calculating *How many grams are in 160 milligrams?*

The easiest way to convert from one unit of measurement to another is to use conversion factors. A **conversion factor** is a ratio of equivalent measurements that is used to convert a quantity expressed in one unit to another unit. Suppose you want to convert the height of Mount Everest, 8848 meters, into kilometers. Based on the prefix *kilo-*, you know that 1 kilometer is 1000 meters. This ratio gives you two possible conversion factors.

$$\frac{1 \text{ km}}{1000 \text{ m}} \qquad \frac{1000 \text{ m}}{1 \text{ km}}$$

Since you are converting from meters to kilometers, the number should get smaller. Multiplying by the conversion factor on the left yields a smaller number.

$$8848 \text{ m} \times \frac{1 \text{ km}}{1000 \text{ m}} = 8.848 \text{ km}$$

Notice that the meter units cancel, leaving you with kilometers (the larger unit).

To convert 8.848 kilometers back into meters, multiply by the conversion factor on the right. Since you are converting from kilometers to meters, the number should get larger.

$$8.848 \text{ km} \times \frac{1000 \text{ m}}{1 \text{ km}} = 8848 \text{ m}$$

In this case, the kilometer units cancel, leaving you with meters.

≡Quick Lab

Comparing Precision

Materials

3 plastic bottles of different sizes, beaker, graduated cylinder

Procedure

1. Draw a data table with three rows and three columns. Label the columns Estimate, Beaker, and Graduated Cylinder.

2. Record your estimate of the volume of a plastic bottle in your data table. Then, fill the bottle with water and pour the water into the beaker. Read and record the volume of the water.

3. Pour the water from the beaker into the graduated cylinder. Read and record the volume of water.

4. Repeat Steps 2 and 3 with two other plastic bottles.

Analyze and Conclude

1. **Analyzing Data** Review your volume measurements for one of the bottles. How many significant figures does the volume measured with the beaker have? How many significant figures does the volume measured with the graduated cylinder have?

2. **Comparing and Contrasting** Which provided a more precise measurement—the beaker or the graduated cylinder?

3. **Inferring** How could you determine the accuracy of your measurements?

Limits of Measurement

Suppose you wanted to measure how much time it takes for you to eat your breakfast. Figure 18 shows two clocks you could use—an analog clock and a digital clock. The analog clock displays time to the nearest minute. The digital clock displays time to the nearest second (or one sixtieth of a minute). Which clock would you choose?

Precision The digital clock offers more precision. **Precision** is a gauge of how exact a measurement is. According to the analog clock, it might take you 5 minutes to eat your breakfast. Using the digital clock, however, you might measure 5 minutes and 15 seconds, or 5.25 minutes. The second measurement has more significant figures. **Significant figures** are all the digits that are known in a measurement, plus the last digit that is estimated. The time recorded as 5.25 minutes has three significant figures. The time recorded as 5 minutes has one significant figure. The fewer the significant figures, the less precise the measurement is.

When you make calculations with measurements, the uncertainty of the separate measurements must be correctly reflected in the final result. ⊂⊃ **The precision of a calculated answer is limited by the least precise measurement used in the calculation.** So if the least precise measurement in your calculation has two significant figures, then your calculated answer can have at most two significant figures.

Suppose you measure the mass of a piece of iron to be 34.73 grams on an electronic balance. You then measure the volume to be 4.42 cubic centimeters. What is the density of the iron?

$$\text{Density} = \frac{34.73 \text{ g}}{4.42 \text{ cm}^3} = 7.857466 \text{ g/cm}^3$$

Your answer should have only three significant figures because the least precise measurement, the volume, has three significant figures. Rounding your answer to three significant figures gives you a density of 7.86 grams per cubic centimeter.

Accuracy Another important quality in a measurement is its accuracy. **Accuracy** is the closeness of a measurement to the actual value of what is being measured. For example, suppose the digital clock in Figure 18 is running 15 minutes slow. Although the clock would remain precise to the nearest second, the time displayed would not be accurate.

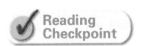 Reading Checkpoint) *What is accuracy?*

Figure 18 A more precise time can be read from the digital clock than can be read from the analog clock. The digital clock is precise to the nearest second, while the analog clock is precise to the nearest minute.

Common Temperatures			
	Fahrenheit (°F)	Celsius (°C)	Kelvin (K)
Water boils	212	100	373
Human body	98.6	37	310
Average room	68	20	293
Water freezes	32	0	273

Figure 19 Temperature can be expressed in degrees Fahrenheit, degrees Celsius, or kelvins.

Measuring Temperature

A **thermometer** is an instrument that measures temperature, or how hot an object is. The How It Works box on page 21 describes how a bulb thermometer measures temperature.

The two temperature scales that you are probably most familiar with are the Fahrenheit scale and the Celsius scale. On the Fahrenheit scale, water freezes at 32°F and boils at 212°F at sea level. On the Celsius (or centigrade) scale, water freezes at 0°C and boils at 100°C. A degree Celsius is almost twice as large as a degree Fahrenheit. There is also a difference of 32 degrees between the zero point of the Celsius scale and the zero point of the Fahrenheit scale. You can convert from one scale to the other by using one of the following formulas.

$$°C = \frac{5}{9}(°F - 32.0°) \qquad °F = \frac{9}{5}(°C) + 32.0°$$

The SI base unit for temperature is the kelvin (K). A temperature of 0 K, or 0 kelvin, refers to the lowest possible temperature that can be reached. In degrees Celsius, this temperature is $-273.15°C$. To convert between kelvins and degrees Celsius, use the following formula.

$$K = °C + 273$$

Figure 19 compares some common temperatures expressed in degrees Celsius, degrees Fahrenheit, and kelvins.

Section 1.3 Assessment

Reviewing Concepts

1. ⬤ Why do scientists use scientific notation?
2. ⬤ What system of units do scientists use for measurements?
3. ⬤ How does the precision of measurements affect the precision of scientific calculations?
4. List the SI units for mass, length, and temperature.

Critical Thinking

5. **Applying Concepts** A bulb thermometer gives an indoor temperature reading of 21°C. A digital thermometer in the same room gives a reading of 20.7°C. Which device is more precise? Explain.

6. **Calculating** Convert −11°F into degrees Celsius, and then into kelvins.

Math **Practice**

7. Write the following measurements in scientific notation. Then convert each measurement into SI base units.
   a. 0.0000000000372 g
   b. 45,000,000,000 km

8. The liquid in a bulb thermometer falls 1.1 cm. Calculate the liquid's change in volume if the inner radius of the tube is 6.5×10^{-3} cm.

Thermometer

A bulb thermometer consists of a sealed, narrow glass tube, called a capillary tube. It has a glass bulb at one end and is filled with colored alcohol or mercury. Because mercury is poisonous, mercury thermometers are rarely used in medicine. The thermometer works on the principle that the volume of a liquid changes when the temperature changes. When warmed, the liquid in the bulb takes up more space and moves up the capillary tube.

Interpreting Diagrams *Why is a thermometer with a narrow tube easier to read than one with a wide tube?*

Measuring temperature
Thermometers are useful scientific instruments. They can be used to measure the static temperature of a material, or to record the change in temperature of a substance being heated, as shown above.

Scale *The scale indicates the temperature according to how far up or down the capillary tube the liquid has moved.*

Celsius (centigrade) temperature scale

Capillary tube

Fahrenheit scale

°C °F

50
120
40
100
30
80
20
60
10
40
0
20
10
20
20
0

Wide or narrow?
The volume of a tube is calculated using the formula $V = \pi r^2 l$, where r is the radius and l is the length. For a given volume, if the radius of a tube is decreased (as in a capillary tube), the length of the liquid column increases. Any change in volume is then easier to see.

Colored liquid *The liquid moves up and down the capillary tube as the temperature changes.*

Bulb *The bulb contains the reservoir of liquid.*

Compressed scale

Liquid rises less in a wide tube for the same temperature change.

Liquid rises more in a narrow tube for the same temperature change.

Expanded, easy-to-read scale

1.4 Presenting Scientific Data

Reading Focus

Key Concepts

- How do scientists organize data?
- How can scientists communicate experimental data?

Vocabulary

- ◆ slope
- ◆ direct proportion
- ◆ inverse proportion

Reading Strategy

Comparing and Contrasting After you read this section, compare types of graphs by completing the table below.

Type of Graph	Description	Used For
Line	a. ?	b. ?
Bar	c. ?	d. ?
Circle	e. ?	f. ?

Much of the information you get every day comes from the news media. Newspapers, television, radio, and the Internet let you access a wealth of information about events going on in the world. But in order for news to be useful, it must be communicated. If a news reporter witnesses an event but doesn't report it, then he might as well not have seen it. If the event is reported, then it must be described in a clear, organized manner for it to be understood and appreciated. Like the news, scientific data become meaningful only when they are organized and communicated.

Organizing Data

Scientists accumulate vast amounts of data by observing events and making measurements. Interpreting these data can be a difficult task if they are not organized. Scientists can organize their data by using data tables and graphs. These tools make it easier to spot patterns or trends in the data that can support or disprove a hypothesis.

Data Tables The simplest way to organize data is to present them in a table. Figure 20 is a data table that shows the average annual precipitation for seven U.S. cities. The table relates two variables—a manipulated variable (location) and a responding variable (average annual precipitation).

Average Annual Precipitation for Selected U.S. Cities	
City	**Average Annual Precipitation (cm)**
Buffalo, N.Y.	98.0
Chicago, Ill.	91.0
Colorado Springs, Colo.	41.2
Houston, Tex.	117.0
San Diego, Calif.	25.1
Tallahassee, Fla.	166.9
Tucson, Ariz.	30.5

Figure 20 Using a table is a simple way to present data visually.

Mass vs. Volume of Water

$$\text{Slope} = \frac{\text{Rise}}{\text{Run}} = \frac{5\text{ g}}{5\text{ cm}^3} = 1\text{ g/cm}^3$$

Rise = 5 g

Run = 5 cm³

Mass (g)

Volume (cm³)

Figure 21 Plotting the mass of water against the volume of water yields a straight line.
Using Graphs *What does the slope represent?*

Time to Fill a 1-gallon Pot With Water

Time (minutes)

Flow Rate (gallons per minute)

Figure 22 In an inverse proportion, the product of two variables remains constant. Each point on the graph above represents the same volume of water: 1 gallon.

Line Graphs A line graph is useful for showing changes that occur in related variables. In a line graph, the manipulated variable is generally plotted on the horizontal axis, or *x*-axis. The responding variable is plotted on the vertical axis, or *y*-axis, of the graph.

Figure 21 is a line graph that shows how the mass of water increases with volume. The data points yield a straight line. The steepness, or **slope,** of this line is the ratio of a vertical change to the corresponding horizontal change. The formula for the slope of a line is

$$\text{Slope} = \frac{\text{Rise}}{\text{Run}}$$

"Rise" represents the change in the *y*-variable. "Run" represents the corresponding change in the *x*-variable. Note that in Figure 21, because mass per unit volume is density, the slope represents the density of water.

The relationship between the mass and volume of water is an example of a direct proportion. A **direct proportion** is a relationship in which the ratio of two variables is constant. For example, suppose you have a 3-cubic-centimeter sample of water that has a mass of 3 grams. Doubling the volume of the sample to 6 cubic centimeters results in doubling the mass of the sample to 6 grams. Tripling the volume to 9 cubic centimeters results in tripling the mass to 9 grams.

Figure 22 shows how the flow rate of a water faucet affects the time required to fill a 1-gallon pot. Figure 22 illustrates an **inverse proportion,** a relationship in which the product of two variables is a constant. If you start with a flow rate of 0.5 gallon per minute, you will fill the pot in 2 minutes. If you double the flow rate to 1.0 gallon per minute, you reduce the time required to fill the pot to 1 minute, or one half of the original time.

Science Skills **23**

Faster Than Speeding Data

A modem is a device used to send and receive data. For example, if you upload an image to a Web site, the modem in your computer converts the data of the image into a different format. The converted data are then sent through a telephone line or cable TV line. The smallest unit of data that can be read by a computer is a binary digit, or "bit." A bit is either a 0 or a 1. Computers process bits in larger units called bytes. A byte is a group of eight bits.

The table shows the data transfer rates for modems used in home computers. Data transfer rates are often measured in kilobits per second, or

Modem Speeds		
Type of Modem	Data Transfer Rate (kbps)	Upload Time for 1 MB (s)
56K dial-up	48	167
Cable (low-speed)	384	21
DSL (medium-speed)	512	16
DSL (high-speed)	768	10
Cable (high-speed)	2000	4

kbps. The time required to upload a 1-megabyte (MB) file is given for each rate listed.

1. **Using Graphs** Use the data in the table to create a line graph. Describe the relationship between data transfer rate and upload time.

2. **Inferring** How would doubling the data transfer rate affect the upload time?

Go Online
NSTA SCLINKS

For: Links on graphing
Visit: www.SciLinks.org
Web Code: ccn-0014

Bar Graphs A bar graph is often used to compare a set of measurements, amounts, or changes. Figure 23 is a bar graph of the data from Figure 20. The bar graph makes it easy to see how the data for one city compare with the data for another.

Circle Graphs If you think of a pie cut into pieces, you have a mental model of a circle graph. A circle graph is a divided circle that shows how a part or share of something relates to the whole. Figure 24 is a circle graph that describes the composition of Earth's crust. The entire circle represents the mass of Earth's crust. Each "slice" of the circle represents a percentage of that mass corresponding to a specific substance.

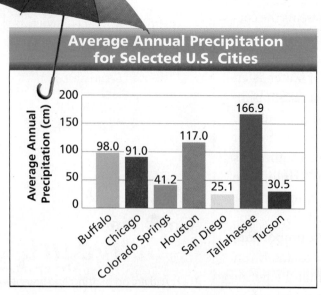

Figure 23 A bar graph is useful for comparing several measurements.

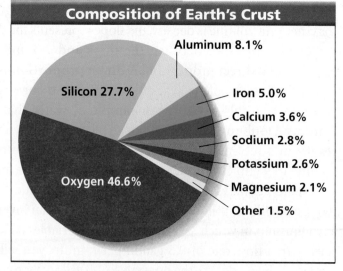

Figure 24 A circle graph is useful for showing how a part of something relates to the whole.

Communicating Data

A crucial part of any scientific investigation is reporting the results. 🔑 **Scientists can communicate results by writing in scientific journals or speaking at conferences.** Scientists also exchange information through conversations, e-mails, and Web sites. Young scientists often present their research at science fairs like the one in Figure 25.

Different scientists may interpret the same data differently. This important notion is the basis for peer review, a process in which scientists examine other scientists' work. Not only do scientists share research with their peers, but they also invite feedback from those peers. Peer review encourages comments, suggestions, questions, and criticism from other scientists. Peer review can also help determine if data were reported accurately and honestly. Based on their peers' responses, the scientists who submitted their work for review can then reevaluate how to best interpret their data.

Figure 25 At a science fair, students communicate what knowledge they have gained by using scientific methods.

Section 1.4 Assessment

Reviewing Concepts

1. 🔑 How do scientists organize data?
2. 🔑 How can scientists communicate experimental results?
3. What does a given point represent on a line graph?
4. The density of copper is 8.92 g/cm³. If you plotted the mass of copper in grams versus the volume in cubic centimeters, what would the slope of the line be?

Critical Thinking

5. **Comparing and Contrasting** When would you choose a line graph to present data? When would you choose a bar graph?

6. **Using Tables and Graphs** Count the number of students in your class with blue eyes, brown eyes, and green eyes. Display these data in a table and bar graph.

> ## Connecting Concepts
>
> **Scientific Methods** Reread the description of scientific methods in Section 1.2. Then write a paragraph explaining which steps in a scientific method might require data to be organized. (*Hint:* You might use information diagrammed in Figure 7.)

Determining the Thickness of Aluminum Foil

Many products such as aluminum foil are too thin to measure easily. However, it is important for manufacturers to know how thick they are. They wouldn't be useful if they were made too thick or too thin. In this lab, you will use the same method that manufacturers use to determine the thickness of aluminum foil.

Problem How can you determine the thickness of aluminum foil?

Materials
- metric ruler
- aluminum foil
- scissors
- balance
- graph paper

Skills Measuring, Calculating, Using Graphs

Data Table

Length (mm)	Area (mm²)	Mass (g)	Volume (mm³)	Thickness (mm)

Density of Alumnium = _____ g/mm³

Procedure

1. On a separate sheet of paper, make a copy of the data table shown. Include the information below the data table.

2. Cut out three squares of aluminum foil with sides of the following lengths: 50 mm, 100 mm, and 200 mm.

3. To determine the area of the 50-mm foil square, measure the length of one of its sides and then square it. Record the length and area in your data table.

4. Place the foil square on the balance to determine its mass. Record the mass of the foil square in your data table.

5. You will need the density of aluminum foil to calculate the volume of the foil square from its mass. The density of aluminum foil is 2.71 g/cm^3. Convert cm^3 to mm^3 and record the density of aluminum foil (in g/mm^3) on the line provided below your data table.

6. To determine the volume of the foil square, divide its mass by its density in g/mm^3. Record the volume in your data table.

7. To determine the thickness of the foil square, divide its volume by its area. Record this thickness in your data table.

8. Repeat Steps 3 through 7 using the 100-mm foil square.

9. Repeat Steps 3 through 7 using the 200-mm foil square.

10. Construct a graph of your data. Plot length on the horizontal axis and thickness on the vertical axis. Draw a straight line connecting all three points.

Analyze and Conclude

1. **Measuring** How many significant figures were there in your measurement of the length of each square of aluminum foil?

2. **Using Graphs** What effect, if any, did the length of the square have on your estimate of the thickness of the foil?

3. **Comparing** Which estimate of thickness was most precise? Explain your answer.

4. **Controlling Variables** What factors limited the precision of your measurements?

Go Further Aluminum is composed of small particles. Each particle has a diameter of 2.86×10^{-10} m. Calculate how many particles make up the thickness of the foil. Then, calculate the number of particles in the 50-mm square. Finally, determine the mass of one particle.

For: Data sharing
Visit: PHSchool.com
Web Code: ccd-0010

Study Guide

1.1 What is Science?

Key Concepts

- Science begins with curiosity and often ends with discovery.
- Science and technology are interdependent. Advances in one lead to advances in the other.
- Natural science is generally divided into three branches: physical science, Earth and space science, and life science.

Vocabulary

science, *p. 3*

technology, *p. 3*

chemistry, *p. 4*

physics, *p. 4*

geology, *p. 4*

astronomy, *p. 4*

biology, *p. 4*

1.2 Using a Scientific Approach

Key Concepts

- The goal of a scientific method is to solve a problem or to better understand an observed event.
- A scientific law describes an observed pattern in nature without attempting to explain it. The explanation of such a pattern is provided by a scientific theory.
- Scientific models make it easier to understand things that might be too difficult to observe directly.

Vocabulary

scientific method, *p. 7*

observation, *p. 8*

hypothesis, *p. 8*

manipulated variable, *p. 8*

responding variable, *p. 8*

controlled experiment, *p. 8*

scientific theory, *p. 9*

scientific law, *p. 9*

model, *p. 10*

1.3 Measurement

Key Concepts

- Scientific notation makes very large or very small numbers easier to work with.
- Scientists use a set of measuring units called SI.
- The precision of a calculation is limited by the least precise measurement used in the calculation.

Vocabulary

scientific notation, *p. 14*

length, *p. 16*

mass, *p. 16*

volume, *p. 16*

density, *p. 17*

conversion factor, *p. 18*

precision, *p. 19*

significant figures, *p. 19*

accuracy, *p. 19*

thermometer, *p. 20*

1.4 Presenting Scientific Data

Key Concepts

- Scientists can organize their data by using data tables and graphs.
- Scientists can communicate results by writing in journals or speaking at conferences.

Vocabulary

slope, *p. 23*

direct proportion, *p. 23*

inverse proportion, *p. 23*

Thinking Visually

Using Tables Use information from the chapter to complete the table below.

Type of Unit	Description	Example
Base	a. ___?___	b. ___?___
Derived	c. ___?___	d. ___?___

Reviewing Content

Choose the letter that best answers the question or completes the statement.

1. The application of knowledge to solve practical problems is known as
   - **a.** science.
   - **b.** curiosity.
   - **c.** technology.
   - **d.** experimentation.

2. Which is not a branch of natural science?
   - **a.** physical science
   - **b.** life science
   - **c.** Earth science
   - **d.** social science

3. What is the purpose of an experiment?
   - **a.** to communicate data
   - **b.** to test a hypothesis
   - **c.** to prove a scientific law
   - **d.** none of the above

4. A representation of an object or event is called
   - **a.** a scientific law.
   - **b.** a model.
   - **c.** a hypothesis.
   - **d.** a variable.

5. Which value is equivalent to 5×10^6?
   - **a.** five thousand
   - **b.** fifty thousand
   - **c.** five million
   - **d.** fifty million

6. What is the SI base unit of mass?
   - **a.** gram
   - **b.** kilogram
   - **c.** milligram
   - **d.** pound

7. An electric generator produces 10 megawatts. This amount is equivalent to
   - **a.** 10,000 watts.
   - **b.** 1,000,000 watts.
   - **c.** 10,000,000 watts.
   - **d.** 0.010 watt.

8. Which of the following is a ratio of equivalent measurements that is used to convert a quantity expressed in one unit to another unit?
   - **a.** slope
   - **b.** conversion factor
   - **c.** derived unit
   - **d.** density

9. When the ratio of two variables is constant, their relationship can be described as
   - **a.** inversely proportional.
   - **b.** interdependent.
   - **c.** directly proportional.
   - **d.** parallel.

10. Which of the following would best suit data that describe how a part relates to the whole?
    - **a.** line graph
    - **b.** bar graph
    - **c.** circle graph
    - **d.** scientific notation

Understanding Concepts

11. Give an example of a case where the branches of natural science appear to overlap.

12. What is the goal of a scientific method?

13. How are controlled experiments useful?

14. Suppose you perform an experiment, and the resulting data do not support your hypothesis. What is the next step you might take?

15. What are some safety precautions that you should follow when working in the laboratory?

16. What is scientific notation?

17. What are the SI base units for length and temperature?

18. How do derived units differ from base units?

19. How is the precision of a calculated result related to the precision of the measurements used in the calculation?

20. How can you convert a temperature expressed in degrees Celsius to kelvins?

21. Which of the following graphs describes a direct proportion?

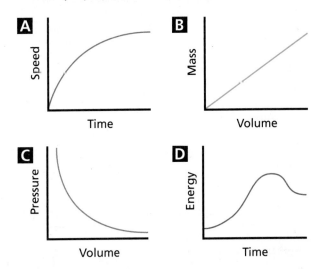

22. Why is it important for scientists to communicate their results?

Critical Thinking

23. Formulating Hypotheses Suppose you want to know if objects with different masses fall to the ground at different rates. State a hypothesis about falling objects.

24. Designing Experiments Explain how you can test the hypothesis in Question 23. What will be the manipulated variable in your experiment? What will be the responding variable?

25. Calculating A triathlete enters a race in which he swims 500 meters, runs 3000 meters, and cycles 10.0 kilometers. What is the total distance of the race in kilometers?

26. Using Models Explain how a map of your town is an example of a model. How does this model help you plan a trip to an unfamiliar place?

27. Using Graphs Use the data in the table below to create a line graph. Plot distance on the vertical axis. Plot driving time on the horizontal axis. Calculate the slope of the line. If speed is the ratio of distance to time, what is the average driving speed of the trip?

Driving Distance and Time

City	Distance From Start (km)	Driving Time From Start (h)
New York City, N.Y.	750	9.5
Cleveland, Ohio	1300	16.25
Chicago, Ill.	1900	23.25
Omaha, Nebr.	2100	26.25
Cheyenne, Wyo.	2900	36.25
Salt Lake City, Utah	3600	45
San Francisco, Calif.	4800	60

Math Skills

28. Calculating If a thermometer outside your classroom indicates a temperature of 61 degrees Fahrenheit, what is the temperature in degrees Celsius? In kelvins?

29. Problem Solving Suppose you have a large coffee can full of pennies. How can you estimate how much money the can contains without counting all the coins? (*Hint:* What is the relationship between the mass of pennies and the number of pennies?)

30. Calculating The Milky Way galaxy contains between 200 and 400 billion stars. Estimate the number of stars in a cluster of 30 galaxies similar in size to the Milky Way. Your answer should consist of a low estimate and a high estimate, both expressed in scientific notation.

Concepts in Action

31. Designing Experiments A zookeeper notices that elephants become restless shortly before an earthquake. The zookeeper forms a hypothesis that, just before an earthquake occurs, an elephant detects a sound that humans are unable to hear. How could this hypothesis be tested?

32. Making Judgments You see an advertisement on television for an over-the-counter medication that has been "scientifically proven to work." How could you find out if this claim is true?

33. Writing in Science Write a paragraph describing how advances in technology have affected your life. (*Hint:* The first sentence should state the paragraph's main idea.)

Performance-Based Assessment

Designing Experiments Grocery stores carry many brands of household detergents. Design an experiment to compare a more expensive brand of detergent with a less expensive one. Is one brand better for some purposes than the other?

For: Self-grading assessment
Visit: PHSchool.com
Web Code: cca-0015

Standardized Test Prep

Test-Taking Tip

Calculating

Checking units is a very important part of problem solving. Keep these tips in mind when solving problems involving unit conversions:

- A conversion factor is a ratio of equivalent measurements.
- Write horizontal fractions to help keep track of conversion factors. For example, write $\frac{32\ g}{cm^3}$ as opposed to 32 g/cm³.
- Line up conversion factors so that the unit you are converting cancels.
- If you have to square or cube a unit, make sure you square or cube the entire conversion factor.
- Make a reality check of your answer. If the units are wrong, your calculations are probably wrong. Also, verify that the numerical answer is reasonable.

Practice using these tips in Questions 2 and 4.

Choose the letter that best answers the question or completes the statement.

1. In a controlled experiment,
   (A) there are multiple responding variables.
   (B) the responding variable is kept constant.
   (C) the manipulated variable is kept constant.
   (D) the responding variable is deliberately changed.
   (E) only one variable at a time is deliberately changed.

2. The speed of an object indicates how far it travels in a given amount of time. If an electron travels 2.42×10^8 meters in 2.00 seconds, what is the speed of this electron in cm/s?
   (A) 1.21×10^8 cm/s
   (B) 4.84×10^8 cm/s
   (C) 1.21×10^{10} cm/s
   (D) 2.42×10^{10} cm/s
   (E) 4.84×10^{10} cm/s

3. A doctor measures the temperature of a patient to be 101°F. What is this temperature in kelvins?
   (A) 38.3 K   (B) 73.8 K
   (C) 214 K   (D) 311 K
   (E) 346 K

4. The density of seawater is 1.024×10^3 kg/m³. What is the density of seawater in g/cm³?
   (A) 102.4 g/cm³
   (B) 1.024×10^{-6} g/cm³
   (C) 1.024 g/cm³
   (D) 3.072×10^3 g/cm³
   (E) 1.024×10^9 g/cm³

5. A student conducts an experiment by dropping a basketball and a box of cereal of the same weight from the top of a building. The student measures the time it takes for each object to strike the ground. What was the student's hypothesis?

   (A) A basketball weighs more than cereal.
   (B) Curved objects travel through the air faster than flat objects.
   (C) Heavier objects travel through the air faster than lighter objects.
   (D) Gravity pulls on objects of the same weight with the same force.
   (E) Heavier objects strike the ground with a greater force than lighter objects.

6. If two variables are directly proportional, then
   (A) an increase in one variable causes a decrease in the other variable.
   (B) the product of the two variables is constant.
   (C) the ratio of the two variables is constant.
   (D) neither variable is the controlled variable.
   (E) both variables are constant.

Chemistry

Focus on the BIG Ideas

Chemistry is the study of the composition, structure, properties, and reactions of matter. Matter that always has exactly the same composition is classified as a substance. Elements are the simplest substances. The smallest particle of an element is an atom.

There are only about 100 elements. In the modern periodic table, elements are arranged by increasing atomic number (number of protons). Based on their chemical and physical properties, elements are classified as metals, nonmetals, and metalloids.

Unlike physical changes, chemical changes involve a change in the composition of matter. During a reaction, chemical bonds in the reactants are broken and chemical bonds in the products are formed. Mass is conserved in chemical reactions.

Nuclear changes (such as radioactivity) involve the conversion of atoms of one element to atoms of another. During nuclear reactions, mass can be created or destroyed, and it is the total sum of mass and energy that is conserved.

Fireworks Display in ▶ Sydney, Australia
When fireworks explode, they produce colorful displays of light.

Careers in Chemistry

What do the people on these pages have in common? They all use chemistry on the job. From toxicologists to firefighters, there are many exciting chemistry careers to choose from.

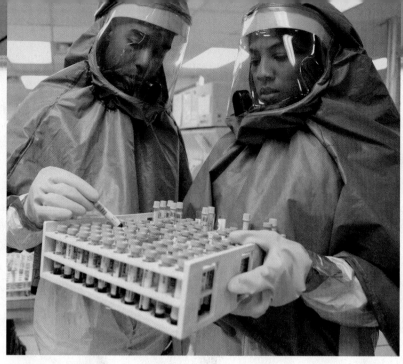

Toxicologist

Toxicologists determine the effects natural and synthetic chemicals may have on people, other organisms, and the environment. Toxicologists conduct experiments to find out whether certain chemicals are dangerous or safe to use. They also determine how much of a given chemical could be harmful.

Educational requirements Four-year bachelor of science degree, majoring in chemistry

Forensic Chemist

Forensic chemists help law enforcement officials solve crimes. At a crime scene, a forensic chemist carefully gathers all the physical evidence and brings it back to the laboratory for analysis and identification. Physical evidence may include fibers, paints, glass, and stains.

Educational requirements Master's degree in chemistry

Food Science Technician

Food science technicians help to ensure that the food you eat is healthful, safe, and flavorful. They use their knowledge of chemistry to develop new or better ways of preserving, processing, packaging, and storing foods. Some food service technicians analyze food content to determine levels of vitamins, fat, carbohydrates, or protein.

Educational requirements Four-year college degree, majoring in chemistry

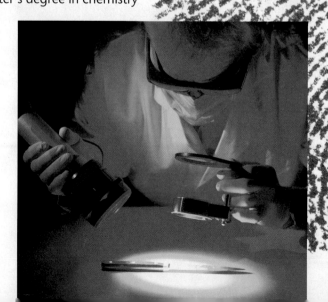

Nuclear Medicine Technologist

Nuclear medicine technologists apply their knowledge of nuclear chemistry to help diagnose diseases and disorders. They prepare and administer radioactive substances and use radiation detection devices to trace these substances in the body. Nuclear medicine technologists work directly with patients and closely with nuclear medicine physicians.

Educational requirements Two-year community or junior college degree, or a one-year certificate in nuclear medicine technology

Firefighter

Firefighters are highly trained professionals who respond to fires, hazardous chemical spills, and medical emergencies. When responding to a fire or spill, firefighters have to know what effects different chemicals have in different situations.

Educational requirements
High-school diploma

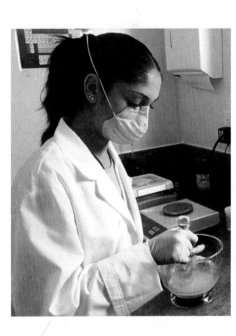

Pharmacist

A pharmacist dispenses drugs prescribed by physicians and dentists and gives information to patients about the drugs and their uses. Pharmacists understand the uses, effects, and composition of drugs, including their chemical properties and biological side effects.

Educational requirements Two years of college, four-year college of pharmacy program, internship, and passage of a state board examination

Go Online
PHSchool.com

For: Career links
Visit: PHSchool.com
Web Code: ccb-1000

CHAPTER

2 Properties of Matter

21st Century Learning

Economic Literacy

What factors influence the cost of metal?

Pots and pans, beverage cans, jewelry, the change in your pocket—these are just a few examples of everyday objects around you that are made of metal. Some metals, due to their properties, are more valuable than others. Select a particular metal and research its properties, uses, and price history. Digitally record a podcast that describes the metal, its current price per unit mass (or weight), and how its price has changed over the years.

How do science concepts apply to your world? Here are some questions you'll be able to answer after you read this chapter.

- **How do the properties of different materials affect the way clothes are cleaned?** *(Section 2.1)*

- **Why doesn't every batch of salsa taste equally "hot"?** *(Section 2.1)*

- **How does fog reduce a driver's ability to see the road ahead?** *(Section 2.1)*

- **Why does a cook use a wooden spoon to stir a pot of soup?** *(Section 2.2)*

- **What methods are used to purify water?** *(page 52)*

- **Why does a banana change color as it ripens?** *(Section 2.3)*

Parts of the Guggenheim Museum Bilbao in Spain are covered with titanium—a strong, elastic metal that reflects light.

Chapter Preview

Inquiry Activity

What Properties Could You Use to Describe Materials?

Procedure

1. Your teacher will provide you with samples of rubber, copper, steel, wood, and carbon. On a sheet of paper, list the materials, leaving room to write your description of each.

2. Determine and record the properties or characteristics of the materials by touching, manipulating, smelling, and looking at them.

Think About It

1. **Comparing and Contrasting** List one or more properties of each material that can be used to distinguish it from the others.

2. **Observing** Write a description of one of the materials that could be used to clearly identify it.

2.1 Classifying Matter

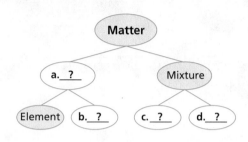

Reading Focus

Key Concepts

- Why are elements and compounds classified as pure substances?
- How do mixtures differ from pure substances?
- What is the main difference among solutions, suspensions, and colloids?

Vocabulary

- pure substance
- element
- atom
- compound
- heterogeneous mixture
- homogeneous mixture
- solution
- suspension
- colloid

Reading Strategy

Summarizing Copy the diagram below. As you read, complete the classification of matter.

Matter
- a. ?
  - Element
  - b. ?
- Mixture
  - c. ?
  - d. ?

Each piece of clothing sold has a care label, which lists recommended cleaning methods for the clothing. For a sweater, the instructions might say to machine wash the sweater using a gentle cycle, and then tumble dry at a low temperature. They might say to hand wash the sweater in cold water and lay the sweater flat to dry. The label might even say, "Dry clean only."

Why is it necessary to put care instructions on a label? The same cleaning method will not work for all materials. For example, a shirt made from 100 percent cotton may need to be ironed after washing. But a shirt made from a cotton and polyester blend may come out of the dryer wrinkle free. A wool jacket often needs to be dry cleaned because wool can shrink when washed in water.

The tendency to wrinkle when washed is a property of cotton. The tendency not to wrinkle when washed is a property of polyester. The tendency to shrink when washed is a property of wool. Cotton, wool, and polyester have different properties because they have different compositions. The word *composition* comes from a Latin word meaning "a putting together," or the combining of parts into a whole. Based on their compositions, materials can be divided into pure substances and mixtures.

Figure 1 You can use the care labels on clothing to sort laundry into batches for cleaning. The care label shown is for a wool sweater that needs to be dry cleaned or washed by hand.

Pure Substances

Matter that always has exactly the same composition is classified as a **pure substance,** or simply a substance. Table salt and table sugar are two examples of pure substances. Every pinch of salt tastes equally salty. Every spoonful of sugar tastes equally sweet. 🔵 **Every sample of a given substance has the same properties because a substance has a fixed, uniform composition.** Substances can be classified into two categories—elements and compounds.

Elements

Although there are millions of known substances, there are only about 100 elements. An **element** is a substance that cannot be broken down into simpler substances. Imagine cutting a copper wire into smaller and smaller pieces. Eventually you would end up with extremely tiny particles called copper atoms. An **atom** is the smallest particle of an element. 🔵 **An element has a fixed composition because it contains only one type of atom.**

No two elements contain the same type of atom. In Chapter 4, you will find out more about atoms, including how the atoms of one element differ from the atoms of every other element.

Examples of Elements At room temperature (20°C, or 68°F), most elements are solids, including the elements aluminum and carbon. You have seen aluminum foil used to wrap food. Most soft drink cans are made from aluminum. Carbon is the main element in the marks you make with a pencil on a piece of paper. Some elements are gases at room temperature. The elements oxygen and nitrogen are the main gases in the air you breathe. Only two elements are liquids at room temperature, bromine and mercury, both of which are extremely poisonous. Figure 2 shows four elements and their symbols.

Figure 2 Aluminum, carbon, and gold are elements that you can see in common objects, such as cans, pencils, and rings. Mixtures containing iodine are used to prevent and treat infections. **Analyzing Data** *Which of these elements has a symbol that is not related to its name in English?*

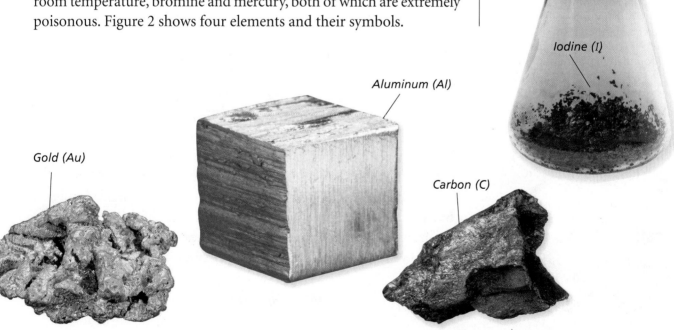

Iodine (I)

Aluminum (Al)

Gold (Au)

Carbon (C)

Silicon

Oxygen

Figure 3 Elements have different properties than their compounds. Silicon is a gray solid and oxygen is a colorless gas, which can be stored in a metal tank. Silicon and oxygen combine to form silicon dioxide—a colorless, transparent solid found in most grains of sand.

Silicon dioxide

Symbols for Elements In 1813, Jöns Berzelius, a Swedish chemist, suggested that chemists use symbols to represent elements. Many of the symbols he assigned to elements are still used. Each symbol has either one or two letters. The first letter is always capitalized. If there is a second letter, it is not capitalized.

It is easy to see why C and Al are used to represent carbon and aluminum. But why does gold have the symbol Au? The symbols that Berzelius chose were based on the Latin names of the elements. The Latin name for gold is *aurum.*

The symbols allow scientists who speak different languages to communicate without confusion. For example, nitrogen is known as *azote* in France, as *stickstoff* in Germany, and as *nitrógeno* in Mexico. But scientists who speak English, French, German, and Spanish all agree that the symbol for the element nitrogen is N.

Sometimes an element's name contains a clue to its properties. For example, the name hydrogen comes from the Greek words *hydro* and *genes,* meaning "water" and "forming."

Compounds

Water is composed of the elements hydrogen and oxygen. When electricity passes through water, bubbles of oxygen and hydrogen gas form and rise to the surface of the water. If the gases are collected in a container and a flame is brought near the mixture, the hydrogen and oxygen react and form water. Water is classified as a compound. A **compound** is a substance that is made from two or more simpler substances and can be broken down into those simpler substances. The simpler substances are either elements or other compounds.

The properties of a compound differ from those of the substances from which it is made. For example, oxygen and hydrogen are gases at room temperature, but water is a liquid. Hydrogen can fuel a fire, and oxygen can keep a fire burning, but water does not burn or help other substances to burn. In fact, water is one of the substances commonly used to put out fires.

Figure 3 shows another example of how properties change when elements join and form compounds. Silicon dioxide is a compound found in most light-colored grains of sand. It is a colorless, transparent solid. Yet, silicon dioxide is made from a colorless gas (oxygen) and a gray solid (silicon). Silicon is used to make chips for computers.

🔑 **A compound always contains two or more elements joined in a fixed proportion.** For example, in silicon dioxide, there are always two oxygen atoms for each silicon atom. (*Di-* means "two.") In water, there are always two hydrogen atoms for each oxygen atom.

 What happens if electricity passes through water?

Figure 4 The ingredients shown are used to make one kind of salsa, which is an example of a heterogeneous mixture.

Salsa

- 4 or 5 plum tomatoes
- 3–5 fresh Serrano chili peppers
- 12 sprigs of cilantro
- large garlic clove
- small white onion
- $1\frac{1}{2}$ teaspoons fresh lime juice
- $\frac{3}{4}$ teaspoon salt

Mixtures

Suppose you are making salsa using the ingredients shown in Figure 4. You have a choice. You can use exactly the amounts listed in the recipe, or you can adjust the ingredients according to your own taste. You might have to prepare the recipe a few times before deciding if you have just the right amount of each ingredient.

Mixtures tend to retain some of the properties of their individual substances. But the properties of a mixture are less constant than the properties of a substance. ⟶ **The properties of a mixture can vary because the composition of a mixture is not fixed.** The type of pepper and the quantity of pepper used in a salsa recipe determine the "hotness" of a batch of salsa. Chili peppers contain a compound called capsaicin (kap SAY uh sin) that can cause a burning sensation in your mouth. The amount of capsaicin varies among types of peppers. Cayenne peppers, for example, contain more capsaicin than do jalapeño peppers.

No matter how well you stir a batch of salsa, the ingredients will not be evenly distributed. There may, for example, be more onion in one portion of the salsa than another. Mixtures can be classified by how well the parts of the mixture are distributed throughout the mixture.

Heterogeneous Mixtures If you look at a handful of sand from a beach, the sand appears to be all the same material. However, if you use a hand lens, you will notice that the sample of sand is not the same throughout. Figure 5 shows that grains of sand vary in size. Also, some grains are light in color and some are dark. Sand is an example of a heterogeneous mixture. Heterogeneous (het uh roh GEE nee us) comes from the Greek words *hetero* and *genus,* meaning "different" and "kind." In a **heterogeneous mixture,** the parts of the mixture are noticeably different from one another.

Figure 5 Sand is a heterogeneous mixture. The spoon is stainless steel, which is a homogeneous mixture. **Interpreting Photographs** *Explain how viewing sand through a hand lens helps show that sand is a heterogeneous mixture.*

Do the Contents of Two Cans of Mixed Nuts Meet FDA Regulations?

The Food and Drug Administration (FDA) has two main areas of concern about food. First, and most important, the FDA ensures that food sold in the United States is safe to eat. Second, the FDA ensures that the information on a food label accurately describes a food product.

What can you assume when you see the label "mixed nuts" on a can of nuts? According to the FDA regulations, a can labeled *mixed nuts* must contain at least four types of shelled nuts other than peanuts. The mass of each type of nut must be not less than 2 percent of the total mass and not more than 80 percent of the total mass.

Contents of Two Cans of Mixed Nuts		
Type of Nut	Mass in Brand A	Mass in Brand B
Peanut	152.39 g	191.96 g
Almond	47.02 g	31.18 g
Brazil nut	57.88 g	19.60 g
Cashew	46.20 g	73.78 g
Hazelnut	19.90 g	16.90 g
Pecan	21.40 g	16.90 g

1. **Comparing and Contrasting** How are the two brands of mixed nuts alike? How are they different?

2. **Calculating** What is the percent by mass of each type of nut in each can?

3. **Drawing Conclusions** Do the contents of each can meet the FDA regulations? Explain.

4. **Inferring** On the Brand A label, the nuts are listed in this order: peanuts, Brazil nuts, almonds, cashews, pecans, and hazelnuts. What do you think determines the order?

Go Online

NSTA SciLINKS

For: Links on mixtures
Visit: www.SciLinks.org
Web Code: ccn-1021

Homogeneous Mixtures If you collect water from both the shallow end and the deep end of a swimming pool, the water samples will appear the same. The water in a swimming pool is a homogeneous (hoh moh GEE nee us) mixture of water and substances that dissolve in water. In a **homogeneous mixture,** the substances are so evenly distributed that it is difficult to distinguish one substance in the mixture from another. A homogeneous mixture appears to contain only one substance. The serving spoon in Figure 5 is made of stainless steel—a homogeneous mixture of iron, chromium, and nickel.

Solutions, Suspensions, and Colloids

It isn't always easy to tell a homogeneous mixture from a heterogeneous mixture. You may need to observe the properties of a mixture before you decide. The size of the particles in a mixture has an effect on the properties of the mixture. **Based on the size of its largest particles, a mixture can be classified as a solution, a suspension, or a colloid.**

Solutions If you place a spoonful of sugar in a glass of hot water and stir, the sugar dissolves in the water. The result is a homogeneous mixture of sugar and water. When substances dissolve and form a homogeneous mixture, the mixture that forms is called a **solution.** The windshield wiper fluid in Figure 6 is a solution. So is tap water.

Figure 6 The liquids shown represent three categories of mixtures. **A** Windshield wiper fluid is a solution. **B** Muddy water collected from a swamp is a suspension. **C** Milk is a colloid.
Comparing and Contrasting *Based on appearance, how are a solution and a colloid similar?*

Liquid solutions are easy to recognize. They do not separate into distinct layers over time. If you pour a liquid solution through a filter, none of the substances in the solution are trapped in the filter. You can see through solutions that are liquids because light passes through them without being scattered in all directions. These three properties of liquid solutions can be traced to the size of the particles in a solution. The particles in a solution are too small to settle out of the solution, be trapped by a filter, or scatter light.

Suspensions Have you ever seen the instruction "Shake well before using" on a bottle? This instruction is a clue that the material in the bottle is a suspension. A **suspension** is a heterogeneous mixture that separates into layers over time. For example, if you shake up a container of sand and water, the sand mixes with the water and forms a suspension. Over time, the suspended particles of sand settle to the bottom of the container.

You could use a filter to separate the sand from the water. The water would pass through the filter, but the sand would remain in the filter paper. Suspended particles settle out of a mixture or are trapped by a filter because they are larger than the particles in a solution. The worker in Figure 7 is using a mask to filter out particles of plastic foam that are suspended in air. Because larger particles can scatter light in all directions, suspensions are cloudy.

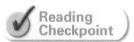 **Reading Checkpoint** *What happens to suspended particles over time?*

Figure 7 When a surfboard is sanded, particles of plastic become suspended in air. The worker wears a mask to keep from breathing in the particles.

Figure 8 The photograph shows how water droplets in fog scatter the light from high beams. The drawing compares the areas lit by high beams and low beams. **Interpreting Diagrams** *Which beams normally make a larger area of a road visible?*

High beam

Low beam

Colloids Milk is a mixture of substances including water, sugar, proteins, and fats. When fresh cow's milk is allowed to stand, a layer of cream rises to the top. This layer contains much of the fat in the milk. In the milk you buy at the store, the cream does not form a separate layer. The milk has been processed so that the fat remains dispersed throughout the milk. The result is homogenized milk, which is a colloid.

A **colloid** contains some particles that are intermediate in size between the small particles in a solution and the larger particles in a suspension. Like solutions, colloids do not separate into layers. You cannot use a filter to separate the parts of a colloid.

Fog is a colloid of water droplets in air. Figure 8 shows how fog affects which headlights a driver uses. Automobiles have headlights with low beams for normal driving conditions and high beams for roads that are poorly lit. With the high beams, a driver can see a bend in the road or an obstacle sooner. But the high beams are not useful on a foggy night because the water droplets scatter light back toward the driver and reduce visibility. With the low beams, much less light is scattered. The scattering of light is a property that can be used to distinguish colloids and suspensions from solutions.

Section 2.1 Assessment

Reviewing Concepts

1. Why does every sample of a given substance have the same properties?

2. Explain why the composition of an element is fixed.

3. Describe the composition of a compound.

4. Why can the properties of a mixture vary?

5. On what basis can mixtures be classified as solutions, suspensions, or colloids?

Critical Thinking

6. **Predicting** If you added salt instead of sugar to a pitcher of lemonade, how would this change the properties of the lemonade?

7. **Interpreting Visuals** Explain why silicon dioxide cannot be the only compound in the sample of sand shown in Figure 5.

8. **Inferring** Fresh milk is a suspension. After fresh milk is homogenized, it is a colloid. What happens to the size of the drops of fat in milk when milk is homogenized?

Writing in Science

Writing Instructions Pick a cereal that is an obvious mixture. Write rules that could be used to control the cereal's composition. Use the FDA rules for mixed nuts as a model.

2.2 Physical Properties

Reading Focus

Key Concepts
- What are some examples of physical properties?
- How can knowing the physical properties of matter be useful?
- What processes are used to separate mixtures?

Vocabulary
- ◆ physical property
- ◆ viscosity
- ◆ conductivity
- ◆ malleability
- ◆ melting point
- ◆ boiling point
- ◆ filtration
- ◆ distillation
- ◆ physical change

Reading Strategy
Building Vocabulary Copy the table. As you read, write a definition for each property.

Physical Property	Definition
Viscosity	a. ?
Malleability	b. ?
Melting point	c. ?

If there are pitchers of ice water and lemonade on a picnic table, how do you know which liquid is in each pitcher? It's easy! The lemonade is yellow. Lemonade also has a tart taste that is hard to miss. A yellow color and a tart taste are two properties of lemonade.

Examples of Physical Properties

A **physical property** is any characteristic of a material that can be observed or measured without changing the composition of the substances in the material. **Viscosity, conductivity, malleability, hardness, melting point, boiling point, and density are examples of physical properties.**

Viscosity Suppose you knock over an open bottle of vinegar and an open jar of honey at exactly the same time. In the time it takes for the vinegar bottle to empty, the honey will scarcely start to flow. The tendency of a liquid to keep from flowing—its resistance to flowing—is called its **viscosity**. The greater the viscosity, the slower the liquid moves. Thick liquids, such as corn syrup and the honey in Figure 9, have a high viscosity. Thin liquids, such as vinegar, have a low viscosity.

The viscosity of a liquid usually decreases when it is heated. For example, a spoonful of cooking oil will spread more quickly across the bottom of a heated frying pan than across the bottom of a cold pan.

Why is the viscosity of a liquid important? Consider the motor oil used to keep the parts of an automobile engine from wearing away as they move past one another. The motor oil must not be too thick in cold weather or too thin in hot weather.

Figure 9 The object in the photograph is called a honey dipper. Honey is an example of a liquid with a high viscosity.

Liquid crystal thermometer
Metal rod
Wooden rod
Foam cups

Quick Lab

Comparing Heat Conductors

Materials

2 plastic foam cups, scissors, metric ruler, metal rod, wooden rod, 2 liquid crystal thermometers, hot water, clock or watch with second hand

Procedure

1. Make a data table with a column for time and a column to record the temperature of each rod.

2. Cut 3 cm off the top of one cup. Turn the cup upside down. Use the metal rod to make two holes about 3 cm apart in the bottom.

3. Attach a thermometer to each rod as shown.

4. Insert both rods so they will just touch the bottom of the second cup. Lay the cup with the rods on the table. Do not touch the rods and thermometers during the experiment.

5. Ask your teacher to add hot water to the intact cup until it is about three fourths full.

6. Hold the cup with the hot water firmly as you place the cup with the rods on top of it. **CAUTION** *Be careful not to overturn the cup.*

7. Observe and record the temperatures every minute for five minutes.

Analyze and Conclude

1. **Comparing and Contrasting** Is metal or wood a better conductor of heat? Explain.

2. **Applying Concepts** Is a metal cup a good container for keeping a drink hot for as long as possible? Give a reason for your answer.

3. **Evaluating** Describe any variables, other than the type of material, that were not controlled in this lab.

Conductivity Which spoon should you choose for stirring a pot of soup heating on the stove—a metal spoon or a wooden spoon? If one end of a metal object is heated, the other end will soon feel hot. A material's ability to allow heat to flow is called **conductivity.**

Materials that have a high conductivity, such as metals, are called conductors. If a material is a good conductor of heat, it is usually also a good conductor of electricity. Wood is not a good conductor of heat. You can stir hot soup with a wooden spoon without worrying about burning your hand because the wooden spoon stays cool to the touch.

Figure 10 Because gold is both malleable and beautiful, it is often used to make jewelry. These ancient gold medallions were made to form a necklace.

Malleability The ancient gold objects in Figure 10 were found in a tomb in Greece. A goldsmith made the medallions by tapping gold with a small hammer and punch. Gold can be shaped in this way because it is malleable. **Malleability** (mal ee uh BIL uh tee) is the ability of a solid to be hammered without shattering. Most metals are malleable. By contrast, an ice cube breaks into small pieces when struck with a hammer. So does ordinary glass when hit by a fast-moving object such as a baseball. Solids that shatter when struck are brittle.

Reading Checkpoint *Why would a cook use a wooden spoon to stir hot soup?*

Hardness One way to compare the hardness of two materials is to see which of the materials can scratch the other. The blade of a typical kitchen knife, for example, can scratch a copper sheet because stainless steel is harder than copper. The stainless steel in a knife blade is a hard solid that can be shaped into a sharp cutting edge. The material used to sharpen the blade must be harder than stainless steel. Diamond is the hardest known material. Some of the grinding wheels used to sharpen steel contain small grains of diamond. The man in Figure 11 is carving a canoe from a soft wood—Western red cedar.

Figure 11 This Tlingit carver is using an adze to carve a canoe from Western red cedar. Red cedar is a relatively soft wood.

Melting and Boiling Points If you leave a tray of ice cubes on your kitchen counter, the ice cubes will melt. The temperature at which a substance changes from solid to liquid is its **melting point.** For water, this change normally occurs at 0°C. If you heat water to cook pasta at sea level, the water will start to boil at 100°C. The temperature at which a substance boils is its **boiling point.** Figure 12 shows the melting point and the boiling point for some substances.

Density Density can be used to test the purity of a substance. Recall that density is the ratio of the mass of a substance to its volume. At room temperature, silver has a density of 10.5 g/cm^3. If a coin has a density of 9.9 g/cm^3 at room temperature, either the coin is not made from silver or the coin contains substances in addition to silver.

Density can be used to test the purity of methanol. Methanol is a fuel burned in some racing motorcycles. The American Motorcycle Association (AMA) requires racers to use fuel that is at least 99.65 percent pure. Race officials may collect a sample of fuel and measure its temperature and density. Then they compare the measured density to the expected density of methanol at that temperature. These spot checks keep racers from adding substances to the fuel that will give them an unfair advantage in a race.

Melting and Boiling Points of Some Substances		
Substance	**Melting Point**	**Boiling Point**
Hydrogen	−259.3°C	−252.9°C
Nitrogen	−210.0°C	−195.8°C
Ammonia	−77.7°C	−33.3°C
Octane (found in gasoline)	−56.8°C	125.6°C
Water	0.0°C	100.0°C
Acetic acid (found in vinegar)	16.6°C	117.9°C
Table salt	800.7°C	1465°C
Gold	1064.2°C	2856°C

Figure 12 The table lists the melting points and boiling points for several substances.
Analyzing Data *Which of these substances are liquids at room temperature (20°C, or 68°F)?*

Using Physical Properties

People use data about physical properties to solve many different types of problems. ⬤ **Physical properties are used to identify a material, to choose a material for a specific purpose, or to separate the substances in a mixture.**

Using Properties to Identify Materials

The steps used to identify a material are similar to the steps used to test for purity. The first step is to decide which properties to test. The second step is to do tests on a sample of the unknown. The final step is to compare the results with the data reported for known materials.

The identification of a material can be a crucial step in solving a crime. A detective collects red paint chips from the scene of a hit-and-run accident. He asks a chemist at the crime lab to use the chips to identify the model of the missing vehicle. Because paint is a mixture of substances, the chemist can do tests that distinguish one type of red paint from another. The technician compares the data she collects to an FBI database. The database contains information about the paints used on different makes and models of cars. Once the detective knows the make and model, he uses a database of registered owners to create a list of possible suspects.

Using Properties to Choose Materials

Properties determine which materials are chosen for which uses. For example, you wouldn't want shoelaces made from wood. Shoelaces must be flexible, that is, they must be able to bend without breaking. They must also be durable, that is, they must be able to withstand repeated use. Laces in hiking boots like those in Figure 13 are usually nylon or leather.

People don't consider just one property when choosing a material for a particular application. They look at a set of properties. For example, the How It Works box on page 49 explains how the properties of wax are used when clay molds are made for casting metal sculptures.

Figure 13 Shoelaces for hiking boots are sometimes made from leather. So are some belts and shoes. **Making Generalizations** *What properties of leather would make it a suitable material for all three types of objects?*

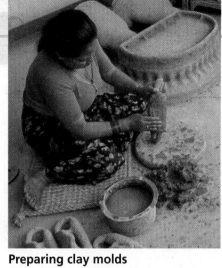

Making a Sculpture

A process called lost-wax casting is used to make metal sculptures. Different stages of the process depend on physical properties of wax, clay, and metal. Wax can be carved and molded. Clay becomes brittle when baked at a high temperature. When melted, most metals form homogeneous mixtures, which can be poured into molds.

Interpreting Diagrams *Why is it important that wax has a low melting point?*

Preparing clay molds
This artist from Nepal in southern Asia is preparing molds for lost-wax casting. She is applying layers of clay to a wax model.

1 Wax model A wax model of the sculpture is built up around a clay core. Wax is used because it is soft enough for carving fine details, but hard enough to retain its shape at room temperature.

Wax model

Layers of clay applied to the wax model

Clay core

Wax model

Melting wax

Cast metal sculpture

Molten metal poured into mold

Broken clay

2 Clay mold Clay is applied to the wax model in layers of increasing coarseness, and left to dry. The inner, finer layers capture every detail of the sculpture in a smooth mold. The outer, coarser layers (clay mixed with sand) provide strength.

3 Melting wax The clay-covered wax model is then baked in a kiln. Because wax has a low melting point, the wax model melts away inside the clay, leaving a hardened shell mold. This clay mold is then used to make the final sculpture.

4 Molten metal Molten (liquid) metal is poured into the clay mold and left to cool and harden. For this sculpture of an African head, a mixture of copper, zinc, and lead was used.

5 Metal sculpture When the metal has cooled, the clay shell is broken open to reveal the finished metal sculpture.

Figure 14 These Americorps students are looking for artifacts at the San Diego Presidio—a fort that was built in 1769. As the students sift dirt through a screen, small objects buried in the dirt collect on the screen. *Applying Concepts How could changing the size of the holes in a screen change the number of objects found?*

Using Properties to Separate Mixtures

Some properties can be used to separate mixtures. ● **Filtration and distillation are two common separation methods.**

Filtration One way to make a pot of tea is to pour hot water over loose tea leaves. Some compounds in the tea leaves, such as caffeine, dissolve in the water. You can separate the hot tea from the loose leaves by pouring the mixture through a strainer. Using a strainer is a type of filtration. **Filtration** is a process that separates materials based on the size of their particles. Particles of the compounds that dissolve are small enough to pass through the strainer, but the tea leaves themselves are too large to pass through the strainer. The drip method of brewing coffee also uses a filter to separate the brewed coffee from the coffee grounds.

The students in Figure 14 are using a wire screen to locate small objects buried in the sand at an archaeological site. Particles of dirt are small enough to pass through the holes in the screen, but objects such as broken bits of pottery are too large to pass through the screen.

Distillation How can you separate the parts of a solution when all the particles in a solution are small enough to pass through a filter? Sometimes distillation can work. **Distillation** is a process that separates the substances in a solution based on their boiling points.

One practical use of distillation is to provide fresh water for submarines. Most submarines can store only enough fresh water to last about ten days. Each submarine has equipment that can convert seawater into fresh water. The water is heated until it changes from a liquid to a gas. The gas is cooled until it changes back to a liquid, which is collected in a separate container. Boiling can separate fresh water from seawater because water has a much lower boiling point than the compounds dissolved in seawater. These compounds are left behind in the original container.

For: Articles on properties of matter

Visit: PHSchool.com

Web Code: cce-1022

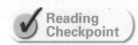
Reading Checkpoint *How can loose tea leaves be removed from a pot of brewed tea?*

Recognizing Physical Changes

The change of water from a liquid to a gas during boiling is a physical change. A **physical change** occurs when some of the properties of a material change, but the substances in the material remain the same. For example, if you slowly heat butter in a pan, it changes from a solid to a liquid, but the substances in the butter do not change. Two other examples of physical changes are crumpling a piece of paper and slicing a tomato. Crumpling and slicing are actions that change the size and shape of a material, but not its composition.

Some physical changes can be reversed. You can freeze water, melt the ice that forms, and then freeze the water again. You can use an iron to remove the wrinkles from a cotton shirt. You can braid hair, unbraid the hair, and then braid it again. Some physical changes cannot be reversed. You would not expect to reconstruct a whole tomato from tomato slices or to replace the peel on a peeled orange. Figure 15 shows one physical change that can be reversed and one that cannot be reversed.

Figure 15 Braiding hair and cutting hair are examples of physical changes. Braiding is a reversible change. Cutting cannot be reversed.

Section 2.2 Assessment

Reviewing Concepts

1. List seven examples of physical properties.
2. Describe three uses of physical properties.
3. Name two processes that are used to separate mixtures.
4. When you describe a liquid as thick, are you saying that it has a high or a low viscosity?
5. Explain why sharpening a pencil is an example of a physical change.
6. What allows a mixture to be separated by distillation?

Critical Thinking

7. **Designing Experiments** How could you find out whether copper is harder or softer than the plastic used in a plastic cup?

8. **Inferring** Why would you expect the materials used to make pot holders to be poor conductors of heat?
9. **Applying Concepts** Silicon dioxide is a solid at room temperature and methanol is a liquid. Which substance has the higher melting point?

Connecting Concepts

Organizing Data In what order are the substances arranged in Figure 12? Use what you studied about organizing data in Section 1.4 to explain why this order is useful. Explain why you might choose a different order if you had similar data for 500 substances.

Getting a Fresh Start

Water found in nature is never 100 percent pure. There are always substances dissolved in the water. Some of these substances, as well as bacteria and particles of dirt, must be removed before the water is fit to drink.

Reservoir

1 Coarse filter A screen prevents large items such as leaves from entering the water treatment plant.

Coarse filter screen

Outlet tower

Aeration tank

2 Aeration During aeration, air may be bubbled into the water or water may be sprayed into the air. Aeration removes substances from water, such as iron compounds, that give water an unpleasant taste.

Alum (aluminum sulfate) added

Colloid forms.

Layer of lumps

Cleaned water spills over into a trough.

3 Forming a colloid Alum is added to the mixing tank. Alum causes small particles in the water to form a type of colloid called a gel. Most of the bacteria in the water are trapped in the gel.

4 Sedimentation In the sedimentation tank, large lumps slowly settle to the bottom of the tank from where they can be removed.

Sedimentation tank

Water from the ground About half of the drinking water in the United States comes from natural underground sources. Although this groundwater is filtered as it passes through rocks and sand, it sometimes contains high levels of dissolved minerals or chemical pollutants. So groundwater is purified using a modified version of surface water filtration.

6 Carbon filter The water is sometimes passed through a carbon filter. This filter removes tiny amounts of dissolved impurities, and improves the water's taste and color.

Water storage tank

Water softener added

Fluorine compound added

Chlorine added

5 Sand and gravel filter Next, the water trickles through sand and gravel filter beds, which trap the remaining suspended particles. Because the filter beds can become clogged, they are washed every 24 hours.

Carbon filter

Gravel layer

Filtered water

Sand layer

7 Additives The fluorine compound prevents tooth decay and the chlorine kills bacteria. The water softener removes some magnesium and calcium compounds.

8 Storage Finally, the water is held in storage tanks before passing into the public water supply.

Going Further

- Some people use a system to purify water at home. Research one of these systems. Gather information from at least two sources. Describe how the system works. Compare the method used to the processes that occur at a water purification plant.

- Evaluate the sources you used and identify any possible biases.

2.3 Chemical Properties

Reading Focus

Key Concepts

- When can chemical properties be observed?
- What observations might indicate that a chemical change has occurred?
- What is the difference between chemical and physical changes?

Vocabulary

- chemical property
- flammability
- reactivity
- chemical change
- precipitate

Reading Strategy

Relating Text and Visuals Copy the table. Find examples of the clues for recognizing chemical changes in Figures 19 and 20.

Clue	Example
Change in color	a.____?____
Production of gas	b.____?____
Formation of precipitate	c.____?____

How would you describe candles like the ones in Figure 16? You might describe their color or their hardness. Or, you might observe that the candles float on water, and conclude that the density of candle wax is less than that of water. Color, hardness, and density are physical properties. But there is something else about the candles that may seem even more obvious to you: the fact that the candles are burning. The ability to burn is not a physical property because you cannot observe burning without changing the composition of the material that is burning. As a candle burns, new substances form.

Observing Chemical Properties

Most candles are made from paraffin, which is a mixture of compounds containing carbon and hydrogen. As a candle burns, the compounds combine with oxygen in the air to form water and carbon dioxide. (Carbon dioxide is the gas that gives a carbonated beverage its fizz.) The ability to burn is a chemical property. A **chemical property** is any ability to produce a change in the composition of matter. **Chemical properties can be observed only when the substances in a sample of matter are changing into different substances.** Flammability and reactivity are two examples of chemical properties.

Flammability Materials that burn can be used as fuel. Sometimes, people use burning newspapers to start a fire in a fireplace. Gasoline is the fuel burned in most automobiles. The chemical property that paper and gasoline share is their flammability. **Flammability** is a material's ability to burn in the presence of oxygen.

Figure 16 When candles burn, new substances form. The ability to burn is a chemical property.

Sometimes flammability is not a desirable property. For example, there are laws that regulate the flammability of fabrics. The fabrics used in children's sleepwear must have a low flammability. These fabrics are described as flame-resistant because they are difficult to ignite. If they do ignite, they burn slowly.

Reactivity The property that describes how readily a substance combines chemically with other substances is **reactivity.** Nitrogen and oxygen are the main gases in air. Oxygen is a highly reactive element. Nitrogen has an extremely low reactivity.

Oxygen reacts easily with most other elements. Figure 17 shows the rust that forms when oxygen reacts with iron and water. Rust is a brittle, reddish-brown compound. A rusty chain or bolt is more likely to break than a new chain or bolt because rust is weaker than iron. Because iron is highly reactive, you would not choose iron to make decorative objects, such as jewelry or coins.

Many uses of nitrogen depend on its low reactivity. For example, seawater is often stored in steel tanks located below the lowest deck of a ship. The seawater helps to keep the ship stable in the water. Over time, rust forms in the tanks because iron in the steel reacts with oxygen dissolved in the water. Researchers in Japan have developed a way to reduce the amount of rust produced. They pump nitrogen gas into the tanks, and the nitrogen displaces the dissolved oxygen.

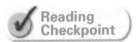 **Reading Checkpoint** *Which element is more reactive—oxygen or nitrogen?*

Go Online
NSTA SciLINKS

For: Links on chemical and physical changes
Visit: www.SciLinks.org
Web Code: ccn-1023

Figure 17 This automobile must have been exposed to air and water for many years.
Drawing Conclusions *What evidence is there that parts of the automobile contained iron?*

Quick Lab

Identifying a Chemical Change

Materials

3 test tubes; test-tube rack; glass-marking pencil; 3 10-mL graduated cylinders; solutions of copper sulfate, calcium chloride, and sodium chloride

Procedure

1. Construct a data table with columns labeled Test Tube, Contents, and Observations.

2. Label the test tubes A, B, and C.

3. Pour 5 mL of copper sulfate solution into test tube A. Pour 5 mL of calcium chloride solution into test tube B. Pour 5 mL of sodium chloride solution into test tube C. **CAUTION** *Do not allow the solutions to touch your skin. They may cause irritation.*

4. Add 5 mL of calcium chloride solution to test tube A. Add 5 mL of sodium chloride solution to test tube B. Add 5 mL of copper sulfate solution to test tube C.

5. Examine the test tubes for evidence of a chemical change. Record your observations.

6. Pour the contents of the test tubes into the sink. Rinse out the test tubes and flush the contents down the drain. **CAUTION** *Wash your hands thoroughly with soap or detergent before leaving the laboratory.*

Analyze and Conclude

1. **Inferring** In which test tube(s) did a chemical change occur? Explain your answer.

2. **Evaluating** Can you be sure that a chemical change occurred? Explain your answer.

Recognizing Chemical Changes

Figure 18 shows what happens to banana peels as bananas ripen. The color change in a banana peel is caused by chemical changes that are taking place in the cells of the banana. A **chemical change** occurs when a substance reacts and forms one or more new substances. Chemical changes occur when a cake bakes in an oven, leaves on trees change color, and food is digested in your stomach.

How can you recognize a chemical change? You have to look for clues. For example, when food spoils, it often gives off an unpleasant odor. 🔑 **Three common types of evidence for a chemical change are a change in color, the production of a gas, and the formation of a precipitate.**

Figure 18 As a banana ripens, chemical changes cause the peel to change color from green to yellow. In a banana that is overly ripe, different chemical changes cause the peel to turn brown. **Observing** *Based on your experience, what other properties of a banana change as it ripens?*

A Change in Color Over time, a shiny silver bracelet that is exposed to air will darken. As a match burns, it shrivels up and turns black. The new copper roof and the old copper roof in Figure 19 have different colors. In each of these examples, a change in color is a clue that a chemical change has produced at least one new substance.

Production of a Gas Figure 20A shows what happens when you mix vinegar with baking soda. Bubbles of carbon dioxide form immediately. A similar chemical change happens when you use baking powder as an ingredient in a cake recipe. Baking powder is a mixture of baking soda and one or more acids that react when wet. As the cake bakes, the bubbles of carbon dioxide expand and cause the cake to rise.

Formation of a Precipitate Another chemical change you can observe in the kitchen is the curdling of milk. If you add lemon juice or vinegar to milk, small bits of white solid will separate from the liquid. Any solid that forms and separates from a liquid mixture is called a **precipitate.** When an acid is added to milk, proteins in the milk undergo a chemical change that alters their structure, causing them to stick together in clumps. They form the precipitate shown in Figure 20B.

Figure 19 When copper is exposed to moist air, it forms a thin coating called a patina. A new copper roof has a reddish color. The green patina on an old copper roof is a mixture of copper compounds.
Predicting *Would a patina form faster in a rainy climate or in a dry climate?*

> **Reading Checkpoint** *What happens when you add vinegar to baking soda?*

A

Figure 20 The formation of a gas or a precipitate can be a clue to chemical change. **A** Carbon dioxide gas forms when vinegar is mixed with baking soda. **B** The curds in cottage cheese form when an acid is added to milk.

B

Figure 21 A blacksmith uses a hammer to shape a horseshoe that has been heated. Although the color of the iron horseshoe changes, no chemical change is occurring. **Inferring** *Other than color, what physical property of iron is affected by heating?*

Is a Change Chemical or Physical?

It is not always easy to distinguish a chemical change from a physical change. Even if you observe a color change, a gas, or a precipitate, you cannot be sure that a chemical change has taken place. When the iron horseshoe in Figure 21 is heated, its color changes from gray to red. Despite this change in color, the iron is still iron. When water boils on a stove, the bubbles of gas that rise to the surface are still water.

Before you decide whether or not a chemical change has occurred, ask yourself this question: Are different substances present after the change takes place? If not, then the change is physical, not chemical. ⬤ **When matter undergoes a chemical change, the composition of the matter changes. When matter undergoes a physical change, the composition of the matter remains the same.**

Section 2.3 Assessment

Reviewing Concepts

1. ⬤ Under what conditions can chemical properties be observed?

2. ⬤ List three common types of evidence for a chemical change.

3. ⬤ How do chemical changes differ from physical changes?

4. Explain why the rusting of an iron bar decreases the strength of the bar.

5. A pat of butter melts and then burns in a hot frying pan. Which of these changes is physical and which is chemical?

Critical Thinking

6. **Comparing and Contrasting** Compare the properties of a raw egg to those of a hard-boiled egg.

7. **Classifying** If you spill household bleach on denim jeans, you will observe that the area of the spill no longer has a blue color. Is this change chemical or physical? Give a reason for your answer.

8. **Inferring** Gold and platinum are often used to make jewelry. What can you infer about the reactivity of these elements?

Connecting C Concepts

Scientific Methods Section 1.2 listed typical steps scientists use. Which steps might you use to decide whether a change is physical or chemical? Explain.

What Should Be Done With Arsenic-Treated Wood?

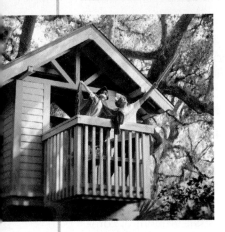

Termites are among the organisms that attack untreated wood. In 1950, United States suppliers of lumber began to treat wood with a mixture of copper, chromium, and arsenic (CCA). The mixture slows the damage to wood by poisoning the attacking organisms. Outdoor structures such as decks and porches were made from CCA-treated wood. By 2002, more than 95 percent of treated lumber sold for use outdoors contained CCA.

Arsenic is a poison that has been linked with certain types of cancer. Arsenic can be absorbed through the skin or ingested in water or food. Consumers were especially concerned about children touching CCA-treated wood and then placing their unwashed fingers in their mouths. Some consumers asked the Environmental Protection Agency (EPA) to ban the use of CCA. In 2002, the chemical and home-improvement industries agreed to stop producing CCA-treated wood for home use.

The Viewpoints

Old CCA-Treated Wood Does Not Need to Be Removed

The EPA did not recommend tearing down existing structures made from CCA-treated wood. A panel of Florida doctors reported that they found no studies linking cancer in children and exposure to CCA-treated wood. They concluded that the amount of arsenic that children could absorb from treated wood is small compared to the amount of arsenic that occurs naturally in soil.

There are risks associated with disposing of treated wood. Burning arsenic-treated wood produces ash with high levels of arsenic. The ash would poison a person who inhaled, ingested, or touched it. The only acceptable method of disposal is in landfills, which are rapidly filling. Also, arsenic from landfills can end up in groundwater.

Old CCA-Treated Wood Needs to Be Removed

A report produced by one state's Department of Environmental Protection concluded that there is a serious risk for children exposed to arsenic from treated wood. The level of arsenic remains high for 20 years in CCA-treated wood. The useful life of most treated wood products is about 20 years.

An area of CCA-treated wood the size of a four-year-old's hand contains about 120 times the amount of arsenic allowed in a 6-ounce glass of water. (The EPA limit for arsenic in drinking water is 10 parts per billion.) Rainwater penetrates wood and dissolves arsenic. The arsenic ends up on the surface of the wood or in the soil near the wood.

Research and Decide

1. **Defining the Issue** In your own words, describe the issue that needs to be resolved about existing structures made from CCA-treated wood.

2. **Analyzing the Viewpoints** List three arguments of those who don't think that existing structures made from CCA-treated wood need to be removed. List three arguments of those who want to remove existing structures made from CCA-treated wood.

3. **Forming Your Opinion** Should existing structures built from CCA-treated wood be removed? Which argument did you find most convincing?

For: More on this issue
Visit: PHSchool.com
Web Code: cch-1020

Using Properties to Identify Materials

Forensic chemists test the physical and chemical properties of materials found at a crime scene. They also do similar tests on the materials found on a suspect's skin or clothing. These materials are often complex mixtures, such as soil, which contain many substances. In this lab, you will compare the properties of three known materials with two samples of "evidence." These samples represent evidence from a crime scene and evidence from a suspect's shoe. Although your materials and equipment are less complex than those used by forensic chemists, your overall method will be similar to the methods they use.

Problem Can the properties of materials that appear similar be used to tell them apart?

Materials
- 2 spot plates
- glass-marking pencil
- 5 laboratory spatulas
- cornstarch
- baking soda
- baking powder
- wash bottle of water
- vinegar
- iodine solution
- sample from crime scene
- sample from suspect's shoe

Skills Observing, Inferring, Predicting

Procedure

Part A: Properties of Known Substances

1. On a separate sheet of paper, copy the data table shown.

2. Use a glass-marking pencil to label 15 wells A through O on the spot plates. Make a mark next to each well, not in the well.

3. Use a spatula to place a small amount of cornstarch in wells A, B, and C. Record any physical properties of the cornstarch that you observe.

4. Use a clean spatula to place a small amount of baking soda in wells D, E, and F. Record any physical properties of baking soda you observe.

5. Using a clean spatula, place a small amount of baking powder in wells G, H, and I. Record any physical properties of baking powder you observe.

6. Fill wells A, D, and G with water. Record any changes you observe.

Data Table				
Sample	Description	Result of Adding Water	Result of Adding Vinegar	Result of Adding Iodine
Cornstarch				
Baking soda				
Baking powder				
Crime scene sample				
Sample from suspect's shoe				

7. Fill wells B, E, and H with vinegar. Record any changes you observe.

8. Add one drop of iodine solution to wells C, F, and I. Record any changes you observe.
CAUTION *Iodine solution is corrosive and poisonous. It can stain skin and clothing. Rinse any iodine spills with water.*

Part B: Properties of Unknown Substances

9. Predicting Look at the sample from the crime scene and the sample from the suspect's shoe. Based on your observations, predict whether testing will show that the samples are identical. Record your prediction.

10. Use a clean spatula to place a small amount of the sample from the crime scene in wells J, K, and L. Record any physical properties of the sample that you observe.

11. Use a clean laboratory spatula to place a small amount of the sample from the suspect's shoe in wells M, N, and O. Record any physical properties of the sample that you observe.

12. Fill wells J and M with water. Record your observations.

13. Fill wells K and N with vinegar. Record your observations.

14. Add one drop of iodine solution to wells L and O. Record your observations.

15. Rinse all materials off the spot plates and flush them down the drain with at least ten times as much water. Dispose of your plastic gloves as directed by your teacher. **CAUTION** *Wash your hands thoroughly with soap or detergent before leaving the laboratory.*

Analyze and Conclude

1. Analyzing Data Were you able to use the ability to dissolve in water to distinguish all three materials? Explain.

2. Drawing Conclusions Are the samples from the suspect and from the crime scene identical?

3. Evaluating and Revising Did the data you collected support your prediction? Explain your answer.

Go Further Design an experiment to determine the effect of heating on the materials you tested in this lab. With your teacher's approval and supervision, carry out your experiment and use the data you collect to identify a sample of an unknown material.

Study Guide

2.1 Classifying Matter

Key Concepts

- Every sample of a given substance has the same properties because a substance has a fixed, uniform composition.
- An element has a fixed composition because it contains only one type of atom.
- A compound always contains two or more elements joined in a fixed proportion.
- The properties of a mixture can vary because the composition of a mixture is not fixed.
- Based on the size of its largest particles, a mixture can be classified as a solution, a suspension, or a colloid.

Vocabulary

pure substance, *p. 39*

element, *p. 39*

atom, *p. 39*

compound, *p. 40*

heterogeneous mixture, *p. 41*

homogeneous mixture, *p. 42*

solution, *p. 42*

suspension, *p. 43*

colloid, *p. 44*

2.2 Physical Properties

Key Concepts

- Viscosity, conductivity, malleability, hardness, melting point, boiling point, and density are examples of physical properties.
- Physical properties are used to identify a material, to choose a material for a specific purpose, or to separate the substances in a mixture.
- Filtration and distillation are two common separation methods.

Vocabulary

physical property, *p. 45*

viscosity, *p. 45*

conductivity, *p. 46*

malleability, *p. 46*

melting point, *p. 47*

boiling point, *p. 47*

filtration, *p. 50*

distillation, *p. 50*

physical change, *p. 51*

2.3 Chemical Properties

Key Concepts

- Chemical properties can be observed only when the substances in a sample of matter are changing into different substances.
- Three common types of evidence for a chemical change are a change in color, the production of a gas, and the formation of a precipitate.
- When matter undergoes a chemical change, the composition of the matter changes. When matter undergoes a physical change, the composition of the matter remains the same.

Vocabulary

chemical property, *p. 54*

flammability, *p. 54*

reactivity, *p. 55*

chemical change, *p. 56*

precipitate, *p. 57*

Thinking Visually

Concept Map Use information from the chapter to complete the concept map below.

Reviewing Content

Choose the letter that best answers the question or completes the statement.

1. Which of these substances is not an element?
   a. water
   b. hydrogen
   c. aluminum
   d. iron

2. Tap water is
   a. an element.
   b. a compound.
   c. a substance.
   d. a mixture.

3. When a homemade oil-and-vinegar salad dressing is left standing, it separates into layers. The salad dressing is a
   a. solution.
   b. suspension.
   c. colloid.
   d. compound.

4. Which of the following is not an example of a physical property?
   a. density
   b. flammability
   c. hardness
   d. melting point

5. Which material is a poor conductor of heat?
   a. iron
   b. silver
   c. wood
   d. copper

6. A material that can be hit without shattering is
   a. viscous.
   b. flammable.
   c. malleable.
   d. hard.

7. At room temperature, a substance with a melting point of 40°C is a
   a. solid.
   b. liquid.
   c. gas.
   d. mixture.

8. Which action involves a chemical change?
   a. making ice cubes
   b. adding sugar to tea
   c. cutting wrapping paper
   d. baking a cake

9. A substance that has little tendency to change into other substances is said to have low
   a. reactivity.
   b. density.
   c. viscosity.
   d. conductivity.

10. Formation of a precipitate is usually evidence of
    a. the separation of a mixture.
    b. a chemical change.
    c. the formation of a mixture.
    d. a physical change.

Understanding Concepts

11. Explain why the properties of a pure substance do not vary from sample to sample.

12. What is the difference between an element and a compound?

13. How does the composition of a mixture of hydrogen and oxygen differ from the composition of a compound containing hydrogen and oxygen?

14. Suppose all the grains in a sample of sand were exactly the same size. Could the sample still be a heterogeneous mixture? Explain your answer.

15. What allows a mixture to be separated by filtration?

16. Explain why viscosity is classified as a physical property.

17. Based on these pieces of pottery found in Grand Canyon National Park, would you describe pottery as a malleable or brittle material?

18. A sample of copper can be drawn into a thin wire. Is this property of copper a physical property or a chemical property? Explain.

19. Name one physical property and one chemical property of wood.

20. Why is breaking down a compound into its elements considered a chemical change?

21. List one physical change and one chemical change that occur when a candle burns.

22. Suppose you need to identify the material in an object without changing the object in any way. Should you use physical or chemical properties to identify the material? Explain your choice.

Critical Thinking

23. Applying Concepts Ammonia is a compound of hydrogen and nitrogen that dissolves easily in water. Can you conclude that hydrogen and nitrogen dissolve in water? Explain your answer.

24. Posing Questions What information would you need to know about a sample of air before you could classify the sample as a solution, suspension, or colloid?

25. Applying Concepts Explain why you cannot use mass or volume alone to identify substances.

Use the table to answer questions 26 and 27.

Melting Points and Densities of Some Substances

Substance	Melting Point	Density
Aluminum	660.3°C	2.70 g/cm³
Table salt	800.7°C	2.17 g/cm³
Isopropyl alcohol	−89.5°C	0.78 g/cm³
Bromine	−7.2°C	3.10 g/cm³
Water	0.0°C	1.00 g/cm³
Gold	1064.2°C	19.3 g/cm³

26. Analyzing Data You have a solid with a density of 0.78 g/cm³. Is it possible that this solid is one of the substances listed in the table? Explain.

27. Using Tables A solid, rectangular block of material floats on water. Is it possible that the block is pure gold? Explain your answer.

28. Drawing Conclusions At room temperature, two white solids have the same density. With just this information, is it possible to conclude that the two solids are the same material? Explain.

29. Designing Experiments How could you use density to show that a gold bracelet contains elements other than gold?

30. Inferring Suppose you mix two colorless liquids together and a green solid settles to the bottom of the container. Explain why you might be confident that a chemical change has taken place.

Concepts in Action

31. Comparing and Contrasting The photo shows maple sap being collected in a bucket. The sap is about 97% water and 3% sugar with traces of other compounds. Cans of 100% pure maple syrup contain about 34% water and 66% sugar. Which would have the greater viscosity—the maple sap or the maple syrup? Give a reason for your answer.

32. Inferring One of the general safety instructions for working in a laboratory is to tie back long hair, especially when using a lab burner. From this instruction, what can you infer about the flammability of hair?

33. Applying Concepts Why might valuable documents be stored in pure nitrogen instead of in air? Recall that air is a mixture of gases, including nitrogen and oxygen.

34. Relating Cause and Effect Explain why painting an iron railing can slow down the rate at which the railing rusts.

35. Writing in Science Cheesecloth is a type of cotton cloth used by cooks. Write a paragraph explaining why a cook might wrap a lemon wedge in cheesecloth before squeezing juice from the lemon. What process for separating mixtures is the cook using?

Performance-Based Assessment

Writing in a Journal Keep a journal for a day. List five physical changes and five chemical changes that you observe. Be sure to describe why you think each change is physical or chemical.

For: Self-grading assessment
Visit: PHSchool.com
Web Code: cca-1020

Standardized Test Prep

Test-Taking Tip

Using Models

For some test questions, you will be asked to decide what a visual model represents. Look at the model below. Notice that there are two types of particles shown and notice how the particles are distributed. Use what you observe to decide which answer is the best choice.

What type of matter does the model represent?
(A) a solution
(B) a colloid
(C) a suspension
(D) an element
(E) a homogeneous mixture

(Answer: C)

Choose the letter that best answers the question or completes the statement.

1. All pure substances
   (A) contain only one type of atom.
   (B) can be broken down into simpler substances.
   (C) cannot be broken down into simpler substances.
   (D) have a fixed composition.
   (E) have a variable composition.

2. Which property can be used to separate a mixture by distillation?
   (A) melting point
   (B) boiling point
   (C) density
   (D) viscosity
   (E) conductivity

3. During which of these events does a chemical change occur?
   (A) Ice cubes melt.
   (B) A pot of water boils.
   (C) A heated iron bar turns red.
   (D) A paper clip is bent.
   (E) A cake rises in the oven.

4. You can be certain that a change is a chemical change if
   (A) the change cannot be reversed.
   (B) new substances form.
   (C) bubbles are produced.
   (D) a precipitate forms.
   (E) there is a color change.

Use the drawings to answer Questions 5 and 6.

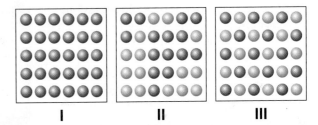

I   II   III

5. Which of the drawings could represent a homogeneous mixture?
   (A) drawing I
   (B) drawing II
   (C) drawing III
   (D) drawings I and III
   (E) drawings II and III

6. Which of the drawings could represent an element?
   (A) drawing I
   (B) drawing II
   (C) drawing III
   (D) drawings I and III
   (E) drawings II and III

3 States of Matter

When temperatures rise in the spring, the ice begins to melt on Bow Lake at Banff National Park in Alberta, Canada.

21st Century Learning

Creativity and Intellectual Curiosity

What can you find out about plasma or Bose-Einstein condensates?

You are probably familiar with three common states of matter—solid, liquid, and gas. But scientists also recognize two states of matter that are more rare: plasma and Bose-Einstein condensate. Choose one of these for a research project. Find out how scientists define this particular state of matter and under what conditions it forms. Present your research to the class by posting on your class blog or wiki.

How do science concepts apply to your world? Here are some questions you'll be able to answer after you read this chapter.

- **How can balloons have many different shapes?** *(Section 3.1)*

- **Why should you check the air pressure of tires before you go for a long drive?** *(Section 3.2)*

- **What controls the movement of air into and out of your lungs as you breathe?** *(Section 3.2)*

- **How is the altitude of a hot-air balloon controlled?** *(page 82)*

- **Why does pasta take longer to cook in Denver than in New Orleans?** *(Section 3.3)*

Chapter Preview

3.1 Solids, Liquids, and Gases

3.2 The Gas Laws

3.3 Phase Changes

Inquiry ⟩ Activity

How Easy Is It to Compress Air and Water?

Procedure

1. Insert a plunger into a syringe that is sealed at the narrow end. Push the plunger into the syringe as far as you can. Use the marks on the side of the syringe to read the volume of the air inside the syringe. Record this volume.

2. Remove the plunger. Fill the syringe with water by holding it under water in a large plastic container of water. **CAUTION** *Wipe up any spilled water right away to avoid slips and falls.*

3. While holding the syringe over the container, repeat Step 1. Record the volume of the water.

Think About It

1. Comparing and Contrasting Which was harder to compress, the air or the water? (To compress means to squeeze into a smaller volume.)

2. Inferring Based on your answer to Question 1, in which material are the particles closer together, in air or in water? Explain your answer.

3.1 Solids, Liquids, and Gases

Reading Focus

Key Concepts
- How can shape and volume be used to classify materials?
- How can kinetic theory and forces of attraction be used to explain the behavior of gases, liquids, and solids?

Vocabulary
- ◆ solid
- ◆ liquid
- ◆ gas
- ◆ kinetic energy

Reading Strategy
Comparing and Contrasting Copy the diagram. As you read, replace each letter with one of these phrases: *definite volume, definite shape, variable volume,* or *variable shape.*

Solid Liquid Gas

a. ? b. ? c. ? d. ?

Do you recognize the object in Figure 1? It is a carpenter's level. A level can be used to see whether a surface is perfectly horizontal. The level has one or more transparent tubes inside a metal or wooden frame. Inside each tube is a clear liquid, such as alcohol, and an air bubble. When a carpenter places the level on a surface that is perfectly horizontal, the air bubble stays in the middle of the horizontal tube. The bubble moves to the high end of the tube if the surface is slanted.

The metal, alcohol, and air in a carpenter's level represent three states of matter. At room temperature, most metals are solids, alcohol is a liquid, and air is a gas. In this chapter, you will learn why the appearance and behavior of solids, liquids, and gases are different.

Describing the States of Matter

If you were asked to classify some materials as solids, liquids, or gases, you would probably find the task fairly easy. But could you describe what method you used to classify the materials? You might notice that some materials have a definite shape and volume and some materials do not. **Materials can be classified as solids, liquids, or gases based on whether their shapes and volumes are definite or variable.** Shape and volume are clues to how the particles within a material are arranged.

Figure 1 Carpenters use a level to find out if a surface is perfectly horizontal. In the level shown, three clear plastic tubes are set into an aluminum frame. Each tube contains a liquid and a gas. **Classifying** *What property could you use to distinguish the liquid or gas from the solids in a level?*

Solids Think about these familiar objects: a pencil, a quarter, a book, and a cafeteria tray. What do these four objects have in common? They all have a recognizable shape and they all take up a certain amount of space. The materials in these objects are all in the solid state. **Solid** is the state of matter in which materials have a definite shape and a definite volume.

The term *definite* means that the shape and volume of a pencil won't change as you move the pencil from a desk drawer to a pencil case to a backpack. Changing the container doesn't change the shape or volume of a solid. However, the term *definite* doesn't mean that the shape or volume can never change. After all, you can change the shape of a pencil by sharpening it. You can change the shape of a copper wire by bending the wire.

Figure 2 shows the arrangement of atoms in a copper wire. The copper atoms are packed close together and are arranged in a regular pattern. Almost all solids have some type of orderly arrangement of particles at the atomic level.

Liquids How good are you at estimating whether the juice remaining in an almost-empty bottle will fit in a glass? If your estimate is not accurate, you will run out of space in the glass before you run out of juice in the bottle.

Appearances can be deceiving. Imagine a narrow glass and a wide bottle side by side. Each contains exactly 350 milliliters of juice (about three quarters of a pint). There will seem to be more juice in the glass because the juice rises almost to the rim of the glass. There will seem to be less juice in the bottle because the juice forms a shallow layer. What can you learn about liquids from this comparison?

A liquid always has the same shape as its container and can be poured from one container to another. **Liquid** is the state of matter in which a material has a definite volume but not a definite shape.

Mercury exists as a liquid at room temperature. The drawing in Figure 3 shows the arrangement of atoms in liquid mercury. Compare this arrangement to the arrangement of copper atoms in Figure 2. The mercury atoms are close together but their arrangement is more random than the arrangement of atoms in copper.

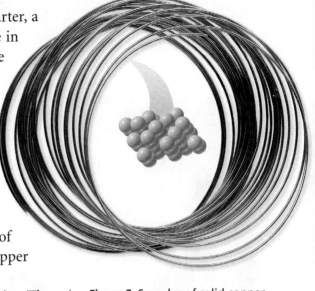

Figure 2 Samples of solid copper have definite volume. Copper atoms are packed close together in an orderly arrangement.

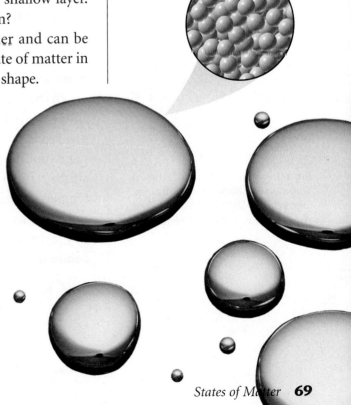

Figure 3 At room temperature, mercury is a liquid. Drops of mercury on a flat, clean surface have a round shape. Mercury in a container has the same shape as its container. **Comparing and Contrasting** *Compare the arrangement of atoms in copper and mercury.*

Gases If you were asked to name a gas, what would you say? Air, which is a mixture of gases, is probably the most obvious example. You might also mention natural gas, which is used as a fuel for heating homes. **Gas** is the state of matter in which a material has neither a definite shape nor a definite volume. (The adjective form of the word *gas* is *gaseous* (GAS e us), as in *gaseous state*.) A gas takes the shape and volume of its container.

The balloons in Figure 4 are filled with helium, a colorless gas that is less dense than air. Two of the balloons are teardrop-shaped and two are disk-shaped. The "shape" of the helium in a balloon is the same as the shape of the balloon itself. The volume of the helium in a balloon is equal to the volume of the balloon.

The helium atoms in a balloon are not arranged in a regular pattern, as shown in the drawing in Figure 4. They are at random locations throughout the balloon. There is more space between two helium atoms in a balloon than between two neighboring atoms in solid copper or liquid mercury.

Because of the space among helium atoms, a large amount of helium can be compressed into a metal cylinder. When helium flows from the cylinder into a balloon, the helium atoms spread out. If 200 balloons are filled from a single cylinder, the total volume of the balloons will be much larger than the volume of the cylinder.

Other States of Matter
On Earth, almost all matter exists in a solid, liquid, or gaseous state. But ninety-nine percent of all the matter that can be observed in the universe exists in a state that is not as common on Earth. At extremely high temperatures, such as those found on the sun or other stars, matter exists as plasma. You will read more about the properties of plasmas in Chapter 10.

In the 1920s Satyendra Bose, a physicist from India, wrote a paper about the behavior of light. After Albert Einstein read the paper, he realized that the behavior described could apply to matter under certain conditions. Einstein made a bold prediction. He predicted that a fifth state of matter would exist at extremely low temperatures. At temperatures near −273°C, groups of atoms would behave as though they were a single particle. In 1995, scientists produced this fifth state of matter, which is called a Bose-Einstein condensate (or BEC). It behaved as Einstein had predicted decades before.

Figure 4 Helium gas takes the volume and shape of its container. **Observing** *Describe the shape of the helium in the blue balloon.*

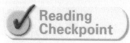 **Reading Checkpoint** *How can atoms behave at temperatures near −273°C?*

Why Was Mercury Used in Thermometers?

Until recently, mercury thermometers were used in homes and schools. When a thermometer broke, people were exposed to mercury. When broken thermometers were thrown away, they ended up in landfills. Mercury is a toxic substance that can harm humans and other organisms. Schools no longer use mercury thermometers and people are encouraged to replace their fever thermometers.

So why did people continue to use mercury thermometers long after they knew the dangers of mercury? Look at the data table. It lists some densities over a temperature range from 0°C to 150°C. The temperatures are given at 30-degree intervals.

1. **Using Tables** How does the density of mercury change as the temperature increases?

2. **Relating Cause and Effect** How does a change in density affect the volume of a mercury sample?

Density of Mercury		
Temperature (°C)	Density (g/mL)	Volume of One Gram (mL)
0	13.60	0.07356
30	13.52	0.07396
60	13.45	0.07436
90	13.38	0.07476
120	13.30	0.07517
150	13.23	0.07558

3. **Calculating** If a thermometer contained a gram of mercury, how much would the volume of the mercury change when the temperature rose from 0°C to 30°C? From 30°C to 60°C? From 60°C to 90°C? From 90°C to 120°C?

4. **Drawing Conclusions** Why was mercury a better choice than water for the liquid in a thermometer? (*Hint:* Between 0°C and 30°C, the volume of a gram of water changes by 0.0042 mL. Between 30°C and 60°C, the volume changes by 0.0127 mL. Between 60°C and 90°C, the volume changes by 0.0188 mL.)

5. **Inferring** Why is the mercury in a thermometer stored in a narrow tube?

Kinetic Theory

Why, under ordinary conditions, is copper a solid, mercury a liquid, and helium a gas? To begin to answer that question, you need to know something about kinetic energy. An object that is moving has kinetic energy. The word *kinetic* comes from a Greek word meaning "to move." **Kinetic energy** is the energy an object has due to its motion.

The faster an object moves, the greater its kinetic energy is. A ball thrown at 85 miles (137 kilometers) per hour by the pitcher in Figure 5 has more kinetic energy than a ball thrown at 78 miles (125 kilometers) per hour. When a baseball is thrown, a batter can see that it is moving. But the batter cannot see that there is also motion occurring within the baseball. According to the kinetic theory of matter, particles inside the solid baseball are moving. Particles in the air that the baseball travels through are moving too.

The kinetic theory of matter says that all particles of matter are in constant motion. The theory was developed in the mid-1800s to explain the behavior of gases. It can also help to explain the behavior of liquids and solids.

Figure 5 The kinetic energy of a baseball depends on the speed at which the pitcher throws the ball.

Figure 6 This photograph of billiard balls was taken just after the cue struck the white ball, which began to move. The white ball moved in a straight line until it collided with the dark blue ball. The collision caused the dark blue ball to start moving. The motion of billiard balls can be compared to the motion of particles in a gas.

Figure 7 A helium atom travels in a straight line until it collides with another helium atom or the side of its container.
Relating Cause and Effect *What can happen to the kinetic energy of two helium atoms when the atoms collide?*

Explaining the Behavior of Gases

You can compare the motion of the particles in a gas to the movement of balls during a game of billiards. When a cue strikes a billiard ball, as shown in Figure 6, the ball moves in a straight line until it strikes the side of the billiard table or another ball. When a moving ball strikes a ball at rest, the first ball slows down and the second ball begins to move. Kinetic energy is transferred during those collisions.

Motion in Gases Unlike billiard balls, the particles in a gas are never at rest. At room temperature, the average speed of the particles in a sample of gas is about 1600 kilometers per hour. The use of the term *average* is a clue that not all particles are moving at the same speed. Some are moving faster than the average speed and some are moving slower than the average speed.

Figure 7 shows the possible paths of two helium atoms in a container of helium gas. Notice that each atom moves in a straight line until it collides with the other atom or with a wall of the container. During a collision, one atom may lose kinetic energy and slow down while the other atom gains kinetic energy and speeds up. However, the total kinetic energy of the atoms remains the same.

The diagram in Figure 7 does not accurately compare the volumes of the atoms and the container. The volume of a helium atom is extremely small compared to the volume of its container. If there were a billion times a trillion helium atoms in a liter bottle, there would still be a large amount of space in the bottle.

Between collisions, why doesn't one particle in a gas affect the other particles in the gas? **There are forces of attraction among the particles in all matter.** If the particles are apart and moving fast, as in a gas, the attractions are too weak to have an effect. Under ordinary conditions, scientists can ignore the forces of attraction in a gas.

Kinetic Theory of Gases The kinetic theory explains the general properties of a gas. **The constant motion of particles in a gas allows a gas to fill a container of any shape or size.** Think about air in a tire. The walls of the tire keep the air contained. What if there is a hole in the tire? Because the particles in the air are in constant motion, some of the particles would travel to the hole and move out of the tire. The kinetic theory as applied to gases has three main points.

- Particles in a gas are in constant, random motion.

- The motion of one particle is unaffected by the motion of other particles unless the particles collide.

- Forces of attraction among particles in a gas can be ignored under ordinary conditions.

✓ Reading Checkpoint *Describe the motion of particles in a gas.*

Explaining the Behavior of Liquids

The particles in liquids also have kinetic energy. So why does a liquid such as mercury have a definite volume at room temperature instead of expanding to fill its container? The average speed of a mercury atom is much slower than the average speed of a helium atom at the same temperature. A mercury atom has about 50 times the mass of a helium atom. This greater mass is only partly responsible for the slower speed. What other factor is responsible?

The particles in a liquid are more closely packed than the particles in a gas. Therefore, attractions between the particles in a liquid do affect the movement of the particles. A mercury atom in liquid mercury is like a student in the crowded hallway in Figure 8. The student's path may be blocked by students moving in the other direction. The student's ability to move is affected by interactions with other students.

In a liquid, there is a kind of tug of war between the constant motion of particles and the attractions among particles. This tug of war explains the general behavior of liquids. **A liquid takes the shape of its container because particles in a liquid can flow to new locations. The volume of a liquid is constant because forces of attraction keep the particles close together.** Because forces of attraction limit the motion of particles in a liquid, the particles in a liquid cannot spread out and fill a container.

For: Links on kinetic theory
Visit: www.SciLinks.org
Web Code: ccn-1031

For: Activity on mercury in the enviroment
Visit: PHSchool.com
Web Code: ccc-1031

Figure 8 Particles in a liquid behave like students moving through a crowded hallway.

Figure 9 These photographs of an audience in a movie theater were taken at different times on the same day. The behavior of the audience can be compared to the behavior of particles in a solid. *Observing* **What stayed the same and what changed between the photographs?**

Explaining the Behavior of Solids

You might compare the particles in a solid to a polite audience in a movie theater. While the movie is running, people stay in their seats. Although people move around in their seats, as shown in Figure 9, each person remains in essentially the same location during the movie. They have "fixed" locations in a total volume that does not change.

⬤ **Solids have a definite volume and shape because particles in a solid vibrate around fixed locations.** Vibration is a repetitive back-and-forth motion. Look back at the orderly arrangement of copper atoms in Figure 2. Strong attractions among the copper atoms restrict their motion and keep each atom in a fixed location relative to its neighbors. Each atom vibrates around its location but it does not exchange places with a neighboring atom.

Section 3.1 Assessment

Reviewing Concepts

1. ⬤ How are shape and volume used to classify solids, liquids, and gases?

2. ⬤ What does the kinetic theory say about the motion of atoms?

3. ⬤ How is a gas able to fill a container of any size or shape?

4. ⬤ Use kinetic theory and attractive forces to explain why a liquid has a definite volume and a shape that can vary.

5. ⬤ Explain why a solid has a definite shape and volume.

6. How does the arrangement of atoms in most solids differ from the arrangement of atoms in a liquid?

Critical Thinking

7. **Using Analogies** Explain how the behavior of popcorn in a popcorn popper can be used as an analogy for the motion of gas particles.

8. **Applying Concepts** A hazardous chemical is leaking from a tank truck. Rescue workers need to evacuate people who live near the accident. Why are more people likely to be affected if the chemical is a gas, rather than a liquid?

Connecting C Concepts

Viscosity Review the description of viscosity in Section 2.2. Use the tug of war between forces of attraction and kinetic energy to explain differences in viscosity among liquids at the same temperature.

3.2 The Gas Laws

Reading Focus

Key Concepts

- What causes gas pressure in a closed container?
- What factors affect gas pressure?
- How are the temperature, volume, and pressure of a gas related?

Vocabulary

- pressure
- absolute zero
- Charles's law
- Boyle's law

Reading Strategy

Identifying Cause and Effect Copy the diagram. As you read, identify the variables that affect gas pressure.

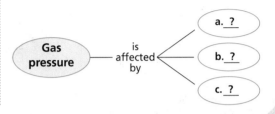

The woman in Figure 10 is taking a deep breath. This action helps reduce her breathing rate and increase the volume of air she inhales. When you inhale, the volume of your chest cavity increases and air moves into your lungs. When you exhale, the volume of your chest cavity decreases and air is pushed out of your lungs.

After you read this section, you will understand how changing the volume of your chest cavity causes air to move into and out of your lungs. Changes in the volume, the temperature, the pressure, and the number of particles have predictable effects on the behavior of a gas.

Figure 10 Taking a deep breath increases the volume of your chest cavity, which causes air to move into your lungs.

Pressure

At many hockey rinks, a layer of shatterproof glass keeps the puck away from the spectators. The force with which the puck hits the glass depends on the speed of the puck. The faster the puck is traveling, the greater the force is. The smaller the area of impact is, the greater the pressure produced. **Pressure** is the result of a force distributed over an area. If the edge of the puck hits the glass, it exerts more pressure than if the face of the puck hits the glass at the same speed.

The SI unit of pressure is derived from SI units for force and area. Force is measured in newtons (N) and area in square meters (m^2). When a force in newtons is divided by an area in square meters, the unit of pressure is newtons per square meter (N/m^2). The SI unit for pressure, the pascal (Pa), is shorthand for newtons per square meter. One pascal is a small amount of pressure. Scientists often express larger amounts of pressure in kilopascals. One kilopascal (kPa) is equal to 1000 pascals.

An object does not need to be as large as a hockey puck to exert pressure when it collides with another object. Recall that the helium atoms in a balloon are constantly moving. The pressure produced by a single helium atom colliding with a wall is extremely small. However, there are more than 10^{22} helium atoms in a small balloon. When so many particles collide with the walls of a container at the same time, they produce a measurable pressure.

🔑 **Collisions between particles of a gas and the walls of the container cause the pressure in a closed container of gas.** The more frequent the collisions, the greater the pressure of the gas is. The speed of the particles and their mass also affect the pressure.

✓ **Reading Checkpoint** *How does the frequency of collisions affect the pressure of a gas?*

Factors That Affect Gas Pressure

Think again about the collisions that produce gas pressure. What changes might affect the pressure of a gas in a container? The particles in the gas could move faster or slower. The gas could be moved into a larger or smaller container. You could add gas or remove gas from the container. 🔑 **Factors that affect the pressure of an enclosed gas are its temperature, its volume, and the number of its particles.**

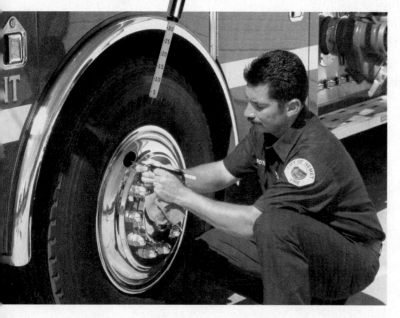

Figure 11 The fire-fighter is using a pressure gauge to check the air pressure in a tire on a firetruck. If the tires on the truck have a 44.5-inch diameter, the pressure on a front tire should be about 125 pounds per square inch (psi).

Temperature Suppose you are about to go on a long drive. The driver suspects that the air pressure in the automobile tires might be low. You check the pressure in each tire, using a pressure gauge like the one in Figure 11. You find that the measurements are well within the automobile manufacturer's guidelines. If you checked the tire pressures again after a few hours on the highway, would you be surprised to find that the pressure in the tires had increased?

The constant motion of tires on the highway causes the tires and the air in the tires to warm up. As the temperature rises, the average kinetic energy of the particles in the air increases. With increased kinetic energy, the particles move faster and collide more often with the inner walls of the tires. The faster-moving particles also hit the walls with greater force. The increase in the number of collisions along with the increase in the force of the collisions causes an increase in the pressure of the air in the tires. 🔑 **Raising the temperature of a gas will increase its pressure if the volume of the gas and the number of particles are constant.**

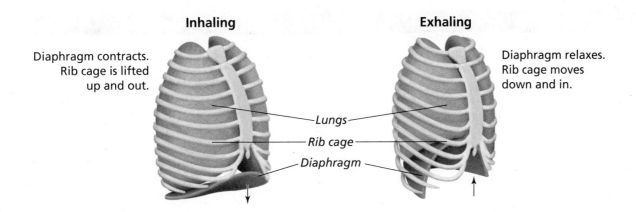

Inhaling

Diaphragm contracts.
Rib cage is lifted
up and out.

Exhaling

Diaphragm relaxes.
Rib cage moves
down and in.

Lungs

Rib cage

Diaphragm

Volume Imagine that you have a plastic bottle that appears empty. If you twist the cap onto the bottle and then squeeze the bottle, what will happen? At first, the plastic will give a little, reducing the volume of the bottle. But soon you will feel pressure from inside the bottle resisting your efforts to further reduce the volume. The pressure you feel is a result of the increased pressure of the air trapped inside the bottle. As the volume is decreased, particles of trapped air collide more often with the walls of the bottle. ⊙ **Reducing the volume of a gas increases its pressure if the temperature of the gas and the number of particles are constant.**

Figure 12 shows how the relationship between volume and pressure explains what happens when you breathe. As you inhale, a muscle called the diaphragm (DY uh fram) contracts. The contraction causes your chest cavity to expand. This temporary increase in volume allows the particles in air to spread out, which lowers the pressure inside the chest cavity. Because the pressure of the air outside your body is now greater than the pressure inside your chest, air rushes into your lungs.

When you exhale, your diaphragm relaxes and the volume of your chest cavity decreases. The particles in the air are squeezed into a smaller volume and the pressure inside your lungs increases. Because the pressure of the air inside your chest is now greater than the pressure of the air outside your body, air is forced out of your lungs.

Number of Particles You can probably predict what will happen to the pressure when you add more gas to a container. Think about a tire. Once the tire is inflated, its volume is fairly constant. So adding more air will increase the pressure inside the tire. The more particles there are in the same volume, the greater the number of collisions and the greater the pressure. At some point the rubber from which the tire is made will not be strong enough to withstand the increased pressure and the tire will burst. ⊙ **Increasing the number of particles will increase the pressure of a gas if the temperature and the volume are constant.**

Figure 12 Movement of a muscle called the diaphragm changes the volume of your chest cavity. The volume increases when you inhale and decreases when you exhale.
Interpreting Diagrams *How does the movement of your rib cage affect the volume of your chest cavity?*

For: Articles on properties of matter
Visit: PHSchool.com
Web Code: cce-1032

Charles's Law

Boyle's Law

Figure 13 These graphs compare the effects of temperature and volume on the pressure of a gas. Charles's law describes the direct relationship between the temperature and the volume. Boyle's law describes the inverse relationship between the volume and the pressure.
Controlling Variables *For each graph, name the manipulated variable and the responding variable.*

Charles's Law

During his lifetime, the French physicist Jacques Charles (1746–1823) was known for his inventions, including the hydrogen balloon. Today, Charles is best known for his investigations of the behavior of gases. Charles collected data on the relationship between the temperature and volume of gases. When he graphed the data, the graph was a straight line, as shown in Figure 13. The graph shows that the volume of a gas increases at the same rate as the temperature of the gas.

Charles extended the line on his graph beyond the measured data to see what the temperature would have to be to produce a volume of 0 L. The temperature at the point where the line crossed the *x*-axis was −273.15°C. This temperature is equal to 0 K on the Kelvin temperature scale. A temperature of 0 K is called **absolute zero.** No scientist has produced a temperature of absolute zero in a laboratory, but some have come extremely close. As a gas cools to temperatures near 0 K, the gas changes to a liquid, a solid, or sometimes a Bose-Einstein condensate.

Charles's law states that the volume of a gas is directly proportional to its temperature in kelvins if the pressure and the number of particles of the gas are constant. Charles's law can be written as a mathematical expression in which T_1 and V_1 represent the temperature and volume of a gas before a change occurs. T_2 and V_2 represent the temperature and volume after a change occurs.

Charles's Law

$$\frac{V_1}{T_1} = \frac{V_2}{T_2}$$

The temperatures must be expressed in kelvins. If temperatures in degrees Celsius are used in the expression, the volume will not be directly proportional to the temperature.

Boyle's Law

Robert Boyle, who was born in Ireland in 1627, was the first to describe the relationship between the pressure and volume of a gas. The graph in Figure 13 shows what happens when the volume of a cylinder containing a set amount of gas is decreased. What happens when the volume of the cylinder is reduced from 2.0 liters to 1.0 liter? The pressure of the gas in the cylinder doubles from 50 kilopascals to 100 kilopascals.

Boyle's Law

$$P_1V_1 = P_2V_2$$

Boyle's law states that the volume of a gas is inversely proportional to its pressure if the temperature and the number of particles are constant. Boyle's law can be expressed mathematically. P_1 and V_1 represent the pressure and volume of a gas before a change occurs. P_2 and V_2 represent the pressure and volume of a gas after a change occurs.

 Reading Checkpoint *How is Boyle's law expressed mathematically?*

Observing the Effect of Temperature on Gas Pressure

Materials

pan, metric ruler, empty beverage can, masking tape, hot plate, clock, tongs

Procedure

1. Fill a pan with cold water to a depth of 3 cm.

2. Use masking tape to cover half the opening of the can. **CAUTION** *Do not cover the entire opening with tape.*

3. Place the can on the hot plate and turn the hot plate to a high setting. Heat the can for 5 minutes and then turn off the hot plate.

4. Use tongs to remove the can from the hot plate and place it upside down in the pan of water as shown. The opening should be below the surface of the water. Observe the can as it cools.

Analyze and Conclude

1. **Inferring** How did the temperature of the air inside the can change when you heated the can? How did it change when you put the can in the water?

2. **Drawing Conclusions** What happened to the pressure of the air inside the can when you put the can in the cold water?

3. **Inferring** Did the air pressure outside the can change during the experiment?

4. **Formulating Hypotheses** What caused the change you observed in Step 4?

The Combined Gas Law

The relationships described by Boyle's law and Charles's law can be described by a single law. The combined gas law describes the relationship among the temperature, volume, and pressure of a gas when the number of particles is constant.

> **Combined Gas Law**
> $$\frac{P_1 V_1}{T_1} = \frac{P_2 V_2}{T_2}$$

The combined gas law is used to solve many problems involving gases.

Math Skills

The Combined Gas Law

A cylinder that contains air at a pressure of 100 kPa has a volume of 0.75 L. The pressure is increased to 300 kPa. The temperature does not change. Find the new volume of air.

1 Read and Understand

What information are you given?

$$P_1 = 100 \text{ kPa} \qquad P_2 = 300 \text{ kPa} \qquad V_1 = 0.75 \text{ L}$$

2 Plan and Solve

What unknown are you trying to calculate?

$$V_2$$

What expression can you use?

$$\frac{P_1 V_1}{T_1} = \frac{P_2 V_2}{T_2}$$

Cancel out the variable that does not change and rearrange the expression to solve for V_2.

$$P_1 V_1 = P_2 V_2 \qquad V_2 = \frac{P_1 V_1}{P_2}$$

Replace each variable with its known value.

$$V_2 = 100 \text{ kPa} \times \frac{0.75 \text{ L}}{300 \text{ kPa}} = 0.25 \text{ L}$$

3 Look Back and Check

Is your answer reasonable?

Volume should decrease as pressure increases. The pressure tripled from 100 kPa to 300 kPa. The answer, 0.25 L, is one third the original volume, 0.75 L.

Math Practice

1. A gas has a volume of 5.0 L at a pressure of 50 kPa. What happens to the volume when the pressure is increased to 125 kPa? The temperature does not change.

2. Gas stored in a tank at 273 K has a pressure of 388 kPa. The safe limit for the pressure is 825 kPa. At what temperature will the gas reach this pressure?

3. At 10°C, the gas in a cylinder has a volume of 0.250 L. The gas is allowed to expand to 0.285 L. What must the final temperature be for the pressure to remain constant? (*Hint:* Convert from degrees Celsius to kelvins using the expression °C + 273 = K.)

It is harder for scientists to do a controlled experiment when they are studying events that occur in natural settings. Scientists need laws like the combined gas law to deal with situations in which multiple variables are changing. Balloons like the one in Figure 14 are used by scientists to gather data about Earth's atmosphere. The balloon is filled with hydrogen or helium. It carries a package of weather instruments up into the atmosphere. The instruments measure temperature, pressure, and water content at different levels in the atmosphere.

What will happen to the volume of the weather balloon as it rises through the atmosphere? Both pressure and temperature decrease as the altitude increases in Earth's atmosphere. A decrease in external pressure should cause the balloon to expand to a larger volume. A decrease in temperature should cause the balloon to contract to a smaller volume. Whether the balloon actually expands or contracts depends on the size of the changes in pressure and temperature.

Figure 14 These scientists are releasing a weather balloon into the atmosphere. The balloon is designed to burst when it reaches an altitude of about 27,400 meters.
Drawing Conclusions *What happens to the pressure inside a weather balloon as it rises?*

Section 3.2 Assessment

Reviewing Concepts

1. How is the gas pressure produced in a closed container of gas?

2. What three factors affect gas pressure?

3. How does increasing the temperature affect the pressure of a contained gas?

4. What happens to the pressure of a gas if its volume is reduced?

5. How does increasing the number of particles of a contained gas affect its pressure?

Critical Thinking

6. **Predicting** What happens to the pressure in a tire if air is slowly leaking out of the tire? Explain your answer.

7. **Comparing and Contrasting** What do Boyle's law and Charles's law have in common? How are they different?

8. **Applying Concepts** Some liquid products are sold in aerosol cans. Gas is stored in a can under pressure and is used to propel the liquid out of the can. Explain why an aerosol can should never be thrown into a fireplace or incinerator.

Math Practice

9. Two liters of hydrogen gas are stored at a pressure of 100 kPa. If the temperature does not change, what will the volume of the gas be when the pressure is decreased to 25 kPa?

10. You know that a gas in a sealed container has a pressure of 111 kPa at 23°C. What will the pressure be if the temperature rises to 475°C?

Riding on Air

Warm air is less dense than cold air. So if enough warm air is confined to a lightweight container, the container can rise through the surrounding colder air. This is the principle that allows a hot-air balloon to get off and stay off the ground.

When air is heated, the particles in the air gain energy and move faster on average. The particles also move farther apart, so a given volume of hot air contains fewer particles and has less mass than the same volume of cold air. This difference in density produces an upward force. In a hot-air balloon, the force is very small, equivalent to lifting about one tenth of a gram for each liter of air. A large volume of air is needed to support the mass of the balloon and any passengers. That is why hot-air balloons need to be large.

To heat the air, the pilot burns propane gas, which is stored under pressure in tanks. The bottom of the balloon's envelope (the skirt) is treated so that it is not flammable.

As the balloon nears the chosen altitude, the pilot turns the burner off so that the balloon will stop rising. The pilot maintains the altitude of the balloon by turning the burner on and off and by opening a valve at the top of the balloon to let hot air escape.

The horizontal movement of the balloon is much harder to control. The wind speed and wind direction vary at different altitudes. The pilot uses the burner and the valve to change the altitude of the balloon and take advantage of favorable winds. A hot-air balloon cannot land at the same spot from which it took off. The ground crew must drive to the landing site to collect the balloon and the passengers.

Taking Off and Landing

Launching and piloting a hot-air balloon is an activity that takes skill and patience.

3 Once up, the pilot maintains altitude by occasionally turning on the burner for a few seconds.

Valve

2 Gas burners are switched on to heat the air and inflate the balloon, which begins to rise.

1 The crew uses fans to fill the envelope with cold air.

Burner

4 To lose altitude, the pilot opens a valve at the top of the envelope to let out some hot air.

Fast-moving hot air particles

Envelope made from tough nylon

Flame-resistant skirt

Jet of flame from burner

Flexible, lightweight, wicker basket

Slower-moving cold air particles

Upward force

Particle Pressure

Particles in hot air move faster and are farther apart than those in cold air, so hot air is less dense than cold air. With lower density, heated air rises over colder air.

Balloon Valve

The valve helps to control the balloon's altitude. When the valve is opened, some hot air is released from the top of the balloon. The hot air is replaced by cold air flowing into the base of the balloon. This exchange of cold air for hot air increases the mass of the balloon, causing it to descend until the pilot closes the valve.

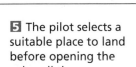

5 The pilot selects a suitable place to land before opening the valve all the way.

6 The balloon slowly falls to the ground and collapses.

7 The crew gathers up the envelope.

Going Further

■ Write a paragraph comparing early hot-air balloons with modern balloons. Include the following information: the kind of materials used, the distances traveled, and the types of fuel used.

■ Cite the sources you used for your paragraph and explain how you knew that these sources were reliable.

3.3 Phase Changes

Reading Focus

Key Concepts

- What are six common phase changes?
- What happens to a substance's temperature and a system's energy during a phase change?
- How does the arrangement of water molecules change during melting and freezing?
- How are evaporation and boiling different?

Vocabulary

- phase change
- endothermic
- heat of fusion
- exothermic
- vaporization
- heat of vaporization
- evaporation
- vapor pressure
- condensation
- sublimation
- deposition

Reading Strategy

Summarizing Copy the diagram. As you read, complete the description of energy flow during phase changes.

Massive chunks of frozen water called icebergs are a common sight off the continent of Antarctica. A large iceberg like the one in Figure 15 contains enough fresh water to supply millions of people with water for a year. During the summer in southern Australia, fresh water is a scarce resource. People have proposed towing icebergs to Australia from Antarctica. The plan has not been implemented because the trip could take months to complete and much of the iceberg would melt along the way. In this section, you will find out what happens when a substance, such as water, changes from one state to another.

Characteristics of Phase Changes

When at least two states of the same substance are present, scientists describe each different state as a phase. For example, if an iceberg is floating in the ocean, there are two phases of water present—a solid phase and a liquid phase. A **phase change** is the reversible physical change that occurs when a substance changes from one state of matter to another.

Figure 15 The solid and liquid phases of water are visible in this photograph of an iceberg in the Amundsen Sea near Antarctica.

In Figure 16, a state of matter is listed at each corner of the triangle. Each arrow in the diagram represents a different phase change. Each pair of arrows represents a set of reversible changes. For example, the arrow starting at the solid phase and ending at the liquid phase represents melting. The arrow starting at the liquid phase and ending at the solid phase represents freezing.

Melting, freezing, vaporization, condensation, sublimation, and deposition are six common phase changes. All phase changes share certain characteristics related to energy and temperature.

Temperature and Phase Changes
One way to recognize a phase change is by measuring the temperature of a substance as it is heated or cooled. **The temperature of a substance does not change during a phase change.**

Naphthalene (NAF thuh leen) is a compound that is sometimes used in mothballs. Figure 17 is a graph of the data collected when a solid piece of naphthalene is slowly heated. Temperature readings are taken at regular intervals. At first the temperature rises as the solid naphthalene warms up. But at 80°C, the temperature of the naphthalene stops rising. The temperature remains at 80°C, which is the melting point of naphthalene, until melting is complete.

If liquid naphthalene is placed in an ice-water bath, the temperature of the liquid will drop until it reaches 80°C. It will remain at 80°C until all the liquid freezes. The temperature at which the substance freezes—its freezing point—is identical to the temperature at which it melts. The freezing and melting points of naphthalene are both 80°C.

If naphthalene is heated after it has completely melted, its temperature begins to rise again. The temperature keeps rising until it reaches 218°C, which is the boiling point of naphthalene. Until boiling is complete, the temperature remains at 218°C.

Figure 16 This diagram lists six physical changes that can occur among the solid, liquid, and gaseous phases of a substance. **Interpreting Diagrams** *Explain why the changes are grouped into the pairs shown on the diagram.*

Go Online
NSTA SciLINKS

For: Links on phase diagrams
Visit: www.SciLinks.org
Web Code: ccn-1030

Figure 17 This graph shows what happens to the temperature of a solid sample of naphthalene as the sample is slowly heated. **Using Graphs** *What happened to the temperature in the interval between four and seven minutes?*

Figure 18 This elaborate ice sculpture was carved in Asahikawa, Japan. The ice sculpture will start to melt if the temperature rises above 0°C or sunlight shines directly on the ice.

Energy released

Figure 19 As ice forms on this strawberry plant, the energy released keeps the plant from freezing at temperatures slightly below 0°C. **Applying Concepts** *Explain why a farmer would need to keep spraying the plant with water while the temperature remains below freezing.*

Energy and Phase Changes During a phase change, energy is transferred between a substance and its surroundings. The direction of the transfer depends on the type of phase change. ◯ **Energy is either absorbed or released during a phase change.**

The ice sculpture in Figure 18 isn't going to last forever. When the temperature of the air rises above 0°C or when sunlight shines directly on the ice, an ice sculpture begins to melt. Melting is an example of an endothermic change. During an **endothermic** change, the system absorbs energy from its surroundings.

The amount of energy absorbed depends on the substance. For example, one gram of ice absorbs 334 joules (J) of energy as it melts. This amount of energy is the **heat of fusion** for water. Fusion is another term for melting. The heat of fusion varies from substance to substance.

One gram of water releases 334 joules of energy to its surroundings as it freezes, the same amount of energy that is absorbed when one gram of ice melts. Farmers use this release of energy to protect their crops. When farmers expect temperatures to drop slightly below 0°C, they spray the crops with water as shown in Figure 19. As water freezes, it releases heat. The flow of heat slows the drop in temperature and helps protect the crops from damage. Freezing is an example of an exothermic change. During an **exothermic** change, the system releases energy to its surroundings.

An understanding of phase changes can be useful in many situations. The How It Works box explains how the design of an ice rink in Utah allows the manager of the rink to control the hardness of the ice.

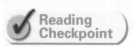 **Reading Checkpoint** *How much energy does one gram of ice absorb as it melts?*

Custom-Tailored Ice

At the Utah Olympic Oval the hardness of the ice can be controlled. The ice must be cold and hard for long speed-skating races, where the length of a skater's glide is important. For shorter races, the skaters need more traction, so the ice is made a little warmer and softer.

Interpreting Diagrams *What is the purpose of the sand layer?*

Speed Skater
This skater is racing at the Utah Olympic Oval, one of the world's most technically advanced ice rinks.

Lubricant

A **Skating surface** The surface is built up from thin layers of ice to a depth of less than 2 cm. The ice can be as cold as −8°C. The temperature and the hardness of the ice are controlled by tiny changes to the temperature of the underlying concrete layer.

B **Chilled concrete slab** The temperature is controlled by cold salt water, which is pumped through pipes embedded in the slab. The salt water remains liquid because its freezing point is lower than that of pure water.

C **Insulating layers** These layers prevent heat from rising up into the concrete slab from the warmer sand layer underneath.

D **Sand layer** To prevent the gravel layer from freezing, which could damage the rink structure, the sand layer is kept at a temperature above 0°C.

E **Gravel layer** This layer provides the foundation for the rink.

Paint layer with markings

Paint layer with logos

Paint layer with background color

Ice layers
The skating surface is formed with as many as 24 layers of ice and paint. Warm water is used for the top layers because it contains less dissolved air, and can produce a denser, harder, frozen surface.

States of Matter **87**

Go Online

SCiLINKS

For: Links on phases of matter
Visit: www.SciLinks.org
Web Code: ccn-1033

Melting and Freezing

In water, hydrogen and oxygen atoms are combined in small units called molecules. Each water molecule contains two hydrogen atoms and one oxygen atom. 🔑 **The arrangement of molecules in water becomes less orderly as water melts and more orderly as water freezes.**

Melting In ice, attractions between water molecules keep the molecules in fixed positions. When ice cubes are removed from a freezer and placed in an empty glass, heat flows from the air to the ice. As the ice gains energy, the molecules vibrate more quickly. At the melting point of water, 0°C, some molecules gain enough energy to overcome the attractions and move from their fixed positions. When all the molecules have enough energy to move, melting is complete. Any energy gained by the water after the phase change increases the average kinetic energy of the molecules, and the temperature rises.

Freezing When liquid water is placed in a freezer, energy flows from the water to the air in the freezer, and the water cools down. As the average kinetic energy of its molecules decreases, they move more slowly. At the freezing point of water, some molecules move slowly enough for the attractions between molecules to have an effect. When all the molecules have been drawn into an orderly arrangement, freezing is complete. Any energy removed from the ice after the phase change decreases the average kinetic energy of the molecules, and the temperature of the ice drops.

Often, people think of cold temperatures when they hear the term *freezing*. But substances that are solids at room temperature can freeze at temperatures that are quite high. For example, silicon freezes at 1412°C (2574°F). As a comparison, you can bake cookies at 177°C (350°F).

Vaporization and Condensation

Figure 20 shows how food cools and stays cold in a refrigerator. The process depends on a substance that changes from a liquid to a gas to a liquid over and over again. During these phase changes, energy flows from the inside of the refrigerator to the outside.

The phase change in which a substance changes from a liquid into a gas is **vaporization.** Vaporization is an endothermic process. That is, a substance must absorb energy in order to change from a liquid to a gas. One gram of water gains 2258 joules of energy when it vaporizes at 100°C. This amount of energy is the **heat of vaporization** for water. The heat of vaporization varies from substance to substance.

Figure 20 In a refrigerator, a pair of phase changes keep the food cold. Energy from inside the food compartment is used to change a liquid to a gas in the evaporator. This energy is released when the compressed gas changes back to a liquid in the condenser.

Evaporator

Energy removed from food compartment

Condenser

Compressor

Energy released to surroundings

Scientists distinguish two vaporization processes—boiling and evaporation. **Evaporation takes place at the surface of a liquid and occurs at temperatures below the boiling point.**

Evaporation If you go outside after a rain shower on a sunny, warm day, you may notice puddles of water. If you return to the same location after a few hours, the puddles may be gone. This disappearance of the puddles is due to evaporation. **Evaporation** is the process that changes a substance from a liquid to a gas at temperatures below the substance's boiling point.

Figure 21 shows what is happening as water evaporates from a small, shallow container. Some molecules near the surface are moving fast enough to escape the liquid and become water vapor. (A vapor is the gaseous phase of a substance that is normally a solid or liquid at room temperature.) The greater the surface area of the container, the faster the water evaporates.

What happens if the water is in a closed container? As the water evaporates, water vapor collects above the liquid. The pressure caused by the collisions of this vapor and the walls of the container is called **vapor pressure.** The vapor pressure of water increases as the temperature increases. At higher temperatures, more water molecules have enough kinetic energy to overcome the attractions of other molecules in the liquid.

Figure 21 Evaporation takes place at the surface of a liquid.

> ✓ **Reading Checkpoint** *How does the surface area of a liquid affect the rate of evaporation?*

Boiling As you heat a pot of water, both the temperature and the vapor pressure of the water increase. When the vapor pressure becomes equal to atmospheric pressure, the water boils. The temperature at which this happens is the boiling point of water.

The kinetic theory explains what happens when water boils. As the temperature increases, water molecules move faster and faster. When the temperature reaches 100°C, some molecules below the surface of the liquid have enough kinetic energy to overcome the attraction of neighboring molecules. Figure 22 shows that bubbles of water vapor form within the liquid. Because water vapor is less dense than liquid water, the bubbles quickly rise to the surface. When they reach the surface, the bubbles burst and release water vapor into the air.

Figure 22 Boiling takes place throughout a liquid. **Applying Concepts** *Explain why the temperature of water does not rise during boiling.*

89

Observing Phase Changes

Materials

250-mL Erlenmeyer flask, graduated cylinder, thermometer, dry ice

Procedure

1. Pour 150 milliliters of water into a 250-mL Erlenmeyer flask. Place a thermometer in the flask. **CAUTION** *Wipe up any spilled water right away to avoid slips and falls.*

2. Observe what happens after your teacher adds a small piece of dry ice to the flask. (Dry ice is solid carbon dioxide.) **CAUTION** *Dry ice can damage skin on contact. Do not touch the dry ice.*

3. Record the temperature of the water just after the dry ice is added and again after it is no longer visible.

Analyze and Conclude

1. **Observing** What happened when the dry ice was added to the water?

2. **Analyzing Data** Did adding the dry ice cause the water to boil? Explain your answer.

3. **Inferring** What was the source of the bubbles in the water?

4. **Formulating Hypotheses** What caused a cloud to form above the flask?

5. **Applying Concepts** What phase changes occurred in the flask?

Figure 23 Water vapor from the air condensed into drops of liquid water on these blades of grass.

The boiling point of a substance depends on the atmospheric pressure. The normal boiling point of water at sea level is 100°C. At higher elevations, the atmospheric pressure is lower. Do you know that Denver, Colorado, is called the mile-high city? This nickname is based on Denver's location at one mile above sea level. In Denver, the vapor pressure of water will equal atmospheric pressure at temperatures below 100°C. The boiling point of water in Denver can be as low as 95°C. Food does not cook as quickly at 95°C as it does at 100°C. Pasta takes longer to cook in Denver than in New Orleans, Louisiana, a city that is located near sea level.

Condensation Have you ever come out of a shower to find your bathroom mirror clouded over? The "cloud" on the mirror is caused by water vapor that cooled as it came in contact with the mirror. The water vapor transferred heat to the mirror and condensed into liquid water. **Condensation** is the phase change in which a substance changes from a gas or vapor to a liquid. This process is also responsible for the morning dew on the blades of grass in Figure 23. Condensation is an exothermic process.

Sublimation and Deposition

Directors of concerts and plays sometimes use dry ice to create a fog-like special effect. Dry ice is the common name for the solid form of carbon dioxide. At room temperature, dry ice can directly change from a solid to a colorless gas. **Sublimation** is the phase change in which a substance changes from a solid to a gas or vapor without changing to a liquid first. Sublimation is an endothermic change. As dry ice sublimes, the cold carbon dioxide vapor causes water vapor in the air to condense and form clouds.

Where does the name dry ice come from? Solid carbon dioxide does not form a liquid as its temperature rises. Suppose 100 steaks are shipped from Omaha, Nebraska, to a supermarket in Miami, Florida. The steaks will spoil unless they are kept cold during the trip. If regular ice is used, water collects in the shipping container as the ice melts. If the steaks are shipped in dry ice, the container and the steaks stay dry during the journey. Figure 24 shows another use of dry ice.

When a gas or vapor changes directly into a solid without first changing to a liquid, the phase change is called **deposition.** This exothermic phase change is the reverse of sublimation. Deposition causes frost to form on windows. When water vapor in the air comes in contact with cold window glass, the water vapor loses enough kinetic energy to change directly from a gas to a solid.

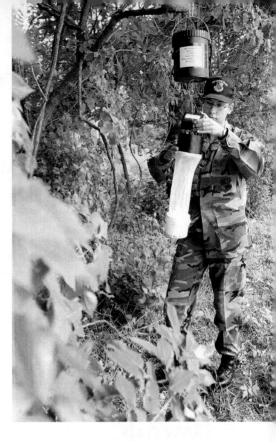

Figure 24 A technician at Tinker Air Force Base in Oklahoma hangs a mosquito trap. The trap is baited with dry ice because mosquitoes are attracted to carbon dioxide.

Section 3.3 Assessment

Reviewing Concepts

1. Name six common phase changes.

2. What happens to the temperature of a substance during a phase change?

3. How does the energy of a system change during a phase change?

4. What happens to the arrangement of water molecules as water melts and freezes?

5. What is the difference between evaporation and boiling?

6. Explain why sublimation and deposition are classified as physical changes.

Critical Thinking

7. **Applying Concepts** How can the mass of a pile of snow decrease on a sunny day when the air temperature does not rise above 0°C?

8. **Drawing Conclusions** At room temperature, table salt is a solid and acetone is a liquid. Acetone is the main ingredient in nail polish remover. What conclusion can you draw about the melting points of these materials?

Writing in Science

Steps in a Process Write a paragraph describing three steps that must occur for a water molecule to start on the surface of hot bath water and end up on the surface of a bathroom mirror. Note whether the phase changes that take place during the process are endothermic or exothermic. (*Hint:* Use words such as *first, next,* and *finally* to show the order of events.)

Investigating Changes in Temperature During Heating of Solids

Lauric acid is a solid that is found in coconuts and processed foods that are made with coconut oil. Lauric acid is also used to make some soaps and cosmetics. In this lab, you will measure the temperature of ice and of lauric acid as these solids are heated and melt. You will graph the data you collect and compare the heating curves for ice and lauric acid.

Problem
What happens to the temperature of a substance during a phase change?

Materials
- 500-mL beaker
- crushed ice
- thermometer
- hot plate
- clock with second hand
- test tube of lauric acid with thermometer
- glass stirring rod
- graph paper

 For the probeware version of this lab, see the Probeware Lab Manual, Lab 1.

Skills
Measuring, Using Graphs

Procedure

Part A: Heating Ice

1. On a sheet of paper, make a copy of the data table shown. Start with 11 blank rows, but leave space below your data table to add more rows, if necessary.

2. Fill a 500-mL beaker halfway with crushed ice.
   CAUTION *Use care when handling glassware to avoid breakage. Wipe up any spilled ice right away to avoid slips and falls.*

3. Place the beaker on a hot plate. Don't turn the hot plate on yet. Insert a thermometer into the ice. Because it takes several seconds for the thermometer to adjust to the temperature of its surroundings, wait 20 seconds and then measure the temperature of the ice. Record this temperature next to the 0 minutes entry in your data table.

4. Turn the hot plate to a low setting.
   CAUTION *Be careful not to touch the hot plate because contact with the hot plate could cause a burn.*

5. Observe and record the temperature at one-minute intervals until all the ice has changed to liquid water. Circle the temperature at which you first observe liquid water and the temperature at which all the ice has changed to liquid water.

Data Table		
Time (minutes)	Temperature of Water (°C)	Temperature of Lauric Acid (°C)
0		
1		

6. After all the ice has melted, make five more measurements of the temperature at one-minute intervals. Turn off the hot plate.

7. Graph your data with time on the horizontal axis and temperature on the vertical axis.

Part B: Heating Lauric Acid

8. Empty the water from the beaker into the sink. Fill the beaker halfway with cool tap water.

9. Place a test tube containing lauric acid and a thermometer into the beaker. If necessary, add or remove water from the beaker so that the surface of the water is above the surface of the lauric acid but below the opening of the test tube.

10. Place the beaker on the hot plate. After 20 seconds, measure the temperature of the lauric acid. Record this temperature next to the 0 minutes entry in your data table.

11. Repeat Steps 4 through 7 using the lauric acid instead of the ice. To keep the temperature the same throughout the water bath, use the glass stirring rod to stir the water after you take each temperature measurement.

Analyze and Conclude

1. **Using Graphs** Describe the shape of your graph for ice.

2. **Analyzing Data** What happened to the temperature of the ice-water mixture during the phase change?

3. **Drawing Conclusions** What happened to the energy that was transferred from the hot plate to the ice during the phase change?

4. **Comparing and Contrasting** Compare the shapes of the graphs for ice and for lauric acid. Compare the melting points of ice and lauric acid.

For: Data sharing
Visit: PHSchool.com
Web Code: ccd-1030

Study Guide

3.1 Solids, Liquids, and Gases

🔑 Key Concepts

- Materials can be classified as solids, liquids, or gases based on whether their shapes and volumes are definite or variable.

- The kinetic theory of matter states that all particles of matter are in constant motion.

- There are forces of attraction among the particles in all matter.

- The constant motion of particles in a gas allows a gas to fill a container of any shape or size.

- A liquid takes the shape of its container because particles in a liquid can flow to new locations. The volume of a liquid is constant because forces of attraction keep the particles close together.

- Solids have a definite volume and shape because particles in a solid vibrate around fixed locations.

Vocabulary

solid, *p. 69;* liquid, *p. 69;* gas, *p. 70;* kinetic energy, *p. 71*

3.2 The Gas Laws

🔑 Key Concepts

- Collisions between particles of a gas and the walls of the container cause the pressure in a closed container of gas.

- Factors that affect the pressure of an enclosed gas are its temperature, its volume, and the number of its particles.

- Raising the temperature of a gas will increase its pressure if the volume of the gas and the number of particles are constant.

- Reducing the volume of a gas increases its pressure if the temperature of the gas and the number of particles are constant.

- Increasing the number of particles will increase the pressure of a gas if the temperature and the volume are constant.

- The combined gas law can be expressed as

$$\frac{P_1 V_1}{T_1} = \frac{P_2 V_2}{T_2}$$

Vocabulary

pressure, *p. 75;* absolute zero, *p. 78;* Charles's law, *p. 78;* Boyle's law, *p. 79*

3.3 Phase Changes

🔑 Key Concepts

- Melting, freezing, vaporization, condensation, sublimation, and deposition are six common phase changes.

- The temperature of a substance does not change during a phase change.

- Energy is either absorbed or released during a phase change.

- The arrangement of molecules in water becomes less orderly as water melts, and more orderly as water freezes.

- Evaporation takes place at the surface of a liquid and occurs at temperatures below the boiling point.

Vocabulary

phase change, *p. 84;* endothermic, *p. 86;* heat of fusion, *p. 86;* exothermic, *p. 86;* vaporization, *p. 88;* heat of vaporization, *p. 88;* evaporation, *p. 89;* vapor pressure, *p. 89;* condensation, *p. 90;* sublimation, *p. 91;* deposition, *p. 91;*

Thinking Visually

Web Diagram Use information from the chapter to complete the web diagram on phase changes.

Assessment

Reviewing Content

Choose the letter that best answers the question or completes the statement.

1. Which state of matter has a definite volume but a variable shape?
    a. solid   **b.** liquid
    c. gas   **d.** vapor

2. In which state(s) of matter can materials take the shape of their containers?
    a. solid and liquid   **b.** solid and gas
    c. liquid and gas   **d.** liquid only

3. Which statement is true about the atoms in helium gas?
    a. They travel in circular paths.
    b. They have strong attractions to one another.
    c. They are not closely packed.
    d. They are arranged in an orderly pattern.

4. If the speed of an object increases, its kinetic energy
    a. decreases.   **b.** increases.
    c. stays the same.   **d.** is unpredictable.

5. The SI unit of pressure is the
    a. pascal.   **b.** newton.
    c. square meter.   **d.** psi.

6. Increasing which variable would decrease the pressure of a contained gas?
    a. temperature   **b.** number of particles
    c. boiling point   **d.** volume

7. Boyle's law relates pressure and
    a. temperature.   **b.** number of particles.
    c. volume.   **d.** mass.

8. Which of the following changes is exothermic?
    a. evaporation   **b.** freezing
    c. boiling   **d.** sublimation

9. The phase change that is the reverse of vaporization is
    a. freezing.   **b.** melting.
    c. condensation.   **d.** evaporation.

10. Which of these phase changes does NOT involve changing a liquid into a gas?
    a. sublimation   **b.** vaporization
    c. evaporation   **d.** boiling

Understanding Concepts

11. Provide an example of each of the three states of matter that exist at room temperature.

12. Compare and contrast liquid water and ice in terms of how definite their shapes and volumes are.

13. What three assumptions about particles in a gas are made by the kinetic theory?

14. Using the kinetic theory, explain why a liquid has a definite volume but a gas does not.

15. How do the way that atoms are arranged in liquid mercury and solid copper affect the movement of mercury and copper atoms?

16. Using the kinetic theory, explain what causes gas pressure.

17. What three factors affect the pressure of a gas in a closed container?

18. If a piston moves downward in a cylinder, what happens to the volume and pressure of the gas in the cylinder? The temperature remains constant.

19. What happens to the speed of the particles inside an air-filled balloon if the temperature of the balloon increases?

20. Using the kinetic theory, explain why the pressure of a gas increases when its temperature increases.

21. How are the pressure and volume of a gas related?

22. How does an endothermic phase change differ from an exothermic phase change?

23. Compare the vapor pressure of water at 10°C with its vapor pressure at 50°C.

24. Explain why water has a different boiling point at an elevation of 3000 meters than it does at sea level.

Assessment (continued)

Critical Thinking

25. Classifying If you take a helium balloon from inside a warm house to outside on a snowy day, what will happen to the balloon? Could you classify this change as a phase change? Explain your answer.

26. Comparing and Contrasting Compare the melting and freezing of water in terms of (a) the temperature at which these processes take place and (b) how energy is involved in these processes.

Use the graphs to answer Questions 27–29.

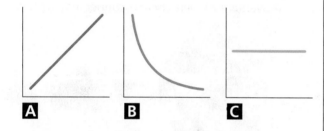

27. Using Graphs Which graph represents what happens to the pressure in a tire as air is added to the tire? Assume the temperature of the gas is constant.

28. Using Graphs Which graph represents what happens to the pressure in an aerosol can if the can is heated?

29. Applying Concepts Which graph represents temperature versus time during a phase change?

Math Skills

30. Making Generalizations The pressure of a gas is directly proportional to its temperature in kelvins. Using P_1, P_2, T_1, and T_2, write a mathematical equation that expresses this relationship.

31. Calculating An automobile tire has a pressure of 325 kPa when the temperature is 10°C. If the temperature of the tire rises to 50°C and its volume is constant, what is the new pressure?

32. Calculating A gas sample occupies 4.2 L at a pressure of 101 kPa. What volume will it occupy if the pressure is increased to 235 kPa?

Concepts in Action

33. Using Models If there is a gas leak in the basement of a building, you will soon notice an odor throughout the house. However, if there is a water leak in the basement, you will need to go to the basement to detect the leak. Use the kinetic theory to explain the differences.

34. Inferring A student examines a thermometer placed in a can containing a substance that is being heated. The temperature remains the same for several minutes, and then it starts to rise. Without looking in the can, how does the student know what is occurring in the can?

35. Relating Cause and Effect In Earth's atmosphere, pressure and temperature both decrease as altitude increases. Weather balloons expand as they rise. Which has more effect on the weather balloon, the decrease in pressure or the decrease in temperature? Explain your answer.

36. Drawing Conclusions In a car engine, air and gasoline vapors are mixed in a cylinder. A piston is pushed into the cylinder before a spark ignites the mixture of gases. When the piston is pushed into the cylinder, what happens to the pressure of the gases in the cylinder?

37. Writing in Science Unpopped popcorn kernels contain a small amount of water. Use what you know about vaporization and how gases behave to explain why popcorn pops when it is heated.

Performance-Based Assessment

Making a Poster The gas laws have many practical applications in cooking. Make a poster, including diagrams, that shows how two factors that affect gases affect cooking. Examples might include explaining why cakes rise while baking or why some recipes specify high-altitude temperatures and cooking times.

For: Self-grading assessment
Visit: PHSchool.com
Web Code: cca-1030

Standardized Test Prep

Watch For Qualifiers

The words *best* and *least* are examples of qualifiers. If a question contains a qualifier, more than one answer will contain correct information. However, only one answer will be complete and correct for the question asked. Look at the question below. Eliminate any answers that are clearly incorrect. Then choose the remaining answer that offers the best explanation for the question asked.

Choose the *best* explanation for why one particle in a gas does not affect other particles in a gas unless the particles collide.
(A) Particles in a gas are constantly moving.
(B) All the particles in a gas have the same kinetic energy.
(C) There are no forces of attraction among particles in a gas.
(D) There are billions of particles in a small sample of a gas.
(E) Particles in a gas are relatively far apart.

(Answer: E)

Choose the letter that best answers the question or completes the statement.

1. A material can be classified as a liquid if
(A) it has a definite shape and a definite volume.
(B) it has a definite shape and a variable volume.
(C) it has a variable shape and a definite volume.
(D) it has a variable shape and a variable volume.
(E) its particles vibrate around fixed locations.

2. Which statement *best* explains what must take place for water to boil?
(A) The water releases energy to its surroundings.
(B) Bubbles rise to the surface of the water.
(C) The vapor pressure of the water becomes equal to atmospheric pressure.
(D) Molecules at the surface of the water overcome the attractions of neighboring molecules.
(E) The temperature of the water increases.

3. Condensation is the phase change in which a substance changes from
(A) a solid to a gas.
(B) a solid to a liquid.
(C) a liquid to a solid.
(D) a liquid to a gas.
(E) a gas to a liquid.

4. Which of these statements about an enclosed gas is true? (Assume all quantities are constant except the two variables described in each statement.)
(A) Raising the temperature of a gas will increase its pressure.
(B) Increasing the volume of a gas will increase its pressure.
(C) Reducing the number of particles of a gas will increase its pressure.
(D) The volume of a gas is inversely proportional to its temperature in kelvins.
(E) The volume of a gas is directly proportional to its pressure.

Use the illustration to answer Question 5. Assume that the number of particles of gas in container A equals the number of particles of gas in container B.

5. If the temperature is constant, the pressure in container B is
(A) one half the pressure in container A.
(B) twice the pressure in container A.
(C) equal to the pressure in container A.
(D) five times the pressure in container A.
(E) one fifth the pressure in container A.

6. During an endothermic phase change,
(A) the temperature of a substance rises.
(B) the temperature of a substance decreases.
(C) energy is transferred from a substance to its surroundings.
(D) a substance absorbs energy from its surroundings.
(E) there is no transfer of energy.

21st Century Learning

Problem Identification, Formulation, and Solution

What are subatomic particles?

Atoms are too small to be seen, but scientists have learned much about their structure. Atoms are made of even smaller particles called subatomic particles. Make a slide-show presentation that describes the structure of an atom. Your presentation should include information about the size, mass, charge, and location of each type of subatomic particle. Show your presentation in class or post it to your class blog.

How do science concepts apply to your world? Here are some questions you'll be able to answer after you read this chapter.

- **What uses are there for objects that are not visible to the unaided eye?** *(page 106)*

- **Which subatomic particle produces the images on many television screens and computer monitors?** *(Section 4.2)*

- **How does the type of hydrogen atom in water affect the properties of water?** *(Section 4.2)*

- **How do fireworks produce the colors you see when the fireworks explode?** *(Section 4.3)*

These images of carbon were magnified as much as 20 million times. Color was added to the images to highlight features.

Chapter Preview

Inquiry > Activity

How Can You Study Objects That Are Not Visible?

Procedure

1. Make and record observations about the contents of two sealed bags. Use your senses of touch, smell, and hearing to help you make your observations.

2. Predicting Based on your observations, make a prediction about what objects could be in each bag. Decide whether there is a single object or more than one object in each bag.

3. Your teacher will list on the chalkboard all of the predictions from the class.

Think About It

1. Inferring What evidence did you use to predict what objects were in the bags and how many objects were in the bags?

2. Evaluating and Revising Record one of the predictions listed that fits your observations as well as or better than your own prediction.

3. Designing Experiments Propose an experiment that would test the prediction.

4.1 Studying Atoms

Key Concepts

- What was Dalton's theory of the structure of matter?
- What contributions did Thomson and Rutherford make to the development of atomic theory?

Vocabulary

- nucleus

Reading Strategy

Summarizing Copy the table. As you read, complete the table about atomic models.

Scientist	Evidence	Model
a. ___?___	Ratio of masses in compounds	b. ___?___
c. ___?___	Deflected beam	d. ___?___
Rutherford	e. ___?___	Positive, dense nucleus

Studying the structure of atoms is a little like studying wind. Because you cannot see air, you must use indirect evidence to tell the direction of the wind. You might notice which way fallen leaves move as they are pushed by the wind, and infer that the leaves and wind are moving in the same direction.

Atoms pose a similar problem because they are extremely small. Even with a microscope, scientists cannot see the structure of an atom. In this chapter, you will find out how John Dalton, J. J. Thomson, Ernest Rutherford, Niels Bohr, and other scientists used evidence from experiments to develop models of atoms.

Ancient Greek Models of Atoms

If you cut a piece of aluminum foil in half, you have two smaller pieces of the same shiny, flexible substance. You could cut the pieces again and again. Can you keep dividing the aluminum into smaller pieces? Greek philosophers debated a similar question about 2500 years ago.

The philosopher Democritus believed that all matter consisted of extremely small particles that could not be divided. He called these particles *atoms* from the Greek word *atomos*, which means "uncut" or "indivisible." He thought there were different types of atoms with specific sets of properties. The atoms in liquids, for example, were round and smooth, but the atoms in solids were rough and prickly.

Aristotle did not think there was a limit to the number of times matter could be divided. Figure 1 shows the model Aristotle used to describe matter. For many centuries, most people accepted Aristotle's views on the structure of matter. But by the 1800s, scientists had enough data from experiments to support an atomic model of matter.

Figure 1 Aristotle thought that all substances were built up from only four elements—earth, air, fire, and water. These elements were a combination of four qualities—hot, cold, dry, and wet. Fire was a combination of hot and dry. Water was a combination of cold and wet.

Dalton's Atomic Theory

John Dalton was born in England in 1766. He was a teacher who spent his spare time doing scientific experiments. Because of his interest in predicting the weather, Dalton studied the behavior of gases in air. Based on the way gases exert pressure, Dalton correctly concluded that a gas consists of individual particles.

Evidence for Atoms Dalton gathered evidence for the existence of atoms by measuring the masses of elements that combine when compounds form. He noticed that all compounds have something in common. No matter how large or small the sample, the ratio of the masses of the elements in the compound is always the same. In other words, compounds have a fixed composition.

For example, when magnesium burns, as shown in Figure 2, it combines with oxygen. The product of this change is a white solid called magnesium oxide. A 100-gram sample of magnesium combines with 65.8 grams of oxygen. A 10-gram sample of magnesium combines with 6.58 grams of oxygen. The ratio of the mass of magnesium to the mass of oxygen is constant in magnesium oxide.

Dalton's Theory Dalton developed a theory to explain why the elements in a compound always join in the same way. ◉ **Dalton proposed the theory that all matter is made up of individual particles called atoms, which cannot be divided.** The main points of Dalton's theory are as follows.

- All elements are composed of atoms.

- All atoms of the same element have the same mass, and atoms of different elements have different masses.

- Compounds contain atoms of more than one element.

- In a particular compound, atoms of different elements always combine in the same way.

In the model of atoms based on Dalton's theory, the elements are pictured as solid spheres like those in Figure 3. Each type of atom is represented by a tiny, solid sphere with a different mass.

Recall that a theory must explain the data from many experiments. Because Dalton's atomic theory met that goal, the theory became widely accepted. Over time, scientists found that not all of Dalton's ideas about atoms were completely correct. But this did not cause later scientists to discard the atomic theory. Instead, they revised the theory to take into account new discoveries.

 Reading Checkpoint *What did Dalton notice that all compounds have in common?*

Figure 2 Magnesium reacts with oxygen to form the compound magnesium oxide. The ratio of magnesium to oxygen, by mass, in magnesium oxide is always about 3 : 2. **Observing** *What color is magnesium oxide?*

Figure 3 Dalton made these wooden spheres to represent the atoms of different elements.

Sticky sides down

Quick Lab

Investigating Charged Objects

Materials

transparent tape, metric ruler, scissors

Procedure

1. Cut two 10-cm pieces of tape. Fold over 1 cm of tape at one end of each piece of tape to form a "handle."

2. Hold the pieces of tape by their folded ends so that they are hanging straight down. Then, without letting the pieces of tape touch, slowly bring their sticky sides close together. Record your observations.

3. Place one piece of tape on a clean surface with the sticky side facing down.

4. Place the second piece, sticky side down, directly over the first piece, as shown. Press down firmly so the pieces stick together.

5. Remove the joined strips from the table. Slowly peel the strips apart.

6. Bring the separated strips close together without touching. Record your observations.

Analyze and Conclude

1. **Drawing Conclusions** What can you conclude about the charges on the two pieces of tape after they are separated?

2. **Inferring** What other objects have you observed that became charged?

Figure 4 Amber is the hardened form of a sticky, viscous liquid that protects trees from insects and disease. If amber is rubbed with wool, it becomes charged and can attract a feather. **Predicting** *What will happen to the feather if the amber loses its charge?*

Thomson's Model of the Atom

When some materials are rubbed, they gain the ability to attract or repel other materials. Glass and the amber in Figure 4 have this property. Based on their behavior, such materials are said to have either a positive or a negative electric charge. Objects with like charges repel, or push apart. Objects with opposite charges attract, or pull together.

Some charged particles can flow from one location to another. A flow of charged particles is called an electric current. When you turn on an appliance such as a hair dryer, a current flows from the wall socket through the appliance. Joseph John Thomson (1856–1940), better known as J. J. Thomson, used an electric current to learn more about atoms.

Thomson's Experiments Thomson used a device like the one shown in Figure 5A. At the center of the device is a sealed glass tube from which most of the air has been removed. There is a metal disk at each end of the tube. Wires connect the metal disks to a source of electric current. When the current is turned on, one disk becomes negatively charged and the other disk becomes positively charged. A glowing beam appears in the space between the disks.

Thomson hypothesized that the beam was a stream of charged particles that interacted with the air in the tube and caused the air to glow. In one experiment Thomson did to test his hypothesis, he placed a pair of charged metal plates on either side of the glass tube, as shown in Figure 5B. The plates caused the beam to deflect, or bend, from its straight path. Thomson observed that the beam was repelled by the negatively charged plate and attracted by the positively charged plate.

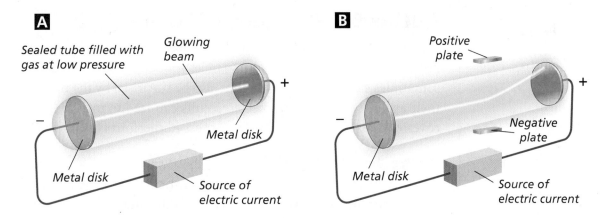

A

Sealed tube filled with gas at low pressure

Glowing beam

−

Metal disk

Metal disk

+

Source of electric current

B

Positive plate

−

Metal disk

Negative plate

+

Source of electric current

Figure 5 Thomson used a sealed tube of gas in his experiments. **A** When the current was on, the disks became charged and a glowing beam appeared in the tube. **B** The beam bent toward a positively charged plate placed outside the tube.
Inferring **What was the charge on the particles in the beam?**

Evidence for Subatomic Particles Thomson concluded that the particles in the beam had a negative charge because they were attracted to the positive plate. He hypothesized that the particles came from inside atoms. He had two pieces of evidence to support his hypothesis. No matter what metal Thomson used for the disk, the particles produced were identical. The particles had about $\frac{1}{2000}$ the mass of a hydrogen atom, the lightest atom.

Thomson's discovery changed how scientists thought about atoms. Before his experiments, the accepted model of the atom was a solid ball of matter that could not be divided into smaller parts. 🔑 **Thomson's experiments provided the first evidence that atoms are made of even smaller particles.** Thomson revised Dalton's model to account for these subatomic particles.

Figure 6 A scoop of chocolate chip ice cream can represent Thomson's model of the atom. The chips represent negatively charged particles, which are spread evenly through a mass of positively charged matter—the vanilla ice cream.

Thomson's Model An atom is neutral, meaning it has neither a negative nor a positive charge. How can an atom contain negative particles and still be neutral? There must be some positive charge in the atom. In Thomson's model of the atom, the negative charges were evenly scattered throughout an atom filled with a positively charged mass of matter. The model is called the "plum pudding" model, after a traditional English dessert.

You might prefer to think of Thomson's model as the "chocolate chip ice cream" model. Think of the chocolate chips in Figure 6 as the negative particles and the vanilla ice cream as the positively charged mass of matter. When the chocolate chips are spread evenly throughout the ice cream, their "negative charges" balance out the "positive charge" of the vanilla ice cream.

 Reading Checkpoint *How do objects with the same charge behave when they come close to one another?*

For: Links on atomic theory
Visit: www.SciLinks.org
Web Code: ccn-1041

Rutherford's Atomic Theory

When you try something new, you may have expectations about the outcome. Does the outcome always meet your expectations or are you sometimes surprised? Scientists can also be surprised by the results of their experiments, but unexpected results can lead to important discoveries. This is what happened to Ernest Rutherford (1871–1937).

Rutherford's Hypothesis In 1899, Ernest Rutherford discovered that uranium emits fast-moving particles that have a positive charge. He named them alpha particles. In 1909, Rutherford asked one of his students, Ernest Marsden, to find out what happens to alpha particles when they pass through a thin sheet of gold.

Recall that in Thomson's model of the atom, the mass and positive charge are evenly spread throughout an atom. Based on this model, Rutherford hypothesized that the mass and charge at any location in the gold would be too small to change the path of an alpha particle. He predicted that most particles would travel in a straight path from their source to a screen that lit up when struck. Those few that did not pass straight through would be deflected only slightly.

The Gold Foil Experiment Marsden used the equipment shown in Figure 7. He aimed a narrow beam of alpha particles at the gold. The screen around the gold was made of a material that produced a flash of light when struck by a fast-moving alpha particle. By observing the flash, Marsden could figure out the path of an alpha particle after it passed through the gold.

Some of the locations of the flashes on the screen did not support Rutherford's prediction. More particles were deflected than he expected. About one out of every 20,000 was deflected by more than 90 degrees. Some of the alpha particles behaved as though they had struck an object and bounced straight back.

Figure 7 The path of an alpha particle can be detected by the location of a flash on a screen. Rutherford expected the paths of the positively charged alpha particles that were aimed at the thin gold foil to be affected only slightly by the gold atoms. But more particles were deflected than expected and some particles bounced straight back.

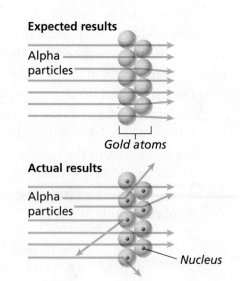

Discovery of the Nucleus The alpha particles whose paths were deflected must have come close to another charged object. The closer they came, the greater the deflection was. But many alpha particles passed through the gold without being deflected. From these results, Rutherford concluded that the positive charge of an atom is not evenly spread throughout the atom. It is concentrated in a very small, central area that Rutherford called the nucleus. The **nucleus** is a dense, positively charged mass located in the center of the atom. (The plural of *nucleus* is *nuclei*.)

Because Thomson's model no longer explained all the evidence, Rutherford proposed a new model. ◯ **According to Rutherford's model, all of an atom's positive charge is concentrated in its nucleus.** The alpha particles whose paths were deflected by more than 90 degrees came very close to a nucleus. The alpha particles whose paths were not bent moved through the space surrounding the nuclei without coming very close to any nucleus.

Figure 8 shows the inside of the Astrodome, a domed stadium in Houston, Texas. The roof of the stadium rises to a height of 202 feet above the center of the field. If an atom had the same volume as the stadium, its nucleus would have the volume of a marble. The total volume of an atom is about a trillion (10^{12}) times the volume of its nucleus.

Figure 8 The Houston Astrodome occupies more than nine acres and seats 60,000 people. If the stadium were a model for an atom, a marble could represent its nucleus. **Using Analogies** *In the model, where would the marble have to be located in the stadium to represent the nucleus?*

Section 4.1 Assessment

Reviewing Concepts

1. ◯ What theory did Dalton propose about the structure of matter?

2. ◯ What evidence did J. J. Thomson provide about the structure of an atom?

3. ◯ What did Rutherford discover about the structure of an atom?

4. What evidence did Thomson have that his glowing beam contained negative particles?

5. Why was Dalton's model of the atom changed after Thomson's experiment?

Critical Thinking

6. **Comparing and Contrasting** Explain why scientists accepted Dalton's atomic theory but not the idea of an atom proposed by the Greek philosophers.

7. **Drawing Conclusions** If you observed a beam of particles being bent toward a negatively charged plate, what might you conclude?

8. **Relating Cause and Effect** In the Rutherford experiment, why weren't all the alpha particles deflected?

Writing in Science

Writing to Persuade Imagine you live in ancient Greece. Assume all you know about matter is what you can observe with your five senses. You have heard the views of both Democritus and Aristotle about matter. Write a paragraph supporting one of their views.

Small-Scale Construction

Some scientists and engineers think of atoms and molecules as construction materials for building very small objects.

The field of science called nanotechnology is named for a unit of measurement—the nanometer. A billion nanometers (10^9 nm) can fit in one meter. The diameter of a human hair is about 80,000 nm. Scientists and engineers who use nanometers as measuring units are building miniature versions of objects such as motors.

There are two general methods for building any object. You can start with more material than you need and shape the object by removing matter or you can build up the object from smaller pieces. When you shape your nails with an emery board, you are using a top-down construction method. When you see "some assembly required" on the side of a box, the manufacturer expects you to use a bottom-up method of construction.

Dust mite

Silicon gear assembly

Building from the top down
Gears are toothed disks that are designed to fit together so that the motion of one gear controls the motion of another. These silicon gears are among the smallest objects ever made from the top down.

Building from the bottom up
With a scanning tunneling microscope, it is possible to move individual atoms or molecules. This figure, made of linked carbon monoxide molecules, is just five nanometers (0.000005 mm) tall. In 1990, scientists built this figure to demonstrate bottom-up construction methods.

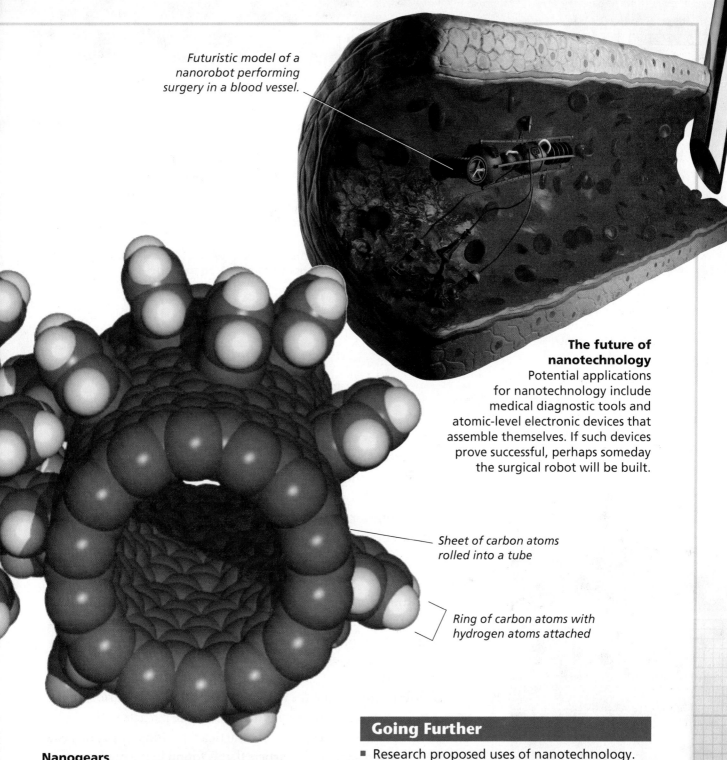

Futuristic model of a nanorobot performing surgery in a blood vessel.

The future of nanotechnology

Potential applications for nanotechnology include medical diagnostic tools and atomic-level electronic devices that assemble themselves. If such devices prove successful, perhaps someday the surgical robot will be built.

Sheet of carbon atoms rolled into a tube

Ring of carbon atoms with hydrogen atoms attached

Nanogears

This image of nanogears was produced with a computer program designed to make models of molecules. Hollow tubes (nanotubes) made from sheets of carbon atoms do exist. So do the rings containing carbon and hydrogen atoms, which are used for the "teeth" of the gears. But researchers need to figure out how to get the "teeth" to attach to the tubes.

Going Further

■ Research proposed uses of nanotechnology. Make a poster describing one proposed use. Explain the advantage of using small objects in this application. What problems must be solved before the application can be used?

4.2 The Structure of an Atom

Reading Focus

Key Concepts

- What are three subatomic particles?

- What properties can be used to compare protons, electrons, and neutrons?

- How are atoms of one element different from atoms of other elements?

- What is the difference between two isotopes of the same element?

Vocabulary

- proton
- electron
- neutron
- atomic number
- mass number
- isotopes

Reading Strategy

Monitoring Your Understanding Before you read, copy the table. List what you know about atoms and what you would like to learn. After you read, list what you have learned.

What I Know About Atoms	What I Would Like to Learn	What I Have Learned

Figure 9 This 45-foot-tall steel sculpture of a clothespin is in Philadelphia, Pennsylvania. Claes Oldenburg made the clothespin in 1976 from 10 tons of steel. If a proton had a mass of 10 tons, then an electron would have a mass of about 5 kilograms.

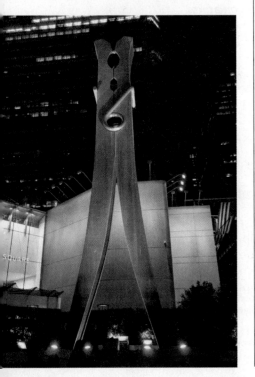

Beams like the ones Thomson produced create the images on many television screens. When a beam sweeps across the screen, spots on the screen light up in the same way the screen in the gold-foil experiment lit up when struck by an alpha particle. In a color television, there are three beams, one for each primary color of light—red, green, and blue. The particles in these beams are subatomic particles.

Properties of Subatomic Particles

By 1920, Rutherford had seen evidence for the existence of two subatomic particles and had predicted the existence of a third particle. **Protons, electrons, and neutrons are subatomic particles.**

Protons Based on experiments with elements other than gold, Rutherford concluded that the amount of positive charge varies among elements. Each nucleus must contain at least one particle with a positive charge. Rutherford called these particles protons. A **proton** is a positively charged subatomic particle that is found in the nucleus of an atom. Each proton is assigned a charge of 1+. Some nuclei contain more than 100 protons.

Electrons The particles that Thomson detected were later named electrons. *Electron* comes from a Greek word meaning "amber." An **electron** is a negatively charged subatomic particle that is found in the space outside the nucleus. Each electron has a charge of 1−.

Properties of Subatomic Particles					
Particle	Symbol	Relative Charge	Relative Mass (proton = 1)	Actual Mass (g)	Model
Electron	e^-	1−	$\dfrac{1}{1836}$	9.11×10^{-28}	
Proton	p^+	1+	1	1.674×10^{-24}	
Neutron	n	0	1	1.675×10^{-24}	

Figure 10 This table lists the symbol, the relative charge, the relative mass, and the actual mass of an electron, a proton, and a neutron. The Model column shows the colors used in this book to represent the subatomic particles. **Calculating** *What is the difference in actual mass between a proton and a neutron?*

Neutrons In 1932, the English physicist James Chadwick designed an experiment to show that neutrons exist. Chadwick concluded that the particles he produced were neutral because a charged object did not deflect their paths. A **neutron** is a neutral subatomic particle that is found in the nucleus of an atom. It has a mass almost exactly equal to that of a proton.

Comparing Subatomic Particles

Figure 10 summarizes some properties of protons, electrons, and neutrons. ⚬ **Protons, electrons, and neutrons can be distinguished by mass, charge, and location in an atom.** Protons and neutrons have almost the same mass. But the data in Figure 10 show that it would take about 2000 electrons to equal the mass of one proton. Electrons have a charge that is equal in size to, but the opposite of, the charge of a proton. Neutrons have no charge. Protons and neutrons are found in the nucleus, but electrons are found in the space outside the nucleus.

Go Online
SCIENCE NEWS

For: Articles on atomic chemistry
Visit: PHSchool.com
Web Code: cce-1042

Problem-Solving ⟩ Activity

Designing an Atomic Exhibit

You work as a volunteer at the local science museum. You are asked to design an exhibit that compares the size of a lithium atom to the size of its nucleus. A lithium atom has a diameter of about 3×10^2 picometers. The nucleus of a lithium atom has a diameter of about 5×10^{-3} picometers. There are a trillion (10^{12}) picometers in a meter.

Defining the Problem State the problem in your own words. What decisions will you need to make before you can proceed?

Organizing Information How many times larger is the lithium atom than its nucleus? Find several objects that could represent the nucleus in your exhibit and measure their diameters.

Creating a Solution Pick one of the objects you measured to represent the nucleus in your atomic exhibit. Figure out how far away from the object you would have to place a marker so that people could visualize the relative sizes of the atom and the nucleus.

Presenting Your Plan Write a proposal to present to the committee that approves projects. Tell them where you would place the nucleus and where you would have to place the marker. Be prepared to explain why your exhibit needs the space you are requesting.

Everything scientists know about the nucleus and subatomic particles is based on how the particles behave. Scientists still do not have an instrument that can show the inside of an atom. But they do have microscopes that can show how atoms are arranged on the surface of a material. The How It Works box on page 111 describes one of those microscopes.

 Reading Checkpoint *Which scientist demonstrated the existence of neutrons?*

Atomic Number and Mass Number

Dalton predicted that the atoms of any element are different from the atoms of all other elements. With the discovery of subatomic particles, scientists were able to describe those differences.

Atomic Number The atoms of any given element always have the same number of protons. For example, there is one proton in the nucleus of each and every hydrogen atom. Therefore, hydrogen is assigned the atomic number 1. The **atomic number** of an element equals the number of protons in an atom of that element.

Hydrogen atoms are the only atoms with a single proton. ⚷ **Atoms of different elements have different numbers of protons.** The sulfur shown in Figure 11A is assigned atomic number 16 because a sulfur atom has 16 protons. You can use atomic numbers to refer to elements, like names and symbols, because each element has a unique atomic number.

Each positive charge in an atom is balanced by a negative charge because atoms are neutral. So the atomic number of an element also equals the number of electrons in an atom. Each hydrogen atom has one electron. Each sulfur atom has 16.

Mass Number The atomic number tells you the number of protons in an atom's nucleus. It does not give you any information about the number of neutrons in an atom. For that information, you need to know the atom's mass number. The **mass number** of an atom is the sum of the protons and neutrons in the nucleus of that atom. An atom of aluminum with 13 protons and 14 neutrons has a mass number of 27. If you know the atomic number and the mass number of an atom, you can find the number of neutrons by subtracting.

Figure 11 Each element has a different atomic number. **A** The atomic number of sulfur (S) is 16. **B** The atomic number of iron (Fe) is 26. **C** The atomic number of silver (Ag) is 47.
Applying Concepts *How many protons are there in each atom of sulfur, iron, and silver?*

Number of Neutrons

Number of neutrons = Mass number − Atomic number

HOW It Works

Scanning Tunneling Microscope

A probe is moved back and forth across the surface of a sample. When electrons jump, or tunnel, across the gap between the sample and the probe, an electric current is produced. A computer uses data about changes in the probe's position to produce an image of the sample's surface. **Interpreting Diagrams** *How is the distance between the probe tip and the sample kept constant?*

Scanning tunneling microscope
Modern scanning tunneling microscopes produce images of metal samples or biological specimens such as DNA.

A **Scanning probe**
As the probe is moved over the sample, current flows between the probe tip and the sample. The processor holds the tip at a constant distance from the sample by keeping the electric current constant. Thus, changes in the vertical position of the probe will follow the contours of the sample's surface.

Electrical signal from processor

Electrical signal from probe

B **Processor**
The processor sends, receives, and records information about the movement of the probe.

Scanning device *This device raises and lowers the probe.*

Electron flow
Electrons flow across a gap of about one nanometer (0.000001 mm) between the probe tip and the sample, producing an electric current.

Gold sample

C **Computer** A computer assembles a map of the sample's surface, using data received from the processor. Color was added to the image shown on the computer screen.

Probe tip *The tip of the probe is only one or two atoms in width.*

Comparing Ordinary Water and Heavy Water		
Property	Ordinary Water	Heavy Water
Melting point	0.00°C	3.81°C
Boiling point	100.00°C	101.42°C
Density (at 25°C)	0.99701 g/cm³	1.1044 g/cm³

Figure 12 Heavy water contains hydrogen-2 atoms, which have twice the mass of hydrogen-1 atoms. **Using Tables** *At what temperature would a sample of heavy water freeze?*

Isotopes

In Dalton's atomic theory, all the atoms of a given element are identical. Every atom of a given element *does* have the same number of protons and electrons. But every atom of a given element *does not* have the same number of neutrons. **Isotopes** are atoms of the same element that have different numbers of neutrons and different mass numbers. ⬤ **Isotopes of an element have the same atomic number but different mass numbers because they have different numbers of neutrons.**

For example, every atom of oxygen has 8 protons. Some oxygen atoms have 8 neutrons and a mass number of 16. Some oxygen atoms have 9 neutrons and a mass number of 17. Some oxygen atoms have 10 neutrons and a mass number of 18. When it is important to distinguish one oxygen isotope from another, the isotopes are referred to as oxygen-16, oxygen-17, and oxygen-18. All three oxygen isotopes can react with hydrogen to form water or combine with iron to form rust.

With most elements, it is hard to notice any differences in the physical or chemical properties of their isotopes. Hydrogen is an exception. Hydrogen-1 has no neutrons. (Almost all hydrogen is hydrogen-1.) Hydrogen-2 has one neutron, and hydrogen-3 has two neutrons. Because a hydrogen-1 atom has only one proton, adding a neutron doubles its mass. Water that contains hydrogen-2 atoms in place of hydrogen-1 atoms is called heavy water. Figure 12 compares some physical properties of ordinary water and heavy water.

Section 4.2 Assessment

Reviewing Concepts

1. ⬤ Name three subatomic particles.
2. ⬤ Name three properties you could use to distinguish a proton from an electron.
3. ⬤ Which characteristic of an atom always varies among atoms of different elements?
4. ⬤ How are the isotopes of an element different from one another?
5. What do neutrons and protons have in common? How are they different?
6. How can atoms be neutral if they contain charged particles?
7. What is the difference between atoms of oxygen-16 and oxygen-17?

Critical Thinking

8. **Comparing and Contrasting** What property do protons and electrons have that neutrons do not?
9. **Applying Concepts** Explain why it isn't possible for an atom to have a mass number of 10 and an atomic number of 12.

Connecting ⊂ Concepts

Elements In Section 2.1, you were told that elements contain only one type of atom. How would you define "type of atom" to account for the existence of isotopes?

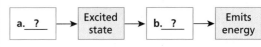

Reading Focus

Key Concepts

- What can happen to electrons when atoms gain or lose energy?
- What model do scientists use to describe how electrons behave in atoms?
- What is the most stable configuration of electrons in an atom?

Vocabulary

- energy levels
- electron cloud
- orbital
- electron configuration
- ground state

Reading Strategy

Sequencing Copy the flowchart. After you read, complete the description of how a gain or loss of energy affects atoms.

Electrons and Energy Levels

| a. ? | → | Excited state | → | b. ? | → | Emits energy |

Have you ever wondered what produces the different colors in a fireworks display? Why does one explosion produce red light and another explosion produce green light? The people who make fireworks know that certain compounds will produce certain colors of light when they are heated. For example, compounds containing the element strontium produce red light when they are heated. Compounds containing barium produce green light.

You have seen two things that can happen when atoms absorb energy—an increase in kinetic energy or a phase change. But there is another possibility. The energy may be temporarily absorbed by the atom and then emitted as light. The colors in a fireworks display are a clue to how electrons are arranged in atoms.

Bohr's Model of the Atom

You may have seen diagrams of an atom that look like a solar system with planets revolving around a sun. These diagrams are based on a model of the atom that was developed by Niels Bohr (1885–1962), a Danish physicist who worked for a while with Rutherford. Bohr agreed with Rutherford's model of a nucleus surrounded by a large volume of space. But Bohr's model did something that Rutherford's model did not do. It focused on the electrons. A description of the arrangement of electrons in an atom is the centerpiece of the modern atomic model.

Figure 13 Fireworks are often displayed above the Lincoln Memorial in Washington, D.C. The red light was produced by a strontium compound.

Energy Levels In Bohr's model, electrons move with constant speed in fixed orbits around the nucleus, like planets around a sun. Each electron in an atom has a specific amount of energy. If an atom gains or loses energy, the energy of an electron can change. The possible energies that electrons in an atom can have are called **energy levels.**

To understand energy levels, picture them as steps in a staircase. As you move up or down the staircase, you can measure how your position changes by counting the number of steps you take. You might take one step up, or you might jump two steps down. Whether you are going up or down, you can move only in whole-step increments. Just as you cannot stand between steps on a staircase, an electron cannot exist between energy levels.

DK SCIENCE and History

Models of the Atom

The development of scientific ideas on the structure of atoms has passed several key milestones during the last 200 years.

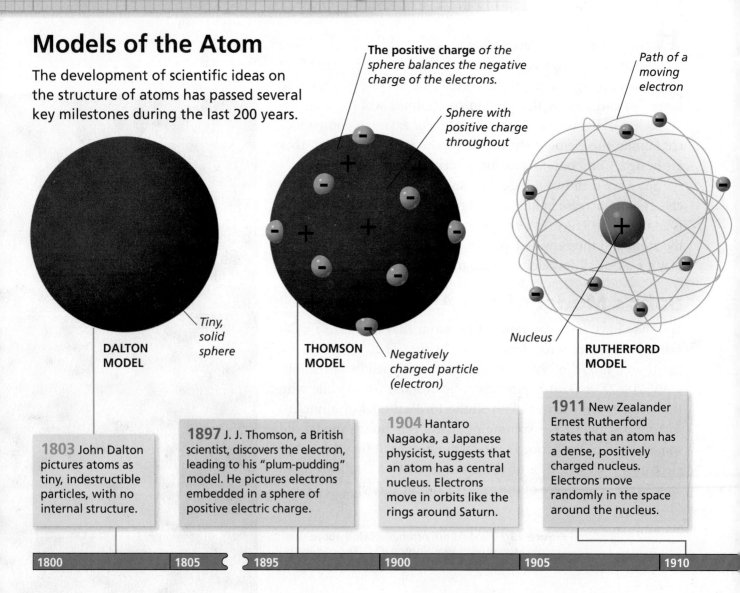

The positive charge *of the sphere balances the negative charge of the electrons.*

Sphere with *positive charge throughout*

Path of a *moving electron*

DALTON MODEL

Tiny, solid sphere

THOMSON MODEL

Negatively charged particle (electron)

Nucleus

RUTHERFORD MODEL

1803 John Dalton pictures atoms as tiny, indestructible particles, with no internal structure.

1897 J. J. Thomson, a British scientist, discovers the electron, leading to his "plum-pudding" model. He pictures electrons embedded in a sphere of positive electric charge.

1904 Hantaro Nagaoka, a Japanese physicist, suggests that an atom has a central nucleus. Electrons move in orbits like the rings around Saturn.

1911 New Zealander Ernest Rutherford states that an atom has a dense, positively charged nucleus. Electrons move randomly in the space around the nucleus.

| 1800 | 1805 | 1895 | 1900 | 1905 | 1910 |

The landing at the bottom of the staircase is like the lowest energy level in an atom. Each step up represents a higher energy level. The distance between two steps represents the difference in energy between two energy levels. To continue the analogy, there would need to be a different staircase for each element because no two elements have the same set of energy levels.

🔑 **An electron in an atom can move from one energy level to another when the atom gains or loses energy.** An electron may move up two energy levels if it gains the right amount of energy. An electron in a higher energy level may move down two energy levels if it loses the right amount of energy. The size of the jump between energy levels determines the amount of energy gained or lost.

Writing in Science

Summary Select a scientist mentioned on the time line. Research and write a paragraph about the scientist's early years. What experiences led to his interest in science? Was he the first in his family to be interested in science? What subjects did he study at school?

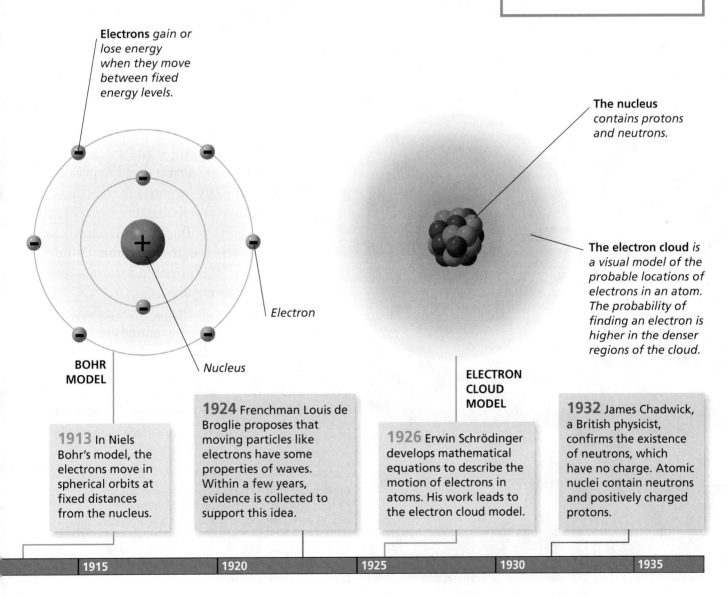

Electrons *gain or lose energy when they move between fixed energy levels.*

Electron

BOHR MODEL

Nucleus

The nucleus *contains protons and neutrons.*

The electron cloud *is a visual model of the probable locations of electrons in an atom. The probability of finding an electron is higher in the denser regions of the cloud.*

ELECTRON CLOUD MODEL

1913 In Niels Bohr's model, the electrons move in spherical orbits at fixed distances from the nucleus.

1924 Frenchman Louis de Broglie proposes that moving particles like electrons have some properties of waves. Within a few years, evidence is collected to support this idea.

1926 Erwin Schrödinger develops mathematical equations to describe the motion of electrons in atoms. His work leads to the electron cloud model.

1932 James Chadwick, a British physicist, confirms the existence of neutrons, which have no charge. Atomic nuclei contain neutrons and positively charged protons.

| 1915 | 1920 | 1925 | 1930 | 1935 |

Evidence for Energy Levels What evidence is there that electrons can move from one energy level to another? Scientists can measure the energy gained when electrons absorb energy and move to a higher energy level. They can measure the energy released when the electron returns to a lower energy level.

The movement of electrons between energy levels explains the light you see when fireworks explode. Light is a form of energy. Heat produced by the explosion causes some electrons to move to higher energy levels. When those electrons move back to lower energy levels, they emit energy. Some of that energy is released as visible light. Because no two elements have the same set of energy levels, different elements emit different colors of light.

 What determines the amount of energy gained or lost when an electron moves between energy levels?

Electron Cloud Model

Like earlier models, Bohr's model was improved as scientists made further discoveries. Bohr was correct in assigning energy levels to electrons. But he was incorrect in assuming that electrons moved like planets in a solar system. Today, scientists know that electrons move in a less predictable way.

Scientists must deal with probability when trying to predict the locations and motions of electrons in atoms. An **electron cloud** is a visual model of the most likely locations for electrons in an atom. The cloud is denser at those locations where the probability of finding an electron is high. **Scientists use the electron cloud model to describe the possible locations of electrons around the nucleus.**

Figure 14 provides an analogy for an electron cloud. When the blades of a windmill are at rest, you can count the number of blades. When they are moving, the blades spin so fast that you see only a blur. You know that the blades are located somewhere in the blur, but at any specific moment in time you can't be exactly sure where each blade is located.

Figure 14 When the blades of a windmill are at rest, you can see their locations. When the blades are spinning, you see only a blur that is similar to a drawing of an electron cloud. **Comparing and Contrasting** *Describe one difference between the motion of windmill blades and the motion of an electron.*

Quick Lab

Comparing Excited States

Materials

fluorescent ("neon") markers, glow-in-the-dark toy, ultraviolet (UV) lamp

Procedure

1. Use the fluorescent markers to draw a picture on a piece of paper.

2. With the room darkened, observe your drawing under a UV lamp. **CAUTION** *Do not look directly at the light.* Remove the drawing from under the UV light and observe it again. Record your observations.

3. Observe the glow-in-the-dark toy under the UV light. Remove the toy from the light and observe it again. Record your observations.

Analyze and Conclude

1. **Observing** How did the glow of the toy differ from the glow of your drawing?

2. **Formulating Hypotheses** Use the concepts of ground and excited states to explain how UV light caused your drawing and the toy to glow.

3. **Drawing Conclusions** In which object, your drawing or the toy, do the atoms have excited states that are more stable, or less likely to change? Explain your answer.

Atomic Orbitals

The electron cloud represents all the orbitals in an atom. An **orbital** is a region of space around the nucleus where an electron is likely to be found. To understand the concept of an orbital, imagine a map of your school. Suppose you mark your exact location with a dot once every 10 minutes over a period of one week. The places you visit the most—such as your classrooms, the cafeteria, and the area near your locker—would have the highest concentration of dots. The places you visit the least would have the lowest concentration of dots.

The dots on your map are a model of your "orbital." They describe your most likely locations. There are some locations in your orbital that you may not visit every week—such as the principal's office or the auditorium. These locations may not be represented by a dot on your map. Despite such omissions, the dots on your map are a good model of how you usually behave in your orbital. 🔵 **An electron cloud is a good approximation of how electrons behave in their orbitals.**

The level in which an electron has the least energy—the lowest energy level—has only one orbital. Higher energy levels have more than one orbital. Figure 15 shows the number of orbitals in the first four energy levels of an atom. Notice that the maximum number of electrons in an energy level is twice the number of orbitals. Each orbital can contain two electrons at most.

Figure 15 The table lists the number of orbitals in the first four energy levels of an atom. It also lists the maximum number of electrons in each energy level. **Inferring** *How many electrons can be in each orbital?*

Energy Levels, Orbitals, and Electrons		
Energy Level	Number of Orbitals	Maximum Number of Electrons
1	1	2
2	4	8
3	9	18
4	16	32

Figure 16 A gymnast on a balance beam is like an atom in an excited state—not very stable.

Electron Configurations

How are the seats in your classroom arranged? Are they lined up neatly in rows, or are they grouped in clusters? A configuration is an arrangement of objects in a given space. Some configurations are more stable than others, meaning that they are less likely to change. The position of the gymnast on the balance beam in Figure 16 is not very stable because the beam is only 10 centimeters wide.

An **electron configuration** is the arrangement of electrons in the orbitals of an atom. 🔑 **The most stable electron configuration is the one in which the electrons are in orbitals with the lowest possible energies.** When all the electrons in an atom have the lowest possible energies, the atom is said to be in its **ground state.**

For example, lithium is a silvery-white metal with an atomic number of 3, which means that a lithium atom has three electrons. In the ground state, two of the lithium electrons are in the orbital of the first energy level. The third electron is in an orbital of the second energy level.

If a lithium atom absorbs enough energy, one of its electrons can move to an orbital with a higher energy. This configuration is referred to as an excited state. An excited state is less stable than the ground state. Eventually, the electron that was promoted to a higher energy level loses energy, and the atom returns to the ground state. Helium, neon, argon, krypton, and xenon atoms returning from excited states to the ground state emit the light you see in "neon" lights.

Section 4.3 Assessment

Reviewing Concepts

1. 🔑 When is an electron in an atom likely to move from one energy level to another?

2. 🔑 What model do scientists use to describe how electrons move around the nucleus?

3. 🔑 Describe the most stable configuration of the electrons in an atom.

4. What did Bohr contribute to modern atomic theory?

5. What does an electron cloud represent?

Critical Thinking

6. **Comparing and Contrasting** A boron atom has two electrons in the first energy level and three in the second energy level. Compare the relative energies of the electrons in these two energy levels.

7. **Making Judgments** Was Rutherford's model of an atom incorrect or incomplete? Explain your answer.

8. **Posing Questions** Apply what you know about charged particles to the modern model of the atom. Is there anything about the behavior of electrons in atoms that is unexpected? Explain your answer.

Writing in Science

Describing Energy Levels Use a bookcase as an analogy for the energy levels in an atom. Use the analogy to write a paragraph about electrons and energy levels. (*Hint:* Reread the staircase analogy on pages 114 and 115.)

Using Flame Tests

Forensic scientists use various approaches to distinguish different substances. In this lab, you will observe the flame colors of several substances and use the data to determine the identity of an unknown substance.

Problem
How can the color of a flame be used to distinguish substances?

Materials

- solutions of calcium chloride, boric acid, potassium chloride, copper(II) sulfate, sodium chloride, and an unknown
- Bunsen burner
- nichrome wire loop
- dilute solution of hydrochloric acid
- wash bottle with distilled water

Skills
Observing, Predicting, Using Data Tables

Procedure

Part A: Observing Flame Colors

1. Make a copy of the data table shown.

Data Table	
Solution	Flame Color
Calcium chloride	
Potassium chloride	
Boric acid	
Copper(II) sulfate	
Sodium chloride	
Unknown	
Identity of Unknown	

2. Light the Bunsen burner. **CAUTION** *Put on safety goggles and a lab apron. Tie back loose hair and clothing before working with a flame.*

3. Dip the wire loop into the calcium chloride solution and then place the loop in the flame as shown. Observe and record the color of the flame.

4. Clean the loop by dipping it into hydrochloric acid. Then, while holding the loop over a sink, rinse away the acid with distilled water. **CAUTION** *Keep hydrochloric acid away from your skin and clothing. Do not breathe in its vapor.*

5. Repeat Steps 3 and 4 with each of the other solutions. Be careful not to transfer any solution from one container to another. **CAUTION** *These chemicals are poisonous. Do not let them get on your skin.*

Part B: Examining an Unknown Solution

6. Obtain the unknown solution from your teacher.

7. Repeat Steps 3 and 4 using the unknown solution. Compare your observations with the other data you recorded to identify the unknown. **CAUTION** *Wash your hands thoroughly before leaving the laboratory.*

Analyze and Conclude

1. **Comparing and Contrasting** Is there a relationship between the color of the flame and the color of the solution?

2. **Formulating Hypotheses** How do these substances produce light of different colors?

3. **Drawing Conclusions** A forensic scientist does a flame test on a substance that was found at a crime scene. What might the scientist conclude if the flame turns green?

Go Further There is another test that you can use to distinguish elements by color. With your teacher supervising, dip a wire loop in borax. Heat the loop in a flame until the borax melts. Remove the loop from the flame and let the borax cool. It will form a clear glass bead. Dip the bead in a tiny sample of solid copper sulfate and return the loop to the flame for a few seconds. Remove the loop and observe the color of the bead as it cools.

Study Guide

4.1 Studying Atoms

Key Concepts

- Dalton proposed the theory that all matter is made up of individual particles called atoms, which cannot be divided.
- Thomson's experiments provided the first evidence that atoms are made of even smaller particles.
- According to Rutherford's model, all of an atom's positive charge is concentrated in its nucleus.

Vocabulary

nucleus, *p. 105*

4.2 The Structure of an Atom

Key Concepts

- Protons, electrons. and neutrons are subatomic particles.
- Protons, electrons, and neutrons can be distinguished by mass, charge, and location in an atom.
- Atoms of different elements have different numbers of protons.
- Isotopes of an element have the same atomic number but different mass numbers because they have different numbers of neutrons.

Vocabulary

proton, *p. 108*
electron, *p. 108*
neutron, *p. 109*
atomic number, *p. 110*
mass number, *p. 110*
isotopes, *p. 112*

4.3 Modern Atomic Theory

Key Concepts

- An electron in an atom can move from one energy level to another when the atom gains or loses energy.
- Scientists use the electron cloud model to describe the possible locations of electrons around the nucleus.
- An electron cloud is a good approximation of how electrons behave in their orbitals.
- The most stable electron configuration is the one in which the electrons are in orbitals with the lowest possible energies.

Vocabulary

energy levels, *p. 114*
electron cloud, *p. 116*
orbital, *p. 117*
electron configuration, *p. 118*
ground state, *p. 118*

Thinking Visually

Table of Properties Use information from the chapter to complete the table below.

Particle	Proton	Electron	Neutron
Symbol	a. __?__	e^-	n
Relative charge	1+	b. __?__	c. __?__
Relative mass	d. __?__	$\dfrac{1}{1836}$	e. __?__

Assessment

Reviewing Content

Choose the letter that best answers the question or completes the statement.

1. One of the first people to state that matter is made up of atoms was
   a. Democritus.   **b.** Aristotle.
   c. Dalton.   **d.** Rutherford.

2. Dalton's model of an atom is best described as
   a. a solar system.   **b.** a solid sphere.
   c. a plum pudding.   **d.** an electron cloud.

3. Who provided the first evidence that atoms contain subatomic particles?
   a. Dalton   **b.** Rutherford
   c. Thomson   **d.** Bohr

4. Almost all the mass of an atom is located in its
   a. protons.   **b.** electrons.
   c. electron cloud. **d.** nucleus.

5. An electron is a particle with
   a. a negative charge, found in the nucleus.
   b. a positive charge, found in the nucleus.
   c. no charge, found outside the nucleus.
   d. a negative charge, found outside the nucleus.

6. Which particle is the least massive?
   a. proton   **b.** electron
   c. neutron   **d.** nucleus

7. All atoms of an element have the same
   a. mass number.   **b.** number of isotopes.
   c. atomic number.   **d.** number of neutrons.

8. The number of neutrons in an atom equals the
   a. mass number minus atomic number.
   b. atomic number plus number of electrons.
   c. mass number plus atomic number.
   d. atomic number minus mass number.

9. The atomic number of sulfur is 16. How many electrons are there in an atom of sulfur-34?
   a. 16   **b.** 34
   c. 18   **d.** 50

10. Atoms emit energy as light when
   a. electrons move to a higher energy level.
   b. electrons move to a lower energy level.
   c. protons move to a higher energy level.
   d. protons move to a lower energy level.

Understanding Concepts

11. Why must indirect evidence be used to study the structure of atoms?

12. What evidence convinced Dalton that elements must be made of individual particles called atoms?

13. In Thomson's experiment, why was the glowing beam repelled by a negatively charged plate?

14. What evidence supported Thomson's hypothesis that the negative particles he observed came from inside atoms?

15. Compare the mass and volume of the nucleus to the total mass and volume of an atom.

16. Compare the relative masses of protons, neutrons, and electrons in an atom.

17. What is the difference between the atomic number of an atom and its mass number?

18. If the atomic number of an atom is 11, how many electrons does the atom have? Explain.

19. If an atom has an atomic number of 6 and a mass number of 14, how many protons, electrons, and neutrons are in the atom?

20. What part of Dalton's theory was modified after the discovery of isotopes?

21. Which isotope of oxygen is represented by the drawing—oxygen-16, oxygen-17, or oxygen-18? Assume that all the protons and neutrons in the nucleus are visible in the drawing. Give a reason for your answer.

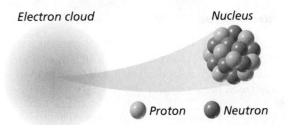

Electron cloud   *Nucleus*

● *Proton*   ● *Neutron*

22. What is the main difference between Bohr's model of the atom and the atomic theory that is currently accepted?

23. What does it mean to say that an atom is in an excited state?

Assessment (continued)

Critical Thinking

24. Controlling Variables Look at the drawing of the experimental setup in Figure 5A. Explain how the setup is a control for the setup in Figure 5B.

25. Predicting How would the results of Thomson's experiment change if the beam were a stream of neutrons instead of a stream of electrons?

26. Interpreting Diagrams The atomic number of carbon is 6. The atomic number of nitrogen is 7. The atomic number of oxygen is 8. Name the isotope represented by the drawing.

Electron cloud   *Nucleus*

 Proton ● Neutron

27. Hypothesizing Why were the proton and electron discovered before the neutron?

28. Applying Concepts Explain why a neutral atom cannot have one proton, one neutron, and two electrons.

29. Classifying The nucleus of an atom contains six neutrons and six protons. The nucleus of a second atom contains six neutrons and five protons. Are they atoms of different elements or isotopes of the same element? Explain your answer.

Math Skills

30. Calculating The atomic number for iron is 26. How many neutrons are in the nucleus of an iron atom with a mass number of 57? How many electrons does the iron atom have?

31. Applying Concepts If a potassium atom has an atomic number of 19 and a mass number of 39, how many protons, electrons, and neutrons are in the atom?

32. Applying Concepts A helium-4 atom has twice as many protons as a hydrogen atom. How many protons and how many neutrons are in the nucleus of a helium-4 atom?

Concepts in Action

33. Comparing and Contrasting The compound in blood that carries oxygen to cells throughout the body contains iron. Iron has an atomic number of 26. Iron-59 is used to diagnose disorders in the blood. How is iron-59 different from all other isotopes of iron? How is it the same?

34. Using Analogies Scientists working in the field of nanotechnology use either a top-down or bottom-up approach to construct tiny objects. Give an example of a visible structure that was made using the bottom-up approach and one that was made using the top-down approach.

35. Inferring If you see a green color when fireworks explode, can you be certain that the fireworks contained a barium compound? Give a reason for your answer.

36. Relating Cause and Effect Brightly colored neon lights consist of tubes filled with a gas. When an electric current passes through the tubes, different colors are emitted. Why might you conclude that the tubes in a multicolored display contain more than one element?

37. Writing in Science Better technology leads to an increase in scientific knowledge. An increase in knowledge allows for the invention of new technology. Write a paragraph discussing these statements. Use a scanning tunneling microscope as your example.

Performance-Based Assessment

Preparing a Survey Write ten questions you could ask to find out what people know about the modern model of an atom. Figure out the best order for the questions to test someone's knowledge fairly. Be prepared to explain your choices.

For: Self-grading assessment
Visit: PHSchool.com
Web Code: cca-1040

Standardized Test Prep

Test-Taking Tip

Using Data Tables

When presented with a question that is related to a data table, read the title of the table to see what type of data it contains. Then look at the headings of the columns and rows to see how the data are organized. The table below lists properties for subatomic particles. There is a row for each particle and a column for each property. Read the question to find out which data you will need to answer the question. In this case, you will need the data on relative charge.

Properties of Subatomic Particles

Particle	Symbol	Relative Charge	Relative Mass (proton = 1)
Electron	e^-	1−	$\dfrac{1}{1836}$
Proton	p^+	1+	1
Neutron	n	0	1

Which of the following statements is true?
(A) The charge on a proton is larger than the charge on an electron.
(B) The charge on a proton is smaller than the charge on an electron.
(C) The charge on a proton is identical to the charge on an electron
(D) The charge on a proton is equal in size but opposite to the charge on an electron.
(E) A proton is a neutral particle.

(Answer: D)

Choose the letter that best answers the question or completes the statement.

1. J. J. Thomson demonstrated that electrons
   (A) have a negative electric charge.
   (B) have a positive electric charge.
   (C) are repelled by a positively charged object.
   (D) are attracted to a negatively charged object.
   (E) do not have an electric charge.

2. According to Dalton's atomic theory, an atom is
   (A) made of smaller particles.
   (B) a particle with a positive charge.
   (C) the smallest particle of an element.
   (D) in constant motion.
   (E) a particle with a negative charge.

3. Electrons in the first energy level of an atom
   (A) have no energy.
   (B) have the lowest possible energy.
   (C) have the highest possible energy.
   (D) are in an excited state.
   (E) are in an unstable state.

4. Most alpha particles pass through a thin layer of gold without deflection because gold atoms
   (A) are filled with positively charged matter.
   (B) have no overall charge.
   (C) have a negatively charged nucleus.
   (D) do not have a nucleus.
   (E) have a dense nucleus surrounded by space.

Use the data table to answer Question 5.

Comparison of Oxygen Isotopes

Property	Oxygen-16	Oxygen-18
Protons	8	8
Neutrons	8	10
Electrons	8	8
Percentage in nature	99.757	0.205

5. What is the mass number of oxygen-18?
   (A) 8
   (B) 10
   (C) 16
   (D) 18
   (E) 0.205

6. An electron configuration describes
   (A) regions of space around the nucleus of an atom.
   (B) possible energies that an electron can have.
   (C) the arrangement of electrons in an atom.
   (D) the emission of light from an excited atom.
   (E) the number of possible orbitals in an atom.

What are periodic trends and why are they important?

The periodic table lists important information about the elements. This information is communicated in the text entries within the table and also in the arrangement of the table's rows and columns. After you have learned how to read the periodic table, create a Web page that explains periodic trends. Include both a graphic description and a written description of each trend. Your finished Web page should serve as a useful reference for someone wanting to find the information quickly.

How do science concepts apply to your world? Here are some questions you'll be able to answer after you read this chapter.

- **How can a card game be a model for organizing elements?** *(Section 5.1)*

- **What do a piano keyboard and a periodic table of the elements have in common?** *(Section 5.2)*

- **Which element makes it possible for plants to capture the energy of sunlight and use it to make sugar?** *(Section 5.3)*

- **Why are aluminum cans such an important part of recycling programs?** *(Section 5.3)*

- **Can an element be both helpful and harmful to the human body?** *(page 146)*

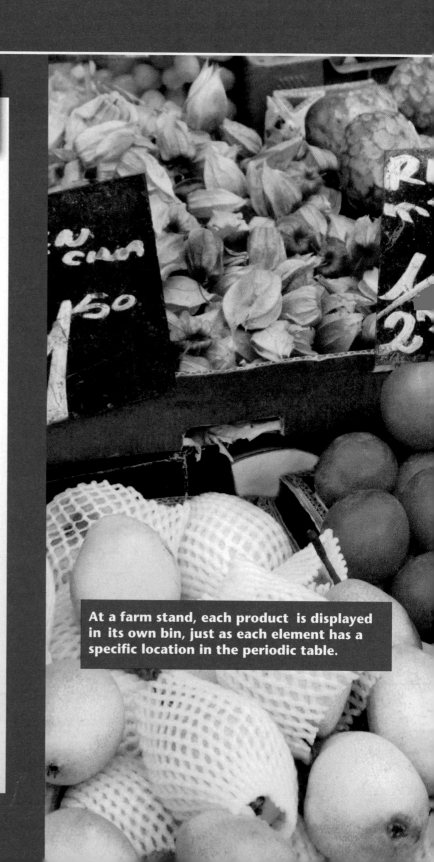

At a farm stand, each product is displayed in its own bin, just as each element has a specific location in the periodic table.

Chapter Preview

Inquiry **Activity**

How Much Data Do You Need to Identify a Pattern?

Procedure

1. Your teacher will give you a stapled stack of paper. Look at the squares on the top sheet of paper. Try to figure out what familiar phrase you would see if all the squares were filled in. Record your prediction on the sheet.

2. Remove the top sheet and look at the second sheet. Again, try to figure out what letters belong in the squares. Record your prediction.

3. Continue this process until you have looked at all the sheets in the stack.

Think About It

1. **Observing** How did the information on the sheets change as you moved from the top to the bottom of the stack?

2. **Drawing Conclusions** How did the number of letters provided affect your ability to predict the phrase?

3. **Using Analogies** Describe another situation in which having more data makes it easier to recognize a pattern.

5.1 Organizing the Elements

Key Concepts

- How did Mendeleev organize the elements in his periodic table?
- What evidence helped verify the usefulness of Mendeleev's table?

Vocabulary

- periodic table

Reading Strategy

Identifying Main Ideas
Copy the table. As you read, write the main idea for each topic.

Topic	Main Idea
Mendeleev's proposal	a. _____?_____
Mendeleev's prediction	b. _____?_____
Evidence supporting Mendeleev's table	c. _____?_____

In a department store, clothes for men, women, and children are in different departments. Within some departments, items are further grouped by size or cost. The store manager has to choose a set of categories and then place each item in the most appropriate location.

Scientists faced a similar challenge when they looked for a logical way to organize the elements. They had to decide what categories to use and where to place each element. An organized table of the elements is one of the most useful tools in chemistry. The placement of elements on the table reveals the link between the atomic structure of elements and their properties.

The Search for Order

Until 1750, scientists had identified only 17 elements. These elements were mainly metals, such as copper and iron. The rate of discovery increased rapidly as chemists began to investigate materials in a systematic way. As the number of known elements grew, so did the need to organize them into groups based on their properties.

In 1789, French chemist Antoine Lavoisier (la VWAH zee ay) grouped the known elements into categories he called metals, nonmetals, gases, and earths. For the next 80 years, scientists looked for different ways to classify the elements. But none of their systems provided an organizing principle that worked for all the known elements. A Russian chemist and teacher, Dmitri Mendeleev (Duh MEE tree Men duh LAY uff), would discover such a principle.

Figure 1 This directory shows how items are organized by floor in one department store.

Mendeleev's Periodic Table

In the 1860s, Mendeleev was working on a textbook to use with his chemistry students. Because he needed to describe 63 elements, Mendeleev was looking for the best way to organize the information. He found a way to approach the problem while playing his favorite card game, a version of solitaire. In this game, the player sorts a deck of cards by suit and value. To finish the game, the player must end up with four columns, as shown in Figure 2. Each column contains cards of a single suit arranged in order by value.

Figure 2 A deck of cards can be divided into four suits—diamonds, spades, hearts, and clubs. In one version of solitaire, a player must produce an arrangement in which each suit is ordered from ace to king. This arrangement is a model for Mendeleev's periodic table.

Mendeleev's Proposal Mendeleev's strategy for organizing the elements was modeled on the card game. Mendeleev made a "deck of cards" of the elements. On each card, he listed an element's name, mass, and properties. He paid special attention to how each element behaved in reactions with oxygen and hydrogen. When Mendeleev lined up the cards in order of increasing mass, a pattern emerged. The key was to break the elements into rows, as shown in Figure 3.

🔑 **Mendeleev arranged the elements into rows in order of increasing mass so that elements with similar properties were in the same column.** The final arrangement was similar to a winning arrangement in solitaire, except that the columns were organized by properties instead of suits. Within a column, the masses increased from top to bottom. Mendeleev's chart was a periodic table. A **periodic table** is an arrangement of elements in columns, based on a set of properties that repeat from row to row.

Figure 3 This is a copy of a table that Mendeleev published in 1872. He placed the elements in groups based on the compounds they formed with oxygen or hydrogen. **Using Tables** *How many elements did Mendeleev place in Group II?*

Group I	Group II	Group III	Group IV	Group V	Group VI	Group VII	Group VIII
H = 1							
Li = 7	Be = 9.4	B = 11	C = 12	N = 14	O = 16	F = 19	
Na = 23	Mg = 24	Al = 27.3	Si = 28	P = 31	S = 32	Cl = 35.5	Fe = 56, Co = 59,
K = 39	Ca = 40	— = 44	Ti = 48	V = 51	Cr = 52	Mn = 55	Ni = 59, Cu = 63.
(Cu = 63)	Zn = 65	— = 68	— = 72	As = 75	Se = 78	Br = 80	Ru = 104, Rh = 104,
Rb = 85	Sr = 87	Yt = 88	Zr = 90	Nb = 94	Mo = 96	— = 100	Pd = 106, Ag = 108.
(Ag = 108)	Cd = 112	In = 113	Sn = 118	Sb = 122	Te = 125	I = 127	
Cs = 133	Ba = 137	Di = 138	Ce = 140	—	—	—	— — —
(—)	—	—	—	Ta = 182	W = 184	—	Os = 195, Ir = 197,
—	—	Er = 178	La = 180				Pt = 198, Au = 199.
(Au = 199)	Hg = 200	Tl = 204	Pb = 207	Bi = 208			
—	—	—	Th = 231	—	U = 240		

≡Quick Lab

Making a Model of a Periodic Table

Materials

plastic bag containing color chips

Procedure

1. Remove the color chips from the bag and place them on a flat surface, color side up.

2. Identify a property that you can use to divide the chips into groups. Then, identify a second property that you can use to order the chips from top to bottom within a group.

3. Use the properties you chose to arrange the chips into a table with rows and columns. Your teacher deliberately left out a chip from each bag. Decide where to leave a gap in your table for the missing chip.

Analyze and Conclude

1. **Classifying** What property did you use to divide the color chips into groups? What property did you use to arrange the chips within a group from top to bottom?

2. **Making Generalizations** What pattern repeats across each row of your table?

3. **Predicting** Based on its location on your table, describe the missing chip.

4. **Comparing and Contrasting** Compare the process you used to construct your table to the process Mendeleev used to make his table. Describe similarities and differences.

For: Links to periodic table
Visit: www.SciLinks.org
Web Code: ccn-1051

Mendeleev's Prediction Mendeleev could not make a complete table of the elements because many elements had not yet been discovered. He had to leave spaces in his table for those elements. For example, Mendeleev placed bromine (Br) in Group VII because bromine and chlorine (Cl) have similar properties. This placement left four spaces in row 4 between zinc (Zn) and bromine. Mendeleev had only two elements, arsenic and selenium, to fill those spaces, based on their masses. He placed arsenic and selenium in the columns where they fit best and left gaps in the columns labeled Groups III and IV.

Mendeleev was not the first to arrange elements in a periodic table. He was not even the first to leave spaces in a periodic table for missing elements. But he was able to offer the best explanation for how the properties of an element were related to its location in his table.

An excellent test for the correctness of a scientific model, such as Mendeleev's table, is whether the model can be used to make accurate predictions. Mendeleev was confident that the gaps in his table would be filled by new elements. He used the properties of elements located near the blank spaces in his table to predict properties for undiscovered elements. Some scientists didn't accept these predictions. Others used the predictions to help in their search for undiscovered elements.

 Reading Checkpoint

Why did Mendeleev place bromine in Group VII of his periodic table?

Evidence Supporting Mendeleev's Table

Mendeleev named missing elements after elements in the same group. He gave the name eka-aluminum to the element that belonged one space below aluminum on the table. (*Eka* is a Sanskrit word meaning "one.") Mendeleev predicted that eka-aluminum would be a soft metal with a low melting point and a density of 5.9 g/cm³.

In 1875, a French chemist discovered a new element. He named the element gallium (Ga) in honor of France. (The Latin name for France is *Gallia*.) Gallium is a soft metal with a melting point of 29.7°C and a density of 5.91 g/cm³. Figure 4 shows a sample of gallium and a traffic signal that uses gallium compounds.

The properties of gallium are remarkably similar to the predicted properties of eka-aluminum. Scientists concluded that gallium and eka-aluminum are the same element. 🔑 **The close match between Mendeleev's predictions and the actual properties of new elements showed how useful his periodic table could be.** The discovery of scandium (Sc) in 1879 and the discovery of germanium (Ge) in 1886 provided more evidence. With the periodic table, chemists could do more than predict the properties of new elements. They could explain the chemical behavior of different groups of elements.

Figure 4 Gallium was discovered in 1875. Heat from a person's hand can melt gallium. In some traffic signals, there are tiny light emitting diodes (LEDs) that contain a compound of gallium. **Comparing and Contrasting** *How does the melting point of gallium (29.7°C) compare to room temperature (about 25°C)?*

Section 5.1 Assessment

Reviewing Concepts

1. 🔑 Describe how Mendeleev organized the elements into rows and columns in his periodic table.

2. 🔑 How did the discovery of new elements such as gallium demonstrate the usefulness of Mendeleev's table?

3. Scientists before Mendeleev had proposed ways to organize the elements. Why were Mendeleev's efforts more successful?

4. What characteristic of solitaire did Mendeleev use as a model for his periodic table?

5. Why did Mendeleev leave spaces in his table?

6. In general, how can a scientist test the correctness of a scientific model?

Critical Thinking

7. **Inferring** Explain why it would not have been possible for a scientist in 1750 to develop a table like Mendeleev's.

8. **Predicting** How was Mendeleev able to predict the properties of elements that had not yet been discovered?

Writing in Science

Writing to Persuade Write a paragraph about Mendeleev's periodic table. Use the paragraph to convince a reader that the periodic table is extremely useful to scientists. (*Hint:* Use specific facts to support your argument.)

Reading Focus

Key Concepts
- How is the modern periodic table organized?
- What does the atomic mass of an element depend on?
- What categories are used to classify elements on the periodic table?
- How do properties vary across a period in the periodic table?

Vocabulary
- period
- group
- periodic law
- atomic mass unit (amu)
- metals
- transition metals
- nonmetals
- metalloids

Reading Strategy
Previewing Copy the table below. Before you read, write two questions about the periodic table on pages 132 and 133. As you read, write answers to your questions.

Questions About the Periodic Table	
Question	Answer
a._____?_____	b._____?_____
c._____?_____	d._____?_____

Figure 5 On this synthesizer keyboard, there is a repeating pattern of notes. The eight-note interval between any two notes with the same name is an octave. **Observing** *How many octaves are visible on the keyboard?*

$\mathbf{F}$igure 5 shows a synthesizer keyboard with labels for the notes that correspond to the white keys. If you strike the key labeled middle C and then play the white keys in order from left to right, you will hear the familiar do-re-mi-fa-sol-la-ti scale. The next white note is a C that is an octave above middle C. An octave is the interval between any two notes with the same name. (The prefix *octa-* means "eight.") Because the scale repeats at regular eight-note intervals, the scale is an example of a periodic pattern.

The sounds of musical notes that are separated by an octave are related, but they are not identical. In a similar way, elements in the same column of the periodic table are related because their properties repeat at regular intervals. But elements in different rows are not identical. You can use the modern periodic table of elements to classify elements and to compare their properties.

A B C D E F G A B *Middle* C D E F G A B C D E

1	H																		He
2	Li	Be											B	C	N	O	F	Ne
3	Na	Mg											Al	Si	P	S	Cl	Ar
4	K	Ca		Sc	Ti	V	Cr	Mn	Fe	Co	Ni	Cu	Zn	Ga	Ge	As	Se	Br	Kr
5	Rb	Sr		Y	Zr	Nb	Mo	Tc	Ru	Rh	Pd	Ag	Cd	In	Sn	Sb	Te	I	Xe
6	Cs	Ba	La Ce Pr Nd Pm Sm Eu Gd Tb Dy Ho Er Tm Yb	Lu	Hf	Ta	W	Re	Os	Ir	Pt	Au	Hg	Tl	Pb	Bi	Po	At	Rn
7	Fr	Ra	Ac Th Pa U Np Pu Am Cm Bk Cf Es Fm Md No	Lr	Rf	Db	Sg	Bh	Hs	Mt	Ds	Rg	Cn	Uut	Uuq	Uup	Uuh		Uuo

The Periodic Law

Mendeleev developed his periodic table before the discovery of protons. He did not know that all atoms of an element have the same number of protons. He did not know that atoms of two different elements could not have the same number of protons. ⟳ **In the modern periodic table, elements are arranged by increasing atomic number (number of protons).** Figure 6 shows one way the known elements can be arranged in order by increasing atomic number.

Periods Each row in the table of elements in Figure 6 is a **period.** Period 1 has 2 elements. Periods 2 and 3 have 8 elements. Periods 4 and 5 have 18 elements. Period 6 has 32 elements. The number of elements per period varies because the number of available orbitals increases from energy level to energy level.

To understand the structure of the table, think about what happens as the atomic number increases. The first energy level has only one orbital. The one electron in a hydrogen atom and the two electrons in a helium atom can fit in this orbital. But one of the three electrons in a lithium atom must be in the second energy level. That is why lithium is the first element in Period 2. Sodium, the first element in Period 3, has one electron in its third energy level. Potassium, the first element in Period 4, has one electron in its fourth energy level. This pattern applies to all the elements in the first column on the table.

Groups Each column on the periodic table is called a **group.** The elements within a group have similar properties. ⟳ **Properties of elements repeat in a predictable way when atomic numbers are used to arrange elements into groups.** The elements in a group have similar electron configurations. An element's electron configuration determines its chemical properties. Therefore, members of a group in the periodic table have similar chemical properties. This pattern of repeating properties is the **periodic law.**

Look at Figure 7 on pages 132 and 133. There are 18 groups in this periodic table. Some elements from Periods 6 and 7 have been placed below Period 7 so that the table is more compact.

Figure 6 This diagram shows one way to display a periodic table of the elements. There are 7 rows, or periods, in the table. There are 32 columns, or groups, in the table. **Comparing and Contrasting** *Compare the numbers of elements in Periods 1, 3, and 5.*

For: Links on periodic law
Visit: www.SciLinks.org
Web Code: ccn-1052

Periodic Table of the Elements

Figure 7 In a modern periodic table of the elements, elements are arranged in order of increasing atomic number.

Nonmetals	Metals	Metalloids	
C	Li	B	Solid
Br	Hg		Liquid
H			Gas
	Tc		Not found in nature

+1
1
1A

| 1 |
| **H** |
| Hydrogen |
| 1.0079 |

+2
2
2A

3	4
Li	**Be**
Lithium	Beryllium
6.941	9.0122

11	12
Na	**Mg**
Sodium	Magnesium
22.990	24.305

+2

| 3 | 4 | 5 | 6 | 7 | 8 | 9 |
| **3B** | **4B** | **5B** | **6B** | **7B** | **8B** | |

19	20	21	22	23	24	25	26	27
K	**Ca**	**Sc**	**Ti**	**V**	**Cr**	**Mn**	**Fe**	**Co**
Potassium	Calcium	Scandium	Titanium	Vanadium	Chromium	Manganese	Iron	Cobalt
39.098	40.08	44.956	47.90	50.941	51.996	54.938	55.847	58.933

37	38	39	40	41	42	43	44	45
Rb	**Sr**	**Y**	**Zr**	**Nb**	**Mo**	**Tc**	**Ru**	**Rh**
Rubidium	Strontium	Yttrium	Zirconium	Niobium	Molybdenum	Technetium	Ruthenium	Rhodium
85.468	87.62	88.906	91.22	92.906	95.94	(98)	101.07	102.91

55	56	71	72	73	74	75	76	77
Cs	**Ba**	**Lu**	**Hf**	**Ta**	**W**	**Re**	**Os**	**Ir**
Cesium	Barium	Lutetium	Hafnium	Tantalum	Tungsten	Rhenium	Osmium	Iridium
132.91	137.33	174.97	178.49	180.95	183.85	186.21	190.2	192.22

87	88	103	104	105	106	107	108	109
Fr	**Ra**	**Lr**	**Rf**	**Db**	**Sg**	**Bh**	**Hs**	**Mt**
Francium	Radium	Lawrencium	Rutherfordium	Dubnium	Seaborgium	Bohrium	Hassium	Meitnerium
(223)	(226)	(262)	(261)	(262)	(263)	(264)	(265)	(268)

57	58	59	60	61	62
La	**Ce**	**Pr**	**Nd**	**Pm**	**Sm**
Lanthanum	Cerium	Praseodymium	Neodymium	Promethium	Samarium
138.91	140.12	140.91	144.24	(145)	150.4

Lanthanide Series

89	90	91	92	93	94
Ac	**Th**	**Pa**	**U**	**Np**	**Pu**
Actinium	Thorium	Protactinium	Uranium	Neptunium	Plutonium
(227)	232.04	231.04	238.03	(237)	(244)

Actinide Series

Go Online
active art

For: Activity on the periodic table
Visit: PHSchool.com
Web Code: ccp-1052

*Name not officially assigned

Atomic number ——— 17
Element symbol ——— Cl
Element name ——— Chlorine
Atomic mass ——— 35.453

Figure 8 This box provides four pieces of information about the element chlorine: its symbol, its name, its atomic number, and its atomic mass.

Atomic Mass

There are four pieces of information for each element in Figure 7: the name of the element, its symbol, its atomic number and its atomic mass. 🔑 **Atomic mass is a value that depends on the distribution of an element's isotopes in nature and the masses of those isotopes.** You will use atomic masses when you study chemical reactions in Chapter 7.

Atomic Mass Units The mass of an atom in grams is extremely small and not very useful because the samples of matter that scientists work with contain trillions of atoms. In order to have a convenient way to compare the masses of atoms, scientists chose one isotope to serve as a standard. Recall that each isotope of an element has a different number of neutrons in the nuclei of its atoms. So the atoms of two isotopes have different masses.

Scientists assigned 12 atomic mass units to the carbon-12 atom, which has 6 protons and 6 neutrons. An **atomic mass unit** (amu) is defined as one twelfth the mass of a carbon-12 atom.

Isotopes of Chlorine In nature, most elements exist as a mixture of two or more isotopes. Figure 8 shows that the element chlorine has the symbol Cl, atomic number 17, and an atomic mass of 35.453 atomic mass units. (The unit for atomic mass is not listed in the periodic table, but it is understood to be the amu.) Where does the number 35.453 come from? There are two natural isotopes of chlorine, chlorine-35 and chlorine-37. An atom of chlorine-35 has 17 protons and 18 neutrons. An atom of chlorine-37 has 17 protons and 20 neutrons. So the mass of an atom of chlorine-37 is greater than the mass of an atom of chlorine-35.

Weighted Averages Your teacher may use a weighted average to determine your grade. In a weighted average, some values are more important than other values. For example, test scores may count more heavily toward your final grade than grades on quizzes or grades on homework assignments.

Figure 9 lists the atomic masses for two naturally occurring chlorine isotopes. If you add the atomic masses of the isotopes and divide by 2, you get 35.967, not 35.453. The value of the atomic mass for chlorine in the periodic table is a weighted average. The isotope that occurs in nature about 75% of the time (chlorine-35) contributes three times as much to the average as the isotope that occurs in nature about 25% of the time (chlorine-37).

Distribution of Chlorine Isotopes in Nature		
Isotope	Percentage	Atomic Mass
Chlorine-35	75.78%	34.969
Chlorine-37	24.22%	36.966

Figure 9 This table shows the distribution and atomic masses for the two natural isotopes of chlorine. **Using Tables** *Which isotope occurs more often in nature?*

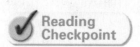

Reading Checkpoint   *What is an atomic mass unit?*

Classes of Elements

The periodic table in Figure 7 presents three different ways to classify elements. First, elements are classified as solids, liquids, or gases, based on their states at room temperature. The symbols for solids are black. The symbols for liquids are purple. The symbols for gases are red.

Second, elements are divided into those that occur naturally and those that do not. All but two elements with atomic numbers 1 through 92 occur on Earth. Elements with atomic numbers of 93 and higher do not occur naturally. The symbols for these elements are white. In Chapter 10, you will find out how elements that do not occur in nature are produced.

The third classification system puts elements into categories based on their general properties. 🔑 **Elements are classified as metals, nonmetals, and metalloids.** In the periodic table, metals are located on the left, nonmetals are on the right, and metalloids are in between.

Metals The majority of the elements on the periodic table are classified as metals. In Figure 7, they are represented by blue boxes. **Metals** are elements that are good conductors of electric current and heat. Except for mercury, metals are solids at room temperature. Most metals are malleable. Many metals are ductile; that is, they can be drawn into thin wires.

Some metals are extremely reactive and some do not react easily. One way to demonstrate this difference is to compare the behavior of gold and the behavior of magnesium when these metals are exposed to the oxygen in air. Gold remains shiny because it does not react with the oxygen. Magnesium reacts with the oxygen and quickly dulls. Figure 10A shows one magnesium coil that is dull and one that is shiny. Figure 10B shows one use for a metal with a shiny surface.

≡Quick ⟩Lab

Defining a Metal
Procedure

1. Use forceps to put a piece of magnesium into a test tube in a test tube rack. Using a graduated cylinder, add 5 mL of hydrochloric acid to the test tube. **CAUTION** *Wear plastic gloves because the acid can burn skin or clothing.* Record your observations.

2. Repeat Step 1 with sulfur, aluminum, and silicon.

Analyze and Conclude

1. **Classifying** Based on their locations in the periodic table, classify the four elements as metals, metalloids, or nonmetals.

2. **Comparing and Contrasting** Compare the behavior of the metals with the acid to the behavior of the other elements with the acid.

3. **Forming Operational Definitions** Use your observations to write a definition of a metal.

Figure 10 Magnesium and aluminum are typical metals. **A** When magnesium reacts with oxygen, a dull layer forms on its surface. The layer can be removed to reveal magnesium's shiny surface. **B** Many telescope mirrors are coated with aluminum to produce a surface that reflects light extremely well.

Figure 11 A compound of erbium (Er) and oxygen is used to tint glass pink.

The metals in groups 3 through 12 are called transition metals. **Transition metals** are elements that form a bridge between the elements on the left and right sides of the table. Transition elements, such as copper and silver, were among the first elements discovered. One property of many transition metals is their ability to form compounds with distinctive colors. The How It Works box on page 137 describes the use of transition elements in the production of colored glass.

Some transition elements have more properties in common than elements in other groups. This is especially true of elements in the lanthanide and actinide series. These elements are so similar that chemists in the 1800s had difficulty separating them when they were found mixed together in nature. A compound of erbium and oxygen was used to tint the lenses shown in Figure 11.

Nonmetals In Figure 7, nonmetals are represented by yellow boxes. As their name implies, nonmetals generally have properties opposite to those of metals. **Nonmetals** are elements that are poor conductors of heat and electric current. Because nonmetals have low boiling points, many nonmetals are gases at room temperature. In fact, all the gases in the periodic table are nonmetals. The nonmetals that are solids at room temperature tend to be brittle. If they are hit with a hammer, they shatter or crumble.

Nonmetals vary as much in their chemical properties as they do in their physical properties. Some nonmetals are extremely reactive, some hardly react at all, and some fall somewhere in between. Fluorine in Group 17 is the most reactive nonmetal. It even forms compounds with some gases in Group 18, which are the least reactive elements in the table. The toothpaste in Figure 12 contains a compound of the nonmetal fluorine and the metal sodium. This compound helps to protect your teeth against decay.

Metalloids In the periodic table in Figure 7, metalloids are represented by green boxes. **Metalloids** are elements with properties that fall between those of metals and nonmetals. For example, metals are good conductors of electric current and nonmetals are poor conductors of electric current. A metalloid's ability to conduct electric current varies with temperature. Pure silicon (Si) and germanium (Ge) are good insulators at low temperatures and good conductors at high temperatures.

Figure 12 Toothpaste contains a compound that helps to protect teeth from tooth decay. The compound is formed from the nonmetal fluorine and the metal sodium.

Reading Checkpoint *Which type of metals tend to form compounds with distinctive colors?*

Making Glass

For more than 4500 years, people have made glass from sand. The float-glass process shown below is used to make large sheets of glass for windows, while molds are used to make glass bottles. **Interpreting Diagrams** *How is air used in making glass bottles?*

Colored glass
Metallic elements are mixed with the raw ingredients to produce colored glass. Iron or chromium is added for green, copper or gold for red, and cobalt for blue.

Cullet (waste glass) *Lime (calcium oxide)*
Sand (silicon dioxide) *Soda ash (sodium carbonate)*

1 **Adding the raw ingredients** Sand, lime, and soda ash are poured into the furnace and heated to 1500°C (2730°F). Recycled waste glass, called cullet, is also added, to reduce the cost of raw materials.

2 **Heating in the furnace** The furnace heats the ingredients, producing liquid glass at 1100°C (2010°F). Rollers move the hot and molten glass to the next stage.

3 **Liquid glass** The glass is floated over a bath of melted tin. The glass emerges at 600°C (1110°F) as a continuous sheet with the same thickness throughout.

4 **Cooling the glass** The glass is cooled slowly in a temperature-controlled oven to keep it from cracking.

Furnace
Rollers

Melted tin *Floating the glass on liquid tin produces a glass surface that is as smooth as the surface of the liquid tin.*

Making bottles
Mass-produced glass bottles are made by adding hot glass to a mold and shaping the glass with air at high pressure.

Air pushes the glass to the bottom of the mold, where the neck of the bottle will form.

Hot glass is placed in the mold.

Air tube

Mold sealed

Air blown through the air tube forces the liquid glass to assume the shape of the bottle mold.

Oven

Glass cutter

5 **Cutting the glass** A diamond-tipped cutter is used to cut the cooled glass.

| Sodium | Magnesium | Aluminum | Silicon | Phosphorus | Sulfur | Chlorine | Argon |

Figure 13 From left to right across Period 3, there are three metals (Na, Mg, and Al), one metalloid (Si), and four nonmetals (P, S, Cl, and Ar). Many light bulbs are filled with argon gas.
Observing *Which other element in Period 3 is a gas?*

Variation Across a Period

The properties within a period change in a similar way from left to right across the table, except for Period 1. **Across a period from left to right, the elements become less metallic and more nonmetallic in their properties.** The most reactive metals are on the left side of the table. The most reactive nonmetals are on the right in Group 17. The Period 3 elements shown in Figure 13 provide an example of this trend.

There are three metals, a metalloid, and four nonmetals in Period 3. If you were unwise enough to hold a piece of sodium in your hand, it would react quickly and violently with the water on your moist skin. But magnesium will not react with water unless the water is hot. Aluminum does not react with water, but it does react with oxygen.

Silicon is the least reactive element in Period 3 (except for argon). Under ordinary conditions, phosphorus and sulfur do not react with water, but they do react with oxygen. They also react with chlorine, which is a highly reactive nonmetal. Chlorine must be handled with as much care as sodium. Argon hardly reacts at all.

Section 5.2 Assessment

Reviewing Concepts

1. What determines the order of the elements in the modern periodic table?

2. Describe the periodic law.

3. What two factors determine the atomic mass of an element?

4. Name three categories that are used to classify the elements in the periodic table.

5. What major change occurs as you move from left to right across the periodic table?

Critical Thinking

6. **Formulating Hypotheses** The atomic mass of iodine (I) is less than the atomic mass of tellurium (Te). But an iodine atom has one more proton than a tellurium atom. Explain how this situation is possible.

7. **Applying Concepts** Explain how you know that no new element with an atomic number less than 100 will be discovered.

8. **Comparing and Contrasting** Compare the reactions with water of the elements sodium and magnesium.

Writing in Science

Explanatory Paragraph The word *isotope* comes from the Greek words *isos,* meaning "equal," and *topos,* meaning "place." Write a paragraph explaining how the isotopes chlorine-35 and chlorine-37 occupy the same place in the periodic table.

5.3 Representative Groups

Reading Focus

Key Concepts
- Why do the elements in a group have similar properties?
- What are some properties of the A groups in the periodic table?

Vocabulary
- valence electron
- alkali metals
- alkaline earth metals
- halogens
- noble gases

Reading Strategy
Monitoring Your Understanding Copy the table below. As you read, record an important fact about each element listed.

Element	Important Fact
Magnesium	a._____?_____
Aluminum	b._____?_____
Chlorine	c._____?_____

Why is hydrogen located on the left side of the periodic table with the active metals? It is a nonmetal gas that seems to have more in common with the nonmetals in Group 17. Hydrogen's location is related to its electron configuration, not its properties.

Valence Electrons

Did you wonder why there are two numbering schemes on the periodic table in Figure 7? When the A groups are numbered from 1 through 8, they provide a useful reminder about the electron configurations of the elements in those groups. The number of an A group matches the number of valence electrons in an electron configuration for an element in that group. A **valence electron** is an electron that is in the highest occupied energy level of an atom. These electrons play a key role in chemical reactions. Properties vary across a period because the number of valence electrons increases from left to right.

Elements in a group have similar properties because they have the same number of valence electrons. These properties will not be identical because the valence electrons are in different energy levels. Valence electrons explain the location of hydrogen. Because hydrogen has a single valence electron, it is grouped with other elements, such as lithium, that have only one valence electron.

Figure 14 Because hydrogen is flammable, it can be used as a fuel in automobiles like this one. An engine that burns hydrogen has a key advantage over an engine that burns gasoline. Only water is produced when hydrogen burns.

139

Figure 15 The element sodium is an alkali metal **A** Unlike most metals, sodium is soft enough to cut with a knife. **B** When sodium reacts with water, enough energy is released to ignite the hydrogen that is produced. **Predicting** *What happens when potassium comes in contact with water?*

The Alkali Metals

The elements in Group 1A are called **alkali metals.** These metals have a single valence electron and are extremely reactive. Because they are so reactive, alkali metals are found in nature only in compounds. The most familiar of these compounds is table salt—a compound of sodium and chlorine (sodium chloride). Sodium chloride can be obtained through the evaporation of seawater or from large salt deposits on the surface of Earth or underground.

Not all the elements in a group are equally reactive. Sodium is more reactive than lithium, potassium is more reactive than sodium, and rubidium is more reactive than potassium. **The reactivity of alkali metals increases from the top of Group 1A to the bottom.**

Sodium is about as hard as cold butter and can be cut with a sharp knife, as shown in Figure 15A. Sodium melts at about 98°C and has a lower density than water. A piece of sodium may be able to float on water, but Figure 15B shows that it won't be there for long. The sodium reacts violently with water and releases enough energy to ignite the hydrogen gas that is produced. Sodium and potassium are stored under oil to keep them from reacting with the oxygen and water vapor in air. Cesium is so reactive that it reacts with water at temperatures as low as −115°C. Cesium is usually stored in a sealed glass tube containing argon gas.

Go Online
SCIENCE NEWS®

For: Articles on elements
Visit: PHSchool.com
Web Code: cce-1053

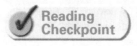
Reading Checkpoint

How many valence electrons does an alkali metal have?

The Alkaline Earth Metals

The elements in Group 2A are called **alkaline earth metals**. All alkaline earth metals have two valence electrons. Metals in Group 2A are harder than metals in Group 1A. The melting point of magnesium is 650°C, which is much higher than the melting point of sodium—98°C.

👁 **Differences in reactivity among the alkaline earth metals are shown by the ways they react with water.** Calcium, strontium, and barium react easily with cold water. Magnesium will react with hot water, but no change appears to occur when beryllium is added to water. Magnesium and calcium have essential biological functions and they provide materials used in construction and transportation.

Magnesium Magnesium plays a key role in the process that uses sunlight to produce sugar in plants like the one in Figure 16. The compound at the center of this process is chlorophyll (KLAWR uh fil), and at the center of chlorophyll is magnesium. A mixture of magnesium and other metals can be as strong as steel, but much lighter. Reducing overall mass without sacrificing strength is an important consideration in transportation. The frames of bicycles and backpacks often contain magnesium.

Calcium Your body needs calcium to keep your bones and teeth strong. Calcium carbonate—a compound of calcium, carbon, and oxygen—is the main ingredient in chalk, limestone, coral, and the pearl in Figure 16. Your toothpaste may contain the compound calcium carbonate because this hard substance can polish your teeth. The plaster cast in Figure 16 contains calcium sulfate, which is a compound of calcium, sulfur, and oxygen.

Group 2A

4	**Be** Beryllium
12	**Mg** Magnesium
20	**Ca** Calcium
38	**Sr** Strontium
56	**Ba** Barium
88	**Ra** Radium

Figure 16 Chlorophyll molecules in spinach contain magnesium. An oyster shell and a pearl are both made from calcium carbonate. A plaster cast contains the compound calcium sulfate.

Spinach plant

Oyster shell with pearl

Plaster cast

The Boron Family

Group 3A contains the metalloid boron, the well-known metal aluminum, and three less familiar metals (gallium, indium, and thallium). All these elements have three valence electrons.

Aluminum is the most abundant metal in Earth's crust. It is often found combined with oxygen in a mineral called bauxite (BAWKS eyet). Aluminum is less reactive than sodium and magnesium. It is strong, lightweight, malleable, and a good conductor of electric current.

More than 10 percent of the aluminum produced is used as packaging. Some aluminum is used in window screens, window frames, and gutters. Parts of cars and airplanes are also made from aluminum. People are encouraged to recycle aluminum because the energy needed to purify recycled aluminum is only about 5 percent of the energy needed to extract aluminum from bauxite.

A compound of boron, silicon, and oxygen is used to make a type of glass that does not shatter easily when it undergoes a rapid change in temperature. Glass that contains boron is used to make laboratory glassware, such as the flasks in Figure 17. It is also used in cookware that can go directly from the oven to the refrigerator.

Figure 17 These students are using flasks made from glass that contains boron. This type of glass does not shatter as easily as glass without boron.

Group 3A

5 **B** Boron
13 **Al** Aluminum
31 **Ga** Gallium
49 **In** Indium
81 **Tl** Thallium

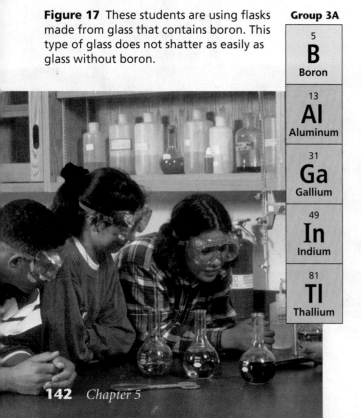

Group 4A

6 **C** Carbon
14 **Si** Silicon
32 **Ge** Germanium
50 **Sn** Tin
82 **Pb** Lead

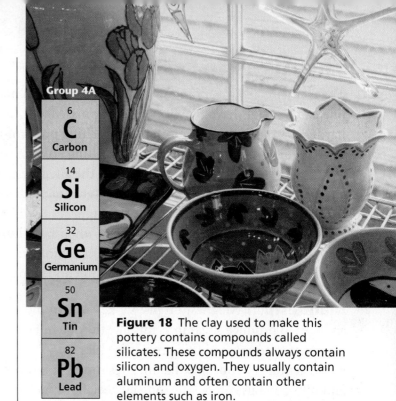

Figure 18 The clay used to make this pottery contains compounds called silicates. These compounds always contain silicon and oxygen. They usually contain aluminum and often contain other elements such as iron.

The Carbon Family

Group 4A contains a nonmetal (carbon), two metalloids (silicon and germanium), and two metals (tin and lead). Each of these elements has four valence electrons. Notice that the metallic nature of the elements increases from top to bottom within the group. In keeping with this trend, germanium is a better conductor of electric current than silicon.

Life on Earth would not exist without carbon. **Except for water, most of the compounds in your body contain carbon.** Reactions that occur in the cells of your body are controlled by carbon compounds. Carbon and its compounds are discussed in Chapter 9, Carbon Chemistry.

Silicon is the second most abundant element in Earth's crust. It is found as silicon dioxide in quartz rocks, sand, and glass. The clay used to produce the pottery in Figure 18 contains silicon compounds called silicates. Silicon carbide, a compound of silicon and carbon, is extremely hard. Saw blades tipped with silicon carbide last many times longer than ordinary steel blades.

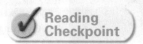 **Reading Checkpoint** *Which Group 3A element is a nonmetal?*

The Nitrogen Family

Group 5A contains two nonmetals (nitrogen and phosphorus), two metalloids (arsenic and antimony), and one metal (bismuth). Like the groups on either side of it, Group 5A includes elements with a wide range of physical properties. Nitrogen is a nonmetal gas, phosphorus is a solid nonmetal, and bismuth is a dense metal. Despite their differences, all the elements in Group 5A have five valence electrons. Nitrogen and phosphorus are the most important elements in Group 5A.

When air is cooled, the oxygen condenses before the nitrogen because nitrogen has a lower boiling point than oxygen. Much of the nitrogen obtained from air is used to produce fertilizers, like the three shown in Figure 19. 🔑 **Besides nitrogen, fertilizers often contain phosphorus.** Your body uses compounds containing nitrogen and phosphorus to control reactions and release energy from food.

Phosphorus exists as an element in several forms with different properties. White phosphorus is so reactive that it bursts into flame when it is in contact with oxygen. Red phosphorus is less reactive and is used to make matches ignite.

Figure 19 The composition of a fertilizer varies with its intended use. The numbers on the bags of fertilizer are, from left to right, the relative amounts of nitrogen, phosphorus, and potassium.
Analyzing Data *Which type of fertilizer contains the most phosphorus?*

Group 5A

7
N
Nitrogen
15
P
Phosphorus
33
As
Arsenic
51
Sb
Antimony
83
Bi
Bismuth

Group 6A

8
O
Oxygen
16
S
Sulfur
34
Se
Selenium
52
Te
Tellurium
84
Po
Polonium

Figure 20 Sulfur is often found in nature in its elemental form—not combined with other elements. **Inferring** *What does this information tell you about the reactivity of sulfur?*

The Oxygen Family

Group 6A has three nonmetals (oxygen, sulfur, and selenium), and two metalloids (tellurium and polonium). All the elements in Group 6A have six valence electrons.

🔑 **Oxygen is the most abundant element in Earth's crust.** Complex forms of life need oxygen to stay alive because oxygen is used to release the energy stored in food. Oxygen can be stored as a liquid under pressure in oxygen tanks. There must be no sparks or flames near an oxygen tank because materials that are flammable burn easily in pure oxygen.

Ozone is another form of the element oxygen. At ground level, ozone can irritate your eyes and lungs. At upper levels of the atmosphere, ozone absorbs harmful radiation emitted by the sun.

Sulfur was one of the first elements to be discovered because it is found in large natural deposits like the one in Figure 20. The main use of sulfur is in the production of sulfuric acid, a compound of sulfur, hydrogen, and oxygen. More sulfuric acid is produced in the United States than any other chemical. About 65 percent of the sulfuric acid produced is used to make fertilizers.

Group 7A

9
F
Fluorine

17
Cl
Chlorine

35
Br
Bromine

53
I
Iodine

85
At
Astatine

Figure 21 At room temperature, chlorine is a gas, bromine is a liquid, and iodine is a solid. Halogens react easily with metals, such as the iron in steel wool. At a swimming pool, the chlorine content must be tested frequently. **Applying Concepts** *What process causes iodine vapor to collect in a flask of solid iodine?*

Chlorine reacting with
steel wool

The Halogens

The elements in Group 7A are called **halogens.** Each halogen has seven valence electrons. Figure 21 shows the range of physical properties among the halogens. Fluorine and chlorine are gases, bromine is a liquid that evaporates quickly, and iodine is a solid that sublimes. **Despite their physical differences, the halogens have similar chemical properties.** They are highly reactive nonmetals, with fluorine being the most reactive and chlorine a close second. Halogens react easily with most metals. Figure 21 shows what happens when heated steel wool is plunged into chlorine.

Recall that a fluorine compound is used to prevent tooth decay. If you use pans with a nonstick coating to make omelets or muffins, you have seen another use of a fluorine compound. Have you ever noticed a sharp smell when adding bleach to a load of clothes? The smell comes from a small amount of chlorine gas that is released from a chlorine compound in the bleach. Chlorine is also used to kill bacteria in drinking water and swimming pools. The woman in Figure 21 is testing the level of chlorine in a swimming pool.

Your body needs iodine to keep your thyroid gland working properly. This gland controls the speed at which reactions occur in your body. Seafood is a good source of iodine. At a time when fresh fish was not available in all parts of the United States, people began to add iodine compounds to table salt. Salt that contains such compounds is called iodized salt.

The Noble Gases

The elements in Group 8A are called **noble gases.** Helium has two valence electrons. Each of the other noble gases has eight valence electrons. ⬤ **The noble gases are colorless and odorless and extremely unreactive.** In Chapter 6, you will study the relationship between the electron configurations of the noble gases and their low reactivity.

It is not easy to discover a colorless, odorless gas. It is even harder if the gas rarely reacts. Scientists discovered argon when they noticed that the density of nitrogen collected from air did not match the density of nitrogen formed during chemical changes. In time, the scientists figured out that the "impurity" in atmospheric nitrogen was an unknown element.

An element that does not react easily with other elements can be very useful. For example, during one stage in the process of making computer chips, pure silicon is heated in a furnace at 1480°C. At this temperature, silicon reacts with both oxygen and nitrogen. So the heating must take place in an argon atmosphere.

Some light bulbs are filled with argon because the glowing filament in the bulb will not react with argon as it would react with oxygen. Using argon increases the number of hours the bulb can be lit before it burns out. All the noble gases except radon are used in "neon" lights like those shown in Figure 22.

Group 8A

| 2 |
| He |
| Helium |

| 10 |
| Ne |
| Neon |

| 18 |
| Ar |
| Argon |

| 36 |
| Kr |
| Krypton |

| 54 |
| Xe |
| Xenon |

| 86 |
| Rn |
| Radon |

Figure 22 When electric current passes through noble gases, they emit different colors. Helium emits pink, neon emits orange-red, argon emits lavender, krypton emits white, and xenon emits blue.

Section 5.3 Assessment

Reviewing Concepts

1. ⬤ Explain why elements in a group have similar properties.

2. ⬤ What is the relationship between an alkali metal's location in Group 1A and its reactivity?

3. ⬤ What element exists in almost every compound in your body?

4. ⬤ Which Group 5A elements are found in fertilizer?

5. ⬤ Which group of elements is the least reactive?

6. Why is hydrogen located in a group with reactive metals?

7. What biological function requires magnesium?

8. Why is aluminum recycled?

9. What is the main use of sulfur?

10. Why is chlorine added to drinking water?

Critical Thinking

11. **Comparing and Contrasting** In which class of elements is there a greater range of properties, the metals or the nonmetals? Give an example to support your answer.

12. **Making Generalizations** What happens to the reactivity of nonmetals within a group from the top of the group to the bottom?

Connecting ⊂ Concepts

Using Physical Properties In Section 2.2, three ways to use physical properties are discussed. Find one example in Section 5.3 that illustrates each use. If necessary, reread pages 48 and 50.

Elemental Friends and Foes

Some elements are essential for your health, and some are extremely harmful. You need to obtain the right amounts of the twenty-five essential elements through a balanced diet, and to reduce your exposure to the harmful elements.

Eating a variety of foods helps to ensure that all the elements needed by your body are available. The required elements can be classified as major, lesser, or trace elements. An element is classified based on its percentage by mass in the body.

The six major elements are hydrogen, oxygen, carbon, nitrogen, phosphorus, and calcium. These six major elements account for almost 99 percent of your body mass. Nearly every compound in your body contains carbon and hydrogen, and many contain oxygen too. The compounds that control all the chemical changes that take place in cells contain nitrogen. Calcium is essential for healthy bones and teeth. Phosphorus is found in your DNA and in the molecules that transfer energy within cells.

The lesser elements are iron, potassium, zinc, sodium, sulfur, chlorine, and magnesium. For each lesser element, there is a recommended amount that needs to be taken in daily. These amounts vary from 15 milligrams for zinc to 400 milligrams for magnesium. Lesser elements help your body build tissues and maintain other cell processes. For example, nerves and muscles require magnesium to function properly.

The trace elements are vanadium, chromium, molybdenum, manganese, cobalt, copper, boron, tin, silicon, selenium, fluorine, and iodine. The quantities required are tiny, but trace elements perform important functions. For example, red blood cells would not mature without cobalt.

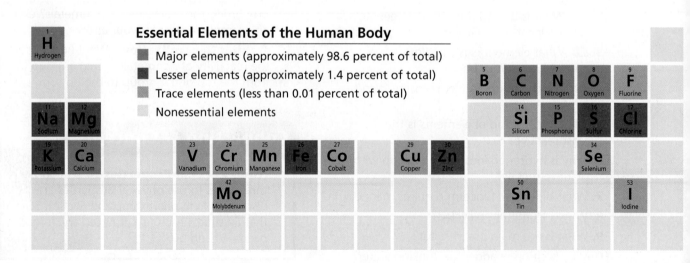

Essential Elements of the Human Body

■ Major elements (approximately 98.6 percent of total)
■ Lesser elements (approximately 1.4 percent of total)
■ Trace elements (less than 0.01 percent of total)
■ Nonessential elements

Essential elements

The 25 elements essential to the human body are generally ingested as part of compounds found in food. The roles and functions of a few of these elements are shown here.

Carbon

Carbon is the second most common element in the human body. It is essential to life, because it is present in almost every compound in the body. If a food contains carbohydrates, proteins, or fats, it contains carbon compounds.

PASTA

Oxygen

This is the most abundant element in your body. The most important function of oxygen is to help release the energy stored in foods. You absorb oxygen from the air you breathe.

Hydrogen

Hydrogen is found in foods and in water, which accounts for more than 60 percent of body mass. Chemical reactions in cells take place in water.

WATER

Iron

Iron is a very important trace element because it is part of hemoglobin. This compound transports oxygen through the blood to every cell in the body. Meat, fish, and leafy green vegetables, such as spinach, are good sources of iron.

SPINACH

Iodine

Iodine is required in small amounts for the production of thyroxine by the thyroid gland. Thyroxine controls the rate of all chemical processes in the body. Fresh fish is a good source of iodine.

RED SNAPPER

GRAPES

Vanadium

Vanadium can help control blood sugar levels. It also plays an important role in the formation of bones and teeth. Vanadium can be found in black peppercorns.

BLACK PEPPERCORNS

Potassium

Potassium is essential to muscle and nerve function, and helps keep the body's fluids in balance. It also stimulates the kidneys to remove body wastes. Potassium can be found in fruit and dairy products.

CHEESES

CONCEPTS in Action

Harmful Elements

Some elements should be avoided completely. These foes include metals, such as lead and mercury, and the metalloid arsenic. Harmful elements may enter the body in water, air, or food. Inside the body, nonessential elements may compete with essential elements and disrupt cell functions. Large amounts of harmful elements can stress the body's normal methods for eliminating toxins. Harmful elements can build up in body tissues.

For decades lead was used in paint and in gasoline to improve engine performance. These products are now lead free. The use of mercury in thermometers has been reduced and arsenic compounds are no longer used in pesticides.

Many trace elements are only helpful if ingested in the small recommended amounts. Larger quantities of most trace elements can be harmful, as can larger-than-required amounts of lesser elements, such as sodium.

82
Pb
Lead

Lead
Too much lead in the bloodstream can lead to organ damage and learning difficulties, especially in young children. For this reason, the use of lead-based paint was banned in 1978. Children may still be a risk if they live in an older house with layers of peeling paint.

80
Hg
Mercury

Mercury
Mercury is used in numerous industrial processes, but it is toxic and can damage the brain and nervous system. For this reason it should be handled with great care. It is particularly important to avoid inhaling mercury vapor.

33
As
Arsenic

Arsenic
Arsenic has been known as a poison for centuries, yet compounds of arsenic were used to treat some diseases before the discovery of penicillin. Arsenic compounds are no longer used to protect crops from insect pests or to preserve wood. Drinking water can absorb arsenic as it flows over rocks. But the amount of arsenic in drinking water is limited by law to less than 50 micrograms in each liter of water.

Arsenic pesticide

BEEF

Zinc

Zinc
This trace element can be found in almost every cell of your body. Among other things, it helps to support a healthy immune system. Beef is a good source of zinc, but no more than 40 milligrams of zinc should be taken daily. Too much zinc can cause anemia by reducing iron uptake.

Too much of a good thing

Many of the elements found in your body are needed in only very small amounts. Too much can often be harmful. The Food and Drug Administration provides guidelines on the safe daily quantities to take through food or supplements.

TABLE SALT

Sodium

Sodium
It is hard to avoid sodium in your diet because table salt contains a sodium compound (sodium chloride). Everybody needs some sodium each day to maintain water balance and nerve function. But too much sodium (more than 3 grams daily) can cause high blood pressure.

Selenium

Selenium
This trace element helps to maintain a healthy immune system. Brazil nuts are a good source of selenium, as are fruits and vegetables. While selenium supplements may be useful for some people, no more than 400 micrograms should be taken daily. Too much selenium can cause nerve damage.

BRAZIL NUTS

Going Further

- Choose a trace element other than vanadium, selenium, or iodine. Find out which foods are good sources of the element. Write a paragraph explaining how your diet meets or could be adjusted to meet your need for this element.

- Evaluate the foods you typically eat to figure out whether your diet includes enough of the essential element potassium.

Predicting the Density of an Element

Density is a useful property for identifying and classifying elements. In this lab, you will determine the densities of three elements in Group 4A—silicon, tin, and lead. Then you will use your data to predict the density of another element in Group 4A—germanium.

Problem
Can the densities of elements within a group be used to help predict the density of another element in the group?

Materials
- unlined white paper
- scissors
- metric ruler
- balance
- forceps
- silicon
- tin
- lead shot
- 50-mL graduated cylinder
- graph paper
- periodic table

 For the probeware version of this lab, see the Probeware Lab Manual, Lab 2.

Skills
Measuring, Observing, Using Graphs, Calculating

Procedure

Part A: Measuring Mass
1. On a sheet of paper, make a copy of the data table shown.
2. Cut out three 10-cm × 10-cm pieces of paper from a sheet of unlined white paper. Label one piece of paper Silicon, the second Tin, and the third Lead. Find the mass of each piece of paper and record it in your data table.

3. Using forceps, place the silicon onto the paper labeled Silicon, as shown. Find the mass of the silicon and the paper. Record this mass in your data table. Then, subtract the mass of the paper from the mass of the silicon and paper. Record the mass of silicon in your data table. Set the paper containing the silicon aside for now.

4. Repeat Step 3 to find the masses of tin and lead.

Part B: Measuring Volume
5. Place 25 mL of water in the graduated cylinder. Measure the volume of the water to the nearest 0.1 mL. Record the volume (in cm^3) in your data table. (*Hint:* 1 mL = 1 cm^3)

6. Tilt the graduated cylinder and carefully pour the silicon from the paper into the graduated cylinder, as shown on page 151. Make sure that the silicon is completely covered by the water. Measure and record the volume of the water and silicon in your data table. Then, subtract the volume of water from the volume of the water and silicon. Record the result in your data table.

7. Repeat Steps 5 and 6 to find the volumes of tin and lead.

Data Table							
Element	Mass of Paper (g)	Mass of Paper and Element (g)	Mass of Element (g)	Volume of Water (cm^3)	Volume of Water and Element (cm^3)	Volume of Element (cm^3)	Density of Element (g/cm^3)
Silicon							
Tin							
Lead							

Part C: Calculating Density

8. To calculate the density of silicon, divide its mass by its volume.

$$\text{Density} = \frac{\text{Mass}}{\text{Volume}}$$

Record the density of silicon in your data table.

9. Repeat Step 8 to find the densities of tin and lead.

10. Make a line graph that shows the relationship between the densities of silicon, tin, and lead and the periods in which they are located in the periodic table. Place the number of the period (from 1 to 7) on the horizontal axis and the density (in g/cm^3) on the vertical axis. Draw a straight line that comes as close as possible to all three points.

11. Germanium is in Period 4. To estimate the density of germanium, draw a dotted vertical line from the 4 on the horizontal axis to the solid line. Then, draw a dotted horizontal line from the solid line to the vertical axis. Read and record the density of germanium.

12. Wash your hands with warm water and soap before you leave the laboratory.

Analyze and Conclude

1. **Classifying** List lead, silicon, and tin in order of increasing density.

2. **Comparing and Contrasting** How does your estimate of the density of germanium compare with the actual density of germanium, which is 5.3 g/cm^3?

3. **Calculating** Use the formula for percent error (PE) to calculate a percent error for your estimate of the density of germanium.

$$PE = \frac{\text{Estimated value} - \text{Accepted value}}{\text{Accepted value}} \times 100$$

4. **Drawing Conclusions** How does the density of the elements change from silicon to lead in Group 4A?

Go Further Use reference books or sites on the Internet to research properties of Group 4A elements. Construct a graph that shows how another property, such as melting point or boiling point, varies among the Group 4A elements you explored. Determine whether knowing the values for three of the elements would allow you to accurately predict a value for the fourth element.

Study Guide

5.1 Organizing the Elements

Key Concepts

- Mendeleev arranged the elements into rows in order of increasing mass so that elements with similar properties were in the same column.

- The close match between Mendeleev's predictions and the actual properties of new elements showed how useful his periodic table could be.

Vocabulary

periodic table, *p. 127*

5.2 The Modern Periodic Table

Key Concepts

- In the modern periodic table, elements are arranged by increasing atomic number (number of protons). Each row on the table is a period. Each column is a group.

- Properties of elements repeat in a predictable way when atomic numbers are used to arrange elements into groups.

- Atomic mass is a value that depends on the distribution of an element's isotopes in nature and the masses of those isotopes.

- Elements are classified as metals, nonmetals, and metalloids. Metals are elements that are good conductors of electric current and heat. Nonmetals are poor conductors of electric current and heat. Metalloids are elements with properties that fall between those of metals and nonmetals.

- Across a period from left to right, the elements become less metallic and more nonmetallic in their properties.

Vocabulary

period, *p. 131*

group, *p. 131*

periodic law, *p. 131*

atomic mass unit (amu), *p. 134*

metals, *p. 135*

transition metals, *p. 136*

nonmetals, *p. 136*

metalloids, *p. 136*

5.3 Representative Groups

Key Concepts

- Elements in a group have similar properties because they have the same number of valence electrons.

- The alkali earth metals in Group 1A are extremely reactive. The reactivity of these metals increases from the top of the group to the bottom.

- Differences in reactivity among the alkaline earth metals in Group 2A are shown by the ways they react with water.

- Group 3A contains the most abundant metal in Earth's crust—aluminum. The energy needed to recycle aluminum is 5 percent of the energy needed to extract aluminum from bauxite.

- Group 4A contains the nonmetal carbon. Most compounds in your body contain carbon. Carbon compounds control reactions that occur in cells.

- Fertilizers usually contain the Group 5A elements nitrogen and phosphorus.

- Oxygen, in Group 6A, is the most abundant element in Earth's crust.

- Despite their physical differences, the halogens in Group 7A are all highly reactive nonmetals.

- The noble gases, in Group 8A, are colorless and odorless and extremely unreactive.

Vocabulary

valence electron, *p. 139*

alkali metals, *p. 140*

alkaline earth metals, *p. 141*

halogens, *p. 144*

noble gases, *p. 145*

Thinking Visually

Web Diagram Use information from the chapter to complete the web diagram below. The web relates states of matter at room temperature to categories of elements.

Reviewing Content

Choose the letter that best answers the question or completes the statement.

1. Mendeleev arranged the elements in his periodic table in order of
  a. atomic number.   **b.** number of electrons.
  c. mass.   **d.** number of neutrons.

2. Mendeleev's decision to leave gaps in his periodic table was supported by the discovery of
  a. electrons.   **b.** protons.
  c. argon.   **d.** gallium.

3. In a modern periodic table, elements are arranged in order of
  a. atomic number.   **b.** number of isotopes.
  c. atomic mass.   **d.** number of neutrons.

4. How many periods does the periodic table have?
  a. 18   **b.** 7
  c. 9   **d.** 8

5. An atomic mass unit is
  a. one twelfth the mass of a carbon-12 atom.
  b. the mass of a carbon-12 atom.
  c. the mass of a neutron.
  d. the mass of a proton.

6. An element that is shiny and conducts electric current is likely to be a
  a. gas.   **b.** metal.
  c. metalloid.   **d.** nonmetal.

7. Copper is an example of
  a. an alkali metal.   **b.** an alkaline earth metal.
  c. a nonmetal.   **d.** a transition metal.

8. Elements that have the same number of valence electrons are
  a. in the same period.
  b. in the same group.
  c. called noble gases.
  d. called transition metals.

9. The most reactive metals are the
  a. transition metals.   **b.** alkaline earth metals.
  c. alkali metals.   **d.** metalloids.

10. Which elements are all gases at room temperature?
  a. Group 1A   **b.** Period 3
  c. Group 7A   **d.** Group 8A

Understanding Concepts

11. What information did Mendeleev have about the elements he organized into a periodic table?

12. How did Mendeleev know where to leave the spaces in his table?

13. Why is the table of the elements shown in Figure 7 called a periodic table?

14. Why does the number of elements vary from period to period?

15. Explain how the atomic mass of an element is affected by the distribution of its isotopes in nature.

16. List three ways that the elements in the periodic table can be classified.

17. In general, what happens to the reactivity of elements in groups labeled A as atomic numbers increase across a period?

18. Why don't the elements within an A group in the periodic table have identical properties?

19. Why was it difficult to discover the noble gases?

Use this portion of the periodic table to answer Questions 20–23.

14	15	16	17
Si	**P**	**S**	**Cl**
Silicon	Phosphorus	Sulfur	Chlorine
28.086	30.974	32.06	35.453
32	33	34	35
Ge	**As**	**Se**	**Br**
Germanium	Arsenic	Selenium	Bromine
72.59	74.922	78.96	79.904

20. How many of the elements shown are metals? How many are nonmetals? How many are metalloids?

21. Which element is a liquid at room temperature and which is a gas at room temperature?

22. Which of the two halogens shown is more reactive? Give a reason for your answer.

23. Does selenium have more in common with sulfur or bromine? Explain your answer.

Assessment (continued)

Critical Thinking

24. Classifying If you know that an element is a solid at room temperature, do you have enough data to classify the element as a metal, metalloid, or nonmetal? If you know that the element is a gas at room temperature, do you have enough data? Explain your answers.

25. Applying Concepts An element on the periodic table has two naturally occurring isotopes. One isotope has an atomic mass of about 10 amu. The other isotope has an atomic mass of about 11 amu. What is the name of this element?

26. Predicting How many valence electrons would an element with atomic number 113 have?

27. Applying Concepts Why are samples of the alkali metal cesium usually stored in argon gas?

28. Applying Concepts Why are halogens found in nature only in compounds?

29. Applying Concepts Which element on the periodic table has chemical properties that are most similar to those of carbon?

30. Designing Experiments If you were trying to make a compound of the noble gas xenon, would you use nitrogen or fluorine? Explain your choice.

Use the table to answer Questions 31–33.

Properties of Elements X, Y, and Z			
Element	Melting Point	Boiling Point	Valence Electrons
X	97.80°C	883°C	1
Y	−259.34°C	−252.87°C	1
Z	−101.5°C	−34.04°C	7

31. Analyzing Data In general, where would you find Elements X, Y, and Z on the periodic table?

32. Classifying Describe the state of each element at room temperature based on its melting and boiling points.

33. Drawing Conclusions Use your answers to Questions 31 and 32 to identify element Y. Explain your reasoning.

Concepts in Action

34. Predicting What might happen to a heated beaker made from glass that does not contain boron if the beaker were placed in a pan of ice water?

35. Inferring Based on the content of most fertilizers, name two elements other than carbon that are found in compounds in plants.

36. Making Generalizations Explain how the amount of a trace element an organism is exposed to affects the element's ability to help or harm an organism. Use the example of selenium. (*Hint:* Refer to the discussion on page 149.)

37. Problem Solving Sometimes old books fall apart when they are stored in air. Use what you know about the reactivity of elements to propose a way that old books could be kept from falling apart.

38. Using Analogies Explain how a calendar is similar to a periodic table and how it is different.

39. Relating Cause and Effect When corn plants have yellow leaves, it is a sign that the plants lack an essential element. Which element must be added to the soil to produce leaves with a healthy green color?

40. Writing in Science You write for a newsletter that has a feature called Element of the Month. It is your turn to write the feature. Pick an element that you think is worthy of attention. Write a brief essay and suggest a photo to be used with your feature.

Performance-Based Assessment

Design Your Own Periodic Table Make a version of the periodic table that presents the information provided in Figure 7 in a different, but useful, way.

For: Self-grading assessment
Visit: PHSchool.com
Web Code: cca-1050

Standardized Test Prep

Choose the letter that best answers the question or completes the statement.

1. Which elements are as reactive as alkali metals?
(A) alkaline earth metals
(B) halogens
(C) noble gases
(D) transition metals
(E) metalloids

2. How many valence electrons do atoms of oxygen and sulfur have?
(A) 2
(B) 4
(C) 6
(D) 8
(E) 10

3. Moving across a period from left to right,
(A) elements become less metallic.
(B) elements become more metallic.
(C) elements become more reactive.
(D) elements become less reactive.
(E) elements have fewer valence electrons.

4. Which statement *best* describes nonmetals?
(A) Nonmetals are good conductors of heat and electric current.
(B) Nonmetals are brittle solids.
(C) Many general properties of nonmetals are opposite to those of metals.
(D) Nonmetals are located on the left side of the periodic table.
(E) All nonmetals are extremely reactive.

Use this portion of the periodic table to answer Questions 5–7.

13	14	15
Al	**Si**	**P**
Aluminum	Silicon	Phosphorus
26.982	28.086	30.974
31	32	33
Ga	**Ge**	**As**
Gallium	Germanium	Arsenic
69.72	72.59	74.922

5. Which list of elements contains only metalloids?
(A) aluminum and gallium
(B) silicon and germanium
(C) phosphorus and arsenic
(D) aluminum, silicon, and phosphorus
(E) gallium, germanium, and arsenic

6. Which elements did Mendeleev leave spaces for in his first periodic table?
(A) aluminum and phosphorus
(B) aluminum and germanium
(C) silicon and arsenic
(D) gallium and germanium
(E) gallium and aluminum

7. Which of the elements are among the most abundant in Earth's crust?
(A) silicon and phosphorus
(B) aluminum and phosphorus
(C) phosphorus and arsenic
(D) gallium and arsenic
(E) aluminum and silicon

CHAPTER

6 Chemical Bonds

21st Century Learning

Self Direction

How can compounds be shown with electron dot diagrams?

Elements that do not have complete sets of valence electrons tend to react. In certain cases, the reaction involves the transfer of electrons between atoms. You can describe this process by using electron dot diagrams. Use the animation tools in presentation software to illustrate the formation of two different ionic compounds. Each animation should show how the transfer of one or more electrons between atoms results in the formation of the compound.

How do science concepts apply to your world? Here are some questions you'll be able to answer after you read this chapter.

- **Why is titanium metal welded in an argon atmosphere?** *(Section 6.1)*

- **What causes a crystal of rock salt to shatter when it is struck?** *(Section 6.1)*

- **Why is water a liquid while carbon dioxide is a gas at room temperature?** *(Section 6.2)*

- **What advantage does jewelry made from a gold silver alloy have over jewelry made from pure gold?** *(Section 6.4)*

- **How does mixing other elements with silicon make silicon a better conductor of electric current?** *(page 182)*

The calcium carbonate in shells and the silicon dioxide in sand are examples of compounds with different types of bonds.

Chapter Preview

Inquiry Activity

What Can the Shape of a Material Tell You About the Material?

Procedure

1. Use a wood splint or small lab spatula to place a small sample of table salt on a sheet of black construction paper.

2. Use a hand lens to examine the sample. On a separate sheet of paper, sketch the shapes of some pieces in the sample.

3. Repeat Steps 1 and 2 with each of the compounds your teacher provides.

Think About It

1. **Observing** Compare the shapes of the pieces in the different compounds.

2. **Predicting** Could any differences you observed be used to identify a compound? Explain your answer.

3. **Formulating Hypotheses** What could be happening at the atomic level in compounds to produce the different shapes you observed?

6.1 Ionic Bonding

Reading Focus

Key Concepts
- When is an atom unlikely to react?
- What is one way in which elements can achieve stable electron configurations?
- How does the structure of an ionic compound affect its properties?

Vocabulary
- electron dot diagram
- ion
- anion
- cation
- chemical bond
- ionic bond
- chemical formula
- crystals

Reading Strategy
Sequencing Copy the concept map. As you read, complete the concept map to show what happens to atoms during ionic bonding.

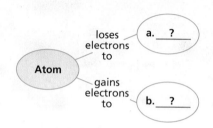

The handle of the titanium mug in Figure 1 was joined to the body by welding. The pieces were heated until their surfaces fused together. The welding of titanium does not take place in air. At the temperature at which welding occurs, titanium becomes hot enough to react with oxygen in the air, forming an oxide. The oxide makes the weld more brittle and likely to break. Because titanium does not react with a noble gas such as argon, the welding of titanium usually takes place in an argon atmosphere.

Argon's name is a reminder of its inactivity. It comes from the Greek word *argos,* which means "idle" or "inert." Why is argon very inactive yet oxygen is highly reactive? Chemical properties, such as reactivity, depend on an element's electron configuration.

Stable Electron Configurations

The highest occupied energy level of a noble gas atom is filled. **When the highest occupied energy level of an atom is filled with electrons, the atom is stable and not likely to react.** The noble gases have stable electron configurations with eight valence electrons (or two in the case of helium).

The chemical properties of an element depend on the number of valence electrons. Therefore, it is useful to have a model of atoms that focuses only on valence electrons. The models in Figure 2 are electron dot diagrams. An **electron dot diagram** is a model of an atom in which each dot represents a valence electron. The symbol in the center represents the nucleus and all the other electrons in the atom.

Figure 1 The handle and body of this titanium mug were welded together in an argon atmosphere. If titanium is allowed to react with oxygen in air, the compound that forms makes the weld more brittle and more likely to break.

Electron Dot Diagrams for Some Group A Elements

Group 1A	2A	3A	4A	5A	6A	7A	8A
H·							He:
Li·	·Be·	·B·	·C·	·N·	:O·	:F·	:Ne:
Na·	·Mg·	·Al·	·Si·	·P·	:S·	:Cl·	:Ar:
K·	·Ca·	·Ga·	·Ge·	·As·	:Se·	:Br·	:Kr:

Figure 2 In an electron dot diagram, each dot represents a valence electron. *Observing How many valence electrons do sodium and chlorine have?*

Ionic Bonds

Elements that do not have complete sets of valence electrons tend to react. By reacting, they achieve electron configurations similar to those of noble gases. **Some elements achieve stable electron configurations through the transfer of electrons between atoms.**

Transfer of Electrons Look at the electron dot diagram for chlorine in Figure 2. A chlorine atom has one electron fewer than an argon atom. If the chlorine atom were to gain a valence electron, it would have the same stable electron arrangement as argon. Look at the electron dot diagram for sodium. A sodium atom has one more electron than a neon atom. If a sodium atom were to lose this electron, its highest occupied energy level would have eight electrons. It would then have the same stable electron arrangement as neon.

What happens at the atomic level when sodium reacts with chlorine? An electron is transferred from each sodium atom to a chlorine atom. Each atom ends up with a more stable electron arrangement than it had before the transfer.

$$Na· \ + \ ·Cl: \longrightarrow Na^+ \ :Cl:^-$$

Formation of Ions When an atom gains or loses an electron, the number of protons is no longer equal to the number of electrons. The charge on the atom is not balanced and the atom is not neutral. An atom that has a net positive or negative electric charge is called an **ion.** The charge on an ion is represented by a plus or a minus sign. Notice the plus sign next to the symbol for sodium and the minus sign next to the symbol for chlorine.

Go Online

For: Links on ionic bonds
Visit: www.SciLinks.org
Web Code: ccn-1061

What Determines the Size of an Atom or Ion?

Scientists use atomic radii to compare the sizes of atoms of different elements. Remember from mathematics that the radius of a sphere is the distance from the center of the sphere to its outer edge. The radius is half the diameter of the sphere. Because atomic radii are extremely small, these distances are expressed in units called picometers (pm). As a comparison, there are one billion (10^9) picometers in a millimeter.

The table shows the atomic radius and ionic radius for six metals and six nonmetals. You will use the data to relate the size of an element's atoms to the element's location on the periodic table. You also will use the data to compare the sizes of atoms and their ions.

1. **Using Tables** Within a period, what happens to the atomic radius as the atomic number of the elements increases?

2. **Using Tables** Within Groups 1A, 2A, 6A, and 7A, what happens to the atomic radius of elements as the atomic number increases?

Atomic and Ionic Radii

1A	2A	6A	7A
152	112	66	64
Li	Be	O	F
1+ 60	2+ 31	2− 140	1− 136
186	160	103	99
Na	Mg	S	Cl
1+ 95	2+ 65	2− 184	1− 181
227	197	117	114
K	Ca	Se	Br
1+ 133	2+ 99	2− 198	1− 195

Atomic radius

Ionic radius

3. **Inferring** How does adding an occupied energy level affect the atomic radius? (*Hint:* Lithium is a Period 2 element and sodium is a Period 3 element.)

4. **Comparing and Contrasting** Compare the atomic and ionic radii for potassium (K), and for bromine (Br).

5. **Making Generalizations** What happens to the radius of an atom when the atom loses electrons? When the atom gains electrons?

6. **Relating Cause and Effect** Explain the difference in size between a metal atom and its cation.

The ion that forms when a chlorine atom gains an electron has 17 protons and 18 electrons. This ion has a charge of 1− because it has one extra electron. The symbol for the ion is written Cl^{1-}, or Cl^- for short. An ion with a negative charge is an **anion** (AN eye un). Anions like the Cl^- ion are named by using part of the element name plus the suffix –*ide*. Thus, Cl^- is called a *chloride* ion.

A sodium ion has 11 protons and 10 electrons. Because it has one extra proton, the sodium ion has a charge of 1+. The symbol for the ion is written Na^{1+}, or Na^+ for short. An ion with a positive charge is a **cation** (KAT eye un). Naming a cation is easy. You just use the element name, as in the *sodium* ion.

Formation of Ionic Bonds Remember that a particle with a negative charge will attract a particle with a positive charge. When an anion and a cation are close together, a chemical bond forms between them. A **chemical bond** is the force that holds atoms or ions together as a unit. An **ionic bond** is the force that holds cations and anions together. An ionic bond forms when electrons are transferred from one atom to another.

Ionization Energy An electron can move to a higher energy level when an atom absorbs energy. Cations form when electrons gain enough energy to escape from atoms. The energy allows electrons to overcome the attraction of the protons in the nucleus. The amount of energy used to remove an electron is called ionization energy. It varies from element to element. The lower the ionization energy, the easier it is to remove an electron from an atom.

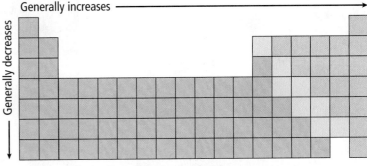

Generally increases ⟶

Generally decreases ↓

Trends in Ionization Energy

Figure 3 shows two trends for ionization energy. Ionization energies tend to increase from left to right across a period. It takes more energy to remove an electron from a nonmetal than from a metal in the same period. Ionization energies tend to decrease from the top of a group to the bottom. In Group 1A, potassium has a lower ionization energy than sodium. So it is easier to remove an electron from potassium than from sodium, and potassium is more reactive than sodium.

Reading Checkpoint   *What is ionization energy?*

Figure 3 Ionization energies generally increase from left to right across a period. **Interpreting Diagrams** *What is the trend for ionization energy within a group?*

Ionic Compounds

Compounds that contain ionic bonds are ionic compounds, which can be represented by chemical formulas. A **chemical formula** is a notation that shows what elements a compound contains and the ratio of the atoms or ions of these elements in the compound. The chemical formula for sodium chloride is NaCl. From the formula, you can tell that there is one sodium ion for each chloride ion in sodium chloride.

Based on the diagram in Figure 4, what would the formula for magnesium chloride be? A magnesium atom cannot reach a stable electron configuration by reacting with just one chlorine atom. It must transfer electrons to two chlorine atoms. After the transfer, the charge on the magnesium ion is 2+ and its symbol is Mg^{2+}. The formula for the compound is $MgCl_2$. The 2 written to the right and slightly below the symbol for chlorine is a subscript. Subscripts are used to show the relative numbers of atoms of the elements present. If there is only one atom of an element in the formula, no subscript is needed.

Figure 4 Magnesium chloride forms when magnesium atoms transfer electrons to chlorine atoms. Magnesium chloride is used to control dust that is stirred up by traffic on unpaved roads.

Figure 5 The structure and shape of a crystal are related. **A** In a sodium chloride crystal, each ion is surrounded by six oppositely charged ions. **B** Sodium chloride crystals are shaped like cubes.

Crystal Lattices A chemical formula for an ionic compound tells you the ratio of the ions in the compound. But it does not tell you how the ions are arranged in the compound. If you looked at a sample of sodium chloride with a hand lens or microscope, you would be able to see that the pieces of salt are shaped like cubes. This shape is a clue to how the sodium and chloride ions are arranged in the compound.

Figure 5A shows that the ions in sodium chloride are arranged in an orderly, three-dimensional structure. Each chloride ion is surrounded by six sodium ions and each sodium ion is surrounded by six chloride ions. Each ion is attracted to all the neighboring ions with an opposite charge. This set of attractions keeps the ions in fixed positions in a rigid framework, or lattice. The repeating pattern of ions in the lattice is like the repeating pattern of designs on the wallpaper in Figure 6.

Solids whose particles are arranged in a lattice structure are called **crystals.** Compare the cubic shape of the sodium chloride crystals in Figure 5B to the arrangement of ions in Figure 5A. The shape of an ionic crystal depends on the arrangement of ions in its lattice. In turn, the arrangement of the ions depends on the ratio of ions and their relative sizes. Crystals are classified into groups based on the shape of their crystals. Crystals of ruby have a six-sided, hexagonal shape. The How It Works box on page 163 describes one way to make rubies.

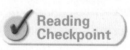 **Reading Checkpoint** *What shape are sodium chloride crystals?*

Figure 6 This wallpaper displays a repeating pattern of flower and fruit designs. **Using Analogies** *How is this arrangement of designs similar to the arrangement of ions in a crystal?*

Synthetic Rubies

Rubies are mainly aluminum oxide, which is white. The substitution of a small percentage of chromium ions for aluminum ions gives rubies their distinctive red color. Because natural rubies are rare, rubies are often manufactured. **Interpreting Diagrams** *What substances are in the mixture used to make rubies?*

SYNTHETIC RUBY BOULE

HEXAGONAL CRYSTAL STRUCTURE

NATURAL RUBY

Synthetic ruby
A synthetic ruby boule has a hexagonal crystal structure identical to the natural ruby gemstone. Its shape is determined by the arrangement of ions in the crystal.

Making synthetic rubies
One way of making synthetic rubies is called the pulled-growth method. It was invented by Polish scientist Jan Czochralski (1885–1953).

Aluminum and chromium oxides

Seed crystal

Rotating rod

Melt

Ruby forming

Ruby boule

Heater

Crucible

Furnace vessel

1 **Seed crystal** Aluminum oxide and chromium(VI) oxide are melted. A tiny piece of ruby, called a seed crystal, is attached to a rod and placed above the molten mixture (melt).

2 **Lowering into the melt** The rod is lowered until the seed crystal touches the melt. The rod is slowly lifted, and ions in the melt begin to attach themselves to the seed crystal to form a ruby.

3 **Forming a boule** As the rod is lifted higher, an oblong-shaped crystal called a boule grows from the end. Once cooled, the boule can be cut into different shapes.

Hammer strikes crystal.

Ionic crystal shatters when struck.

Figure 7 When an ionic crystal is struck, ions are moved from their fixed positions. Ions with the same charge repel one another and the crystal shatters.

Properties of Ionic Compounds The properties of sodium chloride are typical of an ionic compound. It has a high melting point (801°C). In its solid state, sodium chloride is a poor conductor of electric current. But when melted, it is a good conductor of electric current. Sodium chloride crystals shatter when struck with a hammer. ◉ **The properties of an ionic compound can be explained by the strong attractions among ions within a crystal lattice.**

Recall that the arrangement of particles in a substance is the result of two opposing factors. The first factor is the attractions among particles in the substance. The second factor is the kinetic energy of the particles. The stronger the attractions among the particles, the more kinetic energy the particles must have before they can separate.

For an electric current to flow, charged particles must be able to move from one location to another. The ions in a solid crystal lattice have fixed positions. However, when the solid melts, the lattice breaks apart and the ions are free to flow. Melted, or molten, sodium chloride is an excellent conductor of electric current.

Rock salt contains large crystals of sodium chloride. If you tapped a crystal of rock salt sharply with a hammer, it would shatter into many smaller crystals. Figure 7 shows what happens to the positions of the ions when the crystal is struck. Negative ions are pushed into positions near negative ions, and positive ions are pushed into positions near positive ions. Ions with the same charge repel one another and cause the crystal to shatter.

Section 6.1 Assessment

Reviewing Concepts

1. ◉ When is an atom least likely to react?

2. ◉ Describe one way an element can achieve a stable electron configuration.

3. ◉ What characteristic of ionic bonds can be used to explain the properties of ionic compounds?

4. Use ionization energy to explain why metals lose electrons more easily than nonmetals.

5. Why is a rock salt crystal likely to shatter when struck?

Critical Thinking

6. **Making Generalizations** What will the ratio of ions be in any compound formed from a Group 1A metal and a Group 7A nonmetal? Explain your answer.

7. **Drawing Conclusions** Why do ionic compounds include at least one metal?

8. **Predicting** Based on their chemical formulas, which of these compounds is not likely to be an ionic compound: KBr, SO_2, or $FeCl_3$? Explain your answer.

Connecting Concepts

Reactivity of Metals Use what you know about how ionic bonds form to explain the difference in reactivity between potassium and calcium. If necessary, reread the description of Group 1A and Group 2A properties in Section 5.3.

6.2 Covalent Bonding

Reading Focus

Key Concepts

- How are atoms held together in a covalent bond?

- What happens when atoms don't share electrons equally?

- What factors determine whether a molecule is polar?

- How do attractions between polar molecules compare to attractions between nonpolar molecules?

Vocabulary

- covalent bond
- molecule
- polar covalent bond

Reading Strategy

Relating Text and Visuals Copy the table. As you read, look closely at Figure 9. Complete the table by describing each type of model shown.

Model	Description
Electron dot	a. _____?_____
Structural formula	b. _____?_____
Space-filling	c. _____?_____
Electron cloud	d. _____?_____

Plants absorb water through their roots from soil or from a solution containing nutrients, as in Figure 8. Carbon dioxide from the air enters the plants through small openings in their leaves. The plants use the energy from sunlight to convert water and carbon dioxide into a sugar. Energy is stored in the chemical bonds of the sugar.

The elements in sugar are carbon, oxygen, and hydrogen. All three are nonmetals, which have relatively high ionization energies. A transfer of electrons does not tend to occur between nonmetal atoms. So, how are two nonmetals able to form bonds?

Covalent Bonds

You and a friend are participating in a treasure hunt. The rules state that the first person to find all eight items on a list will win a 21-speed bicycle. After about an hour, you have found six of the items on the list and your friend has found the other two. You and your friend have incomplete sets of items. But if you are willing to share your items with your friend, together you will have a complete set of items and qualify for the prize. Of course, you will have to be willing to share the bicycle, too. When nonmetals join together, they display a similar sharing strategy.

Figure 8 When plants are grown in water instead of soil, you can see their roots. Plants absorb water through their roots and carbon dioxide through small openings in their leaves.

Chemical Bonds **165**

Molecular Models

Electron dot diagram	Structural formula
H:H	H–H
Space-filling model	**Electron cloud model**
	H H

Figure 9 As a space shuttle lifts off, it leaves a water vapor trail. A reaction of hydrogen and oxygen produces the water.
Using Models *How is the bond between hydrogen atoms represented in each model of a hydrogen molecule?*

Fluorine (F$_2$)

Nitrogen (N$_2$)

Chlorine (Cl$_2$)

Bromine (Br$_2$)

Iodine (I$_2$)

Figure 10 These space-filling models represent diatomic molecules of five elements.
Using Models *How many atoms are in a diatomic molecule?*

Sharing Electrons A hydrogen atom has one electron. If it had two electrons, it would have the same electron configuration as a helium atom. Two hydrogen atoms can achieve a stable electron configuration by sharing their electrons and forming a covalent bond. A **covalent bond** is a chemical bond in which two atoms share a pair of valence electrons. When two atoms share one pair of electrons, the bond is called a single bond.

Figure 9 shows four different ways to represent a covalent bond. In the electron dot model, the bond is shown by a pair of dots in the space between the symbols for the hydrogen atoms. In the structural formula, the pair of dots is replaced by a line. The electron cloud model and the space-filling model show that orbitals of atoms overlap when a covalent bond forms.

Molecules of Elements Two hydrogen atoms bonded together form a unit called a molecule. A **molecule** is a neutral group of atoms that are joined together by one or more covalent bonds. The hydrogen molecule is neutral because it contains two protons (one from each atom) and two electrons (one from each atom). What keeps the hydrogen atoms together in the molecule? ⊙ **The attractions between the shared electrons and the protons in each nucleus hold the atoms together in a covalent bond.**

A chemical formula can be used to describe the molecules of an element as well as a compound. The element hydrogen has the chemical formula H$_2$. The subscript 2 indicates that there are two atoms in a molecule of hydrogen.

Many nonmetal elements exist as diatomic molecules. *Diatomic* means "two atoms." Four of the models in Figure 10 are of halogens. A halogen atom has seven valence electrons. If two halogen atoms share a valence electron from each atom, both atoms have eight valence electrons.

⧉ Quick Lab

Analyzing Inks

Materials

test paper, metric ruler, felt-tip markers, stapler, beaker, alcohol-water mixture, Petri dish

Procedure

1. Place the test paper on a clean surface. Use the ruler to draw the pencil line shown in the drawing. Use your markers to place color dots at the locations shown in the drawing.

2. With the ink marks on the outside, staple the two ends of the paper together to form a tube.

3. Pour the alcohol-water mixture into the beaker to a depth of 0.5 cm. Stand the paper in the beaker so that the dots are at the bottom. The paper should not touch the sides of the beaker. Invert the Petri dish over the beaker.

4. When the mixture reaches the top of the paper, remove the paper from the beaker. Unstaple the paper and lay it flat. Make a drawing of the results with each colored area labeled.

Analyze and Conclude

1. **Observing** Which markers contained inks that were mixtures of colored substances?

2. **Formulating Hypotheses** How did some molecules in the ink move up the paper?

3. **Predicting** Assume that molecules in the test paper are more polar than molecules in the alcohol-water mixture. Would you expect the most polar molecules in ink to stick tightly to the paper or to move with the liquid? Explain.

4. **Designing Experiments** How could the procedure from this lab be used to identify a black ink whose composition is unknown?

Multiple Covalent Bonds Nitrogen has five valence electrons. If two nitrogen atoms shared a pair of electrons, each one would have only six valence electrons. If they shared two pairs of electrons, each atom would have only seven valence electrons. When the atoms in a nitrogen molecule (N_2) share three pairs of electrons, each atom has eight valence electrons. Each pair of shared electrons is represented by a long dash in the structural formula $N \equiv N$. When two atoms share three pairs of electrons, the bond is called a triple bond. When two atoms share two pairs of electrons, the bond is called a double bond.

 What does the subscript 2 in the formula for a hydrogen molecule indicate?

Unequal Sharing of Electrons

In general, elements on the right of the periodic table have a greater attraction for electrons than elements on the left have (except for noble gases). In general, elements at the top of a group have a greater attraction for electrons than elements at the bottom of a group have. Fluorine is on the far right and is at the top of its group. It has the strongest attraction for electrons and is the most reactive nonmetal.

For: Links on covalent bonding
Visit: www.SciLinks.org
Web Code: ccn-1062

HCl

Figure 11 Shared electrons in a hydrogen chloride molecule spend less time near the hydrogen atom than near the chlorine atom. *Inferring* **Which element has a greater attraction for electrons—hydrogen or chlorine?**

Polar Covalent Bonds In a molecule of an element, the atoms that form covalent bonds have the same ability to attract an electron. Shared electrons are attracted equally to the nuclei of both atoms. In a molecule of a compound, electrons may not be shared equally.

Figure 11 shows models of the molecule that forms when hydrogen reacts with chlorine. A chlorine atom has a greater attraction for electrons than a hydrogen atom does. In a hydrogen chloride molecule, the shared electrons spend more time near the chlorine atom than near the hydrogen atom. A covalent bond in which electrons are not shared equally is called a **polar covalent bond.** (One meaning of the term *polar* is "opposite in character, nature, or direction.")

When atoms form a polar covalent bond, the atom with the greater attraction for electrons has a partial negative charge. The other atom has a partial positive charge. The symbols δ– and δ+ are used to show which atom has which charge. (δ is the lowercase version of the Greek letter delta.)

Polar and Nonpolar Molecules Can you assume that a molecule that contains a polar covalent bond is polar? If a molecule has only two atoms, it will be polar. But, when molecules have more than two atoms, the answer is not as obvious. **The type of atoms in a molecule and its shape are factors that determine whether a molecule is polar or nonpolar.**

Compare the models of carbon dioxide and water in Figure 12. In carbon dioxide, there are double bonds between each oxygen atom and the central carbon atom. Because oxygen has a greater attraction for electrons than carbon does, each double bond is polar. However, the molecule is linear: all three atoms are lined up in a row. The carbon-oxygen double bonds are directly opposite each other. There is an equal pull on the electrons from opposite directions. The pulls cancel out and the molecule as a whole is nonpolar.

There are two single bonds in a water molecule. The bonds are polar because oxygen has a greater attraction for electrons than hydrogen does. Because the water molecule has a bent shape rather than a linear shape, the polar bonds do not cancel out. The two hydrogen atoms are located on the same side of the molecule, opposite the oxygen atom. The oxygen side of the molecule has a partial negative charge. The hydrogen side of the molecule has a partial positive charge.

CO_2

H_2O

Figure 12 In a carbon dioxide (CO_2) molecule, the polar bonds between the carbon atom and the oxygen atoms cancel out because the molecule is linear. In a water (H_2O) molecule, the polar bonds between the oxygen atom and the hydrogen atoms do not cancel out because the molecule is bent.

Attraction Between Molecules

In a molecular compound, there are forces of attraction between molecules. These attractions are not as strong as ionic or covalent bonds, but they are strong enough to hold molecules together in a liquid or solid. **Attractions between polar molecules are stronger than attractions between nonpolar molecules.**

Water molecules are similar in mass to methane (CH_4) molecules. Yet, methane boils at $-161.5°C$ and water boils at $100°C$ because methane molecules are nonpolar and water molecules are polar. Each dashed line in Figure 13 represents an attraction between a partially positive hydrogen atom in one water molecule and a partially negative oxygen atom in another. Molecules on the surface of a water sample are attracted to molecules that lie below the surface and are pulled toward the center of the sample. These attractions increase the energy required for water molecules to evaporate. They raise the temperature at which vapor pressure equals atmospheric pressure—the boiling point.

Attractions among nonpolar molecules are weaker than attractions among polar molecules, but they do exist. After all, carbon dioxide can exist as solid dry ice. Attractions among nonpolar molecules explain why nitrogen can be stored as a liquid at low temperatures and high pressures. Because electrons are constantly in motion, there are times when one part of a nitrogen molecule has a small positive charge and one part has a small negative charge. At those times, one nitrogen molecule can be weakly attracted to another nitrogen molecule.

Figure 13 Each dashed line in the drawing represents an attraction between a hydrogen atom and an oxygen atom.
Interpreting Diagrams *In a water molecule, which atom has a partial negative charge? Which has a partial positive charge?*

Section 6.2 Assessment

Reviewing Concepts

1. What attractions hold atoms together in a covalent bond?

2. What happens to the charge on atoms when they form a polar covalent bond?

3. Name the two factors that determine whether a molecule is polar.

4. Compare the strength of attractions between polar molecules to the strength of attractions between nonpolar molecules.

5. What is a molecule?

Critical Thinking

6. **Applying Concepts** Which of these elements does not bond to form molecules: oxygen, chlorine, neon, or sulfur?

7. **Inferring** Why is the boiling point of water higher than the boiling point of chlorine?

8. **Using Diagrams** Based on their electron dot diagrams, what is the formula for the covalently bonded compound of nitrogen and hydrogen?

Connecting Concepts

Viscosity Review the description of the physical property viscosity in Section 2.2. Then write a paragraph explaining how attractions between molecules might affect the viscosity of a liquid.

6.3 Naming Compounds and Writing Formulas

Reading Focus

Key Concepts

- What information do the name and formula of an ionic compound provide?

- What information do the name and formula of a molecular compound provide?

Vocabulary

- polyatomic ion

Reading Strategy

Predicting Copy the table. Before you read, predict the meaning of the term *polyatomic ion*. After you read, if your prediction was incorrect, revise your definition.

Vocabulary Term	Before You Read	After You Read
Polyatomic ion	a. ___?___	b. ___?___

Thomas Drummond was a Scottish surveyor and inventor. Around 1826, he discovered that a white solid called lime emits a bright light when heated to a high temperature. This discovery was extremely useful in the era before electric lighting. Limelight was used to produce a light that could be focused on a single spot on a stage. It also was used to produce lighthouse beams that could be seen from a great distance.

People have used mixtures of lime and water for centuries to white-wash houses and fences. The flowerpots in Figure 14 were coated with a lime wash to which paint pigments were added. Other names for lime are quicklime and unslaked lime. Having two or more names for a compound can be confusing. Also, names like lime or quicklime don't tell you much about the composition of a compound.

Chemists use a system for naming compounds that is based on rules established by the International Union of Pure and Applied Chemistry (IUPAC). In this system, the chemical name for lime is calcium oxide and its chemical formula is CaO. This formula tells you that there is a one-to-one ratio of calcium ions to oxide ions in calcium oxide. The formula of a compound serves as a reminder of the composition of the compound.

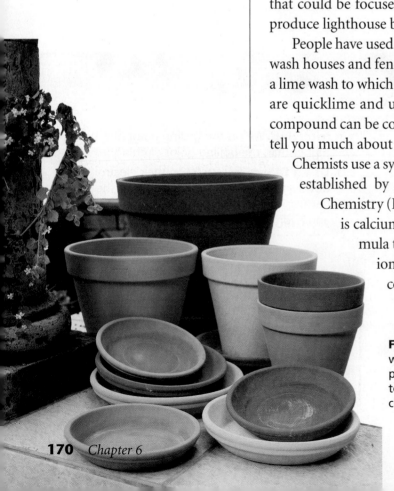

Figure 14 These flowerpots were coated with a solution of lime and water. Paint pigments were mixed with the lime wash to produce the different colors. The chemical name for lime is calcium oxide.

Figure 15 The brass vase on the left is coated with an oxide of copper that is red. Most of the surface of the plate on the right is coated with an oxide of copper that is black.
Classifying *How can you be sure that the oxides of copper are different compounds?*

Describing Ionic Compounds

Both of the objects in Figure 15 are coated with compounds of copper and oxygen. Based on the two colors of the coatings, copper and oxygen must form at least two compounds. One name cannot describe all the compounds of copper and oxygen. There must be at least two names to distinguish red copper oxide from black copper oxide. The name of an ionic compound must distinguish the compound from other ionic compounds containing the same elements. The formula of an ionic compound describes the ratio of the ions in the compound.

Binary Ionic Compounds A compound made from only two elements is a binary compound. (The Latin prefix *bi-* means "two," as in bicycle or bisect.) Naming binary ionic compounds, such as sodium chloride and cadmium iodide, is easy. The names have a predictable pattern: the name of the cation followed by the name of the anion. Remember that the name for the cation is the name of the metal without any change: sodium atom and sodium ion. The name for the anion uses part of the name of the nonmetal with the suffix *–ide:* iodine atom and iodide ion. Figure 16 shows the names and charges for eight common anions.

Figure 16 The table lists the element names, ion names, symbols, and charges for eight anions. The name of an anion is formed by adding the suffix –ide to the stem of the name of the nonmetal.

Common Anions			
Element Name	Ion Name	Ion Symbol	Ion Charge
Fluorine	Fluoride	F^-	1–
Chlorine	Chloride	Cl^-	1–
Bromine	Bromide	Br^-	1–
Iodine	Iodide	I^-	1–
Oxygen	Oxide	O^{2-}	2–
Sulfur	Sulfide	S^{2-}	2–
Nitrogen	Nitride	N^{3-}	3–
Phosphorus	Phosphide	P^{3-}	3–

Some Metal Cations			
Ion Name	Ion Symbol	Ion Name	Ion Symbol
Copper(I)	Cu^+	Chromium(II)	Cr^{2+}
Copper(II)	Cu^{2+}	Chromium(III)	Cr^{3+}
Iron(II)	Fe^{2+}	Titanium(II)	Ti^{2+}
Iron(III)	Fe^{3+}	Titanium(III)	Ti^{3+}
Lead(II)	Pb^{2+}	Titanium(IV)	Ti^{4+}
Lead(IV)	Pb^{4+}	Mercury(II)	Hg^{2+}

Figure 17 Many paint pigments contain compounds of transition metals. These metals often form more than one type of ion. The ion names must contain a Roman numeral. **Using Tables** *How is the Roman numeral in the name related to the charge on the ion?*

Ammonium ion
(NH_4^+)

Figure 18 The atoms in an ammonium ion are joined by covalent bonds. The ion loses a valence electron as it forms. This loss leaves only 10 electrons to balance the charge on 11 protons.

Metals With Multiple Ions The alkali metals, alkaline earth metals, and aluminum form ions with positive charges equal to the group number. For example, the symbol for a potassium ion is K^+, the symbol for a calcium ion is Ca^{2+}, and the symbol for an aluminum ion is Al^{3+}.

Many transition metals form more than one type of ion. Notice the two copper ions listed in Figure 17, a copper(I) ion with a 1+ charge and a copper(II) ion with a 2+ charge. When a metal forms more than one ion, the name of the ion contains a Roman numeral to indicate the charge on the ion. These ion names can distinguish red copper(I) oxide from black copper(II) oxide. The formula for "copper one oxide" is Cu_2O because it takes two Cu^{1+} ions to balance the charge on an O^{2-} ion. The formula for "copper two oxide" is CuO because it takes only one Cu^{2+} ion to balance the charge on an O^{2-} ion.

Polyatomic Ions The electron dot diagram in Figure 18 describes a group of atoms that includes one nitrogen and four hydrogen atoms. It is called an ammonium ion. The atoms are joined by covalent bonds. Why does the group have a positive charge? The nitrogen atom has seven protons, and each hydrogen atom has one proton—eleven in total. But the group has only ten electrons to balance the charge on the protons—eight valence electrons and nitrogen's two inner electrons.

A covalently bonded group of atoms that has a positive or negative charge and acts as a unit is a **polyatomic ion.** The prefix *poly-* means "many." Most simple polyatomic ions are anions. Figure 19 lists the names and formulas for some polyatomic ions. Sometimes there are parentheses in a formula that includes polyatomic ions. For example, the formula for iron(III) hydroxide is $Fe(OH)_3$. The subscript 3 indicates that there are three hydroxide ions for each iron(III) ion.

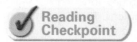 **Reading Checkpoint** *When are Roman numerals used in compound names?*

Quick Lab

Modeling Molecules

Materials

blue plastic-foam ball, black plastic-foam ball, 7 white gumdrops, toothpicks

Procedure

1. To make a model of an ammonia molecule (NH_3), insert a toothpick in each of 3 gumdrops. The gumdrops represent hydrogen atoms and the toothpicks represent bonds.

2. An ammonia molecule is like a pyramid with the nitrogen at the top and the hydrogen atoms at the corners of the base. Insert the toothpicks in the blue foam ball (nitrogen) so that each gumdrop is the same distance from the ball.

3. The hydrogen atoms in a methane molecule (CH_4) are equally spaced around the carbon. Use the black ball to make a model of methane.

Analyze and Conclude

1. **Comparing and Contrasting** Compare the shapes of the methane and ammonia molecules.

2. **Using Models** Why is carbon in the center of the methane molecule?

Writing Formulas for Ionic Compounds If you know the name of an ionic compound, you can write its formula. Place the symbol of the cation first, followed by the symbol of the anion. Use subscripts to show the ratio of the ions in the compound. Because all compounds are neutral, the total charges on the cations and anions must add up to zero.

Suppose an atom that gains two electrons, such as sulfur, reacts with an atom that loses one electron, such as sodium. There must be two sodium ions (Na^+) for each sulfide ion (S^{2-}). The formula for sodium sulfide is Na_2S. The $2-$ charge on one sulfide ion is balanced by the $1+$ charges on two sodium ions.

Some Polyatomic Ions			
Name	**Formula**	**Name**	**Formula**
Ammonium	NH_4^+	Acetate	$C_2H_3O_2^-$
Hydroxide	OH^-	Peroxide	O_2^{2-}
Nitrate	NO_3^-	Permanganate	MnO_4^-
Sulfate	SO_4^{2-}	Hydrogen sulfate	HSO_4^-
Carbonate	CO_3^{2-}	Hydrogen carbonate	HCO_3^-
Phosphate	PO_4^{3-}	Hydrogen phosphate	HPO_4^{2-}
Chromate	CrO_4^{2-}	Dichromate	$Cr_2O_7^{2-}$
Silicate	SiO_3^{2-}	Hypochlorite	OCl^-

Figure 19 This table lists the names and formulas of some polyatomic ions. Except for the ammonium ion, all the ions listed are anions. **Using Tables** *Which element is found in all the anions whose names end in -ate?*

Writing Formulas for Ionic Compounds

What is the formula for the ionic compound calcium chloride?

Math Practice

1. Write the formula for the compound calcium oxide.

2. Write the formula for the compound copper(I) sulfide.

3. Write the formula for the compound sodium sulfate.

4. What is the name of the compound whose formula is NaOH?

1 **Read and Understand**

What information are you given?

The name of the compound is calcium chloride.

2 **Plan and Solve**

List the symbols and charges for the cation and anion.

Ca with a charge of 2+ and Cl with a charge of 1−

Determine the ratio of ions in the compound.

It takes two 1− charges to balance the 2+ charge. There will be two chloride ions for each calcium ion.

Write the formula for calcium chloride.

$CaCl_2$

3 **Look Back and Check**

Is your answer reasonable?

Each calcium atom loses two electrons and each chlorine atom gains one electron. So there should be a 1-to-2 ratio of calcium ions to chloride ions.

Describing Molecular Compounds

Like ionic compounds, molecular compounds have names that identify specific compounds, and formulas that match those names. With molecular compounds, the focus is on the composition of molecules. ⊙ **The name and formula of a molecular compound describe the type and number of atoms in a molecule of the compound.**

Naming Molecular Compounds The general rule is that the most metallic element appears first in the name. These elements are farther to the left in the periodic table. If both elements are in the same group, the more metallic element is closer to the bottom of the group. The name of the second element is changed to end in the suffix *-ide*, as in carbon dioxide.

Go Online

NSTA *SciLINKS*

For: Links on chemical formulas
Visit: www.SciLinks.org
Web Code: ccn-1063

Two compounds that contain nitrogen and oxygen have the formulas N_2O_4 and NO_2. The names of these two compounds reflect the actual number of atoms of nitrogen and oxygen in a molecule of each compound. You can use the Greek prefixes in Figure 20 to describe the number of nitrogen and oxygen atoms in each molecule.

In an N_2O_4 molecule, there are two nitrogen atoms and four oxygen atoms. The Greek prefixes for two and four are *di-* and *tetra-*. The name for the compound with the formula N_2O_4 is dinitrogen tetraoxide. In an NO_2 molecule, there are one nitrogen atom and two oxygen atoms. The Greek prefixes for one and two are *mono-* and *di-*. So a name for the compound with the formula NO_2 is mononitrogen dioxide. However, the prefix *mono-* often is not used for the first element in the name. A more common name for the compound with the formula NO_2 is nitrogen dioxide.

Writing Molecular Formulas Writing the formula for a molecular compound is easy. Write the symbols for the elements in the order the elements appear in the name. The prefixes indicate the number of atoms of each element in the molecule. The prefixes appear as subscripts in the formulas. If there is no prefix for an element in the name, there is only one atom of that element in the molecule.

What is the formula for diphosphorus tetrafluoride? Because the compound is molecular, look for elements on the right side of the periodic table. Phosphorus has the symbol P. Fluorine has the symbol F. *Di-* indicates two phosphorus atoms and *tetra-* indicates four fluorine atoms. The formula for the compound is P_2F_4.

Prefixes For Naming Compounds

Number of Atoms	Prefix
1	mono-
2	di-
3	tri-
4	tetra-
5	penta-
6	hexa-
7	hepta-
8	octa-
9	nona-
10	deca-

Figure 20 These Greek prefixes are used to name molecular compounds. The prefix *octa-* means "eight," as in the eight tentacles of an octopus.

Section 6.3 Assessment

Reviewing Concepts

1. What does the formula of an ionic compound describe?

2. What do the name and formula of a molecular compound describe?

3. What suffix is used to indicate an anion?

4. Why are Roman numerals used in the names of compounds that contain transition metals?

5. What is a polyatomic ion?

Critical Thinking

6. **Applying Concepts** How is it possible for two different ionic compounds to contain the same elements?

7. **Calculating** How many potassium ions are needed to bond with a phosphate ion?

Math Practice

8. What are the names of these ionic compounds: LiCl, BaO, Na_3N, and $PbSO_4$?

9. Name the molecular compounds with these formulas: P_2O_5 and CO.

10. What is the formula for the ionic compound formed from potassium and sulfur?

6.4 The Structure of Metals

Reading Focus

Key Concepts

- What are the forces that give a metal its structure as a solid?
- How do metallic bonds produce some of the typical properties of metals?
- How are the properties of alloys controlled?

Vocabulary

- metallic bond
- alloy

Reading Strategy

Relating Cause and Effect Copy the concept map. As you read, complete the map to relate the structure of metals to their properties.

Figure 21 This photograph of the tungsten filament from a light bulb was taken with a scanning electron microscope. Color was added to the photo. The filament is magnified more than 100 times. The diameter of the wire is about 15 μm, or 0.0015 cm.

Light bulbs are easy to ignore unless a bulb burns out and you are searching for a replacement in the dark. But in the decades just before the year 1900, light bulbs were an exciting new technology. One challenge for researchers was to find the best material for the filaments in light bulbs. The substance had to be ductile enough to be drawn into a narrow wire. It could not melt at the temperatures produced when an electric current passes through a narrow wire. It had to have a low vapor pressure so that particles on the surface were not easily removed by sublimation.

The substance the researchers found was tungsten (W), a metal whose name means "heavy stone" in Swedish. Figure 21 shows a magnified view of the narrow coils in a tungsten filament. Tungsten has the highest melting point of any metal—3410°C—and it has the lowest vapor pressure. The properties of a metal are related to bonds within the metal.

Metallic Bonds

Metal atoms achieve stable electron configurations by losing electrons. But what happens if there are no nonmetal atoms available to accept the electrons? There is a way for metal atoms to lose and gain electrons at the same time. In a metal, valence electrons are free to move among the atoms. In effect, the metal atoms become cations surrounded by a pool of shared electrons. A **metallic bond** is the attraction between a metal cation and the shared electrons that surround it.

Hammer strikes metal.

Metal changes shape but does not break.

🔑 **The cations in a metal form a lattice that is held in place by strong metallic bonds between the cations and the surrounding valence electrons.** Although the electrons are moving among the atoms, the total number of electrons does not change. So, overall, the metal is neutral.

The metallic bonds in some metals are stronger than in other metals. The more valence electrons an atom can contribute to the shared pool, the stronger the metallic bonds will be. The bonds in an alkali metal are relatively weak because alkali metals contribute only a single valence electron. The result is that alkali metals, such as sodium, are soft enough to cut with a knife and have relatively low melting points. Sodium melts at 97.8°C. Transition metals, such as tungsten, have more valence electrons to contribute and, therefore, are harder and have higher melting points. Recall that tungsten melts at 3410°C.

Explaining Properties of Metals

The structure within a metal affects the properties of metals. 🔑 **The mobility of electrons within a metal lattice explains some of the properties of metals.** The ability to conduct an electric current and malleability are two important properties of metals.

Recall that a flow of charged particles is an electric current. A metal has a built-in supply of charged particles that can flow from one location to another—the pool of shared electrons. An electric current can be carried through a metal by the free flow of the shared electrons.

The lattice in a metal is flexible compared to the rigid lattice in an ionic compound. Figure 22 is a model of what happens when someone strikes a metal with a hammer. The metal ions shift their positions and the shape of the metal changes. But the metal does not shatter because ions are still held together by the metallic bonds between the ions and the electrons. Metallic bonds also explain why metals, such as tungsten and copper, can be drawn into thin wires without breaking.

Figure 22 In a metal, cations are surrounded by shared valence electrons. If a metal is struck, the ions move to new positions, but the ions are still surrounded by electrons. **Classifying** *What property of metals is displayed when a hammer strikes a metal?*

 Reading Checkpoint *What two important properties of metals can be explained by their structure?*

Alloys

A friend shows you a beautiful ring that she says is made from pure gold. Your friend is lucky to have such a valuable object. The purity of gold is expressed in units called karats. Gold that is 100 percent pure is labeled 24-karat gold. Gold jewelry that has a 12-karat label is only 50 percent gold. Jewelry that has an 18-karat label is 75 percent gold.

The surface of an object made from pure gold can easily be worn away by contact with other objects or dented because gold is a soft metal. When silver, copper, nickel, or zinc is mixed with gold, the gold is harder and more resistant to wear. These gold mixtures are alloys. An **alloy** is a mixture of two or more elements, at least one of which is a metal. Alloys have the characteristic properties of metals.

DK SCIENCE and History

Milestones in Metallurgy

The science of metallurgy includes ways to extract metals from ores, refine metals, and use metals. Described here are some advances in metallurgy since 1850.

Hot gas flame *The flame from a burning gas melts the surfaces where two metal parts will join.*

BESSEMER CONVERTER

Vanadium steel *This alloy becomes popular in car manufacturing because it is lightweight and strong.*

Gas torch

GAS WELDING

1856 Henry Bessemer develops an efficient process for producing steel by blowing air through molten iron.

1886 Charles Hall and Paul Héroult independently develop a method for using electricity to obtain aluminum from aluminum oxide.

1908 Henry Ford uses vanadium steel (an alloy of iron with carbon and vanadium) extensively in his Model T Fords.

1914 The start of World War I leads to the wide-scale use of welding techniques, such as gas welding with acetylene, for ship building.

| 1850 | 1880 | 1910 |

Copper Alloys The first important alloy was bronze, whose name is associated with an important era in history—the Bronze Age. Metalworkers in Thailand may have been the first to make bronze. But people in other locations probably thought they were the first to make bronze. News didn't travel quickly in that era.

Metalworkers might have noticed that the metal they extracted by heating deposits of copper was not always the same. The difference in properties could be traced to the presence of tin. In its simplest form, bronze contains only copper and tin, which are relatively soft metals. Mixed together in bronze, the metals are much harder and stronger than either metal alone. ● **Scientists can design alloys with specific properties by varying the types and amounts of elements in an alloy.**

Writing in Science

Cause-Effect Paragraph
Write a paragraph about Henry Ford's decision to use vanadium steel for automobile parts. Where did Ford first see parts made from vanadium steel? What properties of this type of steel impressed Ford? Did Ford need to overcome any problems before going ahead with his plan?

Steel-framed structure *The Empire State Building is supported by a framework of steel columns and beams that weigh 60,000 tons.*

EMPIRE STATE BUILDING

1931 The 102-story Empire State Building in New York City is completed. Skyscrapers would be impossible without steel-framed construction.

Metal parts, *such as the gears in this gold watch, are made by applying heat and pressure to powdered metal in a mold.*

METAL PARTS FROM POWDER

1942 Making small, complex parts from metal powders is less wasteful than machining. World War II spurs advances in iron powder metallurgy.

Superalloys containing rhenium are used in jet engines.

1991 New alloys containing rhenium are introduced. These superalloys are capable of retaining their strength at very high temperatures.

1940	1970	2000

Figure 23 This ancient statue of horses from Venice, Italy, and this modern French horn are both made from copper alloys. The statue is made from bronze, an alloy of copper and tin. The French horn is made from brass, an alloy of copper and zinc.

For: Articles on metals
Visit: PHSchool.com
Web Code: cce-1064

Bronze is hard and durable enough to be used for propellers on ships and for statues, such as the statue of horses in Figure 23. A bronze bell has a clear, loud tone that lasts for several seconds.

A brass bell has a duller tone that dies away quickly. Brass is another alloy of copper that has been known for centuries. In its simplest form, brass contains only copper and zinc. Although both bronze and brass are alloys of copper, they have distinctly different properties. Brass is softer than bronze and is easier to shape into forms such as the French horn in Figure 23. Brass is shinier than bronze but is likely to weather more quickly.

Steel Alloys The 1900s could be called the Age of Steel because of the skyscrapers, automobiles, and ships that were built from steel during the 1900s. Steel is an alloy of iron that contains small quantities of carbon, ranging from less than 0.2 percent to about 3 percent by mass. The smaller carbon atoms fit in the spaces between the larger iron atoms in the lattice. The carbon atoms form bonds with neighboring iron atoms. These bonds make the lattice harder and stronger than a lattice that contains only iron.

The properties of any particular type of steel depend on which elements other than iron and carbon are used and how much of those elements are included. Stainless steels contain more than 10 percent chromium by mass, but almost no carbon. Stainless steels are durable because chromium forms an oxide that protects the steel from rusting. But stainless steel is more brittle than steels that contain more carbon. The steel cables in the bridge in Figure 24 have to be strong enough to resist forces that might stretch the cables or cause them to break. The steel used contains sulfur, manganese, phosphorus, silicon, and 0.81 percent carbon.

Figure 24 The Golden Gate Bridge is a landmark in San Francisco, California. Its cables, towers, and deck contain steel. The steel in the cables needs to resist forces that pull on the cables. The steel in the towers needs to resist the compression forces caused by the weight of the cables, the deck, and the vehicles that travel across the bridge.
Drawing Conclusions *Would the steel used for the cables and the steel used for the towers have the same composition? Give a reason for your answer.*

Other Alloys Airplane parts are made of many different alloys that are suited to particular purposes. The body of a plane is large and needs to be made from a lightweight material. Pure aluminum is lighter than most metals, but it bends and dents too easily. If a small amount of copper or manganese is added to aluminum, the result is a stronger material that is still lighter than steel.

For certain aircraft parts, even lighter materials are needed. Alloys of aluminum and magnesium are used for these parts. Magnesium is much less dense than most metals used to build structures. However, pure magnesium is soft enough to cut with a knife, and it burns in air. An aluminum-magnesium alloy keeps the advantages of magnesium without the disadvantages.

Section 6.4 Assessment

Reviewing Concepts

1. What holds metal ions together in a metal lattice?

2. What characteristic of a metallic bond explains some of the properties of metals?

3. How can scientists design alloys with specific properties?

4. Explain why the metallic bonds in some metals are stronger than the bonds in other metals.

5. Why are metals good conductors of electric current?

6. How does adding carbon to steel make the steel harder and stronger?

Critical Thinking

7. **Predicting** Which element has a higher melting point, potassium in Group 1A or calcium in Group 1B? Give a reason for your answer.

8. **Applying Concepts** Can two different elements form a metallic bond together?

Compare-Contrast Paragraph Write a paragraph comparing the properties of ionic compounds and alloys. Relate their properties to the structure of their lattices.

Chipping In

Tasks done by computers that filled an entire room in the 1950s are now done by devices the size of a credit card. This miniaturization in the electronics industry is due to semiconductors.

Semiconductors are solid substances, such as silicon, that have poor electrical conductivity at ordinary temperatures. Silicon has four valence electrons. In pure silicon, each atom forms single bonds with four other atoms. This arrangement leaves no electrons free to move through the silicon. The conductivity of silicon is greatly improved by adding small amounts of other elements to silicon, a process called doping.

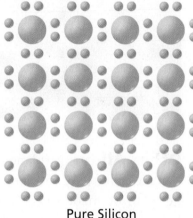

Pure Silicon

Doping

An element with five valence electrons, such as phosphorus, can be added to silicon. After a phosphorus atom bonds with four atoms, there is an extra electron that is free to move. Silicon doped with phosphorus is called *n*-type silicon because electrons have a negative charge. An element with three valence electrons, such as boron, can be added to silicon. Adding boron leaves holes to which electrons can move from neighboring atoms. Because the lack of an electron has the effect of a positive charge, silicon with boron is called *p*-type silicon.

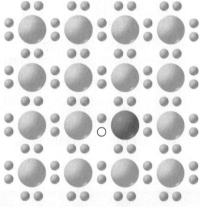

Silicon with boron

Silicon wafer

Silicon crystal

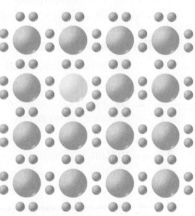

Silicon with phosphorus

Wafers and chips

Silicon crystals are cut into wafer-thin slices. Each wafer can be made into hundreds of silicon chips.

Vacuum tube
Glass vacuum tubes used in early computers were fragile and took up space.

Integrated circuit on a silicon chip

Computer chip
In 1974, the first computer microchip contained 6000 transistors. Today, more than 40 million transistors can be placed on a single computer chip.

Diode
In a diode, a layer of *p*-type silicon is joined to a layer of *n*-type silicon. When the leads on a diode are correctly connected in a circuit, electrons flow toward the junction between the two types of silicon. Electrons from the *n*-type silicon fill holes in the *p*-type silicon. In devices that use batteries, a diode can keep electrons from flowing if the batteries are not inserted correctly. Some diodes emit light when the circuit is complete.

Transistor
In a transistor, there are three layers of doped silicon. There is a layer of *p*-type silicon sandwiched between two layers of *n*-type silicon or a layer of *n*-type silicon between two layers of p-type silicon. Transistors are used to amplify current. A small current applied to the central layer of a transistor can produce a larger current.

Going Further

- Research and write about the development of transistors. Why were researchers looking for a replacement for vacuum tubes? How did replacing vacuum tubes with transistors affect the size of radios and computers?

- Make a table or Venn diagram to compare *n*-type silicon with *p*-type silicon.

Improving the Dyeing of Nonpolar Fabrics

Most natural fibers, such as cotton and wool, consist of large molecules that have regions with a partial positive or partial negative charge. These polar molecules have a strong attraction for dyes that contain either polar molecules or ions.

The molecules in some manufactured fibers, such as nylon, are nonpolar molecules. These synthetic fibers are difficult to dye. Molecules of other synthetic fibers, such as polyester and rayon, have only a few polar regions. As you might suspect, polyester and rayon have intermediate attractions for dyes. In this lab, you will investigate a process for improving a fiber's ability to absorb and retain dye.

Problem How can you increase the dye-holding capacity of nonpolar fibers?

Materials
- tongs
- 2 fabric test strips
- hot dye bath containing methyl orange
- clock or watch
- paper towels
- scissors
- soap
- hot iron(II) sulfate solution

Skills Observing, Drawing Conclusions

Procedure

Part A: Dyeing Without Treatment

1. On a sheet of paper, copy the data table shown.

2. Use the tongs to immerse a fabric test strip in the methyl orange dye bath. **CAUTION** *The dye bath is hot. Do not touch the glass. The dye will stain skin and clothing.*

3. After 7 minutes, remove the strip from the dye bath. Allow as much of the dye solution as possible to drip back into the bath as shown on page 185. Rinse off the excess dye with water in the sink.

4. Place the strip on a paper towel to dry. Be careful to avoid splashes when transferring the strip between the dye bath and paper towel. Record your observations in your data table.

5. After the fabric strip is dry, test it for colorfastness, or the ability to hold dye. Cut the strip in half lengthwise and wash one half of the strip in the sink with soap and water.

Data Table		
Dye Treatment	Dyeing of Fibers	Colorfastness of Fibers
Methyl orange		
Iron sulfate and methyl orange		

6. Allow the washed half-strip to dry and then compare the washed half to the unwashed half. Record your observations in your data table. Staple the half-strips to a sheet of paper and label each half-strip to indicate how you treated it.

Part B: Dyeing With Treatment

7. Use the tongs to place the second fabric strip in the iron(II) sulfate solution for 25 minutes. Then use tongs to lift the strip and allow it to drain into the iron(II) sulfate solution. Wring the strip as dry as possible over the solution. **CAUTION** *The strip will be hot. Allow it to cool before touching it. Wear plastic gloves.*

8. Repeat Steps 2, 3, and 4 using the strip that you treated with iron(II) sulfate.

9. To test the strip for colorfastness, repeat Steps 5 and 6.

10. Clean up your work area and wash your hands thoroughly with warm water and soap before leaving the laboratory.

Analyze and Conclude

1. **Comparing and Contrasting** How did the color of the untreated strip compare with the color of the treated strip?

2. **Comparing and Contrasting** How did the colorfastness of the untreated strip compare to the colorfastness of the treated strip?

3. **Applying Concepts** Silk blouses and shirts can be purchased in many intense colors. Why do you think silk is able to hold a variety of intense dyes?

4. **Drawing Conclusions** How does iron(II) sulfate affect the ability of a fabric to absorb dyes? (*Hint:* What kind of compound is iron(II) sulfate?)

5. **Predicting** A care label might say *Wash in cold water only.* What might happen to the color of a piece of clothing with this label if you washed the clothing in hot water?

Study Guide

6.1 Ionic Bonding

Key Concepts

- When the highest occupied energy level of an atom is filled with electrons, the atom is stable and not likely to react.

- Some elements achieve stable electron configurations through the transfer of electrons between atoms. An ionic bond forms when electrons are transferred from one atom to another.

- The properties of an ionic compound can be explained by the strong attractions among ions within a crystal lattice.

Vocabulary

electron dot diagram, *p. 158*

ion, *p. 159*

anion, *p. 160*

cation, *p. 160*

chemical bond, *p. 160*

ionic bond, *p. 160*

chemical formula, *p. 161*

crystals, *p. 162*

6.2 Covalent Bonding

Key Concepts

- The attractions between the shared electrons and the protons in each nucleus hold the atoms together in a covalent bond.

- When atoms form a polar covalent bond, the atom with the greater attraction for electrons has a partial negative charge. The other atom has a partial positive charge.

- The type of atoms in a molecule and its shape are factors that determine whether a molecule is polar or nonpolar.

- Attractions between polar molecules are stronger than attractions between nonpolar molecules.

Vocabulary

covalent bond, *p. 166*

molecule, *p. 166*

polar covalent bond, *p. 168*

6.3 Naming Compounds and Writing Formulas

Key Concepts

- The name of an ionic compound must distinguish the compound from other ionic compounds containing the same elements. The formula of an ionic compound describes the ratio of the ions in the compound.

- The name and formula of a molecular compound describe the type and number of atoms in a molecule of the compound.

Vocabulary

polyatomic ion, *p. 172*

6.4 The Structure of Metals

Key Concepts

- The cations in a metal form a lattice that is held in place by strong metallic bonds between the cations and the surrounding valence electrons.

- The mobility of electrons within a metal lattice explains some of the properties of metals.

- Scientists can design alloys with specific properties by varying the types and amounts of elements in an alloy.

Vocabulary

metallic bond, *p. 176*

alloy, *p. 178*

Thinking Visually

Concept Map Use information from the chapter to complete the concept map below.

Reviewing Content

Choose the letter that best answers the question or completes the statement.

1. When an atom loses an electron, it forms a(n)
  a. anion.
  b. cation.
  c. polyatomic ion.
  d. neutral ion.

2. The charge on a chloride ion in $AlCl_3$ is
  a. 1+.
  b. 3∓.
  c. 1−.
  d. 3−.

3. Which pair has the same electron configuration?
  a. Cl^- and Ar
  b. Cl^- and Ar^-
  c. Cl and Ar
  d. Cl^+ and Ar

4. A chemical bond that forms when atoms share electrons is always a(n)
  a. polar bond.
  b. ionic bond.
  c. metallic bond.
  d. covalent bond.

5. When two fluorine atoms share a pair of electrons, the bond that forms is a(n)
  a. polar covalent bond.
  b. ionic bond.
  c. nonpolar covalent bond.
  d. double bond.

6. The chemical formula for magnesium bromide is
  a. MgBr.
  b. $MgBr_2$.
  c. $Mg(II)Br_2$.
  d. Mg_2Br.

7. The compound with the formula $SiCl_4$ is
  a. silicon chloride.
  b. silicon chlorine.
  c. silicon(I) chloride.
  d. silicon tetrachloride.

8. The attraction among water molecules is stronger than the attraction among
  a. sodium and chloride ions.
  b. carbon dioxide molecules.
  c. the atoms in a polyatomic ion.
  d. atoms in a diatomic molecule.

9. Which type of solid is likely to be the best conductor of electric current?
  a. ionic compound
  b. covalent compound
  c. metal element
  d. nonmetal element

10. An alloy contains
  a. at least one metallic element.
  b. at least one nonmetallic element.
  c. only metallic elements.
  d. only nonmetallic elements.

Understanding Concepts

11. What is a stable electron configuration?

12. What does each dot in an electron dot diagram represent?

13. What process changes atoms into ions?

14. What keeps the ions in their fixed positions within a crystal lattice?

15. What are subscripts used for in chemical formulas?

16. Explain why a melted ionic compound is a good conductor of electric current, but a solid ionic compound is a poor conductor of electric current.

17. What distinguishes single, double, and triple covalent bonds?

18. Explain why the covalent bonds in molecules of elements are always nonpolar.

19. Explain why, in a covalent bond between oxygen and hydrogen, the hydrogen atom has a partial positive charge and the oxygen atom has a partial negative charge.

20. What is the name of the binary compound formed from potassium and iodine?

21. Write the formulas for the compounds called copper(I) chloride and copper(II) chloride.

22. Name the compounds represented by the space-filling models labeled A, B, and C.

A **B** **C**

☐ Sulfur ■ Oxygen ■ Carbon ■ Nitrogen

23. In general, what determines the strength of metallic bonds?

24. What properties of copper and tin change when these metals are mixed together to form bronze?

25. What advantage of magnesium is retained in magnesium alloys? What disadvantage is reduced?

Assessment (continued)

Critical Thinking

26. Classifying What does a fluoride ion have in common with a neon atom and a sodium ion?

27. Comparing and Contrasting How are molecules and polyatomic ions similar?

28. Classifying Classify the bonds in each of these compounds as ionic, polar covalent, or nonpolar covalent: SO_3, CaO, and I_2.

29. Applying Concepts Write the names for the compounds with these chemical formulas: SCl_2, Ag_2SO_4, LiF, CS_2, and $Ca(OH)_2$.

Use these diagrams to answer Questions 30–34.

30. Using Models Which of the three elements are metals and which are nonmetals?

31. Applying Concepts Element Q forms compounds with element X and with element Z. Write the formulas for these two compounds.

32. Calculating What would the formula be for a compound containing chromium(III) ions and ions of element Z?

33. Applying Concepts Draw an electron dot structure for a compound of fluorine and Z.

34. Predicting If an atom of X reacts with an atom of X, what kind of bond forms?

Math Skills

35. Calculating What is the total number of shared electrons in a carbon dioxide molecule?

36. Making Generalizations What is the ratio of anions to cations in a compound formed by a Group 2A metal and a Group 7A nonmetal?

37. Applying Concepts Write the formulas for barium fluoride, sodium oxide, iron(II) sulfate, and ammonium sulfate.

Concepts In Action

38. Using Models A solution of hydrogen peroxide (H_2O_2) and water is sometimes used to disinfect a cut. Which of the following formulas is the correct structural formula for hydrogen peroxide?

39. Relating Cause and Effect In a carbonated beverage, the main ingredients are water and carbon dioxide. Carbon dioxide gas is released when the bottle is opened. Why is water a liquid but carbon dioxide a gas at room temperature?

40. Classifying The shells shown on page 156 contain the compound calcium carbonate ($CaCO_3$). Explain how this compound can contain both ionic and covalent bonds.

41. Relating Cause and Effect How does adding some phosphorus to silicon make silicon a better conductor of electric current?

42. Writing in Science Compare what happens to the valence electron in a hydrogen atom when the atom bonds with another hydrogen atom and when the atom bonds with an oxygen atom.

Performance-Based Assessment

Designing an Advertisement You own a store that sells bronze bells. Design a quarter-page ad for your store to be published in your local directory of businesses. Write copy for your ad. Describe a photograph to use in the ad. Also supply a sketch showing how you want the copy and the photograph to be laid out on the page.

For: Self-grading assessment
Visit: PHSchool.com
Web Code: cca-1060

Standardized Test Prep

Use the table to answer Questions 4 and 5.

Test-Taking Tip

Paying Attention to the Details

Sometimes two or more answers to a question are almost identical. If you do not read the answers carefully, you may select an incorrect answer by mistake. In the question below, all the answers include the correct elements in the correct order—metal before nonmetal. However, only one of the answers uses the correct rules for naming $CaCl_2$.

The name for the compound with the formula $CaCl_2$ is

(A) calcium(II) chloride.
(B) calcium chlorine.
(C) calcium dichloride.
(D) calcium chloride.
(E) monocalcium dichloride.

(Answer: D)

Choose the letter that best answers the question or completes the statement.

1. How many electrons does a Group 7A atom need to gain in order to achieve a stable electron configuration?
(A) 0
(B) 1
(C) 2
(D) 7
(E) 8

2. What type of bond forms when electrons are transferred from one atom to another?
(A) nonpolar covalent bond
(B) ionic bond
(C) polar covalent bond
(D) polyatomic bond
(E) metallic bond

3. Metallic bonds form between
(A) cations and protons.
(B) anions and protons.
(C) cations and anions.
(D) cations and electrons.
(E) anions and electrons.

Some Ions and Their Symbols			
Ion Name	Ion Symbol	Ion Name	Ion Symbol
Copper(I)	Cu^+	Nitrate	NO_3^-
Copper(II)	Cu^{2+}	Sulfate	SO_4^{2-}
Iron(II)	Fe^{2+}	Carbonate	CO_3^{2-}
Iron(III)	Fe^{3+}	Phosphate	PO_4^{3-}

4. What is the formula for copper(II) nitrate?
(A) $CuNO_3$
(B) $Cu_2(NO_3)_2$
(C) $Cu(NO_3)_2$
(D) Cu_2NO_3
(E) $CuNO_2$

5. In the compound iron(II) carbonate, the ratio of iron(II) ions to carbonate ions will be
(A) one to one.
(B) two to one.
(C) three to one.
(D) one to two.
(E) one to three.

6. All steels contain
(A) copper and zinc.
(B) copper and tin.
(C) iron and chromium.
(D) chromium and carbon.
(E) iron and carbon.

7. What is the reason that water has a higher boiling point than expected?
(A) Attractions among nonpolar water molecules are strong.
(B) Water molecules have a linear shape.
(C) Water molecules are not very massive.
(D) There are strong attractions among polar water molecules.
(E) There are no attractions among water molecules.

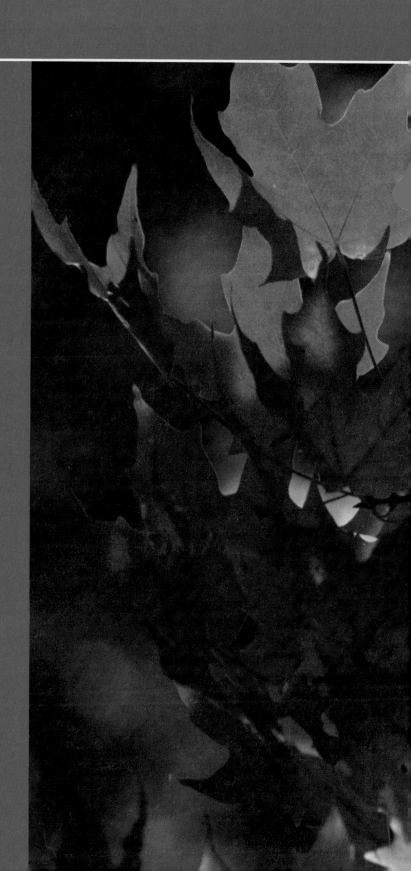

How do scientists classify reactions?

Scientists classify chemical reactions based on the type of reactant or the number of reactants and products. Work in a group to develop a slide-show presentation that summarizes general types of reactions. First, determine how the slide show will be organized. Then work as a group or split up into smaller groups to cover the different reaction types. Present the final slide show in class or publish it on your class Web site.

How do science concepts apply to your world? Here are some questions you'll be able to answer after you read this chapter.

- What happens to a piece of charcoal as it burns? *(Section 7.1)*

- How do air bags inflate? *(Section 7.2)*

- Why does a propane stove need a spark in order for the propane to ignite? *(Section 7.3)*

- How do firefighters put out wildfires? *(page 210)*

- How does a refrigerator keep food fresh? *(Section 7.4)*

- What changes take place inside a closed container of water? *(Section 7.5)*

Chapter Preview

Autumn leaves change color
as a result of a series of
chemical reactions.

Inquiry > Activity

How Is Mass Conserved in a Chemical Change?

Procedure

1. Pour 100 mL of water into a resealable plastic bag. Flatten the bag to remove all of the air and then seal the bag. Measure and record the mass of the bag and the water.

2. Measure and record the mass of a square piece of paper with sides of 10 cm. Place an antacid tablet on the paper. Measure and record the mass of the tablet and the paper together. To find the mass of just the tablet, subtract the mass of the paper from the combined masses of the tablet and the paper.

3. Record the combined masses of the bag, the water, and the antacid tablet.

4. Slightly open one side of the bag and drop the tablet into the water. Quickly reseal the bag. After the bubbling has stopped, measure and record the mass of the bag and its contents.

Think About It

1. **Applying Concepts** How do you know whether a chemical change took place?

2. **Inferring** What happened to the mass of the plastic bag and its contents after the bubbling stopped? What might this information tell you about a chemical change?

7.1 Describing Reactions

Reading Focus

Key Concepts

- What is the law of conservation of mass?
- Why must chemical equations be balanced?
- Why do chemists use the mole?
- How can you calculate the mass of a reactant or product in a chemical reaction?

Vocabulary

- ◆ reactants
- ◆ products
- ◆ chemical equation
- ◆ coefficients
- ◆ mole
- ◆ molar mass

Reading Strategy

Monitoring Your Understanding Preview the Key Concepts, topic headings, vocabulary, and figures in this section. List two things you expect to learn. After reading, state what you learned about each item you listed.

What I Expect to Learn	What I Learned
a. _____?_____	b. _____?_____
c. _____?_____	d. _____?_____

What type of change is happening in Figure 1? When charcoal burns, it changes into other substances while producing heat and light. Burning is a chemical change. When a substance undergoes a chemical change, a chemical reaction is said to take place. In order to understand chemical reactions, you first must be able to describe them.

Chemical Equations

A useful way of describing a change is to state what is present before and after the change. For example, suppose you wanted to show how your appearance changed as you grew older. You could compare a photo of yourself when you were younger with a photo that was taken recently.

A useful description of a chemical reaction tells you the substances present before and after the reaction. In a chemical reaction, the substances that undergo change are called **reactants.** The new substances formed as a result of that change are called **products.** In Figure 1, the reactants are the carbon in the charcoal and the oxygen in the air. The product of the reaction is carbon dioxide gas.

Using Equations to Represent Reactions During a chemical reaction, the reactants change into products. You can summarize this process with a word equation.

$$\text{Reactants} \longrightarrow \text{Products}$$

Figure 1 Burning is an example of a chemical reaction. When charcoal burns, the carbon in the charcoal reacts with oxygen in the air to produce carbon dioxide and heat.

To describe the burning of charcoal, you can substitute the reactants and products of the reaction into the word equation as follows.

$$\text{Carbon} + \text{Oxygen} \longrightarrow \text{Carbon dioxide}$$

You can then simplify the word equation by writing the reactants and products as chemical formulas.

$$C + O_2 \longrightarrow CO_2$$

Now you have a chemical equation. A **chemical equation** is a representation of a chemical reaction in which the reactants and products are expressed as formulas. You can read the equation above as, "Carbon and oxygen react and form carbon dioxide," or, "The reaction of carbon and oxygen yields carbon dioxide."

 Reading Checkpoint *What is a chemical equation?*

Conservation of Mass As a piece of charcoal burns, it gets smaller and smaller until it is finally reduced to a tiny pile of ash. Although the charcoal seems to disappear as it burns, it is actually being converted into carbon dioxide gas. If you measured the mass of the carbon dioxide produced, it would equal the mass of the charcoal and oxygen that reacted.

During chemical reactions, the mass of the products is always equal to the mass of the reactants. This principle, established by French chemist Antoine Lavoisier (1743–1794), is known as the law of conservation of mass. **The law of conservation of mass states that mass is neither created nor destroyed in a chemical reaction.** Recall that mass is a measure of the amount of matter. So, this law is also known as the law of conservation of matter. By demonstrating that mass is conserved in various reactions, Lavoisier laid the foundation for modern chemistry.

Figure 2 illustrates how a chemical equation can be restated in terms of atoms and molecules. The equation reads, "One atom of carbon reacts with one molecule of oxygen and forms one molecule of carbon dioxide." Suppose you have six carbon atoms. If each carbon atom reacts with one oxygen molecule to form one carbon dioxide molecule, then six carbon atoms react with six oxygen molecules to form six carbon dioxide molecules. Notice that the number of atoms on the left side of the equation equals the number of atoms on the right. The equation shows that mass is conserved.

Go Online
NSTA SciLINKS

For: Links on conservation of mass
Visit: www.SciLinks.org
Web Code: ccn-1071

Figure 2 Whether you burn one carbon atom or six carbon atoms, the equation used to describe the reaction is the same. **Using Models** *How do both models of the reaction below show that mass is conserved?*

Burning of Carbon

| C Carbon | + | O_2 Oxygen | $\longrightarrow$ | CO_2 Carbon dioxide |

Reactants — Products

Figure 3 Water is a compound made up of the elements hydrogen and oxygen.

Go Online
active art

For: Activity on balancing equations
Visit: PHSchool.com
Web Code: ccp-1071

Figure 4 In the unbalanced equation, the hydrogen atoms are balanced but the oxygen atoms are not. After changing the coefficients, both the hydrogen and oxygen atoms are balanced. **Applying Concepts** *Why must chemical equations be balanced?*

Balancing Equations

Water is formed by the reaction of hydrogen and oxygen. You can describe the reaction by writing a chemical equation.

$$H_2 + O_2 \longrightarrow H_2O$$

If you examine this equation carefully, you will notice that the number of atoms on the left side does not equal the number of atoms on the right. The equation is not balanced. **In order to show that mass is conserved during a reaction, a chemical equation must be balanced.**

You can balance a chemical equation by changing the **coefficients,** the numbers that appear before the formulas. In the unbalanced equation above, the coefficients are understood to be 1. When you change a coefficient, you change the amount of that reactant or product represented in the chemical equation. As you balance equations, you should never change the subscripts in a formula. Changing the formula changes the identity of that reactant or product.

The first step in balancing an equation is to count the number of atoms of each element on each side of the equation, as shown in Figure 4. The left side of the unbalanced equation has two hydrogen atoms and two oxygen atoms. The right side has two hydrogen atoms and one oxygen atom. The oxygen atoms need to be balanced.

The next step is to change one or more coefficients until the equation is balanced. You can balance the oxygen atoms by changing the coefficient of H_2O to 2.

$$H_2 + O_2 \longrightarrow 2H_2O$$

The oxygen atoms are now balanced. However, the hydrogen atoms have become "unbalanced," with two on the left, and four on the right. To balance the hydrogen atoms, change the coefficient of H_2 to 2.

$$2H_2 + O_2 \longrightarrow 2H_2O$$

The equation is now balanced. Each side of the balanced equation has four hydrogen atoms and two oxygen atoms, as shown in Figure 4. According to the balanced equation, two molecules of hydrogen react with one molecule of oxygen to yield two molecules of water.

Unbalanced Chemical Equation	
H_2 + O_2 ⟶ H_2O	
Reactants	**Product**
2 hydrogen atoms	2 hydrogen atoms
2 oxygen atoms	1 oxygen atom

Balanced Chemical Equation	
$2H_2$ + O_2 ⟶ $2H_2O$	
Reactants	**Product**
4 hydrogen atoms	4 hydrogen atoms
2 oxygen atoms	2 oxygen atoms

Balancing Chemical Equations

Write a balanced equation for the reaction between copper and oxygen to produce copper(II) oxide, CuO.

 1 **Read and Understand**

What information are you given?

Reactants: Cu, O_2 Product: CuO

2 **Plan and Solve**

Write a chemical equation with the reactants on the left side and the product on the right.

$$Cu + O_2 \longrightarrow CuO$$

This equation is not balanced. Change the coefficient of CuO in order to balance the number of oxygen atoms.

$$Cu + O_2 \longrightarrow 2CuO$$

Change the coefficient of Cu in order to balance the number of copper atoms.

$$2Cu + O_2 \longrightarrow 2CuO$$

 3 **Look Back and Check**

Is your answer reasonable?

The number of atoms on the left equals the number of atoms on the right.

1. Hydrogen chloride, or HCl, is an important industrial chemical. Write a balanced equation for the production of hydrogen chloride from hydrogen and chlorine.

2. Balance the following chemical equations.
   a. $H_2O_2 \longrightarrow H_2O + O_2$
   b. $Mg + HCl \longrightarrow$
      $\qquad H_2 + MgCl_2$

3. Ethylene, C_2H_4, burns in the presence of oxygen to produce carbon dioxide and water vapor. Write a balanced equation for this reaction.

Counting With Moles

How many shoes do you own? Because shoes come in twos, you would most likely count them by the pair rather than individually. The counting units you use depend on what you are counting. For example, you might count eggs by the dozen or paper by the ream.

Chemists also need practical units for counting things. Although you can describe a reaction in terms of atoms and molecules, these units are too small to be practical. ⬤ **Because chemical reactions often involve large numbers of small particles, chemists use a counting unit called the mole to measure amounts of a substance.**

A **mole** (mol) is an amount of a substance that contains approximately 6.02×10^{23} particles of that substance. This number is known as Avogadro's number. In chemistry, a mole of a substance generally contains 6.02×10^{23} atoms, molecules, or ions of that substance. For instance, a mole of iron is 6.02×10^{23} atoms of iron.

Figure 5 Shoes are often counted by the pair, eggs by the dozen, and paper by the ream (500 sheets). To count particles of a substance, chemists use the mole (6.02×10^{23} particles).

Figure 6 The molar mass of carbon is 12.0 grams. The molar mass of sulfur is 32.1 grams. *Inferring If each of the carbon and sulfur samples contains one mole of atoms, why do the samples have different masses?*

Molar Mass A dozen eggs has a different mass than a dozen oranges. Similarly, a mole of carbon has a different mass than a mole of sulfur, as shown in Figure 6. The mass of one mole of a substance is called a **molar mass.** For an element, the molar mass is the same as its atomic mass expressed in grams. For example, the atomic mass of carbon is 12.0 amu, so the molar mass of carbon is 12.0 grams.

For a compound, you can calculate the molar mass by adding up the atomic masses of its component atoms, and then expressing this sum in grams. A carbon dioxide molecule is composed of one carbon atom (12.0 amu) and two oxygen atoms (2×16.0 amu $= 32.0$ amu). So carbon dioxide has a molar mass of 44.0 grams.

Mole-Mass Conversions Once you know the molar mass of a substance, you can convert moles of that substance into mass, or a mass of that substance into moles. For either calculation, you need to express the molar mass as a conversion factor. For example, the molar mass of CO_2 is 44.0 grams, which means that one mole of CO_2 has a mass of 44.0 grams. This relationship yields the following conversion factors.

$$\frac{44.0 \text{ g } CO_2}{1 \text{ mol } CO_2} \qquad \frac{1 \text{ mol } CO_2}{44.0 \text{ g } CO_2}$$

Suppose you have 55.0 grams of CO_2. To calculate how many moles of CO_2 you have, multiply the mass by the conversion factor on the right.

$$55.0 \text{ g } CO_2 \times \frac{1 \text{ mol } CO_2}{44.0 \text{ g } CO_2} = 1.25 \text{ mol } CO_2$$

You can check your answer by using the conversion factor on the left.

$$1.25 \text{ mol } CO_2 \times \frac{44.0 \text{ g } CO_2}{1 \text{ mol } CO_2} = 55.0 \text{ g } CO_2$$

Quick Lab

Modeling a Mole

Materials

bolt, 2 nuts, 2 washers, balance

Procedure

1. Measure and record the mass of one bolt, one nut, and one washer. Each piece of hardware will represent an atom of a different element.

2. Assemble the bolt, nuts, and washers together so that they form a model of a molecule known as BN_2W_2.

3. Predict the mass of BN_2W_2.

4. Test your prediction by finding the mass of your model.

Analyze and Conclude

1. **Analyzing Data** Did your prediction match the actual mass of your model? Explain.

2. **Calculating** How many models of your molecule can you make with 20 washers and as many nuts and bolts as you need?

3. **Calculating** How many models of your molecule can you make with 100 grams of nuts and as many bolts and washers as you need?

Chemical Calculations

Think about baking a cake like the one in Figure 7. The directions on a box of cake mix might tell you to add two eggs and one cup of water to the cake mix. Suppose you wanted to make three cakes. Although the directions don't tell you specifically how many eggs and how much water are required for three cakes, you could figure out the amounts. To make three cakes, you would need three times as much of each ingredient—six eggs, three cups of water, and three packages of cake mix.

Chemical equations can be read as recipes for making new substances. Figure 8 shows the balanced equation for the formation of water. You can read this equation as, "Two molecules of hydrogen react with one molecule of oxygen and form two molecules of water." In terms of moles, the equation reads, "Two moles of hydrogen react with one mole of oxygen and form two moles of water." To convert from moles to mass, you need to use the molar masses as conversion factors. Figure 8 shows how the same equation can also be read as, "4.0 grams of H_2 reacts with 32.0 grams of O_2 and forms 36.0 grams of H_2O."

How many grams of oxygen would you need to make 144 grams of water? ☞ **In chemical reactions, the mass of a reactant or product can be calculated by using a balanced chemical equation and molar masses of the reactants and products.** The chemical equation tells you how to relate amounts of reactants to amounts of products. Molar masses let you convert those amounts into masses.

 Reading Checkpoint *How do you convert from moles to mass?*

Converting Mass to Moles To calculate how much oxygen is required to make 144 grams of water, you need to begin with a balanced chemical equation for the reaction.

$$2H_2 + O_2 \longrightarrow 2H_2O$$

The first step in your calculations is to determine how many moles of water you are trying to make. By using the molar mass of water, you can convert the given mass of water into moles.

$$144 \text{ g H}_2\text{O} \times \frac{1 \text{ mol H}_2\text{O}}{18.0 \text{ g H}_2\text{O}} = 8.00 \text{ mol H}_2\text{O}$$

Formation of Water						
Equation	$2H_2$	+	O_2	→	$2H_2O$	
Amount	2 mol		1 mol		2 mol	
Molar Mass	2.0 g/mol		32.0 g/mol		18.0 g/mol	
Mass (Moles × Molar Mass)	4.0 g	+	32.0 g	→	36.0 g	

Figure 7 A cake recipe tells you how much of each ingredient to use for each cake you bake. **Using Analogies** *How is a cake recipe like a chemical equation?*

Figure 8 In a balanced chemical equation, the number of atoms of each element on the left equals the number of atoms of each element on the right. By using molar masses, you can show that the mass of the reactants equals the mass of the products.

Using Mole Ratios Remember the balanced chemical equation for the formation of water. You can read it as, "Two moles of hydrogen react with one mole of oxygen and form two moles of water." Because each mole of oxygen that reacts will yield two moles of water, you can write the following conversion factors, or mole ratios.

$$\frac{1 \text{ mol O}_2}{2 \text{ mol H}_2\text{O}} \qquad \frac{2 \text{ mol H}_2\text{O}}{1 \text{ mol O}_2}$$

The mole ratio on the left allows you to convert moles of water to moles of oxygen. Now you can calculate how many moles of oxygen are required to produce eight moles of water:

$$8.00 \text{ mol H}_2\text{O} \times \frac{1 \text{ mol O}_2}{2 \text{ mol H}_2\text{O}} = 4.00 \text{ mol O}_2$$

Converting Moles to Mass The last step is to convert moles of O_2 to grams of O_2 by using the molar mass of O_2 as a conversion factor.

$$4.00 \text{ mol O}_2 \times \frac{32.0 \text{ g O}_2}{1 \text{ mol O}_2} = 128 \text{ g O}_2$$

So, in order to produce 144 grams of H_2O, you must supply 128 grams of O_2. Notice that you used the concept of a mole in two ways to solve this problem. In the first and last step, you used a molar mass to convert between mass and moles. In the middle step, you used the mole ratio to convert moles of a product into moles of a reactant.

Section 7.1 Assessment

Reviewing Concepts

1. What is the law of conservation of mass?
2. Why does a chemical equation need to be balanced?
3. Why do chemists use the mole as a counting unit?
4. What information do you need to predict the mass of a reactant or product in a chemical reaction?
5. What is a mole ratio?

Critical Thinking

6. **Applying Concepts** The following equation describes how sodium and chlorine react to produce sodium chloride.

$$2Na + Cl_2 \longrightarrow 2NaCl$$

Is the equation balanced? Explain your answer.

7. **Calculating** Ammonia, NH_3, can be made by reacting nitrogen with hydrogen.

$$N_2 + 3H_2 \longrightarrow 2NH_3$$

How many moles of NH_3 can be made if 7.5 moles of H_2 react with enough N_2?

8. **Calculating** What mass of NH_3 can be made from 35.0 g of N_2?

Math Practice

9. Balance the following equation.

$$K + Br_2 \longrightarrow KBr$$

10. Write a balanced chemical equation for the formation of magnesium oxide, MgO, from magnesium and oxygen.

7.2 Types of Reactions

Reading Focus

Key Concepts

- What are the general types of chemical reactions?
- How did the discovery of subatomic particles affect the classification of reactions?

Vocabulary

- synthesis reaction
- decomposition reaction
- single-replacement reaction
- double-replacement reaction
- combustion reaction
- oxidation-reduction reaction

Reading Strategy

Previewing Skim the section and begin a concept map like the one below that identifies types of reactions with a general form. As you read, add the general form of each type of reaction.

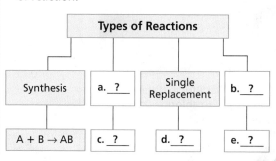

The walls of the cave shown in Figure 9 are solid limestone. When hydrochloric acid is dropped on limestone, a chemical reaction occurs in which a gas is produced. Geologists can use this reaction to determine whether a rock sample contains the mineral calcium carbonate, $CaCO_3$. When a rock that contains calcium carbonate reacts with hydrochloric acid, it fizzes. The gas in the bubbles is carbon dioxide.

Many other reactions produce carbon dioxide. For example, heating limestone produces carbon dioxide. So does burning gasoline. However, just because two reactions have the same product, you cannot assume that they are the same type of reaction.

Classifying Reactions

Just as you can classify matter into different types, you can classify chemical reactions into different types. Reactions are often classified by the type of reactant or the number of reactants and products. Some general types of chemical reactions are synthesis reactions, decomposition reactions, single-replacement reactions, double-replacement reactions, and combustion reactions. Each type describes a different way in which reactants interact to form products.

Figure 9 The walls and other formations of Blanchard Springs Caverns in Arkansas contain the mineral calcium carbonate, $CaCO_3$.

Figure 10 Sodium metal reacts vigorously with chlorine to form sodium chloride, NaCl.
Interpreting Photos *What evidence in this photograph tells you that a chemical reaction is taking place?*

Synthesis A **synthesis reaction** is a reaction in which two or more substances react to form a single substance. The reactants may be either elements or compounds. The product synthesized is always a compound. The general equation for a synthesis reaction is

$$A + B \longrightarrow AB$$

Figure 10 shows what happens when sodium reacts with chlorine. The product of this reaction is the compound sodium chloride, which appears as a whitish cloud of solid particles. You are probably more familiar with sodium chloride as table salt. You can describe the synthesis of sodium chloride with the following equation.

$$2Na + Cl_2 \longrightarrow 2NaCl$$

Another example of a synthesis reaction is hydrogen and oxygen reacting to form water.

$$2H_2 + O_2 \longrightarrow 2H_2O$$

This reaction is used to generate electricity for satellites and spacecraft.

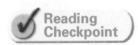 **Reading Checkpoint** *What is a synthesis reaction?*

Decomposition The opposite of synthesis is decomposition. A **decomposition reaction** is a reaction in which a compound breaks down into two or more simpler substances. The reactant in a decomposition reaction must be a compound. The products may be elements or compounds. The general equation for a decomposition reaction is

$$AB \longrightarrow A + B$$

When electricity passes through water, the water decomposes into hydrogen gas and oxygen gas. You can describe the decomposition of water by writing the following equation.

$$2H_2O \longrightarrow 2H_2 + O_2$$

Notice that this reaction is the opposite of the synthesis of water.

Another example of decomposition occurs in the making of cement. Cement factories use a giant kiln, or oven, to heat a mixture of clay and limestone. The heat causes the calcium carbonate in the limestone to decompose into lime, CaO, and carbon dioxide.

$$CaCO_3 \longrightarrow CaO + CO_2$$

The carbon dioxide escapes the kiln through a smokestack. The clay-and-lime mixture is cooled and ground into cement powder.

The How It Works box on page 201 describes a decomposition reaction that is used to make automobiles safer.

Go Online
NSTA *SciLINKS*

For: Links on chemical reactions
Visit: www.SciLinks.org
Web Code: ccn-1076

Automobile Safety: Air Bags

Air bags are inflatable cushions built into a car's steering wheel or dashboard. In a crash, the bags inflate, protecting both the driver and the passenger. The whole process takes 0.04 second. **Interpreting Diagrams** *What is the source of the gas that fills an air bag?*

Testing air bags
Air bags have been shown to reduce the risk of serious injury in a head-on collision by 30 percent. New cars have air bags on both the driver and passenger sides.

1 Collision A collision triggers the car's crash sensors, which send an electrical signal to the igniter in the steering wheel.

Crash sensor

Ignition unit

Igniter

Sodium azide pellets

Air bag folded into steering wheel

Steering wheel

Nitrogen gas leaks through holes

Nitrogen gas

Igniter

Electrical signal from crash sensor

Sodium azide pellets decomposing

2 Air bag inflates The igniter sets off a combustion reaction that heats up the sodium azide (NaN_3) contained in the ignition unit. When it is heated, the sodium azide decomposes into metallic sodium (Na) and nitrogen gas (N_2). The nitrogen gas inflates the air bag. The decomposition reaction is $2NaN_3 \rightarrow 2Na + 3N_2$.

Nontoxic residue of secondary reactions

Deflated air bag

3 Air bag deflates The nitrogen escapes through tiny holes in the bag, causing immediate deflation of the air bag. Because sodium is dangerous (due to its high reactivity), the ignition unit also contains other chemicals that react with sodium to form a nontoxic material.

Chemical Reactions **201**

Figure 11 A single-replacement reaction occurs when copper wire is submerged in a solution of silver nitrate. As the copper replaces the silver in the silver nitrate solution, the solution turns blue, and silver crystals form on the wire.

Figure 12 Potassium reacts with water in a single-replacement reaction that produces hydrogen gas and potassium hydroxide.

Single Replacement

A **single-replacement reaction** is a reaction in which one element takes the place of another element in a compound. Single-replacement reactions have the general form

$$A + BC \longrightarrow B + AC$$

Suppose you dip a coil of copper wire into a solution of silver nitrate and water, as shown in Figure 11. A vivid chemical reaction takes place as the solution turns blue and the submerged part of the wire becomes coated with a silvery metal. In this reaction, the copper replaces the silver in silver nitrate to form copper(II) nitrate. The equation for this reaction is

$$Cu + 2AgNO_3 \longrightarrow 2Ag + Cu(NO_3)_2$$

Notice that one of the products is silver, which you can see adhering to the wire in Figure 12. The other product, copper(II) nitrate, gives the solution its blue color.

Recall that alkali metals are very reactive elements. Figure 12 shows potassium reacting with water. This is another example of a single-replacement reaction, as the element potassium replaces hydrogen in water to form potassium hydroxide, KOH.

$$2K + 2H_2O \longrightarrow H_2 + 2KOH$$

The heat produced by this chemical reaction causes the hydrogen gas to ignite explosively.

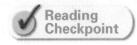 Reading Checkpoint *What is a single-replacement reaction?*

Double Replacement A **double-replacement reaction** is one in which two different compounds exchange positive ions and form two new compounds. The general form of a double replacement reaction is

$$AB + CD \longrightarrow AD + CB$$

Notice that two replacements take place in this reaction. Not only is A replacing C, but C is also replacing A.

Solutions of lead(II) nitrate, $Pb(NO_3)_2$, and potassium iodide, KI, are both colorless. However, when these solutions are mixed, as shown in Figure 13, a yellow precipitate forms as a result of a double-replacement reaction. The equation for this reaction is

$$Pb(NO_3)_2 + 2KI \longrightarrow PbI_2 + 2KNO_3$$

The lead ions in $Pb(NO_3)_2$, trade places with the potassium ions in KI. The products are lead(II) iodide, PbI_2, which precipitates out of solution, and potassium nitrate, KNO_3, which remains in solution.

When geologists test the calcium carbonate content in a rock, they make use of the following double-replacement reaction.

$$CaCO_3 + 2HCl \longrightarrow CaCl_2 + H_2CO_3$$

One of the products of this reaction is calcium chloride, $CaCl_2$. The other product is carbonic acid, H_2CO_3, which decomposes into carbon dioxide gas and water.

$$H_2CO_3 \longrightarrow CO_2 + H_2O$$

Figure 13 When potassium iodide solution is poured into a solution of lead(II) nitrate, a double-replacement reaction takes place. Lead(II) iodide forms as a yellow precipitate.
Comparing and Contrasting *How does a double-replacement reaction differ from a single-replacement reaction?*

☰Quick Lab

Identifying a Type of Reaction

Materials
piece of zinc, copper(II) sulfate ($CuSO_4$) solution, 250-mL beaker, tongs, paper towel

Procedure

1. Place the zinc in the beaker and add enough $CuSO_4$ solution to cover the zinc as shown. **CAUTION** *Be careful when using chemicals. Copper sulfate is toxic.*

2. After 5 minutes, carefully remove the zinc from the solution using the tongs and place the zinc on the paper towel to dry. Observe any changes that have occurred to the zinc and the solution of $CuSO_4$. **CAUTION** *Follow your teacher's instructions for disposal of used chemicals. Wash your hands with soap or detergent before leaving the laboratory.*

Analyze and Conclude

1. **Observing** What clues indicate that a chemical reaction has taken place?

2. **Applying Concepts** What were the reactants in this reaction? What were the products? Write a balanced chemical equation for the reaction.

3. **Classifying** Is this a single-replacement or double-replacement reaction? Explain.

Figure 14 A Bunsen burner generates heat and light by the combustion of natural gas.
Interpreting Photos *What reactants or products are visible in the reaction shown above?*

Combustion A **combustion reaction** is one in which a substance reacts rapidly with oxygen, often producing heat and light. The burning of natural gas, shown in Figure 14, is an example of combustion. The main component of natural gas is methane, CH_4. When methane burns in an unlimited supply of oxygen, the following reaction occurs.

$$CH_4 + 2O_2 \longrightarrow CO_2 + 2H_2O$$

The products of the reaction are carbon dioxide and water. The combustion of methane also generates both heat and light.

By now you know the chemical equation for the combustion of hydrogen.

$$2H_2 + O_2 \longrightarrow 2H_2O$$

Notice that you could also classify this reaction as the synthesis of water. The classifications for chemical reactions sometimes overlap.

Reactions as Electron Transfers

So far, you have learned that chemical reactions can be identified by the type of reactant or by the number of reactants and products. For example, in a combustion reaction one of the reactants must be oxygen. In a synthesis reaction, two or more reactants combine to form a single product.

As scientists learned more about the structure of the atom, they found different ways to describe how reactions take place. **The discovery of subatomic particles enabled scientists to classify certain chemical reactions as transfers of electrons between atoms.** A reaction in which electrons are transferred from one reactant to another is called an **oxidation-reduction reaction,** or redox reaction.

Oxidation For a long time, people have known that metals react with oxygen. Calcium, for instance, reacts with oxygen and forms calcium oxide (CaO), shown in Figure 15. Iron reacts with oxygen and forms rust, or iron(III) oxide (Fe_2O_3). These types of synthesis reactions, in which a metal combines with oxygen, traditionally have been classified as oxidations.

When calcium reacts with oxygen, the following reaction takes place.

$$2Ca + O_2 \longrightarrow 2CaO$$

Notice that while the atoms of both reactants (Ca and O_2) are neutral, the product of the reaction is a compound composed of ions (Ca^{2+} and O^{2-}). When calcium reacts with oxygen, each neutral calcium atom loses two electrons and becomes a calcium ion with a charge of $2+$.

$$Ca \longrightarrow Ca^{2+} + 2e^-$$

Figure 15 Calcium oxide, or lime, is produced when calcium burns in the presence of oxygen. In this reaction, the calcium is oxidized and the oxygen is reduced.

Any process in which an element loses electrons during a chemical reaction is called oxidation. A reactant is oxidized if it loses electrons. Note that the modern definition of oxidation is much broader than the original meaning. Oxygen doesn't always have to be present in order for an element to lose electrons. For example, when sodium reacts with chlorine, each neutral sodium atom loses one electron and becomes a sodium ion, Na^+.

Reduction As calcium atoms lose electrons during the synthesis of calcium oxide, the oxygen atoms gain electrons. As each neutral oxygen atom gains two electrons, it becomes an ion with a charge of $2-$.

$$O + 2e^- \longrightarrow O^{2-}$$

The process in which an element gains electrons during a chemical reaction is called reduction. A reactant is said to be reduced if it gains electrons.

Oxidation and reduction always occur together. When one element loses electrons, another element must gain electrons. Note that oxidation-reduction reactions do not always involve complete transfers of electrons. For example, in the synthesis of water, hydrogen is oxidized as it partially loses electrons. Oxygen is reduced as it partially gains electrons.

Go Online

NSTA SciLINKS

For: Links on oxidation and reduction
Visit: www.SciLinks.org
Web Code: ccn-1072

Section 7.2 Assessment

Reviewing Concepts

1. What are five general types of reactions?
2. How did the discovery of subatomic particles affect the classification of reactions?
3. The synthesis of water is described by the equation $2H_2 + O_2 \longrightarrow 2H_2O$. How is the decomposition of water related to this reaction? Explain, using a chemical equation.
4. Explain the difference between a single-replacement reaction and a double-replacement reaction.
5. Propane, C_3H_8, is frequently used in camping stoves. When propane undergoes combustion, what are the products formed?
6. Is the reaction represented by the following equation a redox reaction? Explain your answer.

$$2Hg + O_2 \longrightarrow 2HgO$$

Critical Thinking

7. **Predicting** What is the product of the synthesis reaction between magnesium and iodine? Explain your answer.
8. **Classifying** Identify these reactions as synthesis, decomposition, single replacement, double replacement, or combustion.
   a. $Pb(NO_3)_2 + 2HCl \longrightarrow PbCl_2 + 2HNO_3$
   b. $2C_2H_6 + 7O_2 \longrightarrow 4CO_2 + 6H_2O$
   c. $Ca + 2HCl \longrightarrow CaCl_2 + H_2$
   d. $2SO_2 + O_2 \longrightarrow 2SO_3$

Writing in Science

Explanatory Paragraph Write a paragraph explaining why the formation of water can be classified as a synthesis, combustion, or oxidation-reduction reaction.

7.3 Energy Changes in Reactions

Reading Focus

Key Concepts

- What happens to chemical bonds during a chemical reaction?
- What happens to energy during a chemical reaction?

Vocabulary

- chemical energy
- exothermic reaction
- endothermic reaction

Reading Strategy

Comparing and Contrasting Copy the Venn diagram. As you read, complete it to show the differences between exothermic and endothermic reactions.

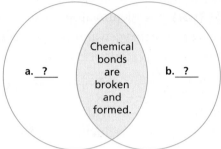

If you've ever had a barbecue, you may have used a gas grill like the one shown in Figure 16. Many types of gas grills use propane, C_3H_8. You can think of a propane grill as the scene of a chemical reaction—specifically, a combustion reaction. The reactants are propane and oxygen, and the products are carbon dioxide and water. However, the description of this reaction is incomplete unless you consider the heat and light produced. Heat, after all, is the reason for using a propane grill.

Chemical Bonds and Energy

The heat produced by a propane grill is a form of energy. When you write the chemical equation for the combustion of propane, you can include "heat" on the right side of the equation.

$$C_3H_8 + 5O_2 \longrightarrow 3CO_2 + 4H_2O + \text{Heat}$$

Figure 16 Many portable barbecue grills burn propane gas.

This equation states that the heat released in the reaction came from the reactants. **Chemical energy** is the energy stored in the chemical bonds of a substance. A propane molecule has ten single covalent bonds (eight C—H bonds and two C—C bonds). The chemical energy of a propane molecule is the energy stored in these bonds. Likewise, oxygen, carbon dioxide, and water molecules all have energy stored in their chemical bonds.

Energy changes in chemical reactions are determined by changes that occur in chemical bonding. 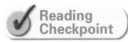 **Chemical reactions involve the breaking of chemical bonds in the reactants and the formation of chemical bonds in the products.** In the combustion of propane, the bonds in propane and oxygen molecules are broken, while the bonds in carbon dioxide and water molecules are formed.

Breaking Bonds As Figure 17 illustrates, each propane molecule reacts with five oxygen molecules. In order for the reaction to occur, eight C—H single bonds, two C—C single bonds, and five O=O double bonds must be broken. Breaking chemical bonds requires energy. This is why propane grills have an igniter, a device that produces a spark. The spark provides enough energy to break the bonds of reacting molecules and get the reaction started.

Forming Bonds Figure 17 also shows you that for each molecule of propane burned, three molecules of carbon dioxide and four molecules of water are formed. This means that six C=O double bonds and eight O—H single bonds are formed in the reaction. The formation of chemical bonds releases energy. The heat and light given off by a propane stove result from the formation of new chemical bonds. The bonds form as the carbon, hydrogen, and oxygen atoms in the propane and oxygen molecules are rearranged into molecules of carbon dioxide and water.

Reading Checkpoint *Does breaking chemical bonds require energy or release energy?*

Propane Combustion

C_3H_8 +	$5O_2$	→	$3CO_2$ +	$4H_2O$ +	Heat
propane	oxygen		carbon dioxide	water	

8 C–H, 2 C–C bonds broken	5 O=O bonds broken	→	6 C=O bonds formed	8 O–H bonds formed	

Figure 17 In order for the combustion of propane to occur, all the chemical bonds in the reactants (propane and oxygen) must be broken. The formation of the chemical bonds in the products completes the reaction.
Inferring *How does the chemical energy of the reactants compare to the chemical energy of the products in this reaction?*

Reaction Energy—Exothermic

Chemical Energy →

Reactants

Energy released by reaction

Products

Reaction Progress →

A

Reaction Energy—Endothermic

Chemical Energy →

Products

Energy absorbed by reaction

Reactants

Reaction Progress →

B

Figure 18 In chemical reactions, energy is either released or absorbed. **A** In an exothermic reaction, energy is released to the surroundings. **B** In an endothermic reaction, energy is absorbed from the surroundings. **Using Graphs** *How do the energy diagrams show that energy is conserved in chemical reactions?*

Exothermic and Endothermic Reactions

Recall that physical changes can release or absorb energy. During an exothermic change, such as freezing, energy is released to the surroundings. During an endothermic change, such as melting, energy is absorbed from the surroundings. Energy also flows into and out of chemical changes. 🔑 **During a chemical reaction, energy is either released or absorbed.**

Exothermic Reactions A chemical reaction that releases energy to its surroundings is called an **exothermic reaction.** In exothermic reactions, the energy released as the products form is greater than the energy required to break the bonds in the reactants.

Combustion is an example of an extremely exothermic reaction. When 1 mole of propane reacts with 5 moles of oxygen, 2220 kJ (kilojoules) of heat is released. You can use this value to replace "heat" in the combustion equation written earlier.

$$C_3H_8 + 5O_2 \longrightarrow 3CO_2 + 4H_2O + 2220 \text{ kJ}$$

Figure 18A shows how chemical energy changes during an exothermic reaction. Notice that the chemical energy of the reactants is greater than the chemical energy of the products. The difference between these amounts of energy equals the amount of heat given off by the reaction.

In any reaction, the chemical energy reaches a peak before the reactants change into products. This peak represents the amount of energy required to break the chemical bonds of the reactants. Unless reacting particles collide with enough energy to break these bonds, the reaction will not occur. For example, at room temperature, the collisions between propane and oxygen molecules are not energetic enough to result in combustion. However, if you increase the temperature by adding a spark, some of the molecules around the spark move faster and are able to collide with enough energy to react.

Endothermic Reactions A chemical reaction that absorbs energy from its surroundings is called an **endothermic reaction.** In an endothermic reaction, more energy is required to break the bonds in the reactants than is released by the formation of the products.

Figure 18B shows the energy diagram for an endothermic reaction. Notice that the energy of the products is greater than the energy of the reactants. The difference between these amounts of energy equals the amount of heat that must be absorbed from the surroundings.

When mercury(II) oxide is heated to a temperature of about 450°C, it breaks down into mercury and oxygen, as shown in Figure 19. The decomposition of mercury(II) oxide is an endothermic reaction that can be described by the following equation.

$$2HgO + 181.7 \text{ kJ} \longrightarrow 2Hg + O_2$$

Because heat is absorbed, the energy term appears on the left side of the equation. For every 2 moles of HgO that decomposes, 181.7 kJ of heat must be absorbed.

Conservation of Energy

In an exothermic reaction, the chemical energy of the reactants is converted into heat plus the chemical energy of the products. In an endothermic reaction, heat plus the chemical energy of the reactants is converted into the chemical energy of the products. In both cases, the total amount of energy before and after the reaction is the same. This principle is known as the law of conservation of energy. You will read more about how energy is conserved later.

Figure 19 The orange-red powder in the bottom of the test tube is mercury(II) oxide. At about 450°C, mercury(II) oxide decomposes into oxygen gas (which escapes from the test tube) and mercury (droplets of which can be seen collecting on the sides of the test tube).

Section 7.3 Assessment

Reviewing Concepts

1. What happens to chemical bonds as a chemical reaction occurs?

2. How do chemical reactions involve energy?

3. Is the combustion of propane endothermic or exothermic?

4. When propane reacts with oxygen, does the surrounding area become warmer or cooler?

5. Is energy created during an exothermic reaction? Explain.

Critical Thinking

6. **Inferring** Explain why methane does not react with oxygen at room temperature.

7. **Calculating** Methane reacts with oxygen in the following combustion reaction.

$$CH_4 + 2O_2 \longrightarrow CO_2 + 2H_2O$$

What bonds are broken when one molecule of methane reacts with two molecules of oxygen?

Connecting Concepts

Chemical Bonds Reread the descriptions of chemical bonds in Sections 6.1 and 6.2. Then, describe the decomposition of mercury(II) oxide. Specify which bonds are ionic and which bonds are covalent.

Firefighting

Uncontrolled fires threaten lives and property and can have a devastating effect on the environment. To fight fires, it is necessary to understand how they start, and what sustains them.

Fire is the result of combustion, a rapid reaction between oxygen and fuel. During combustion, fuel and oxygen react to form carbon dioxide, water, and heat. Most fires in rural areas, called wildfires, are caused by people being careless with campfires or cigarettes. Arson and lightning are also common causes. Usually the fire starts in an area of dry grass, which will ignite at a temperature of 150–200°C. Burning grass can create enough heat to ignite bushes, and these, in turn, may be tall enough to carry the flames into trees. (Wood has a higher ignition temperature, around 260°C.) Environmental conditions, such as drought that has left vegetation dry, and strong winds, can cause a small fire to spread. Wind also carries fire forward into new areas. Burning twigs and branches that become detached from trees can be blown into new areas of vegetation.

Dousing
Planes or helicopters are used to drop water or a fire-retardant slurry on a large fire. The slurry contains ammonium sulfate, $(NH_4)_2SO_4$, which helps smother the fire.

Firefighter
Firefighters wear protective clothing, helmets, and goggles. This firefighter also carries a shovel for digging trenches to stop a fire spreading.

Backburning
One way to stop a big fire is to start a smaller fire. This technique, called backburning, burns off vegetation between the fireline and the main fire. When the two fires meet, the blaze stops spreading because the land on either side has already been burned.

Boundary of
Hanford site

Extent of fire

Smoke plume

Firebreaks
In parts of the world where wildfires are common, strips of land are cleared of combustible vegetation to create firebreaks. Firefighters also dig firebreaks during fires to prevent fires from spreading.

Going Further
- Write a paragraph explaining how dousing, backburning, and firebreaks affect the chemical reactions involved in wildfires.

Wildfire in Washington State
This satellite picture shows a forest fire that raged for two months in 2000 at the Department of Energy's site at Hanford. The fire was started by a vehicle fire and reached more than 500 square kilometers.

7.4 Reaction Rates

Reading Focus

Key Concept
- What does a reaction rate tell you?
- What factors cause reaction rates to change?

Vocabulary
- reaction rate
- catalyst

Reading Strategy
Building Vocabulary
Copy the partially completed web diagram at the right. Then, as you read, complete it with key terms from this section.

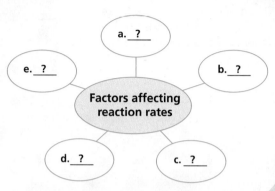

a. ?

b. ?

c. ?

d. ?

e. ?

Factors affecting reaction rates

Figure 20 A cyclist burns the Calories in a banana faster than a person walking would. But burning the banana outside the body would release the energy of the banana even faster.

You may have heard of athletes "burning Calories" when they exercise. A Calorie is a unit of energy used in the field of nutrition. The average banana, for instance, contains about 100 Calories. The cyclist in Figure 20 can use up, or burn, as many as 10,000 Calories during the course of a race. That adds up to a lot of bananas!

If you eat a banana, you provide your body with about 100 Calories to burn. This energy is released in a series of reactions that take place inside your body. A much faster way of releasing the energy contained in a banana is to burn it—outside the body—in a combustion reaction. In both cases, the total amount of energy released is the same. However, the time it takes for the energy to be released is different in each case.

Reactions Over Time

The progress of any chemical reaction can be measured over time. Different reactions have different durations. Some reactions, such as the explosion of TNT, happen almost instantaneously. Other reactions, such as tree leaves changing color during autumn, happen gradually.

Any change that happens over a period of time can be expressed as a rate. For example, speed is the rate that distance changes over time. A **reaction rate** is the rate at which reactants change into products over time. **Reaction rates tell you how fast a reaction is going.** That is, how fast the reactants are being consumed, how fast the products are being formed, or how fast energy is being absorbed or released.

Factors Affecting Reaction Rates

Recall that chemical reactions involve collisions between particles of reactants. The reaction rate depends on how often these particles collide. If the collisions occur more frequently, then the reaction rate increases. If the collisions occur less frequently, then the reaction rate decreases. Almost any reaction rate can be changed by varying the conditions under which the reaction takes place. **Factors that affect reaction rates include temperature, surface area, concentration, stirring, and catalysts.**

Temperature Suppose you are frying an egg in a frying pan. What happens if you increase the heat under the pan? The hotter the pan, the faster the egg will cook. Generally, an increase in temperature will increase the reaction rate, while a decrease in temperature will decrease the reaction rate. For instance, you store milk in a refrigerator to slow down the reactions that cause the milk to spoil. These reactions don't stop completely. Even milk stored in a refrigerator will eventually spoil. But the rate of spoiling decreases if the milk is kept cold.

Increasing the temperature of a substance causes its particles to move faster, on average. Particles that move faster are both more likely to collide and more likely to react. If the number of collisions that produce reactions increases, then the reaction rate increases.

 How does temperature affect reaction rates?

Surface Area Grain may not strike you as a dangerous material, but it can be explosive under the right conditions. The cause of the fire in Figure 21 was a combustion reaction between grain dust (suspended in the air) and oxygen. The rate of combustion was very rapid due to the small particle size of the grain dust.

The smaller the particle size of a given mass, the larger is its surface area. Imagine using a newspaper to cover the floor of a room. If you keep all the sections folded together, you can only cover a small area. However, if you separate the newspaper into pages and lay them out like tiles, you can cover a much larger area with the same mass of paper.

An increase in surface area increases the exposure of reactants to one another. The greater this exposure, the more collisions there are that involve reacting particles. With more collisions, more particles will react. This is why increasing the surface area of a reactant tends to increase the reaction rate.

For: Links on factors affecting reaction rate
Visit: www.SciLinks.org
Web Code: ccn-1074

Figure 21 This grain elevator in Potlatch, Idaho, exploded when grain dust reacted with oxygen in the air.
Applying Concepts *How does surface area affect reaction rates?*

Observing the Action of Catalysts

Materials

5 test tubes, test-tube rack, marking pencil, dropper pipet, wood splint, platinum wire, 0.1 g manganese dioxide (MnO_2), 5 drops of copper(II) chloride ($CuCl_2$) solution, 0.1 g raw potato, graduated cylinder, 25 mL hydrogen peroxide (H_2O_2)

Procedure

1. Label the 5 test tubes from A to E with the marking pencil.

2. Put a small piece of platinum wire in test tube A. Add a tiny amount (about the tip of the wood splint) of MnO_2 to test tube B. Use the dropper pipet to put 5 drops of $CuCl_2$ in test tube C. Put a piece of potato in test tube D. Test tube E should remain empty for now. **CAUTION** *MnO_2 and $CuCl_2$ are toxic.*

3. Carefully add 5 mL of hydrogen peroxide to test tube A. **CAUTION** *Be careful when using chemicals.* Observe how fast the bubbles are produced.

4. Repeat Step 3 with test tubes B through E.

Analyze and Conclude

1. **Observing** What effect did the platinum wire, MnO_2, $CuCl_2$, and the potato have on the rate at which the bubbles were produced in the hydrogen peroxide?

2. **Comparing and Contrasting** Which catalyst(s) caused the reaction to go the fastest? The slowest?

3. **Inferring** Why did you put only hydrogen peroxide in test tube E?

Stirring You can also increase the exposure of reactants to each other by stirring them. For example, when you wash your clothes in a washing machine, particles of detergent react with particles of the stains on your clothes. This reaction would go slowly if you just left your clothes soaking in a tub of water and detergent. A washing machine speeds up the reaction by stirring the contents back and forth. Collisions between the particles of the reactants are more likely to happen. Stirring the reactants will generally increase the reaction rate.

Concentration Another way you can change the reaction rate is to change the concentration of the reactants. Concentration refers to the number of particles in a given volume. The more reacting particles that are present in a given volume, the more opportunities there are for collisions involving those particles. The reaction rate is faster.

Both of the beakers in Figure 22 contain a piece of material dipped in dye solution. Dyeing is a chemical reaction in which dye particles react with the particles of the material being dyed. The material dipped in the more concentrated dye becomes colored more quickly.

For gases, concentration changes with pressure. The greater the pressure of a gaseous reactant, the greater is its concentration, and the faster is the reaction rate.

Figure 22 The dye solution in the left beaker is more concentrated than the solution in the right. Increasing the concentration of the dye increases the rate of color change in the material.

Catalysts Sometimes you can change a reaction rate by using catalysts. A **catalyst** is a substance that affects the reaction rate without being used up in the reaction. Chemists often use catalysts to speed up a reaction or enable a reaction to occur at a lower temperature. In the making of sulfuric acid, one of the steps involved is the reaction of sulfur dioxide with oxygen to form sulfur trioxide. This reaction happens very slowly without a catalyst such as vanadium(V) oxide.

$$2SO_2 + O_2 \xrightarrow{V_2O_5} 2SO_3$$

Since the catalyst is neither a reactant nor a product, it is written over the arrow. Because the catalyst is not consumed, it can be used to speed up the same reaction over and over again.

Recall that in order for a reaction to take place, the reacting particles must collide with enough energy to break the chemical bonds of those particles. As shown in Figure 23, a catalyst lowers this energy barrier. One way that a catalyst can do this is by providing a surface on which the reacting particles can come together. Imagine that you go to a party and make several new friends. By bringing people together, the party has made it easier for you to form those friendships. Similarly, a catalyst can "invite" reacting particles together so that they are more likely to react.

Reaction Energy— Catalyzed and Uncatalyzed

Figure 23 The graph above shows how a catalyst lowers the amount of energy required for effective collisions between reacting particles.
Using Graphs *In an exothermic reaction, how does a catalyst affect the amount of energy released?*

Section 7.4 Assessment

Reviewing Concepts

1. What does a reaction rate tell you?
2. What five factors affect reaction rates?
3. Explain why reactions take place faster at higher temperatures.
4. When you add baking soda to vinegar, the mixture fizzes as carbon dioxide gas is produced. Suppose you added water to the vinegar before you mixed it with the baking soda. What do you think would happen to the rate of carbon dioxide production?
5. How does a catalyst make a reaction go faster?
6. Platinum is a catalyst for the decomposition of hydrogen peroxide into water and oxygen.

$$2H_2O_2 \xrightarrow{Pt} 2H_2O + O_2$$

What would you expect to see if platinum were added to hydrogen peroxide solution?

Critical Thinking

7. **Applying Concepts** Explain why, if you want to store uncooked hamburger meat for a month, you put it in a freezer rather than a refrigerator.
8. **Evaluating** The reaction between magnesium and hydrochloric acid produces hydrogen. If you increase the concentration of HCl, the reaction takes place faster. Could HCl be considered a catalyst for this reaction? Explain your answer.

Writing in Science

Compare and Contrast Paragraph Write a paragraph explaining how temperature, concentration, surface area, and catalysts affect reaction rates.

7.5 Equilibrium

Reading Focus

Key Concepts

- Under what conditions do physical and chemical equilibria occur?
- How do equilibrium systems respond to change?

Vocabulary

- equilibrium
- reversible reaction

Reading Strategy

Outlining As you read, make an outline of the most important ideas in this section.

```
I. Equilibrium
   A. Types of Equilibria
       1. _____
       2. _____
   B. _____
       1. Temperature
       2. Pressure
       3. _____
```

Suppose you're waiting in line for a toll booth at a bridge, like some of the cars shown in Figure 24. You notice that every time a car passes by a toll booth in the direction you are traveling, another car passes through the toll plaza in the opposite direction. The rate of cars entering equals the rate of cars exiting. As a result, the number of cars on either side of the toll plaza remains constant, although cars are continually entering and exiting the bridge.

Types of Equilibria

The traffic at a toll bridge is similar to a system in equilibrium. **Equilibrium** (plural *equilibria*) is a state in which the forward and reverse paths of a change take place at the same rate.

Recall that changes to matter are either physical or chemical. When opposing physical changes take place at the same rate, a physical equilibrium is reached. When opposing chemical changes take place at the same rate, a chemical equilibrium is reached.

Figure 24 About 190,000 vehicles pass through the toll plaza of New York City's Verrazano-Narrows Bridge every day.

Physical Equilibrium

What happens when you pour some water into a jar and then close the lid? You might think that nothing happens at all. But in fact, some of the water undergoes a physical change by evaporating. As more water evaporates, some of the water vapor condenses. Eventually, the rate of evaporation equals the rate of condensation, and the system reaches equilibrium as shown in Figure 25.

When liquid water is in equilibrium with water vapor, you can describe the system by writing this equation.

$$H_2O(l) \rightleftharpoons H_2O(g)$$

Here, l stands for liquid and g stands for gas. The pair of arrows in this equation indicates that the forward change (evaporation) and the reverse change (condensation) are happening simultaneously and at the same rate. Both the forward and reverse changes are physical changes, so this equation represents a physical equilibrium. **When a physical change does not go to completion, a physical equilibrium is established between the forward and reverse changes.**

Chemical Equilibrium

All the chemical equations you have seen so far have been written with single arrows, which suggest that all reactions go to completion in one direction. In reality, however, most reactions are reversible to some extent. A **reversible reaction** is a reaction in which the conversion of reactants into products and the conversion of products into reactants can happen simultaneously.

In the previous section, you read about the synthesis of sulfur trioxide from sulfur dioxide and oxygen. This is actually a reversible reaction that can be expressed as

$$2SO_2(g) + O_2(g) \rightleftharpoons 2SO_3(g)$$

If sulfur dioxide and oxygen are mixed in a closed container, the forward reaction will start to produce sulfur trioxide. However, once molecules of sulfur trioxide form, some of them will change back into the reactants by the reverse reaction. Eventually, the rate of the forward reaction (synthesis) will equal the rate of the reverse reaction (decomposition), and the system will reach equilibrium. **When a chemical reaction does not go to completion, a chemical equilibrium is established between the forward and reverse reactions.** During chemical equilibrium, the reactants change into products just as fast as the products change back into reactants.

 Reading Checkpoint *What happens during chemical equilibrium?*

H₂O molecules

Figure 25 Liquid water left in a closed container eventually reaches equilibrium with its vapor. **Interpreting Diagrams** *What do the arrows represent in the diagram above?*

For: Links on factors affecting equilibrium
Visit: www.SciLinks.org
Web Code: ccn-1075

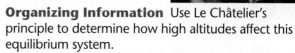

Recreating High Altitudes

An important chemical equilibrium in your blood involves the reaction of hemoglobin (Hb) with oxygen (O_2) to form oxyhemoglobin (HbO_2).

$$Hb + O_2 \rightleftharpoons HbO_2$$

This equilibrium changes with altitude. As you move from lower to higher elevations, the concentration of oxygen in the air decreases, and the equilibrium shifts in the direction that produces less oxyhemoglobin. Your body responds to the shift by producing more hemoglobin. Studies have shown that athletes can improve their performance at sea level by living or training at high altitudes. Some training facilities are designed to recreate high altitudes. Imagine that you are asked to build such a facility.

Defining the Problem In your own words, state the problem you face.

Organizing Information Use Le Châtelier's principle to determine how high altitudes affect this equilibrium system.

Creating a Solution The physical properties of the air inside the training facility include temperature, pressure, and composition. Figure out how to shift the equilibrium in the direction you want by changing one of these properties.

Presenting Your Plan Write a proposal to an athletic team that could benefit from using your training facility. Explain how your facility recreates a high-altitude environment.

Factors Affecting Chemical Equilibrium

Like reaction rates, chemical equilibria can change depending on the conditions of the reaction. While a reaction rate either increases or decreases in response to a change, an equilibrium shifts. That is, the equilibrium favors either the forward or the reverse reaction. **When a change is introduced to a system in equilibrium, the equilibrium shifts in the direction that relieves the change.** This rule was first observed by Henri Le Châtelier, shown in Figure 26. Today, the rule is known as Le Châtelier's principle.

The making of ammonia is an example of a process in which chemists apply Le Châtelier's principle. Ammonia is an important industrial chemical used to make fertilizers, cleaning agents, dyes, and plastics. The following equation describes the synthesis of ammonia.

$$N_2(g) + 3H_2(g) \rightleftharpoons 2NH_3(g) + Heat$$

Suppose you have a system that contains nitrogen, hydrogen, and ammonia in equilibrium. By applying Le Châtelier's principle, you can predict how this system will be affected by changes in temperature, pressure, and concentration. In the ammonia plant shown in Figure 27, chemists must consider these same factors.

Temperature In the equation for the synthesis of ammonia, heat is written as a product. This tells you that the forward reaction is exothermic. In the reverse reaction, heat is a reactant. So the decomposition of ammonia is endothermic.

Figure 26 French Chemist Henri-Louis Le Châtelier (1850–1936) published the first version of his principle of chemical equilibrium in 1884.

What would happen if you increased the temperature of a system that contained nitrogen, hydrogen, and ammonia? According to Le Châtelier's principle, if you added heat to the system, the equilibrium would shift in the direction that removes heat from the system. The system would favor the reverse reaction, which is endothermic. So by increasing the temperature, you would decrease the amount of ammonia.

Pressure Suppose you increased the pressure of the system. According to Le Châtelier's principle, if you increased the pressure, the equilibrium would shift in the direction that decreases the pressure of the system. In order to decrease pressure, the system would favor the reaction that produces fewer gas molecules. You can see that the left side of the equation has four gas molecules, while the right side has two. So by increasing the pressure, you would shift the equilibrium to the right, producing more ammonia.

Concentration A change in concentration of the reactants or products can also affect equilibrium. Suppose you removed ammonia from the nitrogen-hydrogen-ammonia system. Le Châtelier's principle tells you that the equilibrium would shift in the direction that produces ammonia. In order to produce ammonia, the system would favor the forward reaction.

Figure 27 Operating an ammonia plant at relatively low temperature, high pressure, and low ammonia concentration maximizes the amount of ammonia produced.

Section 7.5 Assessment

Reviewing Concepts

1. What happens when a physical change does not go to completion? What happens when a reaction does not go to completion?

2. Once a chemical reaction has reached equilibrium, how does the system respond to change?

3. What does the double-ended arrow indicate in the following chemical equation?

$$CaCO_3 \rightleftharpoons Ca^{2+} + CO_3^{2-}$$

4. For which of the following reactions are both reactants and products likely to be found when the reaction appears to be complete? Explain.

$$Mg + O_2 \longrightarrow 2MgO$$

$$HF + H_2O \rightleftharpoons H_3O^+ + F^-$$

Critical Thinking

5. **Inferring** Suppose the following reaction is allowed to come to equilibrium.

$$2NO_2(g) \rightleftharpoons N_2O_4(g)$$

How will increasing the pressure on this system affect the amount of N_2O_4 formed?

6. **Using Models** At 0°C, liquid water is in equilibrium with ice. Make a drawing of water molecules at this temperature, and describe what is happening.

Connecting C Concepts

Phase Changes Write an equation for a system in which the sublimation and deposition of water have reached equilibrium. Use what you studied in Section 3.3 to explain what changes are happening.

Manipulating Chemical Equilibrium

Chemical reactions tend to go to equilibrium. It is possible to shift the equilibrium by changing the conditions under which the reaction occurs. Factors that can affect chemical equilibrium include the concentration of reactants and products, temperature, and pressure. In this lab, you will observe a chemical reaction and use your observations to predict how one factor will shift the equilibrium of the reaction. Then, you will perform an experiment to test your prediction.

Problem
How can you change the equilibrium of a chemical reaction?

Materials
- iodine-starch solution
- 150-mL beaker
- 4 dropper pipets
- spot plate
- ascorbic acid (vitamin C) solution
- chlorine bleach (sodium hypochlorite, NaOCl) solution

Skills
Formulating Hypotheses, Designing Experiments, Observing

Procedure

Part A: Observing a Reversible Reaction

1. Pour 50 mL of iodine-starch solution into the 150-mL beaker. The dark color of this solution is due to the presence of iodine molecules (I_2) within the grains of starch. **CAUTION** *Handle iodine solutions with care. Iodine is toxic.*

2. Use a dropper pipet to transfer 3 drops of iodine-starch solution from the beaker to one well on the spot plate.

3. Use another clean dropper pipet to add one drop of ascorbic acid solution to the iodine-starch solution on the spot plate. Continue to add ascorbic acid solution to the mixture on the spot plate, one drop at a time, until the mixture becomes clear. When an iodine molecule reacts with ascorbic acid, the iodine molecule is reduced and breaks down into two colorless iodide ions ($2I^-$).

Sample Data Table			
Initial Solution	Solution Added	Quantity Added (mL)	Color of Resulting Mixture

4. Use the third clean dropper pipet to transfer one drop of colorless iodide solution to a second well on the spot plate.

5. Use the last clean dropper pipet to add bleach solution to the drop of colorless iodide solution, one drop at a time. Continue until the dark color of the iodine-starch solution reappears. **CAUTION** *Bleach can damage skin and clothing.* The chlorine bleach (NaOCl) oxidizes iodide ions (I^-), converting them to iodine molecules (I_2).

6. Write a chemical equation showing the equilibrium between iodine molecules and iodide ions. This equation does not need to be balanced. Label the two sides of your equation to indicate which substance appears dark and which appears colorless.

Part B: Design Your Experiment

7. **Predicting** Select one of the solutions used earlier that affects the equilibrium between iodine molecules and iodide ions. Record your prediction of the change you will observe in an iodine-starch solution as you add the solution that you selected.

8. **Designing Experiments** Design an experiment to test your prediction. Your experimental plan should describe in detail how you will perform your experiment.

9. Construct a data table like the sample data table shown, in which to record your observations. (*Note:* Your data table may not be exactly like the sample data table.)

10. Perform your experiment only after your teacher has approved your plan. Record your observations in your data table.
CAUTION *Wash your hands with soap or detergent before leaving the laboratory.*

Analyze and Conclude

1. **Analyzing Data** What factor did you investigate? How did it affect the equilibrium between iodine molecules and iodide ions?

2. **Predicting** How would you expect the equilibrium to change if you added more iodide ions to the mixture? Explain your answer.

3. **Calculating** When chlorine bleach (sodium hypochlorite, NaOCl) oxidizes iodide ions to iodine molecules, sodium hypochlorite is reduced to sodium chloride (NaCl) and water (H_2O). Write a balanced chemical equation for this reaction, beginning with the reactants sodium hypochlorite, iodide ions, and hydrogen ions (H^+).

4. **Drawing Conclusions** How does the addition of more product affect the chemical equilibrium of a reaction?

Go Further Design an experiment to determine whether other substances that are easily oxidized or reduced, such as iron ions, can reduce iodine to iodide, or oxidize iodide to iodine. Then, with your teacher's approval and supervision, perform your experiment.

Study Guide

7.1 Describing Reactions

Key Concepts

- The law of conservation of mass states that mass is neither created nor destroyed.

- In order to show that mass is conserved during a reaction, a chemical equation must be balanced.

- Because chemical reactions often involve large numbers of small particles, chemists use a unit called the mole to measure amounts of a substance.

- In chemical reactions, the mass of a reactant or product can be calculated by using a balanced chemical equation and molar masses.

Vocabulary

reactants, *p. 192;* products, *p. 192;* chemical equation, *p. 193;* coefficients, *p. 194;* mole, *p. 195;* molar mass, *p. 196*

7.2 Types of Reactions

Key Concepts

- The general types of chemical reactions are synthesis reactions, decomposition reactions, single-replacement reactions, double-replacement reactions, and combustion reactions.

- Scientists classify certain chemical reactions as transfers of electrons between atoms.

Vocabulary

synthesis reaction, *p. 200;* decomposition reaction, *p. 200;* single-replacement reaction, *p. 202;* double-replacement reaction, *p. 203;* combustion reaction, *p. 204;* oxidation-reduction reaction, *p. 204*

7.3 Energy Changes in Reactions

Key Concepts

- Chemical reactions involve the breaking of chemical bonds in the reactants and the formation of chemical bonds in the products.

- During a chemical reaction, energy is either released or absorbed.

Vocabulary

chemical energy, *p. 206;* exothermic reaction, *p. 208;* endothermic reaction, *p. 209*

7.4 Reaction Rates

Key Concepts

- Reaction rates tell you how fast a reaction is going.

- Factors that affect reaction rates include temperature, surface area, concentration, stirring, and catalysts.

Vocabulary

reaction rate, *p. 212;* catalyst, *p. 215*

7.5 Equilibrium

Key Concepts

- When a physical change does not go to completion, a physical equilibrium is established between the forward and reverse changes. When a chemical reaction does not go to completion, a chemical equilibrium is established between the forward and reverse reactions.

- When a change is introduced to a system in equilibrium, the equilibrium shifts in the direction that relieves the change.

Vocabulary

equilibrium, *p. 216;* reversible reaction, *p. 217*

Thinking Visually

Concept Map Use information from the chapter to complete the concept map below.

Assessment

Reviewing Content

Choose the letter that best answers the question or completes the statement.

1. In the following equation, what are the reactants?

$NaHCO_3 + HCl \longrightarrow NaCl + H_2O + CO_2$

 a. $NaHCO_3$ and HCl   **b.** $NaHCO_3$ and NaCl
 c. HCl and NaCl   **d.** NaCl, H_2O, and CO_2

2. Which of the following is a statement of the law of conservation of mass?

 a. Mass is created but not destroyed.
 b. Mass is destroyed but not created.
 c. Mass is neither created nor destroyed.
 d. Mass is both created and destroyed, depending on the chemical reaction.

3. The mass of a hydrogen atom is 1.0 amu, and the mass of a carbon atom is 12.0 amu. What is the molar mass of methane, CH_4?

 a. 13.0 amu   **b.** 13.0 g
 c. 16.0 amu   **d.** 16.0 g

4. In what type of reaction does one reactant form two or more products?

 a. synthesis   **b.** decomposition
 c. single replacement   **d.** double replacement

5. What particle is transferred from one atom to another in a redox reaction?

 a. electron   **b.** neutron
 c. proton   **d.** nucleus

6. Which of the following is a single replacement?

 a. $KOH + HCl \longrightarrow KCl + H_2O$
 b. $2Na + 2H_2O \longrightarrow H_2 + 2NaOH$
 c. $2C_2H_6 + 7O_2 \longrightarrow 4CO_2 + 6H_2O$
 d. $H_2O + CO_2 \longrightarrow H_2CO_3$

7. How are reactions related to chemical bonds?

 a. Bonds in the reactants are broken, and bonds in the products are formed.
 b. Bonds in the products are broken, and bonds in the reactants are formed.
 c. Bonds in both the reactants and products are broken.
 d. Bonds are formed in both the reactants and the products.

8. What type of reaction always releases energy?

 a. endothemic   **b.** exothermic
 c. decomposition   **d.** oxidation-reduction

9. In general, an increase in temperature

 a. increases reaction rate.
 b. decreases reaction rate.
 c. does not affect reaction rate.
 d. acts as a catalyst.

10. What takes place at chemical equilibrium?

 a. Reactants form more quickly than products.
 b. Products form more quickly than reactants.
 c. Reactants and products stop forming.
 d. Reactants and products form at the same rate.

Understanding Concepts

11. Write the following chemical equation in words.

$$CaCO_3 + Heat \longrightarrow CaO + CO_2$$

12. Explain how a balanced chemical equation shows that mass is conserved.

13. Explain the following diagram in your own words.

14. Compare oxidation and reduction.

15. Paper burns by combining with oxygen. Why doesn't paper burn every time it contacts oxygen?

16. Give an example of a chemical reaction that occurs slowly. Give another example of a chemical reaction that occurs quickly.

Answer Questions 17–18 based on the equation below.

$$C(s) + H_2O(g) + Heat \rightleftharpoons CO(g) + H_2(g)$$

17. How would you adjust the temperature to increase the amount of product?

18. Does the removal of hydrogen gas as it is produced shift the reaction to the left or the right?

Critical Thinking

19. Observing Explain how you know that a chemical reaction takes place when iron rusts.

20. Inferring As a candle burns, its mass decreases. However, mass is conserved in this reaction. Explain this observation.

21. Making Generalizations In a certain chemical reaction, two reactants undergo change to form two products. Why can't you determine what type of reaction occurred from this information?

22. Applying Concepts Use the reaction that occurs when magnesium burns in oxygen to show how a reaction might be included in more than one category of reaction.

23. Classifying Is breaking bonds an endothermic process or an exothermic process? Explain.

24. Inferring Explain how energy is conserved in an endothermic reaction.

Use the diagram below to answer Questions 25–26.

25. Comparing and Contrasting The volume of the cube in A equals the total volume of the cubes in B. Compare the surface areas of the cubes in A and B.

26. Using Models Use the diagram to explain how surface area affects reaction rates.

27. Predicting You are performing an experiment and want to increase the rate of reaction. You stop stirring the reactants and, instead, increase the concentration of one reactant. Can you expect the reaction to proceed at a faster rate? Explain.

Math Skills

28. Applying Concepts Balance each of the following chemical equations.
  a. $KI \longrightarrow K + I_2$
  b. $Na + H_2O \longrightarrow H_2 + NaOH$
  c. $CH_4 + O_2 \longrightarrow CO_2 + H_2O$

29. Calculating What mass of KBr is contained in 2.50 moles of the compound?

30. Calculating How many moles of Na_2CrO_4 are contained in 74.3 grams of the compound?

Concepts in Action

31. Inferring Kept at room temperature, batteries will eventually lose their charge. Why will keeping batteries in the freezer make them last longer?

32. Drawing Conclusions Octane, C_8H_{18}, is one of the compounds present in gasoline. The products of the burning of octane are water and carbon dioxide. In this reaction, which contain more energy, the bonds in the reactants or the bonds in the products? Explain.

33. Writing in Science Write a paragraph describing a chemical reaction that you have observed recently.

Performance-Based Assessment

Designing an Experiment Choose a chemical reaction that reaches equilibrium and includes at least one gas. Design an experiment that will show the effects of concentration, temperature, and pressure on the system. You will not actually perform the experiment, so you are not limited by the equipment available in your laboratory. Prepare a lab report that includes a hypothesis, all steps of the procedure, and any expected results.

For: Self-grading assessment
Visit: PHSchool.com
Web Code: cca-1070

Standardized Test Prep

Test-Taking Tip

Calculating
When balancing chemical equations, follow these tips:

- Never change the subscript in any formula. Change only the coefficients.
- First, balance the atom that is most obviously unbalanced by placing a coefficient in front of the appropriate formula.
- Next, balance other atoms by placing coefficients in front of appropriate formulas.
- Finally, balance any atom that appears by itself in a formula (such as O_2, H_2, or Ca).
- Count the number of atoms of each element on both sides of the equation. If they are not equal, continue balancing.

Practice using these tips in Questions 1 and 3.

Choose the letter that best answers the question or completes the statement.

1. Balance this chemical equation.

    $MgO + H_3PO_4 \longrightarrow Mg_3(PO_4)_2 + H_2O$
    (A) $3MgO + 2H_3PO_4 \longrightarrow Mg_3(PO_4)_2 + 3H_2O$
    (B) $3MgO + 2H_3PO_4 \longrightarrow Mg_3(PO_4)_2 + 2H_2O$
    (C) $6MgO + 2H_3PO_4 \longrightarrow Mg_3(PO_4)_2 + 3H_2O$
    (D) $6MgO + 2H_3PO_4 \longrightarrow 2Mg_3(PO_4)_2 + 6H_2O$
    (E) $6MgO + 4H_3PO_4 \longrightarrow 2Mg_3(PO_4)_2 + 3H_2O$

Questions 2 and 3 refer to the following reaction.

$$C_4H_{10} + O_2 \longrightarrow CO_2 + H_2O$$

2. What type of reaction is described by this equation?
    (A) synthesis   (B) decomposition
    (C) combustion   (D) double replacement
    (E) single replacement

3. Balance the equation for the reaction between butane (C_4H_{10}) and oxygen, and then determine how many grams of CO_2 are formed when 5.00 grams of C_4H_{10} react.
    (A) 1.65 grams   (B) 3.79 grams
    (C) 15.1 grams   (D) 20.0 grams
    (E) 26.4 grams

4. Which equation describes a synthesis?
    (A) $Ba(OH)_2 + 2HCl \longrightarrow BaCl_2 + 2H_2O$
    (B) $CH_4 + 2O_2 \longrightarrow CO_2 + 2H_2O$
    (C) $Zn + CuSO_4 \longrightarrow Cu + ZnSO_4$
    (D) $2H_2 + O_2 \longrightarrow 2H_2O$
    (E) $CaCO_3 \longrightarrow CaO + CO_2$

Use the energy diagram to answer Question 5.

Reaction Energy for $A_2 + 2B \rightleftharpoons 2AB$

5. What effect would a catalyst have on the reaction $A_2 + 2B \rightleftharpoons 2AB$?
    (A) It gives the products more energy.
    (B) It makes the reaction endothermic.
    (C) It gives the reacting particles more energy.
    (D) It provides a new reaction pathway for the reactants.
    (E) none of the above

6. The following equation shows the formation of ammonia (NH_3) from nitrogen (N_2) and hydrogen (H_2). This reaction is in equilibrium.

    $N_2(g) + 3H_2(g) \rightleftharpoons 2NH_3(g) + $ Heat

    If the pressure of the system is decreased, the equilibrium will shift
    (A) to the right because there are fewer moles of gas on the product side of the equation.
    (B) to the left because there are more moles of gas on the reactant side of the equation.
    (C) to the right because a drop in pressure brings the reactants together so they can react.
    (D) to the left because a drop in pressure pulls the product molecules apart.
    (E) in neither direction because pressure does not affect chemical equilibriums.

8 Solutions, Acids, and Bases

This cave formed gradually as rainwater seeped through limestone rock and dissolved the calcium carbonate in the limestone.

21st Century Learning
Communication Skills

Why is soil acidity important in gardening?

In order for their plants to thrive, gardeners and farmers need to be mindful of the acidity of the soil. Suppose you are planning a small garden for your neighborhood. Use the library or Internet to find out the typical soil acidity for your area and how this affects the variety of plant life. Talk to a local gardener, farmer, or plant nursery worker to find out how soil acidity is measured and maintained. Then write a paragraph that outlines your plan for the garden, making sure to discuss soil pH considerations.

How do science concepts apply to your world? Here are some questions you'll be able to answer after you read this chapter.

- **How do road workers keep ice from building up on streets and highways?** *(Section 8.1)*

- **Why don't oil and water mix?** *(Section 8.2)*

- **What foods contain acids?** *(Section 8.3)*

- **Why do some people consume sports drinks?** *(Section 8.4)*

- **How are nutrients delivered to your body's cells?** *(page 250)*

Chapter Preview

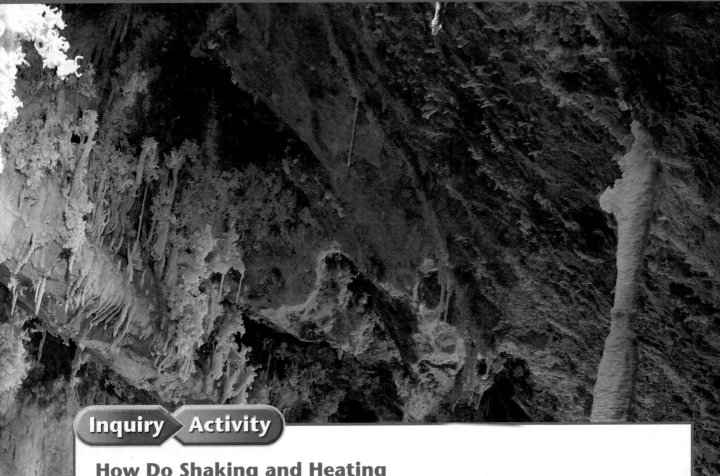

Inquiry Activity

How Do Shaking and Heating Affect a Carbonated Beverage?

Procedure

1. Remove the cap from a plastic bottle of carbonated beverage (a solution of carbon dioxide in water). Observe what happens.

2. Fit a balloon tightly over the top of the bottle. Holding the bottle over a sink, shake it several times from side to side. Observe any changes in the balloon and the liquid.

3. Place the bottle in a bucket of hot water. Observe any further changes in the balloon.

Think About It

1. **Observing** What happened when you removed the cap from the bottle?

2. **Inferring** What caused the balloon to expand?

3. **Drawing Conclusions** How did shaking affect the rate of the change in the beverage?

4. **Applying Concepts** How would storing a carbonated beverage in a refrigerator affect what happens when the cap is removed?

8.1 Formation of Solutions

Reading Focus

Key Concepts

- What are three processes that can occur when substances dissolve?

- What are some properties of a solution that differ from those of its solvent and solutes?

- What happens to energy when a solution forms?

- What factors affect the rate of dissolving?

Vocabulary

- solute
- solvent
- dissociation
- dispersion
- ionization

Reading Strategy

Comparing and Contrasting Copy the Venn diagram below. Contrast dissociation and ionization by listing the ways they differ.

Dissociation   **Ionization**

a. ?

b. ?

can produce ions in solution

c. ?

d. ?

Figure 1 If divers surface too quickly from great depths, the nitrogen that has dissolved in their blood and other tissues bubbles out of solution. These bubbles can become trapped in joints and cause great pain, a condition called "the bends."

Scuba divers, like the one in Figure 1, are able to breathe underwater with the aid of a tank containing compressed air. Like the air you breathe at sea level, the air inside the tank contains about 78 percent nitrogen. As a scuba diver descends to greater depths, the pressure of the air in the diver's lungs increases. At a depth of 10 meters, the air in the diver's lungs is already twice the pressure of the air at sea level.

The human body consists mainly of water. When gases come in contact with water, they dissolve in the water to form a solution. The deeper a scuba diver goes, the greater is the air pressure in her lungs, and the more nitrogen dissolves in the blood and tissues of her body.

The idea of a gas dissolving may seem strange to you. When you hear the word *dissolve*, you probably think of a solid dissolving in a liquid, such as sugar added to tea. However, any states of matter—solid, liquid, and gas—can become part of a solution. For a solution to form, one substance must dissolve in another.

Types of Solutions		
Solute	Solvent	Example
Gas	Gas	Air (oxygen, carbon dioxide in nitrogen)
Liquid	Gas	Water in air
Gas	Liquid	Carbonated beverage (carbon dioxide in water)
Liquid	Liquid	Vinegar (acetic acid in water)
Solid	Liquid	Sugar water (sugar in water)
Solid	Solid	Stainless steel (Chromium and nickel in iron)

Dissolving

Recall that a solution is a homogeneous mixture of two or more substances. Every solution has two types of components. A **solute** is a substance whose particles are dissolved in a solution. The substance in which the solute dissolves is called the **solvent.** For example, seawater is a solution in which salt is the solute and water is the solvent.

Solutes and solvents can take the form of a solid, liquid, or gas. The solution takes the state of the solvent. Figure 2 lists some common solutions and the states of their respective solutes and solvents. Air, for instance, is a solution of several gases dissolved in another gas. Nitrogen, making up about 78 percent of air, is the solvent. Oxygen, carbon dioxide, argon, and other gases are solutes.

You are probably most familiar with solutions in which water is the solvent. Carbonated drinks, hot tea, and seawater are just a few examples of the many water-based solutions you might have encoun-tered. Substances can dissolve in water in three ways—by dissociation, dispersion, and ionization.

Dissociation of Ionic Compounds For a solute to dissolve in water, the solute and solvent particles must attract one another. However, the particles within the solute are attracted to one another, and the particles within the solvent are attracted to one another. So before a solution can form, the attractions that hold the solute together and the solvent together must be overcome.

Figure 3 illustrates how a sodium chloride crystal dissolves in water. Sodium chloride is an ionic compound. Water is a polar molecule, and is attracted to the ions in the solute. The crystal dissolves as the sodium and chlorine ions are pulled into solution, one by one, by the surrounding water molecules. The process in which an ionic compound separates into ions as it dissolves is called **dissociation.**

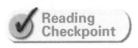
Reading Checkpoint *How does sodium chloride dissolve in water?*

Figure 2 A stainless steel pot or pan is a solution of chromium and nickel in iron. In a solution, the solvent is the substance in the greatest quantity.

Figure 3 When an ionic compound dissolves in water, the charged ends of water molecules surround the oppositely charged ions.

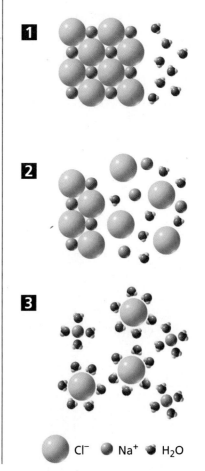

1

2

3

Cl⁻   Na⁺   H₂O

1

2

Sugar

Water

Figure 4 Saliva dissolves the sugar in hard candy by dispersion. As water molecules collide with sugar crystals, attractions develop between the water molecules and sugar molecules at the surface of the solid.

Dispersion of Molecular Compounds

When you place a piece of hard candy on your tongue, the sweet taste spreads, or disperses, throughout your mouth. The water in your saliva dissolves the sugar and flavoring in the candy. Sugar dissolves in water by **dispersion,** or breaking into small pieces that spread throughout the water.

Both sugar and water are polar molecules, so they attract one another. Because the water molecules are constantly moving, they collide frequently with the surface of the sugar crystals, as shown in Figure 4. Attractions form between the water molecules and the exposed sugar molecules. When enough water molecules have surrounded a sugar molecule, the attractions between them are great enough to overcome the attractions holding the sugar molecule to the surface of the crystal. The sugar molecule breaks free, and is pulled into solution by the water molecules.

As more sugar molecules break free of the crystal, another layer of sugar molecules is exposed to the water, and the process repeats. The solute particles become evenly spread throughout the solvent.

Reading Checkpoint *How does sugar dissolve in water?*

Ionization of Molecular Compounds

Hydrogen chloride, HCl, is a molecular compound in which a hydrogen atom and a chlorine atom share a pair of electrons. Recall that a hydrogen atom has only one proton and one electron. When HCl gas dissolves in water, the hydrogen proton from each HCl molecule is transferred to a water molecule. For each HCl molecule that reacts, a hydronium ion, H_3O^+, and a chloride ion, Cl^-, are produced.

Notice that when hydrogen chloride and water form a solution, two molecular compounds react to form two ions. The process in which neutral molecules gain or lose electrons is known as **ionization.** Unlike dissociation and dispersion, which are physical changes, dissolving by ionization is a chemical change. The solution that results contains new substances. When a solute dissolves by dissociation, the ions pulled into solution are the same ions present in the solute. When a solute dissolves by ionization, the ions in solution are formed by the reaction of solute and solvent particles.

Properties of Liquid Solutions

The physical properties of salt are clearly different from the physical properties of water. But how do the properties of a saltwater solution compare to those of its solute and solvent? **Three physical properties of a solution that can differ from those of its solute and solvent are conductivity, freezing point, and boiling point.**

Conductivity Solid sodium chloride is a poor conductor of electric current. But when sodium chloride dissociates in water, the sodium and chloride ions are able to move freely. The ions in solution will then conduct an electric current. Hydrogen chloride gas is also a poor conductor of electric current. However, when hydrogen chloride ionizes in water, the resulting solution conducts an electric current.

Freezing Point and Boiling Point If you live in a cold climate, you are probably familiar with icy roads like the one in Figure 5. You may have seen snowplows or salt trucks spreading magnesium chloride, $MgCl_2$, or a similar ionic compound on these icy roads. When magnesium chloride dissolves in melting ice and snow, it dissociates into magnesium (Mg^{2+}) ions and chloride (Cl^-) ions. As Figure 6A shows, ice forms when water molecules are able to arrange themselves in a rigid, honeycomb-like structure. In Figure 6B, the presence of magnesium and chloride ions, which are attracted to the water molecules, interferes with the freezing process. The freezing point of water at sea level is 0°C. When icy roads are salted with magnesium chloride, the resulting solution can have a freezing point as low as −15°C.

A solute can also raise the boiling point of the solvent. For example, the coolant used in most car radiators is a solution containing water and ethylene glycol, $C_2H_6O_2$. Water at sea level boils at 100°C. Adding ethylene glycol to water raises the boiling point. The resulting solution helps prevent the engine from overheating. Because ethylene glycol also lowers the freezing point of water, the coolant does not freeze during spells of cold weather.

Figure 5 Salt spread on icy roads lowers the freezing point of water.

Figure 6 The presence of solute particles affects how a solvent freezes. **A** Pure water freezes in a hexagonal pattern. **B** In water "salted" with $MgCl_2$, the dissociated Mg^{2+} and Cl^- ions disrupt the formation of ice crystals. **Using Models** *How do the interactions between Mg^{2+} and H_2O differ from the interactions between Cl^- and H_2O?*

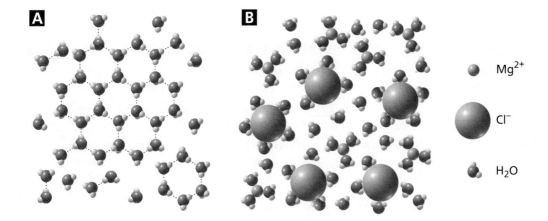

A **B**

Mg^{2+}

Cl^-

H_2O

For: Links on solutions
Visit: www.SciLinks.org
Web Code: ccn-1081

Heat of Solution

When sodium hydroxide, NaOH, dissolves in water, the solution becomes warmer. The solution releases energy to the surroundings. In contrast, when ammonium nitrate, NH_4NO_3, dissolves in water, the solution becomes colder. The solution absorbs energy from the surroundings. **During the formation of a solution, energy is either released or absorbed.**

Like chemical reactions, the solution process can be described as exothermic or endothermic. Dissolving sodium hydroxide in water is exothermic, as it releases heat. Dissolving ammonium nitrate in water is endothermic, as it absorbs heat. The How It Works box on page 233 describes how dissolving ammonium nitrate is used in cold packs.

In order for a solution to form, both the attractions among solute particles and the attractions among solvent particles must be broken. Breaking attractions requires energy. As the solute dissolves, new attractions form between solute and solvent particles. The formation of attractions releases energy. The difference between these energies is known as the heat of solution. For example, dissolving one mole of sodium hydroxide in water releases 44.5 kilojoules of heat. In this exothermic change, energy is released as NaOH and H_2O form new attractions. It is 44.5 kilojoules greater than the energy required to break the attractions among NaOH crystals and among H_2O molecules.

Reading Checkpoint *Does the breaking of attractions among solvent particles release energy or absorb energy?*

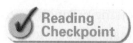

Comparing Heats of Solution

Materials

2 large test tubes, 10-mL graduated cylinder, distilled water, thermometer, 1 g potassium chloride, 5 mL 95% isopropyl alcohol solution, stirring rod

Procedure

1. Add 5 mL of distilled water to each test tube. Measure and record the temperature of the water in each test tube to the nearest 0.2°C.

2. Remove the thermometer. Add the potassium chloride to one of the test tubes. Stir until the potassium chloride dissolves.
   CAUTION: *Use the stirring rod, not the thermometer, to stir the solution.*

3. Measure and record the final temperature of the solution. Rinse the thermometer.

4. Add 5 mL of the alcohol solution to the second test tube. Stir the mixture. Measure and record the final temperature.

Analyze and Conclude

1. **Observing** What happened to the temperature of each solution?

2. **Classifying** Which process was exothermic? Which was endothermic?

3. **Inferring** If there were no change in temperature during the formation of a solution, how would you explain this observation?

Cold Packs

Instant hot and cold packs are often used by athletes to treat injuries. Hot packs are also used in cold weather to warm hands and feet. Both types of pack work through the action of chemicals that either release or absorb heat when they dissolve in water. One type of cold pack is shown below. **Inferring** *How does shaking the pack after squeezing it affect the rate of dissolving?*

Using a cold pack
A cold pack removes heat from the inflammation around an injury. It also decreases the size of capillaries (small blood vessels) in the injured area, which reduces swelling and bruising.

A **Inside the pack** A cold pack consists of two sealed bags, one inside the other. The strong outer bag contains solid ammonium nitrate powder. The thin-walled inner bag contains water.

B **Squeezing the pack** When the pack is squeezed, the inner bag containing the water bursts. The water rushes into the outer bag where it dissolves the ammonium nitrate.

Outer bag

Ammonium nitrate powder

Water in inner bag

Inner bag bursts.

Ammonium nitrate dissolves in water.

C **Heat absorbed** As the ammonium nitrate dissolves, it absorbs energy from the water. This causes the temperature of the solution in the bag to drop rapidly. The pack is then ready for use.

Heat absorbed

Solutions, Acids, and Bases **233**

Crushed solid

Stirring

Heat

Figure 7 The rate of dissolving can be increased by reducing the particle size of the solute, by stirring, and by heating the solvent. **Predicting** *How does changing the temperature setting on a washing machine affect how fast the detergent will dissolve?*

Factors Affecting Rates of Dissolving

You already know that sugar dissolves in water. But what do you know about the rate at which it dissolves? Like rates of chemical reactions, rates of dissolving depend on the frequency and energy of collisions that occur between very small particles. During a chemical reaction, collisions occur between particles of the reactants. During the formation of a solution, collisions occur between particles of the solute and solvent. 🔑 **Factors that affect the rate of dissolving include surface area, stirring, and temperature.**

When a sugar cube dissolves in water, the dissolving takes place at the surfaces of the cube. The greater the surface area of a solid solute, the more frequent the collisions are between solute and solvent particles. More collisions result in a faster rate of dissolving. You can increase the surface area of a solid by dividing it into smaller particles. The more finely divided a solid solute, the faster it dissolves. For example, one gram of granulated sugar dissolves faster in water than a 1-gram sugar cube.

You can also make sugar dissolve faster by stirring the mixture. Stirring moves dissolved particles away from the surface of the solid, and allows for more collisions between solute and solvent particles.

Another way to speed up the rate of dissolving is to increase the temperature of the solvent. For example, sugar dissolves faster in warm water than it does in cold water. Increasing the temperature of a solvent causes its particles to move faster, on average. As a result, both the number of collisions and the energy of these collisions with solute particles increase. The solute goes into solution more quickly.

Section 8.1 Assessment

Reviewing Concepts

1. 🔑 What are three ways that substances can dissolve in water?

2. 🔑 What physical properties of a solution differ from those of its solutes and solvent?

3. 🔑 How does the formation of a solution involve energy?

4. 🔑 What factors affect dissolving rates?

Critical Thinking

5. **Comparing and Contrasting** Compare the processes by which sugar crystals and hydrogen chloride gas dissolve in water.

6. **Predicting** Suppose you put equal amounts of pure water and salt water into separate ice cube trays of the same size and shape. When you put both trays in the freezer, what would you expect to happen?

Connecting ⊂ Concepts

Reaction Rates In Section 7.3, factors affecting chemical reaction rates are discussed. Find out which of these factors also affect rates of dissolving.

8.2 Solubility and Concentration

Reading Focus

Key Concepts

- How are solutions with different amounts of solute described?
- What factors determine the solubility of a solute?
- What are three ways to measure the concentration of a solution?

Vocabulary

- ◆ solubility
- ◆ saturated solution
- ◆ unsaturated solution
- ◆ supersaturated solution
- ◆ concentration
- ◆ molarity

Reading Strategy

Previewing Copy the table below. Before you read the section, rewrite the green topic headings as *how, why,* and *what* questions. As you read, write an answer to each question.

Question	Answer
What is solubility?	a. ___?___
b. ___?___	Solvent, temperature, and pressure
c. ___?___	d. ___?___

Have you ever prepared a pitcher of lemonade or iced tea? Fresh lemonade is a solution of water, lemon juice, and sugar. Water is the solvent. Lemon juice and sugar are the solutes.

You might be surprised at how much sugar can dissolve in water. However, there is a limit to the amount of sugar that can dissolve in a given amount of water. Once that limit is reached, no more sugar will dissolve, and you cannot make the solution taste any sweeter.

Solubility

The maximum amount of a solute that dissolves in a given amount of solvent at a constant temperature is called **solubility.** Solubilities are usually expressed in grams of solute per 100 grams of solvent at a specified temperature. Figure 8 lists the solubilities of some common substances in water at 20°C. Notice that table sugar is more soluble in water than table salt, which is more soluble than baking soda.

Knowing the solubility of a substance can help you classify solutions based on how much solute they contain. ⬤ **Solutions are described as saturated, unsaturated, or supersaturated, depending on the amount of solute in solution.**

Solubility in 100 g of Water at 20°C	
Compound	**Solubility (g)**
Table salt (NaCl)	36.0
Baking soda (NaHCO$_3$)	9.6
Table sugar (C$_{12}$H$_{22}$O$_{11}$)	203.9

Figure 8 At a given temperature, different solutes have different solubilities in water. **Calculating** *At 20°C, how much baking soda can dissolve in 200 grams of water?*

Saturated Solutions Table sugar is very soluble in water. At 20°C, 203.9 grams of table sugar will dissolve in 100 grams of water. What will happen if you try to dissolve more than 203.9 grams of table sugar in the same amount of water? The extra sugar will not go into solution. The solution is already saturated. A **saturated solution** is one that contains as much solute as the solvent can hold at a given temperature. When a solution is saturated, the solvent is "filled" with solute. If you add more solute, it will not dissolve.

Unsaturated Solutions A solution that has less than the maximum amount of solute that can be dissolved is called an **unsaturated solution.** For example, many of the beverages you drink are unsaturated solutions of sugar in water. If you sweeten your lemonade with a spoonful of sugar, and the sugar dissolves, you know that the solution is unsaturated. As long as the amount of solute is less than the solubility at that temperature, the solution is unsaturated.

Supersaturated Solutions Have you ever tried to carry more books than you can easily manage? If you're not careful, you'll drop them all because the load is so unstable. Similarly, a solvent can sometimes dissolve more solute than you might expect, based on its solubility. Solubility is given at a specific temperature, such as 20°C. If you heat a solvent above that temperature, more solute may dissolve. If you then carefully cool the solvent back to 20°C without jarring it, you may be able to keep the extra solute in solution.

A **supersaturated solution** is one that contains *more* solute than it can normally hold at a given temperature. Supersaturated solutions are very unstable. If even a tiny crystal of the solute falls into a supersaturated solution, the extra solute can rapidly deposit out of solution, as shown in Figure 9.

Figure 9 A supersaturated solution is analogous to the overloaded man shown above. One wrong step, and he might drop all the boxes. In the photo sequence below, a single crystal of sodium acetate, $NaC_2H_3O_2$, is added to a supersaturated solution of sodium acetate in water. The excess solute rapidly crystallizes out of the solution.

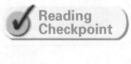 *Reading Checkpoint* *How does a supersaturated solution differ from a saturated solution?*

Factors Affecting Solubility

Have you ever had to clean oil or grease from your hands? If you rinse your hands in water alone, the oil remains on your hands. But if you use soapy water, you can easily rinse the oil off your hands. Oil is soluble in soapy water, but not in pure water. Solubility varies not only with the solvent used, but also with the conditions of the solution process. **Three factors that affect the solubility of a solute are the polarity of the solvent, temperature, and pressure.**

Polar and Nonpolar Solvents Oil does not dissolve in water because oil molecules are nonpolar and water molecules are polar. A common guideline for predicting solubility is "like dissolves like." Solution formation is more likely to happen when the solute and solvent are either both polar or both nonpolar. Figure 11 illustrates how soapy water dissolves oil. A soap molecule has a polar end, which attracts water molecules, and a nonpolar end, which attracts oil. The soap molecules break up the oil into small droplets that are soluble in water.

Temperature When you add a large amount of sugar to cold tea, only a small amount dissolves. If you add the same amount of sugar to the same amount of hot tea, more sugar will dissolve. In general, the solubility of solids increases as the solvent temperature increases.

When a glass of cold water warms up to room temperature, bubbles form on the inside of the glass. These bubbles are gases that were dissolved in the water. They come out of the solution as the water temperature rises. Unlike most solids, gases usually become less soluble as the temperature of the solvent increases.

Pressure How do manufacturers produce a carbonated beverage? They use pressure to force carbon dioxide (CO_2) to dissolve in the liquid. Increasing the pressure on a gas increases its solubility in a liquid. The pressure of CO_2 in a sealed 12-ounce can of soda at room temperature can be two to three times atmospheric pressure.

Figure 10 Generally, a solute is more likely to dissolve in a "like" solvent than an "unlike" solvent. **Classifying** *How is saltwater an example of "like dissolving in like"?*

Solvent-Solute Combinations		
Solvent Type	**Solute Type**	**Will Solution Form?**
Polar	Polar (or ionic)	More likely
Polar	Nonpolar	Not likely
Nonpolar	Polar (or ionic)	Not likely
Nonpolar	Nonpolar	More likely

Figure 11 Soaps and detergents are used to remove grease and oil stains. Soap molecules form attractions to both polar water molecules and nonpolar oil molecules. As the water flows away, it carries the oil with it.

Water molecule
Polar end of soap molecule
Nonpolar end of soap molecule
Grease

SMITH'S
Cranberry Juice
Black River Falls, Wisconsin

Contains 27% Cranberry Juice

INGREDIENTS: Filtered Water, Cranberry Juice (Cranberry Juice from Concentrate and Cranberry Juice), High Fructose Corn Syrup, Ascorbic Acid (Vitamin C)

Figure 12 The juice squeezed from fruit is already a solution. Most bottled or canned juices are less-concentrated solutions of fruit juices, made by adding water. Percent by volume is a way to measure the concentration of one liquid dissolved in another.

Concentration of Solutions

How do you take your tea? Some people prefer their tea very concentrated, so they leave the tea bag in hot water for several minutes. Other people immerse the tea bag for only a minute or two, because they prefer their tea much less concentrated, or dilute. The resulting solutions differ in how much solute is present. The **concentration** of a solution is the amount of solute dissolved in a specified amount of solution. **Concentration can be expressed as percent by volume, percent by mass, and molarity.**

Percent by Volume Fruit juice bottles often have labels, such as the one in Figure 12, that state the percentage of "real juice" in the bottle. For example, if 27 percent of the total volume of liquid is fruit juice, the concentration of fruit juice is 27 percent by volume. Use the following equation to calculate concentration as a percent by volume.

$$\text{Percent by volume} = \frac{\text{Volume of solute}}{\text{Volume of solution}} \times 100\%$$

Percent by Mass Concentration expressed as a percent by mass is more useful when the solute is a solid. Percent by mass is the percent of a solution's total mass that is accounted for by a solute.

$$\text{Percent by mass} = \frac{\text{Mass of solute}}{\text{Mass of solution}} \times 100\%$$

Suppose you have 100 grams of a solution of sugar in water. After allowing the water to evaporate, 15 grams of sugar remain. So, the concentration of sugar in the solution was 15 percent by mass.

Problem-Solving ▶ Activity

Putting the Fizz Into Carbonated Beverages

You have been asked to find a supplier of carbon dioxide for a factory that produces carbonated beverages. You also must find out how to regulate the carbonation levels of the beverages produced.

Defining the Problem Describe your task in your own words.

Organizing Information Find examples of chemical reactions that produce carbon dioxide. What industries use such reactions? In addition, list and review the general factors affecting solubility.

Creating a Solution Choose a business or industry to supply your factory with carbon dioxide. Figure out how the solubility of a gas in a liquid varies under different conditions.

Presenting Your Plan Write a proposal to the manager of your factory. Explain your choice of a carbon dioxide supplier, and describe how to regulate carbonation levels of the beverages produced.

Molarity Suppose you add 10 grams of sodium chloride to 100 milliliters of water. Then, in a different container, you add 10 grams of table sugar to 100 milliliters of water. Do the two solutions contain the same number of solute particles? No, they do not, because the two different solutes have different molar masses.

To compare the number of solute particles in solutions, chemists often use moles to measure concentration. Recall that a mole is the amount of a substance that contains approximately 6.02×10^{23} particles of that substance. **Molarity** is the number of moles of a solute dissolved per liter of solution. Use the following equation to calculate molarity.

$$\text{Molarity} = \frac{\text{Moles of solute}}{\text{Liters of solution}}$$

To make a 1-molar (1M) solution of sodium chloride in water, first calculate the molar mass of the solute. Sodium chloride, NaCl, has a molar mass of 58.5 grams. If 58.5 grams of sodium chloride is mixed with enough water to make one liter of solution, the resulting solution is 1-molar.

Table sugar, $C_{12}H_{22}O_{11}$, has a molar mass of 342 grams. To make a 1-molar solution of table sugar in water, 342 grams of table sugar must be added to enough water to make one liter of solution.

Figure 13 A 1M NaCl solution contains 58.5 grams of NaCl per liter of solution. **Calculating** *How much solute would you need to make to make one liter of a 0.2-molar solution of sodium chloride in water?*

Section 8.2 Assessment

Reviewing Concepts

1. ⬤ What terms are used to describe solutions with different amounts of solute?

2. ⬤ List three factors that affect solubility.

3. ⬤ What are three ways to measure the concentration of a solution?

4. What is the effect of pressure on the solubility of a gas?

5. Compare a 2-molar solution of salt water with a 2-molar solution of sugar water. How are they similar? How are they different?

Critical Thinking

6. **Problem Solving** How would you figure out the solubility of an unknown solid in water?

7. **Inferring** Despite the name, dry cleaning does involve the use of liquid solvents. Why would a dry cleaner use both polar and nonpolar cleaning solvents?

8. **Calculating** Use the periodic table to find the mass of potassium nitrate (KNO_3) needed to make 1 liter of 1-molar solution.

Writing in Science

Compare and Contrast Paragraph Write a paragraph comparing the different ways that concentration can be expressed. (*Hint:* Describe what quantities must be measured for each type of concentration calculation.)

8.3 Properties of Acids and Bases

Reading Focus

Key Concepts

- What are some general properties of acids and bases?
- What are the products of neutralization?
- What are proton donors and proton acceptors?

Vocabulary

- acid
- indicator
- base
- neutralization
- salt

Reading Strategy

Using Prior Knowledge Before you read, copy the table below and write your definition for each vocabulary term. After you read, write the scientific definition of each term and compare it with your original definition.

Term	Your Definition	Scientific Definition
Acid	a. __?__	b. __?__
Base	c. __?__	d. __?__
Salt	e. __?__	f. __?__

Figure 14 Soap making involves the use of a base such as sodium hydroxide or potassium hydroxide.

One of the chemicals used to make the soaps shown in Figure 14 is sodium hydroxide. In traditional soap making, sodium hydroxide is added to a mixture of melted animal or vegetable fats. As the mixture is brought to a boil, the sodium hydroxide reacts with the fats. The products of the reaction are glycerol (a colorless, syrupy liquid) and soap. After the glycerol is separated from the soap, the soap is purified. Other chemicals are then mixed with the soap to give it a particular scent and color.

Sodium hydroxide belongs to a class of compounds, known as bases, that share some physical and chemical properties. Bases are related to another class of compounds called acids. As you will discover, there are several differences among acidic solutions, basic solutions, and solutions that have properties of neither an acid nor a base.

Identifying Acids

An **acid** is a compound that produces hydronium ions (H_3O^+) when dissolved in water. Recall that when hydrogen chloride gas dissolves in water, it ionizes and forms hydronium ions and chloride ions.

$$HCl + H_2O \longrightarrow H_3O^+ + Cl^-$$

The solution that results is called hydrochloric acid. Figure 15 lists some common acids and their uses.

Common Acids		
Name	Formula	Use
Acetic acid	CH_3COOH	Vinegar
Carbonic acid	H_2CO_3	Carbonated beverages
Hydrochloric acid	HCl	Digestive juices in stomach
Nitric acid	HNO_3	Fertilizer production
Phosphoric acid	H_3PO_4	Fertilizer production
Sulfuric acid	H_2SO_4	Car batteries

Figure 15 The table lists names, formulas, and uses for several common acids. **Inferring** *What products are formed when nitric acid ionizes in water?*

Acids have certain chemical and physical properties that are similar. ◉ **Some general properties of acids include sour taste, reactivity with metals, and ability to produce color changes in indicators.**

Sour Taste Foods that taste sour often contain acids. For example, lemons, grapefruits, limes, and oranges all contain citric acid. The vinegar used in salad dressings contains acetic acid, CH_3COOH. Dairy products that have spoiled contain butyric (byoo THIR ik) acid. While many of the foods you eat contain acids, you should never test an acid by tasting it.

Reactivity With Metals When you use aluminum foil to cover a bowl of leftover spaghetti sauce or other foods containing tomatoes, the foil often turns dark. The foil may also develop small holes, and the food may acquire a metallic taste. Tomatoes contain citric acid, which reacts with metals such as aluminum.

The reaction between an acid and a metal is an example of a single-replacement reaction. For example, when zinc is added to a test tube containing hydrochloric acid, bubbles form in the tube. The following equation describes the reaction.

$$Zn + 2HCl \longrightarrow H_2 + ZnCl_2$$

As the zinc replaces hydrogen in hydrochloric acid, hydrogen gas and zinc(II) chloride are produced.

Color Changes in Indicators An **indicator** is any substance that changes color in the presence of an acid or base. One of the most common indicators used is litmus, a kind of dye derived from plants called lichens (LY kens). Litmus paper, shown in Figure 16, is made by coating strips of paper with litmus. Blue litmus paper turns red in the presence of an acid. If you drop an unknown solution onto blue litmus paper and the litmus paper turns red, you can classify the solution as an acid.

Figure 16 Litmus paper is an indicator that changes color in the presence of acids and bases. When blue litmus paper touches an acid, it turns red. Apples contain several acids, including malic acid, ascorbic acid (vitamin C), and citric acid.

For: Links on bases
Visit: www.SciLinks.org
Web Code: ccn-1083

Identifying Bases

Sodium hydroxide, NaOH, is an example of a base. A **base** is a compound that produces hydroxide ions (OH^-) when dissolved in water. When sodium hydroxide dissolves in water, it dissociates into sodium ions and hydroxide ions.

$$NaOH \longrightarrow Na^+ + OH^-$$

Figure 17 lists some common bases and their uses. Like acids, bases have certain physical and chemical properties that you can use to identify them. 🔑 **Some general properties of bases include bitter taste, slippery feel, and ability to produce color changes in indicators.** Unlike acids, bases usually do not react with metals. However, low reactivity with metals is not considered a general property of bases. For example, sodium hydroxide reacts very vigorously with metals such as aluminum and zinc.

Bitter Taste Have you ever tasted unsweetened chocolate (sometimes called baking chocolate)? Without sugar, chocolate tastes bitter. Cacao beans contain a base called theobromine that gives unsweetened chocolate its bitter taste.

Many cough syrups and other liquid medicines contain similar bases. Fruit flavorings are often added to mask the taste of these basic solutions.

Slippery Feel Bases feel slippery. Wet soap and many cleaning products that contain bases are slippery to the touch. When wet, some rocks feel slippery because the water dissolves compounds trapped in the rocks, producing a basic solution.

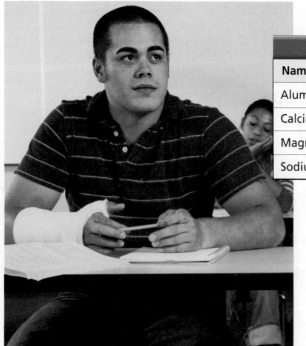

Common Bases		
Name	**Formula**	**Uses**
Aluminum hydroxide	$Al(OH)_3$	Deodorant, antacid
Calcium hydroxide	$Ca(OH)_2$	Concrete, plaster
Magnesium hydroxide	$Mg(OH)_2$	Antacid, laxative
Sodium hydroxide	NaOH	Drain cleaner, soap production

Figure 17 A base is a compound that produces hydroxide ions when dissolved in water. The plaster in this boy's cast contains a base. Bases are also commonly found in products used for cleaning.

Quick Lab

Using an Indicator

Materials

one quarter cup of frozen blueberries, foam cup, spoon, 4 small plastic cups, 2 dropper pipets, lemon juice, white vinegar, window cleaner, baking soda

Procedure

1. Place the blueberries in the foam cup and mash them with the spoon. Try to get as much juice out of the berries as possible. You will use the juice as an indicator.

2. Use the spoon to remove most of the crushed berries and discard them as directed by your teacher. Leave as much juice behind as possible.

3. Use a dropper pipet to place a few drops of lemon juice (which is acidic) in one of the plastic cups. Use a second pipet to add one drop of your indicator to the lemon juice. Swirl the cup. Record your observations.

4. Rinse out the pipets with water. Repeat Step 3, using vinegar and then window cleaner in place of lemon juice. Record your observations.

5. Place several drops of the indicator in the last plastic cup. Add a small pinch of baking soda to the cup. Swirl the cup. Record your observations.

Analyze and Conclude

1. Classifying Use your observations to determine how the color of blueberry juice changes in acids and bases.

2. Drawing Conclusions How does the blueberry indicator help you determine whether a material is an acid or a base?

3. Inferring Why does the color of the blueberry indicator change less when added to acids than when added to bases?

Color Changes in Indicators Bases turn red litmus paper blue. The litmus paper will change back to red if you drop an acidic solution on it.

Phenolphthalein (fee nol THAY leen) is another example of an acid-base indicator. In a solution containing a base, phenolphthalein is red. In a solution containing an acid, phenolphthalein is colorless.

Some flowers, like the hydrangeas shown in Figure 18, contain natural indicators. The color of the flowers depends on whether the plant is growing in acidic or basic soil. When hydrangeas grow in acidic soil, the flowers are bluish-purple. When hydrangeas grow in basic soil, the flowers are pink. By manipulating the acidity of the soil, gardeners can determine the color of the flowers.

 What color does litmus paper turn in a base?

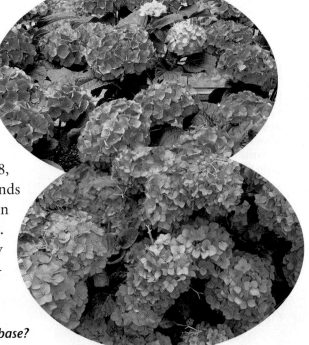

Figure 18 Soil acidity can affect the color of flowers such as hydrangeas.

Solutions, Acids, and Bases **243**

Neutralization and Salts

When people eat fish, they sometimes squeeze lemon juice over the fish. Fish contains bases that can leave a bitter taste. Lemon juice contains acids, such as citric acid. By squeezing lemon juice over the fish, the citric acid reacts with the bases in the fish, and the fish tastes less bitter.

The reaction between an acid and a base is called **neutralization.** During neutralization, the negative ions in an acid combine with the positive ions in a base to produce an ionic compound called a **salt.** At the same time, the hydronium ions from the acid combine with the hydroxide ions from the base to produce water. **The neutralization reaction between an acid and a base produces a salt and water.**

For example, when hydrochloric acid reacts with sodium hydroxide, the following neutralization reaction occurs.

$$(H_3O^+ + Cl^-) + (Na^+ + OH^-) \longrightarrow 2HOH + (Na^+ + Cl^-)$$

$$\text{acid} \qquad\qquad \text{base} \qquad\qquad \text{water} \qquad \text{salt}$$

The products of the reaction are a salt made up of sodium and chloride ions, and water. If you let the water in the resulting solution evaporate, the sodium and chloride ions would begin to crystallize out of solution, forming table salt.

Table salt is the most common example of a salt compound. Other common salts are listed in Figure 19. For instance, baking soda, $NaHCO_3$, is produced during the neutralization reaction between sodium hydroxide and carbonic acid, H_2CO_3. The other product is water. The ocean contains many dissolved salts, including chlorides and sulfates of potassium, calcium, magnesium, and sodium. Many of these salts go into solution as seawater washes against rocks.

Figure 19 The common salts listed in the table can all be made by reacting an acid with a base. One of these salts, sodium carbonate, was used to make the glass for the vases shown below. *Inferring* **Name an acid and a base that could react to form potassium chloride, KCl.**

Common Salts		
Name	**Formula**	**Uses**
Sodium chloride	NaCl	Food flavoring, preservative
Sodium carbonate	Na$_2$CO$_3$	Used to make glass
Potassium chloride	KCl	Used as a salt substitute to reduce dietary intake of sodium
Potassium iodide	KI	Added to table salt to prevent iodine deficiency
Magnesium chloride	MgCl$_2$	De-icer for roads
Calcium carbonate	CaCO$_3$	Chalk, marble floors, and tables
Ammonium nitrate	NH$_4$NO$_3$	Fertilizer, cold packs

Proton Donors and Acceptors

Recall that hydronium ions (H_3O^+) are produced when acids dissolve in water. When an acid and a base react in water, a proton from the hydronium ion from the acid combines with the hydroxide ion (OH^-) from the base to form water (H_2O). Acids lose, or "donate," protons. Bases "accept" protons, forming water, a neutral molecule. ⬤ **Acids can be defined as proton donors, and bases can be defined as proton acceptors.** This definition allows you to classify a wider range of substances as acids or bases.

Based on the definitions of acids and bases that you read earlier in this section, water is neither an acid nor a base. However, using the proton-donor or proton-acceptor definition, water can act as either an acid or a base depending on the compound with which it reacts.

Figure 20 shows the ionization of hydrogen chloride and ammonia as they form solutions. In the first reaction, water acts as a base. It accepts a proton from hydrogen chloride and becomes a hydronium ion. In the second reaction, water acts as an acid. It donates a proton to the ammonia, which acts as a base. The resulting solution contains hydroxide ions and ammonium ions, NH_4^+.

Figure 20 In the first reaction, water acts as a base, accepting a proton from hydrogen chloride. In the second reaction, water acts as an acid, donating a proton to the ammonia. *Applying Concepts* ***What acts as the proton donor in the first reaction?***

Section 8.3 Assessment

Reviewing Concepts

1. ⬤ List three general properties of acids.
2. ⬤ List three general properties of bases.
3. ⬤ What are the two products of a neutralization reaction?
4. ⬤ What are the proton-donor and proton-acceptor definitions of acids and bases?
5. What ion is present in all common acid solutions?

Critical Thinking

6. **Using Analogies** Commercials for antacids often claim these products neutralize stomach acid. Antacids are bases. Think of an analogy for the way in which antacids neutralize acids.

7. **Applying Concepts** In the following equation, which reactant is a proton donor? Which is a proton acceptor?
   $$HNO_3 + H_2O \longrightarrow H_3O^+ + NO_3^-$$

Connecting C Concepts

Classifying Reactions Compare neutralization with the types of chemical reactions described in Section 7.2. To which type of reaction is neutralization most similar? Explain your choice.

8.4 Strength of Acids and Bases

Key Concepts

- How is pH used to describe the concentration of acids and bases?

- How do strong acids and bases differ from weak acids and bases?

- Why are strong acids and bases good electrolytes?

Vocabulary

- pH
- buffer
- electrolyte

Reading Strategy

Comparing and Contrasting Copy the Venn diagram below. As you read, complete the diagram by comparing and contrasting acids and bases.

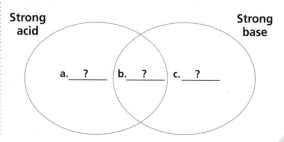

On a hot summer day, you might go swimming in a pool with some of your friends. As the water evaporates from your skin, you feel cooler and refreshed.

Have you ever thought about how the water in a swimming pool is made safe for swimming? You may have noticed the odor of chlorine at a backyard swimming pool or at larger municipal pools. Certain compounds of chlorine are dissolved in the water. These compounds prevent the growth of bacteria that could make you sick.

The concentration of hydronium ions in solution must be carefully controlled in a swimming pool. If there are too many or too few hydronium ions, then the right compounds of chlorine will not be present. Figure 21 shows a pool maintenance worker adding sodium bicarbonate, $NaHCO_3$, to the water. Sodium bicarbonate can be used to lower the concentration of hydronium ions in solution.

How can you describe the acidity or basicity of a solution? One way is to determine the concentration of hydronium or hydroxide ions present in solution. Another way is to describe how readily those hydronium ions or hydroxide ions formed.

Figure 21 Sodium bicarbonate, or baking soda, is often added to swimming pools to regulate the acidity of the water.

Car battery acid   Lemons   Oranges   White bread   Distilled water   Soap   Drain cleaner

0 1 2 3 4 5 6 7 8 9 10 11 12 13 14

Most acidic   Vinegar   Tomato   Milk   **Neutral**   Baking soda   Ammonia   **Most basic**

The pH Scale

Chemists use a number scale from 0 to 14 to describe the concentration of hydronium ions in a solution. It is known as the pH scale. The **pH** of a solution is a measure of its hydronium ion concentration. A pH of 7 indicates a neutral solution. Acids have a pH less than 7. Bases have a pH greater than 7.

Notice in Figure 22 that water falls in the middle of the pH scale. Water ionizes slightly according to the following reaction.

$$2H_2O \rightleftharpoons H_3O^+ + OH^-$$

The arrow pointing to the left is longer than the arrow pointing to the right to show that water contains more molecules than ions. Water is neutral because it contains small but equal concentrations of hydronium ions and hydroxide ions. At 25°C, the concentration of both H_3O^+ and OH^- in water is 1.0×10^{-7} M. Pure water has a pH of 7.

If you add an acid to water, the concentration of H_3O^+ increases and the concentration of OH^- decreases. Suppose you have a hydrochloric acid solution in which the concentration of H_3O^+ is 0.10 M (or 1.0×10^{-1} M). The solution has a pH of 1. **The lower the pH value, the greater the H_3O^+ ion concentrtion in solution is.**

If you add a base to water, the concentration of OH^- increases and the concentration of H_3O^+ decreases. Consider a sodium hydroxide solution in which the concentration of OH^- is 0.10 M. The concentration of H_3O^+ in this solution is 1.0×10^{-13} M, which corresponds to a pH of 13. **The higher the pH value, the lower the H_3O^+ ion concentration is.**

Reading Checkpoint   *What is the pH of pure water?*

Strong Acids and Bases

Recall that some reactions go to completion while others reach equilibrium. When certain acids and bases dissolve in water, the formation of ions from the solute almost goes to completion. Such acids and bases are classified as *strong*.

Figure 22 The pH scale can help you classify solutions as acids or bases.
Comparing and Contrasting *The desired pH range of chlorinated water in swimming pools is 7.2 to 7.8. How does the concentration of hydronium ions in this solution compare to that of lemon juice?*

Go Online

NSTA SCLINKS

For: Links on pH
Visit: www.SciLinks.org
Web Code: ccn-1084

Making a Battery

Materials

1 large fresh lemon, plastic knife, zinc strip, 2 copper strips, multimeter

Procedure

1. Roll the lemon between your hands until it softens.

2. Use the knife to carefully cut two parallel slits in the lemon about 1 cm apart. Push the copper strips into the slits to a depth of 2 to 3 cm. Don't allow the strips to touch.

3. Attach the copper strips to the terminals of the multimeter. Observe the reading and record it.

4. Replace one of the copper strips with the zinc strip and repeat step 3.

Analyze and Conclude

1. **Observing** What was the reading on the multimeter when you used two copper strips? A copper and a zinc strip?

2. **Predicting** Lemon juice is acidic. Would a basic solution provide a similar result?

Strong Acids When hydrogen chloride dissolves in water, almost all of its molecules ionize. After the reaction, there are about the same number of hydronium ions in solution as there were molecules of HCl to begin with. The products do not reform reactant molecules. HCl is an example of a strong acid. **When strong acids dissolve in water, they ionize almost completely.** Other strong acids include sulfuric acid, H_2SO_4, and nitric acid, HNO_3.

Strong Bases When dissolved in water, sodium hydroxide almost completely dissociates into sodium and hydroxide ions. Sodium hydroxide is an example of a strong base. **Strong bases dissociate almost completely in water.** Other strong bases include calcium hydroxide, $Ca(OH)_2$, and potassium hydroxide, KOH.

Weak Acids and Bases

The citric acid in orange juice and the acetic acid in vinegar are *weak* acids. Toothpaste and shampoo contain *weak* bases. **Weak acids and bases ionize or dissociate only slightly in water.**

Weak Acids A solution of acetic acid, CH_3COOH, and water can be described by the following equation.

$$CH_3COOH + H_2O \rightleftharpoons CH_3COO^- + H_3O^+$$

The equilibrium favors the reactants over the products, so few ions form in solution. A weak acid forms fewer hydronium ions than a strong acid of the same concentration. This also means that a weak acid has a higher pH than a strong acid of the same concentration.

It is important to understand the difference between concentration and strength. Concentration is the amount of solute dissolved in a given amount of solution. Strength refers to the solute's tendency to form ions in water. You cannot assume that a strong acid has a low pH, because its concentration also affects pH. For instance, a dilute solution of HCl (a strong acid) can have a pH of 6. But a concentrated solution of acetic acid (a weak acid) can have a pH of 3.

Weak Bases Ammonia, NH_3, is a colorless gas with a distinctive smell. When it dissolves in water, very little of it ionizes. Equilibrium favors the reactants, so few NH_4^+ and OH^- ions are produced.

$$NH_3 + H_2O \rightleftharpoons NH_4^+ + OH^-$$

Buffers Weak acids and bases can be used to make buffers. A **buffer** is a solution that is resistant to large changes in pH. Buffers can be prepared by mixing a weak acid and its salt or a weak base and its salt. Because a buffer can react with both an acid and a base, its pH remains relatively constant.

Electrolytes

Sports drinks, like the one shown in Figure 23, taste salty because they contain salts of elements such as sodium, potassium, and calcium. Salts are examples of electrolytes. An **electrolyte** is a substance that ionizes or dissociates into ions when it dissolves in water. The resulting solution can conduct electric current. The electrolytes in sports drinks help restore the balance of ions in your body.

Electrolytes can be classified as strong or weak. **Strong acids and bases are strong electrolytes because they dissociate or ionize almost completely in water.** For example, sodium hydroxide is a strong electrolyte that produces many ions in water. Salts are also strong electrolytes. When potassium chloride dissolves in water, it dissociates into potassium and chloride ions. In contrast, acetic acid is a weak electrolyte because it only partially ionizes.

Batteries and other portable devices that produce electricity also contain electrolytes. Car batteries use lead plates in combination with the electrolyte sulfuric acid to produce electricity. Space shuttles use devices called fuel cells that provide electricity to power all the crafts' devices. Fuel cells use the strong base potassium hydroxide as an electrolyte. Instead of metal electrodes, the fuel cells use oxygen and hydrogen brought from Earth. At the same time that the fuel cells provide electrical energy to power a space shuttle, they also produce water that the crew can use.

Figure 23 Drinking sports drinks after exercising can restore the balance of ions in your body.

Section 8.4 Assessment

Reviewing Concepts

1. How is pH related to the concentration of hydronium ions in solution?

2. What determines the degree to which an acid or base is weak or strong?

3. Are strong acids and bases good electrolytes? Explain why or why not.

4. Why is pure water neutral?

5. What is a buffer?

Critical Thinking

6. **Comparing and Contrasting** Explain how the concentration of an acid differs from the strength of an acid.

7. **Relating Cause and Effect** Suppose you add another liter of water to 1 liter of a 1-molar solution of hydrochloric acid. What happens to the number of hydronium ions in solution? What happens to the concentration?

Writing in Science

Explanatory Paragraph Explain the concept of a pH scale, and compare the pH values of acids, bases, and pure water. (*Hint:* Use examples from Figure 22 to help you describe the range of the pH scale.)

River of Life

Just as rivers are used to transport products and raw materials, blood connects the body's living cells, delivering nutrients and carrying away wastes. The exact composition of this red liquid changes continuously as it flows through the body.

Liquid tissue
Blood is a mixture of cells—red blood cells, white blood cells, and platelets—suspended in a water-based solution called plasma. Nutrients, vitamins, and minerals also travel in blood, dissolved in the plasma. The cells and other substances remain suspended in the blood because the heart's pumping action keeps the blood moving.

Red blood cell

White blood cell

Blood components
When left to sit, blood separates into its parts. About 55 percent makes up the liquid top layer and 45 percent makes up the cellular layer below.

Plasma *This liquid part of the blood is about 90 percent water. The other 10 percent includes many dissolved substances, such as proteins and glucose.*

White blood cells and platelets *White blood cells help the body fight disease. Platelets help the blood to clot when bleeding occurs.*

Red blood cells *These cells contain the compound hemoglobin, which carries oxygen from the lungs to cells throughout the body.*

Blood flow

The body's circulation system contains two circuits. In the first, blood is pumped by the heart to the lungs. As oxygenated blood returns to the heart, it is pumped to the remaining tissues in the body through the second circuit.

Lungs *In the lungs, carbon dioxide is removed from the blood, and oxygen is taken up by red blood cells.*

Heart *The heart pumps oxygenated blood, shown in red, from the lungs around the body. At the same time, the heart pumps deoxygenated blood, shown in blue, back to the lungs.*

Cells *Oxygen is delivered to each cell in the body, and carbon dioxide is removed.*

Platelet

Maintaining blood pH levels

For the body to function normally, blood pH must be kept within a narrow range. Buffer systems ensure pH levels are maintained within that range. A buffer is a chemical or a combination of chemicals that can absorb either hydrogen ions (H^+) or hydroxide ions (OH^-). Buffers maintain a relatively constant hydrogen ion concentration. Hydrogen ions produced by chemical reactions in the body are the main threat to your blood's pH. A very important blood buffer system consists of hydrogen carbonate ions (HCO_3^-) and carbonic acid (H_2CO_3) as shown in this equation.

$$HCO_3^- + H^+ \rightleftharpoons H_2CO_3$$

Carbon dioxide (CO_2) dissolved in the blood acts as an acid. It forms carbonic acid when dissolved in water, and donates hydrogen ions when they are needed. Hydrogen carbonate, produced by the kidneys, is a base that soaks up hydrogen ions when there are too many of them, and transports them to the lungs where the acid is excreted as carbon dioxide.

Using Blood

Because blood is continuously replenished by the body, it can be taken from healthy people and made available for those who need it—whether because of blood loss in accidents or surgery, or to treat illnesses such as anemia or cancer.

Blood banks store blood from donors, or sometimes from a patient, for use during a planned surgery. Once collected, compounds are added to prevent clotting. Most blood is separated into components. For example, plasma can be stored at −18°C for up to 12 months, while platelets are stored at room temperature and must be used within 5 days.

Charles Drew
During the 1940s, physician and inventor Charles Drew developed methods for separating and storing blood on a large scale, providing the basis for today's Red Cross centers.

1900: Karl Landsteiner
discovers three of the main blood groups (A, B, and O). The fourth group, AB, is discovered in 1902.

1932: First blood bank
is established in Russia, followed in 1937 by the first United States hospital blood bank in Chicago.

1940: Charles Drew
pioneers large-scale separation and storage of blood plasma.

1948: American Red Cross
establishes a national blood collection and distribution program.

Tube containing blood spun at high speed

Centrifuge
A centrifuge works like the spin cycle on a washing machine to separate blood quickly into its different components.

1950: Plastic blood bags are introduced for blood storage, allowing blood to be frozen at lower temperatures and for longer periods.

1985: First HIV testing of donor blood is carried out, followed by other tests to protect transfusion patients from disease.

Blood Transfusion

Each year, more than 4 million people in the United States receive a blood transfusion, either of whole blood or of a blood component, such as plasma or platelets. Before being stored, blood from a donor is tested to make sure it is safe.

Blood bag *The use of whole blood in transfusions has been reduced in recent years but it is retained as a treatment option in cases of massive blood loss.*

Donated blood

Crossmatching blood

Blood groups are used to determine which blood can be given to whom. Antigens, or molecular markers on the surface of red blood cells, determine the type of blood a person can safely receive in a transfusion. If blood of incompatible types is mixed, the red blood cells form clumps instead of mixing properly. These clumps can block blood vessels and even cause death.

Going Further

- Research and write a paragraph about the work of Charles Drew. What methods did he use to prolong the storage time for whole blood? Why did he decide to separate whole blood into plasma and cells for storage?

- Research how the donation of platelets differs from the donation of whole blood. Compare the pros and cons of each process.

Exploration Lab

Preparing a Salt by Neutralization

In this lab, you will prepare table salt by reacting hydrochloric acid (HCl) with sodium hydroxide (NaOH). To be sure that all of the acid and base have reacted, you will use phenolphthalein. You will first have to test the colors of this indicator with a known acid and base. After the acid and base have reacted, you will measure the pH of the solution with pH paper. Finally, you will evaporate the water and collect the sodium chloride.

Problem
How can you produce a salt by neutralization?

Materials
- 3 dropper pipets
- labels
- 10-mL graduated cylinder
- test tube rack
- 2 10-mL test tubes
- distilled water
- hydrochloric acid
- sodium hydroxide solution
- 3 stirring rods
- phenolphthalein solution
- 2 25-mL beakers
- pH paper
- large watch glass
- 100-mL beaker
- hot plate

 For the probeware version of this lab, see Probeware Lab Manual, Lab 3.

Skills
Observing, Measuring, Analyzing Data

Procedure

Part A: Preparing for the Experiment

1. On a separate sheet of paper, copy the data table shown.

Data Table	
Material(s)	Observation
1 mL	_____ drops
HCl + phenolphthalein	_____ (color)
NaOH + phenolphthalein	_____ (color)
Drops of HCl used	_____ drops
mL of HCl used	_____ mL
Drops of NaOH used	_____ drops
mL of NaOH used	_____ mL
pH of final solution	_____

2. Place about 10 mL of distilled water in a 25-mL beaker. Set the graduated cylinder on the table and add distilled water to the 5-mL mark. Be sure that the *bottom* of the meniscus is on the 5-mL line.

3. To determine the number of drops in 1 mL, use a clean dropper pipet to add 1 mL of water to the graduated cylinder. Hold the dropper pipet straight up and down with the tip of the dropper pipet just inside the mouth of the cylinder. As your partner watches the liquid level in the cylinder, add drops of water one at a time while counting the drops. Continue adding drops until the liquid level reaches 6 mL. Record the number of drops in 1 mL.

4. Label one clean dropper pipet *Hydrochloric acid (HCl)* and the other *Sodium hydroxide (NaOH)*.

5. Using the HCl dropper pipet, add 3 mL of hydrochloric acid to a clean test tube. **CAUTION** *Hydrochloric acid is corrosive. In case of spills, clean thoroughly with water.* Add 2 to 3 drops of phenolphthalein to the test tube. Use a clean stirring rod to mix the hydrochloric acid and indicator. Record your observations.

6. Using the dropper pipet labeled NaOH, add 3 mL of sodium hydroxide solution to a clean test tube. **CAUTION** *Sodium hydroxide is corrosive. In case of spills, clean thoroughly with water.* Add 2 to 3 drops of phenolphthalein to the test tube. Use a clean stirring rod to mix the sodium hydroxide solution and indicator. Record your observations.

Part B: Making the Salt

7. Using the HCl dropper pipet, add 4 mL of hydrochloric acid to a clean 25-mL beaker. Record the number of drops you used. Add 2 to 3 drops of phenolphthalein to the beaker.

8. Use the NaOH dropper pipet to add sodium hydroxide drop by drop to the beaker of hydrochloric acid and phenolphthalein, stirring constantly. Count the drops as you add them. As a pink color remains longer, add the drops more slowly.

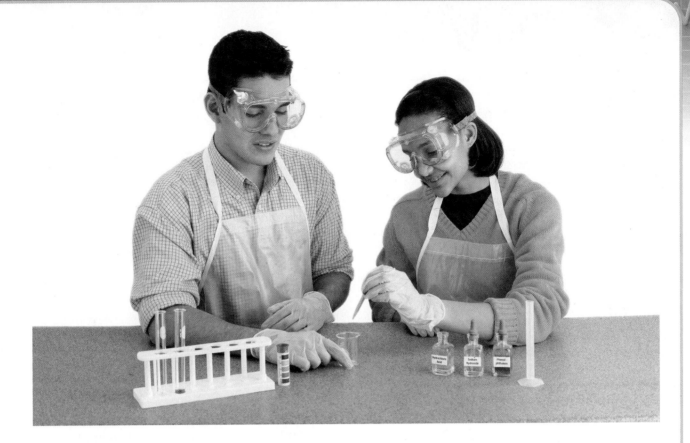

9. Continue to add and count the drops of sodium hydroxide until a light pink color remains for at least 30 seconds. (Note: If you add too much sodium hydroxide, add a few more drops of hydrochloric acid until the color disappears.) Record any additional drops of hydrochloric acid that you added. Then, carefully add sodium hydroxide until one drop produces a lasting pink color. Record the total number of drops of sodium hydroxide used.

10. Use a piece of pH paper to determine the pH of the final solution. Record the pH. If the pH is higher than 7.0, add hydrochloric acid drop by drop, testing the pH with pH paper after each drop, until the pH is equal to 7.0. Record the pH and the total number of drops of HCl you added.

11. Use the solution in the beaker to fill the watch glass halfway.

12. Fill the 100-mL beaker about half full of water. Place the beaker on top of the hot plate.

13. Set the watch glass on top of the beaker.

14. Turn on the hot plate to a low setting. Adjust the heat as the water in the beaker warms. The water should simmer, but not boil.

CAUTION *Do not touch the hot plate or the beaker.* Heat until a solid is visible at the edges of the water in the watch glass and the water is nearly evaporated. Turn off the heat.

15. Allow the remaining water to evaporate. Observe the contents of the watch glass. Record your observations.

16. When the watch glass has cooled, dispose of the contents as directed by your teacher. Clean up your equipment. Wash your hands with soap and water.

Analyze and Conclude

1. **Comparing and Contrasting** What was the total amount of hydrochloric acid used to make the neutral solution? What was the total amount of sodium hydroxide? How do the amounts compare?

2. **Drawing Conclusions** What do you conclude about the concentrations of hydrochloric acid and sodium hydroxide in the solutions?

3. **Predicting** If the acid had been twice as concentrated as the base, how would your data have changed?

8.1 Formation of Solutions

Key Concepts

- Substances can dissolve in water in three ways—through dissociation, dispersion, and ionization.
- Three physical properties of a solution that can differ from those of its solute and solvent are conductivity, freezing point, and boiling point.
- During the formation of a solution, energy is either released or absorbed.
- Factors that affect the rate of dissolving include surface area, temperature, and stirring.

Vocabulary

solute, *p. 229;* solvent, *p. 229;* dissociation, *p. 229;* dispersion, *p. 230;* ionization, *p. 230*

8.2 Solubility and Concentration

Key Concepts

- Solutions are described as unsaturated, saturated, or supersaturated, depending on the amount of solute in solution.
- Three factors that affect the solubility of a solute are the type of bonding in the solute and solvent, temperature, and pressure.
- Concentration can be expressed as percent by volume, percent by mass, and molarity.

Vocabulary

solubility, *p. 235;* saturated solution, *p. 236;* unsaturated solution, *p. 236;* supersaturated solution, *p. 236;* concentration, *p. 238;* molarity, *p. 239*

8.3 Properties of Acids and Bases

Key Concepts

- Acids taste sour, react with certain metals, and turn blue litmus paper red. Bases taste bitter, feel slippery, and turn red litmus paper blue.
- The neutralization reaction between an acid and a base produces a salt and water.
- Acids can be defined as proton donors, and bases can be defined as proton acceptors.

Vocabulary

acid, *p. 240;* indicator, *p. 241;* base, *p. 242;* neutralization, *p. 244;* salt, *p. 244*

8.4 Strength of Acids and Bases

Key Concepts

- The lower the pH value, the greater the H_3O^+ ion concentration is. The higher the pH value, the lower the H_3O^+ ion concentration is.
- The strength of an acid or a base depends on the degree to which it dissociates or ionizes in water.
- Strong acids and bases are good electrolytes because they produce many ions in solution.

Vocabulary

pH, *p. 247;* buffer, *p. 248;* electrolyte, *p. 249*

Thinking Visually

Concept Map Use the information on acids and bases to complete the concept map below.

Reviewing Content

Choose the letter that best answers the question or completes the statement.

1. The parts of a solution are the
    a. salt and vapor.   **b.** solvent and solid.
    c. solute and water.   **d.** solute and solvent.

2. In a solution, the solute is the substance that
    a. dissolves in the solvent.
    b. is in the greatest quantity.
    c. is the liquid.
    d. is a solid.

3. Sugar dissolves in water through
    a. ionization.   **b.** dissociation.
    c. neutralization.   **d.** dispersion.

4. Ionic compounds produce ions in solution by
    a. ionization.   **b.** dissociation.
    c. evaporation.   **d.** dispersion.

5. The process by which some molecular compounds dissolve in water to form ions is
    a. ionization.   **b.** dissociation.
    c. neutralization.   **d.** dispersion.

6. The boiling point of a liquid solution is
    a. the same as the boiling point of the solvent.
    b. the same as the boiling point of the solute.
    c. higher than the boiling point of the solvent.
    d. lower than the boiling point of the solvent.

7. Which of the following is NOT characteristic of an acid?
    a. tastes sour
    b. reacts with metals
    c. turns litmus paper blue
    d. produces H_3O^+ ions in solution

8. The reaction between an acid and a base is called
    a. ionization.   **b.** neutralization.
    c. dissociation.   **d.** dispersion.

9. A solution of sodium hydroxide in water is most likely to have a pH close to
    a. 14.   **b.** 7.
    c. 5.   **d.** 3.

10. Substances that form ions when dissolved in water are
    a. solutions.   **b.** molecules.
    c. polar.   **d.** electrolytes.

Understanding Concepts

11. How does increasing the temperature of a solvent affect the solubility of a gas?

12. Explain why the temperature of water might increase when a solution forms.

13. Explain why crushing a solute increases the rate of solution.

14. Name and describe the three types of solutions.

15. Explain why oil does not dissolve in water.

16. Describe how you might increase the solubility of a solid in a liquid.

17. Explain how a solution can be both dilute and saturated.

18. Describe three different ways in which the concentration of a solution can be reported.

19. Define and give an example of an acid and of a base.

20. List the properties of acids and bases. Which of the properties would you use to safely test whether an unknown substance was an acid or a base?

21. If you add hydrochloric acid (HCl) to magnesium (Mg) metal, what will you observe? What products form in this reaction?

22. Identify each of the following compounds as an acid, base, or salt: LiOH, H_2CO_3, Ba(OH)$_2$, and KCl.

23. What determines the strength of an acid?

24. What happens when a solution of nitric acid (HNO$_3$) is added to a solution of potassium hydroxide (KOH)? What are the products?

25. Which of the following compounds can react with H_2SO_4 to form a salt: NaCl, Ca(OH)$_2$, HF, AlCl$_3$, H_2O, Mg(OH)$_2$? Name the salt(s) that would form.

Critical Thinking

26. Comparing and Contrasting Compare what happens when NaCl and HCl are added to water.

27. Calculating The molar mass of sucrose, or table sugar, is 342 grams. Calculate how many grams of sucrose are required to make 3.0 liters of 0.50 M sucrose solution.

28. Applying Concepts A solution is an acid or a base, and it doesn't react with metal. Is its pH more likely to be 4 or 9? Explain your answer.

29. Inferring You have equal amounts of three colorless liquids, X, Y, and Z. An indicator is yellow in a pH of 8 or less and blue in a pH of 8 or more. The indicator turns blue in X and yellow in Y and Z. When you add liquid Z to X, the indicator turns yellow. When you add Z to Y, the solution remains yellow. Which liquid could be water?

Math Skills

Use the graph to answer Questions 30–32.

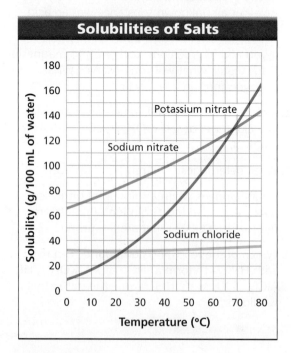

30. Using Graphs Which compound is the most soluble at 75°C?

31. Interpreting Diagrams What kind of solution would you have if it contained 50 grams of sodium chloride in 100 mL of water at 30°C?

32. Calculating How many grams of sodium nitrate would you need to make 100 mL of a saturated solution at 25°C?

Concepts in Action

33. Designing an Experiment Commercials often say that antacids "neutralize excess stomach acid." Stomach acid is hydrochloric acid with a pH of around 1–4 depending on what and how recently you have eaten. Design an experiment to test how effective various brands of antacids are at neutralizing stomach acid.

34. Making Judgments A single dose of antacid A changes the pH of stomach contents from 1 to 3. A single dose of antacid B changes the pH of stomach contents from 1 to 8. Which antacid would you choose to use? Explain your answer.

35. Writing in Science You are in charge of writing the directions for a safety workers' training manual. The manual tells workers what to do if a train carrying nitric acid derails and the acid spills. What are some things they could do to clean up the spill? Write the procedures in steps, explaining why each step is done.

Performance-Based Assessment

Making a Display Prepare a classroom display on the importance of acids and bases in daily life. Include information on the properties of acids and bases, as well as examples of where they are found in daily life. Research ways in which manufacturers use acids and bases to produce common items and include that information in your display.

For: Self-grading assessment
Visit: PHSchool.com
Web Code: cca-1080

Standardized Test Prep

Test-Taking Tip

Some test questions may include a drawing of lab equipment. It is important that you carefully study the information presented in the question as well as the picture provided. Keep these tips in mind when answering a question with lab equipment drawings:

- Identify the equipment shown so you can determine what information the drawing can or cannot give you.

- Think of similar labs or questions you may have seen. These may help you determine the information available from the drawing.

- The drawings may not be drawn to scale. You must read and interpret the scales and increments carefully.

- Carefully read the question. You may not need all the information presented in the drawing or you may need more information than is presented in the drawing.

Practice using these tips in Question 6.

1. Which of the following will NOT increase the rate at which a solute dissolves in a solvent?
   (A) increasing the surface area of the solute
   (B) stirring the solvent
   (C) increasing the temperature
   (D) increasing the particle size of the solute
   (E) agitating the mixture

2. At 20°C, a saturated solution contains 36 g of NaCl and 100 mL of water. All the solid is dissolved. What happens if the solution is slowly cooled to 0°C?
   (A) It freezes.
   (B) It becomes supersaturated.
   (C) The pressure on it increases greatly.
   (D) More NaCl could be dissolved in it.
   (E) The NaCl reacts with the water.

3. Which pH indicates a solution of an acid?
   (A) pH = 3
   (B) pH = 7
   (C) pH = 9
   (D) pH = 14
   (E) pH = 19

4. Which substance is a weak base?
   (A) NaCl
   (B) NH_3
   (C) HCl
   (D) HF
   (E) KOH

5. What reaction occurs when a solution of hydrochloric acid, HCl, is mixed with a solution of calcium hydroxide, $Ca(OH)_2$?
   (A) $Cl + Ca(OH) \longrightarrow HCa + Cl(OH)_2$
   (B) $HCl + Ca(OH)_2 \longrightarrow H(OH)_2 + CaCl$
   (C) $2HCl + Ca(OH)_2 \longrightarrow 2H_2O + CaCl_2$
   (D) $2HCl + Ca(OH)_2 \longrightarrow H_2Ca + 2ClOH$
   (E) $HCl + Ca(OH)_2 \longrightarrow$ no reaction occurs

0.1 M HCl   0.1 M NaOH

6. If the contents of the two beakers shown above are mixed, the resulting solution
   (A) will turn red litmus paper blue.
   (B) will turn blue litmus paper red.
   (C) will resist large changes in pH.
   (D) will react with metals.
   (E) will not change the color of red or blue litmus paper.

21st Century Learning
Global Awareness

What fossil fuels are used to create electricity?

Fossil fuels account for the great majority of the world's energy use. Research online to identify the types of fossil fuels used by power plants to generate electricity. Determine the pros and cons of these fuels, and find out how much electricity is produced in the United States using each type of fossil fuel. Create a multimedia presentation summarizing your research.

How do science concepts apply to your world? Here are some questions you'll be able to answer after you read this chapter.

- **Why do homes that are heated with oil or natural gas often have carbon monoxide detectors?** *(Section 9.1)*

- **How are coal-burning power plants reducing air pollution?** *(page 270)*

- **What makes the odor of rotten fish so different from the odor of roses?** *(Section 9.2)*

- **What do tires, a trash bag, and pasta have in common?** *(Section 9.3)*

- **How does your body release the energy stored in food?** *(Section 9.4)*

Chapter Preview

This drilling platform will be used to pump petroleum from layers of rock beneath the ocean floor.

Inquiry Activity

Do All Carbon Compounds Have Similar Properties?

Procedure

1. Examine samples of sucrose, cellulose, isopropyl alcohol, polystyrene, and polypropylene. All five compounds contain carbon and hydrogen. Sucrose, cellulose, and isopropyl alcohol contain oxygen, too.

2. Record a set of physical properties for each compound. Include some of the properties you studied in Chapter 2.

Think About It

1. **Making Generalizations** Is there any property you observed that you could use to classify a compound as a carbon compound?

2. **Formulating Hypotheses** Why does carbon form many more compounds than other elements do? (*Hint:* How many valence electrons does carbon have and what type of bonds does it form?)

9.1 Carbon Compounds

Reading Focus

Key Concepts

- What are three forms of carbon?
- What factors determine the properties of a hydrocarbon?
- What are the three types of unsaturated hydrocarbons?
- What are the three main fossil fuels and the two primary products of their combustion?

Vocabulary

- organic compound
- network solid
- hydrocarbon
- saturated hydrocarbon
- isomers
- unsaturated hydrocarbon
- aromatic hydrocarbons
- fossil fuels

Reading Strategy

Previewing Copy the table below. Before you read, use the models in Figure 2 to describe the arrangement of carbon atoms in each form of carbon.

Forms of Carbon Compounds	
Diamond	a. ?
Graphite	b. ?
Buckminsterfullerene	c. ?

Figure 1 A whale's survival depends on carbon compounds. Carbon compounds form the structures of a whale's cells and control reactions that take place in those cells. The instructions for these processes are stored in organic compounds.

Until 1828, chemists divided compounds into compounds that chemists could produce and compounds that only organisms could produce. The compounds produced by *organisms* were called *organic* compounds. In 1828, a German chemist, Friedrich Wöhler, mixed silver cyanate, AgOCN, with ammonium chloride, NH_4Cl. He expected to make ammonium cyanate. Instead, he produced urea, $(NH_2)_2CO$, which is a product of reactions that occur in the livers of many organisms. Wöhler had synthesized an organic compound.

An **organic compound** contains carbon and hydrogen, often combined with a few other elements, such as oxygen and nitrogen. There are millions of organic compounds—more than 90 percent of all known compounds. Remember that carbon has four valence electrons. So, a carbon atom can form four single covalent bonds, or a double bond and two single bonds, or a triple bond and a single bond. Most of the bonds in organic compounds are carbon-to-carbon bonds or carbon-to-hydrogen bonds.

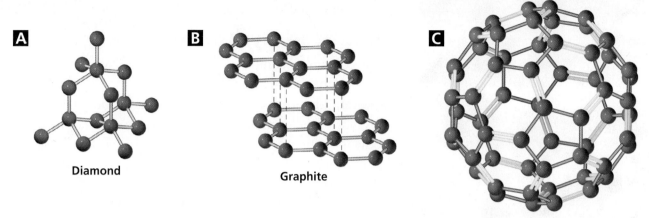

A Diamond

B Graphite

C Buckminsterfullerene

Forms of Carbon

The element carbon exists in several forms with different properties. ⬤ **Diamond, graphite, and fullerenes are forms of carbon.** In each form, there is a different arrangement of bonded carbon atoms.

Diamond Cutting, grinding, and drilling tools are often coated with diamond because no substance is harder than diamond. Diamond is an example of a network solid. In a **network solid,** all the atoms are linked by covalent bonds. A network solid is sometimes described as a single molecule. Figure 2A shows how the carbon atoms are linked in diamond. Covalent bonds connect each carbon atom in diamond to four other carbon atoms. The three-dimensional structure that results is rigid, compact, and strong. Diamond is harder than other substances because cutting a diamond requires breaking many covalent bonds.

Graphite A second form of carbon, graphite, has very different properties from diamond. It is extremely soft and slippery. Figure 2B shows how the carbon atoms in graphite are arranged in widely spaced layers. Within each layer, each carbon atom forms strong covalent bonds with three other carbon atoms. Between graphite layers the bonds are weak, which allows the layers to slide easily past one another. Because graphite is soft and slippery, it is a good lubricant for moving metal parts in machinery. Pencil "lead" is a mixture of graphite and clay. The layered structure of graphite explains why you can make pencil marks on paper and why the marks can be erased easily.

Fullerenes In 1985, researchers discovered a third form of carbon in the soot produced when some carbon compounds burn. Fullerenes are large hollow spheres, or cages, of carbon. These cages have since been found in meteorites. Figure 2C shows a model of a cage made from 60 carbon atoms. On the surface of the cage, the atoms form alternating hexagons and pentagons, like a soccer ball cover. The C_{60} molecule is called buckminsterfullerene after Buckminster Fuller, an architect who designed domes with similar geometric patterns.

Figure 2 There are several forms of carbon. **A** In diamond, carbon atoms are arranged in a rigid, three-dimensional network. **B** In graphite, the atoms are arranged in layers. **C** In fullerenes, carbon atoms are arranged in hollow spheres. **Predicting** *Are the properties of fullerenes more like those of diamond or of graphite? Give a reason for your choice.*

Go **Online**

For: Activity on carbon bonding
Visit: PHSchool.com
Web Code: ccp-1091

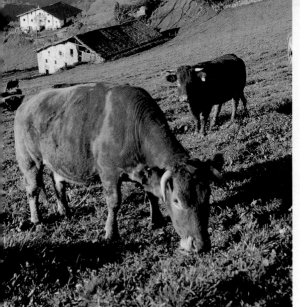

Figure 3 Microorganisms in the stomachs of a cow produce more than 500 liters of methane (CH₄) per day.

Figure 4 Molecules of ethane, propane, pentane, and octane have two, three, five, and eight carbon atoms, respectively. **Making Generalizations** *How does increasing the number of carbon atoms affect the boiling point of a straight-chain alkane?*

Saturated Hydrocarbons

Grass contains a compound called cellulose. Most organisms, including the grazing cows in Figure 3, cannot digest cellulose. However, microorganisms in cows' stomachs break down cellulose into smaller molecules that cows can digest. One of the products of this process is methane, CH_4, which is a hydrocarbon. A **hydrocarbon** is an organic compound that contains only the elements hydrogen and carbon. Methane is a saturated hydrocarbon. In a **saturated hydrocarbon,** all of the bonds are single bonds. A saturated hydrocarbon contains the maximum possible number of hydrogen atoms for each carbon atom. Another name for a saturated hydrocarbon is an alkane. Names of alkane compounds end in –*ane,* as in methane and propane.

 Factors that determine the properties of a hydrocarbon are the number of carbon atoms and how the atoms are arranged. A hydrocarbon molecule can contain one carbon atom, as in methane, or more than 30 carbon atoms, as in asphalt. The carbon atoms can be arranged in a straight chain, a branched chain, or a ring.

Straight Chains Figure 4 lists the names, molecular formulas, structural formulas, and boiling points for four straight-chain alkanes. Recall that a molecular formula shows the type and number of atoms in a molecule of the compound. A structural formula shows how those atoms are arranged. The number of carbon atoms in a straight-chain alkane affects the state of the alkane at room temperature. Methane and propane are gases. Pentane and octane are liquids. The more carbon atoms, the higher the boiling point is.

✓ **Reading Checkpoint** *What is another name for a saturated hydrocarbon?*

Some Straight-Chain Alkanes				
Name	Methane	Propane	Pentane	Octane
Molecular Formula	CH_4	C_3H_8	C_5H_{12}	C_8H_{18}
Structural Formula	H | H−C−H | H	H H H | | | H−C−C−C−H | | | H H H	H H H H H | | | | | H−C−C−C−C−C−H | | | | | H H H H H	H H H H H H H H | | | | | | | | H−C−C−C−C−C−C−C−C−H | | | | | | | | H H H H H H H H
Boiling Point	−161.5°C	−42.1°C	36.0°C	125.6°C

Quick Lab

Comparing Isomers

Materials

30 marshmallows, 70 raisins, 50 toothpicks

Procedure

1. Use marshmallows to represent carbon atoms, and raisins to represent hydrogen atoms, as in the model of propane shown. **CAUTION** *Do not eat anything in the laboratory.* Break the toothpicks in half to represent single bonds. Build models of five different isomers of hexane (C_6H_{14}).

2. For each model, attach all six carbon atoms first. Then attach hydrogen atoms until each carbon atom has four bonds.

Analyze and Conclude

1. **Using Models** Draw a structural formula for each isomer.

2. **Predicting** Would pentane (C_5H_{12}) or heptane (C_7H_{16}) have more isomers than hexane? Explain your answer.

Branched Chains Look at the butane and isobutane formulas in Figure 5. Both compounds have a molecular formula of C_4H_{10}, but their structural formulas are different. In isobutane, there is a branch at the point where a carbon atom bonds to three other carbon atoms.

Compounds with the same molecular formula but different structural formulas are **isomers.** Differences in structure affect some properties of isomers. Butane boils at –0.5°C, but isobutane boils at –11.7°C. The number of possible isomers increases rapidly each time an additional carbon atom is added to the chain. For example, octane (C_8H_{18}) has 18 isomers, while decane ($C_{10}H_{22}$) has 75.

Rings Figure 5 also shows the structural formula for cyclobutane. The carbon atoms in cyclobutane are linked in a four-carbon ring. Because each carbon atom forms bonds with two other carbon atoms, it can bond with only two hydrogen atoms. So cyclobutane (C_4H_8) molecules have two fewer hydrogen atoms than butane (C_4H_{10}) molecules. Most ring alkanes, or cyclic hydrocarbons, have rings with five or six carbons.

Figure 5 Butane, isobutane, and cyclobutane represent three ways that carbon atoms are arranged in an alkane—in a straight chain, in a branched chain, and in a ring. Classifying *Explain why butane and cyclobutane are not isomers.*

Unsaturated Hydrocarbons

A hydrocarbon that contains one or more double or triple bonds is an **unsaturated hydrocarbon.** These hydrocarbons are classified by bond type and the arrangement of their carbon atoms. 🔑 **There are three types of unsaturated hydrocarbons—alkenes, alkynes, and aromatic hydrocarbons.**

Figure 6 There are three types of unsaturated hydrocarbons.
A Ethene is an alkene that controls the ripening of a tomato.
B Ethyne is an alkyne used in torches that cut metals or weld them together. **C** Kekulé figured out the ring structure of the aromatic hydrocarbon benzene.

Alkenes Many fruit-bearing plants produce ethene (C_2H_4), which controls the rate at which fruits, such as the tomato in Figure 6A, ripen. There is a double bond between the two carbon atoms in ethene. Hydrocarbons that have one or more carbon-carbon double bonds are alkenes. The names of alkenes end in *–ene*. Plastics used in trash bags and milk jugs are produced by reactions involving ethene.

Alkynes In 1895, Henry-Louis Le Châtelier reported that a flame produced when ethyne burned had a temperature about 1000°C higher than a flame produced when hydrogen burns. Ethyne (C_2H_2), also known as acetylene, is an alkyne. Alkynes are straight- or branched-chain hydrocarbons that have one or more triple bonds. Alkyne names end in *–yne*.

Alkynes are the most reactive hydrocarbon compounds. The welder in Figure 6B is burning a mixture of oxygen and acetylene in an oxyacetylene torch. The temperature of the flame produced approaches 3500°C. At that temperature, most metals can be melted and welded together. The acetylene and oxygen are stored under pressure in tanks.

Aromatic Hydrocarbons The Belgian stamp in Figure 6C honors Friedrich Kekulé (1829–1896), who figured out that benzene (C_6H_6) is an unsaturated hydrocarbon with a ring structure. Although the formula shows alternating single and double bonds, the six bonds in the ring are identical. Six of the valence electrons are shared by all six carbon atoms. Hydrocarbons that contain similar ring structures are known as **aromatic hydrocarbons.** The name was chosen because many of these compounds have strong aromas or odors.

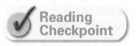

Reading Checkpoint *What is an unsaturated hydrocarbon?*

Fossil Fuels

Some hydrocarbons were formed from plants and animals that lived in Earth's oceans and swamps millions of years ago. After those plants and animals died, they were buried under layers of rock and soil. High temperature and pressure deep in Earth's crust changed those remains into deposits of hydrocarbons called fossil fuels. **Fossil fuels are mixtures of hydrocarbons that formed from the remains of plants or animals.** **Three types of fossil fuels are coal, natural gas, and petroleum.** The type of fossil fuel produced depends on the origin of the organic material and the conditions under which it decays.

Coal The ferns in Figure 7A are similar to those that produced the coal in Figure 7B. Coal is a solid fossil fuel that began to form about 300 million years ago in ancient swamps. Giant tree ferns and other plants were buried in those swamps. After millions of years of pressure, the plant remains produced a mixture of hydrocarbons. Most of the hydrocarbons in coal are aromatic hydrocarbons with high molar masses. These compounds have a high ratio of carbon to hydrogen. So burning coal produces more soot than burning other fossil fuels does.

Natural Gas The second main fossil fuel, natural gas, formed from the remains of marine organisms. Natural gas is mostly methane. It also contains ethane, propane, and isomers of butane. Natural gas is distributed through a network of underground pipes. It is used for heating and cooking, and to generate some electricity. Deposits of natural gas are found with deposits of coal and petroleum. Enormous amounts of unused natural gas resources also exist as methane frozen together with water, called methane hydrate. Methane hydrate is found in Arctic soils and in offshore sediments.

Petroleum The third main fossil fuel, petroleum, also formed from the remains of marine organisms. Petroleum, often known as crude oil, is pumped from deep beneath the Earth's surface. It is a complex liquid mixture of hydrocarbons, comprised mainly of long-branched alkanes and alkenes. For petroleum to be useful, it must be separated into simpler mixtures, or fractions, such as gasoline and heating oil.

Figure 7 Fossil fuels form from the remains of plants and animals. **A** The ferns shown are similar to ferns that lived millions of years ago. **B** The imprints of ferns left on the lump of coal are evidence that the coal formed when plant remains were compressed under layers of rock and soil.

For: Links on fossil fuels
Visit: www.SciLinks.org
Web Code: ccn-1091

The labels show the following fractions:
- Petroleum gas < 40°C C_1 to C_4
- Gasoline 40°–200°C C_5 to C_{12}
- Kerosene, jet fuel 200°–250°C C_{12} to C_{16}
- Heating oil 250°–300°C C_{15} to C_{18}
- Lubricating oil 300°–370°C $\geq C_{19}$
- Residue, asphalt $\geq C_{25}$

Distillation Tower

Crude oil vapors

Crude oil

Heating burner

Figure 8 The petroleum pumped from underground deposits is a complex mixture of hydrocarbons. **A** At a refinery, petroleum is separated into mixtures called fractions. **B** The diagram shows some of the fractions that can be collected from a distillation tower. The labels provide data on the compounds within a fraction. For example, compounds in kerosene have from 12 to 16 carbon atoms and condense at temperatures between 200°C and 250°C. **Interpreting Diagrams** *How many carbon atoms are there in the compounds in the petroleum gas fraction?*

For: Activity on photochemical smog
Visit: PHSchool.com
Web Code: ccc-1090

The diagram in Figure 8B shows how petroleum is separated into fractions through a type of distillation called fractional distillation. When petroleum is heated in a distillation tower, most of the hydrocarbons vaporize. The vapors rise through the tower and condense as the temperature decreases. Compounds with higher boiling points condense first. They are collected near the bottom of the tower.

Combustion of Fossil Fuels

The energy released from fossil fuels through combustion is used to heat buildings, cook food, or for transportation. Recall that energy from the combustion of propane heats the air in a hot-air balloon.

$$C_3H_8 + 5O_2 \longrightarrow 3CO_2 + 4H_2O \text{ (complete combustion)}$$

🔑 **The primary products of the complete combustion of fossil fuels are carbon dioxide and water.** Burning fossil fuels increases the amount of carbon dioxide in the atmosphere. This increase may affect temperatures, amounts of rain, and sea levels worldwide. Some sulfur and nitrogen are in fossil fuels, and air contains nitrogen. So nitrogen oxides and sulfur dioxide are produced during the combustion of fossil fuels.

Incomplete Combustion In stoves and furnaces, there may not be enough oxygen available for complete combustion of all the fuel. So a deadly gas, carbon monoxide, is produced. This colorless, odorless gas can be inhaled and absorbed by blood. It keeps hemoglobin from carrying oxygen to cells. Safety experts recommend that homes heated with natural gas or heating oil have carbon monoxide detectors.

$$2C_3H_8 + 7O_2 \longrightarrow 6CO + 8H_2O \text{ (incomplete combustion)}$$

When fossil fuels undergo incomplete combustion in factories or power plants, they also produce tiny particles of carbon. Inhaling these particles can cause heart and lung problems.

Figure 9 This statue of George Washington was sculpted from marble in 1918. The photograph was taken in the 1990s. The damage was done by calcium carbonate in the marble reacting with sulfuric acid in acid rain.

Acid Rain The combustion of fossil fuels causes the acidity of rain to increase. Rain is always slightly acidic, with a pH of about 5.6, because carbon dioxide dissolves in water droplets and forms carbonic acid, H_2CO_3. Sulfur dioxide and nitrogen oxides released into the atmosphere also dissolve in water, forming sulfuric acid, H_2SO_4, and nitric acid, HNO_3. The pH of rain containing sulfuric acid and nitric acid can be as low as 2.7. These acids damage stone structures like the statue in Figure 9. They also damage metal and concrete.

For: Activity on acid rain
Visit: PHSchool.com
Web Code: ccc-1091

Section 9.1 Assessment

Reviewing Concepts

1. Name three forms of carbon.

2. What two factors can affect the properties of a hydrocarbon?

3. Name the three categories of unsaturated hydrocarbons.

4. Name the three main fossil fuels.

5. What are the two primary products of the complete combustion of fossil fuels?

6. What are three ways that carbon atoms can be arranged in hydrocarbon molecules?

Critical Thinking

7. **Classifying** Why isn't carbon dioxide considered an organic compound?

8. **Applying Concepts** Draw structural formulas for the two branched-chain isomers of pentane, C_5H_{12}.

Connecting Concepts

Saturation Compare the way *saturated* and *unsaturated* are used in describing hydrocarbons to how they were used in describing solutions in Section 8.2.

Breathing Easy

Coal-burning power stations produce more than half the electricity in the United States. An average coal-burning power station emits about 10,000 tons each of sulfur dioxide and nitrogen oxides each year.

Oxides of sulfur and nitrogen cause smog and acid rain, and can irritate your lungs. The Clean Coal Technology Program in the United States encourages the development of technologies that reduce emissions of these harmful gases. The diagram shows how these emissions are reduced. The process begins when sulfur is washed from the surface of coal and ends when cleaner air is released into the atmosphere. Researchers are also exploring ways to capture the carbon dioxide that is produced to keep it from entering the atmosphere.

Hot gases out

Coal

Coal and limestone

FURNACE 1

Cyclone separator

3 Cyclone separator The cyclone separates the unburned fuel from the hot gases.

FURNACE 2

1 Washing coal The coal is crushed and washed to remove sulfur from its surface. When the coal is placed in a water-filled tank, the coal floats to the surface while the sulfur impurities sink to the bottom.

Hot air jets

Air in

Unburned fuel from furnace 1

2 Furnace 1 A mixture of coal and limestone floats on a stream of hot air in the furnace. Calcium carbonate in the limestone reacts with sulfur dioxide to form calcium sulfate. The amount of air is limited and the temperature is held low to keep nitrogen from reacting with oxygen.

More limestone added

Cyclone separator

Air in

4 Furnace 2 Unburned coal from the first furnace is transferred into furnace 2 for further burning. More limestone is added to react with any sulfur dioxide produced.

Electric
generator

Gas turbine

Steam
turbine

Chimney

Particle
filters

Condenser

Steam
out

Boiler

Water in

6 Particle filter
Hot gases from the furnaces
are fed through filters
made of tightly woven
fabric. The filters trap tiny
particles of coal and ash
and prevent them from
entering the gas turbine.

Heat
exchanger

7 Heat exchanger Waste
gases are cooled in the
heat exchanger by a coil
containing cold water. The
cooled and cleaned gases,
containing dramatically
reduced amounts of sulfur
dioxide and nitrogen
oxides, are emitted from
the chimney.

5 Boiler Water from the
condenser flows through pipes
in the boiler. Hot gases from
furnace 2 are fed into the
boiler to heat the water. The
steam created is used to spin a
steam turbine. The hot gases
are fed back to furnace 2 so
unburned fuel can react.

Going Further

- Research the process of coal gasification. Write
  a paragraph describing one of the methods
  used to convert coal into flammable gases.
  What gases are produced? What are the
  benefits of coal gasification? Are there any
  problems with the technology?

- How do the changes that take place in the
  furnaces differ from the changes that take
  place in the cyclone separator and the boiler?

9.2 Substituted Hydrocarbons

Reading Focus

Key Concepts
- What functional groups are found in alcohols, organic acids, and organic bases?
- How are esters formed?

Vocabulary
- substituted hydrocarbon
- functional group

Reading Strategy
Monitoring Your Understanding Copy the table. As you read, complete the table by connecting each functional group with the type of compound that contains the functional group.

Functional Group	Type of Compound
–OH	a. ?
–COOH	b. ?
–NH$_2$	c. ?

The electric drill in Figure 10 can be used to drill holes, tighten a screw, or sand a rough surface. To change the function of the drill, you replace, or substitute, an attachment. A carbon atom in an organic compound can have four attachments. In a methane molecule (CH_4), the carbon atom has four identical attachments—its hydrogen atoms. When methane reacts with chlorine, chlorine atoms replace hydrogen atoms.

$$CH_4 + Cl_2 \longrightarrow CH_3Cl + HCl$$

Chloromethane and hydrogen chloride are products of the reaction between methane and chlorine. So are compounds with two, three, or four chlorine atoms. Organic compounds containing chlorine or other halogens are halocarbons. Almost all the halocarbons found on Earth were released from refrigerators, air conditioners, or aerosol sprays. Researchers have established that halocarbons containing chlorine and fluorine deplete Earth's protective ozone layer. The manufacture of chlorofluorocarbons has been restricted since 1990.

A hydrocarbon in which one or more hydrogen atoms have been replaced by an atom or group of atoms is a **substituted hydrocarbon.** The substituted atom or group of atoms is called a **functional group** because it determines the properties of the compound. Alcohols, organic acids, organic bases, and esters are substituted hydrocarbons.

Figure 10 Hydrocarbons in which some hydrogen atoms have been replaced can be compared to an electric drill with attachments.
Inferring *What determines the function of the drill, the drill itself or the attachments?*

hole saw bit

Forstner drill bit

Phillips screwdriver bit

twist drill bit

drum sander

Exploring Boiling Points of Chlorocarbons

Use the data given to construct a graph with *Number of Chlorine Atoms,* from 0 to 4, on the horizontal axis and *Boiling Point* on the vertical axis. Draw a smooth curve connecting the points.

1. **Using Graphs** Predict the boiling point of dichloromethane.

2. **Relating Cause and Effect** What effect does increasing the number of chlorine atoms have on the boiling point?

Boiling Points of Methane and Its Substituted Chlorocarbons

Name	Formula	Boiling Point (°C)
Methane	CH_4	−161
Chloromethane	CH_3Cl	−24
Dichloromethane	CH_2Cl_2	?
Trichloromethane	$CHCl_3$	61
Tetrachloromethane	CCl_4	77

3. **Formulating Hypotheses** Why is the boiling point of CH_3Br higher than the boiling point of CH_3Cl? (*Hint:* Compare the atomic masses for bromine and chlorine.)

Alcohols

Methanol, CH_3OH, is used as a fuel in some motorcycles. Ethanol, CH_3CH_2OH, is often mixed with gasoline to help the gasoline burn more completely. Methanol and ethanol are alcohols. The name of an alcohol ends in *–ol.* ◯ **The functional group in an alcohol is a hydroxyl group, –OH.** When a halocarbon reacts with a base, the products are an alcohol and salt.

$$CH_3Cl + NaOH \longrightarrow CH_3OH + NaCl$$

An alcohol can also be made by reacting an alkene with water.

| Ethene | Water | Ethanol |

Organic Acids and Bases

The sharp, sour taste of a lemon comes from citric acid, an organic acid. ◯ **The functional group in organic acids is a carboxyl group, –COOH.** Names of organic acids end in *-oic.* Organic acids tend to have sharp tastes and strong odors. The simplest organic acid is methanoic acid, which is also known as formic acid. Vinegar is a solution of water and the organic acid ethanoic acid, which is usually referred to as acetic acid. If the ants in Figure 11 sprayed the formic acid they produce on your skin, your skin would itch or burn.

Methanoic acid　　**Ethanoic acid**

Figure 11 Birds sometimes will sit on an ants' nest and allow the ants to crawl over them. The methanoic acid sprayed by the ants is a natural pesticide that kills mites in the birds' feathers.

Figure 12 Many compounds in rose petals contribute to the fragrance of a rose. Some of these compounds are esters, which tend to have pleasant, sweet odors.

Do you know the smell of rotten fish? Then you've encountered a type of substituted hydrocarbon called an amine. Amines are organic bases. **The functional group in an amine is an amino group, $-NH_2$.** Amines are found in paints, dyes, and disinfectants. In Section 9.3 you will study the role organic bases play in the formation of organic compounds that are essential for life.

Esters

One group of substituted hydrocarbons accounts for the flavors of many foods and the pleasant odor of many flowers. These compounds are known as esters. **Esters form when organic acids react with alcohols.** The second product of the reaction is water. For example, ethanoic acid can react with methanol to produce methyl ethanoate (methyl acetate). The reaction is reversible.

$$\underset{\text{Ethanoic acid}}{\begin{matrix} H & O \\ | & || \\ H-C-C-OH \\ | \\ H \end{matrix}} + \underset{\text{Methanol}}{\begin{matrix} H \\ | \\ HO-C-H \\ | \\ H \end{matrix}} \overset{H^+}{\rightleftharpoons} \underset{\text{Methyl ethanoate}}{\begin{matrix} H & O & H \\ | & || & | \\ H-C-C-O-C-H \\ | & & | \\ H & & H \end{matrix}} + \underset{\text{Water}}{HOH}$$

Esters are used in many processed foods to produce flavors such as strawberry, banana, and grape. Flowers like the roses in Figure 12 produce esters and other compounds with distinctive odors that attract insects for pollination. Sometimes, the compounds produced by the plant mimic compounds produced by the insect.

Section 9.2 Assessment

Reviewing Concepts

1. What functional groups are found in alcohols, organic acids, and organic bases?
2. Which types of compounds can react to produce esters?
3. What is a substituted hydrocarbon?
4. When a halocarbon reacts with a base, what products are produced?
5. What are two properties of organic acids?

Critical Thinking

6. **Classifying** An unknown compound has no noticeable odor. Explain why the compound is unlikely to be an organic acid, an organic base, or an ester.

7. **Inferring** What kind of organic compound gives a vitamin-C tablet its sour taste?
8. **Applying Concepts** Name one kind of substituted hydrocarbon you would expect to find in artificially flavored grape jelly.

Connecting Concepts

Types of Reactions Alcohols can be made by reacting halocarbons with bases, or alkenes with water. Review the general types of reactions presented in Section 7.2. Which types best describe the two methods for producing an alcohol? Explain your choices.

9.3 Polymers

Reading Focus

Key Concepts
- What is one way that polymers can be classified?
- What are three examples of synthetic polymers?
- What are four types of polymers that organisms can produce?

Vocabulary
- polymer
- monomers
- carbohydrates
- nucleic acids
- amino acid
- protein

Reading Strategy
Identifying Main Ideas Before you read, copy the concept map. As you read, complete the map to summarize two main ideas about polymers.

a. ? — form — polymers — which can be — b. ? / c. ?

Freight trains, like those in Figure 13, use different types of cars to transport goods. A flatcar with no sides or roof is used to haul steel beams. Grain is carried in covered hoppers, which have a hatch at the top and a chute at the bottom. Liquids travel in tank cars. The cars on a train may be all the same type or a mixture of different types. On average, about 100 cars are linked together behind the locomotive on a freight train.

Like freight trains, some molecules are built up from smaller units linked together. A **polymer** is a large molecule that forms when many smaller molecules are linked together by covalent bonds. The smaller molecules that join together to form a polymer are **monomers.** *Poly-* means "many." *Mono-* means "one." In some polymers, there is only one type of monomer. Other polymers have two or more kinds of monomers.

Polymers can be classified as natural polymers or synthetic polymers. Many important types of biological molecules are natural polymers. Organisms produce these polymers in their cells. Synthetic polymers are developed by chemists in research laboratories and manufactured in factories. Both types of polymers have industrial uses. For example, silk and cotton fabrics are woven from natural polymer fibers, while polar fleece is made from a synthetic polymer.

Figure 13 Couplers that interlock like the fingers of your hands connect one railroad car to another. Many cars can be joined together to form a train because there is a coupler on both ends of a car. **Using Analogies** *How is a polymer like a train?*

A

B

C

Figure 14 Synthetic polymers are used to make tires, ropes, and plastic objects. **A** About half the rubber produced in the world is used to manufacture tires. **B** Nylon is a good choice for a rope because its fibers are strong and do not wear out easily. **C** The hard plastic shapes are made from a high-density polyethylene polymer.
Inferring *At room temperature, polymers are most likely to exist as which state of matter?*

For: Links on polymers
Visit: www.SciLinks.org
Web Code: ccn-1093

Synthetic Polymers

The properties of a polymer depend on the type and number of monomers in the polymer. ⊙ **Rubber, nylon, and polyethylene are three examples of compounds that can be synthesized.**

Rubber The sap collected from rubber trees in tropical regions contains rubber. So why would a chemist make synthetic rubber? The supply of natural rubber is limited. During World War II, the allies could not obtain natural rubber. Chemists worked hard to produce a synthetic rubber, using hydrocarbons from petroleum. Natural rubber and synthetic rubbers contain different monomers and have different properties. The tires in Figure 14A will resist wear and be less likely to leak if they are made of synthetic rubber. Rubber is used as an adhesive. The How It Works box on page 277 explains how adhesives work.

Nylon In the 1930s, Wallace Carothers was trying to produce a synthetic polymer to replace silk. The polymer he produced was nylon, which has properties not found in natural polymers. Nylon fibers are very strong, durable, and shiny. Nylon is used in parachutes, windbreakers, fishing line, carpets, and ropes like the one in Figure 14B.

Polyethylene Plastic milk bottles, plastic wrap, and the plastic shapes in Figure 14C are made of polyethylene. This polymer forms when ethene (or ethylene) molecules link head to tail. The number of carbon atoms in a polyethylene chain affects the properties of the polymer. The more carbon atoms in the chain, the harder the polymer is.

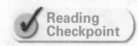

Reading Checkpoint *What determines the hardness of polyethylene?*

Synthetic Adhesives

Adhesion is the force of attraction between molecules of different substances whose surfaces are in contact. These forces are rarely strong enough to bind two surfaces together. An adhesive placed between the surfaces binds them together. Most adhesives are synthetic polymers. The diagram illustrates how some adhesives work. The adhesive remains liquid until the surfaces are in position. Then the adhesive sets. **Interpreting Diagrams** *Explain the purpose of a stabilizer in an adhesive.*

It also sticks handles to teapots.

Permanent adhesion
An epoxy resin was used to attach the automobile to the billboard. Epoxy resins are often stored in two parts that are mixed just before the epoxy is used. Strong binding forces in these adhesives make them heat- and water-resistant.

1 Liquid adhesive
In a typical adhesive, monomer molecules and a stabilizer are in a solvent. The stabilizer stops the monomers from forming a solid polymer.

Tube

Monomer molecule

Stabilizer

Solvent

2 Applying the adhesive Some of the liquid is squeezed onto one of the surfaces to be joined.

Monomers join together.

Temporary adhesion
The sticky strip on a reusable note is an adhesive containing tiny spheres. The spheres limit the amount of surface area that makes contact, so the note sticks lightly and repositions easily.

3 The adhesive sets
Contact with water in the air and on the surfaces being joined makes the stabilizer inactive. The monomers then begin to join together to form a polymer. As the chain lengthens, the adhesive changes from a liquid to a solid.

Types of adhesion
Adhesion can work in three ways. Molecules of the polymer may fill crevices in the surfaces being connected. The molecules may also be attracted to one another by intermolecular forces, or they may react by forming covalent bonds.

Distinguishing Sugars From Starches

Materials

1 slice each of potato, ripe apple, and bread; 15 mL cornstarch; 15 mL table sugar; iodine in dropper bottle; 6 small paper plates

Procedure

1. Place one sample of each food on a paper plate. **CAUTION** *Never eat anything in a lab.*

2. Place 2 to 3 drops of iodine solution on the cornstarch. Record your observations.

3. Repeat Step 2 using sugar instead of cornstarch.

4. Place 2 to 3 drops of iodine on each of the other food samples. Record your observations.

Analyze and Conclude

1. **Classifying** How can an iodine solution be used to distinguish a sugar from a starch?

2. **Drawing Conclusions** Which of the food samples contained starch?

3. **Predicting** What other foods would turn dark when tested with iodine solution?

Natural Polymers

Almost all of the large molecules produced by organisms are polymers. 🔑 **Four types of polymers produced in plant and animal cells are starches, cellulose, nucleic acids, and proteins.**

Starches Many animals are attracted to sweet-tasting foods. The compounds responsible for this sweetness are often sugars. Simple sugars have the formula $C_6H_{12}O_6$. They can exist as straight chains or rings. The simple sugars glucose and fructose can react to form sucrose (table sugar). Glucose monomers join to form starches as shown below.

Figure 15 All the foods shown contain starch, which is a polymer of the simple sugar glucose. **Observing** *Identify foods that you recognize in the photograph.*

Glucose   A type of starch found in plants

Typically, a starch contains hundreds of glucose monomers. Plants store starches for food and to build stems, seeds, and roots. Flour for the bread, pasta, and tortillas shown in Figure 15 is made by grinding the seeds of grains, such as wheat and corn. Simple sugars, slightly more complex sugars such as sucrose, and polymers built from sugar monomers are all classified as **carbohydrates.**

Cellulose The carbohydrate cellulose is the main component of cotton and wood. It is the most abundant of all organic compounds found in nature. Cellulose molecules contain 3000 or more glucose monomers. Cellulose gives strength to plant stems and tree trunks. Most animals cannot digest cellulose.

Nucleic Acids There are molecules in each cell of a plant or animal that store information about its structures and functions. These molecules are nucleic acids. **Nucleic acids** are large, nitrogen-filled polymers found mainly in the nuclei of cells. There are two types of nucleic acid, deoxyribonucleic acid (DNA) and ribonucleic acid (RNA).

The monomers in a nucleic acid are nucleotides. Figure 16A shows the three parts of a DNA nucleotide. The yellow circle represents a phosphate group. The green pentagon represents deoxyribose sugar, which has a five-atom ring. The purple rectangle represents an organic base. The bases in DNA are adenine, thymine, cytosine, and guanine.

When two strands of DNA line up as shown in Figure 16B, an adenine base always pairs up with a thymine base, and a cytosine base always pairs up with a guanine base. These pairs of bases are arranged like the rungs of a ladder. The strands are held together by strong intermolecular attractions between hydrogen atoms on one strand and nitrogen or oxygen atoms on the other strand. Figure 16C shows how the strands twist around each other in a structure called a double helix. The order of the base pairs in a strand is a code that stores information that is used to produce proteins.

Phosphate

Deoxyribose sugar

Adenine

Thymine

Cytosine

Guanine

 Reading Checkpoint *What are the two types of nucleic acids?*

Figure 16 Nucleic acids are polymers that store the genetic information that gives the girls in the photograph their distinct physical characteristics. **A** The monomers in DNA have three components—a phosphate group, a sugar, and one of four organic bases. **B** Two strands of DNA are held together by intermolecular attractions between the organic bases. **C** The shape of DNA is like a twisted ladder. Phosphate-sugar chains form the sides of the ladder. The rungs of the ladder are pairs of bases.

Proteins Recall that organic acids contain a –COOH group and organic bases, or amines, contain an –NH₂ group. There is one substituted hydrocarbon that contains both groups. An **amino acid** is a compound that contains both carboxyl and amino functional groups in the same molecule. There are about 20 amino acids that your body needs to function.

Glycine   Phenylalanine

Your cells can manufacture some, but not all, of the amino acids. For example, your body can make glycine, but not phenylalanine. The essential amino acids that your body cannot make must come from foods like those in Figure 17.

Your cells use amino acids as the monomers for constructing protein polymers. A **protein** is a polymer in which at least 100 amino acid monomers are linked through bonds between an amino group and a carboxyl group. The instructions for making proteins are stored in DNA. Proteins make up the fibers of your muscles, your hair and fingernails, and the hemoglobin in your blood. Your body may contain as many as 300,000 different proteins.

Figure 17 The foods shown are all good protein sources. **Classifying** *Group the foods into three or four categories.*

Section 9.3 Assessment

Reviewing Concepts

1. Describe a way that polymers can be classified.

2. Name three synthetic polymers.

3. What are four types of polymers that can be found in the cells of organisms?

4. What are the three parts of a nucleotide?

5. What holds the bases together in DNA?

6. What two functional groups are found in amino acids?

Critical Thinking

7. **Using Analogies** Which natural polymers are like a train with identical freight cars and which are like a train with a mixture of different cars?

8. **Inferring** There is another system for classifying carbohydrates that uses the categories monosaccharides, disaccharides, and polysaccharides. Where would you place glucose, sucrose, and cellulose in this classification system? Give a reason for your answer.

Writing in Science

Compare-Contrast Paragraph Write a paragraph comparing natural and synthetic polymers in general. How are they similar? How are they different?

Genetically Modified Organisms: Modern Miracles or *Frankenfoods?*

People have been selectively breeding plants and animals for many years. Selective breeding works over generations to enhance or eliminate specific traits in an organism. Today, through genetic engineering, scientists can isolate and combine genes to create a genetically modified organism that would never exist in nature. Crops, such as corn and soy, are sometimes modified to avoid damage from weeds, insects, or viruses.

Here's an example. A bacterium called *Bacillus thurlingensis,* found in soil, creates a type of protein that kills insect larvae. Splicing the genes that encode this protein from that bacterium into corn DNA creates a new strain of corn. This genetically modified corn is protected against the corn borer, a pest that causes billions of dollars of damage to crops each year. This new strain of corn reduces the need to spray corn crops with pesticides.

The Viewpoints

Genetic modification is a beneficial tool.

The population of the world is expected to grow by roughly two billion people in the next 20 years, but the amount of farming land might actually decrease because of development and other factors. Genetic modification allows people to grow food more productively by using helpful gene traits that can make crops and livestock more resistant to pests and diseases.

Genetic modification can also help to reduce certain health issues. For example, golden rice is a type of rice that has added genes that make it rich in beta-carotene, a form of vitamin A. Golden rice can help to reduce vitamin A deficiencies in populations that rely predominantly on rice as their staple food.

Genetic modification is a dangerous practice.

Selective breeding does not create plants or animals that would be impossible in nature. Conversely, genetic modification creates unnatural creatures. Furthermore, it is impossible to predict the effects these new life forms could have on the environment. Inserting a bacterial gene into a plant could have unknown repercussions. Will the inserted gene be harmful to people? Will insects that are not pests also be harmed? In addition, once genetically modified organisms are out in the world, they could be difficult to contain. For example, the pollen from genetically modified plants could pollinate other plants to create new, unknown hybrids, which might have further unexpected effects on the environment.

Research and Decide

1. **Defining the Issue** In your own words, describe why genetically modified organisms are controversial.

2. **Analyzing the Viewpoints** List three arguments that support the use of genetic modification. List three arguments made by people who think that genetic modification is a dangerous idea.

3. **Forming Your Opinion** Traditionally, farmers store and sow the seeds of crops from previous years. However, many genetically modified crops produce sterile seeds. Farmers who grow these genetically modified crops must buy new seeds each year from seed companies. Are there advantages to this type of arrangement? Are there disadvantages? Explain your answer.

For: Links on polymers
Visit: www.SciLinks.org
Web Code: ccn-1093

9.4 Reactions in Cells

Figure 18 Unlike a plant, this runner must get the energy he needs from the food he eats.

For thousands of years, people used whale oil and other animal fats as fuels for their lamps. As fats burn, they combine with oxygen and produce carbon dioxide and water. They also release energy in the form of heat and light. In a lamp, combustion takes place rapidly. In the cells of organisms, a more controlled version of the process releases energy stored in molecules. Some of the energy released helps maintain your internal body temperature at or close to 37°C.

Reactions that take place in cells follow the same rules as reactions that take place in a research laboratory or classroom. Some reactions go to completion and some reach an equilibrium point. Many reactions occur in solution and catalysts are often needed. Energy is transferred and energy is converted from one form to another. Photosynthesis and cellular respiration are two processes that allow organisms to meet their energy needs.

Photosynthesis

The sun is the primary source of energy for most plants and animals. During **photosynthesis,** plants chemically combine carbon dioxide and water into carbohydrates. The process requires light and chlorophyll, a green pigment in plants. This equation summarizes the process.

$$6H_2O + 6CO_2 + \text{Energy (light)} \longrightarrow C_6H_{12}O_6 + 6O_2$$

 During photosynthesis, energy from sunlight is converted into chemical energy. Photosynthesis involves a complex series of chemical reactions. When all the reactions are complete, the energy from sunlight has been stored in the covalent bonds of molecules.

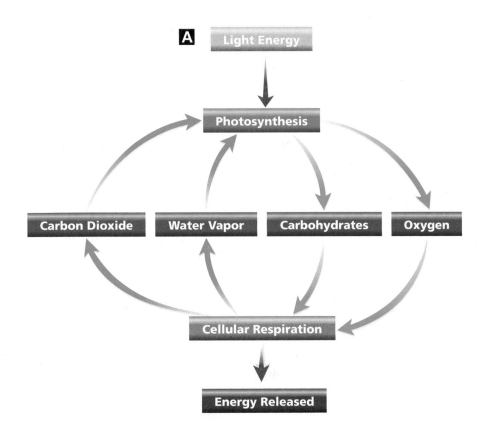

A
Light Energy

Photosynthesis

Carbon Dioxide | Water Vapor | Carbohydrates | Oxygen

Cellular Respiration

Energy Released

Figure 19 Products of cellular respiration are reactants during photosynthesis. **A** Cellular respiration and photosynthesis are two parts of the same cycle. **B** Plants can survive without people, but people cannot survive without plants.

Cellular Respiration

What does your body need energy for, besides maintaining a constant body temperature? Everything! It takes energy to laugh or cry, to heal a bone or a paper cut, to climb a rope or a staircase, or even to sleep. 🔑 **During cellular respiration, the energy stored in the products of photosynthesis is released.** Like photosynthesis, cellular respiration is a complex series of reactions. This equation is a summary of the overall process.

$$C_6H_{12}O_6 + 6O_2 \longrightarrow 6H_2O + 6CO_2 + \text{Energy (heat)}$$

Figure 19 summarizes the relationship between photosynthesis and cellular respiration. Each process produces the reactants for the other process. Carbon dioxide and water are reactants in photosynthesis and products of cellular respiration. Carbohydrates and oxygen are reactants in cellular respiration and products of photosynthesis.

In the equation for cellular respiration, glucose is reacting with oxygen. The glucose can come from simple sugars or from starches, because starch is a polymer of glucose. During digestion, starch breaks down into glucose. This process is an example of depolymerization. Fats are also a good source of energy. One gram of fat produces twice the energy of one gram of a carbohydrate.

Reading Checkpoint *Which produces more energy per gram, a carbohydrate or a fat?*

For: Activity on phytoplankton
Visit: PHSchool.com
Web Code: ccc-1094

Enzymes and Vitamins

Without some help, many of the reactions that take place in your cells would not happen fast enough to keep the cells alive. Your internal temperature should not vary more than a few degrees from 37°C. So you cannot increase the temperature to speed up a reaction in your cells. **Enzymes and vitamins are compounds that help cells function efficiently at normal body temperature.**

Enzymes Without enzymes, cells could not digest food or extract energy from food. **Enzymes** are proteins that act as catalysts for reactions in cells. Enzymes allow reactions to proceed faster at much lower temperatures than would normally happen. Your body uses thousands of enzymes to control reactions within your cells. Pepsin, for example, is an enzyme that breaks apart proteins. It works only in the acidic environment of the stomach. Some enzymes require a co-enzyme to function, often a metal ion or a water-soluble vitamin.

Vitamins In the 1800s, British sailors ate limes on long sea voyages. The limes were protection against scurvy, which causes severe pain and weakness. Limes contain vitamin C. **Vitamins** are organic compounds that organisms need in small amounts, but cannot produce. A vitamin that dissolves in water, such as vitamin C, gets eliminated from the body and must be replaced daily. A vitamin that dissolves in fats, such as vitamin A, can build up over time in body tissues. Taking excess amounts of fat-soluble vitamins may be harmful.

Figure 20 Lemons, limes, and oranges are sources of vitamin C. **Drawing Conclusions** *Is vitamin C soluble in fat or in water?*

For: Articles on biochemistry
Visit: PHSchool.com
Web Code: cce-1094

Section 9.4 Assessment

Reviewing Concepts

1. What happens to sunlight during photosynthesis?

2. Describe the relationship between photosynthesis and cellular respiration.

3. What molecules improve the efficiency of cell functions?

4. What happens to starch during digestion?

5. Why can't an increase in temperature be used to speed up reactions in cells?

Critical Thinking

6. **Formulating Hypotheses** Why must combustion in cells take place in multiple steps?

7. **Drawing Conclusions** Some bacteria do not require oxygen. How would the disappearance of plants affect these bacteria?

8. **Inferring** What affect could a lack of essential amino acids have on reactions in a person's body?

Writing in Science

Explanatory Paragraph Check the label on a package of multivitamins and minerals. Compare the masses of the minerals to the masses of the vitamins included in a single pill. Discuss any trend that you detect.

Comparing Vitamin C in Fruit Juices

Various brands of juices claim to be good sources of vitamin C, but which juices are the best sources? Vitamin C is an organic acid called ascorbic acid. Like other acids, vitamin C reacts with indicators to produce a color change. This reaction can be used to determine the amount of vitamin C present in foods, such as fruit juices. In this lab, you will add an indicator to a sample of apple juice. The indicator will change color when all the vitamin C has reacted. Then you will test and compare the vitamin C content in other juices with the results for apple juice.

Problem Which juice provides the most vitamin C?

Materials
- apple juice
- a variety of other fruit juices
- test tubes and rack
- 10-mL graduated cylinder
- methylene blue indicator in dropper bottle
- stirring rods

Skills Observing, Measuring, Analyzing Data

Procedure

Part A: Measuring Vitamin C in Apple Juice

1. On a sheet of paper, copy the data table.
2. Use a graduated cylinder to measure 10 mL of apple juice. Pour the juice into a test tube.

Data Table	
Type of Juice	**Number of Drops**
Apple	

3. Add a drop of methylene blue indicator to the test tube. Stir until the color of the indicator disappears.
4. Add more indicator, one drop at a time, stirring after each addition. Count the drops you add. Stop adding the indicator when the last drop of indicator does not change color. Record the number of drops you used.

Part B: Measuring Vitamin C in Other Juices

5. Formulate and record a hypothesis about which juice will have the greatest amount of vitamin C. You will need to decide which variables must be kept the same, as well as how to account for bits of solid in some juices.
6. List the steps in your procedure and write the names of each of the juices to be tested in the left column of your data table.
7. Have your teacher check your procedure before you begin your experiment.

Analyze and Conclude

1. **Using Graphs** Make a bar graph of your data. Which juice required the most drops of indicator? Which required the least?
2. **Drawing Conclusions** Based on your data, which juice contained the most vitamin C? How did you reach this conclusion?
3. **Evaluating and Revising** What unexpected problems did you encounter? Explain how you could revise your procedure to avoid these problems.

Study Guide

9.1 Carbon Compounds

Key Concepts

- Diamond, graphite, and fullerenes are forms of carbon. Diamond is a network solid. Graphite forms layers that slide past one another. Fullerenes are large hollow spheres or cages of carbon.

- Factors that determine the properties of a hydrocarbon are the number of carbon atoms and how the atoms are arranged. Hydrocarbons can form a straight chain, a branched chain, or a ring.

- There are three types of unsaturated hydrocarbons— alkenes, alkynes, and aromatic hydrocarbons.

- Three types of fossil fuels are coal, petroleum, and natural gas. The primary products of the complete combustion of fossil fuels are carbon dioxide and water.

Vocabulary

organic compound, *p. 262;* network solid, *p. 263;* hydrocarbon, *p. 264;* saturated hydrocarbon, *p. 264;* isomers, *p. 265;* unsaturated hydrocarbon, *p. 266;* aromatic hydrocarbons, *p. 266;* fossil fuels, *p. 267*

9.2 Substituted Hydrocarbons

Key Concepts

- The functional group in an alcohol is a hydroxyl group, –OH. The functional group in an organic acid is a carboxyl group, –COOH. The functional group in an amine is an amino group, –NH$_2$.

- Esters form when organic acids react with alcohols.

Vocabulary

substituted hydrocarbon, *p. 272* functional group, *p. 272*

9.3 Polymers

Key Concepts

- Polymers can be classified as natural polymers or synthetic polymers.

- Rubber, nylon, and polyethylene are three examples of compounds that can be synthesized.

- Four types of polymers produced in plant and animal cells are starches, cellulose, nucleic acids, and proteins.

Vocabulary

polymer, *p. 275;* monomers, *p. 275;* carbohydrates, *p. 278;* nucleic acids, *p. 279;* amino acid, *p. 280;* protein, *p. 280*

9.4 Reactions in Cells

Key Concepts

- During photosynthesis, energy from sunlight is converted into chemical energy.

- During cellular respiration, the energy stored in the products of photosynthesis is released .

- Enzymes and vitamins help cells function efficiently at normal body temperature.

Vocabulary

photosynthesis, *p. 282;* enzymes, *p. 284;* vitamins, *p. 284*

Thinking Visually

Concept Map Copy the concept map onto a sheet of paper. Use information from the chapter to complete it.

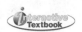
Reviewing Content

Choose the letter that best answers the question or completes the statement.

1. How many bonds can a carbon atom form?
　　a. two　　　　**b.** four
　　c. six　　　　**d.** seven

2. Two compounds that have the same molecular formula but different structural formulas are
　　a. isomers.　　**b.** isotopes.
　　c. alkanes.　　**d.** alkenes.

3. Which compound has a triple bond?
　　a. alkene　　　**b.** alkyne
　　c. alkane　　　**d.** alcohol

4. The primary products of complete combustion of fossil fuels are
　　a. carbon monoxide and water.
　　b. carbon dioxide and water.
　　c. carbon dioxide and carbon monoxide.
　　d. methane and water.

5. What is an organic compound with at least one hydroxyl group called?
　　a. an organic acid
　　b. an alkyne
　　c. an organic base
　　d. an alcohol

6. Amines all contain atoms of
　　a. oxygen.　　　**b.** nitrogen.
　　c. sulfur.　　　**d.** chlorine.

7. The monomers for protein molecules are
　　a. ethene.　　　**b.** nucleic acids.
　　c. amino acids.　　**d.** ethanoic acids.

8. A nucleotide does not contain a(n)
　　a. organic base.
　　b. organic acid.
　　c. sugar.
　　d. phosphate group.

9. Reactions in cells take place at about
　　a. 100°C.　　　**b.** 0°C.
　　c. 40°C.　　　**d.** 60°C.

10. An enzyme is a
　　a. protein.　　　**b.** vitamin.
　　c. lipid.　　　**d.** carbohydrate.

Understanding Concepts

11. How did the synthesis of urea change the definition of an organic compound?

12. Why is diamond extremely hard but graphite is extremely soft?

13. What is a saturated hydrocarbon?

14. Why can an acetylene torch be used to weld metals together?

15. How are fossil fuels formed?

16. How are the hydrocarbons in petroleum separated into fractions?

17. Why is it important to make sure that there is plenty of air around a gas burner such as the one shown below?

18. How is acid rain produced?

19. What is a functional group?

20. Why is ethanol added to gasoline?

21. What types of substituted hydrocarbons can react to form esters?

22. Explain why natural and synthetic rubber have different properties.

23. What do cellulose and starch have in common?

24. What are the products of photosynthesis? What are the products of cellular respiration?

25. What role do enzymes play in cells?

Assessment (continued)

Critical Thinking

26. Predicting Does methane have isomers? Explain your answer.

27. Forming Operational Definitions Present an argument for classifying double and triple bonds as functional groups. (*Hint:* What is the role of a functional group in a compound?)

28. Classifying Based on their names, classify each of these compounds: octacosane, pentyne, and octanol. What information did the names provide that helped you classify the compounds?

29. Classifying Which natural polymers can be eaten for breakfast? Which natural polymers can be worn to school?

30. Applying Concepts When your skin is exposed to sunlight, cells in your skin produce vitamin D. Should vitamin D be classified as a vitamin? Give a reason for your answer.

Math Skills

Use this table to answer Questions 31–33.

Selected Properties of Fuels		
Fuels	**Melting Point (°C)**	**Boiling Point (°C)**
Alcohol 1	6	228
Alcohol 2	26	83
Alkane 1	−183	−162
Alkane 2	−138	0
Alkane 3	−57	126

31. Analyzing Data Which fuel is a liquid across the greatest range of temperature?

32. Using Tables At 20°C, which fuels would be liquid?

33. Analyzing Data Look at the data for the three unknown alkanes. Which alkane is likely to have the fewest carbon atoms? Which is likely to have the most carbon atoms? Give a reason for your choices.

Concepts in Action

34. Designing Experiments You work at a refinery and want to know whether a fraction you have collected from a distillation tower is a single substance or a mixture. What kind of test could you do to find out?

35. Relating Cause and Effect What are two ways that a large forest fire might affect the amount of carbon dioxide in the atmosphere?

36. Making Judgments Why do you think progress in solar energy, wind power, and other alternative forms of energy has been slow?

37. Drawing Conclusions If the cells in your body can manufacture proteins, why are proteins an important part of a balanced diet?

38. Comparing and Contrasting When wood burns, the cellulose in wood is converted to carbon dioxide and water. The same products are produced when a termite digests wood, but the process occurs at a much lower temperature. Explain the difference in temperature.

39. Writing in Science Describe the series of events that starts with the death of a group of ancient ocean organisms and ends with filling the tank of an automobile with gasoline. (*Hint:* Consider making a flow chart of events first.)

Performance-Based Assessment

Animating a Process Make a flip book that begins with the sun providing energy for photosynthesis in a plant. It should proceed through photosynthesis, and then show how the products of photosynthesis are used in cellular respiration. Complete the book by showing the products of cellular respiration about to be used for photosynthesis.

For: Self-grading assessment
Visit: PHSchool.com
Web Code: cca-1090

Standardized Test Prep

Choose the letter that best answers the question or completes the statement.

1. Benzene is classified as an aromatic hydrocarbon because
   (A) it has a strong odor.
   (B) it contains only carbon and hydrogen.
   (C) it is a compound found in coal.
   (D) it has an unsaturated ring structure.
   (E) it has a saturated ring structure.

2. How are photosynthesis and cellular respiration related?
   (A) They both occur in all living organisms.
   (B) They both consume more energy than they produce.
   (C) They both produce water and carbon dioxide.
   (D) Cellular respiration stores energy, and photosynthesis releases it.
   (E) Photosynthesis stores energy, and cellular respiration releases it.

3. Which type of compound forms when amino acids are linked together?
   (A) nucleic acid
   (B) protein
   (C) carbohydrate
   (D) organic acid
   (E) ester

4. What type of substituted hydrocarbon contains the functional group –OH?
   (A) halocarbon
   (B) alcohol
   (C) ester
   (D) organic base
   (E) organic acid

Use the diagram to answer Questions 5 and 6. The diagram shows a combustion apparatus used to identify hydrocarbons.

A   B

5. A sample of a hydrocarbon is in the glass tube. What gas is in the green tank?
   (A) nitrogen
   (B) carbon dioxide
   (C) oxygen
   (D) methane
   (E) acetylene

6. The containers labeled A and B absorb the primary products of the reaction that occurs in the tube. Those products are
   (A) carbon dioxide and water.
   (B) carbon monoxide and water.
   (C) oxides of sulfur and nitrogen.
   (D) sulfuric and nitric acid.
   (E) carbon dioxide and carbon monoxide.

21st Century Learning

Communication Skills

How is radiocarbon dating used to date objects?

The use of radioisotopes to date rocks and artifacts has helped scientists piece together a clearer picture of Earth's past. Use the library or Internet to learn more about an archaeological site that you have heard about in the news. Find out how the age of the site was determined. Digitally record a podcast about the site and the methods used by scientists to date the site and/or its artifacts. Post the podcast on your class Web site.

How do science concepts apply to your world? Here are some questions you'll be able to answer after you read this chapter.

- **Why is radon gas dangerous?** *(Section 10.1)*

- **How can you measure the age of a rock?** *(Section 10.2)*

- **How does a smoke detector work?** *(Section 10.3)*

- **How can doctors diagnose certain types of cancer?** *(page 306)*

- **How does a nuclear reactor generate electricity?** *(Section 10.4)*

This false-color image from a bubble chamber shows the tracks of subatomic particles at high speed.

Chapter Preview

Inquiry Activity

What Happens When an Atom Decays?

Procedure

1. Using green beads to represent protons and purple beads to represent neutrons, make a model of a nucleus of a beryllium atom that contains 4 protons and 4 neutrons.

2. Atomic nuclei such as the one you modeled can decay by losing a particle that contains 2 protons and 2 neutrons. Remove the appropriate number of beads from your model to represent this process.

Think About It

1. **Observing** How many protons and how many neutrons are left in your nuclear model?

2. **Using Models** What element does your nuclear model now represent?

10.1 Radioactivity

Reading Focus

Key Concepts

- What happens during nuclear decay?
- What are three types of nuclear radiation?
- How does nuclear radiation affect atoms?
- What devices can detect nuclear radiation?

Vocabulary

- radioactivity
- radioisotope
- nuclear radiation
- alpha particle
- beta particle
- gamma ray
- background radiation

Reading Strategy

Previewing Copy the table below. Before you read the section, rewrite the topic headings as *how, why,* and *what* questions. As you read, write an answer to each question.

Question	Answer
What is nuclear decay?	a._____?_____
b._____?_____	Alpha, beta, gamma
c._____?_____	d._____?_____
e._____?_____	f._____?_____

Figure 1 Due to rainy weather, Henri Becquerel postponed his intended experiment with uranium salts. **A** Without any exposure to sunlight, the salts still produced a foggy image on a photographic plate. **B** For his discovery of radioactivity, Becquerel shared the 1903 Nobel Prize for Physics with Marie and Pierre Curie.

A

B

In 1896, French physicist Antoine Henri Becquerel (1852–1908) was experimenting with uranium salts. He hypothesized that the salts, which glow after being exposed to light, produced X-rays while they glowed. To test his hypothesis, Becquerel performed an experiment. First, he wrapped a photographic plate in paper. Then, he placed some uranium salts on the plate and set it outside in the sunlight, which caused the salts to glow. When Becquerel developed the plate, he got a foggy image. At the time, Becquerel thought that X-rays from the salts had penetrated the paper and fogged the plate.

Like any good scientist, Becquerel wanted to repeat his experiment, but a spell of bad weather forced him to wait. In the meantime, he left a wrapped photographic plate and uranium salts in a desk drawer. After several days, Becquerel decided to develop the plate without exposing the uranium to sunlight. To his surprise, he got the foggy image shown in Figure 1A. Later, Becquerel determined that the uranium salts had emitted rays that had never been observed before.

Nuclear Decay

Becquerel's experiment marked the discovery of radioactivity. **Radioactivity** is the process in which an unstable atomic nucleus emits charged particles and energy. Any atom containing an unstable nucleus is called a radioactive isotope, or **radioisotope** for short.

Radioisotopes of uranium—primarily uranium-238—were the source of radioactivity in Becquerel's experiment. (Recall that the name of an isotope includes its mass number.) Another common radioisotope is carbon-14, which can be found in fossils like the ones shown in Figure 2.

Unlike stable isotopes such as carbon-12 or oxygen-16, radioisotopes spontaneously change into other isotopes over time. When the composition of a radioisotope changes, the radioisotope is said to undergo nuclear decay. **During nuclear decay, atoms of one element can change into atoms of a different element altogether.** For example, uranium-238 decays into thorium-234, which is also a radioisotope.

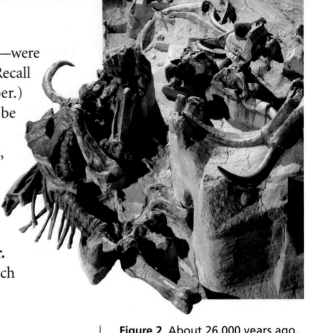

Figure 2 About 26,000 years ago, more than 100 mammoths died at a sinkhole in Hot Springs, South Dakota. Scientists figured out how old the remains were by measuring amounts of the radioisotope carbon-14 contained in the mammoth bones.

Types of Nuclear Radiation

Scientists can detect a radioactive substance by measuring the nuclear radiation it gives off. **Nuclear radiation** is charged particles and energy that are emitted from the nuclei of radioisotopes. **Common types of nuclear radiation include alpha particles, beta particles, and gamma rays.** Figure 3 shows the properties of these three types of radiation.

Alpha Decay When a uranium-238 sample decays, it emits alpha particles. An **alpha particle** is a positively charged particle made up of two protons and two neutrons—the same as a helium nucleus. It has a 2+ charge. The common symbol for an alpha particle is ^4_2He. The subscript is the atomic number (the number of protons). The superscript is the mass number (the sum of the numbers of protons and neutrons). Another symbol for an alpha particle is the Greek letter α.

Alpha decay, which refers to nuclear decay that releases alpha particles, is an example of a nuclear reaction. Like chemical reactions, nuclear reactions can be expressed as equations. The following nuclear equation describes the alpha decay of uranium-238.

$$^{238}_{92}\text{U} \rightarrow \,^{234}_{90}\text{Th} + \,^4_2\text{He}$$

In alpha decay, the product isotope has two fewer protons and two fewer neutrons than the reactant isotope. In the equation above, the mass number on the left (238) equals the sum of the mass numbers on the right (234 + 4). Also, the atomic number on the left (92) equals the sum of the atomic numbers on the right (90 + 2). In other words, the equation is balanced.

Alpha particles are the least penetrating type of nuclear radiation. Most alpha particles travel no more than a few centimeters in air, and can be stopped by a sheet of paper or by clothing.

Figure 3 Within a few years of Becquerel's discovery of radioactivity, Ernest Rutherford classified three types of nuclear radiation based on his own studies of uranium compounds. *Comparing and Contrasting How do alpha particles, beta particles, and gamma rays differ in terms of charge? In terms of mass?*

Characteristics of Nuclear Radiation				
Radiation Type	Symbol	Charge	Mass (amu)	Common Source
Alpha particle	α, ^4_2He	2+	4	Radium-226
Beta particle	β, $^0_{-1}\text{e}$	1−	$\dfrac{1}{1836}$	Carbon-14
Gamma ray	γ	0	0	Cobalt-60

For: Activity on radiation
Visit: PHSchool.com
Web Code: ccc-1101

Figure 4 Alpha particles (shown in red) are the least penetrating type of nuclear radiation. Gamma rays (shown in green) are the most penetrating. A concrete slab can block most but not all of the gamma rays released by a radioactive source.
Interpreting Diagrams *Which type of radiation can penetrate paper but is blocked by aluminum foil?*

Beta Decay When thorium-234 decays, it releases negatively charged radiation called beta particles. A **beta particle** is an electron emitted by an unstable nucleus. In nuclear equations, a beta particle is written as $_{-1}^{0}e$ or β. Because of its single negative charge, a beta particle is assigned an atomic number of -1. In Chapter 4, you learned that an electron has very little mass when compared with a proton. For this reason, a beta particle is assigned a mass number of 0.

How can an atomic nucleus, which has a positive charge, emit a negatively charged particle? During beta decay, a neutron decomposes into a proton and an electron. The proton stays trapped in the nucleus, while the electron is released. The following equation describes the beta decay of thorium-234.

$$_{90}^{234}\text{Th} \rightarrow {}_{91}^{234}\text{Pa} + {}_{-1}^{0}e$$

In beta decay, the product isotope has one proton more and one neutron fewer than the reactant isotope. The mass numbers of the isotopes are equal because the emitted beta particle has essentially no mass.

Due to their smaller mass and faster speed, beta particles are more penetrating than alpha particles. As Figure 4 illustrates, beta particles pass through paper, but can be stopped by a thin sheet of metal.

 What is a beta particle?

Gamma Decay Not all nuclear radiation consists of charged particles. A **gamma ray** is a penetrating ray of energy emitted by an unstable nucleus. The symbol for a gamma ray is γ. Gamma radiation has no mass and no charge. Like X-rays and visible light, gamma rays are energy waves that travel through space at the speed of light.

Radioactive sample

Lead box

Paper

Aluminum

Concrete

— Alpha particles (α)
— Beta particles (β)
— Gamma rays (γ)

Math Skills

Balancing Nuclear Equations

Write a balanced nuclear equation for the alpha decay of polonium-210.

 Read and Understand

What information are you given?

Reactant isotope = polonium-210

Radiation emitted = $^4_2$He (alpha particle)

Use the periodic table to obtain the atomic number of polonium.

Reactant isotope = $^{210}_{84}$Po

2 Plan and Solve

What unknowns are you trying to calculate?

Atomic number of product isotope, Z = ?

Mass number of product isotope, A = ?

Chemical symbol of product isotope, X = ?

What equation contains the given information?

$$^{210}_{84}\text{Po} \rightarrow ^A_Z\text{X} + ^4_2\text{He}$$

Write and solve equations for atomic mass and atomic number.

$210 = A + 4 \qquad 84 = Z + 2$

$210 - 4 = A \qquad 84 - 2 = Z$

$206 = A \qquad\qquad 82 = Z$

According to the periodic table, the element with an atomic number of 82 is lead, Pb. So, X is Pb. The balanced nuclear equation is shown below.

$$^{210}_{84}\text{Po} \rightarrow ^{206}_{82}\text{Pb} + ^4_2\text{He}$$

 Look Back and Check

Is your answer reasonable?

The mass number on the left equals the sum of the mass numbers on the right. The atomic number on the left equals the sum of the atomic numbers on the right. The equation is balanced.

Math Practice

1. Write a balanced nuclear equation for the alpha decay of thorium-232.

2. Write a balanced nuclear equation for the beta decay of carbon-14.

3. Determine the product of alpha decay for americium-241.

4. Determine the product of beta decay for strontium-90.

Figure 5 The mineral autunite is an important source of uranium.

During gamma decay, the atomic number and mass number of the atom remain the same, but the energy of the nucleus decreases. Gamma decay often accompanies alpha or beta decay. For example, thorium-234 emits both beta particles and gamma rays (abbreviated as γ) as it decays.

$$^{234}_{90}\text{Th} \rightarrow\ ^{234}_{91}\text{Pa} +\ ^{0}_{-1}\text{e} + \gamma$$

Gamma rays are much more penetrating than either alpha particles or beta particles. It can take several centimeters of lead or several meters of concrete to stop gamma radiation.

Effects of Nuclear Radiation

You may not realize it, but you are exposed to nuclear radiation every day. Most of this is **background radiation,** or nuclear radiation that occurs naturally in the environment. Radioisotopes in air, water, rocks, plants, and animals all contribute to background radiation. Most rocks, such as the one in Figure 5, contain at least trace amounts of radioactive elements. Another source of background radiation is cosmic rays. Cosmic rays are streams of charged particles (mainly protons and alpha particles) from outer space. Collisions between cosmic rays and Earth's atmosphere shower the surface below with nuclear radiation. All this radioactivity may sound dangerous. However, background radiation levels are generally low enough to be safe.

When nuclear radiation exceeds background levels, it can damage the cells and tissues of your body. ⬤ **Nuclear radiation can ionize atoms.** When cells are exposed to nuclear radiation, the bonds holding together proteins and DNA molecules may break. As these molecules change, the cells may no longer function properly.

Alpha particles, beta particles, and gamma rays are all forms of ionizing radiation. Alpha particles can cause skin damage similar to a burn, but they are not a serious health hazard unless an alpha-emitting substance is inhaled or eaten. For example, radon gas is a potentially dangerous natural source of alpha particles because it can be inhaled. Radon-222 is formed through a series of nuclear decays that begins with uranium-238 in rocks deep underground. As radon-222 is produced, it seeps upward toward the surface. It sometimes collects in the basements of buildings that lack proper ventilation, as shown in Figure 6. Prolonged exposure to radon-222 can lead to lung cancer.

Figure 6 Radon gas is produced underground as the uranium in rocks and soil decays. As the radon seeps up through the ground, it can get into buildings by passing through cracks or holes in their foundations.
Inferring How would ventilation of the basement affect radon levels in the house shown below?

Insulation, modern windows, and modern building materials keep radon from escaping.

Radon gas dissolved in water is released through agitation.

Radon naturally diffuses up through the ground.

Radon enters through pinholes and cracks in the foundation.

Radon is produced by the nuclear decay of uranium found in rocks and soil.

When exposure to nuclear radiation is external, the amount of tissue damage depends on the penetrating power of the radiation. For example, beta particles can damage tissues in the body more than alpha particles, but less than gamma rays. Gamma rays can penetrate deeply into the human body, potentially exposing all organs to ionization damage.

Detecting Nuclear Radiation

Although you can't see, hear, or feel the radioactivity around you, scientific instruments can measure nuclear radiation. **Devices that are used to detect nuclear radiation include Geiger counters and film badges.** A Geiger counter, shown in Figure 7, uses a gas-filled tube to measure ionizing radiation. When nuclear radiation enters the tube, it ionizes the atoms of the gas. The ions produce an electric current, which can be measured. The greater the amount of nuclear radiation, the greater the electric current produced in the tube is.

Recall that in Becquerel's experiment, nuclear radiation left an image on a photographic plate. Today, many people who work with or near radioactive materials wear film badges to monitor their exposure to nuclear radiation. A film badge contains a piece of photographic film wrapped in paper. The film is developed and replaced with a new piece periodically. The exposure on the film indicates the amount of radiation exposure for the person wearing the badge.

Figure 7 Wearing protective clothing, a firefighter uses a Geiger counter to test the ground for radioactivity. Firefighters sometimes help clean up accidents involving radioactive materials.

Section 10.1 Assessment

Reviewing Concepts

1. How does an element change during nuclear decay?

2. What are three types of nuclear radiation?

3. How are atoms affected by nuclear radiation?

4. What devices can be used to detect nuclear radiation?

5. How do types of nuclear radiation differ in electric charge?

6. Describe the penetrating power of each common type of radiation.

7. What is background radiation? List some of its sources.

Critical Thinking

8. **Predicting** What is the effect of beta decay on the composition of a nucleus?

9. **Inferring** Why do you think airplane pilots wear film badges?

Math Practice

10. Write a balanced nuclear equation for the alpha decay of radium-226.

11. Write a nuclear equation that describes the beta decay of hydrogen-3.

10.2 Rates of Nuclear Decay

Reading Focus

Key Concepts

- How do nuclear decay rates differ from chemical reaction rates?

- How do scientists determine the age of an object that contains carbon-14?

Vocabulary

- half-life

Reading Strategy

Identifying Details Copy the concept map below. As you read, complete it to identify details about radiocarbon dating.

Radiocarbon dating

uses the radioisotope

a. ?

can be used to date objects as old as

b. ? years

A well-known theory is that early Americans were people from Siberia who crossed the Bering Strait into Alaska about 13,000 years ago. However, this theory has been challenged by recent scientific discoveries. In the 1990s, archaeologists working at a site in Cactus Hill, Virginia, found stone tools, charcoal, and animal bones that were at least 15,000 years old. Some of the artifacts were as much as 17,000 years old. The age of these artifacts suggests that the first Americans reached the continent much earlier than formerly thought. Some archaeologists have since revised their theories on the origin of America's earliest ancestors. One possible explanation is that the first Americans were people from Europe who crossed the Atlantic Ocean by using boats.

Figure 8 shows some of the artifacts from the Cactus Hill site. They certainly look very old, but the archaeologists needed to find out *how* old. One clue that can reveal the age of an object is how many radioactive nuclei it contains. Because most materials contain at least trace amounts of radioisotopes, scientists can estimate how old they are based on rates of nuclear decay.

Figure 8 These stone tools from the archaeological site in Cactus Hill, Virginia, are at least 15,000 years old. Scientists estimated the age of the site based on rates of nuclear decay.

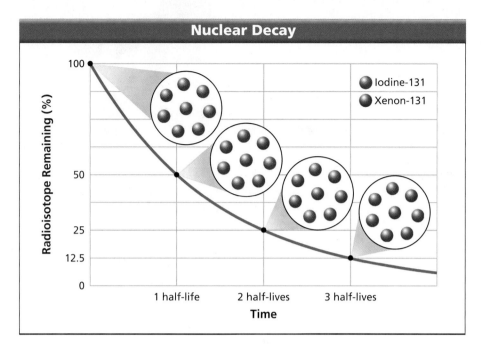

Nuclear Decay

Radioisotope Remaining (%)

100

50

25

12.5

0

1 half-life   2 half-lives   3 half-lives

Time

● Iodine-131
● Xenon-131

Figure 9 The half-life for the beta decay of iodine-131 is 8.07 days. After one half-life (8.07 days), half of a sample of iodine-131 will have decayed into xenon-131. After two half-lives (16.14 days), three quarters of the sample will have decayed.

Half-Life

A nuclear decay rate describes how fast nuclear changes take place in a radioactive substance. Every radioisotope decays at a specific rate that can be expressed as a half-life. A **half-life** is the time required for one half of a sample of a radioisotope to decay. After one half-life, half of the atoms in a radioactive sample have decayed, while the other half remain unchanged. After two half-lives, half of the remaining half decays, leaving one quarter of the original sample unchanged. Figure 9 illustrates the nuclear decay rate of iodine-131. Iodine-131 has a half-life of 8.07 days. After two half-lives, or 16.14 days, the fraction of iodine-131 remaining is one quarter. After three half-lives, or 24.21 days, the fraction of iodine-131 remaining is one half of one quarter, or one eighth.

Half-lives can vary from fractions of a second to billions of years. Figure 10 lists the half-lives of some common radioisotopes. Uranium-238, for instance, has a half-life of 4.5 billion years. This means that in 4.5 billion years, there will be half as much uranium-238 on Earth as there is today. You could also say that 4.5 billion years ago, there was twice as much uranium-238 on Earth as there is today. ⊙ **Unlike chemical reaction rates, which vary with the conditions of a reaction, nuclear decay rates are constant.** Regardless of the temperature, pressure, or surface area of a uranium-238 sample, its half-life is still 4.5 billion years.

 Reading Checkpoint   *What is a half-life?*

Figure 10 Nuclear decay rates are constant. A given radioisotope decays at a specific rate, or half-life. **Calculating** *What isotope is produced by the nuclear decay of radon-222?*

Half-Lives and Radiation of Selected Radioisotopes		
Isotope	**Half-life**	**Nuclear Radiation Emitted**
Radon-222	3.82 days	α
Iodine-131	8.07 days	β
Thorium-234	24.1 days	β, γ
Radium-226	1620 years	α, γ
Carbon-14	5730 years	β
Thorium-230	75,200 years	α, γ
Uranium-235	7.04×10^8 years	α, γ
Potassium-40	1.28×10^9 years	β, γ
Uranium-238	4.47×10^9 years	α

Modeling Half-Life

Procedure

1. Put 100 1-cm squares of wallpaper in a large plastic bag. Construct a data table with 2 columns and 9 blank rows. Label the columns Spill Number and Number of Squares Returned.

2. Close the bag and shake it to mix up the squares. Then, spill them onto a flat surface.

3. Remove the squares that are face-side up. Record the number of squares remaining and return them to the bag.

4. Repeat Steps 2 and 3 until there are no squares left to put back into the bag.

Analyze and Conclude

1. **Analyzing Data** How many spills were required to remove half of the squares? To remove three fourths of the squares?

2. **Using Graphs** Graph your results. Plot spill number on the horizontal axis and the number of squares remaining on the vertical axis.

3. **Using Models** If each spill represents one year, what is the half-life of the squares?

Suppose you have a one-gram sample of iridium-182, which undergoes beta decay to form osmium-182. The half-life of iridium-182 is 15 minutes. After 45 minutes, how much iridium-182 will remain in the sample? To solve this problem, you first need to calculate how many half-lives will elapse during the total time of decay.

$$\text{Half-lives elapsed} = \frac{\text{Total time of decay}}{\text{Half-life}} = \frac{45 \text{ min}}{15 \text{ min}} = 3$$

After three half-lives, the amount of iridium-182 has been reduced by half three times.

$$\frac{1}{2} \times \frac{1}{2} \times \frac{1}{2} = \frac{1}{8}$$

So after 45 minutes, $\frac{1}{8} \times 1$ gram, or 0.125 gram, of iridium-182 remains while 0.875 gram of the sample has decayed into osmium-182.

Radioactive Dating

Now suppose you have a sample that was originally iridium-182, but three quarters of it have since decayed into osmium-182. Based on the fraction of iridium-182 left (one quarter), you can calculate the age of the sample to be two half-lives, or 30 minutes old.

The artifacts from Cactus Hill were dated by measuring levels of carbon-14, which has a half-life of 5730 years. Carbon-14 is formed in the upper atmosphere when neutrons produced by cosmic rays collide with nitrogen-14 atoms. The radioactive carbon-14 undergoes beta decay to form nitrogen-14.

$$^{14}_{6}\text{C} \rightarrow \, ^{14}_{7}\text{N} + \, ^{0}_{-1}\text{e}$$

Go Online

NSTA SciLINKS

For: Links on half-life
Visit: www.SciLinks.org
Web Code: ccn-1102

Carbon reacts with oxygen in the atmosphere and forms carbon dioxide. As plants absorb carbon dioxide during photosynthesis, they maintain the same ratio of carbon-14 to carbon-12 as in the atmosphere. Likewise, animals have the same ratio of carbon isotopes as the plants they eat. When a plant or animal dies, however, it can no longer absorb carbon. From this point on, the organism's carbon-14 levels decrease as the radioactive carbon decays. **In radiocarbon dating, the age of an object is determined by comparing the object's carbon-14 levels with carbon-14 levels in the atmosphere.** For example, if the ratio of carbon-14 to carbon-12 in a fossil is half the ratio in the atmosphere, then the organism lived about 5730 years ago.

Because atmospheric carbon-14 levels can change over time, the calculated age of the fossil is not totally accurate. To get a more accurate radiocarbon date, scientists compare the carbon-14 levels in a sample to carbon-14 levels in objects of known age. Such objects might include trees (which can be dated by counting tree rings) or artifacts from a specific historical period.

Radiocarbon dating can be used to date any carbon-containing object less than 50,000 years old, such as the artifact in Figure 11. Objects older than 50,000 years contain too little carbon-14 to be measurable. To date objects thought to be older than 50,000 years, scientists measure the amounts of radioisotopes with longer half-lives than carbon-14. Geologists, for instance, use the half-lives of potassium-40, uranium-235, and uranium-238 to date rock formations. The older the rock, the lower are the levels of the radioisotope present.

Figure 11 Radiocarbon dating has helped archaeologists learn more about ancient civilizations. Excavations in Abydos, a major archaeological site of ancient Egypt, have unearthed fascinating artifacts. This mummy case, containing the remains of a cat, is 1900 years old.

Section 10.2 Assessment

Reviewing Concepts

1. How are nuclear decay rates different from chemical reaction rates?

2. How can scientists determine the age of an object that contains carbon-14?

3. If a radioactive sample has decayed until only one eighth of the original sample remains unchanged, how many half-lives have elapsed?

4. What type of nuclear radiation is emitted when carbon-14 decays?

Critical Thinking

5. **Predicting** Can radiocarbon dating be used to determine the age of dinosaur fossils? Explain. (*Hint:* Dinosaurs roamed Earth more than 65 million years ago.)

6. **Inferring** All of the isotopes of radon have half-lives shorter than four days, yet radon is still found in nature. Explain why all the radon has not already decayed.

7. **Calculating** A certain isotope of technetium has a half-life of six hours. If it is given to a patient as part of a medical procedure, what fraction of the radioisotope remains in the body after one day?

Writing in Science

Explanatory Paragraph Archaeology is the study of past cultures. Explain how a concept in chemistry led to advances in archaeology.

Should Radon Testing in Schools Be Mandatory?

Radon (Rn) is a radioactive element that forms from the nuclear decay of uranium in rocks and soil. A colorless, odorless gas, radon can enter buildings through drains, cracks in the floors and walls, and even the water supply. Indoor radon levels tend to be highest in places that are close to the soil and have little ventilation, such as basements or crawl spaces.

When a person inhales radon-contaminated air, the lungs trap radioactive particles. As these particles decay, radiation is released into the lung tissue. Over time, repeated exposure to high radon levels can result in lung cancer.

The Environmental Protection Agency (EPA) identifies 4 picocuries per liter (pCi/L) of air as the national "action level" for radon. (A picocurie is a unit of radioactivity.) If an indoor space has a radon level of 4 pCi/L or higher, the EPA recommends that steps be taken to reduce it. Such steps might include installing a ventilation system and sealing cracks in the building's foundation.

The Viewpoints

Radon Testing in Schools Should Be Mandatory

The EPA estimates that indoor radon exposure contributes to 21,000 lung cancer deaths in the United States each year. After smoking, radon is the second-leading cause of lung cancer.

Students and teachers spend extended periods of time indoors at school. A nationwide survey of radon levels in schools found that nearly one in five schools has at least one classroom with radon exceeding the EPA's action level of 4 pCi/L.

Indoor radon can be easily tested. If elevated radon levels are found, they can be reduced using proven techniques. But without mandatory testing, school administrators may not be aware of the potential risk of radon exposure in their schools.

Radon Testing in Schools Should Not Be Mandatory

The EPA's radon guidelines are based mainly on studies of workers in uranium mines. Radon levels in these mines were far greater than those found in homes or schools. In addition, the miners engaged in tiring labor, resulting in heavy breathing of the surrounding air. Lastly, most of the miners were smokers. The data from these studies are appropriate for predicting the risk of radon exposure for uranium miners—but not for the general public.

The EPA's action level of 4 pCi/L is not universally accepted. In Canada and Europe, for example, radon guidelines are much less strict. Until scientists gather more data about the risk of residential radon exposures, radon testing in schools should not be mandatory.

Research and Decide

1. **Defining the Issue** In your own words, explain the issue that needs to be resolved about indoor radon.

2. **Analyzing the Viewpoints** List two arguments of those who think that radon testing should be mandatory in schools. List two arguments of those who think that radon testing should not be mandatory in schools.

3. **Forming Your Opinion** Should there be mandatory radon testing in schools? Which argument did you find more convincing?

For: More on this issue
Visit: PHSchool.com
Web Code: cch-1100

10.3 Artificial Transmutation

Reading Focus

Key Concepts
- How do artificial transmutations occur?
- How are transuranium elements produced?

Vocabulary
- transmutation
- transuranium elements
- quark

Reading Strategy
Monitoring Your Understanding Preview the Key Concepts, topic headings, vocabulary, and figures in this section. List two things you expect to learn. After reading, state what you learned about each item you listed.

What I Expect to Learn	What I Learned
a. ___?___	b. ___?___
c. ___?___	d. ___?___

During the Middle Ages, a number of people, like the ones shown in Figure 12, were obsessed with the idea of changing lead into gold. For centuries, these early scientists, known as alchemists, tried to use chemical reactions to make gold. But no matter how many recipes they tried, the alchemists only succeeded in making compounds that contained lead. What were they doing wrong?

Nuclear Reactions in the Laboratory

The alchemists were trying to achieve transmutation. **Transmutation** is the conversion of atoms of one element to atoms of another. It involves a nuclear change, not a chemical change.

Nuclear decay is an example of a transmutation that occurs naturally. Transmutations can also be artificial. **Scientists can perform artificial transmutations by bombarding atomic nuclei with high-energy particles, such as protons, neutrons, or alpha particles.**

Early experiments involving artificial transmutation led to important clues about atomic structure. In 1919, a decade after he discovered the atomic nucleus, Ernest Rutherford performed the first artificial transmutation. Rutherford had been studying the effects of nuclear radiation on various gases. When Rutherford exposed nitrogen gas to alpha particles, he found that some of the alpha particles were absorbed by the nitrogen nuclei. Each newly formed nucleus then ejected a proton, leaving behind the isotope oxygen-17.

$$^{14}_{7}\text{N} + {}^{4}_{2}\text{He} \rightarrow {}^{17}_{8}\text{O} + {}^{1}_{1}\text{H}$$

Note that $^{1}_{1}\text{H}$ represents a proton. Rutherford's experiment provided evidence that the nucleus contains protons.

Figure 12 This painting of an alchemist's laboratory was made around 1570. The alchemists failed in their attempts to turn lead into gold.

Modeling Transmutation

Materials

periodic table, 2 sheets of unlined white paper, 32 green beads, 32 purple beads

Procedure

1. Use the periodic table to complete the following nuclear reaction. Then, write it on one of the sheets of paper.

$$^{10}_{5}B + ^{4}_{2}He \rightarrow ^{A}_{Z}X + ^{1}_{1}H$$

2. Count the number of protons and neutrons present in each reactant and product.

3. Using the green beads to represent protons and the purple beads to represent neutrons, make a model of each reactant and product below its symbol on the sheet of paper.

4. Repeat Steps 1 to 3 using the following nuclear reaction and the second sheet of paper.

$$^{14}_{7}N + ^{4}_{2}He \rightarrow ^{A}_{Z}X + ^{1}_{1}H$$

Analyze and Conclude

1. **Applying Concepts** What was the missing product in each of the equations? How did you know what the missing product was?

2. **Using Models** Make a model of the nuclear reaction between an alpha particle and an atom of aluminium-27. (*Hint:* One of the two products is a proton.)

Figure 13 In 1977, the National Aeronautics and Space Administration (NASA) launched two identical spacecraft, Voyager 1 and Voyager 2. These spacecraft, which are still exploring the outer solar system, are powered by the alpha decay of plutonium-238. **Inferring** *What isotope is produced by the alpha decay of plutonium-238?*

Transuranium Elements

Elements with atomic numbers greater than 92 (uranium) are called **transuranium elements.** All transuranium elements are radioactive, and they are generally not found in nature. ⬭ **Scientists can synthesize a transuranium element by the artificial transmutation of a lighter element.**

Neptunium was the first transuranium element synthesized. In 1940, scientists at the University of California, Berkeley, bombarded uranium-238 with neutrons, producing uranium-239. The uranium-239 underwent beta decay to form neptunium-239.

$$^{239}_{92}U \rightarrow ^{239}_{93}Np + ^{0}_{-1}e$$

Although most transuranium elements have only been produced for research, some are synthesized for industrial or consumer use. For example, americium-241 is a transuranium element used in smoke detectors. As americium-241 decays, it emits alpha radiation. This radiation ionizes the air inside a smoke detector to allow an electric current to flow. When smoke enters the smoke detector, it disrupts the current and the alarm goes off. Another useful transuranium element is plutonium-238. Figure 13 shows a space probe that runs on electrical energy generated by the decay of plutonium-238.

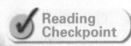 **Reading Checkpoint** *What is a transuranium element?*

Particle Accelerators

In Rutherford's transmutation experiment, the radioactive element radium was used as a source of alpha particles. However, sometimes transmutations will not occur unless the bombarding particles are moving at extremely high speeds. In order to perform such transmutations, scientists use devices called particle accelerators. In a particle accelerator, charged particles can be accelerated to speeds very close to the speed of light. The fast-moving particles are guided toward a target, where they collide with atomic nuclei. With the help of particle accelerators, scientists have produced more than 3000 different isotopes.

Scientists also conduct collision experiments in order to study nuclear structure. Since the proton, neutron, and electron were discovered, more than 200 different subatomic particles have been detected. According to the current model of the atom, protons and neutrons are made up of even smaller particles called quarks. A **quark** is a subatomic particle theorized to be among the basic units of matter. Both protons and neutrons belong to a class of particles that are made up of three quarks. Six types of quarks are currently thought to exist. Two of these types were discovered at Fermi National Accelerator Laboratory, also known as Fermilab. Figure 14 shows one of the devices used at Fermilab to detect subatomic particles.

Figure 14 This particle detector records subatomic particles produced in the Tevatron, the most powerful particle accelerator in the United States. The Tevatron is located at Fermilab in Batavia, Illinois.

Section 10.3 Assessment

Reviewing Concepts

1. How do scientists perform artificial transmutations?

2. How are transuranium elements produced?

3. How does artificial transmutation differ from nuclear decay?

4. Write the equation for the transmutation that occurs when an alpha particle combines with an oxygen-16 atom, emitting a proton.

5. Does fermium-257 undergo nuclear decay? Explain.

Critical Thinking

6. **Predicting** Bombarding a lithium-6 atom with a neutron produces helium-4 and another particle. What is that particle?

7. **Predicting** Curium was first synthesized by bombarding a target isotope with alpha particles, which produced curium-242 and a neutron. What was the target isotope? (*Hint:* Use the symbol $_0^1 n$ to represent a neutron.)

8. **Inferring** Why can't the transuranium elements be made by exposing other elements to naturally occurring alpha radiation?

Writing in Science

Summary Write a brief summary of the first artificial transmutation, performed by Ernest Rutherford. (*Hint:* Your summary should describe an example of a nuclear reaction.)

Nuclear Medicine

Exposure to nuclear radiation is often harmful to the human body. However, scientists have also found nuclear radiation to be a powerful tool in the field of medicine.

Because radioisotopes are detectable by their radiation, they can be used as tracers that map out specific locations in the body. For example, the radioisotope iodine-131 is absorbed by the thyroid gland in the throat in the same way that iodine-127 is. If iodine-131 is injected into the body, the radiation it emits will show how well the thyroid gland is functioning.

Radioactive tracers can also be used to pinpoint the location of cancer cells. Cancer cells multiply rapidly and absorb glucose much faster than normal cells. If the glucose molecules are "tagged" with a radioactive tracer, such as flourine-18, the location of the cancer cells can be found by tracking areas of high glucose concentration.

Radioisotopes with short half-lives are chosen for medical uses. These isotopes decay so rapidly that after only a day or two, practically none of the isotope remains.

PET scanner
PET (positron emission tomography) scans use radioactive tracers to examine parts of the body, such as the brain. The patient receives an injection of radioactive tracer. The tracer produces gamma rays that are detected by the scanner.

Tagged glucose is absorbed slowly in the blue areas, indicating normal tissue.

Red color shows greater glucose absorption in possibly cancerous areas.

PET scan of brain
This scan shows the level of activity in different areas of the brain. Glucose tagged with flourine-18 is absorbed more rapidly in areas of high brain activity and by cancer cells. Here, red shows the greatest activity and blue the least.

Positron

Gamma ray

Electron

Gamma rays

Gamma rays are produced when the tracer emits a positron. A positron is a particle with the mass of an electron but a charge of 1+. The positron is destroyed upon contact with an electron from a nearby atom in the body, and emits two gamma rays in opposite directions.

Gamma-ray detectors

Brain

Atom of tracer isotope

Gamma ray

Producing an image

The scanner detects the gamma rays and produces two-dimensional images like slices through the brain. The scanner's computer then constructs a three-dimensional image based on the scans.

Going Further

- Write a paragraph describing how radioactive tracers are used in medicine. Indicate what qualities make a particular radioisotope useful as a radioactive tracer in the human body.

Strong Nuclear Forces

Neutron

Neutron

Proton

Proton

Electric Forces

Neutron

Neutron

Proton

Proton

Figure 15 Two kinds of forces act upon particles in the nucleus. Strong nuclear forces, which are attractive, act on protons and neutrons alike. Electric forces in the nucleus are repulsive, and act only among protons.
Using Models *What atomic nucleus is represented above?*

Alternative energy sources may someday replace fossil fuels such as coal and oil. One alternative energy source that is widely used today is nuclear energy. Nuclear energy is the energy released by nuclear reactions.

Shortly after the discovery of radioactivity, scientists realized that atomic nuclei contained vast amounts of energy. By the late 1930s, scientists discovered that transmutations involved more than just the conversion of one element into another—they also involved the conversion of mass into energy.

Nuclear Forces

What holds the nucleus together? Remember that the protons in the nucleus are all positively charged, so they tend to repel one another. Clearly, there must be an attractive force that binds the particles of the nucleus. Otherwise, the protons would simply push one another away.

The **strong nuclear force** is the attractive force that binds protons and neutrons together in the nucleus. Because the strong nuclear force does not depend on charge, it acts among protons, among neutrons, and among protons and neutrons. **Over very short distances, the strong nuclear force is much greater than the electric forces among protons.** For example, at distances as short as the width of a proton, the strong nuclear force is more than 100 times greater than the electric force that repels protons. However, the strong nuclear force quickly weakens as protons and neutrons get farther apart. Figure 15 summarizes the forces acting on protons and neutrons in the nucleus.

A Nuclear Forces Acting on a Proton of a Small Nucleus

Strong nuclear forces

Electric force

B Nuclear Forces Acting on a Proton of a Large Nucleus

Strong nuclear forces

Electric forces

The Effect of Size on Nuclear Forces Electric forces in atomic nuclei depend on the number of protons. The greater the number of protons in a nucleus, the greater is the electric force that repels those protons. So in larger nuclei, the repulsive electric force is stronger than in smaller nuclei.

The effect of size on the strong nuclear force is more complicated. On one hand, the more protons and neutrons there are in a nucleus, the more possibilities there are for strong nuclear force attractions. However, as the size of the nucleus increases, the average distance between protons and neutrons increases. Because the strong nuclear force only acts over short ranges, the possibility of many attractions is never realized in a large nucleus. As a result, the strong nuclear force felt by one proton or neutron in a large nucleus is about the same as in a small nucleus, as shown in Figure 16.

Unstable Nuclei A nucleus becomes unstable, or radioactive, when the strong nuclear force can no longer overcome the repulsive electric forces among protons. While the strong nuclear force does not increase with the size of the nucleus, the electric forces do. There is, therefore, a point beyond which all elements are radioactive. All nuclei with more than 83 protons are radioactive.

Fission

In 1938, two German chemists, Otto Hahn and Fritz Strassman, performed a series of important transmutation experiments. By bombarding uranium-235 with high-energy neutrons, Hahn and Strassman hoped to produce more massive elements. Instead, their experiments produced isotopes of a smaller element, barium. Unable to explain their data, Hahn and Strassman turned to a colleague for help. In 1939, Lise Meitner, shown in Figure 17, and Otto Frisch, another physicist, offered a groundbreaking explanation for the experiments. The uranium-235 nuclei had been broken into smaller fragments. Hahn and Strassman had demonstrated nuclear fission. **Fission** is the splitting of an atomic nucleus into two smaller parts.

Figure 16 The size of a nucleus affects how strongly it is bound together. **A** In a nucleus containing two protons and two neutrons, the strong nuclear forces easily overcome the electric force between the protons. **B** In a nucleus containing many protons and neutrons, the larger number of electric forces makes the nucleus less stable.

Figure 17 Austrian physicist Lise Meitner (1878–1968), shown here, and Otto Frisch were the first scientists to describe nuclear fission. Meitner correctly predicted that fission releases large amounts of energy.

Neutron

Krypton-91
$^{91}_{36}$Kr

Energy

$^{235}_{92}$U
Uranium-235

$^{236}_{92}$U
Uranium-236
(very unstable)

$^{142}_{56}$Ba
Barium-142

Figure 18 The fission of uranium-235 yields smaller nuclei, neutrons, and energy. The nuclear equation for this reaction can be written as follows.

$$^{235}_{92}\text{U} + ^{1}_{0}\text{n} \longrightarrow$$

$$^{91}_{36}\text{Kr} + ^{142}_{56}\text{Ba} + 3^{1}_{0}\text{n} + \text{energy}$$

Comparing and Contrasting *How does fission differ from nuclear decay?*

Figure 18 illustrates the fission of a uranium-235 nucleus. Notice that one of the products of the reaction is energy. ☁ **In nuclear fission, tremendous amounts of energy can be produced from very small amounts of mass.** For example, the nuclear energy released by the fission of 1 kilogram of uranium-235 is equivalent to the chemical energy produced by burning more than 17,000 kilograms of coal.

Converting Mass Into Energy In the nuclear equation shown in Figure 18, the mass numbers on the left equal the mass numbers on the right. Yet when the fission of uranium-235 is carried out, about 0.1 percent of the mass of the reactants is lost during the reaction. This "lost" mass is converted into energy.

In 1905, more than 30 years before the discovery of fission, physicist Albert Einstein had introduced the mass-energy equation. It describes how mass and energy are related.

Mass–Energy Equation

$$E = mc^2$$

In the mass-energy equation, E represents energy, m represents mass, and c represents the speed of light (3.0×10^8 m/s). The conversion of a small amount of mass releases an enormous amount of energy. Likewise, a large amount of energy can be converted into a small amount of mass. The explosion of the first atomic bomb in 1945 offered a powerful demonstration of the mass-energy equation. The bomb contained 5 kilograms of plutonium-239. Fission of the plutonium produced an explosion that was equivalent to 18,600 tons of TNT.

Recall how the law of conservation of mass applied to chemical reactions. In nuclear reactions, however, the energies involved are much larger. To account for the conversion of mass into energy, a modified conservation law is used. According to the law of conservation of mass and energy, the total amount of mass and energy remains constant.

Go Online

NSTA SciLINKS

For: Links on fission
Visit: www.SciLinks.org
Web Code: ccn-1104

Figure 19 The fission of one nucleus can trigger a chain reaction. The splitting of a uranium-235 nucleus by a neutron yields two or three neutrons, each of which can cause another fission. **Interpreting Diagrams** *Does the fission of uranium-235 always yield the same isotopes as products? Explain.*

Triggering a Chain Reaction

How fast does a rumor spread? Imagine that you started a rumor by telling it to three of your friends. Then suppose each of those friends told three more friends. If this pattern continued, the rumor would quickly spread to hundreds of people, even though it originally started with just one person, you.

Nuclear fission can follow a similar pattern, in which one reaction leads to a series of others. During the fission of uranium-235, each reactant nucleus splits into two smaller nuclei and releases two or three neutrons. If one of these neutrons is absorbed by another uranium-235 nucleus, another fission can result, releasing more neutrons, as shown in Figure 19. In a **chain reaction,** neutrons released during the splitting of an initial nucleus trigger a series of nuclear fissions.

The speed of a chain reaction can vary. In an uncontrolled chain reaction, all of the released neutrons are free to cause other fissions, resulting in a fast, intense release of energy. Nuclear weapons are designed to produce uncontrolled chain reactions. In a controlled chain reaction, some of the neutrons are absorbed by nonfissionable materials, resulting in only one new fission for each splitting of an atom. The heat from controlled chain reactions can be used to generate electrical energy. Unfortunately, another product of controlled chain reactions is radioactive waste, shown in Figure 20.

In order to sustain a chain reaction, each nucleus that is split must produce, on average, one neutron that causes the fission of another nucleus. This condition corresponds to a specific mass of fissionable material, known as a critical mass. A **critical mass** is the smallest possible mass of a fissionable material that can sustain a chain reaction.

What is a chain reaction?

Figure 20 A crane lowers drums of radioactive waste into a landfill in Hanford, Washington.

Nuclear Chemistry **311**

Nuclear Energy from Fission Today, nuclear power plants generate about 20 percent of the electricity in the United States. In a nuclear power plant, controlled fission of uranium-235 occurs in a vessel called a fission reactor.

Unlike power plants that burn fossil fuels, nuclear power plants do not emit air pollutants such as oxides of sulfur and nitrogen. However, nuclear power plants have their own safety and environmental issues. For example, workers in nuclear power plants need to wear protective clothing to reduce their exposure to nuclear radiation. In addition, the fission of uranium-235 produces many radioactive isotopes with half-lives of hundreds or thousands of years. This radioactive waste must be

SCIENCE and History

Nuclear Chemistry

Over the last 100 years scientists have uncovered many secrets about the atomic nucleus. Developments have ranged from the synthesis of new elements to the harnessing of nuclear power as a viable energy source.

MARIE AND PIERRE CURIE AT WORK IN THEIR LABORATORY

EQUIPMENT USED BY HAHN AND STRASSMANN

HENRI BECQUEREL

1896 French scientist Antoine Henri Becquerel discovers radioactivity in uranium.

1898 Marie and Pierre Curie discover the radioactive elements radium and polonium. By making radium available to other scientists, the Curies helped advance the study of radioactivity.

1905 Albert Einstein's mass-energy equation, $E = mc^2$, provides the basis for nuclear power.

1932 First atom smasher (subatomic particle accelerator) is used by John Cockcroft and Ernest Walton.

1938 Germans Otto Hahn and Fritz Strassmann produce nuclear fission by bombarding uranium-235 atoms with neutrons.

1890   1910   1930

isolated and stored so that it cannot harm people or contaminate the environment while it decays.

Another concern about nuclear power is that the operators of the plant could lose control of the reactor. For instance, if the reactor's cooling system failed, then a meltdown might occur. During a meltdown, the core of the reactor melts and radioactive material may be released. If the structure that houses the reactor is not secure, then the environment can become contaminated. In 1986, one of the reactors at the nuclear power station in Chernobyl, Ukraine, overheated during an experiment. A partial meltdown resulted, and large amounts of radioactive material were released into the atmosphere.

Writing in Science

Summary Write a paragraph about the history of nuclear energy based on some of the events in the time line below. (*Hint:* Before you write, use a flowchart to organize the events you wish to include.)

ENRICO FERMI

ATOM BOMB TEST

IDAHO TESTING STATION

1942 The first controlled, self-sustaining nuclear chain reaction is achieved by Enrico Fermi's research group in Chicago.

1945 United States explodes first atom bomb in a test near Alamagordo, New Mexico.

1951 Electricity from nuclear fission produced at National Reactor Testing Station, Idaho.

1960 Willard Libby wins the Nobel Prize for developing carbon-14 dating. The technique became widely used in archaeology and geology.

1986 Partial meltdown occurs at Chernobyl power plant.

1950   1970   1990

Nuclear Power Station

Since the first nuclear bomb was exploded in 1945, scientists have found ways of utilizing the enormous power of nuclear fission for peaceful purposes. Nuclear power is now a major means of producing electricity. About 20 percent of electricity in the United States is generated this way. **Interpreting Diagrams**

How is water used in a nuclear power station?

Fission control
The fission reaction within the reactor core is controlled by neutron-absorbing control rods. Because they are still radioactive, the used rods are removed from the reactor core and stored in a pool, as shown above.

A **Reactor core**
Fission reactions take place in the reactor core, releasing large amounts of heat.

B **Steam generator**
Heat released in the reactor core is absorbed by water in the steam generator. This transfer of energy produces large amounts of high-pressure steam.

C **Turbines and condenser** The high-pressure steam forces the turbine to rotate at great speed. As it cools, the steam condenses to form liquid water, which is then piped back to the steam generator.

Water pressurizer

High-strength protective shielding

High-pressure turbine

Steam condenses.

Condenser

Control rods

Pump

Fuel rods containing uranium dioxide

Water

Cooling water exits.

Cooling water enters.

Pump

Filter

D **Electric generator** Here the work done by the force turning the turbines produces electrical energy.

Fusion

Another type of nuclear reaction that can release huge amounts of energy is fusion. **Fusion** is a process in which the nuclei of two atoms combine to form a larger nucleus. As in fission, during fusion, a small fraction of the reactant mass is converted into energy.

On any day or night, you can detect the energy released by fusion reactions occurring far away from Earth. The sun and other stars are powered by the fusion of hydrogen into helium. Inside the sun, an estimated 600 million tons of hydrogen undergo fusion each second. About 4 million tons of this matter is converted into energy.

Matter within the sun and other stars exists as plasma. **Plasma** is a state of matter in which atoms have been stripped of their electrons. You can think of plasma as a gas containing two kinds of particles—nuclei and electrons. Although fusion occurs at millions of degrees Celsius, plasma can exist at much lower temperatures. Scientists estimate that more than 99 percent of matter in the universe is plasma.

Fusion may someday provide an efficient and clean source of electricity. Scientists envision fusion reactors fueled by two hydrogen isotopes, deuterium (hydrogen-2) and tritium (hydrogen-3). The fusion of deuterium and tritium produces helium, neutrons, and energy.

$$\,_1^2\text{H} + \,_1^3\text{H} \rightarrow \,_2^4\text{He} + \,_0^1\text{n} + \text{energy}$$

Scientists face two main problems in designing a fusion reactor. They need to achieve the high temperatures required to start the reaction, and they must contain the plasma.

Figure 21 The Tokamak Fusion Test Reactor at the Princeton Plasma Physics Laboratory in Princeton, New Jersey, was one of the very few fusion reactors that have been built. It was retired in 1997, after 15 years of experimentation.

Section 10.4 Assessment

Reviewing Concepts

1. Under what conditions does the strong nuclear force overcome the repulsive effect of electric forces in the nucleus?

2. What property of fission makes it a useful reaction?

3. What particles are affected by strong nuclear forces?

4. What must happen in order for a nuclear chain reaction to occur?

5. Why is a cooling system necessary in a nuclear reactor?

6. How do the products of a fusion reaction differ from the products of a fission reaction?

Critical Thinking

7. **Inferring** How does the strong nuclear force affect an atom's electrons? (*Hint:* Think about where the electrons are located in the atom.)

8. **Inferring** Why do fission chain reactions of uranium-235 not occur in underground uranium deposits?

Connecting Concepts

Fossil Fuels Reread the description of fossil fuels in Section 9.1. Then compare fossil fuel combustion with nuclear fission.

Modeling a Chain Reaction

In a nuclear fission chain reaction, a nucleus is struck by a neutron, which causes the nucleus to split into two smaller nuclei and to release other neutrons. If these neutrons strike other nuclei, a chain reaction can occur. In this lab, you will model a nuclear fission chain reaction using dominoes.

Problem
How can you make a model of a nuclear fission chain reaction?

Materials
- 20 dominoes
- watch with a second hand, or stopwatch
- metric ruler

Skills
Observing, Using Models

Procedure

1. Stand 15 dominoes in a single straight row in such a way that the distance between them is about one half of their height. Knock over the first domino. Measure and record the time it takes for all the dominoes to fall.

2. Repeat Step 1 two more times. Then, average the three time measurements to get a more accurate time.

3. Arrange 15 dominoes as shown below so that each domino will knock over two others. Observe what happens when you knock over the first domino. Measure and record how long it takes for the whole set of dominoes to fall over.

4. Repeat Step 3 two more times. Average the three time measurements to get a more accurate time.

5. Set up 15 dominoes again as you did in Step 3. This time, however, hold a metric ruler on end, in the middle of the arrangement of dominoes, as shown in the photograph on the next page. Knock over the first domino. Observe what happens.

6. Set up 15 dominoes as you did in Step 3, but this time, place 5 additional dominoes behind and at right angles to 5 randomly chosen dominoes for support, as shown below. The 5 supported dominoes represent atoms of a different isotope that must be struck with more energy to undergo fission.

7. Knock over the first domino. Measure and record the time it takes for the dominoes to fall and how many dominoes fall.

8. Repeat Steps 6 and 7 two more times. Then, average the three time measurements to get a more accurate time.

9. Repeat Steps 6 through 8, but this time, place supporting dominoes behind only 3 dominoes.

10. Repeat Steps 6 through 8, but this time, place a supporting domino behind only 1 domino.

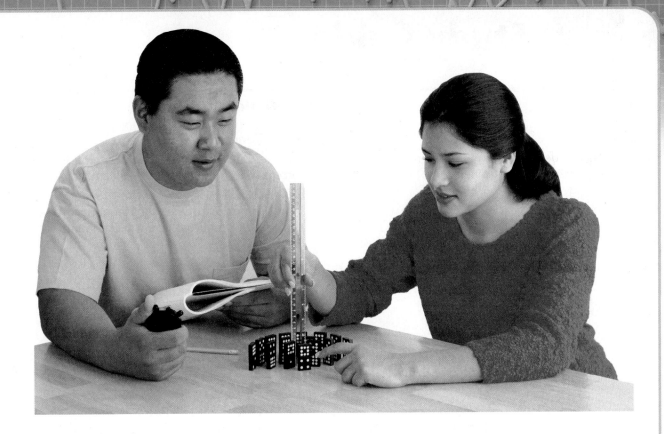

Analyze and Conclude

1. **Calculating** What was the average fall time for the arrangement of dominoes in Steps 1 and 2? In Steps 3 and 4?

2. **Applying Concepts** What type of reaction was modeled in Steps 3 and 4?

3. **Using Models** In your falling-dominoes model of nuclear fission chain reactions, what did a standing domino represent? What did the fall of a domino represent?

4. **Using Models** In your falling-dominoes model of nuclear fission chain reactions, what did the striking of one domino by another represent? What did the metric ruler represent?

5. **Analyzing Data** Before a sample of an easily fissionable isotope is used, it is refined by removing less fissionable isotopes of the same element. On the basis of your observations in Steps 6 through 10, explain why this refinement is necessary.

6. **Inferring** What factors do you think would affect the rate of a nuclear fission chain reaction?

7. **Drawing Conclusions** What do you think would happen to a nuclear fission chain reaction if control rods were not present?

8. **Evaluating and Revising** What are some of the limitations of using falling dominoes to model a nuclear fission chain reaction? Suggest how you might revise this model to make it more representative of a chain reaction.

Go Further Visit the library and find out about the Manhattan Project and how it made history. Use what you have learned from the falling-dominoes model to help you understand the scientific discoveries related to controlled and uncontrolled nuclear chain reactions.

Study Guide

10.1 Radioactivity

Key Concepts

- During nuclear decay, atoms of one element can change into atoms of a different element altogether.
- Common types of nuclear radiation include alpha particles, beta particles, and gamma rays.
- Nuclear radiation can ionize atoms.
- Devices that are used to detect nuclear radiation include Geiger counters and film badges.

Vocabulary

radioactivity, *p. 292;* radioisotope, *p. 292;* nuclear radiation, *p. 293;* alpha particle, *p. 293;* beta particle, *p. 294;* gamma ray, *p. 294;* background radiation, *p. 296*

10.2 Rates of Nuclear Decay

Key Concepts

- Unlike chemical reaction rates, which vary with the conditions of a reaction, nuclear decay rates are constant.
- In radiocarbon dating, the age of an object is determined by comparing the object's carbon-14 levels with carbon-14 levels in the atmosphere.

Vocabulary

half-life, *p. 299*

10.3 Artificial Transmutation

Key Concepts

- Scientists can perform artificial transmutations by bombarding atomic nuclei with high-energy particles such as protons, neutrons, or alpha particles.
- Scientists can synthesize a transuranium element by the artificial transmutation of a lighter element.

Vocabulary

transmutation, *p. 303;* transuranium elements, *p. 304;* quark, *p. 305*

10.4 Fission and Fusion

Key Concepts

- Over very short distances, the strong nuclear force is much greater than the electric forces among protons.
- In nuclear fission, tremendous amounts of energy can be produced from very small amounts of mass.

Vocabulary

strong nuclear force, *p. 308;* fission, *p. 309;* chain reaction, *p. 311;* critical mass, *p. 311;* fusion, *p. 315;* plasma, *p. 315*

Thinking Visually

Concept Map Use information from the chapter to complete the concept map below.

Reviewing Content

Choose the letter that best answers the questions or completes the statement.

1. An alpha particle is identical to
   a. a neutron.
   b. a helium nucleus.
   c. an electron.
   d. a hydrogen nucleus.

2. When a beta particle is emitted, the mass number of a nucleus
   a. increases by one.
   b. decreases by one.
   c. decreases by four.
   d. remains the same.

3. The most penetrating form of nuclear radiation is
   a. an alpha particle.
   b. a beta particle.
   c. a gamma ray.
   d. an electron.

4. The half-life of cobalt-60 is 5.3 years. What fraction of a sample remains after 21.2 years?
   a. one half
   b. one quarter
   c. one eighth
   d. one sixteenth

5. Which of the following is a radioisotope commonly used in dating archeological artifacts?
   a. nitrogen-14
   b. carbon-12
   c. uranium-235
   d. carbon-14

6. Transmutation does not occur in which of these nuclear processes?
   a. nuclear fission
   b. nuclear fusion
   c. alpha decay
   d. gamma decay

7. Based on its location on the periodic table, an element that is not naturally occurring is
   a. terbium (Tb).
   b. curium (Cm).
   c. holmium (Ho).
   d. lutetium (Lu).

8. Nuclear particles are held together by
   a. the strong nuclear force.
   b. electrical attraction.
   c. quarks.
   d. electrical repulsion.

9. Nuclear power plants generate electricity from
   a. nuclear fusion.
   b. nuclear fission.
   c. combustion.
   d. radioactivity.

10. The primary reaction inside stars changes
    a. hydrogen to helium.
    b. helium to hydrogen.
    c. uranium to plutonium.
    d. nitrogen to carbon.

Understanding Concepts

11. How do radioisotopes of an element differ from other isotopes?

12. What is the effect on the mass number and charge of a nucleus when it loses an alpha particle?

13. How do the mass number and charge of a nucleus change when it emits a gamma ray?

14. Which type of radiation—alpha, beta, or gamma—is most dangerous to living things? Explain.

15. Why does a Geiger counter occasionally click even if no artificial radioisotopes are nearby?

16. How does raising the temperature affect the rate of nuclear decay?

17. Why can't carbon-14 be used to determine the age of fossils that are several hundred thousand years old?

18. Write the equation for the transmutation that occurs when an alpha particle combines with a nitrogen-14 atom, emitting a proton.

19. Compare and contrast the processes of fission and fusion.

20. What is necessary to sustain a nuclear chain reaction?

21. Why do nuclear reactions produce more energy per mass of matter than chemical reactions?

22. The diagram below shows a nuclear reactor, including control rods. What is the function of a control rod in a nuclear power plant?

Control rods

Fuel rods

Reactor

Coolant

Assessment (continued)

Critical Thinking

Use the figure below to answer Questions 23 and 24.

Stable isotope

23. **Classifying** In the illustrated uranium-238 decay sequence, classify the type of radiation released in each of the transmutations from uranium-238 to radon-222.

24. **Making Generalizations** Study the sequence of decay from radon-222 to lead-206. Make a generalization as to what type of decay lead, polonium, and bismuth undergo until stable lead-206 is formed.

25. **Inferring** A film badge consists of a piece of film wrapped in a piece of dark plastic or paper. Doses of what kinds of radiation can be measured with this simple piece of equipment? Explain.

26. **Calculating** The first sample of californium was made by bombarding a target isotope with alpha particles. In addition to californium-245, the reaction produced a neutron. What was the target isotope?

Math Skills

27. **Calculating** After 36.9 years, a sample of hydrogen-3 contains one eighth of the amount it contained originally. What is the half-life of the isotope?

28. **Calculating** The half-life of iron-59 is 44.5 days. After 133.5 days, 2.76 g of iron-59 remains. What was the mass of the original sample?

29. **Inferring** The beta emissions from a bone that was found buried in a cave indicate that there are 4.6 carbon-14 decays per gram of carbon per minute. A chicken bone from a fast-food restaurant shows 18.4 emissions per gram of carbon per minute. How old is the bone from the cave?

Concepts in Action

30. **Inferring** Radioisotopes are commonly used in medical tests to diagnose diseases. Do the radioisotopes used for this purpose have long half-lives or short half-lives? Explain.

31. **Applying Concepts** Americium-241 and radon-222 both emit alpha particles. Americium is found in almost every home as a component of smoke detectors. But radon is considered a health hazard. Why is radon more hazardous?

32. **Making Judgments** If a fusion power plant could be constructed, why might it be a better source of energy than a fission plant?

33. **Writing in Science** Write a paragraph explaining how radon gas can collect in buildings. (*Hint:* The first sentence in your paragraph should state the paragraph's main idea.)

Performance-Based Assessment

Evaluating Many transuranium elements were named for the scientists who synthesized them or the location in which they were produced. Choose such a transuranium element, find out how it was created, and evaluate its importance. Write a pamphlet informing your classmates about the element you chose.

For: Self-grading assessment
Visit: PHSchool.com
Web Code: cca-1100

Standardized Test Prep

Choose the letter that best answers the question or completes the statement.

1. Which equation correctly shows beta decay?
    (A) $^{210}_{82}Pb \rightarrow ^{209}_{81}Tl + ^{0}_{-1}e + \gamma$
    (B) $^{210}_{82}Pb \rightarrow ^{209}_{83}Bi + ^{0}_{-1}e + \gamma$
    (C) $^{210}_{82}Pb \rightarrow ^{210}_{83}Tl + ^{0}_{-1}e + \gamma$
    (D) $^{210}_{82}Pb \rightarrow ^{210}_{83}Bi + \gamma$
    (E) $^{210}_{82}Pb \rightarrow ^{210}_{83}Bi + ^{0}_{-1}e + \gamma$

2. The half-life of radon-222 is 3.8 days. If a sample currently has 3.1 grams of radon-222, how much radon-222 did this sample have 15.2 days ago?
    (A) 12.4 grams   (B) 47.1 grams
    (C) 49.6 grams   (D) 57.8 grams
    (E) 92.7 grams

3. Radioactive decay of nuclei often involves several decays before a stable nucleus is formed. This is called a decay chain. What stable isotope is formed when radon-222 undergoes a decay chain of four alpha decays followed by four beta decays?
    (A) tungsten-206   (B) platinum-206
    (C) lead-206   (D) tungsten-214
    (E) lead-214

4. Which nucleus balances the following nuclear equation for the fission of uranium-235?
    $^{235}_{92}U + ^{1}_{0}n \rightarrow ^{90}_{38}Sr + ^{A}_{Z}X + 2^{1}_{0}n + \gamma$
    (A) $^{146}_{54}Xe$ (B) $^{146}_{52}Te$
    (C) $^{144}_{52}Te$ (D) $^{144}_{54}Xe$
    (E) $^{142}_{50}Sn$

5. Uranium-238 is less stable than oxygen-16. What accounts for this difference?
    (A) Uranium is a solid, while oxygen is a gas.
    (B) Unlike oxygen-16, uranium-238 has a nucleus in which repulsive electric forces surpass the strong nuclear forces.
    (C) Oxygen-16 has fewer electrons than uranium-238.
    (D) Uranium-238 has fewer neutrons than oxygen-16.
    (E) Unlike uranium-238, oxygen-16 has a nucleus in which the strong nuclear forces are overcome by repulsive electric forces.

6. The primary source of energy in stars is the fusion of hydrogen into helium. However, another reaction is believed to occur simultaneously. It is called the carbon-nitrogen-oxygen (CNO) cycle. In the diagram below, the symbol $^{0}_{+1}e$ represents a positron. A positron is a particle that has the same mass as an electron but a charge of $1+$.

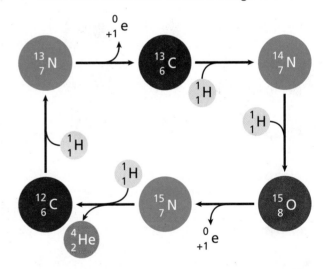

Which equation describes the CNO cycle?
    (A) $^{1}_{1}H \rightarrow ^{4}_{2}He + ^{0}_{+1}e$
    (B) $4^{1}_{1}H \rightarrow ^{4}_{2}He + 2^{0}_{+1}e$
    (C) $^{2}_{1}H + ^{3}_{1}H \rightarrow ^{4}_{2}He + ^{1}_{0}n$
    (D) $^{12}_{6}C \rightarrow ^{12}_{6}C + ^{4}_{2}He$
    (E) $^{12}_{6}C + ^{1}_{1}H \rightarrow ^{12}_{6}C + ^{4}_{2}He$

Vasco da Gama Bridge ▶
The Vasco da Gama Bridge spans the water at Lisbon, Portugal. Large ships can pass under the bridge to reach the port.

Physics

Focus on the BIG Ideas

Physicists investigate the laws that govern space, time, forces, motion, matter, and energy. Newton's laws of motion describe the relationship between the forces acting on a body and its motion. The motion of objects is governed by four universal forces: gravitational forces, electromagnetic forces, strong nuclear forces, and weak nuclear forces.

Energy is defined as the ability to do work. The amount of energy in the universe is constant, and energy is conserved within any closed system. However, energy can change between many different forms of kinetic energy and potential energy. The total potential and kinetic energy of all the microscopic particles in an object make up its thermal energy. Heat is the transfer of thermal energy from one object to another because of a temperature difference.

Careers in Physics

Many exciting career opportunities involve physics. Whether you want to become an electrician or an architect, you can put the ideas you read about in this unit to work toward a great career.

Computer Repair Technician
Computer repair technicians repair, maintain, and install mainframes, network servers, and personal computers. They also must be familiar with electronics, the technology that includes components such as electron tubes and photoelectric cells.
Educational requirements
Two-year community or junior college program in computer repair technology

Aerospace Engineer
If you have ever flown in an airplane, you have first-hand experience of the work of aerospace engineers. These professionals understand the principles of flight and are able to design, analyze, model, simulate, and test aircraft, spacecraft, missiles, and rockets. Aerospace engineers often specialize in areas such as propulsion, guidance, or navigation and control.
Educational requirements
Master's degree in physics, aerodynamics, or astronautics

Camera Operator
Lights—Camera—Action—Many motion picture camera operators hear this almost every day. Camera operators use lenses in their cameras and set up lights to photograph scenes. They also adjust the controls on the camera to produce high quality footage.
Educational requirements
High-school diploma

HVAC Technician

HVAC (heating, ventilation, and air conditioning) technicians install, maintain, and repair heating and cooling systems in homes and commercial buildings. HVAC technicians also make sure that ozone-depleting chemicals are not released into the environment.

Educational requirements Two-year community or junior college degree, with courses in mathematics, physics, chemistry, and mechanical drawing; refrigeration handler's license

Architect

To find out what an architect does, all you have to do is look around you. Architects design all types of buildings, from houses to airport terminals to entire developments. Architects have to be able to predict how a building and its materials will hold up to a variety of forces.

Educational requirements Five-year bachelor of architecture program, three- to four-year master of architecture program for those with a degree in another discipline, internship, and passage of Architect Registration Examination

Go Online
PHSchool.com

For: Career links
Visit: PHSchool.com
Web Code: ccb-2000

Electrician

Electricians are responsible for installing, testing, and maintaining electrical systems. They also must adhere to the National Electrical Code and obey state and local building codes to safely install electrical systems.

Educational requirements Four- or five-year apprenticeship program and state license

The time-lapse photo shows how the position of a gymnast changes from moment to moment.

CHAPTER
11 Motion

21st Century Learning

Critical Thinking and Systems Thinking

What is the relationship between displacement, velocity, and acceleration?

Search for an online simulation tool that generates graphs of displacement vs. time and velocity vs. time. Work in a small group to study examples of motion in a straight line using the simulation tool. First, simulate motion at a constant velocity. Then change the settings to simulate motion at a constant acceleration. Take screen-shots of the motion graphs generated and arrange them in a presentation. Use the graphs to describe the history of the motion that you simulated.

How do science concepts apply to your world? Here are some questions you'll be able to answer after you read this chapter.

- How can two people look at the same object, and only one of them see the object as moving? *(Section 11.1)*

- One person says that your school is 5 blocks from the library, and another person says the two buildings are 7 blocks apart. How can both people be right? *(Section 11.1)*

- What does a car's speedometer measure? *(Section 11.2)*

- How do ships stay on course? *(page 338)*

- When you drop a stone off a cliff, how fast does the stone fall? *(Section 11.3)*

- How can something that is slowing down be accelerating? *(Section 11.3)*

Chapter Preview

Inquiry > Activity

How Does a Ramp Affect a Rolling Marble?

Procedure

1. Form a ramp by placing one end of a 1-meter-long board on a stack of six identical books.

2. Have your partner release a marble at the top of the ramp. Use a stopwatch to measure the time the marble takes to reach the bottom. Record this time.

3. **Predicting** How many books tall would the stack have to be to double the time needed for the marble to reach the ramp's bottom? Record your prediction.

4. Test your prediction. Remove one book from the stack and repeat Step 2. Continue this process until the time needed for the marble to roll down the ramp doubles.

Think About It

1. **Predicting** What would happen to the time needed for the marble to roll down the ramp if the ramp were nearly horizontal?

2. **Formulating Hypotheses** If you keep adding books to the stack, will the time needed for the marble to roll down the ramp decrease indefinitely? Explain your answer.

11.1 Distance and Displacement

Reading Focus

Key Concepts

- What is needed to describe motion completely?
- How are distance and displacement different?
- How do you add displacements?

Vocabulary

- ◆ frame of reference
- ◆ relative motion
- ◆ distance
- ◆ vector
- ◆ resultant vector

Reading Strategy

Predicting Copy the table below and write a definition for *frame of reference* in your own words. After you read the section, compare your definition to the scientific definition and explain why the frame of reference is important.

Frame of reference probably means	Frame of reference actually means
a. ___?___	b. ___?___

On a spring day a butterfly flutters past. First it flies quickly, then slowly, and then it pauses to drink nectar from a flower. The butterfly's path involves a great deal of motion.

How fast is the butterfly moving? Is it flying toward the flower or away from it? These are the kinds of questions you must answer to describe the butterfly's motion. To describe motion, you must state the direction the object is moving as well as how fast the object is moving. You must also tell its location at a certain time.

Choosing a Frame of Reference

How fast is the butterfly in Figure 1 moving? Remember that the butterfly is moving on Earth, but Earth itself is moving as it spins on its axis and revolves around the sun. If you consider this motion, the butterfly is moving very, very fast!

To describe motion accurately and completely, a frame of reference is necessary. The necessary ingredient of a description of motion—a **frame of reference**—is a system of objects that are not moving with respect to one another. The answer to "How fast is the butterfly moving?" depends on which frame of reference you use to measure motion. How do you decide which frame of reference to use when describing the butterfly's movement?

Figure 1 You must choose a frame of reference to tell how fast the butterfly is moving.
Applying Concepts *Identify a good frame of reference to use when describing the butterfly's motion.*

Figure 2 To someone riding on a speeding train, others on the train don't seem to be moving.

How Fast Are You Moving? How fast are the train passengers in Figure 2 moving? There are many correct answers because their motion is relative. This means it depends on the frame of reference you choose to measure their motion. **Relative motion** is movement in relation to a frame of reference. For example, as the train moves past a platform, people standing on the platform will see those on the train speeding by. But when the people on the train look at one another, they don't seem to be moving at all.

Which Frame Should You Choose? When you sit on a train and look out a window, a treetop may help you see how fast you are moving relative to the ground. But suppose you get up and walk toward the rear of the train. Looking at a seat or the floor may tell you how fast you are walking relative to the train. However, it doesn't tell you how fast you are moving relative to the ground outside. Choosing a meaningful frame of reference allows you to describe motion in a clear and relevant manner.

Measuring Distance

Distance is the length of a path between two points. When an object moves in a straight line, the distance is the length of the line connecting the object's starting point and its ending point.

It is helpful to express distances in units that are best suited to the motion you are studying. The SI unit for measuring distance is the meter (m). For very large distances, it is more common to make measurements in kilometers (km). One kilometer equals 1000 meters. For instance, it's easier to say that the Mississippi River has a length of 3780 kilometers than 3,780,000 meters. Distances that are smaller than a meter are measured in centimeters (cm). One centimeter is one hundredth of a meter. You might describe the distance a marble rolls, for example, as 6 centimeters rather than 0.06 meter.

For: Links on comparing frames of reference
Visit: www.SciLinks.org
Web Code: ccn-2111

Procedure

1. Draw a dot at the intersection of two lines near the bottom edge of a sheet of graph paper. Label the dot "Start."

2. Draw a second, similar dot near the top of the paper. Label this dot "End."

3. Draw a path from the Start dot to the End dot. Choose any path that stays on the grid lines.

4. Use a ruler to determine the distance of your path.

5. Use a ruler to determine the displacement from start to end.

Analyze and Conclude

1. **Observing** Which is shorter, the distance or the displacement?

2. **Evaluating and Revising** How could you have made the distance shorter?

3. **Inferring** If you keep the Start and End points the same, is it possible to make the displacement shorter? Explain your answer.

Measuring Displacements

To describe an object's position relative to a given point, you need to know how far away and in what direction the object is from that point. Displacement provides this information. ➾ **Distance is the length of the path between two points. Displacement is the direction from the starting point and the length of a straight line from the starting point to the ending point.**

Displacements are sometimes used when giving directions. Telling someone to "Walk 5 blocks" does not ensure they'll end up in the right place. However, saying "Walk 5 blocks north from the bus stop" will get the person to the right place. Accurate directions give the direction from a starting point as well as the distance.

Think about the motion of a roller coaster car. If you measure the path along which the car has traveled, you are describing distance. The direction from the starting point to the car and the length of the straight line from the starting point to the car describe displacement. After completing one trip around the track, the roller coaster car's displacement is zero.

Combining Displacements

Displacement is an example of a vector. A **vector** is a quantity that has magnitude and direction. The magnitude can be size, length, or amount. Arrows on a graph or map are used to represent vectors. The length of the arrow shows the magnitude of the vector. Vector addition is the combining of vector magnitudes and directions. ➾ **Add displacements using vector addition.**

Displacement Along a Straight Line When two displacements, represented by two vectors, have the same direction, you can add their magnitudes. In Figure 3A, the magnitudes of the car's displacements are 4 kilometers and 2 kilometers. The total magnitude of the displacement is 6 kilometers. If two displacements are in opposite directions, the magnitudes subtract from each other, as shown in Figure 3B. Because the car's displacements (4 kilometers and 2 kilometers) are in opposite directions, the magnitude of the total displacement is 2 kilometers.

Figure 3 When motion is in a straight line, vectors add and subtract easily. **A** Add the magnitudes of two displacement vectors that have the same direction. **B** Two displacement vectors with opposite directions are subtracted from each other.

4 km + 2 km = 6 km

4 km − 2 km = 2 km

Displacement That Isn't Along a Straight Path

When two or more displacement vectors have different directions, they may be combined by graphing. Figure 4 shows vectors representing the movement of a boy walking from his home to school. He starts by walking 1 block east. Then he turns a corner and walks 1 block north. He turns once again and walks 2 blocks east. For the last part of his trip to school, he walks 3 blocks north. The lengths of the vectors representing this path are 1 block, 1 block, 2 blocks, and 3 blocks.

The boy walked a total distance of 7 blocks. You can determine this distance by adding the magnitudes of each vector along his path.

The vector in red is called the **resultant vector,** which is the vector sum of two or more vectors. In this case, it shows the displacement. The resultant vector points directly from the starting point to the ending point. If you place a sheet of paper on the figure and mark the length of the resultant vector, you see that it equals the length of 5 blocks. Vector addition, then, shows that the boy's displacement is 5 blocks approximately northeast, while the distance he walked is 7 blocks.

Figure 4 Measuring the resultant vector (the diagonal red line) shows that the displacement from the boy's home to his school is two blocks less than the distance he actually traveled.

Section 11.1 Assessment

Reviewing Concepts

1. What is a frame of reference? How is it used to measure motion?

2. How are distance and displacement similar and different?

3. How are displacements combined?

4. A girl who is watching a plane fly tells her friend that the plane isn't moving at all. Describe a frame of reference in which the girl's description would be true.

Critical Thinking

5. **Using Analogies** Is displacement more like the length of a rope that is pulled tight or the length of a coiled rope? Explain.

6. **Making Judgments** Would you measure the height of a building in meters? Give reasons for your answer.

7. **Problem Solving** Should your directions to a friend for traveling from one city to another include displacements or distances? Explain.

8. **Inferring** The resultant vector of two particular displacement vectors does not equal the sum of the magnitudes of the individual vectors. Describe the directions of the two vectors.

Writing in Science

Compare-Contrast Paragraph Write a paragraph describing how the distance you travel from home to school is different from your displacement from home to school. (*Hint:* Make a simple sketch similar to Figure 4 and refer to it as you write.)

11.2 Speed and Velocity

Key Concepts

- How are instantaneous speed and average speed different?
- How can you find the speed from a distance-time graph?
- How are speed and velocity different?
- How do velocities add?

Vocabulary

- speed
- average speed
- instantaneous speed
- velocity

Reading Strategy

Monitoring Your Understanding After you have finished reading this section, copy the table below. Identify several things you have learned that are relevant to your life. Explain why they are relevant to you.

What Is Relevant	Why It Is Relevant
a. ?	b. ?
c. ?	d. ?
e. ?	f. ?

Figure 5 The speed of an in-line skater is usually described in meters per second. The speed of a car is usually described in kilometers per hour.

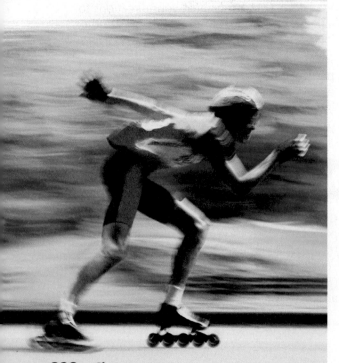

ook out a window for a few minutes, and you will see things in motion. Some things are moving slowly. Perhaps you see a leaf floating through the air. Other things, such as a car or a bird, are moving fast. The growth rate of trees and grass is so slow that their motion cannot be detected with the unaided eye. The differences among these types of motion can be described in terms of speed.

Speed

To describe the speed of a car, you might say it is moving at 45 kilometers per hour. **Speed** is the ratio of the distance an object moves to the amount of time the object moves. The SI unit of speed is meters per second (m/s). However, just as with distances, you need to choose units that make the most sense for the motion you are describing. The in-line skater in Figure 5 may travel 2 meters in one second. The speed would be expressed as 2 m/s. A car might travel 80 kilometers in one hour. Its speed would be expressed as 80 km/h.

Two ways to express the speed of an object are average speed and instantaneous speed. **Average speed is computed for the entire duration of a trip, and instantaneous speed is measured at a particular instant.** In different situations, either one or both of these measurements may be a useful way to describe speed.

Average Speed Describing the speed of a hiker isn't as easy as describing constant speed along a straight line. A hiker may travel slowly along rocky areas but then travel quickly when going downhill. Sometimes it is useful to know how fast something moves for an entire trip. **Average speed,** $\bar{v}$, is the total distance traveled, d, divided by the time, t, it takes to travel that distance. This can be written as an equation:

For: Links on motion
Visit: www.SciLinks.org
Web Code: ccn-2112

Average Speed

$$\text{Average speed} = \frac{\text{Total distance}}{\text{Total time}}, \text{ or } \bar{v} = \frac{d}{t}$$

During the time an object is moving, its speed may change, but this equation tells you the average speed over the entire trip.

 Skills

Calculating Average Speed

While traveling on vacation, you measure the times and distances traveled. You travel 35 kilometers in 0.4 hour, followed by 53 kilometers in 0.6 hour. What is your average speed?

1 **Read and Understand**

What information are you given?

Total Distance (d) = **35 km + 53 km = 88 km**

Total Time (t) = **0.4 h + 0.6 h = 1.0 h**

2 **Plan and Solve**

What unknown are you trying to calculate?

Average Speed $(\bar{v})$ = ?

What formula contains the given quantities and the unknown?

$$\bar{v} = \frac{d}{t}$$

Replace each variable with its known value.

$$\bar{v} = \frac{88 \text{ km}}{1 \text{ h}} = 88 \text{ km/h}$$

3 **Look Back and Check**

Is your answer reasonable?

Yes, 88 km/h is a typical highway speed.

 Practice

1. A person jogs 4.0 kilometers in 32 minutes, then 2.0 kilometers in 22 minutes, and finally 1.0 kilometer in 16 minutes. What is the jogger's average speed in kilometers per minute?

2. A train travels 190 kilometers in 3.0 hours, and then 120 kilometers in 2.0 hours. What is its average speed?

For: Activity on the movement of Earth's plates
Visit: PHSchool.com
Web Code: ccc-2112

Figure 6 The speedometer in a car measures the car's instantaneous speed. Note the scale markings are given both in km/h and miles per hour, mph.

Instantaneous Speed Average speed is useful because it lets you know how long a trip will take. Sometimes however, such as when driving on the highway, you need to know how fast you are going at a particular moment. The car's speedometer gives your instantaneous speed. **Instantaneous speed,** v, is the rate at which an object is moving at a given moment in time. For example, you could describe the instantaneous speed of the car in Figure 6 as 55 km/h.

> **Reading Checkpoint** *What does a car's speedometer measure?*

Graphing Motion

A distance-time graph is a good way to describe motion. Figure 7 shows distance-time graphs for the motion of three cars. Recall that slope is the change in the vertical axis value divided by the change in the horizontal axis value. On these graphs, the slope is the change in the distance divided by the change in time. **The slope of a line on a distance-time graph is speed.** In Figure 7A, the car travels 500.0 meters in 20.0 seconds, or 25.0 meters per second. In Figure 7B, another car travels 250.0 meters in 20.0 seconds at a constant speed. The slope of the line is 250.0 meters divided by 20.0 seconds, or 12.5 meters per second. Notice that the line for the car traveling at a higher speed is steeper. A steeper slope on a distance-time graph indicates a higher speed.

Figure 7C shows the motion of a car that is not traveling at a constant speed. This car travels 200.0 meters in the first 8.0 seconds. It then stops for 4.0 seconds, as indicated by the horizontal part of the line. Next the car travels 300.0 meters in 8.0 seconds. The times when the car is gradually increasing or decreasing its speed are shown by the curved parts of the line. The slope of the straight portions of the line represent periods of constant speed. Note that the car's speed is 25 meters per second during the first part of its trip and 38 meters per second during the last part of its trip.

Figure 7 The slope of the line on a distance–time graph indicates the speed of the object. **Using Graphs** *If the car in Figure 7A required less time to travel a given distance, how would the slope change?*

A

B

C

Measuring Distance and Speed

Every car has a speedometer, which measures the car's speed, and an odometer, which measures the distance it has traveled. These devices work by counting the number of times the car's wheels turn (to give distance) and their rate of turning (speed).

Interpreting Diagrams *What is the purpose of the worm gears?*

Digital Odometer
Some cars have a magnetic sensor that detects turns of the transmission shaft. The signal is transmitted to a computer, which calculates and displays the car's distance traveled.

Coil spring *This spring holds the pointer at zero when the car and the magnet are at rest.*

Cable *A cable linked to the transmission rotates at a rate directly proportional to the road speed.*

Pointer *The pointer is attached to the drag cup. The faster the magnet spins, the greater the angle the drag cup turns. The higher speed is shown by the pointer.*

Worm gears *The worm gears reduce the cable's rotational speed and move the odometer dials.*

Drag cup *The drag cup turns from its resting position through an angle that increases with the magnet's spin rate.*

Dial

Measurement
For each full turn of the worm gear the odometer moves up one digit, indicating that the car has traveled one tenth of a mile.

Odometer

Magnet *The magnet is attached to the shaft. As the shaft spins the magnet, a magnetic field exerts force on the drag cup.*

Figure 8 A cheetah's speed may be as fast as 90 km/h. To describe the cheetah's velocity, you must also know the direction in which it is moving.

Velocity

The cheetah is the fastest land animal in the world. Suppose a cheetah, running at 90 kilometers per hour, is 30 meters from an antelope that is standing still. How long will it be before the cheetah reaches the antelope? Do you have enough information to answer the question? The answer is no. Sometimes knowing only the speed of an object isn't enough. You also need to know the direction of the object's motion. Together, the speed and direction in which an object is moving are called **velocity.** To determine how long it will be before the cheetah reaches the antelope, you need to know the cheetah's velocity, not just its speed. **Velocity is a description of both speed and direction of motion. Velocity is a vector.**

Figure 8 shows a cheetah in motion. If you have ever seen a video of a cheetah chasing its prey, you know that a cheetah can change speed and direction very quickly. To represent the cheetah's motion, you could use velocity vectors. You would need vectors of varying lengths, each vector corresponding to the cheetah's velocity at a particular instant. A longer vector would represent a faster speed, and a shorter one would show a slower speed. The vectors would also point in different directions to represent the cheetah's direction at any moment.

A change in velocity can be the result of a change in speed, a change in direction, or both. The sailboat in Figure 9 moves in a straight line (constant direction) at a constant speed. The sailboat can be described as moving with uniform motion, which is another way of saying it has constant velocity. The sailboat may change its velocity simply by speeding up or slowing down. However, the sailboat's velocity also changes if it changes its direction. It may continue to move at a constant speed, but the change of direction is a change in velocity.

Figure 9 As the sailboat's direction changes, its velocity also changes, even if its speed stays the same.
Inferring *If the sailboat slows down at the same time that it changes direction, how will its velocity be changed?*

Combining Velocities

Sometimes the motion of an object involves more than one velocity. 🔑 **Two or more velocities add by vector addition.** The velocity of the river relative to the riverbank (X) and the velocity of the boat relative to the river (Y) in Figure 10A combine. They yield the velocity of the boat relative to the riverbank (Z). This velocity is 17 kilometers per hour downstream.

In Figure 10B, the relative velocities of the current (X) and the boat (Y) are at right angles to each other. Adding these velocity vectors yields a resultant velocity of the boat relative to the riverbank of 13 km/h (Z). Note that this velocity is at an angle to the riverbank.

Figure 10 Vector addition is used when motion involves more than one velocity. **A** The velocity of the boat in the reference frame of the riverbank (17 km/h) is a combination of the relative velocities of the boat and the river. **B** You can determine the resultant velocity of the boat relative to the riverbank (13 km/h) by measuring from the tail of one vector to the head of the other.

Section 11.2 Assessment

Reviewing Concepts

1. 💬 What does velocity describe?

2. 💬 What shows the speed on a distance-time graph?

3. 💬 What is the difference between average speed and instantaneous speed?

4. 💬 How can two or more velocities be combined?

Critical Thinking

5. **Applying Concepts** Does a car's speedometer show instantaneous speed, average speed, or velocity? Explain.

6. **Designing Experiments** Describe an experiment you could perform to determine the average speed of a toy car rolling down an incline.

7. **Applying Concepts** Explain why the slope on a distance-time graph is speed. (*Hint:* Use the definition of *speed* on page 332 and the graphs in Figure 7.)

Math ⬧ Practice

8. An Olympic swimmer swims 50.0 meters in 23.1 seconds. What is his average speed?

9. A plane's average speed between two cities is 600 km/h. If the trip takes 2.5 hours, how far does the plane fly? (*Hint:* Use the average speed formula in the form $d = \bar{v}t$.)

Navigation at Sea

For centuries, crossing the oceans was extremely perilous. There are few landmarks at sea to guide the sailor, and methods of measuring direction, speed, and distance were crude and often inaccurate.

The invention of the magnetic compass brought major advancement in navigation in the early 1100s. Although the compass allowed a sailor to maintain an accurate course, it did nothing to tell him where he actually was. For this, a frame of reference was needed, and the one adopted was the system of latitude and longitude. This system measures location in degrees north or south of the equator, and degrees east or west of Greenwich, England. Using a device called a sextant, latitude in the northern hemisphere was relatively easy to determine. Finding longitude was more difficult. The solution was to combine celestial observation and the use of a highly accurate sea-going clock that kept track of the time at a fixed location on Earth.

Sextant
This instrument was once an essential aid to navigation. With it, a sailor could accurately measure the angles of celestial bodies above the horizon. To take a reading, the observer looks through the telescope and moves the sextant's arm until an image of a star or the sun lines up with the horizon. The angle is then read off the scale.

Sun's rays

Fixed mirror

Rotating mirror

Telescope

Eyepiece

Movable arm

Scale

Magnetic compass
The magnetic compass contains a magnetized needle which, due to the Earth's magnetic field, points roughly toward the North Pole.

Finding location

Regular calculations of latitude and longitude have been the cornerstone of ocean navigation for about 300 years. A sextant and an accurate sea-going clock were needed to calculate both.

Determining latitude

To determine latitude is to find out how far north or south you are from the equator. In the northern hemisphere, latitude is measured with reference to Polaris. Using a sextant, you measure the angle of Polaris above the horizon, and this gives you your latitude, expressed in degrees. If Polaris is directly overhead, you must be at the North Pole (90° north latitude); if it is on the horizon, you must be at the equator (0°).

Determining longitude

To determine longitude is to find out how far east or west you are from Greenwich, England. To do this, while you are still in your home port, you set your sea-going clock for noon when the sun is at its highest point. Then, while you are at sea, you check the clock again when the sun is at its highest point. If the clock says 3 P.M., then you must have traveled 3 hours west of the port. Since the sun moves 15° per hour, 3 hours corresponds to 45° west.

CONCEPTS in Action

Modern navigation

Today's sea navigators are fortunate by comparison with their predecessors. Instead of having to make complex calculations involving times and sextant angles, they can buy a global positioning system receiver. This modern receiver not only provides quick and accurate readings of latitude and longitude, but it also displays the ship's position on a digital chart.

Satellite network The global network consists of 24 satellites in six different circular orbits around Earth.

The satellites orbit 20,200 km above Earth's surface.

Range of positions *Each satellite transmits a range of possible positions for the ship (shown here by colored circles).*

GPS satellite *Each satellite emits precisely timed radio signals.*

On-board GPS receiver

Global Positioning System (GPS)
A GPS receiver calculates its distance from a minimum of three satellites by analyzing the different travel times of their signals. The distance from each satellite gives a range of possibilities for the receiver's location. To find its exact position, a microchip in the on-board receiver calculates where the signals intersect.

Master control
Located in Colorado, the master control communicates with all the satellites.

340 *Chapter 11*

Charting a course

A navigator normally keeps a record of the ship's movements on a chart. Positions obtained by GPS or other means are plotted on the chart, which can also be used to work out a compass bearing or a course for the next part of the voyage.

Transparent compass

Nautical dividers
Dividers are used for making chart measurements.

Ship's position

Coast

GPS receiver

Today, receivers are made in a range of sizes down to handheld models. They usually give a position accurate to 100 meters, but enhanced units are accurate within 10 meters.

Open sea

Using radar

A radar set displays nearby land, boats, and other surface objects. It is useful for both navigation and collision avoidance, especially in foggy conditions.

Going Further

■ Research the term *knots,* which is used for measuring a ship's speed. Write a paragraph to explain how speed was originally estimated on a ship by using knots.

11.3 Acceleration

Reading Focus

Key Concepts

- How are changes in velocity described?
- How can you calculate acceleration?
- How does a speed-time graph indicate acceleration?
- What is instantaneous acceleration?

Vocabulary

- ◆ acceleration
- ◆ free fall
- ◆ constant acceleration
- ◆ linear graph
- ◆ nonlinear graph

Reading Strategy

Summarizing Read the section on acceleration. Then copy and complete the concept map below to organize what you know about acceleration.

Figure 11 The basketball constantly changes velocity as it rises and falls.

A basketball constantly changes velocity during a game. The player in Figure 11 dribbles the ball down the court, and the ball speeds up as it falls and slows down as it rises. As she passes the ball, it flies through the air and suddenly stops when a teammate catches it. The velocity of the ball increases again as it is thrown toward the basket.

But the rate at which velocity changes is also important. Imagine a basketball player running down the court and slowly coming to a stop. Now imagine the player running down the court and stopping suddenly. If the player stops slowly, his or her velocity changes slowly. If the player stops suddenly, his or her velocity changes quickly. The ball handler's teammates must position themselves to assist the drive or to take a pass. Opposing team members want to prevent the ball handler from reaching the basket. Each player must anticipate the ball handler's motion.

Velocity changes frequently, not only in a basketball game, but throughout our physical world. Describing changes in velocity, and how fast they occur, is a necessary part of describing motion.

What Is Acceleration?

The rate at which velocity changes is called **acceleration.** Recall that velocity is a combination of speed and direction. **Acceleration can be described as changes in speed, changes in direction, or changes in both. Acceleration is a vector.**

Changes in Speed We often use the word *acceleration* to describe situations in which the speed of an object is increasing. A television newscaster describing the liftoff of a rocket-launched space shuttle, for example, might exclaim, "That shuttle is really accelerating!" We understand that the newscaster is describing the spacecraft's quickly increasing speed as it clears its launch pad and rises through the atmosphere. Scientifically, however, acceleration applies to any change in an object's velocity. This change may be either an increase or a decrease in speed. Acceleration can be caused by positive (increasing) change in speed or by negative (decreasing) change in speed.

For example, suppose that you are sitting on a bus waiting at a stoplight. The light turns green and the bus moves forward. You feel the acceleration as you are pushed back against your seat. The acceleration is the result of an increase in the speed of the bus. As the bus moves down the street at a constant speed, its acceleration is zero. You no longer feel pushed toward your seat. When the bus approaches another stoplight, it begins to slow down. Again, its speed is changing, so the bus is accelerating. You feel pulled away from your seat. Acceleration results from increases or decreases in speed. As the bus slows to a stop, it experiences negative acceleration, also known as deceleration. Deceleration is an acceleration that slows an object's speed.

An example of acceleration due to change in speed is **free fall,** the movement of an object toward Earth solely because of gravity. Recall that the unit for velocity is meters per second. The unit for acceleration, then, is meters per second per second. This unit is typically written as meters per second squared (m/s^2). Objects falling near Earth's surface accelerate downward at a rate of 9.8 m/s^2. Each second an object is in free fall, its velocity increases downward by 9.8 meters per second. Imagine the stone in Figure 12 falling from the mouth of the well. After 1 second, the stone will be falling at about 9.8 m/s. After 2 seconds, the stone will be going faster by 9.8 m/s. Its speed will now be downward at 19.6 m/s. The change in the stone's speed is 9.8 m/s^2, the acceleration due to gravity.

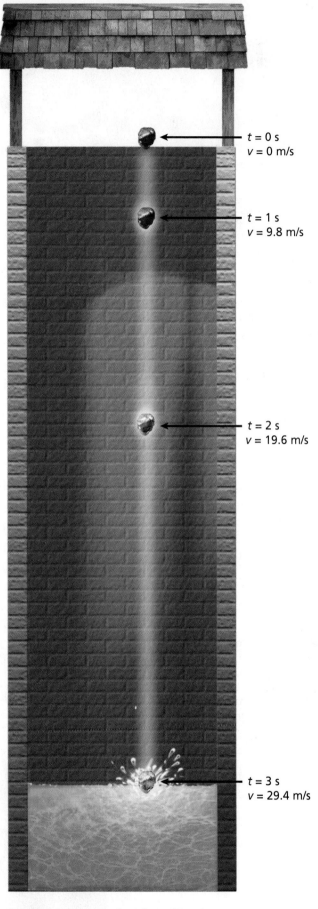

$t = 0$ s
$v = 0$ m/s

$t = 1$ s
$v = 9.8$ m/s

$t = 2$ s
$v = 19.6$ m/s

$t = 3$ s
$v = 29.4$ m/s

Figure 12 The velocity of an object in free fall increases 9.8 m/s each second.

Changes in Direction Acceleration isn't always the result of changes in speed. You can accelerate even if your speed is constant. You experience this type of acceleration if you ride a bicycle around a curve. Although you may have a constant speed, your change in direction means you are accelerating. You also may have experienced this type of acceleration if you have ridden on a carousel like the one in Figure 13. A horse on the carousel is traveling at a constant speed, but it is accelerating because its direction is constantly changing.

Figure 13 When you ride on a carousel, you accelerate because of the changing direction.

Changes in Speed and Direction Sometimes motion is characterized by changes in both speed and direction at the same time. You experience this type of motion if you ride on a roller coaster like the one in Figure 14. The roller coaster ride starts out slowly as the cars travel up the steeply inclined rails. The cars reach the top of the incline. Suddenly they plummet toward the ground and then whip around a curve. You are thrown backward, forward, and sideways as your velocity increases, decreases, and changes direction. Your acceleration is constantly changing because of changes in the speed and direction of the cars of the roller coaster.

Similarly, passengers in a car moving at the posted speed limit along a winding road experience rapidly changing acceleration. The car may enter a long curve at the same time that it slows to maintain a safe interval behind another car. The car is accelerating both because it is changing direction and because its speed is decreasing.

Figure 14 A roller coaster produces acceleration due to changes in both speed and direction. **Applying Concepts** *Describe the acceleration occuring at this instant on the rollercoaster ride.*

Constant Acceleration The velocity of an object moving in a straight line changes at a constant rate when the object is experiencing constant acceleration. **Constant acceleration** is a steady change in velocity. That is, the velocity of the object changes by the same amount each second. An example of constant acceleration is illustrated by the jet airplane shown in Figure 15. The airplane's acceleration may be constant during a portion of its takeoff.

 What is constant acceleration?

Figure 15 Constant acceleration during takeoff results in changes to an aircraft's velocity that are in a constant direction.

Calculating Acceleration

Acceleration is the rate at which velocity changes. **You calculate acceleration for straight-line motion by dividing the change in velocity by the total time.** If a is the acceleration, v_i is the initial velocity, v_f is the final velocity, and t is total time, then this equation can be written as follows.

Acceleration

$$\text{Acceleration} = \frac{\text{Change in velocity}}{\text{Total time}} = \frac{(v_f - v_i)}{t}$$

Notice in this formula that velocity is in the numerator and time is in the denominator. If the velocity increases, the numerator is positive and thus the acceleration is also positive. For example, if you are coasting downhill on a bicycle, your velocity increases and your acceleration is positive. If the velocity decreases, then the numerator is negative and the acceleration is also negative. For example, if you continue coasting after you reach the bottom of the hill, your velocity decreases and your acceleration is negative.

Remember that acceleration and velocity are both vector quantities. Thus, if an object moving at constant speed changes its direction of travel, there is still acceleration. In other words, the acceleration can occur even if the speed is constant. Think about a car moving at a constant speed as it rounds a curve. Because its direction is changing, the car is accelerating.

To determine a change in velocity, subtract one velocity vector from another. If the motion is in a straight line, however, the velocity can be treated as speed. You can then find acceleration from the change in speed divided by the time.

For: Links on acceleration
Visit: www.SciLinks.org
Web Code: ccn-2113

Calculating Acceleration

A ball rolls down a ramp, starting from rest. After 2 seconds, its velocity is 6 meters per second. What is the acceleration of the ball?

1 **Read and Understand**

What information are you given?

> **Time** = 2 s
>
> **Starting velocity** = 0 m/s
>
> **Ending velocity** = 6 m/s

2 **Plan and Solve**

What unknown are you trying to calculate?

> **Acceleration** = ?

What formula contains the given quantities and the unknown?

$$a = \frac{(v_f - v_i)}{t}$$

Replace each variable with its known value.

$$\text{Acceleration} = \frac{(6 \text{ m/s} - 0 \text{ m/s})}{2 \text{ s}}$$

$$= 3 \text{ m/s}^2 \text{ down the ramp}$$

3 **Look Back and Check**

Is your answer reasonable?

Objects in free fall accelerate at a rate of 9.8 m/s². The ramp is not very steep. An acceleration of 3 m/s² seems reasonable.

 Math **Practice**

1. A car traveling at 10 m/s starts to decelerate steadily. It comes to a complete stop in 20 seconds. What is its acceleration?

2. An airplane travels down a runway for 4.0 seconds with an acceleration of 9.0 m/s². What is its change in velocity during this time?

3. A child drops a ball from a bridge. The ball strikes the water under the bridge 2.0 seconds later. What is the velocity of the ball when it strikes the water?

4. A boy throws a rock straight up into the air. It reaches the highest point of its flight after 2.5 seconds. How fast was the rock going when it left the boy's hand?

Graphs of Accelerated Motion

You can use a graph to calculate acceleration. For example, consider a downhill skier who is moving in a straight line. After traveling down the hill for 1 second, the skier's speed is 4 meters per second. In the next second the speed increases by an additional 4 meters per second, so the skier's acceleration is 4 m/s². Figure 16 is a graph of the skier's speed. ● **The slope of a speed-time graph is acceleration.** This slope is change in speed divided by change in time.

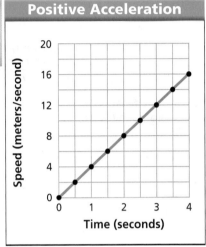

Positive Acceleration

Speed-Time Graphs The skier's speed increased at a constant rate because the skier was moving down the hill with constant acceleration. Constant acceleration is represented on a speed–time graph by a straight line. The graph in Figure 16 is an example of a **linear graph,** in which the displayed data form straight-line parts. The slope of the line is the acceleration.

Constant negative acceleration decreases speed. A speed-time graph of the motion of a bicycle slowing to a stop is shown in Figure 17. The horizontal line segment represents constant speed. The line segment sloping downward represents the bicycle slowing down. The change in speed is negative, so the slope of the line is negative.

Figure 16 The slope of a speed-time graph indicates acceleration. A positive slope shows that the skier's acceleration is positive.

Negative Acceleration

Figure 17 The horizontal part of the graph shows a biker's constant speed. The part of the graph with negative slope shows negative acceleration as the mountain biker slows to a stop.

Acceleration Over Time

Distance (meters) vs. Time (seconds)

Figure 18 A distance-time graph of accelerated motion is a curve.

Distance-Time Graphs Accelerated motion is represented by a curved line on a distance-time graph. In a **nonlinear graph,** a curve connects the data points that are plotted. Figure 18 is a distance-time graph. The data in this graph are for a ball dropped from rest toward the ground.

Compare the slope of the curve during the first second to the slope of the curve during the fourth second. Notice that the slope is much greater during the fourth second than it is during the first second. Because the slope represents the speed of the ball, an increasing slope means that the speed is increasing. An increasing speed means that the ball is accelerating.

Instantaneous Acceleration

Acceleration is rarely constant, and motion is rarely in a straight line. A skateboarder moving along a half-pipe changes speed and direction. As a result, her acceleration changes. At each moment she is accelerating, but her instantaneous acceleration is always changing. **Instantaneous acceleration is how fast a velocity is changing at a specific instant.**

Acceleration involves a change in velocity or direction or both, so the vector of the skateboarder's acceleration can point in any direction. The vector's length depends on how fast she is changing her velocity. At every moment she has an instantaneous acceleration, even if she is standing still and the acceleration vector is zero.

Section 11.3 Assessment

Reviewing Concepts

1. Describe three types of changes in velocity.
2. What is the equation for acceleration?
3. What shows acceleration on a speed-time graph?
4. Define instantaneous acceleration.

Critical Thinking

5. **Comparing and Contrasting** How are deceleration and acceleration related?
6. **Applying Concepts** Two trains leave a station at the same time. Train A travels at a constant speed of 16 m/s. Train B starts at 8.0 m/s but accelerates constantly at 1.0 m/s². After 10.0 seconds, which train has the greater speed?

7. **Inferring** Suppose you plot the distance traveled by an object at various times and you discover that the graph is not a straight line. What does this indicate about the object's acceleration?

Math Practice

8. A train moves from rest to a speed of 25 m/s in 30.0 seconds. What is the magnitude of its acceleration?
9. A car traveling at a speed of 25 m/s increases its speed to 30.0 m/s in 10.0 seconds. What is the magnitude of its acceleration?

Investigating the Velocity of a Sinking Marble

In this lab, you will graph the motion of a marble falling through shampoo.

Problem What does a distance-time graph look like for a marble falling through shampoo?

Materials

- clear shampoo
- 100-mL graduated cylinder
- 2 small marbles
- stopwatch
- forceps
- masking tape
- metric ruler
- 10-mL graduated cylinder
- long glass stirring rod
- dropper pipet
- graph paper

Skills Measuring, Observing, Using Tables and Graphs

Procedure

1. On a separate sheet of paper, make a copy of the data table shown.

Data Table		
Distance (mm)	First Marble Time (s)	Second Marble Time (s)

2. Wrap a small amount of masking tape around the tips of the forceps. This will allow you to grip the marble with them.

3. Measure the distance between the 10-mL gradations on the 100-mL graduated cylinder. Record the new distance in the first row of your data table.

4. Multiply this distance by 2 and write the result in the second row. For the third row, multiply the distance by 3. Continue until you have written distances in 10 rows.

5. Slowly pour 100 mL of clear shampoo into the 100-mL graduated cylinder.

6. Be ready to observe the marble as it falls through the shampoo. Grasp the marble with the forceps and hold the marble just above the shampoo-filled graduated cylinder.

7. Say "Go!" as you drop the marble into the shampoo. At the same moment, your partner should start the stopwatch.

8. Each time the lower edge of the marble reaches a 10-mL mark on the cylinder, say "Now." Your partner should note and record the time on the stopwatch.

9. Continue calling out "Now" each time the marble reaches a 10-mL mark until it comes to rest on the bottom of the cylinder. Say "Stop!"

10. Use the 10-mL graduated cylinder to add about 8 mL of water to the 100-mL graduated cylinder. Use the glass stirring rod to mix the water and shampoo gently but thoroughly.

11. With the dropper pipet, remove enough liquid from the graduated cylinder to decrease the volume to 100 mL.

12. Repeat Steps 6 through 9 using another marble.

13. Wash all supplies as instructed by your teacher.

Analyze and Conclude

1. **Using Tables and Graphs** Use the data you collected to make a distance-time graph for each of the two marbles.

2. **Observing** Explain the motion of the marbles as they fell through the shampoo. How did you show this motion on your graphs?

3. **Inferring** Based on your graphs, were the marbles accelerating? Explain your answers.

4. **Calculating** Use your data table to calculate the average speed of each marble.

For: Data sharing
Visit: PHSchool.com
Web Code: ccd-2110

Study Guide

11.1 Distance and Displacement

Key Concepts

- To describe motion accurately and completely, a frame of reference is needed.
- Distance is the length of the path between two points. Displacement is the direction from the starting point and the length of a straight line from the starting point to the ending point.
- Add displacements by using vector addition.

Vocabulary

frame of reference, *p. 328*

relative motion, *p. 329*

distance, *p. 329*

vector, *p. 330*

resultant vector, *p. 331*

11.2 Speed and Velocity

Key Concepts

- Average speed is computed for the entire duration of a trip, and instantaneous speed is measured at a particular instant.

- $\text{Average speed} = \dfrac{\text{Total distance}}{\text{Total time}}$

- The slope of a line on a distance-time graph is speed.
- Velocity is a description of both speed and direction of motion. Velocity is a vector.
- Two or more velocities add by vector addition.

Vocabulary

speed, *p. 332*

average speed, *p. 333*

instantaneous speed, *p. 334*

velocity, *p. 336*

11.3 Acceleration

Key Concepts

- Acceleration can be described as changes in speed, changes in direction, or changes in both. Acceleration is a vector.
- You calculate acceleration by dividing the change in velocity by the total time.

$$\text{Acceleration} = \frac{v_f - v_i}{t}$$

- The slope of a speed-time graph is the acceleration.
- Instantaneous acceleration is how fast a velocity is changing at a specific instant.

Vocabulary

acceleration, *p. 342*

free fall, *p. 343*

constant acceleration, *p. 345*

linear graph, *p. 347*

nonlinear graph, *p. 348*

Thinking Visually

Concept Map Copy the concept map below onto a sheet of paper. Use information from the chapter to complete the concept map.

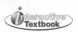
Reviewing Content

Choose the letter that best answers the question or completes the statement.

1. Motion is described with respect to a
   a. graph.
   b. displacement.
   c. slope.
   d. frame of reference.

2. Displacement is distance combined with
   a. direction.
   b. speed.
   c. velocity.
   d. magnitude.

3. Displacement vectors of 3 m and 5 m in the same direction combine to make a displacement vector that is
   a. 2 m.
   b. 0 m.
   c. 8 m.
   d. 15 m.

4. Average speed is the total distance divided by the
   a. average distance.
   b. average acceleration.
   c. total time.
   d. slope.

5. The slope of a distance-time graph is equal to the
   a. speed.
   b. acceleration.
   c. displacement.
   d. motion.

6. Velocity is
   a. the slope of a linear graph.
   b. acceleration divided by displacement.
   c. speed with direction.
   d. the same in all reference frames.

7. Two or more velocities can be combined by
   a. graphing the slope.
   b. using vector addition.
   c. calculating the instantaneous speed.
   d. determining the rate.

8. A ball just dropped is an example of
   a. constant speed.
   b. instantaneous speed.
   c. combining displacements.
   d. free fall.

9. Acceleration is equal to
   a. distance divided by time.
   b. change in speed divided by time.
   c. the slope of a distance-time graph.
   d. change in speed multiplied by time.

10. The rate at which velocity is changing at a given instant is described by
   a. instantaneous acceleration.
   b. average speed.
   c. constant speed.
   d. vector addition.

Understanding Concepts

11. Why is it necessary to choose a single frame of reference when measuring motion?

12. For what kinds of distances would you choose to make measurements in millimeters? In kilometers?

13. Light from a star travels to Earth in a straight line at a constant speed of almost 300,000 km/s. What is the acceleration of the light?

14. If two displacement vectors add to yield a total displacement of zero, what do you know about the two displacements?

15. How will the total distance traveled by a car in 2 hours be affected if the average speed is doubled?

16. How do you know that a speedometer tells you the instantaneous speed of a car?

17. On a distance-time graph, what would the curve describing constant speed look like?

18. A spider is crawling on a wall. First it crawls 1 meter up, then 1 meter to the left, and then 1 meter down. What is its total displacement?

19. A jogger travels 8.0 kilometers in 1.25 hours. What is the jogger's average speed?

20. You see a lightning bolt in the sky. You hear a clap of thunder 3 seconds later. The sound travels at a speed of 330 m/s. How far away was the lightning? (*Hint:* Assume you see lightning instantly.)

21. If a river current is 8.0 m/s, and a boat is traveling 10.0 m/s upstream, what is the boat's speed relative to the riverbank?

22. If an object is moving with constant velocity, what do you know about its acceleration?

23. If the plotted points on a speed-time graph do not form a straight line, what do you know about the object's acceleration?

24. Explain a situation in which you can accelerate even though your speed doesn't change.

Assessment (continued)

Critical Thinking

25. Applying Concepts A girl moves at 2 m/s delivering newspapers. She throws a newspaper directly behind her at 2 m/s. In the frame of reference of someone standing nearby, what is the motion of the newspaper?

26. Designing an Experiment Design an experiment to measure the speed of a toy train going around a circular track.

27. Analyzing Data A raft floats downstream. After 1 minute it has moved 50.0 meters. After 2 minutes it has moved 100.0 meters. After 3 minutes it has moved 150.0 meters. Could the raft's speed be constant? Explain.

28. Problem Solving A rocket ship is moving through space at 1000 m/s. It accelerates in the same direction at 4 m/s². What is its speed after 100 seconds?

Math Skills

Use the following graph to answer Questions 29 and 30.

A Record of Typical Motion

29. Using Graphs The graph above shows the motion for a person walking down a street. Describe the history of the motion.

30. Using Graphs How fast is the person walking during the first 10 seconds?

31. Calculating A car starts from rest and increases its speed to 15 m/s in 20 seconds. What is the car's acceleration?

Concepts in Action

32. Predicting The propulsion system of the rocket ship described in problem 28 is tested. Its rockets are fired and the ship accelerates from rest at 5 m/s² for 2 minutes. How does the ship's final velocity compare with the ship's initial velocity in problem 28?

33. Comparing and Contrasting Compare the case of a rubber ball falling through the air and a rubber ball bouncing up and down on a hard floor. For which of these cases is the instantaneous acceleration always the same as the constant acceleration?

34. Calculating Two trains on parallel tracks are traveling in the same direction. One train starts 10 km behind the other. It overtakes the first train in 2 hours. What is the relative speed of the second train with respect to the first train?

35. Writing in Science Write a paragraph explaining how different reference frames affect descriptions of motion in the following scenario. A basketball player dribbles down the court at a constant speed and then shoots the ball into the basket. Describe the motion of the ball from the reference frame of a camera mounted directly behind the basket. Then, describe the motion of the ball from the reference frame of the basketball player. (*Hint:* Sketch displacement versus time graphs of the ball's motion based on each reference frame.)

Performance-Based Assessment

Creating a Table Use a table to present the distances and displacements between familiar places. In a third column include the average speed at which you travel between these places. Be sure to list the places in pairs, such as home and school, a park and the library, or your bed and front door. Estimate the displacement if you can't measure it.

Go Online
PHSchool.com

For: Self-grading assessment
Visit: PHSchool.com
Web Code: cca-2110

Standardized Test Prep

Test-Taking Tip

When answering a question with a graph, keep these tips in mind:

- Read the question thoroughly to identify what the question is asking.
- Study the name of the graph, if applicable. This may help you identify what information is available from the graph.
- Carefully examine the graph and take note of the axes labels.
- Identify the scale of the axes.
- Recall information, equations, definitions, relationships, and so forth that may be required to interpret the graph. For example, the slope of a distance-time graph is the speed of the object.
- Once you have chosen your answer, check it against the graph.

Determining Distance

The graph above depicts motion in a straight line. During which time periods does acceleration occur?

(A) 0 s–2 s only
(B) 0 s–2 s and 6 s–8 s only
(C) 16 s–18 s only
(D) 0 s–2 s, 6 s–8 s, and 16 s–18 s only
(E) Acceleration occurs during the entire time period shown.

(Answer: D)

1. A delivery truck driver's round-trip route from the warehouse takes her 3 km east, then 1 km north, then 3 km west, and then 1 km south. Which of the following statements is FALSE?
   (A) The displacement of the round trip is zero.
   (B) The distance of the round trip is 8 km.
   (C) After driving 3 km east, the magnitude of the distance and displacement are the same.
   (D) After driving 3 km east and 1 km north, the magnitude of the distance and displacement are the same.
   (E) none of the above

2. A runner completes a 10.0-km race in exactly 30 minutes. What is the runner's average speed in km/h? (60 minutes = 1 hour)
   (A) 30.0 km/h   (B) 20.0 km/h
   (C) 15.0 km/h   (D) 10.0 km/h
   (E) 5.00 km/h

3. Which of the following is NOT a vector quantity?
   (A) velocity
   (B) displacement
   (C) distance
   (D) acceleration
   (E) none of the above

4. Based on the speed-time graph shown at the left, what is the acceleration during the first 2 seconds?
   (A) 1 m/s^2
   (B) 2 m/s^2
   (C) 4 m/s^2
   (D) 5 m/s^2
   (E) 10 m/s^2

5. A race car drives around a circular race track at constant speed. Which of the following statements is TRUE?
   (A) A speed-time graph of the car's motion would be a horizontal line.
   (B) A distance-time graph of the car's motion would be a straight line with a positive slope.
   (C) The velocity of the car is constantly changing.
   (D) The car is constantly accelerating.
   (E) all of the above

12 Forces and Motion

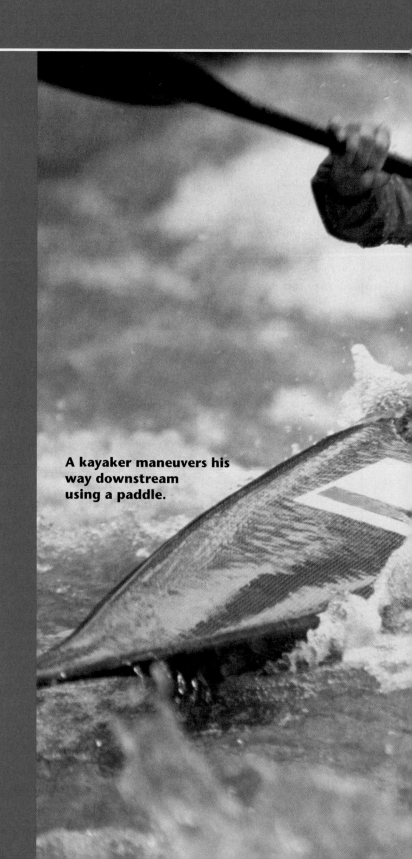

What forces are in a car crash?

When a car is in a collision, the forces on the car and on the people inside can be dangerously unbalanced. Go online and research video simulations of car crashes. Pick a crash simulation that you can use as a basis for a video presentation about forces. Plan to show the video during your presentation, and to pause it in at least three places to identify and describe both the balanced and unbalanced forces at that moment.

How do science concepts apply to your world? Here are some questions you'll be able to answer after you read this chapter.

- **Why doesn't the pulling by each team in a tug of war always result in motion?** *(Section 12.1)*

- **Why do flying squirrels spread their arms and legs when they jump through the air?** *(Section 12.1)*

- **What happens to the forward motion of a passenger in a head-on auto accident?** *(Section 12.2)*

- **What factors affect the fall of a sky diver?** *(page 370)*

- **What brings the head of a hammer to a stop when you drive a nail into a board?** *(Section 12.3)*

- **What causes tides?** *(Section 12.4)*

A kayaker maneuvers his way downstream using a paddle.

Chapter Preview

Inquiry ▶ Activity

What Starts an Object Moving?

Procedure

1. On a flat surface, arrange four pennies in a row so that they are touching one another.

2. Using your index finger, slide a fifth penny across the surface in line with the row of pennies so that it strikes a penny at one end of the row.

Think About It

1. **Observing** Describe how the row of pennies moves in response to the collision.

2. **Formulating Hypotheses** What do you think caused the pennies to move after the collision? Why didn't the pennies move before the collision?

12.1 Forces

Key Concepts

- How do forces affect the motion of an object?
- What are the four main types of friction?
- How do gravity and air resistance affect a falling object?
- In what direction does Earth's gravity act?
- Why does a projectile follow a curved path?

Vocabulary

- force
- newton
- net force
- friction
- static friction
- sliding friction
- rolling friction
- fluid friction
- air resistance
- gravity
- terminal velocity
- projectile motion

Reading Strategy

Relating Text and Visuals Copy the table below. As you read, look carefully at Figures 2, 3, and 5. Complete the table by describing the forces and motion shown in each figure.

Figure	Is Net Force 0?	Effect on Motion
2A	a. ___?___	b. ___?___
2B	c. ___?___	d. ___?___
3	e. ___?___	f. ___?___
5A	g. ___?___	h. ___?___
5B	i. ___?___	j. ___?___

Figure 1 The wind pushes against the man and his umbrella. The push from the wind is a force.

A powerful storm is approaching. The weather forecast calls for gale-force winds. Many people in the city decide to leave work early in order to get home before things get worse. As shown in Figure 1, a man pushes ahead into a strong wind and shields himself from the driving rain with an umbrella. The strong wind makes it very difficult for him to hold onto his umbrella. To keep the umbrella from being pulled from his hands, he tightly squeezes the umbrella handle. Elsewhere, a store owner attempts to bring in a folding sign that hasn't blown away because it is chained to a pole.

Wind is but one example of the many forces you experience every day. The study of forces is a very important part of physics. As you read this section you'll learn what forces are and how they make things move.

What Is a Force?

The man out in the storm is battling the forces of wind. A **force** is a push or a pull that acts on an object. **A force can cause a resting object to move, or it can accelerate a moving object by changing the object's speed or direction.** The force of the wind pushing against the man slows his speed. A strong gust could even change the direction in which he was moving.

Measuring Force Forces are often easy to measure. In fact, if you've ever shopped at a grocery store, you may have measured forces using a spring scale like the one shown in Figure 2. The stretch of the spring in the scale depends on the amount of weight (a type of force) acting on it. As more fruit is placed on the scale, the spring is stretched farther and the scale reading increases.

Units of Force Force is measured in newtons, abbreviated as N. One **newton** is the force that causes a 1-kilogram mass to accelerate at a rate of 1 meter per second each second (1 m/s^2). In fact, 1 newton is equal to 1 kilogram-meter per second squared ($1 \text{ N} = 1 \text{ kg·m/s}^2$). The newton is named after Sir Isaac Newton (1642–1727), the English scientist who explained how force, mass, and acceleration are related. You'll learn more about forces and mass in the next section.

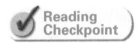 **Reading Checkpoint** *What amount of force accelerates a 1-kilogram mass at 1 m/s²?*

Representing Force You can use an arrow to represent the direction and strength of a force. The direction of the arrow represents the direction of the force. The length of the arrow represents the strength, or magnitude, of the force.

In Figure 2, the force arrows represent the weight of the items on the scale. Both arrows point down because weight always acts downward. The lengths of the arrows show you that more weight acts on the scale in Figure 2B than the one in Figure 2A.

Combining Forces

Have you ever helped to push a car that has run out of gas? If you have, you were taking advantage of the fact that forces can be combined. The individual force of each person's push adds with the others into a larger force that allows you to move the car.

You can combine force arrows to show the result of how forces combine. That is, forces in the same direction add together and forces in opposite directions subtract from one another. The **net force** is the overall force acting on an object after all the forces are combined.

Figure 2 The downward force arrows represent the weight (a type of force) on the scales. The dial indicator gives a visual measure of the weight. **Calculating** *What is the approximate weight difference between the two scale readings?*

Figure 3 In this tug of war, the two groups pull with equal forces in opposite directions. The forces combine by subtracting from each other.
Interpreting Photos *What is the net force acting on the rope?*

A Adding forces

B Subtracting forces

C Equal and opposite forces

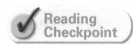

Figure 4 Forces can add together or subtract from one another.
A Two forces acting in the same direction add together. **B** Forces in opposite directions subtract from each other. C Forces that are equal in size and opposite in direction result in no net force.

Balanced Forces Sometimes, the net force acting on an object is zero. Look at the tug of war in Figure 3. Each group pulls on the rope with the same amount of force, but they pull in opposite directions. Neither group wins the tug of war because the forces on the rope are balanced. Balanced forces are forces that combine to produce a net force of zero. **When the forces on an object are balanced, the net force is zero and there is no change in the object's motion.**

Examples of balanced forces are common. For example, imagine two people locked in an arm wrestling match. Although neither person's arm may be moving, a pair of equal and opposite balanced forces are acting. An unlimited number of individual forces can act on an object and still produce a net force of zero. As shown in Figure 3, the individual force exerted by each person still results in a zero net force on the rope.

Unbalanced Forces Often, the forces on an object are unbalanced. If you push hard against the side of a book that is resting on a table, the book will begin to move. This is an example of an unbalanced force. An unbalanced force is a force that results when the net force acting on an object is not equal to zero. **When an unbalanced force acts on an object, the object accelerates.**

Forces acting in opposite directions can also combine to produce an unbalanced force. When a team of people win a tug of war, they win by pulling with a greater force than the losing team. The two unequal forces act in opposite directions but combine to produce an unbalanced net force. The net force equals the size of the larger force minus the size of the smaller force. This unbalanced force causes the rope, the winning team, and the losing team to accelerate in the direction of the unbalanced force. Figure 4 shows several examples of how forces combine.

Reading Checkpoint *What is the net force of a pair of balanced forces?*

Friction

All moving objects are subject to **friction,** a force that opposes the motion of objects that touch as they move past each other. Without friction, the world would be a very different place. In a frictionless world, every surface would be more slippery than a sheet of ice. Your food would slide off your fork. Walking would be impossible. Cars would slide around helplessly with their wheels spinning.

Friction acts at the surface where objects are in contact. Note that "in contact" includes solid objects that are directly touching one another as well as objects moving through a liquid or a gas. ◯ **There are four main types of friction: static friction, sliding friction, rolling friction, and fluid friction.**

Static Friction Imagine trying to push a large potted tree across a patio. Although you apply force to the pot by pushing on it, you can't get the pot to move. As shown in Figure 5A, the force of static friction opposes your push. **Static friction** is the friction force that acts on objects that are not moving. Static friction always acts in the direction opposite to that of the applied force.

You experience static friction every time you take a step. As you push off with each step, static friction between the ground and your shoe keeps your shoe from sliding.

Sliding Friction With the help of a friend, you push on the pot with enough force to overcome the static friction. The pot slides across the patio as shown in Figure 5B. Once the pot is moving, static friction no longer acts on it. Instead, a smaller friction force called sliding friction acts on the sliding pot. **Sliding friction** is a force that opposes the direction of motion of an object as it slides over a surface. Because sliding friction is less than static friction, less force is needed to keep an object moving than to start it moving.

For: Links on forces
Visit: www.SciLinks.org
Web Code: ccn-2121

Figure 5 Different types of friction act on moving and nonmoving objects. **A** Static friction acts opposite the direction of the force you apply to move the plant. The potted tree does not move. **B** When you push with more force, the potted tree begins to slide. Sliding friction acts to oppose the direction of motion.

Rolling Friction When a round object rolls across a flat floor, both the object and the floor are bent slightly out of shape. This change in shape at the point of rolling contact is the cause of **rolling friction,** the friction force that acts on rolling objects. For a given set of materials, the force of rolling friction is about 100 to 1000 times less than the force of static or sliding friction. Because of this, professional movers often use wheeled dollies to move heavy objects.

Ball bearings like those shown in Figure 6 are often used to reduce friction in machines. A ball bearing is made up of a set of round balls located between two smooth surfaces. The balls roll as the surfaces move past each other. Friction is greatly reduced between the surfaces because rolling friction replaces sliding friction. Inline skates, skateboards, bicycles, and automobiles are just a few of the many machines that use ball bearings.

Fluid Friction Friction also acts on a submarine moving through water and on an airplane flying through air. Water and a mixture of gases such as air are known as fluids. The force of **fluid friction** opposes the motion of an object through a fluid. You feel fluid friction when stirring thick cake batter. The motion of the spoon through the batter is slowed by fluid friction. Fluid friction increases as the speed of the object moving through the fluid increases. Thus the faster you stir, the greater the friction is.

Fluid friction acting on an object moving through the air is known as **air resistance.** At higher speeds, air resistance can become a significant force. For this reason, bicyclists and speed skaters often wear slick racing suits to reduce air resistance.

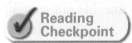 Reading Checkpoint *What are two common examples of fluid friction?*

Figure 6 Ball bearings in these wheels greatly reduce friction by replacing sliding friction with rolling friction.

Gravity

Why do leaves fall to the ground? The answer is gravity. **Gravity** is a force that acts between any two masses. Gravity is an attractive force, that is, it pulls objects together. Earth's gravitational force exerts a force of attraction on every other object that is near Earth. That includes you—the force of Earth's gravity holds you on the ground. Note that the force of gravity does not require objects to be in contact for it to act on them. Unlike friction, gravity can act over large distances.

🔑 **Earth's gravity acts downward toward the center of Earth.** Fortunately, an upward force usually balances the downward force of gravity. What forces act on the boulder in Figure 7? Gravity pulls down on the boulder. An upward force supplied by the supporting rock acts upward and balances the downward gravitational force. Because the forces on the boulder are balanced, it remains at rest as it has for thousands of years.

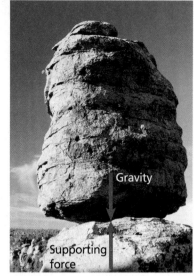

Figure 7 Earth exerts an attractive, downward force on this boulder.
Inferring *Because the boulder is at rest, what do you know about the net force acting on it?*

Falling Objects What forces affect the motion of a dollar bill dropped from the top of a tall building? Both gravity and air resistance affect the motion of a falling object. 🔑 **Gravity causes objects to accelerate downward, whereas air resistance acts in the direction opposite to the motion and reduces acceleration.**

In Figure 8, a flying squirrel has jumped from a tree and is falling toward the ground. As you can see, the squirrel has positioned its body parallel to Earth's surface and spread its arms and legs. By doing this, the squirrel creates a very large surface area. The large area maximizes the force of air resistance acting to slow the squirrel's downward acceleration. Because of the squirrel's slower downward acceleration, it is able to travel farther through the air than would otherwise be possible.

As objects fall to the ground, they accelerate and gain speed. With increasing speed comes increasing air resistance. If an object falls for a long time, the upward force of air resistance becomes equal to the downward force of gravity. At this point, the forces acting on the object are balanced. Acceleration is zero and the object continues falling at a constant velocity. **Terminal velocity** is the constant velocity of a falling object when the force of air resistance equals the force of gravity. Read the Concepts in Action pages later in this chapter to learn how sky divers reach terminal velocity.

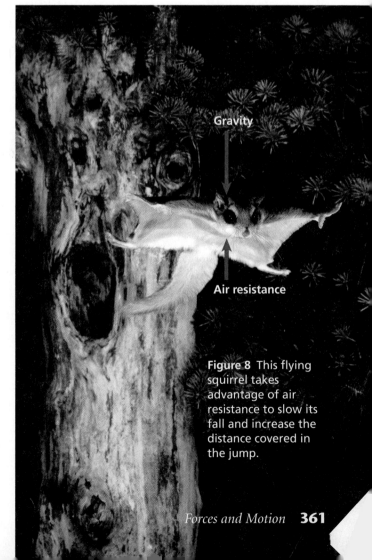

Figure 8 This flying squirrel takes advantage of air resistance to slow its fall and increase the distance covered in the jump.

Forces and Motion **361**

Figure 9 Gravity acts on falling objects. **A** Although their masses are different, the blue and green balls fall at the same rate. **B** The yellow ball is a projectile, following a curved path. **Applying Concepts** *What forces act on each of the falling balls?*

Projectile Motion

When you throw a ball forward, you'll notice that it actually follows a curved path. This curved path is an example of **projectile motion,** the motion of a falling object (projectile) after it is given an initial forward velocity. Air resistance and gravity are the only forces acting on a projectile.

Figure 9 shows the motion of two balls released at the same time. Figure 9A shows that balls of different mass fall at the same rate. In Figure 9B the curved path of the yellow ball is the result of the force of gravity and the initial horizontal velocity. **The combination of an initial forward velocity and the downward vertical force of gravity causes the ball to follow a curved path.** The two balls fall with the same acceleration and strike the ground at the same time.

Section 12.1 Assessment

Reviewing Concepts

1. How is the motion of an object affected when a force acts on it?

2. List the four types of friction.

3. How does air resistance affect the acceleration of a falling object?

4. Earth's gravitational force acts in what direction?

5. Describe why a projectile follows a curved path.

Critical Thinking

6. **Comparing and Contrasting** Compare the strengths of static, sliding, and rolling friction.

7. **Applying Concepts** Explain why falling leaves often do not fall in a straight-line path to the ground.

8. **Predicting** Two coins are knocked off a table at the same time by different forces. Which coin will hit the floor first?

Connecting Concepts

Velocity and Acceleration Make sketches of Figures 9A and 9B. Use them to relate the concepts of velocity and acceleration from Section 11.3 to falling objects. Add velocity and acceleration arrows at three locations on each sketch.

12.2 Newton's First and Second Laws of Motion

Reading Focus

Key Concepts

- How does Newton's first law relate change in motion to a zero net force?
- How does Newton's second law relate force, mass, and acceleration?
- How are weight and mass related?

Vocabulary

- ♦ inertia
- ♦ mass
- ♦ weight

Reading Strategy

Building Vocabulary Copy the table below. Then as you read the section, write a definition for each vocabulary term in your own words.

Vocabulary	Definition
Inertia	a. ___?___
b. ___?___	c. ___?___
d. ___?___	e. ___?___

Why do some cars accelerate faster than others? How does an ice skater glide far across the ice after pushing off only once? The answers to these questions involve the concepts of mass and inertia.

Aristotle, Galileo, and Newton

Modern scientists understand the relationships between force and motion. However, it took about 2000 years to develop this understanding.

Aristotle The ancient Greek scientist and philosopher Aristotle (384 B.C.–322 B.C.) made many scientific discoveries through careful observation and logical reasoning. He was not always correct. Aristotle incorrectly proposed that force is required to keep an object moving at constant speed. This error held back progess in the study of motion for almost two thousand years.

Galileo Italian scientist Galileo Galilei (1564–1642) experimented to find out about the world. By rolling balls down wooden ramps, he studied how gravity produces constant acceleration. Galileo concluded that moving objects that were not subjected to friction or any other force would continue to move indefinitely. Galileo's portrait and the title page from the book that presented his work are shown in Figure 10.

Figure 10 Galileo's work helped correct misconceptions about force and motion that had been widely held since Aristotle's time.

Figure 11 Isaac Newton published his work on force and motion in the book entitled *Principia*.

Newton In 1665, the plague broke out in London, forcing Isaac Newton to leave Trinity College in Cambridge, England, where he was a student. Over the next two years, Newton built on the work of scientists such as Galileo. He published his results many years later in a book entitled *Principia*. In this important work, Newton first had to define mass and force. He then introduced his laws of motion. Newton's portrait and the title page of *Principia* are shown in Figure 11.

Newton's First Law of Motion

Newton summarized his study of force and motion in several laws of motion. **According to Newton's first law of motion, the state of motion of an object does not change as long as the net force acting on the object is zero.** Thus, unless an unbalanced force acts, an object at rest remains at rest, and an object in motion remains in motion with the same speed and direction. For example, a soccer ball resting on the grass remains motionless until a force is applied to it in the form of a kick. The kicked ball begins rolling. Because friction between the grass and the ball acts on the ball as it rolls, the ball slows. The force of friction slows the ball and brings it to a stop.

Newton's first law of motion is sometimes called the law of inertia (in UR shuh). **Inertia** is the tendency of an object to resist a change in its motion. In other words, an object at rest tends to remain at rest, and an object in motion tends to remain in motion with the same direction and speed. Note that as the soccer ball sat motionless in the grass, the forces acting on it were balanced. The ball remained at rest until an unbalanced force acted on it. The ball has inertia.

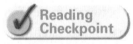 *How does a zero net force affect an object's motion?*

Figure 12

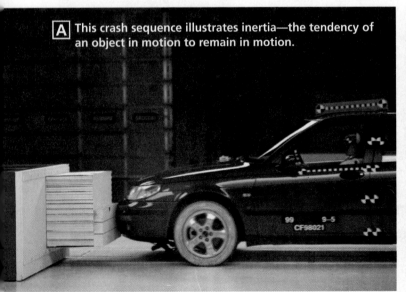

A This crash sequence illustrates inertia—the tendency of an object in motion to remain in motion.

B At impact, the air bag deploys. Note that the test dummy continues its forward motion as the collision begins to slow the car.

Think about what happens if you are in a moving car that is involved in a front-end collision. The collision makes the car stop suddenly. What happens to you? Because you have inertia, you continue moving forward. The series of photos in Figure 12 shows you how dangerous a front-end collision can be. If a seat belt and airbag had not restrained the test dummy, it would have crashed into the steering wheel and windshield with great force. The seat belt and airbag work by exerting force against the body of the dummy, opposing its forward motion.

Newton's Second Law of Motion

How do unbalanced forces affect the motion of an object? An unbalanced force causes an object's velocity to change. In other words, the object accelerates. For example, you apply a net force to a ball when you throw it. The harder you throw, the more the ball accelerates. In fact, the acceleration of the ball is directly proportional to the net force acting on it. If you double the force, the acceleration of the ball doubles as well. Newton also learned that the acceleration of an object depends upon its mass. **Mass** is a measure of the inertia of an object and depends on the amount of matter the object contains.

👓 **According to Newton's second law of motion, the acceleration of an object is equal to the net force acting on it divided by the object's mass.** Thus, doubling the mass of an object cuts its acceleration in half. Newton was able to put these ideas into a single formula.

Newton's Second Law

$$\text{Acceleration} = \frac{\text{Net force}}{\text{Mass}}, \quad \text{or} \quad a = \frac{F}{m}$$

Quick Lab

Investigating Inertia
Procedure
1. Place an index card on a flat table. Place a coin in the middle of the card. As quickly as you can, try to pull the card out from under the coin. Observe what happens to the coin.

2. Repeat Step 1 while moving the card slowly.

3. Repeat Step 1 again. This time, slowly accelerate the card, and then suddenly bring it to a stop.

Analyze and Conclude

1. **Applying Concepts** Use the concepts of inertia and friction to explain the behavior of the coin each time you moved the card.

2. **Predicting** How would your observations be different with a coin of greater mass? Test your predictions.

C As the car comes to a stop, the air bag prevents the test dummy from striking the steering wheel.

D Interpreting Photographs What objects and devices absorb the energy of the crash?

Crash-Test Dummies

Dummies are used in simulated car crashes to study what might happen to passengers in a real crash. They are fitted with a range of measuring devices that track the motion of the dummies throughout the crash. By analyzing the data, scientists learn how injuries occur and how they can be prevented. **Interpreting Diagrams** *What forces act on the crash-test dummy to slow its forward movement?*

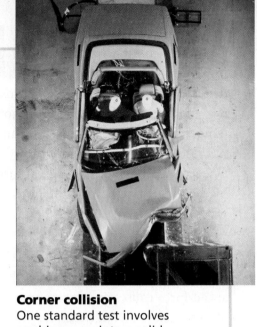

Corner collision
One standard test involves crashing a car into a solid concrete wall at nearly 60 kilometers an hour. Other tests involve crashing a sled into the side or corner of the car.

Impact
Upon initial impact, the front of the car stops abruptly, but inertia keeps the dummy moving forward.

Seatbelt The seatbelt immediately tightens to slow down the dummy and to absorb energy.

Markers Cameras focus on the markers to record how the body moves during the collision.

Paint Layers of different colored paints on the dummy record the direction and effects of impact forces.

Sensors Computers connected to sensors on the legs, chest, abdomen, and head measure and record movement and acceleration.

 Car's initial velocity

Inflating air bag The air bag exerts a force that slows down the dummy's forward motion, absorbs its energy, and prevents it from hitting the steering wheel.

The acceleration of an object is always in the same direction as the net force. In using the formula for Newton's second law, it is helpful to realize that the units N/kg and m/s² are equivalent. The Math Skills box reinforces this relationship.

Note that Newton's second law also applies when a net force acts in the direction opposite to the object's motion. In this case, the force produces a deceleration that reduces the speed. This is the principle used by automobile seat belts. In a collision, the seat belt applies a force that opposes a passenger's forward motion. This force decelerates the passenger in order to prevent serious injury.

Math > Skills

Newton's Second Law

An automobile with a mass of 1000 kilograms accelerates when the traffic light turns green. If the net force on the car is 4000 newtons, what is the car's acceleration?

 Read and Understand

What information are you given?

Mass, m = 1000 kg

Force, F = 4000 N **(in the forward direction)**

 Plan and Solve

What unknown are you trying to calculate?

Acceleration, a = ?

What formula contains the given quantities and the unknown?

$$\text{Acceleration} = \frac{\text{Net force}}{\text{Mass}}, a = \frac{F}{m}$$

Replace each variable with its known value and solve.

$$a = \frac{4000 \text{ N}}{1000 \text{ kg}} = \frac{4 \text{ N}}{\text{kg}} = \frac{4 \frac{\text{kg·m}}{\text{s}^2}}{\text{kg}} = 4 \text{ m/s}^2$$

$a = 4$ m/s² in the forward direction

3 Look Back and Check

Is your answer reasonable?

Powerful sports cars can accelerate at 6 m/s² or more. Thus, a smaller acceleration of 4 m/s² seems reasonable.

Math > Practice

1. A boy pushes forward a cart of groceries with a total mass of 40.0 kg. What is the acceleration of the cart if the net force on the cart is 60.0 N?

2. What is the upward acceleration of a helicopter with a mass of 5000 kg if a force of 10,000 N acts on it in an upward direction?

3. An automobile with a mass of 1200 kg accelerates at a rate of 3.0 m/s² in the forward direction. What is the net force acting on the automobile? (*Hint:* Solve the acceleration formula for force.)

4. A 25-N force accelerates a boy in a wheelchair at 0.5 m/s² What is the mass of the boy and the wheelchair? (*Hint:* Solve Newton's second law for mass.)

Force

Acceleration

Force

Acceleration

Figure 13 Acceleration depends directly on force and inversely on mass. Neglecting friction, when the same force acts, the single cart accelerates eight times faster than the chain of eight carts.
Predicting *How would the acceleration of a chain of two carts compare with the acceleration of a single cart if the same force acted on both?*

The shopping carts in Figure 13 further illustrate Newton's second law. What happens if you push on a single shopping cart? The unbalanced force causes the cart to accelerate. What happens when you push with the same force on a chain of eight shopping carts? The acceleration of the chain of carts is much less than that of the single cart. The chain of carts accelerates less because it has more mass.

Weight and Mass

Do you sometimes talk about weight and mass as if they were the same thing? Although related to each other, mass and weight are not the same. **Weight** is the force of gravity acting on an object. An object's weight is the product of the object's mass and acceleration due to gravity acting on it.

Weight Formula

Weight = Mass × Acceleration due to gravity

$$W = mg$$

The weight formula is basically Newton's second law. However, weight (W) is substituted for force (F) and acceleration due to gravity (g) is substitutued for acceleration (a). In other words, $W = mg$ is a different form of $a = \frac{F}{M}$, that is when the equation is solved for force, $F = ma$. The value of g in the formula is 9.8 m/s^2.

In using the weight formula or Newton's second-law formula, make sure you use the correct units. The force (F or W) should be in newtons, the acceleration (a or g) in meters per second squared, and the mass (m) in kilograms. The following example shows how to use the weight formula.

If an astronaut has a mass of 112 kilograms, what is his weight on Earth where the acceleration due to gravity is 9.8 m/s^2?

Weight = Mass × Acceleration due to gravity

$$= 112 \text{ kg} \times 9.8 \text{ m/s}^2$$

$$= 1100 \text{ kg·m/s}^2 = 1100 \text{ N}$$

A **Astronaut on Earth**
Mass = 88.0 kg; Weight = 863 N

B **Astronaut on Moon**
Mass = 88.0 kg; Weight = 141 N

Figure 14 Weight is a measure of the force of gravity acting on an object. **A** An astronaut with a mass of 88 kg weighs 863 N on Earth. **B** An astronaut with a mass of 88 kg weighs 141 N on the moon. **Calculating** *If the same astronaut stood on Mars where the acceleration due to gravity is about 3.7 m/s², how much would the astronaut weigh?*

If you study the weight formula, you'll see that mass and weight are proportional. Doubling the mass of an object also doubles the object's weight. ⬤ **Mass is a measure of the inertia of an object; weight is a measure of the force of gravity acting on an object.** Consider the same astronaut shown on Earth and on the moon in Figure 14. On the moon, the acceleration due to gravity is only about one sixth that on Earth. Thus, the astronaut weighs only about one sixth as much on the moon as on Earth. In both locations, the mass of the astronaut is the same.

Section 12.2 Assessment

Reviewing Concepts

1. ⬤ State Newton's first law of motion in your own words.

2. ⬤ What equation states Newton's second law of motion?

3. ⬤ How is mass different from weight?

Critical Thinking

4. **Applying Concepts** Describe several examples of Newton's first and second laws that you observe during a normal day.

5. **Making Judgments** A steel ball is the same size as a wooden ball, but weighs twice as much. If both balls are dropped from an airplane, which of them will reach terminal velocity more quickly? Explain.

Math **Practice**

6. During a test crash, an air bag inflates to stop a dummy's forward motion. The dummy's mass is 75 kg. If the net force on the dummy is 825 N toward the rear of the car, what is the dummy's deceleration?

7. A bicycle takes 8.0 seconds to accelerate at a constant rate from rest to a speed of 4.0 m/s. If the mass of the bicycle and rider together is 85 kg, what is the net force acting on the bicycle? (*Hint:* First calculate the acceleration.)

CONCEPTS in Action

Terminal Speed

Imagine you are a sky diver about to step out of a plane and fall through the air. What forces will you experience during your fall? How can you use these forces to combine an exhilarating experience with a safe landing?

Upward drag force

Helmet for protection

Sky diving relies on two principles of physics. First, if there is nothing to support you, the force of gravity will cause you to accelerate downward. Second, all fluids—including air—produce a drag force that opposes the motion of an object moving through the fluid. The speed of a falling object increases until the drag force equals the force of gravity. At this point, the net force is zero and the sky diver falls at a constant, terminal speed.

The actual terminal speed depends on several factors. For example, an object with greater mass has a greater gravitational force on it, increasing its terminal speed. Thinner air, such as air at very high altitudes, increases velocity by decreasing the drag force. A sky diver can also partially control the drag force, and terminal speed, by changing shape. Opening the parachute dramatically increases the drag force and lowers the terminal speed to about 4.5 meters per second—a speed suitable for landing.

Harness

Downward force of gravity

The Sky Diving Sequence

No matter what the starting altitude, any sky dive consists of the same basic stages, starting with the jump from the plane.

Altimeter showing altitude

1 Jumping out Upon jumping, the sky diver begins accelerating at a rate of 9.8 meters per second per second in free fall. Within a few seconds she will reach maximum speed.

Parachute

2 Falling freely Sky divers usually jump from a height of about 3000 meters and fall freely for about 45 seconds before opening the parachute. The top speed reached, known as terminal speed, is about 52 meters per second. Falling from very high altitudes, where the air is thinner and the drag force is less, can produce higher terminal speeds.

3 Slowing the fall Usually the parachute is fully open by the time the sky diver is 300 meters above the ground. The parachute causes rapid deceleration and allows the sky diver to make a steady descent, using the control lines to steer.

Going Further

- Research the development and use of the parachute and prepare a poster presentation of your findings. Be sure to include a development time line listing names and dates of significant contributions and advances.

Sky diver lands standing up

4 Landing The sky diver pulls down on the control lines to achieve a safe and steady low-speed landing.

12.3 Newton's Third Law of Motion and Momentum

Key Concepts

- What is Newton's third law of motion?
- What is needed for an object to have a large momentum?
- How is momentum conserved?

Vocabulary

- momentum
- law of conservation of momentum

Reading Strategy

Summarizing Read the section on momentum. Then copy and complete the concept map below to organize what you know about momentum.

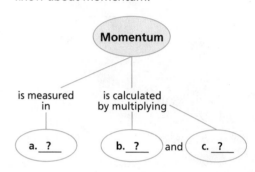

Momentum

is measured in

is calculated by multiplying

a. ?

b. ? and c. ?

Think physics the next time you go to an amusement park. There is no better place than an amusement park to see Newton's laws in action. As you experience sudden starts, stops, changes in direction, and possibly even free fall, you can be sure that the laws of physics control your motion. The bumper cars in Figure 15 illustrate momentum and Newton's third law of motion, the subjects of this section.

If you have ever driven a bumper car, you know your goal is to slam into another car head on. When you collide with the other car, you do so with enough force to jolt the other driver almost out of the seat. There are two parts to this collision, however—the collision also causes your own car to rebound sharply. Newton's third law of motion explains the behavior of the bumper cars during a collision.

Figure 15 When this bumper car collides with another car, two forces are exerted. Each car in the collision exerts a force on the other.

Newton's Third Law

A force cannot exist alone. Forces always exist in pairs. **According to Newton's third law of motion, whenever one object exerts a force on a second object, the second object exerts an equal and opposite force on the first object.** These two forces are called action and reaction forces.

Go Online

NSTA *SciLINKS*

For: Links on Newton's laws
Visit: www.SciLinks.org
Web Code: ccn-2123

Action and Reaction Forces The force your bumper car exerts on the other car is the action force. The force the other car exerts on your car is the reaction force. These two forces are equal in size and opposite in direction.

Pressing your hand against a wall also produces a pair of forces. As you press against the wall, your hand exerts a force on the wall. This is the action force. The wall exerts an equal and opposite force against your hand. This is the reaction force.

A similar situation occurs when you use a hammer to drive a nail into a piece of wood. When the hammer strikes the nail, it applies a force to the nail. This action force drives the nail into the piece of wood. Is there a reaction force? According to Newton's third law there must be an equal and opposite reaction force. The nail supplies the reaction force by exerting an equal and opposite force on the hammer. It is this reaction force that brings the motion of the hammer to a stop.

Action-Reaction Forces and Motion

Can you determine the action and reaction forces occurring in Figure 16? The swimmer uses her arms to push against the water and create an action force. The action force causes the water to move in the direction of the action force. However, the water also exerts its equal and opposite reaction force on the swimmer. The reaction force acts on the swimmer and pushes her forward through the water.

Unlike the swimmer in Figure 16, not all action and reaction forces produce motion. Pushing against the wall with your hand is an example of an action-reaction force pair that does not result in motion.

Action-Reaction Forces Do Not Cancel You may be wondering why the action and reaction forces acting on the swimmer in Figure 16 do not cancel each other and produce a net force of zero. The reason is that the action and reaction forces do not act on the same object. The action force acts on the water, and the reaction force acts on the swimmer. Only when equal and opposite forces act on the same object do they result in a net force of zero.

Figure 16 Action-reaction forces propel the swimmer through the water. The swimmer pushes against the water, and the water pushes the swimmer ahead.
Comparing and Contrasting
Describe the magnitude and direction of the action and reaction forces acting on the swimmer.

Reading Checkpoint *Why don't action and reaction forces cancel each other out?*

Momentum

Imagine a loaded shopping cart and a small glass marble are both slowly rolling toward you at the same speed. The marble is easier to stop. Intuitively, you know that a loaded shopping cart is harder to stop because it has a greater mass. If the marble were moving 100 times faster than the shopping cart, which would be easier to stop? **Momentum** is the product of an object's mass and its velocity. An object with large momentum is hard to stop. ⬅ **An object has a large momentum if the product of its mass and velocity is large.** The momentum for any object at rest is zero. A huge rocket such as the space shuttle has zero momentum as it sits on the launch pad. A small 1-kilogram meteor traveling at the very high speed of 20 kilometers per second has a very large momentum.

DK SCIENCE and History

Amusement Park Rides

For more than one hundred years, engineers have been designing rides that subject riders to jarring motions, large accelerations, terrifying heights, soakings, or free falls.

Acceleration *Riders experience an acceleration toward the loop's center as they move around it.*

Start turret, 13 meters above the ground

Maximum height *The first Ferris wheel is 80.5 m tall.*

Wood-paneled car *Each car has a mass of 13 tons and holds as many as 60 people.*

The ride *Passengers move at a speed of about 0.5 m/s.*

LOOPING GRAVITY RAILWAY

FERRIS WHEEL

1846 The first railway to turn its passengers upside down opens at a park in Paris, France.

1884 The first true roller coaster in America appears at Coney Island, New York.

1893 The George Ferris Giant Wheel, named after the inventor, debuts at the Columbian Exposition in Chicago. A ride costs 50 cents.

1900 Trolley companies build amusement parks to encourage weekend travel.

1845	1875	1905

You can calculate momentum by multiplying an object's mass (in kilograms) and its velocity (in meters per second).

Momentum Formula

$$\text{Momentum} = \text{Mass} \times \text{Velocity}$$

Momentum is measured in units of kilogram-meters per second.

Which has more momentum, a 0.046-kilogram golf ball with a speed of 60.0 meters per second, or a 7.0-kilogram bowling ball with a speed of 6.0 meters per second?

$$\text{Momentum}_{\text{golf ball}} = 0.046 \text{ kg} \times 60.0 \text{ m/s} = 2.8 \text{ kg·m/s}$$

$$\text{Momentum}_{\text{bowling ball}} = 7.0 \text{ kg} \times 6.0 \text{ m/s} = 42 \text{ kg·m/s}$$

The bowling ball has considerably more momentum than the golf ball.

Writing in Science

Explain a Sequence Write a paragraph about one of the amusement park rides shown on the time line. Describe the motion of the ride using Newton's laws of motion. (*Hint:* Before you write, use a diagram to analyze the forces acting on the ride at a particular moment.)

Roller coaster
This version, about three kilometers long, catapults riders to about 25 m/s in the first 4 seconds.

THEME PARK

Sun wheel, a modern twist on the Ferris wheel.

Rubber bumper
This prolongs the time of impact and decreases the force of the collisions.

Sharp drop
Riders reach a maximum speed of about 25 m/s during the drop.

BUMPER CAR

FREE FALL RIDE

1928 The first fully steerable bumper car is invented.

1934 The first wild mouse coaster, with sharp turns and abrupt drops, is built in Germany.

1955 The first cartoon-themed amusement park opens in Anaheim, California.

1963 The world's first log-in-water ride is an instant success at a park in Texas. Similar rides are soon being built around the world.

1996 A free-fall ride with a drop of 46 meters opens in Maryland.

| 1935 | 1965 | 1995 |

A Both cars moving.

Before collision

10 m/s →

Momentum = 300,000 kg·m/s

5 m/s →

Momentum = 150,000 kg·m/s

Momentum before collision = 450,000 kg·m/s

Cars bounce off each other.

After collision

5 m/s →

Momentum = 150,000 kg·m/s

10 m/s →

Momentum = 300,000 kg·m/s

Momentum after collision = 450,000 kg·m/s

B One car moving.

Before collision

10 m/s →

Momentum = 300,000 kg·m/s

0 m/s

Momentum = 0

Momentum before collision = 300,000 kg·m/s

Cars bounce off each other.

After collision

0 m/s

Momentum = 0

10 m/s →

Momentum = 300,000 kg·m/s

Momentum after collision = 300,000 kg·m/s

C One car moving.

Before collision

10 m/s →

Momentum = 300,000 kg·m/s

0 m/s

Momentum = 0

Momentum before collision = 300,000 kg·m/s

Cars couple.

After collision

5 m/s →

Momentum = 300,000 kg·m/s

Momentum after collision = 300,000 kg·m/s

Figure 17 Three different collisions between equal-mass train cars are shown above. In each collision, the total momentum of the train cars does not change—momentum is conserved. **Calculating** *What is the mass of each train car?*

Go Online
active art

For: Activity on momentum
Visit: PHSchool.com
Web Code: ccp-2123

Conservation of Momentum

What happens to momentum when objects collide? Look at the collisions in Figure 17. Under certain conditions, collisions obey the law of conservation of momentum. In physics, the word *conservation* means that something has a constant value. That is, conservation of momentum means that momentum does not increase or decrease.

Imagine two trains colliding as shown in Figure 17A. If the two cars are part of a closed system, then momentum is conserved. A closed system means other objects and forces cannot enter or leave a system. Objects within the system, however, can exert forces on one another. According to the **law of conservation of momentum,** if no net force acts on a system, then the total momentum of the system does not change.

Thus, if we consider the two train cars as a closed system, the cars can exert forces on each other. But overall, the total momentum of the system is conserved. **In a closed system, the loss of momentum of one object equals the gain in momentum of another object—momentum is conserved.**

Momentum

A class studied the speed and momentum of a 0.25-kilogram ball dropped from a bridge. The graph shows the momentum of the ball from the time it was dropped until the time it hit the river flowing below the bridge.

1. **Applying Concepts** At what time did the ball have zero momentum? Describe this point in the ball's motion.

2. **Using Graphs** At what time did the ball have the greatest momentum? What was the peak momentum value?

3. **Calculating** What is the ball's speed after 1.25 seconds? (*Hint:* Use the graph and the momentum formula.)

Momentum of a 0.25-kg Ball

Three different closed systems are shown in Figure 17. Each system consists of two train cars with the same mass that collide. In Figures 17A and 17B, the train cars collide and then bounce apart. In Figure 17C, the cars collide and then join together. Examine the momentum of each train car before and after the collision. Note that the total momentum before and after each collision does not change. The momentum is conserved.

Section 12.3 Assessment

Reviewing Concepts

1. Using Newton's third law, explain what is meant by action and reaction pairs of forces.

2. State in your own words the formula for momentum.

3. What is a necessary condition for the conservation of momentum?

4. If an eagle and a bumblebee are traveling at 8 km/hr, which has more momentum? Explain.

Critical Thinking

5. **Applying Concepts** A friend tells you that a rowboat is propelled forward by the force of its oars against the water. First, explain whether the statement is correct, and then identify the action and reaction forces.

6. **Inferring** Explain how Newton's third law of motion is at work when you walk.

7. **Applying Concepts** Explain in terms of Newton's third law why someone who tries to jump from a canoe to a riverbank may fall into the water.

Writing in Science

Explanatory Paragraph Write a paragraph explaining why it is impossible to identify a single isolated force. State in your first sentence the main idea of Newton's third law of motion.

12.4 Universal Forces

Reading Focus

Key Concepts

- What force can attract and repel?
- What force holds the nucleus together?
- What is Newton's law of universal gravitation?

Vocabulary

- electromagnetic force
- strong nuclear force ◆ weak nuclear force ◆ gravitational force ◆ centripetal force

Reading Strategy

Comparing and Contrasting Copy the table below. After reading the section, compare the two universal nuclear forces by completing the table.

Force	Acts on Which Particles?	Acts Over What Distance?	Relative Strength
Strong nuclear	a. ?	b. ?	c. ?
Weak nuclear	d. ?	e. ?	f. ?

If you could travel to a distant planet in another galaxy, what would you expect to find? The scene shown in Figure 18 is one possibility. Although this world looks so different from the one you know, some things on this distant planet would be familiar—the forces.

Observations of planets, stars, and galaxies strongly suggest four different forces exist throughout the universe. These forces are known as universal forces. The four universal forces are the electromagnetic, strong nuclear, weak nuclear, and gravitational. All the universal forces act over a distance between particles of matter, which means that the particles need not be in contact in order to affect one another. In addition, each of these forces is affected by the distance between the particles of matter.

Figure 18 An artist's depiction of a planet's surface shows a world very different from Earth. Regardless of location, however, certain universal forces are present.

Electromagnetic Forces

Electric and magnetic force are two different aspects of the electromagnetic force. **Electromagnetic force** is associated with charged particles. ◢ **Electric force and magnetic force are the only forces that can both attract and repel.** To understand electric and magnetic forces, recall what you learned about charged particles in Chapter 4.

Electric Forces Electric forces act between charged objects or particles such as electrons and protons. Objects with opposite charges—positive and negative—attract one another. Objects with like charges repel one another. Figure 19 shows that clothes often cling together when they are removed from a dryer. Some clothes, such as cotton socks, lose electrons easily and become positively charged. Other clothes, such as polyester shirts, gain electrons easily and become negatively charged. Because the oppositely charged particles attract one another, the clothes cling together.

Magnetic Forces Magnetic forces act on certain metals, on the poles of magnets, and on moving charges. Magnets have two poles, north and south, that attract each other. Two poles that are alike repel each other. If you have handled magnets, you know that when opposite magnetic poles are brought close, they almost seem to jump together. On the other hand, when two similar poles approach each other, you can feel them pushing apart.

Figure 20 shows a child's wooden train set whose cars are linked with magnets. Each car has a north pole on one end and a south pole on the other. Children quickly learn that if a train car won't stick to the one in front of it, the car must be turned around.

 Reading Checkpoint *What type of force acts between particles with the same electrical charge?*

Nuclear Forces

Think about the nucleus of an atom, with its protons crammed into an incredibly small space. Because protons are positively charged, you would expect that an electric force of repulsion would break the nucleus apart. Scientists believe the nucleus would fly apart if there were not another, much stronger, attractive force holding the protons within the nucleus.

🔑 **Two forces, the strong nuclear force and the weak nuclear force, act within the nucleus to hold it together.** The strong nuclear force overcomes the electric force of repulsion that acts among the protons in the nucleus. The weak nuclear force is involved in certain types of radioactive processes.

Strong Nuclear Force The **strong nuclear force** is a powerful force of attraction that acts only on the neutrons and protons in the nucleus, holding them together. The range over which the strong nuclear forces acts is approximately equal to the diameter of a proton (10^{-15} m). Although this force acts over only extremely short distances, it is 100 times stronger than the electric force of repulsion at these distances.

Figure 19 Clothes often acquire electric charges in the dryer. Clothes with opposite charges tend to cling together.

Figure 20 A magnetic force of attraction holds the two train cars together.
Applying Concepts *How are the two magnetic poles of the magnets related?*

Materials

balloon, bubble solution, bubble wand

Procedure

1. Inflate a balloon and then make a knot in its neck to close it. Rub the balloon back and forth against your hair to charge it.

2. Blow several bubbles into the air and hold the charged balloon above them. Observe how the distance between the balloon and the bubbles affects the speed at which the bubbles fall. **CAUTION** *Quickly wipe up any spilled bubble solution to avoid slips and falls.*

3. Try to temporarily suspend a bubble in the air without touching it with the balloon.

Analyze and Conclude

1. **Drawing Conclusions** How does the distance between two objects affect the force of attraction between them?

2. **Predicting** If a bubble were suspended below the balloon, what do you think would happen when you moved the balloon closer to the bubble?

Weak Nuclear Force The other powerful force in the nucleus is the weak nuclear force. As the name implies, the weak force is weaker in strength than the strong nuclear force. The **weak nuclear force** is an attractive force that acts only over a short range. The short range over which the weak nuclear force acts, about 10^{-18} meters, is less than the range of the strong nuclear force.

Gravitational Force

Gravity, the weakest universal force, is so much a part of your life that you probably take it for granted. You know from experience that objects fall toward Earth. It was Newton who discovered that gravity affects all objects in the universe. The same force acting on a falling apple is also acting on the moon to keep it in its orbit.

Gravitational force involves much more than just Earth's gravitational field. **Gravitational force** is an attractive force that acts between any two masses. **Newton's law of universal gravitation states that every object in the universe attracts every other object.**

Thus, Earth exerts a force on an apple, and the apple exerts an equal force on Earth. You exert a gravitational force on your textbook, and your textbook exerts an equal gravitational force on you. The reason you don't notice gravity pulling your textbook toward you is that your mass and the mass of the textbook are so small. It takes a huge mass such as Earth's to exert a large gravitational force. The attractive force of gravity acting between two objects is shown in Figure 21.

Figure 21 Gravitational force depends upon mass and distance. **A** Two masses, X and Y, attract each other. **B** The larger mass of X results in a larger gravitational force. **C** Increasing the distance between the masses significantly reduces the gravitational force.

Gravity Acts Over Large Distances The gravitational force between two objects is proportional to their masses and decreases rapidly as the distance between the masses increases. The greater the mass of the objects, the greater is the gravitational force. Gravitational force decreases with the square of the distance between the objects. As shown in Figures 21A and 21C, if the distance between masses doubles, the force of gravity is only one fourth as strong.

Gravity is the weakest universal force, but it is the most effective force over long distances. Gravity holds you on Earth. It keeps the moon in orbit around Earth, the planets in orbit around the sun, and the stars in orbit in their galaxies. The sun's mass is about 300,000 times the mass of Earth, so the sun's gravitational force is much stronger than that of Earth. The influence of the sun's gravitational force extends well beyond Earth. Pluto, which is almost 40 times farther from the sun than Earth is, has its orbit determined by the gravitational pull of the sun.

 Reading Checkpoint *What factors affect gravitational force?*

 Go Online
SCI LINKS

For: Links on gravity
Visit: www.SciLinks.org
Web Code: ccn-2124

The Earth, Moon, and Tides How is the moon kept in orbit around Earth? Recall that the moon has inertia, so according to Newton's first law, it should continue to move along a straight path until acted upon by a force. That force is Earth's gravitational force, which acts continuously to pull the moon toward it, as shown in Figure 22.

Earth's gravitational attraction keeps the moon in an elliptical orbit around Earth. It works in much the same way that a string tied to an eraser allows you to twirl the eraser in a circle over your head. As you twirl the eraser, the string exerts a centripetal force on the eraser. A **centripetal force** is a center-directed force that continuously changes the direction of an object to make it move around the center. This center-directed force causes a continuous change in the direction of the eraser. In a similar way, the center-directed force of Earth's gravity pulls the moon into an elliptical orbit around Earth.

If you have spent time at the seashore, you have probably noticed that the level of the tide changes throughout the day. The gravitational pull from the moon produces two bulges in Earth's oceans. One bulge is on the side of Earth closest to the moon. The other bulge is on the side of Earth farthest from the moon. Earth rotates once per day beneath theses two bulges. This rotation results in two high and two low tides per day on Earth.

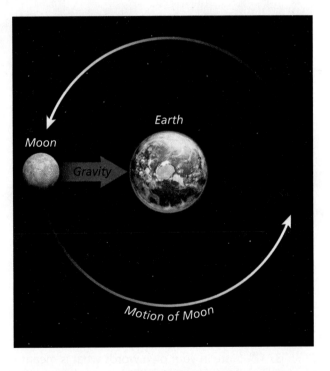

Figure 22 The moon's inertia and the gravitational pull of Earth result in an elliptical orbit. The gravitational pull of the moon is the primary cause of Earth's ocean tides.

Satellites in Orbit Artificial satellites are launched into orbit by a rocket or space shuttle. Why doesn't a satellite in a high orbit need to fire rocket engines continuously to remain in orbit? Much like the moon, the satellite needs only the centripetal force provided by gravity and its inertia to maintain its orbit. Satellites in a low orbit, however, are slowed by friction with Earth's atmosphere. As a satellite loses speed, it loses altitude. Eventually, the satellite reenters Earth's atmosphere and burns up.

Uses of Satellites Currently, there are thousands of artificial satellites orbiting Earth. These satellites perform many functions. They monitor Earth's weather, create detailed radar maps of Earth's surface, use telescopes to gaze deep into space, and study Earth's climate. Some satellites, like the one shown in Figure 23, receive and transmit radio and microwave signals. Numerous communication satellites are used to receive and transmit cell phone and satellite television signals.

The next time you watch an event on television transmitted by satellite from another part of the world, you should thank Isaac Newton. His work to discover the laws of motion and universal gravitation have led to the development of countless modern technologies.

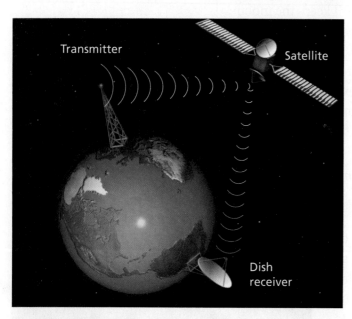

Figure 23 Satellites are used to receive and transmit electromagnetic waves over great distances.

Section 12.4 Assessment

Reviewing Concepts

1. Which universal force can repel as well as attract?

2. Which universal force acts to hold the nucleus together?

3. State in your own words what is meant by Newton's law of universal gravitation.

4. How does friction with the atmosphere affect the speed of an artificial satellite?

Critical Thinking

5. **Using Models** The moon in its orbit around Earth behaves like a ball at the end of a string being swung above your head. Explain the forces involved.

6. **Predicting** If the speed of an orbiting satellite decreases, how might you expect its orbit to change?

7. **Inferring** Explain how Newton's third law and his law of universal gravitation are connected.

Writing in Science

Descriptive Paragraph Write a short paragraph describing why you think the outcomes of scientific investigations related to universal laws would be similar regardless of what part of the world they might be conducted.

Exploration > Lab

Investigating a Balloon Jet

In this lab, you will examine the relationships among force, mass, and motion.

Problem
How does a jet-powered device move?

Materials
- string, 3 m in length
- drinking straw
- 4 long balloons
- masking tape
- stopwatch
- meter stick
- 2 threaded nuts
- 2 chairs

 For the probeware version of this lab, see the Probeware Lab Manual, Lab 4.

Skills Applying Concepts

Procedure

1. On a separate sheet of paper, make a copy of the data table shown.

2. Insert the string through the straw and tie each end of the string to the back of a separate chair. Pull the chairs apart until the string is tight and horizontal.

3. Blow up the balloon and then hold the balloon's opening closed. Record the length of the balloon. Have a classmate attach the balloon lengthwise to the straw using tape.

4. While continuing to hold the balloon's opening closed, slide the balloon jet to the end of the string as shown.

5. Release the balloon. Measure the time during which the balloon jet moves. Measure the distance that the balloon jet travels along the

string. Record the distance and time values in the data table for 0 Nuts Used, Trial 1.

6. Repeat Steps 3 through 5 with a new balloon. Make sure to inflate the balloon to the same size as in Step 3. Record your results in the data table for 0 Nuts Used, Trial 2.

7. Repeat Steps 3 through 6 twice more with a new balloon. This time, tape two nuts to the balloon before releasing it. Record your results in the data table for 2 Nuts Used, Trials 1 and 2.

8. Calculate and record the average speed for each trial. The average speed is equal to the distance divided by the time.

Analyze and Conclude

1. **Applying Concepts** Use Newton's second and third laws to explain the motion of the balloon jet.

2. **Analyzing Data** How did adding mass (nuts) to the balloon jet affect its motion?

Data Table				
Number of Nuts Used	Trial Number	Time (seconds)	Distance (centimeters)	Average Velocity (cm/s)
0	1			
0	2			
2	1			
2	2			
Length of Inflated Balloon (centimeters)				

Study Guide

12.1 Forces

Key Concepts

- A force can cause a resting object to move, or it can accelerate a moving object by changing the object's speed or direction.

- When the forces on an object are balanced, there is no change in the object's motion. When an unbalanced force acts on an object, the object accelerates.

- There are four main types of friction: static friction, sliding friction, rolling friction, and fluid friction.

- Earth's gravity acts downward toward the center of Earth. Gravity causes objects to accelerate downward, whereas air resistance acts in the direction opposite to the motion and reduces acceleration.

- The combination of initial forward velocity and downward vertical force of gravity cause a projectile to follow a curved path.

Vocabulary

force, *p. 356;* newton, *p. 357;* net force, *p. 357;* friction, *p. 359;* static friction, *p. 359;* sliding friction, *p. 359;* rolling friction, *p. 360;* fluid friction, *p. 360;* air resistance, *p. 360;* gravity, *p. 361;* terminal velocity, *p. 361;* projectile motion, *p. 362*

12.2 Newton's First and Second Laws of Motion

Key Concepts

- According to Newton's first law of motion, the state of motion of an object does not change as long as the net force acting on the object is zero.

- According to Newton's second law of motion, the acceleration of an object is equal to the net force acting on it divided by the object's mass.

- Acceleration = $\frac{\text{Net force}}{\text{Mass}}$

- Weight = Mass × Acceleration due to gravity

- Mass is a measure of the inertia of an object; weight is a measure of the force of gravity acting on an object.

Vocabulary

inertia, *p. 364;* mass, *p. 365;* weight, *p. 368*

12.3 Newton's Third Law of Motion and Momentum

Key Concepts

- According to Newton's third law of motion, forces exist as equal and opposite force pairs.

- Momentum = Mass × Velocity
  An object has a large momentum if the product of its mass and velocity is large.

- Momentum is conserved in a closed system.

Vocabulary

momentum, *p. 374;* law of conservation of momentum, *p. 376*

12.4 Universal Forces

Key Concepts

- Electric and magnetic forces are the only forces that can both attract and repel.

- The strong and weak nuclear forces hold the nucleus together.

- Newton's law of universal gravitation states that every object in the universe attracts every other object.

Vocabulary

electromagnetic force, *p. 378;* strong nuclear force, *p. 379;* weak nuclear force, *p. 380;* gravitational force, *p. 380;* centripetal force, *p. 381*

Thinking Visually

Concept Map Use the information on forces from the chapter to complete the concept map below.

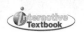
Reviewing Content

Choose the letter that best answers the question or completes the statement.

1. Which is not a force?
  a. friction   **b.** gravity
  c. momentum   **d.** weight

2. You push on a box and are unable to move it. What force opposes your push?
  a. static friction   **b.** rolling friction
  c. sliding friction   **d.** air resistance

3. Air resistance depends on
  a. the velocity of a moving object.
  b. the weight of a moving object.
  c. the mass of a moving object.
  d. the inertia of a moving object.

4. What force besides gravity acts on a projectile?
  a. weak nuclear   **b.** electrical
  c. magnetic   **d.** air resistance

5. Newton's first law of motion is sometimes called the law of
  a. inertia.   **b.** conservation.
  c. momentum.   **d.** resistance.

6. A change in which of the following affects the weight of an object?
  a. momentum
  b. velocity
  c. acceleration due to gravity
  d. friction

7. Which represents Newton's second law?
  a. $v = \frac{d}{t}$ **b.** $a = \frac{F}{m}$

  c. $F = mv$ **d.** $F = 0$

8. For every action force there is a
  a. reaction force.   **b.** net force.
  c. friction force.   **d.** unbalanced force.

9. Momentum depends upon
  a. force only.   **b.** velocity and friction.
  c. weight and mass. **d.** mass and velocity.

10. What force holds the nucleus together?
  a. magnetic
  b. strong nuclear
  c. gravitational
  d. centripetal

Understanding Concepts

11. Three forces act on a wooden crate that is initially at rest as shown below. Determine the net force acting on the crate and describe the resulting motion of the crate.

12. Suppose two 4-newton forces act on an object in the same direction. What is the net force on the object?

13. Five different forces act on an object. Is it possible for the net force on the object to be zero? Explain.

14. What happens to an object when an unbalanced force acts on it?

15. You push harder and harder on a box until it begins sliding across the floor. Which was the stronger of the forces acting on the box, static friction or sliding friction?

16. How do ball bearings reduce friction in machinery?

17. Explain why a falling object subjected to Earth's gravity does not continue to accelerate forever.

18. What is the difference between mass and weight?

19. What is an action-reaction pair?

20. What must you know to determine which of two vehicles traveling at the same velocity, has the greater momentum?

21. What force is responsible for your socks sticking together after they have been in a clothes dryer?

22. What particles do the strong and weak nuclear forces act on?

23. What force is responsible for the orbits of the planets in the solar system?

Assessment (continued)

Critical Thinking

24. Applying Concepts When shooting an arrow at a target, why is it advisable to aim above the bull's-eye rather than directly at it?

25. Inferring When a tennis player practices by hitting a ball against a wall, which of Newton's laws of motion is the player making use of?

26. Comparing and Contrasting The moon's gravity is only one sixth that of Earth's. Explain how the weight and mass of an object differ between the two locations.

27. Interpreting Graphs The graph below shows the relationship between the force acting on an object and the acceleration of the object. What is the acceleration of the object when a 3-newton force acts on it? What is the object's mass?

28. Comparing and Contrasting Consider two rocks with masses of 1 and 10 kilograms. What is the relation between their inertias? Between their masses? Between their weights on Earth?

29. Relating Cause and Effect During a fuel-economy test of a sports car, the car achieved more miles per gallon of gasoline when its convertible top was up. Explain how the convertible top being up or down is related to the car's fuel economy.

30. Applying Concepts What are the two ways in which the acceleration of an object can be increased?

Math Skills

31. Using Formulas A 100-kg crate, sliding on a floor, is brought to a stop by 25-N force. What is the deceleration of the crate?

32. Calculating What is the momentum of an 80-kg runner moving at the speed of 2.5 m/s?

33. Using Formulas What is the weight on Earth of a girl with a mass of 30 kg? The acceleration due to gravity on Earth is 9.8 m/s^2.

Concepts in Action

34. Inferring Hovercraft, which move over water on a cushion of air, can achieve greater speeds than ordinary boats. Explain why this is possible.

35. Making Judgments Imagine that you have designed clothing for professional bicycle racers. How could you judge the effectiveness of the clothing at improving a racer's speed?

36. Designing an Experiment Explain how you could determine the force of static friction acting on a box that is resting on a rough floor.

37. Writing in Science Consider an automobile cruising at a constant speed on the highway. Write a paragraph summarizing the forces acting on the car. Be sure to include the force supplied by the engine and at least two types of friction acting on the car.

Performance-Based Assessment

Communicating Results Draw a cartoon that illustrates one of Newton's laws in an amusing way. You and your classmates might display your cartoons for the whole school to enjoy.

For: Self-grading assessment
Visit: PHSchool.com
Web Code: cca-2120

Standardized Test Prep

Choose the letter that best answers the question or completes the statement.

1. Which of the following correctly lists friction types (excluding fluid friction) from weakest to strongest?
   (A) sliding, static, magnetic
   (B) static, rolling, sliding
   (C) weak, strong, nuclear
   (D) rolling, sliding, static
   (E) static, sliding, rolling

2. Which statement about an object falling at terminal velocity is TRUE?
   (A) Unbalanced forces act on the object.
   (B) The net force acting on the object is zero.
   (C) The object is accelerating.
   (D) The object is traveling in a circular path.
   (E) No fluid friction acts on the object.

3. An object changes direction as it moves. Which of the following is FALSE?
   (A) The acting net force is not zero.
   (B) An unbalanced force acts on the object.
   (C) The object is accelerating.
   (D) A centripetal force must act on the object.
   (E) The object's inertia remains unchanged.

4. Which has the greatest momentum?
   (A) a huge boulder at rest
   (B) a small pebble that is tossed into the air
   (C) a baseball after it is hit with a bat
   (D) a small pebble at rest
   (E) a car traveling on a highway

Use the diagram below to answer Questions 5 and 6. The diagram shows how five forces act on a wooden crate as it slides across the floor.

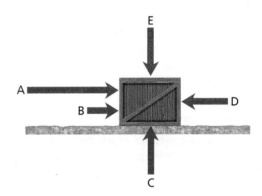

5. If A = 60 N, B = 20 N, C = 30 N, D = 30 N, and E = 30 N, which of the following statements is FALSE?
   (A) A net force of 50 N acts on the crate and the crate moves to the right.
   (B) The crate accelerates to the right.
   (C) The net force in the vertical direction is zero.
   (D) Force C represents the weight of the crate.
   (E) Forces C and E represent balanced forces acting in the vertical direction.

6. Which force represents the sliding friction force?
   (A) A
   (B) B
   (C) C
   (D) D
   (E) E

CHAPTER
13 Forces in Fluids

21st Century Learning
Creativity and Intellectual Curiosity

What are some useful applications of air pressure?

A number of common technologies—including aerosol cans, drinking straws, and fire extinguishers—function by making use of a difference in gas pressure. Use the library or Internet to identify some other devices that make use of a pressurized gas. Choose one device and then create a multimedia presentation that explains how the device works. Your presentation should describe in detail the role of gas pressure in the operation if the device.

How do science concepts apply to your world? Here are some questions you'll be able to answer after you read this chapter.

- **Why is a bicycle seat uncomfortable to sit on for long periods of time?** *(Section 13.1)*

- **Why do your ears pop when you drive up a mountain or fly in a plane?** *(Section 13.1)*

- **How are airplanes that weigh many tons able to fly through the air?** *(Section 13.2)*

- **Why are airplane wings curved on the top?** *(page 398)*

- **Why do heavily loaded cargo ships float lower in the water than unloaded cargo ships?** *(Section 13.3)*

A kite is held aloft by the forces of the wind.

Chapter Preview

Inquiry ‣ Activity

What Makes Something Sink or Float?

Procedure

1. **Predicting** Record your prediction of whether a wooden toothpick and a piece of clay will float on water.

2. To test your predictions, fill a bowl almost to its rim with water.

3. Place a wooden toothpick in the water. Shape a piece of clay into a cup and place it in the water. Record your observations.

4. Remove the clay from the water, dry it with a paper towel, and then tightly roll it into a small ball. Place the ball of clay in the water and record your observations.

Think About It

1. **Evaluating** Which of your predictions were correct?

2. **Observing** What effect did rolling the clay into a ball have on its ability to float?

3. **Formulating Hypotheses** What property of the clay did you change by rolling it into a small ball? Explain how this change affected the clay's ability to float.

13.1 Fluid Pressure

Reading Focus

Key Concepts

- How is pressure calculated?
- How does water pressure change with depth?
- How is pressure distributed at a given level in a fluid?
- How does air pressure change with altitude?

Vocabulary

- pressure
- pascal
- fluid

Reading Strategy

Using Prior Knowledge Before reading the section, copy the table below. In it, write the common definition of the word *pressure*. After you have read the section, write the scientific definition of *pressure* and contrast it to your original definition.

Meanings of *Pressure*	
Common definition	a._____?_____
Scientific definition	b._____?_____

Why is a theater seat so much more comfortable than a bicycle seat? One of the main reasons any seat is comfortable is the pressure it exerts on your body. As you read this chapter, you'll learn about pressure, and how fluids such as air and water can exert and transmit pressure.

Pressure

The comfort of the plush theater seats shown in Figure 1 is related to **pressure**—the result of a force distributed over an area. A theater seat's large padded seat and back offer a larger area to support your weight than a bicycle seat does. Thus, the theater seat exerts less pressure on you and is more comfortable than the bicycle seat.

Many other everyday situations also involve pressure. A sharp pencil easily pokes a hole through a sheet of paper, whereas the eraser end of the pencil does not. Why is this? The reason is the same—pressure.

Figure 1 Because the theater seat exerts a supporting force over a larger area, it is more comfortable than the bicycle seat. **Comparing and Contrasting** *What force acts on both seats?*

The pencil point has a much smaller area than the eraser, so it exerts much greater pressure than the eraser. The greater pressure exerted by the pencil point allows it to pierce the paper easily.

👈 **To calculate pressure, divide the force by the area over which the force acts.**

Pressure

$$\text{Pressure} = \frac{\text{Force}}{\text{Area}}$$

In the formula, force should be in newtons (N) and area should be in square meters (m^2). The resulting unit, newtons per square meter (N/m^2), is the SI unit of pressure, also known as a **pascal** (Pa). The pascal is named for French scientist Blaise Pascal (1623–1662). Pressures are often stated in units of kilopascals (kPa). Note that 1 kPa is 1000 Pa.

Consider a box with a weight of 2700 newtons resting on the ground. If the area of the box touching the ground is 1.5 square meters, what pressure does the box exert on the ground?

$$\text{Pressure} = \frac{\text{Force}}{\text{Area}} = \frac{2700 \text{ N}}{1.5 \text{ m}^2} = 1800 \text{ N/m}^2 = 1800 \text{ Pa} = 1.8 \text{ kPa}$$

Pressure in Fluids

A **fluid** is a substance that assumes the shape of its container. Both liquids and gases are fluids. Water, oil, gasoline, air, and helium are fluids. The particles that make up liquids and gases are shown in Figure 2.

Just as a person sitting in a seat exerts force and pressure, so does a fluid. Imagine a glass filled with water. The water flows to take the same shape as that of the glass. Because the water is in contact with the walls and bottom of the glass, it exerts pressure on these surfaces. The amount of pressure exerted depends on several factors.

Have you ever noticed what happens to the pressure exerted on your body as you swim downward in a pool? 👈 **Water pressure increases as depth increases. The pressure in a fluid at any given depth is constant, and it is exerted equally in all directions.** Surprisingly, the shape of a container and the area of its bottom surface do not affect fluid pressure. For a fluid that is not moving, depth and the type of fluid are the two factors that determine the pressure the fluid exerts.

Reading Checkpoint *How is fluid pressure related to fluid depth?*

Figure 2 Both liquids and gases can flow and take on the shape of their containers. **A** Particles in a liquid are tightly packed together but are able to slide past one another. **B** Particles in a gas are far apart and travel in straight lines until they collide with another particle or object.
Inferring *Based on the illustrations, can a gas be compressed into a smaller space?*

Planetary Atmospheres

The layer of gases surrounding a planet is known as its atmosphere. All of the planets in our solar system have some form of atmosphere. The weight of an atmosphere creates atmospheric pressure at the planet's surface.

The table at the right gives data about the atmospheric composition and pressure for several of the planets.

1. **Interpreting Tables** Which planet listed in the table has the greatest atmospheric pressure?

2. **Interpreting Tables** What chemical substance exists in all but one of the atmospheres?

Planetary Atmospheres		
Planet	Composition of Atmosphere	Atmospheric Pressure (kPa)
Mercury	Mixture of helium, sodium, and oxygen	10^{-12}
Earth	77% nitrogen, 21% oxygen, 1% argon	101.3
Venus	96% carbon dioxide, 3.5% nitrogen	9120
Mars	95% carbon dioxide, 2.7% nitrogen, 1.6% argon	0.71

3. **Converting Units** The bar is another unit of pressure (1 bar = 101.3 kPa). Convert each of the given pressures into bars.

4. **Using Formulas** How much force is exerted on a 2.00-square-meter area of Venus's surface?

5. **Predicting** On which planet would a helium-filled balloon have the smallest volume?

As you just learned, fluid pressure is determined by the type of fluid and its depth. Thus the amount of fluid, measured in terms of volume or weight, does not affect pressure. To prove this, imagine a large lake and a bathtub. Although they contain very different amounts of water, the pressure at a depth of 25 centimeters is the same in both the lake and the bathtub.

Note that each of the connected vases in Figure 3 contains a different amount of liquid. Yet, the liquid levels are all the same. Why is this? It is because pressure depends on depth, not amount. If the pressure at the bottom of all the vases were not the same, the water would flow until the pressures equalized.

Air Pressure and the Atmosphere

You live at the bottom of a vast ocean of fluid. Unlike fish, however, you live in an ocean of air. Air is a mixture of gases that make up Earth's atmosphere. Just as ocean water exerts pressure, so does Earth's atmosphere. The weight of Earth's atmosphere exerts a pressure of about 101 kPa at sea level.

Just as water pressure in a beaker increases with depth, air pressure increases with the depth of the atmosphere. Instead of saying they are at a certain depth in the atmosphere, however, people refer to their altitude above sea level. **Air pressure decreases as the altitude increases.**

Figure 3 This Pascal vase is made up of several oddly shaped vases that are connected to one another at their base. **Drawing Conclusions** *What can you conclude from the fact that all of the fluid levels are the same?*

Have your ears ever popped while you were riding in an elevator, flying in a plane, or driving up to the mountains? In situations such as these, the outside air pressure changes more quickly than your ears can adjust. This creates a difference in pressure between the inside of your ear and the air outside. These unbalanced pressures equalize when air passes through a small tube within your ear. This is the popping sensation you feel.

You may be surprised to learn that as you read this, the atmosphere is exerting more than 1000 newtons of force on the top of your head. As shown in Figure 4, this is enough force to crush a can! Why then aren't you crushed by air pressure? Fortunately, the inside of your body also exerts pressure. You are not crushed like the can in Figure 4 because the pressure inside your body balances the air pressure outside. The balanced forces cancel, resulting in a net force of zero.

Figure 4 This series of photos (1–4) illustrates that the atmosphere can exert enough force to crush a metal can. A can containing a small amount of water is heated until the water boils. Then the can is capped, the hot plate is switched off, and the can is allowed to cool. As the can cools, the pressure inside the can becomes less than the pressure outside the can. The difference in pressure crushes the can.

Section 13.1 Assessment

Reviewing Concepts

1. What must you know to calculate pressure?

2. What is the relationship between the depth of water and the pressure it exerts?

3. How is pressure distributed at a given level in a fluid?

4. How does the pressure exerted by the atmosphere change as altitude increases?

5. Why don't you feel the pressure exerted by the atmosphere?

Critical Thinking

6. **Inferring** Some deep-sea fish have been known to explode as they are brought to the ocean's surface. How do pressure changes cause this to happen?

7. **Applying Concepts** A 500-N student stands on one foot. A 750-N student stands on two feet. If both students wear the same size shoe, which exerts the greater pressure?

Math Practice

8. A circus performer on a pair of stilts exerts a pressure of 32 kPa on the ground. If the performer stands on one stilt, what pressure does the stilt exert on the ground?

9. A book with a weight of 12 N rests on its back cover. If the back cover measures 21 cm by 28 cm, how much pressure does the book exert?

13.2 Forces and Pressure in Fluids

Reading Focus

Key Concepts

- How does Pascal's principle describe the transmission of pressure through a fluid?

- How does a hydraulic system work?

- How is the speed of a fluid related to the pressure within the fluid?

Vocabulary

- hydraulic system
- lift

Reading Strategy

Predicting Copy the table below. Then imagine two small foam balls hanging from strings at the same height with about three centimeters of space between them. Before you read the section, write a prediction about what will happen to the balls when you blow air through the space between them. Identify your reasons. After you have read the section, check the accuracy of your prediction.

Prediction	a._____?_____
Reason for prediction	b._____?_____

Figure 5 The fast-moving stream of air from the blow dryer creates a column of low-pressure air. The table tennis ball is suspended in an area of low pressure.

Suppose your teacher held a table tennis ball on an upward-pointing hair dryer. He then asked you to predict what would happen when the hair dryer was turned on and the ball was released. Did you predict that the ball would be blown up and away? If you did, you were wrong!

As shown in Figure 5, when the hair dryer was turned on, the table tennis ball was not blown away. Instead, it was lifted up and suspended in the air stream above the hair dryer. Suppose your teacher then made the ball bob in the air stream by gently moving the hair dryer up and down. How was that possible? Read on to learn how fluids are able to transmit pressure and how moving fluids produce the pressure changes and forces that explain this demonstration.

Transmitting Pressure in a Fluid

As you learned in the previous section, a fluid exerts pressure equally in all directions at a given depth. You also know that the amount of pressure exerted by a fluid depends on the type of fluid and its depth. Apply these two concepts in the following thought experiment. Imagine a two-liter plastic soda bottle completely filled with water, with its cap tightly screwed on. The bottle is sitting upright on a table. Can you visualize and describe how the pressure forces act against the inside of the bottle?

Pascal's Principle

The pressure forces acting on the bottle are shown in Figure 6A. Note that at any given depth, equal pressures act against the inside of the bottle. Note also that the pressure increases with depth. Now imagine what happens to the pressure inside the bottle if you tightly squeeze it at the middle. Will the pressure be greater at the point where you squeeze?

The pressure inside the squeezed bottle is shown in Figure 6B. Note that the pressure increases with depth, as it did before the bottle was squeezed. More important, note that the pressure increases equally throughout the water, not just at the point where you squeeze. Pascal discovered this phenomenon in the 1600s. His observation led to a general principle. ⚙ **According to Pascal's principle, a change in pressure at any point in a fluid is transmitted equally and unchanged in all directions throughout the fluid.**

Hydraulic Systems

Hydraulics is the science of applying Pascal's principle. The dump truck in Figure 7A makes use of a hydraulic lift system. A **hydraulic system** is a device that uses pressurized fluid acting on pistons of different sizes to change a force.

Look at the diagram of a hydraulic system shown in Figure 7B. An input force is applied to the small piston, which pushes against the fluid sealed in the hydraulic system. Applying Pascal's principle, you know that the pressure produced by the small piston is transmitted through the fluid to the large piston. Thus, the pressure on both pistons is the same.

However, the pressure pushing against the large piston acts on a much larger area, which is the key to how the system works. ⚙ **In a hydraulic lift system, an increased output force is produced because a constant fluid pressure is exerted on the larger area of the output piston.** This large output force is used to lift and dump the load. The amount the input force is increased depends on the areas of the pistons. If the large piston has eight times the area of the small piston, then the output force is eight times greater than the input force. Why is this? Recall that force is equal to the product of pressure and area. Because the pressure on each piston is the same, the difference in forces is directly related to the difference in areas.

Figure 6 A change in pressure at any point in a fluid is transmitted equally and unchanged in all directions throughout the fluid. **A** Note that the forces exerted against the walls of the container are equal at a given depth. **B** When squeezed, the pressure is transmitted equally throughout the fluid.

Force   Force

Figure 7 A The truck uses hydraulic-powered struts to lift its load and dump it on the ground. **B** The larger area of the output piston produces the increased force used to lift the load.

Output force

Large piston

Small piston

Hydraulic fluid

Input force

Forces in Fluids **395**

Figure 8 The airplane wing changes the flow pattern of the air it passes through. Note how air flowing over the top of the wing is diverted up and over the wing's curved surface.
Comparing and Contrasting *How does the flow of air over the top of the wing (green arrows) compare with the flow of air under the wing (blue arrows)?*

Bernoulli's Principle

Try this simple experiment. Pick up a single sheet of paper and hold its top corners using both of your hands. Now position the paper directly in front of your mouth and blow as hard as you can over the top surface of the paper. Even though you are blowing over its top, the far end of the paper lifts upward.

The Swiss scientist Daniel Bernoulli (1700–1782) discovered the reason why the sheet of paper behaves as it does. **According to Bernoulli's principle, as the speed of a fluid increases, the pressure within the fluid decreases.** As the air blows across the top of the paper, the pressure exerted by the air decreases. Because the air below the paper is nearly motionless, it exerts a greater pressure. The difference in pressure forces the paper upward.

Bernoulli's principle explains the table tennis ball demonstration discussed earlier. The air from the dryer strikes the bottom of the ball and lifts it into the air. The pressure in this fast-moving air stream, however, is less than the pressure in the surrounding air. If the ball moves sideways out of the air stream, it encounters higher-pressure, slower-moving air. The higher-pressure air forces the ball back into the air stream coming from the hair dryer.

Bernoulli's principle has many applications in industry and explains many things in nature as well.

Reading Checkpoint *How is a fluid's speed related to the pressure it exerts?*

Wings and Lift The ability of birds and airplanes to fly is largely explained by Bernoulli's principle. As shown in Figure 8, the air traveling over the top of an airplane wing moves faster than the air passing underneath. This creates a low-pressure area above the wing. The pressure difference between the top and the bottom of the wing creates an upward force known as **lift.** The lift created in this way is a large part of what keeps the airplane aloft.

For: Links on Bernoulli's principle
Visit: www.SciLinks.org
Web Code: ccn-2132

The wings of birds produce lift in much the same way as an airplane wing. Unlike airplane wings, birds can flap their wings to produce forward movement and some lift.

Sometimes wings are used to create a downward force. Race cars often have an upside-down wing known as a spoiler mounted on the rear of the car. The downward force created by the spoiler pushes the tires down onto the road, giving the car better traction. Increased traction allows the car to go around corners at higher speeds.

Spray Bottles Figure 9 shows the design of a typical hose-end sprayer. This type of sprayer is often used to apply fertilizers and pesticides to lawns, plants, and trees. A concentrated solution of the chemical that is to be sprayed is placed in the solution chamber. The sprayer is then attached to a garden hose.

As water streams through the sprayer, it passes over the top of a small tube that reaches down into the solution chamber. The fast-moving water creates a low-pressure area at the top of the tube. The pressure difference between the solution chamber and the tube forces the concentrated solution up the tube. The solution then mixes with the water and is sprayed out of the end of the sprayer.

Figure 9 The design of a hose-end sprayer is based on Bernoulli's principle. Pressure differences draw the concentrated solution up into the fast-moving water stream.

1 Water moves through sprayer at high speed (low pressure).

2 Water and fertilizer mix here.

3 Mixture sprays out tip.

Concentrated fertilizer solution (atmospheric pressure)

Section 13.2 Assessment

Reviewing Concepts

1. ⬤ Describe Pascal's principle in your own words.

2. ⬤ How is a hydraulic system able to increase force?

3. ⬤ How are fluid speed and fluid pressure related?

4. How does an airplane wing produce lift?

Critical Thinking

5. **Predicting** Water is nearly incompressible. Air is easily compressed. Predict what will happen when an air-filled balloon is pulled to the bottom of a swimming pool.

6. **Applying Concepts** The area of an output piston is 25 times greater than the area of the input piston. If the input force is 40 newtons, what is the output force?

7. **Relating Cause and Effect** Two table tennis balls are suspended from strings so they hang at the same height with a small space between them. When a hair dryer is used to blow air between the two balls, the balls come together and touch. Explain why this occurs.

8. **Inferring** When cars pass one another in opposite directions on the highway, they tend to be forced together. Use Bernoulli's principle to explain why this happens.

Connecting ⊂ Concepts

Net Force Review unbalanced forces in Section 12.1 and their relation to net force. Relate Bernoulli's principle to air flowing over an airplane wing and the creation of a net upward force.

Airplane Motion

Four forces act on an airplane in flight. They are thrust, drag, lift, and weight. Lift and drag are known as aerodynamic forces because they result entirely from the plane's movement through the air.

Of the aerodynamic forces, lift is the least familiar. One source of lift is Bernoulli's principle. According to Bernoulli's principle, the pressure of a fluid such as air decreases as its speed increases. Because the air moving over the top of an airplane wing moves faster than the air moving beneath the wing, it creates a pressure difference that lifts the wing and hence the plane. Another source of lift is the slant of the wing. As the wing moves through the air, the wing forces air downward. According to Newton's third law of motion, this action must have a reaction. The reaction force also exerts an upward force on the wing.

Thrust

Flight controls

In addition to the engines, the pilot has control over a number of other parts of the airplane that affect its motion through the air. These include the spoilers and flaps, and other parts of the wings and tail. These parts affect yaw (turning to left or right), pitch (tilting from back to front) and roll (one wing tilting up, and the other down).

Flap affects lift and drag.

Rudder controls yaw.

Elevator controls pitch.

Aileron controls roll.

Spoiler increases drag.

YAW

PITCH

ROLL

Air flow around wing

The movement of an airplane wing through the air causes air passing over the top of the wing first to be accelerated upward (upwash) and then rapidly downward (downwash). Overall, the wing produces a downward movement of the air, and the wing itself is pushed upward. The air flowing over the top of the wing has the lowest pressure. The result is an overall pressure difference that pushes the wing up.

Initial upwash

Downwash along wing

More air moves downward (to fill void)

Fast-moving, low-pressure air

Air below wing under pressure

Direction in which the plane is traveling

Lift due to pressure imbalance

Engine generates thrust.

Lift

Wing generates lift.

Drag

Weight

Four forces acting on a plane

The engine produces thrust, which pushes the plane forward. Thrust is opposed by drag (air resistance), which increases with the airplane's speed. The thrust must create enough speed to generate lift. Lift is the upward force on the airplane caused by movement of its wings through the air. For the plane to become airborne, the lift must exceed the plane's weight.

Going Further

- Research the development of airplane engines since the early 1900s. Prepare a poster to present your findings. Include information on engine type, power or thrust produced, and a description of the plane the engine was used in.

13.3 Buoyancy

Reading Focus

Key Concepts

- What is the effect of buoyancy on the apparent weight of an object?
- How can you determine if an object will float or sink in a fluid?

Vocabulary

- buoyancy
- buoyant force
- Archimedes' principle

Reading Strategy

Summarizing Copy the table below. As you read about buoyancy, write a brief summary of the text following each green heading. Your summary should include only the most important information.

Section 13.3 Buoyancy
Buoyant Force Buoyant force is the apparent loss of weight of an object submerged in a fluid.
a._____?_____
b._____?_____

ave you ever stood in a pool and tried lifting a friend who was submerged in the water? If you have, you may recall how surprisingly easy your friend was to lift. Or perhaps you have gone swimming in a lake or bay where the very salty water made it easy to float on the surface. What forces make these two situations possible? In this section you'll learn the answers to these questions.

Buoyant Force

You are easily able to lift a friend submerged in water because of buoyancy. **Buoyancy** is the ability of a fluid to exert an upward force on an object placed in it. **Buoyancy results in the apparent loss of weight of an object in a fluid.** In fact, every object in a fluid experiences buoyancy. When an object is submerged in water, the water exerts an upward force on the object, making it easier to lift. This upward force, which acts in the opposite direction of gravity, is called a **buoyant force.**

How is a buoyant force produced? To answer this question, examine the forces pressure exert on the submerged object in Figure 10. Because water pressure increases with depth, the forces pushing up on the bottom of the object are greater than the forces from pressure pushing down on the top of the object. All of the other non-vertical forces cancel one another out. The result is a net upward force—the buoyant force.

Figure 10 The forces from pressure acting on the bottom of this golf ball are greater than those acting on the top. This produces a net force—called the buoyant force—that acts upward on the ball.

Archimedes' Principle

Archimedes, an ancient Greek mathematician who died in 212 B.C., is credited with an important discovery that bears his name. According to **Archimedes' principle,** the buoyant force on an object is equal to the weight of the fluid displaced by the object.

When an object is submerged, it pushes aside, or displaces, a volume of fluid equal to its own volume. When an object floats on the surface of a fluid, it does not displace its entire volume. The floating object does, however, displace a volume equal to the volume of the part of the object that is submerged.

Density and Buoyancy

Density and buoyancy are closely related. Recall that density is the ratio of an object's mass to its volume. Densities are often expressed in the non-SI units of grams per cubic centimeter (g/cm^3). Water, for example, has a density of $1 \ g/cm^3$, whereas steel has a density of $7.8 \ g/cm^3$.

If an object is less dense than the fluid it is in, it will float. If the object is more dense than the fluid it is in, it will sink. Different fluids can also float or sink in one another. Oil, for example, floats on water because oil is less dense than water.

You can also determine if an object will float by analyzing the forces acting on it. As you can see in Figure 11, two forces act on every object in a fluid—weight and the buoyant force. The force of gravity, equal to the object's weight, acts downward on the object. The buoyant force, equal to the weight of the volume of displaced fluid, acts upward on the object. **When the buoyant force is equal to the weight, an object floats or is suspended. When the buoyant force is less than the weight, the object sinks.**

Figure 11 The weight and buoyant force determines if an object sinks or floats. **A** The metal cube sinks because its weight is greater than the buoyant force. **B** Equal forces acting on this submerged cube allow it to be suspended in the fluid. **C** The partially submerged wood cube floats at a depth where the buoyant force and weight are equal.

≡Quick Lab

Changing Buoyancy

Procedure

1. Fill a plastic bottle with water up to its neck. Squeeze a dropper pipet's bulb and draw water into the pipet until it is about half full. Insert the pipet, bulb end up, into the bottle. The pipet should float at the water's surface.

2. Add water to the bottle until it is full. Tightly twist the cap onto the bottle. Trap as little air as possible in the bottle.

3. Observe what happens to the pipet as you squeeze, hold, and then release the bottle.

Analyze and Conclude

1. **Applying Concepts** Describe the changes in pressure during Step 3.

2. **Inferring** How did the volume of the air trapped inside the pipet change when the bottle was squeezed?

3. **Drawing Conclusions** Explain how squeezing and releasing the bottle caused the pipet to move up and down in the water.

Forces in Fluids

Suspended An object that has the same density as the fluid it is submerged in will be suspended (it will float at any level) in the fluid. The buoyant force acting on the suspended object exactly equals the object's weight. Submarines and some fish are able to suspend themselves in water partly by adjusting their density. To learn more about submarines, read the How It Works box below.

Sinking If the shape of a ship's hull allows it to float, what causes a ship to sink? As you know, when the ship's weight becomes greater than the buoyant force acting on it, the ship will sink. This may occur when the ship damages its hull and takes on water. As water enters the hull, the ship displaces less water and the buoyant force decreases. If the damage is not fixed, the ship will eventually sink.

DK HOW It Works

Submarine

According to Archimedes' principle, the buoyant force on an object is equal to the weight of the fluid displaced by the object. Whereas the weight of an object acts downward, the buoyant force acts upward. **Interpreting Diagrams** *When diving and surfacing, how do submarines make use of Archimedes' principle?*

Steering a submarine
The crew alters the buoyancy of the submarine to make it rise or sink. To steer the submarine through the water, crewmen also use the propeller and the rudder, and adjust the angle of the diving planes.

Rudder

Propeller

Part of submarine shown in cross-section below

Air being blown out

Vent

Compressed air tank

Outer hull

Inner hull

Ballast tanks flooding

Rear diving planes angled upward

Forward diving planes angled downward

Water being taken in

SUBMARINE DIVING

A **Negative buoyancy** As long as it remains submerged, a submarine experiences a constant buoyant force. To overcome the buoyant force so the submarine can dive—that is, to achieve negative buoyancy—its weight must increase. This is done by flooding the ballast tanks, replacing air with water.

Floating You may be wondering why a piece of steel sinks, whereas a huge steel ship floats. A heavy steel ship floats because of the shape of its hull. The hull is shaped so that it displaces a large volume of water, creating a large buoyant force. The buoyant force created by the ship's hull is large enough to counteract the ship's tremendous weight.

Objects also float more easily in dense fluids. Why is this? As you know, the buoyant force acting on the object equals the weight of the volume of the fluid it displaces. For a given displacement, the denser the fluid is, the greater is the weight displaced. This greater displaced weight results in a greater buoyant force. This is why it is easier for a person to float in very salty water. The dense salty water produces a larger buoyant force when displaced by the person's body.

Go Online
NSTA SciLINKS

For: Links on buoyancy
Visit: www.SciLinks.org
Web Code: ccn-2133

B **Neutral buoyancy** Once the submarine's ballast tanks hold enough water for the submarine's weight to equal the buoyant force, the submarine is said to have neutral buoyancy. It now has no tendency to rise or sink.

Diving planes angled upward

Air being pumped into ballast tanks

Diving planes horizontal

Rear diving planes angled downward

Ballast tanks emptying of water

SUBMARINE RISING

SUBMARINE FLOATING LEVEL

Ballast tanks partially filled with water

C **Positive buoyancy** To rise again, the submarine's weight must be decreased. Air is pumped into the ballast tanks to force the water out. The buoyant force acting on the submarine now exceeds the submarine's weight. With positive buoyancy, the submarine rises.

Figure 12 The exposed green and red stripes on the ship's hull indicate that the ship is riding high in the water.
Applying Concepts *How will the ship's level in the water change if it takes on additional cargo?*

The ability of a huge steel ship to float in water can also be explained in terms of density. As you know, a solid piece of steel sinks in water. A ship's shape, however, allows it to displace a very large volume of water relative to its weight. That is, the ship's shape increases its volume and decreases its density. As long as the ship's effective density is less than that of water, the ship floats.

The heavier the ship, the more water it must displace in order to float. The relationship between weight and the level a ship rides at in the water can be seen in Figure 12. If the cargo ship were completely loaded, it would need to displace more water in order to float.

Why do some balloons float in air whereas others do not? The answer has to do with density differences. Helium and hot air are both less dense than normal-temperature air. When a balloon is filled with either helium or hot air, a buoyant force from the displaced normal-temperature air acts on the balloon. If the size of the buoyant force is large enough, the balloon rises into the air.

Section 13.3 Assessment

Reviewing Concepts

1. 🔵 How does buoyancy affect the apparent weight of an object in a fluid?

2. 🔵 What determines if an object will float or sink in a fluid?

3. How does Archimedes' principle relate the buoyant force acting on an object and the volume of fluid displaced by the object?

4. How is the density of a floating object related to the density of the fluid it is floating in?

Critical Thinking

5. **Applying Concepts** An empty oil tanker displaces enough water to support its weight. Why doesn't the tanker sink when loaded with thousands of tons of oil?

6. **Inferring** A small object is able to float at any level when placed in water. What does this observation tell you about the object's density?

7. **Applying Concepts** A 350-N block of wood is thrown into a lake, where it floats. What is the buoyant force acting on it?

Writing in Science

Compare and Contrast Paragraph Write a paragraph comparing the forces acting on an object that floats in water and an object that sinks in water. Be sure to describe the relative sizes of the forces acting on each object. (*Hint:* Before you write, review the forces shown in Figure 11.)

Determining Buoyant Force

In this lab, you will analyze recorded data to determine the buoyant forces acting on objects.

Problem How does the buoyant force determine whether an object sinks?

Materials

string, rock, spring scale, can, plastic tub, sponge, paper towels, 100-g standard mass, wooden block tied to a fishing weight, 250-mL graduated cylinder

 For the probeware version of this lab, see the Probeware Lab Manual, Lab 5.

Skills Measuring, Calculating

Procedure

1. Make a copy of the data table shown.

2. Tie one end of the string around the rock. Tie the other end to the spring scale. Suspend the rock from the spring scale and measure and record its weight in air in your data table.

3. Place the can in an upright position in the plastic tub. Completely fill the can with water. Wipe up any water that spills into the tub. **CAUTION** *Wipe up any water that spills on the floor to avoid slips and falls.*

4. Lower the rock into the water until it is completely submerged. Record in your data table the apparent weight in water of the submerged rock. Remove the rock from the can.

5. Without spilling any water, carefully remove the can from the tub. Pour the water from the

tub into the graduated cylinder. Record the volume of displaced water in your data table.

6. Repeat Steps 2 through 5, first with the 100-g standard mass and then with the wooden block that is tied to a fishing weight.

7. To determine the buoyant force on each object, subtract its apparent weight in water from its weight in air. Record these values.

8. Calculate the weight of the water each object displaces. (*Hint:* 1.0 mL of water has a weight of 0.0098 N.) Record these weights.

Analyze and Conclude

1. **Observing** What force is responsible for the difference between the weight of each object in the air and its apparent weight in water?

2. **Analyzing Data** How is the buoyant force related to the weight of water displaced?

3. **Forming Operational Definitions** Define buoyant force and describe two ways you can measure it or calculate it.

4. **Drawing Conclusions** Explain what causes an object to sink or to float, using the terms *buoyancy, weight, force, density,* and *gravity.*

Data Table					
Object	Weight in Air (N)	Apparent Weight in Water (N)	Buoyant Force (weight in air − apparent weight in water, N)	Volume of Displaced Water (mL)	Weight of Displaced Water (N)
Rock					
100-g standard mass					
Wood block with fishing weight					

13.1 Fluid Pressure

🐟 Key Concepts

• Pressure = $\dfrac{\text{Force}}{\text{Area}}$

• Water pressure increases as depth increases.

• The pressure in a fluid at any given depth is constant and is exerted equally in all directions.

• Air pressure decreases as altitude increases.

Vocabulary

pressure, *p. 390*
pascal, *p. 391*
fluid, *p. 391*

13.2 Forces and Pressure in Fluids

🐟 Key Concepts

• According to Pascal's principle, a change in pressure at any point in a fluid is transmitted equally and unchanged in all directions throughout the fluid.

• In a hydraulic lift system, an increased output force is produced by a constant fluid pressure exerted on the larger area of the output piston.

• According to Bernoulli's principle, as the speed of a fluid increases, the pressure within the fluid decreases.

Vocabulary

hydraulic system, *p. 395*
lift, *p. 396*

13.3 Buoyancy

🐟 Key Concepts

• Buoyancy results in the apparent loss of weight of an object in a fluid.

• If an object is less dense than the fluid it is in, it will float. If the object is more dense than the fluid it is in, it will sink.

• When the buoyant force is equal to the weight, an object floats or is suspended. When the buoyant force is less than the weight, the object sinks.

Vocabulary

buoyancy, *p. 400*
buoyant force, *p. 400*
Archimedes' principle, *p. 401*

Thinking Visually

Use the information from the chapter to complete the concept map below.

Reviewing Content

Choose the letter that best answers the question or completes the statement.

1. A resting object exerts pressure equal to
   a. its mass times its contact area.
   b. its weight times its contact area.
   c. its mass divided by its contact area.
   d. its weight divided by its contact area.

2. Compared to the pressure exerted by a brick standing on its end, the pressure exerted by a brick resting on its side is
   a. the same.   b. less.
   c. more.   d. twice as much.

3. The amount of water pressure you experience while swimming in a pool depends on
   a. your buoyancy.
   b. the area of the pool.
   c. the volume of water in the pool.
   d. how deep you are in the water.

4. Which of the following is NOT true about the SI unit of pressure?
   a. It is used for fluids only.
   b. It is called a pascal.
   c. It is equal to one newton per square meter.
   d. It represents force per unit area.

5. Blaise Pascal discovered that changes in pressure
   a. are transmitted equally throughout a fluid.
   b. increase with depth of fluid.
   c. decrease with depth of fluid.
   d. depend on area.

6. In a hydraulic lift system, the output force is greater than the input force because
   a. a larger pressure acts on the output piston.
   b. a larger pressure acts on the input piston.
   c. the fluid pressure acts on areas of different sizes.
   d. of Bernoulli's principle.

7. Which of the following is NOT true about Bernoulli's principle?
   a. The pressure within a moving fluid is greater than the pressure within a nonmoving fluid.
   b. As a fluid's speed increases, the pressure within it decreases.
   c. When a moving fluid slows, the pressure within it increases.
   d. It helps explain the lift of an airplane.

8. The buoyant force acting on a submerged object is equal to
   a. the object's mass.
   b. the object's volume.
   c. the mass of the fluid displaced by the object.
   d. the weight of the fluid displaced by the object.

9. A partially submerged object floats when
   a. the object's weight is equal to the buoyant force.
   b. the object's mass is equal to the buoyant force.
   c. the object's weight is greater than the buoyant force.
   d. the buoyant force is downward.

10. A submarine changes depth by altering its
    a. speed.   b. density.
    c. total area.   d. shape.

Understanding Concepts

11. How is pressure different from force?

12. What are two characteristics of fluids?

13. State Archimedes' principle in your own words.

14. What two forces determine whether an object floats or sinks?

15. Why is it easier to float in salt water than in fresh water?

16. Why do helium-filled balloons rise in air?

17. Explain how a hydraulic lift operates.

18. Why is it easier to pull a submerged boat anchor to the surface than it is to lift it onto the boat?

19. Three different liquids and two equal-size cubes are placed in a beaker as shown. Which of the objects has the greater buoyant force acting on it?

Critical Thinking

20. Applying Concepts In order to save someone who has fallen through the ice of a frozen lake, rescuers often reach the victim by crawling across the ice on their stomachs. Explain why the rescuers use this technique.

21. Designing an Experiment Your lab has two pressurized gas cylinders, each containing a different gas. Describe an experiment that could be used to determine whether each gas is less dense than air.

22. Applying Concepts For patients with muscles weakened due to injury, physical therapists recommend exercising in a swimming pool. Why is pool exercise preferred to exercise in a gym?

23. Using Models The high-speed winds of a hurricane sometimes cause houses to explode. Use a drawing to model the pressures acting on the house. Explain the areas of high and low pressure using Bernoulli's principle.

Math Skills

Use the illustration to answer Questions 24 and 25. The results of adding a small stone to a beaker that was filled to the brim with water is shown below.

24. Converting Units What is the volume of the stone in cm^3? (*Hint:* 1.0 mL = 1.0 cm^3)

25. Calculating If 1.0 cm^3 equals 1.0 mL, and 1.0 cm^3 of water has a mass of 1.0 g, calculate the buoyant force acting on the stone.

26. Using Formulas A 520-N ballet dancer is balanced on the toe of her shoe. If the toe has an area of 0.0010 m^2, what pressure does she exert on the floor?

27. Using Formulas A small hydraulic jack exerts a force of 2200 N. If the area of the jack's output piston is 0.0060 m^2, what is the pressure of the hydraulic fluid inside the jack?

Concepts in Action

28. Comparing and Contrasting Water exerts pressure on all sides of a submerged submarine. Compare and contrast the pressures acting on the submarine at a depth of 50 m to the pressures at a depth of 200 m.

29. Predicting An empty metal can is capped, attached to weights, and thrown into a deep ocean trench. A second, identical metal can is left uncapped, attached to weights, and thrown into the same trench. Both cans sink. Predict what will happen to each can and explain your reasons.

30. Applying Concepts When a driver presses on the brake pedal of a car, the car is easily brought to a stop. Explain how the car's hydraulic braking system transmits and increases the force applied to the brake pedal.

31. Writing in Science Explain how airplane wings and the wings of birds affect the air flowing over them to produce lift.

Performance-Based Assessment

Using Models Use what you have learned from this chapter to make a model boat out of a 10-cm-square piece of foil. Test your model boat in a tank of water to see how many pennies it can support before sinking. Compare the performance of your boat with those of your classmates. Suggest several design improvements based on your results.

For: Self-grading assessment
Visit: PHSchool.com
Web Code: cca-2130

Standardized Test Prep

Test-Taking Tip

Simplify the Question

When reading a problem, it is important not to be confused by unnecessary information. It helps to rephrase the problem by ignoring the irrelevant information. Start with the question you are asked to answer. Then reread the problem and list only the information you need to answer the question. In the example below, you do not need to know water volume.

Beaker A contains 100 mL of water. Beaker B, which is smaller, contains 75 mL of water. The depth of water is the same in both beakers. Which of the following is TRUE?

(A) The volume is greater in beaker B.
(B) The pressure is greater at the bottom of beaker B than at the bottom of beaker A.
(C) The volume is equal in both beakers.
(D) The pressure is equal at the bottom of both beakers.
(E) The pressure is greater at the bottom of beaker A than at the bottom of beaker B.

(Answer: D)

Choose the letter that best answers the question or completes the statement.

1. During a storm, the wind exerts a 150-N force on a window that measures 1.00 m by 0.50 m. The outside air pressure is 101 kPa. What pressure, in pascals, does the wind exert on the window?
   (A) 75 Pa
   (B) 150 Pa
   (C) 1.5×10^3 Pa
   (D) 3.0×10^2 Pa
   (E) 3.0×10^5 kPa

2. Two identical beakers are both half filled with a liquid. Beaker A contains water and Beaker B contains a liquid that is denser than water. Which of the following is FALSE?
   (A) The pressure at the bottom of Beaker B is greater than that at the bottom of Beaker A.
   (B) The pressure within each fluid is exerted equally in all directions.
   (C) The mass of fluid in Beaker B is greater than the mass of fluid in Beaker A.
   (D) The mass of fluid in Beaker A is greater than the mass of fluid in Beaker B.
   (E) The volume of fluid in Beaker B is equal to the volume of fluid in Beaker A.

3. When air is blown between two balls suspended from strings, the balls come together and touch. This is explained by
   (A) Archimedes' principle.
   (B) Pascal's principle.
   (C) the Pauli exclusion principle.
   (D) Bernoulli's principle.
   (E) the hydraulic principle.

4. In a hydraulic system, the area of the output piston is three times larger than the area of the input piston. How is the output force related to the input force?
   (A) It is nine times smaller.
   (B) It is three times smaller.
   (C) They are both zero.
   (D) It is three times larger.
   (E) It is nine times larger.

Questions 5 and 6 refer to the diagram of an unknown substance in a beaker of water shown below.

Buoyant force

5. How are the weight of the unknown object and the buoyant force acting on it related?
   (A) They are the same.
   (B) They are both equal to zero.
   (C) The weight is less than the buoyant force.
   (D) The buoyant force is more than the weight.
   (E) The weight is more than the buoyant force.

6. Which of the following is TRUE?
   (A) Forces from pressure act equally on all sides of the cube.
   (B) The unknown substance has a density greater than 1.0 g/cm^3.
   (C) The buoyant force equals the pressure.
   (D) The buoyant force is more than the weight.
   (E) The weight is equal to the buoyant force.

CHAPTER 14 Work, Power, and Machines

This powerful strip-mining shovel is able to remove tons of earth in a single load of its bucket.

21st Century Learning

Problem Identification, Formulation, and Solution

How can you improve the efficiency of a machine?

Look for some examples of simple machines in your school or at home. Form a small group and discuss with your classmates how these machines make it easier to do work. Discuss possible ways to increase the efficiency of one of these machines. Work with your group to produce a short video about your ideas. In the video, offer suggestions on how to maximize the work that can be done by the machine.

How do science concepts apply to your world? Here are some questions you'll be able to answer after you read this chapter.

- **Why can a snow blower remove snow faster than a person using a shovel?** *(Section 14.1)*

- **How can you lift a car using your hands?** *(Section 14.2)*

- **How does a nutcracker make it easier to crack a nut?** *(Section 14.3)*

- **Why are the trails up mountains constructed to be long and winding?** *(Section 14.4)*

- **Why do bicycles have gears?** *(page 436)*

Chapter Preview

Inquiry Activity

How Do Ramps Help You Raise Objects?

Procedure

1. Make a stack of five books.

2. Make a ramp by leaning a short board against the top of the book stack. Place a sixth book against the bottom edge of the board to keep the ramp from sliding down.

3. Measure and record the height and length of the ramp.

4. Use a spring scale to pull a laboratory cart up the ramp at constant speed. Record the force indicated on the spring scale.

5. Repeat Steps 2 through 4 using a longer board.

Think About It

1. **Comparing and Contrasting** Which ramp required a greater force to pull the cart? Which ramp required the cart to travel a greater distance?

2. **Predicting** How do you think the force needed to pull the cart would change if the cart accelerated up the length of the ramp?

3. **Formulating Hypotheses** Explain why a box that is too heavy to lift can often be pushed up a ramp.

Reading Focus

Key Concepts

- When does a force do work?
- How are work and power related?

Vocabulary

- work
- joule
- power
- watt
- horsepower

Reading Strategy

Relating Text and Visuals Copy the table shown at the right. As you read, look carefully at Figures 1 and 2 and read their captions. Complete the table by describing the work shown in each figure.

Figure	Direction of Force	Direction of Motion	Is Work Done?
1	a. ___?	b. ___?	c. ___?
2A	d. ___?	e. ___?	f. ___?
2B	g. ___?	h. ___?	i. ___?
2C	j. ___?	k. ___?	l. ___?

Figure 1 The weight lifter applies a large force to hold the barbell over his head. However, because the barbell is motionless, no work is done on the barbell. **Applying Concepts** *Did the weight lifter do work on the barbell to lift it over his head?*

You are already familiar with the everyday meaning of work. Working at an after-school job, doing yard work at home, and completing your homework may all be common events in your life. In science, however, "work" means something very different.

Look at the weight lifter shown in Figure 1. He is exerting a large force in order to hold the heavy barbell over his head. You can tell from the look on his face that holding up the weight is hard work. However, a scientist would tell you that at this instant the weight lifter is actually doing no work on the nonmoving barbell. Read on to learn about the work that was done to lift the barbell overhead.

What Is Work?

Recall that an object begins moving only when an unbalanced force acts on it. In science, **work** is the product of force and distance. Work is done when a force acts on an object in the direction the object moves. For example, work is done by the weight lifter when he exerts an upward force to raise the barbell over his head.

Work Requires Motion Though it may seem surprising, the weight lifter in Figure 1 does no work on the barbell as he holds it over his head. Why is that? Because although force is applied to the barbell, the force does not cause the barbell to move. ⬤ **For a force to do work on an object, some of the force must act in the same direction as the object moves. If there is no movement, no work is done.**

Force

Direction of motion

A Force and motion in same direction

This force does work.

This force does no work.

Force

Direction of motion

B Part of force in direction of motion

Force

Direction of motion

C Lifting force not in direction of motion

Work Depends on Direction The amount of work done on an object, if any, depends on the direction of the force and the direction of the movement. For example, though you would never do this, imagine pulling a suitcase as shown in Figure 2A. Note that all of the force acts in the same direction as the suitcase moves—all of the force does work on the suitcase.

A force does not have to act entirely in the direction of movement to do work. Look at the forces and direction of motion shown as the suitcase is pulled in Figure 2B. The force acts upward and to the right along the handle, whereas the suitcase moves only to the right along the ground. Figure 2B shows that there is a horizontal portion of the force acting in the direction of motion. Only the horizontal part of the applied force—the part in the direction of movement—does work.

👄 **Any part of a force that does not act in the direction of motion does no work on an object.** As shown in Figure 2C, the vertical lifting force does not act in the direction of motion. Thus, this vertical force does no work on the suitcase.

Calculating Work

Although the weight lifter in Figure 1 does no work while holding the barbell over his head, he did do work in lifting the barbell to the overhead position. The work done is calculated by multiplying the constant force acting in the direction of motion by the distance that the object moves.

> **Work**
>
> **Work = Force × Distance**

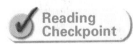
Reading Checkpoint *How do you calculate work?*

Figure 2 The work done on an object depends on the size of the force acting in the direction of motion and on the distance the object moves. **A** When force and motion are in the same direction, the work done is maximized. **B** Only the horizontal part of the force does work to move the suitcase to the right. **C** Because the lifting force is not in the direction the suitcase moves, the force does no work on the suitcase.

For: Links on work
Visit: www.SciLinks.org
Web Code: ccn-2141

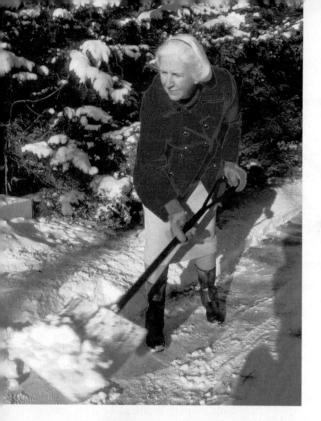

Units of Work When using SI units in the work formula, the force is in newtons, and distance is in meters. The product of force and distance results in the units of newton-meters, also known as joules. The **joule** (J) is the SI unit of work. When a force of 1 newton moves an object 1 meter in the direction of the force, 1 joule of work is done. The joule is named after James Prescott Joule (1818–1889), a British scientist famous for researching the relationship between work and heat.

Using the Work Formula It is easy to calculate the work done by a weight lifter who lifts a 1600-newton barbell over his head. Assume that the barbell is lifted to a height of 2.0 meters. To use the work formula, simply substitute the correct values into the formula and multiply.

$$\text{Work} = \text{Force} \times \text{Distance}$$

$$\text{Work} = 1600 \text{ N} \times 2.0 \text{ m}$$

$$\text{Work} = 3200 \text{ N·m} = 3200 \text{ J}$$

What Is Power?

Often people are not just concerned about getting work done. They want it done fast, and that requires power. Power, like work, has a precise meaning in science.

Power is the rate of doing work. ◯ **Doing work at a faster rate requires more power. To increase power, you can increase the amount of work done in a given time, or you can do a given amount of work in less time.**

Figure 3 shows an example of what a difference in power means when performing a task such as snow removal. Work is required to move snow from one location to another. As you can see in Figure 3, a person using a shovel and a person using a snow blower can both do the work needed to remove the snow. Clearly, the snow blower can do the job much faster. The fact that the snow blower can do more work in less time means that it has more power.

You may have noticed that the size of the engine used by a machine is often an indication of its power. For example, compare the snow blower's small engine with the engine used by a truck pushing a snowplow. The truck's powerful engine allows it to remove snow at a very fast rate.

Figure 3 Power is the rate of doing work. Because the snow blower can remove more snow in less time, it requires more power than hand shoveling does.
Comparing and Contrasting *What is the source of power in each of the above photos?*

Reading Checkpoint *How does doing work at a faster rate affect the power required?*

Calculating Power

You can calculate power by dividing the amount of work done by the time needed to do the work.

> **Power**
>
> $$\text{Power} = \frac{\text{Work}}{\text{Time}}$$

When using SI units in the power formula, work is in joules (J) and time is in seconds (s). The SI unit of power is the **watt** (W), which is equal to one joule per second. Thus, a 40-watt light bulb requires 40 joules each second that it is lit. This amount of power is also approximately equal to lifting your textbook a height of one meter in half a second.

 Math Skills

Calculating Power

You exert a vertical force of 72 newtons to lift a box to a height of 1.0 meter in a time of 2.0 seconds. How much power is used to lift the box?

 1 Read and Understand

What information are you given?

Force = 72 N   Distance = 1.0 m

Time = 2.0 s

2 Plan and Solve

What formula contains the given quantities and the unknown?

$$\text{Power} = \frac{\text{Work}}{\text{Time}} = \frac{\text{Force} \times \text{Distance}}{\text{Time}}$$

Replace each variable with its known value and solve.

$$\text{Power} = \frac{72\,\text{N} \times 1.0\,\text{m}}{2.0\,\text{s}} = 36\,\text{J/s} = 36\,\text{W}$$

 3 Look Back and Check

Is your answer reasonable?

36 watts is not a lot of power, which seems reasonable considering the box was lifted slowly, through a height of only 1 meter.

Math Practice

1. Your family is moving to a new apartment. While lifting a box 1.5 m straight up to put it on a truck, you exert an upward force of 200 N for 1.0 s. How much power is required to do this?

2. You lift a book from the floor to a bookshelf 1.0 m above the ground. How much power is used if the upward force is 15.0 N and you do the work in 2.0 s?

3. You apply a horizontal force of 10.0 N to pull a wheeled suitcase at a constant speed of 0.5 m/s across flat ground. How much power is used? (*Hint:* The suitcase moves 0.5 m/s. Consider how much work the force does each second and how work is related to power.)

James Watt and Horsepower

Besides the watt, another common unit of power is the horsepower. One **horsepower** (hp) is equal to about 746 watts. The horsepower was first defined by Scottish scientist James Watt (1736–1819). Watt was looking for a way to compare the power outputs of steam engines he had designed. Horses were a logical choice for comparison as they were the most commonly used source of power in the 1700s. Watt did not want to exaggerate the power of his steam engines. Thus, after many experiments, he defined the horsepower based on the power output of a very strong horse. Figure 4 shows a comparison of two equivalent power sources.

Figure 4 Although the horse-drawn plow and the gasoline-powered engine get their power from different sources, both are capable of doing work at a rate of about four horsepower.

Section 14.1 Assessment

Reviewing Concepts

1. What conditions must exist in order for a force to do work on an object?

2. What formula relates work and power?

3. How much work is done when a vertical force acts on an object moving horizontally?

Critical Thinking

4. **Applying Concepts** A desk exerts an upward force to support a computer resting on it. Does this force do work? Explain.

5. **Predicting** Two cars have the same weight, but one of the cars has an engine that provides twice the power of the other. Which car can make it to the top of a mountain pass first? Which car does more work to reach the pass?

6. **Comparing and Contrasting** You carry two heavy bags of groceries upstairs to your kitchen. Will you do more work on the bags if you carry them up one at a time? Explain.

Math Practice

7. How much work does a 25-newton force do to lift a potted plant from the floor to a shelf 1.5 meters high?

8. You lift a large bag of flour from the floor to a 1-meter-high counter, doing 100 joules of work in 2 seconds. How much power do you use to lift the bag of flour?

14.2 Work and Machines

Reading Focus

Key Concepts

- How do machines make work easier?
- How are work input and work output related for a machine?

Vocabulary

- machine
- input distance
- output force
- work output
- input force
- work input
- output distance

Reading Strategy

Summarizing Copy the table shown. As you read, complete the table for each machine. After you read, write a sentence summarizing the idea that your table illustrates.

Machine	Increases or Decreases Input Force	Increases or Decreases Input Distance
Tire jack	a. _____?_____	b. _____?_____
Lug wrench	c. _____?_____	d. _____?_____
Rowing oar	e. _____?_____	f. _____?_____
Summary:	g. _____?_____	

T wo good friends, each one wearing her most glamorous dress, are on their way to a school dance when disaster strikes. Their car gets a flat tire! To fix it, they'll have to remove the flat tire and put on the spare tire. But won't loosening the lug nuts and lifting the car off of the ground require more force than they can exert just using their hands? How can they change the tire?

As shown in Figure 5, machines come to the rescue. Fortunately, all cars come with the tools designed to help you change a tire. With the help of a lug wrench and jack, which are actually simple machines, they'll have no problem changing the tire. Read on to learn how a car jack and a lug wrench alter forces to make changing a tire a relatively easy task.

Machines Do Work

A **machine** is a device that changes a force. When using the jack, you apply a force to the jack handle. The jack changes this force and applies a much stronger force to lift the car. Because the jack increases the force you exert, it is a machine. **Machines make work easier to do. They change the size of a force needed, the direction of a force, or the distance over which a force acts.** Both the lug wrench and the jack allow a single person to apply enough force to accomplish tasks they would normally not be able to.

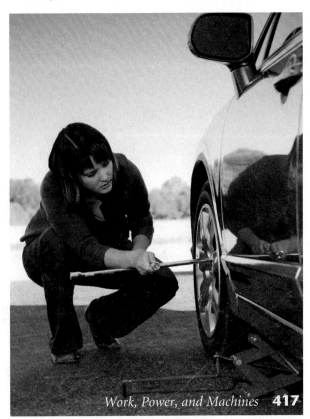

Figure 5 All cars come equipped with simple machines designed to make changing a tire a fairly easy task.
Inferring *Does the jack used to lift the car increase or decrease the force applied to it?*

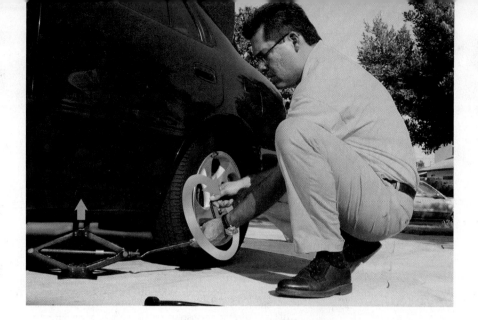

Figure 6 Turning the jack handle allows the man to raise the car. The distance moved by the handle is much greater than the distance the car is raised.
Comparing and Contrasting *How does the force exerted on the jack handle compare with the force exerted by the jack on the car?*

Increasing Force How is a machine able to increase a force? Study what is happening in Figure 6. Each complete rotation of the jack handle applies a small force over a large distance. However, each rotation lifts the car only a very short distance. Thus a small force exerted over a large distance becomes a large force exerted over a short distance.

Raising a car using a machine such as a jack is similar to moving a stack of books by picking them up one at a time. Lifting the books one at a time takes less force. But there's a tradeoff—the total distance traveled is much greater. If a machine increases the distance over which you exert a force, then it decreases the amount of force you need to exert.

Increasing Distance Some machines decrease the applied force, but increase the distance over which the force is exerted. Look at the rowing shell in Figure 7. Each oar operates as a machine that pushes the boat through the water. The arrows show how pulling the end of each oar through a small distance moves the end of the oar in the water through a large distance. Increasing the distance the oar travels through the water helps you go fast. But again, there is a tradeoff. The increased travel of the oar through the water requires you to exert a greater force. A machine that decreases the distance through which you exert a force increases the amount of force required.

Changing Direction Some machines change the direction of the applied force. An example is shown in Figure 7. Pulling back on the handle of the oar causes its other end to move in the opposite direction. So not only can machines change the amount of force and the distance the force acts through, but they can also change the direction of the force.

 Give an example of a machine that changes the direction of an applied force.

Go Online
NSTA SciLINKS

For: Links on machines
Visit: www.SciLinks.org
Web Code: ccn-2142

Work Input and Work Output

To row the boat in Figure 7, the rower pulls back on each oar handle and the other end of each oar pushes against the water. Work is done on the oars (the machine) by pulling on them, and the oars do work on the water to move the boat. Recall from Chapter 12 that friction acts against the motion of any object. **Because of friction, the work done by a machine is always less than the work done on the machine.**

Work Input to a Machine The force you exert on a machine is called the **input force.** The distance the input force acts through is known as the **input distance.** The work done by the input force acting through the input distance is called the **work input.** The work input equals the input force multiplied by the input distance.

Each oar in Figure 7 is a machine. For the oar, the input force is the force exerted on the handle and the input distance is the distance the handle moves. The work input is the work you do to move the handle. You can increase the work input by increasing the input distance, increasing the input force, or increasing both at once.

Figure 7 The oars of the boat act as machines that increase the distance over which the force acts. **Predicting** *If the oar is pushed farther away from the boat, how will the force needed to pull the oar through the water change?*

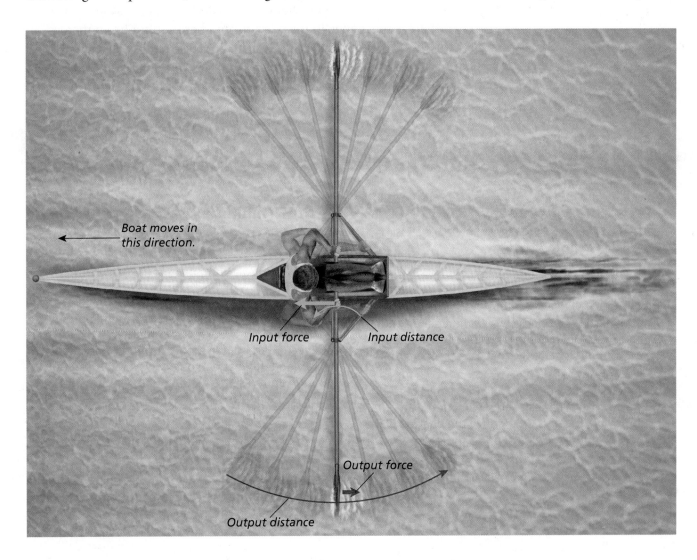

Boat moves in this direction.

Input force

Input distance

Output force

Output distance

Figure 8 The output work of the oars results from the oars pushing against the water so that the water pushes back against the oars.
Observing *What evidence can you see in the photo that a force is acting on the water?*

Work Output of a Machine The force that is exerted by a machine is called the **output force.** The distance the output force is exerted through is the **output distance.** The **work output** of a machine is the output force multiplied by the output distance. Look back at Figure 7 one more time to see the output force, distance, and work for the oars. How are the input work and output work related? Although nearly equal, the output work is less than the input work because of friction. All machines use some amount of input work to overcome friction.

As the rowers pull on one end of each oar, the other ends push against the water as shown in Figure 8. The force of the oar on the water causes an equal and opposite reaction force to be exerted by the water on the oar. It is this reaction force that propels the boat through the water.

Can you increase the work output of the oar by positioning it differently? Unless the new position decreases friction, the answer is no. If there is no change in the work input, there cannot be an increase in the work output. The only way to increase the work output is to increase the amount of work you put into the machine. You cannot get more work out of a machine than you put into it!

Section 14.2 Assessment

Reviewing Concepts

1. How can using a machine make a task easier to perform?
2. How does the work done on a machine compare to the work done by a machine?
3. What changes can a machine make to a force?
4. A machine produces a larger force than you exert to operate the machine. How does the input distance of the machine compare to its output distance?
5. You do 200 J of work pulling the oars of a rowboat. What can you say about the amount of work the oars do to move the boat? Explain.
6. How can you increase the work output of a machine?

Critical Thinking

7. **Inferring** When you swing a baseball bat, how does the output distance the end of the bat moves compare with the distance you move your hands through? Why might this difference be useful?
8. **Applying Concepts** An advertisement for a new type of wrench claims it reduces the force needed to tighten a bolt. If the advertisement is correct, what do you know to be true about the input distance?

Connecting Concepts

Forces Recall what you learned about forces in Chapter 12. Explain how friction and Newton's third law of motion influence the movement of the oar as it is pulled by the rower shown in Figure 7.

14.3 Mechanical Advantage and Efficiency

Reading Focus

Key Concepts

- How does the actual mechanical advantage of a machine compare to its ideal mechanical advantage?

- Why is the efficiency of a machine always less than 100 percent?

Vocabulary

- mechanical advantage
- actual mechanical advantage
- ideal mechanical advantage
- efficiency

Reading Strategy

Building Vocabulary Copy the table below. Then as you read the section, write a definition for each vocabulary term in your own words.

Vocabulary	Definition
Mechanical advantage	a. ___?___
b. ___?___	c. ___?___
d. ___?___	e. ___?___
f. ___?___	g. ___?___

Try cracking a walnut by squeezing it in your hand. You'll find that you can't apply enough force to break the shell. Next try cracking the shell using a nutcracker. A nutcracker, which is a type of machine, is shown in Figure 9. If you squeeze the nutcracker near its pivot end, you still won't be able to crack the nut. When you squeeze the ends of the handles, however, a fairly small force cracks the shell apart. In this section you'll learn why a machine like the nutcracker is so sensitive to the location of the input force.

Mechanical Advantage

The relation of input force used to operate a machine and the output force exerted by the machine depends on the type of machine and how it is used. Thus the location of the nut in the nutcracker affects the force the nutcracker is able to exert.

The **mechanical advantage** of a machine is the number of times that the machine increases an input force. Suppose a nut is in the nutcracker at position A in Figure 9. In this position the nutcracker exerts a force on the nut about seven times greater than the force you exert on the nutcracker. In position A the nutcracker's mechanical advantage is about 7. However, if the nut is moved to position B, the mechanical advantage decreases to about 3.

Figure 9 A nutcracker is a machine capable of converting the input force applied to it into a larger force capable of cracking a nut. Because it increases force, the nutcracker has a mechanical advantage greater than 1. **Inferring** *What might be the reason that the nutcracker has two different areas (A and B) to use for nut cracking?*

For: Links on mechanical advantage

Visit: www.SciLinks.org

Web Code: ccn-2143

Actual Mechanical Advantage The mechanical advantage determined by measuring the actual forces acting on a machine is the actual mechanical advantage. The **actual mechanical advantage** (AMA) equals the ratio of the output force to the input force.

> **Actual Mechanical Advantage**
>
> $$\text{Actual mechanical advantage} = \frac{\text{Output force}}{\text{Input force}}$$

A loading ramp is a machine used to move heavy items into a truck. For instance, a long inclined ramp decreases the input force needed to lift a refrigerator into a truck. The mechanical advantage of a ramp with a rough surface is less than that of a similar smooth ramp because a greater force is needed to overcome friction.

DK SCIENCE and History

Innovations of the Industrial Revolution

From the 1700s to the early 1900s, a stream of new machines and other inventions changed patterns of work and commerce forever.

Seed-free cotton collects here.

Waste material

COTTON GIN

Threads are interwoven here.

POWER LOOM

Chimney

Boiler

STEPHENSON'S ROCKET

1765 James Watt modifies the existing Newcomen steam engine to create a more efficient machine.

1793 Eli Whitney's cotton gin efficiently and quickly separates harvested cotton fiber from seeds. The process makes cotton manufacturing easier, and cotton farming profitable.

1807 The *Clermont*, Robert Fulton's river steamboat, makes its maiden voyage on the Hudson River.

1813 Francis Lowell and Paul Moody create the first power loom in America, based on an English design.

1829 Stephenson's Rocket, an early steam locomotive, wins a competition for locomotive speed in England.

| 1750 | 1775 | 1800 | 1825 |

Ideal Mechanical Advantage What can be done to increase the actual mechanical advantage of a ramp? One way is to reduce the friction of the ramp. In fact, if any machine were frictionless, its mechanical advantage would be the maximum possible value. The **ideal mechanical advantage** (IMA) of a machine is the mechanical advantage in the absence of friction. 🔑 **Because friction is always present, the actual mechanical advantage of a machine is always less than the ideal mechanical advantage.** Because friction reduces mechanical advantage, engineers often design machines that use low-friction materials and lubricants.

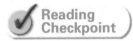
Reading Checkpoint *How does increased friction affect the actual mechanical advantage of a machine?*

Writing in Science

Explanatory Paragraph
Study the photo of one of the inventions shown in the time line. Write a paragraph in which you identify the simple machines used in the device and explain how these machines are used in the operation of the device.

SINGER SEWING MACHINE

Straight needle moves up and down.

Workers install an engine on an assembly line.

FORD CAR FACTORY

TOY REPRODUCTION OF A MECHANICAL REAPER

1834 Virginian farmer Cyrus McCormick patents the first mechanical reaper, leading to huge gains in farm efficiency and productivity.

1851 New Yorker Isaac Merrit Singer improves on existing sewing machine designs. The Singer becomes the first commercially successful sewing machine.

1869 Completion of the first trans-continental railroad leads to the rise of rail transportation and westward expansion.

1908 Henry Ford uses an assembly line to mass produce affordable cars.

1850　　　1875　　　1900

Quick Lab

Using Friction to Change Mechanical Advantage

Materials

6 books, board, 3 different kinds of shoes, 1-kilogram mass, spring scale

Procedure

1. Create a stack of five books. Make a ramp by leaning the end of a board against the top of the stack. Place a sixth book at the bottom of the ramp to keep the board from sliding down off the stack of books.

2. Attach the spring scale to a shoe. Place the mass in the shoe. Suspend the shoe with the mass from the spring scale. Observe and record the force reading on the scale.

3. Place the shoe containing the mass on the bottom of the ramp as shown.

4. Use the spring scale to pull the shoe up the ramp at a slow constant speed. Observe and record the force reading on the spring scale.

5. **Predicting** Record your prediction of the force needed to pull the mass up the ramp in each of the other shoes. Investigate your predictions by repeating Steps 2 through 4 for each shoe.

Analyze and Conclude

1. **Calculating** Determine and record the actual mechanical advantage of the ramp for each shoe. To do this, divide the force measured in Step 2 by the force measured in Step 4.

2. **Comparing** Which shoe resulted in the largest mechanical advantage? The smallest mechanical advantage? Explain these results.

3. **Drawing Conclusions** Which shoe required the most force to pull it up the ramp? What did this additional force accomplish? Explain.

Figure 10 The cable supporting the gondola forms an inclined plane, a type of machine. The inclined plane is used to move people up to the top of the mountain.

Calculating Mechanical Advantage

Ideal mechanical advantage is easier to measure than actual mechanical advantage because it depends only on the locations of the forces and the distances over which they act. To calculate the ideal mechanical advantage of any machine, divide the input distance by the output distance. Remember that the effects of friction are neglected when calculating ideal mechanical advantage.

> ### Ideal Mechanical Advantage
> $$\text{Ideal mechanical advantage} = \frac{\text{Input distance}}{\text{Output distance}}$$

The gondola in Figure 10 makes use of the inclined plane formed by its supporting cable to more easily move people uphill. The increased horizontal distance (input distance) is greater than the vertical gain in height (output distance). Thus the inclined cable gives the gondola a mechanical advantage greater than 1.

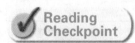

Reading Checkpoint *What two quantities must you know in order to calculate ideal mechanical advantage?*

Math Skills

Calculating IMA

A woman drives her car up onto wheel ramps to perform some repairs. If she drives a distance of 1.8 meters along the ramp to raise the car 0.3 meter, what is the ideal mechanical advantage (IMA) of the wheel ramps?

1 **Read and Understand**

What information are you given?

$$\text{Input distance} = 1.8 \text{ m}$$

$$\text{Output distance} = 0.3 \text{ m}$$

2 **Plan and Solve**

What unknown are you trying to calculate?

$$\text{IMA} = ?$$

What formula contains the given quantities and the unknown?

$$\text{IMA} = \frac{\text{Input distance}}{\text{Output distance}}$$

Replace each variable with its known value and solve.

$$\text{IMA} = \frac{1.8 \text{ m}}{0.3 \text{ m}} = 6$$

3 **Look Back and Check**

Is your answer reasonable?

The IMA must be greater than 1 because the input distance is greater than the output distance. The calculated IMA of 6 seems reasonable.

Math Practice

1. A student working in a grocery store after school pushes several grocery carts together along a ramp. The ramp is 3 meters long and rises 0.5 meter. What is the ideal mechanical advantage of the ramp?

2. A construction worker moves a crowbar through a distance of 0.50 m to lift a load 0.05 m off of the ground. What is the IMA of the crowbar?

3. The IMA of a simple machine is 2.5. If the output distance of the machine is 1.0 m, what is the input distance?

Efficiency

Because some of the work input to a machine is always used to overcome friction, the work output of a machine is always less than the work input. The percentage of the work input that becomes work output is the **efficiency** of a machine. **Because there is always some friction, the efficiency of any machine is always less than 100 percent.**

> **Efficiency**
>
> $$\text{Efficiency} = \frac{\text{Work output}}{\text{Work input}} \times 100\%$$

Figure 11 The flow pattern of a smoke trail is analyzed by computers to determine the fluid friction forces (air resistance) acting on the vehicle. Engineers use these test data to optimize a vehicle's shape for maximum fuel efficiency.

Efficiency is usually expressed as a percentage. For example, if the efficiency of a machine is 75 percent, then you know that 75 percent of the work input becomes work output. If a machine requires 10.0 J of work input to operate, then the work output is 75% of 10.0 J.

$$\text{Work output} = \frac{\text{Work input} \times \text{Efficiency}}{100\%}$$

$$\text{Work output} = \frac{10.0\text{ J} \times 75\%}{100\%} = 7.5\text{ J}$$

Reducing friction increases the efficiency of a machine. Automobiles, for example, are designed so their wheels roll on bearings that contain many small steel rollers. Recall that rolling friction is less than sliding friction. Thus, the roller bearings reduce the friction of the rotating wheels. To further reduce the rolling friction, the roller bearings are also lubricated with grease.

As shown in Figure 11, the shapes of many cars are designed to minimize air resistance. The lower the air resistance, the more easily a car passes through the air. At highway speeds, more than 50% of the output work of the engine is used to overcome air resistance. Streamlining the car's body reduces the amount of work the engine must do to move the car at any speed.

Section 14.3 Assessment

Reviewing Concepts

1. Why is the actual mechanical advantage of a machine always less than its ideal mechanical advantage?

2. Why can no machine be 100% efficient?

3. You test a machine and find that it exerts a force of 5 N for each 1 N of force you exert operating the machine. What is the actual mechanical advantage of the machine?

4. How can two machines appear identical and yet not have the same actual mechanical advantage?

5. What information would you use to calculate the efficiency of a machine?

Critical Thinking

6. Making Generalizations When is the ideal mechanical advantage of a machine greater than 1?

7. Applying Concepts Suppose you are an inventor in 1900. You are constructing a bicycle of your own design. What could you do to ensure your bicycle efficiently changes the work input into forward motion?

Math Practice

8. You have just designed a machine that uses 1000 J of work from a motor for every 800 J of useful work the machine supplies. What is the efficiency of your machine?

9. If a machine has an efficiency of 40%, and you do 1000 J of work on the machine, what will be the work output of the machine?

14.4 Simple Machines

Key Concepts

- What are the six types of simple machines?
- What determines the mechanical advantage of the six types of simple machines?

Vocabulary

- ◆ lever
- ◆ fulcrum
- ◆ input arm
- ◆ output arm
- ◆ wheel and axle
- ◆ inclined plane
- ◆ wedge
- ◆ screw
- ◆ pulley
- ◆ compound machine

Reading Strategy

Summarizing After reading the section on levers, complete the concept map below to organize what you know about first-class levers. Construct and complete similar concept maps for second- and third-class levers.

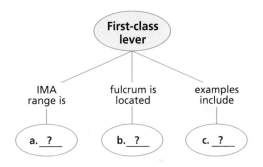

What can you say about the workings of the strange contraption shown in Figure 12? Notice that a series of devices are arranged so that output of one device acts as the input of the next.

Many mechanical devices are combinations of two or more of the six different simple machines. **The six types of simple machines are the lever, the wheel and axle, the inclined plane, the wedge, the screw, and the pulley.** As you'll learn, you can tell a lot about a simple machine by its appearance. For several machines, you can even calculate the ideal mechanical advantage based solely on the locations of the forces involved.

Figure 12 The idea for this labor-saving auto jack comes from Rube Goldberg (1883–1970), a sculptor, author, and Pulitzer Prize-winning cartoonist.

Figure 13

Three Classes of Levers

A | First-Class Lever

Output force Input force

Fulcrum

The screwdriver is being used as a first-class lever with a mechanical advantage greater than 1. (Diagram is not drawn to scale.)

B | Second-Class Lever

Input force Output force

Fulcrum

The wheelbarrow has its output force located between the input force and the fulcrum. (Diagram is not drawn to scale.)

C | Third-Class Lever

Fulcrum

Input force

Output force

The output distance of the broom is greater than the input distance the hands move through. (Diagram is not drawn to scale.)

Levers

Suppose you need to pry the lid off a can of paint. How can you make the task easier? A common solution is to slip the flat end of a screwdriver under the lid of the paint can and then to pry the lid off by pushing down on the screwdriver. This is an example of a **lever,** a rigid bar that is free to move around a fixed point. The fixed point the bar rotates around is the **fulcrum.** Levers are classified into three categories based on the locations of the input force, the output force, and the fulcrum.

The **input arm** of a lever is the distance between the input force and the fulcrum. The **output arm** is the distance between the output force and the fulcrum. 🔑 **To calculate the ideal mechanical advantage of any lever, divide the input arm by the output arm.**

First-Class Levers Figure 13A shows a screwdriver being used as a first-class lever to open a paint can. The fulcrum in this case is actually the inside edge of the paint can. The position of the fulcrum identifies a first-class lever—the fulcrum of a first-class lever is always located between the input force and the output force.

Depending on the location of the fulcrum, the mechanical advantage of a first-class lever can be greater than 1, equal to 1, or less than 1. Examples of first-class levers include a seesaw, scissors, and tongs.

Second-Class Levers In a second-class lever the output force is located between the input force and the fulcrum. The wheelbarrow shown in Figure 13B is a second-class lever.

When you lift the handles of a wheelbarrow, it rotates around its fulcrum. Parts of the wheelbarrow near the fulcrum move through a smaller distance than those closer to the handle. Thus the input distance your hands move to lift the wheelbarrow is larger than the output distance the wheelbarrow moves to lift its load. The increased input distance means it takes less force from you to lift the load. The mechanical advantage of a second-class lever is always greater than 1.

Third-Class Lever The input force of a third-class lever is located between the fulcrum and the output force. As shown in Figure 13C, the output distance over which the third-class lever exerts its force is always larger than the input distance you move the lever through. Because of this, the mechanical advantage of a third-class lever is always less than 1. Baseball bats, hockey sticks, and golf clubs are all third-class levers.

 Reading Checkpoint *Which classes of levers can have a mechanical advantage less than 1?*

For: Links on simple machines
Visit: www.SciLinks.org
Web Code: ccn-2144

Quick Lab

Comparing Lever Arms

Materials

pencil, masking tape, spring scale, 500-g mass, meter stick

Procedure

1. Construct a data table with columns labeled Output Force, Output Arm, Input Force, Input Arm, and Mechanical Advantage.

2. Suspend the 500-g mass from the spring scale. Observe the force on the scale and record it as the output force.

3. Tape a pencil parallel to and near the edge of a table as shown. Tape the 500-g mass to the meter stick so it's centered on the 10-cm mark.

4. Position the 20-cm mark of the meter stick on the pencil as shown. Record the distance from the pencil to the center of the mass as the output arm.

5. Attach the spring scale at the 90-cm mark of the meter stick. Record the distance from the pencil to this mark as the input arm.

6. Pull straight down on the spring scale so the 500-g mass is lifted off of the table. Record the force on the spring scale as the input force.

7. Repeat Steps 5 and 6 with the spring scale located at the 80-cm, 70-cm, 60-cm, and 50-cm marks on the meter stick.

Analyze and Conclude

1. **Calculating** Calculate and record the mechanical advantage of the lever for each input arm.

2. **Using Graphs** Plot a graph of mechanical advantage versus the length of the input arm.

3. **Analyzing Data** How does changing the input arm affect the mechanical advantage?

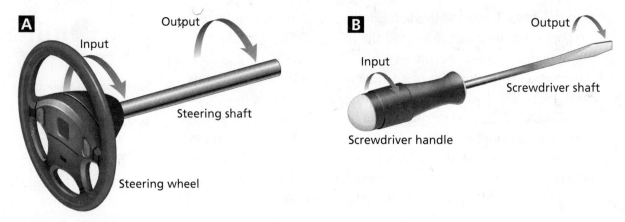

A Input • Output • Steering shaft • Steering wheel

B Input • Output • Screwdriver shaft • Screwdriver handle

Figure 14 A wheel and axle is a type of simple machine consisting of two disks or cylinders with different radii. **A** The steering mechanism used in a car is a wheel and axle. **B** When turning a screw with a screwdriver, the input force is applied to the larger-radius handle and the screw is turned by the smaller-radius shaft.

Figure 15 This long and winding road acts like a type of simple machine known as an inclined plane. Applying Concepts *As the road becomes steeper, how does its mechanical advantage change?*

Wheel and Axle

Are you excited about "getting behind the wheel" of a car in a few years? To be scientifically correct, you'll actually be getting behind a wheel and axle, a type of simple machine. A **wheel and axle** is a simple machine that consists of two disks or cylinders, each one with a different radius. A steering wheel, as shown in Figure 14A, consists of a large wheel attached to a narrow axle.

The outer disk is the wheel and the inner cylinder is the axle. The wheel and the axle rotate together as a unit. In a car, the steering wheel the driver turns is the wheel, and the shaft that rotates with it is the axle.

Depending on the purpose of the machine, the input force can be exerted on the wheel or the axle. ⟳ **To calculate the ideal mechanical advantage of the wheel and axle, divide the radius (or diameter) where the input force is exerted by the radius (or diameter) where the output force is exerted.** Though it may not appear so, a wheel and axle is similar to a lever, with the center of the two cylinders acting as the fulcrum.

A wheel and axle machine can have a mechanical advantage greater than 1 or less than 1. For a steering wheel, the driver applies force to the larger radius of the wheel. Because the input distance is larger than the output distance, a steering wheel has a mechanical advantage greater than 1.

Inclined Planes

Imagine how hard it would be to walk straight up the side of a steep hill. By following the gentler slope of a winding trail, it is easier to walk up the hill. Why is that so? It is because the required input force is decreased when the input distance is greater than the output distance. Remember, however, that although it is easier to reach the top of a hill using the trail, you'll have to walk a longer distance. As shown in Figure 15, switchback roads are often used to make steep mountain passes easier for automobiles to climb.

Gently sloping trails and roads are also a type of simple machine—an inclined plane. An **inclined plane** is a slanted surface along which a force moves an object to a different elevation. The ramp that makes a refrigerator easier to lift into a truck is an inclined plane. So are the wheelchair ramps used in front of buildings. The distance along the ramp is its input distance, whereas the change in height of the ramp is its output distance. 🔑 **The ideal mechanical advantage of an inclined plane is the distance along the inclined plane divided by its change in height.** For example, a 6-meter-long ramp that gains 1 meter of height has an ideal mechanical advantage of 6.

Wedges and Screws

Wedges and screws are similar to inclined planes because both involve sloping surfaces. A key difference, however, is that wedges and screws have sloping surfaces that move.

Wedges A **wedge** is a V-shaped object whose sides are two inclined planes sloped toward each other. Figure 16 shows a type of wedge often used to split wood. A sledgehammer drives the wedge into the log. As the wedge is driven in, its sloping sides push the wood on either side a small distance apart. This gives a wedge a mechanical advantage greater than 1. The thinner a wedge is relative to its length, the less the wedge separates the wood fibers as it moves through the log. 🔑 **A thin wedge of a given length has a greater ideal mechanical advantage than a thick wedge of the same length.** Other examples of wedges are a knife blade, which cuts best when its edge is sharp, and a zipper, which uses a wedge to separate and join the zipper's teeth.

Screws A **screw,** as shown in Figure 17, is an inclined plane wrapped around a cylinder. For two screws of the same length, the one whose threads are closer together moves forward less for each turn of the screw. 🔑 **Screws with threads that are closer together have a greater ideal mechanical advantage.**

The thread on a screw is usually measured in threads per inch or threads per centimeter. A screw with fewer threads per inch takes fewer turns to drive into a piece of wood or other material. But the smaller mechanical advantage of the screw requires you to exert a greater input force in order to drive it in. Other common examples of the screw include nuts, which have the threads on the inside, and bolts.

Reading Checkpoint *How is a screw similar to an inclined plane?*

Figure 16 The wedge being used to split the log consists of two inclined planes that slope toward each other. The inclined planes force the wood fibers apart as the wedge is driven into the log.
Relating Cause and Effect *What is the cause of the forces, exerted by the wedge, that split the log apart?*

Figure 17 A screw is a simple machine made up of an inclined plane wrapped around a cylinder.

Work, Power, and Machines **431**

Figure 18 A worker watches as a pulley moves a large fabricated part through a factory. **Interpreting Photos** *Based on what can be seen in the photograph, what is the approximate mechanical advantage of the pulley being used?*

Pulleys

A construction worker needs to lift a load of roofing materials onto the roof where he is working. Because it is easier and safer, he uses a pulley system to lift the load. The pulley system allows him to pull with less force than is needed to lift the load directly upward.

A **pulley** is a simple machine that consists of a rope that fits into a groove in a wheel. Pulleys produce an output force that is different in size, direction, or both, from that of the input force. 🔑 **The ideal mechanical advantage of a pulley or pulley system is equal to the number of rope sections supporting the load being lifted.** Part of a pulley system is shown in Figure 18.

Fixed Pulleys A fixed pulley is a wheel attached in a fixed location. Fixed pulleys are only able to rotate in place. The direction of the exerted force is changed by a fixed pulley, but the size of the force is not. If you use the fixed pulley shown in Figure 19A, the rope or chain lifts the load up as far as you pull down the rope. Thus, the ideal mechanical advantage of a fixed pulley is always 1. Assuming friction forces are small, the input force and output force will be the same. Examples of fixed pulleys include the pulley at the top of a flagpole and the pulleys used to pull up blinds.

Figure 19
Three Types of Pulleys

A Fixed Pulley

B Movable Pulley

C Pulley System

A fixed pulley changes only the direction of the input force.

Movable pulleys change both the direction and the size of the input force.

Pulley systems are made up of both fixed and movable pulleys.

Pulley System Performance

A shipyard has many different pulleys and pulley systems in use. The pulleys are used to move large, heavy, fabricated ship sections through the manufacturing process. During an annual safety and performance inspection of three of the company's systems, a facility engineer collected the data shown in the graph. The data give the measured output forces for a range of given input forces.

1. **Using Graphs** What system requires the smallest input force to lift a 2500-N load?

2. **Calculating** Determine the actual mechanical advantage for each of the systems for a 2000-N input force.

3. **Applying Concepts** Which of the three systems shown in the graph consists of a single fixed pulley? Explain how you know.

Performance of Three Pulley Systems

4. **Inferring** Describe what happens to system B's output force as the input force increases above 4000 N. How does this affect the mechanical advantage of the system at higher loads? Offer a possible cause for the performance shown in the graph.

5. **Applying Concepts** Using the mechanical advantage value from Question 2, determine the output force of system A for an input force of 8000 N.

Movable Pulley As you can see in Figure 19B, a movable pulley is attached to the object being moved rather than to a fixed location. If you are pulling up on the rope on the right with a force of 10 newtons, then both sections of the rope pull up with the same force of 10 newtons. Thus, the pulley exerts a 20-newton output force from a 10-newton input force. The movable pulley in Figure 19B has a mechanical advantage of 2. Movable pulleys are used to reduce the input force needed to lift a heavy object. Sailors use movable pulleys to pull in sails, and skyscraper window washers stand on platforms suspended by movable pulleys.

Pulley System By combining fixed and movable pulleys into a pulley system, a large mechanical advantage can be achieved. The mechanical advantage that results depends on how the pulleys are arranged. The pulley system shown in Figure 19C has four segments of supporting rope. Ignoring friction, each one of the four segments supplies a lifting force as strong as the force you exert on the rope. Thus the output force is four times stronger than the input force. The pulley system has a mechanical advantage of 4. Using pulley systems in combination with other simple machines, large cranes are able to lift railroad locomotives!

How is it possible to achieve a large mechanical advantage using pulleys?

For: Activity on types of pulleys
Visit: PHSchool.com
Web Code: ccp-2144

Elevator

Skyscrapers are vital to the economies of large cities with limited area for buildings. Stacking one floor on top of another produces a lot of floor space for offices. However, skyscrapers would be impractical without elevators. Elevators allow people to be transported hundreds of feet in the air. The cable elevator is the most popular type today. **Interpreting Diagrams** *What is the purpose of the counterweight?*

Elevator motor
The elevator motor is needed to accelerate the car and compensate for the varying load.

Motor

Sheave (pulley)

Cables

Car empty *The motor is needed to lower the car.*

Counterweight

Car half full *When the weights are balanced, the work done by the motor is minimized.*

Car full *The motor is needed to raise the car.*

Governor *This device regulates the speed of the car.*

Motor

Sheave *A pulley carries the cables attached to the car and the counterweight.*

Steel cables

Counterweight *The counterweight is made of cast iron, or concrete in a steel frame.*

Outer shaft doors

Elevator car *As the motor turns the sheave, the car moves up or down the shaft on guide rails.*

Safety brakes *The brakes slow the car if it moves too fast.*

Guide rails

Shock absorber *This piston stops the car if it falls.*

ELEVATOR SHAFT

Compound Machines

Look closely at a pair of scissors. You'll notice they consist of a couple of simple machines. The edges are sharpened like wedges. The blades and the handles together function as levers. In fact, most of the machines you use every day are actually a combination of simple machines working together. A **compound machine** is a combination of two or more simple machines that operate together. Many familiar compound machines, such as a car, a washing machine, or a clock, are combinations of hundreds or thousands of simple machines.

Look at the complex mechanisms of the watch shown in Figure 20. How do these simple machines interact to accomplish their task of keeping time? In a compound machine, the output force of one simple machine becomes the input force for another machine. Inside the watch, a complex series of gears is designed so that one gear drives the next. Each gear acts as a continuous lever. These gears help keep accurate track of days, hours, minutes, and seconds.

Figure 20 The complex workings of this watch consist of a series of machines. The output of one machine acts as the driving input for the next machine in the series.

Section 14.4 Assessment

Reviewing Concepts

1. Name six kinds of simple machines. Give an example of each.

2. Describe how to determine the ideal mechanical advantage of each type of simple machine.

3. How are the lever and the wheel and axle related to each other?

4. What is the ideal mechanical advantage of a ramp if its length is 4.0 m and its higher end is 0.5 m above its lower end?

5. Tightening a screw with a larger spacing between its threads requires fewer turns of a screwdriver than tightening a screw with smaller thread spacing. What is a disadvantage of the screw with larger thread spacing?

6. What class or classes of lever always have a mechanical advantage greater than 1?

Critical Thinking

7. **Making Generalizations** If you want to pry the lid off a paint can, will it require less force to use a long screwdriver or a short screwdriver? Explain.

8. **Calculating** When the pedals of a bicycle move through a distance of 0.25 m, the rear wheel of the bicycle moves 1.0 m. What is the ideal mechanical advantage of the bicycle?

9. **Applying Concepts** Explain why it could be useful for the mechanical advantage of a bicycle to be less than 1.

Writing in Science

Steps in a Process Write a paragraph describing the series of events that occur in the operation of a complex machine that you have used today.

Gearing Up for Better Bikes

The different gears on a bike allow you to change the distance the bike moves for each turn of the pedals. Cyclists use a low gear to climb hills and to accelerate. In a low gear, the chain connects a small front gear to a large back gear. A high gear is used for speed on level roads or for going downhill. In a high gear, the chain connects a large front gear to a small back gear.

Freewheels *These allow the bike to roll forward without the cyclist pedaling. When the bike is pedaled forward, a ratchet engages to drive the rear wheel.*

Sprockets, or cogs

Derailleur Gears

The chain connecting the front chainwheel to the rear wheel sprocket serves as a belt to make the wheel turn faster than your feet. Wheel sprockets of various sizes are used to obtain different speeds. Derailleurs are used to move the chain from one sprocket to another.

Guide pulley

Chain *The chain needs to be the correct width to operate smoothly over the sprockets and chainwheels, and the correct length for optimum shifting performance.*

Rear derailleur *The guide pulley feeds the chain to the selected rear wheel sprocket. The tension pulley uses a spring to keep the entire chain assembly tight.*

Tension pulley

Bicycle gear ratios

The lowest gear ratio on the bike might be a front chainwheel with 13 teeth and a rear gear with 52 teeth. In this case, the rear wheel will turn once for every four turns of the chainwheel. Working up through the gears gradually changes this ratio, allowing the bike to travel farther with every turn of the pedals.

DISTANCE

Back gear   Front gear

RATIOS

Low gear

Middle gear

High gear

Distance traveled in one turn of the pedals

Front derailleur *The chain passes through this cage as it feeds onto the front chainwheels. By moving from side to side, the front derailleur is able to shift the chain among the chainwheels.*

Spider *The spider is the multi-armed part of the crank.*

Chainwheels *These are also called chainrings or front sprockets. The larger the chainwheel, the higher the gear is.*

Crank *The crank connects the pedal to the front chainwheel.*

Gearless bikes

Before the bicycle chain was invented, bicycle pedals were fixed to the axle of the front wheel. Today's track racers are also gearless (and brakeless), but only for the sake of fairness. This means that all of the bikes have the same mechanical advantage.

Going Further

- Write an instruction manual to explain how a new cyclist can make the best use of gear ratios. Use terms from this feature to describe which gear ratios are best for different situations and why.

Determining Mechanical Advantage

Many complex machines have an adjustable mechanical advantage. In this lab, you will learn how adjusting the mechanical advantage of a bicycle affects the bicycle's performance.

Problem How does mechanical advantage affect the performance of a bicycle?

Materials
- board with two nails
- 4 thread spools, 3 with different diameters
- rubber band
- masking tape
- multispeed bicycle (one or more per class)
- meter stick
- thick leather glove

Skills Measuring, Calculating

Procedure

Part A: Modeling the Mechanical Advantage of a Bicycle

1. On a separate sheet of paper, make a copy of the Data Table for part A.

2. Use a piece of masking tape to label each nail on the board. Label one nail *Pedals* and the other nail *Wheel*. To model the pedals and rear wheel of a bicycle, place a spool on each nail in the board and join the spools with a rubber band as shown.

3. Use a pencil to make a reference mark on the edge of each spool. These marks will help you observe the motion of the spools as they turn.

4. **Measuring** Use a ruler to measure the radius of each spool in your model. Record these measurements in your data table.

5. The pedal spool represents the pedals and the gears attached to them. The wheel spool represents the rear wheel and its gears. Using the reference marks, observe the wheel spool as you turn the pedal spool through five complete revolutions. Record the number of revolutions of the wheel spool in your data table.

Data Table: Part A				
Pedal Spool Radius (cm)	Revolutions of Pedal Spool	Wheel Spool Radius (cm)	Revolutions of Wheel Spool	IMA
	5			
	5			
	5			

6. Replace the wheel spool with a spool of a different diameter. Repeat Steps 3 through 5 for each diameter of wheel spool.

7. **Calculating** The ideal mechanical advantage (IMA) of a bicycle is equal to the distance the pedals move divided by the distance the rear wheel moves. For your model,

$$IMA = \frac{5 \times \text{Pedal radius}}{\left(\begin{array}{c}\text{Revolutions}\\\text{of wheel}\end{array}\right) \times \left(\begin{array}{c}\text{Wheel}\\\text{radius}\end{array}\right)}$$

Calculate the mechanical advantage of each spool combination you used. Record these values in your data table.

Part B: Analyzing Bicycle Gears

8. On a separate sheet of paper, make a copy of the Data Table for part B.

9. **Measuring** Work in groups of three. Use a meter stick to measure the radius of the pedals and the rear wheel as shown. Record these measurements in your data table.

10. One person should hold the bicycle with its rear wheel slightly off the floor. While a second person turns the pedals, a third person should use the bicycle's gear shifters to place the chain on the smallest pedal gear and the largest rear wheel gear. **CAUTION** *Keep your hands out of the spokes, chain, and gears.*

11. One person should put on a heavy leather glove, while a second person holds the bicycle with its rear wheel slightly off the floor.

12. The third person should slowly turn the pedals through five complete revolutions. The person who is wearing the glove should gently hold the rear tire tread so that the wheel turns only as fast as the pedals force it to move. This person should also observe the position of the valve stem to count the number of revolutions of the rear wheel. Record the number of revolutions of the rear wheel in your data table.

Rear wheel radius

Pedal radius

13. Repeat Steps 10 through 12, once using the smallest pedal gear and a mid-sized rear-wheel gear, and then again using the largest pedal gear and the smallest rear-wheel gear.

14. **Calculating** Use the equation in Step 7 to calculate the mechanical advantage of the bicycle for each gear combination you used. Record these values in your data table.

Analyze and Conclude

1. **Analyzing Data** Which combination of pedal and rear wheel gears provided the greatest mechanical advantage? The least advantage?

2. **Applying Concepts** To ride quickly on a level road, would you select a gear combination with a large mechanical advantage or a small one? Explain your answer.

3. **Drawing Conclusions** To decrease the force needed to ride a bicycle up a steep hill, would you select a gear combination with a large mechanical advantage or a small one? What size rear-wheel gear would you use to race on a flat road? Explain.

Data Table: Part B			
Size of Pedal Gear	Smallest	Smallest	Largest
Size of Rear Wheel Gear	Largest	Medium	Smallest
Pedal Radius (cm)			
Revolutions of Pedal	5	5	5
Rear Wheel Radius (cm)			
Revolutions of Rear Wheel			
IMA			

For: Data Sharing
Visit: PHSchool.com
Web Code: ccd-2140

Study Guide

14.1 Work and Power

🔑 Key Concepts

- Work = Force × Distance. Work is done on an object when a force acts in the same direction as the object moves.
- Power = Work ÷ Time. Power is the rate of doing work. Doing work faster requires more power.

Vocabulary

work, *p. 412*

joule, *p. 414*

power, *p. 414*

watt, *p. 415*

horsepower, *p. 416*

14.2 Work and Machines

🔑 Key Concepts

- Machines make work easier by changing the force needed, the direction of the force, or the distance over which the force acts.
- Work output (done by a machine) is always less than the work input (done on the machine).

Vocabulary

machine, *p. 417*

input force, *p. 419*

input distance, *p. 419*

work input, *p. 419*

output force, *p. 420*

output distance, *p. 420*

work output, *p. 420*

14.3 Mechanical Advantage and Efficiency

🔑 Key Concepts

- Friction is present in all machines. Because of friction, the actual mechanical advantage is always less than the ideal mechanical advantage.

- Actual mechanical advantage = $\dfrac{\text{Output force}}{\text{Input force}}$

- Ideal mechanical advantage = $\dfrac{\text{Input distance}}{\text{Output distance}}$

- Efficiency = $\dfrac{\text{Work output}}{\text{Work input}} \times 100\%$

- Because of friction, the efficiency of any machine is always less than 100 percent.

Vocabulary

mechanical advantage, *p. 421*

actual mechanical advantage, *p. 422*

ideal mechanical advantage, *p. 423*

efficiency, *p. 425*

14.4 Simple Machines

🔑 Key Concept

- The six types of simple machines are the lever, the wheel and axle, the inclined plane, the wedge, the screw, and the pulley.

Vocabulary

lever, *p. 428*

fulcrum, *p. 428*

input arm, *p. 428*

output arm, *p. 428*

wheel and axle, *p. 430*

inclined plane, *p. 431*

wedge, *p. 431*

screw, *p. 431*

pulley, *p. 432*

compound machine, *p. 435*

Thinking Visually

Concept Map Use information from the chapter to complete the concept map below.

Reviewing Content

Choose the letter that best describes the question or completes the statement.

1. Work is the product of
  a. speed and force.
  b. force and distance.
  c. power and force.
  d. motion and force.

2. Which of the following is a unit of work?
  a. joule
  b. watt
  c. horsepower
  d. newton

3. How much work, in N•m, is done when a 10.0-N force moves an object 2.5 m?
  a. 0.25 N•m
  b. 2.5 N•m
  c. 25 N•m
  d. 4.0 N•m

4. Power is equal to work divided by
  a. time.
  b. force.
  c. distance.
  d. mechanical advantage.

5. If a machine has a mechanical advantage much larger than 1, its output force is
  a. much larger than its input force.
  b. much less than its input force.
  c. about the same as its input force.
  d. in the same direction as its input force.

6. How is the work output of a machine related to its work input?
  a. always less
  b. always greater
  c. always equal
  d. always zero

7. A machine with a 5-N input force and a 25-N output force has a mechanical advantage of
  a. 2.
  b. 5.
  c. 20.
  d. 125.

8. The mechanical advantage of a pulley system depends upon
  a. the diameter of the pulley wheels.
  b. the length of the rope.
  c. the number of sections of rope.
  d. the direction of the input force.

9. A screw can be considered a type of
  a. lever.
  b. inclined plane.
  c. pulley.
  d. compound machine.

10. Which is not a simple machine?
  a. wedge
  b. screw
  c. lever
  d. fulcrum

Understanding Concepts

11. Does an athlete do work on a trophy as she lifts it overhead? Is work done on the trophy as she stands still holding the trophy overhead? Explain.

12. What is the scientific definition of power?

Questions 13–15 refer to the illustration below.

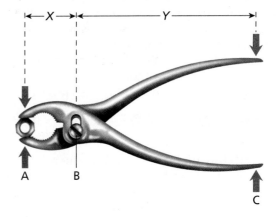

13. Identify the position of the fulcrum.

14. If X = 3.0 cm and Y = 15.0 cm, what is the ideal mechanical advantage of the pliers?

15. If the output force is 50.0 N and the input force is 12.5 N, what is the actual mechanical advantage of the pliers?

16. A machine you designed has input and output arms that pivot around a fulcrum. When the input arm is pushed down through a short distance, the output arm moves down through a longer distance. Is the output force less than, equal to, or greater than the input force?

17. A machine has an efficiency of 60%. What happens to 60% of the work put into the machine, and what happens to the other 40%?

18. Identify the simple machines in a pair of scissors.

19. Why would you use a single fixed pulley to lift a box if the pulley's mechanical advantage is 1?

20. What determines the class of a lever?

21. Is a screw with fewer or more threads per centimeter easier to drive into a piece of wood? Explain.

Critical Thinking

22 Applying Concepts Give an example of a useful machine you have seen that has a mechanical advantage less than 1. State how the machine is useful in terms of changing forces, distances, or directions.

23. Comparing and Contrasting A ramp 20 m long and 4 m high is used to lift a heavy box. A pulley system with 4 rope sections supporting the load is used to lift an identical box to a height of 4 m. Assume that friction can be ignored. Compare and contrast the input force and input distance needed to lift each box.

24. Generalizing In a pulley system, where is there likely to be friction that reduces the efficiency?

25. Classifying Classify each of these items as a type of simple machine: a steel bolt, an iron nail, and a screwdriver.

Math Skills

Use the illustration below to answer Questions 26 and 27.

26. Using Equations The figure above shows the distances from the fulcrum to the input and output forces of a lever. Use these distances to calculate the ideal mechanical advantage of the lever.

27. Using Equations If the actual mechanical advantage is 2.9 and the input force is 10.0 N, what is the output force?

28. Using Equations How much work does a 50-N force do when lifting a box 2 meters?

29. Calculating How much work does a 1-kW motor do in one minute?

Concepts in Action

30. Applying Concepts Which would be the better choice for driving a screw into a board, a long screwdriver with a narrow handle, or a short screwdriver with a wide handle? Explain.

31. Classifying What type of simple machine is a water faucet handle? Is the output force larger or smaller than the input force?

32. Comparing and Contrasting A man weighing 1000 newtons walks from the ground floor to the fifth floor of a building, gaining 20 meters of height in 200 seconds. The next day he returns to the building, but this time uses the elevator. The elevator takes 20 seconds to reach the fifth floor. Compare and contrast the power and time requirements to reach the fifth floor.

33. Relating Cause and Effect In a bicycle, the output of one simple machine is the input of another. Why might you expect the efficiency of the bicycle to be less than the efficiency of each of the simple machines that is part of it?

34. Writing in Science Explain why you might shift into a lower gear to climb a hill on a bike. Your explanation should include a discussion of the input force and distance.

Performance-Based Assessment

Using Models Imagine you have a younger brother who weighs half as much as you do. Design a seesaw you could use together. Create a model of your seesaw design and label it to show the distances that you and your brother must sit from the fulcrum. Explain why you chose the fulcrum position as you did.

For: Self-grading assessment
Visit: PHSchool.com
Web Code: cca-2140

Standardized Test Prep

Choose the letter that best answers the question or completes the statement.

1. An applied force acts upward on a moving wooden crate as shown below. Which of the following statements is TRUE?
   (A) The power used to move the crate is 150 W.
   (B) The force does no work on the crate.
   (C) The force does 150 J of work on the crate.
   (D) The force does 66 J of work on the crate.
   (E) The force accelerates the crate.

100-N applied force

Direction of motion

Speed = 1.5 m/s

2. A machine is used to lift boxes in a warehouse. Which change will increase the power of the machine?
   (A) decreasing the distance the boxes are lifted
   (B) decreasing the force exerted by the machine
   (C) increasing the friction inside the machine
   (D) decreasing the time it takes to lift the boxes
   (E) decreasing the work done by the machine

3. Which statement is NEVER true for a machine?
   (A) The output force is greater than the input force.
   (B) The machine changes a force.
   (C) The machine changes the direction of a force.
   (D) The machine changes the distance over which a force acts.
   (E) The work output equals the work input.

4. Which of the following will increase the actual mechanical advantage of a machine?
   (A) decreasing the output force
   (B) decreasing the friction
   (C) increasing the input force
   (D) decreasing the time required
   (E) increasing the time required

5. The diagram below represents a first-class lever. Which point(s) could be the fulcrum for this lever?
   (A) A only
   (B) B only
   (C) C only
   (D) A or C only
   (E) A, B, or C only

● ——————●———————————————————●
A   B   C

6. What information is required to calculate the actual mechanical advantage of a lever?
   (A) input arm and output arm
   (B) input distance and output distance
   (C) input force and output force
   (D) Work input and work output
   (E) internal friction

CHAPTER

15 Energy

What is the most effective energy resource for your state?

In Section 15.3, you will learn about various energy resources used around the world. Work in a small group to research effective energy resources in your state. Identify the pros and cons of each energy source, and develop an overall energy strategy for your state. Post your group's strategy and research on a Web page, and create an online discussion board to invite feedback from state residents. Use the feedback to help troubleshoot and refine your proposed energy strategy.

How do science concepts apply to your world? Here are some questions you'll be able to answer after you read this chapter.

- **Why does a basketball bounce higher than a slice of bread?** *(Section 15.1)*

- **How can an object from space damage a car?** *(Section 15.2)*

- **How do gulls use energy conversion to obtain food?** *(Section 15.2)*

- **How do pole vaulters propel themselves high into the air?** *(Section 15.2)*

- **How are roller coasters designed to be both safe and thrilling?** *(page 460)*

- **How can the wind be used to light a bulb?** *(Section 15.3)*

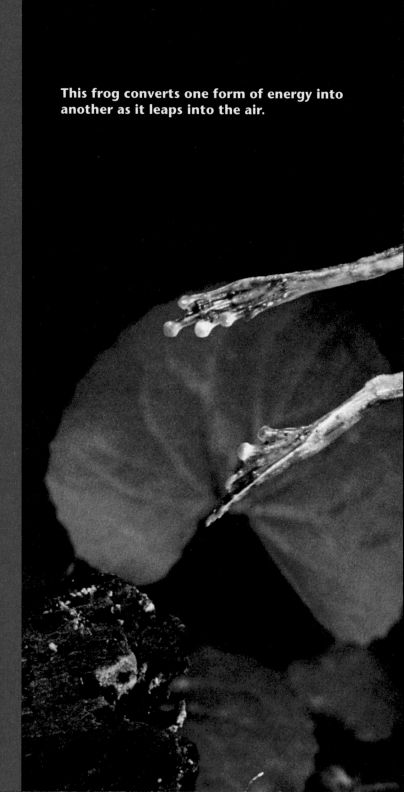

This frog converts one form of energy into another as it leaps into the air.

Chapter Preview

15.1 Energy and Its Forms

15.2 Energy Conversion and Conservation

15.3 Energy Resources

Inquiry Activity

How Can Energy Change Form?

Procedure

1. Examine a flashlight, a solar calculator, and a wind-up toy. Determine how each object operates.

2. Record the name of each object, the source of the energy that it requires, and the kind of energy it produces. For example, does the object require or produce electricity or light?

Think About It

1. **Classifying** What was the source of energy for each object?

2. **Inferring** What form of energy did each object produce?

3. **Drawing Conclusions** How did energy change form in each object? For example, did any of the objects convert light into another form of energy?

15.1 Energy and Its Forms

Reading Focus

Key Concepts

- How are energy and work related?
- What factors does the kinetic energy of an object depend on?
- How is gravitational potential energy determined?
- What are the major forms of energy?

Vocabulary

- energy
- kinetic energy
- potential energy
- gravitational potential energy
- elastic potential energy
- mechanical energy
- thermal energy
- chemical energy
- electrical energy
- electromagnetic energy
- nuclear energy

Reading Strategy

Building Vocabulary Copy the partially completed concept map below. Then, as you read, complete it with vocabulary terms and definitions from this section.

The road that winds through the mountain valley was closed. Skiers were banned from the area. The sound of artillery fire echoed from the mountains. It seemed out of place in this picturesque scene of snow-covered peaks surrounding the valley. A moment of quiet followed the blast. Suddenly, the snow broke loose with a menacing roar. Tumbling down the mountainside, the snow buried everything in its path. You can see in Figure 1 the enormous mass of accumulated snow that had hung above the valley. After the avalanche, the valley was quiet again. It is safe for skiers and hikers to return to the area.

This is the work of researchers at the Avalanche Control Section in Glacier National Park, Canada. These scientists monitor the snow as it builds up layer by layer on the park's upper peaks. They can predict when an avalanche is about to happen. With well-timed artillery shots, they make the avalanche happen at a time when the released energy cannot harm anyone.

Figure 1 In an avalanche, a mass of loose snow, soil, or rock suddenly gives way and slides down the side of a mountain.

Energy and Work

Where did the energy of the avalanche come from? Where did it go? Energy is known by the changes it causes. You can hear the roar of an avalanche and see the movement of the snow. Sound and motion are examples of energy in action. In order to define energy, you need to return to the definition of a related topic, work. Recall that work is done when a force moves an object through a distance. **Energy** is the ability to do work. In other words, energy is transferred by a force moving an object through a distance.

Figure 2 Energy has many different forms. **A** The sun gives off energy in the form of heat and light. **B** Plants convert sunlight into food that we can process and eat. **C** People convert food energy into muscle movement.
Applying Concepts *How did the skiers in the photo obtain the energy to climb the mountain slope?*

Work and energy are closely related. When work is done on an object, energy is transferred to that object. ⊙ **Work is a transfer of energy.** Both work and energy are typically measured in joules (J). Recall that 1 joule equals 1 newton-meter, the work done when an object is moved 1 meter by a 1-newton force. Although energy can take many different forms, it can always be measured in joules.

Think about the work and energy involved in doing something as simple as carrying your backpack up a flight of stairs. You do work on the backpack by lifting it against the force of gravity. This work requires energy. The energy to do the work comes from your muscles. Your muscles receive energy from the food you eat. The energy contained in your food comes from plants that have used the energy of sunlight, or animals that have eaten such plants. Figure 2 shows some of the many forms of energy.

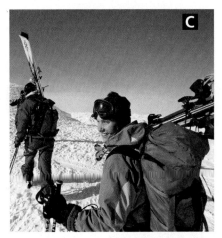

Kinetic Energy

Many forms of energy can be classified into two general types: kinetic energy and potential energy. The energy of motion is called **kinetic energy.** The word kinetic comes from the Greek word *kinetos,* meaning "moving."

⊙ **The kinetic energy of any moving object depends upon its mass and speed.** To calculate the kinetic energy of an object in joules, multiply $\frac{1}{2}$ by the object's mass (m) in kilograms and the square of its speed (v) in meters per second.

Kinetic Energy

$$\text{Kinetic energy (KE)} = \frac{1}{2}mv^2$$

Notice that doubling the mass in the formula would double the kinetic energy. However, doubling the speed would quadruple the kinetic energy, since kinetic energy is proportional to the square of an object's speed.

Math Skills

Calculating Kinetic Energy

A 0.10-kilogram bird is flying at a constant speed of 8.0 m/s. What is the bird's kinetic energy?

1 Read and Understand

What information are you given?

Mass, $m = 0.10$ kg   Speed, $v = 8.0$ m/s

What unknown are you trying to calculate?

Kinetic energy of the bird, KE

2 Plan and Solve

What equation contains the given quantities and the unknown?

$$KE = \tfrac{1}{2}mv^2$$

Substitute the known values in the formula for KE.

$$KE = \tfrac{1}{2}(0.10 \text{ kg})(8.0 \text{ m/s})^2$$
$$= 3.2 \text{ kg} \cdot \text{m}^2/\text{s}^2 = 3.2 \text{ J}$$

3 Look Back and Check

Is your answer reasonable?

It seems reasonable because the bird has a low mass, so it would not have much kinetic energy.

Math Practice

1. A 70.0-kilogram man is walking at a speed of 2.0 m/s. What is his kinetic energy?

2. A 1400-kilogram car is moving at a speed of 25 m/s. How much kinetic energy does the car have?

3. A 50.0-kilogram cheetah has a kinetic energy of 18,000 J. How fast is the cheetah running? (*Hint:* Rearrange the equation to solve for *v*.)

Figure 3 When this musician pulls the string of her cello to one side, the string is stretched and gains potential energy.

Potential Energy

Potential energy is energy that is stored as a result of position or shape. The musician in Figure 3 adds energy to the cello string by plucking it. The energy is stored in the stretched string when the musician pulls it to one side. Then she releases the string and allows it to vibrate. The stored energy is converted into kinetic energy. You can also store energy just by picking up a book and holding it in the air. Let go of the book and that stored energy will turn into the kinetic energy of motion as the book falls to the floor. Plucking a string and lifting a book are two examples of stored energy—energy with the potential to do work. Two forms of potential energy are gravitational potential energy and elastic potential energy.

Gravitational Potential Energy When you lift your gym bag up to the top seat of the bleachers, you do work to increase the potential energy of your bag. Potential energy that depends upon an object's height is called **gravitational potential energy.** This type of potential energy increases when an object is raised to a higher level.

The diver shown in Figure 4 is standing motionless at the end of a diving board, so she has no kinetic energy. But she does have energy—gravitational potential energy. She gained this potential energy by doing work—by climbing up the steps to the diving board. As always, the work done equals force (her weight) multiplied by distance (the height she climbs). You can use this work to calculate how much potential energy is gained.

⚷ **An object's gravitational potential energy depends on its mass, its height, and the acceleration due to gravity.** The gravitational potential energy an object gains is equal to its weight (mg) multiplied by its height (h).

Gravitational Potential Energy

Potential energy (PE) = mgh

To calculate gravitational potential energy in joules, the mass of the object is expressed in kilograms and the height of the object is expressed in meters. The acceleration due to gravity, g, has a value in SI units of 9.8 m/s^2 on Earth. Note that height is measured from the ground or floor or some other reference level. Therefore, gravitational potential energy is measured relative to that same reference level.

Gravitational potential energy is directly related to the mass of the object and its height relative to a reference level. Thus, doubling either the mass of the object or its height doubles its gravitational potential energy.

Suppose the diver at the top of a 10.0-meter-high diving platform has a mass of 50.0 kilograms. You can calculate her potential energy relative to the ground as follows.

$$\begin{aligned} PE &= mgh \\ &= (50.0 \text{ kg})(9.8 \text{ m/s}^2)(10.0 \text{ m}) \\ &= 4900 \text{ kg·m}^2\text{/s}^2 = 4900 \text{ J} \end{aligned}$$

If, instead, the diver was standing on the ground, her height above the ground would be zero. Therefore, her gravitational potential energy relative to the ground would also be zero.

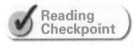

Reading Checkpoint *What is gravitational potential energy?*

Figure 4 This diver has gravitational potential energy as she stands at the end of a diving board. **Predicting** *How would the diver's potential energy change if she stood on a platform twice as high as the one shown in the photo?*

Go Online
NSTA *SciLINKS*

For: Links on potential and kinetic energy
Visit: www.SciLinks.org
Web Code: ccn-2151

Energy **449**

Figure 5 A compressed bicycle shock absorber and a wound-up toy robot both have elastic potential energy.

Elastic Potential Energy The potential energy of an object that is stretched or compressed is known as **elastic potential energy.** Something is said to be elastic if it springs back to its original shape after it is stretched or compressed. Think back to the last time you stretched a rubber band between your fingers. By stretching the rubber band, you did work on it. Just like the musician did with her cello string, the energy you added was stored in the rubber band as potential energy. If you've ever broken a stretched rubber band, you may have felt a painful snap on your hand. The rubber band's elastic potential energy was converted into kinetic energy.

Elastic potential energy can also be stored in objects that are compressed, such as springs. Drop a slice of bread on the floor and it does not bounce noticeably. Why doesn't it? The bread is not very elastic. Drop a basketball on the floor and the basketball bounces back up. The compressed air in the ball forces the ball to spring back into shape after hitting the ground, propelling the ball back up. Other examples of elastic potential energy are shown in Figure 5.

Forms of Energy

All energy can be considered to be kinetic energy, potential energy, or the energy in fields such as those produced by electromagnetic waves. Some familiar examples are the chemical energy in fireworks, electrical energy in lightning bolts, and nuclear energy within the sun. **The major forms of energy are mechanical energy, thermal energy, chemical energy, electrical energy, electromagnetic energy, and nuclear energy.** Each of these forms of energy can be converted into other forms of energy.

Mechanical Energy The energy associated with the motion and position of everyday objects is **mechanical energy.** Don't be confused by the name, however. Mechanical energy is not limited to machines. Mechanical energy is the sum of an object's potential energy and kinetic energy. Speeding trains, bouncing balls, and sprinting athletes all have mechanical energy.

Mechanical energy does not include thermal energy, chemical energy, or other forms of energy associated with the motion or the arrangement of atoms or molecules. Most of these other forms of energy do involve kinetic or potential energy, but on an atomic scale. However, the mechanical energy of a speeding train and a sprinting athlete comes from the chemical energy of the train's fuel and the sprinter's body cells.

Thermal Energy Almost all of the matter around you contains atoms. These particles are always in random motion and thus have kinetic energy. The total potential and kinetic energy related to the motion of all the microscopic particles in an object make up its **thermal energy.** When an object's atoms move faster, its thermal energy increases and the object becomes warmer. As Figure 6 shows, when objects are hot enough, they can emit visible light.

Chemical Energy The campers in Figure 7 are toasting marsh-mallows over a campfire. The source of energy for the fire is the energy stored in wood. When the wood is burned, energy is released and heats the marshmallows as well as the area around the campfire. The energy stored in wood is chemical energy. **Chemical energy** is the energy stored in chemical bonds. When bonds are broken, the released energy can do work. All chemical compounds, including fuels such as coal and gasoline, store energy. For example, cars can use the chemical energy stored in gasoline to move about. The gasoline is burned in the car's engine and some of its chemical energy is converted into mechanical energy to move the car.

 Reading Checkpoint *What is chemical energy?*

Figure 6 Energy occurs in many forms. This molten metal is extremely hot. It contains a great deal of thermal energy. **Observing** *What other kinds of energy are evident in this photograph?*

Figure 7 This family is using the chemical energy of burning wood to produce thermal energy for heating marshmallows.

Figure 8 Two major forms of energy are electrical energy and electromagnetic energy. **A** Lightning bolts transfer electric charge. **B** Galaxies are giant structures in space that typically contain billions of stars. The stars give off enormous amounts of electromagnetic energy.

Electrical Energy Many devices you use every day use electricity, or electrical energy. **Electrical energy** is the energy associated with electric charges. Electric charges can exert forces that do work. Batteries, which convert chemical energy to electrical energy, are used to operate portable CD players, flashlights, and calculators. Electrical energy also occurs in nature. The powerful bolts of lightning shown in Figure 8A are produced by electrical energy.

Electromagnetic Energy The sun radiates electromagnetic energy into space and is the source, either directly or indirectly, of most of the world's energy supplies. **Electromagnetic energy** is a form of energy that travels through space in the form of waves. Visible light and X-rays are examples of electromagnetic energy. Because electromagnetic waves can travel long distances through air and space, they are often used for communication. The glowing galaxy in Figure 8B is emitting electromagnetic energy of many kinds.

Nuclear Energy The nucleus of an atom is held together by strong and weak nuclear forces, which can store an enormous amount of potential energy. The energy stored in atomic nuclei is known as **nuclear energy.** A nuclear power plant uses nuclear fission reactions to generate electricity. Nuclear fission is a process that releases energy by splitting nuclei apart. A second type of nuclear reaction, nuclear fusion, releases energy when less massive nuclei combine to form a more massive nucleus. The heat and light of the sun are produced by the fusion of hydrogen nuclei into helium nuclei.

Section 15.1 Assessment

Reviewing Concepts

1. Describe the relationship between work and energy.

2. How is the kinetic energy of an object determined?

3. What factors determine the gravitational potential energy of an object?

4. Give an example of each of the major forms of energy.

5. When you heat a pot of water over a flame, what form of energy is added to the water?

Critical Thinking

6. **Applying Concepts** What kind of energy is represented by an archer stretching a bow string?

7. **Applying Concepts** Can an object have both kinetic energy and potential energy at the same time? Explain.

Math Practice

8. A 60.0-kg person walks from the ground to the roof of a 74.8-m-tall building. How much gravitational potential energy does she have at the top of the building?

9. A pitcher throws a 0.145-kg baseball at a velocity of 30.0 m/s. How much kinetic energy does the ball have?

15.2 Energy Conversion and Conservation

Reading Focus

Key Concepts
- Can energy be converted from one form into another?
- What is the law of conservation of energy?
- What energy conversion takes place as an object falls toward Earth?
- How are energy and mass related?

Vocabulary
- energy conversion

Reading Strategy
Relating Cause and Effect Copy the flow-chart below. As you read, complete the chart to explain an energy conversion. Make two similar charts for pendulums and pole vaults.

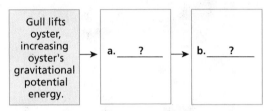

Gull lifts oyster, increasing oyster's gravitational potential energy. → a. _____? → b. _____?

On October 9, 1992, people from Kentucky to New York reported seeing a bright streak of white light shooting across the night sky. Most observers, having seen "shooting stars" before, expected this one to quickly burn out and disappear. However, that did not happen. The shooting star, or meteor, continued streaking across the sky. After a few seconds, pieces of the meteor broke off, creating a series of smaller streaks of light. Eventually, the streaks disappeared from view. Although the event was interesting, most witnesses probably soon forgot about it.

However, the meteor was not soon forgotten by the owners of a red automobile in Peekskill, New York. Unfortunately for them, a large chunk of the meteor made it through Earth's atmosphere and struck their parked car. The car was badly damaged, as shown in Figure 9. Luckily, no one was in the car at the time, and so no one was hurt.

As the Peekskill meteor traveled through the atmosphere, some of its kinetic energy was converted into light and heat. The light made the meteor visible in the sky. The heat caused a large portion of the meteor to vaporize in the atmosphere. Upon impact, much of the meteor's remaining kinetic energy went into smashing the metal body of the car.

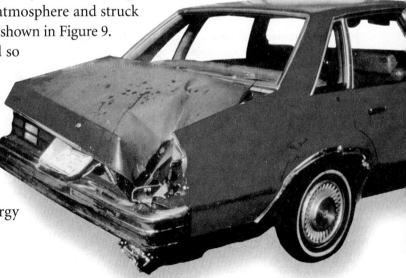

Figure 9 A meteor crashed into the rear of this car, causing considerable damage.

Energy Conversion

The Peekskill meteor clearly shows that energy can change forms. Energy can be converted from one form to another. The process of changing energy from one form to another is **energy conversion.**

Not all energy conversions are as dramatic as the Peekskill meteor. Energy conversions are constantly taking place all around you, often without you noticing. Wind-up toys store elastic potential energy in a compressed spring. When the spring unwinds, potential energy is converted into the kinetic energy of the toy's moving parts. Light bulbs convert electrical energy into thermal energy and electromagnetic energy.

In some cases, energy is converted from one form into another in a series of steps. The striking of the match shown in Figure 10 is a good example. In lighting a match, your muscles use chemical energy moving your hand to strike the match against a rough area on the matchbox. Friction between the match and the matchbox converts some of the match's kinetic energy into thermal energy. The thermal energy triggers a chemical reaction on the match tip, releasing some of the match's stored chemical energy. The stored chemical energy is then converted into thermal energy and electromagnetic energy in the flame.

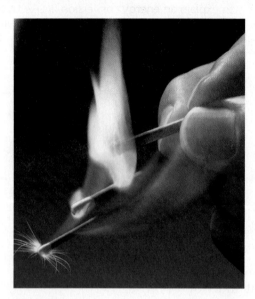

Figure 10 Energy is converted from one form to another as this match is lit.
Applying Concepts *What energy conversions take place when you turn on a battery-powered portable radio?*

Reading Checkpoint *What energy conversions occur in lighting a match?*

≡Quick Lab

Exploring Energy Conversion

Materials

small steel ball of known mass, box lined with soft modeling clay, meter stick, graph paper

Procedure

1. Construct a data table with 3 blank rows and 5 columns labeled Mass, Height, Diameter, Potential Energy, and Kinetic Energy.

2. Drop the ball into the box of clay from a height of 30 cm. Record this height.

3. Measure and record the diameter of the crater that the ball formed.

4. Repeat Steps 2 and 3, dropping the ball from 60 cm and 90 cm.

5. Graph your data. Plot the crater diameter on the vertical axis and height on the horizontal axis.

Analyze and Conclude

1. **Using Graphs** According to your graph, how are crater diameter and the height of the ball related?

2. **Calculating** For each height, calculate and record the initial potential energy of the ball.

3. **Drawing Conclusions** How are kinetic energy and crater diameter related? (*Hint:* The ball's kinetic energy when it hits the clay equals the potential energy it started with, *mgh*.)

Figure 11 Although speed skaters slide quickly over smooth ice, they are still slowed down by friction with the air and the surface of the ice.
Inferring *What are two ways that skaters can reduce friction?*

Conservation of Energy

When energy changes from one form to another, the total energy remains unchanged even though many energy conversions may occur. This is one of the most important concepts in science, the law of conservation of energy. ☐ **The law of conservation of energy states that energy cannot be created or destroyed.** According to the law of conservation of energy, energy can be converted from one form to another. However, in a closed system, the amount of energy present at the beginning of a process is the same as the amount of energy at the end. (In a closed system, nothing can enter or leave.)

You know that if you stop pedaling when you're riding a bike on a flat path, the bike will eventually come to a stop. The moving bike had kinetic energy. Where did the bike's kinetic energy go? The bike slowed down and stopped because of frictional forces acting over a distance. The work done by friction changes kinetic energy into thermal energy.

As a bicycle moves, it encounters friction with the ground and the air. Such friction causes a continual conversion of kinetic energy into thermal energy. Thus, as the bicycle slows, it gains thermal energy. So do the ground and the air. When the energy lost to frictional forces is accounted for, energy is conserved overall.

Recall that friction within machinery reduces efficiency. Friction is a major cause of energy consumption in cars and factories. All moving parts are subject to friction.

You can reduce friction but you can't avoid it. Friction is everywhere. Even the skaters in Figure 11 are subject to friction. Recall that objects moving through the air are slowed by air resistance. In many cases, most of a falling object's potential energy is converted into thermal energy because of air resistance.

You can ignore the effects of friction in many everyday situations. A marble dropped from one meter above the ground, for example, encounters so little air resistance that it can be ignored.

For: Links on energy
Visit: www.SciLinks.org
Web Code: ccn-2152

Figure 12 Some gulls use energy conversion to obtain food by dropping oysters onto rocks. **Applying Concepts** *Where is the oyster's potential energy greatest? Where is its kinetic energy greatest?*

Energy Conversions

One of the most common energy conversions is between potential energy and kinetic energy. **The gravitational potential energy of an object is converted to the kinetic energy of motion as the object falls.** That's what happens when an avalanche brings tons of snow from the top of a mountain to the valley floor. Similarly, when you release a compressed spring, the elastic potential energy of the spring is converted into kinetic energy as the spring expands. Conversions between kinetic and potential energy can happen in both directions, that is, from kinetic to potential energy, or from potential to kinetic energy.

Some gulls use energy conversion to obtain food. Oysters are a food source for gulls. However, it is difficult for a gull to break open an oyster's hard shell with its beak. Unfortunately for the oyster, gulls have learned a clever way to use gravitational potential energy, as shown in Figure 12. A hungry gull picks up an oyster and flies high into the air directly over some rocks. The gull does work on the oyster by raising it against the force of gravity, thereby increasing the oyster's potential energy. While over the rocks, the gull lets the oyster fall. As the oyster falls, its gravitational potential energy is converted into kinetic energy. The oyster picks up speed until it hits the rocks. The impact breaks open the shell. The gull then swoops down to enjoy its meal.

Energy Conversion in Pendulums At the lake, you grab a rope hanging from a tree branch. With a yell, you swing down toward the lake, and pick up speed until you land with a giant splash. A rope swing is an example of a pendulum. A pendulum consists of a weight swinging back and forth from a rope or string.

Pendulums were used in the first truly accurate clocks. The Dutch scientist Christiaan Huygens (1629–1695) made the first pendulum clock in 1656. Pendulum clocks such as the one shown in Figure 13 make use of the fact that the time it takes for a pendulum to swing back and forth once is precisely related to its length.

Kinetic energy and potential energy undergo constant conversion as a pendulum swings. At the highest point in its swing, the pendulum is momentarily motionless as it changes direction. At this point, the weight at the end of the pendulum has zero kinetic energy and maximum potential energy.

As the pendulum swings downward, potential energy is converted to kinetic energy. At the bottom of the swing, the pendulum has maximum kinetic energy and zero potential energy. The pendulum then moves upward again, repeating the process. Eventually, frictional forces slow down the pendulum. In a clock, a spring mechanism or hanging weights provide energy to keep the pendulum swinging despite the effects of friction.

Figure 13 Pendulum clocks use pendulums to maintain accurate time.

Energy Conversion in the Pole Vault The pole vault is a difficult track and field event that requires a combination of speed, strength, timing, and energy conversion. In the pole vault, an athlete uses a flexible pole to propel himself over a high bar. Look at the pole-vaulter's jump in Figure 14 and think about how energy changes during the jump.

In order to start the jump with as much kinetic energy as possible, the pole-vaulter sprints down the runway as fast as he can. At the end of his sprint, he plants the end of a long pole at the base of the high bar and propels himself into the air. The pole-vaulter's kinetic energy is partially converted into elastic potential energy as the pole bends. The pole springs back into shape, propelling the pole-vaulter upward, hopefully high enough to clear the bar.

As the pole-vaulter soars, his kinetic energy decreases while he gains gravitational potential energy. Once the highest point has been reached, his gravitational potential energy begins to convert back to kinetic energy. The pole-vaulter picks up speed as he falls back to the ground.

 Reading Checkpoint *What energy changes occur in a pole vault?*

Figure 14 A pole-vaulter converts kinetic energy into potential energy in order to propel himself high into the air. **Applying Concepts** *At which point does a pole-vaulter have the most gravitational potential energy?*

Energy Conversion Calculations When friction is small enough to be ignored, and no mechanical energy is added to a system, then the system's mechanical energy does not change. Recall that mechanical energy is the total kinetic and potential energy of an object.

$$\text{Mechanical energy} = \text{KE} + \text{PE}$$

You can apply the law of conservation of energy to any mechanical process. A mechanical process can be any action, such as the motion of a pendulum, water falling in a waterfall, or a diver propelled by a diving board. In all of these processes, if friction can be neglected, the mechanical energy at the beginning equals the mechanical energy at the end. That is, total mechanical energy remains constant. This equality can be stated as follows.

Conservation of Mechanical Energy
$$(\text{KE} + \text{PE})_{\text{beginning}} = (\text{KE} + \text{PE})_{\text{end}}$$

The Math Skills box on the following page shows how the conservation of mechanical energy equation can be used.

Math > Skills

Conservation of Mechanical Energy

At a construction site, a 1.50-kg brick is dropped from rest and hits the ground at a speed of 26.0 m/s. Assuming air resistance can be ignored, calculate the gravitational potential energy of the brick before it was dropped.

1 Read and Understand

What information are you given?

> **Mass, $m = 1.50$ kg**   **Final speed, $v = 26.0$ m/s**

What unknown are you trying to calculate?

> **Gravitational potential energy of the brick before it was dropped, PE**

2 Plan and Solve

What equations or formulas contain the given quantities and the unknown?

Because the brick falls without air resistance, the conservation of mechanical energy equation can be used.

$$(KE + PE)_{beginning} = (KE + PE)_{end}$$

You will also need to use the formula for kinetic energy (KE).

$$KE = \frac{1}{2}mv^2$$

Note that the KE at the beginning is zero because the brick has not yet begun to fall. Also, when the brick hits the ground, its potential energy is zero. Substitute these values into the conservation of energy formula.

$$(PE)_{beginning} = (KE)_{end}$$

Substitute the formula for KE.

$$PE = KE = \frac{1}{2}mv^2$$

Substitute the known values and calculate the PE.

$$PE = \frac{1}{2}(1.50 \text{ kg})(26.0 \text{ m/s})^2 = 507 \text{ kg·m}^2/\text{s}^2 = 507 \text{ J}$$

3 Look Back and Check

Is your answer reasonable?

Check the answer by finding the initial height of the brick, using PE = 507 J = *mgh*. Substituting in *m* and *g* gives *h* = 34.5 m. This is a reasonable height for an object in free fall to reach a speed of 26.0 m/s.

Math > Practice

1. A 10-kg rock is dropped and hits the ground below at a speed of 60 m/s. Calculate the gravitational potential energy of the rock before it was dropped. You can ignore the effects of friction.

2. A diver with a mass of 70.0 kg stands motionless at the top of a 3.0-m-high diving platform. Calculate his potential energy relative to the water surface while standing on the platform, and his speed when he enters the pool. (*Hint:* Assume the diver's initial vertical speed after diving is zero.)

3. A pendulum with a 1.0-kg weight is set in motion from a position 0.04 m above the lowest point on the path of the weight. What is the kinetic energy of the pendulum at the lowest point? (*Hint:* Assume there is no friction.)

Energy and Mass

Physicist Albert Einstein (1879–1955), shown in Figure 15, developed his special theory of relativity in 1905. This theory included the now-famous equation $E = mc^2$. In Einstein's equation, E is energy, m is mass, and c is the speed of light. This seemingly ordinary equation has surprising consequences. ⬤ **Einstein's equation, $E = mc^2$, says that energy and mass are equivalent and can be converted into each other.** In other words, energy is released as matter is destroyed, and matter can be created from energy.

Notice that the speed of light is squared in Einstein's equation. The speed of light is an extremely large number, 3.0×10^8 meters per second. Thus, a tiny amount of matter can produce an enormous amount of energy. Suppose 1 gram of matter were entirely converted into energy.

$$E = mc^2 = (10^{-3} \text{ kg}) \times (3 \times 10^8 \text{ m/s}) \times (3 \times 10^8 \text{ m/s})$$

$$= 9 \times 10^{13} \text{ kg·m}^2/\text{s}^2 = 9 \times 10^{13} \text{ J}$$

In comparison, 1 gram of TNT produces only 2931 joules of energy. In nuclear fission and fusion reactions, however, large amounts of energy are released by the destruction of very small amounts of matter. Therefore, the law of conservation of energy has been modified to say that mass and energy together are always conserved.

Figure 15 Albert Einstein made important contributions to many areas of physics. His theory of special relativity showed that energy and mass are equivalent.

Section 15.2 Assessment

Reviewing Concepts

1. ⬤ Describe how energy can be converted from one form to another in a wind-up toy.

2. ⬤ What does the law of conservation of energy state?

3. ⬤ As an object falls in free fall, what energy change is taking place?

4. ⬤ What did Einstein conclude about the relationship between energy and mass?

5. What type of energy change results when friction slows down an object?

6. Describe the energy of a playground swing at its highest position.

Critical Thinking

7. **Inferring** Why does a bouncing ball rise to a lower height with each bounce? What energy conversion is taking place?

8. **Applying Concepts** To begin a dive, a diver jumps into the air and then lands on the diving board, causing it to bend. What type of energy conversions occur as the board springs back and propels the diver up into the air?

Math ▶ Practice

9. A 0.15-kg ball is thrown into the air and rises to a height of 20.0 m. How much kinetic energy did the ball initially have?

10. A 125-g steel ball with a kinetic energy of 0.25 J rolls along a horizontal track. How high up an inclined track will the ball roll if friction can be ignored?

Roller Coasters

A roller coaster is a train powered by gravity. An initial store of potential energy is released dramatically during the ride.

A roller coaster's first hill, called the lift hill, is the highest point of the ride. As the coaster plunges down the first drop, its potential energy is converted into kinetic energy, the energy of motion. Later, some of this kinetic energy is converted back into potential energy as the coaster's speed decreases during a climb. Over the course of the ride, the coaster's total mechanical energy (potential plus kinetic energy) gradually decreases. This change occurs due to friction from the rails and the air, which causes the coaster's mechanical energy to be converted into heat. By the end of the ride, all the potential energy created on the lift hill has been lost as heat.

As it falls, the coaster converts potential energy into kinetic energy.

Releasing energy

A roller coaster goes through a series of exchanges between potential and kinetic energy.

A cable *pulls cars to the top of the lift hill. During the climb, the coaster builds up potential energy.*

Potential energy *rapidly turns into kinetic energy during the first plunge.*

Kinetic energy *reaches a maximum as the coaster reaches the bottom of the first hill.*

The second loop *has a lower peak than the first because the coaster's energy is reduced by friction.*

Design and safety

The job of a roller coaster designer is to make sure that a ride is terrifying but safe. Some people are concerned that designers are providing riders with greater thrills at the expense of their safety. Safety experts say that the risk of injury is small, but it is important to pay attention to restrictions regarding height and medical conditions.

Coaster forces
During a ride, you are kept in your seat by the safety bar and by the force of the seat pushing on you. The coaster also exerts large forces on the track, which must be inspected daily for structural damage.

Acceleration
An early loop ride at Coney Island subjected riders to about 12 g's (12 times the acceleration due to gravity). For safety reasons, most modern rides do not exceed 5 g's.

Going Further

- Select an amusement park ride that you enjoy. Use library or Internet resources to discover the principles of physics that allow this ride to work. Write a paragraph or draw a diagram explaining what you have learned.

15.3 Energy Resources

From the alarm clock that wakes you up each morning to the light that you turn off before you sleep, you depend on energy resources to operate many different devices to get you through each day. Energy resources can be classified as either renewable or nonrenewable.

Figure 16 Crude oil is pumped out of the ground or ocean floor. It is then refined and turned into gasoline, fuel oil, and other oil products.

Nonrenewable Energy Resources

Nonrenewable energy resources exist in limited quantities and, once used, cannot be replaced except over the course of millions of years. **Nonrenewable energy resources include oil, natural gas, coal, and uranium**. Such resources are currently being used much faster than they can be replaced, creating concern about how long they will last.

Oil, natural gas, and coal are known as **fossil fuels** because they were formed underground from the remains of once-living organisms. Currently, fossil fuels account for the great majority of the world's energy use. These fuels are not distributed evenly throughout the world. For example, about 60 percent of known oil supplies are located in a small area in the Middle East. The United States has just 2 percent of the world's oil supplies but about 25 percent of the world's coal supplies. Fossil fuels are relatively inexpensive and are usually readily available, but their use creates pollution.

Renewable Energy Resources

Renewable energy resources are resources that can be replaced in a relatively short period of time. Most renewable energy resources originate either directly or indirectly from the sun. The sun and Earth are constantly releasing large amounts of energy. This energy can be used for generating electric power, heating buildings or other purposes. 🔑 **Renewable energy resources include hydroelectric, solar, geothermal, wind, biomass, and, possibly in the future, nuclear fusion.** The challenge for engineers and scientists is to find efficient ways to make these energy resources inexpensive and convenient.

Hydroelectric Energy Energy obtained from flowing water is known as **hydroelectric energy.** Hydroelectric energy is an indirect form of solar energy. Energy from the sun causes evaporation of water, which later falls back to Earth as precipitation. The water from this precipitation often collects to form rivers. As river water flows downhill, its gravitational potential energy is converted into kinetic energy. This kinetic energy can be used to turn turbines that are connected to electric generators in a power plant, such as the one shown in Figure 17. The major advantages of hydroelectric energy include its low cost to produce and lack of pollution. Dams, however, cause a variety of environmental problems. For example, dams hamper the run of fish upriver for spawning. Also, in the United States, many of the most suitable sites for hydroelectric plants are already in use.

Figure 17 Hoover Dam was built across the Colorado River on the Arizona-Nevada border. This 221-meter-tall structure can generate over 2 million kilowatts of power. **Applying Concepts** *What type of energy conversion is involved in a hydroelectric plant?*

Data Analysis

World Energy Use

Which energy resources are most commonly used around the world? How is energy use changing over time? The table shows total world energy use in 2000 and 2007. Energy use can be measured in British thermal units, or Btu (1 Btu = 1055 J). Note that petroleum includes oil and related fuels.

1. **Using Tables** What was the world's largest source of energy in 2000? In 2007?

2. **Analyzing Data** In general, how did usage change from 2000 to 2007?

3. **Graphing** Make a circle graph of world energy use by source for the year 2007.

World Energy Use (×10^{15} Btu)		
Source	2000	2007
Petroleum	155.52	173.87
Coal	92.37	132.47
Natural gas	90.95	111.21
Hydroelectric power	26.73	29.64
Nuclear fission	25.65	27.06
Other	2.99	5.32

4. **Analyzing Data** What percentage of world energy use in 2007 was accounted for by fossil fuels?

5. **Predicting** How might total world energy use be different in 2020? Explain.

Figure 18 Solar and geothermal energy plants use renewable resources to generate electricity.
A A concentrating solar power (CSP) plant uses solar cells to convert sunlight into electricity.
B A geothermal plant in California uses Earth's thermal energy to generate electricity.
Comparing and Contrasting *What are some similarities and differences between solar energy and geothermal energy?*

For: Articles on energy and energy resources
Visit: PHSchool.com
Web Code: cce-2153

Solar Energy The amount of energy from the sun that reaches Earth in one hour is more than the amount of energy used by the world's population in a year. Sunlight that is converted into usable energy is called **solar energy.** Passive solar designs use sunlight to heat a building without using machinery. Sunlight passing through the windows of a house may be absorbed by walls that then radiate thermal energy to warm the house.

In an active solar energy system, sunlight heats flat collection plates through which water flows. The heated water may be used directly, or it may be used to heat the house. Sunlight can also be converted into electrical energy by solar cells, also known as photovoltaic cells, like those shown in Figure 18A. Concentrating solar power (CSP) plants use mirrors to focus sunlight to produce electricity.

The benefits of solar energy depend on the climate. Solar energy is nonpolluting, but for areas where cloudy days are frequent, solar energy is less practical.

Geothermal Energy **Geothermal energy** is thermal energy beneath Earth's surface. In some regions, especially near volcanoes, geothermal energy is used to generate electicity. The geothermal power plant in Figure 18B pumps water into the ground, where it turns into steam. The steam is then used to drive electric generators. Geothermal energy is nonpolluting, but is not widely available.

Other Renewable Resources Sunlight causes plants to grow, converting electromagnetic energy into chemical energy. The chemical energy stored in living things is called **biomass energy.** Biomass can be converted directly into thermal energy. For example, many people around the world burn wood or peat to heat their homes or for cooking. Also, agricultural wastes such as corn stalks can be converted into a high-energy alcohol fuel that can be added to gasoline for cars.

Wind energy is another renewable energy source. Wind turbines convert the kinetic energy of wind into electrical energy. Wind energy is actually a form of solar energy. Energy from the sun causes uneven heating of air, which, in turn, causes differences in air pressure. Winds blow from areas of higher pressure to areas of lower pressure.

A form of hydrogen is also the most likely raw material for another future source of energy, nuclear fusion. The process of fusion will probably produce little pollution or radioactive waste. Scientists have been working on sustained fusion for years, but many challenges remain.

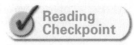 *What is biomass energy?*

Wind Turbine

Wind turbines convert the kinetic energy in the horizontal movement of wind into rotational energy of the turbine's rotor shaft. Rotational energy is then converted into electrical energy using an electric generator. The output of a wind turbine depends on the turbine's size and the wind's speed. **Interpreting Diagrams** *What is the purpose of the gearbox?*

Wind farm
Enormous wind farms like this one in California can generate as much power as a large power plant (without any air pollution).

Blades The shape and angle of the blades are designed to extract as much energy as possible from the horizontal movement of the wind.

Gearbox The rotor shaft itself rotates fairly slowly at about 20–30 revolutions per minute. The gearbox converts this to a rotation some 50 times faster—about 1500 revolutions per minute.

Generator The shaft from the gearbox enters the generator, which converts the kinetic energy of the shaft into electrical energy.

The anemometer measures wind speed.

Wind vane

Rotor shaft

Direction of rotation

Wind direction

A yaw ring changes the direction of the turbine.

Electrical energy passes to the local grid.

Yaw drive mechanism

Control unit This computer-operated unit controls the yaw drive mechanism, ensuring that the turbine always faces directly into the wind.

Conserving Energy Resources

Fossil fuel supplies may become increasingly scarce and expensive in the future. An important way to make these energy resources last longer is to use them more slowly. 🔑 **Energy resources can be conserved by reducing energy needs and by increasing the efficiency of energy use.** Finding ways to use less energy or to use energy more efficiently is known as **energy conservation.**

It's easy to forget that the energy you use often comes at the expense of resources that are being used up forever. People can reduce the use of these resources by making energy-saving decisions, for example turning off lights when they are not being used. Because conventional cars consume an enormous amount of energy, the decisions that people make about transportation are very important. Walking or biking on short trips and carpooling can save considerable energy. Using mass transportation, such as the streetcar shown in Figure 19, can also reduce energy use.

Making appliances, cars, and even light bulbs more energy efficient is a way of reducing energy use while still enjoying its benefits. Much has already been done to make appliances more energy efficient. Light bulbs have been developed that provide superior lighting at a lower energy cost. The technology for further improvement, including more fuel-efficient cars, is already known in many cases. However, the initial cost of energy efficiency can be an obstacle for manufacturers and for consumers. Energy-efficient purchases often cost more initially, but can save money in fuel costs over time.

Figure 19 Mass transportation systems include buses, trains, and streetcars such as the one shown here. **Inferring** *How can the use of mass transportation save energy?*

Section 15.3 Assessment

Reviewing Concepts

1. 🔘 List the major nonrenewable and renewable sources of energy.

2. 🔘 What could be done to make present energy resources last longer?

3. Why are coal, oil, and natural gas called fossil fuels?

Critical Thinking

4. **Applying Concepts** You are looking for the best place to build a hydroelectric plant along a river. Would you locate the plant along a steep or flat section of the river? Explain.

5. **Comparing and Contrasting** How are passive and active solar energy systems different?

6. **Applying Concepts** Describe three ways that you used energy resources today.

Writing in Science

Writing to Persuade Suppose you are an energy planner who is concerned about the possibility of future shortages of electricity. Write a paragraph describing one or two proposals that you think would help to avoid this potential problem.

Investigating a Spring Clip

There are many ways to use potential energy. A spring clip is a device used to hold weights on a barbell. The spring clip stores energy when you compress it. In this lab, you will determine how the distance you compress a spring clip is related to the force you apply and to the spring's potential energy.

Problem How does the force you apply to a spring clip affect its elastic potential energy?

Materials

- clamp
- spring clip
- masking tape
- metric ruler
- 50-newton spring scale
- graph paper

 For the probeware version of this lab, see the Probeware Lab Manual, Lab 6.

Skills Measuring, Using Tables and Graphs

Procedure

1. Make a data table with three columns. Label the columns Force (N), Position of Handle (cm), and Total Distance Moved (cm).

2. Using the clamp, firmly attach one handle of the spring clip to a tabletop, with the other handle facing up and away from the table as shown. **CAUTION** *Be careful not to pinch your fingers with the clamp or spring clip.*

3. Remove the plastic cover from the upper handle of the spring clip. Hook the spring scale to the spring clip handle as shown and use masking tape to secure it. Have your teacher check your setup for safety before proceeding.

4. Have a classmate hold the ruler next to the spring clip as shown. Record the starting position of the handle. (The reading on the spring scale should be zero.)

5. Slowly pull the spring scale down at a right angle to the upper handle until the upper handle moves 0.1 cm. Record the force and the position of the upper handle. Slowly release the scale back to the starting position.

6. Repeat Step 5, this time pulling the handle 0.2 cm from the starting position.

7. Repeat Step 5 a few more times, pulling the handle 0.1 cm farther each time. Continue until the spring scale reaches its maximum force.

8. Calculate the total distance the handle moved each time you pulled it and record these values in your data table. Graph your data. Place distance on the horizontal axis and force on the vertical axis.

Analyze and Conclude

1. **Using Graphs** What is the approximate relationship between the total distance you compressed the spring clip and the force you applied to it?

2. **Classifying** What type of energy transfer did you use to compress the spring clip? What type of energy did the spring clip gain when it was compressed?

3. **Drawing Conclusions** What relationship exists between the distance the spring clip was compressed and its potential energy? (*Hint:* The elastic potential energy of the spring clip equals the work done on it.)

For: Data sharing
Visit: PHSchool.com
Web Code: ccd-2150

15.1 Energy and Its Forms

Key Concepts

- Work is the transfer of energy.
- The kinetic energy of any moving object depends on its mass and speed.
- An object's gravitational potential energy depends on its mass, its height, and the acceleration due to gravity.
- The major forms of energy are mechanical energy, thermal energy, chemical energy, electrical energy, electromagnetic energy, and nuclear energy.

Vocabulary

energy, *p. 447*

kinetic energy, *p. 447*

potential energy, *p. 448*

gravitational potential energy, *p. 449*

elastic potential energy, *p. 450*

mechanical energy, *p. 450*

thermal energy, *p. 451*

chemical energy, *p. 451*

electrical energy, *p. 452*

electromagnetic energy, *p. 452*

nuclear energy, *p. 452*

15.2 Energy Conversion and Conservation

Key Concepts

- Energy can be converted from one form to another.
- The law of conservation of energy states that energy cannot be created or destroyed.
- The gravitational potential energy of an object is converted to the kinetic energy of motion as the object falls.
- Einstein's equation shows that energy and mass are equivalent, and can be converted into each other.

Vocabulary

energy conversion, *p. 454*

15.3 Energy Resources

Key Concepts

- Nonrenewable energy resources include oil, natural gas, coal, and uranium.
- Renewable energy resources include hydroelectric, solar, geothermal, wind, biomass, and, possibly in the future, nuclear fusion.
- Energy resources can be conserved by reducing our energy needs and by increasing the efficiency of energy use.

Vocabulary

nonrenewable energy resources, *p. 462*

fossil fuels, *p. 462*

renewable energy resources, *p. 463*

hydroelectric energy, *p. 463*

solar energy, *p. 464*

geothermal energy, *p. 464*

biomass energy, *p. 464*

energy conservation, *p. 466*

Thinking Visually

Comparing and Contrasting Copy the partially completed table below. Complete it to compare the major forms of energy.

Form of Energy	Definition	Example
Mechanical	Energy of motion and position of everyday objects	Bouncing ball
a. ___?___	b. ___?___	Lightning
c. ___?___	Energy stored in chemical bonds	d. ___?___
Electromagnetic	e. ___?___	f. ___?___
Nuclear	g. ___?___	Fission
Thermal	h. ___?___	i. ___?___

Reviewing Content

Choose the letter that best answers the question or completes the statement.

1. The energy of a moving object is
   a. kinetic energy.
   b. potential energy.
   c. chemical energy.
   d. nuclear energy.

2. If the speed of an object doubles, its kinetic energy
   a. doubles.
   b. quadruples.
   c. stays the same.
   d. is halved.

3. An example of an object having elastic potential energy is
   a. a stretched spring.
   b. books on a shelf.
   c. a moving arrow.
   d. a falling oyster.

4. An example of electromagnetic energy is
   a. a falling rock.
   b. a stretched spring.
   c. a speeding train.
   d. sunlight.

5. Energy stored in the bonds between atoms is called
   a. kinetic energy.
   b. mechanical energy.
   c. chemical energy.
   d. thermal energy.

6. Mechanical energy is
   a. found in machinery only.
   b. usually measured at the atomic level.
   c. the sum of the chemical and thermal energy of an object.
   d. the sum of the kinetic and potential energy of an object.

7. An example of the conversion of gravitational potential energy into kinetic energy is
   a. a falling raindrop.
   b. a gasoline-powered engine.
   c. striking a match.
   d. a hockey puck sliding on ice.

8. The law of conservation of energy states that
   a. energy cannot be converted from one form to another.
   b. energy cannot be created or destroyed.
   c. energy resources must be used efficiently.
   d. energy is constantly being lost to friction.

9. Which of the following energy resources accounts for most of the world's present energy use?
   a. uranium
   b. solar energy
   c. fossil fuels
   d. wind energy

10. Most renewable energy originates from
    a. fossil fuels.
    b. the ground.
    c. the sun.
    d. uranium.

Understanding Concepts

11. What is energy?

12. How are kinetic energy and potential energy different?

13. How does the potential energy of an object change when its height is tripled?

14. Look at the graphs below. One of the graphs is a plot of kinetic energy vs. mass for a set of objects with different masses, all moving at the same speed. The other graph is a plot of kinetic energy vs. speed for a set of objects with the same mass, all moving at different speeds. Identify each graph and explain how can you tell which graph is which.

15. What happens to the atoms of an object if its thermal energy is increased?

16. Explain the energy conversions that occur as a basketball falls, hits the ground, and bounces back up. Ignore frictional forces.

17. What force is acting when the kinetic energy of a moving object is converted into thermal energy?

18. Explain how energy is converted as a pendulum swings.

19. Is mechanical energy always conserved? Explain why or why not.

20. Explain the meaning and the importance of the formula $E = mc^2$.

21. Why are coal, oil, and natural gas considered to be nonrenewable energy resources?

22. What is the source of geothermal energy?

Critical Thinking

23. Calculating A small meteoroid is approaching Earth. It has a mass of 100.0 kg and a speed of 10.0 km/s. How much kinetic energy does the meteoroid have? (*Hint:* 1 km = 1000 m)

24. Designing an Experiment Design an experiment to find out how much elastic potential energy is in a compressed spring. In addition to the spring, you may use a small metal ball, a ruler, and a scale for measuring mass.

25. Calculating A 0.15-kg ball is dropped from the top of a 150-m building. What is the kinetic energy of the ball when it passes the sixteenth floor at a height of 63 m? (Ignore air resistance.)

Math Skills

26. Converting Units Using mass in kg, velocity in m/s, and height in m, show that the formulas for kinetic energy and gravitational potential energy result in energy values with the same units. What is the energy unit called?

Questions 27–29 refer to the data in the table below.

Three balls are thrown vertically into the air from different heights above the ground. The data for each ball are shown in the table below.

Data Table			
Object	Mass (kg)	Initial Upward Speed (m/s)	Initial Height Above Ground (m)
Ball 1	1.00	8.00	15.00
Ball 2	2.00	1.00	10.00
Ball 3	3.00	4.00	5.00

27. Calculating How much kinetic energy does each ball have when it is thrown?

28. Analyzing Data Which ball has the greatest gravitational potential energy when it reaches its maximum height? (*Hint:* Find the total energy for each ball.)

29. Predicting Which ball hits the ground with the most kinetic energy?

Concepts in Action

30. Using Graphs A soccer ball is kicked from the ground into the air. Describe two graphs that show how the potential energy and kinetic energy change between the time the ball is kicked and when it lands. (*Hint:* Make time the *x*-axis.)

31. Inferring When a falling object reaches a speed called terminal velocity, its speed no longer increases. The object is losing gravitational potential energy but not gaining kinetic energy. Since energy must be conserved, where must the gravitational potential energy be going?

32. Calculating Suppose a 200.0-kilogram dolphin is lifted in the air to be placed into an aquarium tank. How much energy is needed to lift the dolphin 3.00 meters into the air?

33. Applying Concepts How is energy converted as a car moves between the top and the bottom of a roller coaster loop?

34. Making Judgments What are some advantages and disadvantages of solar energy?

35. Applying Concepts How can electricity be obtained from the wind?

36. Writing in Science Using your own words, write a brief summary of the law of conservation of energy. Include an example from your everyday life.

Performance-Based Assessment

Applying Concepts Identify one practical way that your family or school could reduce energy use. Find out how much energy is currently being used for the purpose you choose, and estimate how much energy your suggestion could save. Write a brief summary of your recommendations.

For: Self-grading assessment
Visit: PHSchool.com
Web Code: cca-2150

Standardized Test Prep

Choose the letter that best answers the question or completes the statement.

1. Which form of energy does a plant store when light is transformed during photosynthesis?
(A) chemical energy
(B) thermal energy
(C) mechanical energy
(D) electrical energy
(E) nuclear energy

2. Which of the following is NOT an example of kinetic energy being converted to potential energy?
(A) a basketball player jumping for a rebound
(B) releasing a compressed spring
(C) squeezing a rubber ball
(D) pulling a sled up a hill
(E) a swing moving upward

3. A 50.0-kg wolf is running at 10.0 m/sec. What is the wolf's kinetic energy?
(A) 5 J   (B) 500 J
(C) 5000 J   (D) 250 J
(E) 2500 J

4. Friction causes kinetic energy to be converted into
(A) potential energy.
(B) thermal energy.
(C) mechanical energy.
(D) electrical energy.
(E) chemical energy.

5. Which of the following is NOT considered a renewable energy resource?
(A) geothermal energy
(B) biomass
(C) hydroelectric energy
(D) uranium
(E) wind energy

Use the figure below to answer Questions 6 and 7.

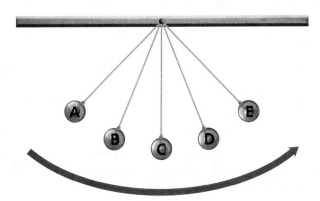

A pendulum weight is released in position A. The weight moves through positions B, C, D, and E.

6. At which location(s) does the pendulum have maximum potential energy?
(A) A and B
(B) B and D
(C) C only
(D) D and E
(E) A and E

7. At which location(s) does the pendulum have maximum kinetic energy?
(A) A and B
(B) B and D
(C) C only
(D) D and E
(E) A and E

CHAPTER 16

Thermal Energy and Heat

21st Century Learning

Accountability and Adaptability

What is thermal pollution and how can it be reduced?

Research thermal pollution on the Internet. Find out why all heat engines produce thermal pollution, and identify sources of thermal pollution in your area. Use this information to post a comment to a local blog or an online news article about the environment. Explain thermal pollution in a way that the general public will understand, and suggest how individuals and organizations can help reduce thermal pollution.

How do science concepts apply to your world? Here are some questions you'll be able to answer after you read this chapter.

- **When a car has been warmed by the sun, why is the metal door hotter than the plastic bumper?** *(Section 16.1)*

- **Why doesn't hot air burn your unprotected arm when you reach into an oven?** *(Section 16.2)*

- **Why does a bicycle pump heat up when you pump up a tire?** *(Section 16.2)*

- **What energy-saving strategies are used in a solar-heated home?** *(page 484)*

- **Why must a car engine have a cooling system?** *(Section 16.3)*

- **Can you cool a kitchen by leaving the refrigerator door open?** *(Section 16.3)*

Chapter Preview

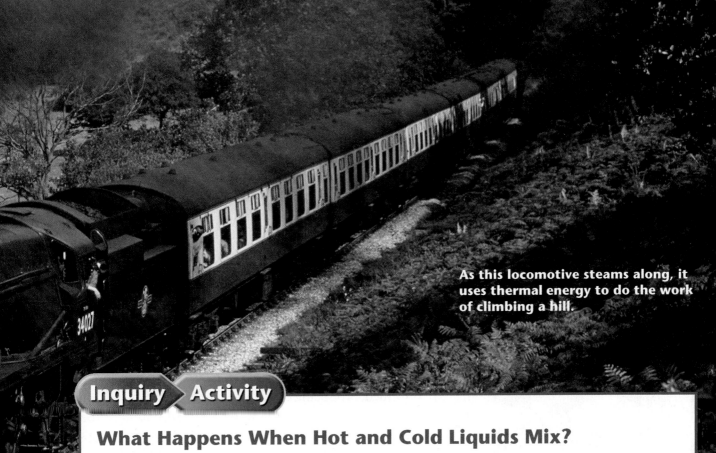

As this locomotive steams along, it uses thermal energy to do the work of climbing a hill.

Inquiry > Activity

What Happens When Hot and Cold Liquids Mix?

Procedure

1. Fill one graduated cylinder with hot water and another with cold water. **CAUTION** *Be careful when handling hot liquids.* Use a thermometer to measure the temperature of the water in each graduated cylinder. Record the temperatures.

2. Pour 100 mL of hot water into a plastic foam cup. Add 100 mL of cold water to the cup. Stir the water with a glass rod, and measure and record its temperature.

3. Repeat Step 2, this time adding 50 mL of cold water to 100 mL of hot water.

Think About It

1. **Comparing and Contrasting** How did the final temperatures in Steps 2 and 3 compare?

2. **Relating Cause and Effect** What factors can you identify that determine the final temperature when you mix hot water with cold water?

3. **Controlling Variables** Why do you think it was important to use the same graduated cylinders in Step 3 that you used in Step 2?

16.1 Thermal Energy and Matter

Reading Focus

Key Concepts

- In what direction does heat flow spontaneously?
- What is the temperature of an object related to?
- What two variables is thermal energy related to?
- What causes thermal expansion?
- How is a change in temperature related to specific heat?
- On what principle does a calorimeter operate?

Vocabulary

- heat
- temperature
- absolute zero
- thermal expansion
- specific heat
- calorimeter

Reading Strategy

Previewing Copy the table below. Before you read, preview the figures in this section and add two more questions to the table. As you read, write answers to your questions.

Questions About Thermal Energy and Matter	Answers
Which has more thermal energy, a cup of tea or a pitcher of juice?	a. ___?___
b. ___?___	c. ___?___
d. ___?___	e. ___?___

Figure 1 Count Rumford supervised the drilling of brass cannons in a factory in Bavaria. From his observations, Rumford concluded that heat is not a form of matter.

In the 1700s, most scientists thought heat was a fluid called *caloric* that flowed between objects. In 1798, the American-born scientist Benjamin Thompson (1753–1814), also known as Count Rumford, challenged this concept of heat. Rumford managed a factory that made cannons. Figure 1 shows how a brass cylinder was drilled to make the cannon barrel. Water was used to cool the brass so that it did not melt. Rumford observed that the brass became hot as long as the drilling continued, producing enough heat to boil the water. Soon after the drilling stopped, however, the water stopped boiling. When the drilling resumed, the water again came to a boil. Based on his observations, Rumford concluded that heat could not be a kind of matter, but instead was related to the motion of the drill.

Work and Heat

A drill is a machine that does work on the cannon. Remember that no machine is 100 percent efficient. Some of the work done by the drill does useful work, but some energy is lost due to friction. Friction causes the moving parts to heat up. The more work done by the drill, the more that friction causes the cannon to heat up.

Heat is the transfer of thermal energy from one object to another because of a temperature difference. **Heat flows spontaneously from hot objects to cold objects.** Heat flows from the cannon to the water because the cannon is at a higher temperature than the water.

Temperature

How do you know something is hot? You might use a thermometer to measure its temperature. **Temperature** is a measure of how hot or cold an object is compared to a reference point. Recall that on the Celsius scale, the reference points are the freezing and boiling points of water. On the Kelvin scale, another reference point is **absolute zero**, which is defined as a temperature of 0 kelvins.

🌡 **Temperature is related to the average kinetic energy of the particles in an object due to their random motions through space.** As an object heats up, its particles move faster, on average. As a result, the average kinetic energy of the particles, and the temperature, must increase.

Why does heat flow from a high to a low temperature? One way that heat flows is by the transfer of energy in collisions. On average, high-energy particles lose energy, and low-energy particles gain energy in collisions. Overall, collisions transfer thermal energy from hot to cold objects.

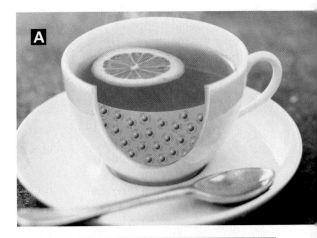

Thermal Energy

Recall that thermal energy is the total potential and kinetic energy related to the motion of all the particles in an object. 🌡 **Thermal energy depends on the mass, temperature, and phase (solid, liquid, or gas) of an object.**

Thermal energy, unlike temperature, depends on mass. Suppose you compare a cup of tea and a teapot full of tea. Both are at the same temperature, so the average kinetic energy of the particles is the same in both containers. However, there is more thermal energy in the teapot because it contains more particles.

Now consider how thermal energy varies with temperature. You can do this by comparing a cup of hot tea with a cup of cold tea. In both cases, the tea has the same mass, and the same number of particles. But the average kinetic energy of particles is higher in the hot tea, so it also has greater thermal energy than the cold tea.

Figure 2 shows the particles in a cup of hot tea and in a pitcher of lemonade. The tea is at a higher temperature because its particles move a little faster, on average. But they are only moving slightly faster, and the pitcher of lemonade has many more particles than the tea. As it turns out, the pitcher of lemonade has more thermal energy than the cup of hot tea.

Figure 2 Thermal energy depends on mass and temperature. **A** The tea is at a higher temperature than the lemonade because its particles have a higher average kinetic energy. **B** The lemonade is at a lower temperature, but it has more thermal energy because it has many more particles. **Inferring** *In which liquid are water particles moving faster, on average?*

Reading Checkpoint *What is thermal energy?*

Thermal Contraction and Expansion

If you take a balloon outside on a cold winter day, it shrinks. Can you explain why? As temperature decreases, the particles that make up the air inside the balloon move more slowly, on average. Slower particles collide less often and exert less force, so gas pressure decreases and the balloon contracts. This is called thermal contraction.

If you bring the balloon inside, it expands. **Thermal expansion** is an increase in the volume of a material due to a temperature increase. **Thermal expansion occurs when particles of matter move farther apart as temperature increases.** Gases expand more than liquids and liquids usually expand more than solids. A gas expands more easily than a liquid or a solid because the forces of attraction among particles in a gas are weaker.

Thermal expansion is used in glass thermometers. As temperature increases, the alcohol in the tube expands and its height increases. The increase in height is proportional to the increase in temperature. In an oven thermometer, a strip of brass and a strip of steel are bonded together and wound up in a coil. As the coil heats up, the two metals expand at different rates, and the coil unwinds. This causes the needle to rotate on the temperature scale.

 What is thermal expansion?

Specific Heat

When a car is heated by the sun, the temperature of the metal door increases more than the temperature of the plastic bumper. Do you know why? One reason is that the iron in the door has a lower specific heat than the plastic in the bumper. **Specific heat** is the amount of heat needed to raise the temperature of one gram of a material by one degree Celsius. If equal masses of iron and plastic absorb the same heat, the iron's temperature rises more. **The lower a material's specific heat, the more its temperature rises when a given amount of energy is absorbed by a given mass.**

Specific heat is often measured in joules per gram per degree Celsius, or J/g·°C. Figure 3 gives specific heats for a few common materials. It takes 4.18 joules of energy to raise the temperature of 1.00 gram of water by 1.00 degree Celsius. How much energy is needed to heat 2.00 grams of water to the same temperature? You would have to add twice as much energy, or 8.36 joules.

Specific Heats of Selected Materials	
Material (at 100 kPa)	**Specific Heat (J/g·°C)**
Water	4.18
Plastic (polypropylene)	1.84–2.09
Air	1.01
Iron	0.449
Silver	0.235

Figure 3 Specific heat is the heat needed to raise the temperature of 1 gram of material by 1°C. **Analyzing Data** *Which material in the table has the highest specific heat? The lowest?*

The heat (Q) absorbed by a material equals the product of the mass (m), the specific heat (c), and the change in temperature (ΔT).

Go Online

For: Links on specific heat
Visit: www.SciLinks.org
Web Code: ccn-2161

Specific Heat

$$Q = m \times c \times \Delta T$$

In this formula, heat is in joules, mass is in grams, specific heat is in J/g•°C, and the temperature change is in degrees Celsius.

 Skills

Calculating Specific Heat

An iron skillet has a mass of 500.0 grams. The specific heat of iron is 0.449 J/g•°C. How much heat must be absorbed to raise the skillet's temperature by 95.0°C?

1 Read and Understand

What information are you given?

Mass of iron, m = 500.0 g

Specific heat of iron, c = 0.449 J/g•°C

Temperature change, ΔT = 95.0°C

2 Plan and Solve

What unknown are you trying to calculate?

Amount of heat needed, Q = ?

What formula contains the given quantities and the unknown?

$$Q = m \times c \times \Delta T$$

Replace each variable with its known value.

$$Q = 500.0 \text{ g} \times 0.449 \text{ J/g•°C} \times 95.0°C$$

$$= 21,375 \text{ J} = 21.4 \text{ kJ}$$

3 Look Back and Check

Is your answer reasonable?

Round off the data to give a quick estimate.

Q = 500 g × 0.5 J/g•°C × 100°C = 25 kJ

This is close to 21.4 kJ, so the answer is reasonable.

 Practice

1. How much heat is needed to raise the temperature of 100.0 g of water by 85.0°C?

2. How much heat is absorbed by a 750-g iron skillet when its temperature rises from 25°C to 125°C?

3. In setting up an aquarium, the heater transfers 1200 kJ of heat to 75,000 g of water. What is the increase in the water's temperature? (*Hint:* Rearrange the specific heat formula to solve for ΔT.)

4. To release a diamond from its setting, a jeweler heats a 10.0-g silver ring by adding 23.5 J of heat. How much does the temperature of the silver increase?

5. What mass of water will change its temperature by 3.0°C when 525 J of heat is added to it?

Calorimeter

Stirrer   Thermometer

Lid

Water

Aluminum
sample

Figure 4 A calorimeter is used to measure
specific heat. A sample to be tested is heated
and placed in the calorimeter. The lid is put on
and the temperature change is observed.
Hypothesizing *Why does the calorimeter
need a stirrer?*

Measuring Heat Changes

A **calorimeter** is an instrument used to measure changes in
thermal energy. 🔑 **A calorimeter uses the principle that heat
flows from a hotter object to a colder object until both reach
the same temperature.** According to the law of conservation
of energy, the thermal energy released by a test sample is equal
to the thermal energy absorbed by its surroundings. The
calorimeter is sealed to prevent thermal energy from escaping.

Figure 4 shows how a calorimeter can be used to measure
the specific heat of aluminum. A known mass of water is
added to the calorimeter. The mass of the sample of aluminum
is measured. The aluminum is heated and then placed in the
water. The calorimeter is sealed. As the aluminum cools off,
the water is stirred to distribute thermal energy evenly. The
water heats up until both the aluminum and the water are at the
same temperature. The change in temperature of the water is
measured. The thermal energy absorbed by the water is calculated using the specific heat equation. Since this same amount
of thermal energy was given off by the sample of aluminum,
the specific heat of aluminum can be calculated.

Section 16.1 Assessment

Reviewing Concepts

1. 🔑 In what direction does heat flow on its
   own spontaneously?

2. 🔑 How is the temperature of an object
   related to the average kinetic energy of
   its particles?

3. 🔑 Name two variables that affect the
   thermal energy of an object.

4. 🔑 What causes thermal expansion of an
   object when it is heated?

5. 🔑 How do the temperature increases
   of different materials depend on their
   specific heats?

6. 🔑 What principle explains how a calorimeter
   is used to measure the specific heat of a
   sample material?

Critical Thinking

7. **Applying Concepts** Why is it necessary to
   have regularly spaced gaps between sections
   of a concrete sidewalk?

8. **Predicting** An iron spoon and silver spoon
   have the same mass. Which becomes hotter
   when both are left in hot tea for one minute?
   (*Hint:* Use the specific heats given in Figure 3.)

9. **Calculating** If it takes 80.0 joules to raise the
   temperature of a material by 10.0°C, how
   much heat must be added to cause an
   additional increase of 20.0°C?

Math ◆ Practice

10. The specific heat of copper is
    0.39 J/g•°C. How much heat is needed
    to raise the temperature of 1000.0 g of
    copper from 25.0°C to 45.0°C?

11. A peanut burned in a calorimeter
    transfers 18,200 joules to 100.0 g of
    water. What is the rise in the water's
    temperature? (*Hint:* Rearrange the
    specific heat formula to solve for Δ*T*.)

16.2 Heat and Thermodynamics

Reading Focus

Key Concepts

- Why is conduction slower in gases than in liquids or solids?

- In what natural cycles do convection currents occur?

- How does an object's temperature affect radiation?

- What are the three laws of thermodynamics?

Vocabulary

- conduction
- thermal conductor
- thermal insulator
- convection
- convection current
- radiation
- thermodynamics
- heat engine
- waste heat

Reading Strategy

Building Vocabulary Copy the table below. As you read, add definitions and examples to complete the table.

Definitions	Examples
Conduction: transfer of thermal energy without transfer of matter	Frying pan handle heats up.
Convection: **a.** _____ ? _____	**b.** ____ ? ____
Radiation: **c.** _____ ? _____	**d.** ____ ? ____

To bake cookies, you put cookie dough on a baking sheet and pop it in the oven. When the timer goes off, you use oven mitts to pull out the baking sheet. Why isn't your bare arm burned by the hot air in the oven? One reason is that air is not a very good conductor of thermal energy.

Conduction

Conduction is the transfer of thermal energy with no overall transfer of matter. Conduction occurs within a material or between materials that are touching. To understand conduction, look at the Newton's cradle in Figure 5. When a ball is pulled back and released, you might expect all of the balls to move to the right after the impact. Instead, most of the kinetic energy is transferred to one ball on the end. Similarly, in conduction, collisions between particles transfer thermal energy, without any overall transfer of matter.

Recall that forces are weak among particles in a gas. Compared to liquids and solids, the particles in gases are farther apart. **Conduction in gases is slower than in liquids and solids because the particles in a gas collide less often.** In most solids, conduction occurs as particles vibrate in place and push on each other. In metals, conduction is faster because some electrons are free to move about. These free electrons collide with one another and with atoms or ions to transfer thermal energy.

Figure 5 Conduction is the transfer of thermal energy without transferring matter. This device, called Newton's cradle, helps to visualize conduction. After one ball strikes the rest, most of the kinetic energy is transferred to one ball on the end.

Figure 6 The arrows show how thermal energy is conducted away from the heat source in a metal frying pan. **Predicting** *Would it be safe to touch the handle of the wooden spoon?*

Figure 7 Convection is the transfer of thermal energy by the movement of particles in a fluid. **A** Passing sandbags along a line is like transferring thermal energy by convection. **B** The arrows show convection of air in an oven. **Predicting** *Which part of the oven should have the highest temperature?*

Thermal Conductors Figure 6 shows a frying pan on a hot stove. The bottom of the pan heats up first. The metal handle heats up last. You can see that the flames do not directly heat the handle. The handle heats up because the metal is a good thermal conductor.

A **thermal conductor** is a material that conducts thermal energy well. A wire rack in a hot oven can burn you because the metal conducts thermal energy so quickly. Pots and pans often are made of copper or aluminum because these are good conductors.

A thermal conductor doesn't have to be hot. Why does a tile floor feel colder than a wooden floor? Both floors are at room temperature. But the tile feels colder because it is a better conductor and transfers thermal energy rapidly away from your skin.

Thermal Insulators Why is it safe to pick up the wooden spoon shown in Figure 6? Wood heats up slowly because it is a poor conductor of thermal energy. A material that conducts thermal energy poorly is called a **thermal insulator.**

Air is a very good insulator. A double-pane window has an air space contained between two panes of glass. The air slows down conduction to reduce heat loss in winter and to keep heat out of a building in summer. More expensive windows use argon gas, which is an even better insulator than air. Wool garments and plastic foam cups are two more examples of insulators that use trapped air to slow down conduction.

Convection

Convection is the transfer of thermal energy when particles of a fluid move from one place to another. Look at the people building a wall with sandbags in Figure 7A. The moving sandbags are like the particles in a fluid. The wall grows taller as more and more sandbags arrive. In much the same way, particles in a fluid can transfer thermal energy from a hot area to a cold area.

Baking instructions sometimes tell you to use the top rack of an oven. Figure 7B shows why the temperature is lower at the top of the oven. When air at the bottom of the oven heats up, it expands and becomes less dense than the surrounding air. Due to the difference in density, the hot air rises. The rising air cools as it moves away from the heat source. As a result, the coolest air is at the top of the oven.

Air circulating in an oven is an example of a convection current. A **convection current** occurs when a fluid circulates in a loop as it alternately heats up and cools down. In a heated room, convection currents help keep the temperature uniform throughout the room. 🔑 **Convection currents are important in many natural cycles, such as ocean currents, weather systems, and movements of hot rock in Earth's interior.**

Radiation

At a picnic, you might use a charcoal grill to cook food. When you stand to the side of the grill, heat reaches you without convection or conduction. In much the same way, the sun warms you by radiation on a clear day. The space between the sun and Earth has no air to transfer thermal energy. **Radiation** is the transfer of energy by waves moving through space. Heat lamps used in restaurants are a familiar example of radiation.

🔑 **All objects radiate energy. As an object's temperature increases, the rate at which it radiates energy increases.** In Figure 8, the electric heating coil on a stove radiates so much energy that it glows. If you are close to the heating coil, you absorb radiation, which increases your thermal energy. In other words, it warms you up. The farther you are from the heating coil, the less radiation you receive, and the less it warms you.

✓ **Reading Checkpoint**   *What is radiation?*

≡Quick⟩Lab

Observing Convection
Procedure 🖐️ 🧪

1. Fill a 100-mL beaker halfway with cold water.

2. Fill a dropper pipet with hot water colored with food coloring. Wipe the pipet with a paper towel so no food coloring is on the outside of the pipet.

3. Insert the tip of the pipet into the cold water, halfway between the surface of the water and the bottom of the beaker.

4. Slowly squeeze the pipet bulb. Observe the water in the beaker from the side.

Analyze and Conclude

1. **Observing** Describe the motion of the colored hot water in the beaker.

2. **Inferring** Explain why the hot water behaved as it did.

3. **Predicting** How would colored cold water move in a beaker of hot water?

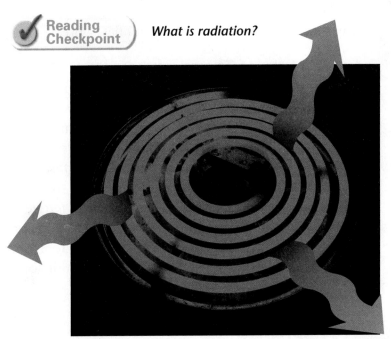

Figure 8 A heating coil on a stove radiates thermal energy. The changing color of the red arrows indicates that the farther you are from the coil, the less radiation you receive.

Thermal Energy and Heat   **481**

Go Online

NSTA SciLINKS

For: Links on thermodynamics
Visit: www.SciLinks.org
Web Code: ccn-2162

Thermodynamics

The study of conversions between thermal energy and other forms of energy is called **thermodynamics.** Count Rumford made a good start in this field. But many scientists still believed that heat was a kind of matter. Then in 1845, James Prescott Joule (1818–1889) published his results from a convincing experiment.

Joule carefully measured the energy changes in a system. Recall that a system is any group of objects that interact with one another. Joule's system included a falling weight that turned a paddle wheel in a container of water. As the weight fell, the paddle churned a known mass of water. The water heated up due to friction from the turning paddle. Joule carefully measured the work done by the falling weight. He found that the work almost exactly equaled the thermal energy gained by the water. Joule is often given credit for discovering the first law of thermodynamics. That is the law of conservation of energy applied to work, heat, and thermal energy.

First Law of Thermodynamics Recall that energy cannot be created or destroyed. But energy can be converted into different forms. ⟳ **The first law of thermodynamics states that energy is conserved.** If energy is added to a system, it can either increase the thermal energy of the system or do work on the system. But no matter what happens, all of the energy added to the system can be accounted for. Energy is conserved.

Look at the bicycle pump in Figure 9. You can consider the tire, the pump, and the air inside to be a system. The force exerted on the pump does work on the system. Some of this work is useful; it compresses air into the tire. The rest of the work is converted into thermal energy. That is why a bicycle pump heats up as you inflate a tire.

Second Law of Thermodynamics If you take a cold drink from the refrigerator and leave it out in a warm room, will the drink become colder? Of course it won't. You know that the drink will warm up. Thermal energy flows spontaneously only from hotter to colder objects.

⟳ **The second law of thermodynamics states that thermal energy can flow from colder objects to hotter objects only if work is done on the system.** A refrigerator, for example, must do work to transfer thermal energy from the cold food compartment to the warm room air. The thermal energy is released by coils at the bottom or in the back of the refrigerator.

Figure 9 You can consider the bicycle pump, the tire, and the air inside of both to be a system. The person does work on the system by pushing on the pump. Some of the work is converted into thermal energy, which heats the air in the pump and the tire.

A **heat engine** is any device that converts heat into work. One consequence of the second law of thermodynamics is that the efficiency of a heat engine is always less than 100 percent. The best an engine can do is to convert most of the input energy into useful work. Thermal energy that is not converted into work is called **waste heat.** Waste heat is lost to the surrounding environment. In fact, a heat engine can do work only if some waste heat flows to a colder environment outside the engine.

Spontaneous changes will always make a system less orderly, unless work is done on the system. For example, if you walk long enough, your shoelaces will become untied. But the opposite won't happen; shoelaces don't tie themselves. Disorder in the universe as a whole is always increasing. You can only increase order on a local level. For instance, you can stop and tie your shoelaces. But this requires work. Because work always produces waste heat, you contribute to the disorder of the universe when you stop to tie a shoelace!

Third Law of Thermodynamics The efficiency of a heat engine increases with a greater difference between the high temperature inside and the cold temperature outside the engine. In theory, a heat engine could be 100 percent efficient if the cold outside environment were at absolute zero (0 kelvins). But this would violate the third law of thermodynamics. 🔑 **The third law of thermodynamics states that absolute zero cannot be reached.** Scientists have been able to cool matter almost all of the way to absolute zero. Figure 10 shows the equipment used to produce the record lowest temperature, just 3 billionths of a kelvin above absolute zero!

Figure 10 The third law of thermodynamics states that absolute zero cannot be reached. This physicist is adjusting a laser used to cool rubidium atoms to 3 billionths of a kelvin above absolute zero. This record low temperature was produced by a team of scientists at the National Institute of Standards and Technology.

Section 16.2 Assessment

Reviewing Concepts

1. 🔑 Why is conduction in gases slower than conduction in liquids or solids?
2. 🔑 Give three examples of convection currents that occur in natural cycles.
3. 🔑 What happens to radiation from an object as its temperature increases?
4. 🔑 State the first law of thermodynamics.
5. 🔑 In your own words, what is the second law of thermodynamics?
6. 🔑 State the third law of thermodynamics.
7. Why does a metal spoon feel colder than a wooden spoon at room temperature?
8. Why is solar energy transferred to Earth by radiation?

Critical Thinking

9. **Applying Concepts** If your bedroom is cold, you might feel warmer with several thin blankets than with one thick one. Explain why.
10. **Relating Cause and Effect** If every object is radiating constantly, why aren't all objects getting colder?

Connecting 🅒 Concepts

Conservation of Energy Review energy conservation in Section 15.2. Describe how the first and the second laws of thermodynamics are consistent with the law of conservation of energy.

Solar Home

Huge amounts of radiant energy from the sun constantly fall on the surface of our planet. How can this energy be harnessed to help make a home that is warm and comfortable in all seasons?

Heating a home with solar energy means making the best use of available sunlight. To provide warmth, large windows are placed on the south side of the house to trap sunlight, while north-facing walls have good insulation and few windows. On the roof, solar collectors absorb energy from the sun's rays to heat water, while solar panels convert the sun's energy to electrical energy for use in household appliances. High-quality insulation is used in all outside walls to reduce heat lost through convection, conduction, and radiation. But because the sun does not shine continuously, solar-heated homes also use energy from conventional sources to keep the home heated day and night, year-round.

Large area of glass to trap radiant energy from the sun

Automated louvers for cooling when needed

Trees on south and west sides for summer shade

Positioning for sunlight
Windows should face south to trap as much light as possible from the winter sun, with few windows on the west side to reduce overheating in summer.

Summer sun

Winter sun

Evergreens provide a year-round windbreak.

Deciduous trees give summer shade.

Planting trees and shrubs
Trees placed away from the house act as a wind-break to reduce heat loss. Deciduous trees, planted closer, prevent overheating in summer, and allow sunlight to pass through in winter.

Solar panel to generate electricity

Solar collector to heat water

Well-insulated timber-framed walls

Small windows to reduce heat loss

Solar panels
Solar panels use the sun's energy to generate electricity for the home. The panels are made up of a series of linked photovoltaic cells. Light from the sun releases electrons from silicon atoms in the cells, producing an electric current. Rechargeable batteries can store electrical energy to provide power when there is no sunlight.

Sun's rays

Rechargeable battery

Entertainment or communication appliance

Solar panel on roof

Air conditioning system

Lighting

Electric circuit

Cooking appliance

Heating system

Stud frame

Plasterboard

Insulating material

Wall insulation
Wood is a natural insulator, so timber construction reduces heat flow through the walls. Filling the wall cavity with insulating material seals the walls against drafts, and greatly reduces heat loss.

Wood siding

Going Further

- Research solar-heated pools in the library or on the Internet. Make a poster display explaining how solar heating differs from a typical pool heating system. Include diagrams that explain how radiation, absorption, insulation, and convection are used in a solar-heated pool.

S team locomotives were one of the most important early uses of the steam engine. Prior to the locomotive, steam engines provided power for coal mines and mills. But don't think that steam engines are only a thing of the past. In fact, most electric power plants today use steam turbines, a very efficient kind of steam engine.

Heat Engines

Heat engines played a key role in the development of the modern industrial world. **The two main types of heat engines are the external combustion engine and the internal combustion engine.**

External Combustion Engine A steam engine is an **external combustion engine**—an engine that burns fuel outside the engine. Thomas Newcomen developed the first practical steam engine in 1712. His engine was used to pump water out of coal mines. In 1765, James Watt designed an engine that was more efficient, in part because it operated at a higher temperature.

Figure 11 shows one type of steam engine. Hot steam enters the cylinder on the right side. When the valve slides to the left, hot steam is trapped in the cylinder. The steam expands and cools as it pushes the piston to the left. Thus heat is converted into work. The piston moves back and forth as hot steam enters first on one side and then on the other side.

Figure 11 In an external combustion engine, combustion occurs outside of the engine.

Internal Combustion Engine Most cars use internal combustion engines that burn gasoline. An **internal combustion engine** is a heat engine in which the fuel burns inside the engine. Most internal combustion engines use pistons that move up and down inside cylinders. Each upward or downward motion of a piston is called a stroke. The linear motion of each stroke is converted into rotary motion by the crankshaft. The crankshaft is connected to the transmission, which is linked to the vehicle's wheels through the drive shaft.

Figure 12 shows the sequence of events in one cylinder of a four-stroke engine. In the intake stroke, a mixture of air and gasoline vapor enters the cylinder. Next, in the compression stroke, the piston compresses the gas mixture. At the end of compression, the spark plug ignites the mixture, which heats the gas under pressure. In the power stroke, the hot gas expands and drives the piston down. During the exhaust stroke, gas leaves the cylinder, and the cycle repeats.

Recall that a heat engine must discharge some waste energy in order to do work. In an internal combustion engine, the cooling system and exhaust transfer heat from the engine to the environment. A coolant—usually water and antifreeze—absorbs some thermal energy from the engine and then passes through the radiator. A fan blows air through the radiator, transferring thermal energy to the atmosphere. Without a cooling system, an engine would be damaged by thermal expansion. If you are ever in a car that overheats, stop driving and allow the engine to cool. Otherwise, there is a risk of serious damage to the engine.

Gasoline engines are more efficient than old-fashioned steam engines, but they still are not very efficient. Only about one third of the fuel energy in a gasoline engine is converted to work. Auto makers have tried several ways to make engines more efficient. One design, called a hybrid design, uses a heat engine together with an electric motor. This design is explained in the How It Works box on the next page.

For: Activity on four-stroke engines
Visit: PHSchool.com
Web Code: ccp-2163

Figure 12 In an internal combustion engine, fuel is burned inside the engine. Most cars have a four-stroke internal combustion engine. This diagram shows only one of the cylinders during each stroke. **Classifying** *In which of the strokes does the piston do work that can be used by the car?*

A Intake stroke   **B** Compression stroke   **C** Power stroke   **D** Exhaust stroke

Cylinder
Piston
Intake valve
Air-fuel mixture
Spark plug
Exhaust valve
Exhaust gases

Hybrid Automobile

Internal combustion engines produce harmful emissions from the combustion of gasoline. Recently, cleaner electric cars have been developed, but these need frequent recharging. Hybrid cars solve these problems by using a combination of smaller gasoline engines and electric motors. **Interpreting Diagrams** *Which features of the hybrid automobile help to reduce fuel consumption?*

A new breed of car
This hybrid car was first produced in 1999. It is light, aerodynamic, and has a small, efficient engine.

Lightweight materials *A small engine and synthetic materials, such as carbon fiber, reduce the car's weight to improve fuel efficiency.*

Aerodynamic body *The teardrop shape reduces air resistance, improving efficiency.*

Battery *The battery stores energy for the electric motor.*

Gasoline engine *This small heat engine is most efficient for cruising at constant speed. It is assisted by the electric motor during acceleration.*

Fuel tank

Electric motor *The electric motor is more efficient than a heat engine for accelerating at low speeds. When the brakes are used, the electric motor acts as a generator, recharging the batteries. This way of generating power is called regenerative braking.*

Transmission *This converts the rotation of shafts in the electric motor and the gas engine into wheel rotation. In this model, both the electric motor and the engine can directly drive the transmission.*

Tires *These tires are inflated to a higher pressure than conventional tires to reduce friction.*

Heating Systems

At the start of the industrial revolution, wood-burning fireplaces were the principal method of heating buildings. Rumford was keenly aware of the drawbacks of fireplaces. They were smoky and not very efficient. Too much heat went up the chimney. In 1796, Rumford designed a fireplace that now bears his name. His fireplace was not as deep as standard fireplaces, and it had slanted walls to reflect heat into the room. His improvements were quickly accepted and used throughout England.

Today, fireplaces are often used to supplement central heating systems. A **central heating system** heats many rooms from one central location. The central location of a heating system often is in the basement. The most commonly used energy sources for central heating systems are electrical energy, natural gas, oil, and coal. Heating systems differ in how they transfer thermal energy to the rest of the building. 🔑 **Most heating systems use convection to distribute thermal energy.**

Hot-Water Heating Figure 13 shows the main components of a hot-water heating system. At the boiler, heating oil or natural gas burns and heats the water. The circulating pump carries the hot water to radiators in each room. The hot water transfers thermal energy to the radiator by conduction. As the pipes heat up, they heat the room air by conduction and radiation. Hot air rises and sets up a convection current in each room. After transferring much of its thermal energy to the room, the cooled water returns to the boiler and the cycle begins again.

Temperature is controlled by a thermostat. One kind of thermostat is like a thermometer, with a strip of brass and steel wound up in a coil. When the heating system is on, the coil heats up. The two metals in the coil expand at different rates, and the coil rotates. This trips a switch to turn off the heat. As the room cools, the coil rotates in the opposite direction, until it trips the switch to turn the heat back on.

Steam Heating Steam heating is very similar to hot-water heating except that steam is used instead of hot water. The transfer of heat from the steam-heated radiator to the room still occurs by conduction and radiation. Steam heating often is used in older buildings or when many buildings are heated from one central location.

Reading Checkpoint *How are fireplaces often used today?*

Figure 13 Within the pipes of this hot-water heating system, the water circulates in a convection current. In each room, the air moves in a convection current. **Relating Cause and Effect** *Why has the water returning to the boiler cooled down?*

Thermostat

Radiator

Exhaust vent

Expansion tank

Boiler

Circulating pump

Figure 14 In a forced-air central heating system, the hot air enters the room through a supply vent in the floor. The hot air rises as cooler, denser air in the room sinks. The cooler air returns to the furnace through the return vent. **Inferring** *If the hot air supply vent were located near the ceiling, what would be the warmest part of the room?*

Cool air sinks

Hot air rises

Supply vent

Chimney

Return vent

Duct

Furnace

Electric Baseboard Heating An electric baseboard heater uses electrical energy to heat a room. A conductor similar to the heating element in an electric stove is used to convert electrical energy to thermal energy. The hot coil heats the air near it by conduction and radiation. Then convection circulates the warm air to heat the room.

Radiant heaters are similar to electric baseboard heating. They are often sold as small portable units, and are used to supplement a central heating system. These "space heaters" are easy to turn on and off and to direct onto cold toes or other areas where heat is needed most. Sometimes these heaters have a fan that helps to circulate heat.

Forced-Air Heating To maintain even room temperatures, forced-air heating systems use fans to circulate warm air through ducts to the rooms of a building. In a forced-air heating system, shown in Figure 15, convection circulates air in each room. Because the warm air entering the room rises toward the ceiling, the warm-air vents are located near the floor. Cool room air returns to the furnace through floor vents on the other side of the room. One advantage of forced-air heating is that the air is cleaned as it passes through filters located near the furnace.

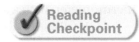 **Reading Checkpoint** *How do forced-air heating systems circulate air?*

Cooling Systems

Most cooling systems, such as refrigerators and air conditioners, are heat pumps. A **heat pump** is a device that reverses the normal flow of thermal energy. Heat pumps do this by circulating a refrigerant through tubing. A **refrigerant** is a fluid that vaporizes and condenses inside the tubing of a heat pump. When the refrigerant absorbs heat, it vaporizes, or turns into a gas. When the refrigerant gives off heat, it condenses, or turns back into a liquid.

Recall that thermal energy flows spontaneously from hot objects to cold objects. 🔑 **Heat pumps must do work on a refrigerant in order to reverse the normal flow of thermal energy.** In this process, a cold area, such as the inside of a refrigerator, becomes even colder.

What Is the Real Cost of a Washing Machine?

If you ever shop for a new washing machine, you'll notice the bright yellow Energy Guide sticker on each machine. The sticker gives the machine's operating cost per year as estimated by the U.S. Department of Energy. The largest part of the cost for cleaning clothes is heating the water that goes into the washing machine. So a machine that uses less water is more efficient.

Comparing Washing Machines

1. **Using Graphs** One family uses an electric water heater. What is their cost per year for machine A? For machine D?

2. **Calculating** How much money does this family save each year using machine A compared to using machine D?

3. **Calculating** The price of machine A is $300 more than the price of machine D. If the family uses a machine for 10 years, which

one costs less overall? (*Hint:* Add the price to the operating cost for 10 years.)

4. **Calculating** Another family uses a gas water heater. Which machine should this family choose? Explain your thinking.

5. **Evaluating and Revising** A washing machine advertisement states that the annual cost assumes an electric water heater is used. Why would an advertisement include only this cost?

Refrigerators A refrigerator is a heat pump—it transfers thermal energy from the cold food compartment to the warm room. To move heat from a colder to a warmer location, a motor must do work to move refrigerant through tubing inside the refrigerator walls. Could you cool your kitchen on a hot day by leaving the refrigerator door open? It might seem so, but an open refrigerator would actually heat the kitchen! You may have noticed the hot coils underneath or behind the refrigerator. The coils not only release heat absorbed from the food compartment; they also release thermal energy produced by the work the motor does. That is why a refrigerator with an open door adds more heat to the room than it removes.

 What is a heat pump?

Figure 15 When a refrigerator door is open, some thermal energy from the room enters the refrigerator. But more thermal energy leaves the refrigerator through the coils underneath the food compartment.
Interpreting Photos *Why can't you cool a room by leaving the refrigerator door open?*

Temperature in room: 25°C

Temperature inside refrigerator: 3°C

Warm air out

Condenser coil
Vapor cools to liquid
as heat is removed.

Cold
air out

Compressor

Warm
air in

Expansion valve
Pressure drops, causing liquid
refrigerant to become cold.

Evaporator coil
Liquid absorbs heat
to become vapor.

Figure 16 In a window air conditioner, outside air is heated as a fan blows it through the condenser coil. Inside the room, a fan draws in warm air through the evaporator coil. The fan blows cooled air out into the room. **Interpreting Diagrams** *What work is done by the compressor?*

Air Conditioners Have you ever been outside on a hot day and stood near a room air conditioner? The air conditioner is actually heating the outdoor air. Near the air conditioner is the last place you'd want to be on a hot day!

Where does the hot air come from? It must come from inside the house. But as you know from the second law of thermodynamics, heat only flows from a lower temperature (indoors) to a higher temperature (outdoors) if work is done on the system.

Figure 16 shows how a room air conditioner operates. The compressor raises the temperature and pressure of the refrigerant, turning it into a hot, high-pressure gas. The temperature of the condenser coil is higher than the outside air temperature, so heat flows spontaneously from the coil to the outside air. A fan increases the rate at which heat flows. As thermal energy is removed from the coil, the refrigerant cools and condenses into a liquid.

The liquid refrigerant then flows through the expansion valve and decreases in temperature. As the cold refrigerant flows through the evaporator coil, it absorbs thermal energy from the warm room air. The fan sends cold air back into the room. The refrigerant becomes a vapor, and the process starts all over again.

Section 16.3 Assessment

Reviewing Concepts

1. List the two main types of heat engines.

2. How is thermal energy distributed in most heating systems?

3. How does a heat pump move thermal energy from a cold area to a warm area?

4. If the efficiency of a gasoline engine is 25 percent, what happens to the missing 75 percent of the energy in the fuel?

Critical Thinking

5. **Predicting** A diesel engine runs at a higher temperature than a gasoline engine. Predict which engine would be more efficient. Explain your answer.

6. **Applying Concepts** Why would it be a mistake to locate a wood-burning stove on the second floor of a two-story house?

Writing in Science

Writing to Persuade Imagine that you are a marketing executive in a company that sells HVAC (heating, ventilation, and air conditioning) equipment. Write a one-page flyer comparing four kinds of heating systems. Organize the flyer so it is easy for customers to see the benefits of each system.

Using Specific Heat to Analyze Metals

In this lab, you will determine the specific heat of steel and aluminum. Then you will use specific heat to analyze the composition of a metal can.

Problem
How can you use specific heat to determine the composition of a metal can?

Materials
- 10 steel bolts
- balance
- 50-cm length of string
- clamp
- ring stand
- boiling water bath (shared with class)
- thermometer
- 500-mL graduated cylinder
- ice water
- foam cup with lid
- aluminum nails
- crushed can

 For the probeware version of this lab, see the Probeware Lab Manual, Lab 7.

Skills
Calculating, Designing Experiments

Procedure

Part A: Determining Specific Heat

1. Copy the data table shown below.

Data Table		
	Water	Steel Bolt
Mass (g)		
Initial temperature (°C)		
Final temperature (°C)		
Specific heat (J/g•°C)	4.18	

2. Measure and record the mass of 10 steel bolts.

3. Tie the bolts to the string. Use a clamp and ring stand to suspend the bolts in the boiling water bath. **CAUTION** *Be careful not to splash boiling water.* After a few minutes, record the water temperature as the initial temperature of the bolts.

4. Use a graduated cylinder to pour 200 mL of ice water (without ice) into the foam cup. Record the mass and temperature of the ice water. (*Hint:* The density of water is 1 g/mL.)

5. Use the clamp to move the bolts into the cup of ice water. Cover the cup and insert the thermometer through the hole in the cover.

6. Gently swirl the water in the cup. Record the highest temperature as the final temperature for both the water and the steel bolts.

7. Calculate and record the specific heat of steel. (*Hint:* Use the equation $Q = m \times c \times \Delta T$ to calculate the energy the water absorbs.)

8. Repeat Steps 3 through 7 with aluminum nails to determine the specific heat of aluminum. Start by making a new data table. Use a mass of aluminum that is close to the mass you used for the steel bolts.

Part B: Design Your Own Experiment

9. **Designing Experiments** Design an experiment that uses specific heat to identify the metals a can might be made of.

10. Construct a data table in which to record your observations. After your teacher approves your plan, perform your experiment.

Analyze and Conclude

1. **Comparing and Contrasting** Which metal has a higher specific heat, aluminum or steel?

2. **Drawing Conclusions** Was the specific heat of the can closer to the specific heat of steel or of aluminum? What can you conclude about the material in the can?

3. **Evaluating** Did your observations prove what the can was made of? If not, what other information would you need to be sure?

4. **Inferring** The can you used is often called a tin can. The specific heat of tin is 0.23 J/g•°C. Did your data support the idea that the can was made mostly of tin? Explain your answer.

Study Guide

16.1 Thermal Energy and Matter

Key Concepts

- Heat flows spontaneously from hot objects to cold objects.
- Temperature is related to the average kinetic energy of an object's particles due to their random motion through space.
- Thermal energy depends on the mass, temperature, and phase (solid, liquid, or gas) of an object.
- Thermal expansion occurs because particles of matter tend to move farther apart as temperature increases.
- The lower a material's specific heat is, the more its temperature rises when a given amount of energy is absorbed by a given mass.
- A calorimeter uses the principle that heat flows from a hotter object to a colder object until both reach the same temperature.

Vocabulary

heat, *p. 474*
temperature, *p. 475*
absolute zero, *p. 475*
thermal expansion, *p. 476*
specific heat, *p. 476*
calorimeter, *p. 478*

16.2 Heat and Thermodynamics

Key Concepts

- Conduction in gases is slower than in liquids and solids because the particles in a gas collide less often.
- Convection currents are important in many natural cycles, such as ocean currents, weather systems, and movements of hot rock in Earth's interior.
- All objects radiate energy. As an object's temperature increases, the rate at which it radiates energy increases.
- The first law of thermodynamics states that energy is conserved.
- The second law of thermodynamics states that thermal energy can flow from colder objects to hotter objects only if work is done on the system.
- The third law of thermodynamics states that absolute zero cannot be reached.

Vocabulary

conduction, *p. 479*
thermal conductor, *p. 480*
thermal insulator, *p. 480*
convection, *p. 480*
convection current, *p. 481*
radiation, *p. 481*
thermodynamics, *p. 482*
heat engine, *p. 483*
waste heat, *p. 483*

16.3 Using Heat

Key Concepts

- The two main types of heat engines are the external combustion engine and the internal combustion engine.
- Most heating systems use convection to distribute thermal energy.
- Heat pumps must do work on a refrigerant in order to reverse the normal flow of thermal energy.

Vocabulary

external combustion engine, *p. 486*
internal combustion engine, *p. 487*
central heating system, *p. 489*
heat pump, *p. 490*
refrigerant, *p. 490*

Thinking Visually

Concept Map Copy the concept map below onto a sheet of paper. Use the information from the chapter to complete the diagram.

Reviewing Content

Choose the letter that best answers the question or completes the statement.

1. When a drill is used to bore a hole in an object,
   a. no useful work is done.
   b. no energy is lost due to friction.
   c. the drill is 100 percent efficient.
   d. friction causes the object to heat up.

2. Why does liquid rise in a thermometer?
   a. convection
   b. thermal expansion
   c. condensation
   d. radiation

3. To heat 1 g of water by 1°C requires
   a. 1 calorie.
   b. 1 Calorie.
   c. 1 joule.
   d. 1 watt.

4. The best thermal insulators
   a. conduct heat well.
   b. are gases.
   c. are metals.
   d. have free electrons.

5. A blow dryer transfers thermal energy mainly by
   a. conduction.
   b. convection.
   c. radiation.
   d. specific heat.

6. Which statement is NOT true about radiation?
   a. All objects radiate.
   b. Hot objects radiate faster than cold objects.
   c. Radiation only transfers energy in matter.
   d. The sun's energy reaches Earth by radiation.

7. Energy added to a system
   a. does work or increases thermal energy.
   b. cannot heat the environment.
   c. is converted to radiation.
   d. reduces the kinetic energy of the system.

8. All engines operate at less than 100 percent efficiency because they
   a. absorb heat.
   b. conduct heat.
   c. burn gasoline.
   d. emit heat.

9. Which occurs just before ignition?
   a. intake stroke
   b. compression stroke
   c. exhaust stroke
   d. power stroke

10. Which of the following is a FALSE statement about a heat pump?
    a. It requires no work.
    b. It moves heat from a cold to a hot area.
    c. It uses a refrigerant.
    d. Air conditioners are heat pumps.

Understanding Concepts

11. In what direction does heat flow? Why do particles of matter transfer thermal energy in this direction?

12. How can one object feel warmer than another object if the two objects are at the same temperature?

13. Why does a balloon filled with air expand when it is heated?

14. Power lines sag more between telephone poles in summer than in winter. Explain why this is so.

15. Why does a piece of steel heat up more than an equal mass of plastic when both absorb the same energy?

16. In a calorimeter, what determines how much energy is absorbed by the water?

17. Why are metals generally good thermal conductors?

18. How does sunlight reach an astronaut on the International Space Station?

19. How can the efficiency of a heat engine be improved?

20. What is waste heat?

21. What is the most important difference between an internal combustion engine and an external combustion engine?

22. Why does a heat pump need an external source of energy (such as electrical energy)?

23. Describe convection in a room heated by a radiator.

Critical Thinking

24. **Controlling Variables** You can tell if your sister has a low fever by feeling her forehead with your hand. Can you detect your own fever with your hand? Explain why or why not.

25. **Comparing and Contrasting** How are conduction, convection, and radiation similar to one another? How are they different?

26. **Applying Concepts** Why would an engine be less efficient on Venus than on Earth? (*Hint:* On Venus, the surface temperature is 460°C.)

27. **Predicting** Just after a heating system turns on, what part of a room will be warmest? When the heat turns off and the radiators are cold, what part of the room will be warmest? Explain.

Math Skills

Use the following graph to answer Questions 28–30.

Temperature Rise of 1 Gram of Different Materials

28. **Using Graphs** The same energy was added to each sample. Which material has the highest specific heat? Explain your answer.

29. **Calculating** The specific heat of aluminum is 0.90 J/g•°C and of iron is 0.45 J/g•°C. How much energy was absorbed by each 1-gram sample?

30. **Posing Questions** A friend infers from the graph that the temperature of a 10.0-g sample of iron would rise 110°C. What should she ask before using the graph this way?

Concepts in Action

31. **Applying Concepts** When you are outside on a cold winter day, which would you expect to be warmer, blood flowing toward your heart or blood flowing toward your fingers? Explain.

32. **Using Analogies** If you put a cover on a casserole at dinner, it will stay warm longer. In what way can this help you to explain why a calorimeter is more accurate if it is well insulated?

33. **Formulating Hypotheses** Some recipes say that while a pie is baking, aluminum foil should be put on the edges to keep the crust from burning. Hypothesize how the aluminum foil helps keep the crust from burning.

34. **Making Judgments** Suppose you try to heat an apartment using a portable heater in one of the rooms. Would a fan be helpful? Explain why or why not.

35. **Inferring** In a home heated only by solar energy, why is it especially important to have very good insulation?

36. **Writing in Science** Explain why a school might ask teachers to keep windows closed and the shades down during a heat wave.

Performance-Based Assessment

Making a Computer Presentation Make a computer slideshow presentation about conductors and insulators. Start by identifying various materials around your home as either good conductors or good insulators. Plan the organization of the slideshow. Finish the show with a summary table that classifies all of the materials in your presentation. Present your show to your class.

For: Self-grading assessment
Visit: PHSchool.com
Web Code: cca-2160

Standardized Test Prep

Choose the letter that best answers the question or completes the statement.

1. Which statement describes the direction of spontaneous heat flow?
   (A) Heat flows between two objects at the same temperature.
   (B) Heat flows in a vacuum by conduction.
   (C) Heat flows from an object at high temperature to one at low temperature.
   (D) Heat flows from an object at low temperature to one at high temperature.
   (E) Thermal energy can only be absorbed by cool objects.

2. How are refrigerants used to remove heat in a refrigerator?
   (A) The refrigerant vaporizes as it absorbs heat from the food.
   (B) The refrigerant vaporizes as it supplies heat to the food.
   (C) The refrigerant condenses as it absorbs heat from the food.
   (D) The refrigerant condenses and turns into a liquid, giving off heat to the food.
   (E) The refrigerant condenses and turns into a gas, giving off heat to the food.

3. The table below shows the average high and low temperatures in January and July for two cities at the same latitude. Both cities receive about the same amount of sunlight. Which city is on an island in the ocean and which city is in a desert?
   (A) City A is on an island; City B is in the desert.
   (B) Both cities are in the desert.
   (C) Both cities are on an island.
   (D) City B is on an island; City A is in the desert.
   (E) Not enough information is given.

City Temperatures				
	January High	January Low	July High	July Low
City A	26°C	18°C	28°C	20°C
City B	32°C	10°C	44°C	27°C

4. Which of the following best explains why gases expand more readily than liquids or solids?
   (A) Gases have less density than solids or liquids.
   (B) Gases are lighter than solids or liquids.
   (C) Gases have a higher average kinetic energy than solids or liquids.
   (D) Gas particles have weaker attractive forces than solids or liquids.
   (E) Gases are more compressible than solids or liquids.

5. Which substance will have the greatest increase in temperature when equal masses absorb equal amounts of thermal energy? (Specific heats are given in parentheses.)
   (A) water (4.18 J/g•°C)
   (B) ammonia gas (2.1 J/g•°C)
   (C) ethyl alcohol (2.43 J/g•°C)
   (D) aluminum (0.90 J/g•°C)
   (E) lead (0.46 J/g•°C)

6. Which of the following illustrates the first law of thermodynamics?
   (A) Refrigerators make objects colder.
   (B) A bicycle pump gets warm when used.
   (C) Stoves radiate energy.
   (D) Soft drinks served with ice melt the ice.
   (E) Absolute zero cannot be reached.

CHAPTER 17 Mechanical Waves and Sound

Ocean waves, like all mechanical waves, carry energy through a medium.

21st Century Learning

Information and Media Literacy

What are some useful applications of refraction?

One interesting example of wave behavior is refraction, which is the bending of a wave as it enters a new medium at an angle. Do Internet research on refraction and find out about some of the useful applications of this behavior. Create a multimedia presentation on refraction that includes text, diagrams, and photos, and deliver the presentation to the class.

How do science concepts apply to your world? Here are some questions you'll be able to answer after you read this chapter.

- Why does a wave topple over on itself when it approaches the shore? *(Section 17.1)*

- How does a surfer know when the next wave is coming? *(Section 17.2)*

- Why does a gymnast on a trampoline time her jumps to match the movement of the trampoline surface? *(Section 17.3)*

- How much faster is a sound wave than a car traveling on the highway? *(Section 17.4)*

- How can headphones reduce noise without interfering with sounds you want to hear? *(page 522)*

Chapter Preview

Inquiry Activity

How Does a Disturbance Produce Waves?

Procedure

1. Fill a clear plastic container and a dropper pipet with water.

2. Observe the surface of the water by looking down at an angle into the container. Use the dropper pipet to release a drop of water from a height of about 3 cm above the surface of the water.

3. Repeat Step 2 with a drop released from each of these heights: 10, 20, 50, and 70 cm.

Think About It

1. **Observing** Which drop produced the highest waves?

2. **Making Generalizations** In general, how would you expect the distance a drop falls to affect the wave it produces? Explain your answer.

3. **Formulating Hypotheses** Why does the distance a drop falls affect the height of the waves it produces? Explain your answer.

17.1 Mechanical Waves

Reading Focus

Key Concepts
- What causes mechanical waves?
- What are the three main types of mechanical waves?

Vocabulary
- mechanical wave
- medium
- crest
- trough
- transverse wave
- compression
- rarefaction
- longitudinal wave
- surface wave

Reading Strategy
Previewing Copy the web diagram below. Use Figure 2 to complete the diagram. Then use Figures 3 and 4 to make similar diagrams for longitudinal waves and surface waves.

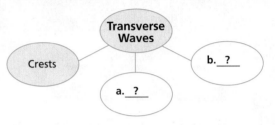

Have you ever gone to a wave pool at an amusement park? You can hear the laughter and screams as wave after wave passes by, giving the people a wild ride. It's obvious that waves are moving through the water, but you may not realize that the screams and laughter are also carried by waves. In this chapter, you will learn about the different kinds of mechanical waves, including sound waves.

What Are Mechanical Waves?

A **mechanical wave** is a disturbance in matter that carries energy from one place to another. Recall that energy is the ability to do work. In a wave pool, each wave carries energy across the pool. You can see the effects of a wave's energy when the wave lifts people in the water.

Mechanical waves require matter to travel through. The material through which a wave travels is called a **medium.** Solids, liquids, and gases all can act as mediums. In a wave pool, waves travel along the surface of the water. Water is the medium. Waves travel through a rope when you shake one end of it. In that case, the medium is the rope.

A **mechanical wave is created when a source of energy causes a vibration to travel through a medium.** A vibration is a repeating back-and-forth motion. When you shake a rope, you add energy at one end. The wave that results is a vibration that carries energy along the rope.

Figure 1 In a wave pool, the waves carry energy across the pool.

Types of Mechanical Waves

Mechanical waves are classified by the way they move through a medium. The three main types of mechanical waves are transverse waves, longitudinal waves, and surface waves.

Transverse Waves When you shake one end of a rope up and down, the vibration causes a wave. Figure 2 shows a wave in a rope at three points in time. Before the wave starts, every point on the rope is in its rest position, represented by the dashed line. The highest point of the wave above the rest position is the **crest.** The lowest point below the rest position is the **trough** (TRAWF). You can see from the ribbon attached to the rope that crests and troughs are not fixed points on a wave. In Figure 2A, the ribbon is at a crest. In Figure 2C, the ribbon is at a trough. The motion of a single point on the rope is like the motion of a yo-yo. The point vibrates up and down between a maximum and minimum height.

Notice that the wave carries energy from left to right, in a direction perpendicular to the up-and-down motion of the rope. This is a transverse wave. A **transverse wave** is a wave that causes the medium to vibrate at right angles to the direction in which the wave travels.

Have you ever shaken crumbs off a picnic blanket? This is another example of a transverse wave. Shaking one end of the blanket up and down sends a transverse wave through the blanket. The up and down motion of the blanket helps to shake off the crumbs.

Go Online

SciLINKS

For: Links on vibrations and waves
Visit: www.SciLinks.org
Web Code: ccn-2171

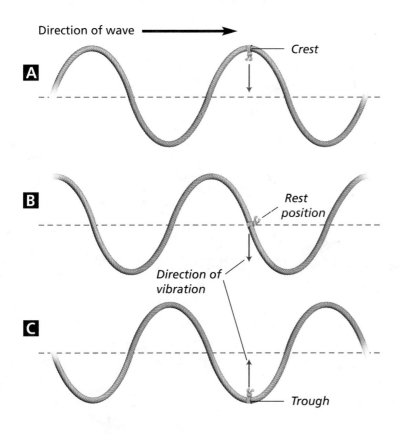

Figure 2 A transverse wave causes the medium to vibrate in a direction perpendicular to the direction in which the wave travels. In the wave shown here, each point on the rope vibrates up and down between a maximum and minimum height. **A** The ribbon is at a crest. **B** The ribbon is at the rest position. **C** The ribbon is at a trough.
Comparing and Contrasting *How does the direction of the wave compare with the direction in which the ribbon moves?*

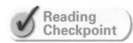

Quick Lab

Observing Waves in a Medium

Procedure

1. Fill a large, clear, square or rectangular container halfway with water. Add a drop of food coloring in the center of the container.

2. At the side of the container, submerge a ruler lengthwise. Move the ruler up and down to make waves.

3. Observe and record how the waves and the food coloring move.

Analyze and Conclude

1. **Comparing and Contrasting** Compare the movement of the waves with the movement of the food coloring.

2. **Formulating Hypotheses** Generate one or more hypotheses to explain the observed motion of the food coloring.

Longitudinal Waves Figure 3 shows a wave in a spring toy at two points in time. To start the wave, add energy to the spring by pushing and pulling the end of the spring. The wave carries energy along the spring from left to right. You can see in Figure 3A that when the wave starts, some of the coils are closer together than they would be in the rest position. An area where the particles in a medium are spaced close together is called a **compression** (kum PRESH un). As the compression moves to the right in Figure 3B, coils behind it are spread out more than they were in the rest position. An area where the particles in a medium are spread out is called a **rarefaction** (rehr uh FAK shun).

Look at the ribbon tied to one of the coils. The ribbon is first in a compression and then in a rarefaction. However, the ribbon and the coil it is tied to do not move along the spring. As compressions and rarefactions travel along the spring toward the right, each coil vibrates back and forth around its rest position. In this wave, the vibration is a back-and-forth motion of the coil that is parallel to, or in the same direction as, the direction in which the wave moves. This is a longitudinal wave. A **longitudinal wave** (lawn juh TOO duh nul) is a wave in which the vibration of the medium is parallel to the direction the wave travels.

Waves in springs are not the only kind of longitudinal waves. P waves (originally called primary waves) are longitudinal waves produced by earthquakes. Because P waves can travel through Earth, scientists can use these waves to map Earth's unseen interior.

Reading Checkpoint *What are compressions and rarefactions?*

Figure 3 A longitudinal wave causes the medium to vibrate in a direction parallel to the direction in which the wave travels. Each point on the spring vibrates back and forth about its rest position. **A** When the end of the spring is pushed, a compression starts to move along the spring. **B** When the end of the spring is pulled, a rarefaction follows the compression along the spring.

Surface Waves If you ask people to describe waves, most likely they will describe ocean waves before they think of the waves that travel in a rope or a spring. Ocean waves are the most familiar kind of surface waves. A **surface wave** is a wave that travels along a surface separating two media.

The ocean wave in Figure 4 travels at the surface between water and air. The floating fishing bobber helps to visualize the motion of the medium as the wave carries energy from left to right. When a crest passes the bobber, the bobber moves up. When a trough passes, the bobber moves down. This up-and-down motion, like the motion of a transverse wave, is perpendicular to the direction in which the wave travels. But the bobber also is pushed back and forth by the surface wave. This back-and-forth motion, like the motion of a longitudinal wave, is parallel to the direction in which the wave travels. When these two motions combine in deep water, the bobber moves in a circle.

If you watched the bobber for ten minutes, it would not move closer to shore. Most waves do not transport matter from one place to another. But when ocean waves approach the shore, they behave differently. Perhaps you have seen seaweed washed ashore by breaking waves. As a wave enters shallow water, it topples over on itself because friction with the shore slows down the bottom of the wave. The top of the wave continues forward at its original speed. As a result, the wave carries the medium, along with anything floating in it, toward the shore.

Wave direction →

Figure 4 As the ocean wave moves to the right, the bobber moves in a circle, returning to its original position.
Making Generalizations *If these were breaking waves near the shore, what would happen to the bobber over time?*

Section 17.1 Assessment

Reviewing Concepts

1. ☁ Describe how mechanical waves are produced.

2. ☁ List the three main types of mechanical waves.

3. For each type of wave, compare the vibration of the medium to the direction of the wave.

4. Name one example of each type of wave.

Critical Thinking

5. **Comparing and Contrasting** How are transverse and longitudinal waves similar? How are they different?

6. **Applying Concepts** A spring hangs from the ceiling. Describe how a single coil moves as a longitudal wave passes through the spring.

7. **Interpreting Diagrams** In Figure 4, why is the first position of the bobber the same as the fifth position of the bobber?

Connecting ⊂ Concepts

Energy Review potential and kinetic energy in Section 15.1. Then, describe the energy changes in a single coil of a spring as longitudinal waves pass through it.

17.2 Properties of Mechanical Waves

Reading Focus

Key Concepts

- What determines the frequency of a wave?
- How are frequency, wavelength, and speed related?
- How is the amplitude of a wave related to the wave's energy?

Vocabulary

- periodic motion
- period
- frequency
- hertz
- wavelength
- amplitude

Reading Strategy

Building Vocabulary Copy and expand the table below. As you read, write a definition in your own words for each term.

Vocabulary Term	Definition
Period	a. ___?___
Frequency	b. ___?___
Wavelength	c. ___?___
Amplitude	d. ___?___

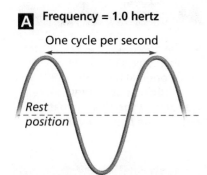

A Frequency = 1.0 hertz

One cycle per second

Rest position

B Frequency = 2.0 hertz

Two cycles per second

Figure 5 Frequency is the number of complete cycles in a given time. **A** A wave vibrating at one cycle per second has a frequency of 1.0 Hz. **B** A wave vibrating at two cycles per second has a frequency of 2.0 Hz.

Will it be a good day for surfing? You might not think that a surfer would check the Internet to find out. But some Web sites now update ocean wave data every hour. Of course, fishing boats and naval vessels also need this information. Usually, the properties used to describe waves are period, frequency, wavelength, speed, and amplitude.

Frequency and Period

How do surfers know when the next wave is coming? If they count the time between two successive crests, the next crest usually will come after this same time interval. Any motion that repeats at regular time intervals is called **periodic motion.** The time required for one cycle, a complete motion that returns to its starting point, is called the **period.** For an ocean wave, the period is the time between two successive crests.

Any periodic motion has a **frequency,** which is the number of complete cycles in a given time. For a wave, the frequency is the number of wave cycles that pass a point in a given time. Frequency is measured in cycles per second, or **hertz** (Hz).

A wave's frequency equals the frequency of the vibrating source producing the wave. The rope in Figure 5A is shaken with a frequency of one vibration per second, so the wave frequency is one cycle per second, or 1 hertz. In Figure 5B, the vibration is twice as fast, so the frequency is two cycles per second, or 2 hertz.

Comparing Frequency and Wave Speed

Materials

3-m rope, tape measure, stopwatch

Procedure

1. Tie one end of the rope to a chair. Shake the other end to send waves down the rope.

2. With a partner, measure the time it takes your hand to move back and forth ten times. Then, measure and record the distance from your hand to the chair and the time it takes a wave crest to travel this distance.

3. Repeat Step 2, but this time shake the rope more rapidly. Record your data.

Analyze and Conclude

1. **Calculating** What was the frequency of the waves in Steps 2 and 3? (*Hint:* Divide 10 waves by the time it took to make them.)

2. **Calculating** What was the wave speed in Steps 2 and 3? (*Hint:* Divide distance by time.)

3. **Drawing Conclusions** How was wave speed affected by increasing the frequency?

Wavelength

Wavelength is the distance between a point on one wave and the same point on the next cycle of the wave. For a transverse wave, wavelength is measured between adjacent crests or between adjacent troughs. For a longitudinal wave, wavelength is the distance between adjacent compressions or rarefactions. Notice in Figure 6 that when wavelength is shorter, crests are closer together. They must occur more frequently. **Increasing the frequency of a wave decreases its wavelength.**

Reading Checkpoint *What is wavelength?*

Wave Speed

Recall that the speed of an object equals distance divided by time. To calculate a swimmer's speed, for example, you can measure the length of one lap in a pool and the time it takes to swim one lap. This is like measuring the wavelength (one lap) and period (time to swim one lap) of the swimmer's motion. In much the same way, you can calculate the speed of a wave by dividing its wavelength by its period. You can also calculate wave speed by multiplying wavelength by frequency.

Speed of Waves

$$\text{Speed} = \text{Wavelength} \times \text{Frequency}$$

When the wavelength is in meters and the frequency is in hertz, the units for speed are meters per second. If you know any two of the values in this formula, you can solve for the third value.

A

B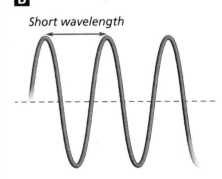

Figure 6 Wavelength can be measured from any point on a wave to the same point on the next cycle of the wave. **A** The wavelength of a transverse wave equals the distance from crest to crest or from trough to trough. **B.** The wavelength of this wave is half the wavelength of the wave in A. **Inferring** *Which wave has a greater frequency?*

Math Skills

Speed of Mechanical Waves

One end of a rope is vibrated to produce a wave with a wavelength of 0.25 meters. The frequency of the wave is 3.0 hertz. What is the speed of the wave?

1. Read and Understand

What information are you given?

Wavelength = 0.25 m

Frequency = 3.0 Hz

2. Plan and Solve

What unknown are you trying to calculate?

Speed = ?

What formula contains the given quantities and the unknown?

Speed = Wavelength × Frequency

Replace each variable with its known value.
(Hint: $1 Hz = \frac{1}{s}$)

Speed = 0.25 m × 3.0 Hz

$= 0.25 \text{ m} \times 3.0 \frac{1}{s}$

Speed = 0.75 m/s

3. Look Back and Check

Is your answer reasonable?

Because the frequency is 3.0 hertz, the wave should travel a distance of 3 wavelengths in 1 second. This distance is 0.75 meters, which agrees with the calculated speed of 0.75 m/s.

Math Practice

1. A wave on a rope has a wavelength of 2.0 m and a frequency of 2.0 Hz. What is the speed of the wave?

2. A motorboat is tied to a dock with its motor running. The spinning propeller makes a surface wave in the water with a frequency of 4 Hz and a wavelength of 0.1 m. What is the speed of the wave?

3. What is the speed of a wave in a spring if it has a wavelength of 10 cm and a period of 0.2 s? (*Hint:* Use the equation Speed = $\frac{\text{Wavelength}}{\text{Period}}$.)

4. What is the wavelength of an earthquake wave if it has a speed of 5 km/s and a frequency of 10 Hz?

For: Links on wave properties
Visit: www.SciLinks.org
Web Code: ccn-2172

The speed of a wave can change if it enters a new medium or if variables such as pressure and temperature change. However, for many kinds of waves, the speed of the waves is roughly constant for a range of different frequencies. **If you assume that waves are traveling at a constant speed, then wavelength is inversely proportional to frequency.** What does this mean for two waves with different frequencies? The wave with the lower frequency has a longer wavelength.

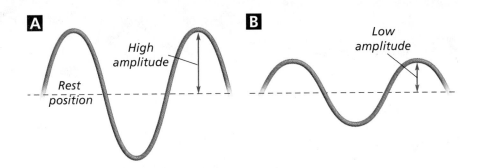

A

High amplitude

Rest position

B

Low amplitude

Figure 7 The more energy a wave has, the greater is its amplitude. **A** The amplitude of a transverse wave equals the distance to the highest point above the rest position. **B** This wave's amplitude is one half the amplitude of the wave in A. **Applying Concepts** *Which wave has more energy?*

Amplitude

If you drop a pebble into a pond, the wave is not very high. If you do a "cannonball" jump into the water, you know the wave will be much higher. These two waves have different amplitudes. The **amplitude** (AM pluh tood) of a wave is the maximum displacement of the medium from its rest position.

Figure 7 shows the amplitudes of two transverse waves in a rope. The amplitude of a transverse wave is the distance from the rest position to a crest or a trough. It takes more energy to produce a wave with higher crests and deeper troughs. ◯ **The more energy a wave has, the greater is its amplitude.**

How do you measure the amplitude of a longitudinal wave? In this case, the amplitude is the maximum displacement of a point from its rest position. The more energy the wave has, the more the medium will be compressed or displaced.

-Go Online
PLANETDIARY

For: Activity on tsunamis
Visit: PHSchool.com
Web Code: ccc-2172

Section 17.2 Assessment

Reviewing Concepts

1. ◯ How is the vibration of the source related to a wave's frequency?

2. ◯ How is wavelength related to frequency for waves moving at a constant speed?

3. ◯ How is the energy of a wave related to its amplitude?

4. Describe two ways you could measure the wavelength of a longitudinal wave.

5. Describe how you measure the amplitude of a transverse wave.

Critical Thinking

6. **Applying Concepts** If a wave's period doubles, how does the wave's frequency change? (*Hint:* Period $= \frac{1}{\text{Frequency}}$)

7. **Designing Experiments** Describe an experiment to measure the frequency of a longitudinal wave in a spring.

8. **Predicting** If you double the frequency of a wave, what is the effect on its wavelength (assuming speed does not change)?

Math Practice

9. A wave on a rope has a frequency of 3.3 Hz and a wavelength of 1.2 m. What is the speed of the wave?

10. A spring toy vibrates at 2 Hz to produce a wave. What is the period of the wave?

17.3 Behavior of Waves

Reading Focus

Key Concepts

- How does reflection change a wave?
- What causes the refraction of a wave when it enters a new medium?
- What factors affect the amount of diffraction of a wave?
- What are two types of interference?
- What wavelengths will produce a standing wave?

Vocabulary

- reflection
- refraction
- diffraction
- interference
- constructive interference
- destructive interference
- standing wave
- node
- antinode

Reading Strategy

Identifying Main Ideas Copy and expand the table below. As you read, write the main idea of each topic.

Topic	Main Idea
Reflection	a. _____?_____
Refraction	b. _____?_____
Diffraction	c. _____?_____
Interference	d. _____?_____
Standing waves	e. _____?_____

Have you ever noticed bright lines like those shown in Figure 8 dancing on the bottom of a pool? These lines are produced when light shines through waves on the surface of the water. The lines don't seem to have a pattern because there are so many waves interacting. Imagine following just one of these waves. What will happen when it strikes the side of the pool? When it encounters another wave or an obstacle like a person? As the waves crisscross back and forth, many interactions can occur, including reflection, refraction, diffraction, and interference.

Figure 8 The ripples visible on the bottom of the pool are caused by light shining through surface waves.

Reflection

The next time you are in a pool, try to observe ripples as they hit the side of the pool. **Reflection** occurs when a wave bounces off a surface that it cannot pass through. The reflection of a wave is like the reflection of a ball thrown at a wall. The ball cannot go through the wall, so it bounces back.

If you send a transverse wave down a rope attached to a wall, the wave reflects when it hits the wall. **Reflection does not change the speed or frequency of a wave, but the wave can be flipped upside down.** If reflection occurs at a fixed boundary, then the reflected wave will be upside down compared to the original wave.

Refraction

Refraction is the bending of a wave as it enters a new medium at an angle. Imagine pushing a lawnmower from grass onto gravel, as shown in Figure 9. The direction of the lawnmower changes because one wheel enters the gravel before the other one does. The wheel on the gravel slows down, but the other wheel is still moving at a faster speed on the grass. The speed difference between the two wheels causes the lawnmower to change direction. Refraction changes the direction of a wave in much the same way. ◖ **When a wave enters a medium at an angle, refraction occurs because one side of the wave moves more slowly than the other side.**

Figure 10 shows the refraction of an ocean wave as it flows into a shallow area. The shallower water can be considered a new medium. The lines on the photograph show the changing direction of the wave. These lines, called wave fronts, are parallel to the crests of the wave.

Notice that the wave fronts approach the shore at an angle. The left side of each wave enters shallower water before the right side does. As the left side of the wave slows down, the wave bends toward the left.

If a wave front is parallel to the shoreline, the wave enters the shallower water all at once. The wave will slow down but it will not change direction. Refraction of the wave occurs only when the two sides of a wave travel at different speeds.

 Reading Checkpoint *What is refraction?*

Figure 9 A lawnmower turns when it is pushed at an angle from the grass onto the gravel. **Relating Cause and Effect** *Explain why the lawnmower straightens out after both wheels are on the gravel.*

Labels on Figure 9: Grass — Gravel — Left wheel is still rolling faster on grass. — Direction changes. — Mower pivots because the right wheel moves more slowly when it reaches gravel.

Figure 10 As an ocean wave approaches the shore at an angle, the wave bends, or refracts, because one side of each wave front slows down before the other side does.

Mechanical Waves and Sound **509**

Figure 11 A Mechanical waves, like the water waves shown here, diffract as they move past an obstacle or through an opening. **A** This wave diffracts, or spreads out, after it passes through a narrow opening. **B** Diffraction also occurs when a wave encounters an obstacle.

Diffraction

Diffraction (dih FRAK shun) is the bending of a wave as it moves around an obstacle or passes through a narrow opening. Figure 11A shows how water waves spread out as they pass through a narrow opening. The pattern produced is very similar to the circular ripples you see when a pebble is tossed into a pond. Diffraction also occurs when waves bend around an obstacle, as shown in Figure 11B.

🔑 **A wave diffracts more if its wavelength is large compared to the size of an opening or obstacle.** If the wavelength is small compared to the opening or obstacle, the wave bends very little. The larger the wavelength is compared to the size to the opening or obstacle, the more the wave diffracts.

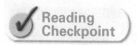 **Reading Checkpoint** *What is diffraction?*

Interference

If two balls collide, they cannot continue on their original paths as if they had never met. But waves can occupy the same region of space and then continue on. **Interference** occurs when two or more waves overlap and combine together. 🔑 **Two types of interference are constructive interference and destructive interference.** The displacements of waves combine to increase amplitude in constructive interference and to decrease amplitude in destructive interference.

Go Online

NSTA *SciLINKS*

For: Links on diffraction and interference
Visit: www.SciLinks.org
Web Code: ccn-2173

Constructive Interference Imagine a child being pushed on a swing by her mother. If the mother times her pushes correctly, she will push on the swing just as the child starts to move forward. Then the mother's effort is maximized and the child gets a boost to go higher. In the same way, the amplitudes of two waves can add together. **Constructive interference** occurs when two or more waves combine to produce a wave with a larger displacement.

What happens if you and a friend send waves with equal frequencies toward each other on a jump rope? Figure 12A shows how constructive interference produces a wave with an increased amplitude. The crests of waves 1 and 2 combine to make a higher crest in wave 3. At the point where two troughs meet, wave 3 has a lower trough.

Destructive Interference What happens if the mother has bad timing while pushing on the swing? Instead of working to boost her daughter upward, some of her effort is wasted, and the girl will not swing as high. In much the same way, destructive interference can reduce the amplitude of a wave. **Destructive interference** occurs when two or more waves combine to produce a wave with a smaller displacements.

In Figure 12B, two waves with the same frequency meet, but this time the crest of wave 1 meets the trough of wave 2. The resulting wave 3 has a crest at this point, but it is lower than the crest of wave 1. Destructive interference produces a wave with a reduced amplitude.

Go Online
active art

For: Activity on interference
Visit: PHSchool.com
Web Code: ccp-2173

Figure 12 Two waves with equal frequencies travel in opposite directions. The motions are graphed here to make it easier to see how the waves combine. **A** When a crest meets a crest, the result is a wave with an increased amplitude. **B** When a crest meets a trough, the result is a wave with a reduced amplitude.
Making Generalizations *How is the amplitude of wave 3 related to the amplitudes of waves 1 and 2?*

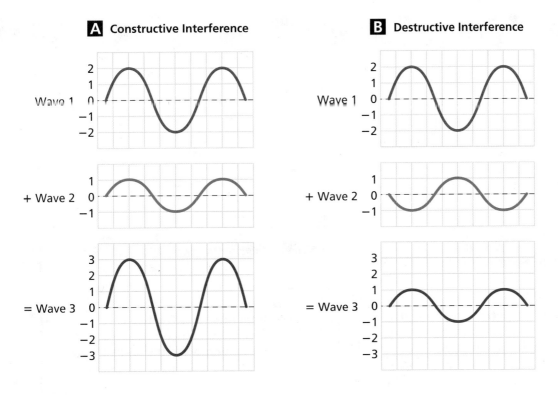

A Constructive Interference

B Destructive Interference

Mechanical Waves and Sound **511**

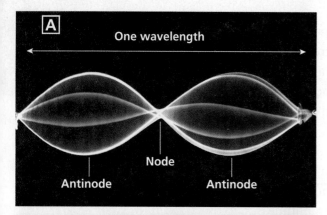

A One wavelength

Antinode

Node

Antinode

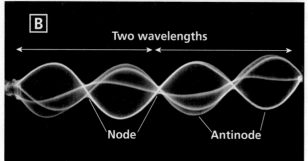

B Two wavelengths

Node

Antinode

Figure 13 These photos show standing waves for two different frequencies. **A** One wavelength equals the length of the cord. **B** Two wavelengths equal the length of the cord.
Interpreting Photos *In which photo do the waves have a longer wavelength?*

Standing Waves

If you tie one end of a rope to a chair and shake the other end, waves travel up the rope, reflect off the chair, and travel back down the rope. Interference occurs as the incoming waves pass through the reflected waves. At certain frequencies, interference between a wave and its reflection can produce a standing wave. A **standing wave** is a wave that appears to stay in one place—it does not seem to move through the medium.

You can observe a standing wave if you pluck a guitar string or any elastic cord. Only certain points on the wave, called nodes, are stationary. A **node** is a point on a standing wave that has no displacement from the rest position. At the nodes, there is complete destructive interference between the incoming and reflected waves. An **antinode** is a point where a crest or trough occurs midway between two nodes.

Why does a standing wave happen only at particular frequencies? **A standing wave forms only if half a wavelength or a multiple of half a wavelength fits exactly into the length of a vibrating cord.** In Figure 13A, the wavelength equals the length of the cord. In Figure 13B, the wavelength is halved. You can adjust the wavelength by changing the frequency of the waves. Once you find a frequency that produces a standing wave, doubling or tripling the frequency will also produce a standing wave.

Section 17.3 Assessment

Reviewing Concepts

1. How is a wave changed by reflection?

2. What causes refraction when a wave enters a medium at an angle?

3. What determines how much a wave diffracts when it encounters an opening or an obstacle?

4. List the types of interference.

5. At what wavelengths can a standing wave form in an elastic cord?

Critical Thinking

6. **Comparing and Contrasting** How does the frequency of a reflected wave compare to the frequency of the incoming wave?

7. **Comparing and Contrasting** How are diffraction and refraction similar? How are they different?

8. **Applying Concepts** What is the amplitude of the wave that results when two identical waves interfere constructively?

Writing in Science

Explain a Sequence Imagine you are floating in a wave pool. The crest of one wave hits you from the left just as the crest of another hits you from the right. The two waves are otherwise identical. A friend takes a series of five photos starting when the crests hit you. Write a paragraph describing the photos.

Are Regulations Needed to Protect Whales from Noise Pollution?

Researchers have known for decades that humpback whales sing complicated songs. Their songs can be as long as 30 minutes, and a whale may repeat the song for two or more hours. Songs can be heard at distances of hundreds of kilometers. There is evidence that whales use variations in the songs to tell other whales about the location of food and predators. Only the male humpbacks sing, which has led some researchers to think that songs are also used to attract a mate.

The whale songs may be threatened by noise pollution. In the past 50 years, ocean noise has increased due to human activity. Goods are transported across the ocean in larger ships than ever before. Large ships use bigger engines. They produce low-frequency noise by stirring up air bubbles with their propellers. Unfortunately, whales also use low-frequency sound in their songs, perhaps because these sounds carry farther than high-frequency sounds in the ocean. Propeller noise from large ships is loud enough to interfere with whale songs at a distance of 20 kilometers.

The Viewpoints

Regulations Are Needed to Reduce Noise Pollution From Large Ships

Whales use their songs in ways that affect their survival—eating, mating, and avoiding predators. Studies often focus on the effects of noise from a single ship, but in routes taken by ocean freighters, noise from many ships combines to produce a higher volume. Ocean freighters often travel near whale migration routes, so even noise that affects whales at a distance of 20 kilometers may have an impact on whale survival. If regulations are delayed until research can prove that noise pollution affects whales, it may be too late to help the whales. Many kinds of whales are on the endangered species list, so it is important to err on the side of safety.

Regulations Are Not Needed to Reduce Noise Pollution From Large Ships

Whale songs can be lengthy and are often repeated, so the effect of noise from ships is limited because ships quickly move out of an area. One study showed that whales changed the rhythm and tempo of their songs in response to noise from large ships, but there was no evidence that the communication was less effective. Also, it is expensive to modify ship propellers to reduce low-frequency noise. If less-developed countries cannot afford to modify ships, regulations will not be effective in reducing ocean noise levels.

Research and Decide

1. **Defining the Issue** In your own words, describe the major issue that needs to be resolved about ocean noise pollution.

2. **Analyzing the Viewpoints** List three arguments for those who think regulations should require large ships to reduce noise pollution. List three arguments for those who think regulations are not necessary.

3. **Forming Your Opinion** Explain which argument you find most convincing.

For: More on this issue
Visit: PHSchool.com
Web Code: cch-2173

17.4 Sound and Hearing

Reading Focus

Key Concepts

- What properties explain the behavior of sound?
- How is ultrasound used?
- How does frequency of sound change for a moving source?
- What are the functions of the three main regions of the ear?
- How is sound recorded?
- How do musical instruments vary pitch?

Vocabulary

- sound waves
- intensity
- decibel
- loudness
- pitch
- sonar
- Doppler effect
- resonance

Reading Strategy

Using Prior Knowledge Copy the web diagram below. Before you read, add properties you already know about. Then add details about each property as you read.

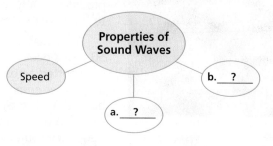

Take a moment to listen. Even in a quiet room you can usually hear many different sounds. You might hear someone opening a book, people talking in the hall, cars and trucks driving outside, and maybe even an airplane flying overhead. You can identify sounds without seeing them because sound waves carry information to your ears.

Properties of Sound Waves

Sound waves are longitudinal waves—compressions and rarefactions that travel through a medium. Have you ever stopped to question why sounds can hurt your ears? Why there is a delay before you hear an echo down a long, empty hallway at school? **Many behaviors of sound can be explained using a few properties—speed, intensity and loudness, and frequency and pitch.**

Speed Why is there a delay when you hear an echo? It takes time for sound to travel from place to place. In dry air at 20°C, the speed of sound is 342 meters per second. That's more than ten times faster than your speed in a car on a highway!

Figure 14 shows how the speed of sound varies in different media. In general, sound waves travel fastest in solids, slower in liquids, and slowest in gases. This is partly due to the fact that particles in a solid tend to be closer together than particles in a liquid or a gas. The speed of sound depends on many factors, including the density of the medium and how elastic the medium is.

Figure 14 The speed of sound is shown here for a variety of materials.
Making Generalizations *How does temperature affect the speed of sound?*

Speed of Sound	
Medium (at 1 atm)	Speed (m/s)
Dry air, 0°C	331
Dry air, 20°C	342
Fresh water, 0°C	1401
Fresh water, 30°C	1509
Salt water, 0°C	1449
Salt water, 30°C	1546
Lead, 25°C	1210
Cast iron, 25°C	4480
Aluminum, 25°C	5000
Borosilicate glass, 25°C	5170

Intensity and Loudness Intensity is the rate at which a wave's energy flows through a given area. Sound intensity depends on both the wave's amplitude and the distance from the sound source. If someone whispers in your ear, the sound intensity may be greater than when someone shouts at you from the other end of a field.

Sound intensity levels are measured in units called decibels. The **decibel** (dB) is a unit that compares the intensity of different sounds. The decibel scale is based on powers of ten. For every 10-decibel increase, the sound intensity increases tenfold. Figure 15 shows the intensity levels of some common sounds. A 0-decibel sound can just barely be heard. A 20-decibel sound has 100 times more energy per second than a 0-decibel sound. A 30-decibel sound delivers 1000 times more energy per second than a 0-decibel sound.

Unlike intensity, loudness is subjective—it is subject to a person's interpretation. **Loudness** is a physical response to the intensity of sound, modified by physical factors. The loudness you hear depends, of course, on sound intensity. As intensity increases, loudness increases. But loudness also depends on factors such as the health of your ears and how your brain interprets the information in sound waves.

Frequency and Pitch Try plucking a stretched rubber band. Then, stretch the rubber band farther and pluck again. You should be able to see the vibration become faster as you hear the sound frequency become higher. The frequency of a sound wave depends on how fast the source of the sound is vibrating.

The size of a musical instrument tells you something about the frequencies it can produce. The trumpet in Figure 16 can produce higher frequencies than the French horn. Both instruments produce different frequencies by changing the length of tubing through which air moves. The air in the tubing forms a standing wave. The longer the tubing, the longer is the wavelength of the standing wave, and the lower is the frequency of the note produced.

Pitch is the frequency of a sound as you perceive it. Pitch does depend upon a wave's frequency. High-frequency sounds have a high pitch, and low-frequency sounds have a low pitch. But pitch, like loudness, also depends on other factors such as your age and the health of your ears.

Sound Intensity Level	
Sound	**Intensity Level (decibels)**
Threshold of human hearing	0
Whisper	15–20
Normal conversation	40–50
Street noise	60–70
Inside a bus	90–100
Operating heavy machinery	80–120
Rock concert (in audience)	110–120
Threshold of pain	120
Jet plane (taking off)	120–160

Figure 15 Lengthy exposure to sounds more intense than 90 decibels can cause hearing damage. **Analyzing Data** *Which sounds are potentially dangerous?*

Figure 16 The French horn can produce lower notes than the trumpet because it can make a longer tube for a standing wave.

French Horn

Trumpet

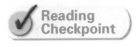 **Reading Checkpoint** *What is loudness?*

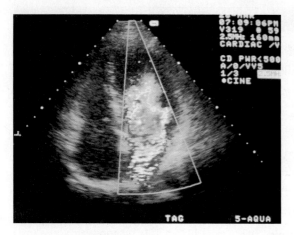

Figure 17 Ultrasound can be used to make images of the heart, which help doctors diagnose disease.

For: Activity on sonar and marine mammals
Visit: PHSchool.com
Web Code: ccc-2174

Ultrasound

Most people hear sounds between 20 hertz and 20,000 hertz. Infrasound is sound at frequencies lower than most people can hear, and ultrasound is sound at frequencies higher than most people hear. ◯ **Ultrasound is used in a variety of applications, including sonar and ultrasound imaging.**

Sonar is a technique for determining the distance to an object under water. Sonar stands for *sound na*vigation and *r*anging. The distance to the object is calculated using the speed of sound in water and the time that the sound wave takes to reach an object and the echo takes to return.

Ultrasound imaging is an important medical technique. Figure 17 shows an image of the heart made by sending ultrasound pulses into a patient. A pulse is a very short burst of a wave. Each ultrasound pulse is short—about $\frac{1}{8000}$ of a second—so that it doesn't interfere with the reflected pulse. Computer software uses the reflected pulses to make a detailed map of structures and organs inside the body.

The Doppler Effect

Perhaps you have heard the pitch of a siren change as it passed you. This is the **Doppler effect**—a change in sound frequency caused by motion of the sound source, motion of the listener, or both. The Doppler effect was discovered by the Austrian scientist Christian Doppler (1803–1853).

◯ **As a source of sound approaches, an observer hears a higher frequency. When the sound source moves away, the observer hears a lower frequency.** Figure 18 shows a single frequency emitted by the ambulance siren. As the ambulance moves toward observer B, the wave fronts bunch together. Observer B hears a higher frequency than the frequency of the source. For observer A, however, the wave fronts are spread out, and the frequency is lower than the source frequency.

Figure 18 Observer A hears a lower-pitch sound than observer B because the wave fronts are farther apart for observer A. **Inferring** *What can you infer about the pitch the ambulance driver hears?*

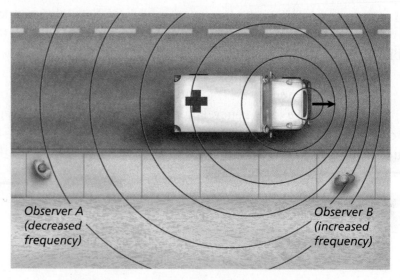

Observer A (decreased frequency)

Observer B (increased frequency)

Hearing and the Ear

Can you feel sound waves with your hand at this very moment? Probably you can't. But suppose you hold a balloon. Then your hand can feel sounds because the balloon membrane vibrates. Just like the balloon, your ear has a membrane that vibrates when sound waves strike it.

Your ear is a complex system that consists of three main regions—the outer ear, the middle ear, and the inner ear—as shown in Figure 19. 🔑 **The outer ear gathers and focuses sound into the middle ear, which receives and amplifies the vibrations. The inner ear uses nerve endings to sense vibrations and send signals to the brain.**

Go Online
SCIENCE NEWS®

For: Articles on sound
Visit: PHSchool.com
Web Code: cce-2174

Figure 19
The Anatomy of the Ear

Outer Ear The part of the ear you can see funnels sound waves down the ear canal, a tunnel about 2.5 cm long. There, sound waves strike the eardrum, a tightly stretched membrane between the outer and middle ear. The eardrum vibrates at the same frequency as the sound waves striking it.

Middle Ear The middle ear contains three tiny bones—the hammer, the anvil, and the stirrup. When the eardrum vibrates, the hammer vibrates at the same frequency. The hammer strikes the anvil, which in turn moves the stirrup back and forth. The three bones act as a lever system to amplify the motion of the eardrum.

Inner Ear Vibrations from the stirrup travel into the cochlea, a spiral-shaped canal filled with fluid. The inside of the cochlea is lined with thousands of nerve cells with tiny hair-like projections. As the fluid in the cochlea vibrates, the projections sway back and forth and send electrical impulses to the brain.

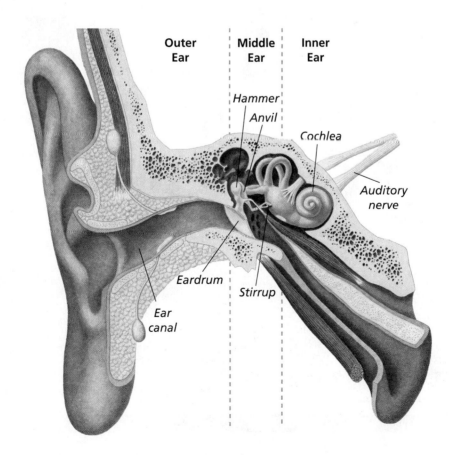

How Sound Is Reproduced

Sound has been reproduced in many ways, from old-fashioned records to modern digital technologies. But no matter how sound is recorded or stored, in the end it must be converted back into sound waves by loudspeakers. ● **Sound is recorded by converting sound waves into electronic signals that can be processed and stored. Sound is reproduced by converting electronic signals back into sound waves.**

A modern speaker produces sound waves in much the same way that a drum does. A drum skin vibrates up and down like a trampoline. As the drum vibrates, it sends a series of compressions and rarefactions through the air across the room. They carry energy to your ears in the form of sound waves.

DK SCIENCE and History

Sound Recording

Recording technology has come a long way since Thomas Edison made the first sound recording of the human voice at his New Jersey laboratory in 1877.

Funnel *The funnel is used for recording and playback.*

Horn *The horn channels sounds from an iron diaphragm.*

As wire recording gives way to magnetic tape, portable reel-to-reel recorders, like this 1950s model, become very popular.

Metal cylinder *This is wrapped with a layer of tinfoil.*

Mouthpiece *The mouthpiece records sounds as scratches on the tinfoil.*

Steel needle

Hand crank

PHONOGRAPH

GRAMOPHONE

REEL-TO-REEL RECORDER

1877 American inventor Thomas Edison records his voice on a tinfoil cylinder phonograph.

1885 The wax-coated cylinder is introduced as an improvement on Edison's first design.

1887 German-born American Emile Berliner invents the Gramophone, which stores sounds as grooves in the wax surface of a flat disc.

1900 Danish inventor Valdemar Poulsen unveils a magnetic recording device, called the Telegraphone.

1928 Tape with a magnetic coating is developed in Germany. Further refinements and a 1930s tape recorder called the Magnetophone make reel-to-reel recording popular.

1875	1900	1925

In a speaker, an electronic signal causes a magnet to vibrate. The magnet is attached to a membrane. The vibrating membrane sends sound waves through the air. Larger-diameter speakers, like a large bass drum, are better at reproducing lower frequencies of sound. Smaller-diameter speakers, like a small bongo drum, are better for reproducing higher frequencies of sound.

When a singer sings into a microphone, the reverse process happens. Sound waves from the singer's voice vibrate a membrane inside the microphone. The membrane causes a magnet to vibrate, which produces an electronic signal in the microphone wires. The energy of sound waves has been converted into an electronic signal that can be processed and stored.

Audio cassettes, a compact version of reel-to-reel magnetic tapes, are soon in demand.

VINYL LONG PLAYING

CASSETTE TAPE RECORDER

MP3 PLAYER

1948 Columbia introduces the first 12-inch vinyl records. Relatively cheap to make, these allow for a longer playing time.

1962 Philips, based in the Netherlands, demonstrates its first compact audio cassette. It is sold the following year with dictation machines. A stereo version is introduced in 1967.

1982 The first digital audio compact discs (CDs) are sold in Japan.

1998 MP3 technology becomes popular. This format allows music to be compressed, stored, and transferred digitally over computer networks.

1950   1975   2000

The Piano

The piano is a highly versatile musical instrument. Usually there are 88 separate keys, which produce a range of notes and volume. The sounds are made by wire strings that vibrate against a soundboard inside the piano.

Interpreting Photos *What causes the strings in a piano to vibrate?*

Grand piano
Pianos can be upright or, like this grand, horizontal. A grand piano makes a rich and powerful sound.

Bridge *Each string passes over a curved piece of wood called a bridge, which transmits the string's vibrations to the soundboard.*

Cast iron frame *This rigid frame is strong enough to allow huge force to be exerted on the strings.*

Bass bridge

Key

Damper

Treble strings *Short, thin strings produce higher pitches.*

Bass strings *Long, thick strings produce lower pitches. The bass strings cross over the mid-range strings to use space efficiently.*

Pins for tuning

Wire string   *Damper*

Felt-tipped hammer

Soundboard *Made from a large, thin piece of wood (usually spruce), the soundboard resonates and amplifies the sound from the vibrating wires.*

Keyboard action
As a key is pressed down, the section beyond the pivot moves up. This activates a series of levers that flick a hammer upward to strike the string and make it vibrate. The damper is released, which allows the string to continue vibrating.

Interconnected levers

Key

Damper lever

Pivot

Music

Musical instruments can produce a wide variety of sounds. In a wind instrument, such as a flute or trumpet, holes are closed using fingers or valves. This changes the length of the column of air in which a standing sound wave is produced. For some stringed instruments, such as a violin, musicians change the length of the strings by pressing down with their fingers. For other instruments, such as a piano, they use a fixed set of strings of different lengths. **Most musical instruments vary pitch by changing the frequency of standing waves.**

Musical instruments often use resonance to amplify sound. **Resonance** (REZ uh nuhns) is the response of a standing wave to another wave of the same frequency. Think of a child being pushed on a swing. If the pushes are timed at the right frequency, the child can swing higher and higher. In the same way, one wave can "push" another wave to a higher amplitude. Resonance can produce a dramatic increase in amplitude. A piano, for example, amplifies sound with a soundboard. The soundboard resonates in response to the vibrating strings.

Once sound waves leave an instrument, they can take several routes to a listener. In a large concert hall, interference with reflected sound waves can be a problem. Theaters such as the one in Figure 20 are designed with reflecting panels and sound-absorbing tiles. These are located with great care to prevent "dead spots" where the volume is reduced by destructive interference of reflected sound waves.

Figure 20 The Central Michigan University Music Building, like many concert halls, was designed by acoustic engineers. Sound-absorbing tiles (on the sides and rear) reduce unwanted reflections. The curved reflecting panels above the stage help gather and direct sound waves toward the audience.

Section 17.4 Assessment

Reviewing Concepts

1. List five properties used to explain the behavior of sound waves.

2. Name two uses for ultrasound.

3. What is the Doppler effect?

4. What are the ear's three main regions? Describe the function of each region.

5. How is sound recorded?

6. How does a musical instrument produce notes at different pitches?

Critical Thinking

7. **Applying Concepts** If workers in a distant stone quarry are blasting, why can you feel the explosion in your feet before you hear it?

8. **Comparing and Contrasting** How does the intensity of a 40-decibel sound compare to the intensity of a 20-decibel sound?

9. **Applying Concepts** How could a bat use reflections of sound waves to determine distance to an insect?

Connecting Concepts

Frames of Reference Review what you learned about combining velocities in Section 11.2. Then explain why the Doppler effect depends on the velocity of the sound source in the observer's frame of reference.

Now Hear This

Imagine eliminating all unwanted noise and only hearing the sounds you need to hear. That is the goal of noise-cancellation technology.

Noise-cancelling headset *This headset removes noise but allows communication with co-workers.*

In the modern world, there is plenty of unwanted noise from jet aircraft engines, construction equipment, and factory machinery. Traditionally, the way to deal with noise has been to put a barrier, such as an ear plug or ear muffler, between the source of the noise and your ears. This type of ear protection has the drawback, however, that it blocks out most sound, not just unwanted noise. That makes communication with co-workers difficult. Now, new technology is available that selectively removes unwanted noise, but transmits the sounds you need to hear.

Sound Control
Airport workers, jet pilots, rock musicians, and some factory workers all have a need for noise reduction.

Noise-cancellation technology

In noise-cancellation technology, a headset is fitted with a tiny microphone. This microphone is linked to an electronic device that can analyze the amplitude and frequency of sounds. When an undesirable noise is picked up by the microphone, a tiny speaker generates an anti-noise wave. The two waves cancel each other in destructive interference.

Wall of ear cup cuts out some noise.

Unwanted noise wave

Desirable sounds pass through to the ear.

The anti-noise generator *creates an anti-noise wave.*

Noise wave

Destructive Interference
The anti-noise wave is generated in such a way that its peaks coincide exactly with the troughs of the noise wave, and vice versa. All that is left of both waves is a faint hiss.

Music or speech can be channeled electronically through a wire.

Eardrum

Faint hiss

Microphone

Anti-noise wave

Car racing
Noise-cancellation technology has numerous applications. It is used in the army, on building sites, and in noisy sports like car racing.

Going Further

- Research in the library or on the Internet products that use noise cancellation, such as car stereos that reduce road noise, mobile phones, stereo headphones, or headsets for customer service operators. Write a paragraph explaining how one of these products works.

Investigating Sound Waves

Sound is produced when a vibrating source causes a medium to vibrate. In this lab, you will investigate how the vibrating source affects characteristics of the sound produced.

Problem
What determines the frequency and amplitude of the sound produced by a vibrating object?

Materials
- meter stick
- two cardboard tubes
- scissors or scalpel
- two rubber bands
- wax paper
- balloon
- small mirror
- transparent tape
- flashlight

Skills
Observing, Inferring, Drawing Conclusions, Controlling Variables

Procedure

Part A: Investigating How Length Affects Pitch

1. Hold one end of a meter stick down firmly on a table so that 20 centimeters of the meter stick extends past the edge of the table. Pluck the end of the meter stick that extends past the table to produce a vibration and a sound as shown. Observe the vibration and sound of the meter stick.

2. Repeat Step 1, but this time allow 40 centimeters of the meter stick to extend past the edge of the table. Observe and record how the length of the vibrating part of the meter stick affects the pitch.

3. Repeat Step 1, but this time allow 60 centimeters of the meter stick to extend past the edge of the table. Record your observations.

4. Investigate the relationship between length and frequency for a vibrating column of air, as you did with the vibrating meter stick. Make a kazoo by cutting a hole in the middle of one of the cardboard tubes. Make the hole approximately 1 centimeter in diameter. Use a rubber band to fasten the piece of wax paper over one end of the tube. **CAUTION** *Be careful when cutting with sharp instruments; always cut away from yourself and away from nearby people.*

5. Make a second kazoo by cutting the second tube 10 centimeters shorter than the first tube. Using the short tube, repeat Step 4.

6. Hold the shorter kazoo in front of your mouth and hum into the open end, keeping your pitch steady. Repeat this action with the longer kazoo, making sure to hum exactly as you did before. Observe and record how the length of the kazoo affects the pitch of the sound.

Part B: Investigating How Frequency Affects Pitch and How Amplitude Affects Loudness

7. Cut the neck off of the balloon. Replace the wax paper on the longer kazoo with the cut-open balloon. Wrap the rubber band several times around the end of the cardboard tube. The rubber band should hold the balloon tightly stretched over the end of the tube. Use tape to attach the small mirror onto the balloon on the end of the tube.

8. Have a classmate shine a flashlight on the mirror as shown while you hum into the kazoo. Your classmate should position the flashlight so that a spot of light is reflected on the wall. It may be necessary to darken the room. Observe how the spot of light moves when you hum into the kazoo. Make a note of your position and the position and angle of the kazoo and the flashlight.

9. Without changing how loudly you hum, use your voice to raise the pitch of your humming. Observe and record how the movement of the spot of light differs from your observations in Step 8. Make sure you do not change your distance from the wall or the angle at which the light from the flashlight strikes the mirror attached to the kazoo.

10. Repeat Step 9, but this time hum at a lower pitch than you did in Step 8.

11. Repeat Steps 9 and 10, but this time vary the loudness of your humming while keeping the pitch constant.

Analyze and Conclude

1. **Observing** What happened to the frequency of the meter stick's vibration when you made the overhanging part longer?

2. **Inferring** How did the frequency of the meter stick's vibration affect the pitch of its sound?

3. **Inferring** How did the kazoo's length affect its pitch?

4. **Analyzing Data** When you changed the pitch of your humming, how did it affect the frequency of vibration of the mirror?

5. **Analyzing Data** How is the amplitude of the kazoo's vibration related to its loudness?

6. **Controlling Variables** Explain why it was important to keep loudness constant when you changed the pitch of your humming in Step 9.

Go Further Design an experiment to investigate what variables affect the pitch and loudness of vibrating strings. Use an instrument such as a guitar or violin. After your teacher approves your plan, carry out your experiment.

17.1 Mechanical Waves

Key Concepts

- A wave is created when a source of energy causes a vibration to move through a medium.
- The three main types of mechanical waves are transverse, longitudinal, and surface waves.

Vocabulary

mechanical wave, *p. 500;* medium, *p. 500;* crest, *p. 501;* trough, *p. 501;* transverse wave, *p. 501;* compression, *p. 502;* rarefaction, *p. 502;* longitudinal wave, *p. 502;* surface wave, *p. 503*

17.2 Properties of Mechanical Waves

Key Concepts

- A wave's frequency equals the frequency of the vibrating source producing the wave.
- For waves traveling at a constant speed, wavelength is inversely proportional to frequency.
- As energy of a wave increases, amplitude increases.

Vocabulary

periodic motion, *p. 504;* period, *p. 504;* frequency, *p. 504;* hertz, *p. 504;* wavelength, *p. 505;* amplitude, *p. 507*

17.3 Behavior of Waves

Key Concepts

- Reflection does not change the speed or frequency of a wave, but the wave can be flipped upside down.
- Refraction occurs because one side of a wave moves more slowly than the other side.
- A wave diffracts more if its wavelength is large compared to the size of an opening or obstacle.
- Interference can be constructive or destructive.
- A standing wave forms only if the length of a vibrating cord is a multiple of one half wavelength.

Vocabulary

reflection, *p. 508;* refraction, *p. 509;* diffraction, *p. 510;* interference, *p. 510;* constructive interference, *p. 511;* destructive interference, *p. 511;* standing wave, *p. 512;* node, *p. 512;* antinode, *p. 512*

17.4 Sound and Hearing

Key Concepts

- Many behaviors of sound can be explained using a few properties—speed, intensity and loudness, and frequency and pitch.
- Ultrasound is used in a variety of applications, including sonar and ultrasound imaging.
- As a source of sound approaches, an observer hears a higher frequency. When the sound source moves away, the observer hears a lower frequency.
- The outer ear gathers and focuses sound into the middle ear, which receives and amplifies the vibrations. The inner ear uses nerve endings to sense vibrations and send signals to the brain.
- Sound is recorded by converting sound waves into electronic signals that can be processed and stored. Sound is reproduced by converting electronic signals back into sound waves.
- Most instruments vary pitch by changing the frequency of standing waves.

Vocabulary

sound waves, *p. 514;* intensity, *p. 515;* decibel, *p. 515;* loudness, *p. 515;* pitch, *p. 515;* sonar, *p. 516;* Doppler effect, *p. 516;* resonance, *p. 521*

Thinking Visually

Web Diagram Copy the web diagram below onto a sheet of paper. Use information from the chapter to complete the diagram.

Reviewing Content

Choose the letter that best answers the question or completes the statement.

1. Which of the following is NOT true about mechanical waves?
   a. They carry energy.
   b. They transfer matter.
   c. They can be longitudinal.
   d. They require a medium.

2. In a transverse wave, the medium vibrates
   a. at right angles to the wave direction.
   b. in the same direction as the wave.
   c. in a direction opposite that of the wave.
   d. at a 45° angle to the wave direction.

3. The height of a wave crest is called
   a. wavelength.   b. frequency.
   c. amplitude.   d. energy.

4. For waves moving at a constant speed, if wavelength is doubled, then frequency is
   a. doubled.   b. halved.
   c. unchanged.   d. quadrupled.

5. When a wave is reflected, its speed
   a. increases.   b. increases or decreases.
   c. decreases.   d. is unchanged.

6. When a wave bends around an obstacle, it is called
   a. reflection.   b. refraction.
   c. diffraction.   d. interference.

7. When two waves interfere, the displacement where two troughs meet is
   a. positive.   b. negative.
   c. zero.   d. a crest.

8. A large speaker is better than a small speaker for producing sounds with
   a. low frequency.   b. high frequency.
   c. low intensity.   d. high intensity.

9. The highest-frequency sound human ears can usually hear is about
   a. 20 Hz.   b. 10,000 Hz.
   c. 20,000 Hz.   d. 30,000 Hz.

10. Sonar can make use of
    a. the Doppler effect. b. ultrasound.
    c. infrasound.   d. resonance.

Understanding Concepts

11. Name two kinds of longitudinal waves and explain how you know they are longitudinal.

12. How are some surface waves similar to both transverse and longitudinal waves?

Copy the diagram below on a separate piece of paper and use it to answer Questions 13–15.

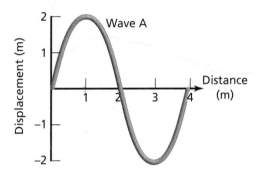

13. On your diagram, draw wave B with the same wavelength as wave A, but twice the amplitude.

14. On your diagram, draw wave C with the same amplitude as wave A, but twice the wavelength.

15. How does the frequency of wave C compare with the frequency of wave A, assuming they travel at the same speed?

16. What causes refraction of a wave as it enters a new medium at an angle?

17. Regardless of the direction of waves far from an island, waves close to the island move toward the shore on all sides. Explain.

18. Why does a node in a standing wave have zero displacement?

19. How is intensity different from loudness?

20. Explain why a fire engine's siren sounds lower in pitch after the fire engine passes you.

21. What is the function of the eardrum?

22. What are the names of the three small bones in the middle ear, and what is their purpose?

23. Why are the materials used in construction of a concert hall important?

Critical Thinking

24. **Making Generalizations** A friend says that all mechanical waves must lose energy as they move through a medium because some energy is lost due to friction. Explain why this is true.

25. **Forming Operational Definitions** Two sound waves with different frequencies travel through a steel rod at the same speed. Explain by giving an operational definition of wave speed.

26. **Relating Cause and Effect** Can two waves traveling in the same direction form a standing wave? Explain why or why not.

27. **Inferring** The buzzing sound of a mosquito flying around your head has a higher pitch than the buzz of a bumblebee. What can you infer about the mosquito's wings compared to the bee's wings?

28. **Relating Cause and Effect** At the same time, you hear a kitten's purr and a clap of thunder. The kitten's purr is louder. Explain how this is possible.

29. **Applying Concepts** How much greater is the intensity of a 25-dB sound than a 15-dB sound? What would be the intensity in dB for a sound that is 100 times louder than the 25-dB sound?

Math Skills

Use the illustration below to answer Questions 30–32.

Ocean wave

30. **Interpreting Diagrams** What is the wavelength of the ocean wave shown in the figure?

31. **Evaluating Expressions** Three complete wavelengths pass a fixed point once every 2 seconds. What is the frequency of the wave?

32. **Calculating** What is the speed of the ocean wave in Question 31?

33. **Calculating** A deep-water wave has a wavelength of 10.0 meters. If it travels at 3.9 m/s, what is the wave's period?

Concepts in Action

34. **Applying Concepts** Some gardeners protect their gardens from animals by using sound that animals find irritating. Explain how the gardeners can tolerate the sound, while the animals cannot.

35. **Formulating Hypotheses** Generate a hypothesis about how the frequency of noise made by a machine changes as the machine operates at higher speeds.

36. **Writing in Science** Write a paragraph describing the motion of a lily pad as several waves from a boat pass by. Explain why the motion would be the same or different if the lily pad were floating free instead of attached by roots to the pond floor. (*Hint:* Before you write, draw a series of diagrams to show the motion.)

Performance-Based Assessment

Using Models Try blowing across the top of a bottle to produce a tone. Experiment to see how adding water of different heights affects the pitch. See if you can arrange a series of eight bottles to produce a musical scale. Learn to play a simple tune on your musical bottles. Summarize your results in a computer presentation that explains the relationship between the height of the air column and the pitch produced.

For: Self-grading assessment
Visit: PHSchool.com
Web Code: cca-2170

Standardized Test Prep

Test-Taking Tip

Controlling Variables

Some test questions ask which variables must be controlled in an experiment. It helps to start by writing an equation for the variables you are given. For the question below, write an equation that includes wavelength and frequency.

Speed = Wavelength × Frequency

This equation gives you one variable to control: the wave speed. Next, think of any conditions that might affect this variable. You know that wave speed changes in a different medium, so the medium must be controlled. Other conditions that are often controlled include conditions in the lab, such as temperature and pressure, or quantities of matter, such as mass or volume.

Which variables must be held constant in an experiment to determine how the frequency of a sound wave affects wavelength?
  I. time
  II. wave speed
  III. temperature

(A) I only
(B) II only
(C) I and II only
(D) II and III only
(E) I, II, and III

(Answer: D)

Choose the letter that best answers the question or completes the statement.

1. Which of the following is required to transmit energy using mechanical waves?
   (A) medium   (B) crest
   (C) trough   (D) reflection
   (E) period

2. How are wavelength and frequency related for a wave moving at constant speed?
   (A) Wavelength equals frequency.
   (B) Wavelength is greater than frequency.
   (C) Frequency is greater than wavelength.
   (D) Wavelength is proportional to frequency.
   (E) Wavelength is inversely proportional to frequency.

3. Which of the following statements is generally true for the musical instrument (panpipes) below?

   (A) The longest pipe has the highest pitch.
   (B) The shortest pipe has the highest pitch.
   (C) The pipe in the middle has the highest pitch.
   (D) The pitch cannot be changed.
   (E) Any of the pipes could produce the highest pitch.

4. Which conditions best describe what happens when a transverse wave is reflected?
   (A) Some of a wave does not pass through a boundary or surface.
   (B) A wave enters a new medium at an angle.
   (C) A wave becomes longitudinal.
   (D) A wave combines with another wave.
   (E) A wave interferes with another wave.

5. Which of the following variables can affect the wavelength of a sound wave?
   I. the medium
   II. the frequency of the wave
   III. the amplitude of the wave

   (A) I only   (B) II only
   (C) I and II only   (D) II and III only
   (E) I, II, and III

6. Ocean waves flow past a concrete support for a bridge. The support is 30 meters wide and it sits in very deep water. Which of the following is LEAST likely to occur?
   (A) The waves will reflect.
   (B) The waves will diffract.
   (C) The waves will lose some energy.
   (D) The waves will continue past the support.
   (E) The waves will refract.

CHAPTER 18 The Electromagnetic Spectrum and Light

21st Century Learning
Health Literacy

What are the health risks of radiation?

As you read this page, you are being bombarded by radiation from the sun and distant stars, as well as from rocks deep in the ground beneath your feet. Although radiation is a natural part of your world, too much exposure to certain types of radiation can be harmful. Visit the Web site of the Environmental Protection Agency and search for information on radiation exposure. Create a short video or digital presentation to explain radiation risks to someone without a background in science.

How do science concepts apply to your world? Here are some questions you'll be able to answer after you read this chapter.

- **Why does a lamp seem brighter the closer you are to it?** *(Section 18.1)*

- **How does a microwave oven cook food?** *(Section 18.2)*

- **How is a mirage formed?** *(Section 18.3)*

- **How can you make millions of colors from only three?** *(Section 18.4)*

- **How can you tell if a painting is a forgery?** *(Page 554)*

- **Why are fluorescent lights commonly used in large buildings?** *(Section 18.5)*

Colorful neon lights brighten up a walkway in Chicago's O'Hare Airport.

Chapter Preview

Inquiry > Activity

How Do Color Filters Work?

Procedure

1. Place a piece of cardboard that has a slit cut into it in sunlight so that a beam of light passes through the slit. **CAUTION** *Never look directly at the sun.*

2. Create a rainbow by positioning a prism in the beam of light that has passed through the slit. Project the rainbow onto white paper.

3. Use colored markers to draw the colors in the order in which they appear on the paper.

4. Replace the paper. Place a red filter between the slit and the prism and draw the colors you see projected onto the paper.

5. Repeat Step 4 with a blue filter and then with a green filter.

Think About It

1. **Inferring** What happens to sunlight when it passes through a prism?

2. **Observing** Which colors did you see projected onto the paper while using each filter? Which colors didn't you see while using each filter?

3. **Drawing Conclusions** What can you conclude about what happens to sunlight as it passes through a filter?

18.1 Electromagnetic Waves

Reading Focus

Key Concepts

- How are electromagnetic waves different from mechanical waves?
- What is the maximum speed of light?
- How do electromagnetic waves differ from one another?
- What is the dual nature of electromagnetic radiation?
- What happens as light travels farther from its source?

Vocabulary

- electromagnetic waves
- electric field
- magnetic field
- electromagnetic radiation
- photoelectric effect
- photons
- intensity

Reading Strategy

Comparing and Contrasting Copy the table below. As you read about electromagnetic waves, fill in the table to compare them with mechanical waves. Use E for properties of electromagnetic waves, M for mechanical waves, and B for both.

Travels through vacuum	E
Travels through medium	a. ?
Fits wave model	B
Fits particle model	b. ?
Transverse wave	c. ?
Longitudinal wave	d. ?

What do X-ray machines, microwave ovens, and heat lamps have in common with police radar, television, and radiation therapy? They all use waves. You are surrounded by such waves all the time. But you may not realize it, because most waves are invisible.

With X-rays, you can take pictures of your bones. Your dentist uses X-rays to examine the inner structure of your teeth. Microwaves cook or reheat your meals and carry cell phone conversations between you and your friends. Radio waves bring your favorite music to your radio from the radio station. Ultraviolet rays can give you a sunburn. Without waves, the girl in Figure 1 wouldn't be able to talk with her friends on a cell phone. Without waves, you wouldn't be able to watch your favorite TV show. You wouldn't be able to see colors. In fact, without waves you wouldn't be able to see anything at all.

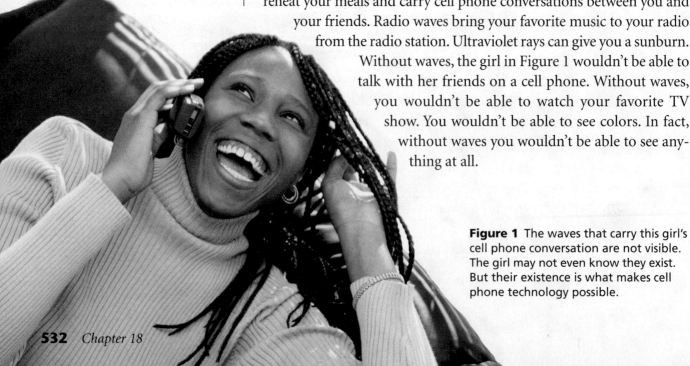

Figure 1 The waves that carry this girl's cell phone conversation are not visible. The girl may not even know they exist. But their existence is what makes cell phone technology possible.

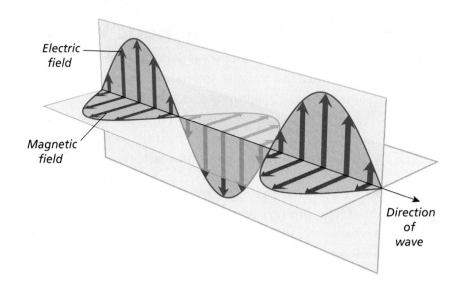

Figure 2 Electromagnetic waves consist of changing electric fields and magnetic fields. The fields are at right angles to each other and to the direction of the wave. **Interpreting Diagrams** *How can you tell that electromagnetic waves are transverse waves?*

What Are Electromagnetic Waves?

The visible and invisible waves you will learn about in this chapter exhibit some of the same behaviors as mechanical waves. Other behaviors are unique to electromagnetic waves. **Electromagnetic waves** are transverse waves consisting of changing electric fields and changing magnetic fields. Like mechanical waves, electromagnetic waves carry energy from place to place. Electromagnetic waves differ from mechanical waves in how they are produced and how they travel.

How They Are Produced Electromagnetic waves are produced by constantly changing fields. An **electric field** in a region of space exerts electric forces on charged particles. Electric fields are produced by electrically charged particles and by changing magnetic fields. A **magnetic field** in a region of space produces magnetic forces. Magnetic fields are produced by magnets, by changing electric fields, and by vibrating charges. ⊙ **Electromagnetic waves are produced when an electric charge vibrates or accelerates.** Figure 2 shows that the fields are at right angles to each other. You can tell this is a transverse wave because the fields are also at right angles to the direction in which the wave travels.

How They Travel Because changing electric fields produce changing magnetic fields, and changing magnetic fields produce changing electric fields, the fields regenerate each other. As the fields regenerate, their energy travels in the form of a wave. Unlike mechanical waves, electromagnetic waves do not need a medium. ⊙ **Electromagnetic waves can travel through a vacuum, or empty space, as well as through matter.** The transfer of energy by electromagnetic waves traveling through matter or across space is called **electromagnetic radiation.**

What are electromagnetic waves?

For: Links on waves
Visit: www.SciLinks.org
Web Code: ccn-2181

The Speed of Electromagnetic Waves

A thunderstorm is approaching. The sky is dark, and lightning flashes in the distance. Within a few seconds, you hear thunder's low rumble. As the storm approaches, the lightning gets brighter and the thunder louder. The lightning flashes and the sound of thunder come closer in time. Still, you see the lightning before you hear the thunder, because light travels faster than sound. But how much faster is light?

Michelson's Experiment In ancient times, people tried to measure the speed of light but no instrument was accurate enough. Light moves so fast that people thought its speed was infinite. Several experiments in the 1800s proved it was not infinite and gave approximate values. Then, in 1926, the American physicist Albert Michelson (1852–1931) measured the speed of light more accurately than ever before.

Figure 3 shows an experimental setup similar to Michelson's. On top of Mount Wilson in California, Michelson placed an eight-sided rotating mirror. He placed another mirror, this one stationary, on Mount San Antonio, 35.4 kilometers away. Michelson shined a bright light at one face of the rotating mirror. The light reflected to the stationary mirror on the other mountain and then back to Mount Wilson, where it struck another face of the rotating mirror. Michelson knew how fast the eight-sided mirror was rotating and how far the light traveled from mountain to mountain and back again. With those values he was able to calculate the speed of light quite accurately. His findings were similar to modern measurements.

The Speed of Light Since Michelson, many other scientists have measured the speed of light. Their experiments have confirmed that light and all electromagnetic waves travel at the same speed when in a vacuum, regardless of the observer's motion. **The speed of light in a vacuum, *c*, is 3.00×10^8 meters per second.**

Figure 3 Michelson timed a light beam as it traveled from one mountain to another and back again. His experiment measured the speed of light more accurately than it had been measured before. **Inferring** *Why must the light beam travel so far for its speed to be measurable?*

Mt. San Antonio

Mirror

35.4 km

Octagonal rotating mirror

Telescope

Light source

Mt. Wilson

Wavelength and Frequency

In a vacuum, all electromagnetic waves travel at the same speed. But not all electromagnetic waves are the same. 🔑 **Electromagnetic waves vary in wavelength and frequency.**

The speed of an electromagnetic wave is the product of its wavelength and its frequency. Because the speed of electromagnetic waves in a vacuum is constant, the wavelength is inversely proportional to the frequency. As the wavelength increases, the frequency decreases. If you know the wavelength of an electromagnetic wave, you can calculate its frequency.

Math Skills

Calculating Wave Speed

A radio station broadcasts a radio wave with a wavelength of 3.0 meters. What is the frequency of the wave?

 Read and Understand

What information are you given?

$$\text{Speed} = c = 3.00 \times 10^8 \text{ m/s}$$

$$\text{Wavelength} = 3.0 \text{ m}$$

 Plan and Solve

What unknown are you trying to calculate?

$$\text{Frequency} = ?$$

What formula contains the given quantities and the unknown?

$$\text{Speed} = \text{Wavelength} \times \text{Frequency}$$

$$or, \text{Frequency} = \frac{\text{Speed}}{\text{Wavelength}}$$

Replace each variable with its known value.

$$\text{Frequency} = \frac{3.00 \times 10^8 \text{ m/s}}{3.0 \text{ m}}$$

$$= 1.0 \times 10^8 \text{ Hz}$$

 Look Back and Check

Is your answer reasonable?

Check that product of wavelength and frequency gives a speed of 3.0×10^8 m/s.

$$\text{Speed} = 3.0 \text{ m} \times (1.0 \times 10^8 \text{ Hz}) = 3.0 \times 10^8 \text{ m/s}$$

Math Practice

1. A global positioning satellite transmits a radio wave with a wavelength of 19 cm. What is the frequency of the radio wave? (*Hint:* Convert the wavelength to meters before calculating the frequency.)

2. The radio waves of a particular AM radio station vibrate 680,000 times per second. What is the wavelength of the wave?

3. Radio waves that vibrate 160,000,000 times per second are used on some train lines for communications. If radio waves that vibrate half as many times per second were used instead, how would the wavelength change?

Wave or Particle?

Scientists know that electromagnetic radiation travels as a wave. Scientists also have evidence that electromagnetic radiation behaves like a stream of particles. In the late 1600s, the English physicist Isaac Newton was the first to propose a particle explanation. He based this hypothesis on two pieces of evidence: light travels in a straight line and it casts a shadow, as shown in Figure 4. But not all evidence supports Newton's hypothesis. So which is light, wave or particle? It is both. **Electromagnetic radiation behaves sometimes like a wave and sometimes like a stream of particles.**

Evidence for the Wave Model

In 1801, the English physicist Thomas Young (1773–1829) showed that light behaves like a wave. Look at Figure 5. Young passed a beam of light first through a single slit and then through a double slit. Where light from the two slits reached a darkened screen, Young observed alternating bright and dark bands. The bands were evidence that the light had produced an interference pattern. Bright bands indicated constructive interference, and dark bands indicated destructive interference. Interference occurs only when two or more waves overlap. Therefore, Young's experiment showed that light behaves like a wave.

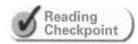
Reading Checkpoint *What is the evidence that light travels like a wave?*

Figure 4 The fact that light casts a shadow has been used as evidence for both the wave model of light and the particle model of light.

Figure 5 This diagram illustrates Young's experiment, which showed that light behaves like a wave. When light passes through a single slit and then a double slit, it produces an interference pattern. Constructive interference produces bright bands of light. Destructive interference produces dark bands.
Predicting *What would you expect to see on the screen if light behaved like a stream of particles?*

Interference pattern appears on screen.

Card with two slits

Card with one slit

Light source

Dark bands show destructive interference.

Bright bands show constructive interference.

Light from single slit produces coherent light at second card.

A No electrons are emitted.

Bright red light or infrared rays

Metal plate

B Electrons are emitted.

Dim blue light or ultraviolet rays

Metal plate

Figure 6 The emissions of electrons from a metal caused by light striking the metal is called the photoelectric effect. **A** Red light or infrared rays, no matter how bright, does not cause electrons to be emitted from this metal surface. **B** When blue light or ultraviolet rays strike the metal surface, electrons are emitted, even if the light is dim.

Evidence for the Particle Model

When dim blue light hits the surface of a metal such as cesium, an electron is emitted. A brighter blue light causes even more electrons to be emitted, as you can see in Figure 6. But red light, no matter how bright it is, does not cause the emission of any electrons in this particular metal.

The emission of electrons from a metal caused by light striking the metal is called the **photoelectric effect.** Discovered in 1887, the photoelectric effect was puzzling. Scientists did not understand why dim blue light caused electrons to be emitted from metal but even bright red light did not.

In 1905, Albert Einstein (1879–1955) proposed that light, and all electromagnetic radiation, consists of packets of energy. These packets of electromagnetic energy are now called **photons** (FOH tawnz). Each photon's energy is proportional to the frequency of the light. The greater the frequency of an electromagnetic wave, the more energy each of its photons has.

Blue light has a higher frequency than red light, so photons of blue light have more energy than photons of red light. Blue light consists of photons that have enough energy to cause electrons to be emitted from a metal surface. So blue light can cause emission of electrons.

Red light has a lower frequency than blue light, so photons of red light have less energy than photons of blue light. Red light consists of photons that have too little energy to cause any electrons to be emitted from a metal surface. So red light does not cause emission of electrons.

Reading Checkpoint *What is the photoelectric effect?*

Figure 7 The closer you are to a surface when you spray paint it, the smaller the area the paint covers and the more intense the paint color looks. **Using Models** *How does a can of spray paint help you model a change in light intensity?*

A

B

Intensity

The closer you are to a source of light, the brighter the light appears. If you want to read at night, you must sit near a lamp. At night, as you walk away from a street light, the area around you becomes darker. A street light doesn't give off less light when you move farther from it. It just provides you with less light the farther away you are. Photons travel outward from a light source in all directions. Near the light source, the photons spread through a small area, so the light is intense. **Intensity** is the rate at which a wave's energy flows through a given unit of area. You can think of intensity as brightness. Farther from the source, the photons spread over a larger area. ⟳ **The intensity of light decreases as photons travel farther from the source.**

A can of spray paint can help you model a change in light intensity. Look at Figure 7. When the nozzle is close to a piece of paper, the paint forms a small, dense spot. When the nozzle is farther from the paper, the paint forms a larger, fainter spot because the paint is sprayed over a larger area. Like paint on paper, light intensity decreases as distance from the light source increases.

A wave model for light also explains how intensity decreases with distance from a source. As waves travel away from the source, they pass through a larger and larger area. Because the total energy does not change, the wave's intensity decreases.

Section 18.1 Assessment

Reviewing Concepts

1. ⟳ What produces electromagnetic waves?
2. ⟳ How fast does light travel in a vacuum?
3. ⟳ What makes electromagnetic waves different from one another?
4. ⟳ Explain how light behaves like a stream of particles.
5. ⟳ What happens to the intensity of light as photons move away from the light source?
6. How does photon energy relate to frequency?

Critical Thinking

7. **Applying Concepts** Why does blue light cause emission of electrons from metal while red light does not?

8. **Observing** Describe what happens as you get closer to a light source. Explain this observation.

Math **Practice**

9. What is the wavelength of an AM radio wave in a vacuum if its frequency is 810 kilohertz?

10. A global positioning satellite (GPS) transmits a signal at a frequency of 1575 megahertz. What is the wavelength? (*Hint:* Assume the wave speed is the same as in a vacuum.)

18.2 The Electromagnetic Spectrum

Reading Focus

Key Concepts

- What waves are included in the electromagnetic spectrum?
- How is each type of electromagnetic wave used?

Vocabulary

- electromagnetic spectrum
- amplitude modulation
- frequency modulation
- thermograms

Reading Strategy

Summarizing Copy the chart below and add four more rows to complete the table for the electromagnetic spectrum. After you read, list at least two uses for each kind of wave.

Type of Waves	Uses	
Radio Waves	Communications	a. ?
Infrared Rays	b. ?	Keeping food warm

How do you investigate something that is invisible? First you have to suspect that it exists. Then you have to figure out a way to detect what is invisible and collect data about it. Such was the way the German-born astronomer William Herschel (1738–1822) discovered infrared radiation.

The Waves of the Spectrum

In England in 1800, with a technique discovered earlier, Herschel used a prism to separate the wavelengths present in sunlight. He produced a band of colors: red, orange, yellow, green, blue, and violet. He wondered if the temperature of each color of light was different from the temperature of the other colors of light. As you can see in Figure 8, Herschel placed thermometers at various places along the color band and measured the temperatures. Herschel observed that the temperature was lower at the blue end and higher toward the red end.

This discovery made Herschel pose a new question: Would the temperature increase even more beyond the red end, in an area that showed no color? He measured the temperature just beyond the red end of the color band. This area recorded an even higher temperature than the red area. Herschel concluded there must be invisible radiation beyond the red end of the color band.

Figure 8 Herschel measured the temperature of different colors of light. The temperature was lowest at the blue end and highest at the red end. Curiosity led Herschel to discover evidence of radiation past the red end of the band of visible light.

Figure 9 The electromagnetic
spectrum consists of radio waves,
infrared rays, visible light,
ultraviolet rays, X-rays, and
gamma rays.
Interpreting Diagrams *Which
waves of the electromagnetic
spectrum have the longest
wavelengths?*

Today, radiation beyond the red end of the color band is called infrared radiation. Herschel experimented with infrared radiation and found it had many of the same properties as visible light. With these experiments, Herschel opened the door to the study of invisible types of electromagnetic radiation.

The full range of frequencies of electromagnetic radiation is called the **electromagnetic spectrum.** Figure 9 shows the spectrum of electromagnetic radiation in order of increasing frequency from left to right. Visible light is the only part of the electromagnetic spectrum that you can see, but it is just a small part. 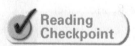 **The electromagnetic spectrum includes radio waves, infrared rays, visible light, ultraviolet rays, X-rays, and gamma rays.** Each kind of wave is characterized by a range of wavelengths and frequencies. All of these waves have many useful applications.

Reading Checkpoint *What is the full range of frequencies of electromagnetic radiation called?*

Radio Waves

Radio waves have the longest wavelengths in the electromagnetic spectrum, from 1 millimeter to as much as thousands of kilometers or longer. Because they are the longest waves, radio waves also have the lowest frequencies in the spectrum—300,000 megahertz (MHz) or less. **Radio waves are used in radio and television technologies, as well as in microwave ovens and radar.**

Go Online

NSTA *SciLINKS*

For: Links on the
electromagnetic
spectrum
Visit: www.SciLinks.org
Web Code: ccn-2182

Radio In a radio studio such as the one in Figure 10, music and voices that have been changed into electronic signals are coded onto radio waves and then broadcast. There are two ways that radio stations code and transmit information on radio waves. Both ways are based on a wave of constant frequency and amplitude. To code the information onto this wave so that it can be broadcast, one of two characteristics of the wave must be varied, or modulated.

In **amplitude modulation,** the amplitude of the wave is varied. The frequency remains the same. AM radio stations broadcast by amplitude modulation. In **frequency modulation,** the frequency of the wave is varied. The amplitude remains the same. FM stations broadcast by frequency modulation. Whichever way the radio wave is transmitted, your radio receives it, decodes it, and changes it back into sound waves you can hear.

Have you ever traveled a long distance in a car and "lost" a station on the radio? A station is lost when its signal becomes too weak to detect. An FM radio station is more likely to be lost than an AM station because FM radio signals do not travel as far as AM signals along Earth's curved surface. AM radio stations use frequencies between 535 kilohertz and 1605 kilohertz. FM stations use frequencies between 88 megahertz and 108 megahertz. Particles in Earth's upper atmosphere reflect the lower-frequency AM radio waves much better than the higher-frequency FM radio waves. The reflection helps transmit AM signals farther.

Television Radio waves also carry signals for television programming. The process is like transmitting radio signals. But one difference is that the radio waves carry information for pictures as well as for sound. Once they have been broadcast, the signals are received by an antenna, and sent to the TV set.

Location and weather can affect the reception of television signals by an antenna. For that reason, many people prefer to receive television signals that have been transmitted by satellite. With this type of transmission, TV broadcasts are sent to satellites, which then retransmit the signals back to Earth.

If you have a satellite dish, you can receive the signals directly. If not, a cable service can receive the signals and resend them to your home.

Radio Broadcasting

Figure 10 The announcer's voice and the music on CD leave the radio studio as electronic signals. Those signals are used to produce a wave with either a varying amplitude or a varying frequency.
A AM waves have a varying amplitude.
B FM waves have a varying frequency.

A Amplitude modulation

B Frequency modulation

Data › Analysis

How Long Does an Antenna Need to Be?

Have you ever noticed how the lengths of antennas vary from quite short (cell phones) to very long (radio transmitters)? The length of an antenna depends in part on the length of the waves it transmits. Each letter in the graph (A–E) represents an antenna of a different length. The graph shows the wavelengths that can be transmitted by antennas of a few different lengths.

1. **Calculating** What is the frequency of the wave that antenna B transmits? (*Hint:* Assume the wave travels at the speed of light.)

2. **Drawing Conclusions** What relationship is there between antenna length and wavelength?

3. **Inferring** At an outdoor concert, a singer is using a wireless microphone with antenna C. Speakers broadcast her performance. Now and then the speakers also broadcast an employee taking an order at a fast food restaurant nearby. What is the approximate wavelength of the transmissions from the restaurant? How do you know?

4. **Predicting** If you used a microphone that transmitted waves at 600 MHz, approximately how long would its antenna need to be?

Microwaves The shortest-wavelength radio waves are called microwaves. Microwaves have wavelengths from about 1 meter to about 1 millimeter. Their frequencies vary from about 300 megahertz to about 300,000 megahertz.

Microwaves cook and reheat food. When water or fat molecules in the food absorb microwaves, the thermal energy of these molecules increases. But microwaves generally penetrate foods only a few centimeters, so heating occurs only near the surface of the food. That is why instructions tell you to let the food stand for a few minutes—so thermal energy can reach the center by conduction. Microwaves also carry cell phone conversations. The process works much like the radio broadcast.

Figure 11 A speed-monitoring trailer uses radar to measure the speed of an approaching car. It reminds motorists of the posted speed limit and makes them aware of their actual speed.

Radar The word *radar* is an acronym for *ra*dio *d*etection *a*nd *r*anging. Radar technology uses a radio transmitter to send out short bursts of radio waves. The waves reflect off the objects they encounter, and bounce back toward where they came from. The returning waves are then picked up and interpreted by a radio receiver.

Recall that the Doppler effect is an apparent change in the frequency of a wave. The Doppler effect can be used to find the speed of a moving car. Radio waves are sent from a stationary source, such as the radar trailer in Figure 11, toward a moving car. The faster a car is moving toward the source, the higher is the frequency of the radio waves returning to the source.

Figure 12 A thermogram can be used to diagnose problems in a utility line. **A** When viewed in visible light, the wires all look the same. **B** The colors in the thermogram image show that the electric current in the center wire is not flowing as it should.

Infrared Rays

Infrared rays have higher frequencies than radio waves and lower frequencies than red light. Infrared wavelengths vary from about 1 millimeter to about 750 nanometers. (A nanometer is 10^{-9} meters, or one millionth of a millimeter.) **Infrared rays are used as a source of heat and to discover areas of heat differences.**

You cannot see infrared radiation, but your skin senses it as warmth. Reptile habitats at zoos are often kept warm with infrared lamps. Restaurants use infrared lamps to keep buffet-style foods at a safe temperature for consumption.

Warmer objects give off more infrared radiation than cooler objects. A device called a thermograph uses infrared sensors to create thermograms. **Thermograms** (THUR moh gramz) are color-coded pictures that show variations in temperature. They are used to find places where a building loses heat to the environment. Thermograms can also locate problems in the path of electric current, as shown in Figure 12.

The human body is usually warmer than its surroundings. After a natural disaster such as an earthquake, search-and-rescue teams use infrared cameras to locate victims quickly—even underground.

Visible Light

The visible part of the electromagnetic spectrum is light that the human eye can see. Each wavelength in the visible spectrum corresponds to a specific frequency and has a particular color. Figure 13 shows the wavelength and frequency ranges of different colors of light in a vacuum.

People use visible light to see, to help keep them safe, and to communicate with one another. Light enables people to read. It is what makes flowers, boxes, signs, and all other objects visible. Automobiles have headlights and taillights that make night driving safer. Traffic lights communicate information to drivers about what is expected of them—to stop, for example, when the light is red.

Go Online
PLANETDIARY

For: Activity on the greenhouse effect
Visit: PHSchool.com
Web Code: ccc-2182

Figure 13 Each color of light corresponds to a different range of wavelengths. The wavelengths of visible light are quite small. Wavelengths of red light, for example, are about one hundredth the thickness of a human hair.
Using Tables *As the wavelength decreases from the red end of the spectrum to the violet end, what happens to the frequency?*

The Visible Spectrum		
Color	Wavelength (nm)	Frequency (× 10¹⁴ Hz)
Red	610–750	4.9–4.0
Orange	590–610	5.1–4.9
Yellow	570–590	5.3–5.1
Green	500–570	6.0–5.3
Blue	450–500	6.7–6.0
Violet	400–450	7.5–6.7

Reading Checkpoint *What is the visible part of the electromagnetic spectrum?*

Quick Lab

Evaluating Sunscreen

Procedure

1. Insert a black paper strip inside each of two plastic petri dishes to cover the sides. Place six ultraviolet-detecting beads in each dish. Cover each dish with its lid.

2. On one of the lids, spread a thin layer of sunscreen.

3. Place the dishes in direct sunlight. Record the time it takes for the beads in each dish to change color.

Analyze and Conclude

1. **Comparing and Contrasting** Compare the times the beads in the two dishes took to change color.

2. **Using Models** Explain how this lab models the use of sunscreen. What does the color change of the beads represent?

3. **Predicting** How might a sunscreen with a higher SPF (sun protection factor) affect the time needed for the beads to change color?

Go **O**nline

For: Activity on electromagnetic waves
Visit: PHSchool.com
Web Code: ccp-2182

Figure 14 Airport security screeners use X-rays to search baggage for potentially dangerous objects.
Inferring *Why are there dark areas in this X-ray image?*

Ultraviolet Rays

The wavelengths of ultraviolet rays vary from about 400 nanometers to about 4 nanometers. Ultraviolet radiation has higher frequencies than violet light. **Ultraviolet rays have applications in health and medicine, and in agriculture.**

In moderation, exposure to ultraviolet rays helps your skin produce vitamin D. Vitamin D helps the body absorb calcium from foods to produce healthy bones and teeth. Excessive exposure can cause sunburn, wrinkles, and eventually skin cancer. It can also damage your eyes.

Ultraviolet rays are used to kill microorganisms. In heating and cooling systems of large buildings, ultraviolet rays disinfect the air that flows through the systems. In winter, plant nurseries use ultraviolet lights to help plants grow.

X-Rays

X-rays have very short wavelengths, from about 12 nanometers to about 0.005 nanometers. They have higher frequencies than ultraviolet rays. X-rays have high energy and can penetrate matter that light cannot. **X-rays are used in medicine, industry, and transportation to make pictures of the inside of solid objects.**

Your teeth and bones absorb X-rays. X-ray photographs show softer tissue as dark, highly exposed areas. Bones and teeth appear white. Too much exposure to X-rays can kill or damage living tissue.

The lids on aluminum cans are sometimes inspected with X-rays to make sure they are sealed properly. X-rays can be used to identify the contents of entire truck trailers. Packages and suitcases, such as the one in Figure 14, are X-rayed in search of dangerous contents.

 Reading Checkpoint *What are X-rays used for?*

Looking

Listening

Speaking

Thinking and Speaking

Gamma Rays

Gamma rays have the shortest wavelengths in the electromagnetic spectrum, about 0.005 nanometer or less. They have the highest frequencies and therefore the most energy and the greatest penetrating ability of all the electromagnetic waves. Exposure to tiny amounts of gamma rays are tolerable, but overexposure can be deadly. **Gamma rays are used in the medical field to kill cancer cells and make pictures of the brain, and in industrial situations as an inspection tool.**

Gamma rays are used in radiation therapy to kill cancer cells without harming nearby healthy cells. Gamma rays are also used to make pictures of the human brain, with different levels of brain activity represented by different colors. Four brain scans are shown in Figure 15.

Pipelines are checked with machines that travel on the inside of a pipe, taking gamma ray pictures along the entire length. Technicians examine the pictures for rusting, cracks, or other signs of damage.

Figure 15 Gamma rays emitted by radioactive tracers in the brain are used to produce color-coded images. Areas of high activity show up in red. These images show where the brain is active when the patient is (from left to right) looking at something, listening, speaking, and thinking and speaking. The more involved the task, the more parts of the brain are activated.

Section 18.2 Assessment

Reviewing Concepts

1. List the kinds of waves included in the electromagnetic spectrum, from longest to shortest wavelength.

2. Name three uses for each type of wave.

3. How is radar used to determine the speed of a car?

4. How can X-rays make pictures of the inside of solid objects?

Critical Thinking

5. **Comparing and Contrasting** How are AM radio waves similar to FM radio waves? How are they different?

6. **Classifying** What type of electromagnetic wave are microwaves and radar?

7. **Predicting** Which do you think will penetrate farther into a block of lead, X-rays or gamma rays? Explain your reasoning.

Writing in Science

Explanatory Writing Write one paragraph each about three different kinds of electromagnetic waves that you will encounter today. Use a single characteristic, such as wavelength or frequency, to describe each wave. Explain how life might be different without each kind of wave.

18.3 Behavior of Light

Reading Focus

Key Concepts

- What three types of materials affect the behavior of light?

- How does light behave when it enters a new medium?

Vocabulary

- transparent
- translucent
- opaque
- image
- regular reflection
- diffuse reflection
- mirage
- polarized light
- scattering

Reading Strategy

Monitoring Your Understanding Copy the flowchart below. As you read, complete it to show how different materials affect light.

Figure 16 Water is transparent. You can see through it. That characteristic makes it possible to photograph these fish and other animals living in the ocean.

What would you see if you were snorkeling in warm ocean waters over a coral reef? You might see fish of bright colors, clown fish, sea stars, sponges, and clams. You might see sharks or turtles, and of course, coral. But why can you see these animals so clearly? Why can you see the reef through the water but not, for example, through the bottom of the boat that brought you to the reef?

Light and Materials

Without light, nothing is visible. When you look at the reef animals, what you are really seeing is light. You can see the reef through the water, because light passes through the water between the reef and your eyes. But you can't see the reef through the bottom of the boat because light doesn't pass through the boat.

How light behaves when it strikes an object depends on many factors, including the material the object is made of. **Materials can be transparent, translucent, or opaque.** Each type of material affects the behavior of light in different ways.

A material through which you can see clearly is transparent. A **transparent** material transmits light, which means it allows most of the light that strikes it to pass through it. For example, the water where the fish and coral in Figure 16 live is transparent. While riding on a bus, you can see buildings and trees outside because the bus windows are transparent.

If you can see through a material, but the objects you see through it do not look clear or distinct, then the material is translucent (trans LOO sunt). A **translucent** material scatters light. The soaps in Figure 17A are translucent. When you look into a room through a frosted glass door, you can make out shapes of people and objects, but the shapes are fuzzy and lack detail.

Most materials are opaque (oh PAYK). An **opaque** material either absorbs or reflects all of the light that strikes it. The fruit in Figure 17B is opaque. An opaque object does not allow any light to pass through it. You can't see through a wooden table or a metal desk. Wood and metal are examples of opaque materials.

Interactions of Light

When light encounters matter, some or all of the energy in the light can be transferred to the matter. And just as light can affect matter, matter can affect light. 🔑 **When light strikes a new medium, the light can be reflected, absorbed, or transmitted. When light is transmitted, it can be refracted, polarized, or scattered.**

Reflection When you look in a mirror, you see a clear image of yourself. An **image** is a copy of an object formed by reflected (or refracted) waves of light. Similarly, when you look at a still lake, you can see a sharp reflected image of the far shore. But what happens to the reflected image in the lake if the wind suddenly gusts, causing ripples in the surface of the water? The image is blurred, or fuzzy-looking. When light reflects from a smooth surface, you see a clear, sharp image. When light reflects from a rough surface, you see a blurred reflected image or no image at all.

Regular reflection occurs when parallel light waves strike a surface and reflect all in the same direction. Regular reflection happens when light hits a smooth, polished surface, like a mirror or the surface of a still body of water such as in Figure 18.

Diffuse reflection occurs when parallel light waves strike a rough, uneven surface, and reflect in many different directions. If you could look at this page of your book through a microscope, you would see that the paper has a rough surface. The rough surface causes diffuse reflection of the light that shines on it.

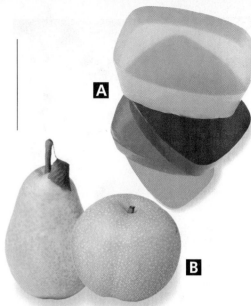

Figure 17 When light strikes a new medium, it can be reflected, absorbed, refracted, polarized, or scattered. **A** The translucent bars of soap scatter light, making the soaps and what you can see through them appear fuzzy. **B** You cannot see through the fruit because opaque materials do not transmit any light.

Figure 18 Almost all objects reflect light. **A** In regular reflection, a smooth surface reflects a clear image because parallel light waves reflect all in the same direction. **B** In diffuse reflection, parallel light waves reflect in many directions.

A Regular reflection

B Diffuse reflection

Figure 19 Light refracts, or bends, when it moves from one medium to another. Because the light bends, the image you see appears to be bent as well.
Relating Cause and Effect *Why does the underwater part of the pencil appear to be closer to you than the part above water?*

Refraction A light wave can refract, or bend, when it passes at an angle from one medium into another. You can easily observe two common effects of refraction when light travels from air into water. Refraction makes underwater objects appear closer and larger than they really are. Refraction can also make an object, such as a pencil, appear to break at the surface of the water, as shown in Figure 19.

Refraction can also sometimes cause a mirage. A **mirage** is a false or distorted image. Mirages occur because light travels faster in hot air than in cooler, denser air. On a sunny day, air tends to be hotter just above the surface of a road than higher up. Normally, light travels from the sun all the way to the ground before being reflected. But on a hot day, light is gradually refracted as it moves into layers of hotter and hotter air. This gradual refraction causes some of the light to follow a curved path, rather than a straight path to the ground. Light that reaches your eyes after traveling in this manner can look as if it was reflected from a layer of water. Mirages also form this way above the hot sand in deserts.

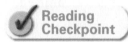 *What is a mirage?*

Polarization Light with waves that vibrate in only one plane is **polarized light.** Polarizing filters transmit light waves that vibrate in this way. Look at Figure 20. Unpolarized light vibrates in all directions. A vertical polarizing filter stops waves vibrating on a horizontal plane. Waves vibrating on a vertical plane pass through. A horizontal polarizing filter then blocks the waves vibrating on a vertical plane. To understand how a polarizing filter works, think of a light wave as being like a postcard that you push through a mail slot in a door. If you hold the postcard so that it lines up with the mail slot, then you can easily push it through. But if the postcard is at an angle to the mail slot, it has trouble passing through. In the same way, a polarizing filter blocks waves with electric fields vibrating in one direction.

Figure 20 This simplified model shows how polarizing filters behave. A vertical polarizing filter blocks light that is horizontally polarized.
Applying Concepts *What would happen if you looked at light through a horizontally polarizing filter and a vertically polarizing filter at the same time?*

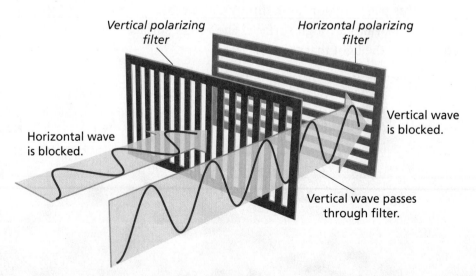

Vertical polarizing filter

Horizontal polarizing filter

Horizontal wave is blocked.

Vertical wave is blocked.

Vertical wave passes through filter.

Light reflecting from a nonmetallic flat surface, such as a window or the surface of a lake, can become polarized. When sunlight reflects from a horizontal surface, horizontally polarized light reflects more strongly than the rest of the sunlight. This reflection produces glare. To block the glare, polarized sunglasses have vertically polarized filters, which block the horizontally polarized light.

Scattering Earth's atmosphere contains many molecules and other tiny particles. These particles can scatter sunlight. **Scattering** means that light is redirected as it passes through a medium. Look at Figure 21. A scattering effect reddens the sun at sunset and sunrise. Most of the particles in the atmosphere are very small. Small particles scatter shorter-wavelength blue light more than light of longer wavelengths. The sunlight encounters more of the molecules and tiny particles that scatter the shorter-wavelength colors. By the time the sunlight reaches your eyes, most of the blue and even some of the green and yellow have been scattered. Most of what remains for your eyes to detect are the longer wavelengths of light, orange and red.

When the sun is high in the sky, its light travels a shorter distance through Earth's atmosphere. It scatters blue light in all directions much more than other colors of light. Scattering explains why the sky appears blue on a sunny day, even though air itself is colorless.

Figure 21 The lower the sun is on the horizon, the more of the atmosphere the light travels through before it reaches Earth's surface. In certain weather conditions, the blue, green, and yellow wavelengths of sunlight are heavily scattered. What's left to enjoy are the beautiful reds and oranges of sunrise and sunset.

Section 18.3 Assessment

Reviewing Concepts

1. 🌐 Explain the differences among opaque, transparent, and translucent materials. Name two objects made from each type of material.

2. 🌐 List and explain three things that can happen to a light wave when it enters a new medium.

3. What is the difference between diffuse reflection and regular reflection?

4. What happens to light that passes through a horizontal polarizing filter?

Critical Thinking

5. **Predicting** A black car reflects much less light than a white car. Which car's surface will be warmer after 1 hour of sunshine? Explain.

6. **Formulating Hypotheses** A mountain climber finds that her sunglasses are not blocking glare from a vertical rock wall. What can you hypothesize about the polarizing filters in her sunglasses?

7. **Applying Concepts** On a foggy night, you can see a car's headlight beams but you may not be able to see the car itself. Explain why.

Connecting Concepts

Mechanical Waves Review the behaviors of mechanical waves discussed in Section 17.2, such as reflection and refraction. Compare them with the behaviors of light.

18.4 Color

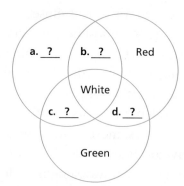

Reading Focus

Key Concepts
- How does a prism separate white light?
- What determines the color of an object?
- What are the primary colors of light?
- What are the primary colors of pigments?

Vocabulary
- dispersion
- primary colors
- secondary color
- complementary colors of light
- pigment
- complementary colors of pigments

Reading Strategy
Venn Diagram Copy the Venn diagram below. After you read, label the diagram for mixing primary colors of light. Make a similar diagram for mixing primary colors of pigments.

a. ?   b. ?   Red

White

c. ?   d. ?

Green

Have you ever zoomed in on a color photograph displayed on a computer screen? If you have, you've seen that the photograph is made up of many tiny squares, called *pixels,* as shown in Figure 22. Your computer screen might be set to display 256 colors, thousands of colors, or even millions of colors. All of these colors are generated using various combinations of only three colors of light. If you were to print the same photograph, your printer would also use only three colors, plus black, to create the image out of tiny dots of ink. The three colors the computer uses are different from the three the printer uses. How can that be?

Figure 22 This student is looking at many colors on his computer screen. What he is actually seeing, however, are combinations of only three colors of light.

Figure 23 White light is dispersed by prisms and water droplets. **A** When white light passes through a prism, the shorter wavelengths are bent more than the longer wavelengths. The colors are separated. When red light enters the second prism, it is refracted but the color does not change. **B** Water droplets separate the colors of sunlight, producing a rainbow.

Separating White Light Into Colors

In 1666, the English physicist Isaac Newton investigated the visible spectrum. First, he used a glass prism to produce a visible spectrum from sunlight. With screens, he then blocked all colors of light except blue. Next, he placed a second prism where the blue light was visible. The second prism refracted the blue light but had no further effect on the color. Newton's experiments showed that white sunlight is made up of all the colors of the visible spectrum.

How does a prism separate white light into a visible spectrum? **As white light passes through a prism, shorter wavelengths refract more than longer wavelengths, and the colors separate.** Look at Figure 23A. When red light, with its longer wavelength, enters a glass prism, it slows down the least of all the colors, and so is bent the least. Violet light is bent the most. The process in which white light separates into colors is called **dispersion.**

A rainbow gives a beautiful example of dispersion. Droplets of water in the air act like prisms. They separate sunlight into the spectrum. When light enters a raindrop, it slows down and refracts. Then it reflects off the far inner surface of the raindrop. It refracts again as it exits the raindrop, speeds up, and travels back toward the source of the light.

What process causes a rainbow?

The Colors of Objects

Would it surprise you to learn that an object of any color does not have a definite color? An object's color is the color of light that reaches your eye when you look at the object. **The color of any object depends on what the object is made of and on the color of light that strikes the object.** Sunlight contains all the colors of the visible spectrum. But when you look, for example, at a red car in sunlight, the red paint reflects mostly red light. Most of the other colors in white light are absorbed at the surface of the paint.

For: Links on color
Visit: www.SciLinks.org
Web Code: ccn-2184

Figure 24 Under white light, the pots appear white, green, yellow, red, and blue. **Observing** *How does the red pot appear under red, green, and blue light?*

What happens if you change the color of the light shining on an object? Look at Figure 24, which shows the same stack of flower pots in several different colors of light. The pots appear to be different colors when viewed in different colors of light. For example, the red pot looks black when viewed in blue light because the red plastic absorbs all of the light striking it. No red light reaches the object, so none can be reflected from it.

Mixing Colors of Light

Figure 25 shows how equal amounts of three colors of light—red, green, and blue—combine to produce white light. **Primary colors** are three specific colors that can be combined in varying amounts to create all possible colors. ⊙ **The primary colors of light are red, green, and blue.**

When red light strikes a white surface, red light is reflected. Similarly, when blue light strikes a white surface, blue light is reflected. What happens if both red light and blue light strike a white surface? Both colors are reflected and the two colors add together to make a third color, magenta. When colors of light are mixed together, the colors add together to form a new color.

The secondary colors of light are cyan, yellow, and magenta. Each **secondary color** of light is a combination of two primary colors. Therefore, if you add a primary color to the proper secondary color, you will get white light. Any two colors of light that combine to form white light are **complementary colors of light.** A complementary color pair is a combination of one primary color and one secondary color. Blue and yellow are complementary colors of light, as are red and cyan, and green and magenta.

Figure 25 The three primary colors of light are red, green, and blue. When any two primary colors combine, a secondary color is formed. **Observing** *What color of light is produced when all three primary colors combine in equal amounts?*

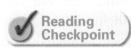 *How is a secondary color of light formed?*

Mixing Pigments

Paints, inks, photographs, and dyes get their colors from pigments. A **pigment** is a material that absorbs some colors of light and reflects other colors. Stone Age cave paintings were made with natural pigments from colored earth and clay. Over the centuries, natural pigments have been obtained from many sources, including metal oxide compounds, minerals, plants, and animals. Today's artists use paints made from natural pigments as well as from synthetic, or manufactured, pigments.

The primary colors of pigments are cyan, yellow, and magenta. Perhaps you have noticed that color printers and photocopiers use these three colors, plus black. You can mix varying amounts of these primary pigment colors to make almost any other color. Each pigment reflects one or more colors. As pigments are mixed together, more colors are absorbed and fewer colors are reflected. When two or more pigments are mixed together, the colors absorbed by each pigment are subtracted out of the light that strikes the mixture.

Look at Figure 26. The light filters absorb light in much the same way pigments do. When cyan and magenta are combined, blue is formed. Cyan and yellow combine to form green. Yellow and magenta combine to form red. The secondary colors of pigments are red, green, and blue. Any two colors of pigments that combine to make black pigment are **complementary colors of pigments.**

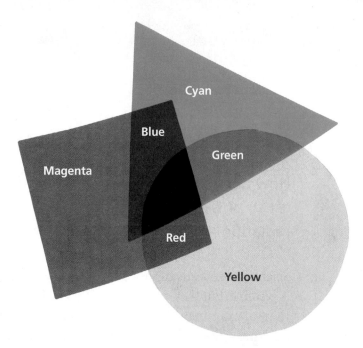

Figure 26 The three primary colors of pigments are cyan, yellow, and magenta. When the three primary colors of pigments are combined, the secondary colors of pigments are formed. **Interpreting Diagrams** *Which colors of pigments combine to make black?*

Section 18.4 Assessment

Reviewing Concepts

1. Explain how a prism separates white light into the colors of the spectrum.

2. What determines the color of an object?

3. What three colors of light can combine to form any other color?

4. What three colors of pigments can combine to form any other color?

5. Explain how the process of dispersion of light forms a rainbow.

6. What are pigments? Explain how different pigments affect light.

Critical Thinking

7. **Predicting** What color would a blue wall appear under green light?

8. **Applying Concepts** Why does combining equal amounts of cyan, yellow, and magenta paints form black?

Writing in Science

Explain a Concept Write a letter to a friend who is not in class with you. Explain how an object gets its color. Give evidence and use examples to support your explanation.

New Light on Old Art

How does an expert know if a painting is by a famous artist, or is a fake? Scientific methods use electromagnetic radiation—visible light, ultraviolet, infrared, and X-rays.

Scientific methods cannot prove that a painting is genuine, but they can prove that it is a forgery. Careful examination may reveal aspects of the painting—the artist's methods or the materials used—that come from a time period later than the supposed date of the painting.

The simplest techniques used to examine paintings are those involving visible light. Looking at a cross section of a paint sample with a microscope or hand lens shows how the artist built up the layers of paint.

Scientists are able to examine the structure of the paint pigment in detail using high-powered microscopes. The structure can reveal whether the pigment is natural or has been made synthetically. Because synthetic paint pigments were not developed until the 1800s, the presence of synthetic pigment indicates the earliest date for the painting.

VISIBLE LIGHT

Interpreting visible light
This is the part of the electromagnetic spectrum to which human eyes are sensitive. Paint pigments reflect some parts of the visible spectrum and absorb others, so the eye perceives them as colored.

Examining samples
Using scalpels and tweezers, experts take tiny samples from a painting to examine the painted surface.

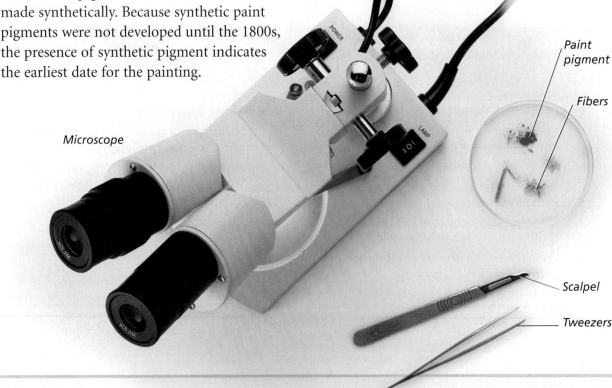

Paint pigment

Fibers

Microscope

Scalpel

Tweezers

Examining the Paint Surface

Identifying the pigments used in a painting usually requires taking one or more tiny samples from the painting. This sampling must be done with extreme care.

Carmine pigment

COCHINEAL BEETLES

Yellow lake pigment

BUCKTHORN BERRIES

Natural materials

Before the 1800s, most pigments used by artists were from natural sources. Many, including yellow lake, were obtained from plants. Some, such as carmine or cochineal, were of animal origin. Others, like ultramarine, came from minerals.

Lapis lazuli *was ground to a powder to make ultramarine pigment.*

Powdered pigment

Ultramarine pigment

Synthetic pigment has round, fine particles

Natural pigment has rough, crystalline particles

Under the microscope
High magnifications (100 to 500 times) show the physical structure of pigment particles. Here, the particles in the sample of synthetic ultramarine are different from those in the natural sample. Synthetic ultramarine was introduced in 1828, so paintings using this pigment could not have been made earlier than that year.

Looking Beneath the Paint Surface

Rather than removing samples of the paint layer, non-invasive methods examine an intact painting by using the nonvisible regions of the electromagnetic spectrum. Ultraviolet, infrared, and X-rays can reveal many secrets that are invisible to the human eye.

Ultraviolet rays are best at showing surface features. The varnish that is the top layer of most paintings will fluoresce when exposed to ultraviolet. This fluorescence shows whether the original varnish has been disturbed.

Infrared rays can penetrate the layers of paint, so infrared imaging can be used to detect charcoal sketches and other images that are often hidden beneath the painted surface.

X-rays are used to look through a painting. X-rays are absorbed by dense materials and pass through others. Pigments that include metal atoms, such as white lead, show up clearly, as do metal objects used in the painting's construction. One forger was caught when X-rays revealed a machine-made nail in the wooden panel under a painting that was supposedly painted in the 1500s! Machine-made nails were not manufactured until the 1800s.

ULTRAVIOLET RAYS

Interpreting ultraviolet radiation

Although transparent to visible light, the varnish layer on the surface of most paintings can be seen using ultraviolet rays. In this copy of Cranach's painting, the ultraviolet makes the varnish layer fluoresce. Dark regions show areas that have been retouched or painted over.

Darker areas have been retouched or painted over.

Art forgery detection
A technician operates an infrared scanner. He is examining a copy of a painting by the German painter Lucas Cranach the Elder (1472–1553).

INFRARED RAYS

Interpreting infrared imaging

The penetrating power of infrared most often uncovers preliminary sketches. But infrared imaging can also reveal surprising changes in the development of a work of art. In this self-portrait by Judith Leyster about 1630, the infrared image reveals that the artist originally included a portrait of herself on the easel. But later she changed the portrait to a musician.

Merry musician in the final painting

Infrared rays penetrate layers of paint, revealing an underlying self-portrait.

X-RAYS

Interpreting X-rays

X-rays can reveal the creative process at work. In this portrait of Pope Julius II, painted by Raphael in 1511–1512, the X-ray image shows a pattern of crossed keys on the wall behind the seated figure. The keys do not appear in visible light. Because oil paints are opaque to visible light, the artist probably simply painted over the keys.

Part of the overpainted pattern of crossed keys

Horizontal wooden battens used to strengthen the panel

Going Further

■ Choose one of these painting styles to research: impressionism, surrealism, pointillism, or op art. Prepare an oral report to share with the class, including an explanation of the painting style, how light and color are used in the style, and three samples of the painting style.

18.5 Sources of Light

Reading Focus

Key Concepts

- What are the six common sources of light?
- How does each type of light source generate light?

Vocabulary

- ◆ luminous
- ◆ incandescent
- ◆ fluorescence
- ◆ phosphor
- ◆ laser
- ◆ coherent light

Reading Strategy

Sequencing Copy and complete the flowchart below. As you read, pick two other light sources and complete a similar flowchart showing how each source generates light.

Incandescent Bulb

Electrons flow through filament.

↓

a. _____?_____

↓

Filament radiates light.

Figure 27 An incandescent bulb contains a filament. As electrons flow through the filament, the filament gets hot and emits light. **Formulating Hypotheses** *Why is a 100-watt bulb generally brighter than a 75-watt bulb?*

As sunlight fades toward the end of the day, objects around you become less and less visible. When the sun has completely set, you can no longer see your surroundings. Objects are invisible in the dark because no light is available to reflect off them. But some things, such as flashlights and fireflies, produce their own light. Objects that give off their own light are **luminous.** The sun is luminous, as are all light sources.

⊙ **Common light sources include incandescent, fluorescent, laser, neon, tungsten-halogen, and sodium-vapor bulbs.** Each type of bulb produces light in a different way.

Incandescent Light

The light produced when an object gets hot enough to glow is **incandescent.** Figure 27 shows an incandescent light bulb. Inside, you can see the filament, a thin coil of wire stretched between two thicker wires. ⊙ **When electrons flow through the filament of an incandescent bulb, the filament gets hot and emits light.**

The filaments in incandescent light bulbs are made of a substance called tungsten. Incandescent light bulbs are filled with a mixture of nitrogen gas and argon gas at very low pressure. These gases do not react with the filament as oxygen would, and so the filament lasts longer. Incandescent bulbs give off most of their energy as heat, not light.

Fluorescent Light

In a process called **fluorescence** (floo uh RES uns), a material absorbs light at one wavelength and then emits light at a longer wavelength. A **phosphor** is a solid material that can emit light by fluorescence. **Fluorescent light bulbs emit light by causing a phosphor to steadily emit photons.** A fluorescent bulb, such as the one in Figure 28, is a glass tube that contains mercury vapor. Inside, the glass is coated with phosphors.

When electric current flows through a fluorescent bulb, small pieces of metal called electrodes heat up and emit electrons. The electrons hit atoms of the mercury vapor, causing the mercury atoms to emit ultraviolet rays. The ultraviolet rays strike the phosphor coating on the inside of the tube and the atoms emit visible light.

You may have noticed that office buildings and schools use mostly fluorescent lights. Fluorescent tubes do not get as hot as incandescent bulbs because they emit most of their energy as light. This means that they use energy very efficiently. One 18-watt fluorescent tube provides the same amount of light as a 75-watt incandescent bulb, and the fluorescent tube lasts ten times longer.

Reading Checkpoint *What happens during fluorescence?*

Glass tube filled with mercury vapor

Electrode

Electrical contacts

Figure 28 The electrodes in a fluorescent bulb emit electrons that cause the mercury atoms to emit ultraviolet rays. These rays cause the phosphor coating to emit light.

≡Quick Lab

Comparing Fluorescent and Incandescent Light

Materials

spectroscope, clear incandescent bulb, fluorescent bulb, colored pencils

Procedure

1. Turn on a clear, incandescent bulb. **CAUTION** *Incandescent bulbs get quite hot after they have been on for some time.* Observe the spectrum of the light coming from the incandescent bulb through a spectroscope.

2. Use colored pencils to draw this spectrum. Label the source of the spectrum.

3. Repeat Steps 1 and 2 with a fluorescent bulb.

Analyze and Conclude

1. **Comparing and Contrasting** How do the spectra produced by incandescent and fluorescent lights compare?

2. **Drawing Conclusions** During fluorescence, electrons absorb energy and move to specific higher energy levels. As they move back to a lower energy level, they release energy in the form of light. How does this fact help explain the appearance of the spectrum of fluorescent light?

Laser Light

A **laser** is a device that generates a beam of coherent light. The word *laser* stands for *l*ight *a*mplification by *s*timulated *e*mission of *r*adiation. 🔑 **Laser light is emitted when excited atoms of a solid, liquid, or gas emit photons.** Light in which waves have the same wavelength, and the crests and troughs are lined up, is **coherent light.** A beam of coherent light doesn't spread out significantly from its source, so the light has a relatively constant intensity. The energy it carries may be focused on a small area.

Lasers can cut through metals and make computer chips. Surgeons use lasers to cut or repair damaged tissue. Lasers carry information through optical fibers. Laser light is used to measure distances precisely.

📖 HOW It Works

Gas Laser

Laser light is produced by exciting the atoms of a solid, liquid, or gas so that they emit photons. Some of these photons collide with other excited atoms and stimulate the emission of more photons. Eventually some photons are released as an intense beam of light. The gas laser shown here uses a mixture of helium and neon gases. **Interpreting Photographs** *How does a laser produce coherent light?*

A **Gas mixture** Helium and neon gases are held in a sealed glass tube. Additional tubes, containing electrodes, are attached at the sides.

Fully reflective mirror *Photons bounce between this and a second, semi-reflective mirror.*

Using lasers Hand-held devices incorporating lasers are used in stores for reading bar codes. In the home, they are at the heart of many devices such as DVD and CD players.

Laser beam scans the label.

Neon Light

A big city at night is likely aglow in neon lights. **Neon lights emit light when electrons move through a gas or a mixture of gases inside glass tubing.** Many lights called neon lights contain gases other than neon. Often, other gases including helium, argon, and krypton are used in neon lights. Helium gas gives off a pink light. A mixture of argon gas and mercury vapor produces greenish-blue light. Krypton gas produces a pale violet light. Pure neon emits red light when electrons flow through the gas. Each kind of gas emits photons of different energies, and therefore different colors. The different photons emitted combine to give each glowing gas a distinctive color. The color of glass used to make the tube can also affect the color of the light.

Go Online
SCIENCE NEWS

For: Articles on light and optics
Visit: PHSchool.com
Web Code: cce-2185

B **Electrode** An electric current passes between this electrode and its twin on the other side of the tube, raising gas atoms to an excited state. This causes the atoms to release photons.

C **Photon multiplication** The photons begin to bounce back and forth off the mirrors at either end. Some hit other excited atoms, stimulating the emission of additional photons.

D **Semi-reflective mirror** Because it is only semi-reflective, this mirror reflects most of the photons but lets a few of them through.

E **Laser beam** A straight, narrow, intense beam of coherent light emerges at this end.

Neon atom — Tube wall — Mirror

Mirror — Helium atom — Coherent waves — Laser beam

Coherent light
The waves in laser light all have the same wavelength and direction of travel, and their peaks coincide. Light with these properties is called coherent light.

Sodium-Vapor Light

Sodium-vapor lights contain a small amount of solid sodium, as well as a mixture of neon and argon gases. 🔑 **As electric current passes through a sodium-vapor bulb, it ionizes the gas mixture. The mixture warms up and the heat causes the sodium to change from a solid into a gas.** The current of electrons knocks electrons in sodium to higher energy levels. When the electrons move back to lower energy levels, the sodium atoms emit light. Sodium-vapor lights are energy efficient and give off very bright light. Many streets and parking lots are illuminated with sodium-vapor lights. Figure 29 shows how sodium-vapor light produced with neon and argon can alter the color of the objects it illuminates.

Figure 29 The yellow color of sodium-vapor light makes objects look different than they look in sunlight.

Tungsten-Halogen Light

Tungsten-halogen light is produced in much the same way as incandescent light. But unlike incandescent lights, a tungsten-halogen's bulb has a small amount of a halogen gas, such as iodine, bromine, or fluorine. 🔑 **Inside a tungsten-halogen bulb, electrons flow through a tungsten filament. The filament gets hot and emits light.** The halogen gas reduces wear on the filament, so tungsten-halogen bulbs last longer than incandescent bulbs. The bulb of a tungsten-halogen light is made of quartz, because quartz has a high melting point. If glass were used, it would start to melt when the bulb got hot.

Section 18.5 Assessment

Reviewing Concepts

1. 🔑 Name six common sources of light.
2. 🔑 Describe how each type of bulb produces visible light.
3. Why are fluorescent light bulbs often used in office buildings and schools?
4. List three uses for lasers.
5. How are tungsten-halogen bulbs different from incandescent bulbs?

Critical Thinking

6. **Comparing and Contrasting** How are the six main types of lights similar? How are they different?

7. **Applying Concepts** Why do some bulbs heat up more than others?

8. **Formulating Hypotheses** A friend rubs a compact fluorescent bulb on her shirt on a dry day, and the bulb lights up for a moment. Propose a hypothesis to explain why.

Connecting Concepts

Energy Review the types of energy in Section 15.1: mechanical, chemical, thermal, electrical, electromagnetic, and nuclear. Then pick two light sources and describe the energy changes in each after you turn on the light.

Mixing Colored Lights

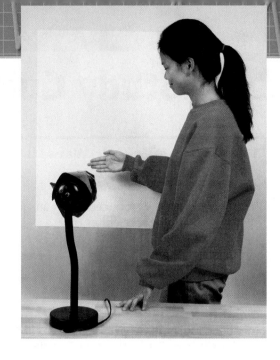

What is color? How many different colors can be formed from a combination of only three colors? In this exploration, you will examine what happens when lights of three different colors are mixed.

Problem
How can you produce a range of colors from three lights of different colors?

Materials
- sources of red, blue, and green light
- tape
- large sheet of white paper

Skills
Observing

Procedure

1. On a separate sheet of paper, make a copy of the data table shown.

Data Table

Light Sources	Colors of Lights	Colors of Shadows
Red only		
Blue only		
Green only		
Red and blue		
Red and green		
Blue and green		
Red, blue, and green		

2. Dim the room lights. Turn on the red light source and shine it on a large sheet of white paper. In your data table, record the colors you observe on the paper. **CAUTION** *Do not touch lamps when they are on. They may be hot.*

3. Place your hand between the light source and the paper as shown. Record the color of your hand's shadow.

4. Repeat Steps 2 and 3 with the blue and then with the green light source.

5. Now turn on the red and blue light sources and allow their beams to partially overlap. Record your observations in your data table.

6. Place your hand in the overlapping beams of light. Note the colors of any shadows that your hand makes. Record your observations.

7. Repeat Steps 5 and 6 with the red and green light sources. Then repeat Steps 5 and 6 with the blue and green light sources.

8. Turn on all three light sources and allow their beams to overlap. Record your observations.

9. Place your hand in the overlapping red, green, and blue beams. Note the colors of any shadows that your hand makes on the white paper. Record your observations.

Analyze and Conclude

1. **Observing** What happened when two colored lights overlapped?

2. **Analyzing Data** How did the combination of two colored lights produce the shadows you observed?

3. **Applying Concepts** Explain how combining three colored lights produced the colors you observed.

4. **Drawing Conclusions** From the shadows you observed when using three colored lights, what can you conclude about how colors of light combine? Explain your answer.

Go Further Examine the effects of red, green, and blue lights on the appearance of familiar objects, such as red apples and green grass. Prepare a report explaining your observations and present the report to the class.

18.1 Electromagnetic Waves

Key Concepts

- Electromagnetic waves are produced when an electric charge vibrates or accelerates.
- Electromagnetic waves can travel through a vacuum as well as through matter. The speed of light in a vacuum, c, is 3.00×10^8 m/s.
- Electromagnetic waves vary in wavelength and frequency.
- Electromagnetic radiation behaves sometimes like a wave and sometimes like a stream of particles.
- Light spreads out as it moves away from its source.

Vocabulary

electromagnetic waves, *p. 533;* electric field, *p. 533;* magnetic field, *p. 533;* electromagnetic radiation, *p. 533;* photoelectric effect, *p. 537;* photons, *p. 537;* intensity, *p. 538*

18.2 The Electromagnetic Spectrum

Key Concepts

- The electromagnetic spectrum includes radio waves, infrared waves, visible light, ultraviolet rays, X-rays, and gamma rays.
- Electromagnetic waves are used in communications, medicine, and industry.

Vocabulary

electromagnetic spectrum, *p. 540;* amplitude modulation, *p. 541;* frequency modulation, *p. 541;* thermograms, *p. 543*

18.3 Behavior of Light

Key Concepts

- Materials can be transparent, translucent, or opaque.
- When light strikes a new medium, it can be reflected, absorbed, or transmitted.

Vocabulary

transparent, *p. 546;* translucent, *p. 547;* opaque, *p. 547;* image, *p. 547;* regular reflection, *p. 547;* diffuse reflection, *p. 547;* mirage, *p. 548;* polarized light, *p. 548;* scattering, *p. 549*

18.4 Color

Key Concepts

- As white light passes through a prism, shorter wavelengths refract more than longer wavelengths, and the colors separate.
- The color of any object depends on what the object is made of and on the color of light that strikes the object.
- The primary colors of light are red, green, and blue.
- The primary colors of pigments are cyan, yellow, and magenta.

Vocabulary

dispersion, *p. 551;* primary colors, *p. 552;* secondary color, *p. 552;* complementary colors of light, *p. 552;* pigment, *p. 553;* complementary colors of pigments, *p. 553*

18.5 Sources of Light

Key Concepts

- Common light sources include incandescent, fluorescent, laser, neon, tungsten-halogen, and sodium-vapor bulbs.
- Each light source produces light in a different way.

Vocabulary

luminous, *p. 558;* incandescent, *p. 558;* fluorescence, *p. 559;* phosphor, *p. 559;* laser, *p. 560;* coherent light, *p. 560*

Thinking Visually

Web Diagram Copy the web diagram below onto a sheet of paper. Use information from the chapter to complete the diagram.

Reviewing Content

Choose the letter that best answers the question or completes the statement.

1. Electromagnetic waves
   a. all have the same wavelength.
   b. do not carry energy.
   c. can travel through empty space.
   d. all have the same frequency.

2. The particle model describes light as
   a. a stream of photons.
   b. an interference pattern.
   c. a wave.
   d. an electric field.

3. The electromagnetic waves with the highest frequency are
   a. infrared rays.   b. gamma rays.
   c. ultraviolet rays.   d. radio waves.

4. Microwaves and radar are
   a. infrared rays.   b. X-rays.
   c. radio waves.   d. ultraviolet rays.

5. Light that vibrates in only one direction is
   a. scattered.   b. reflected.
   c. refracted.   d. polarized.

6. Objects appear fuzzy through a material that is
   a. polarized.   b. translucent.
   c. transparent.   d. opaque.

7. Combining equal intensities of red light, green light, and blue light makes
   a. a secondary color.
   b. a complementary color.
   c. black light.
   d. white light.

8. A green object
   a. absorbs green light.
   b. reflects green light.
   c. absorbs yellow and blue light.
   d. reflects red and blue light.

9. An object that produces its own light is
   a. luminous.   b. coherent.
   c. opaque.   d. translucent.

10. Which type of light bulb uses phosphors?
    a. neon   b. incandescent
    c. tungsten-halogen   d. fluorescent

Understanding Concepts

11. How do electric and magnetic fields interact in an electromagnetic wave?

12. What behavior of light is evidence for a wave model of light?

13. Why are infrared rays useful in search-and-rescue operations?

14. How are ultraviolet rays harmful? How can they be helpful?

15. X-rays can take pictures of your bones but visible light cannot. Explain why.

16. Explain why you can see through the glass walls of the terrarium below.

17. How do polarized sunglasses work?

18. What does a prism do to white light?

19. How are the secondary colors of light related to the primary colors?

20. What are complementary colors of pigments?

21. When mixing colors of light, why does combining a secondary color with its complementary color give white light?

22. Explain why fluorescent lights are more efficient than incandescent lights.

23. Explain how laser light is different from ordinary visible light.

24. What is the purpose of halogen gas in a tungsten-halogen lamp?

Critical Thinking

25. Comparing and Contrasting How are microwaves and infrared rays similar? How are they different?

26. Applying Concepts How does the frequency of a car's returning radar signal change if the car moves away from the radar source?

27. Applying Concepts What color would the sunset be if you observed it on the moon? (*Hint:* the moon has no atmosphere.)

28. Comparing and Contrasting List the three primary colors of light and the three primary colors of pigments. What is the result if the three primary colors of light are mixed? What is the result if the three primary colors of pigments are mixed?

Use the illustration below to answer Questions 29–31.

29. Interpreting Photos Describe each combination of colors in A, B, and C.

30. Applying Concepts If you had green paint, such as produced in mixture A in the illustration, what is the fewest number of colors you could mix with it to get black? What would the color or colors be?

31. Predicting What color would you expect to make if you combined cyan and yellow from A, magenta and yellow from B, and only the magenta from C? Explain why.

32. Inferring Why might it be unsafe to look directly at laser light?

Math Skills

33. Calculating An FM radio station broadcasts on a frequency of 91 MHz. What is the wavelength of the wave that carries the coded information?

34. Calculating What is the frequency of a microwave that has a wavelength of 0.050 m?

35. Converting Units Convert the speed of light to miles per second and miles per hour. (*Hint:* 1 mile = 1610 meters)

Concepts in Action

36. Problem Solving What can you do to ensure even heating of microwaved food? Why does that work?

37. Predicting Are you more likely to see a mirage in the desert when the temperature is 32°C or 23°C? Explain why.

38. Relating Cause and Effect You are working the lights for a school play. The red jacket on the main character looks red, but her green pants look black. What is happening? How can you make both her jacket and her pants look their true color?

39. Writing in Science Write an advertisement for a sunscreen product. Make sure to explain to consumers why ultraviolet rays are dangerous.

Performance-Based Assessment

Comparing and Contrasting Visit a store that sells a variety of light bulbs including incandescent bulbs, tungsten-halogen bulbs, and fluorescent bulbs. Gather information from the packages on price and expected hours of service and display the data in a table. Conclude from your data which kind of bulb provides the most economical lighting for a particular purpose. Write your conclusions in a paragraph and share it with your family and classmates.

For: Self-grading assessment
Visit: PHSchool.com
Web Code: cca-2180

Standardized Test Prep

Test-Taking Tip

Analyzing Data

Some test questions are based on graphs. Take about 20 seconds to scan the graph. Read the labels. Describe the graph to yourself. *The graph gives information on wavelength, from shorter to longer, and frequency, from lower to higher.* Use the information to select which choice best answers the question.

Wavelength

What relationship is represented by the graph?

(A) Frequency is directly proportional to wavelength.
(B) Frequency is inversely proportional to wavelength.
(C) Comparing wavelength and frequency shows photon energy.
(D) Waves with lower frequencies and longer wavelengths exhibit the photoelectric effect.
(E) Wavelength is greater than frequency.

(Answer: B)

Choose the letter that best answers the question or completes the statement.

1. In order of increasing frequency, the electromagnetic waves are radio waves, infrared rays,
   (A) microwaves, visible light, X-rays, and gamma rays.
   (B) visible light, ultraviolet rays, X-rays, and gamma rays.
   (C) ultraviolet rays, X-rays, visible light, and radar.
   (D) gamma rays, X-rays, ultraviolet rays, and visible light.
   (E) gamma rays, X-rays, visible light, and ultraviolet rays.

2. A light source that emits light partly because of its phosphor coating is
   (A) an incandescent bulb.
   (B) a tungsten-halogen lamp.
   (C) a neon tube.
   (D) a fluorescent tube.
   (E) a laser.

3. A material that reflects or absorbs all of the light that strikes it is
   (A) translucent.   (B) opaque.
   (C) black.   (D) transparent.
   (E) incandescent.

4. An electromagnetic wave in space has a frequency of 0.5×10^8 Hz. Its wavelength is
   (A) 0.6 m.   (B) 6 m.
   (C) 60 m.   (D) 600 m.
   (E) 6000 m.

Both a source of red light and a source of blue light shine on a metal, as shown in the diagram below.

Red light   Blue light   Electron

5. What scientific concept does the diagram represent?
   (A) interference
   (B) the photoelectric effect
   (C) polarization
   (D) diffuse reflection
   (E) refraction

6. Why was no electron emitted when the red light hit the metal?
   (A) Photons of red light have too little energy.
   (B) There were not enough photons available.
   (C) All electrons had already been emitted when the blue light hit the metal.
   (D) Red light is absorbed by metal.
   (E) Red light is reflected by metal.

CHAPTER

19 Optics

21st Century Learning

Interpersonal and Collaborative Skills

How do fiber optics work?

Everything that you say over the phone or send over the Internet at some point travels as pulses of light through strands of glass called fiber optic cables. Collaborate with a team to research the field of fiber optics. Create a multimedia presentation that explains the role of total internal reflection in fiber optic transmissions. Review and comment on other presentations by your classmates.

How do science concepts apply to your world? Here are some questions you'll be able to answer after you read this chapter.

- Why do some large trucks have a sign that reads, "If you can't see my mirrors, then I can't see you"? *(Section 19.1)*

- Why do automobile manufacturers place warnings on some side-view mirrors saying that objects seen in the mirror are closer than they appear? *(Section 19.1)*

- Why is movie film placed upside down in a movie projector? *(Section 19.2)*

- How is it possible to see something that no longer exists? *(Section 19.3)*

- How can a television signal be transmitted using light? *(Page 587)*

- How can you relax your eyes? *(Section 19.4)*

Each of these small water droplets acts like a lens and forms an image of the flowers in the background.

Chapter Preview

Inquiry > Activity

How Can You Make Glass Disappear?

Procedure

1. Pour vegetable oil into a container until it is half full. Repeat this procedure using water in a second container.

2. Insert a section of glass tubing into each container.

3. Look at the glass tubing through the side of the container with vegetable oil. Then look at the glass tubing through the side of the container with water.

Think About It

1. **Observing** What did you see when you looked at the glass tubing through the container with the vegetable oil? Through the container with the water?

2. **Inferring** Based on your observations, what can you infer about how light travels through the vegetable oil and the glass tubing? Through the water and the glass tubing?

19.1 Mirrors

Reading Focus

Key Concepts

- What is the law of reflection?
- What type of image is produced by each of the three types of mirrors?

Vocabulary

- ray diagram
- angle of incidence
- angle of reflection
- plane mirror
- virtual image
- concave mirror
- focal point
- real image
- convex mirror

Reading Strategy

Comparing and Contrasting After reading this section, compare mirror types by copying and completing the table.

Mirror	Shape of Surface	Image (virtual, real, or both)
Plane	Flat	Virtual
Concave	a. ?	b. ?
Convex	c. ?	d. ?

It is a bright, sunny day and you are enjoying a peaceful afternoon by a lake. The air is still and the surface of the lake looks just like a sheet of glass. In fact, it is so smooth that you can see your reflection in it.

The Law of Reflection

Optics includes the study of how mirrors and lenses form images. In your study of optics, assume that light is made up of rays that travel in straight lines. A **ray diagram** shows how rays change direction when they strike mirrors and pass through lenses.

Figure 1 shows a simple ray diagram of the law of reflection. The incoming ray, called the incident ray, approaches the mirror. The **angle of incidence** is the angle the incident ray makes with a line drawn perpendicular to the surface of the mirror. The mirror reflects the incident ray. The **angle of reflection** is the angle the reflected ray makes with the perpendicular line. ◗ **The law of reflection states that the angle of reflection is equal to the angle of incidence.**

Figure 1 The flat (plane) mirror and the mirror-like lake surface both obey the law of reflection. According to the law of reflection, the angle of an incident ray equals the angle of the reflected ray.

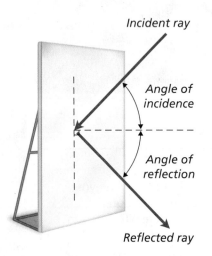

Incident ray

Angle of incidence

Angle of reflection

Reflected ray

Next time you are in a car behind a large truck, look for a sign that reads, "If you can't see my mirror, then I can't see you." Light travels from you to the mirror to the driver's eyes and also from the driver to the mirror to your eyes. If you do not have a line of vision to the truck's side-view mirror, then the truck driver does not have a line of vision to you. It can be dangerous to drive too close to large trucks!

Plane Mirrors

Mirrors are usually made of a sheet of glass that is coated with a thin layer of shiny metal on one surface. A mirror with a flat surface is a **plane mirror.** The large mirror in your bathroom is a plane mirror. When you look into a plane mirror, you see your reversed reflection—a right-left reversed image of yourself. An image is a copy of an object formed by rays of light.

Figure 2 shows how a plane mirror forms an image. To produce your image in a mirror, rays of light strike you and reflect. These reflected rays then strike the mirror and are reflected into your eyes. The dashed lines show how your brain interprets where the rays are coming from. The rays appear to come from behind the mirror. Your image appears the same distance behind the mirror as you are in front, and the image is right side up. If you walk toward the mirror, you'll see your image also move toward the mirror. ☞ **A plane mirror always produces a virtual image.** Although you can see a virtual image, this type of image cannot be projected onto any surface. A **virtual image** is a copy of an object formed at the location from which the light rays appear to come. It is important, however, to realize that the rays do not really come from behind the mirror.

Figure 2 The girl sees a virtual image of herself in the plane mirror. Virtual images such as this cannot be projected onto a screen. Note also how light rays from the object (the girl) reflect from the mirror's surface and obey the law of reflection. **Interpreting Photos** *What do the dashed lines represent?*

Quick Lab

Measuring the Height of Your Mirror Image

Materials

plane mirror, meter stick, newspaper, masking tape

Procedure

1. Have a classmate measure and record your height in centimeters.

2. Stand directly in front of the mirror, 1 m away from it.

3. Look at your image in the mirror. Have a classmate tape newspaper over those parts of the mirror (above and below your image) where you do not see any part of yourself.

4. Measure and record the height of your image by measuring the uncovered part of the mirror.

5. Repeat Steps 3 and 4 for distances of 2 m, 3 m, and 4 m.

Analyze and Conclude

1. **Analyzing Data** How did the height of your image change as you moved farther away from the mirror?

2. **Drawing Conclusions** What is the relationship between your height and the height of your image in the plane mirror?

Concave and Convex Mirrors

Sometimes you see images that are very distorted. Look into both sides of a polished metal spoon. The images you see are quite different from the image formed by a plane mirror. Each side of the spoon produces a different image because each side is curved differently. The curved surface of the spoon changes the way light is reflected.

Concave Mirrors When the inside surface of a curved mirror is the reflecting surface, the mirror is a **concave mirror.** Figure 3A shows how a concave mirror reflects light rays that are parallel to the optical axis. The curvature of the reflecting surface causes the rays to come together. The point at which the light rays meet is called the **focal point.**

Look again at your reflection in the bowl of a spoon. The upside-down image you see is a real image. A **real image** is a copy of an object formed at the point where light rays actually meet. Unlike a virtual image, a real image can be viewed on a surface such as a screen.

👁 **Concave mirrors can form either real or virtual images.** The type of image formed depends upon where the object is in relation to the mirror. Figure 3B shows how a concave mirror forms a real image. When the object is farther from the mirror than the focal point, the reflected rays meet in front of the mirror. Figure 3C shows how a concave mirror forms a virtual image. When the object is closer to the mirror than the focal point is the reflected rays spread out and appear to come from behind the mirror.

Concave mirrors are often used in automobile headlights and flashlights to direct the illumination from a single light bulb into a beam. If the bulb is placed at the focal point of a concave mirror, the reflected light rays will be parallel to one another. This results in a brighter beam of light.

✓ **Reading Checkpoint** *At what location does a real image form?*

Figure 3 Concave mirrors can form either real or virtual images. **A** When parallel incoming rays strike a concave mirror, they are reflected through the focal point. **B** Concave mirrors form real images when the reflected light rays converge. **C** Concave mirrors form virtual images when the reflected rays appear to come from a point behind the mirror.
Interpreting Diagrams
What determines the type of the image formed by a concave mirror?

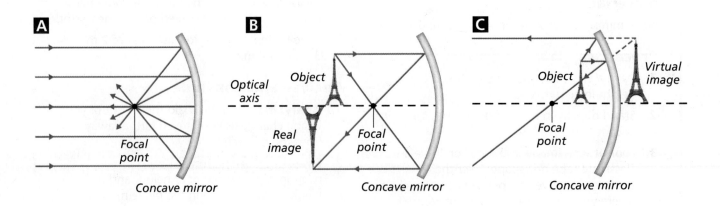

A Concave mirror — Focal point

B Optical axis, Object, Real image, Focal point — Concave mirror

C Object, Focal point, Virtual image — Concave mirror

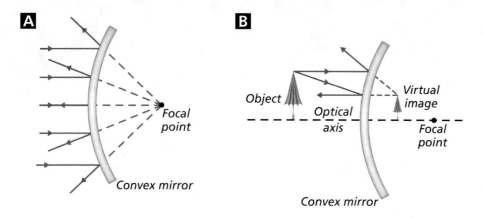

A

Focal point

Convex mirror

B

Object

Optical axis

Virtual image

Focal point

Convex mirror

Figure 4 Convex mirrors can only form virtual images. **A** When parallel incoming rays strike a convex mirror, they are reflected away from one another. **B** Convex mirrors always form virtual images that are upright and smaller than the object. Because of their reduced image size, convex mirrors on automobiles warn that "Objects are closer than they appear."

Convex Mirrors When the outside surface of a curved mirror is the reflecting surface, the mirror is a **convex mirror.** Figure 4A shows how a convex mirror reflects parallel light rays. Note how the curvature of the convex mirror causes the reflected rays to spread out.

⚷ **Convex mirrors always cause light rays to spread out and can only form virtual images.** Figure 4B shows how a convex mirror forms a virtual image. As the rays from the object reflect from the mirror, the rays spread out. Because they appear to be coming from a point behind the mirror, that is where the image appears. The image formed by a convex mirror is always upright and smaller than the object. This allows the mirror to show a wide angle of view. Because of their wide angle of view, round, convex mirrors are often used in store aisles, at hazardous traffic intersections, and for side mirrors on automobiles.

Go **O**nline

active art

For: Activity on mirrors
Visit: PHSchool.com
Web Code: ccp-2191

Section 19.1 Assessment

Reviewing Concepts

1. ⚷ How is the angle of incidence of a light ray related to the angle of reflection?

2. ⚷ What type of image does a plane mirror form?

3. ⚷ What types of image can be produced by a concave mirror? A convex mirror?

4. How are real images different from virtual images?

5. Why can convex mirrors form only one type of image?

Critical Thinking

6. **Applying Concepts** Explain why a plane mirror cannot form a real image.

7. **Inferring** If you place an object 10 cm from a particular concave mirror, a virtual image forms behind the mirror. What can you infer about the focal point of the mirror?

8. **Applying Concepts** If you look inside the bowl of a shiny metal spoon, your image is upside down. If you look at the outside of the bowl, your image is right side up. Explain.

Writing in Science

Compare-Contrast Paragraph Write a paragraph comparing convex mirrors and concave mirrors. (*Hint:* Use the information from your completed Reading Strategy on page 570.)

19.2 Lenses

Key Concepts

- What causes light to refract?
- What type of images do concave and convex lenses form?
- In what types of materials is total internal reflection likely to occur?

Vocabulary

- index of refraction
- lens
- concave lens
- convex lens
- critical angle
- total internal reflection

Reading Strategy

Building Vocabulary Copy the table below. As you read the section, define in your own words each vocabulary word listed in the table.

Vocabulary Term	Definition
Index of refraction	a. _____?_____
Critical angle of refraction	b. _____?_____
Total internal reflection	c. _____?_____

You may wear eyeglasses or contact lenses and you have probably used a hand lens like the one shown in Figure 5. If so, you have seen how the bending, or refracting, of light can change the way you see something. The enlarged image seen through the lens in Figure 5 is due to refraction. The lens material changes the path of the light rays passing through it. The amount the light rays change direction determines the appearance of the image you see.

Index of Refraction of Light

Light usually travels in straight lines. In a vacuum, light travels at a speed of 3.00×10^8 meters per second. Once light passes from a vacuum into any other medium, it slows down. The speed of light in the new medium depends on the material of the new medium.

Some media, such as air, allow light to pass through almost as fast as it would through a vacuum. In fact, air slows the speed of light only by about three ten-thousandths of one percent (0.0003%). Other media cause light to slow down much more. For instance, the speed of light in water and in glass slows to 2.25×10^8 meters per second and 2.00×10^8 meters per second respectively.

Figure 5 Light rays slow and bend as they pass through the curved glass lens. In this case, the result is a magnified image.

When light enters a new medium at an angle, the change in speed causes the light to bend, or refract. For example, when light passes from air into glass or water, it slows down. When light passes from glass or water into air, it speeds up. The amount by which the light refracts as it passes from one medium to another depends upon the difference between the speeds of light in the two media.

Figure 6 shows how the path of a light ray changes as it passes from one medium into another. The incident ray of light, traveling through air, first strikes the boundary between the air and the water. As the light ray enters the water, it is refracted. You can see in Figure 6 that the light ray is now traveling in a new direction. As the ray enters the glass, it is refracted even more. Finally, when the ray reenters air, its path is bent again, but back to its original direction. Note that regardless of the refraction that occurs in the water and glass layers, the ray again travels in its original direction when it reenters the air.

How much the speed of a light ray slows as it enters a new material depends on the material's index of refraction. The **index of refraction** for a material is the ratio of the speed of light in a vacuum to the speed of the light in the material. A material with a low index of refraction (near 1) causes light to slow and refract very little. Air, with an index of refraction of 1.0003, is such a material. Diamond, however, with an index of refraction of 2.42, causes light to slow and refract significantly.

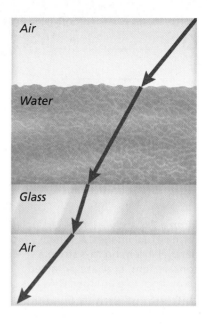

Figure 6 A light ray bends (refracts) as it passes through media with different indices of refraction. **Inferring** *Based on the path of the light ray, which medium has the greatest index of refraction?*

Data Analysis

Properties of Gemstones

Gemstones used in jewelry are known for several of their physical properties—primarily luster and optical brilliance. Luster is a measure of the amount of light that strikes a gemstone's surface and is reflected. Flat and smooth surfaces increase a gemstone's luster.

Like luster, the brilliance of a gemstone involves reflected light. Light that is not reflected by a gem's lustrous surface passes into the stone. The brilliance of a gemstone is a measure of the amount of light entering the gem that is reflected back to the viewer. Precise techniques are used to cut gemstones into shapes that produce maximum brilliance. The combination of a specialized shape and the gemstone's inherent high index of refraction gives gems their brilliance.

The table summarizes the index of refraction and luster of several common gemstones. Note that moissanite is a manufactured material used to simulate diamond.

Properties of Natural and Synthetic Gemstones

Material	Index of Refraction	Luster
Diamond	2.42	17.2%
Moissanite	2.65	20.4%
Ruby	1.77	7.4%
Sapphire	1.77	7.4%
Emerald	1.58	4.8%

1. **Interpreting Tables** Which material is the most lustrous? The least lustrous?

2. **Calculating** What percentage of light striking a sapphire gemstone enters it?

3. **Applying Concepts** If a light ray strikes each material at an angle, in which material would the light ray bend the most?

4. **Applying Concepts** The speed of light through an unknown gemstone is 1.69×10^8 m/s. Identify the gemstone.

A Optical axis

Focal point

Concave lens

B Object

Focal point

Virtual image

Focal point

Concave lens

Figure 7 Concave lenses can only form virtual images. **A** When parallel incoming rays strike a concave lens, they are refracted away from one another. **B** As the light rays diverge after passing through the concave lens, they form a virtual image of the object.

Figure 8 A housefly has two large compound eyes. Each eye is made up of thousands of tiny individual eyes called facets. The outer surface of each facet is convex in shape. The eyes give the fly a nearly 360-degree field of view.

Concave and Convex Lenses

Lenses are used to change the path of light rays before they enter your eyes. A **lens** is an object made of transparent material that has one or two curved surfaces that can refract light. The curvature and thickness of a lens affect the way it refracts light.

Concave Lenses A **concave lens** is curved inward at the center and is thickest at the outside edges. Figure 7A shows how a concave lens refracts light rays. As the rays pass through the lens, each one is refracted due to the change of medium. The rays enter the lens at different angles and so they emerge from the lens at different angles. Concave lenses cause incoming parallel rays to spread out, or diverge. (Concave lenses are a type of diverging lens.) The diverging rays appear to come from a single point, the focal point, on the same side of the lens as the object.

Concave lenses always cause light rays to spread out and can only form virtual images. Figure 7B shows how a concave lens forms a virtual image. The image is formed at the point from which the refracted rays appear to come. The image formed by a concave lens is always smaller than the object.

Concave lenses are often used in the viewfinders of cameras. The small virtual image you see through the viewfinder lens is similar to what the photograph will show. Concave lenses are also combined with mirrors or other lenses to form images in optical instruments such as telescopes.

Convex Lenses Note how the shape of each of the fly's eyes in Figure 8 resembles the exterior surface of a sphere. A shape like this is known as convex. Figure 9A shows that a **convex lens** is curved outward at the center and is thinnest at the outer edges. Figure 9A also shows how light is refracted by a convex lens. As the rays pass through the lens, each one is refracted, and they emerge at different angles. Convex lenses cause incoming parallel rays to come together, or converge. (Convex lenses are also called converging lens.) The converging rays meet at a single point, the focal point, on the side of the lens opposite to the object.

A

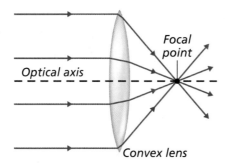

Optical axis

Focal point

Convex lens

Figure 9 Convex lenses can form either real or virtual images. **A** When parallel incoming rays strike a convex lens, they are refracted toward each other and pass through the focal point. **B** When an object is located beyond the focal point of a convex lens, a real image is formed. **C** A magnified, virtual image is formed when the object is located between the focal point and the lens.

B

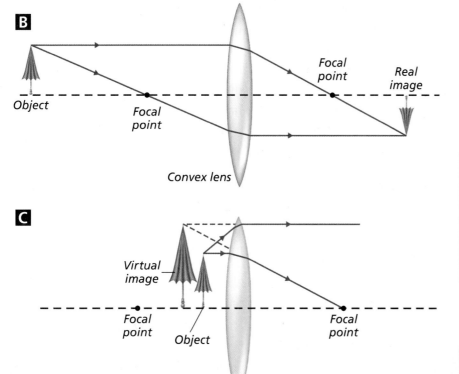

Object

Focal point

Focal point

Real image

Convex lens

Go **O**nline
active art

For: Activity on lenses
Visit: PHSchool.com
Web Code: ccp-2192

Figure 10 In the past, lighthouses used a light source placed at the focal point of a convex lens or series of convex lenses to form a beam of parallel light rays. **Comparing and Contrasting** *How does the setup shown in Figure 9A compare with that used in old lighthouses?*

C

Virtual image

Focal point

Object

Focal point

Convex lens

🔑 **Convex lenses form either real or virtual images.** Whether an image is real or virtual depends upon how far the object is from the lens. Figures 9B and 9C show a convex lens forming real and virtual images.

Convex lenses are used in slide and movie projectors, cameras, and lighthouses like the one in Figure 10. Of course, you don't see an upside-down real image at the movie theatre because the film is placed upside down in the projector. When the rays of light from the upside-down film pass through the projector's convex lens, the real image is projected onto the screen right side up.

Reading Checkpoint *How is a convex lens shaped?*

Total Internal Reflection

A relatively new and very important application of refraction is fiber optics. Light rays are generally unable to exit through the sides of the curving fiber optic strands. Because of this, fiber optics are very useful for carrying information in the form of light. Figures 11A through 11C explain how fiber optics work.

As shown in Figure 11A, a light ray exiting from glass into air is refracted. Figure 11B shows that as the angle of incidence of the exiting ray increases, an angle known as the critical angle of refraction is reached. The **critical angle** is the angle of incidence that produces an angle of refraction of 90 degrees. At the critical angle the light ray bends so much that it takes a path along the glass-air boundary. Figure 11C shows that at angles larger than the critical angle, the light ray bends so much that it is reflected back into the glass. This situation is known as total internal reflection. **Total internal reflection** is the complete reflection of a light ray back into its original medium.

Figure 11 Fiber optics make use of total internal reflection. **A** When a ray hits the glass-air boundary at an angle less than the critical angle, it is partly refracted and partly reflected. **B** At the critical angle, the angle of refraction is 90 degrees. **C** When the critical angle is exceeded, all of the light is reflected—total internal reflection occurs.

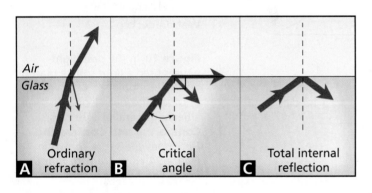

Materials that have small critical angles are likely to cause most of the light entering them to be totally internally reflected. Such materials include diamond and the type of glass used in fiber optic strands. By making use of total internal reflection, fiber optics are able to transmit data in the form of light pulses over large distances with little loss in signal strength. To learn more about fiber optics, see page 586.

Section 19.2 Assessment

Reviewing Concepts

1. What causes light rays to bend?
2. Why can concave lenses form only one type of image?
3. What type of images are formed by concave lenses? By convex lenses?
4. Most of the light entering what type of material is likely to be totally internally reflected?

Critical Thinking

5. **Comparing and Contrasting** How is a convex lens different from a concave lens? How are they the same?

6. **Applying Concepts** Explain how a convex lens is similar to a concave mirror.

Connecting Concepts

Speed of Light In Chapter 18, you learned that light travels at 3.00×10^8 m/s through the air. This speed is the product of frequency and wavelength (Speed = Frequency × Wavelength). Use this equation to show that the wavelength of the light changes when it passes from air to water. (*Hint:* The speed decreases and the frequency does not change.)

Is Video Surveillance an Invasion of Privacy?

Not long ago, video cameras were cumbersome pieces of equipment. They required long cables and stored images on bulky magnetic tape cassettes. Recent advances in optics, digital imaging, and electronic technology have revolutionized video equipment. High-quality digital video cameras that are able to store their images in a variety of convenient formats are now very affordable. Extremely small, battery-powered video cameras are also available to the public.

However, not everyone is excited about the spread of affordable video technology. The explosion in the number of cameras being used for surveillance purposes is a huge concern to many Americans. Is your right to privacy being violated?

The Viewpoints

Video Surveillance Is Not an Invasion of Privacy

Video surveillance is an existing and proven technology that is very effective for many purposes. Traffic cameras on highways help motorists avoid accidents and traffic jams. Video cameras in stores have been used for years to deter and help capture shoplifters. Many major cities have installed cameras at large intersections, to photograph drivers who run red lights. Citations from such systems have cut down on traffic violations and on pedestrian accidents. Sophisticated video systems at some airports can identify known criminals before they board an airplane. The common thing in all of these examples is that the general public is safer because of the use of video surveillance cameras. Having some of our actions recorded on video is a small price to pay for our greatly increased safety.

Video Surveillance Violates a Person's Right to Privacy

Video surveillance comes at a very high price—the loss of personal privacy. Our society is quickly heading toward the day when any individual can be tracked throughout an entire day. Do you want the government and private companies to know every aspect of your life? The United States Supreme Court has stated that some acts that violate a person's reasonable expectation of privacy constitute an illegal search. Yet these actions are going on every day! Video surveillance, which is currently out of control, is just one of many threats to a person's right to a private life. Strict laws designed to protect a person's right to privacy need to be enacted as soon as possible.

Research and Decide

1. **Defining the Issue** Use your own words to describe at least two of the major issues involved in the use of video surveillance cameras.

2. **Analyzing the Viewpoints** List the arguments for and against the use of video surveillance cameras. What are the advantages? What are the disadvantages or risks?

3. **Forming Your Opinion** Is video surveillance an invasion of your right to privacy? If so, in what situations, if any, is it acceptable?

4. **Going Further** Research a recent court case involving video surveillance and privacy. Write a short report summarizing the case. Explain why you agree or disagree with the decision.

For: More on this issue
Visit: PHSchool.com
Web Code: cch-2193

19.3 Optical Instruments

Reading Focus

Key Concepts

- What are the two main types of telescopes?
- How does a camera form an image on film?
- What type of lenses does a compound microscope use to form an image?

Vocabulary

- telescope
- reflecting telescope
- refracting telescope
- camera
- microscope

Reading Strategy

Using Prior Knowledge Copy the diagram below and add to it the names and descriptions of other optical instruments you know. Revise the diagram after reading the section.

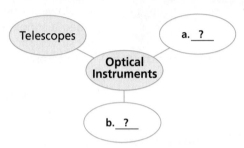

Figure 12 Shown below is one of the two Keck telescopes located on the summit of Hawaii's dormant Mauna Kea volcano. The telescopes, one optical and one infrared, are the largest in the United States. **Inferring** *What might be a reason for the telescopes being located on a mountain top?*

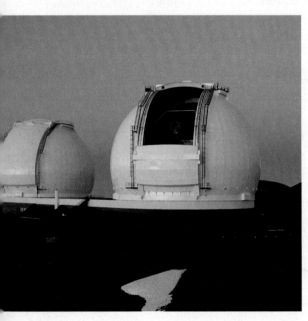

Your view of the world is not shaped solely by what you can see with the unaided eye. From the most distant star in the galaxy to the tiniest cell of your skin, optical instruments improve your ability to see objects. With telescopes, you can see images of astronomical, far-away objects—some of which may no longer exist. With microscopes, you can see detailed images of objects too tiny to otherwise be seen. With cameras, you can fill your photo album with images of your family and friends, or places you have visited.

Telescopes, microscopes, and cameras are all examples of optical instruments that enhance your ability to see. All of these optical instruments have something in common—they all use lenses or mirrors, or a combination of the two, to reflect and refract light.

Telescopes

The universe is so vast that the light coming from the farthest stars has traveled billions of years before it reaches Earth. Some of the light takes so long to reach Earth that by the time it gets here, the source of the light—the star—has long since burned out. With a telescope you can see images of the star even though it no longer exists. A **telescope** is an instrument that uses lenses or mirrors to collect and focus light from distant objects. In Greek, the word *teleskopos* means "seeing from a distance."

Most historians credit Dutch eyeglass maker Hans Lippershey with inventing the first telescope in 1608. In 1671, Isaac Newton invented a telescope that formed images by reflecting light with a curved mirror. By the end of the 1800s, scientists were looking farther and farther into the universe. Today's telescopes map the universe past and present, helping astronomers figure out its history and its future. **There are two main types of telescopes, reflecting telescopes and refracting telescopes.**

Reflecting Telescopes The **reflecting telescope** uses mirrors and convex lenses to collect and focus light. Figure 13A shows the path of light through a reflecting telescope. Light from a distant object strikes a large concave mirror and is brought to a focus. This focused light is reflected by an angled mirror and forms a real image. The convex lens of the eyepiece then enlarges the image.

Refracting Telescopes The **refracting telescope** uses convex lenses to collect and focus light. Light from a distant object enters the telescope by passing through a convex lens called the objective lens. The convex lens forms a real image at its focal point inside the telescope. A convex lens in the eyepiece then magnifies this real image. As you look through the eyepiece, you see an enlarged, upside-down, virtual image of the real image. Figure 13B shows the path of light through a refracting telescope.

Go Online
SCIENCE NEWS®

For: Articles on light and optics
Visit: PHSchool.com
Web Code: cce-2193

Figure 13 The two main types of telescopes use combinations of mirrors and lenses to magnify images of distant objects. **A** The reflecting telescope uses a large concave mirror to focus the incoming light rays. **B** The refracting telescope uses a series of lenses to focus light from distant objects.

A Reflecting Telescope

Viewing direction

Eyepiece lens system

Incoming light

Plane mirror at 45-degree angle

Large concave mirror

Viewing direction

B Refracting Telescope

Incoming light

Convex objective lens

Eyepiece

Viewing direction

Cameras

A **camera** is an optical instrument that records an image of an object. No matter the type of camera, it uses the same basic principle of focusing light rays to form real images. ⬤ **Light rays enter a camera through an opening, are focused by the opening or lens, and form an image that is recorded on film or by a sensor.**

Pinhole Camera Did you know that the word *camera* is Latin for "room?" The earliest cameras were in fact the size of an entire room, and were known as *camera obscura*, or "dark room." One of the earliest uses of a camera obscura is credited to Leonardo da Vinci.

DK SCIENCE and History

Photography

Photography has come a long way since the 1800s, although the basic apparatus is still the same—a box with a hole to let in light.

THREE-COLOR PROJECTOR SYSTEM

Simple wooden box

Holders for black-and-white slides

Holders for red, blue, and green color filters

Hole for lens

FIRST CAMERA

ORIGINAL KODAK CAMERA

1861 Scottish physicist James Clerk Maxwell exhibits a color photographic system involving three black-and-white photos, taken through red, blue, and green filters. When the photos are turned into slides, projected on a screen using the same filters, and superimposed, the original scene is recreated, in color.

1826 Nicéphore Niepce makes the first permanent positive photograph of a landscape.

1840 William Fox Talbot develops the first negative-to-positive process, making multiple black-and-white prints possible.

1888 George Eastman launches the Kodak camera, the first successful roll-film camera. It is preloaded with a 6-meter roll of film at the factory.

1913 German inventor Oscar Barnack develops the UR Leica camera, the first 35 mm camera. It uses the 24 mm x 36 mm frame format.

1820   1855   1890

Da Vinci, an Italian scientist, constructed his camera by making a pinhole opening in the shutter of a window of a darkened room. Images of the outside scenery were projected onto the wall opposite the window. Pinhole cameras do not have to be the size of a room. A simple pinhole camera can consist of a cardboard box with a small hole in one side. Light rays from the top and bottom of an object pass through the pinhole and cross paths. The rays form an upside-down, real image on the back wall of the box. For firsthand experience with a pinhole optical device, build and use the pinhole viewer in the QuickLab later in this section.

Reading Checkpoint *What type of image does a pinhole camera form?*

Focusing magnifier

Focusing ring

Standard lens (one of five options)

KINE-EXAKTA CAMERA

INSTANT PICTURES

LED indicator (indicates low light conditions to activate flash)

MODERN COMPACT DIGITAL CAMERA

Auto-focus zoom lens

1936 German company Ihagee launches the Kine-Exakta, the first single-lens reflex (SLR) camera for 35 mm film.

1942 Kodak announces a film for color prints, Koda-color, the world's first true color negative film.

1947 American inventor Edwin H. Land demonstrates a new one-step photographic system. It develops and produces finished pictures in a few seconds.

1986 Pentax produces the first fully automatic compact camera with a built-in zoom lens.

2000 High resolution, compact, multi-featured, affordable digital cameras are available and popular.

1925

1960

1995

Figure 14 Shown here is a typical single lens reflex (SLR) camera. The mirror reflects the image through the viewfinder so the photographer can bring it into focus. When the shutter release button is pushed, the mirror flips up. This allows the focused light rays to pass straight through the lens system and onto the film.

Viewfinder
Prism
Shutter release button
Shutter
Mirror
Lens elements
Film
Diaphragm
Incoming light

Modern Film Camera Figure 14 shows a typical modern film camera. The lens elements focus the incoming light rays. The focused rays then pass through the diaphragm, a device that controls the amount of light passing through the lens. When the shutter release button is pressed, the mirror flips up and the shutter briefly opens to let the focused light rays strike the film.

To bring an object into focus, the lens must be moved toward or away from the film. This focusing, which can be done manually or automatically, is needed to form a sharp image. The focused light reacts with a light-sensitive chemical coating on the film that records the real image. The image is upside down and smaller than the object. After the film is developed and printed, you have photographs for your album.

Microscopes

A **microscope** is an optical instrument that uses lenses to provide enlarged images of very small, near objects. One common type of microscope is called a compound microscope. 🔑 **The compound microscope uses two convex lenses to magnify small objects.**

Figure 15 shows the structure of a compound microscope. To view an enlarged image of an object, you place the object on a glass slide. You then place the slide on a platform located above a light source. Light rays from below pass up through the object and then pass through a convex lens called the objective. The lens produces an enlarged, upside-down, real image. This image then becomes the "object" for a second convex lens called the eyepiece. The eyepiece enlarges the image. When you look through the eyepiece, you see an enlarged, virtual image of the object. Under the best conditions, modern light microscopes can magnify images more than 1000 times.

Figure 15 This compound microscope uses a mirror to reflect light up and into the microscope.
Comparing and Contrasting *How is the way in which a focused image is formed the same in both a camera and a microscope?*

Eyepiece lens
Objective lens
Slide with specimen
Mirror

≡Quick ⟩ Lab

Building a Pinhole Viewer

Cardboard tube — Wax paper — Rubber bands — Aluminum foil — Pinhole — Rolled tube of black construction paper

Materials

- cardboard tube
- black construction paper
- aluminum foil
- wax paper
- 4 rubber bands
- pin

Procedure

1. Place aluminum foil over one end of the cardboard tube and use a rubber band to hold the foil in place.

2. Place wax paper over the other end of the tube and hold the paper in place with a rubber band. There should be no wrinkles in the wax paper covering the opening of the tube.

3. Roll a piece of black construction paper lengthwise around the tube. The foil end should be flush with one end of the construction paper as shown. Use two more rubber bands to hold the construction paper in place.

4. Verify that the wax paper end is now in the middle of the black construction paper tube.

5. Use a pin to make a hole in the center of the aluminum foil. You may have to enlarge the hole slightly to see an image clearly.

6. Point the pinhole toward a light source and look through the other end of the viewer. Observe several objects inside your classroom (chairs, tables, and books) and outside of your classroom (houses, trees, and cars). **CAUTION** *Do not use the viewer to look at the sun, as you may injure your eyes.*

Analyze and Conclude

1. **Observing** Describe the images that appeared on the wax paper.

2. **Relating Cause and Effect** What caused the images to appear on the wax paper the way they did?

Section 19.3 Assessment

Reviewing Concepts

1. 🌐 Name the two main types of telescopes.
2. 🌐 How does a film camera work?
3. 🌐 Describe the system of lenses in a compound microscope.
4. What is the purpose of the lens in a camera?

Critical Thinking

5. **Inferring** High-speed film is very sensitive to light. Explain how this could be useful for dim-light photography.

6. **Applying Concepts** Can the image seen in the eyepiece of a compound microscope be projected on a screen?

Connecting ⟨ Concepts

Speed of Light From Chapter 18 you know that light travels at an extremely high speed. Explain how the images of deep-space objects you see through telescopes are images of the past.

Optics **585**

Fiber Optics

Optical fibers have caused a revolution in information technology by making it possible to transmit huge amounts of information along slender strands of glass.

Inside a fiber optic cable
One cable contains several fibers. Each fiber consists of a core and an outer layer made from glass of a lower refractive index. The light is kept within the fiber by total internal reflection.

Strengthening steel core

Optical fiber

Protective layer for cable

Protective sheath

Optical fiber core

Outer layer

Internal reflection
Total internal reflection carries light around sharp bends.

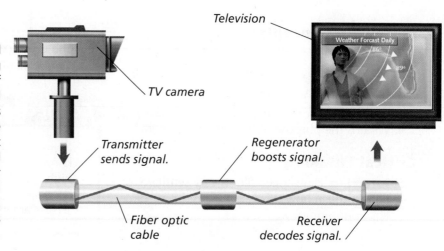

Transmitting a TV signal
TV signals can be sent along optical cables in the form of light. The electrical signal produced by the camera is turned into a digital code by the transmitter, and sent along the cable as rapid pulses of light. The receiver then converts this signal back into an electrical signal, which in turn forms a picture on the TV screen.

TV camera

Transmitter sends signal.

Fiber optic cable

Regenerator boosts signal.

Receiver decodes signal.

Television

Weather Forcast Daily

Optical fibers in medicine

As well as carrying digital information, optical fibers are useful in medicine. This is because they can bend around corners, allowing otherwise inaccessible parts of the body to be viewed.

Tip of the endoscope is inserted first into the body.

A light source is attached here.

Depth scale shows how far the endoscope is inserted into the body.

Eyepiece

ENDOSCOPE

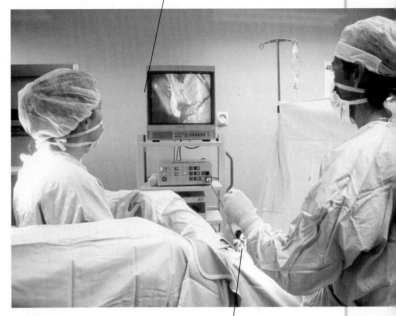

Internal organs is viewed on a computer screen.

Surgeons use an endoscope to look at internal organs.

Endoscope
Endoscopes are used to view the interior of the body. They are often used for investigations —such as checking for a stomach ulcer—and during surgery, to guide the surgeon.

Eye of a sewing needle

Single optical fiber

Strand of glass
Optical fibers are made from ultra-pure glass. Each fiber is thin enough to pass through the eye of a needle. Some top-quality fibers can carry a light beam with just a 10 percent loss of intensity over a kilometer.

Going Further

- Research how fiber optic strands are manufactured. Prepare a poster to present your findings to your class. Include a detailed description of the manufacturing process and the materials used.

19.4 The Eye and Vision

Reading Focus

Key Concepts
- What are the main parts of the eye?
- What are some common vision problems?

Vocabulary
- cornea
- pupil
- iris
- retina
- rods
- cones
- nearsightedness
- farsightedness
- astigmatism

Reading Strategy

Outlining As you read, make an outline of the important ideas in this section. Use the green headings as the main topics and the blue headings as subtopics.

> **I. The Eye and Vision**
>   **A. Structure of the Eye**
>   1. _____
>   2. _____
>   **and so on . . .**
>   **B.** _____
>   **and so on . . .**

Have you ever stopped to appreciate how remarkable your eyes are? They play a very important role in your perception of the world around you. Your eyes, like the one shown in Figure 16, are optical instruments that perform the same tasks of bending and focusing light as telescopes, cameras, and microscopes.

Your eyes form images every moment they are exposed to light. They receive and focus visible light from objects near and far. Your brain then interprets the images of the objects formed by your eyes.

Figure 16 The lens of the eye focuses incoming light rays onto light-sensitive nerve endings located inside and at the back of your eye.

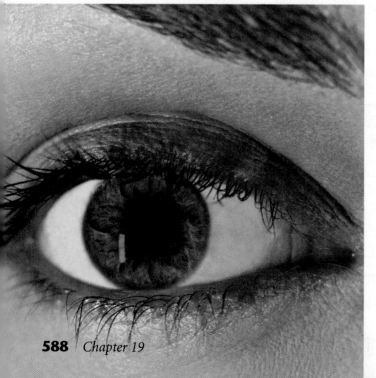

Structure of the Eye

You can read this page because light reflected from the page enters your eye. But how does this light get transformed into images of objects you recognize? Various parts of the eye, each one having its own specific function, work to make your sense of vision possible. Figure 17 shows the structure of the human eye. **The main parts of the eye are the cornea, the pupil and iris, the lens, and the retina.**

Cornea Light rays enter your eyes through the transparent outer coating of the eye, called the **cornea.** The cornea's curved surface helps to focus light entering your eye.

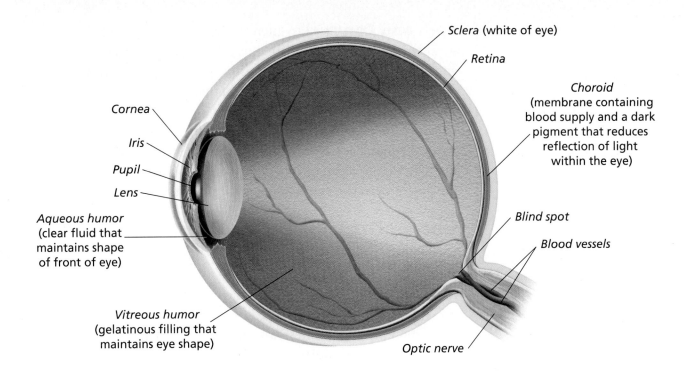

Cornea

Iris

Pupil

Lens

Aqueous humor
(clear fluid that
maintains shape
of front of eye)

Vitreous humor
(gelatinous filling that
maintains eye shape)

Sclera (white of eye)

Retina

Choroid
(membrane containing
blood supply and a dark
pigment that reduces
reflection of light
within the eye)

Blind spot

Blood vessels

Optic nerve

Pupil and Iris After the cornea, light rays pass through the pupil, the part of your eye that looks black. The **pupil** is the opening that allows light rays to enter your eye. The colored part of your eye, the **iris,** contracts and expands to control the amount of light that enters your eye. The controlled movement of the iris is regulated by signals from your brain.

Lens After passing through the pupil, light enters the convex lens in your eye. The lens is a sealed capsule containing a clear fluid. This lens focuses the light onto the light sensor cells at the back of the eye. As you change your focus from near to distant objects, muscles inside the eye change the shape of the flexible lens. The muscles relax and the lens becomes thinner and flatter. If you read for a long time, you'll notice that your eyes become tired and feel strained. This is because the muscles have been contracting for a long time. The best way to relax your eyes is to look far away.

Retina The focused, refracted light is collected at the retina. The **retina** is the inner surface of the eye. Its surface is covered by light-sensitive nerve endings called **rods** and **cones.** The rods and cones convert the light into electrical signals that are sent to the brain through the optic nerve. The area of the retina where the nerve endings come together to form the optic nerve creates a blind spot. This blind spot has no rods or cones and cannot sense light.

 Reading Checkpoint **Which part of the eye controls how much light enters?**

Figure 17 The eye is the organ that provides you with sight. Light passes through the cornea, pupil, and lens before striking the retina. Signals from light-sensitive nerves on the retina are sent through the optic nerve to the brain. **Predicting** *What may result if the eyeball has an elongated (too long) shape?*

Rods and Cones Low-intensity light is sensed by rods. The brain uses signals from rods to distinguish among white, black, and different shades of gray. Cones are sensitive to color, but are less sensitive than rods; that is, they need more light than rods in order to function. The decreased light sensitivity of cones explains why you can't make out the colors of objects in very dim light. There are three different types of cones. Each type of cone is able to sense only a single color—red light, green light, or blue light. People who are colorblind have missing or defective cones of one or more of the three kinds.

Correcting Vision Problems

You have probably heard the expression "20/20 vision." Having 20/20 vision means that you can clearly see things of a certain size from 20 feet. 20/20 vision is considered normal. Not everybody, however, has 20/20 vision. **Several common vision problems are near-sightedness, farsightedness, and astigmatism.** They result in people having vision that is worse than 20/20. In many cases, less-than-perfect vision can be corrected with eyeglasses or contact lenses. Corrective eyeware is not new—eyeglasses were used in China and Italy as early as the 1200s.

✔ **Reading Checkpoint**   *What does it mean to have 20/20 vision?*

Problem: Nearsightedness (Eyeball is too long.)

Image forms in front of retina.

Correction: Eyeglasses with concave lenses

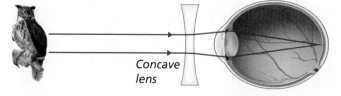

Concave lens

Image forms on retina.

Figure 18 When the eyeball is too long, the focused image forms in front of the retina. By the time the image reaches the retina, it is no longer in focus. This common condition, called nearsightedness, can be corrected with a diverging (concave) lens.

Nearsightedness If you have normal vision, the images you see are clear and undistorted. The light rays that enter your eyes are focused on your retinas. However, for approximately one out of four people, the rays focus before they reach the retina. This condition, called **nearsightedness,** causes distant objects to appear blurry. Nearsightedness occurs either because the cornea is too curved or the eyeball is too long. In either case, the rays of light focus too close to the lens. A nearsighted person can see nearby objects clearly, but distant objects seem blurred. Nearsightedness can be corrected by placing a diverging (concave) lens in front of the eye. The lens spreads the rays out a little before they enter the eye. This causes the image to form farther back, at the retina, instead of in front of it. Some cases of nearsightedness can now be treated with surgery. Figure 18 shows a diagram of a nearsighted eye and how it can be corrected with a diverging (concave) lens.

Laser Eye Surgery

The laser has become a sight-saving tool. In laser eye surgery, a laser beam makes small incisions, half the thickness of a human hair, in the eye. Surgeons correct and control different types of vision problems by careful positioning of the laser incisions. As shown below, a laser can be used to destroy abnormal blood vessels that cause failing vision in patients with diabetes. **Interpreting Diagrams** *On what part of the eye do the abnormal blood vessels form?*

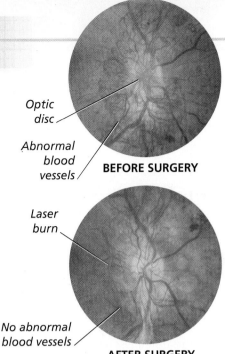

Optic disc

Abnormal blood vessels

BEFORE SURGERY

Laser burn

No abnormal blood vessels

AFTER SURGERY

Results of surgery
Taken through the pupil of the eye, these pictures show how abnormal blood vessels on the retina are burned away by laser treatment. After surgery, the retina appears paler.

Retina

Lens of eye

Pupil

Cornea

Laser burn

Optic disc

Abnormal blood vessels
Due to diabetes, abnormal blood vessels form on the retina, impairing vision.

Laser beam *By destroying parts of the outer layer of the retina and the abnormal blood vessels, it is possible to prevent further deterioration of the patient's vision.*

Mirror

Viewing lens *The lens neutralizes the refractive power of the cornea and focuses the laser beam.*

Problem: Farsightedness (Eyeball is too short.)

Image forms behind retina.

Correction: Eyeglasses with convex lenses

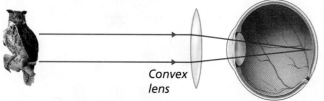

Convex lens

Image forms on retina.

Figure 19 Farsightedness occurs when an image is not focused before it reaches the retina. Farsightedness can be corrected by using a converging (convex) lens in front of the eye.
Comparing and Contrasting *In what ways are farsightedness and nearsightedness similar?*

Farsightedness Blurred images can also be a result of farsightedness. **Farsightedness** is a condition that causes nearby objects to appear blurry. Common causes of farsightedness are either a cornea that is not curved enough or an eyeball that is too short. In either case, the rays of light focus too far from the lens. As a result, the image focuses beyond the retina. A farsighted person can see distant objects clearly, but nearby objects seem blurred. Farsightedness is usually corrected by placing a converging (convex) lens in front of the eye. The lens bends the light rays toward each other before they enter the eye. Because the rays entering the eye are converging, the image is formed on the retina instead of behind the retina. Figure 19 shows a diagram of a farsighted eye and how it can be corrected.

Astigmatism For clear vision, the lens of the eye and the cornea must be properly shaped. When the cornea or lens is misshapen, a defect in vision called astigmatism results. **Astigmatism** is a condition in which objects at any distance appear blurry because the cornea or lens is misshapen. Just as with an eyeball that is too long or too short, this irregularity can prevent light from focusing properly on the retina. The result is that the lens has two different focal points, causing distortion or blurring of the image. Specialized eyeglass lens shapes are used to correct astigmatism.

Section 19.4 Assessment

Reviewing Concepts

1. 🌐 List, in order, the parts of the eye that light encounters.
2. 🌐 What are three common problems that affect vision?
3. What is the eye's blind spot?
4. Which kind of lens can correct nearsightedness? Farsightedness?

Critical Thinking

5. **Inferring** Why is the cornea transparent?
6. **Comparing and Contrasting** How is the structure of the eye similar to that of a simple camera?

7. **Making Judgments** Suppose that when you sit at the back of the room, you can't read the chalkboard. What vision problem might you have?
8. **Connecting Concepts** The index of refraction of the cornea is about the same as that of water. Use this fact to explain why you cannot see as well in water as in air.

Writing in Science

Steps in a Process Write a paragraph describing how a light ray passes through the eye and results in vision.

Selecting Mirrors

In this lab, you will compare several mirrors and select the type that is best for a specific use.

Problem
What mirror shape is best for magnifying images? For providing a wide view?

Materials
plane, convex, and concave mirrors; 2 metric rulers; roll of string; protractor

Skills
Observing, Measuring

Procedure

Part A: Comparing Magnification

1. Construct a data table with three rows and four columns. Label the columns Mirror, Size of Image, Magnification, and Field of View. In the column labeled Mirror, label the three rows Plane, Concave, and Convex.

2. Place the plane mirror on a tabletop with its mirror side facing up. Position a metric ruler horizontally across the center of the mirror.

3. Hold the other metric ruler horizontally against your nose, just below your eyes, as shown below. Make sure the ruler's markings face away from you. Look down at the mirror.

4. Use the ruler resting on the mirror to measure the actual length of the image of a 3-cm-long portion of the ruler you are holding. Record the size of the image in your data table.

5. Repeat Steps 2 through 4 using concave and convex mirrors. Observe each image from the same distance.

6. Divide each image size you measured by 3 cm to determine its magnification. Record the magnification in your data table.

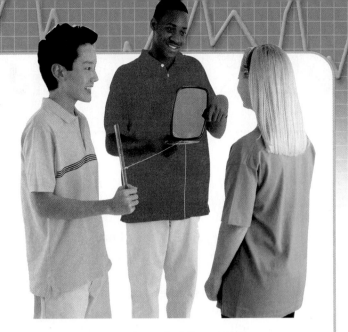

Part B: Comparing Fields of View

7. Tie a string to a ruler. Hold the protractor, mirror, and free end of the string. Have a classmate hold the ruler vertically off to one side of the mirror. Position a third classmate (the observer) directly in front of and about 2 meters away from the mirror as shown.

8. Have the classmate holding the ruler slowly move toward the observer while keeping the string tight. The observer should look directly into the mirror and say "Stop!" as soon as the reflection of the ruler can be seen.

9. Measure the angle the string makes with the protractor. Multiply this angle by 2 and record it as the field of view in your data table.

10. Repeat Steps 7 through 9 using concave and convex mirrors. Observe each mirror from the same distance.

Analyze and Conclude

1. **Observing** Which mirror provided the greatest magnification? The widest view?

2. **Applying Concepts** Which mirror shape would work best for a dentist who needs to see a slightly magnified image of a tooth? Explain your answer.

3. **Drawing Conclusions** Could one of the mirrors be used both to view a wide area and to magnify? Explain your answer.

Study Guide

19.1 Mirrors

Key Concepts

- The law of reflection states that the angle of reflection is equal to the angle of incidence.
- A plane mirror always produces a virtual image.
- Concave mirrors can form either real or virtual images.
- Convex mirrors always cause light rays to spread out and can only form virtual images.

Vocabulary

ray diagram, *p. 570*

angle of incidence, *p. 570*

angle of reflection, *p. 570*

plane mirror, *p. 571*

virtual image, *p. 571*

concave mirror, *p. 572*

focal point, *p. 572*

real image, *p. 572*

convex mirror, *p. 573*

19.2 Lenses

Key Concepts

- When light enters a new medium at an angle, the change in speed causes the light to bend, or refract.
- Concave lenses always cause light rays to spread out and can only form virtual images.
- Convex lenses can form either real or virtual images.
- Materials that have small critical angles of refraction are likely to cause most of the light entering them to be totally internally reflected.

Vocabulary

index of refraction, *p. 575*

lens, *p. 576*

concave lens, *p. 576*

convex lens, *p. 576*

critical angle, *p. 578*

total internal reflection, *p. 578*

19.3 Optical Instruments

Key Concepts

- There are two main types of telescopes, reflecting telescopes and refracting telescopes.

- Light rays enter a camera through an opening, are focused by the opening or lens, and form an image that is recorded on film or by a sensor.
- The compound microscope uses two convex lenses to magnify small objects.

Vocabulary

telescope, *p. 580*

reflecting telescope, *p. 581*

refracting telescope, *p. 581*

camera, *p. 582*

microscope, *p. 584*

19.4 The Eye and Vision

Key Concepts

- The main parts of the eye are the cornea, the pupil and iris, the lens, and the retina.
- Some common vision problems are nearsightedness, farsightedness, and astigmatism.

Vocabulary

cornea, *p. 588*

pupil, *p. 589*

iris, *p. 589*

retina, *p. 589*

rods, *p. 589*

cones, *p. 589*

nearsightedness, *p. 590*

farsightedness, *p. 592*

astigmatism, *p. 592*

Thinking Visually

Concept Map Use the information from the chapter to complete the concept map below.

Reviewing Content

Choose the letter that best answers the question or completes the statement.

1. A reflected ray of light is one that
   a. bends as it enters a new medium.
   b. bounces off a surface.
   c. always forms an image.
   d. travels faster after it is reflected.

2. Which law states that the angle of incidence equals the angle of reflection?
   a. law of refraction
   b. law of diffraction
   c. law of reflection
   d. law of images

3. A plane mirror is
   a. curved outward.
   b. flat.
   c. curved inward.
   d. always round.

4. A virtual image
   a. can never be seen.
   b. cannot be projected.
   c. is always enlarged.
   d. is formed in front of a plane mirror.

5. Concave lenses cause rays to
   a. come together.
   b. spread apart.
   c. reflect.
   d. form real images.

6. Which forms where light rays converge?
   a. imaginary image
   b. real image
   c. virtual image
   d. blind image

7. A ray is incident on a material at the material's critical angle. At what angle does the ray refract?
   a. 0 degrees
   b. 45 degrees
   c. 90 degrees
   d. 180 degrees

8. Which optical device uses mirrors and lenses to magnify images of distant objects?
   a. reflecting telescope
   b. pinhole camera
   c. microscope
   d. refracting telescope

9. The two areas in the eye in which light rays are refracted are
   a. the cornea and the lens.
   b. the pupil and the lens.
   c. the retina and the lens.
   d. the rods and the cones.

10. Which corrects nearsightedness?
    a. concave lens
    b. converging lens
    c. diverging mirror
    d. astigmatism

Understanding Concepts

11. According to the law of reflection, the angle of incidence is equal to what other angle?

12. Describe the image formed by a plane mirror.

13. Why can convex mirrors produce only virtual images?

14. Under what conditions does light bend when it enters a new medium?

15. How is the index of refraction of a medium related to the speed of light in the medium?

16. Explain why a concave lens cannot form a real image.

17. What occurs when the critical angle is exceeded?

18. A student-drawn ray diagram for a lens is shown below. Identify the errors the student made in the diagram.

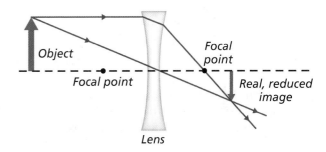

19. Which part of the camera shown in Figure 14 controls the amount of light that strikes the film?

20. Explain how the human eye changes focus from near objects to faraway objects.

21. Explain why rods are more effective than cones for seeing objects at night.

22. Explain how diverging and converging lenses are effective for treating nearsightedness and farsightedness.

Critical Thinking

23. Applying Concepts Which type of mirror would you use to view an enlarged image of an object?

24. Designing Experiments Can the position of an object on the bottom of a swimming pool be accurately determined when viewed from above and at an angle to the water? Design an experiment to find out if refraction affects the apparent position of a submerged object.

25. Applying Concepts How could you convert the pinhole viewer used in the Quick Lab on page 585 into a device that could take a permanent picture?

26. Comparing and Contrasting What are the differences between a reflecting telescope and a refracting telescope?

27. Using Models Draw a ray diagram showing three rays of light traveling in air and striking the surface of water. Show one ray being reflected, one being refracted, and one entering the water without bending.

28. Predicting The illustration below shows a flashlight aimed down into a tub of water with a flat mirror lying on the bottom. Copy and complete the illustration by predicting the path of the light beam. (*Hint:* Remember to consider the effects of refraction and reflection.)

Flashlight

Water

Mirror

29. Inferring Many maps of the moon are printed showing the moon flipped upside down. What can you infer about the optical instruments used to view the moon?

Concepts in Action

30. Using Models How can you use the law of reflection to model a game of billiards?

31. Applying Concepts What kind of lens would you use to help you see a splinter in your finger?

32. Interpreting Diagrams The ray diagram below shows the formation of an image using a lens. Is the image a real or virtual image? What kind of lens is producing the image? Give a possible application for this type of lens.

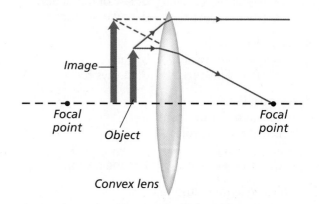

Image

Focal point

Object

Focal point

Convex lens

33. Writing in Science Classify plane, convex, and concave mirrors in terms of image type or image size. Write a paragraph citing examples for each classification.

Performance-Based Assessment

Make a telescope using two convex lenses and a cardboard tube from a finished roll of paper towels. Attach the lenses using tape. If possible, get two tubes of slightly different diameters so that one can fit inside the other. Wrap the smaller tube with tape or cardboard to make the smaller tube fit snugly inside the larger tube. How can you focus your telescope?

For: Self-grading assessment
Visit: PHSchool.com
Web Code: cca-2190

Standardized Test Prep

Choose the letter that best answers the question or completes the statement.

1. Which statement correctly describes a property of mirrors?
   (A) Plane mirrors always form real images.
   (B) Concave mirrors can form real and virtual images.
   (C) The law of reflection only applies to convex mirrors.
   (D) Real images formed by concave mirrors are right side up.
   (E) All mirrors refract light rays to form images.

2. If a light ray slows down as it enters a medium at an angle, the ray is
   (A) totally reflected.
   (B) refracted.
   (C) diffracted.
   (D) evenly dispersed in the new medium.
   (E) travelling faster than 3.0×10^8 m/s.

3. When a ray strikes a plane mirror at an angle,
   (A) the light ray slows down and bends.
   (B) an inverted virtual image is formed.
   (C) the light ray is refracted.
   (D) the angle of incidence of the ray equals the angle of reflection of the ray.
   (E) the image formed is real.

4. Which of the following statements about convex lenses is FALSE?
   (A) They cause light rays to refract.
   (B) They can form real and virtual images.
   (C) They cause incoming parallel rays to converge.
   (D) They are thickest at the outside edges.
   (E) They are used in lighthouses.

5. Which description correctly matches the type of optical instrument?
   (A) Microscope—forms enlarged images of distant objects.
   (B) Camera—focuses incoming light using a series of mirrors.
   (C) Refracting telescope—is made up of two convex lenses.
   (D) Reflecting telescope—is made up of one convex lens and one concave lens.
   (E) Pinhole camera—focuses incoming light using a series of lenses.

Question 6 refers to the ray diagram shown below.

6. Which of the following statements is TRUE?
   (A) The mirror shown is concave.
   (B) The converging light rays form a real image.
   (C) The diverging rays form a real image.
   (D) The diverging rays form a virtual image.
   (E) The reflected light rays are parallel.

CHAPTER

20 Electricity

Lightning provides a powerful display of electrical energy.

21st Century Learning
Economic Literacy

How much does it cost to operate common appliances?

After reading Sections 20.2 and 20.3, you should be able to calculate the energy cost of operating electric appliances. Choose an electrical device that you use at home (for example, a computer or hair dryer), and find out its power rating. Estimate how many hours per day you use it, and calculate the energy consumed in kilowatt-hours. Look up the cost of a kilowatt-hour in your area to determine how much the device costs to operate each day. Post your results on a class blog or wiki.

How do science concepts apply to your world? Here are some questions you'll be able to answer after you read this chapter.

- **Why do you sometimes feel a shock if you walk across carpet on a winter day and then touch a metal door handle?** *(Section 20.1)*

- **What causes lightning?** *(Section 20.1)*

- **How does a battery enable a flashlight to light?** *(Section 20.2)*

- **Why do some appliances use three-prong plugs?** *(Section 20.3)*

- **How do computers process data?** *(page 614)*

- **How is information stored on a DVD?** *(Section 20.4)*

Chapter Preview

Inquiry > Activity

How Can You Reverse the Battery Direction in a Flashlight?

Procedure

1. Remove a battery from a two-battery flashlight. Notice that one end of the battery is labeled + (positive).

2. Return the battery to the flashlight in the same position it was in before. Turn the flashlight on and then off. Observe what happens.

3. Remove the battery and replace it so that it faces the opposite direction. Predict what will happen if you turn the flashlight on. Test your prediction.

Think About It

1. **Comparing and Contrasting** Describe your results when the batteries faced the same direction and when they faced opposite directions. How are these results the same or different?

2. **Inferring** What do your results indicate about how batteries might work?

3. **Predicting** Do you think that the flashlight will work if you reverse the direction of both batteries? Explain your answer.

20.1 Electric Charge and Static Electricity

Reading Focus

Key Concepts

- What produces a net electric charge?
- What determines whether an electric force is attractive or repulsive?
- What determines the strength of an electric field?
- What are three ways in which charge is transferred?
- How does a static discharge occur?

Vocabulary

- electric charge
- electric force
- electric field
- static electricity
- law of conservation of charge
- induction

Reading Strategy

Identifying Main Ideas Copy the table below. As you read, write the main idea for each topic.

Topic	Main Idea
Electric Charge	An excess or shortage of electrons produces a net electric charge.
Electric Forces	a._____
Electric Fields	b._____
Static Electricity	c._____

T hink back to the last time a thunderstorm swept through your area. A bolt of lightning streaked across the sky, followed moments later by the crash of thunder. Have you ever wondered what causes lightning? Perhaps you've observed something similar on a smaller scale closer to home. When you take clothes out of a dryer, some of them can stick together, like the sock and shorts in Figure 1. If you pull the clothes apart in a darkened room, you can see sparks that are like tiny bolts of lightning. This shouldn't be surprising once you realize that lightning and "static cling" have a similar cause—the movement of electric charges.

Figure 1 Electric charge is responsible for clothes that stick together when they are removed from a dryer.

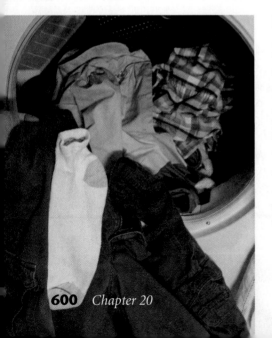

Electric Charge

Recall that electrical energy is the energy associated with electric charges. But what exactly is electric charge? **Electric charge** is a property that causes subatomic particles such as protons and electrons to attract or repel each other. There are two types of electric charge, positive and negative. Protons have a positive charge and electrons have a negative charge. Electric charges move in a flash through a lightning bolt. Electric charges attract one another in clothes taken from the dryer. Although charged particles are too small to see, just about everything in your daily life is affected by charge in one way or another.

Figure 2 shows how charges are arranged in an atom. A cloud of negatively charged electrons surrounds the positively charged nucleus. The atom is neutral because it has an equal number of positive and negative charges. If an atom gains one or more electrons, it becomes a negatively charged ion. If an atom loses electrons, it becomes a positively charged ion. ⊖ **An excess or shortage of electrons produces a net electric charge.**

The SI unit of electric charge is the coulomb (C). It takes about 6.24×10^{18} electrons to produce a single coulomb. A lightning bolt is about 10 to 20 coulombs of charge. In comparison, a flash camera uses the energy from 0.025 coulombs of charge to produce each flash.

Proton

Neutron

Electric Forces

Rub an inflated rubber balloon on your clean, dry hair. If it's a dry day, you can use the balloon to pick up bits of paper. The balloon attracts the paper because the balloon is negatively charged and the paper is positively charged. Now rub a second balloon on your hair and bring the two balloons close together. You can feel the balloons repel. The two balloons repel because they are negatively charged. ⊖ **Like charges repel, and opposite charges attract.** The force of attraction or repulsion between electrically charged objects is **electric force.**

The French scientist Charles-Augustin de Coulomb (1736–1806) discovered that electric forces obey a law similar to the law of universal gravitation. The electric force between two objects is directly proportional to the net charge on each object and inversely proportional to the square of the distance between them. As you can see in Figure 3, doubling the net charge on one object doubles the electric force. If instead you double the distance between the objects, the electric force is one fourth as strong.

Inside an atom, electric forces are much stronger than gravitational forces. Electric forces form chemical bonds, which must be overcome in chemical changes. Electric forces also cause friction and other contact forces. But on a large scale, matter is mostly neutral and in that case, electric forces are close to zero.

Figure 2 A neutral atom has equal numbers of protons and electrons.
Drawing Conclusions *What is the overall charge if the atom loses an electron?*

Electric force exerted on object X by object Y

Electric force exerted on object Y by object X

Figure 3 Electric force depends on charge and distance. **A** Opposite charges attract each other. **B** Doubling one charge doubles the force on both charges. **C** Like charges repel. Doubling the distance makes the force one fourth as great.

Reading Checkpoint   *What is electric force?*

Figure 4 The strength of an electric field depends on the amount of charge that produces the field and on the distance from the charge. **A** The electric field around a positive charge points outward. **B** The electric field around a negative charge points inward.

Electric Fields

The effect an electric charge has on other charges in the space around it is the charge's **electric field.** Figure 4 shows the fields of positive and negative charges. **The strength of an electric field depends on the amount of charge that produces the field and on the distance from the charge.** The lines representing the field are closer together near the charge, where the field is stronger.

An electric field exerts forces on any charged object placed in the field. The force depends on the net charge in the object and on the strength and direction of the field at the object's position. The more net charge an object has, the greater is the force on it. The direction of each field line shows the direction of the force on a positive charge.

Static Electricity and Charging

Static electricity is the study of the behavior of electric charges, including how charge is transferred between objects. There are several ways that a net charge can build up on an object or move from one object to another. **Charge can be transferred by friction, by contact, and by induction.** Keep in mind that whenever there is a charge transfer, the total charge is the same before and after the transfer occurs. This is the **law of conservation of charge**—the total charge in an isolated system is constant.

Charging by Friction The balloon in Figure 5A attracts hair because opposite charges attract. But how do balloons and hair pick up a net charge? Rubbing a balloon on your hair is an example of charging by friction. Electrons move from your hair to the balloon because atoms in rubber have a greater attraction for electrons than atoms in hair. The balloon picks up a net negative charge. Because your hair loses electrons, it becomes positively charged. Even simple everyday activities like walking across a carpet can build up charge this way.

Charging by Contact Why do the girl's hairs repel each other in Figure 5B? In this case, charge is transferred by contact. A Van de Graaff generator has charged the metal sphere. When the girl touches the sphere, she acquires a charge large enough to make her hairs stand on end. The sphere is still charged, but its net charge is reduced.

Figure 5 Charge can be transferred by friction and by contact. **A** Friction transferred electrons from the hair to the balloon. The balloon then attracts the hair because opposite charges attract. **B** A Van de Graaff generator has charged the metal sphere. Touching the sphere transfers charge. The hairs repel each other because like charges repel.

A

B

Charging by Induction Suppose you reach for a doorknob after walking across a carpet. You have picked up extra electrons from the carpet, so your hand is negatively charged. The net negative charge in your hand repels electrons in the metal doorknob. Figure 6 shows that electrons move to the base of the doorknob, leaving a net positive charge in the part of the doorknob closest to the hand. Overall, the doorknob is still neutral, but charge has moved within it. This is **induction,** a transfer of charge without contact between materials.

Static Discharge

Why do you get a shock from a doorknob? The spark you feel is a static discharge. ⊖ **Static discharge occurs when a pathway through which charges can move forms suddenly**. Charges will not travel through air from your hand to the doorknob. But air becomes charged suddenly when the gap between your finger and the doorknob is small. This air provides a path for electrons to flow from your hand to the doorknob. If the room is dark, you can even see this spark.

Lightning is a more dramatic discharge. Charge can build up in a storm cloud from friction between moving air masses. Negative charge in the lower part of the cloud induces a positive charge in the ground below the cloud. As the amount of charge in the cloud increases, the force of attraction between charges in the cloud and charges in the ground increases. Eventually the air becomes charged, forming a pathway for electrons to travel from the cloud to the ground.

Figure 6 Induction occurs when charge is transferred without contact between materials. Negative charges in the hand induce charges to move within the metal doorknob.
Predicting *What would happen if the hand had a net positive charge?*

For: Activity on thunder and lightning
Visit: PHSchool.com
Web Code: ccc-2201

Section 20.1 Assessment

Reviewing Concepts

1. ⊖ How is a net electric charge produced?
2. ⊖ What determines whether charges attract or repel?
3. ⊖ Name two factors that affect the strength of an electric field.
4. ⊖ List three methods of charge transfer.
5. ⊖ Explain how static discharge occurs.
6. How does electric force depend on the amount of charge and the distance between charges?
7. What is the law of conservation of charge?

Critical Thinking

8. **Forming Hypotheses** Why does plastic food wrap cling better to some materials than to others?

9. **Inferring** When a glass rod is rubbed with neutral silk, the glass becomes positively charged. What charge does the silk now have? Explain.

10. **Relating Cause and Effect** Many lightning strikes occur within a cloud, rather than between clouds and the ground. Explain why. (*Hint:* Assume a cloud has no net charge.)

Writing in Science

Explanatory Paragraph Write a paragraph explaining the series of events that may cause you to receive a shock from a metal doorknob on a dry winter day. (*Hint:* Use a flowchart to organize your ideas before writing your paragraph.)

20.2 Electric Current and Ohm's Law

Reading Focus

Key Concepts

- What are the two types of current?
- What are some examples of conductors and insulators?
- What factors affect electrical resistance?
- What causes an electric current?
- How are voltage, current, and resistance related?

Vocabulary

- electric current
- direct current
- alternating current
- electrical conductor
- electrical insulator
- resistance
- superconductor
- potential difference
- voltage
- battery
- Ohm's law

Reading Strategy

Predicting Copy the table below and write a prediction of what electric current is. After you read the section, if your prediction was incorrect or incomplete, write what electric current actually is.

Electric Current Probably Means	Electric Current Actually Means
a. ?	b. ?

If you've ever tried to fix a flashlight, you know there are several parts to check. The batteries may be dead, or the bulb may have burned out. The switch could be broken, or the spring might be corroded. If even one part isn't functioning, the flashlight won't light.

Electric Current

As you can see in Figure 7, the parts of a flashlight form a continuous path through which charge can flow. This continuous flow of electric charge is an **electric current.** The SI unit of electric current is the ampere (A), or amp, which equals 1 coulomb per second.

The two types of current are direct current and alternating current. Charge flows only in one direction in **direct current** (DC). A flashlight and most other battery-operated devices use direct current. Electric current in your home and school is mostly alternating current. **Alternating current** (AC) is a flow of electric charge that regularly reverses its direction.

In a flashlight, electrons flow from the negative terminal of one battery to the positive terminal of the other battery. But notice that the current is in the opposite direction. This is because scientists define current as the direction in which positive charges would flow.

Figure 7 A complete path is required for charge to flow in a flashlight. Batteries must be placed so that charge can flow from negative to positive, passing through the bulb.
Interpreting Diagrams *What purpose does the spring at the base of a flashlight have?*

Flow of current
Negative terminals
Switch
Spring
Positive terminals

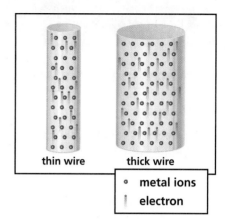

thin wire   thick wire

○ metal ions
| electron

Conductors and Insulators

Why is a metal wire usually coated with plastic or rubber? The metal wire is an electrical conductor. The rubber and plastic are electrical insulators. An **electrical conductor** is a material through which charge can flow easily. A material through which charge cannot flow easily is called an **electrical insulator.** The coating around a wire helps to control the current and keep it where it is needed.

A metal is made up of ions in a lattice. The ions are not free to move. But each ion has one or more electrons that are not tightly bound to it. These free electrons can conduct charge. Most materials do not easily conduct charge because they don't have free electrons. ⚿ **Metals such as copper and silver are good electrical conductors. Wood, plastic, rubber, and air are good electrical insulators.**

Resistance

As electrons move through a conducting wire, they collide with electrons and ions. These collisions convert some kinetic energy into thermal energy. Because less energy is available to move electrons through the wire, the current is reduced. **Resistance** is opposition to the flow of charges in a material. The SI unit of resistance is the ohm.

When you drink a milkshake as shown in Figure 8, it is easier if you use a thicker straw. In the same way, resistance is lowered if you make a wire thicker because more electrons can flow through a thicker wire. ⚿ **A material's thickness, length, and temperature affect its resistance.** Resistance is greater in a longer wire because the charges travel farther. As temperature increases, a metal's resistance increases because electrons collide more often.

If resistance increases as temperature increases, what happens as you cool a conductor? Could you reduce the resistance to zero? This is the idea behind superconductors. A **superconductor** is a material that has almost zero resistance when it is cooled to low temperatures. The best superconductor found thus far must be cooled to about 138 K.

Figure 8 Using a thick straw to drink a milkshake is easier than using a thin straw. Similarly, electrons flow more easily through a thick wire than they flow through a thin wire, assuming the wires are made of the same material.
Applying Concepts *Why should the wire in light bulb filaments be very thin?*

For: Links on conductors and insulators
Visit: www.SciLinks.org
Web Code: ccn-2202

Modeling Resistance in a Wire

Materials

white paper, metric ruler, number 2 pencil, multimeter

Procedure

1. Draw a narrow rectangle 1 cm wide by 5 cm long on the paper. Draw a wide rectangle, 3 cm by 5 cm. Use the pencil to completely fill in both rectangles with graphite.

2. Place the multimeter electrodes at opposite ends of the narrow rectangle. Record the resistance. Keep one electrode in place and slowly drag the other one toward it. Record your observations.

3. Repeat Step 2 using the wide rectangle.

Analyze and Conclude

1. **Observing** In which rectangle is the resistance greater? How does resistance change as the electrodes move together?

2. **Using Models** Explain why a thick wire has lower resistance than a thin wire if all else is equal. Why does resistance decrease as a wire's length decreases?

Voltage

If you remove the batteries from a flashlight, the light will not shine. Why? Because there is resistance in the wires and the bulb, charges do not flow on their own without a source of energy. **In order for charge to flow in a conducting wire, the wire must be connected in a complete loop that includes a source of electrical energy.**

Potential Difference Recall that potential energy is related to position. In Figure 9, water at the top of the fountain has more gravitational potential energy than water at the bottom. That is why water falls spontaneously from a higher to a lower height. In the same way, charges flow spontaneously from a higher to a lower potential energy.

The potential energy of a charge depends on its position in an electric field. **Potential difference** is the difference in electrical potential energy between two places in an electric field. Potential difference is measured in joules per coulomb, or volts. Because it is measured in volts, potential difference is also called **voltage.**

Voltage Sources How does water get to the top of the fountain? A pump inside the fountain does work on the water to increase its potential energy. In the same way, a source of voltage such as a battery does work to increase the potential energy of electric charges.

Three common voltage sources are batteries, solar cells, and generators. A **battery** is a device that converts chemical energy to electrical energy. Batteries, like other voltage sources, have terminals that can connect to wires in a circuit. One terminal is positive and the other is negative. A voltage drop, or potential difference, is maintained across the terminals. In a 9-volt battery, for example, the voltage drop is about 9 volts.

Figure 9 A water fountain has a pump inside that lifts water to the top, increasing the gravitational potential energy of the water. In the same way, a voltage source increases the electrical potential energy of electric charges.

Ohm's Law

The unit of resistance, the ohm, is named after the German scientist Georg Ohm (1789–1854). It was Ohm who first determined how resistance and current affect voltage. He discovered that voltage is not the same everywhere in a circuit. Ohm hypothesized that resistance reduces the voltage. He published his research in 1826, but his findings were so controversial that he lost his job. Eventually his work became widely accepted.

Ohm found a mathematical relationship between voltage, current, and resistance. This relationship became known as Ohm's law. According to **Ohm's law,** the voltage (V) in a circuit equals the product of the current (I) and the resistance (R).

Ohm's Law

$$V = I \times R \text{ or } I = \frac{V}{R}$$

When the current is in amperes and the resistance is in ohms, the voltage is in volts. What is the voltage if the resistance is 3 ohms and the current is 3 amps?

$$V = I \times R = 3 \text{ amps} \times 3 \text{ ohms} = 9 \text{ volts}$$

🔑 **Increasing the voltage increases the current. Keeping the same voltage and increasing the resistance decreases the current.** A multimeter, shown in Figure 10, is a device used to measure current, voltage, and resistance.

Figure 10 A multimeter can be used to measure current, voltage, or resistance. Here the voltage of a 9-volt battery is measured.

Section 20.2 Assessment

Reviewing Concepts

1. 🔑 List the two types of current.
2. 🔑 Name two good electrical conductors and two good electrical insulators.
3. 🔑 What variables affect the resistance of a material?
4. 🔑 What causes charge to flow?
5. 🔑 According to Ohm's law, how is voltage related to resistance and current?
6. What is a superconductor?

Critical Thinking

7. **Problem Solving** Suppose you have two wires of equal length made from the same material. How is it possible for the wires to have different resistances?

8. **Applying Concepts** Use Ohm's law to explain how two circuits could have the same current but different resistances.

Writing in Science

Compare-Contrast Paragraph Write a paragraph comparing and contrasting conductors and insulators and the ways in which they might be used. (*Hint:* Identify materials that are good conductors and materials that are good insulators.)

issues in SCIENCE

Which Technology Should Be Used to Power Electric Cars?

Auto manufacturers have developed technologies for several kinds of alternative-fuel vehicles, including electric cars. Two promising types of electric cars are battery electric vehicles (BEVs) and hydrogen fuel cell cars. However, in both cases, the technology under the hood has some drawbacks.

BEVs are already available. Instead of a fuel tank, a BEV contains a large rechargeable battery pack that powers an electric motor. You can recharge the vehicle's battery pack by using a household electrical outlet. One major problem with BEVs is that they rely on the power grid for energy, and the power plants that generate this energy often burn fossil fuels.

Unlike BEVs, hydrogen fuel cell cars have a fuel tank—but the gas inside is hydrogen, not gasoline. A hydrogen fuel cell is a device that produces electrical energy from a controlled reaction between hydrogen and oxygen. Inside the fuel cell, compressed hydrogen is combined with oxygen from the air. The current generated by the fuel cell is used to power an electric motor. (Fuel cell cars also contain a battery to provide additional power to the motor when needed.) The only by-product of hydrogen fuel cells is water. A major disadvantage of fuel cell cars is that isolating hydrogen is an expensive, energy-intensive process. In order for fuel cell cars to become widely used, engineers will need to find cheaper ways to produce hydrogen and also improve the efficiency of fuel cell technology.

The Viewpoints

Electric Cars Should Use Fuel Cells

Hydrogen fuel cells run on hydrogen, the most abundant element in the universe. Although both hydrogen production and fuel cell technology are very costly, they will become more affordable through technological innovation. Since the only by-product of hydrogen fuel cells is water, the technology is clean and environmentally friendly. In contrast, BEVs are only as "clean" as the power plant used to generate the electricity. Furthermore, BEVs can travel only a limited distance before needing to be recharged (a process that can take several hours). BEVs might seem more practical in the short term, but fuel cell cars offer a better long-term solution.

Electric Cars Should Use Batteries

Batteries are a proven and relatively inexpensive technology that is already being used in electric and hybrid cars. The cost to make a BEV is about one tenth that of a comparable fuel cell car. Although not practical for long road trips, BEVs are well suited for commuters who drive. In addition, many commuters do not use their cars at night; there is plenty of time to recharge the battery of a BEV as long as you remember to plug it in. It is much easier to recharge a BEV than it is to refuel a hydrogen car. For a BEV, you just need an electrical outlet. For hydrogen cars to be practical, we need to build an infrastructure of hydrogen refueling stations from scratch, which would be very time-consuming and costly. In addition, the cost of manufacturing the hydrogen fuel is high.

Research and Decide

1. **Defining the Issue** List some of the advantages and disadvantages of BEVs. Do the same for hydrogen fuel cell vehicles.

2. **Analyzing the Viewpoints** Think about the factors you listed in your answer to the first question. Which of those are likely to be most important to a supporter of BEVs? Of hydrogen fuel cell technology? Can you make any generalizations about the difference in their viewpoints?

3. **Forming Your Opinion** Are BEVs or hydrogen fuel cell vehicles a more promising transportation technology for the future? Explain and defend your position.

4. **Writing in Science** In 2009, the U.S. Department of Energy announced that it would cut off funding for development of a hydrogen fuel cell vehicle, because other technologies can lead to greater reductions in emissions in a shorter time. Write an essay in which you support or criticize this decision.

20.3 Electric Circuits

Reading Focus

Key Concepts
- What is included in a circuit diagram?
- How do series and parallel circuits differ?
- How do you calculate electric power and electrical energy use?
- What devices make electricity safe to use?

Vocabulary
- electric circuit
- series circuit
- parallel circuit
- electric power
- fuse
- circuit breaker
- grounding

Reading Strategy
Relating Text and Visuals Copy the table below. As you read, look at Figure 13 on page 610. List three things that the diagram helps you understand about circuits.

What Can Be Seen in the Circuit Diagram?
Wire bringing current from outside
a. ?
b. ?
c. ?

If you've ever seen a house being built, you know that wires hidden inside the walls connect to every electrical outlet and to every light switch. If you were responsible for wiring a house, like the electrician in Figure 11, how would you do it? A good place to start would be the circuit diagrams supplied by the builder or contractor.

Circuit Diagrams

An **electric circuit** is a complete path through which charge can flow. Wires in a house form a complex network of circuits. It may look like a maze of wires, but each connection has a purpose. An electrician uses circuit diagrams to keep track of how elements in a circuit are connected. ⬢ **Circuit diagrams use symbols to represent parts of a circuit, including a source of electrical energy and devices that are run by the electrical energy.** In a simple circuit, for example, a battery provides the energy to operate a device such as a bell or a light bulb.

A circuit diagram shows one or more complete paths in which charge can flow. Switches show places where the circuit can be opened. If a switch is open, the circuit is not a complete loop, and current stops. This is called an open circuit. When the switch is closed, the circuit is complete and charge can flow. This is called a closed circuit.

Figure 11 To bring electric current into a building, an electrician installs wiring. In a house, all of the wires usually come from one main box.

 Reading Checkpoint *What is an open circuit?*

A Series Circuit

Direction of current

Battery

Bulb

B Parallel Circuit

Figure 12 Circuits can be represented with circuit diagrams. Symbols correspond to each element. **A** A series circuit has one path that each charge can follow. **B** A parallel circuit has more than one path each charge can follow.
Interpreting Diagrams *Which symbol represents a light bulb?*

Figure 12 shows two circuit diagrams. The + and − on the battery symbol indicate the positive and negative terminals. Arrows show the direction of current, from positive to negative. Recall that the direction of current is defined as the direction in which positive charges would flow. Electrons in a wire flow in the opposite direction.

Reading Checkpoint *How is the direction of current defined?*

Series Circuits

In a **series circuit,** charge has only one path through which it can flow. Look at the series circuit in Figure 12A. If one light bulb burns out in a series circuit, it becomes an open circuit. 🔑 **If one element stops functioning in a series circuit, none of the elements can operate.** The bulbs in a circuit are a source of resistance. Adding bulbs to a series circuit increases the resistance. As a result, the current decreases, and each bulb shines less brightly.

Parallel Circuits

Imagine what would happen if circuits in your home were wired in series. If a light bulb burned out, the television would turn off. To avoid this problem, circuits in the home are mostly wired in parallel. A **parallel circuit** is an electric circuit with two or more paths through which charges can flow. If one bulb in Figure 12B burns out, charge still flows along the other path, and the other bulb stays lit. 🔑 **If one element stops functioning in a parallel circuit, the rest of the elements still can operate.**

Figure 13 shows a network of circuits connecting electrical devices in a home. These circuits are wired in parallel so they can operate independently.

Figure 13 Most circuits in a house are parallel. This way, even if one device stops working, the others will still work.

Light circuit

Dryer circuit

Fuse box or circuit breaker

Light switch

TV

Meter

Dryer

Ground

Desk with computer

Lamp

Wall socket

Power and Energy Calculations

Recall that power is the rate of doing work. The rate at which electrical energy is converted to another form of energy is **electric power.** The unit of electric power is the joule per second, or watt (W). Power often is measured in thousands of watts, or kilowatts (kW). **Electric power can be calculated by multiplying voltage by current.**

Go Online

For: Links on electric circuits
Visit: www.SciLinks.org
Web Code: ccn-2203

Electric Power

$$P\,(\text{watts}) = I\,(\text{amps}) \times V\,(\text{volts})$$

Every time you use a 1875-watt hair dryer or turn on a 75-watt light bulb you use electric power. Appliances vary in the amount of power they use.

Math Skills

Calculating Electric Power
An electric oven is connected to a 240-volt line, and it uses 34 amps of current. What is the power used by the oven?

1 **Read and Understand**

What information are you given?

$$\text{Current} = I = 34 \text{ amps}$$

$$\text{Voltage} = V = 240 \text{ volts}$$

2 **Plan and Solve**

What unknown are you trying to calculate?

$$\text{Power} = P = ?$$

What formula contains the given quantities and the unknown?

$$P = I \times V$$

Replace each variable with its known value.

$$P = 34 \text{ amps} \times 240 \text{ volts}$$

$$= 8200 \text{ watts}$$

3 **Look Back and Check**

Is your answer reasonable?

The answer is reasonable because an electric oven should use much more power than a 1875-watt hair dryer.

Math Practice

1. A clothes dryer uses about 27 amps of current from a 240-volt line. How much power does it use?

2. A camcorder has a power rating of 2.3 watts. If the output voltage from its battery is 7.2 volts, what current does it use?

3. A power tool uses about 12 amps of current and has a power rating of 1440 watts. What voltage does the tool require?

Modeling a Fuse

Materials

6-volt battery, two wires with stripped ends, aluminum foil, scissors, wooden block, unpainted metal thumbtacks

Procedure

1. Connect the two wires to the two battery terminals.

2. Cut a strip of aluminum foil about 0.5 cm by 3 cm. In the center, cut the width down to 1 mm. Attach the ends of the foil strip to the wooden block with the thumbtacks.

3. Touch one of the wires to each end of the foil strip to form a circuit.

4. Observe what happens to the foil strip. **CAUTION** *If the wire and the battery become very hot, remove the wires from the foil.*

Analyze and Conclude

1. **Observing** What happened to the foil strip when the wires were attached to it?

2. **Using Models** How is the foil like a fuse? Explain.

Figure 14 Fuses have an internal wire that burns out if a current is too great.

An appliance's power rating lets you know how much power it uses under normal conditions. An electric stove uses about 6000 watts, and a microwave oven uses about 1000 watts. To find the electrical energy used by an appliance, multiply power by time.

Electrical Energy

$$E = P \times t$$

For example, the power rating of a typical clothes dryer is 5400 watts, or 5.4 kilowatts. If you use the clothes dryer for 2 hours, the energy use is 5.4 kilowatts multiplied by 2 hours, or 10.8 kilowatt-hours. Electric power companies usually determine charges on your electric bill using kilowatt-hours as a unit of energy. A kilowatt-hour equals 3,600,000 joules.

Electrical Safety

Inspectors check all new houses to make sure electrical wiring is installed safely. All wires must be able to carry the maximum expected current. But correct wiring is not enough to prevent electrical accidents. **Correct wiring, fuses, circuit breakers, insulation, and grounded plugs help make electrical energy safe to use.**

In the United States, most household circuits usually have an average voltage of 120 volts. The amount of current in a circuit can vary, depending on the number of devices that are in the circuit. Each device that is turned on increases the current. If the current exceeds the circuit's safety limit, the wire may overheat and start a fire.

Home Safety A **fuse** prevents current overload in a circuit. A wire in the center of the fuse melts if too much current passes through it. This melting is known as "blowing a fuse." After a fuse like one of those shown in Figure 14 blows, it must be replaced with a new fuse before the circuit can carry a current again.

Most houses today use circuit breakers instead of fuses to prevent overloads. A **circuit breaker** is a switch that opens when current in a circuit is too high. The circuit breaker must be reset before the circuit can be used again.

Personal Safety Imagine what could happen if your body became part of an electric circuit. Figure 15 shows some effects that current may have on a person. You might not notice a current of 1 milliamp, but higher currents can be quite dangerous.

Electrical wiring in a home is insulated to protect people. If the insulation is damaged, you may accidentally touch the bare wire and get a shock. Avoid touching electrical devices with wet hands because your hands conduct current more readily when they are wet.

Effect of Current on Human Body	
Current Level	**Effect**
1 mA	Slight tingling sensation
5 mA	Slight shock
6–30 mA	Painful shock; loss of muscular control
50–150 mA	Extreme pain; severe muscular contractions. Breathing stops; death is possible.
1000–4300 mA	Nerve damage; heart stops, death is likely.
10,000 mA	Severe burns; heart stops, death is probable.

Figure 15 Even a small current in your body can cause a painful shock or injury. **Analyzing Data** *What is the lowest level of current that causes serious injury?*

Ground-fault circuit interrupter (GFCI)

Insulation also prevents short circuits. In a short circuit, current finds a short path through the circuit with less resistance than the full path through the circuit. A three-prong plug can prevent shocks caused by short circuits. In Figure 15 you can see the circular third prong, which connects to ground. These plugs are used on devices with metal exteriors, such as an electric drill. If a short circuit develops, you might get a shock by holding the drill. But instead of entering your body, the current takes an easier path to ground through the grounding wire. The transfer of excess charge through a conductor to Earth is called **grounding.**

A ground-fault circuit interrupter (GFCI) like the one shown in Figure 15 is an electrical safety outlet. It monitors current flowing to and from an outlet or appliance. If these two currents are not equal, it means current is escaping. The GFCI opens the circuit to prevent serious electric shocks.

Section 20.3 Assessment

Reviewing Concepts

1. Name two elements included in a circuit diagram.
2. What is the difference between a series circuit and a parallel circuit?
3. Write the equations for calculating electric power and electrical energy.
4. Name five safety devices used with electric current.

Critical Thinking

5. **Problem Solving** Two bulbs connected in parallel shine more brightly than when they are connected to the same voltage source in series. Explain why this doesn't violate the law of conservation of energy.

6. **Applying Concepts** You plug in a string of holiday lights and notice that the entire string turns off when you remove one bulb. Explain why this happens.

Math Practice

7. A stereo receiver uses a current of 2.2 amps from a 120-volt line. What is its power?

8. A television connected to a 120-volt line uses 102 watts of power. How much current flows through it?

Getting Personal with Computers

Millions of people use personal computers every day for activities such as writing letters, browsing the Internet, or playing games.

Disk drive

Monitor or display

Keyboard

Computer

Mouse

Basic Components
A computer system is made up of a monitor or display, a keyboard, a mouse, and a computer. Input devices, such as the mouse and keyboard, feed information into the computer. Output devices, such as the monitor, display information that has been taken in by the input devices and processed by the central processing unit (CPU). The computer contains the CPU, memory chips, hard disk, and motherboard.

Inside a Computer
The CPU and other chips in a computer contain integrated circuits. The circuits consist of millions of miniaturized electronic components deposited onto a thin slice of silicon. Computers use the electric signals and circuits within these chips to represent and process data. A binary number system is used, in which data are stored digitally as strings of 1's and 0's. The digits of a binary number are transmitted as electrical pulses. Each digit is called a bit, with 8 bits making up a byte.

Components formed from layers of silicon

Magnified section of part of the surface of a silicon chip through which data are transmitted

Microprocessor chip

Manipulating Bits and Bytes

Computer programs and data, such as word processing files, are stored for the long term on magnetic storage devices such as the hard disk. It is only during actual use of a program and work on data files that they are moved to RAM. Both the hard disk and RAM store data in bytes.

1 Program startup The file to be worked on and the program that allows it to be worked on are stored on the hard disk. Copies of both are moved, via circuits in the motherboard and cables, from hard disk storage to RAM.

2 Work in progress Under the user's control, the CPU works through program instructions. It makes changes to the copy of the data held in RAM.

3 End of session The updated data are saved back to the hard disk, and the program that was being used is erased from RAM.

Hard disk

File and program

CPU

RAM

1

2

3

OPENED COMPUTER

DVD/CD writer

Power supply

Fan housing

Hard disk

Video card houses specially designed graphics chips.

RAM *Random-access memory (RAM) is used to store programs that are being run. Information is temporarily stored in RAM as a series of 1's and 0's. When the computer is switched off, any information stored in RAM is lost.*

Heat Sink *Heat is generated by the flow of electricity inside the computer. A heat sink is needed to dissipate the heat. It draws heat away from the components to protect them.*

CPU *The central processing unit carries out program instructions and controls all the information flowing around the computer.*

Motherboard *This large circuit board houses the CPU, RAM, and ROM (read-only memory). ROM is permanent memory that includes startup instructions.*

Using Computers

Even before there were personal computers, digital computing was put to use in a variety of different ways. Today, computer technology has been miniaturized to create mobile phones, and expanded to allow supercomputers to work at high speed. Virtual reality, a relatively recent development, now allows for realistic simulations in a three-dimensional, computer-generated world.

Mini Computers

Mobile phones and other small electronic devices, such as hand-held computers, use smaller and smaller chips to allow for portability and convenience.

Supercomputers

By cooling the components so that they conduct electricity more efficiently, supercomputers are able to process information at a very fast rate. These computers gain speed by multi-tasking, performing several processes at once. The computer shown here is used in the study of particle physics.

Virtual Reality

Virtual reality is a three-dimensional computer-generated world. Programs such as the NASA flight simulator shown here train students through interactive simulations.

3-D image projector

Instruments and controls

Computer Games
In human-movement tracking technology, computers simulate human movement for realistic computer games. As shown here, markers are placed on a person and used to track his movements. A computer analyzes the path shown by each marker. The computer then recreates the paths for the simulated figures in a computer game, as shown above.

Illuminated markers

Going Further

- Use the library or the Internet to research how making computer circuits smaller allows a computer to operate at a faster speed. Write a paragraph describing one technology that has increased processing speed.

20.4 Electronic Devices

Reading Focus

Key Concepts

- How do electronic signals convey information?
- How do vacuum tubes control electron flow?
- What are two types of semiconductors?
- How are semi-conductors used?
- What are the benefits of using microchips in communication devices?

Vocabulary

- electronics
- electronic signal
- analog signal
- digital signal
- semiconductor
- diode
- transistor
- integrated circuit
- computer

Reading Strategy

Summarizing Copy the table below. As you read, complete the table to summarize what you learn about solid-state components.

Solid-State Component	Description	Uses
Diode	a. ?	b. ?
Transistor	c. ?	d. ?
Integrated circuit	e. ?	f. ?

How do a toaster and a lamp use electric current differently than a computer or a mobile phone? The toaster and lamp are *electrical* devices. They change electrical energy into heat or light. The computer and mobile phone are *electronic* devices, which use electric current to process or send information.

Electronic Signals

The science of using electric current to process or transmit information is **electronics.** The information is carried by an electronic signal. An **electronic signal** is information sent as patterns in the controlled flow of electrons through a circuit.

To understand how this works, think about circuits. If a voltage source is connected to a circuit by a wire, electrons will flow through the wire. Controlling the electron flow—by either altering the voltage or turning the current on and off—produces a coded signal. **Electronics conveys information with electrical patterns called analog and digital signals.**

Figure 16 A computer uses electric current to process information. A toaster uses electric current to change electrical energy into thermal energy.

Analog Signals An **analog signal** is a smoothly varying signal produced by continuously changing the voltage or current in a circuit. Information is encoded in the strength or frequency of the analog signal. Figure 17A shows one familiar example—a signal used by an AM radio station. The music is encoded as a smoothly changing pattern of the voltage.

Digital Signals A **digital signal** encodes information as a string of 1's and 0's. Figure 17B shows how pulsing a current on and off can produce a digital signal. When the current is off, it represents a "0." When the current is on, it represents a "1." You may be familiar with Morse code, which in a similar way uses two signals. A dot and a dash are all you need to represent the 26 letters of the alphabet and the digits 0 through 9.

Digital signals are more reliable than analog signals. For example, a DVD, or digital video disc, encodes digital signals as a series of pits in the DVD surface. If a pit is damaged, it is often still readable as a 0 or a 1. The quality of video is not affected unless the damage is severe. In comparison, damage to an analog videotape adds noise to the signal.

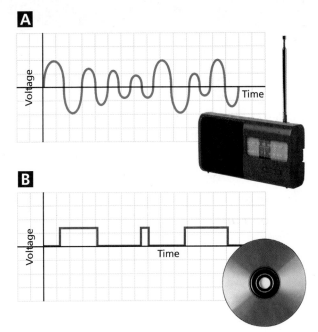

Figure 17 Electronic signals convey information by changing voltage or current in a circuit. **A** An analog signal can be produced by smoothly changing voltage. **B** A digital signal can be produced by pulsing a current on and off. **Applying Concepts** *Could a portable radio, in theory, receive and process a digital signal?*

Vacuum Tubes

To create an electronic signal, you must be able to control the flow of electrons. A vacuum tube was used to control electron flow in early electronic devices. **Vacuum tubes can change alternating current into direct current, increase the strength of a signal, or turn a current on or off.**

One useful type of vacuum tube is a cathode-ray tube (CRT) shown in Figure 18. Many computer monitors and televisions contain CRTs. One side of the CRT has three metal plates that emit electron beams. The electrons are emitted at one end of an airless tube and strike a glass surface on the other end. The glass is coated with phosphors that glow red, green, or blue in response to the electron beams. An electronic signal controls the strength and position of the beams to produce images with the light from the phosphors.

Although vacuum tubes have many useful features, some types burn out frequently and need to be replaced. They are also much too large for use in small electronic devices.

Figure 18 A cathode-ray tube is still used in many computer monitors and television sets.

Reading Checkpoint *What is a CRT?*

Digital Camera

When light enters an analog camera, it strikes a strip of light-sensitive film behind the lens. In a digital camera, the pattern of light is sensed electronically and turned into digital code.

Interpreting Diagrams *What controls the sharpness of a digital image?*

Miniature digital camera
Digital cameras can be much smaller than traditional cameras because high resolution CCDs do not need to use large lenses.

Lens *The lens focuses light from the scene onto the CCD.*

CCD (charged-coupled device) *The CCD has millions of light-sensitive cells, called photosites. The more photosites per unit area, the sharper the image is.*

Analog-to-digital converter *The analog-to-digital converter turns the output of each photosite into digital code.*

Microprocessor *The microprocessor calculates color values for each part of the image.*

Memory chip *Data about the image are stored on this non-removable chip.*

Memory card *This removable card stores the image as a digital file.*

Light from scene

Digital-to-analog converter *Here the digital data are turned into a form that allows the image to be displayed on the LCD screen.*

Cable to computer

Computer output port *This port allows the digital image to be transferred to a computer.*

How the CCD works
In a CCD, a lens focuses light onto a photosite, which converts the light intensity into an electric current. To create a full color image, the CCD contains a color filter. The filter separates incoming light into one of the three primary colors at each photosite. The microprocessor creates a color image by evaluating the color data for groups of photosites.

Lens   *Color filter*   *Photosite*

LCD (liquid crystal display) screen *The LCD screen displays an image of the scene that the camera is aimed at. Images that have been previously saved can also be displayed on the screen.*

Semiconductors

A **semiconductor** is a crystalline solid that conducts current only under certain conditions. Most semiconductors are made with silicon or germanium. In pure form, these elements are poor conductors. But when trace amounts of other elements are added, it becomes possible to control the current inside of the crystals. Figure 19 shows two types of semiconductors. ◯ **In n-type semiconductors, the current is a flow of electrons. In p-type semiconductors, it appears as though positive charge flows.**

A p-type semiconductor can be made by adding a trace amount of boron to silicon. In Figure 19A, you can see spaces, called holes, at each boron atom. The holes are positively charged. Figure 19B shows an n-type semiconductor made by adding phosphorus to silicon. Phosphorus atoms provide weakly bound electrons that can flow.

By themselves, n-type and p-type semiconductors cannot do much. But when joined together, electrons in the n-type semiconductor are attracted toward the positively charged holes in the p-type semiconductor. As electrons jump from hole to hole, it looks like a flow of positive charge because the locations of the holes change.

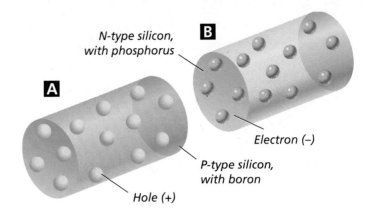

N-type silicon, with phosphorus

Electron (–)

P-type silicon, with boron

Hole (+)

Figure 19 A semiconductor becomes a good conductor of charge if trace amounts of elements are added to it.

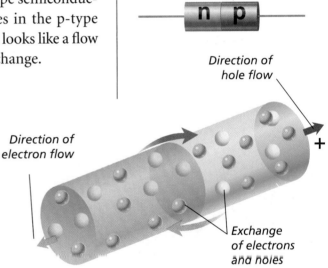

Direction of hole flow

Direction of electron flow

Exchange of electrons and holes

Solid-State Components

Semiconductor devices were first used in the late 1940s. These devices were named solid-state components because they used solids rather than vacuum tubes to control current. ◯ **Most modern electronic devices are controlled by solid-state components.** Three of the most useful solid-state components are diodes, transistors, and integrated circuits.

Diodes A **diode** is a solid-state component that combines an n-type and p-type semiconductor. When a voltage is applied across a diode, electrons flow from the n-type to the p-type semiconductor. There is no current if voltage is applied in the opposite direction. Because the current can be in only one direction, a diode can change alternating current to direct current.

Transistors Figure 20B shows a **transistor,** a solid-state component with three layers of semiconductors. A small current flowing through its center layer changes its resistance. A transistor can be used as a switch because the small current can turn another current on or off. It can also be used as an amplifier. A small voltage applied to one side of the transistor produces a large voltage on the other side.

Figure 20 A A diode is two different semiconductors joined in one component. **B** A transistor is three semiconductors with the middle one different from the outer ones. **Applying Concepts** *In addition to the arrangement of the transistor in B, how else might you arrange the transistor?*

Integrated Circuits An **integrated circuit** is a thin slice of silicon that contains many solid-state components. The components are carefully built layer by layer on the silicon base. Integrated circuits are sometimes called chips or microchips. They perform as well as a network of vacuum tubes, but they need only a tiny fraction of the space. Mobile phones, pagers, and computers all use microchips.

Electronic devices today are so small because hundreds of millions of components fit on a microchip smaller than your fingertip. Integrated circuits are also blindingly fast compared to vacuum tubes. One reason is that current does not have to travel far to get from point to point in the circuit. So it shouldn't be surprising that as technology improves, and chips get smaller, the chips operate at higher speeds.

Communications Technology

A **computer** is a programmable device that can store and process information. Today you find microchips in all sorts of devices that you wouldn't call computers. **Communication devices use microchips to make them more portable, reliable, and affordable.**

Figure 21 shows the inside a mobile phone, which contains many solid-state components. Transistors amplify the phone's incoming signal. Electronic devices called capacitors store electric charge. They allow a mobile phone to store data such as phone numbers, even if the battery is removed for a short time. Diodes maintain proper voltage levels in the circuits. Without solid-state components, none of this would be possible.

Figure 21 A mobile phone uses many solid-state components. **Drawing Conclusions** *Would it be possible to make a mobile phone using vacuum tubes rather than solid-state components?*

Section 20.4 Assessment

Reviewing Concepts

1. How are electronic devices used to process information?
2. Describe how electron flow is controlled in vacuum tubes.
3. What are two types of semiconductors?
4. How are solid-state components used?
5. How are microchips beneficial for communication devices?

Critical Thinking

6. **Comparing and Contrasting** How are solid-state components like vacuum tubes? How are they different?

7. **Applying Concepts** Explain how a diode can be used to change alternating current into direct current.
8. **Using Analogies** Explain how a diode is like a one-way street.

> ## Connecting ⊂ Concepts
>
> **Conservation of Energy** Review Section 15.2. How is energy conserved when a heat sink is used to protect electronic components in a computer?

Forensics Lab

Evaluating Electrical Safety

Electrical appliances must be safely insulated to protect users from injury. In this lab, you will play the role of a safety engineer determining whether an electric power supply is safely insulated.

Problem
How much resistance is needed in series with a known resistance to reduce the voltage by 99 percent?

Materials
- 9-volt battery
- battery clip
- multimeter
- 3 alligator clips
- 4 resistors: 1-ohm, 10-ohm, 100-ohm, 1000-ohm

 For the probeware version of this lab, see Probeware Lab Manual, Lab 8.

Skills
Calculating, Using Tables

Procedure

1. On a separate sheet of paper, make a copy of the data table shown below.

Data Table			
Resistance (ohms)		Voltage difference (volts)	
Current-Carrying	Insulating	Current-Carrying	Insulating
1	1000		
1	100		
10	1000		
10	100		

2. Attach the battery clip to the battery. **CAUTION** *The circuit may become hot.*

3. Use an alligator clip to attach one wire of the 1-ohm resistor to one of the battery clip's wires as shown.

4. Clip one wire of the 1000-ohm resistor to the free end of the 1-ohm resistor. Clip the other wire of the 1000-ohm resistor to the free wire of the battery clip.

5. The 1-ohm resistor represents the current-carrying part of the appliance. The 1000-ohm resistor represents the insulation for the current-carrying part. Place one of the multimeter's electrodes on each wire of the 1-ohm resistor. Record the voltage difference.

6. Place the multimeter's electrodes on the wires of the 1000-ohm resistor. Record the voltage difference.

7. To model a reduction in the resistance of the insulation, repeat Steps 5 and 6, replacing the 1000-ohm resistor with a 100-ohm resistor. Disconnect the resistors from the battery clip.

8. **Predicting** Record your prediction of how increasing the resistance of the current-carrying part of the appliance will affect the voltage difference across the insulating part.

9. To test your prediction, repeat Steps 3 through 7, using a 10-ohm resistor to represent the current-carrying part of the appliance.

Analyze and Conclude

1. **Calculating** When the resistance of the current-carrying part was 1 ohm and the resistance of the insulating part was 100 ohms, what was the ratio of the voltage differences across the current-carrying part and the insulating part?

2. **Drawing Conclusions** In the circuit you built, what is the voltage difference across each resistor proportional to?

3. **Applying Concepts** You know the resistance of the current-carrying part of an appliance. What should the resistance of the insulation be to reduce the voltage by 99 percent?

20.1 Electric Charge and Static Electricity

Key Concepts

- An excess or shortage of electrons produces a net electric charge.
- Like charges repel and opposite charges attract.
- Electric field strength depends on the net charge and distance from the charge.
- Charge can be transferred by friction, by contact, and by induction.
- Static discharge occurs when electric charge is transferred suddenly.

Vocabulary

electric charge, *p. 600;* electric force, *p. 601;* electric field, *p. 602;* static electricity, *p. 602;* law of conservation of charge, *p. 602;* induction, *p. 603*

20.2 Electric Current and Ohm's Law

Key Concepts

- The two types of current are direct current and alternating current.
- Metals such as copper and silver are good conductors. Wood, plastic, rubber, and air are good insulators.
- A material's thickness, length, and temperature affect its resistance.
- In order for charge to flow in a conducting wire, the wire must be connected in a complete loop that includes a source of electrical energy.
- Increasing the voltage increases the current. Keeping the same voltage and increasing the resistance decreases the current.

Vocabulary

electric current, *p. 604;* direct current, *p. 604;* alternating current, *p. 604;* electrical conductor, *p. 605;* electrical insulator, *p. 605;* resistance, *p. 605;* superconductor, *p. 605;* potential difference, *p. 606;* voltage, *p. 606;* battery, *p. 606;* Ohm's law, *p. 607*

20.3 Electric Circuits

Key Concepts

- An electric circuit has a source of electrical energy and devices run by electrical energy.
- If one element stops functioning in a series circuit, none of the elements can operate, but in a parallel circuit, the rest of the elements still can operate.
- Electric power is voltage multiplied by current. Electrical energy is power multiplied by time.
- A variety of devices make electrical energy safe.

Vocabulary

electric circuit, *p. 609;* series circuit, *p. 610;* parallel circuit, *p. 610;* electric power, *p. 611;* fuse, *p. 612;* circuit breaker, *p. 612;* grounding, *p. 613*

20.4 Electronic Devices

Key Concepts

- Electronics convey information with electrical patterns called analog and digital signals.
- Vacuum tubes and solid-state components are two kinds of devices that can control electron flow.
- Solid-state components use semiconductors.

Vocabulary

electronics, *p. 618;* electronic signal, *p. 618;* analog signal, *p. 619;* digital signal, *p. 619;* semiconductor, *p. 621;* diode, *p. 621;* transistor, *p. 621;* integrated circuit, *p. 622;* computer, *p. 622*

Thinking Visually

Web Diagram Copy the web diagram below and use information from the chapter to complete it.

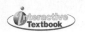
Reviewing Content

Choose the letter that best answers the question or completes the statement.

1. A material has a net electric charge because it
   a. discharges.
   b. has an alternating current.
   c. has an excess or shortage of electrons.
   d. has a direct current.

2. Static electricity is the study of
   a. buildup of charge.
   b. electric discharges.
   c. electric fields.
   d. all of the above.

3. A strong electric field is
   a. directed toward a charge.
   b. directed away from a charge.
   c. caused by a large quantity of charge.
   d. caused by a small quantity of charge.

4. What is a material called that easily carries a current?
   a. insulator   b. semiconductor
   c. electric potential d. conductor

5. A superconducting material
   a. requires very high current.
   b. has no resistance at room temperature.
   c. has no resistance at low temperatures.
   d. has high resistance at low temperatures.

6. What does Ohm's law state?
   a. Current equals voltage times resistance.
   b. Voltage equals resistance divided by current.
   c. Voltage equals current divided by resistance.
   d. Voltage equals current times resistance.

7. Which melts to protect a circuit?
   a. three-prong plug
   b. wiring
   c. diode
   d. fuse

8. What does " I " represent in the equation $P = I \times V$?
   a. voltage   b. resistance
   c. current   d. kilowatts

9. The output of a diode can be
   a. direct current.   b. a superconductor.
   c. resistance.   d. alternating current.

10. Three layers of semiconductor material can form
    a. a transistor only.
    b. a diode only.
    c. either a transistor or a diode.
    d. neither a transistor nor a diode.

Understanding Concepts

11. How does the electric force between two charged objects change if you double the distance between the objects?

12. What determines the direction of the electric field near a charge?

13. How can a charged object cause charges to move within an uncharged object?

14. If the current in a circuit is clockwise, what is the direction of electron flow?

15. Explain why a wire becomes warmer when charges flow through it.

16. Does voltage flow in a circuit? Explain.

Use the following diagram to answer Questions 17 and 18. The three bulbs are identical.

17. Does the same current pass through each bulb? Explain why or why not.

18. What happens to the other bulbs if bulb A burns out? If bulb B burns out?

19. A battery and a light bulb are connected in a simple circuit. What is the source of electrons that flow through the wire?

20. Explain why a light bulb does not change its brightness when another bulb is added in parallel.

21. What are digital and analog signals?

Assessment (continued)

Critical Thinking

22. Applying Concepts In a science museum demonstration, a person on an insulated stand touches a metal sphere. The sphere has a large charge. Explain why the person's hair stands on end.

23. Applying Concepts Explain why a battery is always connected so that one wire goes to the battery's positive terminal and one to the negative terminal.

24. Relating Cause and Effect A person plugs a fan into a wall socket and turns it on. Suddenly, the lights go out in several rooms of the house. Explain what has probably happened and what can be done to fix it.

25. Applying Concepts Explain why a hair dryer has a high-heat setting with a lower resistance than the low-heat setting. (*Hint:* Use the equation $P = IV$.)

26. Comparing and Contrasting How are n-type semiconductors and p-type semiconductors alike. How are they different?

Math Skills

27. Calculating On a wet day, your skin's resistance may be as low as 1000 ohms. On a dry day, it may be as high as 100,000 ohms. How much current moves through your fingers if you touch the terminals of a 9-volt battery on a wet day? On a dry day?

28. Calculating Six light bulbs are connected in series with a 9.0-volt battery. What is the voltage across each bulb?

29. Calculating A freezer has a power rating of 105 watts. How much current does it use if it is plugged into a 120-volt line?

30. Calculating The power rating on an electric oven is 9300 watts. If the oven is plugged into a 240-volt line, how much current does it use? What is the resistance of the oven?

Concepts in Action

31. Relating Cause and Effect You turn a television on and notice a faint crackling sound. If you touch the screen, you get a small shock. What is the source of this electric charge?

32. Inferring Plugs used for connecting an electrical appliance such as a toaster to a wall socket have two prongs. Explain why plugs have two prongs instead of one prong.

33. Inferring The photograph below shows ceramic insulators holding the power lines at each pole. What is the purpose of the insulators?

34. Making Judgments Explain why you think builders should or should not be required to install GFCI (ground-fault circuit interrupter) outlets in all new homes.

35. Writing in Science Write a paragraph explaining in detail why you could be struck by lightning if you stand outside during a thunderstorm. Include a sketch that illustrates the ideas in your paragraph.

Performance-Based Assessment

Designing an Experiment Design and conduct an experiment that uses a light-emitting diode in a simple circuit to demonstrate that current flows only one way through a diode. Before beginning, research the properties and limitations of your diode.

For: Self-grading assessment
Visit: PHschool.com
Web Code: cca-2200

Standardized Test Prep

When a question refers to a diagram, start by scanning the whole diagram. See if you can remember what each symbol means.

In a circuit diagram, determine if the circuit is series or parallel. Check to make sure that each part of the circuit is complete. In the question below, a wire goes to device #2, but no wire leaves it, so no current enters the device.

The direction of current is from the positive terminal to the negative terminal of the voltage source. Note that the direction of current is opposite the direction of electron flow. In the circuit below, current is in a clockwise direction.

In what order does current flow in the circuit above?

(A) 5 – 6 – 7 – 1 – 5 – 3 – 4
(B) 6 – 7 – 8 – 2 – 5 – 1 – 3 – 4
(C) 4 – 3 – 5 – 7 – 6
(D) 3 – 2 – 5 – 6 – 4 – 7
(E) 4 – 3 – 1 – 5 – 8 – 7 – 6

(Answer: E)

1. In the diagram above, the battery is replaced by an AC voltage source. Which of the following is now true?
   (A) The current enters and leaves device #2.
   (B) The current is always clockwise.
   (C) There is not net movement of charge in the circuit.
   (D) The current is always counterclockwise.
   (E) There is no current in the circuit.

2. If you rub a neutral glass rod with silk, the silk acquires a negative charge. If you rub a neutral glass rod with a rubber rod, the rubber acquires a negative charge. If you rub a neutral rubber rod with silk, the rubber rod acquires a negative charge. Which of the three materials has the strongest attraction for electrons?
   (A) glass
   (B) silk
   (C) rubber
   (D) not enough data to answer
   (E) none, because they have equal attractions for electrons

3. A 1.5-m wire carries a 5.0-A current when a potential difference of 3.7 V is applied. What is the resistance of the wire?
   (A) 0.49 ohms
   (B) 0.74 ohms
   (C) 1.1 ohms
   (D) 1.4 ohms
   (E) 2.0 ohms

4. A space heater is connected to a standard 120-V line. If the resistance of the operating heater is 15 ohms, what power does the heater use? (*Hint*: First calculate the current.)
   (A) 8.0 W
   (B) 64 W
   (C) 960 W
   (D) 1800 W
   (E) 220 kW

5. A 1700-W machine operates at 120 V. What is the resistance in the machine?
   (A) 7.1 x 10^{22} ohms
   (B) 1.2 x 10^{21} ohms
   (C) 1.4 ohms
   (D) 8.5 ohms
   (E) 14 ohms

6. A lamp with three 40-W bulbs connected in parallel is plugged into a 120-V outlet. What is the current in the lamp?
   (A) 1 A
   (B) 3 A
   (C) 9 A
   (D) 40 A
   (E) 120 A

CHAPTER
21 Magnetism

How does an electric motor work?

An electric motor is a device that converts electrical energy into mechanical energy. You will learn how electric motors work in Section 21.2. Use the library or Internet to research how to build a simple kind of electric motor called a stripped-down motor. Document your progress by making a video or photo journal to post on a blog. Explain how each part of the stripped-down motor works.

How do science concepts apply to your world? Here are some questions you'll be able to answer after you read this chapter.

- **What causes two magnets to push and pull each other, even when they aren't touching?** *(Section 21.1)*

- **How do electric motors work?** *(Section 21.2)*

- **How do loudspeakers use magnets to change electrical signals into sound?** *(Section 21.2)*

- **How do doctors use magnetic fields to see inside the human body?** *(page 640)*

- **How is electric current generated?** *(Section 21.3)*

- **How does electric current get to your home?** *(Section 21.3)*

When charged particles from the sun are pulled toward the North or South Pole, they may cause colorful lights in the night sky.

Chapter Preview

Inquiry Activity

How Do Magnets Interact With One Another?

Procedure

1. Bring the north pole of one bar magnet close to the south pole of another bar magnet. Observe and record what happens.

2. Bring the north pole of one bar magnet close to the north pole of another bar magnet. Observe and record what happens.

3. **Predicting** Predict what will happen if you bring the north pole of one bar magnet close to the center of another bar magnet. Test your prediction.

Think About It

1. **Observing** Describe the similarities and differences between the interactions of the north and south poles and the two north poles.

2. **Inferring** How do you think distance affects the way magnets interact?

3. **Posing Questions** Write a question about how magnets interact with other materials such as glass, plastic, paper, and cloth.

21.1 Magnets and Magnetic Fields

Key Concepts

- How do magnetic poles interact?
- How can a magnetic field affect a magnet that enters the field?
- Why are some materials magnetic while others are not?

Vocabulary

- magnetic force
- magnetic pole
- magnetic field
- magnetosphere
- magnetic domain
- ferromagnetic material

Reading Strategy

Using Prior Knowledge Copy the diagram below and add what you already know about magnets. After you read, revise the diagram based on what you learned.

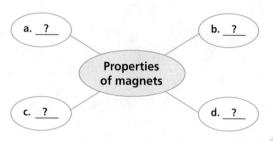

Ancient Greeks observed that magnetite, or lodestone, attracts iron. Some time before 200 A.D., the Chinese sculpted magnetite into spoon-shaped compasses. They called these stones "south pointers." By 1150 A.D., Chinese navigators used compasses with magnetized iron needles. But properties of magnets were not well explained until 1600. In that year, the English physician William Gilbert published *De Magnete*.

Magnetic Forces

You can explore properties of magnets on your own. Either side of a magnet sticks to a refrigerator. Yet if you push two magnets together, they may attract or repel. **Magnetic force** is the force a magnet exerts on another magnet, on iron or a similar metal, or on moving charges. Recall that magnetic force is one aspect of electromagnetic force.

Magnetic forces, like electric forces, act over a distance. Look at the suspended magnets in Figure 1. If you push down on the top two magnets, you can feel the magnets repel. Push harder, and the force increases. Magnetic force, like electric force, varies with distance.

Gilbert used a compass to map forces around a magnetite sphere. He discovered that the force is strongest at the poles. All magnets have two **magnetic poles,** regions where the magnet's force is strongest. One end of a magnet is its north pole; the other end is its south pole. The direction of magnetic force between two magnets depends on how the poles face. Like magnetic poles repel one another, and opposite magnetic poles attract one another.

Figure 1 The green magnet and lower red magnet attract each other. The lower red magnet and the yellow magnet repel each other. **Predicting** *What would happen if the upper red magnet on the pencil were flipped over?*

Magnetic Fields

A **magnetic field** surrounds a magnet and can exert magnetic forces. In Figure 2, iron filings are used to show the shape of the magnetic field around a bar magnet. ◖▬ **A magnetic field, which is strongest near a magnet's poles, will either attract or repel another magnet that enters the field.** The field lines begin near the magnet's north pole and extend toward its south pole. The arrows on the field lines indicate what direction a compass needle would point at each point in space. Where lines are close together, the field is strong. Where lines are more spread out, the field is weak.

Magnetic Fields Around Magnets You can use iron filings to visualize how magnetic fields of two magnets interact. Figure 3A shows the north pole of one magnet facing the north pole of another magnet. Notice that there are no iron filings in the gap between the magnets. Iron filings are not attracted to this area because the combined magnetic field is very weak. Figure 3B shows the combined field of two magnets with opposite poles facing each other. The field lines start at the north pole of one magnet and extend to the south pole of the other magnet. The field in the gap between the magnets is very strong, as you can see from the dense crowding of iron filings in this area.

Figure 2 A magnetic field surrounds every magnet. Iron filings reveal the field lines, which start near the north pole and extend toward the south pole. **Interpreting Diagrams** *In which two areas of a bar magnet is the field strongest?*

Figure 3 Iron filings reveal the combined magnetic field of two interacting magnets. **A** When like poles of two magnets come together, the magnets repel each other. **B** When opposite poles of magnets come together, the magnets attract each other.

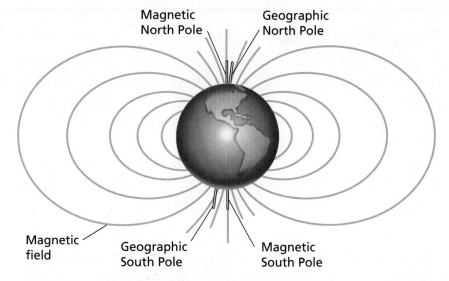

Figure 4 Earth is surrounded by magnetic field lines. These lines are densest at the poles.

Magnetic North Pole
Geographic North Pole
Magnetic field
Geographic South Pole
Magnetic South Pole

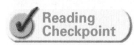

Observing Magnetic Field Lines

Materials

small container of iron filings, 2 bar magnets, paper, 2 textbooks, masking tape

Procedure

1. Place two textbooks side by side, about 7 cm apart.

2. Place the magnets between the books, with north poles facing, about 2 cm apart. Tape the magnets in place.

3. Place the paper over the magnets to form a bridge.

4. Sprinkle iron filings on the paper until you can see the magnetic field lines. Sketch your observations.

5. Carefully return the filings to their container.

6. Repeat Steps 2 through 5 with opposite poles facing.

Analyze and Conclude

1. **Inferring** Where was the magnetic field the strongest? The weakest?

2. **Analyzing Data** How did the fields of like poles facing differ from those of unlike poles facing?

3. **Predicting** What result would you expect if you used sawdust instead of iron filings?

Magnetic Field Around Earth Earth is like a giant magnet surrounded by a magnetic field. The area surrounding Earth that is influenced by this field is the **magnetosphere** (mag NET oh sfeer).

A compass points north because it aligns with Earth's magnetic field. However, as Figure 4 shows, Earth's magnetic poles are not at the geographic poles. The geographic North Pole is at 90° N latitude, but the magnetic North Pole is at about 84° N latitude. Because of this, a compass may point east or west of north. The angle between the direction to true north and to magnetic north is called magnetic declination. Magnetic declination varies with your location on Earth.

Reading Checkpoint *Why does a compass point toward north?*

Magnetic Materials

Within an atom, electrons move around the nucleus. This movement, along with a property of electrons called "spin," causes electrons to act like tiny magnets. In many materials, each electron is paired with another having an opposite spin. Magnetic effects mostly cancel each other. As a result, these materials have extremely weak magnetic fields.

Many other materials have one or more unpaired electrons. The unpaired electrons produce magnetic fields. But the fields usually don't combine because the arrangement of the atoms isn't quite right. These materials have weak magnetic fields. In a few materials, such as iron, nickel, and cobalt, the unpaired electrons make a strong magnetic field. Then the fields combine to form magnetic domains. A **magnetic domain** is a region that has a very large number of atoms with aligned magnetic fields. A **ferromagnetic material** (fehr oh mag NET ik), such as iron, can be magnetized because it contains magnetic domains. **When a material is magnetized, most of its magnetic domains are aligned.**

Nonmagnetized Materials The fact that a material is ferromagnetic does not mean it is a magnet. If the domains of a ferromagnetic material are aligned randomly, the magnetization of the domains is cancelled, and it is not a magnet. An iron nail is an example of a nonmagnetized material. It is ferromagnetic, so the domains have the potential to be aligned, but normally they are not. Figure 5A shows the random orientation of domains in nonmagnetized iron.

Magnetized Materials You can easily magnetize a nonmagnetized ferromagnetic material by placing it in a magnetic field. For example, if you put a nonmagnetized iron nail near a magnet, you will turn the nail into a magnet. Figure 5B shows the alignment of magnetic domains in magnetized iron. The applied magnetic field causes magnetic domains aligned with the field to grow larger. This magnetization can be temporary. If the magnet is moved away from the nail, the motion of the atoms in the nail causes the magnetic domains to become randomly oriented again. In some ferromagnetic materials, the domains stay aligned for a long time. These materials are called permanent magnets. They are not truly permanant, because heat or a jarring impact can realign the domains.

If you cut a magnet in half, each half will have its own north pole and south pole because the domains will still be aligned. If you cut the pieces in half again, each half will again have a north pole and a south pole. No matter how many times you cut the magnets, each piece will have two different poles. A magnet can never have just a north pole or just a south pole.

Figure 5 A magnetic field can magnetize ferromagnetic materials. **A** Before magnetization, domains are random. **B** Domains aligned with the field grow during magnetization. Unaligned domains can shrink.

Section 21.1 Assessment

Reviewing Concepts

1. Describe the interaction of magnetic poles.
2. What two things can happen to a magnet entering a magnetic field?
3. What makes a material magnetic?
4. Describe what happens to the fields of two bar magnets when you bring their north poles together.

Critical Thinking

5. **Predicting** What happens if you suspend a bar magnet so that it can swing freely?
6. **Relating Cause and Effect** How are electrons responsible for magnetism?

7. **Predicting** What will happen if you hit a magnet with a hammer? Explain.
8. **Designing Experiments** How could you test the effects of heating and cooling on the magnetization of a bar magnet?

Connecting C **Concepts**

Electric Charge Review electric charge in Section 20.1. Compare the attraction and repulsion of positive and negative charges with the behavior of two bar magnets placed near one another.

Anti-Theft Security Devices

Anti-theft security devices are found in stores across the world. One of the best of these devices is the electro-magnetic (EM) tag system. This system is based on the interaction between a small piece of magnetic material (a tag) and an EM field created between two pedestals at the store exit. **Applying concepts** *Which is more highly magnetized, an activated or a deactivated tag?*

Library security
Powerful magnets are used to deactivate tags in library books before borrowing. If the tag is not deactivated, the alarm will go off at the library exit.

A **Activated tag** An activated tag is slightly demagnetized. When it passes through the pedestal's EM field, the tag's magnetic domains line up with the field. This change in magnetic domain emits a signal that is picked up by the receiver, which sets off the alarm.

Activated tag (demagnetized)

Magnetic domain

Changing electromagnetic field

B **Deactivated tag**
A deactivated tag is fully magnetized. When it passes through the exit, the tag's domains do not change. Because no signal is emitted, the alarm is not set off.

Deactivated tag (fully magnetized)

Receiver pedestal

Flashing alarm light

Transmitter pedestal

Tag signal

Wire loop carrying alternating current

Activated tag attached to item

Changing electromagnetic field

C **The pedestals** The transmitter pedestal contains a wire loop that produces a changing EM field in the region between the pedestals. The receiver pedestal picks up any signal produced by the tag.

21.2 Electromagnetism

Reading Focus

Key Concepts

- How can an electric charge create a magnetic field?
- How is an electromagnet controlled?
- How do galvanometers, electric motors, and loudspeakers work?

Vocabulary

- electromagnetic force
- solenoid
- electromagnet
- galvanometer
- electric motor

Reading Strategy

Identifying Main Idea Copy the table below. As you read, write the main idea of the text that follows each topic.

Topic	Main Idea
Electricity and magnetism	a. ?
Direction of magnetic fields	b. ?
Direction of electric currents	c. ?
Solenoids and electromagnets	d. ?
Electromagnetic devices	e. ?

Y ou know that unlike electric charges attract one another and that like electric charges repel one another. It is easy to discover a similar effect with the north and south poles of two magnets. However, it's much more difficult to figure out the relationship between electricity and magnetism. In fact, the connection was discovered accidentally by the Danish scientist Hans Christian Oersted in 1820.

One evening Oersted, pictured in Figure 6, was conducting scientific demonstrations for his friends and students in his home. One demonstration used electric current in a wire, and another used a compass needle attached to a wooden stand. As Oersted turned on the current for the electricity demonstration, he saw the compass needle move. When he turned off the current, the needle moved back to its original position. Further investigation showed that the current in the wire produced a magnetic field. Oersted had discovered a relationship between electricity and magnetism.

Electricity and Magnetism

Electricity and magnetism are different aspects of a single force known as the **electromagnetic force.** The electric force results from charged particles. The magnetic force usually results from the movement of electrons in an atom. Both aspects of the electromagnetic force are caused by electric charges.

Figure 6 In 1820 Hans Oersted discovered how magnetism and electricity are connected. A unit of measure of magnetic field strength, the oersted, is named after him.

Figure 7 If you point the thumb of your right hand in the direction of the current, your fingers curve in the direction of the magnetic field. **Inferring** *How can you determine the magnetic field direction from the direction of electron flow?*

Direction of current

Direction of electron flow

Current-carrying wire

Direction of magnetic field

Magnetic Fields Around Moving Charges Oersted's discovery about the relationship between a current-carrying wire and a magnet established an important physics principle. 🔑 **Moving electric charges create a magnetic field.** These moving charges may be the vibrating charges that produce an electromagnetic wave. They may also be, as in Oersted's experiment, the moving charges in a wire. Figure 7 shows how to remember the direction of the magnetic field that is produced. The magnetic field lines form circles around a straight wire carrying a current.

Forces Acting on Moving Charges Recall that an electric field exerts a force on an electric charge. The force is either in the same direction as the electric field or in the opposite direction, depending on whether it is a positive or negative charge.

The effect of a magnetic field on a moving charge is different, as shown in Figure 8. A charge moving in a magnetic field will be deflected in a direction perpendicular to both the magnetic field and to the velocity of the charge. If a current-carrying wire is in a magnetic field, the wire will be pushed in a direction perpendicular to both the field and the direction of the current. Reversing the direction of the current will still cause the wire to be deflected, but in the opposite direction. If the current is parallel to the magnetic field, the force is zero and there is no deflection.

Reading Checkpoint *What are two kinds of moving charges that can create a magnetic field?*

Force deflecting the charge

Velocity of charge

Figure 8 A moving positive charge is deflected at a right angle to its motion by a magnetic field. **Inferring** *In what direction would the particle be deflected if it had a negative charge instead of a positive charge?*

Making an Electromagnet

Materials

iron nail, 20 small metal paper clips, 20-cm length and 1-m length of insulated wire with stripped ends, 6-volt battery, switch

Procedure

1. Make a circuit using the nail, wire, battery, and switch. Use the shorter wire to connect one terminal of the battery to the switch. Connect the longer wire to the other terminal of the battery. Wrap this wire around the nail 10 times. Then connect the longer wire to the switch.

2. Hold the head of the nail over the pile of paper clips. Close the switch. Record how many paper clips the nail can pick up.

3. Open the switch. **CAUTION** *If the switch is left closed, the wire will become very warm.* Wrap the longer wire 40 more times around the nail in the same direction as before.

4. Close the switch. Record how many paper clips the nail can pick up now.

5. Open the switch and disconnect the circuit.

Analyze and Conclude

1. **Observing** How did your ability to pick up paper clips with the nail change when you increased the number of turns in the coil?

2. **Drawing Conclusions** Why did the nail become a magnet when a current-carrying wire was wrapped around it?

Solenoids and Electromagnets

Before you can use electromagnetic force, you need to be able to control it. Using electromagnetic force requires some simple tools. Figure 9A shows a current-carrying wire with a loop in it. The magnetic field in the center of the loop points right to left through the loop, as shown in Figure 9A.

Suppose you loop the wire many times to make a coil, as shown in Figure 9B. Then the magnetic fields of the loops combine so that the coiled wire acts like a bar magnet. The field through the center of the coil is the sum of the fields from each turn of the wire. A coil of current-carrying wire that produces a magnetic field is called a **solenoid.**

If you place a ferromagnetic material, such as an iron rod, inside the coil of a solenoid, the strength of the magnetic field increases. The magnetic field produced by the current causes the iron rod inside the coil of the solenoid to become a magnet. An **electromagnet** is a solenoid with a ferromagnetic core. ● **Changing the current in an electromagnet controls the strength and direction of its magnetic field.** You can also use the current to turn the magnetic field on and off. People use many devices every day, such as hair dryers, telephones, and doorbells, that utilize electromagnets.

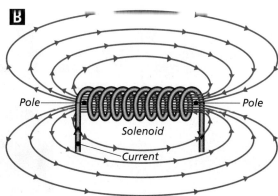

Figure 9 The magnetic field lines around a solenoid are like those of a bar magnet. **Applying Concepts** *Which of the poles is north?*

The strength of an electromagnet depends on the current in the solenoid, the number of loops in the coil in the solenoid, and the type of ferromagnetic core. To increase the strength of an electromagnet, increase the current flowing through the solenoid. A greater current produces a stronger magnetic field. Increasing the number of turns, while keeping the same current, will also increase the field strength. Cores that are easily magnetized, such as "soft" iron, make stronger electromagnets.

Reading Checkpoint *What does the strength of an electromagnet depend on?*

Electromagnetic Devices

Electromagnets can convert electrical energy into motion that can do work. **Electromagnetic devices such as galvanometers, electric motors, and loudspeakers change electrical energy into mechanical energy.** A galvanometer measures current in a wire through the deflection of a solenoid in an external magnetic field. An electric motor uses a rotating electromagnet to turn an axle. A loudspeaker uses a solenoid to convert electrical signals into sound waves you can hear.

Galvanometers Figure 10 shows a **galvanometer,** a device that uses a solenoid to measure small amounts of current. A solenoid is attached to a spring and is free to rotate about an iron core. The solenoid is placed between the poles of two permanent magnets. When there is a current in the solenoid's coils, the resulting magnetic field attempts to align with the field of the permanent magnets. The greater the current, the more the solenoid rotates, as shown by the pointer on the scale. In an automobile fuel gauge, for example, a sensor in the gas tank reduces the current as the gas level decreases. This causes the needle to rotate towards the "empty" mark.

Figure 10 A galvanometer uses an electromagnet to move a pointer. One common application is in an automobile gas gauge. The pointer indicates the amount of current in the wire. The wire is connected to a sensor in the gas tank.

Electric Motors An **electric motor** is a device that uses an electromagnet to turn an axle. Figure 11 shows how an electric motor works. In this figure, the wire is connected to a battery. An actual motor has many loops of wire around a central iron core to make the motor stronger. In the motor of an electric appliance, the wire would be connected to an electrical circuit in a building.

Loop of wire

Current

Commutator

Brush

Direction of rotation

What makes a motor turn? When current flows through a loop of wire, one side of the loop is pushed by the field of the permanent magnet. The other side of the loop is pulled. These forces rotate the loop. If there were no commutator ring, the coil would come to rest. But as the loop turns, each C-shaped half of the commutator connects with a different brush, reversing the current. The forces now change direction, so the coil continues to rotate. As long as current flows, rotation continues.

Loudspeakers A loudspeaker contains a solenoid placed around one pole of a permanent magnet. The current in the wires entering the loudspeaker changes direction and increases or decreases to reproduce music, voices, or other sounds. The changing current produces a changing magnetic field in the solenoid coil. The magnetic force exerted by the permanent magnet moves the coil back and forth. As the coil moves, it causes a thin membrane to vibrate, producing sound waves that match the original sound.

Figure 11 A battery supplies current to a loop of wire through the commutator. As the commutator turns, the direction of current switches back and forth. As a result, the coil's magnetic field keeps switching direction, and this turns the coil about an axle.
Predicting *What would happen if you reversed the positive and negative connections on the battery?*

Section 21.2 Assessment

Reviewing Concepts

1. Besides a magnet, what can create a magnetic field?

2. How is the magnetic field of an electromagnet controlled?

3. How are solenoids and electromagnets used in galvanometers, electric motors, and loudspeakers?

4. How does a ferromagnetic rod inside a solenoid affect the strength of an electromagnet?

Critical Thinking

5. **Comparing and Contrasting** What is the effect of a magnetic field on a stationary electric charge? On a moving electric charge?

6. **Applying Concepts** Why is it a good idea to have the coil of a solenoid wound closely with many turns of wire?

7. **Inferring** What is the purpose of the commutator in an electric motor?

8. **Relating Cause and Effect** What causes the membrane in a loudspeaker to vibrate?

Connecting ⊂ Concepts

Insulators In Section 20.2 you learned that electric charge doesn't flow easily through electrical insulators. Use this to explain why a solenoid has insulated wires.

Peeking Inside the Human Body

Magnetic Resonance Imaging (MRI) is used by doctors to create more detailed images of the human body than are possible with X-rays.

Body tissues vary in their concentration of hydrogen atoms. Fat has a high concentration, as do tissues containing water, because of the hydrogen in H_2O. The concentration of hydrogen atoms in bone is very low. MRI reveals these differences in great detail, with fat and fluids (including blood) showing up as bright areas and bone as dark areas. MRI scans can even depict the brain. It produces images of such detail that they are used by researchers studying how the brain works, as well as by doctors investigating diseases.

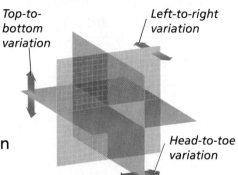

Top-to-bottom variation

Left-to-right variation

Head-to-toe variation

Creating an MRI image
The scanner uses three magnetic fields to read data up and down and along slices of the body. This produces an image that is viewed and interpreted by doctors and radiographers.

Head-to-toe field magnets

Top-to-bottom field magnets

Main magnet *This powerful magnet immerses the patient in a stable, intense magnetic field—the other three magnets create a variable field.*

Radio-frequency source

Motorized bed

Left-to-right field magnets

Inside the scanner
The varying magnetic fields can make images of "slices" through the body in different planes. The main magnet produces a magnetic field as much as 30,000 times stronger than that of Earth.

Each scan can take several minutes, so the patient must lie very still.

How MRI works

MRI affects the nuclei of hydrogen atoms in the body. The nuclei are made to absorb and then re-emit energy by a combination of strong magnetic fields and radio wave pulses. The emitted signals are then used to map concentrations of hydrogen in the body.

1. Random axes

The spins of hydrogen nuclei point in random directions. Like tiny magnets, each nucleus has a north pole and a south pole.

Hydrogen nucleus

Spin axis

2. Aligning axes

When the main MRI magnet is switched on, the magnetic field makes the spins of hydrogen nuclei mostly point in the same direction.

Spin axes line up.

3. Wobbling axes

A pulse of radio waves from the MRI scanner knocks the hydrogen nuclei out of alignment.

Pulse of radio waves from scanner

Spin axes change direction.

4. Realigning axes

When the pulse stops, hydrogen nuclei emit radio waves as they return to alignment with the main magnetic field. With the lesser magnets switched on as necessary to alter the magnetic field at a local level, these waves are picked up by the scanner, which builds up an image of different tissues.

Spin axes realign with magnetic field.

Radio waves emitted by nuclei.

MRI spinal cord scan

The bright red patch here indicates a tumor on the dark green spinal cord. While bone tissue itself is not visible, the vertebrae can be seen because of the marrow they contain.

Spinal cord tumor highlighted by MRI

Going Further

- Items such as jewelry, watches, coins, keys, and credit cards must be removed before beginning an MRI. Research in the library or on the Internet why these items interfere with the procedure or pose a risk to the patient.

21.3 Electrical Energy Generation and Transmission

Reading Focus

Key Concepts

- How is voltage induced in a conductor?
- Name two types of generators.
- How can a transformer change voltage and current?
- What are some sources of electrical energy in the United States?

Vocabulary

- electromagnetic induction
- generator
- transformer
- turbine

Reading Strategy

Sequencing Copy the flowchart below. As you read, complete it to show how a step-up transformer works. Then make a similar flowchart for a step-down transformer.

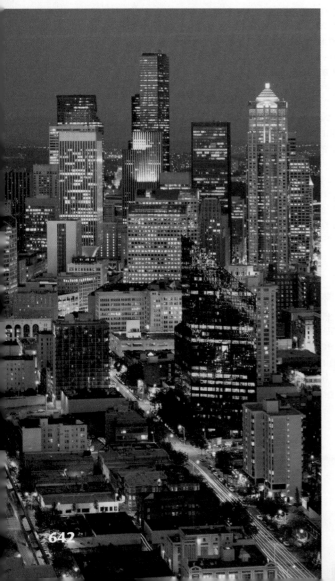

Think about how electrical energy affects a city. Traffic lights change colors to control the flow of cars. Flashing neon lights advertise businesses. Subways use electrical energy to move from place to place. People use electrical energy to warm their homes, cook their suppers, and wash their clothes. At night, lights shine from the windows of tall buildings as shown in Figure 12. Where does all the electrical energy come from?

Generating Electric Current

All of the electrical energy that moves subway trains, lights buildings, and powers factories comes from the two aspects of the electromagnetic force. You already know that an electric current produces a magnetic field. However, you may not know that a magnetic field can be used to produce an electric current. **Electromagnetic induction** is the process of generating a current by moving an electrical conductor relative to a magnetic field. Recall that electrical conductors are materials through which charge can easily flow.

Figure 12 Photographs of large cities, such as Seattle, Washington, are visible reminders of how much people rely on electrical energy.

The English scientist Michael Faraday (1791–1867) discovered electromagnetic induction in 1831, opening the way for many practical uses of electromagnetism. ☞ **According to Faraday's law, a voltage is induced in a conductor by a changing magnetic field.** For example, changing the magnetic field through a coil of wire induces a voltage in the coil. But a current results only if the coil is part of a complete circuit.

You can see this process at work by placing a magnet inside a coil of wire attached to a galvanometer, as shown in Figure 13. If you hold the magnet still, the galvanometer will detect no current in the wire. However, if you quickly move the magnet out of the coil, the current flows briefly, and then immediately drops back to zero. Moving the magnet in and out of the coil causes an electric current first in one direction and then in the other. The same alternating current occurs if you move the coil and keep the magnet still. As long as the magnet and coil are moving relative to one another, the galvanometer will record a current.

Movement of magnet

Coil

Galvanometer shows that the current is flowing.

Figure 13 According to Faraday's law, the moving magnetic field induces a current in the coil. **Predicting** *If you increase the number of turns in the coil, and move the magnet at the same speed, will the current increase or decrease?*

Generators

Moving the magnet in the coil shown in Figure 13 produces only a small amount of electric current. Most of the electrical energy used in homes and businesses is produced at large power plants using generators. A **generator** is a device that converts mechanical energy into electrical energy by rotating a coil of wire in a magnetic field. Electric current is generated by the relative motion of a conducting coil in a magnetic field. ☞ **The two types of generators are AC generators and DC generators.** Although both types have been used, most power plants today use AC generators.

AC Generators Figure 14 shows a simplified AC generator. An actual generator has many loops of wire. The generator produces alternating current, in which charges flow first in one direction and then in the other direction. As you can see, the generator looks very similar to the electric motor you previously studied. While a motor converts electrical energy into mechanical energy, a generator does the opposite.

A wire coil in the generator is attached to metal bands called slip rings. The slip rings are in contact with metal brushes that are in turn attached to a circuit. As the loop of wire is rotated, perhaps by someone turning it, the magnetic field induces a current in the wire. This current is in one direction, and then when the loop turns halfway around, the current reverses direction.

Figure 14 In a simple AC generator, an external force rotates the loop of wire in the magnetic field. This induces a current in the wire. **Forming Hypotheses** *Could you also induce a current if you rotated the magnets instead of the wire loop?*

Wire loop

Slip rings

Brushes

Direction in which the loop is turned

Figure 15 Small generators provide power in areas that are not served by power companies. These generators may also be used to provide electrical energy during a power outage.

You can buy a small AC generator to power electrical devices during a power outage or to use in areas not served by a power company. Figure 15 shows an AC generator that can produce 3300 watts of power. This is enough for a household or small business to use. Power plants use AC generators that are huge compared to the generator shown here.

DC Generators A DC generator produces a direct current. Its design is very much like the design of an AC generator except that a commutator replaces the slip rings. As the loop rotates, an alternating current is induced in the wire. First, one side of the commutator contacts a brush. When the loop rotates, current is induced in the other direction, but now the other side of the commutator contacts that brush. For this reason, the current that leaves the generator flows in only one direction.

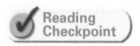 *What kind of current does a DC generator produce?*

Transformers

The electrical energy produced by power plants is transmitted through power lines at very high voltages. These voltages are too high to be used safely in homes. The voltage must first be changed, or transformed. A **transformer** is a device that increases or decreases the voltage and current of two linked AC circuits. A series of transformers changes high-voltage current in power lines into 240-volt current that can be used safely in your home.

A transformer works only with alternating current because only alternating current induces a constantly changing magnetic field. **A transformer changes voltage and current by inducing a changing magnetic field in one coil. This changing field then induces an alternating current in a nearby coil with a different number of turns.**

Why Transformers Are Needed Early power plants used DC generators because the power plants were close to the customers. As the demand for electric power increased, power plants had to transmit power much farther. Remember that an electric charge moving through a wire heats the wire. Over long distances, the resistance of the wire causes large losses of power. Power losses can be reduced by using lower current transmitted at a higher voltage. However, voltage and current can be transformed only with alternating current.

For: Links on transformers
Visit: www.SciLinks.org
Web Code: ccn-2213

Changing Voltage and Current Figure 16 shows two types of transformers. Notice that each transformer has two sets of coils wrapped around a ring-shaped iron core. When there is an alternating current in the primary coil, the current creates a changing magnetic field in the iron core. Because the iron core is also inside the secondary coil, the changing field induces an alternating current in the secondary coil.

The number of turns in the primary and secondary coils determines the voltage and current. To calculate the voltage, divide the number of turns in the secondary coil by the number of turns in the primary coil. The result is the ratio of the output voltage to the input voltage.

Transformers are very efficient because very little energy is lost as heat. Assuming 100% efficiency, the power ($I \times V$) must be the same in the primary and secondary coils. Therefore, if voltage increases in the secondary coil, the current must decrease in the same ratio.

Types of Transformers A step-down transformer decreases voltage and increases current. Notice in Figure 16A that the primary coil has 400 turns, and the secondary coil has 100 turns. If the input voltage in the primary coil is 120 volts, then the output voltage is reduced to 30 volts.

A step-up transformer increases voltage and decreases current. In Figure 16B, the primary coil has 100 turns, and the secondary coil has 400 turns. If the input voltage is 20 volts, the output voltage is 80 volts.

Figure 16 Transformers, such as those at substations of power plants, change voltage. **A** A step-down transformer decreases voltage and increases current. **B** A step-up transformer increases voltage and decreases current.

A Step-down Transformer

Soft iron core
High voltage
Low voltage
400 turns
Secondary coil
100 turns
AC Source
Primary coil

B Step-up Transformer

Low voltage
High voltage
100 turns
Primary coil
400 turns
AC Source
Secondary coil

Transmitting Electricity to a New School

You have been hired as an electrical engineer at your local power plant. Your first task is to plan how electrical energy can be transmitted from the power plant to a school that will soon be built. There are many things you need to investigate. What is the voltage generated at the power plant? How should it be stepped up for transmission? How can it be stepped down for use in the new school?

Defining the Problem Write a few sentences that describe your task and the steps you can take to complete it.

Organizing Information Research the steps that are taken to transmit electrical energy from the power plant to other schools in your area.

Creating a Solution Decide what steps you would take to transmit electrical energy to the new school.

Presenting Your Plan Create a poster showing how electrical energy can be transmitted to the new school. Include descriptions of the types of transformers you could use.

Figure 17 A turbine turns the magnet inside the coil of a generator. **Predicting** *What would happen if a turbine turned faster?*

Electrical Energy for Your Home

A single electric light uses relatively little electrical energy by itself. A massive amount of electrical energy, however, is needed for the lights and other electrical devices that are used by people in an entire city. Consumption on that scale requires equally huge production of electrical energy to meet the demand.

 Most of the electrical energy generated in the United States is produced using coal as an energy source. Some other sources are water (hydroelectric), nuclear energy, wind, natural gas, and petroleum. Below each of the generators shown in Figure 17 is a large turbine, which can convert energy from one of these sources into electrical energy. A **turbine** is a device with fanlike blades that turn when pushed, for example, by water or steam. Burning fossil fuels or nuclear reactions can heat water to produce steam that spins a turbine. Water from a reservoir behind a dam can also turn a turbine. To produce electrical energy, the turbine may turn the coils of a generator or it may spin magnets around the coils of wire.

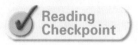 **Reading Checkpoint** *What can push the blades of a turbine?*

Generating plant

11,000 V

240,000 V

High-voltage transmission lines

7200 V

Step-down transformer

Step-up transformer

Step-down transformer (substation)

220–240 V

Follow the steps shown in Figure 18 from the point where electrical energy is generated. The power plant on the left generates electrical energy that is stepped up to hundreds of thousands of volts. Transformers, which are shown in the middle of the diagram, make it possible to bring electrical energy efficiently from the power plant to users. After traveling along the high-voltage transmission lines, the voltage is stepped down at a substation, to a few thousand volts. The electrical energy is then distributed to neighborhoods. Just before the electrical energy reaches people's homes, the voltage is stepped down to between 220 and 240 volts. Heavy duty appliances, like an electric stove, use 240-volt circuits. Most other appliances in the home use 120 volts.

Figure 13 Voltage is increased for long-distance transmission, and then decreased near homes, schools, and businesses.
Interpreting Diagrams *How many step-down transformers are shown in the figure?*

Section 21.3 Assessment

Reviewing Concepts

1. How is voltage induced in a conductor?
2. Name two types of generators.
3. How does a transformer work?
4. Name six sources of electrical energy in the United States.

Critical Thinking

5. **Relating Cause and Effect** Explain how water can be used to create electrical energy.
6. **Applying Concepts** What is the connection between Faraday's law and the generation of electrical energy?
7. **Comparing and Contrasting** Describe how AC generators and DC generators are alike and how they are different.

8. **Drawing Conclusions** Why can't you use electrical energy directly from a high-voltage line?
9. **Calculating** An electronic device contains a transformer. Its primary coil has 200 turns, and its secondary coil has 20 turns. If the device is plugged into a 120-volt line, what is the output voltage of the device?

Writing in Science

Compare-Contrast Paragraph Write a paragraph comparing and contrasting what step-up and step-down transformers do. (*Hint:* Use the terms *voltage, primary coil, secondary coil, input,* and *output.*)

Investigating an Electric Generator

All generators have two main parts—a magnet and a wire that is wrapped into a coil. The arrangement of these parts varies, depending on the size and power of the generator and whether it produces direct or alternating current. In this lab, you will determine how several variables affect the current produced by a simple generator.

Problem
How do the direction in which the magnet moves and the number and direction of the turns in the coil affect the current that a generator produces?

Materials
- cardboard tube
- 5-m length of insulated wire
- metric ruler
- multimeter
- bar magnet
- graph paper

 For the probeware version of this lab, see the Probeware Lab Manual, Lab 9.

Skills
Observing, Using Graphs

Procedure

Part A: Changing the Number of Turns

1. On a separate sheet of paper, make a copy of the data table shown below.

Data Table			
Number of Turns	Direction of Turns	Pole Inserted	Current (mA)
10	Clockwise	North	
20	Clockwise	North	
30	Clockwise	North	
30	Clockwise	South	
30	Counterclockwise	North	

2. Slip the wire between your hand and the cardboard tube so that 15 cm of wire extends from the tube. Use your other hand to wrap the long end of the wire around the tube 10 times in a clockwise direction. Make sure all the turns are within 10 cm of the end of the tube. **CAUTION** *Be careful not to cut yourself on the sharp ends of the wire.*

3. Connect both ends of the wire to the multimeter. Set the multimeter to measure current.

4. Hold the bar magnet by its south pole. Observe the multimeter as you quickly insert the bar magnet into the open end of the cardboard tube that is wrapped with the wire coil. Repeat this step if necessary as you adjust the scale of the multimeter. Record the maximum current in your data table.

5. Disconnect the multimeter from the end of the wire that is farther from the turns.

6. **Predicting** Record your prediction of how increasing the number of turns in the coil will affect the current.

7. To test your prediction, wrap the wire around the end of the tube 10 more times in the same direction as you did previously—clockwise. You should now have a total of 20 turns. Reconnect the wire to the multimeter.

8. Repeat Step 4.

9. Again, disconnect the multimeter from the same end of the wire. Wrap the wire clockwise around the tube 10 more times for a total of 30 turns. Reconnect the wire to the multimeter.

10. Repeat Step 4 and then disconnect the multimeter from the same end of the wire.

Part B: Changing Other Properties of the Generator

11. **Predicting** Record your prediction of how reversing the direction of the magnet will affect the current.

12. To test your prediction, reconnect the wire to the multimeter exactly as you did before. Repeat Step 4, but this time, hold the magnet by its north pole.

13. **Predicting** Record your prediction of how reversing the direction of the turns in the coil will affect the current if you hold the magnet by its south pole.

14. To test your prediction, remove the wire from the tube. Now wrap 30 turns of wire in the opposite direction—counterclockwise.

15. Repeat Step 4, holding the magnet by its south pole.

16. Construct a graph using the data from the first three rows of your data table. Plot the number of turns on the horizontal axis and the current on the vertical axis.

Analyze and Conclude

1. **Inferring** What caused a current in the wire?

2. **Using Graphs** Based on your graph, what is the relationship between the number of turns and the amount of current?

3. **Analyzing Data** Explain the effect that reversing the direction of the magnet or the direction of the turns had on the direction of the current.

4. **Predicting** Explain whether a generator could be built with a stationary magnet and a coil that moved.

5. **Evaluating and Revising** Did your observations support your predictions? If not, evaluate any flaws in the reasoning you used to make the predictions.

For: Data sharing
Visit: PHSchool.com
Web Code: ccd-2210

21.1 Magnets and Magnetic Fields

Key Concepts

- Like magnetic poles repel one another, and opposite magnetic poles attract one another.
- A magnetic field, which is strongest near a magnet's poles, will either attract or repel another magnet that enters the field.
- When a material is magnetized, most of its magnetic domains are aligned.

Vocabulary

magnetic force, *p. 630*

magnetic pole, *p. 630*

magnetic field, *p. 631*

magnetosphere, *p. 632*

magnetic domain, *p. 632*

ferromagnetic material, *p. 632*

21.2 Electromagnetism

Key Concepts

- Moving electric charges create a magnetic field.
- Changing the current in an electromagnet controls the strength and direction of its magnetic field.
- Electromagnetic devices such as galvanometers, electric motors, and loudspeakers change electrical energy into mechanical energy.

Vocabulary

electromagnetic force, *p. 635*

solenoid, *p. 637*

electromagnet, *p. 637*

galvanometer, *p. 638*

electric motor, *p. 639*

21.3 Electrical Energy Generation and Transmission

Key Concepts

- According to Faraday's law, a voltage is induced in a conductor by a changing magnetic field.
- The two types of generators are AC generators and DC generators.
- A transformer changes voltage and current by inducing a changing magnetic field in one coil. This changing field then induces an alternating current in a nearby coil with a different number of turns.
- Most of the electrical energy generated in the United States is produced using coal as an energy source. Some other sources are water (hydroelectric), nuclear energy, wind, natural gas, and petroleum.

Vocabulary

electromagnetic induction, *p. 642*

generator, *p. 643*

transformer, *p. 644*

turbine, *p. 646*

Thinking Visually

Concept Map Copy the concept map below onto a sheet of paper. Use information from the chapter to complete the chart.

Reviewing Content

Choose the letter that best answers the question or completes the statement.

1. Where is the field of a magnet strongest?
   a. near the north pole
   b. near the south pole
   c. near both poles
   d. near the middle

2. If you cut a magnet in half, you have
   a. no magnets.
   b. two half magnets.
   c. one magnet.
   d. two magnets.

3. A magnet's field lines always start near the magnet's
   a. middle.   **b.** south pole.
   c. north pole.   **d.** side.

4. A ferromagnetic material is
   a. always a magnet.
   b. a magnet if its domains are aligned.
   c. a magnet if its domains are not aligned.
   d. never a magnet.

5. An iron bar is placed in a solenoid to
   a. decrease the voltage.
   b. increase the voltage.
   c. increase the magnetic field strength.
   d. decrease the magnetic field strength.

6. Which of these cannot increase the strength of an electromagnet?
   a. making the loops smaller in the coil
   b. placing an iron bar in the coil
   c. winding more loops in the coil
   d. increasing the current in the coil

7. An electric generator converts
   a. electrical energy into mechanical energy.
   b. power into energy.
   c. mechanical energy into electrical energy.
   d. energy into power.

8. What effect does a magnetic field have on a charge moving perpendicular to the field?
   a. It has no effect.
   b. It pulls the charge forward.
   c. It pushes the charge backward.
   d. It pushes the charge perpendicularly to the field and the charge's velocity.

9. A galvanometer is a device used to measure
   a. current.
   b. resistance.
   c. voltage.
   d. magnetic field strength.

10. A transformer increases or decreases
    a. energy.
    b. resistance.
    c. voltage.
    d. direct current.

Understanding Concepts

11. What part of an atom is responsible for producing magnetic fields?

12. Why is iron easy to magnetize when used in an electromagnet?

13. How are magnetic domains in nonmagnetized materials different from the magnetic domains in magnetized materials?

14. Explain how you can determine the direction of a magnetic field produced by a wire if you know the direction of current through the wire.

15. The figure below shows a current-carrying wire between the poles of two magnets. In which direction is charge deflected by the magnetic field?

Current direction

16. How can a change in the voltage of a transformer's primary coil create a change in the secondary coil's voltage, without the coils touching?

17. A transformer is connected to a 9-volt battery. A student tries to use this setup to double the voltage for an experiment. However, the output voltage is zero. Explain why.

Assessment *(continued)*

Critical Thinking

18. Inferring Using the concept of magnetic domains, explain why a magnet will attract an iron nail but not a plastic button.

19. Comparing and Contrasting How does the force that an electric field exerts on a moving charged particle differ from the force exerted by a magnetic field? Assume both fields point in the same direction.

20. Inferring You know that if you point the thumb of your right hand in the direction of the current, your fingers curve in the direction of the magnetic field. Could you use your left hand to demonstrate this rule correctly? Explain your answer. (*Hint:* See Figure 7 on page 636.)

21. Applying Concepts A beam of electrons travels from left to right between the poles of a horseshoe magnet. The north pole is on the top, and the south pole is on the bottom. In which direction will the beam be deflected when it passes through the poles of the magnet?

22. Predicting Would a permanent magnet be a good core for a transformer? Explain.

Math Skills

23. Calculating A transformer has 20 turns in its primary coil and 60 turns in its secondary coil. The input voltage for the transformer is 25 volts. What is the output voltage?

24. Calculating A transformer has an input voltage of 10 volts and an output voltage of 60 volts. If the input voltage is changed to 15 volts, what will the output voltage be?

25. Calculating A toy train uses a step-down transformer with 500 turns on its primary coil and 50 turns on its secondary coil. If it is connected to a 120-volt line, what voltage does the toy train use?

26. Calculating A transformer has 12 turns on its primary coil and 60 turns on its secondary coil. If the current in the primary coil is 5 amps, what is the current in the secondary coil?

Concepts in Action

27. Applying Concepts In a tape recorder, the tape is coated with iron oxide that has been magnetized in patterns corresponding to sounds. To play recorded sounds, the tape moves past a tiny coil of wire. Explain how this produces an electrical signal.

28. Problem Solving A child's toy has a magnet hidden inside. How can you determine where the north and south poles of the magnet are, without damaging the toy?

29. Applying Concepts A power plant generates electricity at 1200 volts. The electricity is transmitted at 180,000 volts and then reduced to 2400 volts at a substation. Finally, it is reduced to 120 volts for use in a home. For each transformer, describe the ratio of the number of turns in the primary and secondary coils.

30. Inferring Credit cards have a magnetic strip on them that contains information in a pattern. When a cashier runs the card through a card reader, the magnetic strip passes by a small wire coil. Why is motion necessary for the coil to read the card?

31. Writing in Science Write a paragraph explaining why alternating current is used for power generation and distribution instead of direct current.

Performance-Based Assessment

Creating an Educational Booklet Write a booklet for elementary students describing how electricity is brought from the power plant to their homes. Include simple illustrations and caution statements that young children can understand.

For: Self-grading assessment
Visit: PHschool.com
Web Code: cca-2210

Standardized Test Prep

1. Two solenoids are nested one inside the other. The inner solenoid is connected to a 12 V AC voltage source. The outer solenoid is part of a complete circuit. Will the setup function as a transformer?
   (A) No, there is no core.
   (B) No, there needs to be a ring.
   (C) No, both sides need a voltage source.
   (D) It is unclear, because current is not given.
   (E) Yes, AC induces a current in the outer coil.

2. What causes a ferromagnetic material to become magnetic?
   (A) unpaired electrons
   (B) paired electrons
   (C) unpaired protons
   (D) paired protons
   (E) none of the above

3. A transformer has 22 coils in its primary coil and 132 coils in its secondary coil. If the input voltage is 112 V, what is the secondary voltage?
   (A) 6.00 V   (B) 18.7 V
   (C) 222 V   (D) 266 V
   (E) 672 V

4. The figure below is a transformer used in lighting dimmer switches. It has one coil wrapped around an iron core. Three moveable taps (T_1, T_2, and T_3) are connected to the wire. When a tap is moved, the number of coils between that tap and the next tap changes. The coils between T_1 and T_2 form the primary coil. The coils between T_2 and T_3 form the secondary coil. To lower the output voltage for this transformer (to dim a light), how should one tap be moved?

   (A) Move T_1 closer to T_2.
   (B) Move T_2 closer to T_3.
   (C) Move T_2 farther from T_3.
   (D) Move T_3 farther from T_2.
   (E) Move T_1 closer to T_3.

5. Particle accelerators use electromagnets to change the direction in which charged particles travel. How does a charged particle move within a magnetic field?
   (A) It moves in the same direction as the magnetic field lines.
   (B) It moves in the direction opposite to the magnetic field lines.
   (C) It comes to a stop.
   (D) It moves in a direction perpendicular to the magnetic field lines.
   (E) none of the above

6. Is it possible for a magnetic field to slow down a charged particle moving through the field?
   (A) Yes, if the charge is moving perpendicular to the field at all times.
   (B) Yes, if the charge is moving in the direction of the magnetic field lines.
   (C) Yes, if the charge is moving in the direction opposite to the magnetic field lines.
   (D) Yes, if the charge is moving very slowly.
   (E) No, a magnetic field can only deflect a charged particle.

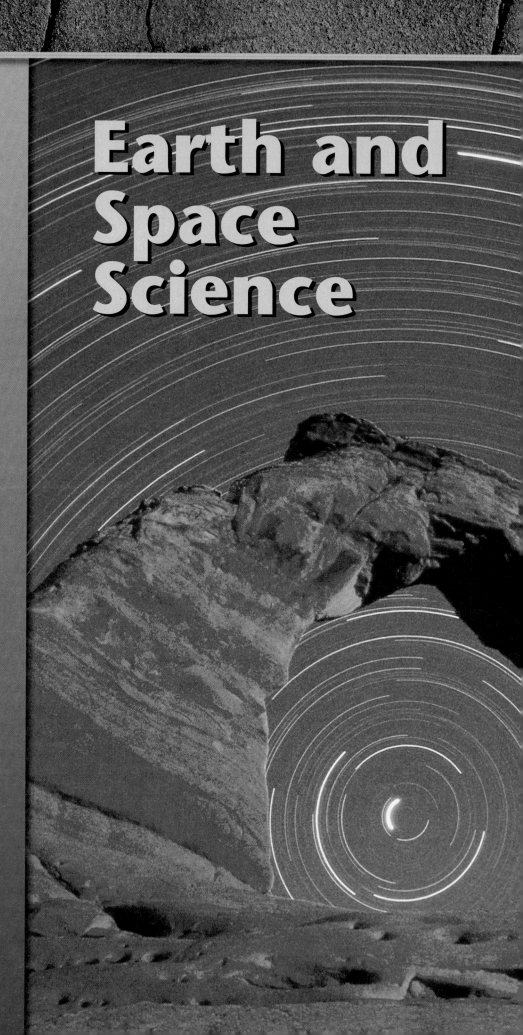

Earth and Space Science

Stars Over Arches National Park, Utah ▶
Both Earth science and space science are represented in this time exposure photo, taken at night. Stars appear as long curved trails of light circling the north celestial pole. The apparent motion of the stars is due to Earth's rotation on its axis.

Chemistry and physics describe the laws governing matter, energy, and their interactions. Earth and space science explores how these rules play out on Earth and beyond—in the solar system, the Milky Way galaxy, and the universe.

Earth is in constant motion, not only in relation to the sun and the Milky Way, but internally as well. Vigorous convection occurs at all levels within the planet, including the mantle, the oceans, and the atmosphere. Earth's high level of geologic activity is the result of two energy sources: the sun and the decay of underground radioactive elements. Sunlight powers the water cycle, and in turn the weathering and erosion processes that tear down land. Radioactivity drives the convection currents in Earth's mantle that control plate motions and create new land. These two processes are in constant battle over control of Earth's surface.

The universe began with the big bang 13.7 billion years ago. Since then, the universe has expanded at the speed of light or faster, and is now tens of billions of light years across. The universe contains hundreds of billions of galaxies, each of which can contain hundreds of billions of stars.

Careers in Earth and Space Science

The career opportunities available in Earth and space science are far reaching—from exploring distant galaxies to investigating deep inside Earth. Here are a few of these exciting careers.

Meteorologist

Meteorologists study how the physical characteristics, processes, and movements of the atmosphere affect the environment. They use this information to forecast the weather and study the patterns of weather change, such as droughts and global warming.

Educational requirements Four-year college degree, majoring in meteorology or atmospheric science

Seismologist

Seismologists are Earth scientists who investigate earthquakes. They determine the location and size of earthquakes, and use seismic waves to study Earth's interior. Some seismologists help the building industry design earthquake-proof structures. Others search for oil and natural gas.

Educational requirements Four-year college degree, majoring in geology, geophysics, or mathematics

Surveying Technician

Helping to measure and map Earth's surface are the responsibilities of surveying technicians. They assist land surveyors who measure distances, directions, and contours on, above, or below Earth's surface. Surveying technicians use surveying instruments to collect data and then enter the data into computers.

Educational requirements Two-year junior or community college program, one to three years of technical school

Go Online
PHSchool.com

For: Career links
Visit: PHSchool.com
Web Code: ccb-3000

Commercial Diver

Just about anywhere there is water, there is a need for commercial divers. Their work ranges from operating submersibles to helping map the ocean floor. They may perform underwater surveys or carry out underwater rescue and salvage operations.

Educational requirements High-school diploma, diving-school certification or naval training

Archaeologist

Archaeologists excavate, preserve, study, and classify objects and structures from past cultures. In order to interpret what they see at a particular site, archaeologists must be able to identify different types of soil and notice the smallest of changes in soil characteristics.

Educational requirements Master's degree in anthropology or archeology

Astronomer

Astronomers use the laws of physics and mathematics to study the universe. They may specialize to investigate the moon, sun, planets, stars, or galaxies, such as the Andromeda Galaxy shown in the photo at the left. They also may use what they know about astronomy to help develop satellites and spacecraft.

Educational requirements Doctoral degree in physics, astrophysics, or space physics

22 Earth's Interior

21st Century Learning

Interpersonal and Collaborative Skills

How can you play the rock cycle?

The rock cycle is important to understanding how parts of the geosphere are formed and destroyed. The rock cycle is also important in cycles that affect life on Earth. Work in a group to design a board game that teaches the concepts of the rock cycle. In addition to presenting the cycle, the game should use examples of the names and types of rocks in the cycle. When your group has finished its work, exchange games with another group to play and provide feedback. Use the feedback to improve your game.

How do science concepts apply to your world? Here are some questions you'll be able to answer after you read this chapter.

- **How is Earth's interior like a hard-boiled egg?** *(Section 22.1)*

- **What does a precious gem have in common with table salt?** *(Section 22.2)*

- **How can one kind of rock change into another kind of rock?** *(Section 22.3)*

- **Where is the longest mountain range in the world?** *(Section 22.4)*

- **Where was the largest earthquake ever recorded?** *(Section 22.5)*

- **Is there really a "Ring of Fire" around the Pacific Ocean?** *(Section 22.6)*

- **How were the Hawaiian islands formed?** *(page 694)*

In this photo, a fishing port in Iceland is threatened by volcanic ash and lava from the nearby Eldfell volcano.

Chapter Preview

Inquiry Activity

How Are Rocks and Minerals Different?

Procedure

1. Place several mineral and rock samples on a flat surface that has been covered with newspaper. Use a hand lens to examine each sample closely. Describe the color of each sample and the appearance of any visible particles that make it up. Record your observations.

2. Place one mineral sample in a plastic bag and put the bag on the newspaper.

3. Gently tap the sample with a hammer until the sample breaks. **CAUTION** *Always wear safety goggles and a lab apron when breaking minerals and rocks.* Use a hand lens to examine the texture and color of the pieces of the sample. Record your observations.

4. Repeat Steps 2 and 3 using the remaining mineral and rock samples.

Think About It

1. **Comparing and Contrasting** Compare the texture and color of each unbroken sample with the texture and color of the broken pieces of that sample. What similarities and differences do you observe? Are these similarities and differences consistent for both types of samples?

2. **Forming Operational Definitions** How would you define a mineral? How would you define a rock?

22.1 Earth's Structure

Figure 1 These workers are drilling a hole that will be more than two kilometers deep. Later they will lower instruments into the hole to record data at that depth.

In many ways, scientists know more about the structure of the universe and the workings of microscopic cells than they do about the ground beneath their feet. With a telescope, an astronomer can see stars at the farthest edges of the universe. With a microscope, a biologist can see the inner structure of cells. But there is no instrument that allows geologists to look deep inside Earth. The reason is both simple and profound: light does not travel through most rocks.

Though scientists cannot see into Earth, in a sense they can listen to it. The waves from earthquakes travel through Earth in a manner similar to the way that sound waves travel to our ears. These waves vibrate within Earth and are recorded at Earth's surface. Scientists are able to interpret these waves to learn about the structure and composition of Earth's interior. Scientists have also drilled holes to a depth of about 12 kilometers to collect data on the uppermost portion of Earth's interior. Figure 1 shows one such drilling effort.

The Science of Geology

Geology is the study of planet Earth, including its composition and structure. Scientists who study Earth and the processes that have shaped Earth over time are called **geologists**. Geologists such as the one shown in Figure 2 divide the forces that change Earth's surface into two groups: constructive forces and destructive forces. Constructive forces shape the surface by building up mountains and other land areas. Destructive forces slowly wear away mountains and, eventually, every other feature on Earth's surface.

The modern science of geology began in the late 1700s. James Hutton, a Scottish physician and farmer, made observations of rocks that he could explain only if Earth were far older than most people had imagined. He observed that some rocks were made of particles that came from older rocks. Hutton realized that Earth's surface had changed gradually over time.

From his observations, Hutton developed the principle of uniformitarianism. **Uniformitarianism** is the idea that the geologic processes that operate today also operated in the past. Thus, ancient rocks can be understood by observing present-day geologic processes. According to the principle of uniformitarianism, dramatic features such as mountains and canyons are the result of geologic processes that work very slowly over long periods of time.

  What do geologists study?

Figure 2 This geologist is examining the rocks that make up the side of a canyon.

A Cross Section of Earth

Since Hutton's time, geologists have learned a great deal about Earth's structure. Earth's surface and interior can be compared to a hard-boiled egg, such as the one shown in Figure 3. Beneath an egg's hard outer shell is a layer of egg white that surrounds the yolk at the center. Earth has a similar layered structure. 🔍 **Earth can be divided into three main layers—the crust, mantle, and core—based on the materials that make up each layer.** This layering is largely due to differences in density.

Physical conditions in Earth's interior vary from layer to layer. Temperature and pressure in Earth's interior increase with depth. As the temperature and pressure increase, the properties of the materials inside Earth also change.

The Crust The rocky outer layer of Earth is the **crust.** Like the shell of an egg, Earth's crust is thin compared to its other layers. Much of the crust is made up of **silicates,** rocks made of compounds of silicon and oxygen. Silicates often contain metals such as aluminum, iron, or calcium.

There are two different types of crust: continental crust and oceanic crust. Continental crust, the rock that makes up the continents, consists mainly of less-dense rocks such as granite. Continental crust averages about 40 kilometers in thickness, although it ranges in thickness from about 8 to 75 kilometers. It is thickest under mountain chains such as the Himalayas. The rock that makes up the ocean floor is oceanic crust. Oceanic crust is composed mostly of dense rocks like basalt. Oceanic crust is about 7 kilometers thick on average, and so is much thinner than continental crust.

Figure 3 Earth's structure is similar to that of a hard-boiled egg. **Using Analogies** *Which of Earth's layers corresponds to the shell of the egg?*

The Mantle Beneath the crust is the **mantle,** a thick layer of hot but solid rock. As Figure 4 shows, the mantle extends about 2850 kilometers, from beneath the crust to the top of the core. Both pressure and temperature increase tremendously the deeper you go into the mantle. Like the crust, the mantle is composed mainly of silicates. The mantle is rich in iron and magnesium, and so is denser throughout than the crust.

Geologists divide the mantle into three layers based on the physical properties of the rock. The **lithosphere** (LITH uh sfeer) is a layer of relatively cool, rigid rock that includes the uppermost part of the mantle as well as Earth's crust. On average, the lithosphere measures about 100 kilometers thick, although it is thicker below the continents and thinner beneath the oceans. Beneath the lithosphere in the mantle is the **asthenosphere** (as THEN uh sfeer), a layer of softer, weaker rock that can flow slowly, the way taffy does. Beneath the asthenosphere is the stronger lower part of the mantle called the **mesosphere.** The stiffer rock of the mesosphere extends all the way down to the upper surface of Earth's core.

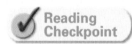 **Reading Checkpoint** *What is the asthenosphere?*

Figure 4 Earth's interior is composed of three main layers—the crust, the mantle, and the core. Earth's rocky crust is its thinnest layer. Most of the interior is occupied by the hot, solid mantle, the molten metal outer core, and the solid metal inner core.
Interpreting Diagrams *Which layer is thickest, the crust, mantle, or outer core?*

Atmosphere

Crust
5–75 km

Mantle
2850 km

Outer core
2260 km

Inner core
1220 km

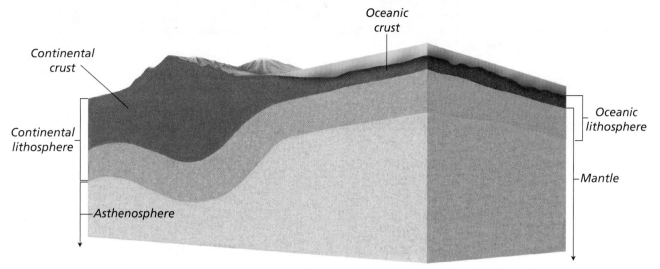

Continental crust

Oceanic crust

Continental lithosphere

Oceanic lithosphere

Mantle

Asthenosphere

Figure 5 The structure of Earth's upper layers is complex. The lithosphere includes the crust and the rigid, uppermost layer of Earth's mantle. Notice that the continental crust is thicker beneath mountain ranges. **Applying Concepts** *What is the relationship between the lithosphere and the mantle?*

The Core Beneath the mantle is the **core,** a large sphere of metal that occupies Earth's center. Scientists think that the core is composed mostly of iron, with lesser amounts of nickel and some lighter elements. Within the core, pressure increases greatly with depth. At Earth's center, the pressure is estimated to be 3.6 million times the pressure at Earth's surface! The temperature at the center of Earth is estimated to be about 5500°C, nearly equal to the temperature of the sun's surface.

The core is divided into two parts—the outer core and the inner core. In the outer core, high temperatures keep the metal liquid. Because of Earth's rotation, the flowing iron of the outer core produces an electric current and creates Earth's magnetic field. In the inner core, very high pressure is a more important factor than temperature. As a result, the inner core is solid.

Section 22.1 Assessment

Reviewing Concepts

1. 🔵 What are the two types of forces studied by geologists? How does each process affect Earth's surface?

2. 🔵 What are the three main layers of Earth? What are the characteristics of each layer?

3. What is the principle of uniformitarianism?

4. Describe the mesosphere.

Critical Thinking

5. **Comparing and Contrasting** What are the two types of crust, and how are they different?

6. **Relating Cause and Effect** Why is Earth's outer core liquid while its inner core is solid? Explain your answer.

Writing in Science

Creative Writing Suppose that you have a vehicle in which you travel to the center of Earth. Write 3 or 4 logbook entries for your trip, describing each of Earth's layers.

22.2 Minerals

Reading Focus

Key Concepts
- What is a mineral?
- What are some important properties of minerals?

Vocabulary
- rock
- inorganic
- streak
- luster
- hardness
- fracture
- cleavage

Reading Strategy

Outlining Before you read, make an outline of this section. Use the green headings as the main topics and the blue headings as subtopics. As you read, add supporting details.

Minerals
I. Minerals and Rocks
II. The Properties of Minerals
A. Crystal Structure
B. _____
C. _____
D. _____

Have you ever imagined finding a sunken treasure? In September 2002, a diver in Florida did just that. His job was to dive for objects from the *Santa Margarita*, a Spanish galleon, or treasure ship, that sank off the Florida Keys nearly 400 years ago. While rinsing sand off a conch shell found near the shipwreck, the diver spotted a shiny green stone. The stone proved to be a large and valuable emerald, like the ones in Figure 6.

Of course, the conch did not produce the emerald. The precious gem was almost certainly from the *Santa Margarita*. Scientists who have studied the emerald think that it originally came from mountains in South America where substances produced deep inside Earth have been brought toward the surface. Emeralds are a variety of the mineral beryl. The magnificent green color that makes emeralds so highly valued as gemstones is probably due to the presence of small amounts of chromium.

Figure 6 Emeralds are a form of the mineral beryl. These gems form deep beneath Earth's surface and are found in relatively few locations.

Figure 7 This portrait of Abraham Lincoln on Mt. Rushmore in South Dakota was sculpted in a granite cliff.

Minerals and Rocks

Plants and soil cover much of Earth's land surface. Beneath the plants and soil, however, is a layer of solid rock. You can see this rock where it is exposed on mountains and canyons, or where a highway cuts through a hillside. What is this material? A **rock** is a solid combination of minerals or mineral materials. **A mineral is a naturally occurring, inorganic solid with a crystal structure and a characteristic chemical composition.**

Minerals are naturally occurring, which means they are made either geologically or biologically, but not artificially by humans. The term **inorganic** means that minerals are formed primarily of compounds other than carbon and hydrogen, even though these elements may be present. Minerals are also solid, and so while ice is a mineral, water is not.

Each mineral is a unique substance with its own chemical composition and crystal structure. For most minerals, the proportion of elements can vary slightly while the mineral still retains a similar set of characteristics. Within each mineral crystal, the chemical composition is nearly constant.

Minerals are the building blocks of rocks. Only a fraction of the more than 4000 known minerals are common. These common minerals are called the rock-forming minerals because they make up most of Earth's rocks. For example, granite is made up of the rock-forming minerals quartz, feldspar, mica, and hornblende. If you were to look closely at a piece of granite like that in Figure 8, you would see that it is made up of different-colored particles. Each particle is a separate mineral crystal. As you learned in chemistry, a crystal is a solid in which atoms are arranged in a regular repeating pattern.

For: Links on minerals
Visit: www.SciLinks.org
Web Code: ccn-3222

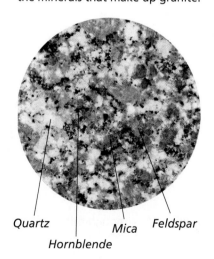

Figure 8 A magnified view reveals the individual crystals of the minerals that make up granite.

Quartz   *Mica*   *Feldspar*
      Hornblende

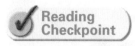

Reading Checkpoint   *What does it mean to say that a mineral is inorganic?*

The Properties of Minerals

Each mineral has a characteristic set of properties that results from its chemical composition and crystal structure. 🔑 **The properties by which minerals can be identified include their crystal structure, color, streak, luster, density, hardness, fracture, and cleavage.** The properties of many common minerals are summarized in Appendix D.

Crystal Structure In each type of mineral, the atoms are arranged in a particular geometric shape, or crystal structure. Each mineral always has the same crystal structure. However, the size of a mineral's crystals can vary. Some crystals are too small to be seen without a microscope. Others can be the size of telephone poles! Many crystals form long prisms with a specific number of sides. For example, quartz crystals, shown in Figure 9, have six sides. Other minerals have crystals shaped like cubes, sheets, needles, or threads. Halite, the mineral form of table salt, forms cubic crystals. Garnet, a red, semiprecious gem, often forms 12-sided crystals.

Color Some minerals can be identified by a characteristic color. Pyrite, also known as fool's gold, is always golden in color. Crystals of pure sulfur are always yellow. But a mineral's color can often be deceptive, because slight changes in composition can cause significant changes in a mineral's color. For example, Figure 9 shows crystals of different colors, but they are all quartz.

Streak The color of a mineral's powder is known as its **streak.** A mineral's streak can be found by scraping the mineral on a piece of unglazed porcelain called a streak plate. The color of a mineral's streak is not always the same as the color of the mineral itself. For example, the hematite shown in Figure 10 looks black or silvery, but has a red-brown streak.

 Reading Checkpoint *What is a mineral's streak?*

Figure 9 Quartz that is pure silicon dioxide is clear or white. Slight impurities produce a range of colors, including the violet quartz (amethyst) specimen shown here.

Figure 10 Although this piece of hematite is silver-gray, it can be identified by its red-brown streak.

Galena

Pyrite

Sulfur

Luster The **luster** of a mineral is the way in which its surface reflects light. Luster refers to the general appearance of a mineral, or how shiny it is. As seen in Figure 11, galena and pyrite have a metallic luster, and sulfur has a resinous-to-greasy luster. Geologists use a variety of terms to describe a mineral's luster. For example, a mineral with a rough, crumbly surface is said to have an earthy luster. Other terms used to describe luster include silky, pearly, and vitreous (glassy.)

Density The density of a mineral depends on its chemical composition. In general, minerals made up of elements with higher atomic masses have higher densities than minerals made up of atoms with lower atomic masses. For example, galena contains much lead, which has a relatively high atomic mass of 207. Galena's density is about 7.5 grams per cubic centimeter. In contrast, quartz is made up of silicon and oxygen, which have relatively low atomic masses of 28 and 16 respectively. Quartz's density is only about 2.6 grams per cubic centimeter.

Figure 11 Galena has a metallic luster and a density of about 7.5 g/cm^3. Pyrite, also known as "fool's gold," has a metallic luster and a density of 5.0 g/cm^3. Sulfur has a resinous-to-greasy luster and a density of 2.0–2.1 g/cm^3. **Designing Experiments** *How could you distinguish a sample of galena from a sample of pyrite?*

Data Analysis

Density of Minerals

The density of minerals varies, depending on what elements the minerals contain. Samples of the minerals in the data table were analyzed for density, silicon and oxygen content, and the presence of metals. Study the data table, and then answer the questions.

1. **Using Tables** Which mineral has the lowest density? The highest density?

2. **Using Tables** Which minerals have the lowest percentage of silicon and oxygen? Which has the highest?

Mineral Properties			
Mineral	Density (g/cm^3)	Percent Si and O	Metals Present
Olivine	3.3	65	Mg, Fe
Augite	3.2	65	Mg, Fe, Ca
Hornblende	3.0	67	Mg, Fe, Ca, Al
Muscovite	2.8	71	K, Al, Mg, Fe
Quartz	2.6	100	None

3. **Formulating Hypotheses** Olivine and augite are abundant in oceanic crust and in the mantle. Quartz, muscovite, and hornblende are abundant in continental crust. Formulate a hypothesis to explain why continental crust floats higher on the mantle than oceanic crust.

4. **Drawing Conclusions** How is a mineral's density related to its silicon and oxygen content?

Mohs Hardness Scale

1	2	3	4	5	6	7	8	9	10
Talc	Gypsum	Calcite	Fluorite	Apatite	Orthoclase	Quartz	Topaz	Corundum	Diamond

Figure 12 Mohs hardness scale ranks minerals according to hardness on a scale from 1 to 10. **Inferring** *Which of the minerals in the table would scratch a glass plate, which has a hardness of 5.5?*

Hardness The atoms of minerals are held together by chemical bonds of different kinds and strengths. As a result, minerals have different hardnesses. **Hardness** is the resistance of a mineral to scratching. A hard mineral can scratch a softer mineral, but not the other way around. The hardness of minerals is ranked on a scale from 1 to 10, called Mohs hardness scale. Diamond is the hardest mineral, with a hardness of 10. Talc is one of the softest minerals, with a hardness of 1. Figure 12 shows the hardness of some minerals according to Mohs scale.

Geologists use scratch tests systematically to determine the hardness of mineral specimens. First, a geologist may try to scratch a glass plate, which has a hardness of 5.5, with the mineral. Having determined that the mineral is either harder or softer than 5.5, the geologist can continue to perform scratch tests. Everyday materials can also be used to compare the hardness of minerals. For example, a copper penny, which has a hardness of about 3.5, can scratch talc but it cannot scratch quartz. A fingernail, with a hardness of 2.5, and a streak plate, with a hardness of 6.5, can also be used to test hardness.

Fracture and Cleavage The **fracture** of a mineral is how the mineral breaks. When a piece of quartz is broken, it has a curved, shell-shaped fracture. Other minerals fracture unevenly along curved or jagged surfaces. Fracture is determined by the crystalline structure of the mineral and the bonds between the atoms in the crystals.

Some minerals split evenly when they break apart. **Cleavage** is a type of fracture in which the mineral tends to split along regular, well-defined planes (flat surfaces) where the bonds are weakest. For example, mica and graphite form sheets. Each sheet of mica contains chemical bonds that are very strong. However, the sheets are held together with weak bonds, so they can easily be peeled apart from each other. In contrast, halite, shown in Figure 13, can be split into block-like pieces that reflect the cubic structure of halite crystals.

Other Properties

Other Properties Some minerals have unusual properties. For example, acids dissolve calcite easily. If you put a few drops of dilute hydrochloric acid on calcite, the calcite will bubble vigorously. In this way, calcite can be distinguished from the similar-looking mineral quartz. Another mineral with an unusual property is magnetite, which is strongly attracted by a magnet. Fluorescent minerals like fluorite give off visible light when they are held under an ultraviolet light. Certain minerals produce small flashes of light when rubbed with a metal point. For example, a form of quartz called rock crystal emits these flashes when it is sawed.

Some minerals have unusual electrical properties. Quartz and tourmaline, for example, become electrically charged when heated and cooled or subjected to pressure. Quartz's electrical properties have applications in electronics equipment.

Iceland spar is a transparent form of the mineral calcite that has the property of refracting light into two separate rays. If you looked at these words through a piece of Iceland spar, you would see a double image of the words. This property is useful in certain optical instruments.

Figure 13 Mica (left) forms in thin, flat sheets that can be easily peeled apart. When halite (right) is broken apart, it forms small cubes that show its crystal structure. *Interpreting Photos Which mineral property do these photos illustrate?*

Section 22.2 Assessment

Reviewing Concepts

1. 🔵 What is a mineral?
2. 🔵 Describe three properties of minerals that can be used to identify them.
3. What determines the crystal shape of a mineral?
4. What determines how a mineral fractures? Explain.

Critical Thinking

5. **Designing Experiments** Suppose you are given two mineral samples that have the same color and luster. What tests could you conduct to determine whether the two samples are the same mineral?

6. **Formulating Hypotheses** Like diamond, graphite is a mineral composed of pure carbon. But its hardness is only between 1 and 2 on the Mohs scale. Formulate a hypothesis to explain the difference in hardness of these minerals.

Connecting Concepts

Covalent Bonds Recall what you learned in Chapter 6 about the characteristics of molecules held together by covalent bonds. Predict a characteristic of quartz (SiO_2), which is covalently bonded.

22.3 Rocks and the Rock Cycle

Reading Focus

Key Concepts

- What are the three major groups of rocks?
- How do igneous rocks form?
- How are sedimentary rocks classified?
- How do metamorphic rocks form?
- How can one type of rock change into another?

Vocabulary

- igneous rock
- magma
- lava
- intrusive rock
- extrusive rock
- sediment
- sedimentary rock
- clastic rocks
- metamorphic rock
- foliated rocks
- rock cycle

Reading Strategy

Comparing and Contrasting Copy the table below. After you read, compare groups of rocks by completing the table.

Rock Group	Formed by	Example
Igneous	a. ___?___	b. ___?___
c. ___?___	d. ___?___	Sandstone
e. ___?___	Heat and pressure	f. ___?___

Figure 14 Lynn Hill is climbing the face of this rock.

Towering more than 1000 meters above Yosemite Valley, California, the steep rock face of El Capitan attracts rock climbers from around the world. In 1993, climber Lynn Hill accomplished the first "free climb" of El Capitan. That is, she climbed without the aid of a rope, except to provide safety in case of a fall. Over four days, Hill ascended El Capitan's steep "nose route," with its sheer cliffs and many overhangs. For an encore, she climbed the same route in 1994 in less than 24 hours!

El Capitan is one of the largest and most impressive chunks of granite on Earth. Yet each of the much smaller rocks that we pass every day also has a fascinating story to tell. Was it formed deep inside a volcano, or crushed by tremendous forces deep within Earth? A few easy-to-observe properties can reveal much about a rock's history.

Classifying Rocks

The properties that geologists use to identify rocks include color and crystal size. The color of a rock indicates the minerals it contains. However, because the colors of most minerals can vary, a rock's color is not always a reliable way to identify it. A better way to identify rocks is by the size of the crystals or other particles they contain.

The size, shape, and arrangement of the crystals and other particles that make up a rock give the rock its texture. A rock's texture reveals what the rock is made from and how and where it formed. **Rocks are classified into three major groups—igneous, sedimentary, and metamorphic—based on how they form.**

Igneous Rock

An **igneous rock** is a rock that forms from magma. **Magma** is a mixture of molten rock and gases, including water vapor, which forms underground. Magma that flows out of volcanoes is called **lava.** ☞ **Igneous rock forms when molten material cools and solidifies either inside Earth or at the surface.** An igneous rock that forms underground from hardened magma is called an **intrusive rock.** An igneous rock that forms at Earth's surface is called an **extrusive rock.**

Extrusive rocks and intrusive rocks have differences in texture caused by differences in how the rocks formed. Intrusive rocks cool slowly underground, allowing their crystals to grow large. Large crystals give intrusive rocks a coarse-grained texture. Extrusive igneous rocks cool very quickly at the surface. Their crystals do not grow much before the rock cools. This gives extrusive rocks a fine-grained texture.

An igneous rock's color gives a clue to its mineral composition. The rock's composition depends on the composition of the magma from which it was formed. Magma that is rich in iron and magnesium produces rocks that are dark and dense, such as gabbro, an intrusive rock, and basalt, an extrusive rock. Some igneous rocks are less dense and lighter in color than basalt and gabbro. These rocks have a high silica content. One such rock is granite, a coarse-grained, intrusive rock.

Figure 15 Basalt is a fine-grained, extrusive rock. As this basalt cooled, the rock formed into hexagonal columns.

Quick Lab

Observing the Size of Crystals

Materials

salol, plastic spoon, 2 watch glasses, tongs, hot plate, hand lens, Petri dish, ice cube, watch with second hand

Procedure

1. Use the spoon to place just enough salol on two watch glasses to cover an area 0.5 cm in width. **CAUTION** *Handle the watch glasses with care to avoid breakage. Salol is poisonous. Don't get it on your skin or breathe its vapor.*

2. Turn the hot plate on to medium heat. Use tongs to place one watch glass on the hot plate.

3. When the salol is almost fully melted, use tongs to place the watch glass on the table. Use the spoon to gently sprinkle a few crystals of salol on the melted salol. Record the time.

4. Use a hand lens to observe the salol as it cools. Record the time when salol crystals begin to reform and how large they are.

5. Place the ice cube on the Petri dish. Repeat Steps 2 to 4 with the second watch glass, but this time, place the watch glass of melted salol on the ice cube instead of the table. Wash your hands with soap and warm water.

Analyze and Conclude

1. **Analyzing Data** How did the rate of cooling affect the size of the crystals that formed?

2. **Using Models** What characteristic of igneous rocks did this lab model? Explain.

3. **Predicting** Pegmatite is an igneous rock that forms when magma cools deep beneath Earth's surface. In contrast, rhyolite is an igneous rock that forms when magma escapes onto the surface. In which rock would you expect to find larger crystals? Explain your answer.

Figure 16 Colorful layers of sandstone, like those in this Utah canyon, formed over millions of years as water and wind laid down sediment.

Sedimentary Rock

The process of weathering breaks down rock at Earth's surface, turning it into smaller pieces. Some rocks are dissolved by rainwater. Other rocks are broken apart by water, wind, or ice. (Weathering will be covered in detail in Chapter 23.)

Sediment consists of small, solid pieces of material that comes from rocks or living organisms. Minerals dissolved in water are also sediment. As in Figure 16, sediment is often carried away by running water or wind to a new location, where it is deposited in layers. This process occurs mainly in the oceans, but it also occurs on river beds, on the bottoms of lakes, and in deserts. Rivers carry sand, mud, and dissolved minerals into the oceans, where these materials are deposited as layers of sediment on the ocean floor.

As more and more sediment piles up, the pressure causes the deeper sediment to be compressed. Dissolved minerals in the water seep into the space between particles of sediment and form a kind of cement. A **sedimentary rock** is a rock that forms over time as sediment is squeezed and cemented together. ⬤ **Geologists classify sedimentary rocks into three main groups according to how they form: clastic rocks, chemical rocks, and organic rocks.**

Clastic Rock Sedimentary rocks that form from the broken fragments of other rocks are called **clastic rocks.** The fragments that make up clastic rocks are usually held together by cement. Otherwise, the fragments would fall apart, like a handful of sand. Clastic rocks are classified mainly based upon the average size of the fragments that they contain. If the rock fragments consist of gravel and pebbles, then the rock is called conglomerate. Like the example in Figure 17, conglomerate usually contains rounded pieces that have been worn smooth in a river or stream. In contrast, breccia is a clastic rock made up of sharp-edged fragments, such as those produced in a volcanic explosion.

Other clastic rocks are made of smaller particles. Sandstone is formed from grains of sand. (Sand itself is made up mostly of small particles of quartz.) If the sediment is primarily mud or silt, the clastic rock is called mudstone. The clay minerals that form mudstone are flat minerals, similar to mica. If these clay minerals are aligned so that the rock can split into sheets, the rock is called shale.

Figure 17 Conglomerate is a sedimentary rock in which rounded pieces of other rocks are cemented together. **Classifying** *What type of sedimentary rock is conglomerate?*

Figure 18 The strangely shaped rocks in Mono Lake, California, are made of tufa, a chemical rock composed of calcium carbonate.

Chemical Rock Chemical sedimentary rocks form when minerals precipitate out of solution. Rainwater dissolves many minerals on the land. These dissolved minerals are then carried down rivers and into the ocean. These minerals remain in solution in ocean water as water evaporates from the ocean surface. The process of evaporation increases the concentration until the minerals precipitate out and sink to the ocean floor. A common type of limestone forms from the precipitation of calcium carbonate in the oceans.

Chemical rocks can also form on land. Many dry basins in the western United States, such as the great salt flats of Utah, are covered with thick layers of precipitated salt. Figure 18 shows chemical rocks that formed in Mono Lake, California.

Organic Rock Some rocks form as the result of organic processes. Marine animals such as coral, clams, and mussels extract calcium carbonate from ocean water to form their shells and skeletons. After these organisms die, their shells and skeletons sink to the ocean floor. Over time, the fragments compact and cement together, forming limestone. Organic limestone is one of the most common sedimentary rocks. Chalk, shown in Figure 19, is a fine-grained, white limestone that formed on the bottom of ancient seas.

Go Online

NSTA *SciLINKS*

For: Links on rocks
Visit: www.SciLinks.org
Web Code: ccn-3223

Figure 19 The cliffs of Dover on the southern coast of England are composed of chalk, a type of fine-grained organic limestone.

✓ **Reading Checkpoint** *How does organic limestone form?*

Shale

Slate

Schist

Gneiss

Figure 20 Heat, pressure, and chemical reactions change the form of rocks. In this sequence, shale changes to slate. Additional heat and pressure may change slate into schist or gneiss.
Comparing and Contrasting *How does gneiss appear to be similar to schist? How is it different?*

Metamorphic Rock

The word *metamorphic* comes from the Greek for "changing form." **Metamorphic rock** is rock that has been changed by temperature, pressure, or reactions with hot water. Geologists call this process of change metamorphism. 🔑 **Metamorphic rock forms when a rock is transformed by heat, pressure, or chemical reactions. Most metamorphic rocks form under high temperatures and pressures deep underground.** The original rock could have been any kind of rock: igneous, sedimentary, or even another metamorphic rock. The result is a new kind of rock.

Metamorphism can result in a rock with a mineral content that is different from that of the original rock. The process begins when heat deep inside Earth allows the minerals to recrystallize, and small crystals to enlarge. As chemical changes occur, new minerals may replace the original minerals. For example, shale is a fine-grained clastic rock that contains clay. During metamorphism, some of the clay changes to the mineral mica, forming the metamorphic rock slate, as you can see in Figure 20.

Metamorphism also changes the texture of rocks. The particles that make up sedimentary and igneous rocks tend to be distributed randomly through the rock. But when pressure is applied from one direction, the particles may line up and lock together in layers or bands. Metamorphic rocks with crystals arranged in parallel layers or bands are **foliated rocks.** Some foliated rocks have a striped appearance. For example, when schist is subjected to heat and pressure, the result is gneiss (nys). Other metamorphic rocks have a nonfoliated texture. Nonfoliated rocks don't have bands. Their crystals are arranged randomly.

The Rock Cycle

Earth is a dynamic planet. Constructive forces form new igneous rock. Destructive forces break down rock, forming sediment. Other forces push rock deep beneath the surface, where heat and pressure form metamorphic rock.

These changes form a cycle—a set of events that repeats again and again. The **rock cycle** is a series of processes in which rocks continuously change from one type to another. 🔑 **In the rock cycle, forces within Earth and at the surface cause rocks to change form.**

To follow the rock cycle in Figure 21, imagine a newly formed igneous rock such as granite. In one path through the rock cycle, the granite is pushed to the surface where it is broken into sand. A river then carries the sand to the ocean floor. There, the sand becomes part of the sedimentary rock sandstone.

The rock cycle doesn't necessarily end with the formation of sandstone. Over millions of years, the sandstone could be pushed deep underground and form the metamorphic rock quartzite. The quartzite could be heated past its melting point and then cool to form a new igneous rock.

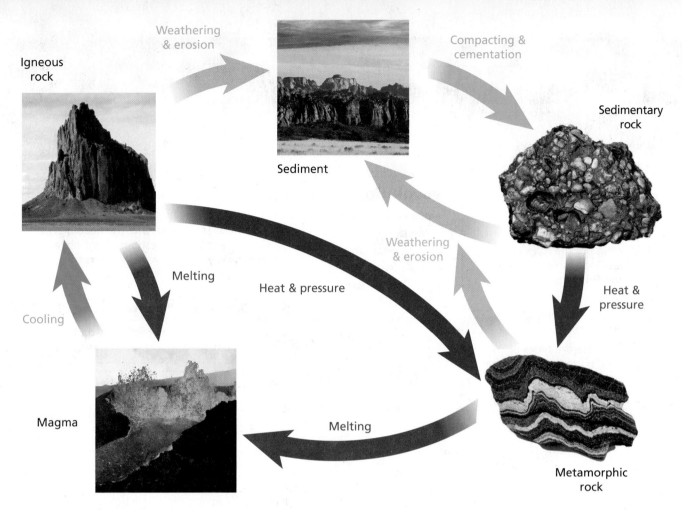

Igneous rock

Weathering & erosion

Sediment

Compacting & cementation

Sedimentary rock

Cooling

Melting

Heat & pressure

Weathering & erosion

Heat & pressure

Magma

Melting

Metamorphic rock

Figure 21 There are many different paths in the rock cycle. Depending on their pathway through the cycle, rocks can wear away, undergo metamorphism, or melt and form new igneous rock.

Section 22.3 Assessment

Reviewing Concepts

1. ⬤ What are the three groups into which geologists classify rocks?

2. ⬤ What are the two ways in which igneous rocks can form?

3. ⬤ What are the three main groups of sedimentary rocks, and how does each group form?

4. ⬤ How are metamorphic rocks formed?

5. ⬤ Describe a path through the rock cycle that begins with magma and ends with a sedimentary rock.

Critical Thinking

6. **Comparing and Contrasting** How is conglomerate different from sandstone?

7. **Applying Concepts** What do the crystal sizes of granite and basalt tell you about where they formed?

8. **Predicting** Forces inside Earth may push granite, a coarse-grained igneous rock, deep below the surface. Predict how the granite could be changed by heat and pressure.

Writing in Science

Steps in a Process Write a paragraph describing the steps in the rock cycle by which an igneous rock could become a sedimentary rock and then a metamorphic rock.

22.4 Plate Tectonics

Reading Focus

Key Concepts
- What are plate tectonics and continental drift?
- What are the roles of sea-floor spreading and subduction in plate tectonics?
- Why do tectonic plates move?
- What are the types of plate boundaries and what are their characteristics?
- Where do most mountains form?

Vocabulary
- plate tectonics
- Pangaea
- continental drift
- mid-ocean ridge
- sea-floor spreading
- subduction
- trench
- divergent boundary
- convergent boundary
- transform boundary

Reading Strategy
Previewing Copy the table below. Before you read this section, rewrite the headings as how, why, and what questions about plate tectonics. As you read, write answers to the questions.

Questions on Plate Tectonics
What is the hypothesis of continental drift?
a._____?_____
b._____?_____
c._____?_____

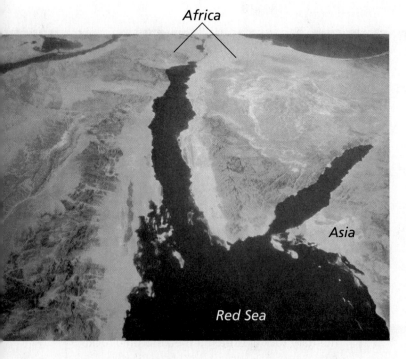

Africa

Asia

Red Sea

Sometimes a single idea can revolutionize an entire field of study. Many observations that previously made little sense will suddenly fit together. Plate tectonics is such an idea. The discovery of plate tectonics revolutionized the field of geology. **Plate tectonics** (tek TAHN iks) is the theory that pieces of Earth's lithosphere, called plates, move about slowly on top of the asthenosphere. **The theory of plate tectonics explains the formation and movement of Earth's plates.**

As recently as the 1960s, many aspects of geology were not well understood. Geologists could not explain why there were mountains in some places and oceans in others. Nor could they explain how fossils of ocean creatures could be found on top of some of the highest mountains. Plate tectonics helps geologists to answer these questions. As you will learn later in this chapter, plate tectonics also does much to explain patterns in the locations of earthquakes and volcanoes.

Figure 22 The Red Sea between Africa and the Arabian peninsula in Asia marks a region where two pieces of the lithosphere are slowly moving apart. Over the next 100 million years, the Red Sea could become an ocean.

Figure 23 Fossils of *Glossopteris* and other plants and animals on widely separated land masses led Alfred Wegener to hypothesize that the continents had once been joined.

Continental Drift

Although the process of plate tectonics was not fully understood until the 1960s, many clues were observed earlier. For instance, when the early explorers began to discover the shapes of the continents, mapmakers noticed how well the shapes of North and South America fit together with Europe and Africa. It seemed almost as if the continents were pieces of a giant jigsaw puzzle that had been broken apart.

Later on, geologists discovered fossils of species of land-based plants and animals on continents separated by large oceans. For example, fossils of the same species of *Glossopteris* (glaw SAHP tuh ris) plant, shown in Figure 23, were found in South America, Africa, Antarctica, India, and Australia. These fossils puzzled geologists because their locations are widely separated.

In 1912, a German scientist named Alfred Wegener (1880–1930) proposed a hypothesis to explain these puzzling observations. ⊂ **Wegener hypothesized that the continents were once joined in a single supercontinent, which then broke into pieces that moved apart.** Wegener called this ancient supercontinent **Pangaea** (pan JEE uh), which means "all land." According to Wegener's hypothesis, the continents move slowly across Earth's surface in a process called **continental drift,** as shown in Figure 24. Continental drift explains why the continents seem to fit together. It also explains why the fossils of plants and animals that once lived in a single region are now scattered across the globe.

However, there were many problems with Wegener's hypothesis. Wegener was unable to explain how the continents could plow through the solid rock of the sea floor. Also, he was unable to give a convincing explanation of what force could move entire continents. As a result, most geologists rejected continental drift.

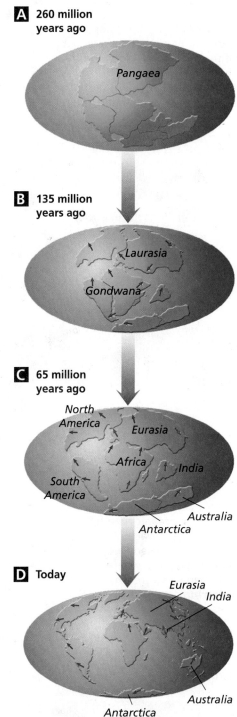

A 260 million years ago

Pangaea

B 135 million years ago

Laurasia

Gondwana

C 65 million years ago

North America
Eurasia
Africa
India
South America
Australia
Antarctica

D Today

Eurasia
India
Australia
Antarctica

Figure 24 The continents move slowly across Earth's surface over time.
A Earth's continents had joined to form the supercontinent Pangaea by 260 million years ago. **B** Pangaea gradually split into two separate land masses, Laurasia and Gondwana. **C** Laurasia split into North America and Eurasia, and South America moved away from Africa. **D** India has now combined with Eurasia, and Australia has broken off from Antarctica.

Figure 25 This false-color satellite image shows a segment of the mid-ocean ridge found in the Atlantic Ocean. Known as the Mid-Atlantic Ridge, it is part of a larger ridge system that winds through all of Earth's oceans.

Sea-floor Spreading

Several decades after Wegener proposed his hypothesis, new evidence led geologists to reconsider his ideas. Some of this evidence came from mapping the sea floor and studying the characteristics of oceanic crust. This evidence helped scientists propose the theory of plate tectonics.

The Mid-Ocean Ridge If you go swimming in a lake, you expect the water in the middle to be deeper than near the shore. Surprisingly, this is often not the case in oceans. When scientists mapped the ocean floor during the mid-1900s, they found a chain of underwater mountains which they called the **mid-ocean ridge.** Like the seams on a baseball, the mid-ocean ridge extends into all of Earth's oceans. It forms the world's longest mountain chain. A segment is shown in Figure 25.

As scientists mapped the Atlantic mid-ocean ridge, they found that it had a remarkable feature: a deep valley running the length of its crest. Scientists also discovered that the rocks of the ocean floor were youngest near the mid-ocean ridge. At first, scientists were puzzled by this new information.

Formation of Oceanic Crust In 1960, geologist Harry Hess proposed the theory of sea-floor spreading to explain these discoveries about the ocean floor. **Sea-floor spreading** is the process by which new oceanic crust is created at mid-ocean ridges as older crust moves away. The mid-ocean ridge is a huge crack in the crust where magma is pulled upward. As shown in Figure 26, the pieces of ocean floor on each side of the central valley are slowly moving apart. As they move, magma from the mantle wells up and solidifies to form new oceanic crust.

Figure 26 During sea-floor spreading, oceanic crust forms at the mid-ocean ridge. This crust gradually moves toward a subduction zone, where old crust sinks beneath a trench.
Inferring *Where is the oldest oceanic crust found?*

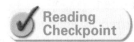 **Reading Checkpoint** *What is sea-floor spreading?*

Subduction of Oceanic Plates As sea-floor spreading occurs, old oceanic plates sink into the mantle in the process of **subduction.** Subduction occurs near the edges of oceanic plates in regions called subduction zones. As a plate sinks through a subduction zone, it bends, forming a depression in the ocean floor called a **trench.** Subduction occurs because as an oceanic plate moves away from the mid-ocean ridge, it gradually cools and becomes more dense. During subduction, the force of gravity slowly pulls the dense edges of oceanic plates into the mantle, destroying old ocean floor. Sea-floor spreading and subduction together act like a giant conveyor belt. **Sea-floor spreading creates new oceanic crust at mid-ocean ridges. Subduction destroys old oceanic crust at subduction zones.** As a result, the ocean floor is renewed about every 200 million years. Over time, these processes change the size and shape of the oceans.

Evidence for Sea-floor Spreading

Other scientists soon provided convincing evidence for Hess's theory. They sampled rocks on both sides of the mid-ocean ridge. They found patterns of parallel magnetic "stripes" that were identical on the two sides. The stripes exist because Earth's magnetic field has reversed itself many times in the past. The stripes formed when Earth's magnetic field caused rock crystals to line up in a certain way before the rock fully solidified. The stripes showed that new ocean floor was being added to both sides of the mid-ocean ridge at roughly the same rate. This pattern of stripes is shown in Figure 27.

Geologists used radioactive dating to determine the ages of rock samples from the ocean floor. They found that rocks nearer the mid-ocean ridge were younger, and the rocks farther from the ridge were older.

The Theory of Plate Tectonics

The evidence of sea-floor spreading provided what was missing from Wegener's hypothesis—a way for pieces of the crust to move. With this knowledge, geologists developed the theory of plate tectonics during the 1960s. According to the theory, Earth's plates are constantly moving, each with a different rate and direction.

What force is powerful enough to move the heavy continents? Look at Figure 28 on page 680. Convection currents form in the mantle as hot rock rises at mid-ocean ridges, cools and spreads out horizontally as ocean lithosphere, and then sinks back into the mantle at subduction zones. These sinking slabs of cold and dense lithosphere, combined with the rising heat from within Earth, drive the circulation of convection currents in the mantle. **Plate motions are the visible part of the process of mantle convection.**

Go Online
SCIENCE NEWS

For: Articles on earthquakes, volcanoes, and plate tectonics
Visit: PHSchool.com
Web Code: cce-3224

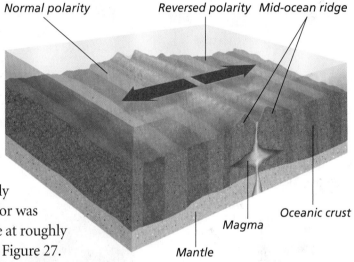

Normal polarity   *Reversed polarity*   *Mid-ocean ridge*

Magma   *Oceanic crust*

Mantle

Figure 27 The pattern of magnetic stripes in the rock of the ocean floor is the same on both sides of the mid-ocean ridge. **Relating Cause and Effect** *Why is the pattern of stripes the same on both sides of the ridge?*

Convection currents
Lithosphere
Outer core
Inner core
Mantle

Figure 28 Heat flows from Earth's hot interior toward the cooler surface mainly through large convection currents in the mantle. Plates are the uppermost part of a global convection system.

The process that drives plate movement on Earth's surface is similar to convection in a pot of boiling soup. The soup is heated from below and rises to the top of the pot, moves across the top and cools, and then sinks back down.

The heat that drives convection in the mantle comes from two sources. Earth was very hot when it first formed, and some of the heat moving upward in convection currents is due to the gradual cooling of its interior. A second source of heat is the result of the decay of radioactive isotopes that are distributed throughout the mantle and crust.

DK SCIENCE and History

Milestones in Geology

Scientific knowledge about Earth's age and geological history has mostly been gathered since the late 1700s. Some of the major advances are described here.

Ammonites *come in many forms, each specific to a particular rock layer and time in the past. They are used as index fossils for the Jurassic period.*

CHARLES DARWIN

JAMES HUTTON

AMMONITE FOSSIL

TITLE PAGE OF *ON THE ORIGIN OF SPECIES*

1795 James Hutton publishes his *Theory of the Earth*, which proposes that our planet is much older than previously thought.

1815 William Smith completes the first geological map of England and Wales. He observes that each layer in a column of sedimentary rock contains index fossils.

1830 British geologist Charles Lyell publishes the first of three volumes of his *Principles of Geology*. The book proposes that Earth has gradually changed over time and that processes still acting today have shaped its surface.

1859 Charles Darwin publishes his groundbreaking work *On the Origin of Species*. The book encourages geologists to begin interpreting their fossil collections in terms of the evolution of life.

| 1790 | 1820 | 1850 | 1880 |

Plate Boundaries

There are about a dozen major tectonic plates, shown in Figure 29 on page 682. Most major plates contain both continental and oceanic crust. The edges of plates meet at plate boundaries. 🔑 **There are three types of plate boundaries: divergent boundaries, convergent boundaries, and transform boundaries.** At each type of boundary, plates move in a different way. As the plates move apart, collide, or slide past each other, they cause changes in Earth's surface.

The motions of Earth's plates have been measured directly using global positioning system (GPS) sensors. The plates move very slowly, about 0.1 to 10 centimeters per year. This speed is similar to the rate at which your fingernails grow—about 4 centimeters per year.

Writing in Science

Summary Research the life and career of one of the geologists in the time line. Write two or three paragraphs that sum up the geologist's major contribution to geology.

Astronauts conduct experiments on the surface of the moon

EDWIN "BUZZ" ALDRIN, JR. WALKING ON THE MOON DURING THE *APOLLO 11* MISSION

TYRANNOSAURUS REX

URANIUM ORE

1907 Bertram Boltwood uses recent discoveries about radioactivity to date uranium-containing rocks. He shows that some are at least 2 billion years old.

1912 Alfred Wegener proposes that the continents were once joined in a supercontinent called Pangaea and have since drifted apart.

1969 Apollo mission astronauts bring rocks back from the moon, a giant leap for lunar geology.

1979 Walter Alvarez discovers a mineral layer containing the element iridium in 65-million-year-old rocks worldwide. He proposes that the iridium came from a huge comet or asteroid that hit Earth. It caused many plant and animal species, including the dinosaurs, to become extinct.

| 1910 | 1940 | 1970 |

Earth's Interior **681**

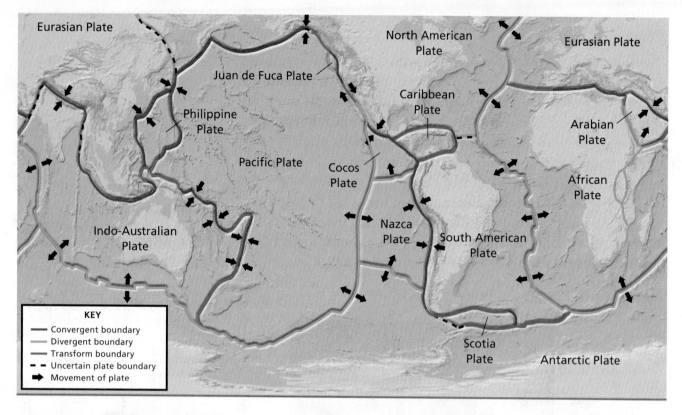

The lithosphere is broken into about a dozen large plates, which move slowly over Earth's surface.

KEY
— Convergent boundary
— Divergent boundary
— Transform boundary
- - Uncertain plate boundary
➤ Movement of plate

Figure 29 The lithosphere is broken into about a dozen large plates, which move slowly over Earth's surface.
Interpreting Maps *What type of boundary exists between the Pacific plate and the Cocos plate?*

Figure 30 Plates meet at three types of boundaries: divergent boundaries, convergent boundaries, and transform boundaries.

Plates move away from each other along a **divergent boundary,** shown in Figure 30. The mid-ocean ridge forms a divergent boundary. Divergent boundaries can also be found on land, for instance, in Africa. When plates move apart, magma rises from the mantle to fill the gap. The magma cools to form new rock at the edge of each plate.

Plates come together, or collide, at a **convergent boundary.** The most common convergent boundary is one where an oceanic plate is subducted beneath a trench. When oceanic crust collides with continental crust, the denser oceanic crust slides under the less dense continental crust. At a **transform boundary,** plates slide past each other, moving in opposite directions. Rock is neither created nor destroyed at a transform boundary.

Divergent Boundary   **Convergent Boundary**   **Transform Boundary**

Lithosphere   *Asthenosphere*   *Lithosphere*

Mountain Building

The theory of plate tectonics helped geologists understand why mountains form in some regions but not in others. ⚷ **Geologists found that most mountains form along plate boundaries.**

Some mountains form when two plates with continental crust at their edges collide along a convergent boundary. Neither plate is subducted during such collisions. Instead, the crust buckles, folds, and thickens, pushing up tall mountains. The collision of the Indo-Australian and Eurasian plates produced Earth's highest mountain range, the Himalayas. Mountains may also form when an oceanic plate collides with a continental plate. The collision of the Nazca and South American plates produced the Andes, shown in Figure 31.

Mountains can also form along diverging plate boundaries. The mid-ocean ridge system forms one long chain of mountains on the ocean floor. In places, the mountains of the mid-ocean ridge rise above sea level. One example is the island of Iceland in the North Atlantic Ocean. As you will read in the next two sections, plate tectonics explains not only mountain building, but many other changes on Earth's surface as well.

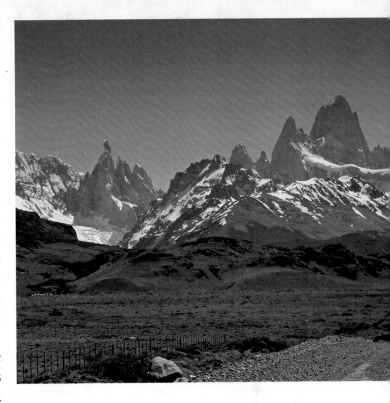

Figure 31 The Andes, which extend along the western side of the South American plate, have risen as a result of a collision between that plate and the Nazca Plate. **Inferring** *What type of plate boundary exists between the South American and Nazca plates?*

Section 22.4 Assessment

Reviewing Concepts

1. ⚷ What is the theory of plate tectonics and what evidence supports it?

2. ⚷ How is the rock of the ocean floor formed?

3. ⚷ What force powers the movement of the continents?

4. ⚷ Describe three main ways in which plates move along plate boundaries.

5. ⚷ Where do most mountains form and how do they form?

6. What was Pangaea and when did it form?

7. How and where is old oceanic crust destroyed?

Critical Thinking

8. **Applying Concepts** Why are trenches usually located at the edges of oceans?

9. **Predicting** The African plate is slowly moving north toward the Eurasian plate. What could eventually happen if the two plates continue to converge?

Connecting ⊂ Concepts

Convection Currents Recall what you learned about convection currents in Chapter 16. Explain how differences in density and temperature could drive convection currents in Earth's mantle.

22.5 Earthquakes

Reading Focus

Key Concepts

- What causes faults and folds?
- What causes earthquakes?
- How are earthquakes measured?
- Where do most earthquakes occur?

Vocabulary

- ◆ earthquake
- ◆ seismic waves
- ◆ tsunami
- ◆ stress
- ◆ fault
- ◆ fold
- ◆ focus
- ◆ epicenter
- ◆ P waves
- ◆ S waves
- ◆ surface waves
- ◆ seismograph

Reading Strategy

Building Vocabulary Make a table like the one below that includes all the vocabulary terms for this section. As you read, define each term in your own words.

Vocabulary Term	Definition
Earthquake	a. _____?_____
Seismic waves	b. _____?_____
Stress	c. _____?_____

It happened on December 26, 2004, at 7:59 A.M. About 35 kilometers beneath the northern tip of the Indonesian island of Sumatra, the ground began to tear as part of the Indian Plate slipped a few meters down into mantle. The tearing continued northward for more than five minutes. When it was over, the process of subduction had unleashed the deadliest earthquake the world had seen in almost 30 years.

An **earthquake** is a movement of Earth's lithosphere that occurs when rocks in the lithosphere suddenly shift, releasing stored energy. A small portion of the energy released during an earthquake is carried by vibrations called **seismic waves**. During the Sumatra earthquake, seismic waves began spreading away from the rupture at about 8 kilometers per second. Within a few seconds, buildings in Sumatra began to crack and collapse.

Figure 32 The tsunami triggered by the 2004 Sumatra earthquake caused extensive damage to coastal areas in Southeast Asia. Earthquakes of similar magnitudes have occurred in the Pacific Northwest in the past and could still occur today.

As a result of the earthquake, nearly 230,000 people died in Asia and Africa. Many people were killed or injured when coastal areas were hit by a tsunami. A **tsunami** is a large sea wave generated by an underwater earthquake, volcano, or landslide. When the 2004 Sumatra earthquake ruptured the sea floor, it pushed up a large volume of water, resulting in a tsunami. Figure 32 shows flood damage caused by the deadly tsunami that followed the Sumatra earthquake.

Stress in Earth's Crust

Earthquakes happen because of the ways that plate movements affect the lithosphere. The forces of plate movement cause deformation, or changes in the shape or volume of a mass of rock. Deformation acting on the rocks of the crust is an example of stress. **Stress** is a force that squeezes rocks together, stretches or pulls them apart, or pushes them in different directions.

One way of applying stress to a material is to try to bend it. If you try to bend a brittle material, such as chalk, it will break. Other sorts of materials, such as copper wire, can bend without breaking. ⬡ **As tectonic plates move, they cause stress in the crust, which in turn produces faults and folds.**

A **fault** is a break in a mass of rock along which movement occurs. The two slabs of rock on either side of a fault move in relation to each other. Many faults occur along plate boundaries. The San Andreas fault, shown in Figure 33, is part of a transform boundary between the Pacific and North American plates. Along this fault, the crust slides in opposite horizontal directions.

A **fold** is a bend in layers of rock. Folds form where rocks are squeezed together, but do not break. Rocks tend to fold rather than break when they are under high temperature or pressure. The folds in rock can vary greatly in size. For example, the wavy patterns in some metamorphic rocks that you can hold in your hand are folds. Folds can also be seen in the rock layers that make up a mountain range, as in Figure 34.

 Reading Checkpoint *What is a fault?*

Figure 33 This portion of the San Andreas fault runs through the Carrizo Plain in south-central California. **Classifying** *What type of plate boundary forms the San Andreas fault?*

Figure 34 Stress can squeeze rock together, producing folds in layers of rock.

685

Figure 35 When an earthquake occurs on a fault, seismic waves move out from the focus. The epicenter lies on the surface, directly above the focus.

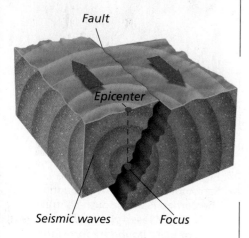

Fault

Epicenter

Seismic waves   Focus

Earthquakes and Seismic Waves

The buildup of stress along a fault provides the energy that powers an earthquake. ⟁ **Earthquakes occur because stress forces have exceeded the strength of rock.**

As you can see in Figure 35, the location beneath Earth's surface where an earthquake begins is called the **focus** (also known as the hypocenter). The location on Earth's surface directly above the focus is called the **epicenter** (EHP uh sen tur). As an earthquake occurs, seismic waves move out in all directions from the focus.

The Physics of Earthquakes Within Earth's crust, forces are at work along faults. They cause the two sides of a fault to move past each other. Sometimes the rocks along the two sides of a fault may snag and remain locked because of friction between the two fault surfaces. As a result, tremendous stress builds up in these areas.

Any material has a limit to how much stress it can absorb. When rocks are strained beyond their limit, they break and grind past each other, releasing huge amounts of energy in the form of an earthquake. As the rocks break and move, potential energy is transformed into kinetic energy in the form of seismic waves.

Types of Seismic Waves Earthquakes produce three main types of seismic waves: P waves, S waves, and surface waves. Each type of seismic wave has different characteristics.

P waves (originally called primary waves) are longitudinal waves similar to sound waves. Recall that, as longitudinal waves move through a material, they cause particles in the material to vibrate in the direction of the waves' motion. Thus, P waves compress and expand the ground like an accordion, as you can see in Figure 36. Because P waves are the fastest seismic waves, they are the first to be detected at a distance. P waves can travel through both solids and liquids.

Figure 36 P waves and S waves are seismic waves that travel through Earth's interior. P waves are longitudinal waves that compress and expand the ground. S waves are transverse waves in which particles vibrate at right angles to the waves' direction of movement.

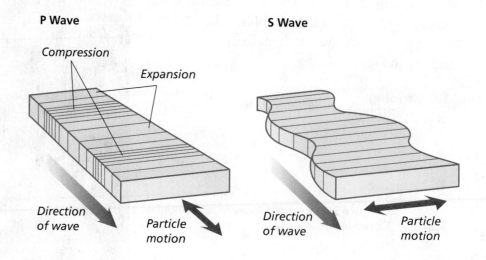

P Wave

Compression

Expansion

Direction of wave   Particle motion

S Wave

Direction of wave   Particle motion

S waves (originally called secondary waves) are transverse waves, like light and other electromagnetic radiation. S waves cause the particles in the materials they pass through to vibrate at right angles to the direction the waves move. You can see how S waves move in Figure 36. Unlike P waves, S waves cannot travel through liquids.

Surface waves are waves that develop when seismic waves reach Earth's surface. Surface waves move more slowly than P waves and S waves, but usually produce larger ground movements and greater damage. Some surface waves are transverse waves, and others have a rolling motion at Earth's surface that is similar to ocean waves.

Measuring Earthquakes

When an earthquake occurs, the first things people want to know are how big it was and where it was centered. **To measure earthquakes and pinpoint their epicenters, geologists record seismic waves using seismographs.** A device that can detect and record seismic waves is called a **seismograph.** The How It Works box on page 688 illustrates a seismograph. The record of an earthquake on a seismograph is called a **seismogram.** Earthquakes can be located using the seismic waves recorded by many different seismographs.

The range in recorded earthquake sizes is enormous. Most earthquakes are too small to be felt by humans. The largest earthquakes release more energy than the United States consumes in a year.

Richter Scale The most well-known scale is the Richter scale. The Richter scale rates earthquakes based on measurements of the times and amplitudes of seismic waves by certain seismographs. However, the Richter scale is no longer used by geologists.

Moment Magnitude Scale The most useful scale for geologists is the moment magnitude scale (M_w). This scale gives a measure of the amount of energy released by an earthquake. Each unit increase on this scale represents about a 32-times increase in the energy released. The largest earthquake ever recorded was a M_w 9.5 earthquake that occurred in southern Chile in 1960.

Modified Mercalli Scale The effects of earthquakes can also be rated using the modified Mercalli scale. This scale, which ranges from 1 to 12, is based on observations of the intensity of ground shaking and damage in the areas affected by an earthquake. For example, an earthquake rated 7 on the Mercalli scale would knock over some chimneys. A rating of 12 applies to earthquakes that cause total destruction of nearby towns or cities.

Reading Checkpoint *What is the moment magnitude scale?*

Go Online
PLANETDIARY

For: Activity on earthquakes
Visit: PHSchool.com
Web Code: ccc-3225

Quick Lab

Modeling a Seismograph

Procedure

1. Obtain cash register paper from your teacher. Roll it up and place a pencil through the center of the roll so the roll turns freely around the pencil.

2. Hold the pencil and paper roll horizontally on a flat surface so that a classmate can slowly pull the free end of the paper across the surface. Have a second classmate hold a felt-tip pen so that it marks a line on the paper as it is pulled across the surface.

3. While the paper is being pulled and marked, have a third classmate do each of the following for 5 seconds: shake the desk gently, shake the desk more vigorously, and hold the desk still.

Analyze and Conclude

1. **Observing** How did shaking affect the ink line?

2. **Using Models** What did the shaking represent?

Measuring Earthquakes

Modern seismometers have been placed all around the world. Some are permanently installed hundreds of feet below ground to avoid noise. Others can be temporarily placed anywhere on land. Many seismometers transmit seismograms via satellite, allowing geologists to analyze earthquakes as they are occurring.

Interpreting Diagrams *Why must the base of a seismometer be cemented to bedrock?*

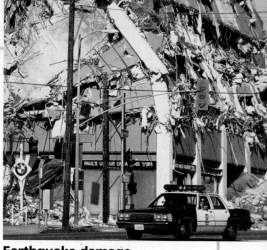

Earthquake damage
An earthquake can shake a building off its foundation. In 1994 an earthquake caused this damage in Northridge, California.

1 Seismometers
These sensitive instruments detect tiny movements in the ground and convert them into electrical signals. Three or more seismometers work together to sense vertical and horizontal movements.

2 Computer
A computer receives the signals from the seismometers and stores the data digitally.

Solar panel providing electrical energy to charge the battery

3 Seismogram Digital data are sent to a survey office, where they are turned into a seismogram. The example below shows a M_W 5 aftershock of the Northridge, California, earthquake. The time interval between the P and S waves indicates how far the seismometer was from the quake center.

Pipe for cables

Soil

Bedrock

Base cemented to bedrock

Battery powering seismometers and computer

Cement base

Ground displacement (usually in millimeters)

P wave

S wave

Time scale

Seismographic Data

A worldwide network of seismographs has provided scientists with a wealth of data on earthquakes. These data have enabled geologists to map the distribution of earthquakes. In addition, seismographic data have been used to probe the structure of Earth's interior. Unfortunately, so far these data have not resulted in a method that can be used to predict when earthquakes will occur.

Every day, earthquakes occur all around the world. **Most earthquakes are concentrated along plate boundaries, where many faults are found.** Some earthquakes occur in the interior of plates, far away from plate boundaries. As a plate moves, it undergoes deformation. The resulting stresses are released as earthquakes.

Scientists have mapped Earth's interior, analyzing how seismic waves move through its layers. The speeds of seismic waves and the paths they take are affected by the temperature, composition, and density of the rocks they pass through. Seismic waves are much like other kinds of waves. When they interact with boundaries between different kinds of rock within Earth, they can be reflected, refracted, or diffracted. Look at Figure 37. Geologists infer that Earth's outer core is liquid because S waves cannot pass through it. They can also tell that the core is mostly iron because P waves travel through it at a speed that matches laboratory experiments on iron.

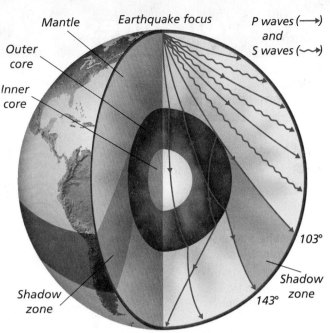

Figure 37 Earth's liquid outer core blocks S waves and bends P waves. The result is a shadow zone on the surface where no direct seismic waves from an earthquake are detected. **Comparing and Contrasting** *Compare where P waves and S waves can be detected on Earth's surface. What does this reveal about Earth's layers?*

Section 22.5 Assessment

Reviewing Concepts

1. Describe how faults and folds form in Earth's crust.
2. What happens along a fault before and during an earthquake?
3. How can the magnitude and location of earthquakes be measured?
4. Where do earthquakes occur most often?

Critical Thinking

5. **Comparing and Contrasting** Compare and contrast P waves, S waves, and surface waves.

6. **Relating Cause and Effect** How can layers within Earth be identified by means of seismic waves?

Math Practice

7. How much more energy is released by a M_W 8 earthquake than a M_W 6 earthquake?

8. P waves move through the crust at a speed of about 6.5 km/s. How far will a P wave move in 5 seconds?

22.6 Volcanoes

Reading Focus

Key Concepts

- How do volcanoes form?
- Why are some volcanic eruptions quiet and others explosive?
- Where are volcanoes found?
- What landforms are formed from lava and magma?

Vocabulary

- volcano
- magma chamber
- pipe ◆ vent
- crater
- caldera
- hot spot
- shield volcano
- cinder cone
- composite volcano
- batholith
- sill ◆ dike
- volcanic neck

Reading Strategy

Sequencing Copy the flowchart. As you read, complete it to show how a volcano forms.

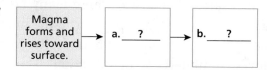

From northern California through the state of Washington, a chain of snow-capped, cone-shaped mountains rises majestically above the surrounding evergreen forests. These peaks form the backbone of the Cascade Range, which is made up of volcanoes. A **volcano** is a mountain that forms when magma reaches the surface.

Most of the time, the volcanoes of the Cascade Range are inactive. Occasionally, however, one of these volcanoes erupts with great violence. That's what happened in May 1980, when Mount St. Helens in Washington exploded. This eruption blew away the top of the mountain. It flattened trees as far as 17 kilometers away, and spewed a cloud of ash more than 20 kilometers into the sky, as shown in Figure 38.

Halfway across the Pacific Ocean, on the island of Hawaii, is another volcano called Kilauea. Unlike Mount St. Helens, Kilauea is often active. Lava bubbles out of the ground and quietly flows down gentle slopes. Although Mount St. Helens and Kilauea are both volcanoes, they are quite different from each other. Volcanoes can result from several different geological processes, and can take a variety of forms.

Figure 38 When Mount St. Helens erupted, trapped gases caused the north side of the mountain to explode. Volcanic ash was ejected high into the atmosphere.

Formation of a Volcano

The process that leads to a volcanic eruption begins deep inside Earth. ➡ **Under certain conditions, small amounts of mantle rock can melt, forming liquid magma. The magma rises upward through the crust, erupting at the surface as a volcano.** Magma rises because it is less dense than the solid rock around and above it.

How a Volcano Erupts What causes a volcanic eruption? The process is similar to what happens when you quickly open a bottle of soda that has been shaken. Like the soda in the bottle, magma is under pressure and contains dissolved gases. In the case of magma, the gases include carbon dioxide and water vapor. As magma approaches the surface, lower pressure allows the gases in magma to expand rapidly. An eruption occurs when the gases bubble out through a crack in the crust, propelling magma to the surface.

Structure of a Volcano Before an eruption, magma often collects in a pocket called a **magma chamber,** shown in Figure 39. Magma slowly accumulates in the magma chamber until enough pressure builds up to start an eruption. Then, magma rises to the surface in a narrow, vertical channel called a **pipe.**

An opening in the ground where magma escapes to the surface is called a **vent.** Often there is one central vent at the top of a volcano. Sometimes there are other vents that open along a volcano's side. At the top of the central vent in most volcanoes is a bowl-shaped pit called a **crater.**

After an eruption, a volcano's magma chamber and main vent may empty of magma, creating a hollow shell. If this shell collapses inward, it creates a huge depression, called a **caldera,** at the top of the volcano.

Figure 39 When a volcanic mountain erupts, magma under pressure is forced upward from the magma chamber. It passes through the pipe, and out the vent. Magma flows onto the surface as lava. **Predicting** *What might happen to a volcano if its pipe became plugged with hardened magma?*

Crater

Lava

Vent

Pipe

Magma chamber

Quiet and Explosive Eruptions

A volcanic eruption like that of Mount St. Helens has the force of a powerful explosion. But in other volcanic eruptions, lava flows gently over the surface. **Volcanoes erupt explosively or quietly, depending on the characteristics of the magma.**

Magma can vary in viscosity, the resistance to flow. Magma with high viscosity is thick and resists flowing. Magma with low viscosity is thin and flows easily.

There are three main factors that determine the viscosity of magma: temperature, water content, and silica content. Higher temperatures lower the viscosity of magma, so it flows more easily. The presence of water in magma also helps it flow more easily. Magma that is high in silica has high viscosity. The silicon and oxygen atoms in silica are held together with strong bonds. The silica in magma acts like glue, preventing the magma from flowing easily.

Quiet Eruptions Volcanoes that have very hot, low-silica magma generally erupt quietly. In a quiet eruption, lava erupts in a stream of low-viscosity lava, called a lava flow. Lava flows from a quiet eruption can travel for great distances. Quiet eruptions produce two different kinds of lava, as shown in Figure 40. Hot, fast-moving lava with a ropelike surface is called pahoehoe (pah HOH ee hoh ee). Cooler, slow-moving lava with a chunky, crumbly appearance is called aa (AH ah).

Explosive Eruptions High-silica magma produces explosive eruptions. Thick magma can clog a volcanic pipe, causing enormous pressure to build up. Trapped steam inside the volcano adds to the pressure, as was the case in the eruption of Mount St. Helens. When the volcano finally explodes, lava and hot gases are hurled outward. The lava solidifies very quickly and shatters into pieces of different sizes. These particles range in size from fine dust and ash, to pebble-sized cinders, to bombs—chunks of lava that can be the size of a small car.

pahoehoe   aa

Figure 40 Lava may flow in the form of rough chunks called aa, or smooth coils called pahoehoe. **Formulating Hypotheses** *Develop a hypothesis to account for the difference in texture between pahoehoe and aa.*

Figure 41 Mt. Kilauea in Hawaii erupts quietly, producing low-viscosity lava flows.

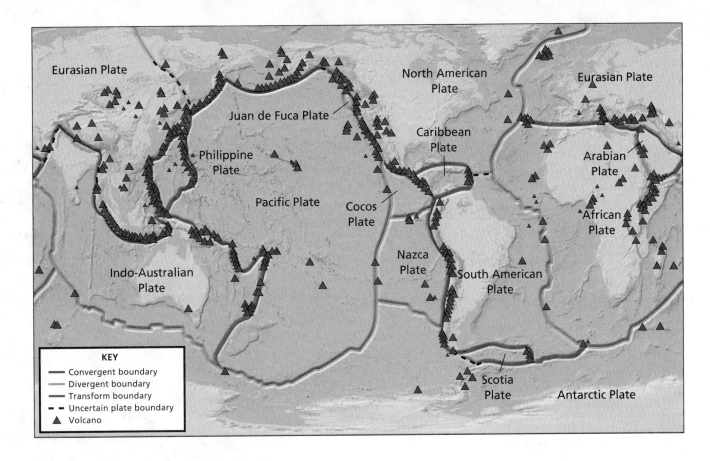

KEY
— Convergent boundary
— Divergent boundary
— Transform boundary
- - Uncertain plate boundary
▲ Volcano

Location and Types of Volcanoes

Most volcanoes occur along plate boundaries or at hot spots in the crust. Volcanoes often form along a converging plate boundary where an oceanic plate is subducted into the mantle. As it sinks through the mantle, the plate causes melting. Magma forms and rises to the surface. As Figure 42 shows, many volcanoes have formed along the trenches that rim the Pacific Ocean. This region is called the "Ring of Fire." Volcanoes also form along a diverging plate boundary where magma rises to fill the gap between two separating plates.

Some volcanoes occur at hot spots, as shown in the Concepts in Action pages. A **hot spot** is a region where hot rock extends from deep within the mantle to the surface.

Different types of volcanic eruptions produce different types of volcanoes. Each type is named for its shape or interior structure. The three major types of volcano are shield volcanoes, cinder cones, and composite volcanoes. A quiet eruption of low-viscosity lava produces a wide, flat volcano called a **shield volcano.** If an eruption is entirely ash and cinders, the result will be a small, steep-sided volcano called a **cinder cone.** A volcano that forms from explosive eruptions that produce a combination of lava and ash is called a **composite volcano.**

Reading Checkpoint   *What is a shield volcano?*

Figure 42 Except for hot-spot volcanoes, most of the world's volcanoes form near plate boundaries.
Relating Cause and Effect *Why are there volcanoes in the middle of the Atlantic Ocean?*

For: Activity on volcanoes
Visit: PHSchool.com
Web Code: ccc-3226

Types of Volcanoes

Volcanoes have different types of magma. The viscosity of the magma plays a large part in determining a volcano's ultimate shape and appearance.

Volcanoes most commonly occur at three major locations on Earth—mid-ocean ridges, subduction zones, and hot spots. Each type of volcanic region produces a different kind of volcano because of the type of magma that exists there. The three main types of volcano are shield volcanoes, composite volcanoes, and cinder cones. Most volcanoes that form above subduction zones, for example, are composite volcanoes. In contrast, many volcanoes that form above hot spots are shield volcanoes.

Shapes of Volcanoes

Each type of volcano has a different shape. The shape is determined by the kind of lava, ash, and cinders that erupt from the volcano's vent, and especially the viscosity of the lava.

Shield volcano
Shield volcanoes are broad, gently sloping volcanic mountains. Their eruptions consist of hot, flowing basaltic lava that travels a long way before it solidifies.

Composite volcano
Composite volcanoes are tall with steep sides that are built up from layers of viscous lava, ash, and volcanic bombs. They often have secondary vents.

Cinder cone
Cinder cones are small with steep sides. They form from ash and cinders that are ejected into the air and fall back onto the volcano.

Volcanic Rocks

The silica and water content of magma help to determine whether an eruption is quiet or explosive and how viscous the lava is when hot. When the lava cools, different types of rock are formed.

Obsidian
Obsidian is a dense, volcanic glass formed from lava that has cooled too quickly for minerals to crystallize.

Lava bombs
Lava bombs form from a glob of magma that is blown explosively into the air. Bombs are usually at least 10 cm in diameter, and can be much larger.

Pumice
Pumice is a light, sponge-like rock usually found at the surface of a lava flow. It consists of a mass of gas bubbles frozen in fragile volcanic glass and minerals.

Hot-spot Volcanoes

A hot spot is a rising column of hot rock that extends from deep within the mantle to the surface. Hot spots often exist in the middle of plates. Because the hot spot stays in one place while the plate moves over it, a chain of volcanoes is formed over time.

A very ancient hot spot under the Pacific plate has, over millions of years, produced the Hawaiian Islands.

Extinct volcanoes form chains of islands

Vent

Plate carries active volcanoes away and they become extinct as new island begins to form.

Rising magma

Volcano erupts over stationary hot spot and creates an island.

Kilauea erupting
A shield volcano, Kilauea is the youngest volcano on the island of Hawaii and one of the most active in the world.

Going Further

- Use library or Internet resources to research a volcano located on another planet or moon. Write a one-page report describing the volcano that you select. Include an explanation of how this volcano compares with volcanoes on Earth.

Figure 43 Ship Rock in New Mexico is a volcanic neck. It formed when the soft rock around a volcano's pipe wore away, revealing hard, igneous rock. The long ridge extending from the volcanic neck is a dike.

Other Igneous Features

Sometimes magma does not reach the surface, but cools and hardens in the crust. This magma forms intrusive igneous rock that may eventually be forced upward and exposed at Earth's surface. 🔵 **Igneous features formed by magma include batholiths, sills, dikes, and volcanic necks.** Lava plateaus are features formed of extrusive igneous rock.

A **batholith** is the largest type of intrusive igneous rock mass. Batholiths often form the core of a mountain range, such as the Sierra Nevada range in California. Magma sometimes squeezes into a crack between layers of rock and then hardens. If the crack is parallel to existing rock layers, the magma hardens into a structure called a **sill.** If the crack cuts across rock layers, the hardened magma forms a **dike.** When magma hardens in a volcano's pipe, a structure called a **volcanic neck** may form, as shown in Figure 43.

The largest lava flows don't come from individual volcanoes. Rather, large amounts of easily-flowing lava sometimes erupt from a cluster of long, thin cracks in the crust. This lava may spread out over an enormous area before solidifying. After many years, layers of hardened lava may form a high, level area called a lava plateau. An example is the Columbia Plateau, which has an average thickness of more than 1 kilometer and covers an area of nearly 200,000 square kilometers in the Pacific Northwest.

Section 22.6 Assessment

Reviewing Concepts

1. 🔵 Describe the process that leads up to the eruption of a volcano.
2. 🔵 How does the silica content of magma affect how explosive an eruption is?
3. 🔵 Explain why volcanoes form in certain regions of Earth's surface.
4. 🔵 Describe four types of intrusive igneous rock features.

Critical Thinking

5. **Relating Cause and Effect** What condition must exist in a volcano for a caldera to form?

6. **Predicting** What would eventually happen, as a result of plate movement, to a volcano that formed over a hot spot?
7. **Comparing and Contrasting** What is the difference between a dike and a sill?

Writing in Science

Descriptive Paragraph Use library or Internet resources to research a major volcanic eruption. Write a paragraph about the eruption including when and where it took place and the type of volcano involved.

Using Earthquakes to Map Plate Boundaries

In this lab, you will analyze data from several earthquakes to determine how the plates in the northwestern United States are moving.

Problem How can you use earthquake data to infer the movement of tectonic plates?

Materials
- graph paper

Skills Inferring, Analyzing Data

Procedure

1. Examine the map of Oregon and Washington states. Earthquakes occur in the western parts of these states as a result of the movements of two plates—the Juan de Fuca Plate, which lies under the Pacific Ocean, and the North American plate.

2. Examine the table of earthquake data. Record any patterns that you observe.

3. Draw a diagram showing how the edges of the Juan de Fuca and North American plates would move if they formed a convergent boundary. Use Figure 30 on page 682 to help you draw this diagram.

4. Draw a diagram showing how the edges of the two plates would move if they formed a transform boundary. Use Figure 30 again to help you draw this diagram.

5. Use the information in the data table to construct a graph showing the location and depth of earthquakes. Plot the distance from the coast on the horizontal axis and the depth of the focus on the vertical axis. Label the vertical axis with zero at the top and maximum depth at the bottom.

6. Draw a curve as close as possible to all the points you plotted on your graph. The curve shows the shape and position of the boundary between the Juan de Fuca and North American plates. Compare your graph to the two diagrams you drew in Steps 3 and 4.

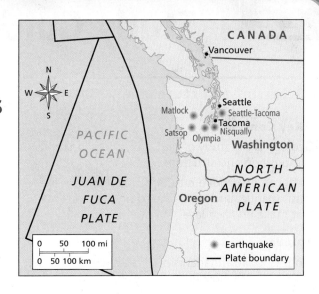

Data Table			
Year	Location of Epicenter	Distance From Coast (km)	Depth of Focus (km)
1949	Olympia	116	53
1965	Seattle-Tacoma	141	63
1999	Satsop	58	41
2001	Nisqually	108	52
2001	Matlock	60	41

Analyze and Conclude

1. **Using Graphs** What kind of boundary do the Juan de Fuca and North American plates form? Explain how your graph supports your answer.

2. **Inferring** What does your graph suggest about the direction in which the Juan de Fuca and North American plates are moving?

3. **Predicting** In California, the Pacific plate and the North American plate meet along a transform boundary called the San Andreas fault. Would you expect to observe a similar curve in a graph of the earthquake data from the San Andreas fault? Explain.

4. **Drawing Conclusions** Based on your data, how is earthquake depth related to distance from a convergent plate boundary? Explain.

Go Further Use resources in the library or on the Internet to learn how geologists estimate the depth of an earthquake's focus. Report your findings to the class.

22.1 Earth's Structure

🔑 Key Concepts

- Geology is the study of planet Earth, including its composition and structure.
- Earth can be divided into three main layers—the crust, mantle, and core—based on the materials that make up each layer.

Vocabulary

geologists, uniformitarianism, silicates, crust, mantle, lithosphere, asthenosphere, mesosphere, core

22.2 Minerals

🔑 Key Concepts

- A mineral is a naturally ocurring, inorganic solid with a crystal structure and a characteristic composition.
- The properties by which minerals can be identified include their crystal structure, color, streak, luster, density, hardness, fracture, and cleavage.

Vocabulary

rock, inorganic, streak, luster, hardness, fracture, cleavage

22.3 Rocks and the Rock Cycle

🔑 Key Concepts

- Rocks are classified into three major groups—igneous, sedimentary, and metamorphic.
- In the rock cycle, forces within Earth and at the surface cause rocks to change form.

Vocabulary

igneous rock, magma, lava, intrusive rock, extrusive rock, sediment, sedimentary rock, clastic rocks, metamorphic rock, foliated rocks, rock cycle

22.4 Plate Tectonics

🔑 Key Concepts

- The theory of plate tectonics explains the formation and movement of Earth's plates.
- Sea-floor spreading creates new oceanic crust at mid-ocean ridges. Subduction destroys old oceanic crust at subduction zones.

- Plate motions are the visible part of the process of mantle convection.
- There are three types of plate boundaries: divergent, convergent, and transform.
- Most mountains form along plate boundaries.

Vocabulary

plate tectonics, Pangaea, continental drift, mid-ocean ridge, sea-floor spreading, subduction, trench, divergent boundary, convergent boundary, transform boundary

22.5 Earthquakes

🔑 Key Concepts

- As tectonic plates move, they cause stress in the crust, which in turn produces faults and folds.
- Earthquakes occur because stress forces have exceeded the strength of rock.
- To measure earthquakes and pinpoint their epicenters, geologists record seismic waves using seismographs.
- Most earthquakes occur along plate boundaries.

Vocabulary

earthquake, seismic waves, stress, fault, fold, focus, epicenter, P waves, S waves, surface waves, seismograph

22.6 Volcanoes

🔑 Key Concepts

- Under certain conditions, small amounts of mantle rock can melt, forming liquid magma. The magma rises upward through the crust, erupting at the surface as a volcano.
- Volcanoes erupt explosively or quietly, depending on the characteristics of the magma.
- Most volcanoes occur along plate boundaries, or at hot spots in the crust.
- The three major types of volcano are shield volcanoes, cinder cones, and composite volcanoes.
- Igneous features formed by magma include batholiths, sills, dikes, and volcanic necks.

Vocabulary

volcano, magma chamber, pipe, vent, crater, caldera, hot spot, shield volcanoes, cinder cone, composite volcano, batholith, sill, dike, volcanic neck

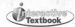
Reviewing Content

Choose the letter that best answers the question or completes the statement.

1. The lithosphere includes the crust and portions of the
   a. mantle.   b. asthenosphere.
   c. mesosphere.   d. outer core.

2. The layer of Earth consisting of weak, soft rock that can flow easily is called the
   a. crust.   b. core.
   c. lithosphere.   d. asthenosphere.

3. Which of the following properties is NOT useful in identifying a mineral?
   a. size   b. cleavage
   c. density   d. hardness

4. The way that the surface of a mineral reflects light is called
   a. density.   b. hardness.
   c. luster.   d. streak.

5. Sedimentary rocks that form from the broken fragments of other rocks are called
   a. chemical rocks.   b. organic rocks.
   c. intrusive rocks. d. clastic rocks.

6. A long, deep depression in the ocean floor is called a
   a. mid-ocean ridge.   b. trench.
   c. caldera.   d. batholith.

7. What type of plate boundary occurs when two plates move away from each other?
   a. divergent   b. convergent
   c. transform   d. subduction

8. Which type of earthquake wave moves the fastest?
   a. surface wave   b. S wave
   c. P wave   d. transverse wave

9. The location inside Earth where an earthquake begins is called the
   a. fold.   b. epicenter.
   c. focus.   d. hot spot.

10. Magma that hardens in a pipe of a volcano may form a
    a. volcanic neck.   b. sill.
    c. batholith.   d. dike.

Understanding Concepts

11. What is the major difference between Earth's inner and outer cores?

12. Use the table below to choose two tests that you would perform to distinguish gold from pyrite and chalcopyrite. Describe how you would perform each test.

Mineral Characteristics			
Mineral	Gold	Pyrite	Chalcopyrite
Color	Rich yellow	Light yellow	Rich yellow
Density (g/cm³)	19.3	5.0	4.3
Hardness	2.5–3.0	6.0–6.5	3.5–4.0
Streak	Yellow	Greenish black	Greenish black

13. Which of the following is a mineral: coal, brick, talc, and granite?

14. What is the difference between an intrusive rock and an extrusive rock?

15. How do metamorphic rocks form?

16. What is continental drift?

17. What evidence is there for sea-floor spreading?

18. What is the importance of convection currents in the theory of plate tectonics?

19. What determines the viscosity of magma?

20. How do hot-spot volcanoes form?

21. Sometimes water is considered a mineral and sometimes it is not. Explain.

22. Coquina is a rock made of fragments of small shells cemented together. What type of rock is coquina?

23. What is the major difference between Wegener's original hypothesis of continental drift and the theory of plate tectonics? How are they similar?

Critical Thinking

24. Applying Concepts New oceanic crust is being produced in the Pacific Ocean due to a mid-ocean ridge that runs along the ocean floor. But the Pacific Ocean is not getting bigger. What must be happening in the Pacific Ocean?

25. Inferring How do scientists know about the structure and composition of Earth's interior?

26. Comparing and Contrasting What is the difference between magma and lava?

Analyzing Data

Use the graph below to answer Questions 27–29.

Seismic Wave Travel Time

27. Using Graphs An earthquake occurs 2000 km from seismograph station A. How much later does the first P wave arrive at the station? How much later does the first S wave arrive?

28. Calculating What is the difference in time between the arrivals of the first P wave and the first S wave at station A?

29. Drawing Conclusions The first P waves of the earthquake arrived at seismograph station B about 2 minutes before the first S waves arrived. How far is seismograph station B from the epicenter of the earthquake?

Concepts in Action

30. Classifying A piece of the metamorphic rock gneiss is formed when a chain of mountains is created. The pressure and temperature surrounding the rock increase so that the gneiss melts completely and then hardens again. Is the new rock still considered a metamorphic rock? Explain.

31. Hypothesizing The fossils of tropical plants and animals have been found in Antarctica. Using your knowledge of plate tectonics, provide a possible explanation for this observation.

32. Applying Concepts When the volcano Krakatoa erupted in the 1880s, the eruption released so much volcanic ash into the atmosphere that temperatures temporarily cooled worldwide. Do you think that Krakatoa's eruption involved low-silica magma or high-silica magma? Explain.

33. Writing In Science Imagine you had to give a presentation on plate tectonics to a group of scientists who were still skeptical about the theory. Organize your talk into sections with the main points and evidence to support them. Be convincing.

Performance-Based Assessment

Classifying Gather about a dozen different local rock and mineral samples. Classify and identify each sample. Present your findings about your collection of rocks and minerals to the class. Indicate how you identified some of the more difficult samples.

Go Online
PHSchool.com

For: Self-grading assessment
Visit: PHSchool.com
Web Code: cca-3220

Standardized Test Prep

Choose the letter that best answers the question or completes the statement.

1. In which part of the mantle would you expect temperature and pressure to be greatest?
(A) asthenosphere   (B) lithosphere
(C) lower crust   (D) mesosphere
(E) outer core

2. Which are examples of how a sedimentary rock can form?
  I. Heat and pressure form banded layers inside a rock.
  II. Magma cools and hardens beneath the surface.
  III. Sediment hardens through compaction and cementation.

(A) I only   (B) III only
(C) I and II only   (D) II and III only
(E) I, II, and III

3. Which is NOT evidence for the theory of plate tectonics?
(A) the buildup of sedimentary rock layers
(B) the way the shapes of some continents fit together
(C) the location of Earth's volcanoes
(D) the distribution of certain fossils
(E) magnetic stripes in ocean-floor rock

4. A subduction zone, where oceanic crust sinks into the mantle, is an example of a
(A) diverging boundary.
(B) fold.
(C) transform boundary.
(D) mid-ocean ridge.
(E) converging boundary.

5. Which of these statements is (are) true of P waves?
  I. They travel only across the surface.
  II. The liquid iron of the outer core blocks them.
  III. They are longitudinal waves.

(A) I only   (B) III only
(C) I and II only   (D) I and III only
(E) I, II, and III

6. Which intrusive igneous rock feature is formed when magma cuts across rock layers?
(A) batholith   (B) dike
(C) caldera   (D) sill
(E) shield volcano

Hardness	
Mineral	**Hardness**
Gypsum	2
Fluorite	4
Quartz	7

7. Which test would be most helpful in identifying the three minerals in the table above?
(A) Try to scratch each one with a penny.
(B) Try to scratch each one with a diamond.
(C) Try to scratch quartz with gypsum.
(D) Try to scratch gypsum and quartz with fluorite.
(E) Try to scratch each one with a streak plate.

23 Earth's Surface

How old are the rocks where you live?

Use the Internet or your local library to learn about a river system in your area. Search for information on the topography, climate, and history of the watershed. Using images from online mapping sites and photo sharing sites, create a narrated slide show that gives a virtual tour of the watershed's features. Post your slide show to a class blog and collect feedback from classmates and other residents in your area.

How do science concepts apply to your world? Here are some questions you'll be able to answer after you read this chapter.

- **Where is most of Earth's fresh water found?** *(Section 23.1)*

- **What are hoodoos, and how are they formed?** *(Section 23.2)*

- **How is a river like a dump truck?** *(Section 23.3)*

- **When was the Chicago region covered by a sheet of ice more than a kilometer thick?** *(Section 23.4)*

- **How would Earth's surface look if the oceans were drained?** *(Section 23.5)*

- **How do scientists explore the ocean floor?** *(page 730)*

- **How can scientists determine the age of a fossil or a rock?** *(Section 23.6)*

At Gooseneck State Park in Utah, the San Juan River winds through deep canyons it has cut into layers of sedimentary rocks.

EARTH AND SPACE SCIENCE

Chapter Preview

23.1 Fresh Water

23.2 Weathering and Mass Movement

23.3 Water Shapes the Land

23.4 Glaciers and Wind

23.5 The Restless Oceans

23.6 Earth's History

Inquiry Activity

How Do Freezing and Thawing Affect Rocks?

Procedure

1. Your group will receive 5 similar rocks to examine for signs of damage. First, look closely at rock A, which was not treated. It is the control. Record your observations.

2. Examine rocks B through E. (Rock B was soaked, frozen, and thawed once; rock C was soaked, frozen, and thawed twice; rock D was soaked, frozen, and thawed three times; and rock E was soaked, frozen, and thawed four times.) Record your observations.

Think About It

1. **Observing** What effect did one freezing and thawing cycle have on rock B? How did repeated freezing and thawing cycles affect rocks C through E?

2. **Inferring** What property of water do you think causes the changes you observed?

3. **Predicting** How would frequent freezing and thawing be likely to affect rocks exposed on the tops of mountains?

Earth's Surface **703**

23.1 Fresh Water

Reading Focus

Key Concepts

- What processes are involved in the water cycle?

- Where is Earth's fresh water found?

Vocabulary

- groundwater
- water cycle
- transpiration
- glacier
- runoff
- tributaries
- watershed
- saturated zone
- water table
- permeable
- aquifer
- impermeable

Reading Strategy

Building Vocabulary Make a table like the one below that includes all the vocabulary terms for the section. As you read, add definitions.

Vocabulary Term	Definition
Groundwater	a. _____?_____
Water cycle	b. _____?_____
Transpiration	c. _____?_____

How would you describe Earth's surface? Would you mention mountains and valleys, or cities and farms? Most people would describe the landscape. But if you could look at Earth from space, you would see that most of its surface—about 71 percent— is covered with water. For this reason, Earth is sometimes called the "water planet." For billions of years, the presence of water has shaped the geology and biology of Earth's surface.

The temperature range on Earth allows water to occur in three states: liquid, solid, and gas. As shown in Figure 1, most of Earth's water is the salt water found in the oceans. Only about three percent of Earth's water is fresh. Most of this fresh water occurs as ice and snow in Earth's high mountains and polar regions. Most of Earth's liquid fresh water is in the form of **groundwater,** the water found underground within cracks and between particles of rock and soil. Smaller amounts of fresh water are found in lakes and streams and as water vapor or clouds in the atmosphere.

Earth's Water

Oceans
97.2%

Glaciers
2.1%

Other
0.7%
(including water vapor, groundwater, lakes, and rivers)

Figure 1 Earth is the only planet with liquid water at its surface. **Using Graphs** *What percentage of Earth's water can be found in glaciers?*

The Water Cycle

Water moves among the oceans, atmosphere, and land in a cycle that covers the entire surface of Earth and even extends below the ground. This continuous movement of water, called the **water cycle,** is shown in Figure 2. **The water cycle is made up of several processes, including evaporation, transpiration, condensation, precipitation, and the eventual return of flowing water to the ocean.** The energy of sunlight and the force of gravity power the water cycle.

Evaporation Solar energy causes water on Earth's surface to evaporate. Recall that evaporation is the process that changes a liquid into a gas. Sunlight heats water and causes it to change into water vapor in the air. This warm, moist air expands and rises, carrying the water vapor higher into the atmosphere. Most evaporation occurs over the ocean and large lakes. Smaller amounts of water evaporate from streams, ponds, and other sources. Some water vapor also enters the atmosphere when it is released from the leaves of trees and other plants in a process called **transpiration.**

Condensation Water vapor does not stay in the atmosphere for long. As warm air rises, it expands and cools. Because colder air can hold less water vapor than warm air, condensation occurs. In condensation, water vapor forms droplets on small particles in the air. At lower temperatures, ice crystals form. Billions of these droplets or ice crystals make up clouds.

Precipitation When the water droplets or ice crystals in clouds get too heavy, gravity causes them to fall to the ground as precipitation—rain, snow, sleet, hail, or freezing rain. Worldwide, the rates of evaporation and precipitation are balanced.

The Water Cycle

Condensation

Precipitation

Transpiration

Evaporation

Runoff

Groundwater

Quick Lab

Modeling the Water Cycle

Procedure

1. Place 100 mL of water in a 250-mL beaker. Cover the beaker with an evaporating dish or a large watch glass.

2. Put the beaker on a hot plate. **CAUTION** *Be careful not to spill the water.* Fill the evaporating dish with ice.

3. Turn the hot plate on to medium. Observe the contents of the beaker for 10 minutes. Record your observations. Be sure to turn off the hot plate.

Analyze and Conclude

1. **Using Models** What source of energy drives the water cycle in your model? What energy source does this correspond to in Earth's water cycle?

2. **Using Models** What is the effect of the ice in your model? What part of the water cycle does the ice help to model?

3. **Predicting** As water evaporates, what will happen to the concentration of any substances dissolved in the water? How does evaporation affect the concentration of salts in the ocean?

Figure 2 Water is constantly moving through the water cycle. **Interpreting Diagrams** *In which step of the water cycle is liquid water converted to water vapor?*

Figure 3 The Mississippi River watershed covers most of the central United States.
Interpreting Maps *Name two tributary rivers that flow into the Mississippi River.*

KEY

—— Watershed boundary

0 km   500
0 miles   500

Completing the Cycle A single molecule of water moves between the surface and atmosphere many times. About 90 percent of the water that evaporates from the oceans falls back into the oceans. Most precipitation that falls on land quickly returns to the atmosphere through evaporation and transpiration. Much of the remaining water seeps into the soil as groundwater or becomes frozen in glaciers. A **glacier** is a large mass of moving ice and snow on land. Some water that falls on land flows into streams before it returns to the ocean.

Fresh Water

Only a small portion of the water on Earth exists as fresh water. Fresh water is relatively free of minerals and salts. ⬤ **A small portion of Earth's fresh water is located in the atmosphere, streams, and lakes. Most is located in groundwater and glaciers.**

The Atmosphere A tiny percentage of Earth's fresh water is found in the atmosphere in the form of water vapor or clouds. Water enters the atmosphere by evaporation, mostly from the oceans. Water vapor stays in the atmosphere for just a short time—a few hours or a few days—before it falls to the surface as precipitation.

Streams and Rivers Streams and rivers contain even less fresh water than the atmosphere. However, a great deal of water passes through streams, making them very important in shaping the surface of the land.

When rain falls on land, much of it enters the ground, but some becomes runoff. **Runoff** is water that flows over Earth's surface. Runoff and some groundwater flows into streams. A stream is any natural channel of flowing water. Streams flow together to form a network, called a river system, that resembles a tree. There is no clear distinction between a large stream and a river. A major river has many smaller streams, called **tributaries,** that flow into it. Tributaries collect runoff from the surrounding land and channel it into rivers.

The area of land that contributes water to a river system is called a **watershed.** Watersheds, also called drainage basins, can be small or large. For example, the Mississippi River watershed drains most of the central United States. As you can see in Figure 3, this watershed extends from the Rocky Mountains in the west to the Appalachian Mountains in the east.

Ponds and Lakes Ponds and lakes form in depressions in the land. Lakes form in large, deep depressions. Ponds, like the one in Figure 4, form in smaller depressions and tend to be smaller and shallower than lakes. Both lakes and ponds usually drain into streams.

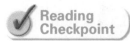 **Reading Checkpoint** *What is the difference between a pond and a lake?*

Water Beneath the Surface About a quarter of all fresh water is groundwater. Close to the surface, the pore spaces in rock and soil are filled with air. Deeper below the surface is the **saturated zone,** a region where the pore spaces are entirely filled with groundwater. The top of the saturated zone is called the **water table.** Look at Figure 5 to see the saturated zone and the water table. The shape of the water table is usually similar to the ground surface above it. Water flows slowly from high elevations of the water table to low elevations. Lakes and streams are usually found where the ground is below the water table. The level of the water table rises and falls, depending in part on the amount of rainfall. During droughts, the water table can drop significantly.

Water flows more easily through some rocks than others. A rock is **permeable** if water can easily pass through it. Rocks like sandstone and limestone are permeable. A permeable rock layer that is saturated with water is called an **aquifer.** In many parts of the world, people rely on aquifers as a source of water for drinking and for agriculture. They can withdraw water from an aquifer by drilling a well below the water table. Aquifers are refilled, or recharged, as rainwater seeps into them.

Rocks are **impermeable** if water cannot easily pass through them. Shale and unbroken granite are examples of impermeable rock. In places where an impermeable rock layer is exposed on a hillside, water may seep to the surface. Groundwater in loose rock or soil above the impermeable layer flows out of the hillside as a spring.

Figure 4 Ponds like this one form when water collects in small, shallow depressions. Many ponds support lush plant growth and animal life.

Figure 5 Groundwater makes up about one quarter of all fresh water. In the saturated zone, groundwater flows in the pore spaces in underground rock. **Interpreting Diagrams** *What is the source of the water in a spring?*

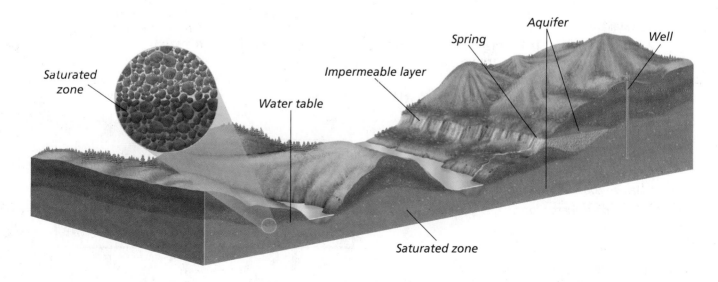

Saturated zone

Water table

Impermeable layer

Spring

Aquifer

Well

Saturated zone

Glaciers and Icebergs Glaciers form in areas where more snow falls than melts each year. As snows build up, the weight of the snow presses on the layers below, changing them to ice. When the weight of the snow is great enough, glaciers begin to flow slowly downhill. Ice is added at the top of the glacier through snowfall. Ice is removed from the glacier by melting, sublimation, and the formation of icebergs. Recall that sublimation is the process of converting a solid directly into a gas.

Icebergs are large pieces of ice that break off when a glacier reaches the ocean. Many icebergs drift great distances from glaciers each year, creating a hazard to ships and ocean drilling platforms. Icebergs eventually melt as they drift into warmer water.

Figure 6 Icebergs are formed when a piece of a glacier breaks off into the ocean. Although this iceberg may drift thousands of kilometers in the salty ocean, it is made of fresh water.

For: Activity on glaciers
Visit: PHSchool.com
Web Code: ccc-3231

Fresh Water Resources As the number of people on Earth increases, the limited supply of fresh water is becoming increasingly important. Nearly a billion people already go to sleep thirsty each night due to insufficient or inadequate water supplies. People in some parts of the world rely on groundwater aquifers that are drying up. Other people depend on runoff from glaciers that are melting. Some rivers, such as the once-mighty Colorado River, rarely make it to the ocean because most of the water is used by humans. One solution, though expensive, is to make fresh water from ocean salt water in a process called desalination.

Section 23.1 Assessment

Reviewing Concepts

1. What are five major processes that move water through Earth's environment?
2. Identify five places where fresh water can be found on Earth. In what two places is most of it located?
3. What energy source powers the water cycle?
4. Starting with runoff, describe the flow of water through a watershed.
5. What is the water table?
6. How do permeable and impermeable rock layers contribute to the formation of a spring?
7. How do icebergs form?

Critical Thinking

8. **Applying Concepts** What might cause a well that draws water from an aquifer to run dry? In your answer, refer to the parts of the groundwater system.
9. **Predicting** How would the path of a water molecule moving through the water cycle be different in Antarctica than in Brazil?

Connecting Concepts

Buoyancy Use what you learned about buoyancy in Section 13.3 to explain why icebergs float very low in ocean water.

23.2 Weathering and Mass Movement

Reading Focus

Key Concepts
- What are the agents of erosion?
- What causes mechanical and chemical weathering?
- What factors affect the rate at which rocks weather?
- What force causes mass movement?

Vocabulary
- erosion
- weathering
- mechanical weathering
- abrasion
- chemical weathering
- mass movement

Reading Strategy
Concept Map As you read, draw a concept map showing the key factors that affect the rate of weathering.

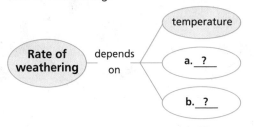

Imagine walking through a pine forest in southern Utah. Suddenly your trail twists, leading you to the edge of a canyon. The curved end of the canyon is shaped like a huge football stadium. But instead of cheering sports fans, this stadium is full of strange columns of rock in yellow, brilliant orange, and rusty red. You are looking at Bryce Canyon, which is famous for its fantastic rock formations, called "hoodoos." The hoodoos are made of different types of sedimentary rock.

Millions of years ago, what is now Bryce Canyon was solid layers of rock. Very slowly, much of this rock was broken down and worn away until only the hoodoos were left standing.

Erosion

Bryce Canyon formed by **erosion,** the process that wears down and carries away rock and soil. Erosion cuts canyons through solid rock and wears away the cliffs above beaches.

Erosion is the destructive process that has shaped Earth's surface over hundreds of millions of years. **Erosion acts through weathering, the force of gravity, and through the movement of streams, groundwater, glaciers, wind, and waves.** Over time, erosion breaks down even the tallest mountains. The end product of erosion is sediment. Recall that sediment is composed of particles of rock and soil and the remains of living things.

Figure 7 Incredible rock formations called hoodoos can be seen at Bryce Canyon National Park in Utah.

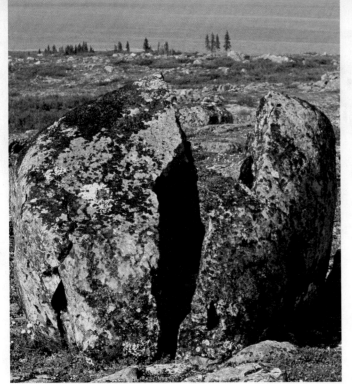

Weathering

Erosion starts with weathering. **Weathering** is the process by which rocks are chemically altered or physically broken down into fragments at or near Earth's surface. 🔑 **There are two forms of weathering: mechanical and chemical. They cause rocks to disintegrate or decompose.**

Mechanical Weathering Under the right conditions, even the hardest rock can be broken into smaller pieces. **Mechanical weathering** is the process of physically breaking rock into smaller fragments. Mechanical weathering occurs through frost wedging, abrasion, growth of plant roots, and other processes.

The most common form of mechanical weathering is frost wedging, shown in Figure 8. When water freezes to form ice, the water expands. This expansion pries open any cracks that the water has seeped into. Frost wedging is an important cause of weathering in mountains, where water often freezes at night and melts during the day. Frost wedging pries rocks apart a little bit every night. If you live in a region that has cold winters, you may see how frost wedging damages roads. Many of the potholes that form in roads during winter are the result in part of frost wedging.

Another form of mechanical weathering, called **abrasion,** occurs when rocks scrape or grind against one another. For example, abrasion occurs when sand carried by water or wind causes bits of rock to break off as if they were being sandblasted.

Mechanical weathering also occurs in other ways. Plant roots can grow into cracks in a rock. Roots exert a powerful force that can slowly pry the rock apart. In another form of weathering, erosion removes material from the surface of a mass of rock, reducing pressure on the rock that remains. This release of pressure allows the rock to expand, causing the outside of the rock to crack and flake off like layers of pastry.

Chemical Weathering **Chemical weathering** is a process in which rock is broken down by chemical reactions. Chemical weathering involves chemical reactions that dissolve the minerals making up rock or change them into new minerals. Over time, the effects of chemical weathering can be dramatic. Pits or holes may form in the rock surface. Eventually, the rock crumbles and disintegrates.

Water is the main agent of chemical weathering. Water is an effective solvent. All minerals dissolve in water, though most do so very slowly.

Figure 8 When water expands to form ice, it can pry open cracks in rock. This is called frost wedging. **Classifying** *Is frost wedging a form of mechanical weathering or chemical weathering?*

For: Links on weathering
Visit: www.SciLinks.org
Web Code: ccn-3232

Chemical weathering also occurs because rain is slightly acidic. Water and carbon dioxide naturally combine to form carbonic acid. The carbonic acid in rainwater dissolves many minerals, such as calcite. The statue of the lion in Figure 9 has been weathered by carbonic acid in rain. Carbonic acid and water react with other minerals, such as the feldspar in granite, to produce clay minerals.

Another type of chemical weathering, the rusting of minerals that are rich in iron, involves oxidation. This results in the formation of new minerals that often have a red or brown color, such as the rusted bicycle in Figure 9.

Reading Checkpoint *What is the main agent of chemical weathering?*

Rates of Weathering

The rate at which mechanical and chemical weathering take place depends on three main factors: temperature, the availability of water, and the type of rock. Chemical weathering occurs more rapidly in places with high temperatures and abundant rainfall. These conditions generally speed up chemical reactions. For example, granite weathers slowly in cool regions, but more rapidly in regions that are hot and wet. Mechanical weathering occurs faster in places where temperature conditions frequently alternate between freezing and thawing.

The rate of weathering also depends upon the kind of rock that is exposed at the surface. Some rocks, such as limestone and marble, undergo rapid chemical weathering. These rocks are composed primarily of calcite, a mineral that reacts readily with carbonic acid. One of the tombstones in Figure 10 shows the effects of chemical weathering on marble. In contrast, the other tombstone is made of slate, which is composed of minerals, such as quartz and mica, that are much more resistant to chemical weathering than calcite.

Figure 9 In chemical weathering, rock is broken down by chemical reactions. **A** One form of chemical weathering occurs through oxidation. Iron-rich minerals become rusted like this old bicycle. **B** Chemical weathering also occurs when rainwater dissolves or reacts with the minerals in rocks, as with this statue of a lion.

Figure 10 Different rocks weather at different rates. Even though the slate tombstone (right) is older, it is much less weathered than the marble one (left). **Inferring** *What type of weathering was likely responsible for wearing away the lettering on the marble tombstone?*

Figure 11 Creep can be caused by the alternate freezing and thawing of water in soil. Slumping often occurs when soil that is rich in clay is soaked by water.
Predicting *How would the steepness of the slope of the hillside affect the amount of creep or slumping?*

Creep

Slumping

Mass Movement

Once weathering loosens particles of rock, the particles, or sediment, do not stay in the same place. **Mass movement** is the downward movement of rock and soil due to gravity. ◔ **Through the process of mass movement, gravity moves loose material down a slope.** There are several types of mass movement.

Landslides The rapid movement of large amounts of rock and soil is a landslide. Landslides often occur after heavy rains or after earthquakes loosen materials on a steep slope. Landslides that occur on the sides of mountains can destroy entire towns.

Mudflows Rapid mass movements of soil and other sediment mixed with water are called mudflows. Mudflows tend to occur in areas where fine sediment has collected in thick layers. When it rains, water loosens the sediment and increases its weight. After a heavy rainfall, the sediment mixed with water washes down the slope.

Creep Creep occurs when soil gradually moves down a slope. Creep often occurs because of the formation of ice. Each time the ground freezes, the soil expands outward. When the ground thaws, the soil moves a small distance downhill. Creep, shown in Figure 11, happens so slowly that it's hard to notice. But over time the results of creep become evident.

Slumping Slumping occurs when weak layers of soil or rock suddenly move downslope as a single unit. Gravity acting on water-saturated soil and rock causes slumping. Slumping often leaves a curved scar.

Section 23.2 Assessment

Reviewing Concepts

1. ◔ What is erosion? List five agents of erosion.
2. ◔ How are mechanical weathering and chemical weathering similar? How do they differ?
3. ◔ What three factors are most significant in determining the rate at which rocks weather?
4. ◔ How does gravity cause erosion?
5. Identify three processes that cause mechanical weathering.
6. What is the role of rainwater in chemical weathering?

Critical Thinking

7. **Predicting** Would you expect chemical weathering to occur more rapidly in a desert or in a rainforest? Explain.
8. **Relating Cause and Effect** What conditions can cause landslides and mudflows?

Connecting Concepts

Chemical and Physical Changes Use what you learned in Chapter 2 to classify each of the following as a chemical or physical change: a cracked sidewalk, a rusty nail, a hard-to-read marble tombstone.

23.3 Water Shapes the Land

Reading Focus

Key Concepts

- What is the most important factor influencing the ability of a stream to cause erosion?
- What features are formed by surface water erosion?
- What features are deposited by running water?
- What causes groundwater erosion?

Vocabulary

- deposition
- saltation
- flood plain
- meander
- oxbow lake
- alluvial fan
- delta
- stalactite
- stalagmite
- sinkhole

Reading Strategy

Concept Map As you read, draw a concept map showing how moving water shapes the land. Begin with the map below.

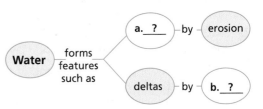

The Mississippi River is like an enormous convoy of dump trucks. Every year it carries more than 300 million tons of sediment to the ocean. This amount of sediment would fill a line of dump trucks wrapped nearly three times around Earth! This sediment has been washed away from the surface of the land. As mountains are made by volcanoes or the motions of tectonic plates, erosion begins to wear them away.

The primary force of erosion is gravity. Gravity pulls sediment and water downhill. The end result of erosion is the deposition of sediment. **Deposition** is the process in which sediment is laid down in new locations.

Most sediment is moved and deposited by flowing water. Flowing water is the major agent of erosion responsible for shaping Earth's surface. Everywhere you look on land, there are features formed by water erosion and deposition.

Figure 12 Streams play an important role in the process of erosion. This stream has cut a deep channel in the soil. The stream banks collapse in mass movement. The soil is then carried away by the stream as sediment.

Forming Sedimentary Layers

Materials

clay; gravel; sand; small dish; tall, narrow jar with cover; tablespoon; clock or watch

Procedure

1. Crumble the clay into a fine powder over a small dish.

2. Fill the jar three quarters full of water. Add one spoonful each of gravel, sand, and clay.

3. Put the cover on the jar tightly and invert the jar several times. Then, place the jar on a flat surface and record the time.

4. For 5 minutes, observe the layers of sediment as they pile up on the bottom of the jar. Record what you observe.

5. Observe the appearance of the water in the jar. Record your observations.

Analyze and Conclude

1. **Observing** In what order did the sediment layers form?

2. **Inferring** Why did the water look the way it did after the sediment layers formed?

3. **Using Models** Was the water in the jar similar to the water in a lake or the water in a fast-moving river? Explain your answer.

4. **Predicting** Would the order of the sediment layers be different if you had stirred the water as the layers accumulated? Under what circumstances would this happen in nature?

Running Water Erodes the Land

Water from rain or melted snow may soak into the ground, evaporate, or flow over the surface as runoff. Erosion begins when runoff carries small particles of soil downhill. Runoff gradually forms small channels in the soil. These channels join together to form larger channels called gullies. As water flows down a hillside through gullies, the water can erode large quantities of soil. Gullies, in turn, flow together to form streams. Unlike gullies, streams flow year-round, except in dry areas or during droughts.

Streams continue the process of erosion by transporting sediment, as shown in Figure 13. Most of the sediment in streams is carried in suspension, in which tiny sediment grains move along with the water. Larger particles of sediment slide, roll, or bounce along the bottom of a stream. The process of particles bouncing along a stream bottom is called **saltation.** During floods, a fast-moving river can move boulders the size of a small car. A large amount of sediment is also carried in solution. Faster streams carry more sediment, which increases abrasion.

Figure 13 Small grains of sediment are carried in suspension by a stream. Large grains move by sliding or rolling, and medium-sized grains move by saltation. Material is also carried in dissolved form. **Predicting** *How might the speed of the stream affect the amount and size of particles it can carry?*

Direction of flow

Suspended sediment is carried by flowing water.

Dissolved sediment moves with flowing water.

Large particles are pushed or rolled along the streambed.

Medium-sized particles move by saltation.

Waterfall

V-shaped valley

Meander

Oxbow lake

Sediment

River mouth

🔑 **A stream's ability to erode depends mainly on its speed.** The water in a mountain stream moves quickly because it is flowing down a steep slope. Fast streams carry more sediment than slow streams of equal size. Fast streams can also carry large sediment grains. As a stream flows toward the sea, its slope decreases. This can make the stream move more slowly, causing larger sediments to settle on the stream bottom.

Features Formed by Water Erosion

Erosion by flowing water reshapes entire watersheds—all the land along and between streams and rivers. 🔵 **Water erosion forms V-shaped valleys, waterfalls, meanders, and oxbow lakes.** Figure 14 shows the features formed along the course of a river.

V-Shaped Valleys Near a stream's source, the stream flows fast as it plunges down steep slopes. As a stream erodes the rock of its streambed, it causes the valley's sides to become steeper. Mass movement on the stream slopes causes a V-shaped valley with sharply angled sides to form.

V-shaped valleys often contain rapids and waterfalls. A waterfall may develop where a stream crosses rock layers that differ in hardness. The harder layers resist erosion, forming the top of the waterfall. The softer rock layers downstream are worn away, leaving the cliff over which the waterfall tumbles.

 Reading Checkpoint *How do waterfalls form?*

Figure 14 As a river winds its way from the mountains to the ocean, it changes the surrounding landscape through erosion and deposition.
Comparing and Contrasting *Which features formed by river erosion typically form near a river's source?*

For: Articles on Earth's surface: weathering, erosion, and deposition
Visit: PHSchool.com
Web Code: cce-3233

Figure 15 Rivers often form winding meanders across their flood plain. This photo shows an oxbow lake in Montana's Blackfoot River Valley.

Figure 16 Alluvial fans and deltas form from sediment deposited by moving water. **A** This alluvial fan in Death Valley, California, formed from sediment deposited when a mountain stream reached flat land. **B** When a large river empties into the ocean, the deposited sediment often forms a delta.

Flood Plains Where a river or stream crosses gently sloping land, a flood plain forms. A **flood plain** is the flat area along a stream that is entirely covered only during times of flood. As a river flows across its flood plain, it deposits sediment, making the flood plain flat. Over time, this sediment builds up into long, low ridges called natural levees. These natural levees help prevent a river from spilling over its banks. During very large floods, however, a river may overflow its levees and erosion may further widen the valley.

Where a river curves slightly, the water on the outside of the curve moves more rapidly than the water on the inside. Fast-moving water causes more erosion. Therefore, the river tends to remove soil from the outside of the curve. Sediment is deposited on the inside of the curve, where water moves more slowly. Over time, this process forms a loop-like bend in the river called a **meander.**

Sometimes during a flood, the river erodes through a narrow neck of land at the base of a meander and forms a new path. Sediments build up along the new channel, cutting the old meander off from the rest of the river. The result is a separate, curved lake, called an **oxbow lake.** Figure 15 shows an oxbow lake formed in the Blackfoot River Valley.

Features Formed by Water Deposition

As a stream or river slows down, it begins to deposit sediment. The slower water cannot carry larger particles of sediment, so these particles fall to the bottom first. As the water slows down even more, smaller particles of sediment are deposited. **Features deposited by flowing water include alluvial fans and deltas.**

As a stream flows out of the mountains and onto the plains, it slows down and sediment settles out. The result is a fan-shaped deposit of sediment on land called an **alluvial fan.** As shown in Figure 16, alluvial fans often grow into thick deposits of sediment.

When a stream flows into a lake or an ocean, the water slows down. The sediment that the stream was carrying is deposited in the form of a delta. A **delta** is a mass of sediment deposited where a river enters a large body of water. Some deltas have a roughly triangular shape.

Groundwater Erosion

Erosion and deposition occur below ground as well as at the surface. ◯ **The processes of chemical weathering causes much groundwater erosion, including the formation of caves and sinkholes.** Recall that carbon dioxide in the air combines with rainwater to form carbonic acid. As the acidic rainwater moves down through the ground, it reacts with some rocks and may become more acidic.

Limestone easily erodes away through this process, forming caves, or caverns. Most caves are small, narrow passages, but some are hundreds of feet high and wide. Caves usually form when they are in the saturated zone, below the water table. When the water table drops, the water flows downward, leaving dry caves like the one in Figure 17.

Sometimes water drips into the cavern from the rock layers above, carrying dissolved minerals. When this mineral-laden water reaches the air of the cave, some of the dissolved carbon dioxide escapes and the minerals are left behind. If the water drips from the cavern ceiling, an icicle-like formation called a **stalactite** (stuh LAK tyt) grows. If the water drips down to the floor, a pillar of minerals called a **stalagmite** (stuh LAG myt) forms.

If erosion weakens a layer of limestone, entire portions of the ground can suddenly collapse. The resulting hole is called a **sinkhole.** Areas of the southern and central United States have many sinkholes. Sinkholes can appear suddenly, swallowing buildings and roads.

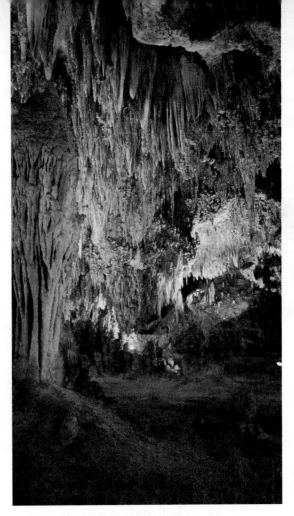

Figure 17 Carlsbad Caverns in New Mexico contain spectacular formations, such as the stalactites and stalagmites shown here.

Section 23.3 Assessment

Reviewing Concepts

1. ◯ What is the major factor that affects the ability of a stream to erode land?

2. ◯ As a stream erodes the land, what features are likely to form in steep areas? What features form in more level areas?

3. ◯ Compare and contrast deltas and alluvial fans.

4. ◯ What process forms caves and sinkholes?

5. What force provides the energy for the erosion caused by running water?

Critical Thinking

6. **Applying Concepts** What determines how much sediment flowing water can carry?

7. **Relating Cause and Effect** How does an oxbow lake form?

8. **Comparing and Contrasting** What is the difference between a stalactite and a stalagmite?

Writing in Science

Describing a Process Imagine that you are a particle of sediment on a mountaintop. Write a paragraph describing your journey to the ocean. (*Hint:* Be sure to mention at least three steps in the transportation of sediment.)

Human Impact on the Environment

Many natural processes, including weathering and erosion, change the shape of the landscape. But there is another powerful agent of geologic change—people! The activities of humans have a great impact on the natural forces that shape Earth's surface. For example, acid rain caused by air pollution increases erosion rates. Humans also change the course of rivers, which can affect natural flooding patterns.

People also shape the land directly through mining and construction. For example, about 12,000 kilograms of minerals are removed from the ground each year for each person in the United States. We also dig up the land to make room for new homes, carve up the land with roads, and pave it over with parking lots. In fact, the amount of land in the U.S. that is covered with roads and parking lots is larger than the size of the state of Georgia; the amount of land developed into towns and cities is larger than the size of the state of California.

The Viewpoints

Reduce Human Activites

Proponents of reducing human activities that impact the land argue that humans have shaped the lands to their own needs, sometimes with extreme consequences. More than a third of land surface on Earth not covered with ice is now used to raise or grow food for people. We continue to change forests to fields and wetlands to housing developments.

Humans are now altering the land surface faster than any other natural process. The human population has doubled in the time since we landed space probes on the moon. Unless human activities are reduced, the surface of the earth will soon bear no resemblance to the lands of our ancestors. We need to reduce the impacts on the land before the damage can't be reversed.

Human Activities Are "Natural"

Throughout geologic history, the surfaces of the land have changed drastically, sometimes catastrophically. Proponents of continuing humans activities unabated point out that these activities are similar to the geologic processes that have greatly altered Earth's surface. Humans are part of nature too.

Earth, as we know it, is not the way it has always been. During the last Ice Age, 15,000 years ago, much of North America was covered with thick ice. Rising sea levels during warm periods flooded regions of the continents with shallow oceans. The rate of human change to the land is fast, but not as fast as that of volcanic eruptions and asteroid impacts that have changed Earth. The impact of human activity is only a small part of the natural processes that change the land.

Research and Decide

1. **Defining the Issue** In your own words, explain the major issues involved in whether or not humans should reduce the impacts they have on the land.

2. **Analyzing the Viewpoints** What risks to the land are posed by human activities? What are the benefits to the land?

3. **Forming Your Opinion** Should there be laws to reduce human changes to the land? What criteria would you use to make such decisions? Give reasons for your opinions.

4. **Persuasive Writing** Choose one way that humans are changing the land. Suppose your state's senator is going to vote on this issue in Congress. Write a letter to your senator presenting your position on this issue.

For: Articles on forces that shape Earth's surface
Visit: PHSchool.com
Web Code: cce-3233

23.4 Glaciers and Wind

Reading Focus

Key Concepts
- How do glaciers form?
- What landscape features are created by glacial erosion and deposition?
- What are the effects of wind erosion and deposition?

Vocabulary
- continental glacier
- valley glacier
- plucking
- cirques
- till
- moraines
- deflation
- dunes
- loess

Reading Strategy
Sequencing Copy the flowchart below. As you read, complete it to show how a glacier forms and moves, and how it erodes and deposits sediment. Add more steps to the chart if necessary.

Snow is compacted to form glacial ice. → a. _____? → b. _____?

Today, the city of Chicago, Illinois, is one of America's largest and busiest cities. But about 15,000 years ago, the land that is now Chicago was buried under a huge glacier more than one kilometer thick! At that time, an enormous ice sheet covered much of the midwestern and northeastern United States and almost all of Canada. That ice sheet changed the landscape of a large portion of North America.

How Glaciers Form and Move

Glaciers form in places where more snow falls than melts or sublimates. As the layers of snow pile up, the weight on the underlying snow increases. Eventually, this weight packs the snow so tightly that glacial ice is formed.

Even though glaciers may appear to be stationary, they are constantly moving. The force of gravity pulls the ice downhill. The ice flows slowly, like honey dripping down a spoon. Sometimes the pressure is great enough to melt the ice at the base of the glacier. This melting can aid the motion of the glacier, with the ice sliding along the bottom. Like a river, a glacier flows fastest in the middle and slowest along the sides.

There are two types of glaciers: continental glaciers and valley glaciers. A **continental glacier** is a thick sheet of ice that covers a huge area, such as a continent or large island. Most of Earth's fresh water is frozen in the continental glaciers that cover Antarctica and Greenland. A glacier that occurs in a high mountain valley is called a **valley glacier.** Like the glacier in Figure 18, a valley glacier usually begins near a mountain peak and winds down through a valley formed originally by a stream.

Figure 18 This valley glacier in Alaska has bands that look like ripples. The dark bands, which include rock debris, show the glacier's slower growth in summer. The light bands form in the winter.
Interpreting Photos *Which part of the glacier moves faster, its center or its sides?*

Glacial Erosion and Deposition

Though glaciers move much more slowly than rivers, they are very effective at eroding and depositing sediment. This is because glaciers tear away the underlying rock as they move. Glaciers erode rock through abrasion and plucking. In **plucking,** shown in Figure 19, glacial ice widens cracks in bedrock beneath the glacier. Pieces of loosened rock are then frozen to the bottom of the glacier, which carries them away. The pieces of rock that are stuck to the bottom and sides of the glacier act like sandpaper. As the glacier moves, it scrapes the bedrock and soil under it and along its sides.

Figure 19 As a glacier moves downhill, it loosens and lifts pieces of rock from the ground underneath in a process known as plucking. **Predicting** *What evidence of plucking would you expect to find after a glacier has melted?*

Features Formed by Glacial Erosion

Glaciers cause **many distinctive features in the landscape, including cirques, horns, U-shaped valleys, and glacial lakes.** Valley glaciers cause erosion high in the mountains where such glaciers begin. For example, a glacier can carve large bowl-shaped valleys out of a mountainside. These valleys, called **cirques,** look as if they were made by a giant ice cream scoop. If several cirques form close together, a ridge may be left between them. If several ridges connect to form a pyramid-shaped peak, the peak is called a horn. The peaks in the Swiss Alps, including the famous Matterhorn, were sculpted by glaciers. Figure 20 shows several of these features.

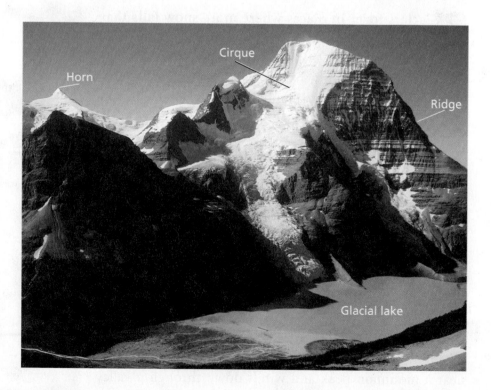

Figure 20 The distinctive landscape near Mount Robson in British Columbia, Canada, was formed by glaciers.

Figure 21 Glaciers can carve out large U-shaped valleys, such as this one in Glacier National Park, Montana.

Glaciers also widen and deepen the valleys through which they flow. When glaciers flow through V-shaped valleys cut by running water, they widen them into U-shaped valleys. Glacial valleys are U-shaped because the moving ice scours the entire valley, eroding rock from the valley's bottom and sides. Glacier National Park, shown in Figure 21, contains many U-shaped valleys that were carved by glaciers.

Unlike valley glaciers, continental glaciers tend to level large surface areas through the scraping and grinding of thick ice. Continental glaciers can enlarge and deepen natural depressions in the surface. These depressions then fill with water when the glaciers retreat. The Great Lakes and the Finger Lakes in New York are examples of glacial lakes that formed by this process.

Features Formed by Glacial Deposition A glacier gathers and transports a huge amount of rock and soil as it moves. ☛ **When a glacier melts, it deposits its load of sediment, creating a variety of landforms.** Glacial sediment is called **till.** Till is an unsorted mixture of sediment containing fragments of many sizes. Giant boulders, gravel, sand, and pulverized rock dust are all found in till. Glaciers deposit till as they melt. The till forms **moraines,** mounds of sediment at the downhill end of the glacier and along its sides. As the How It Works box on page 722 explains, glacial deposits leave many traces in the landscape.

 Reading Checkpoint *What are moraines?*

For: Links on glaciers and landforms
Visit: SciLinks.org
Web Code: ccn-3234

Glacial Deposition

Melting glaciers leave behind a landscape full of glacial deposits. The material from which most of these deposits are created is called till, which is a mixture of different-sized rock particles. In parts of the northern United States, the deposits provide clues to the land's glacial history. **Inferring** *Explain why erratics are often composed of a different type of rock than the surrounding bedrock.*

Kettle lake
As a glacier retreats, large blocks of glacial ice become buried in till and other deposits, where they slowly melt, forming pits in the outwash plain. Water often fills these bowl-shaped depressions, creating kettle lakes.

Drumlins *Drumlins are long teardrop-shaped mounds of till that have been smoothed in the direction of the glacier's flow. Drumlins often occur in groups.*

Eskers *Eskers are ridges made from sand and gravel that were deposited in the bed of a stream that flowed within the glacier.*

Retreating glacier

Glacial lake

Glacial stream

The outwash plain
This broad, flat plain is made of particles of sand and gravel that were deposited from streams that flowed from the glacier.

Erratics *These are boulders that a glacier has carried away from their place of origin.*

Kettle lake

End moraine *An end moraine is a broad, rounded ridge of till marking the farthest point of a glacier's advance.*

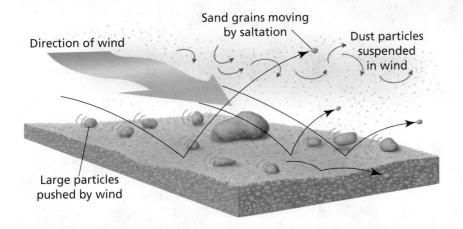

Figure 22 Wind erosion moves particles of different sizes. Small dust particles suspended in the air are blown about by the wind. Heavier sand grains move by saltation. Large particles slide or roll along the surface.

Wind Erosion and Deposition

Wind can also cause erosion and deposition. As with running water, the speed of the wind determines the size of the materials it carries. Slower winds carry only small particles, like dust. Faster winds have more energy and can lift larger particles, such as sand grains. A constant, strong wind can produce a large cloud of dust or sand.

Most wind erosion occurs in the dry areas of the world, such as deserts. Wind erosion also occurs in areas where drought has caused the ground to dry out and the soil is not held in place by plants.

How Wind Causes Erosion As you can see in Figure 22, the wind moves small particles such as sand grains in a series of leaps called saltation. In saltation, wind lifts sand grains a short distance into the air. Gravity pulls the grains back down to the ground, where they collide with and loosen other grains. The result is that the sand grains leap-frog along.

🔑 **Wind erodes the land by deflation and abrasion.** The process of **deflation** occurs when wind picks up and carries away loose surface material. In dry regions where winds are strong, sand and dust are lifted from the surface and carried away. Over time, the surface of the ground is lowered. Larger rocks are left behind, forming a rocky surface that covers much of the land in dry regions.

Recall that abrasion is a type of mechanical weathering. Abrasion by wind occurs in much the same way as abrasion by flowing water. Wind blows sand against other rocks, slowly sandblasting them away and removing the weathered particles.

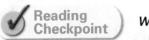 *What is deflation?*

Figure 23 Wind deposits sand in the form of dunes. These large sand dunes are found in the Namib Desert in Africa.

Figure 24 This large dust storm blew through downtown Phoenix, Arizona, in 1999.

Effects of Wind Deposition When wind slows down, it drops the sediment it is carrying. ☞ **Features deposited by wind include sand dunes and loess deposits.** Deposits formed from windblown sand are called **dunes.** Over time, sand dunes can move great distances. A dune moves as the wind picks up sand from the back of the dune and blows it to the front. Sand dunes can take many different forms, depending on wind direction and how much sand is available.

Deposits formed from windblown dust are called **loess** (LES). Loess consists mainly of finely ground particles. The two major sources of loess are deserts and glacial deposits. A dust storm like the one in Figure 24 can transport tons of dust for long distances. Dust from the Sahara Desert in Africa regularly blows across the Atlantic Ocean.

Section 23.4 Assessment

Reviewing Concepts

1. ☞ What conditions are necessary for a glacier to form?

2. ☞ Identify three features caused by glacial erosion.

3. ☞ Describe three features caused by glacial deposition.

4. ☞ What are the two ways that wind erodes particles of rock?

5. ☞ What features can form as wind deposits sediment?

6. What is plucking?

7. How does deflation affect the land surface in dry regions?

8. How do sand dunes form and move?

Critical Thinking

9. **Relating Cause and Effect** How are both glaciers and wind involved in the formation of loess deposits?

10. **Comparing and Contrasting** How is the way wind carries sediment similar to the way a stream carries sediment? How are these processes different? Explain.

Writing in Science

Compare and Contrast Paragraph Write a paragraph comparing how V-shaped valleys and U-shaped valleys are formed. Include an explanation of how a V-shaped valley could turn into a U-shaped valley.

23.5 The Restless Oceans

Oceans surround all of the continents. Earth's ocean waters are divided into four major oceans: the Pacific Ocean, Atlantic Ocean, Indian Ocean, and Arctic Ocean. These oceans also include smaller bodies of water, such as the Gulf of Mexico and the Mediterranean Sea.

Exploring the Ocean

Most of Earth's water exists as salt water in the oceans. Ocean water is a mixture that includes dissolved salts and gases. **Salinity** is the proportion of dissolved salts in water. On average, there are about 35 grams of dissolved salts in each kilogram of ocean water. The most abundant salt in ocean water is table salt, sodium chloride (NaCl).

Salt is added to the oceans by rivers and volcanoes. Rain slowly dissolves salts out of surface rocks. These salts are washed into rivers which then carry them to the ocean. In addition, volcanic eruptions send elements such as sulfur and chlorine into the atmosphere and the oceans. At the same time, salt is removed from seawater by animals and plants as they build hard parts and also by deposition as sediment.

Figure 25 Wave action is the primary means of erosion along coastlines. Here, waves are breaking onto rocks at Cape Kiwanda State Park along the Oregon coast.

Changes With Depth Conditions in the ocean, such as the amount of sunlight, temperature, and pressure, change as you move from the surface to the ocean floor. **Light and temperature decrease with depth, whereas pressure increases.**

Sunlight decreases with depth in the ocean. The deep ocean is totally dark. Light cannot penetrate deeper than about 200 meters.

Water temperature decreases with depth. The top 100 to 500 meters of the ocean are well mixed and relatively warm in the temperate and equatorial zones. Deeper water is much colder and denser. Deep water moves very slowly, and does not interact much with the surface layer.

Pressure increases continuously with depth in the ocean. At a depth of 500 meters, the pressure is about 50 times greater than atmospheric pressure at sea level. Few forms of life can tolerate such great pressures.

The Ocean Floor What would the ocean floor look like if all the water were drained from the oceans? First you would see the **continental shelf.** This gently sloping plain forms an apron of shallow water along the edges of most continents. Beyond the continental shelf, the continental slope descends more steeply to the floor of the deep ocean. In places, you would see deep canyons cutting through the continental shelf and slope.

The ocean floor itself is a vast, flat plain dotted with volcanic peaks. You would also see the mid-ocean ridges winding through the ocean basins, and deep trenches along the edges of some oceanic plates. The deepest point in the ocean is in the Mariana Trench, more than 11 kilometers below sea level. Overall, the oceans have an average depth of 3.8 kilometers!

Figure 26 Kelp forests such as this one off the coast of California occur in coastal waters swept by cold ocean currents. Light can penetrate to the floor of the continental shelf in this region, allowing the long strands of kelp to grow in nutrient-rich waters.

Ocean Currents

Ocean currents, shown in Figure 27, are the patterns of flow in Earth's oceans. Because of these currents, water flows from one ocean to another. Ocean currents are affected by winds, Earth's rotation, and the positions and shapes of the continents.

Surface Currents Have you ever tried to cool a cup of hot chocolate by blowing across it? If you have, then you have imitated the way that winds move currents near the ocean's surface. A **surface current** is a large stream of ocean water that moves continuously in about the same path. **Winds blowing across the surface of the ocean cause the continuous flow of surface currents.**

Global surface currents reflect the effects of wind patterns in the atmosphere. In general, currents of warm water flow away from the equator along the east side of continents. Currents of cold water flow away from the polar regions along the west side of continents. One major current is the Gulf Stream, which carries warm water from the Gulf of Mexico to the North Atlantic Ocean. Figure 28 shows a satellite image of the Gulf Stream. Another is the California current, which carries cool water from the Gulf of Alaska south along the west coast of the United States.

Figure 27 Prevailing wind patterns drive the ocean's surface currents.
Interpreting Maps *What current flows south along the west coast of North America? Is it warm or cold?*

Deep Currents Unlike surface currents, deep currents are not caused by winds. 🔵 **Deep ocean currents are caused by differences in the density of ocean water.** Denser water results from colder temperatures or higher salinity. Because deep ocean currents are affected by density, they are called **density currents.** Density currents are responsible for a slow mixing of water between the surface and deeper ocean. For example, a density current flows south through the Atlantic Ocean. This density current forms near Greenland in an area where very cold, salty water sinks into the deep ocean. Another density current in the Atlantic forms near Antarctica and flows north.

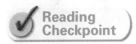 Reading Checkpoint   *What are density currents?*

Figure 28 This satellite image of the Atlantic Ocean shows the Gulf Stream, which carries warm water northward from the Gulf of Mexico toward the British Isles. The image has been enhanced so that the colors indicate water temperature (Red indicates warmer water and blue indicates cooler water.)

Surface wind

Warm surface water

Cold water upwelling

Figure 29 Upwelling of deeper ocean water occurs along some coastlines.
Relating Cause and Effect Why are areas of upwelling often excellent areas for commercial fishing?

Upwelling At certain places in the oceans, water from the deep ocean moves upward toward the surface. The movement of water from the deep ocean to the surface is called **upwelling.** Much upwelling occurs along the western coasts of continents. 🔵 **In upwelling, winds blow warm surface water aside. This allows cold water from the deep ocean to rise and take the place of the warmer water.** You can see how upwelling works in Figure 29. Another major area of upwelling lies along the equator. Here, currents and winds pull surface water on both sides of the equator toward the poles. Upwelling occurs in the strip of ocean where the surface currents move apart.

Upwelling brings nutrients from deep in the ocean to the surface. The nutrients support large populations of algae, which serve as food for tiny ocean animals. These animals, in turn, are eaten by fishes. Areas of upwelling often support large populations of fishes and whales.

Wave Erosion and Deposition

Waves can pound a coastline with a tremendous amount of energy. So it's not surprising that waves are the major cause of erosion along coastlines. On a rocky coast, wave erosion creates cliffs, arches, caves, and tall rock towers called sea stacks, as shown in Figure 30. 🔵 **Two physical processes, hydraulic action and abrasion, are responsible for much wave erosion.** Over time, wave erosion and deposition work together to straighten a coastline.

How Waves Cause Erosion The process of **hydraulic action** occurs when waves pound on cracks in rocks. First, a wave fills a crack with water. Before the water drains from the crack, another wave forces more water into the crack. This pressure causes the crack to get bigger. Waves also compress air as they slam into a cracked rock. This compressed air contributes to wave erosion. Eventually, the rock breaks apart into smaller pieces that are further eroded by waves. Abrasion also breaks up rocks into smaller pieces. The sediment carried by waves acts like sandpaper, rubbing away at the rocks.

Figure 30 Waves produce distinctive geological features.
A A sea cliff with a sea stack and arch in Etretat, France **B** A barrier beach in South Carolina **C** A sand spit along the Red Sea in Egypt

Direction of longshore drift

Movement of sand grains

Direction of incoming waves

Figure 31 Longshore drift can carry sediment great distances along the shore, creating long sandbars or spits that grow parallel to the shoreline.

Sand is continuously eroded and deposited along the shore by waves and currents. **Longshore drift** is the process that moves sand along a shore. Look at Figure 31 to see how longshore drift occurs. Waves carrying sediment approach the shore at an angle. As the waves break, they carry sand up the beach at that angle. The water and sand then flow directly back toward the water. In this way, longshore drift produces a zigzag motion that moves sand great distances along a shore.

Deposition by Currents and Waves The sediment that is eroded from a coastline or brought to the ocean by rivers is also deposited. Currents and waves deposit sediment in bays and inlets as the water slows down. Over time, sediment can collect along the shore. A shoreline covered with sand or other sediment is a beach. In many areas, rivers that discharge into the ocean are the main source of the sand on ocean beaches.

Currents move large amounts of sediment parallel to the shore. When these currents meet a bend in the shoreline, they slow down and deposit the sediment. This deposit is called a spit.

Section 23.5 Assessment

Reviewing Concepts

1. How do temperature and pressure change with depth within the ocean?

2. Compare and contrast how surface currents and density currents form.

3. What causes upwelling?

4. What happens to rock as waves hit the shore?

5. What process moves sand down a coastline?

Critical Thinking

6. **Predicting** El Niño is a weather event in the Pacific Ocean. It pushes warm water over the cold current that flows along the western coast of South America, where upwelling normally occurs. How might El Niño affect the fishing industry in this area?

7. **Developing Hypotheses** A dam is built on a major river that flows into the ocean. Several years later, people observe that nearby ocean beaches have less sand than before. Develop a hypothesis to explain this phenomenon.

Connecting Concepts

Energy Conversion Use what you learned about energy conversion in Section 15.2 to explain how surface currents are produced.

Exploring the Ocean

About 71 percent of Earth's surface is covered by oceans and seas. Within the last century, deep-sea explorations have revealed amazing features of the ocean floor. These include continental slopes, undersea mountains, and the mid-ocean ridges that form between Earth's plates.

Snorkeling
Snorkeling allows great freedom of movement. However, a diver must constantly return to the surface to breathe.

Continental shelf *Continental shelves are gradually sloping zones that extend outward from each of the major land masses.*

Guyot *Some seamounts are guyots—extinct volcanoes with flat tops. Guyots were once islands, but are now below water because the entire ocean floor sinks as it gets older.*

Continental slope *This steep incline extends downward from the edge of a continental shelf.*

Seamount *Seamounts are submarine mountains whose peaks do not break the ocean's surface.*

Abyssal plain *Thick layers of sediment, formed by dust and the remains of microscopic organisms, cover these broad, flat expanses of sea floor.*

SURFACE

AVERAGE DEPTH OF OCEAN: 3.8 km

1 km

2 km

3 km

4 km

(NOT TO SCALE)

B

Deep-sea diver

Surface areas of the ocean (50 m or less in depth) can be explored by scuba divers, who breathe from tanks of compressed air. However, advanced deep sea diving suits allow divers to operate at depths as great as 700 m. The type shown here includes propellors that are operated by the diver's feet.

C

Deep-sea exploration

Submersibles—small, maneuverable submarines with data-collecting equipment—enable researchers to explore the ocean depths. *Alvin* (shown above) can dive to a maximum depth of about 4 km. Scientists aboard *Alvin* discovered the first hydrothermal vents in the Pacific Ocean in 1977. These vents are underwater hot springs located along ocean ridges, where new oceanic crust is forming. The vents spew dark, heated, mineral-rich fluids which support a unique group of organisms.

Going Further

- New technologies allow scientists to discover and explore many sunken ships, including the *Titanic,* Roman trading ships, and pirate vessels. Research how scientists are able to locate and explore such ships. Write a short essay summarizing what you have learned.

Mid-ocean ridge *This line of mountains marks a boundary between diverging tectonic plates. New oceanic crust forms at the mid-ocean ridge.*

Magma

23.6 Earth's History

Reading Focus

Key Concepts

- How do geologists determine the relative and absolute ages of rock layers?
- What forms the basis for the geologic time scale?
- What are the major divisions of Earth's history?

Vocabulary

- fossils
- relative age
- law of superposition
- extinct
- index fossils
- absolute age
- era
- periods
- mass extinction

Reading Strategy

Previewing Copy the table below. Before you read, examine Figures 34 and 36 to help you understand about geologic time. Write at least two questions about them in the table. As you read, write answers to your questions.

Questions on Geologic Time
a. _____ ? _____
b. _____ ? _____

The Grand Canyon slices down nearly two kilometers through many horizontal layers of rock. Each layer formed millions of years ago, as a shallow sea repeatedly flooded this part of North America. The sea slowly filled up with a flat layer of sediment that had eroded from the nearby land. The next time the sea flooded the land, a new, flat sedimentary layer formed on top of the older layer beneath it. As the layers of sediment increased, they slowly changed to rock. At the same time, the remains of living things trapped in the sediment became fossils. **Fossils** are the preserved remains or traces of once living things.

Determining the Age of Rocks

Suppose that a geologist finds a fossil in a sedimentary rock near the rim of the Grand Canyon. Is this fossil older or younger than a fossil found near the canyon bottom? The geologist is trying to determine the relative age of the fossil as well as that of the rock containing it. The **relative age** of a rock is its age compared to the ages of other rocks above or below it in a sequence of rock layers. Figure 33 shows the sequence of rock layers in the Grand Canyon.

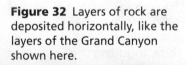

Figure 32 Layers of rock are deposited horizontally, like the layers of the Grand Canyon shown here.

Kaibab-Toroweap limestone

Coconino sandstone

Hermit shale

Supai sandstone

Redwall limestone

Muav limestone

Bright Angel shale

Tapeats sandstone

Vishnu schist

Younger

Older

Colorado River

Figure 33 The walls of the Grand Canyon consist of many different layers of rock.
Interpreting Diagrams *Which of the sedimentary layers shown here is older, the Bright Angel shale or the Tapeats sandstone? Explain your answer.*

The Law of Superposition

Sedimentary rocks form as horizontal layers. Geologists have used this fact to establish a principle for determining the relative ages of rocks. The **law of superposition** states that if rock layers are undisturbed, younger rocks lie above older rocks, and the oldest rocks are at the bottom. 🔑 **Geologists use the law of superposition to determine the relative ages of sedimentary rocks from the sequence of rock layers and the fossils within each layer.** Rock layers often extend over large regions. Geologists have examined sedimentary rocks from locations around the world to develop a relative time scale for many rock layers.

Index Fossils and Relative Dating

Geologists can also determine the relative ages of sedimentary rocks by examining the fossils that are found in them. Most types of organisms preserved as fossils are now extinct. An **extinct** type of organism is one that no longer exists.

Fossils of organisms that are easily identified, occurred over a large area, and lived during a well-defined period of time are called **index fossils.** With index fossils, geologists can determine the relative ages of rocks. If a rock contains examples of an index fossil, then the rock must have formed during the time that that organism lived.

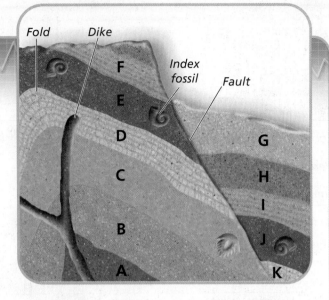

Interpreting Rock Layers

The law of superposition states that in undisturbed beds, younger sedimentary rocks lie on top of older sedimentary layers. But over time, layers of sedimentary rock can change. Deformation can produce faults and folds. Erosion can remove some layers of rock entirely. Igneous dikes may cut across the layers. As you determine the relative ages of rock layers, remember these rules:

- Sedimentary rock layers are horizontal before they deform.

- A fault or dike did not exist when the sedimentary layers formed, so it is younger than the layers it cuts across.

Study the rock layers in the diagram, and then answer the following questions.

1. **Inferring** Which rock layer is older, B or E? J or G?

2. **Analyzing Data** Would a fossil in layer F be older or younger than fossils from layer J?

3. **Inferring** If the dike is 430 million years old, what can you say about the age of layer D?

4. **Drawing Conclusions** Make a table showing the relative ages of all the layers in the diagram, from oldest to youngest.

Radioactive Dating 🔵 Geologists use radioactive dating to **determine the absolute ages of rocks.** A rock's **absolute age** is the time that has passed since the rock formed. When a rock forms, it has a known ratio of radioactive and stable isotopes. Because a radioisotope decays into a stable isotope at a steady rate as the rock ages, scientists can measure this ratio to find the rock's absolute age. Recall from chemistry that the time for half of a radioisotope to decay is called its half-life. Many igneous rocks are very old, so radioisotopes with a very long half-life are used to find their absolute age. A common radioisotope for dating older rocks is potassium-40, which has a half-life of 1.3 billion years.

A Brief History of Earth

Geologists have used information about the relative and absolute ages of rocks to develop a time line for the history of Earth. 🔵 **The geologic time scale is based on the relative ages of rock layers and the use of radioactive dating to find the absolute ages of rocks.** The geologic time scale, shown in Figure 34, is a way of dividing Earth's history.

Figure 34 The geologic time scale shows the major intervals in Earth's history.
Interpreting Diagrams *What three periods make up the Mesozoic Era?*

GEOLOGIC TIME SCALE
Millions of years ago

Earth's history is divided into several large units, called eras. Each **era** is one major stage in Earth's history. An era is further divided into smaller units called **periods.** Eras and periods help scientists locate changes and events in Earth's history.

Some boundaries between eras mark a time when many different kinds of organisms became extinct within a relatively short time. Such an event is called a **mass extinction.** Scientists have developed several theories to explain what caused mass extinctions. These theories include asteroid impacts, volcanic activity, disease, and climate change.

For nearly 4 billion years, changes in Earth's surface, atmosphere, and oceans have effected the development of living things. Living things, in turn, have changed Earth. **The major divisions of Earth's history are Precambrian time and the Paleozoic, Mesozoic, and Cenozoic Eras.**

For: Articles on Earth's history
Visit: PHSchool.com
Web Code: cce-3236

Precambrian Time: 4.6 Billion–542 Million Years Ago

The earliest portion of Earth's history, known as Precambrian time, includes the formation of Earth and the early development of life. At first, Earth's surface was largely molten and was continually bombarded by meteorites. By 4 billion years ago, the forces that cause plate movement were already at work. Soon after, one-celled organisms appeared in the oceans. Tiny photosynthetic organisms took up carbon dioxide from the atmosphere and released oxygen. Later in the Precambrian, simple soft-bodied animals developed. Since soft bodies don't usually form fossils, there are few fossils from Precambrian time.

Paleozoic Era: 542–251 Million Years Ago
Early in the Cambrian period (the first period of the Paleozoic Era), a variety of animals developed in the oceans. Scientists think that some of these animals were related to the clams and worms found in the oceans today. Many other types of early animals, such as those shown in Figure 35, became extinct. But more than 450 million years ago, fishes evolved in the oceans. Plants and animals, including early reptiles, began to live on land. Dense forests of mosses and cone-bearing plants covered much of the land.

At times during the Paleozoic, parts of many continents were flooded by seas. Thick layers of sediment deposited in these seas formed much of the sedimentary rock found on the continents today. During the last period of the Paleozoic Era, the Permian period, the supercontinent Pangaea formed.

Figure 35 During the early Paleozoic Era, life began to evolve into many different forms. This scene shows how life might have looked on the sea floor during the Cambrian Period.

 Reading Checkpoint *When did fishes first appear?*

299	251	200	145	65	23	0	
PERMIAN	TRIASSIC	JURASSIC	CRETACEOUS	PALEOGENE	NEO-GENE		PERIOD
	MESOZOIC			CENOZOIC			ERA

Mesozoic Era: 251–65 Million Years Ago The Mesozoic Era was the time of the dinosaurs. The first dinosaurs appeared about 225 million years ago. About this same time, Pangaea began to break up. The first mammals, which evolved from warm-blooded reptiles, also appeared in the Mesozoic. Many areas had a warm, wet climate. Another major development was the appearance of flowering plants.

All the dinosaurs and many other types of organisms were killed at the end of the Mesozoic Era. What caused this mass extinction?

Figure 36 This spiral diagram provides an overview of Earth's history. Start at the bottom left, which begins with Earth's formation approximately 4.6 billion years ago. Then follow the spiral upward to see many of the major events in the history of life and geology on Earth. **Interpreting Diagrams** *During what era did small mammals first appear?*

Cretaceous

Small mammals appeared (e.g., *Crusafontia*).

Dinosaurs became extinct.

Multicellular soft-bodied animals appeared (e.g., worms and jellyfish).

Shelled invertebrates appeared (e.g., trilobites).

Marine animals and plants flourished.

Ordovician

Cambrian

Precambrian Time

Land plants appeared (e.g., *Cooksonia*).

Photosynthetic organisms appeared (e.g., blue-green algae).

Silurian

Earth formed.

Coral reefs appeared.

Vertebrates appeared (e.g., *Hemicyclapsis*).

More complex types of unicellular life appeared.

Amphibians appeared (e.g., *Ichthyostega*).

The leading hypothesis is that the cause was the impact of one or more large asteroids. Such an impact would have filled the atmosphere with ejected rock and dust and the smoke from enormous fires, blocking out sunlight worldwide. It is possible that volcanic activity at this time had already cooled global climates, worsening the effects of the impact.

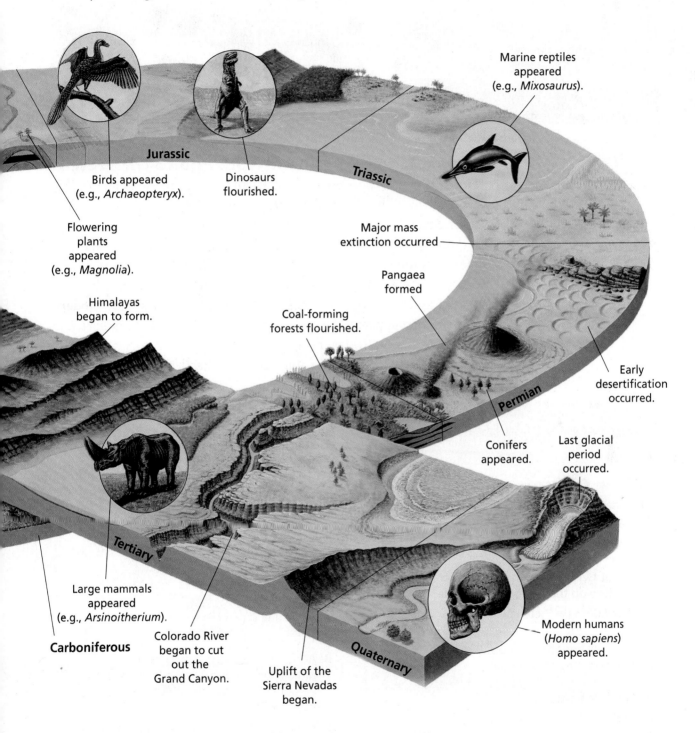

Marine reptiles appeared (e.g., *Mixosaurus*).

Birds appeared (e.g., *Archaeopteryx*).

Dinosaurs flourished.

Jurassic

Triassic

Flowering plants appeared (e.g., *Magnolia*).

Major mass extinction occurred

Pangaea formed

Himalayas began to form.

Coal-forming forests flourished.

Early desertification occurred.

Permian

Conifers appeared.

Last glacial period occurred.

Large mammals appeared (e.g., *Arsinoitherium*).

Tertiary

Carboniferous

Colorado River began to cut out the Grand Canyon.

Uplift of the Sierra Nevadas began.

Quaternary

Modern humans (*Homo sapiens*) appeared.

Figure 37 The two most recent eras of Earth's history are the Mesozoic Era and the Cenozoic Era. **A** During the Mesozoic Era, dinosaurs such as Baryonyx (center) and Brachiosaurus (right) roamed Earth's surface. **B** During the Cenozoic Era the diversity and size of mammals increased greatly.

Cenozoic Era: 65 Million Years Ago to the Present

Since the end of the Mesozoic Era, Earth has been in the Cenozoic Era. During this time, Earth's climate has generally become cooler and drier. Several ice ages have come and gone in the last 5 million years.

Although small mammals existed during the Mesozoic Era, mammals became very diverse and widespread during the Cenozoic Era. Some of these mammals, like those in Figure 37B, were much larger than modern land mammals. About 150,000 years ago, modern humans first appeared in Africa. Since then, humans have migrated to every continent. Today, humans are the dominant form of life on Earth. They have a significant influence on Earth's environments.

Section 23.6 Assessment

Reviewing Concepts

1. What evidence do geologists use to determine the relative age of rocks?

2. How can the absolute age of a rock be determined?

3. What types of information did geologists use to develop the geologic time scale?

4. How does the geologic time scale divide Earth's history?

5. What is one hypothesis about the cause of the dinosaurs' extinction?

Critical Thinking

6. **Inferring** Geologists in two widely separated locations find rocks that contain fossils of an extinct organism that lived for only a brief time. What can the geologists conclude about the ages of the rocks?

7. **Drawing Conclusions** Using radioactive dating, geologists determine that a layer of igneous rock from a lava flow is 60 million years old. What can you conclude about the age of a layer of sedimentary rock that lies just below the igneous rock? Explain.

Math **Practice**

8. A fossil contains 10.0 milligrams of radioactive carbon-14. How much carbon-14 will remain after two half-lives?

9. How long will it take for the amount of potassium-40, which has a half-life of 1.3 billion years, in a rock to decay from 50.0 milligrams to 12.5 milligrams?

Modeling Erosion

Moving water is the major cause of erosion on Earth. In this lab, you will investigate some factors that affect the rate of erosion by moving water.

Problem What are some of the factors that affect the rate of water erosion?

Materials

- metric ruler
- large sheet of cardboard
- plastic wrap
- newspaper
- soil
- blocks
- pencil
- paper cup
- scissors
- drinking straw
- modeling clay
- paper towels
- small rocks

Skills Using Models, Inferring

Procedure

1. On a separate sheet of paper, make a data table with 4 columns and 4 rows. Label the columns Elevation of Cardboard, Slope of Cardboard, Rocks, and Observations.

2. Measure and record the length of the cardboard in centimeters. Wrap the cardboard with plastic wrap to keep it dry.

3. Put several sheets of newspaper on a flat surface. Place cardboard on the newspaper and spread a thin layer of soil over the cardboard.

4. To model a hillside, raise one end of the cardboard about 5 cm from the flat surface by placing blocks under one end.

5. Using a pencil, make a hole in a paper cup 1 cm from the bottom.

6. Cut the straw in half with the scissors and insert the end of one of the halves 2 cm into the hole in the cup.

7. Use modeling clay to seal the hole around the straw. Make sure that the clay forms a tight seal around the straw.

8. Place the cup in the middle of the raised end of the cardboard, so that the straw is pointing downhill as shown.

9. Place your finger over the straw's opening as another student fills the cup with water.

10. Remove your finger. Record your observations in your data table.

11. Clean the cardboard with paper towels and cover it again with soil. Put used soil in the trash.

12. Now use blocks to raise the end of the cardboard 15 cm above the flat surface. Repeat Steps 8 through 11.

13. Lower the end of the cardboard to 5 cm above the flat surface. Repeat Steps 8 through 11 again, but this time place a small rock on the cardboard directly in front of the straw. In your data table, record your observations about how water moves around the rock.

14. Repeat Step 13, but this time place a pile of several small rocks on the cardboard directly in front of the straw. In your data table, record your observations about how water moves around the rocks.

Analyze and Conclude

1. **Observing** Does water erosion create smooth curves or sharp angles?

2. **Analyzing Data** How did increasing the elevation of the cardboard affect the speed of the water?

3. **Calculating** The slope of a hillside is equal to its height divided by the horizontal distance it covers. Using the length of the table under the cardboard and the height it was raised, calculate and record the slope of the model hillside in each row of your data table.

4. **Inferring** What is the relationship between the slope of a hillside and the rate of erosion?

5. **Analyzing Data** Compare the movement of the water with one rock and several rocks in front of the straw. Explain any differences you observed.

Study Guide

23.1 Fresh Water

Key Concepts

- The water cycle is made up of several processes, including evaporation, transpiration, condensation, precipitation, and the eventual return of flowing water to the ocean.
- A small portion of Earth's fresh water is located in the atmosphere, streams, and lakes. Most is located in groundwater and glaciers.

Vocabulary

groundwater, water cycle, transpiration, glacier, runoff, tributaries, watershed, saturated zone, water table, permeable, aquifer, impermeable

23.2 Weathering and Mass Movement

Key Concepts

- Erosion acts through weathering, the force of gravity, and through the movement of streams, groundwater, glaciers, wind, and waves.
- There are two forms of weathering: mechanical weathering and chemical weathering. Both cause rocks to disintegrate.
- The rate at which mechanical and chemical weathering take place depends on three main factors: temperature, the availability of water, and the type of rock.
- Through the process of mass movement, gravity moves loose material down a slope.

Vocabulary

erosion, weathering, mechanical weathering, abrasion, chemical weathering, mass movement

23.3 Water Shapes the Land

Key Concepts

- A stream's ability to erode depends mainly on its speed.
- Water erosion forms V-shaped valleys, waterfalls, flood plains, meanders, and oxbow lakes.
- Features deposited by flowing water include alluvial fans and deltas.
- The process of chemical weathering causes much groundwater erosion, including the formation of caves and sinkholes.

Vocabulary

deposition, saltation, flood plain, meander, oxbow lake, alluvial fan, delta, stalactite, stalagmite, sinkhole

23.4 Glaciers and Wind

Key Concepts

- Glaciers form in places where more snow falls than melts or sublimates.
- Glacial erosion causes many distinctive features in the landscape, such as cirques, horns, U-shaped valleys, and glacial lakes.
- Most till is deposited at the front of a glacier.
- Wind erodes the land by deflation and abrasion.
- Features deposited by wind include sand dunes and loess deposits.

Vocabulary

continental glacier, valley glacier, plucking, cirques, till, moraines, deflation, dunes, loess

23.5 The Restless Oceans

Key Concepts

- Light and temperature decrease with the depth of the ocean, whereas pressure increases.
- Winds blowing across the surface of the ocean cause the continuous flow of surface currents.
- Deep ocean currents are caused by differences in the density of ocean water.
- In upwelling, winds blow warm surface water aside. This allows cold water to rise.
- Two physical processes, hydraulic action and abrasion, are responsible for much wave erosion.

Vocabulary

salinity, continental shelf, surface current, density currents, upwelling, hydraulic action, longshore drift

23.6 Earth's History

Key Concepts

- Geologists use the law of superposition to determine the relative ages of rocks.
- Geologists use radioactive dating to determine the absolute ages of rocks.
- The geologic time scale is based on the relative ages of rock layers and the use of radioactive dating to find the absolute ages of rocks.
- The four major divisions of Earth's history are Precambrian time and the Paleozoic, Mesozoic, and Cenozoic Eras.

Vocabulary

fossils, relative age, law of superposition, extinct, index fossils, absolute age, era, periods, mass extinction

Reviewing Content

Choose the letter that best answers the question or completes the statement.

1. The greatest supply of fresh water on Earth is found in
   a. the oceans.
   b. glaciers.
   c. the atmosphere.
   d. rivers and lakes.

2. The release of water into the atmosphere by plants is called
   a. transpiration.
   b. evaporation.
   c. precipitation.
   d. sublimation.

3. Which of the following is NOT an example of mechanical weathering?
   a. frost wedging
   b. oxidation
   c. plucking
   d. abrasion

4. The type of mass movement that occurs when soil gradually moves down a slope is called (a)
   a. landslide.
   b. mudflow.
   c. creep.
   d. slumping.

5. Which of the following is the most important factor influencing the ability of a stream to erode?
   a. salinity
   b. depth
   c. speed
   d. volume of flow

6. As rivers flow from mountains to the ocean, they tend to
   a. move more quickly.
   b. get narrower.
   c. get steeper.
   d. become less steep.

7. A feature formed by chemical weathering is
   a. a cave.
   b. a dune.
   c. loess.
   d. till.

8. The sediment deposited at the front of a glacier is called a
   a. stalagmite.
   b. slump.
   c. moraine.
   d. meander.

9. Which feature is the result of wind deposition?
   a. horn
   b. delta
   c. sand dune
   d. cirque

10. Absolute ages of rocks are found from
    a. the law of superposition.
    b. the relative order of rock layers.
    c. index fossils.
    d. radioactive dating.

Understanding Concepts

11. Why is less than 1 percent of Earth's water available for human use?

12. Describe the path that one rain drop would take through the water cycle.

13. What is the role of gravity in the water cycle?

14. A simplified diagram of the water cycle is shown below. Identify the process associated with the movement of water in each arrow.

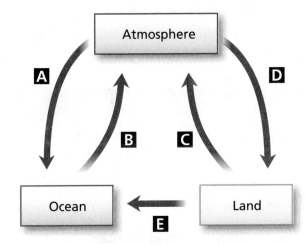

15. Explain how the saturated zone is related to the water table. How might the water table change during a drought?

16. Give one example of mass movement that occurs quickly, and one example of mass movement that occurs slowly.

17. What is saltation?

18. Why are caves most often found in regions where the bedrock is composed of limestone?

19. How can you tell if a mountain valley was formed by a stream or by a glacier?

20. How does the wind-driven process of deflation alter the surface?

21. How are waves responsible for both erosion and deposition?

22. What is an index fossil?

Critical Thinking

23. Hypothesizing The Appalachian Mountains, which stretch from Alabama to Maine, were much higher in the past. Provide an explanation for how these mountains could have become lower.

24. Comparing and Contrasting What is the difference between a valley glacier and a continental glacier? How are they similar?

25. Designing an Experiment Design an experiment that could be used to track ocean currents.

26. Inferring Why are there few fossils from the Precambrian Era?

Analyzing Data

The chart below represents the radioactive decay of 100 milligrams of carbon-14. The colors show the percentage of carbon-14 that has decayed after each half-life. Carbon-14 has a half-life of 5700 years. Use this graph to answer Questions 27–30 below.

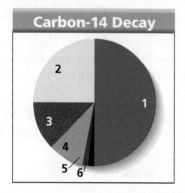

Carbon-14 Decay

27. Using Graphs What percent of the original carbon-14 has decayed after one half-life? After the second half-life?

28. Calculating How much time is needed for three half-lives to pass?

29. Calculating Your sample now has 25 milligrams of carbon-14. How many half-lives have passed?

30. Making Judgments Would carbon-14 dating be an effective tool to determine whether a dinosaur bone is from the Mesozoic Era? Explain.

Concepts in Action

31. Drawing Conclusions You are going to dig a well. You have the choice of digging it into sandstone or into shale. Which type of rock would probably be a better source of water? Explain your answer.

32. Inferring Why do roads in northern states such as Maine or Michigan need to be repaired more often than roads in southern states such as Florida or Louisiana?

33. Predicting Suppose you are building an outdoor sculpture in an area where it rains frequently. Explain whether it would be better to use marble or granite. (*Hint:* Granite is rich in the mineral quartz.)

34. Inferring Given your knowledge of minerals, why does it make sense that beach sand is mostly made of quartz grains?

35. Observing Sinkholes are familiar hazards in areas such as southwestern Virginia or Florida. They can sometimes damage highways, houses, and even farms. Explain how this happens.

36. Comparing and Contrasting The continental shelf and the abyssal plain are very different environments. Compare the conditions of these two regions with regard to light, pressure, and temperature.

37. Writing in Science Select one era or period of geologic time. Write a paragraph describing the environment and common organisms of that time.

Performance-Based Assessment

Classifying Take a walk around your neighborhood. List and describe as many examples of chemical and physical weathering as you can find. Present your findings with a map of the area to your class.

For: Self-grading assessment
Visit: PHSchool.com
Web Code: cca-3230

Standardized Test Prep

Test-Taking Tip

Multiple-Part Answer Choices
Multiple-choice questions may have answer choices that include two or more parts. In such cases, each part of the answer must be true for the entire answer choice to be correct. Even if you are uncertain of the correct answer, you can still improve your chances by eliminating any answer choices that you know are incorrect. For example, consider the following question:

Which of the following accurately describes how ocean conditions change with greater depth?

    I. pressure decreases
    II. density increases
    III. temperature decreases

(A) I only   (B) III only
(C) I and II   (D) II and III
(E) I, II, and III

If you know that pressure increases with greater depth, you know that I is wrong. Therefore, you can eliminate choices A, C, and E, since each includes I as part of the answer. If you know that II is correct, you can also eliminate choice B.

(Answer: D)

Choose the letter that best answers the question or completes the statement.

1. In the water cycle, water is returned to the atmosphere through
    I. condensation
    II. evaporation
    III. precipitation

(A) I only   (B) III only
(C) I and II   (D) II and III
(E) II only

2. Which of the following features is NOT formed by water erosion?
(A) meanders   (B) oxbow lakes
(C) deltas   (D) V-shaped valleys
(E) waterfalls

3. The rate at which rock is weathered depends on which of the following factors?
    I. temperature
    II. rate of deposition
    III. availability of water

(A) I only   (B) I and III
(C) I and II   (D) II and III
(E) I, II, and III

The table below shows the yearly rates of erosion and deposition at four different stream locations. Use the table to answer questions 4 and 5.

Stream Erosion & Deposition		
Location	Rate of Erosion (tons per year)	Rate of Deposition (tons per year)
A	3.00	3.25
B	4.75	4.00
C	4.50	4.65
D	5.60	5.20

4. At which locations is sediment building up?
(A) A and B   (B) C and D
(C) A and C   (D) B and D
(E) A and D

5. In total, how much sediment is gained or lost at Location D?
(A) 0.40 tons per year gained
(B) 0.40 tons per year lost
(C) 10.80 tons per year gained
(D) 10.80 tons per year lost
(E) 5.60 tons per year gained

6. The fact that younger rock layers lie above older rock layers if the rocks remain undisturbed is known as the law of
(A) superposition.   (B) deflation.
(C) deposition.   (D) absolute dating.
(E) relative dating.

7. Dinosaurs became extinct at the end of which division of geologic time?
(A) Precambrian time (B) Cambrian period
(C) Paleozoic Era   (D) Mesozoic Era
(E) Cenozoic Era

CHAPTER
24 Weather and Climate

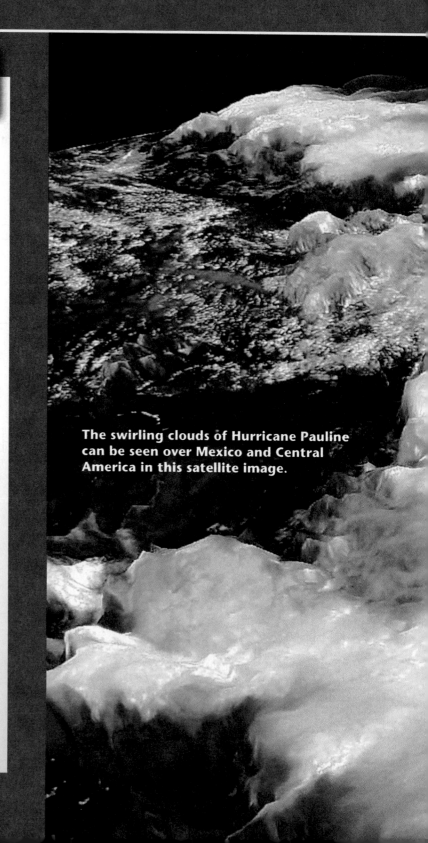

How does latitude affect climate around the world?

Several factors affect the climate where you live, including latitude, distance from large bodies of water, altitude, and prevailing winds. Do an Internet search to find mean monthly temperature data for your city or town. Then look up the mean monthly temperatures for a city on another continent that is at approximately the same latitude as your city or town. Plot both sets of data on the same graph, and post the graph on your class blog. Indicate the locations of the two sites on a map. Then write a short paragraph explaining the similarities or differences in the two sets of temperature data.

How do science concepts apply to your world? Here are some questions you'll be able to answer after you read this chapter.

- **What would Earth be like without an atmosphere?** *(Section 24.1)*

- **What causes the seasons?** *(Section 24.2)*

- **Why is there often a cool breeze at the beach?** *(Section 24.3)*

- **How can the air cause a bad hair day?** *(Section 24.4)*

- **What causes thunder and lightning?** *(Section 24.5)*

- **What happens when a hurricane reaches land?** *(page 772)*

- **How reliable are weather forecasts?** *(Section 24.6)*

- **How do human activities affect climate?** *(Section 24.7)*

The swirling clouds of Hurricane Pauline can be seen over Mexico and Central America in this satellite image.

Chapter Preview

Inquiry › Activity

Why Do Cold Surfaces Become Wet?

Procedure

1. Fill a metal pitcher halfway with warm water. Use paper towels to dry off the outside of the pitcher. With a thermometer, measure the temperature of the air in the classroom and the temperature of the water in the pitcher. Record these temperatures. **CAUTION** *Wipe up any spilled water right away to avoid slips and falls.*

2. Fill a 100-mL beaker with crushed ice. Then, pour the ice into the pitcher and stir the ice with a long-handled spoon.

3. Repeat Step 2 until water begins to appear on the outside of the pitcher. When this occurs, measure and record the temperature of the water in the pitcher.

Think About It

1. **Analyzing Data** Compare the temperature at which drops of water appeared on the outside of the pitcher to the temperature of the air in the classroom.

2. **Formulating Hypotheses** How do you think the water appeared on the outside surface of the pitcher?

24.1 The Atmosphere

Key Concepts

- How does the atmosphere affect conditions on Earth?
- What is Earth's atmosphere composed of?
- How do pressure and density vary with altitude?
- What are the characteristics of the major layers of the atmosphere?

Vocabulary

- atmosphere
- air pressure
- barometer
- troposphere
- weather
- stratosphere
- ozone layer
- mesosphere
- thermosphere
- ionosphere
- aurora

Reading Strategy

Relating Text and Diagrams As you read, refer to Figure 5 and the text to complete the table on the layers of the atmosphere below.

Layer	Altitude Range	Temperature Change
Troposphere	a. ?	b. ?
c. ?	12–50 km	d. ?
e. ?	f. ?	Decreases as altitude increases
Thermosphere	g. ?	h. ?

At 8848 meters (29,030 feet) above sea level, Mount Everest is the highest mountain in the world. In 1953 Edmund Hillary, a New Zealand mountaineer, and Tenzing Norgay, a mountain guide from Nepal, became the first humans to reach the top. The climb was very dangerous for several reasons, including the extremely low temperature and low level of oxygen at the summit. When they finally made it to the top, the two men cheered and embraced. Then Hillary did something to prove a point—he took off his oxygen mask. He wanted to show that a person could stay alive while breathing naturally at that high altitude. But after a few minutes, his vision began to fail. When Hillary replaced his mask, his vision improved. Then the two men started back down the mountain.

Why did Hillary and Tenzing need to carry oxygen to the top of Mount Everest? And why was it so cold there? The answers to these questions depend on how the air around Earth changes with altitude.

Figure 1 Edmund Hillary (left) and Tenzing Norgay were the first to climb Mount Everest, the world's highest mountain.

Earth's Protective Layer

What you commonly call air, scientists call the atmosphere. The **atmosphere** (AT muh sfeer) is the layer of gases that surrounds Earth. ◯ **The atmosphere forms a protective boundary between Earth and space and provides conditions that are suitable for life.** The atmosphere protects Earth's surface from continual pounding by meteoroids, chunks of rock and metal from space. The atmosphere also protects Earth from much of the high-energy radiation from space.

The atmosphere holds in heat and helps to moderate Earth's temperatures. Without the atmosphere, Earth's surface would be similar to the moon's, boiling hot during the day and freezing cold at night. Earth's relatively constant temperatures allow life to flourish.

The atmosphere also provides the gases that are essential for life. Carbon dioxide in the atmosphere is essential for plants and some other organisms to carry out photosynthesis. Photosynthesis is the process of capturing the sun's energy to make food. Oxygen is produced during photosynthesis and released into the atmosphere. Your body uses oxygen to carry out many life functions.

Composition of the Atmosphere

The atmosphere is a mixture of different gases. The composition of the atmosphere is fairly uniform up to an altitude of about 80 kilometers. ◯ **Earth's atmosphere is a mixture of nitrogen, oxygen, water vapor, and many other gases, in which tiny solid and liquid particles are suspended.** As Figure 2 shows, two gases—nitrogen and oxygen—make up more than 99 percent of clean, dry air. The amount of water vapor in air varies from 0.02 percent in cold, dry air to more than 4.0 percent in warm, moist air.

Various amounts of water droplets and solid particles are suspended in the atmosphere. Some solid particles can be seen as floating dust, but most particles are microscopic. These solid particles come from various sources, including smoke from fires, ash and dust from volcanic eruptions, and salt from ocean spray.

Composition of Earth's Atmosphere (Dry Air)

Gas	Percentage by Volume
Nitrogen (N_2)	78.084
Oxygen (O_2)	20.946
Argon (Ar)	0.934
Carbon dioxide (CO_2)	0.039
Neon (Ne)	0.00182
Helium (He)	0.00052
Methane (CH_4)	0.00015
Krypton (Kr)	0.00011
Hydrogen (H_2)	0.00005

Figure 2 Dry air is a mixture of many gases. Air also contains water vapor, which makes up between 0.02 percent and 4.0 percent of air's volume. **Using Tables** *What is the most abundant gas in dry air?*

10 km — Standard cruising altitude for jet liners 10,000–12,000 m

9 km

— **Mt. Everest**
Asia
8848 m

8 km

7 km

— **Mt. McKinley**
Alaska
6194 m

6 km

— **Mt. Kilimanjaro**
Africa
5963 m

5 km

4 km

3 km

2 km — **Mexico City**
2240 m

— **Denver, Colorado**
1600 m

1 km

0 km — **Washington, D.C.**
9 m

Figure 3 The atmosphere is densest close to Earth's surface. **Applying Concepts** *How does air pressure change as altitude increases?*

Air Pressure

The atmosphere has weight because of Earth's gravity. As a result of this weight, the atmosphere exerts pressure. Recall that pressure is the force exerted on a surface divided by the area over which the force is exerted. **Air pressure** is the force exerted by the weight of a column of air on a surface. At sea level, air pressure is about 101,325 newtons per square meter, more commonly expressed as 1013.25 millibars. One millibar equals 100 newtons per square meter.

Effect of Altitude
Air pressure changes with altitude. The atmosphere is densest near Earth's surface and becomes less dense as altitude increases, as shown in Figure 3. Why is this? Air can be compressed, as it is when you pump air into a tire or a basketball. Near Earth's surface, the column of air includes the entire depth of the atmosphere, so the pressure and density are high. As altitude increases, the depth of the column of air above decreases, so the pressure decreases. At high altitudes there is very little air in the column above, so air pressure is lower. 🗨 **As altitude increases, air pressure and density decrease.**

About half of the total mass of the atmosphere is found below an altitude of 5.6 kilometers. When Hillary and Tenzing climbed Mount Everest, they went well above this halfway point. As they climbed, the air became less dense. Hillary had trouble breathing without an oxygen mask because there were many fewer oxygen molecules per cubic meter of air at the summit than at sea level.

Measuring Air Pressure
Scientists measure air pressure with an instrument called a **barometer.** The first barometer was invented in 1643 by the Italian scientist Evangelista Torricelli. Torricelli invented a mercury barometer, similar to the one shown in Figure 4. As air pressure increases, the column of mercury in the barometer rises. As air pressure decreases, the column of mercury falls. Thus, a measurement of the height of a column of mercury is a measurement of air pressure. At sea level, the average air pressure is about 760 millimeters of mercury or, more commonly, 29.92 inches of mercury.

An aneroid (AN uh royd) barometer is a smaller, more portable type of barometer. The word *aneroid* means "not using liquid." Aneroid barometers use a metal chamber that expands and contracts with changes in air pressure.

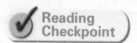
Reading Checkpoint

What instrument is used to measure air pressure?

Layers of the Atmosphere

Temperature changes dramatically as you move up from Earth's surface high into the atmosphere. Scientists use variations in temperature to divide the atmosphere into four vertical layers. 🔑 **The four layers of the atmosphere are the troposphere, the stratosphere, the mesosphere, and the thermosphere.**

The Troposphere You, along with many other living things, live in the layer of the atmosphere called the troposphere. The **troposphere** (TROH puh sfeer) is the lowest layer of Earth's atmosphere. This layer contains almost all of the atmosphere's water vapor and suspended particles, which are important in the formation of clouds and precipitation. Most weather takes place in the troposphere. **Weather** is the condition of the atmosphere in a particular place at a particular time.

The height of the troposphere ranges from about 9 kilometers above the poles to 16 kilometers above the tropics. The average height of the troposphere is about 12 kilometers.

In the troposphere, temperature generally decreases as altitude increases. Though it varies somewhat, the rate of decrease averages about 6.5 Celsius degrees per kilometer. For example, if it is 20°C where you are on Earth's surface, then it is probably about 7°C at an altitude of 2 kilometers above you. This characteristic of the troposphere accounts for the extremely low temperatures that Hillary and Tenzing had to withstand when they scaled Mount Everest.

A **B**

Figure 4 Barometers measure air pressure. **A** Changes in air pressure cause the airtight chamber of this aneroid barometer to flex in and out. **B** Changes in air pressure cause the level of mercury in the open glass tube of this antique mercury barometer to move up or down.

Quick Lab

Demonstrating the Effect of Air Pressure

Materials

plastic cup, index card, plastic tub

Procedure

1. Completely fill the plastic cup with water. Then place the index card on the cup. Make sure that no air is trapped between the water and the card. **CAUTION** *Quickly wipe up any spilled water to avoid slips and falls.*

2. **Predicting** Record your prediction of what will happen when the cup is inverted.

3. To test your prediction, place the palm of one hand on the card. Then use your other hand to invert the cup so that the cup rests upside-down on the card in your hand.

4. Hold the cup and card over the plastic tub and slowly remove your hand from the card. Observe what happens.

Analyze and Conclude

1. **Applying Concepts** What two forces acted on the card after you inverted the cup?

2. **Inferring** After you inverted the cup, which surface of the card experienced a greater force due to air pressure?

3. **Drawing Conclusions** How can you explain what happened when you removed your hand from the card?

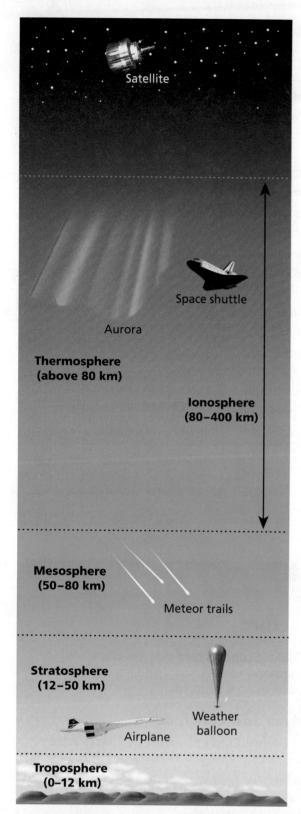

Satellite

Space shuttle

Aurora

Thermosphere
(above 80 km)

Ionosphere
(80–400 km)

Mesosphere
(50–80 km)

Meteor trails

Stratosphere
(12–50 km)

Airplane

Weather
balloon

Troposphere
(0–12 km)

Figure 5 The atmosphere has four principal layers—the troposphere, the stratosphere, the mesosphere, and the thermosphere. The ionosphere overlaps the lower thermosphere. **Interpreting Diagrams** *In which layer do auroras appear?*

The Stratosphere Above the troposphere, as shown in Figure 5, is the stratosphere. The **stratosphere** (STRAT uh sfeer) extends from an altitude of about 12 kilometers to about 50 kilometers. The temperature of the stratosphere remains nearly the same from the boundary with the troposphere to an altitude of about 20 kilometers. Above that height, temperature increases as altitude increases. The temperature in the lower stratosphere remains about −57°C. Above 20 kilometers, the temperature rises to about 0°C.

The upper stratosphere is warmer than the lower stratosphere because of the presence of the **ozone layer,** a region of high ozone concentration. Recall that ozone is a highly reactive gas whose molecules are composed of three oxygen atoms (O_3). Most of the oxygen molecules you breathe are composed of two oxygen atoms (O_2). In the stratosphere, the energy of sunlight is great enough to split O_2 molecules into single oxygen atoms (O). When an oxygen atom (O) collides with a molecule of oxygen (O_2), ozone (O_3) is formed.

Ozone absorbs ultraviolet (UV) radiation in sunlight and filters much of it out before such radiation can reach Earth's surface. The energy absorbed from UV radiation is converted into thermal energy, warming the upper stratosphere.

Because UV radiation can be harmful to living things, the presence of the ozone layer is extremely important to life on Earth. In humans, UV radiation can cause a deadly form of skin cancer. Certain chemical pollutants have been depleting ozone in the stratosphere, permitting more UV radiation to reach Earth's surface. However, the release of such chemicals was limited by international agreements and national policies adopted in the 1990s. As a result, ozone levels in the stratosphere appear to have stabilized.

The Mesosphere The layer above the stratosphere is the mesosphere. The **mesosphere** (MEZ oh sfeer) begins at an altitude of about 50 kilometers and extends to about 80 kilometers. In the mesosphere, temperature decreases as altitude increases. At the top of the mesosphere, the temperature approaches −90°C.

The air is very thin in the mesosphere. Studies in the 1990s discovered that air in this layer may move at speeds of more than 320 kilometers per hour. Most meteoroids that enter the atmosphere burn up in the mesosphere.

 Reading Checkpoint *In which layer of the atmosphere do most meteoroids burn up?*

The Thermosphere The outermost layer of the atmosphere, the **thermosphere** (THUR moh sfeer), begins at an altitude of about 80 kilometers and extends outward into space. No boundary marks the end of the atmosphere. Instead, the thin air of the thermosphere gradually merges with space. In the thermosphere, temperature increases rapidly with altitude, from about −90°C to more than 1000°C. Recall from physics that temperature is a measure of the average kinetic energy of molecules. Because gas molecules in the thermosphere absorb solar radiation and move very fast, the temperature is quite high.

The Ionosphere The **ionosphere** (eye AHN uh sfeer) is not a distinct layer of the atmosphere. Rather, it is a region of charged particles, or ions, that overlaps the lower thermosphere. In the ionosphere, molecules of nitrogen and oxygen lose one or more electrons as they absorb high-energy wavelengths of solar radiation. The molecules become positively charged ions. These ions are most dense between the altitudes of 80 and 400 kilometers. At these high altitudes, certain radio waves sent from Earth's surface, such as AM radio waves, bounce off ions and travel back to Earth. You can often hear AM radio stations from very far away at night because the sun's radiation is blocked by Earth. The ions start to recombine at night, allowing AM radio waves to travel farther.

One of nature's most spectacular displays occurs in the ionosphere. An **aurora,** shown in Figure 6, is a colorful display of light in the sky, produced when charged particles from the sun are attracted to Earth's magnetic poles. There, these particles cause ions in the ionosphere to glow. In the Northern Hemisphere, these displays are called the aurora borealis, or Northern Lights.

For: Articles on the ozone layer
Visit: PHSchool.com
Web Code: ccc-3241

Figure 6 Auroras provide spectacular displays of light in the polar regions. Auroras are produced by glowing ions in the ionosphere.

Section 24.1 Assessment

Reviewing Concepts

1. How does the atmosphere protect life on Earth?
2. What are the two major gases in Earth's atmosphere?
3. How does air pressure change with altitude?
4. List the major layers of the atmosphere in order, beginning with the layer closest to Earth's surface.

Critical Thinking

5. **Predicting** How might human health be affected if the ozone layer suddenly became thinner?

6. **Comparing and Contrasting** Compare the way temperature changes with altitude in the mesosphere and in the thermosphere.

Math Practice

7. If the temperature is 10°C at an altitude of 1000 meters, what would the temperature be on top of a nearby 5000-meter mountain? (*Hint:* Assume that temperature falls 6.5°C per kilometer.)
8. About how much oxygen would there be in a 1000-m^3 volume of dry air?

24.2 The Sun and the Seasons

Reading Focus

Key Concepts

- What are two ways in which Earth moves?
- How is Earth's surface divided into zones based on latitude?
- What causes the seasons?

Vocabulary

- ◆ rotation
- ◆ revolution
- ◆ tropic zone
- ◆ temperate zones
- ◆ polar zones
- ◆ solstice
- ◆ equinox

Reading Strategy

Building Vocabulary Draw a table like the one below that includes all the vocabulary terms listed for the section. As you read, define each vocabulary term in your own words.

Vocabulary Term	Definition
Rotation	a. _____?_____
Revolution	b. _____?_____

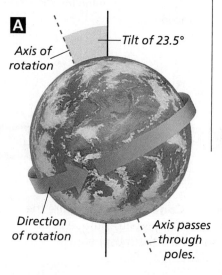

Figure 7 Earth is constantly moving in two ways. **A** Earth rotates around its axis once a day. **B** Earth revolves around the sun once a year.

A

—Tilt of 23.5°

Axis of rotation

Direction of rotation

Axis passes through poles.

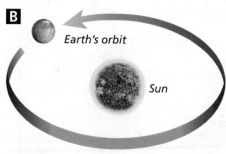

B

Earth's orbit

Sun

No one can feel it, yet Earth is constantly moving in space. **Earth moves in two major ways: rotation and revolution.** As shown in Figure 7A, Earth spins like a top around an imaginary line, or axis, that connects the north and south geographic poles. The poles are the two points at opposite ends of Earth where Earth's axis intersects the surface. The spinning of Earth on its axis is called **rotation.** Earth's rotation causes day and night. As Earth rotates from west to east, the sun appears to move from east to west across the sky. As Earth continues to spin toward the east, the sun sets in the west and night falls. It takes one day, or just under 24 hours, for Earth to complete one rotation.

As Earth rotates on its axis, it also travels around the sun, as shown in Figure 7B. **Revolution** is the movement of one body in space around another. It takes Earth one year, about $365\frac{1}{4}$ days, to complete a full revolution around the sun. Earth revolves around the sun in a broad path, or orbit.

Earth's Latitude Zones

Different parts of Earth receive different amounts of sunlight depending on their latitude. Latitude measures distance in degrees north or south of the equator. For example, the equator is at 0° and the North Pole is at 90° north latitude. As you can see in Figure 8, regions near the equator receive more direct sunlight than the poles. As a result, Earth is generally warmer near the equator and colder toward the poles.

Scientists use lines of latitude to mark out three different types of regions within which temperatures are generally similar: the tropic, temperate, and polar zones. Between the latitudes of 23.5° south and 23.5° north is the **tropic zone,** where Earth is generally warm. From 23.5° north to 66.5° north and from 23.5° south to 66.5° south are the **temperate zones,** which are generally cooler than the tropics. From 66.5° north to the North Pole and from 66.5° south to the South Pole are the **polar zones,** which are generally cold.

Polar zone

Temperate zone

Equator

Tropical zone

Temperate zone

Polar zone

Sun's slanted rays

Sun's direct rays

Sun's slanted rays

Reading Checkpoint) *Which is the coldest type of latitude zone?*

Figure 8 The angle that sunlight strikes Earth's surface varies with latitude. As a result, it is generally warmer near the equator than near the poles.
Interpreting Diagrams *Which latitude zone receives the most direct sunlight?*

The Seasons

Most of the United States is in the temperate zone. In much of the country, therefore, temperature and other weather conditions change over the year with the cycle of the seasons. What causes these seasonal changes? The answer is related to Earth's rotation and its revolution.

Earth's axis of rotation is not straight up and down. Instead, the axis tilts at an angle of about 23.5° relative to a line perpendicular to its orbital path. As Earth orbits the sun, the north end of Earth's axis points in the same direction—toward the North Star. But the orientation of Earth's axis changes relative to the sun over the course of a year. The seasons are caused by the tilt of Earth's axis as it moves around the sun.

Solstices Because Earth's axis is tilted, the latitude at which the noon sun appears directly overhead changes each day according to a yearly cycle. A **solstice** (SOHL stis) occurs on the two days each year when the sun is directly overhead at latitude 23.5° north or 23.5° south. In the Northern Hemisphere, the summer solstice, which marks the beginning of summer, occurs around June 21. At this time, the Northern Hemisphere is tilted toward the sun, so it receives more sunlight than the Southern Hemisphere. On this day, daylight hours are longest in the Northern Hemisphere and shortest in the Southern Hemisphere.

Six months later, on about December 21, the winter solstice, which marks the beginning of winter, occurs in the Northern Hemisphere. On the winter solstice, the Northern Hemisphere is tilted away from the sun. As a result, the Northern Hemisphere now receives less sunlight than the Southern Hemisphere. At this time, the daylight hours are shortest in the Northern Hemisphere, but longest in the Southern Hemisphere.

Figure 9 In the temperate zones, the beginning of autumn brings cooler weather and colorful leaves.

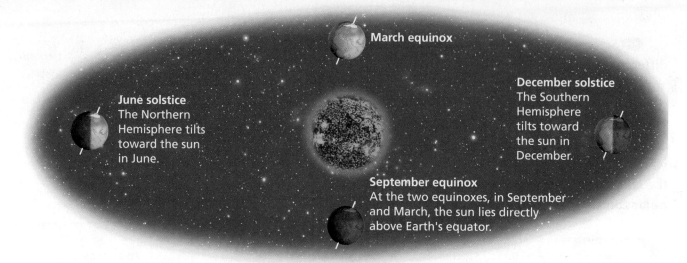

March equinox

June solstice
The Northern
Hemisphere tilts
toward the sun
in June.

December solstice
The Southern
Hemisphere
tilts toward
the sun in
December.

September equinox
At the two equinoxes, in September
and March, the sun lies directly
above Earth's equator.

Figure 10 The seasons are caused by the tilt of Earth's axis as it revolves around the sun. **Interpreting Visuals** *When is the south end of Earth's axis tilted most toward the sun?*

The seasons are not affected by Earth's changing distance from the sun. In fact, in the Northern Hemisphere, Earth is closer to the sun during winter than it is during summer.

Equinoxes Look at Figure 10. Notice that halfway between the solstices are two days, called equinoxes. The equinoxes mark the beginning of spring and autumn. At an **equinox,** neither hemisphere is tilted toward the sun, and the lengths of daylight and of darkness are approximately equal. The vernal equinox, which occurs about March 21 in the Northern Hemisphere, marks the start of spring. The autumnal equinox, which occurs about September 22 in the Northern Hemisphere, marks the start of autumn. On these two days, the noon sun is directly overhead at the equator. Sunlight reaches the Northern Hemisphere and Southern Hemisphere in equal amounts on the equinoxes.

Section 24.2 Assessment

Reviewing Concepts

1. Describe two ways in which Earth moves in space.

2. What are three zones on Earth's surface that are based on latitude? What are their characteristics?

3. What determines the change in seasons?

4. Describe one effect of Earth's rotation.

Critical Thinking

5. **Classifying** Classify each of the following latitudes as part of the tropic, temperate, or polar zones: 15° north, 29° south, and 70° north.

6. **Inferring** What is Earth's orientation at the time of the winter solstice in the Southern Hemisphere? Explain.

7. **Comparing and Contrasting** How are solstices and equinoxes similar? How are they different?

Writing in Science

Cause and Effect Write a paragraph describing how life in your community might be different if Earth's axis were not tilted. (*Hint:* Consider how the tilt of Earth's axis affects the seasons.)

24.3 Solar Energy and Winds

Reading Focus

Key Concepts

- What happens to the energy Earth receives from the sun?
- How is energy transferred within the troposphere?
- What causes winds?
- What are some examples of local winds and global winds?

Vocabulary

- greenhouse effect
- wind
- local wind
- sea breeze
- land breeze
- global winds
- Coriolis effect
- monsoon
- jet stream

Reading Strategy

Comparing and Contrasting Copy the table below. After you read, compare sea and land breezes by completing the table.

Type of Wind	Day or Night?	Direction of Air Movement
Sea breeze	a. ?	b. ?
Land breeze	c. ?	d. ?

The heat you feel when you're out in the sun is one effect of solar energy. You might think that sunlight heats the air directly, just as it heats you directly. But the process is more complicated than that.

Energy in the Atmosphere

Some solar energy that reaches Earth's atmosphere is reflected back, some is absorbed by the atmosphere, and some is absorbed by Earth's surface. About 30 percent of the incoming solar energy is reflected back into space by clouds, dust in the air, gases, and Earth's surface. About 20 percent of the sun's energy is absorbed by clouds and gases. But the greatest amount of solar energy—about half—passes through the atmosphere and is absorbed by the surface.

The atmosphere is heated primarily by energy that is reradiated by Earth's surface. Unlike incoming solar energy, which has much of its energy in the visible spectrum, the energy radiated back into the atmosphere is mostly infrared radiation. Certain gases in the atmosphere, including water vapor and carbon dioxide, allow visible light to pass through but absorb most infrared radiation. These gases radiate some of this absorbed energy back to Earth's surface, warming the lower atmosphere in a process called the **greenhouse effect**. Without the greenhouse effect, Earth's surface would be much cooler than it is.

Energy is transferred within the troposphere in three ways: radiation, convection, and conduction. As the How It Works box on page 756 explains, these processes work together to heat the troposphere.

20% of incoming sunlight absorbed by clouds and gases

25% reflected by clouds, dust, and gases

50% absorbed by surface

5% reflected by surface

Most energy absorbed by the surface is reradiated back into the atmosphere.

Figure 11 About half of the sunlight that reaches Earth is absorbed by the surface. The rest is either reflected back into space or absorbed in the atmosphere.

Energy Transfer in the Troposphere

Energy is transferred within the troposphere by radiation, conduction, and convection. Radiation from the sun heats Earth's surface, which then radiates heat skyward. The air in direct contact with Earth's surface is heated by conduction. Warm air near the surface expands and rises and cooler, denser air sinks, forming convection currents that move heat through the troposphere.

Interpreting Diagrams *Where does most of the energy in the troposphere originally come from?*

Solar radiation

Infrared radiation

Greenhouse effect
When Earth's surface is heated, much of this energy is radiated back as infrared radiation. Some of this radiation is absorbed by gases in the atmosphere. The process by which gases hold heat in the air is called the greenhouse effect.

A **Radiation** Much of the sun's radiation reaches Earth's surface, where it heats the land and water. Land and water radiate heat back into the atmosphere.

B **Conduction** The conduction process transfers heat from land and water directly to the few meters of air nearest Earth's surface.

C **Convection** Convection moves heat through the troposphere. As surface air is heated by radiation and conduction, rising warm air is replaced by denser, downward-flowing cool air.

Wind

What happens when you open a vacuum-packed can of chips? You hear a rush of air, which is the sound of air moving from the high-pressure area outside the can to the low-pressure area inside the can. A similar process occurs in the atmosphere.

Air naturally flows from areas of higher pressure to areas of lower pressure. This flow is **wind,** which is the mainly horizontal movement of air. 👄 **Winds are caused by differences in air pressure.** Larger pressure differences produce stronger winds.

Differences in air pressure are often caused by the unequal heating of Earth's surface. As you've learned, the atmosphere is warmed largely by reradiation from Earth's surface below it. As air is heated, it expands. As it becomes less dense, air rises. Cooler, denser air flows in to replace it. This process occurs on both local and global scales, producing local and global winds.

For: Links on winds
Visit: www.SciLinks.org
Web Code: ccn-3243

Local Winds

On a hot summer day, there is often a cool breeze blowing in from the water to the beach. This breeze is an example of a **local wind,** a wind that blows over a short distance. Local winds are caused by the unequal heating of Earth's surface within a small region.

👄 **The breezes that occur where land meets a large body of water are examples of local winds.** Water has a higher specific heat than land, and therefore takes longer to heat up and cool down. During the day, the sun heats the land more quickly than it heats the water. The air above the land becomes warmer than the air above the water. The warm air expands and rises, creating a lower-pressure area above the land. The cooler air over the water flows toward the land, creating a **sea breeze.**

At night, these temperature and pressure conditions are reversed, as Figure 12 shows. Land cools off more quickly than water. The cooler air over land has a higher density than the warmer air over water. The result is a **land breeze,** where cooler air over land moves toward water. Winds are named for the direction from which they originate—sea breezes begin over the ocean and land breezes begin over land.

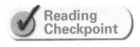 *In which direction does a land breeze blow?*

A Sea Breeze

Warm air rising

Cooler air moving toward the land

B Land Breeze

Cooler air moving toward the water

Warm air rising

Figure 12 Sea breezes and land breezes are local winds. **A** During the day, air pressure differences due to unequal heating cause a sea breeze. **B** At night, pressure differences are reversed, causing a land breeze. **Comparing and Contrasting** *How are land breezes and sea breezes different?*

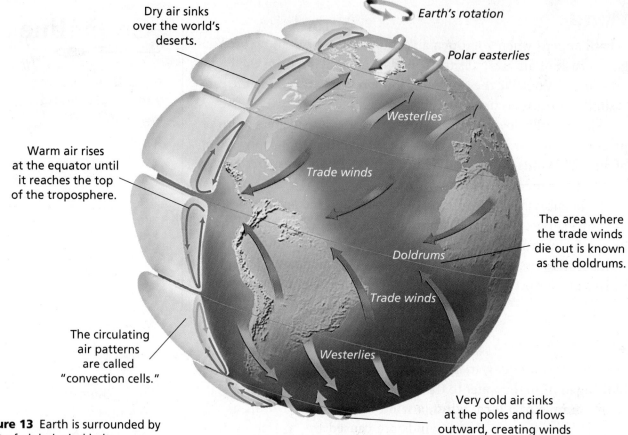

Dry air sinks over the world's deserts.

Earth's rotation

Polar easterlies

Westerlies

Trade winds

Warm air rises at the equator until it reaches the top of the troposphere.

The area where the trade winds die out is known as the doldrums.

Doldrums

Trade winds

The circulating air patterns are called "convection cells."

Westerlies

Very cold air sinks at the poles and flows outward, creating winds called polar easterlies.

Figure 13 Earth is surrounded by a set of global wind belts.

Figure 14 For hundreds of years, sailing ships have relied on global winds to transport cargo across the oceans.
Interpreting Visuals *Which band of global winds would a sailing ship use to move cargo from Canada to Europe?*

Global Winds

Winds that blow over long distances from a specific direction are called **global winds.** These winds are part of a worldwide pattern of air circulation. Global winds are caused by the unequal heating of Earth's surface across a large region.

Convection Cells Global winds move in a series of huge bands called convection cells. As you can see in Figure 13, these bands look like loops from the side. These bands are caused by temperature variations across Earth's surface. At the equator, for example, temperatures tend to be warmer than at other latitudes. Warm air rises at the equator, creating a low-pressure region. This warm air is replaced by cooler air brought by global winds blowing near the surface. Higher in the atmosphere, air blows away from the equator toward the poles. Similar convection cells cover large bands of latitude across Earth.

The trade winds are wind belts just north and south of the equator. In the Northern Hemisphere, they blow from the northeast to the southwest. The prevailing westerlies occur between 30° and 60° latitude in both hemispheres. These winds generally blow from west to east over much of North America. The polar easterlies extend from 60° latitude to the poles in both hemispheres. **Trade winds, westerlies, and polar easterlies are examples of global winds.**

If Earth were not rotating on its axis, global winds would move in roughly straight paths from the poles to the equator. However, because Earth rotates, global winds move in a curved path between the poles and the equator. Notice in Figure 13 that global winds curve to the right in the Northern Hemisphere and to the left in the Southern Hemisphere. The curving effect that Earth's rotation has on all free-moving objects, including global winds, is called the **Coriolis effect.** If Earth were not rotating, a rocket launched from the North Pole toward the equator would move in a straight line, as shown in Figure 15. However, because Earth is rotating underneath the rocket, the rocket would appear to an observer on Earth to curve to the right. Similarly, Earth's rotation causes global winds to curve.

Monsoons Seasonal changes in the heating of Earth's surface affect the circulation of the atmosphere. A **monsoon** is a wind system that is characterized by seasonal reversal of direction. Monsoons are similar to land and sea breezes except that they occur on a much wider scale and longer time frame. For example, the summer monsoon that occurs over much of South and Southeast Asia blows warm, humid air from the ocean onto land. As this air rises over land, it cools and brings heavy rainfall to parts of that region. In winter the monsoon reverses, blowing from land onto water and bringing drier weather.

Jet Stream Global wind patterns are also affected by fast-moving streams of air at high altitudes. A belt of high-speed wind in the upper troposphere is called a **jet stream.** Jet streams are caused by great differences in air pressure that develop at high altitudes.

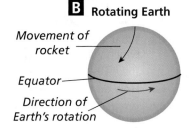

A Non-rotating Earth

Movement of rocket

Equator

B Rotating Earth

Movement of rocket

Equator

Direction of Earth's rotation

Figure 15 The Coriolis effect causes free-moving objects, such as rockets and global winds, to move in a curved path. **A** A rocket launched from the North Pole toward the equator would move in a straight line if Earth were not rotating. **B** The Coriolis effect causes such a rocket to appear to curve to the right. Similarly, the Coriolis effect causes global winds to curve to the right in the Northern Hemisphere.

Section 24.3 Assessment

Reviewing Concepts

1. ⬭ What happens to solar energy when it reaches Earth's atmosphere?
2. ⬭ Explain how energy is transferred within the troposphere.
3. ⬭ What causes the wind to blow?
4. ⬭ How are local winds and global winds similar? How are they different?
5. What are monsoons, and what causes them?

Critical Thinking

6. **Relating Cause and Effects** How does the Coriolis effect influence global wind patterns?

7. **Applying Concepts** You and your family vacation at a cabin on the shore of a large lake. At night, you notice that a breeze blows over your cabin toward the lake. Explain what causes the wind to blow in that direction.

Connecting C Concepts

Thermal Energy Recall what you learned in Chapter 16 about the specific heat of water. Use this information to explain why land and sea breezes undergo daily reversals in direction.

24.4 Water in the Atmosphere

Reading Focus

Key Concepts

- What are some ways in which water condenses in the atmosphere?
- How do clouds form?
- What are the major types of clouds?
- What are the major forms of precipitation?

Vocabulary

- humidity
- relative humidity
- dew point
- cloud
- fog
- stratus clouds
- cumulus clouds
- cirrus clouds

Reading Strategy

Sequencing Copy the flowchart below. As you read, complete it to show how a cloud forms. Add more steps to the chart if necessary.

Cloud Formation

What do fogged-up windows on a cold winter morning and a bad hair day have in common? Both result from high levels of water vapor in the air. The atmosphere contains only about 0.001 percent of the total water in the world. Yet this relatively small amount of water has a great effect on the processes that occur in the atmosphere, including cloud formation and precipitation. It can also cause your windows to fog up and your hair to become limp or frizzy.

Humidity

The amount of water in the atmosphere can vary greatly. Dry air contains much less water vapor than the air above a rainforest. The amount of water vapor in the air is called **humidity.** Warm, tropical air tends to contain more water vapor than cold, polar air does.

When you hear someone talking about the "humidity" of the air, that person is probably talking about relative humidity. **Relative humidity** is the ratio of the amount of water vapor in the air to the maximum amount of water vapor that can exist at that temperature.

Relative humidity is always expressed as a percentage. When the relative humidity is 60 percent, for example, air contains 60 percent of the maximum amount of water vapor that can exist at that temperature. When relative humidity reaches 100 percent, air is said to be saturated.

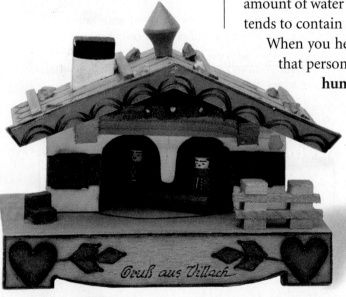

Figure 16 This antique "weather house" shows the humidity, or moisture content, of the air. If the air is humid, a hair inside the house expands and allows the man to come out of the door. When the air is dry, the hair contracts and the woman comes out.

The maximum amount of water that can exist as a gas is greater at high temperatures than at low temperatures. Therefore, if the air temperature decreases, the atmosphere can hold less water vapor. After sunset, the temperature often decreases, and so the maximum amount of water vapor that the atmosphere can hold also decreases. The relative humidity rises, although the amount of water vapor in the air remains the same. Eventually, the air may become saturated with water vapor. The temperature at which air becomes saturated is called its **dew point.** If the temperature drops further, water vapor will condense.

Water vapor typically condenses as dew, frost, clouds, or fog. Dew, shown in Figure 17A, is water vapor that condenses on Earth's surface. Frost, shown in Figure 17B, forms when the dew point of air is below freezing. Frost isn't frozen dew. Rather, frost is formed when water vapor in air changes directly from a gas to solid ice crystals.

When the air warms, as can happen during the day, the amount of water vapor that air can contain increases. As a result, the relative humidity decreases.

 Reading Checkpoint *What is the dew point of air?*

Figure 17 Dew and frost are two forms of condensation. **A** Dew can often be seen on spider webs early in the morning after a cool night. **B** Frost is visible on this pane of glass.
Comparing and Contrasting *How are dew and frost similar? How are they different?*

Cloud Formation

The most noticeable features of the atmosphere are clouds. Some are high and wispy; others are thick and dark. A **cloud** is a dense, visible mass of tiny water droplets or ice crystals that are suspended in the atmosphere. The droplets or crystals that form a cloud are extremely small—one cloud might consist of billions of such droplets and crystals.

Clouds form as warm, moist air rises and water vapor condenses in the atmosphere. Water vapor condenses when air cools to a temperature below its dew point. Such cooling occurs naturally as warm air rises through the atmosphere. As air rises, air pressure decreases. As a result, the air expands and cools, and condensation occurs. Cloud formation, then, is the result of the expansion of air and the resulting drop in temperature.

For a cloud to form, solid particles such as dust and salt must be present for the water vapor to condense upon. When air is cooled below its dew point, water vapor changes into tiny water droplets or ice crystals on these solid particles. This process is similar to the way water vapor condenses onto the bathroom mirror when you take a hot shower.

For: Links on clouds and fog
Visit: www.SciLinks.org
Web Code: ccn-3244

Cirrostratus clouds

◄ Cirrus clouds

Cumulonimbus clouds

Stratus clouds

Classifying Clouds

Clouds seem to come in an endless variety of forms, constantly shifting shapes as they move through the sky. Yet, different clouds have some similarities. Scientists classify clouds on the basis of form and height.

The first cloud classification system was developed in 1803 by the British naturalist Luke Howard. His classification system and the terms he coined for different types of clouds are the basis for what scientists use today. **There are three basic cloud forms: stratus, cumulus, and cirrus.** Scientists use these three forms to name and describe a variety of common cloud types. Notice that clouds are generally grouped into families by the altitude at which they occur. Photos of common types of clouds are shown on this and the following page.

Fog is a cloud that is near or touching the ground. Fogs often form when warm, moist air passes over land. Other fogs form when the ground cools at night, cooling the humid air immediately above the ground to the dew point.

Stratus Clouds Flat layers of clouds that cover much or all of the sky are known as **stratus clouds** (STRAT us). The word *stratus* comes from the Latin word meaning "to spread out." Nimbostratus clouds are low stratus clouds that produce steady and widespread rain or snow. When *nimbo-* or *-nimbus* is added to a cloud's name, it means that the cloud produces precipitation.

◀ Altostratus clouds

▼ Cumulus clouds

Altostratus clouds, which are middle-level clouds, often form a layer that covers most of the sky. These clouds can produce light rain or snow. Middle-level clouds, which occur at altitudes between 2000 and 6000 meters, are given the prefix *alto-*.

Cumulus Clouds Puffy white clouds that look like piles of cotton balls with flat bottoms are **cumulus clouds** (KYOO myuh lus). The word *cumulus* comes from the Latin for "heap." Cumulus clouds are the "fair-weather clouds" that you often see on sunny days. Cumulonimbus clouds are dark, towering clouds that produce heavy precipitation, often together with thunder and lightning. Cumulus clouds and cumulonimbus clouds develop vertically. They form less than 2 kilometers from the ground and grow upward. Cumulonimbus clouds usually have a flat base and a billowing tower rising above. They are sometimes called thunderheads.

Cirrus Clouds Thin, white, wispy clouds, often with a feathery or veil-like appearance, are **cirrus clouds** (SEER us). You can see cirrus clouds high in the sky on a clear, sunny day. The prefix *cirro-* is used to describe high-altitude clouds. Because temperatures at high altitudes are so low, cirrus clouds are mostly ice crystals. Cirrus and cirrostratus clouds generally produce no rain. But such high-altitude clouds often blow into an area just ahead of rain-producing clouds.

 Reading Checkpoint   ***What are cirrus clouds made of?***

▼ Nimbostratus clouds

Forms of Precipitation

Precipitation occurs when water droplets or ice crystals in clouds join together and become large enough to fall to the ground without evaporating. Clouds are the source of all precipitation. 🔑 **The most common types of precipitation are rain, snow, hail, sleet, and freezing rain.**

Rain and Snow Rain is liquid precipitation that usually forms in either nimbostratus clouds or cumulonimbus clouds. Snow is precipitation in the form of ice crystals called snowflakes. The size and shape of snowflakes depend on the temperature at which they form.

Hail, Sleet, and Freezing Rain Hail is precipitation in the form of round, solid pieces of ice more than 5 millimeters in diameter. Hail forms within cumulonimbus clouds when small ice pellets are tossed up and down by rising and falling air. As the ice is tossed about, it collides and combines with water droplets that then freeze, creating more and more layers of ice. Eventually, the ice becomes heavy enough to fall to the ground as hail. Hail can sometimes cause tremendous damage to crops, vehicles, and buildings.

Sleet is precipitation in the form of ice particles that are usually smaller than 5 millimeters in diameter. Sleet is rain that freezes as it falls. Sleet rarely damages crops or vehicles directly, but it can make driving extremely hazardous.

Freezing rain is rain that freezes after hitting the surface. Freezing rain produces beautiful effects, as Figure 18 shows, but it can be dangerous. Roads become very slippery, and branches or power lines can fall from the weight of the ice.

Figure 18 Freezing rain creates beautiful effects but can be dangerous.

Section 24.4 Assessment

Reviewing Concepts

1. 🔑 List the ways in which water vapor condenses in the atmosphere

2. 🔑 Explain how clouds form.

3. 🔑 Describe each of the three main cloud forms.

4. 🔑 What are the most common types of precipitation?

Critical Thinking

5. **Classifying** A winter storm produced precipitation in the form of ice particles that averaged about 4 millimeters in diameter. What kind of precipitation was it?

6. **Applying Concepts** Suppose the dew point of the air in your area is 20°C. The temperature outside is supposed to drop from 25°C to about 15°C by midnight. What weather condition will probably occur by morning? Explain why.

Connecting Concepts

Condensation Use what you learned about phase changes and condensation in Section 3.3 to explain how clouds form.

24.5 Weather Patterns

Reading Focus

Key Concepts
- How do air masses form?
- What are the four types of fronts?
- What types of weather are associated with cyclones and anticyclones?
- How do thunderstorms and tornadoes form?

Vocabulary
- air mass
- front
- cold front
- warm front
- stationary front
- occluded front
- cyclone
- anticyclone
- thunderstorm
- lightning
- thunder
- tornado
- hurricane

Reading Strategy

Outlining Before you read, make an outline of this section. Use the green headings as the main topics and the blue headings as subtopics. As you read, add supporting details.

Weather Patterns
I. Air Masses
II. Fronts
A. Cold Fronts
B. _____
C. _____
D. _____

"**W**e've been basking in this high-pressure system for a week," says the weather reporter on a local TV station, pointing to a large weather map of the country. "But here comes trouble in the form of a cold front moving in from the northwest."

What does it mean to be "basking in a high-pressure system"? Why is a cold front "trouble"? What, in fact, is a "cold front"? In this section, you'll find out the answers to these questions, as well as the meanings of many terms you've heard weather reporters use.

Air Masses

The weather that you experience from day to day is the result of the movement and interactions of air masses in Earth's atmosphere. An **air mass** is a large body of air that has fairly uniform physical properties, such as temperature and moisture content, at any given altitude. Air masses can cover large portions of continents. **An air mass forms when a large body of air becomes fairly stationary over a region of Earth's surface or as air moves over a large, uniform region like an ocean.** The air is strongly influenced by the properties of the region.

Figure 19 A cold front moving in brings stormy weather. The arrow shows the direction that the front is moving.

Direction of front

Modeling Air Masses

Materials: plastic or cardboard divider, clear plastic tank, warm colored sugar solution, cold sugar solution

Procedure

1. Use the divider to separate the clear plastic tank into two equal parts.

2. To model a front between warm and cool air masses, pour the warm, colored sugar solution into one part of the tank. At the same time, have a classmate pour an equal amount of the cold sugar solution into the other part.

3. Observe the two solutions through the side of the tank as you quickly lift the divider straight up and out of the tank.

Analyze and Conclude

1. **Applying Concepts** What caused the solutions to move as they did? Explain your answer.

2. **Using Models** How is this model similar to the behavior of air masses when they meet?

Air masses can vary greatly. Think of the differences in the air above the Gulf of Mexico and the air above northwestern Canada. The first property you might think of is temperature. It's usually a lot warmer near the Gulf of Mexico than it is in Canada. You might also think of humidity. The air above the Gulf of Mexico contains more water vapor than the air above northwestern Canada. Each type of air mass reflects the characteristics of the region where it formed. An air mass that forms over water, for example, contains more water vapor than one that forms over land. An air mass that forms over the Arctic is much colder than one that forms over the tropics.

Air masses are classified according to whether they form over water or land, and the latitude where they form. A maritime air mass forms over water. A continental air mass forms over land. An air mass that forms north of 50° north latitude or south of 50° south latitude, where it is often extremely cold, is called a polar air mass. An air mass that originates in the tropics, where it is warm, is called a tropical air mass.

The air masses that most affect weather in North America include maritime polar air masses, continental polar air masses, maritime tropical air masses, and continental tropical air masses. As shown in Figure 20, maritime polar air masses originate over the frigid North Pacific and North Atlantic oceans. They are cool and moist, and often bring heavy precipitation to coastal areas. Continental polar air masses form over northern Canada and bring cold, dry air to the central and eastern United States. Maritime tropical air masses originate over the Gulf of Mexico and warm oceans to the south. They bring warm, moist air and are often accompanied by fog or rain. Continental tropical air masses form over northern Mexico and dry areas of the Southwest. They bring hot, dry air to the southern Great Plains.

Figure 20 Air masses that form in different regions affect North American weather.
Interpreting Diagrams *What type of air mass is moving toward the northwestern United States? What type of air does it contain?*

Fronts

Air masses don't stay where they form. They move with the circulation of air throughout the world. Recall that convection currents cause warm air near the equator to move toward the poles and cold air at the poles to move toward the equator. Polar air masses, therefore, tend to move toward the equator, and tropical air masses tend to move toward the poles. These air masses collide in the middle latitudes.

As an air mass moves, it tends to retain the properties of the region where it formed. So, a continental polar air mass retains the low temperatures and dryness of its source region as it moves south. Likewise, a maritime tropical air mass retains the high temperatures and moisture of its source region as it moves north. When such different air masses meet, they ordinarily don't mix. Instead, a boundary forms between them.

The sharply defined boundary that forms when two unlike air masses meet is called a **front.** For example, when a continental polar air mass moves southeast and collides with a maritime tropical air mass, a front forms between the two. Clouds and precipitation often accompany fronts. 🔑 **There are four types of fronts: cold fronts, warm fronts, stationary fronts, and occluded fronts.**

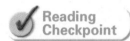 **Reading Checkpoint** *What is a front?*

Cold Fronts In North America, a cold continental polar air mass often moves southeastward into the Midwest. There, it may collide with a maritime tropical air mass from the Gulf of Mexico. At the boundary between the two air masses, a cold front forms. A **cold front** occurs when a cold air mass overtakes a warm air mass.

Figure 21 shows what happens when a cold front forms. Because cold air is denser than warm air, the cold air mass remains close to the ground and moves underneath the warm air mass. The cold air mass forces the warm air mass to rise. Cold fronts usually move quickly and are relatively steep, so the warm air mass is often lifted rapidly.

The rapid rise of warm air often produces cumulus and cumulonimbus clouds. Strong winds, severe thunderstorms, and large amounts of precipitation are often associated with cold fronts. However, because the slope of a cold front is steep and such fronts travel quickly, the severe weather usually lasts for only a short time. Then, as the front passes, the cold air mass settles in, the skies clear, and temperatures drop.

Rising warm air

Cold air mass sinks under the warm air mass.

Direction of front

Precipitation

Figure 21 A cold front forms when a cold air mass overtakes a warm air mass.

Clouds form as rising moist, warm air condenses.

Rising warm air

Direction of front

Cold air mass sinks under the warm air mass.

Precipitation

Figure 22 A warm front occurs when a warm air mass overtakes a cold air mass. **Applying Concepts** *What types of weather are associated with cold fronts and warm fronts?*

Go Online
active art

For: Activity on fronts
Visit: PHSchool.com
Web Code: ccp-3245

Warm Fronts Imagine that a continental polar air mass has settled in the Midwest and a maritime tropical air mass moves toward it from the southeast. As the air masses collide, a warm front results. A **warm front** occurs when a warm air mass overtakes a cold air mass.

Figure 22 shows what happens when a warm front forms. Because the cold air is denser, it remains close to the ground. The advancing warm air mass rises up over the cold air mass. The surface of a warm front is usually less steep than that of a cold front, as you can see by comparing Figures 21 and 22. A warm front has a gentle slope because the advancing warm air mass gradually moves up and over the cold air mass.

As the warm air rises, stratus clouds form. If the warm air mass contains a large amount of moisture, there will be a steady rain. Occasionally heavy showers or thunderstorms occur. Once the front has passed, the warm air mass settles in. The skies are mostly clear, often with some cumulus clouds present, and temperatures rise.

Stationary Fronts The clash of air masses is not always as simple as those that produce cold fronts and warm fronts. Sometimes when two air masses converge, neither air mass overruns the other. Rather, a front forms, and either stays where it formed or moves slowly. When two unlike air masses have formed a boundary but neither is moving, the front is called a **stationary front.** Stationary fronts often result in clouds and steady rain or snow for several days.

Occluded Fronts Another kind of front can occur because cold fronts generally move faster than warm fronts. An **occluded front** forms when a warm air mass is caught between two cooler air masses. The colder air masses force the warm air mass to rise, cutting it off from the ground and trapping it between the two cold air masses. As this warm air rises and cools, its water vapor typically condenses. As a result, occluded fronts are generally accompanied by cloudy skies and precipitation.

Low- and High-Pressure Systems

Air masses are part of larger weather systems. Weather systems are organized around either a center of high air pressure or a center of low air pressure, and may include more than one type of air mass. Weather systems can be huge. Centers of high air pressure may have diameters of 1500 kilometers and centers of low air pressure often have diameters of more than 1000 kilometers.

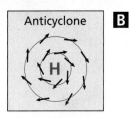

Cyclones A weather system with a center of low air pressure is called a **cyclone,** or sometimes simply a low. As Figure 23 shows, winds in a cyclone circulate counterclockwise in the Northern Hemisphere.

As the warm air at the center of a cyclone rises, pressure decreases. Because air moves from high-pressure areas to low-pressure areas, air spirals in toward the center of a cyclone. Clouds form and precipitation develops. ⟨⟩ **Cyclones are associated with clouds, precipitation, and stormy weather.** Because air is converging in a cyclone, air masses collide and fronts develop.

Cyclones don't stay in one place. A cyclone generally moves in the direction of global winds, and the weather of the cyclone moves along with it. In the middle latitudes of the Northern Hemisphere, the global winds are the westerlies. The westerly winds typically cause fronts and storms to move across the United States from west to east.

Anticyclones A weather system with a swirling center of high air pressure is called an **anticyclone,** or sometimes simply a high. As Figure 23 shows, winds in an anticyclone circulate clockwise in the Northern Hemisphere. Because the center of an anticyclone has high pressure, air flows away from that center. As air flows away from the center, air from higher in the troposphere descends and replaces it. When air descends, it warms and its relative humidity decreases. ⟨⟩ **The weather associated with an anticyclone includes clear skies, very little precipitation, and generally calm conditions.**

 How does air move in an anticyclone?

Figure 23 Cyclones and anticyclones are large weather systems. **A** In the Northern Hemisphere, winds in a cyclone blow counterclockwise and converge. **B** In an anticyclone, winds blow clockwise and diverge.

Figure 24 Winds and heavy rain are common in cyclones.

Storms

You've probably read a mystery or seen a horror film in which the setting is an old house on a stormy night. The winds howl, lightning flashes, and rain pounds the roof. Storms feature strong winds and heavy precipitation. The major types of storms are thunderstorms, tornadoes, and tropical storms, including hurricanes.

Figure 25 Thunderstorms are associated with tall cumulonimbus clouds where there are strong updrafts of warm air. Thunderstorms produce thunder and lightning.

Thunderstorms A **thunderstorm** is a small weather system that includes thunder and lightning. It is usually accompanied by strong winds and heavy rain or hail. **Thunderstorms form when columns of air rise within a cumulonimbus cloud.** These rising columns are often the result of colliding air masses. When a cold front forms, the cold air mass quickly lifts the warm air mass up, and thunderstorms often result. Thunderstorms can also occur on hot summer days when buoyant air rises as part of a convection current within an air mass. If the rising air is cooled to the dew point and the convection is strong enough, a thunderstorm can result. Figure 25 shows how this process occurs.

One striking feature of a thunderstorm is **lightning,** which is a sudden electrical discharge in the atmosphere. Recall from physics that there must be separated positive and negative charges for an electrical discharge to occur. Positive charges tend to develop near the top of a cumulonimbus cloud, while negative charges tend to develop near the base of the cloud. When the potential difference between the positive and negative charges becomes great enough, a discharge occurs. You see the discharge as a lightning flash.

When you think of lightning, you probably also think of thunder. **Thunder** is the sound produced by rapidly expanding air along the path of a lightning discharge. When lightning occurs, the air around it is heated to as much as 33,000°C. The heated air expands explosively, producing sound waves that you hear as thunder. Although thunder and lightning occur at the same time, you hear thunder after you see lightning because light travels much faster than sound.

Tornadoes Twister—even the mere mention of one of these violent storms is enough to make most people shudder. Twister is a common name for a **tornado,** a small but intense windstorm that takes the form of a rotating column of air that touches the ground.

Tornadoes most often form at the leading edge of an advancing cold front or along a line of thunderstorms where winds are converging to a center of very low pressure. **A tornado forms when a vertical cylinder of rotating air develops in a thunderstorm.**

Figure 26 A tornado crosses a farm field. **Applying Concepts** *Why do most tornadoes occur in the spring?*

A tornado appears as a twisting funnel cloud descending from the bottom of a cumulonimbus cloud, as shown in Figure 26. A tornado's winds can sometimes be more than 500 kilometers per hour, although they are more typically about 150 kilometers per hour. A large tornado can cause death and tremendous destruction.

For a tornado to develop, there must be great differences between the properties of colliding air masses. Air masses in the spring tend to have the most contrasting properties, and therefore it is during this season that most tornadoes occur. In the United States, where most of the world's tornadoes develop, these storms occur mainly in the Midwest and the South.

Tropical Storms and Hurricanes Thunderstorms and tornadoes are often associated with cyclones of the middle latitudes. Cyclones also develop in the tropics, where they can develop into tropical storms or hurricanes. A **hurricane** is a large tropical cyclone with winds of at least 119 kilometers per hour (74 miles per hour).

For: Activity on hurricanes
Visit: PHSchool.com
Web Code: ccc-3245

Section 24.5 Assessment

Reviewing Concepts

1. How does an air mass form?
2. What are the four types of fronts?
3. What types of weather do cyclones and anticyclones bring?
4. Compare and contrast how a typical thunderstorm forms with how a tornado forms.

Critical Thinking

5. **Applying Concepts** Why do continental polar air masses have different properties than maritime tropical air masses?

6. **Predicting** A weather reporter says that a warm air mass is caught between two cooler air masses in your area. What kind of weather can you expect in the near future, and why?

Connecting Concepts

Electricity Use what you learned about static electricity in Chapter 20 to explain what lightning is and how it is caused.

Hurricanes

A hurricane is a huge column of spiraling air with winds blowing at speeds of at least 119 kilometers per hour. Hurricanes are highly destructive if they reach land.

All hurricanes start as storms over warm tropical seas where the water temperature is at least 27°C. As the sun heats the ocean's surface, masses of moist, warm air accumulate and rise up, forming huge clouds. More air is sucked into the region from all directions and spirals toward the center. As the hurricane grows stronger, it moves westward, pushed by prevailing winds. Eventually, hurricanes in the Northern Hemisphere move northward, where the cooler temperatures reduce the supply of warm air and moisture needed to maintain the storm. If the hurricane hits land, it is no longer fed by heat and moisture from the ocean, so it loses energy and dissipates.

Typical path of a hurricane.

Life of a Hurricane

These satellite images show hurricanes at four stages of development.

1. The hurricane begins as a swirling cloud of rising air.
2. By day 3, the storm has developed an eye, which is a sign that the hurricane has strengthened.
3. Within 6 days the hurricane has reached its greatest intensity.
4. As the hurricane reaches land, it begins to weaken.

Eye starting to form

Sharply defined eye

Hurricane starting to weaken as it moves over land

Clouds dissipating

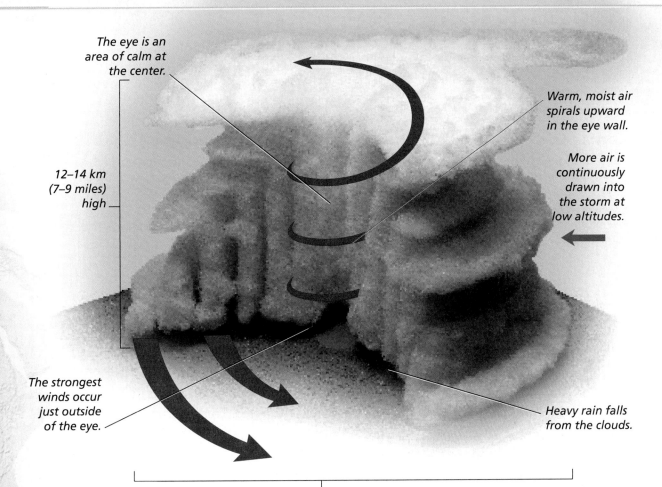

The eye is an area of calm at the center.

12–14 km (7–9 miles) high

Warm, moist air spirals upward in the eye wall.

More air is continuously drawn into the storm at low altitudes.

The strongest winds occur just outside of the eye.

Heavy rain falls from the clouds.

Hurricanes are typically about 600 km (370 miles) across.

Inside a Hurricane

At the center of a hurricane is a calm region called the eye. The eye is a region of very low pressure. Surrounding the eye is a wall of thick clouds, rain, and spiraling winds. Outside of this wall there are often additional bands of clouds and rain. Hurricanes spin in a counterclockwise direction in the Northern Hemisphere, and clockwise in the Southern Hemisphere.

Going Further

- Hurricanes are often remembered for the damage they cause. Some hurricanes may even have changed the course of history. Use library or Internet resources to research a past hurricane. Prepare a poster summarizing what you have learned.

Storm Surge

As it moves across the ocean, the low-pressure eye of the hurricane sucks water into a mound or swell, which can be as high as 8 m (26 ft). When the hurricane hits land, this water surges over coastal regions. The surge may destroy homes and wash boats inland, as in the Mississippi photo above, following Hurricane Katrina in 2005.

24.6 Predicting the Weather

Reading Focus

Key Concepts

- What technologies help meteorologists predict the weather?
- How do meteorologists show information on weather maps?

Vocabulary

- meteorologists
- isotherm
- isobar

Reading Strategy

Identifying the Main Idea Copy the table below. As you read the text, write the main idea for each topic heading.

Heading	Main Idea
Weather forecasting	a. _____?
Weather maps	b. _____?

An old folk rhyme includes this line: "The moon in halos hid her head. . . ." The rhyme suggests that a halo around the moon is a sign that rain or snow should be expected. This bit of folk wisdom has some scientific validity. When you see a halo around the moon, what you're seeing is moonlight shining through cirrostratus clouds. Because cirrostratus clouds often move in before storm clouds, a halo around the moon might indeed indicate precipitation in the near future.

Now consider another bit of weather wisdom from long ago: If a cat scratches itself while sitting on a fence, expect rain before night. Would you look for rain if you saw a cat do that? Probably not. That's the trouble with folk wisdom. Some of it makes sense, and some of it doesn't. Luckily, there are now more reliable ways of forecasting the weather.

Figure 27 Moonlight reflecting off ice crystals in cirrostratus clouds can cause a halo to appear around the moon. Such a halo often indicates that precipitation is on the way.

Weather Forecasting

The study of Earth's atmosphere is called meteorology. **Meteorologists** (mee tee uh RAWL uh jists) are scientists who study weather. **Meteorologists use many technologies to help predict the weather, including Doppler radar, automated weather stations, weather satellites, and high-speed computers.**

Doppler Radar Doppler radar is a technology based on use of the Doppler effect. Recall from physics that the Doppler effect is the apparent change in frequency of waves as either the source of the waves moves or the observer moves. Doppler radar works by bouncing radio waves off particles of precipitation in moving storms and then measuring the frequency of the waves that return.

The frequency changes as the storm moves, so the speed of the storm can be calculated from how much the frequency changes. With Doppler technology, meteorologists can now track the paths of thunderstorms and potential tornadoes with much greater accuracy than in the past.

Weather Stations and Satellites

Automated weather stations are important in gathering weather data. These stations gather information without a human observer being present. A typical weather station is shown in Figure 28. It includes sensors that measure weather data such as temperature, precipitation, and wind speed and direction. The information collected is transmitted as radio signals to a weather center, where it can be displayed on a computer monitor.

Since the early 1960s, weather satellites have been placed in orbit around Earth to collect information about weather, including cloud cover, humidity, temperature, and wind speed. Meteorologists combine data from various weather stations and satellites to form a comprehensive view of a region's weather.

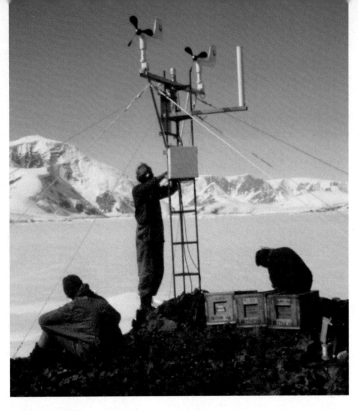

Figure 28 These scientists are setting up an automatic weather station on an island in the Bigourdan Fjord, Antarctica.

Data Analysis

Tracking the Weather

Meteorologists track weather data closely to help produce accurate short-term forecasts and to understand longer-term variations in weather. The table at the right provides the actual daily average temperature and daily precipitation for Minneapolis and St. Paul, Minnesota, for a seven-day period. Use the table and your knowledge of weather to answer the questions below.

1. **Using Tables** On which day was the average daily temperature highest? On which day was it lowest?

2. **Calculating** The average daily temperature on Day 7 was 11°C below normal. What is the normal temperature for that date?

3. **Using Tables** What were the maximum and minimum average daily temperatures over the week? What was the temperature range?

November Weather							
Day	1	2	3	4	5	6	7
Average Daily Temp. (°C)	−7	−7	−4	−4	−6	−5	−13
Daily Precip. (cm)	0	0	11	1	3	16	3

4. **Inferring** What was the total precipitation over the seven days? What was the likely form of this precipitation? (*Hint:* Recall that the freezing point of water is 0°C.)

5. **Predicting** What type of front most likely passed through the region on Day 6 or Day 7? Predict the weather conditions that followed.

6. **Making Generalizations** Suppose you were visiting Minneapolis during this period. Describe how the weather changed during your visit.

Weather Map Key

Low pressure	High pressure
Cold front	
Stationary front	
Warm front	
Occluded front	

Hurricane	Tropical storm
Rain	Thunderstorm
Sunny	Partly cloudy

-10s -0s 0s 10s 20s 30s 40s 50s 60s 70s 80s 90s 100s 110s

Figure 29 The isobars on this weather map encircle the centers of low-pressure and high-pressure systems. You can also see a cold front, a warm front, and a stationary front as well as a hurricane and a tropical storm. **Interpreting Visuals** *According to the weather map, what are the weather conditions in New Orleans, Louisiana?*

Go Online

SCIENCE NEWS

For: Articles on weather and climate
Visit: PHSchool.com
Web Code: cce-3246

High-Speed Computers High-speed computers help meteorologists compile and analyze the tremendous amount of weather data collected every day. With these data, scientists make both short-term and long-term forecasts. How accurate are these forecasts? Most forecasts can be quite accurate in the short term, from 12 hours to 3 days. Meteorologists can also accurately forecast the movement of large weather systems, such as cyclones, over a period of 3 to 7 days. Predicting beyond a week, however, remains extremely difficult, even with modern technology. The movement of weather systems depend on too many variables for meteorologists to forecast the weather reliably over longer periods.

Reading Checkpoint *How accurate are most weather forecasts?*

Weather Maps

To help analyze weather data, meteorologists make maps that show weather patterns of different regions. You've probably seen weather maps in newspapers or on TV weather reports. **Weather maps typically show predicted temperatures and include sun or cloud symbols to indicate cloud cover. They have drawings of rain or snow to show areas of precipitation.** They also usually include symbols for the different kinds of fronts and areas of high and low pressure.

Although the weather maps you see in newspapers or on TV are useful to most people, meteorologists need additional information on maps. For example, temperatures might be plotted and analyzed on a map using isotherms. An **isotherm** is a line on a map that connects points of equal air temperature. With this kind of map, a meteorologist can quickly see temperature patterns.

A comprehensive weather map that meteorologists prepare and use is a summary of weather conditions at a given moment for a given region. This kind of weather map typically includes information about weather systems and fronts. It also includes specific locations where weather data have been collected. More information on this type of map is included in Appendix F.

Figure 29 shows a simplified weather map smilar to what you might find in your local newspaper. Notice that temperature data are displayed using a series of colored bands that group regions in ten-degree temperature intervals. Also notice that there is a tropical storm near New Orleans and a hurricane near Cuba on the weather map. Both are low-pressure centers. To the left of the map is a key for weather symbols used on such maps.

The lines on this weather map are isobars. An **isobar** is a line that connects points of equal air pressure. Notice that the isobars on this map are plotted at intervals of 4 millibars. Isobars help meteorologists, such as the woman shown in Figure 30, to identify the centers of high- and low-pressure systems and the locations of fronts.

Figure 30 Meteorologists use computers to help forecast the weather.

For: Activity on weather maps
Visit: PHSchool.com
Web Code: ccc-3246

Section 24.6 Assessment

Reviewing Concepts

1. What are some of the technologies meteorologists use to collect weather data?

2. How do meteorologists show differences in temperature and pressure on weather maps?

3. Explain how meteorologists use Doppler radar to track and predict the weather.

4. How do meteorologists use high-speed computers to help forecast the weather?

5. Describe the type of information that is typically shown on the weather maps prepared by meteorologists.

Critical Thinking

6. **Inferring** Why might a meteorologist want to compare today's weather map with yesterday's weather map?

7. **Applying Concepts** Why can't meteorologists accurately forecast the weather beyond a period of about a week?

Writing in Science

Solving a Problem Suppose you live in "Tornado Alley," a region in the central United States that is frequently hit by tornadoes. What technology discussed in the text would you recommend to warn residents of your area about an approaching tornado? Write a brief proposal describing the potential benefits of this technology.

24.7 Climate

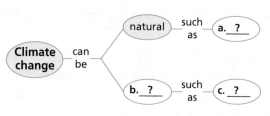

Reading Focus

Key Concepts
- How is climate different from weather?
- What factors determine the climate of a region?
- How do scientists study past climates?
- What natural forces contribute to climate change?
- How are human activities affecting Earth's climate?

Vocabulary
- climate
- desert
- ice ages
- El Niño
- global warming

Reading Strategy

Building Vocabulary Copy the partially completed concept map below. Then, as you read, complete it with terms from this section.

Climate change → can be → natural → such as → a. ?

Climate change → can be → b. ? → such as → c. ?

A friend from another state wants to visit you during school vacation. She's never been to your area, and wants to know what type of clothes to bring. Should she bring her heavy coat or her rain gear? How would you answer her? You could look outside to check the current weather, but that can change quickly. What your friend really needs to know is the typical weather for your area at that time of year. She needs to know about the **climate,** which is the long-term weather conditions of a place or region. **Climate is a description of the pattern of weather over many years.** It includes average weather conditions as well as how weather varies over time, rather than day-to-day changes in the condition of the atmosphere.

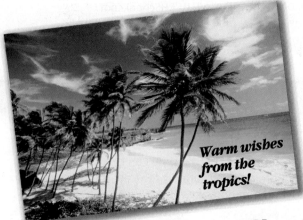

Warm wishes from the tropics!

Figure 31 This postcard shows a warm coastal climate.
Classifying *How might a postcard for your town illustrate its climate?*

Classifying Climates

Scientists divide the world's climates into several different types. What is the climate like in your part of the world? To find out, look at the world map in Figure 32. The map is divided into six major climate groups: tropical, temperate marine, temperate continental, polar, dry, and highlands. One of the six major groups, the dry climates, is determined mainly by precipitation. Another group, the highland climates, is determined mainly by elevation. The four remaining groups are determined mostly on the basis of temperature. Scientists further divide the major climate groups into many different specific climates. It is important to realize, however, that this map is not static. It changes with changing global temperatures and patterns of precipitation.

Climate Regions

——	National Boundary

Tropical—Temperatures 18 °C or above

■	Tropical wet—Hot and rainy all year round
■	Tropical wet-and-dry—Hot with wet and dry seasons

Dry – Potential evaporation exceeds precipitation.

■	Semiarid—Dry but about 25–50 cm/yr of precipitation
■	Arid—Desert with little precipitation

Temperate Marine—Humid with mild winters

■	Mediterranean—Warm, dry summers and rainy winters
■	Humid subtropical—Hot summers and cool to mild winters
■	Marine west coast—Cool summers and mild winters

Temperate Continental—Cold, snowy winters

■	Humid continental—Hot summers and cold winters
■	Subarctic—Short summers and long, cold winters

Highlands

■	Mountains—Cool, wet, and mountainous

Polar—Averages below 10 °C in warmest month

■	Tundra—Always cold and dry with short summer
□	Ice cap—Always cold, averaging below 0 °C

Figure 32 This map illustrates the major climates of the world. **Interpreting Diagrams** *What type of climate do you live in?*

In their study and classification of climates, scientists consider many factors, including soil, vegetation, and animal life. Two factors, however, are most important. ☞ **The two main factors that determine a region's climate are temperature and precipitation.** Scientists consider average temperature and precipitation over the year, as well as how these factors vary from day to day and season to season.

Factors Affecting Temperature

A region's pattern of temperature depends on several factors. ☞ **Factors that affect a region's temperature include its latitude, distance from large bodies of water, ocean currents, and altitude.** The latitude of a region is perhaps the most important factor affecting temperature. Places at the same latitude experience the same seasonal changes in solar radiation and therefore generally have similar temperatures throughout the year.

Another important factor affecting the temperature of a region is its distance from a large body of water. The air above large bodies of water has much less variation in temperature than the air over land. The moderating effects of water are felt in coastal regions. These regions typically have less variation in temperature over the course of a year than do regions located at the same latitude within continents. The temperature of coastal regions is also influenced by nearby ocean currents.

Figure 33 Giraffes inhabit the grasslands near Mount Kilimanjaro, Tanzania. Although Mount Kilimanjaro is near the equator, its top is covered by snow all year because of its high altitude.

Figure 34 A mountain range can form a barrier to the movement of humid air.
Applying Concepts *Where does the heaviest rainfall occur?*

Not all locations at the same latitude have similar temperatures. As you've learned, temperature decreases as altitude increases. As Figure 33 shows, areas that are high above sea level, such as parts of East Africa, have lower average temperatures than areas at the same latitude that are closer to sea level.

Factors Affecting Precipitation

Like temperature, a region's pattern of precipitation depends on several factors. ◯ **Factors that affect a region's precipitation include its latitude, the distribution of air pressure systems and global winds, and the existence of a mountain barrier.** Recall that the maximum amount of water vapor that the air can hold is greater at high temperatures than at low temperatures. Thus, the warm air over the equator usually contains more moisture than the cold air over the poles. As a result, precipitation is generally higher near the equator than near the poles.

A **desert** is an extremely dry region, receiving less than 25 centimeters of rain per year. Deserts may be hot or cold. Many deserts receive almost no rain because they are located within high-pressure belts. A series of deserts can be found around 30° north and south of the equator.

The direction of prevailing winds can play an important role in the amount of precipitation a region receives. For example, a coastal region where the wind generally blows from the ocean onto land will receive a large amount of precipitation. However, if prevailing winds blow from the land toward the ocean, the region will receive much less precipitation.

The very dry high plains of western North America are the result of a mountain barrier. The moist air from the Pacific Ocean loses its moisture as it rises over the mountains of the West, as shown in Figure 34. As the air rises, it cools and its water vapor condenses. Rain or snow falls on the ocean side of the mountains. The air that reaches the far side of the mountains is much drier.

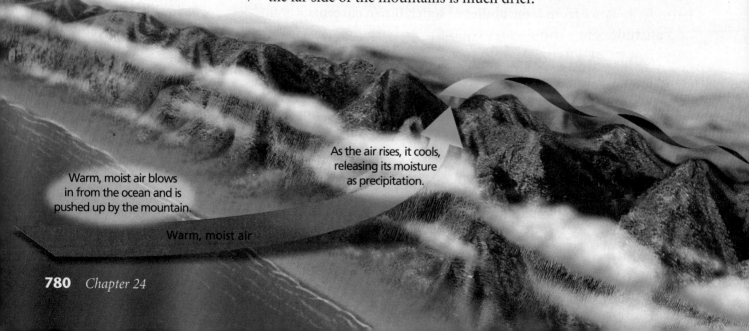

As the air rises, it cools, releasing its moisture as precipitation.

Warm, moist air blows in from the ocean and is pushed up by the mountain.

Warm, moist air

Studying Climate Change

As far back as can be seen in the geologic record, global and regional climates have continually undergone change. For example, some areas in the state of Nebraska used to be desert, but now the sand dunes are covered with a thin layer of vegetation. In other parts of the world, such as the Middle East, a temperate climate became much drier over time. Thousands of years ago, Iraq was a lush, fertile land, and today it is mostly desert.

In order to describe trends in climate change, scientists need climate information from the past. **Scientists study past climates by analyzing data from ice cores, fossils, the pollen record, and tree rings.**

Ice Cores Figure 35 shows one of the best tools for studying climate change: ice cores. In very cold regions such as Antarctica, snow falls each year, forming a new layer of the glacier. By drilling down into the glacier and extracting a core of ice, scientists can obtain a record that spans up to hundreds of thousands of years. The composition of each layer in the ice core reveals how cold it was, how dry and dusty it was, and how much carbon dioxide was in the atmosphere when the layer formed.

Fossils The most abundant isotope of oxygen is oxygen-16. Oxygen-18, which has two more neutrons, is much rarer. During periods of cold climates, ocean water becomes richer in oxygen-18. Plants and animals living in the water incorporate that ratio of isotopes in their body parts. By analyzing the oxygen content in marine fossils, scientists can study climate change over long time periods, ranging from tens of millions of years to hundreds of millions of years.

Pollen and Tree Rings Scientists use pollen records and tree rings to assess climate changes over shorter time periods, ranging from decades to centuries. Different kinds of plants thrive in hot or cold temperatures or in wet or dry climates. By identifying the kinds of pollen found in ice cores or lake sediments, scientists can learn about the climate history. Tree rings also reveal information about past climates. Depending on how favorable the climate is, trees grow by different amounts. Thick tree rings indicate warm and moist climates. Thin rings indicate cold and dry climates.

Figure 35 Ice cores from Antarctica reveal a climate record that goes back more than 800,000 years.

Dry, hot air

Figure 36 Chemical weathering of the Himalayas contributes to the removal of CO_2 from the atmosphere.

Natural Climate Change

A number of natural forces contribute to changes in climate. Natural causes of climate change include plate tectonics, variations in Earth's position relative to the sun, and variations in solar radiation, ocean circulation, and volcanic activity. These factors affect climates over different time frames. For example, a major volcanic eruption can have an immediate effect on climates. But changes in Earth's orbit occur much more gradually, affecting global climates over a 100,000-year period.

Plate Tectonics In Section 22.4, you learned about the movement of Earth's plates. Tectonic-plate activity alters ocean circulation patterns and land erosion rates. These geographic changes, in turn, affect climates over ultra-long periods of tens, or even hundreds, of millions of years.

The Himalayas, shown in Figure 36, offer an example of how scientists have linked plate movement to long-term climate change. The Himalayas formed as a result of the collision of the Indo-Australian and Eurasian plates. As the mountains have risen, they have weathered relatively rapidly. The carbonic acid in rainwater reacts with minerals in the rock, forming carbon-containing compounds that wash down rivers and into the ocean. Eventually, the carbon is deposited in the form of carbonate rocks such as limestone. Over time, these processes have gradually reduced atmospheric carbon dioxide (CO_2) levels and contributed to a long-term cooling of global climates over the past 60 million years.

Earth's Position Relative to the Sun Earth travels in an elliptical orbit around the sun. But the shape of the ellipse varies due to the gravitational pull of other planets. When its orbit is more elliptical, Earth spends more time farther from the sun and receives less sunlight during the year. This contributes to the occurrence of an **ice age**, a period when Earth's climates are colder than usual and glaciers cover large portions of the continents. Ice ages alternate with shorter warm periods, when Earth's orbit is more circular. Each cycle—an ice age interrupted by a warm period—lasts about 100,000 years. The cycle is also influenced by changes in the angle of Earth's axis. The most recent ice age ended between 10,000 and 20,000 years ago.

Figure 37 The shape of Earth's orbit around the sun changes due to the gravitational forces of other planets in the solar system. *Interpreting Diagrams In which orbit does less sunlight reach Earth? How does this change affect Earth's climate?*

Solar Activity Variations in the sun's radiation have been linked to climate changes on Earth over periods ranging from decades to hundreds of years. The amount of solar energy received by Earth fluctuates over a roughly 11-year cycle that corresponds to changing patterns within the sun. In addition, the intensity of these cycles can vary over hundreds of years. The Little Ice Age, a period of cooling from about 1400 to about 1900, was caused by a decrease in solar output.

Ocean Circulation Ocean circulation plays a major role in transferring heat around the globe, and thus in controlling regional climates. Water circulates among the oceans in the form of currents. When these currents change over time, they cause climate change. For example, in the Pacific Ocean, water at the equator usually flows westward. But every three to eight years, prevailing winds weaken, and warm equatorial Pacific water moves eastward in an event called **El Niño**. In the United States, El Niño causes warmer-than-average winters in northern states and wetter-than-average winters in southeastern states.

Volcanic Activity Major volcanic eruptions emit huge amounts of ash and aerosols into the atmosphere. Aerosols are tiny solid particles or liquid drops that stay suspended in the air. Volcanic ash and aerosols in the atmosphere can partially reflect incoming solar radiation, resulting in sudden cooling of global climates. For example, eruptions of the Icelandic volcano Laki from 1783 to 1784 were followed by unusually cold winters in Europe and North America.

For: Activity on El Niño
Visit: PHSchool.com
Web Code: ccc-3247

Data Analysis

Tracking Climate Change

The graph shows how global surface temperatures since 1980 have changed relative to previous years. The blue curve shows the deviation in monthly average surface temperatures. The red curve shows a smoothed five-year average of the monthly data. The year is plotted on the x-axis. Just above the x-axis, two sets of colored bars indicate the durations of two different geologic events: El Niño and the volcanic eruptions of Mount Pinatubo in the Philippines.

Surface Temperature Record

1. **Calculating** Use the five-year average temperature deviation curve to determine how much Earth's surface temperature increased between 1980 and 2005. What was the average increase in surface temperature over this period in degrees Celsius per year?

2. **Using Graphs** How does El Niño affect the monthly average surface temperature? Is the same effect observed during every El Niño event since 1980? Explain.

3. **Inferring** What do you think might have caused monthly average surface temperatures to decline during El Niño events that occurred around 1992 and 1994?

Human Activities and Climate Change

Human populations alter the land, air, and water of Earth's surface faster than most geologic processes. A number of human activities—including agriculture, deforestation, urbanization, wetlands removal, and river management—have an impact on both regional and global climates. Perhaps the most significant human activity that causes climate change is fossil fuel combustion. The burning of coal, oil, and natural gas produces carbon dioxide, a gas that contributes to the greenhouse effect.

Greenhouse Gases Earlier in this chapter, you read about how the greenhouse effect keeps the lower atmosphere warm. In this process, certain gases in the atmosphere absorb energy that has been re-radiated by Earth's surface. Greenhouse gases help insulate Earth's surface, keeping it warm enough to support life.

Three important greenhouse gases are water vapor (H_2O), carbon dioxide (CO_2), and methane (CH_4). Human activity has little effect on the amount of water vapor in the atmosphere. However, activities such as fossil fuel burning and deforestation release billions of tons of CO_2 into the atmosphere each year. In addition, livestock farming releases methane into the air. **Many human activities are increasing the levels of greenhouse gases in the atmosphere. This increase is causing global temperatures to rise.** Between 1910 and 2010, average global temperatures increased by about 1°C. The process by which emissions from human activities increase the greenhouse effect is known as **global warming**.

To see how greenhouse gas levels vary over the long term, scientists can refer to Earth's climate record. For example, ice core samples indicate that atmospheric CO_2 levels over the past 800,000 years typically fluctuated between 170 and 280 parts per million (ppm). But over the last 200 years, CO_2 levels have increased sharply, as shown in Figure 38. Today, the concentration of CO_2 in the atmosphere is 390 ppm—and on the rise.

With the aid of climate models, scientists can predict the extent of global warming. Climate models are sophisticated computer programs that take into account natural and human causes to model both past and future climate changes. Current climate models predict that global temperatures will increase 2 to 5°C over the next century.

Figure 38 The graph shows how CO_2 levels in the atmosphere have changed over time.
Inferring *Why do you think atmospheric CO_2 levels increased dramatically after the year 1800?*

Reading Checkpoint *What kinds of human activities release carbon dioxide into the atmosphere?*

Effects of Global Warming An increase in global temperatures by just a few degrees may not seem like a lot. In the past, however, such increases caused significant changes to Earth's surface. The effects of global warming include droughts and forest fires, as shown in Figure 39. Other significant problems include desertification, changes to the biosphere, melting glaciers, rising sea levels, and regional changes in temperature and precipitation.

When Earth's climate gets warmer, the effects can vary greatly from region to region. Ocean and air currents can change, greatly heating some places and even cooling others. For example, the Antarctic Peninsula has been warming at the rapid rate of 0.5°C every 10 years, but much of the interior of Antarctica has actually been cooling. In general, however, land temperatures are rising much faster than ocean temperatures because more energy is needed to raise the temperature of water than that of rock.

When environments change slowly over millions of years, plant and animal life evolves to adapt. If these environments change too much, too quickly, many species will become extinct. In the case of global warming, only species that can adapt to warmer conditions will survive.

As you already know, when temperatures rise, ice tends to melt. There is evidence of this happening on a global scale: mountain glaciers worldwide are melting at an increasing rate; ice sheets in Antarctica are breaking up and flowing to the ocean; and the amount of Arctic winter sea ice at the North Pole is shrinking. At the same time, sea levels are rising, because of both the melting of continental ice and the thermal expansion of seawater as it warms. Since the end of the last ice age, sea levels have risen 122 meters. As glaciers continue to melt, sea levels will continue to rise. This rise poses a threat to the many people who live in coastal areas. In Figure 40, you can identify many low-lying parts of the eastern United States that are vulnerable to rising sea levels.

Figure 39 When global temperatures rise, some regions get very warm and dry. This can lead to water shortages, which make the land more vulnerable to forest fires.

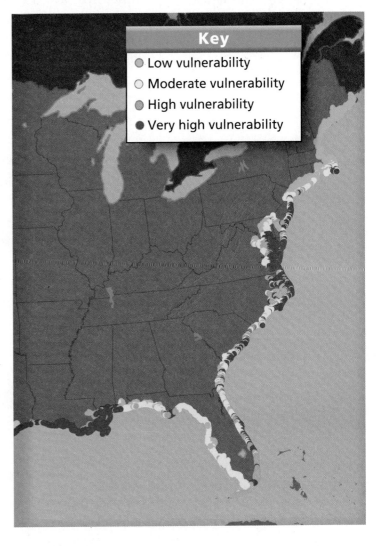

Key
- Low vulnerability
- Moderate vulnerability
- High vulnerability
- Very high vulnerability

Figure 40 This satellite image shows how sea level rise could affect the eastern United States.

Figure 41 The carbon capture system of this power plant in West Virginia helps to reduce the CO_2 emissions from burning coal.

Limiting Global Warming Despite the known effects of greenhouse gas emissions, fossil fuels remain a widespread energy resource. More than 85 percent of the world's energy needs are supplied by fossil fuels. Power plants burn coal; cars burn gasoline or diesel. How, then, can we reduce greenhouse gas emissions? There is no single easy solution, but we have a number of options available to us.

One of the simplest ways to reduce greenhouse gas emissions is to conserve energy. By eliminating bad habits that waste electricity, you consume less energy, which means less fossil fuel burned and less CO_2 emitted. Another option is to improve the efficiency of energy-consuming technologies. For example, developing more fuel-efficient cars will allow drivers to get more miles per gallon of fuel. At home, you can save energy by using more efficient lighting technologies, such as compact fluorescent lights (CFLs) or light emitting diodes (LEDs).

Clean energy sources offer a more groundbreaking solution to the global warming problem. *Clean energy* refers to energy sources that release very low amounts of greenhouse gases. Examples include solar, wind, hydroelectric, biomass, geothermal, tidal, and nuclear energy. Switching to clean energy for even a small portion of your daily energy consumption—such as heating hot-water or recharging electronic devices—can add up to a substantial reduction in CO_2 emissions.

Another technological solution is carbon capture, shown in Figure 41. In conventional coal-burning power plants, the CO_2 produced during combustion escapes into the atmosphere as exhaust. However, CO_2 can be removed either during or after the combustion process. The collected CO_2 then is pumped back into the ground. This process greatly reduces the "carbon footprint" of coal-burning power plants.

Section 24.7 Assessment

Reviewing Concepts

1. How do climate and weather differ?
2. What are the two main factors that determine a region's climate?
3. How can past climates be studied?
4. What natural forces cause climate change?
5. How do human activities impact Earth's climate?

Critical Thinking

6. **Applying Concepts** Why do you think there is more precipitation in southern Florida than there is in northern Alaska?

7. **Inferring** Would a single unusually hot summer prove that global warming is occurring? Explain your answer.

Connecting Concepts

Energy Resources Recall what you learned about nuclear energy, renewable energy resources, and conservation in Chapters 10 and 15. Choose one of those resources and describe how its use might help to reduce global warming.

Determining Relative Humidity

To measure relative humidity, you can use a sling psychrometer. This device contains two thermometers. An absorbent wick keeps the bulb of one thermometer wet. As you spin the psychrometer, air flows over the wet bulb, increasing the rate of evaporation. In this lab, you will discover how a sling psychrometer measures the relative humidity of the air.

Problem How can you measure the relative humidity of the air?

Materials
- sling psychrometer
- relative humidity chart from Appendix G
- clock or watch with second hand

 For the probeware version of this lab, see the Probeware Lab Manual, Lab 10.

Skills Using Tables, Formulating Hypotheses

Procedure

	Data Table		
Location	Dry Bulb Temp. (°C)	Wet Bulb Temp. (°C)	Relative Humidity (%)
Classroom			

1. On a separate sheet of paper, make a copy of the data table shown above.

2. Wet the cotton wick of the sling psychrometer with water.

3. Observe the temperature of the wet-bulb thermometer. Then, spin the psychrometer for 30 seconds. **CAUTION** *Take care not to spin the psychrometer near anyone or anything.*

4. Repeat Step 3 until the temperature of the wet-bulb thermometer remains constant. Then, record the temperatures of both thermometers in your data table.

5. Calculate the difference between your dry-bulb and wet-bulb temperatures.

6. In the relative humidity chart, find the row and column that list the dry-bulb temperature and the difference in temperature that you calculated. The number located where this row and column meet is the relative humidity of the classroom. Record the relative humidity in your data table.

7. Place the psychrometer on a flat surface. Observe the temperature of the wet-bulb thermometer every 30 seconds until it remains constant. Then, repeat Steps 2 through 5 at the location your teacher indicates.

Analyze and Conclude

1. **Analyzing Data** Why did the two thermometers have different temperatures?

2. **Formulating Hypotheses** Explain how the relative humidity of the air affected the difference between the temperatures of the two thermometers.

3. **Drawing Conclusions** What do you think caused the difference in relative humidity between the two locations?

4. **Predicting** How would the relative humidity change if you cooled the air in the classroom?

Go Further Measure and record the temperature and relative humidity outside your school or at home at various times of day for several days. Graph these data and explain any patterns that you observe.

For: Data sharing
Visit: PHSchool.com
Web Code: ccd-3240

24.1 The Atmosphere

 Key Concepts

- Earth's atmosphere forms a protective boundary and provides conditions that are suitable for life.
- Earth's atmosphere is a mixture of many gases in which tiny solid and liquid particles are suspended.
- As altitude increases, pressure and density decrease.
- Scientists use variations in temperature to divide the atmosphere into four vertical layers.

Vocabulary atmosphere, air pressure, barometer, troposphere, weather, stratosphere, ozone layer, mesosphere, thermosphere, ionosphere, aurora

24.2 The Sun and the Seasons

 Key Concepts

- Earth moves by rotation and revolution.
- Scientists use lines of latitude to mark out regions within which temperatures are similar.
- The seasons are caused by the tilt of Earth's axis.

Vocabulary rotation, revolution, tropic zone, temperate zones, polar zones, solstice, equinox

24.3 Solar Energy and Winds

Key Concepts

- Solar energy may be reflected, absorbed by the atmosphere, or absorbed by the surface.
- Energy is transferred within the troposphere in three ways: radiation, convection, and conduction.
- Winds are caused by differences in air pressure.
- Sea breezes and land breezes are local winds. Trade winds and westerlies are global winds.

Vocabulary greenhouse effect, wind, local wind, sea breeze, land breeze, global winds, Coriolis effect, monsoon, jet stream

24.4 Water in the Atmosphere

Key Concepts

- Water vapor condenses as dew, frost, clouds, or fog.
- Clouds form as warm, moist air rises and water vapor condenses in the atmosphere. The basic cloud forms are stratus, cumulus, and cirrus.
- The most common types of precipitation are rain, snow, hail, sleet, and freezing rain.

Vocabulary humidity, relative humidity, dew point, cloud, fog, stratus clouds, cumulus clouds, cirrus clouds

24.5 Weather Patterns

 Key Concepts

- An air mass forms when a large body of air becomes fairly stationary over Earth's surface or as air moves over a large uniform area.
- There are four types of fronts: cold fronts, warm fronts, stationary fronts, and occluded fronts.
- Cyclones are associated with stormy weather. Anticyclones are associated with clear, calm weather.
- Thunderstorms form when columns of air rise within a cumulonimbus cloud. A tornado forms when an area of rotating air develops in a thunderstorm.

Vocabulary air mass, front, cold front, warm front, stationary front, occluded front, cyclone, anticyclone, thunderstorm, lightning, thunder, tornado, hurricane

24.6 Predicting the Weather

 Key Concepts

- Meteorologists use technologies such as Doppler radar to help predict the weather.
- Weather maps often show predicted temperatures, cloud cover, and precipitation.

Vocabulary meteorologists, isotherm, isobar

24.7 Climate

Key Concepts

- Climate is a pattern of weather over many years.
- The two main factors that determine a region's climate are temperature and precipitation.
- Factors that affect a region's temperature include its latitude, distance from large bodies of water, ocean currents, and altitude.
- Factors that affect a region's precipitation include its latitude, the distribution of air pressure systems and global winds, and the existence of a mountain barrier.
- Scientists study past climates by analyzing data from ice cores, fossils, the pollen record, and tree rings.
- Natural causes of climate change include plate tectonics, variations in Earth's position relative to the sun, and variations in solar radiation, ocean circulation, and volcanic activity.
- Many human activities are increasing the levels of greenhouse gases in the atmosphere. This increase is causing global temperatures to rise.

Vocabulary climate, desert, ice ages, El Niño, global warming

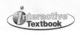
Reviewing Content

Choose the letter that best answers the question or completes the statement.

1. The most abundant gas in air is
   a. oxygen.
   b. nitrogen.
   c. carbon dioxide.
   d. hydrogen.

2. Earth's weather occurs primarily in the
   a. thermosphere.
   b. stratosphere.
   c. troposphere.
   d. mesosphere.

3. Wind is caused by differences in
   a. air pressure.
   b. altitude.
   c. humidity.
   d. condensation.

4. The amount of water vapor in the air is called
   a. dew.
   b. rain.
   c. humidity.
   d. precipitation.

5. A type of cloud that is commonly associated with fair weather is
   a. cumulus.
   b. cumulonimbus.
   c. altostratus.
   d. nimbostratus.

6. When the temperature equals the dew point, the relative humidity is
   a. zero.
   b. about 25%.
   c. about 50%.
   d. 100%.

7. When a warm air mass overtakes a cold air mass, the result is a (an)
   a. cold front.
   b. stationary front.
   c. warm front.
   d. occluded front.

8. Lines connecting areas of equal pressure on a weather map are called
   a. isotherms.
   b. barometers.
   c. isobars.
   d. weather symbols.

9. Generally, climates located farther from the equator have
   a. warmer ocean currents.
   b. lower temperatures.
   c. more rain.
   d. higher relative humidity.

10. A periodic warming of water in the central and eastern Pacific Ocean is called a (an)
    a. monsoon.
    b. jet stream.
    c. global warming.
    d. El Niño.

Understanding Concepts

11. Describe three functions of the atmosphere that make life on Earth possible.

12. How does temperature vary with altitude in the troposphere?

13. Why does Earth have seasons?

14. Describe three ways that the troposphere is heated.

15. Identify the type of front shown on the weather map below. What type of weather will this front likely bring?

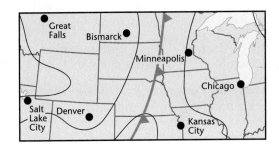

16. What causes global winds?

17. How does hail form?

18. What is the difference between sleet and freezing rain?

19. What is an air mass, and how do air masses form?

20. What are the major types of air masses that influence the weather in North America?

21. Explain how a warm front forms, and describe the weather that is usually associated with a warm front.

22. What is a stationary front, and how does one form?

23. Why do you hear thunder after you see a bolt of lightning?

24. Decribe two technologies that help meteorologists to forecast the weather.

25. Describe two ways in which oceans affect the climate of coastal areas.

26. What are ice ages, and why do they occur?

Critical Thinking

27. Inferring How might Earth be different if there were no ozone layer?

28. Applying Concepts Imagine that you measured air pressure with a mercury barometer at the bottom of a mountain and at the top of that mountain. At which location would the column of mercury be shorter? Explain your answer.

29. Inferring Scientists sometimes refer to one of the layers of the atmosphere as the "weather sphere." Which layer do you think this is, and why?

30. Designing an Experiment Design an experiment that could be used to determine how air pressure changes with altitude.

31. Predicting How might Earth's weather be different if Earth were not tilted on its axis?

32. Applying Concepts Sometimes, when you rise in the morning, you'll see fog over a large area. The fog is often gone by noon. Explain why the fog forms and why it disappears.

33. Classifying In just a few minutes, the weather in your neighborhood changes from sunny and warm to cool and windy, and rain begins to fall. What type of front has probably moved in?

34. Comparing and Contrasting Air masses collide and fronts develop in a cyclone, while air masses don't collide in an anticyclone. What causes this difference?

35. Inferring How would you expect the reading on a barometer to change as a storm moves into your area?

36. Applying Concepts Describe what happens to a hurricane when it passes over land, and why.

37. Inferring Would you expect a land area where the prevailing winds blow from the land to the ocean to receive very much or very little precipitation? Explain your answer.

38. Formulating Hypotheses Portland, Oregon, which is located near the Pacific coast, has milder winters than St. Louis, Missouri, which is located deep in the interior of North America. Yet Portland is farther north than St. Louis. How can you explain this difference in climate?

Analyzing Data

Use the graph below to answer Questions 39 and 40.

Maximum Water Vapor Content

39. Using Graphs What is the maximum number of grams of water vapor that can exist in a kilogram of air at −20°C, 0°C, 20°C, and 40°C?

40. Making Generalizations Use the graph to make a general statement about temperature and water vapor in the atmosphere.

Concepts in Action

41. Inferring Why don't hurricanes form over the Arctic Ocean?

42. Applying Concepts What factors discussed in this chapter affect the climate where you live?

43. Writing in Science Write a descriptive paragraph about a storm that you have experienced. What kind of storm was it?

Performance-Based Assessment

Predicting Use weather maps to interpret weather data for a city of your choice for three consecutive days. Record these data in a table, and predict what the weather will be for the city on the fourth day.

For: Self-grading assessment
Visit: PHSchool.com
Web Code: cca-3240

Standardized Test Prep

Choose the letter that best answers the question or completes the statement.

1. The stratosphere helps to protect Earth's surface from too much ultraviolet radiation because it contains a layer of
   (A) nitrogen.
   (B) carbon dioxide.
   (C) ozone.
   (D) ions.
   (E) water vapor.

2. Which of the following is NOT a type of precipitation?
   (A) dew
   (B) sleet
   (C) snow
   (D) hail
   (E) freezing rain

3. Which of the following is NOT generally associated with large amounts of precipitation?
   (A) anticyclone
   (B) hurricane
   (C) cold front
   (D) occluded front
   (E) thunderstorm

4. The two main factors that determine a region's climate are
   (A) air pressure and relative humidity.
   (B) temperature and precipitation.
   (C) air pressure and temperature.
   (D) precipitation and relative humidity.
   (E) temperature and relative humidity.

Use the graph below to answer questions 5 and 6.

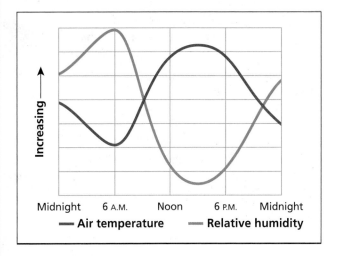

5. Relative humidity is at a minimum at about
   (A) midnight
   (B) 6 A.M.
   (C) 9 A.M.
   (D) 3 P.M.
   (E) 10 P.M.

6. At about what time is condensation most likely to occur?
   (A) 6 A.M.
   (B) 9 A.M.
   (C) noon
   (D) 3 P.M.
   (E) 6 P.M.

7. Isobars are lines on a weather map that connect points of equal
   (A) air temperature.
   (B) wind speed.
   (C) air pressure.
   (D) air density
   (E) precipitation.

25 The Solar System

What planet or moon is currently the target of a space mission and why?

Use library resources and the Internet to research an ongoing space mission to one of the planets or moons discussed in this chapter. Create a poster that details the goals, timeline, findings, and current status of the mission. Use a diagram of the solar system to chart the path of the spacecraft. Present your poster to the class, and then provide status updates on the mission by posting to your class blog.

How do science concepts apply to your world? Here are some questions you'll be able to answer after you read this chapter.

- **How does a spacesuit work?** *(Section 25.1)*

- **Why shouldn't you park a car too close to the ocean's edge?** *(Section 25.2)*

- **Why isn't Earth covered by craters?** *(Section 25.3)*

- **Did Mars once have liquid water?** *(Section 25.3)*

- **Where, besides Earth, is life most likely to occur in our solar system?** *(Section 25.4)*

- **What lies at the outer edges of the solar system?** *(Section 25.4)*

- **Why do comets have tails?** *(page 816)*

- **Are there planets around other stars?** *(Section 25.5)*

Chapter Preview

This composite photo shows Saturn and four of its moons.

Inquiry Activity

Why Does the Sun Seem to Move?

Procedure

1. Tape a pencil to a sunny window with its point facing up.

2. Tape a sheet of paper to a desk or the floor so that the shadow of the pencil point falls on the paper. Use a compass to find east, and mark an arrow on the paper pointing to the east. **CAUTION** *Do not look directly at the sun.*

3. Mark the position of the pencil point's shadow on the paper. Record the time of day.

4. After 10 minutes, repeat Step 3.

Think About It

1. **Observing** In which direction did the shadow move between your two observations?

2. **Inferring** What can you infer about the apparent motion of the sun from the movement of the shadow?

3. **Drawing Conclusions** How must Earth be moving to explain the apparent movement of the sun?

25.1 Exploring the Solar System

Reading Focus

Key Concepts

- How are the geocentric and heliocentric models of the solar system different?
- What keeps the planets in orbit around the sun?
- What bodies make up the solar system?
- How is the solar system being explored today?

Vocabulary

- geocentric
- heliocentric
- ecliptic plane
- moon
- astronomical unit
- space probe

Reading Strategy

Comparing and Contrasting After you read, compare the geocentric and heliocentric systems by completing the table below.

	Location of Earth	Location of Sun	Developer(s) of Theory
Geocentric System	Center of universe	a. ___?___	b. ___?___
Heliocentric System	c. ___?___	d. ___?___	Aristarchus, Copernicus

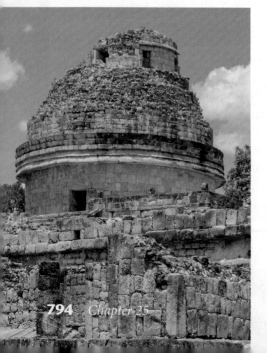

Figure 1 The Mayan ruin of El Caracol, also known as "The Observatory," is located on the Yucatan peninsula. It is thought that the Mayans used El Caracol for astronomical observations.

For thousands of years, people have used the sky to track the passage of time. Farmers in ancient Egypt watched for the first morning appearance of the bright star Sirius to know when to prepare for planting. Stonehenge, in England, consists of a group of large stones set in a circular pattern long ago. The locations of certain stones mark the spots where the sun rises or sets on the longest and shortest days of the year. About 1000 years ago in Central America, the Mayans built observatories such as the one shown in Figure 1. They used their observations to develop calendars and even predict astronomical events.

Models of the Solar System

Ancient observers noticed that most objects in the sky seem to be in a state of slow but steady motion. Every day the sun appears to rise in the east and set in the west. The moon, too, rises and sets every day. Similarly, the stars move across the sky in a fixed pattern.

Camp out for a few nights and you'll notice, as the ancients did, that the stars appear to circle around a fixed point in the sky. In the Northern Hemisphere, the stars circle around Polaris, the North Star. Most ancient people concluded that Earth was stationary and the sun, moon, and stars moved around Earth.

Ancient observers noticed that a few bright starlike objects seemed to wander slowly among the fixed patterns of stars. These objects were called planets, from the Greek word for "wanderers." Besides Earth itself, the ancients knew of the five planets that can be seen with the unaided eye: Mercury, Venus, Mars, Jupiter, and Saturn.

Figure 2 Andreas Cellarius drew these maps of the geocentric model (left) and heliocentric model (right) in the 1660s.
Comparing and Contrasting *Where does Earth appear in each diagram?*

Geocentric Model Most ancient Greeks thought that Earth was at the center of the universe. They believed that all the stars and planets lay on the inside of a giant sphere that revolved around Earth once a day. Since *geo* is the Greek word for "Earth," such a model is called a **geocentric** (jec oh SEN trik) model. 🔑 **In a geocentric model, Earth is stationary while objects in the sky move around it.** The original geocentric model was modified about A.D. 140 by the Egyptian astronomer Ptolemy (TAHL uh mee) to more accurately predict positions of the planets. Ptolemy's geocentric model was widely accepted for nearly 1400 years.

Heliocentric Model Even in ancient times, not everyone thought that Earth was at the center of the universe. The Greek astronomer Aristarchus developed a **heliocentric** (hee lee oh SEN trik) model. 🔑 **In a heliocentric model, Earth and the other planets revolve around the sun.** Figure 2 illustrates the geocentric and heliocentric models. Although today we know that Aristarchus was correct, his model was not accepted by most ancient Greeks. The geocentric model could explain all observations made at that time. Moreover, Earth's motions are not obvious to observers on Earth.

In the early 1500s, the heliocentric model was revived by the Polish scientist Nicolaus Copernicus. Copernicus realized that the motion of the planets could be more simply expained if they are revolving around the sun rather than around the Earth. The observations of Italian scientist Galileo Galilei and other scientists later proved that the heliocentric model was correct.

The apparent motions of the sun, moon, and stars result from Earth's daily rotation on its axis. As Earth rotates, it seems that we are stationary and all of the objects in the sky are spinning around us. The northern stars appear to circle around the North Star because Earth's axis points toward a spot in the sky close to that star.

For: Links on early astronomers
Visit: www.SciLinks.org
Web Code: ccn-3251

For: Activity on defining the planets
Visit: PHSchool.com
Web Code: ccc-3251

Figure 3 The planets orbit mostly in the same plane, though they do not line up as shown here. This figure shows the average distance from the sun to each of the planets. Pluto, now classified as a dwarf planet, is included for comparison. The sizes of the objects shown are not to scale. **Calculating** *Which planet is closest to Earth?*

Planetary Orbits

In the year 1600, Johannes Kepler, a German mathematician, began to analyze the paths of the planets around the sun. Kepler used data that had been collected for more than twenty years by the Danish astronomer Tycho Brahe.

Kepler discovered that the orbit of a planet around the sun is not a circle, but an ellipse. An ellipse looks like an oval, or a circle that has been stretched out along one axis. Most planets' orbits are nearly circular, and so are only slightly elliptical. Imagine that the path of Earth's orbit is traced on the top of a giant table. The plane of this imaginary tabletop containing Earth's orbit is called the **ecliptic plane.**

The force that holds the planets in orbit around the sun wasn't understood until Isaac Newton's discoveries about gravity. Recall that Newton's first law of motion states that an object in motion continues to move in a straight line at a constant speed unless acted upon by a force. This property of matter is known as inertia. Newton realized that the sun must be exerting a gravitational force on the planets that keeps them in orbit. Otherwise, the planets' inertia would cause them to fly off into space. **Gravity and inertia combine to keep the planets in orbit around the sun.**

Components of the Solar System

Our solar system consists of the sun, the planets, their moons, and a variety of smaller objects that mostly revolve in the same plane around the sun. Recall that the ancients knew of six planets. Three more were discovered with the aid of telescopes: Uranus in 1781, Neptune in 1846, and Pluto in 1930. (Pluto was later reclassified as a dwarf planet.) Except for Mercury and Venus, all of the planets have moons. A **moon** is a relatively small natural body in space that revolves around a planet.

Suppose you were surveying the solar system from a great distance. You might be tempted to say that it consists mainly of a single star, the sun, with a few small objects revolving around it all in the same plane. You would not be far wrong, since the sun's mass is about 750 times greater than the mass of the rest of the solar system combined.

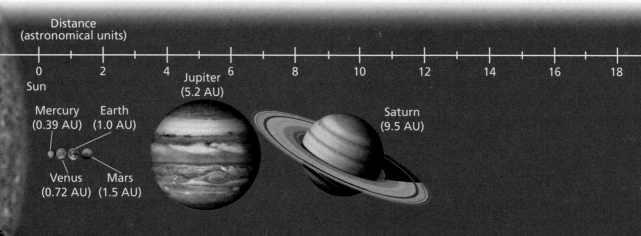

Distance (astronomical units)

0 — Sun
Mercury (0.39 AU)
Earth (1.0 AU)
Venus (0.72 AU)
Mars (1.5 AU)
Jupiter (5.2 AU)
Saturn (9.5 AU)

Unlike the sun, planets and moons don't produce their own light. The nearby planets and moons are visible because sunlight is reflected from their surfaces. In Figure 3 you can see that the orbits of the first four planets—Mercury, Venus, Earth, and Mars—are relatively close to the sun. The orbits of the outer planets, Jupiter, Saturn, Uranus, and Neptune, are much farther from the sun.

Distances between objects in the solar system are much smaller than distances to the stars, but are much larger than distances on Earth. As a result, astronomers often use astronomical units to describe distances within the solar system. One **astronomical unit** (AU) equals the average distance from Earth to the sun—149,598,000 kilometers. In comparison, Neptune is an average of about 30.1 AU from the sun.

 Reading Checkpoint *What is an astronomical unit?*

Exploring the Solar System

Modern technology, including complex telescopes, piloted spacecraft, and space probes, has allowed scientists to explore the solar system. The first rockets powerful enough to escape Earth's atmosphere and enter space were developed in the 1940s and 1950s. The Soviet Union launched the first artificial satellite, Sputnik 1, into orbit in 1957. Sputnik stirred the United States to start its own space program. The so-called space race was underway. On April 12, 1961, Soviet cosmonaut Yuri Gagarin became the first human to orbit Earth. Astronaut Alan Shepard became the first American in space on May 5, 1961.

Travel to the Moon Following Shepard's flight, President John F. Kennedy directed the National Aeronautics and Space Administration (NASA) to launch a major effort to place an astronaut on the moon. The quest to reach the moon progressed through a series of increasingly complex missions. The final step in this effort was a series of space flights called the Apollo program. On July 20, 1969, Neil Armstrong, commander of the *Apollo 11* spacecraft, became the first person to set foot on the moon.

Modeling Orbits

Procedure

1. Cut a 200-cm piece of string. Tie one end of the string securely to a whiffle ball.

2. Wrap the string's other end around your hand, leaving 50 cm of string between your hand and the ball.

3. To model a planet's orbit, swing the ball above your head with just enough force to keep the ball moving parallel to the ground. **CAUTION** *Make sure the ball cannot hit anyone or anything.* Record the number of orbits the ball makes in 10 s.

4. Repeat Step 3, increasing the string's length to 150 cm from the ball.

Analyze and Conclude

1. **Calculating** How long did a single orbit take in Step 3? In Step 4?

2. **Analyzing Data** How did the radius of the ball's orbit affect the time to complete one orbit?

3. **Using Models** How does this lab model the orbits of the planets?

A

B

Figure 4 Modern technology is used to send spacecraft into orbit and to explore the planets. **A** The space probe Cassini launches a probe to explore Saturn's largest moon, Titan, in this illustration. **B** A space shuttle is docked to the International Space Station in this computer-generated illustration.

Over the next few years, five more moon landings took place. Astronauts performed many scientific experiments and brought back to Earth 382 kilograms of rock and soil samples. The last lunar mission, *Apollo 17*, was completed in 1972.

Recent Space Missions Although humans have not yet travelled across the solar system, scientists have gathered much new information about various planets and moons. In the decades since the Apollo program, nearly all of the planets and moons of the solar system have been photographed by space probes. A **space probe** is an unpiloted vehicle that carries scientific instruments into space and transmits information back to Earth. In 2004, NASA successfully landed two space probes, named Spirit and Opportunity, on Mars. Later that year, the space probe Cassini, shown in Figure 4, began exploring the Saturn system of rings and moons from orbit.

The Hubble Space Telescope, launched into orbit around Earth in 1990, has also provided many new views of the solar system and beyond. Today, scientists rely mainly on space probes and telescopes to gather new information about the solar system.

Recent human space flight has centered on the near-Earth missions of the space shuttle. The shuttle is a reusable space vehicle that is launched like a rocket but lands like an airplane. Today, a new era of cooperation exists in the exploration of space. An important step has been the development of the International Space Station, shown in Figure 4. The space station is a permanent laboratory designed for research in space. Astronauts from various countries are currently living aboard the partially completed structure, which is scheduled to be finished in 2010.

Section 25.1 Assessment

Reviewing Concepts

1. What is the difference between the geocentric and heliocentric models of the solar system?

2. Why don't planets travel in straight lines?

3. What are the four types of bodies in the solar system?

4. What are some ways that scientists are currently learning more about the solar system?

Critical Thinking

5. **Comparing and Contrasting** How has the focus of the U.S. space program changed since the time of the Apollo program?

6. **Applying Concepts** Why do some stars seem to rotate around Polaris at night?

Math Practice

7. Using Figure 3, find the average distance of Mars from the sun, in km.

8. Orbiting 2.77 AU from the sun, Ceres is the largest of a group of objects called asteroids. How far from the sun is Ceres in km? Between the orbits of which two planets does the orbit of Ceres lie?

Spacesuit

A spacesuit allows an astronaut to live in space. It provides a pressurized environment, a supply of oxygen, and protection against tiny rock particles called micrometeoroids. **Interpreting Diagrams** *Which part of the spacesuit keeps the astronaut cool?*

Outside the space shuttle
A space suit allows an astronaut to perform extra-vehicular activities (EVAs). This astronaut is attached to the space shuttle.

Helmet and visor *These parts allow the astronaut to breathe and see while protecting against radiation.*

Lights

Communications
A fabric cap supports a set of earphones and a microphone.

In-suit drink bag
This bag contains almost 1 liter of water.

Control module
This module contains the switches needed to operate the life-support systems.

Electric harness
This harness monitors the astronaut's vital signs, and allows for communication.

Glove *Each glove has rubber fingertips for grip, and wrist bearings for ease of movement.*

Pressure bladder
This layer prevents the escape of breathing gases that circulate inside the suit.

Primary life-support system *This system contains oxygen tanks, water, and a machine that removes carbon dioxide from air in the suit.*

Thermal micrometeoroid garment *This layer provides insulation and protection against micrometeoroids.*

Water tubing

Input and output hoses for tube network

Undergarment
This close-fitting garment contains tubes that circulate water to keep the astronaut cool.

25.2 The Earth-Moon System

Reading Focus

Key Concepts

- Why does the moon's temperature vary widely?
- What features are found on the moon's surface?
- How did the moon form?
- What causes the phases of the moon?
- What causes solar and lunar eclipses?
- What causes the tides?

Vocabulary

- maria
- crater
- meteoroids
- phases
- eclipse
- umbra
- penumbra
- tides
- spring tide
- neap tide

Reading Strategy

Building Vocabulary Copy the concept map below. Then, as you read, complete it with terms from this section. Make similar concept maps for eclipses and tides.

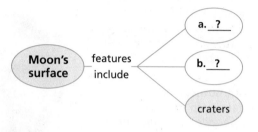

Astronaut Alan Shepard, shown in Figure 5, was commander of the *Apollo 14* mission. He was not a golf pro, but he loved golf so much that he brought the game all the way to the moon. Shepard wondered how far he could hit a golf ball on the moon. So he attached the head of a golf club to the handle of an instrument for collecting rocks. Swinging with just one arm, he hit a golf ball a few hundred meters, much farther than it would have gone on Earth.

Why did the golf ball go so far on the moon? The moon is only about one quarter of Earth's diameter and has much less mass than Earth. As a result, the force of gravity on its surface is only one sixth that on Earth. Also, the moon has virtually no atmosphere to slow the ball down.

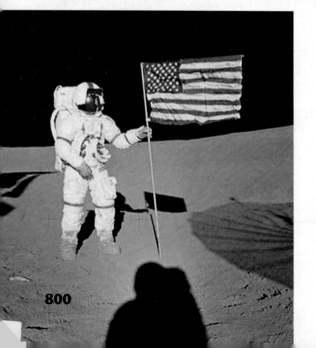

Figure 5 *Apollo 14* commander Alan Shepard planted an American flag on the moon's surface in 1971. **Inferring** *Why did the flag need to be supported by a horizontal rod?*

Earth's Moon

At an average distance of about 384,400 kilometers, the moon is our nearest neighbor in space. Unlike Earth, the moon has no atmosphere. The moon's gravity is too weak to hold onto gas molecules, which simply float away into space. ◐ **The lack of an atmosphere allows the moon's surface temperature to vary tremendously.** In direct sunlight, the average surface temperature of the moon is very high, about 130°C. At night, however, the average surface temperature plummets to a chilly −180°C.

Rocks on the moon's surface date back 3.2–4.5 billion years. Studying such ancient rocks, which are rare on Earth, give scientists clues about the early history of our planet.

Because there is no atmosphere, any liquid water would have long ago evaporated into space. Any water remaining on the moon must be frozen. Evidence of ice near the moon's north and south poles was detected by space craft observations. Sunlight at the poles is less intense, so temperatures are low enough there to keep ice from sublimating (changing directly from a solid to a gas).

Surface Features

Exploration of the moon's surface has revealed the existence of a variety of geological features. **The major surface features of the moon are maria, highlands, and craters.**

Maria and Highlands Do you sometimes think you can see a face when you look up at the Moon? What you are really seeing is a pattern of lighter and darker regions on the moon's surface, as shown in the top photo of Figure 6.

One of the first people to look at the moon with a telescope was Galileo. When Galileo aimed his telescope at the moon 400 years ago, he thought that the dark, smooth regions on the moon's surface resembled the seas on Earth. So, he called them maria (MAH ree uh), the Latin word for "seas." In reality, **maria** are low, flat plains formed by ancient lunar lava flows. They cover about 15 percent of the moon's surface. The maria are surrounded by light-colored areas called lunar highlands. The lunar highlands, which cover most of the moon's surface, are rough, mountainous regions.

Craters Much of the moon's surface is covered with impact craters, such as those shown in Figure 6. These **craters** are round depressions in the surface caused by the impact of high-speed meteoroids. **Meteoroids** are chunks of rock that move through the solar system. Although meteoroid collisions still occur, most craters formed more than 3.8 billion years ago.

The thousands of craters on the moon are evidence that the moon is geologically dead. On Earth, most old craters disappeared as the surface was altered by erosion or collisions between tectonic plates. On the moon, however, there is little erosion and no plate motion to alter craters. Notice in the top photo of Figure 6 that the lunar highlands are much more heavily cratered than the maria. Older craters within the maria were covered by more recent lava flows. The few craters within the maria formed after the lava that covered them had solidified.

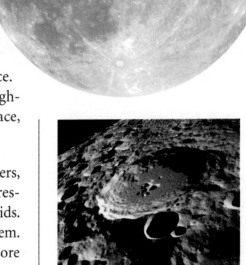

Figure 6 The photos above show features of the moon. The large, dark areas in the top photo are maria. The lighter areas surrounding the maria are lunar highlands. The moon is covered with craters that formed from the impacts of smaller objects.

 Reading Checkpoint   *Why are the lunar highlands more heavily cratered than the maria?*

Not drawn to scale

Figure 7 The moon is thought to have formed in a spectacular collision between the early Earth and a Mars-sized object. **A** The collision knocked part of Earth's mantle into space. **B** Much of the ejected material began to revolve around Earth. It soon began to clump together to form the moon. **C** Earth and the moon today.

Formation of the Moon

Scientists hypothesize that the moon formed after an enormous collision early in Earth's history. At that time, about 4.6 billion years ago, the solar system was full of pieces of rocky debris, some of which were the size of small planets. This debris frequently collided with the planets, creating many large craters. While Earth was still forming, a Mars-sized object probably collided with it off-center, as shown in Figure 7. This collision ejected a large amount of material into space. This material orbited Earth until it eventually came together to form the moon.

Phases of the Moon

The moon doesn't produce its own light. You can see the moon because it reflects light from the sun. When you look at the moon, it sometimes appears full and bright, and sometimes appears as only a sliver. The different shapes of the moon visible from Earth are called **phases.**

The moon's phases are caused by changes in the relative positions of the moon, sun, and Earth as the moon revolves around Earth. Sunlight illuminates half of the moon. The phase of the moon depends on how much of the sunlit portion of the moon is facing Earth.

If you were to track the appearance of the moon from day to day, you would notice that the moon's phases change according to a regular cycle. Figure 8 shows the positions of the moon during its phases. A full moon occurs when the moon is on the opposite side of Earth from the sun, and the whole side of the moon facing Earth is lit by the sun. A new moon occurs when the moon is directly between the sun and Earth. A new moon cannot be seen from Earth because the sunlit side of the moon is facing away from us.

It takes about 29.5 days for the moon to complete a full cycle of phases from full moon to new moon and back again. This period of time is known as a lunar month.

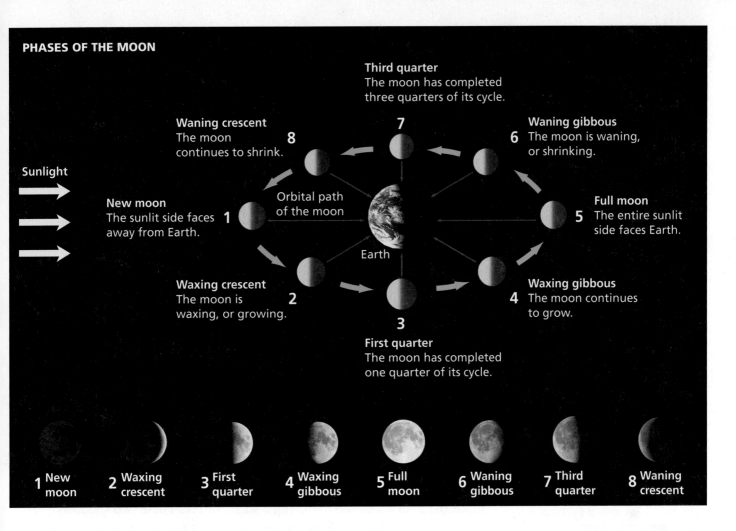

PHASES OF THE MOON

Third quarter
The moon has completed three quarters of its cycle.

Waning crescent
The moon continues to shrink.

Waning gibbous
The moon is waning, or shrinking.

Sunlight

New moon
The sunlit side faces away from Earth.

Orbital path of the moon

Earth

Full moon
The entire sunlit side faces Earth.

Waxing crescent
The moon is waxing, or growing.

First quarter
The moon has completed one quarter of its cycle.

Waxing gibbous
The moon continues to grow.

1 New moon
2 Waxing crescent
3 First quarter
4 Waxing gibbous
5 Full moon
6 Waning gibbous
7 Third quarter
8 Waning crescent

The same side of the moon always faces Earth. This is because the moon makes one full rotation around its axis while making one full revolution around Earth. For this reason, whenever you look at the moon, its surface features are always nearly in the same place. Some parts of the moon may be in shadow, depending upon the particular phase, but the features you can see on its surface hardly move.

Eclipses

Imagine that it is the middle of a sunny day. Suddenly, the sky darkens and the sun appears to shrink. Animals act as if night has fallen. In ancient times, people were terrified of such occurrences, which are known as solar eclipses. An **eclipse** (ih KLIPS) occurs when the shadow of one body in space, such as a planet or moon, falls on another. For an eclipse to occur on Earth, the sun, moon, and Earth must all lie along a straight line.

You might wonder why eclipses do not occur twice each month, whenever there is a new or full moon. Eclipses occur much less often because the plane of the moon's orbit is tilted about 5 degrees with respect to the ecliptic. An eclipse occurs only when the moon crosses Earth's ecliptic plane at the time of a new moon or full moon.

Figure 8 Two different views of the phases of the moon are shown in this diagram. The circular diagram shows how the moon and Earth would appear to an observer in space as the moon orbits Earth. Note that the sun is shining from the left. The photos below the diagram show how the phases of the moon appear to an observer on Earth.
Interpreting Diagrams *During which phase is the dark half of the moon facing Earth?*

Go Online

For: Activity on moon phases and eclipses
Visit: PHSchool.com
Web Code: ccp-3252

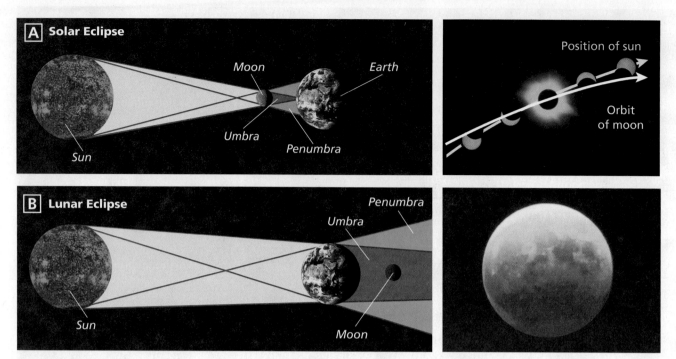

A Solar Eclipse

Moon   Earth

Umbra
Penumbra

Sun

Position of sun

Orbit
of moon

B Lunar Eclipse

Penumbra
Umbra

Sun

Moon

Not drawn to scale

Figure 9 Eclipses occur only at the new moon or the full moon. **A** Solar eclipses occur at the new moon, when Earth can move through the moon's shadow. The multiple- exposure photo on the right has circles added to show several stages of a total solar eclipse. **B** Lunar eclipses occur at the full moon, when the moon can move through Earth's shadow. The moon has a reddish tint during a full lunar eclipse because some sunlight refracted by Earth's atmosphere reaches the moon.
Comparing and Contrasting
Why are total lunar eclipses more frequently seen than total solar eclipses?

For: Activity on eclipses
Visit: PHSchool.com
Web Code: ccc-3252

Solar Eclipse During a new moon, when the moon is between the sun and Earth, Earth may pass through the shadow of the moon. 🔑 **A solar eclipse occurs when the moon casts a shadow on a portion of Earth's surface.** As shown in Figure 9A, the moon casts two kinds of shadows on Earth during a solar eclipse. These two shadows occur because the sun is quite wide. It doesn't cast a sharp-edged shadow, as it would if it were a point of light. The small cone-shaped **umbra** (UM bruh) is the darkest part of the moon's shadow. Within the umbra, the sun's light is completely blocked by the moon. Only people in a very narrow path across Earth's surface are able to see a total solar eclipse. Surrounding the umbra is the larger **penumbra** (pih NUM bruh), a region of shadow that is less dark than the umbra. People within the penumbra see a partial solar eclipse.

Lunar Eclipse During a full moon, when Earth is between the sun and moon, the moon may pass through Earth's shadow, as shown in Figure 9B. 🔑 **A lunar eclipse occurs when Earth casts a shadow on the moon.** Like the moon's shadow, Earth's shadow has an umbra and penumbra.

If the moon passes completely into Earth's umbra, you see a total lunar eclipse. If instead of passing fully into Earth's umbra the moon passes partially through the umbra, you see a partial lunar eclipse.

Unlike a total solar eclipse, a total lunar eclipse can be seen from anywhere on Earth that the moon is visible. Thus, total lunar eclipses are much more frequently seen than total solar eclipses.

Tides on Earth

In Daytona Beach, Florida, people often drive cars along the flat, wide beaches. Occasionally, a driver parks on the beach and returns to find the car covered by the waters of the Atlantic Ocean. The driver is the victim of a rising tide. **Tides** are the regular rise and fall of ocean waters.

🔑 **Tides are caused mainly by differences in the moon's gravitational pull on Earth.** Recall that the force of gravity between two objects decreases as the distance between them increases. The gravitational force of the moon pulls more strongly on the side of Earth that faces it, and less strongly on the side that is away from it. This difference causes the entire Earth to be stretched. Because water flows easily, the effect of the moon's gravity on the oceans is much greater than on the solid Earth.

The gravitational pull of the moon causes the oceans to bulge at the locations closest to and farthest from it. As Earth rotates on its axis, high tides occur when an area moves through either of these two bulges. Most coastal areas experience two high tides and two low tides each day.

The sun also has a gravitational effect on the oceans, but its tidal effects are only about half those of the moon. During a new or full moon, the sun, moon, and Earth are in a straight line. The gravitational pulls of the sun and moon then add together, as shown in Figure 10A. The combined forces produce a **spring tide,** where the change between daily high and low tides is the greatest. When the moon is in its first or third quarter, the moon and the sun are pulling the Earth at right angles, as shown in Figure 10B. The result is a **neap tide,** where there is the least change between daily high and low tides.

A Spring Tides

Full moon

New moon

Sun

Moon's orbit

B Neap Tides

First-quarter moon

Sun

Third-quarter moon

Not drawn to scale

Figure 10 A During spring tides, the pulls of the moon and sun add together. **B** During neap tides, the moon and sun pull Earth and its oceans at right angles.

Section 25.2 Assessment

Reviewing Concepts

1. 🔑 Explain why temperatures vary widely between day and night on the moon.
2. 🔑 How did lunar craters and maria form?
3. 🔑 What do scientists hypothesize about how the moon formed?
4. 🔑 Why do the phases of the moon change?
5. 🔑 What is the difference between a lunar eclipse and a solar eclipse?
6. 🔑 What causes tides on Earth?

Critical Thinking

7. **Comparing and Contrasting** What is the difference between the umbra and the penumbra of a solar eclipse?

8. **Comparing and Contrasting** Why are spring tides larger than neap tides?

Math ▶ Practice

9. The gravitational pull on the moon's surface is about one sixth of that on Earth. If a person weighs 700 newtons on Earth, how much would he or she weigh on the moon?

10. Due to friction caused by the tides, Earth's days are getting longer at a rate of 0.00002 second per year. How much longer will a day be in a million years?

Should the Moon Be Developed?

Decades after the last astronauts explored the moon, various governments and companies are beginning to show interest in the moon's development. There are many different ideas about how the moon should be developed, or whether it should be developed at all. Some think that the moon should be preserved for all mankind, and that its development should be limited to scientific research. Others favor development of the moon by private firms.

Some see the development of the moon beginning with tourism. According to this idea, groups of tourists would pay to be shuttled to a resort on the moon. The moon is also a potential source of minerals such as aluminum and titanium and energy resources such as helium-3, which could fuel fusion reactors. Once enough buildings and equipment are in place on the moon, the mining of such resources could begin and a larger-scale colony could be built.

The Viewpoints

Develop the Moon

Developing the moon will have many advantages. One is to gain scientific knowledge, especially about the early history of the solar system. The moon will be the ultimate tourist destination. Although the cost would be high, many people would be willing to pay for the unique chance to experience the moon's low gravity and airless environment.

The moon is rich in iron, aluminum, calcium, and helium-3. Helium-3 may one day serve as a source of fuel for nuclear fusion. Resources from the moon could potentially be used in a lunar base, on Earth, or for future colonization of space.

The moon is a logical stepping stone for future missions to Mars. A lunar base would provide a valuable testing ground for technology that could eventually be useful on Mars. Such technology will also have applications on Earth, where it will improve people's lives and create new jobs.

Do Not Develop the Moon

The development of the moon would be a waste of time and money. Scarce government funds would be better spent on projects with a more immediate benefit, such as feeding the hungry, improving schools, and building better housing. In the short run, government funding for space should be focused on space probes and telescopes. These technologies allow us to learn more about the solar system and the universe beyond at a relatively low cost. In the long run, a mission sending a crew to Mars would be of much greater interest and scientific value.

The proposed development of the moon would be too expensive and risky to receive private funding. Few tourists are likely to be able to pay the high costs of visiting a resort on the moon. The techniques for mining mineral and energy resources on the moon are uncertain, and any such resources would probably be very costly to produce.

Research and Decide

1. **Defining an Issue** In your own words, explain the major issues involved in the debate about the future development of the moon.

2. **Analyzing the Viewpoints** What are the key arguments expressed by the proponents and critics of developing the moon? What are the benefits? What are the risks?

3. **Forming Your Opinion** Should the moon be developed? If so, explain how. If not, explain why not.

4. **Persuasive Writing** Suppose you have been appointed chair of a presidential commission on the moon's future. Prepare a letter to the President explaining the commission's recommendations.

For: More on this issue
Visit: PHSchool.com
Web Code: cch-3252

25.3 The Inner Solar System

Reading Focus

Key Concepts

- How are the inner planets similar?
- What are the characteristics of each of the four inner planets?
- What are asteroids and how were they formed?

Vocabulary

- terrestrial planets
- asteroids
- asteroid belt

Reading Strategy

Summarizing Make a table like the one below that includes all the headings for the section. Write a brief summary of the text for each heading.

> **I. The Terrestrial Planets**
> • **Four planets closest to the sun**
> • **Small, dense, with rocky surfaces**
> **II. Mercury**
>   a. _____
> **III. Venus**
>   b. _____

$\mathbf{S}$uppose that you wanted to set up a colony on another planet. Which planet would you choose? Venus is the nearest planet and is similar to Earth in size. But Venus is extremely hot and has an atmosphere that is so thick it would crush any potential colonists. Mercury is closest to the sun, but it has no atmosphere. Temperatures there are either far too high or far too low to support life.

Your best choice would be Mars. However, a permanent colony on Mars, like the one pictured in Figure 11, would face very difficult conditions. Mars is usually extremely cold and has a very thin atmosphere with no oxygen. Huge dust storms blow across the planet. Although NASA is considering sending astronauts to Mars, it would take an incredible effort to set up a permanent colony under such harsh conditions.

Figure 11 This imaginative painting shows a possible future human settlement on Mars. Settlers might live in domes to protect themselves from the harsh climate and to provide an atmosphere for breathing.

The Terrestrial Planets

The four planets closest to the sun—Mercury, Venus, Earth, and Mars—are often called the terrestrial planets. The **terrestrial planets** are planets similar in structure to Earth. (*Terra* is the Latin word for "Earth.") **The four inner planets are all relatively small and dense, and have rocky surfaces. Like Earth, they all have a crust, mantle, and iron core.**

All of the terrestrial planets have rocky crusts. Mercury and Mars have surfaces that are pockmarked by craters. On Earth and Venus, most craters have disappeared because the surface is continually being altered. The surfaces of the other terrestrial planets change much more slowly, so more craters are visible.

The Inner Planets					
Planet	Equatorial Diameter (kilometers)	Average Distance to Sun (AU)	Period of Rotation (Earth days)	Period of Revolution (Earth years)	Number of Moons
Mercury	4,880	0.39	59	0.24	0
Venus	12,104	0.72	243	0.62	0
Earth	12,756	1.00	1.00	1.00	1
Mars	6,794	1.52	1.03	1.88	2

Figure 12 The inner planets are all small, dense, and rocky. **Using Tables** *Which of the four inner planets is most similar in size to Earth?*

Figure 13 Mercury's surface is heavily cratered from meteoroid collisions. This false-color image was made by combining a series of smaller images taken by the Mariner 10 space probe. Orange areas for which no images are available are blank. **Comparing and Contrasting** *How does Mercury's surface compare with the surface of Earth's moon?*

Because they are closer to the sun, the terrestrial planets are much warmer on average than the outer planets. Unlike most of the outer planets, the inner planets have few (if any) moons. There are no rings around any of the terrestrial planets. Figure 12 summarizes the main characteristics of the inner planets.

Mercury

Mercury is the smallest of the terrestrial planets, and the closest planet to the sun. Mercury, shown in Figure 13, is a dense planet with a very large iron core. Mercury is geologically quiet. There is little mantle convection within the planet, and little erosion on its surface.

Like its namesake, the swift messenger of the gods, Mercury is the fastest-moving planet. It takes only 88 Earth days for Mercury to complete one revolution. This is the shortest period of revolution of any planet.

Temperature and Atmosphere Mercury's surface temperature ranges between two extremes. The time between sunrise and sunset equals the time it takes for Mercury to revolve around the sun, about 88 days. During this time, the heat from the sun causes the surface to become intensely hot. The temperatures at the equator reach about 430°C, hot enough to melt lead. At night, the temperature becomes extremely cold, as low as −170°C.

Mercury has virtually no atmosphere. Its high daytime temperatures cause gas particles to move very fast. Because Mercury is so small, its gravity is weak, making it easy for such fast-moving gas particles to escape into space.

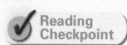 *Why does Mercury lack a substantial atmosphere?*

Exploring Mercury Because Mercury is so close to the sun, it's hard for astronomers on Earth to see. Images are taken by space probes, such as the Mariner and Messenger. As Figure 13 shows, the surface looks like that of Earth's moon. Numerous craters indicate that Mercury has been largely unchanged for billions of years. The Messenger space probe made three flybys of Mercury from 2008–2009, revealing a magnetic field, volcanism, and water ice within some of its craters.

Venus

Venus is called the "evening star" or "morning star" because it is only seen in the west after sunset or in the east before sunrise. With the exception of the moon, it is the brightest object in Earth's night sky. Venus's rotation is unusual in that it rotates in the direction opposite to which it revolves. The rotation rate is also very slow—Venus takes 243 days to rotate around its axis. Venus's day is longer than its year!

Venus's Atmosphere Venus is difficult to study from space because clouds hide its surface, as shown in Figure 14A. Venus's atmosphere is so thick that the pressure at its surface is 90 times that on Earth. **Venus's thick atmosphere is composed mostly of carbon dioxide, which traps heat and raises the planet's temperature.** Venus's atmosphere also contains droplets of sulfuric acid. Spacecraft that landed on Venus's surface in the 1970s found the average surface temperature to be 460°C. Any water that may have once existed on Venus has long since boiled away.

Exploring Venus The high sulfur content of Venus's atmosphere probably results from numerous volcanoes, like the one shown in Figure 14B. The outpouring of lava from volcanoes has frequently resurfaced the planet, erasing craters as well. As a result, Venus's surface has only a small number of impact craters. Though Venus probably has active volcanoes, it shows no evidence of plate tectonics.

Earth

When you compare Earth to the other terrestrial planets using the data in Figure 12, Earth does not seem unusual. But Earth is unique in several important respects. **Earth's surface has a suitable atmosphere and temperature range for water to exist as a liquid.** The presence of liquid water makes Earth, shown in Figure 15, very different from the other planets. Water makes it possible for Earth to support millions of different species of living things. Water also causes erosion, which has shaped Earth's land surface in many ways.

Figure 14 Venus's surface is not visible from space because of its very thick atmosphere.
A Photographs in visible light only show Venus's clouds. **B** Radar is able to penetrate Venus's atmosphere. Radar data were used to produce this false-color image of a volcano on Venus.
Formulating Hypotheses *Why is Venus the brightest planet as seen from Earth?*

Not to scale

Figure 15 Earth is unique among the planets in having liquid-water ocean at its surface.

Go Online

NSTA SciLINKS

For: Links on the solar system
Visit: www.SciLinks.org
Web Code: ccn-3253

Unlike most smaller planets and moons, Earth has enough gravity to hold most gas molecules. This allows Earth to maintain a thick atmosphere. Why isn't Earth's atmosphere composed mostly of carbon dioxide, like the atmospheres of Venus and Mars? On Earth, some living organisms use carbon dioxide and produce oxygen. Earth's oceans also remove carbon dioxide from the atmosphere by dissolving it. The formation of limestone, which contains calcium carbonate ($CaCO_3$), then locks away the carbon underground.

The moon, Mercury, and Mars are all so small that over time they have lost much of their internal heat and have become geologically dead. Earth is large enough that it has not had a chance to cool down much. As a result, Earth has moving tectonic plates that continually change its surface.

DK SCIENCE and History

Exploring the Solar System

Since the 1950s, several countries have made incredible progress in space exploration. Exploration technology and capabilities have changed dramatically since the first satellite launch in 1957.

SURFACE OF MARS

A dog called Laika survived for a few hours in space aboard Sputnik 2.

SPUTNIK 2

Apollo 11 lunar module approaches the surface of the moon.

YURI GAGARIN

APOLLO 11 **MISSION**

1957 The Soviet Union launches the first artificial Earth satellite, Sputnik 1, into space. Sputnik 2 follows a few weeks later.

1961 Russian Yuri Gagarin becomes the first person to orbit Earth, aboard *Vostok 1.*

1969 American astronauts Neil Armstrong and Edwin "Buzz" Aldrin, Jr. are the first people to step onto the moon, as part of the *Apollo 11* mission.

1972 The space probe Pioneer 10 blasts off to study Jupiter and its moons.

1976 Viking I and Viking II space probes land on Mars and send back photos of the red planet's surface.

1950   1960   1970

Mars

Mars is the most Earthlike of all of the planets. The weathering of iron-rich rocks on its surface gives the planet a reddish color. This is why Mars is called the "red planet."

Though the surface of Mars is very old, as shown by the presence of many impact craters, it once had many volcanic eruptions. However, the most recent volcanic activity was possibly less than 100 million years ago. Olympus Mons on Mars is the largest volcano in the solar system. The height of Olympus Mons is nearly three times that of Mount Everest, the tallest mountain on Earth. If this volcano were located on Earth, its base could cover the distance from Cleveland to Washington, D.C.!

Writing in Science

Creative Writing Suppose you are a reporter who is going to interview the chief scientist or astronaut responsible for one of the space missions described in the time line. Prepare at least five questions about the mission. Then write a brief news story, including the responses that you would expect to each of your questions.

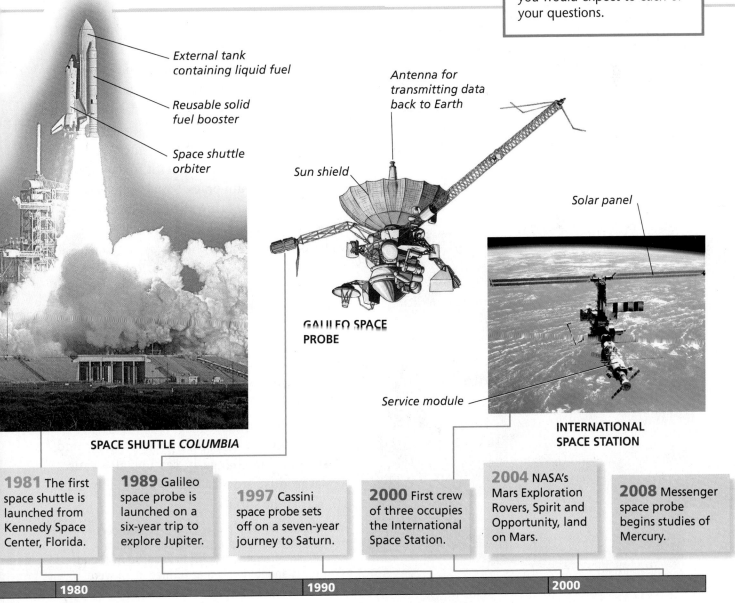

External tank containing liquid fuel

Reusable solid fuel booster

Space shuttle orbiter

Antenna for transmitting data back to Earth

Sun shield

SPACE SHUTTLE COLUMBIA

GALILEO SPACE PROBE

Solar panel

Service module

INTERNATIONAL SPACE STATION

1981 The first space shuttle is launched from Kennedy Space Center, Florida.

1989 Galileo space probe is launched on a six-year trip to explore Jupiter.

1997 Cassini space probe sets off on a seven-year journey to Saturn.

2000 First crew of three occupies the International Space Station.

2004 NASA's Mars Exploration Rovers, Spirit and Opportunity, land on Mars.

2008 Messenger space probe begins studies of Mercury.

1980   1990   2000

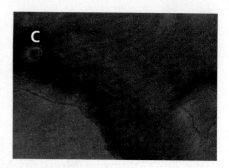

Figure 16 Mars has a thin atmosphere that permits a clear view of its surface from space.
A Mars has ice caps at both poles.
B Olympus Mons is the largest volcano in the solar system.
C These Martian valleys are thought to have been formed at least in part by large flows of liquid water in the distant past.

Mars's Atmosphere Mars has a very thin atmosphere, which allows astronomers to see its surface with a telescope. The thin Martian atmosphere and its distance from the sun make the surface very cold. Temperatures vary from $-140°C$ to $20°C$. Mars's atmosphere is more than 95 percent carbon dioxide, similar to the atmosphere of Venus, but much thinner.

Water on Mars Mars shows evidence of once having a great deal of liquid surface water. Some geologists think Mars's northern lowlands were once covered by an ocean. Features shown in Figure 16C may have been stream channels and gullies. In fact, changes in surface features over the past several years indicate that water may still flow on the surface, if only for brief periods of time.

Why is liquid water rare on Mars's surface? Some water vapor has escaped into space. Some water is stored, along with frozen carbon dioxide, in ice caps at the north and south poles. Some water is frozen underground, just below the Martian surface.

Because Mars had large amounts of liquid water on its surface in the past, many scientists wonder if life once existed there. Robotic probes have carried out experiments on the Martian surface to look for signs of life. None of these probes found clear evidence for the existence of life on Mars.

Martian Seasons Like Earth, Mars has distinct seasons. Mars's seasons are caused by the tilt of its axis. Over the course of a Martian year, Mars's ice caps grow and shrink. The change in seasons also causes large dust storms that occasionally rage across the surface.

Figure 17 This photo of a dark boulder on Martian sand was taken by the Mars Exploration Rover Spirit in 2006. Spirit found rocks and minerals that formed in, or were altered by, water.

Asteroids

Beyond Mars is a region of the solar system where small, rocky bodies called **asteroids** can be found orbiting the sun. This region is referred to as the **asteroid belt.** Astronomers have discovered more than 10,000 asteroids, and many more are thought to exist. Most asteroids are less than 1 kilometer in diameter; only three are larger than 500 kilometers across. Although most asteroids are found in the asteroid belt, others orbit near Jupiter or range through the inner solar system.

The largest asteroids have enough gravity to have pulled themselves into nearly spherical or oval shapes while forming. Smaller asteroids, however, can have very irregular forms, as seen in Figure 18. These odd shapes are a result of impacts with other asteroids and meteoroids. If these small asteroids were solid, they would be likely to shatter during such collisions. Because they haven't shattered, scientists think that some asteroids are like floating rubble heaps, held together by weak gravity.

In the past, scientists thought that asteroids were the remnants of a shattered planet. ☁ **Scientists now hypothesize that asteroids are remnants of the early solar system that never came together to form a planet.** This hypothesis is supported by the lack of mass in the asteroid belt. If all of the asteroids were put together, they would form a planetary body only about 1500 kilometers in diameter. This would hardly qualify as a planet.

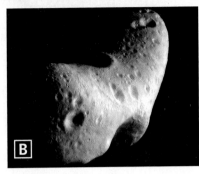

Figure 18 Asteroids come in a variety of sizes and shapes. **A** The asteroid Ida was photographed by the Galileo probe on its way to Jupiter. **B** In 2001, the NEAR Shoemaker space probe landed on the asteroid Eros.
Comparing and Contrasting *How do the shapes of the small asteroids shown compare to the shapes of the planets?*

Section 25.3 Assessment

Reviewing Concepts

1. ☁ What are the common features of the inner planets?

2. ☁ What are the four inner planets? Identify a distinguishing characteristic for each.

3. ☁ What do scientists hypothesize about the formation of the asteroids?

4. Why is there little erosion on Mercury's surface?

5. What is unusual about the rotation of Venus?

6. What is most unusual about Earth, compared to the other terrestrial planets?

7. What is the evidence that Mars once had running water on its surface?

Critical Thinking

8. **Calculating** What is the range of temperatures that occur on Mercury's equator during one full revolution around the sun?

9. **Comparing and Contrasting** How is the composition of Venus's atmosphere different from that of Earth's atmosphere?

Writing in Science

Descriptive Paragraph Suppose you are a member of the first crew of astronauts to land on Mars. Write a paragraph describing your first walk on Mars's surface.

25.4 The Outer Solar System

Reading Focus

Key Concepts
- How are the gas giants similar?
- What are the characteristics of each of the outer planets?
- What is a dwarf planet?
- What are comets and meteoroids?
- What lies in the outer solar system beyond Neptune?

Vocabulary
- gas giants
- ring
- Kuiper belt
- Oort cloud

Reading Strategy

Summarizing Copy the table below and fill it in as you read to summarize characteristics of the outer planets. Expand the table to 4 rows.

Outer Planets	Characteristics
Jupiter	largest; most mass; most moons; Great Red Spot
a. ___?___	b. ___?___
c. ___?___	d. ___?___

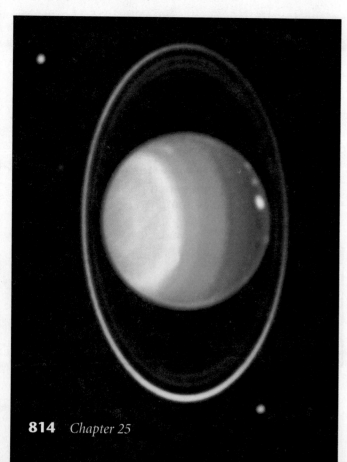

Figure 19 Uranus was discovered in 1781, but its rings were not found until 1977. Like Uranus itself, the rings were discovered by accident. This false-color infrared image was taken by the Hubble Space Telescope.

Scientific discovery happens in different ways. Sometimes things are discovered by accident. At other times, theories predict phenome na that scientists then try to find. The discoveries of Uranus (YOOR uh nus) and Neptune are examples of these two different methods. Unlike Jupiter and Saturn, which appear very bright in the night sky and have been observed for thousands of years, Uranus and Neptune were unknown to ancient observers.

Uranus, shown in Figure 19, was discovered by chance. In 1781, astronomer William Herschel was studying the sky with a telescope when he saw a fuzzy object that he first thought was a comet. Other astronomers had observed Uranus before but had incorrectly identified it as a dim star. Herschel tracked Uranus's position for almost a year before he realized it was a planet.

Over the next 50 years, astronomers noticed that Uranus was not following its predicted orbit. Working independently, mathematicians John Adams of England and Urbain Le Verrier of France concluded that there must be another planet, farther from the sun, whose gravity was affecting Uranus. Each predicted the location in the sky where this new planet should be. In 1846, the planet Neptune was discovered, very near where they had predicted.

The Outer Planets					
Planet	Equatorial Diameter (kilometers)	Average Distance to Sun (AU)	Period of Rotation (Earth days)	Period of Revolution (Earth years)	Number of Moons[†]
Jupiter	142,984	5.20	0.41	11.86	63+
Saturn	120,536	9.54	0.44	29.46	62+
Uranus	51,118	19.19	0.72	84.10	27
Neptune	49,528	30.06	0.67	164.86	13
Pluto*	2,300	39.53	6.39	248.60	3

*Pluto is included for purposes of comparison.   [†]Moons of Jupiter and Saturn are still being discovered.

Gas Giants

Jupiter, Saturn, Uranus, and Neptune are very different from the terrestrial planets. They are much colder because of their greater distance from the sun. All four planets are much larger and more massive than the terrestrial planets. They are composed mainly of hydrogen and helium, which is why they are often referred to as the **gas giants.**

None of the gas giants have solid surfaces. If you tried to land a spaceship on one, you would sink into the planet until the intense pressure of the atmosphere crushed the ship. In fact, the pressure is so great inside each planet that hydrogen and helium exist mostly in liquid form. **The four gas giants are thought to have small, dense cores, and thick atmospheres that are mostly hydrogen and helium.**

Each gas giant resembles a miniature solar system. They have many moons, most of which revolve in the same direction that the planets rotate. Each of the gas giants is surrounded by rings. A **ring** is a disk made of many small particles of rock and ice in orbit around a planet. Such rings are so close to the planet that gravitational forces are very large. These forces may have prevented the ring particles from clumping together to form moons. The characteristics of the gas giants and the dwarf planet Pluto are summarized in Figure 20.

Jupiter

Jupiter, shown in Figure 21, is the first planet beyond the asteroid belt. Named for the ruler of the Roman gods, Jupiter is large enough to hold more than 1300 Earths. **Jupiter is the largest and most massive planet in our solar system.** Like the other gas giants, Jupiter is composed mainly of hydrogen and helium.

Figure 20 The outer planets consist of the four gas giants. Pluto, formerly considered a planet, was reclassified as a dwarf planet in 2006.
Using Tables *What trends do you notice going from Jupiter to Neptune?*

Figure 21 This model of Jupiter is based on photos taken by Voyager 1. The Great Red Spot, visible in the lower half, is a giant storm much larger than Earth.

Figure 22 Two of Jupiter's larger moons are Io (top) and Europa (bottom). Io is the most volcanically active body in the solar system. Io's volcanic eruptions consist mainly of liquid sulfur. Europa may have a liquid water ocean beneath its icy surface. The dark lines are wide fractures in Europa's crust.
Formulating Hypotheses *Would you expect many impact craters on Io's surface? Explain why or why not.*

Jupiter's Atmosphere With many colorful bands of clouds, Jupiter has a striking appearance. Jupiter's clouds move rapidly because Jupiter itself rotates rapidly—one day on Jupiter is less than 10 Earth hours. The brown cloud bands are colder and move faster around the planet than the white bands.

Sometimes storms occur at the boundaries between these brown and white bands. One example is the Great Red Spot, a huge storm that rotates around its own center like a hurricane. It is caught between two bands of winds blowing in opposite directions. On Earth, a hurricane changes and dissipates when it travels from water to land. Because there is no land on Jupiter, such storms can last for many years. The Great Red Spot, for example, was first observed in 1664, but may be much older.

Jupiter's Moons Jupiter has at least 63 moons. Most of them are small, less than 200 kilometers in diameter. However, two of them, Ganymede and Callisto, are similar in size to Mercury. Two others, Io and Europa, are somewhat smaller, about the size of our moon. Ganymede, Io, and Europa have metal cores and rocky mantles. Io, shown in Figure 22, is covered with actively erupting volcanoes. Ganymede, Europa, and Callisto are covered with ice. On Europa, also shown in Figure 22, the icy crust appears to rest on top of a liquid salt-water ocean. Because of this, scientists hypothesize that Europa is the most likely place in the solar system, other than Earth, to support life.

Saturn

Saturn, the second largest planet in the solar system, is best known for its rings. 🔾 **Saturn's rings are the largest and most visible from Earth.** The rings are made of particles of ice and ice-coated rock. These particles are generally between a few micrometers and 10 meters across, with most particles being snowball-sized. The rings are about 274,000 kilometers in diameter, yet are only tens of meters thick.

Figure 23 Saturn has a thick atmosphere. It is surrounded by a spectacular set of rings, the largest in the solar system.

Saturn's Atmosphere Like Jupiter, Saturn has colorful banding in its atmosphere, as shown in Figure 23. Saturn's atmosphere is the largest of any planet in the solar system. Saturn also has the lowest average density. In fact, if there were a bathtub big enough, Saturn would float in the water. Saturn's atmosphere is made mostly of hydrogen and helium, with small amounts of other elements. Scientists think that the helium in Saturn's atmosphere condenses, creating helium "raindrops" that fall into the middle of the planet. As the helium drops fall, their potential energy is converted into heat. This keeps the planet warm, and explains why Saturn releases more heat than Jupiter.

Saturn's Moons Astronomers have found at least 62 moons orbiting Saturn. Most of these moons are very small. However, one moon, Titan, is larger than Mercury. Titan is the only planetary moon with a thick atmosphere and active streams and lakes. In 2004, the space probe Cassini began a series of flybys of Titan, and detected what appear to be lakes of liquid methane on the surface.

Uranus

Because Uranus is so far from the sun, it is very cold. Uranus's atmosphere is mostly hydrogen and helium. It also has a large amount of methane, which gives the planet a distinct blue-green appearance.

Structure of Uranus Like Jupiter and Saturn, Uranus has a dense core. This core is thought to be surrounded by a thick mantle layer of liquid water and dissolved ammonia, somewhat similar to a bottle of window-cleaning solution. A layer of liquid hydrogen and helium surrounds the mantle.

Uranus has rings, although they are not as visible as Saturn's. The particles that make up these rings are very dark, about as reflective as lumps of coal. Uranus has at least 27 moons, though most are quite small.

A Tilted Planet The most unusual characteristic of Uranus is that it lies nearly on its side, as shown in Figure 24. **The axis of Uranus's rotation is tilted more than 90°.** Uranus rotates in a direction opposite to the direction of its revolution around the sun. Uranus's rings and moons revolve about the same tilted axis. Because of the tilt of Uranus's axis, its northern and southern hemispheres alternate being exposed to the sun for many years. This causes immense storms that disturb the planet's otherwise smooth appearance. No one knows for sure why Uranus's axis is so tilted. Scientists hypothesize that the tilt may have been caused by a collision with another large planetary body early in its history.

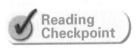 **Reading Checkpoint** *What do scientists hypothesize about the cause of Uranus's tilt?*

Go Online
SCIENCE NEWS®

For: Articles on the solar system
Visit: PHSchool.com
Web Code: cce-3254

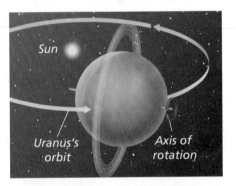

Figure 24 Uranus is unusual in that its axis is tilted so that the planet rotates nearly on its side. Uranus's rings and moons revolve around its greatly tilted axis of rotation. **Inferring** *In what way must the seasons on Uranus be unusual?*

Figure 25 This photo of Neptune was taken by the Voyager 2 spacecraft. The Great Dark Spot, visible near the center, was similar in size to Earth. The white clouds are thought to be made of methane ice crystals.
Formulating Hypotheses *Why is the color of Neptune different from Jupiter, Saturn, and Uranus?*

Figure 26 The New Horizons space probe will reach the dwarf planet Pluto and its three moons in the year 2015.

Neptune

Neptune is so far from the sun that it takes a very long time—165 Earth years—for it to make one revolution. Neptune has about the same composition and is about the same size as Uranus.

Unlike Uranus, Neptune has clearly visible cloud patterns in its atmosphere. Thin, wispy clouds form high within Neptune's atmosphere, similar to cirrus clouds in Earth's atmosphere. Earth's clouds are made of liquid water or ice crystals, but Neptune's clouds are made of methane ice crystals. **Neptune's bluish color comes from the methane in its atmosphere.**

Neptune also has large storms in its atmosphere. One of these, observed by the Voyager 2 space probe in 1989, was called the Great Dark Spot, shown in Figure 25. But by 1994, the storm was gone.

Neptune has thin rings of dark particles, very similar to the rings of Uranus. In addition, Neptune has at least 13 moons. Triton, the only large moon, has a thin atmosphere and an icy surface.

Dwarf Planets

In 2006, astronomers established a new classification for certain objects in the solar system that share some, but not all, of the characteristics of a planet. Pluto, which for many years had been considered the ninth and most distant planet in the solar system, was reclassified as a dwarf planet. **A dwarf planet, like a planet, is spherical and orbits the sun directly. But unlike a planet, a dwarf planet has not cleared the neighborhood around its orbit.** In order for an object to clear out its orbit, it must be massive enough for its gravity to attract all the nearby debris. A dwarf planet is too small for this to happen. As a result, dwarf planets tend to orbit in zones that contain many other objects.

Pluto, shown in Figure 26, is much smaller than the inner or outer planets. Its diameter (2390 km) is about half that of Mercury's. The density of Pluto is similar to that of Triton, suggesting a mixture of ice and rock. Pluto's orbit around the sun is more elliptical than those of the planets. In fact, for a small portion of its orbit, Pluto actually swings closer to the sun than Neptune. Like Uranus, Pluto has a rotation axis that is tilted more than 90°. Pluto also has three moons, Charon, Nix, and Hydra.

Other known dwarf planets include Eris and the asteroid Ceres. Many more solar system objects will likely be named dwarf planets once their shapes can be verified as being spherical. Note, however, that not all astronomers agree on what defines a planet, and the classification of dwarf planet may be subjected to further debate.

Comets and Meteoroids

As the craters on the surfaces of the terrestrial planets and moons show, there are many smaller objects moving through the inner solar system. These objects take two forms: comets and meteoroids. **Comets are dusty pieces of ice and rock that partially vaporize when they pass near the sun. Meteoroids are pieces of rock, usually less than a few hundred meters in size, that travel through the solar system.**

Certain ancient meteoroids have been largely unaltered since the birth of the solar system. These meteoroids are the oldest remnants of the early solar system. Scientists have used radioactive dating to determine their absolute age. This has allowed them to determine that the solar system is about 4.6 billion years old.

The Edge of the Solar System

Astronomers estimate that thousands of solar system objects exist beyond Neptune's orbit. These objects are found largely in two regions, the Kuiper belt and the Oort cloud. The **Kuiper belt** extends from Neptune's orbit out to about 100 AU or more from the sun. Objects in the Kuiper belt are mostly made of ice, dust, and rock. **Most of the objects in the Kuiper belt lie in a doughnut-shaped region close to the ecliptic.** Pluto is an example of a Kuiper-belt object.

Incredible as it may seem, the solar system extends much farther out than the Kuiper belt. **Beyond the Kuiper belt lies a great reservoir of comets called the Oort cloud.** Figure 27 shows the **Oort Cloud,** a very sparse sphere of comets thought to encircle the solar system out to a distance of about 50,000 AU. Occasionally objects from the Oort cloud enter the inner solar system, where they appear as comets.

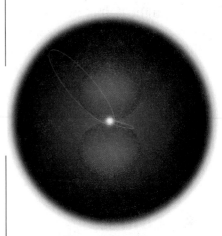

Figure 27 Located in the outer reaches of the solar system, the Oort cloud is a sphere of comets surrounding the sun and planets.

25.4 Assessment

Reviewing Concepts

1. How do the size and density of the gas giants from the terrestrial planets?

2. Name the outer planets and identify a distinguishing characteristic for each.

3. How are planets and dwarf planets similar? How are they different?

4. Compare and contrast comets and meteoroids.

5. What are some differences between the Kuiper belt and the Oort cloud?

Critical Thinking

6. **Inferring** Why might the gas giants be more appropriately called the "liquid giants"?

7. **Comparing and Contrasting** How are Jupiter's four large moons similar? How are they different?

Connecting Concepts

The Scientific Method Write a paragraph explaining how the discoveries of Uranus and Neptune show two different aspects of the process of scientific discovery.

Comets and Meteoroids

Comets and meteoroids are two groups of objects that travel through the solar system. Sometimes they can be seen from Earth as spectacular sights in the night sky.

Comets are dirty snowballs—chunks of rock and ice. They originate in the Kuiper Belt and the Oort Cloud, both of which lie beyond the orbit of Pluto. If a comet comes close to the sun it vaporizes, producing clouds of gas and dust. These clouds appear as tails, which can be millions of kilometers long. If a comet is close enough to Earth, it can be seen as a bright object in the night sky. Meteoroids consist of rock or metal and they can be any size from tiny particles to huge boulders. Most meteoroids burn up as they enter Earth's atmosphere. They appear as streaks of light in the night sky, called meteors. Meteoroids that reach Earth's surface are called meteorites.

Ion tail

Dust tail

Coma

Nucleus is deep inside the coma.

Comets

Most comets travel in highly elliptical orbits around the sun. Their orbital periods vary dramatically. Short-period comets, so called because they take less than 200 years to make one orbit, are the most predictable. Long-period comets may take thousands or millions of years to return to our sky.

Gas and dust jets

A comet's nucleus
A comet has a small nucleus (usually less than 20 km across) that consists of ice and rock. At the comet's surface, jets of gas and dust spray out under pressure, creating a huge cloud called a coma.

Rock *Ice*

Ion tail is pushed away from the sun by the solar wind.

Sun

Coma and tails grow as the comet nears the sun.

A comet's tails
Most comets have two tails: a white dust tail and a bluish ion tail. The dust tail is made of dust pushed outward by photons of light from the sun. The ion tail consists of charged gas particles that are pushed away from the comet by the solar wind (charged particles from the sun). Thus, the tails always face away from the sun.

In spite of its brightness, a comet does not give off any light of its own. What seems to be light from the comet is actually a reflection of the sun's light.

Meteoroids

Most meteoroids are made of rock. Others are made of metal, or a mixture of rock and metal. Sometimes, many meteors flash across the night sky within a short span of time. This event is known as a meteor shower. A meteor shower occurs when Earth passes through the dust and debris from the tail of a comet. The majority of meteoroids are no bigger than grains of sand.

Meteor
A meteor is the light from a meteoroid as it vaporizes in the atmosphere.

METEORITE

This meteorite is made of iron and nickel.

Meteorites
Relatively few meteoroids ever make it to the surface of the Earth. Those that do, called meteorites, can have very different shapes and sizes. Some are fragments broken from a larger space object.

Going Further

■ Use library or Internet resources to find out more about Halley's Comet, a regular visitor to the inner solar system. Include information on the comet's orbit, when it was discovered and when it is expected to return, and what scientists learned from its last appearance in 1986.

Barringer Meteorite Crater, Arizona
50,000 years ago, a meteorite 45 meters across crashed into Earth, producing this huge crater.

25.5 The Origin of the Solar System

Reading Focus

Key Concepts

- What is the nebular theory?
- How does the nebular theory explain the composition and size of the planets?

Vocabulary

solar nebula, protoplanetary disk, planetesimals, accretion

Reading Strategy

Identifying Main Ideas
Copy the incomplete table at the right. As you read, write the main idea for each topic.

Topic	Main Idea
The Nebular Theory	a. _____?_____
Formation of the protoplanetary disk	b. _____?_____
Planetesimals and protoplanets	c. _____?_____
Composition and size of the planets	d. _____?_____

Figuring out how the solar system formed is a bit like detective work. You can't go back 4.6 billion years in time to see exactly what happened. But there are many clues that scientists have used to form a theory about what must have occurred. Any such theory must explain why all of the planets' orbits lie more or less in a single plane and why all of the planets orbit the sun in the same direction. It must also explain the difference in size and composition between the terrestrial planets and the gas giants.

The Nebular Theory

The generally accepted explanation for the formation of the solar system is the nebular theory, illustrated in Figure 28. **The nebular theory states that the solar system formed from a rotating cloud of dust and gas.** A large, thin cloud of dust and gas like the one that eventually formed our solar system is called a **solar nebula.** According to the nebular theory, the solar nebula formed from the material expelled by previous stars.

Figure 28 The contraction of the solar nebula, a large cloud of dust and gas, led to a disk-shaped protoplanetary disk, from which the sun and planets formed. Illustrations are not shown to scale with respect to one another. **Applying Concepts** *What force caused the solar nebula to contract?*

Solar nebula

The sun forms at the center of a protoplanetary disk.

It is likely that a shock wave from the explosion of a nearby star caused the solar nebula to collapse. The nebula most likely began with a slight overall rotation. As the cloud contracted, it began to spin faster. The gravitational attraction between particles became stronger as the solar nebula shrank, accelerating the process.

Formation of the Protoplanetary Disk

As the solar nebula rotated faster, it began to flatten out. Over about 100,000 years, a large disk-shaped cloud of dust and gas called a **protoplanetary disk** formed. Looking like a giant fried egg rotating in space, the disk was densest in the center and thinner toward the edges. The planets would eventually form from the outer parts of the disk.

Nearly all of the mass of the solar nebula, about 99.9 percent, became concentrated near the center. The sun would eventually form in this region. The enormous density at the center of the disk increased until the temperature reached a few million degrees. Then, about 10 million years after the formation of the solar nebula, nuclear reactions began to fuse hydrogen into helium. Our sun was born.

Planetesimals and Protoplanets

The nebular theory also explains how the planets could have formed. Within the contracting protoplanetary disk, dust grains collided frequently. Weak surface forces held these dust grains together, forming loose balls of dust. As these balls of dust collided, they grew larger and larger.

Scientists estimate that, after a few million years, there were about a billion planetesimals revolving around the sun. **Planetesimals** were asteroid-like bodies that eventually combined to form planets. Planetesimals grew by **accretion,** the process of adding mass by colliding with other planetesimals. Once planetesimals became larger than about a kilometer in diameter, they began to exert a significant gravitational attraction on nearby objects. The planetesimals attracted more material, causing them to grow even faster. The result was the accretion of planetesimals into a much smaller number of moon-sized protoplanets. These protoplanets eventually joined to form the current planets in a series of immense collisions. The nebular theory provides an explanation for the current motions of the sun, planets, and most moons. Nearly all are now revolving in the direction that the protoplanetary disk was spinning.

Reading Checkpoint *What were planetesimals?*

Planetesimals form.

Protoplanets form.

Composition and Size of the Planets

At low pressures, such as those found in space, cooling materials generally condense directly from a gas into a solid. Different materials change into a solid at different temperatures. Ice-forming materials, such as water, ammonia, and methane, condense at low temperatures. Rock-forming materials condense at much higher temperatures.

When the solar system formed, the temperatures near the sun were very high. The temperature near Mercury's orbit was about 1200 K, and near Mars's orbit it was roughly 500 K. Water and other ice-forming materials vaporize at these temperatures, so they did not play a role in the early formation of the terrestrial planets. **The terrestrial planets are relatively small and rocky. In part, that is because the inner solar system was too hot during their formation for ice-forming compounds to condense.**

In contrast, ice-forming materials could condense in the outer solar system because it was much colder. Much more material was available, and these planets grew to many times the size of Earth. As these planets grew, their gravity increased, and they were able to capture the extremely abundant hydrogen and helium gas from the surrounding space. **The gas giants are large and have low densities because the outer solar system was cool enough for ice-forming compounds to condense.**

As Figure 29 shows, astronomers have been able to observe protoplanetary disks around distant newborn stars. Astronomers have also detected more than a hundred planets in orbit around distant stars. This evidence of planets forming around other stars, plus the results of computer simulations, provides support for the nebular theory.

Figure 29 The Hubble Space Telescope took this photo of what are thought to be protoplanetary disks around several young stars. These stars are located about 1500 light-years away in the Orion Nebula, a region of intense star formation. **Predicting** *According to the nebular theory, what will these protoplanetary disks eventually become?*

Section 25.5 Assessment

Reviewing Concepts

1. List the major steps in the formation of the solar system according to the nebular theory.

2. Why are compounds such as ammonia most common in the outer solar system?

3. What happened to the planetesimals that once orbited the sun?

4. What was the protoplanetary disk?

Critical Thinking

5. **Applying Concepts** Why do all of the planets revolve around the sun within the same plane and in the same direction?

6. **Inferring** Astronomers are able to detect planets around distant stars because of the gravitational effects of the planets as they orbit the star. Why do you think most of the planets found so far have been very massive?

Writing in Science

Cause-Effect Paragraph Write a paragraph explaining why the terrestrial planets formed mostly from metal and rock, and not hydrogen and helium like the gas giants.

Modeling the Solar System

You may have seen models and illustrations that compare the sizes of the planets, but do not accurately show their relative distances from the sun. In this lab, you will compare the sizes of the planets to their distances from the sun.

Problem
How can you model both the relative sizes and distances of the planets in the solar system?

Materials
- calculator
- large sheet of unlined paper
- meter stick
- scale models of the sun and planets

Skills
Calculating, Using Models

Procedure

1. To model the relative sizes of the planets' orbits, convert the distances of the planets from the sun in astronomical units to kilometers, using Figure 3 on pages 792–793. Record these distances in scientific notation.

2. Use the meter stick to draw a straight line down the entire length of the large sheet of unlined paper. Measure and record the length of this line in centimeters.

3. Label one end of the line *sun* and the other end *Pluto.*

4. To calculate the scale of your model, divide the length of the line in centimeters by Pluto's average distance from the sun in kilometers.

5. To determine Neptune's position, multiply Neptune's average distance from the sun by the scale of your model. Mark Neptune's position on the line in your model.

6. Repeat Step 5 for each of the remaining planets in the solar system.

7. Your teacher will provide a set of scale models of the sun and planets. Use a meter stick to measure and record the diameter of the model of Jupiter.

8. To determine the scale of the planet models, divide the diameter of the model of Jupiter in centimeters by the actual diameter of Jupiter, which can be found in Figure 20 on page 811.

9. To determine the size of the solar system at the scale of the planet models, multiply the actual distance from Pluto to the sun by the scale of the planet models. Convert the result from centimeters to meters and record this distance.

Analyze and Conclude

1. **Using Models** How big would a model of the solar system be at the scale of the planet models you used? Explain your answer.

2. **Analyzing Data** What difficulty would you have including the relative sizes of the planets on the paper model you made in Steps 1 through 6?

3. **Drawing Conclusions** Explain why it is difficult to model the sizes and distances of the planets at the same scale.

Go Further Calculate the distance from the sun to each planet in a model with the same scale as the planet models. Under your teacher's supervision and with the help of your classmates, take the planet models outdoors and position them to model their distances from the sun.

Study Guide

25.1 Exploring the Solar System

Key Concepts

- In a geocentric model, Earth is stationary while objects in the sky move around it.
- In a heliocentric model, Earth and the other planets revolve around the sun.
- Gravity and inertia combine to keep the planets in orbit around the sun.
- Our solar system consists of the sun, the planets, their moons, and a variety of smaller objects that revolve around the sun.
- Modern technology, including complex telescopes, piloted spacecraft, and space probes, has allowed scientists to explore the solar system.

Vocabulary

geocentric, *p. 791;* heliocentric, *p. 791;* ecliptic plane, *p. 792;* moon, *p. 792;* astronomical unit, *p. 793;* space probe, *p. 794*

25.2 The Earth-Moon System

Key Concepts

- The lack of an atmosphere allows the moon's surface temperature to vary tremendously.
- The major surface features of the moon are maria, highlands, and craters.
- Scientists hypothesize that the moon formed after an enormous collision early in Earth's history.
- The moon's phases are caused by changes in the relative positions of the moon, sun, and Earth as the moon revolves around Earth.
- A solar eclipse occurs when the moon casts a shadow on a portion of Earth's surface.
- A lunar eclipse occurs when Earth casts a shadow on the moon.
- Tides are caused mainly by differences in the moon's gravitational pull on Earth.

Vocabulary

maria, *p. 797;* crater, *p. 797;* meteoroids, *p. 797;* phases, *p. 798;* eclipse, *p. 799;* umbra, *p. 800;* penumbra, *p. 800;* tides, *p. 801;* spring tide, *p. 801;* neap tide, *p. 801*

25.3 The Inner Solar System

Key Concepts

- The four inner planets are all relatively small and dense, and have rocky surfaces.
- Scientists now hypothesize that asteroids are remnants of the early solar system.

Vocabulary

terrestrial planets, *p. 803;* asteroids, *p. 809;* asteroid belt, *p. 809*

25.4 The Outer Solar System

Key Concepts

- The four gas giants are thought to have small, dense cores, and thick atmospheres that are mostly hydrogen and helium.
- A dwarf planet is spherical and orbits the sun, but has not cleared the neighborhood around its orbit.
- Comets are dusty pieces of ice and rock. Meteoroids are pieces of rock moving through space.
- The Kuiper belt is a doughnut-shaped region near the ecliptic. The Oort cloud is a reservoir of comets.

Vocabulary

gas giants, *p. 811;* ring, *p. 811;* Kuiper belt, *p. 815;* Oort cloud, *p. 815*

25.5 The Origin of the Solar System

Key Concepts

- The nebular theory states that the solar system formed from a rotating cloud of dust and gas.
- The terrestrial planets are small and rocky because the inner solar system was too hot during their formation for ice-forming compounds to condense. The gas giants are large and have low densities because the outer solar system was much cooler.

Vocabulary

solar nebula, *p. 818;* protoplanetary disk, *p. 819;* planetesimals, *p. 819;* accretion, *p. 819*

Thinking Visually

Compare-and-Contrast Table Make a table comparing and contrasting the terrestrial planets, gas giants, and Pluto.

Assessment

Reviewing Content

Choose the letter that best answers the question or completes the statement.

1. In the geocentric model,
   a. Earth travels around the sun.
   b. the planets travel around Earth.
   c. the planets travel around the sun.
   d. the planets travel around the stars.

2. Which of the following scientists discovered that each planet orbits the sun in an ellipse?
   a. Isaac Newton   b. Nicolaus Copernicus
   c. Galileo Galilei   d. Johannes Kepler

3. Most of the mass of the solar system is contained in
   a. the outer planets.   b. the moons.
   c. the sun.   d. Earth.

4. Dark, smooth regions on the moon are called
   a. maria.   b. highlands.
   c. craters.   d. meteoroids.

5. All the terrestrial planets have
   a. liquid oceans.   b. liquid helium.
   c. rocky surfaces.   d. at least one moon.

6. On Venus and Mars, the major component of the atmosphere is
   a. oxygen.   b. carbon dioxide.
   c. nitrogen.   d. hydrogen.

7. Asteroids are most likely to be
   a. remnants of the early solar system.
   b. former moons of Jupiter.
   c. the remains of a shattered planet.
   d. captured comets.

8. The gas giants are made mostly of
   a. helium gas.
   b. methane ice crystals.
   c. carbon dioxide.
   d. liquid hydrogen and helium.

9. The most likely place in the solar system besides Earth to support life is
   a. Jupiter.   b. Titan.
   c. Venus.   d. Europa.

10. The process by which planetesimals combine with other planetesimals is called
    a. condensation.   b. accretion.
    c. contraction.   d. fusion.

Understanding Concepts

11. Why was the heliocentric model of the solar system not readily accepted at first?

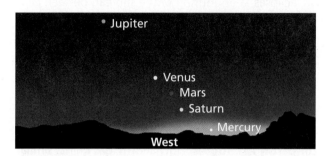

12. Explain why on some occasions you can see the planets line up in the sky.

13. Why are space probes used to explore the solar system?

14. Why does the moon lack an atmosphere?

15. What causes the moon to go through a regular cycle of phases?

16. Why doesn't a solar eclipse occur every time the moon passes between the sun and Earth?

17. In most coastal areas there are two high tides every day. What causes the two tides?

18. What does it mean to say that Mercury is "geologically quiet"?

19. Why is there no liquid water on the surface of Venus?

20. Where would you go to find the largest volcano in the solar system?

21. What is the Great Red Spot in the atmosphere of Jupiter?

22. Why are hydrogen and helium within the gas giant planets largely in a liquid state?

23. How are clouds on Neptune different from those on Earth?

24. What is unusual about the orbit of Pluto around the sun?

25. How were temperatures distributed across the protoplanetary disk that formed our solar system?

Critical Thinking

26. Inferring During some solar eclipses, the moon completely hides the sun. During other solar eclipses, a bright ring of the sun can be seen all the way around the moon. What does this tell you about the shape of the moon's orbit?

27. Drawing Conclusions A thin layer of dust and rock fragments covers the surface of the moon. This lunar soil did not form from weathering, as on Earth, because there is no liquid water on the moon. How do you think the lunar soil formed?

28. Using Analogies How are the gas giants similar to miniature solar systems?

29. Applying Concepts Put the following objects in order from the oldest to the youngest: protoplanets, solar nebula, protoplanetary disk, planetesimals, and planets.

Analyzing Data

Use the table below to answer Questions 30–33.

Largest Moons of the Solar System

Name	Diameter (km)	Period of Revolution (Earth days)	Distance from Planet (× 10³ km)
Callisto	4800	16.69	1883.0
Ganymede	5268	7.16	1070.0
Io	3642	1.77	421.6
Earth's moon	3476	27.32	384.4
Titan	5150	15.95	1221.9

30. Using Tables Which moon in the table is farthest from its planet?

31. Using Tables Which moon is the largest in the solar system? How much larger is it than Earth's moon?

32. Calculating How many times does Io revolve around Jupiter for each time Earth's moon revolves around Earth?

33. Making Generalizations Which planet do most of the large moons revolve around?

Concepts in Action

34. Applying Concepts You see on the news that a hurricane is approaching the coast of North Carolina. The weather service is concerned over the timing of a spring tide. What impact could such a tide have on damage from the hurricane?

35. Inferring If you were on the surface of Venus with a telescope and a friend was on the surface of Mars with a telescope, which one of you would have a better view of Earth? Explain.

36. Applying Concepts Besides Earth, what planets or moons in our solar system are the most likely candidates for life? Explain why.

37. Applying Concepts Why do comets' ion tails always stream away from the sun?

38. Comparing and Contrasting Explain the differences among a meteor, a meteorite, and a meteoroid.

39. Making Judgments In 2006, Pluto's status as a planet was changed to that of a dwarf planet. Why do you think this happened? Do you think Pluto should be kept as a dwarf planet?

40. Writing in Science Imagine you are a television reporter and you are observing the formation of the solar system. Write the script for your broadcast, documenting what you are seeing and offering clues as to why it may be happening.

Performance-Based Assessment

Observing Over the course of a month, keep a record of the moon's phases and position in the sky. Be sure to make your observations at the same time and from the same place each night. Use a tree or other landmark as a reference point. Also record when the sky is cloudy or the moon cannot be seen on a clear night. At the end of the month, prepare a summary of your observations.

Go Online
PHSchool.com

For: Self-grading assessment
Visit: PHSchool.com
Web Code: cca-3250

Standardized Test Prep

Test-Taking Tip

Eliminating Unreasonable Answers

When you answer a multiple-choice question, you can often eliminate at least one answer choice because it is clearly incorrect. If you eliminate one or more choices, you increase your odds of choosing the correct answer.

In the question below, you can immediately eliminate choice A because stars do not revolve around Earth. Clearly, choices D and E cannot both be true. On reflection, you can eliminate both of these choices, as Polaris's distance from Earth is not related to the apparent movement of stars around Polaris. Choices B and C are both factual. However, Earth's revolution around the sun takes one year, and is not related to the apparent daily motion of the stars. The remaining choice must be the correct answer.

In the Northern Hemisphere, certain stars appear to circle around Polaris, the North Star, because

(A) these stars revolve around Earth.
(B) Earth revolves around the sun.
(C) Earth rotates on its axis.
(D) Polaris is the closest star.
(E) Polaris is the most distant visible star.

(Answer: C)

Choose the letter that best answers the question or completes the statement.

1. The planets remain in stable orbits around the sun as a result of a balance between
   (A) gravity and pressure from nuclear fusion.
   (B) thermal energy and electromagnetic energy.
   (C) inertia and pressure from nuclear fusion.
   (D) gravity and inertia.
   (E) pressure from nuclear fusion and electromagnetic energy.

2. Which of the following contributes most to the size of tides on Earth?
   (A) rotation of Earth
   (B) gravitational pull of the moon
   (C) gravitational pull of the sun
   (D) gravitational pull of the planets
   (E) rotation of the sun

3. The asteroid belt can be found between the orbits of
   (A) Neptune and Pluto.
   (B) Mars and Jupiter.
   (C) Earth and Mars.
   (D) Mercury and Venus.
   (E) Jupiter and Saturn.

4. Which of the following is NOT a characteristic of each of the gas giant planets?
   (A) high density
   (B) encircled by rings
   (C) very low surface temperatures
   (D) many moons
   (E) composed mainly of hydrogen and helium

Use the illustration below to answer Questions 5–7.

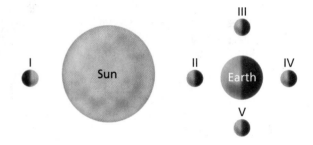

Not to scale

5. In which location could a lunar eclipse occur?
   (A) I
   (B) II
   (C) III
   (D) IV
   (E) V

6. In which location could the moon be during a solar eclipse?
   (A) I
   (B) II
   (C) III
   (D) IV
   (E) V

7. In which location(s) is the moon when half of the side facing Earth is illuminated?
   (A) III only
   (B) IV only
   (C) II and IV
   (D) III and V
   (E) II and V

26 Exploring the Universe

21st Century Learning

Problem Identification, Formulation, and Solution

What can you find out about extrasolar planets in our galaxy?

You are already familiar with the planets that orbit the sun. But astronomers also have discovered planets that orbit other stars. Planets outside our solar system are called extrasolar planets. Use the Internet to search for information on currently known extrasolar planets. Identify the planets that orbit the three closest stars to the sun, and post a summary of each solar system on your class blog. Use the blog to facilitate an online discussion with your classmates about extrasolar planets and how they are discovered.

How do science concepts apply to your world? Here are some questions you'll be able to answer after you read this chapter.

- How can the sun disrupt radio and TV signals on Earth? *(Section 26.1)*

- How do we know what stars are made of? *(Section 26.2)*

- What has such strong gravity that not even light can escape from it? *(Section 26.3)*

- Where were the atoms that make up your body formed? *(Section 26.3)*

- What is at the center of our galaxy? *(Section 26.4)*

- What is the large-scale structure of the universe? *(page 850)*

- Is the universe expanding? *(Section 26.5)*

This cloud of dust and gas is located in the constellation Sagittarius.

Chapter Preview

Inquiry > Activity

Can You Tell How Bright a Light Really Is?

Procedure

1. Work in groups of three or four. Obtain two flashlights, one brighter than the other.

2. **Predicting** If the dimmer flashlight moves close enough to you, will it appear brighter than the other flashlight? Record your prediction.

3. Darken the room. Have two group members stand side by side about 3 meters from the rest of your group. Each one should shine a flashlight at the group.

4. Direct the person with the dimmer flashlight to slowly move closer to the group, keeping the flashlight level.

Think About It

1. **Observing** Was your prediction correct?

2. **Drawing Conclusions** How does the distance from you to a light affect how bright the light appears to you?

3. **Applying Concepts** If one star appears to be brighter than another star, can you tell which one is actually brighter just by looking at them? Explain your answer.

26.1 The Sun

Figure 1 The sun gives off tremendous amounts of energy. Plants on Earth use sunlight directly in photosynthesis.

You know that flowers like the ones in Figure 1 need sunlight. In fact, almost all life on Earth depends on sunlight. Without the sun's radiation, Earth would be a cold, dark, and lifeless planet. But what exactly is the sun? Scientists have learned that the sun is a glowing ball of gas. The sun is extremely hot, about 15 million K at its center and 5800 K at its surface. At such temperatures, most of the atoms in the sun have lost most of their electrons, forming a plasma of ionized gas. About 70 percent of the sun's mass is hydrogen and 28 percent is helium.

Energy From the Sun

The sun gives off tremendous amounts of energy in the form of electromagnetic radiation. But what is the source of this energy? Does the sun burn some type of fuel? If so, how long will it continue to burn before all its fuel is used up? Because the sun and Earth formed together, the answers to these questions can be used to estimate the age of Earth. As a result, scientists from many different fields began a debate that lasted more than 100 years.

In the late 1700s, the German philosopher Immanuel Kant wondered whether the sun produced its energy from an ordinary chemical reaction. He calculated that if it did, it could last only a few thousand years. In the mid-1800s, two physicists, Hermann von Helmholtz and William Thomson (better known as Lord Kelvin), proposed another idea. They hypothesized that gravity was causing the sun to shrink over time, converting its potential energy into thermal energy. According to their calculations, the sun was no more than 20 to 30 million years old.

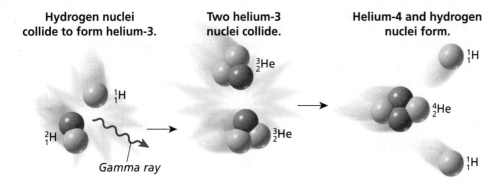

Hydrogen nuclei collide to form helium-3.

^1_1H

^2_1H

Gamma ray

Two helium-3 nuclei collide.

^3_2He

^3_2He

Helium-4 and hydrogen nuclei form.

^1_1H

^4_2He

^1_1H

Figure 2 Nuclear fusion within the sun's central region converts mass into energy. The green particles in the diagram are protons and the purple particles are neutrons.
Interpreting Diagrams *What new isotope is produced by this fusion reaction?*

Scottish geologist Charles Lyell disagreed. Lyell argued that geological processes on Earth had taken hundreds of millions of years. Therefore, Earth and the sun must be far older than other scientists had thought. Evidence from various branches of science eventually led scientists to conclude that the sun is actually about 4.6 billion years old.

How could the sun produce energy for so long? Clearly, the hypotheses about chemical reactions and the sun shrinking were incorrect, as they could not account for the actual age of the sun. It wasn't until the early 1900s that scientists discovered the real source of the sun's energy—nuclear fusion in its central region. Here the temperature and pressure are high enough for fusion to take place. In the process of fusion, as shown in Figure 2, less massive nuclei combine into more massive nuclei, releasing enormous amounts of energy. **The sun's energy is produced in its central region by the fusion of hydrogen nuclei into helium nuclei.**

Forces in Balance

The fossil record of life on Earth shows that the sun has been a fairly stable energy source for billions of years. For the sun to be stable, inward and outward forces within the sun must be in equilibrium. The forces are balanced so that temperature, pressure, and density at any depth remain fairly constant over time.

The energy from nuclear fusion in the center of the sun causes ions to move faster, exerting an outward thermal pressure. At the same time, gravity pulls the gas inward, as shown in Figure 3. **The sun remains stable because the inward pull of gravity balances the outward push of thermal pressure from nuclear fusion.** The sun will remain stable as long as there is a steady energy source within it. Astronomers estimate that the sun will remain stable for another 5 billion years.

Figure 3 Gravity and the outward thermal pressure from nuclear fusion are balanced throughout the sun. Both the force of gravity and the pressure are greater deep within the sun than near the sun's surface.
Predicting *What would happen to the sun if it began to run out of fuel?*

Pressure out

Gravity in

Reading Checkpoint *How long will the sun remain stable?*

For: Links on the sun
Visit: www.SciLinks.org
Web Code: ccn-3261

The Sun's Interior

Astronomers cannot see inside the sun. However, they are able to infer the structure of the sun's interior. They use mathematical models and observe vibrations of the sun that are similar to vibrations caused by earthquakes on Earth. The sun's interior and atmosphere are divided into several layers with distinct characteristics. 👁 **The sun's interior consists of the core, the radiation zone, and the convection zone.** Figure 4 illustrates the structure of the sun.

Core The sun's **core** is its central region, where nuclear fusion occurs. The core has a diameter of about 400,000 kilometers, a little more than a quarter of the diameter of the entire sun.

Radiation Zone You are able to see the sun because some of the energy produced in its core travels outward and escapes into space as visible light. Energy moves through the sun in two main ways: by radiation and by convection. As energy moves outward from the sun's core, it first enters the radiation zone. The **radiation zone** is a region of highly compressed gas. Here, energy is transferred by the absorption and reradiation of electromagnetic waves. Because this region is so dense, energy can take more than 100,000 years to pass through it.

Figure 4 The sun has an interior and an atmosphere. The interior consists of the core, radiation zone, and convection zone. The atmosphere consists of the photosphere, chromosphere, and corona.
Interpreting Diagrams *What is the diameter of the sun's core?*

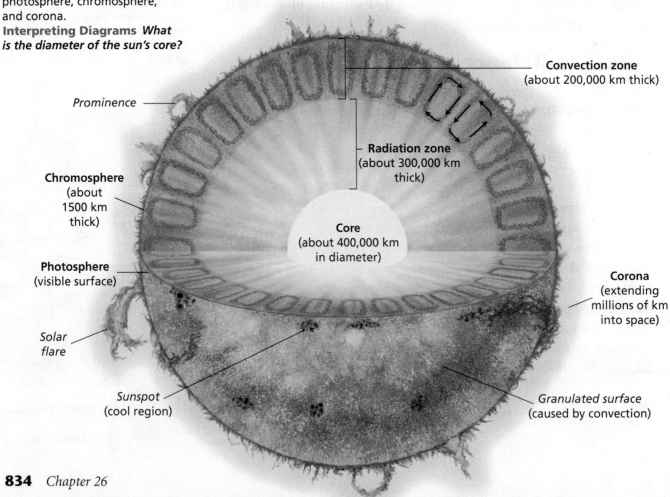

Prominence

Convection zone
(about 200,000 km thick)

Radiation zone
(about 300,000 km thick)

Chromosphere
(about 1500 km thick)

Core
(about 400,000 km in diameter)

Photosphere
(visible surface)

Corona
(extending millions of km into space)

Solar flare

Sunspot
(cool region)

Granulated surface
(caused by convection)

Convection Zone Energy from the radiation zone passes into the **convection zone,** the outer layer of the sun's interior. In the convection zone, energy is transferred outward mainly by convection currents. Hot gases in the convection zone rise toward the sun's atmosphere while cooler gases sink downward.

The Sun's Atmosphere

Outside the convection zone is the sun's atmosphere. The sun's atmosphere consists of three layers: the photosphere, the chromosphere, and the corona.

Photosphere The innermost layer of the sun's atmosphere, which is the visible surface of the sun, is the **photosphere** (FOH tuh sfeer). It is about 500 kilometers thick and has an average temperature of about 5800 K. Although the photosphere is not solid, it is called the sun's surface. Astronomers can't see through it to the sun's interior. The photosphere's surface has a bubbly appearance. The bubbles, called granules, are the tops of convection currents that carry energy from the sun's interior.

Chromosphere Just outside the photosphere is the **chromosphere** (KROH muh sfeer), the middle layer of the sun's atmosphere. Temperature increases to nearly 10,000 K as you move upward through the chromosphere. At such high temperatures, hydrogen gas emits a reddish light. This light gives the chromosphere its name, which means "sphere of color." The faint chromosphere is normally visible only when the brighter photosphere is blocked, such as during a total solar eclipse.

Corona The chromosphere merges with the **corona,** the outermost layer of the sun's atmosphere. The gases in the corona are so thin that the corona, like the chromosphere, is usually seen only during solar eclipses. Gases in the corona are very hot, about 1 million kelvins. But the corona has such a low density that the total amount of thermal energy in it is relatively small.

The corona, shown in Figure 5, extends millions of kilometers above the chromosphere. It gradually thins into the **solar wind,** a stream of electrically charged particles that flows outward from the sun through the solar system. As the solar wind approaches Earth, Earth's magnetic field deflects the charged particles. These particles enter the atmosphere only near Earth's magnetic poles. There they can interact with molecules in the atmosphere, producing auroras.

 Reading Checkpoint *What is the solar wind?*

Figure 5 The corona can only be seen from Earth during a total solar eclipse or when viewed with a special telescope.

For: Activity on sunspots
Visit: PHSchool.com
Web Code: ccc-3262

To sun

Quick Lab

Calculating the Sun's Power

Materials

portable socket with clear light bulb, paraffin-block photometer, meter stick, calculator

Procedure

1. You can estimate the sun's power by comparing it to the known power of a light bulb. Because a bulb's efficiency is about 10 percent, its actual power (P_{bulb}) is the rated power in watts divided by 10.

2. Place the socket on a table so that the bulb filament is perpendicular to the direction of the sun. Turn the bulb on. **CAUTION** *The bulb will become very hot. Do not touch it.*

3. A photometer is used to measure light levels. Hold the photometer directly between the bulb and the sun as shown. **CAUTION** *Do not look directly at the sun.*

4. Look at the narrow edge of the photometer. Move the photometer toward or away from the bulb until the slabs of paraffin on the two sides of the foil seem equally bright.

5. Have a partner measure the distance (D_{bulb}) in centimeters from the foil to the filament.

Analyze and Conclude

1. **Calculating** Earth is about 150 million km from the sun. What is the distance (D_{sun}) between Earth and the sun in centimeters?

2. **Calculating** How bright a light source appears depends directly on its actual power and inversely on the square of its distance from the observer. When the photometer is positioned so that the bulb and the sun appear equally bright, the following ratios are equal:

$$\frac{P_{bulb}}{D^2_{bulb}} = \frac{P_{sun}}{D^2_{sun}}$$

Square your values for D_{bulb} and D_{sun}. Then insert these values and your value for P_{bulb} into the formula. Use the formula to calculate the actual power of the sun (P_{sun}) in watts.

Figure 6 Sunspots are relatively cool areas on the sun's surface. **Interpreting Photos** *How do sunspots appear different from the surrounding photosphere?*

Features of the Sun's Atmosphere

The sun's magnetic field produces striking features on and above its surface. 🔵 **Features of the sun's atmosphere include sunspots, prominences, and solar flares.**

Sunspots Look at Figure 6. The relatively small, dark-looking regions on the sun's surface are called sunspots. **Sunspots** are areas of gas in the photosphere that are cooler than the surrounding gases. However, sunspots aren't really small. Some are larger than Earth! They are also not really dark. If sunspots could be seen apart from the rest of the sun, they would shine brightly. But because they are cooler, sunspots give off less energy than the surrounding photosphere, and so they appear dark by comparison. Sunspots are often found in groups and are associated with intense magnetic fields on the sun. Sunspots last from a few hours to a few months. The number of sunspots varies in cycles, with about 11 years separating one sunspot peak from the next. During peak periods, there may be a hundred sunspots on the sun.

Sunspots provide astronomers with insights into the motions of the sun. The Italian scientist Galileo Galilei discovered that the sun rotates by observing the motion of sunspots. Later observations showed that the sun doesn't spin as a solid body the way Earth does. Instead, sunspots near the sun's equator move faster than sunspots near the sun's poles. This means that the sun rotates faster at its equator than near its poles.

Prominences Prominences are spectacular features of the sun's atmosphere that occur near sunspots. As shown in Figure 7A, **prominences** are huge loops of gas that erupt from sunspot regions. They extend upward from the photosphere into the chromosphere and sometimes into the corona. Prominences travel along the magnetic field lines that connect sunspots. Some prominences reach heights of more than 100,000 kilometers above the sun's surface.

Solar Flares The sun's surface sometimes erupts dramatically, producing X-rays and hurling charged particles into space at speeds of 1000 km/s or more. Such a sudden release of energy from the sun is called a **solar flare.** Like prominences, solar flares usually occur near sunspots. Solar flares heat the corona to a temperature near 20 million K and greatly increase the solar wind. When the additional high-energy particles and radiation from a solar flare reach Earth, they can cause magnetic storms in Earth's upper atmosphere. These storms disrupt electric power transmission as well as radio, television, and telephone signals.

Figure 7 The sun's magnetic field produces prominences and flares visible with special red filters. **A** This prominence forms a huge twirling loop connecting sunspot regions. **B** A solar flare erupts on the edge of the sun.

Section 26.1 Assessment

Reviewing Concepts

1. ⬤ What is the source of the sun's energy?
2. ⬤ What two forces in the sun interact to produce a stable structure?
3. ⬤ List the layers of the sun's interior from the center outward and briefly describe each one.
4. ⬤ Describe each of the layers of the sun's atmosphere from the surface outward.
5. ⬤ Describe three features that exist on or above the sun's surface.

Critical Thinking

6. **Applying Concepts** How have scientists learned about the sun's interior?

7. **Calculating** The sun's mass is more than 300,000 times the mass of Earth. The sun's volume is about 1,000,000 times that of Earth. How much denser is Earth than the sun?

Writing in Science

Describing the Sun Describe in a few paragraphs an imaginary journey to the center of the sun, beginning from its outermost layer. Include a description of each layer and at least two prominent features.

26.2 Stars

Key Concepts

- How can the distance to a star be measured?
- How do astronomers categorize stars?
- What elements are found in stars?
- How do astronomers use H-R diagrams?

Vocabulary

- star
- light-year
- parallax
- apparent brightness
- absolute brightness
- absorption lines
- H-R diagram
- main sequence
- supergiants
- giants
- white dwarf

Reading Strategy

Using Prior Knowledge Copy the concept map below. Add what you already know about stars. After you read, complete your concept map, adding more ovals as needed.

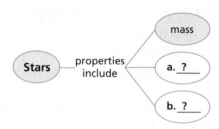

If you look up at the sky at night, you'll see that stars look like points of light. You will probably also notice that some stars are brighter than others. If you look closely, you'll see that some stars have different colors, as shown in Figure 8. However, you can't tell how large or how far away a star is simply by looking at it. You can't poke a star, crawl around inside it, or take its temperature with a thermometer. To explore the stars, modern astronomers use spectrographs and other instruments mounted on telescopes.

A **star** is a large, glowing ball of gas in space, which generates energy through nuclear fusion in its core. The closest star to Earth is the sun, which is considered to be a fairly average star.

Distances to the Stars

Although the sky seems full of stars, most of the universe is nearly empty space. This seeming contradiction exists because most stars are separated by vast distances.

The Light-Year You wouldn't measure the distance between two distant cities in centimeters. Similarly, because stars are so far apart, it's not practical to measure their distances in units that might be used on Earth, such as kilometers. Instead, astronomers use much larger units, including the light-year. A **light-year** is the distance that light travels in a vacuum in a year, which is about 9.5 trillion kilometers. Proxima Centauri, the closest star to the sun, is about 4.3 light-years away.

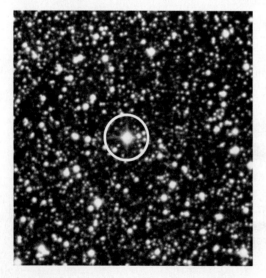

Figure 8 Proxima Centauri, the red star at the center, is the closest star to the sun.

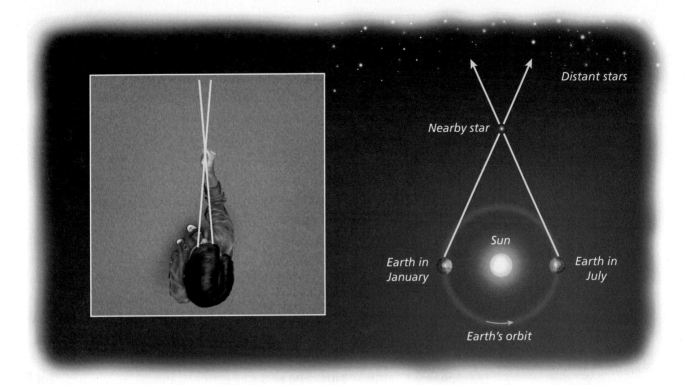

Parallax Stars are so far away that astronomers cannot measure their distances directly. Astronomers have developed various methods of determining the distances to stars. Different methods are used for stars at different distances.

To understand how astronomers can measure distances to nearby stars, hold your thumb up at arm's length in front of you, as the student is doing in Figure 9. Close your left eye and look at your thumb with just your right eye open. Then cover your right eye and look with just your left eye open. Even though you didn't move your thumb, it appeared to move relative to the background because you looked at it from slightly different angles. The apparent change in position of an object with respect to a distant background is called **parallax.**

As Earth moves in its orbit, astronomers are able to observe stars from two different positions. Imagine looking at the stars in winter and then six months later in summer. During this time, Earth has moved from one side of its orbit to the other—a distance of about 300 million kilometers. Because people on Earth are looking from a different angle, the nearby star appears to move against the more-distant background stars.

Before the invention of the telescope, astronomers couldn't measure a star's position very accurately. They couldn't detect the apparent movement of even a single nearby star as Earth moved around the sun.

With the invention of the telescope, astronomers could measure the positions of stars with much greater accuracy. 🔑 **Astronomers measure the parallax of nearby stars to determine their distance from Earth.** The closer a star is to Earth, the greater is its parallax.

Figure 9 You can observe parallax by holding your thumb in front of you. Compare its positions when you look at it first with one eye and then with the other. Astronomers can measure the parallax of nearby stars by measuring their position relative to distant stars as the Earth revolves around the sun.
Observing *Is the parallax of your thumb greater when it is closer to your eyes or when it is farther from your eyes?*

Astronomers have measured the parallax of many nearby stars and determined their distances from Earth. However, if a star is too far away, its parallax is too small to be measured. With present technology, the parallax method gives reasonably accurate distance measurements for stars within a few hundred light-years. Astronomers have developed other ways to estimate distances to more-distant stars.

Properties of Stars

There are many different types of stars. ● **Astronomers classify stars by their color, size, and brightness. Other important properties of stars include their chemical composition and mass.**

Color and Temperature Have you ever looked closely at a candle flame? The hottest part of the flame near the wick is blue or white, while the cooler flame tip is orange. A propane torch flame is blue. Dying campfire embers are red. You can estimate the temperature of a flame from its color. In the same way, a star's color indicates the temperature of its surface. The hottest stars, with surface temperatures above 30,000 K, appear blue. The surfaces (photospheres) of relatively cool red stars are still a toasty 3000 K or so. Stars with surface temperatures between 5000 and 6000 K appear yellow, like the sun. As shown in Figure 10, the color differences between hot blue stars and cool red stars can be seen with the unaided eye. More precise measurements of stars' temperatures can be made by studying stars' spectra.

Brightness When you are outside at night in a city, look for a row of street lights like the one in Figure 11. The closer lights look bright and the more distant lights look dim. However, the more distant lights are not really dimmer. They appear dim to you because, at a greater distance, their light is spread out over a greater area, so a smaller portion enters your eyes. The same is true for the light emitted by stars.

You might think that closer stars will always appear brighter than more-distant stars. Astronomers have discovered, however, that the brightness of stars can vary by a factor of more than a billion. So, stars that look bright may actually be farther away than stars that appear dim.

Although the sun appears to be the brightest star in our sky, it is really a star of only average brightness. The sun appears very bright to us because it is much closer than other stars. The brightness of a star as it appears from Earth is called its **apparent brightness.** The apparent brightness of a star decreases as its distance from you increases.

Figure 10 The "Winter Triangle" can be seen in the late fall and winter in the eastern sky. It is made up of three of the brightest stars in the sky: Betelgeuse, Procyon, and Sirius A. Betelgeuse and the star Rigel belong to the constellation Orion.
Applying Concepts *Which star has a higher surface temperature, Betelgeuse or Sirius A?*

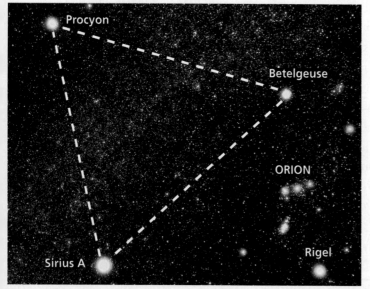

If you move away from a street light or a star, it shines just as brightly as before—but to you it appears fainter. **Absolute brightness** is how bright a star really is. A star's absolute brightness is a characteristic of the star and does not depend on how far it is from Earth. You can calculate a star's absolute brightness if you know its distance from Earth and its apparent brightness.

Size and Mass Once astronomers know a star's temperature and absolute brightness, they can estimate its diameter and then calculate its volume. However, there is no direct way of finding the mass of an isolated star. Instead, astronomers are able to calculate the masses of many stars by observing the gravitational interaction of stars that occur in pairs. From such observations, astronomers have determined that, for most stars, there is a relationship between mass and absolute brightness. Astronomers have found that many stars are similar to the sun in size and mass.

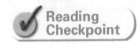 **Reading Checkpoint** *How can astronomers determine a star's mass?*

Figure 11 These streetlights all have about the same absolute brightness. **Inferring** *Why do the nearby streetlights appear brighter than the distant ones?*

Composition A spectrograph is an instrument that spreads light from a hot glowing object, such as a light bulb or a star, into a spectrum. Astronomers can use spectrographs to identify the various elements in a star's atmosphere.

Each star has its own spectrum. The elements within a star's atmosphere absorb light from the star's photosphere. Each element absorbs light of different wavelengths, removing these wavelengths from the star's continuous spectrum. The result is a bright spectrum, such as the one shown in Figure 12. It contains a set of dark lines called **absorption lines** that show where light has been absorbed. Just as fingerprints can be used to identify a person, a star's absorption lines can be used to identify different elements in the star.

Absorption lines of most elements have been identified in the spectra of stars. Observations of such lines in many stars have shown that the composition of most stars is fairly similar. 🔑 **Most stars have a chemical makeup that is similar to the sun, with hydrogen and helium together making up 96 to 99.9 percent of the star's mass.**

Figure 12 This is the spectrum of a star. The dark absorption lines indicate the presence of various elements in the star.

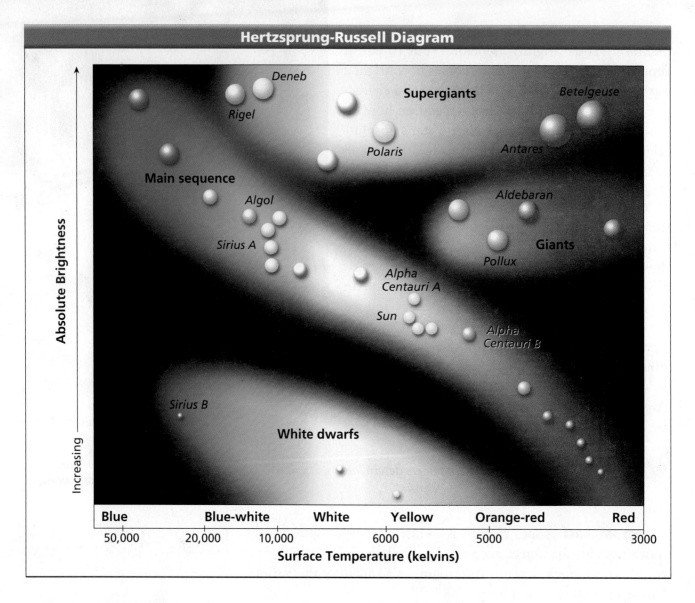

Figure 13 A star's placement on an H-R diagram indicates its absolute brightness and surface temperature (or color).
Interpreting Diagrams
Compare the sun and Aldebaran. Which is hotter and which has a greater absolute brightness?

The Hertzsprung-Russell Diagram

In the early 1900s, two astronomers working independently, Ejnar Hertzsprung and Henry Norris Russell, made a similar observation. Both discovered that stars can be classified by locating them on a graph showing two easily determined characteristics. Such a graph is called a Hertzsprung-Russell diagram, or H-R diagram. An **H-R diagram** is a graph of the surface temperature, or color, and absolute brightness of a sample of stars. These diagrams are one of modern astronomy's most important tools. **H-R diagrams are used to estimate the sizes of stars and their distances, and to infer how stars change over time.**

Look closely at the H-R diagram in Figure 13. The horizontal axis shows the surface temperatures of stars. Recall that a star's color is directly related to its surface temperature. The hottest blue stars are on the left and the coolest red stars are on the right. Surface temperatures of stars range from less than 3000 K to more than 30,000 K.

The vertical axis of the H-R diagram shows absolute brightness, with the brightest stars at the top and the faintest at the bottom. The absolute brightnesses of stars vary even more than temperature, ranging from about one ten-thousandth to a million times that of the sun!

Main-Sequence Stars Notice that stars occur only in certain places on the H-R diagram. Most stars are found along a diagonal band running from the bright hot stars on the upper left to the dim cool stars on the lower right. Astronomers call this diagonal band on the H-R diagram the **main sequence.** About 90% of all stars are found on the main sequence. The sun lies near the middle of this band.

Giants and Dwarfs In general, two factors determine a star's absolute brightness: its size and its surface temperature. Since an H-R diagram shows a star's absolute brightness and surface temperature, you can use the diagram to estimate the star's size. If you compare two stars at the same temperature, the brighter one must be larger. Similarly, hotter stars are brighter than cooler stars of the same size.

The very bright stars at the upper right of the H-R diagram are called **supergiants.** Supergiants are much brighter than main-sequence stars of the same temperature. To be so bright, these supergiants must be very large compared with main-sequence stars. In fact, supergiants range in size from 100 to 1000 times the diameter of the sun. Just below the supergiants on the H-R diagram are the **giants**—large, bright stars that are smaller and fainter than supergiants.

Below the main sequence in the lower part of the H-R diagram are white dwarfs. A **white dwarf** is the small, dense remains of a low- or medium-mass star. You can see from the diagram that white dwarfs are hot but dimmer than main-sequence stars of the same temperature.

Figure 14 The diameter of a red giant is typically 10–100 times that of the sun and more than 1000 times that of a white dwarf.

Sun

Red giant

White dwarf

Section 26.2 Assessment

Reviewing Concepts

1. What method do astronomers use to measure the distances of nearby stars?

2. What are some common properties used to classify stars?

3. Describe the chemical composition of a star like the sun.

4. What is an H-R diagram? How is one useful to an astronomer?

Critical Thinking

5. **Applying Concepts** What causes the dark lines in a star's spectrum?

6. **Comparing and Contrasting** Describe the locations of giants, supergiants, and white dwarfs on an H-R diagram.

Math Practice

7. The bright star Spica is located about 2.49×10^{15} kilometers from Earth. How many light-years is this?

8. Betelgeuse is about 427 light-years from Earth. How many kilometers is this?

26.3 Life Cycles of Stars

Reading Focus

Key Concepts

- How do stars form?
- What determines how long a star remains on the main sequence?
- What happens to a star when it runs out of fuel?

Vocabulary

- nebula
- protostar
- planetary nebula
- supernova
- neutron star
- pulsar
- black hole

Reading Strategy

Sequencing Copy the flowchart below. As you read, extend and complete it to show how a low-mass star evolves. Make a similar flowchart for high-mass stars.

Evolution of a Low-Mass Star

Main sequence → a. ? → b. ?

Do stars change over time? If so, how do they change? To help answer these questions, think about predicting how a baby will look when it grows up. Pictures of the baby's relatives, like Figure 15, would probably help. Astronomers use a similar approach to understand how stars evolve. When astronomers look at an image of a single star, they see a snapshot from a life story that often lasts for billions of years. To learn how a star might change over time, astronomers observe many stars of different ages. These observations provide clues about how stars form, how long they last, and what happens when their fuel runs out.

Most stars fall on the main sequence of the H-R diagram. Among nearby stars, about 10 percent are white dwarfs and fewer than 1 percent are giants or supergiants. Astronomers have inferred that these different types of stars represent different stages of a star's evolution. For most of their lives, stars are very stable. But a star must change when nuclear fusion has used up the supply of hydrogen in its core.

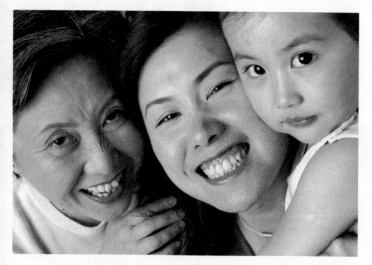

Figure 15 You can often predict how a baby will look as an adult by looking at other family members. In a similar way, astronomers observe stars of different ages to infer how stars evolve.

How Stars Form

The space around stars contains gas and dust. In some regions this matter is spread thinly; in others it is packed densely. A **nebula** is a large cloud of gas and dust spread out over a large volume of space. Some nebulas are glowing clouds lit from within by bright stars. Other nebulas are cold, dark clouds that block the light from more-distant stars beyond the nebulas.

Stars form in the densest regions of nebulae, as shown in Figure 16. Stars are created by gravity. Gravity pulls a nebula's dust and gas into a denser cloud. As the nebula contracts, it heats up. A contracting cloud of gas and dust with enough mass to form a star is called a **protostar.** As a protostar contracts, its internal pressure and temperature continue to rise. **A star is formed when a contracting cloud of gas and dust becomes so dense and hot that nuclear fusion begins.** Pressure from fusion supports the star against the tremendous inward pull of gravity. This new energy source stabilizes the young star, and it joins the main sequence.

Adult Stars

Stars spend about 90 percent of their lives on the main sequence. In all main-sequence stars, nuclear fusion converts hydrogen into helium at a stable rate. There is an equilibrium between the outward thermal pressure from fusion and gravity's inward pull. **A star's mass determines the star's place on the main sequence and how long it will stay there.**

The amount of gas and dust available when a star forms determines the mass of each young star. The most massive stars have large cores and therefore produce the most energy. In a large, young star with 30 times the sun's mass, gravity exerts a huge inward force, increasing the star's internal temperature and pressure. High-mass stars become the bluest and brightest main-sequence stars. Typically, these blue stars are about 300,000 times brighter than the sun. But, like gas-guzzling hot rods, large stars pay a price. Because blue stars burn so brightly, they use up their fuel relatively quickly and last only a few million years.

Stars similar to the sun occupy the middle of the main sequence. A yellow star like the sun has a surface temperature of about 6000 K and will remain stable on the main sequence for about 10 billion years.

Small nebulas produce small, cool stars that are long-lived. A star can have a mass as low as a tenth of the sun's mass. The gravitational force in such low-mass stars is just strong enough to create a small core where nuclear fusion takes place. This lower energy production results in red stars, which are the coolest and least bright of all visible stars. A red main-sequence star, with a surface temperature of about 3500 K, may stay on the main sequence for more than 100 billion years.

 Why do red main-sequence stars last longer than blue main-sequence stars?

Figure 16 A group of bright young stars can be seen in the hollowed-out center of the Rosette Nebula.

Go Online
SCIENCE NEWS

For: Articles on stars, galaxies, and the universe
Visit: PHSchool.com
Web Code: cce-3263

The Death of a Star

Stars don't last forever. When a star's core begins to run out of hydrogen, gravity gains the upper hand over pressure and the core starts to shrink. Soon, the core temperature rises enough to cause the hydrogen in a shell outside the core to begin fusion. The energy flowing outward increases, causing the outer regions of the star to expand. The expanding atmosphere moves farther from the hot core and cools to red. The star becomes a red giant. Eventually, the collapsing core will grow hot enough for helium fusion to occur, producing carbon, oxygen, and heavier elements. In helium fusion, the star stabilizes and its outer layers shrink and warm up. In this period, the star remains in the upper right part of the H-R Diagram. 🔑 **The dwindling supply of fuel in a star's core ultimately leads to the star's death as a white dwarf, neutron star, or black hole.** As Figure 17 shows, the final stages of a star's life depend on its mass.

Low- and Medium-Mass Stars Low-mass and medium-mass stars, which can be as much as eight times as massive as the sun, eventually turn into white dwarfs. Such stars remain in the giant stage until their hydrogen and helium supplies dwindle and there are no other elements to fuse. Then the energy coming from the star's interior decreases. With less outward pressure to support the star against gravity's inward pull, the star collapses. The dying star is surrounded by a glowing cloud of gas. Such a cloud is called a **planetary nebula,** because the first ones found looked like planets when viewed through a small telescope. Figure 18A shows a planetary nebula.

Figure 17 The mass of a star determines the path of its evolution.
Interpreting Diagrams *What are two possible end-stages of a high-mass star?*

EVOLUTION OF STARS

Later stages of
a low-mass star

Nebula

Protostar

Main
sequence star

Red giant

Red supergiant

Early stages of a star

Later stages of
a high-mass star

As the dying star blows off much of its mass, only its hot core remains. This dense core is a white dwarf. A white dwarf is about the same size as Earth but has about the same mass as the sun. White dwarfs don't undergo fusion, but glow faintly from leftover thermal energy. It takes about 20 billion years for a white dwarf to cool down completely. The universe hasn't been here long enough for this to happen yet.

High-Mass Stars The life cycle of high-mass stars (those with a mass of more than eight times that of the sun) is very different from the life cycle of lower-mass stars. As high-mass stars evolve from hydrogen fusion to the fusion of other elements, they grow into brilliant supergiants. This creates new elements, the heaviest being iron. A high-mass star dies quickly because it consumes fuel very rapidly.

As fusion slows in a high-mass star, pressure decreases. Gravity eventually overcomes the lower pressure, leading to a dramatic collapse of the star's outer layers. This collapse produces a **supernova,** an explosion so violent that the dying star becomes more brilliant than an entire galaxy. Supernovas produce enough energy to create elements heavier than iron. These elements, and lighter ones such as carbon and oxygen, are ejected into space by the explosion. The heavier elements in our solar system, including the atoms in your body, came from a supernova that occurred in our galaxy billions of years ago.

 Reading Checkpoint *What is a supernova?*

Figure 18 Nebulas are associated with the birth and death of stars. **A** Planetary nebulas, such as the Hourglass Nebula, are clouds of gas that surround a collapsing red giant. **B** The Crab Nebula is the remnant of a supernova explosion that was observed on Earth in A.D. 1054. The supernova was so bright that people could see it in the daytime.

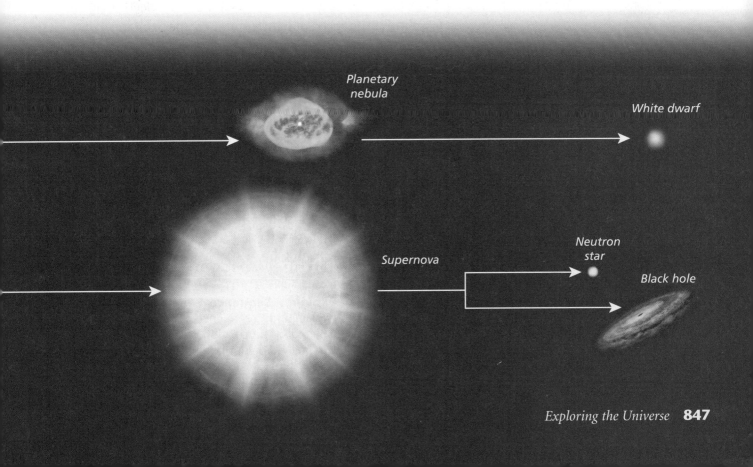

Planetary nebula

White dwarf

Supernova

Neutron star

Black hole

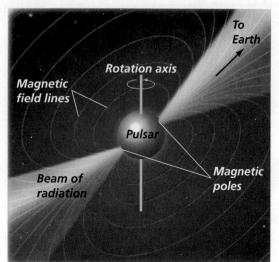

Figure 19 Pulsars emit steady beams of radiation that appear to pulse when the spinning beam sweeps across Earth.

As a supernova spews material into space, its core continues to collapse. If the remaining core has a mass less than about three times the sun's mass, it will become a neutron star. A **neutron star** is the dense remnant of a high-mass star that has exploded as a supernova. In a neutron star, electrons and protons are crushed together by the star's enormous gravity to form neutrons. Neutron stars are much smaller and denser than white dwarfs. A spoonful of a neutron star would weigh nearly a billion tons on Earth! A neutron star with the mass of the sun would be only about 25 kilometers across, the size of a large city.

Like a spinning ice skater pulling in his arms, a neutron star spins more and more rapidly as it contracts. Some neutron stars spin hundreds of turns per second! As shown in Figure 19, neutron stars emit steady beams of radiation in narrow cones. If the neutron star is spinning, these emissions appear to pulse on and off at regular intervals, like the spinning beacon on a lighthouse. Each time one of these beams of radiation sweeps across Earth, astronomers can detect a pulse of radio waves. A spinning neutron star that appears to gives off strong pulses of radio waves is called a **pulsar.**

As impressive as pulsars are, very massive stars can have even more dramatic ends. If a star's core after a supernova explosion is more than about three times the sun's mass, its gravitational pull is very strong. Gravity causes the core to collapse beyond the neutron-star stage. As the collapse continues, the pull of gravity increases and the speed required to escape the star's core reaches the speed of light. Beyond this point, nothing can escape and a black hole is formed. A **black hole** is an object whose surface gravity is so great that even electromagnetic waves, traveling at the speed of light, cannot escape from it.

Section 26.3 Assessment

Reviewing Concepts

1. How does a star form?
2. What factor determines the length of a star's life?
3. Why do some stars become white dwarfs while others become neutron stars or black holes?

Critical Thinking

4. **Predicting** A main-sequence star has a mass 5 times that of the sun. What will be its final stages?

5. **Comparing and Contrasting** How are a protostar and a star different?

6. **Comparing and Contrasting** Why do low-mass stars remain on the main sequence longer than high-mass stars?

Writing in Science

Explain a Sequence Write a paragraph explaining the sequence of events that resulted in the creation of the elements that make up your body.

Black Hole

A black hole is a region of space containing so much matter that it collapses to an infinitely dense point. The force of gravity in a black hole is so great that anything falling into it, including electromagnetic waves, becomes trapped. **Interpreting Diagrams** *What happens to an object trapped by a black hole?*

Detecting a black hole
As matter swirls into a black hole, it can emit X-rays, gamma rays, and other radiation. Astronomers analyze this radiation to discover more about black holes.

Warped space *According to Einstein's theory of general relativity, gravity is a distortion of space and time. The warping of space near a black hole is shown here by the gray plane and white lines.*

A **B** **C** **D** **E**

Objects Nearing a Black Hole

Objects or electromagnetic waves approaching a black hole can suffer various fates.

A is only slightly deflected from its path.
B is strongly deflected.
C almost orbits the hole but escapes.
D goes into orbit around the hole.
E falls into the hole. An object following this path is crushed by the force of gravity.

Downward spiral *Objects or electromagnetic waves spiral downward, following the distortion of space.*

Event horizon *This is the boundary of the black hole and is the point of no return for anything that enters, even electromagnetic waves moving at the speed of light.*

Inside a black hole *In theory, beyond the event horizon light spirals down toward the center of the black hole, a point of infinite density.*

26.4 Groups of Stars

Reading Focus

Key Concepts

- How are stars distributed in space?
- What are the characteristics of each type of star cluster?
- What are the types of galaxies?

Vocabulary

- constellation
- star system
- binary star
- globular cluster
- galaxy
- spiral galaxies
- barred-spiral galaxies
- elliptical galaxies
- irregular galaxies
- quasars

Reading Strategy

Comparing and Contrasting Copy the table below. After you read, compare types of star clusters by completing the table.

Cluster Type	Appearance	Age and Type of Stars
Open cluster	a. ___?___	b. ___?___
c. ___?___	d. ___?___	Bright, young stars
e. ___?___	Spherical, densely packed	f. ___?___

Figure 20 When Giovanni Riccioli used a telescope like this one to observe a star in the handle of the Big Dipper, he discovered two stars that orbit each other.

Ancient observers saw a night sky that was full of stars. They imagined that groups of stars formed pictures of people or animals in the sky. A group of stars that appears to form a pattern as seen from Earth is called a **constellation.** The Big Dipper, for example, is part of the constellation Ursa Major. The stars in a constellation are generally not close to one another. They just happen to lie in the same general direction of the sky as seen from Earth. Constellations are important to astronomy because they help to form a map of the sky. Modern astronomers divide the sky into 88 constellations. You can find a set of star maps in Appendix H at the end of this book.

Star Systems

When you wake up each morning and look out your window, a single star, the sun, greets you with its bright light. However, if you were somewhere else in the universe, the view might be quite different. Imagine what the sky would look like if your solar system had two, three, or even four stars. The stars might all be visible in the sky at the same time, or some might be visible while others were below the horizon. It would be hard to say exactly what a "day" would be on such a planet. You might think that this sounds like a scene from a science fiction movie. But, in fact, most stars occur in groups of two or more.

In 1650, the Italian astronomer Giovanni Baptista Riccioli used a telescope like the one shown in Figure 20 to observe Mizar and Alcor, a double star in the Big Dipper. He saw that Mizar itself was two stars that were very close together. This was the first of thousands of star systems to be discovered. A **star system** is a group of two or more stars that are held together by gravity. Astronomers have determined that more **than half of all stars are members of star systems.** A star system with two stars is called a **binary star.** The two stars orbit each other, held together by gravity.

Sometimes the smaller star in a binary star is too dim to be seen easily from Earth, but can still be detected from the motion of the other star. The bright star Sirius A, for example, wobbles back and forth. Astronomers have discovered that this wobble is caused by the gravitational pull of a faint companion star, Sirius B. In some binary star systems, one star passes in front of the other, blocking some of the light from reaching Earth. Such a star system is called an eclipsing binary. The brightness of an eclipsing binary varies over time in a regular pattern.

Star Clusters

In the winter sky, you can see a faint group of stars called the Pleiades, shown in Figure 21A. Studying star clusters is useful because all the stars formed together in the same nebula. Therefore, they are about the same age and the same distance from Earth. Astronomers plot the stars of a cluster on an H-R diagram to estimate the cluster's age.

There are three basic kinds of star clusters: open **clusters, associations, and globular clusters.** An open cluster, like the Pleiades, has a disorganized or loose appearance and contains no more than a few thousand stars that are well spread out. Open clusters often contain bright supergiants and gas and dust clouds. Associations are temporary groupings of bright, young stars. In time, gravity from nearby stars breaks these groups apart. Associations are typically larger than open clusters.

In contrast, a **globular cluster** is a large group of older stars. Globular clusters usually lack sufficient amounts of gas and dust to form new stars. They are spherical and have a dense concentration of stars in the center, as shown in Figure 21B. Globular clusters can contain more than a million stars. Globular clusters usually do not have short-lived blue stars because these stars have already died out. If Earth revolved around a star in the middle of a globular cluster, the night sky would blaze with the light from thousands of bright stars. Astronomers estimate that the oldest globular clusters are about 12 billion years old. Thus, the universe must be at least that old.

Figure 21 Open clusters contain young blue stars, which are usually absent in globular clusters. **A** The Pleiades are an open star cluster that is visible to the unaided eye. **B** 47 Tucanae is a spectacular globular cluster that is visible in southern skies. **Comparing and Contrasting** *Use these photos to describe the differences between open clusters and globular clusters.*

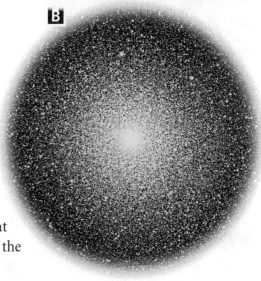

Figure 22 Galaxies have a variety of shapes. **A** A spiral galaxy in the constellation Coma Berenices **B** A barred-spiral galaxy in the Fornax cluster **C** Elliptical galaxy M87 **D** An irregular galaxy with many areas of star formation

Galaxies

A **galaxy** is a huge group of individual stars, star systems, star clusters, dust, and gas bound together by gravity. Our own galaxy is called the Milky Way. In the 1800s and early 1900s, many astronomers thought that the universe did not extend beyond the Milky Way. However, observations of odd spiral-shaped objects sparked a spirited scientific debate. The debate focused on whether these so-called "spiral nebulae" were within or outside the Milky Way. The question was settled only in the 1920s, after a large new telescope was built on Mt. Wilson in California. Astronomers could see individual stars, proving that spiral nebulae were actually distant galaxies consisting of billions of individual stars.

Astronomers now know that there are billions of galaxies in the universe. The largest galaxies consist of more than a trillion stars. Galaxies vary widely in size and shape. ⬦ **Astronomers classify galaxies into four main types: spiral, barred-spiral, elliptical, and irregular.**

Spiral and Barred-Spiral Galaxies Galaxies like the Milky Way are called spiral galaxies. **Spiral galaxies** have a bulge of stars at the center, with arms extending outward like a pinwheel. These spiral arms contain gas, dust, and many bright young stars. Figure 22A shows the spiral galaxy M100. It belongs to the Virgo Cluster of galaxies, which is the nearest major cluster to our own Local Group of galaxies.

Some spiral galaxies, like the one in Figure 22B, have a bar through the center with the arms extending outward from the bar on either side. These are called **barred-spiral galaxies.**

Elliptical Galaxies **Elliptical galaxies** are spherical or oval, with no trace of spiral arms. M87, shown in Figure 22C, is one of the largest and brightest of all galaxies. Elliptical galaxies come in a wide range of sizes. They have very little gas or dust between stars. For this reason, new stars are not forming in older elliptical galaxies. They contain only old stars.

Irregular Galaxies A small fraction of all galaxies are known as irregular galaxies. As shown in Figure 22D, **irregular galaxies** have a disorganized appearance. They have many young stars and large amounts of gas and dust. Irregular galaxies come in many shapes, but are typically smaller than other types of galaxies. They are often located near larger galaxies, whose strong gravity may be causing their shape to become irregular. One of the closest galaxies to our own, the Large Magellanic Cloud, is an irregular galaxy.

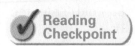 Reading Checkpoint *What are some characteristics of irregular galaxies?*

The Milky Way Galaxy On a clear, dark night far from city lights, you can see a faint white band stretching across the night sky. This is the Milky Way. The Milky Way galaxy has an estimated 200 to 400 billion stars and a diameter of more than 100,000 light years. Every individual star that you can see with the unaided eye is in our galaxy. As Figure 23 shows, the solar system lies in the Milky Way's disk within a spiral arm, about two thirds of the way from the center. From Earth we are looking at the rest of the Milky Way edgewise, so it appears as a band in our night sky, rather than a spiral.

The Milky Way's flattened disk shape is caused by its rotation. The sun takes about 220 million years to complete one orbit around the galaxy's center. At the center of the galaxy is a bulge of stars surrounded by an immense halo of globular clusters. Recent evidence suggests that there is a massive black hole at our galaxy's center. Extending outward and winding through the galaxy's disk are spiral arms of gas, dust, and young stars. Stars are forming in these spiral arms.

Quasars In the 1950s astronomers were mystified by the discovery of distant objects they called quasars. By studying their spectra, astronomers have determined that **quasars** (KWAY zahrz) are the enormously bright centers of distant, young galaxies. Quasars produce more light than hundreds of galaxies the size of the Milky Way. What makes a quasar so bright? The most likely explanation involves matter spiraling into a super-massive black hole with the mass of a billion suns. The gravitational potential energy of this matter is transformed into electromagnetic radiation as it falls into the black hole.

Side View of Our Galaxy

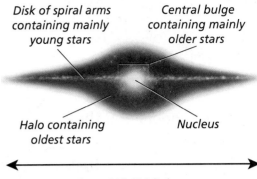

Disk of spiral arms containing mainly young stars

Central bulge containing mainly older stars

Halo containing oldest stars

Nucleus

About 100,000 light-years

Overhead View of Our Galaxy

Location of solar system

Central bulge

Nucleus

Figure 23 In a side view, the Milky Way appears as a flat disk with a central bulge. An overhead view of the Milky Way shows its spiral shape.

Section 26.4 Assessment

Reviewing Concepts

1. �"How are the majority of stars grouped?
2. 🔜 How are open clusters and associations different?
3. 🔜 What are the four major types of galaxies?
4. Describe the Milky Way and its characteristics.
5. What is a quasar?

Critical Thinking

6. **Inferring** Why were telescopes needed to discover star systems?

7. **Classifying** Which type of star cluster has the greatest percentage of old stars?
8. **Inferring** How would you use an H-R diagram to distinguish an elliptical galaxy from a spiral or irregular galaxy?

Connecting Concepts

Gravity Use what you learned about the gravitational attraction that acts between two masses in Section 12.4 to explain why the star Sirius A wobbles.

Scale of the Universe

To understand the immensity of space, astronomers organize the universe into different structures at different scales. Earth, for example, is part of the solar system, which forms part of the Milky Way Galaxy, which in turn is part of the Local Group of galaxies.

SPIRAL GALAXIES

1.6 light-years

Earth

Solar system

100,000 light-years

Milky Way

5 million light-years

120 million light-years

Oort Cloud   Sun

Solar System
Earth and all the planets lie close to the sun. The outer boundary of the solar system is marked by the spherical Oort cloud of comets.

Milky Way Galaxy
Our galaxy contains 200–400 billion stars, most of which are dimmer than the sun. On this scale, the solar system is insignificant.

Local Group
The Local Group contains more than 30 galaxies, including one member larger than the Milky Way, the Andromeda Galaxy. Most galaxies are much smaller than this.

Local Group

Virgo Cluster

Local Supercluster
The Local Supercluster contains dozens of small galaxy clusters, including the Local Group. The Local Supercluster is centered on the giant Virgo Cluster, a collection of more than 2000 galaxies about 65 million light-years from the Milky Way.

Distance measurement

Distances to other galaxies can be measured by observing stars in them called Cepheid variables. Cepheids are stars whose brightness varies over a regular cycle. Because the period of a Cepheid's cycle and its average absolute brightness are related, astronomers can work out how bright a Cepheid really is from its period. Comparing this to its apparent brightness, they can estimate its distance.

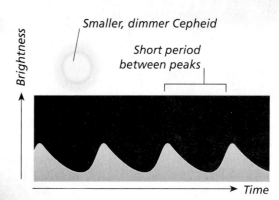

Brightness

Smaller, dimmer Cepheid

Short period between peaks

Time

Brightness

Bigger, brighter Cepheid

Long period between brightness peaks

Time

Nearby universe

Superclusters of galaxies are strung together in vast filaments, which are the largest known structures in the universe. These can stretch across hundreds of millions of light-years. They are separated by huge voids containing very few galaxies. These empty regions are often 100 to 200 million light-years across.

Local Supercluster

Filament of galaxy superclusters

Void

1 billion light-years

Going Further

- Research the Local Group in the library or on the Internet. Make an accurate drawing showing the relative sizes and distances among these three Local Group galaxies: Milky Way, Andromeda Galaxy, and M33.

26.5 The Expanding Universe

Reading Focus

Key Concepts

- How do astronomers know that the universe is expanding?

- What is the big bang theory, and what evidence supports it?

- How can dark matter be detected?

Vocabulary

- ◆ red shift
- ◆ Hubble's Law
- ◆ big bang theory
- ◆ dark matter

Reading Strategy

Previewing Before reading, examine Figure 26 and write at least two questions to help you understand the information in it. As you read, write answers to your questions.

Questions on the Evolution of the Universe
a. _____ ?
b. _____ ?

Have you ever wanted to use a time machine to travel back in time? Telescopes are like time machines because they show what happened in other parts of the universe in the distant past. When you observe a star that is ten light-years away, you are seeing the star as it was ten years ago. This is because light took ten years to travel from the star to Earth. Images of galaxies that are billions of light-years away show how these galaxies looked billions of years ago.

Hubble's Law

Recall from physics that as a sound or light source moves toward or away from an observer, its frequency and wavelength appear to change. This apparent change in frequency and wavelength is known as the Doppler effect. The Doppler effect can be used to determine how fast stars or galaxies are approaching or moving away from Earth. When a star or galaxy is approaching Earth, the lines in its spectrum are shifted toward the shorter (bluer) wavelengths, as shown in Figure 24. When the star or galaxy is moving away, the lines in its spectrum shift toward the longer (redder) wavelengths. The larger the observed shift, the greater is the speed of this movement.

In the mid-1920s, the American astronomer Edwin Hubble studied many galaxies at different distances from Earth. In 1929, Hubble announced his discovery: the light from most galaxies undergoes a **red shift**—that is, their light is shifted toward the red wavelengths. This red shift showed that, remarkably, nearly all galaxies are getting farther away from Earth.

Figure 24 Absorption lines of a galaxy shift toward the blue end of the spectrum when it moves toward Earth. The lines shift to the red end of the spectrum when a galaxy moves away from Earth. **Inferring** *How would the spectrum of a galaxy that is slowly moving away from Earth compare to one that is moving away much more quickly?*

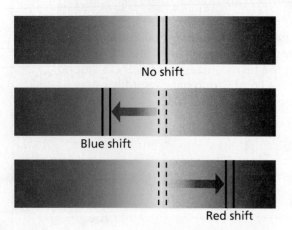

No shift

Blue shift

Red shift

Hubble also found that more-distant galaxies have greater red shifts. This larger shift means that distant galaxies are moving away from Earth faster than closer galaxies. This relationship, called **Hubble's Law,** says that the speed at which a galaxy is moving away is proportional to its distance from us. The most distant observed galaxies are moving away at more than 90 percent of the speed of light!

To visualize the movement of galaxies, imagine the dough for a loaf of raisin bread as it rises. The raisins represent individual galaxies or groups of galaxies, and the dough represents the universe. As shown in Figure 25, when the dough rises, the distance between raisins increases, but the raisins stay the same size. As the dough expands, the distance between raisins that are far apart increases more than the distance between nearby raisins. In the same way, the most distant galaxies are moving away from us more quickly.

🔑 **The observed red shift in the spectra of galaxies shows that the universe is expanding.** Like the dough between the raisins, the space between the galaxies is expanding in all directions, and the universe as a whole is becoming larger.

Figure 25 The raisins in this rising bread dough are all moving away from one another as the dough expands. In a similar way, galaxies move away from one another as the universe expands.

Reading Checkpoint *What is Hubble's Law?*

Hubble's Constant

Hubble's law expresses the relationship between the velocity that a galaxy is moving away from Earth and its distance from us. The ratio of these variables is a constant called Hubble's constant. Hubble's constant can be estimated by finding the slope of a graph of velocity versus distance for a set of galaxies. Data for six galaxies are provided in the table at the right.

Hubble's constant is one of the most important and debated numbers in astronomy. It expresses how fast the universe is expanding, and can be used to estimate the age of the universe.

Velocity and Distance of Galaxies		
Galaxy	Velocity (km/s)	Distance ($\times 10^6$ light-years)
1	4,200	200
2	7,800	390
3	10,500	520
4	17,000	850
5	21,000	1110
6	24,000	1170

1. **Using Tables** Which galaxy is moving away the fastest? Which galaxy is closest to Earth?

2. **Graphing** Graph the data shown in the table. Place velocity on the vertical axis and distance on the horizontal axis. What is the general shape of the graph?

3. **Calculating** Estimate Hubble's constant by measuring the slope of your graph. (*Hint:* Draw a line through the data points. Recall that Slope = Rise ÷ Run.)

4. **Inferring** About how fast is a galaxy receding if its distance is 2000×10^6 light-years? (*Hint:* Use your estimate of Hubble's constant from Question 3.)

5. **Predicting** Use your value for Hubble's constant to estimate the distance of a galaxy that has a velocity of 30,000 km/s.

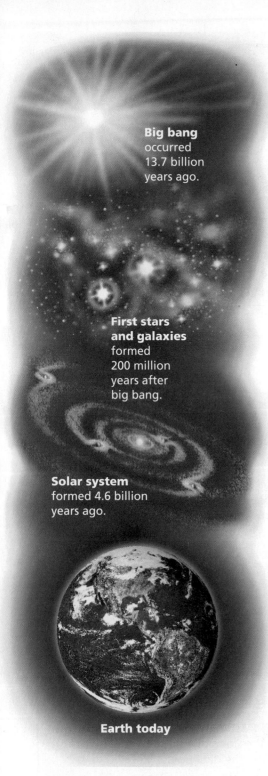

Big bang occurred 13.7 billion years ago.

First stars and galaxies formed 200 million years after big bang.

Solar system formed 4.6 billion years ago.

Earth today

Figure 26 The universe began with the big bang 13.7 billion years ago. The first stars and galaxies formed 200 million years later. The solar system, and Earth, formed about 9 billion years after the big bang.

The Big Bang Theory

If the universe is expanding, where were the galaxies in the distant past? Hubble observed that in every direction you look, galaxies at a given distance are moving away at the same rate. This is what you would expect if the universe were expanding uniformly.

 Astronomers theorize that the universe came into being at a single moment, in an event called the big bang. According to this theory, all the matter and energy of the universe were at one time concentrated in an incredibly hot region smaller than the period at the end of this sentence. The **big bang theory** states that the universe began in an instant, billions of years ago, in an enormous explosion.

After the Big Bang

The universe expanded quickly and cooled down after the big bang. After a few hundred thousand years of expansion, the universe was still much smaller and hotter than it is now, but cool enough for atoms to form. Gravity pulled atoms together into gas clouds that eventually evolved into stars in young galaxies. As shown in Figure 26, the sun and solar system formed about 4.6 billion years ago, when the universe was about two thirds of its present size.

Evidence for the Theory

In 1965, two American physicists, Arno Penzias and Robert Wilson, noticed a signal on their radio telescope that they couldn't explain. They eventually realized that they were detecting a faint distant glow in every direction. Today this glow is called the cosmic microwave background radiation. This glow is energy produced during the big bang, still traveling throughout the universe. **The existence of cosmic microwave background radiation and the red shift in the spectra of distant galaxies strongly support the big bang theory.**

The big bang theory describes how the expansion and cooling of the universe over time could have led to the present universe of stars and galaxies. It offers the best current scientific explanation of the expansion of the observable universe. Variations of the theory continue to be proposed and are being tested with new observations.

Age of the Universe

Since astronomers know how fast the universe is expanding now, they can infer how long it has been expanding. If you traveled backward in time, all of the matter in the universe would be at its starting point 13 to 14 billion years ago. Recent measurements of the microwave background radiation have led to a more precise age. Astronomers now estimate that the universe is 13.7 billion years old.

Continued Expansion

What will happen to the universe in the distant future? Will the galaxies rush apart forever, or is there enough gravitational attraction to pull the galaxies back together? The answer depends on the mass of the entire universe. To have a gravitational force strong enough to reverse the expansion, there must be sufficient mass in the universe. If there is less than this amount of mass, the universe will continue to expand.

How can the amount of matter in the universe be determined? Some matter, like stars, glows. The mass of matter can be seen. However, much of the matter in the universe can't be seen. **Dark matter** is matter that does not give off radiation. **Dark matter cannot be seen directly, but its presence can be detected by observing its gravitational effects on visible matter.** American astronomer Vera Rubin found that galaxies like ours may contain as much as ten times more dark matter than visible matter. Without this dark matter, there would not be enough gravitational force to keep groups of galaxies from flying apart.

There are many unanswered questions about dark matter. Astronomers don't know what it is made of or how it is distributed in the universe. Some astronomers hypothesize that dark matter consists of WIMPs, which stands for weakly interacting massive particles. Currently, experiments are underway to detect WIMPs.

In the past few years, astronomers have discovered that the rate of expansion of the universe may be increasing. Galaxies appear to be moving apart faster now than expected. The reason for this is uncertain. A mysterious force called dark energy is theorized to be causing the rate of expansion to increase. If the expansion is accelerating, it's likely that the universe will expand forever.

Quick Lab

Modeling Expansion of the Universe

Procedure

1. Cut open a rubber band. Lay it flat next to a meter stick with one end, which represents Earth, at 0 cm.

2. Mark 1-cm intervals along the whole length of the rubber band. These marks represent galaxies.

3. Hold one end of the rubber band at 0 cm. Stretch it to twice its original length to model how much the universe expands in a certain time period.

4. Record the distance of each galaxy from Earth, along with its original distance.

Analyze and Conclude

1. **Inferring** Based on how far each galaxy moved in the same time, which galaxy moved the fastest?

2. **Drawing Conclusions** How is a galaxy's speed related to its distance?

Section 26.5 Assessment

Reviewing Concepts

1. What evidence shows that the universe is expanding?

2. According to the big bang theory, how did the universe begin?

3. What evidence supports the big bang theory?

4. What is dark matter, and how have astronomers inferred its existence?

Critical Thinking

5. **Using Analogies** How is a telescope like a time machine?

6. **Comparing and Contrasting** Compare the speeds at which most nearby galaxies and distant galaxies are moving away from Earth.

Connecting Concepts

Scientific Theories Do you think it is correct to call the big bang theory a theory rather than a hypothesis? Explain why. (*Hint:* Review the meaning of these terms in Chapter 1.)

Investigating Parallax

Astronomers use parallax to measure the distances to nearby stars. In this lab, you will investigate the effect of distance on parallax. You will observe how an object appears to move against a distant background as you look at it first through one eye, and then through the other.

Problem
How is parallax related to the distance to a star?

Materials
- unlined paper
- tape
- marker
- pencil
- meter stick
- index card
- graph paper

Data Table			
Distance to Star (m)	Right Eye (cm)	Left Eye (cm)	Parallax (cm) (Difference)
1.0	0		

Skills
Measuring, Using Models

Procedure

1. Tape three sheets of unlined paper to the wall horizontally, at eye level. Use a marker to draw 11 vertical marks 5 centimeters apart on the paper, as shown in the photo on the following page. The marks represent a distant background against which you will view a closer star. Label the marks in multiples of five from left to right, starting with 0 and ending with 50.

2. Construct a copy of the data table shown above.

3. Facing the sheets of paper, stand directly in front of the 25-cm mark. Then, use a meterstick to measure a perpendicular distance of 7 m from the mark. Move to that spot and face toward the 25-cm mark. You must remain at this position until you have finished collecting all data.

4. Have a partner hold a pencil vertically at your eye level as shown in the photo. The pencil should be 1 m in front of you. Your partner should use a meter stick to measure this distance. The pencil represents a nearby star.

5. Hold an index card over your left eye and look at the pencil with your right eye. Your right eye represents Earth's position at one point in its orbit. Move your head so the pencil lines up with the mark labeled 0.

6. Now, without moving your head, hold the index card over your right eye and look at the pencil with your left eye. Your left eye represents Earth's position at the opposite end of its orbit six months later. Note the number of the mark that lines up with the pencil. If the pencil is between two marks, estimate its position to the nearest whole number. Your partner should record this number in the appropriate place in your data table.

7. To determine the parallax, subtract the right eye measurement (zero, in this case) from the left-eye measurement. Record the parallax in the appropriate place in your data table.

8. **Predicting** How do you and your partner think the parallax will change as your partner moves the pencil away from you? Your partner should record your prediction.

9. Have your partner use a meter stick to move the pencil 0.5 m toward the marks. Without moving your head, cover your left eye and look at the pencil with your right eye. Your partner should record the number of the mark the pencil lines up with.

10. Without moving your head, cover your right eye and look at the pencil with your left eye. Your partner should record the number of the mark the pencil lines up with.

11. To determine the parallax, subtract the right-eye measurement from the left-eye measurement. Record the parallax in the appropriate place in your data table.

12. Repeat Steps 9 through 11 until the parallax is less than 1 cm.

13. Construct a graph of the distance to the star (pencil) against the parallax you calculated. Plot the parallax on the horizontal axis and the distance on the vertical axis.

Analyze and Conclude

1. **Using Graphs** What does your graph show is the relationship between the distance to the pencil and the pencil's parallax?

2. **Analyzing Data** Was your prediction in Step 8 correct? Explain your answer.

3. **Drawing Conclusions** Assume that a parallax of less than 1 cm is too small to be measured. What is the maximum distance at which the pencil would still have a parallax you can measure?

4. **Applying Concepts** Parallax can only be used to measure the distances to nearby stars. Why can't this method be used to find the distances to far-away stars?

5. **Inferring** Astronomers usually make two measurements of the position of a star six months apart, when Earth is at opposite sides of its orbit. How is this useful in determining the star's parallax?

Go Further Use the library or the Internet to research how distances to stars are actually measured using parallax. What kinds of telescopes and other technology are used? What is the greatest distance to a star that has been measured using parallax? How do astronomers determine the distances of stars that are too far away from Earth to have a measurable parallax?

26.1 The Sun

🔑 Key Concepts

- The sun's energy is produced in its core by fusion.
- The sun remains stable because the inward pull of gravity balances the outward pressure from fusion.
- The sun's interior consists of the core, radiation zone, and convection zone. Layers of the sun's atmosphere are the photosphere, chromosphere, and corona.
- Features of the sun's atmosphere include sunspots, prominences, and solar flares.

Vocabulary

core, *p. 830;* radiation zone, *p. 830;* convection zone, *p. 831;* photosphere, *p. 831;* chromosphere, *p. 831;* corona, *p. 831;* solar wind, *p. 831;* sunspots, *p. 832;* prominences, *p. 833;* solar flare, *p. 833*

26.2 Stars

🔑 Key Concepts

- Astronomers measure the parallax of nearby stars to determine their distance from Earth.
- Astronomers use several properties to classify stars.
- Most stars have a composition similar to the sun.
- H-R diagrams are used to estimate the sizes and distances of stars and to infer how stars change.

Vocabulary

star, *p. 834;* light-year, *p. 834;* parallax, *p. 835;* apparent brightness, *p. 836;* absolute brightness, *p. 837;* absorption lines, *p. 837;* H-R diagram, *p. 838;* main sequence, *p. 839;* supergiants, *p. 839;* giants, *p. 839;* white dwarf, *p. 839*

26.3 Life Cycles of Stars

🔑 Key Concepts

- A star is formed when nuclear fusion begins.
- A star's mass determines the star's place on the main sequence and how long it will stay there.
- A star ends up as a white dwarf, neutron star, or black hole once it exhausts its fuel supply.

Vocabulary

nebula, *p. 840;* protostar, *p. 841;* planetary nebula, *p. 842;* supernova, *p. 843;* neutron star, *p. 844;* pulsar, *p. 844;* black hole, *p. 844*

26.4 Groups of Stars

🔑 Key Concepts

- Astronomers have determined that more than half of all stars are members of star systems.
- There are three basic kinds of star clusters: open clusters, associations, and globular clusters.
- Astronomers classify galaxies into four main types: spiral, barred-spiral, elliptical, and irregular.

Vocabulary

constellation, *p. 846;* star system, *p. 847;* binary star, *p. 847;* globular cluster, *p. 847;* galaxy, *p. 848;* spiral galaxies, *p. 848;* barred-spiral galaxies, *p. 848;* elliptical galaxies, *p. 848;* irregular galaxies, *p. 848;* quasars, *p. 849*

26.5 The Expanding Universe

🔑 Key Concepts

- The observed red shift in the spectra of galaxies shows that the universe is expanding.
- Astronomers theorize that the universe came into being in an event called the big bang.
- Dark matter can only be detected by observing its gravitational effects on visible matter.

Vocabulary

red shift, *p. 852;* Hubble's Law, *p. 853;* big bang theory, *p. 854;* dark matter, *p. 855*

Thinking Visually

Comparing and Contrasting Use information from the chapter to complete the table below.

Property	Sun	Supergiant
Lifetime on main sequence	a. ____?____	A few million years
Current location on H-R diagram	b. ____?____	c. ____?____
Next stage in evolution	Red giant	d. ____?____
Final stage in evolution	e. ____?____	Neutron star or black hole

Reviewing Content

Choose the letter that best answers the question or completes the statement.

1. The sun produces most of its energy from
   - **a.** chemical reactions.
   - **b.** nuclear fission.
   - **c.** gravitational contraction.
   - **d** nuclear fusion.

2. Where does the sun's visible light come from?
   - **a.** the photosphere
   - **b.** the corona
   - **c.** the chromosphere
   - **d.** the radiation zone

3. Astronomers have learned about the elements in stars by analyzing their
   - **a.** parallax.
   - **b.** apparent brightness.
   - **c.** absorption lines.
   - **d.** red shift.

4. Most stars are
   - **a.** giants.
   - **b.** main-sequence stars.
   - **c.** supergiants.
   - **d.** white dwarfs.

5. Which of the following has the highest surface temperature?
   - **a.** red main sequence star
   - **b.** red supergiant
   - **c.** blue main sequence star
   - **d.** black dwarf

6. The lifetime of a star on the main sequence is determined by its
   - **a.** mass.
   - **b.** apparent brightness.
   - **c.** color.
   - **d.** surface temperature.

7. The sun will eventually use up its hydrogen fuel and become a
   - **a.** neutron star.
   - **b.** white dwarf.
   - **c.** black hole.
   - **d.** supernova.

8. Which of the following is likely to have the highest proportion of old stars?
   - **a.** open cluster
   - **b.** globular cluster
   - **c.** association
   - **d.** spiral galaxy

9. The Milky Way is an example of a (an)
   - **a.** nebula.
   - **b.** elliptical galaxy.
   - **c.** spiral galaxy.
   - **d.** irregular galaxy.

10. Hubble's Law relates the speed at which a galaxy is moving away to its
    - **a.** shape.
    - **b.** mass.
    - **c.** distance.
    - **d.** absolute brightness.

Understanding Concepts

11. Explain the two major ways that energy is transferred from the sun's core through its interior.

12. What are the inward and outward forces that act on the sun? Which force is stronger?

13. Which parts of the sun are visible during a total solar eclipse? Why can't they usually be seen at other times?

14. What is a light-year?

15. The image on the left below shows stars as seen in July. The image on the right below shows the same stars in January. Which star is closest to Earth? Explain.

 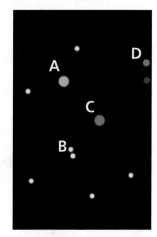

16. Suppose two stars have the same absolute brightness, but one star is twice as far from Earth as the other star. Which star has the greater apparent brightness?

17. When a star enters the red giant stage, what causes its outer layers to expand?

18. How does a black hole form?

19. How does Hubble's Law relate to the big bang theory?

20. How can astronomers measure the speed at which a galaxy is moving away from Earth?

21. Why are dark matter and dark energy so important in predicting the future of the universe?

Critical Thinking

22. Applying Concepts Two stars are the same color, but one looks much brighter in the sky. Give two possible explanations for the difference in apparent brightness.

23. Inferring Explain why a cool star with a high absolute brightness must be a giant or a supergiant.

24. Inferring Arrange the following in order of increasing density: neutron star, main-sequence star, red giant, and black hole.

25. Comparing and Contrasting Compare and contrast star clusters and galaxies.

26. Inferring Astronomers have observed that quasars have huge red shifts. What does this indicate about the distance and speed of quasars?

Math Skills

Use the diagram below to answer Questions 27–29.

27. Using Graphs Which star is brighter, Vega or Betelgeuse?

28. Using Graphs Which stars have higher surface temperatures than the sun?

29. Predicting Which star is likely to last the longest on the main sequence? Explain.

30. Calculating Vega, a star in the constellation Lyra, is located about 25 light-years from Earth. How many kilometers is this?

31. Calculating Another unit used by astronomers for measuring distances in space is the parsec (1 parsec is 3.26 light-years). The Andromeda Galaxy is about 890,000 parsecs from our own galaxy. How many light-years is this? How does this distance compare to the diameter of the Milky Way?

Concepts in Action

32. Applying Concepts How can we learn about the lives of stars, given that stars last much longer than human beings live?

33. Relating Cause and Effect How have supernovas made life on Earth possible?

34. Making Generalizations Give directions for traveling to Earth for an alien coming from the Virgo Cluster.

35. Inferring If astronomers cannot see dark matter, how do they know it exists?

36. Applying Concepts How old is the universe and how do we know?

37. Writing in Science Write a paragraph explaining how astronomers are able to measure the distance to other galaxies using observations of Cepheid variables.

Performance-Based Assessment

Using Models Construct a cutaway model of the sun. Use different colors of paper or clay to represent each layer of the sun's interior and atmosphere. Label each layer and include a brief description of each.

For: Self-grading assessment
Visit: PHSchool.com
Web Code: cca-3260

Standardized Test Prep

Test-Taking Tip

Sequencing a Series of Events

When a test question requires you to sequence a series of events, first try to predict the correct sequence before looking at the answer choices. Then compare your sequence to those listed. Be sure to pay attention to qualifiers in the question such as first, earliest, increasing, or decreasing, as these may help you eliminate choices.

Which sequence of events describes the big bang theory? Begin with the earliest event.

(A) Explosion; atoms form; stars form; all matter concentrated at a single point.
(B) All matter concentrated at a single point; explosion; atoms form; stars form.
(C) Explosion; stars form; all matter concentrated at a single point; atoms form.
(D) Atoms form; all matter concentrated at a single point; explosion; stars form.
(E) Stars form; atoms form; all matter concentrated at a single point; explosion.

(Answer: B)

Choose the letter that best answers the question or completes the statement.

1. The sun's source of energy is nuclear fusion in its
   (A) radiation zone.   (B) core.
   (C) corona.   (D) photosphere.
   (E) convection zone.

2. The most abundant element in most stars is
   (A) helium.   (B) nitrogen.
   (C) argon.   (D) hydrogen.
   (E) oxygen.

3. Stars form from
   (A) planets.   (B) nebulas.
   (C) black holes.   (D) quasars.
   (E) white dwarfs.

4. The two characteristics of stars used to plot a Hertzprung-Russell diagram are
   (A) color and apparent brightness.
   (B) apparent brightness and temperature.
   (C) absolute brightness and mass.
   (D) color and size.
   (E) absolute brightness and temperature.

Use the graph below to answer Questions 5 and 6.

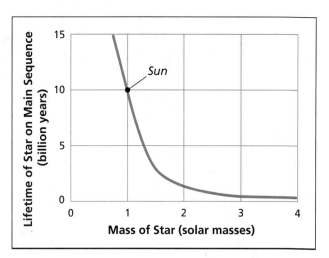

5. About how long will the sun spend on the main sequence?
   (A) 10 million years
   (B) 500 million years
   (C) 1.0 billion years
   (D) 10 billion years
   (E) 15 billion years

6. A star with 3 times the sun's mass has a main sequence lifetime of about
   (A) 500 million years.
   (B) 1.5 billion years.
   (C) 7.5 billion years.
   (D) 10 billion years.
   (E) 15 billion years.

7. Place the following events in the evolution of a sun-like star in the correct sequence, beginning with the earliest event.
   (A) planetary nebula; protostar; white dwarf; main-sequence star; red giant
   (B) protostar; main-sequence star; red supergiant; supernova; neutron star or black hole
   (C) planetary nebula; main-sequence star; red giant; white dwarf; protostar
   (D) protostar; main-sequence star; red giant; planetary nebula; white dwarf
   (E) white dwarf; main-sequence star; red giant; planetary nebula; protostar

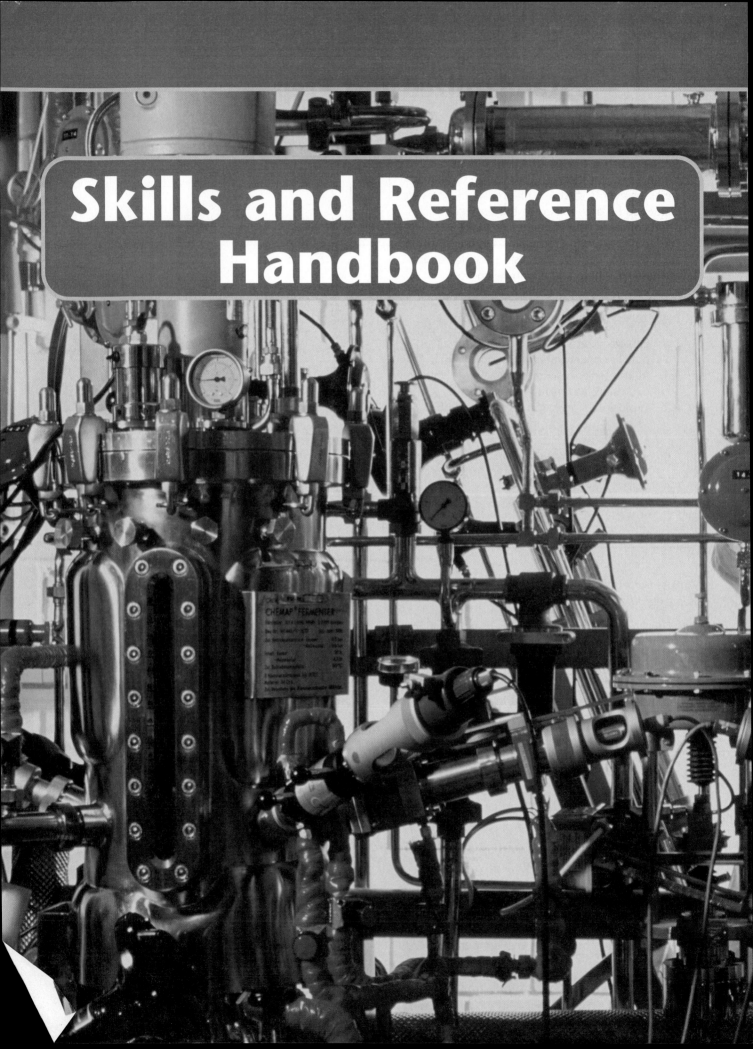

Skills and Reference Handbook

Basic Process Skills

During a physical science course, you often carry out some short lab activities as well as more detailed experiments. Here are some skills that you will use as you work.

Observing

In every science activity, you make a variety of observations. **Observing** is using one or more of the five senses to gather information. Many observations involve the senses of sight, hearing, touch, and smell.

Sometimes you will use tools that increase the power of your senses or make observations more precise. For example, hand lenses enable you to see things in greater detail. Tools may help you eliminate personal opinions or preferences.

In science it is customary to record your observations at the time they are made, usually by writing or drawing in a notebook. You may occasionally make records by using computers, cameras, videotapes, and other tools. As a rule, scientists keep complete accounts of their observations, often using tables to help organize their observations in a regular way.

Inferring

In science as in everyday life, observations are usually followed by inferences. **Inferring** is interpreting an observation or statement based on prior knowledge. For example, you can make several observations using the strobe photograph below. You can observe that the

ball is moving. Based on the motion of the ball, you might infer that the ball was thrown downward at an angle by an experimenter. In making that inference, you would use your knowledge about the motion of projectiles. Someone who knew more about projectile motion might infer that the ball loses energy with each bounce. That is why the height decreases with each bounce.

Notice that an inference is an act of reasoning, not a fact. That means an inference may be logical but not true. It is often necessary to gather further information before you can be confident that an inference is correct. For scientists, that information may come from further observations or from research into the work done by others.

| Comparing Observations and Inferences ||
Sample Observation	Sample Inference
The ball moves less and less vertical distance in the time between each flash of the strobe light.	Gravity is slowing down the ball's upward motion.
The ball moves the same distance to the right in the time between each flash of the strobe light.	Air resistance is so small that it does not slow down the ball's horizontal motion.

Predicting

People often make predictions, but their statements about the future could be either guesses or inferences. In science, a **prediction** is an inference about a future event based on evidence, experience, or knowledge. For example, you can say, *On the first day next month, it will be sunny all day.* If your statement is based on evidence of weather patterns in the area, then the prediction is scientific. If the statement was made without considering any evidence, it's just a guess.

Predictions play a major role in science because they offer scientists a way to test ideas. If scientists understand an event or the properties of a particular object, they should be able to make accurate predictions about that event or object. Some predictions can be tested simply by making observations. For others, carefully designed experiments are needed.

Measuring

Measurements are important in science because they provide specific information and help observers avoid bias. **Measuring** is comparing an object or process to a standard. Scientists use a common set of standards, called the International System of Units, abbreviated as SI (for its French name, *Système International d'Unités*).

What distance does the ball travel in each time interval in the strobe photograph? You can make measurements on the photograph to make more precise statements about the ball's motion.

Calculating

Once scientists have made measurements, calculations are a very important part of analyzing data. How fast is a ball moving? You could directly measure the speed of a ball using probeware such as a motion sensor. But you can also calculate the speed using distance and time measurements. **Calculating** is a process in which a person uses mathematical operations to manipulate numbers and symbols.

Classifying

Classifying is grouping items according to some organizing idea or system. Classifying occurs in every branch of science but it's especially important in chemistry because there are so many different ways that elements can combine to form compounds.

Sometimes you place objects into groups using an established system. Other times you create a system by observing a variety of objects and identifying their properties. For example, you could group household cleaners into those that are abrasive and those that are not. Or you could categorize cleaners as toxic or nontoxic. Ammonia is toxic, whereas vinegar is not.

Using Tables and Graphs

Scientists represent and organize data in tables and graphs as part of experiments and other activities. Organizing data in tables and graphs makes it easier to see patterns in data. Scientists analyze and interpret data tables and graphs to determine the relationship of one variable to another and to make predictions based on the data.

Space-filling model

Electron dot model

Using Models

Some cities refuse to approve new tall buildings if they would cast shadows on existing parks. As architects plan buildings in such locations, they use models to show where a proposed building's shadow will fall at any time of day at any season of the year. A **model** is a mental or physical representation of an object, process, or event. In science, models are usually made to help people understand natural objects and the processes that affect these objects.

Models can be varied. Mental models, such as mathematical equations, can represent some kinds of ideas or processes. For example, the equation for the surface area of a sphere can model the surface of Earth, enabling scientists to determine its size. Models can be two-dimensional (flat) or three-dimensional (having depth). In chemistry, for example, there are several ways to model the arrangement of atoms in a molecule. Two models for a water molecule are shown above. The electron dot model is two-dimensional. It has the advantage of clearly showing how electrons are shared among atoms in the molecule. The space-filling model cannot show the number of electrons inside the atoms or between atoms, but it does show the arrangement of atoms in space.

Experimental Methods

A science experiment is a procedure designed so that there is only one logical explanation for the results. Some types of experiments are fairly simple to design. Others may require ingenious problem solving.

Posing Questions

As a gardener harvested corn in her vegetable garden, she noticed that on one side of the garden the plants produced very few ears of corn. The gardener wondered, *Why didn't the plants on one side of the garden produce as much corn?*

An experiment may begin when someone like the gardener asks a specific question or wants to solve a particular problem. Sometimes the original question leads directly to an experiment, but often researchers need to restate the problem before they can design an appropriate experiment. The gardener's question about the corn, for example, is too broad to be tested by an experiment, since there are so many possible different answers. To narrow the topic, the gardener might think about several related questions: *Were the seeds the same on both sides of the garden? Was the sunlight the same? Is there something different about the soil?*

Formulating Hypotheses

In science, a question about an event is answered by developing a possible explanation called a **hypothesis**. The hypothesis may be developed after long thought and research or come to a scientist "in a flash." To be useful, a hypothesis must lead to predictions that can be tested.

In this case, the gardener decided to focus on the quality of the soil on each side of her garden. She did some tests and discovered that the soil had a lower pH on the side where the plants did not produce well. That led her to propose this hypothesis: *If the pH of the soil is too low, the plants will produce less corn.* The next step is to make a prediction based on the hypothesis, for example, *If the pH of the soil is increased using lime, the plants will yield more corn.* Notice that the prediction suggests the basic idea for an experiment.

Designing Experiments

A carefully designed experiment can test a prediction in a reliable way, ruling out other possible explanations. As scientists plan their experimental procedures, they pay particular attention to the variables that must be controlled and the procedures that must be defined.

The gardener decided to study three groups of plants:
Group 1—20 plants on the side of the garden with a low pH;
Group 2—20 plants on the side of the garden with a low pH, but with lime added; and
Group 3—20 plants on the side of the garden with a high pH.

Controlling Variables

As researchers design an experiment, they identify the **variables**, factors that can change. Some common variables include mass, volume, time, temperature, light, and the presence or absence of specific materials. An experiment involves three categories of variables. The factor that scientists purposely change is called the **manipulated variable**. The factor that may change because of the manipulated variable and that scientists want to observe is called the **responding variable**. And the factors that scientists purposely keep the same are called the **controlled variables**. Controlling variables helps make researchers confident that the observed changes in the responding variable are due to changes in the manipulated variable.

For the gardener, the manipulated variable is the pH of the soil. The responding variable is the number of ears of corn produced by the plants. Among the variables that must be controlled are the amount of sunlight received each day, the time of year when seeds are planted, and the amount of water the plants receive.

What Is a "Control Group"?

When you read about certain experiments, you may come across references to a control group (or "a control") and the experimental groups. All of the groups in an experiment are treated exactly the same except for the manipulated variable. In an experimental group, the manipulated variable is being changed. The control group is used as a standard of comparison. It may consist of objects that are not changed in any way or objects that are being treated in the usual way. For example, in the gardener's experiment, Group 1 is the control group, because for these plants nothing is done to change the low pH of the soil.

Forming Operational Definitions

In an experiment, it is often necessary to define one or more variables explicitly so that any researcher could measure or control the variable in exactly the same way. An **operational definition** describes how a particular variable is to be measured or how a term is to be defined. In this context, the term *operational* means "describing what to do."

The gardener, for example, has to decide exactly how much lime to add to the soil. Can lime be added after the seeds are planted or only before planting? At what pH should no more lime be added to the soil? In this case, the gardener decided to add lime only before planting, and to add enough lime to make the pH equal in Groups 2 and 3.

Analyzing Data

The observations and measurements that are made in an experiment are called **data**. Scientists customarily record data in an orderly way. When an experiment is done, the researcher analyzes the data for trends or patterns, often by doing calculations or making graphs, to determine whether the results support the hypothesis.

For example, the gardener regularly measured and recorded data such as the soil moisture, daily sunlight, and pH of the soil. She found that the soil pH in Groups 2 and 3 started the same, but after two months the soil pH for Group 3 was a little higher than the soil pH for Group 2.

After harvesting the corn, the gardener recorded the numbers of ears of corn produced by each plant. She totaled the number of ears for each group. Her results were the following.

Group 1: 67 ears of corn
Group 2: 102 ears of corn
Group 3: 126 ears of corn

The overall trend was clear: The gardener's prediction was correct.

Drawing Conclusions

Based on whether the results confirm or refute the hypothesis, researchers make a final statement that summarizes the experiment. That final statement is called the **conclusion**. For example, the gardener's conclusion was, *Adding lime to soil with a low pH will improve the production of corn plants.*

Communicating Results

When an experiment has been completed, one or more events may follow. Researchers may repeat the experiment to verify the results. They may publish the experiment so that others can evaluate and replicate their procedures. They may compare their conclusion with the discoveries made by other scientists. And they may raise new questions that lead to new experiments. For example, *Why does the pH level decrease over time when soil is treated with lime?*

Evaluating and Revising

Scientists must be flexible about the conclusions drawn from an experiment. Further research may help confirm the results of the experiment or make it necessary to revise the initial conclusions. For example, a new experiment may show that lime can be effective only when certain microbes are present in the soil. Scientists continuously evaluate and revise experiments based on the findings in new research.

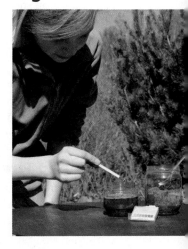

Science Skills

Science Safety

Laboratory work can be exciting, but it can be dangerous if you don't follow safety rules. Ask your teacher to explain any rules you don't understand. Always pay attention to safety symbols and **CAUTION** statements.

General Safety Rules and First Aid

1. Read all directions for an experiment several times. Follow the directions exactly as they are written. If you are in doubt, ask your teacher for assistance.
2. Never perform unauthorized or unsupervised labs, or handle equipment without specific permission.
3. When you design an experiment, do not start until your teacher has approved your plan.
4. If a lab includes physical activity, use caution to avoid injuring yourself or others. Tell your teacher if there is a reason that you should not participate.
5. Never eat, drink, or bring food into the laboratory.
6. Report all accidents to your teacher immediately.
7. Learn the correct ways to deal with a burn, a cut, and acid splashed in your eyes or on your skin.
8. Be aware of the location of the first-aid kit. Your teacher should administer any required first aid.
9. Report any fire to your teacher immediately. Find out the location of the fire extinguisher, the fire alarm, and the phone where emergency numbers are listed.

Dress Code

10. Always wear safety goggles to protect your eyes when working in the lab. Avoid wearing contact lenses. If you must wear contact lenses, ask your teacher what precautions you should take.
11. Wear a laboratory apron to protect your skin and clothing from harmful chemicals or hot materials.
12. Wear disposable plastic gloves to protect yourself from contact with chemicals that can be harmful. Keep your hands away from your face. Dispose of gloves according to your teacher's instructions.
13. Tie back long hair and loose clothing. Remove any jewelry that could contact chemicals or flames.

Heating and Fire Safety

14. Hot plates, hot water, and hot glassware can cause burns. Never touch hot objects with your bare hands. Use an oven mitt or other hand protection.
15. Use a clamp or tongs to hold hot objects. Test an object by first holding the back of your hand near it. If you feel heat on the back of your hand, the object may be too hot to handle.
16. Tie back long hair and loose clothing, and put on safety goggles before using a burner. Follow instructions from your teacher for lighting and extinguishing burners. If the flame leaps out of a burner as you are lighting it, turn the gas off. Never leave a flame unattended or reach across a flame. Make sure your work area is not cluttered with materials.
17. If flammable materials are present, make sure there are no flames, sparks, or exposed sources of heat.
18. Never heat a chemical without your teacher's permission. Chemicals that are harmless when cool can be dangerous when heated. When heating a test tube, point the opening away from you and others in case the contents splash or boil out of the test tube.
19. Never heat a closed container. Expanding hot gases may cause the container to explode.

Using Electricity Safely

20. To avoid an electric shock, never use electrical equipment near water, or when the equipment or your hands are wet. Use ground fault circuit interrupter (GFCI) outlets if you or your equipment may come into contact with moisture.
21. Use only sockets that accept a three-prong plug. Never use two-prong extension cords or adapters. When removing an electrical plug from a socket or extension cord, grasp the plug, not the cord.
22. Disconnect equipment that is not in use. Be sure cords are untangled and cannot trip anyone.
23. Do not use damaged electrical equipment. Look for dangerous conditions such as bare wires or frayed cords. Report damaged equipment immediately.

Using Glassware Safely

24. Handle fragile glassware, such as thermometers, test tubes, and beakers, with care. Do not touch broken glass. Notify your teacher if glassware breaks. Never use chipped or cracked glassware.
25. Never force glass tubing into a stopper. Your teacher will demonstrate the proper methods.
26. Never heat glassware that is not thoroughly dry. Use a wire screen to protect glassware from flames.
27. Hot glassware may not appear hot. Never pick up glassware without first checking to see if it is hot.
28. Never eat or drink from laboratory glassware.

Using Chemicals Safely

29. Do not let any corrosive or poisonous chemicals get on your skin or clothing, or in your eyes. When working with poisonous or irritating vapors, work in a well-ventilated area and wash your hands thoroughly after completing the activity.

30. Never test for an odor unless instructed by your teacher. Avoid inhaling a vapor directly. Use a wafting motion to direct vapor toward your nose.

31. Never mix chemicals "for the fun of it." You might produce a dangerous, possibly explosive substance.

32. Never touch, taste, or smell a chemical that you do not know for certain to be harmless.

33. Use only those chemicals listed in an investigation. Keep the lids on the containers when chemicals are not being used. To avoid contamination, never return chemicals to their original containers.

34. Take extreme care not to spill any chemicals. If a spill occurs, immediately ask your teacher about the proper cleanup procedure. Dispose of all chemicals as instructed by your teacher.

35. Be careful when working with acids or bases. Pour these chemicals over the sink, not over your workbench. If an acid or base gets on your skin or clothing, rinse it off with plenty of cold water. Immediately notify your teacher about an acid or base spill.

36. When diluting an acid, pour the acid into water. Never pour water into the acid.

Using Sharp Instruments

37. Use sharp instruments only as directed. Scissors, scalpels, pins, and knives are sharp and can cut or puncture your skin. Always direct sharp edges and points away from yourself and others.

38. Notify your teacher immediately if you cut yourself when in the laboratory.

End-of-Experiment Rules

39. All chemicals and any other materials used in the laboratory must be disposed of safely. Follow your teacher's instructions.

40. Clean up your work area and return all equipment to its proper place. Thoroughly clean glassware before putting it away.

41. Wash your hands thoroughly with soap, or detergent, and warm water. Lather both sides of your hands and between your fingers. Rinse well.

42. Check that all burners are off and the gas supply for the burners is turned off.

Safety Symbols

 General Safety Awareness
Follow all safety instructions.

 Physical Safety
Use caution in physical activities.

 Safety Goggles
Always wear goggles in the laboratory.

 Lab Apron
Always wear a lab apron in the laboratory.

 Plastic Gloves
Protect your hands from unsafe chemicals.

 Heating
Be careful using sources of heat.

 Heat-Resistant Gloves
Do not touch hot objects with bare hands.

 Flames
Work carefully around open flames.

 No Flames
Flammable materials may be present.

 Electric Shock
Take precautions to avoid electric shock.

 Fragile Glassware
Handle glassware carefully.

 Corrosive Chemical
Work carefully with corrosive chemicals.

 Poison
Avoid contact with poisonous chemicals.

 Fumes
Avoid inhaling dangerous vapors.

 Sharp Object
Use caution with sharp or pointed tools.

 Disposal
Follow instructions for disposal.

 Hand Washing
Wash your hands before leaving the lab.

Reading and Study Skills

At the beginning of each section, you will find a reading strategy to help you study. Each strategy uses a graphic organizer to help you stay organized. The following strategies and graphic organizers are used throughout the text.

Reading Strategies

Using Prior Knowledge

This strategy helps you think about your own experience before you read a section. Research has shown that you learn new material better if you can relate it to something you already know.

Previewing

Previewing a lesson can give you a sense of how the textbook is organized and what lies ahead. One technique is to look at the section topics (in green and blue type). You also can preview by reading captions. Sometimes previewing helps you simply because you find out a topic isn't as hard as you thought it might be.

Predicting

You can preview a section and then make a prediction. For example, you might predict the meaning of an important concept. Then, as you read, check to see if your prediction was correct. Often you find out that you knew more about a topic than you realized.

Building Vocabulary

Start building new vocabulary by previewing a section and listing boldface terms you don't recognize. Then look for each term as you read. Writing a sentence with a term, and defining a term in your own words are two techniques that will help you remember definitions.

Identifying the Main Idea

The key symbols next to boldface sentences identify the main ideas in a section. You can use topic sentences to find the main idea in a paragraph. Often, a topic sentence is the first or second sentence in a paragraph.

Identifying Cause and Effect

Cause-and-effect relationships are very important in science. A flowchart will help you identify cause-and-effect relationships as you read about a process.

Comparing and Contrasting

Comparing and contrasting can help you understand how concepts are related. Comparing is identifying both similarities and differences, while contrasting focuses on the differences. Compare-and-contrast tables and Venn diagrams work best with this strategy.

Sequencing

When you sequence events, it helps you to visualize the steps in a process and to remember the order in which they occur. Sequences often involve cause-and-effect relationships. Use flowcharts for linear sequences and cycle diagrams for repeating sequences.

Relating Text and Figures

You can use diagrams and photographs to focus on the essential concepts in a section. Then find text that extends the information in the figures. You can also reinforce concepts by comparing different figures.

Summarizing

Summarizing requires you to identify key ideas and state them briefly in your own words. You will remember the content of an entire section better even if you summarize only a portion of the section.

Outlining

You can quickly organize an outline by writing down the green and blue headings in a section. Then add phrases or sentences from the boldface sentences to expand the outline with the most important concepts.

Monitoring Your Understanding

You can evaluate your progress with graphic organizers such as a Know-Write-Learn (KWL) table. To make a KWL table, construct a table with three columns, labeled K, W, and L. Before you read, write what you already know in the first column (K). In the middle column, write what you want to learn (W). After you read, write what you learned (L).

Graphic Organizers

Concept Maps and Web Diagrams

A **concept map** is a diagram that contains concept words in ovals and connects the ovals with linking words. Often the most general concept is placed at the top of the map. The content of the other ovals becomes more specific as you move away from the main concept. Linking words are written on a line between two ovals.

A **web diagram** is a type of concept map that shows how several ideas relate to one central idea. Each subtopic may also link to subtopics, creating the visual effect of a spider web. Linking words are usually not included.

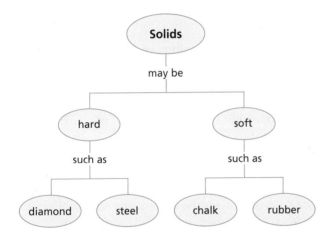

Compare-and-Contrast Tables

A **compare-and-contrast table** is a way of showing the similarities and differences between two or more objects or processes. The table provides an organized framework for making comparisons based on specific characteristics.

The items to be compared are usually column headings across the top of the table. Characteristics for comparison are listed in the first column. You complete the table by filling in information for each item.

Compare-and-Contrast Table		
Contents	Book	CD-ROM
Paper pages	Yes	No
Photographs	Yes	Yes
Videos	No	Yes

Venn Diagrams

A **Venn diagram** consists of two or more ovals that overlap. Each oval represents a particular object or idea. Unique characteristics are shown in the part of each oval that does not overlap. Shared characteristics are shown in the area of overlap.

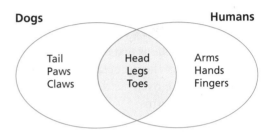

Flowcharts

A **flowchart** is used to represent the order in which a set of events occurs. Each step in the sequence is described in a box. Each box is linked to the next box with an arrow. The flowchart shows a sequence from beginning to end.

Cycle Diagrams

A **cycle diagram** shows boxes representing a cyclical sequence of events. As in a flowchart, boxes are linked with arrows, but the sequence does not have a beginning or end. The boxes are usually arranged in a clockwise circle.

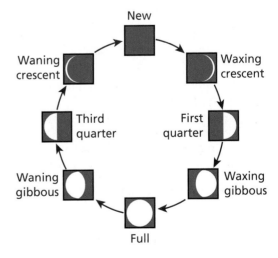

Math Skills

Throughout your study of physical science, you will often need to solve math problems. This appendix is designed to help you quickly review the basic math skills you will use most often.

Fractions

Adding and Subtracting Fractions

To add or subtract fractions that have the same denominator, add or subtract the numerators, and then write the sum or difference over the denominator. Express the answer in lowest terms.

Examples

$$\frac{3}{10} + \frac{1}{10} = \frac{3+1}{10} = \frac{4}{10} = \frac{2}{5}$$

$$\frac{5}{7} - \frac{2}{7} = \frac{5-2}{7} = \frac{3}{7}$$

To add or subtract fractions with different denominators, find the least common denominator. Write an equivalent fraction for each fraction using the least common denominator. Then add or subtract the numerators. Write the sum or difference over the least common denominator and express the answer in lowest terms.

Examples

$$\frac{1}{3} + \frac{3}{5} = \frac{5}{15} + \frac{9}{15} = \frac{5+9}{15} = \frac{14}{15}$$

$$\frac{7}{8} - \frac{1}{4} = \frac{7}{8} - \frac{2}{8} = \frac{7-2}{8} = \frac{5}{8}$$

Multiplying Fractions

When multiplying two fractions, multiply the numerators to find the product's numerator. Then multiply the denominators to find the product's denominator. It helps to divide any numerator or denominator by the greatest common factor before multiplying. Express the answer in lowest terms.

Examples

$$\frac{3}{5} \times \frac{2}{7} = \frac{3 \times 2}{5 \times 7} = \frac{6}{35}$$

$$\frac{4}{14} \times \frac{6}{9} = \frac{2 \times 2}{7 \times 2} \times \frac{2 \times 3}{3 \times 3} = \frac{2 \times 2}{7 \times 3} = \frac{4}{21}$$

Dividing Fractions

To divide one fraction by another, invert and multiply. Express the answer in lowest terms.

Examples

$$\frac{2}{5} \div \frac{3}{4} = \frac{2}{5} \times \frac{4}{3} = \frac{2 \times 4}{5 \times 3} = \frac{8}{15}$$

$$\frac{9}{16} \div \frac{5}{8} = \frac{9}{16} \times \frac{8}{5} = \frac{9 \times 1}{2 \times 5} = \frac{9}{10}$$

Ratios and Proportions

A ratio compares two numbers or quantities. A ratio is often written as a fraction expressed in lowest terms. A ratio also may be written with a colon.

Examples

The ratio of 3 to 4 is written as 3 to 4, $\frac{3}{4}$, or 3 : 4.

The ratio of 10 to 5 is written as $\frac{10}{5} = \frac{2}{1}$, or 2 : 1.

A proportion is a mathematical sentence that states that two ratios are equivalent. To write a proportion, place an equal sign between the two equivalent ratios.

Examples

The ratio of 6 to 9 is the same as the ratio of 8 to 12.

$$\frac{6}{9} = \frac{8}{12}$$

The ratio of 2 to 4 is the same as the ratio of 7 to 14.

$$\frac{2}{4} = \frac{7}{14}$$

You can set up a proportion to determine an unknown quantity. Use x to represent the unknown. To find the value of x, cross multiply and then divide both sides of the equation by the number that comes before x.

Example

Two out of five students have blue notebooks. If this same ratio exists in a class of twenty students, how many students in the class have blue notebooks?

$$\frac{2}{5} = \frac{x}{20} \quad \leftarrow \textbf{Cross multiply.}$$

$$2 \times 20 = 5x \quad \leftarrow \textbf{Divide.}$$

$$8 = x$$

Percents and Decimals

Calculating Percents

A percent is a ratio that compares a number to 100. The word *percent* (%) means "parts of 100" or "per 100 parts." Another way to think of a percent is as a part of a whole expressed in hundredths. Thus, the number 0.41 ("41 hundredths") can also be expressed as 41%, or "41 per 100 parts."

$$0.41 = \frac{41}{100} = 41\%$$

You can calculate a percent by multiplying the ratio of the part to the whole by 100%.

$$\text{Percent} = \frac{\text{Part}}{\text{Whole}} \times 100\%$$

Examples

The fraction $\frac{7}{10}$ is equivalent to 70%.

The fraction $\frac{5}{8}$ is equivalent to 62.5%.

The fraction $\frac{15}{200}$ is equivalent to 7.5%.

You have probably seen data expressed in the form of a percent. For instance, nutrition labels on packaged foods include a column titled "% Daily Value." In this column, the nutrients (such as fat, cholesterol, and fiber) contained in a single serving are compared to the recommended daily intake. You also encounter percents when you go shopping (items on sale might be labeled "20% off") or when you receive test scores.

Example

A student answers 34 questions correctly on a 40-question exam. What is the student's score expressed as a percent?

$$\text{Percent} = \frac{\text{Part}}{\text{Whole}} \times 100\%$$

$$= \frac{\text{Number of correct answers}}{\text{Number of questions asked}} \times 100\%$$

$$= \frac{34}{40} \times 100\%$$

$$= 85\%$$

Converting Between Percents and Decimals

To convert a percent to a decimal value, write the number without the percent sign and move the decimal point two places to the left. Add a zero before the decimal point.

Examples

$$38\% = 0.38$$
$$13.92\% = 0.1392$$

You can convert a decimal value to a percent value by moving the decimal point two places to the right and adding the percent sign.

Examples

$$0.46 = 46\%$$
$$0.8215 = 82.15\%$$

Converting between percents and decimals is often necessary when solving word problems involving composition or concentration.

Example

A nighttime cold medicine is 22% alcohol by volume. How many milliliters of alcohol are in a 250-mL bottle of this medicine?

$$22\% = 0.22 \leftarrow \textbf{Convert percent to a decimal.}$$

$$\frac{\text{Part}}{\text{Whole}} = \frac{\text{Part}}{250 \text{ mL}} = 0.22$$

$$\text{Part} = 250 \text{ mL} \times 0.22$$

$$\text{Part} = 55 \text{ mL}$$

Example

During a flu epidemic, 28% of the students at a school were absent. If 238 students were absent, what was the school's enrollment?

$$28\% = 0.28 \leftarrow \textbf{Convert percent to a decimal.}$$

$$\frac{\text{Part}}{\text{Whole}} = \frac{238 \text{ students}}{\text{Whole}} = 0.28$$

$$\text{Whole} = \frac{238 \text{ students}}{0.28}$$

$$\text{Whole} = 850 \text{ students}$$

Math Skills

Scientific Notation

Very large and very small numbers are often expressed in scientific notation. In scientific notation, a number is written as the product of two numbers: a coefficient that is greater than or equal to one and less than ten, and 10 raised to a power. For example, the number 710,000 written in scientific notation is 7.1×10^5. The coefficient in this number is 7.1. The power of ten, or the exponent, is 5. The exponent indicates how many times the coefficient must be multiplied by 10 to equal the number 710,000.

To convert a large number to scientific notation, move the decimal point to the left until it is located just to the right of the first nonzero number. The number of places that you move the decimal point becomes the positive exponent of 10.

Example

$18{,}930{,}000 = 1.893 \times 10^7$

To write a number less than 1 in scientific notation, move the decimal point just to the right of the first nonzero number. Use the number of places you moved the decimal point as the negative exponent of 10.

Example

$0.0027 = \dfrac{2.7}{10 \times 10 \times 10} = 2.7 \times 10^{-3}$

When you convert a number to scientific notation, remember that you are not changing the value of the number. You are only changing the way that it is written.

Examples

$500{,}000 = 5 \times 10^5$

$0.000\,000\,042 = 4.2 \times 10^{-8}$

$0.030\,06 = 3.006 \times 10^{-2}$

$285.2 = 2.852 \times 10^2$

$0.0002 = 2 \times 10^{-4}$

$83{,}700{,}000 = 8.37 \times 10^7$

Adding and Subtracting

To add or subtract numbers in scientific notation, the exponents must be the same. If they are different, rewrite one of the numbers to make the exponents the same. Then write the answer so that only one number is to the left of the decimal point.

Examples

$$(3.20 \times 10^3) + (5.1 \times 10^2) = (32.0 \times 10^2) + (5.1 \times 10^2)$$
$$= 37.1 \times 10^2$$
$$= 3.71 \times 10^3$$

$$(3.42 \times 10^{-5}) - (2.5 \times 10^{-6})$$
$$= (34.2 \times 10^{-6}) - (2.5 \times 10^{-6})$$
$$= 31.7 \times 10^{-6}$$
$$= 3.17 \times 10^{-5}$$

Multiplying and Dividing

To multiply or divide numbers in scientific notation, the exponents are added or subtracted.

Examples

$$(1.2 \times 10^3) \times (3.4 \times 10^4) = (4.1 \times 10^{3\,+\,4})$$
$$= 4.1 \times 10^7$$

$$(5.0 \times 10^9) \div (2.5 \times 10^6) = (2.0 \times 10^{9\,-\,6})$$
$$= 2.0 \times 10^3$$

$$\frac{(1.2 \times 10^{-3})^2}{(10^{-2})^3 \times (2.0 \times 10^{-3})} = \frac{1.2^2 \times (10^{-3})^2}{(10^{-6}) \times (2.0 \times 10^{-3})}$$

$$= \frac{1.44 \times 10^{-6}}{2.0 \times 10^{-6\,+\,3(-3)}}$$

$$= \frac{1.44 \times 10^{-6}}{2.0 \times 10^{-9}}$$

$$= 0.72 \times 10^{-6\,-\,(-9)}$$

$$= 0.72 \times 10^3$$

$$= 7.2 \times 10^2$$

Significant Figures

When measurements are combined in calculations, the uncertainty of each measurement must be correctly reflected in the final result. The digits that are accurate in the answer are called significant figures. When the result of a calculation has more significant figures than needed, the result must be rounded off. If the first digit after the last significant digit is less than 5, round down. If the first digit after the last significant digit is 5 or more, round up.

Examples

1577 rounded to three significant figures is 1580.
1574 rounded to three significant figures is 1570.
2.458462 rounded to three significant figures is 2.46.
2.458462 rounded to four significant figures is 2.458.

Examples

Each of the measurements listed below has three significant figures. The significant figures are underlined.

<u>456</u> mL
0.<u>305</u> g
<u>70.4</u> mg
0.000<u>457</u> g
<u>5.64</u> × 10^3 km
<u>444</u>,000 ng
<u>1.30</u> × 10^{-2} m
0.004 <u>06</u> dm

Adding and Subtracting

In addition and subtraction, the number of significant figures in the answer depends on the number with the largest uncertainty.

Example

$$
\begin{array}{r}
25.34 \text{ g} \\
152 \text{ g} \\
+ \quad 4.009 \text{ g} \\
\hline
181 \text{ g}
\end{array}
$$

The measurement with the largest uncertainty is 152 g, and it is measured to the nearest gram. Therefore, the answer is given to the nearest gram.

Example

189.427 g − 19.00 g = 170.427 g ≈ 170.43 g

The measurement with the larger uncertainty is 19.00 g, which is measured to the nearest hundredth of a gram. Therefore, the answer is given to the nearest hundredth of a gram.

Multiplying and Dividing

In multiplication and division, the measurement with the smallest number of significant figures determines the number of significant figures in the answer.

Example

(5.3 m) × (1.54 m) = 8.162 m^2 ≈ 8.2 m^2

Because 5.3 m has only two significant figures, the answer must be rounded to two significant figures.

Example

$$
\begin{aligned}
\text{Density} &= \frac{\text{Mass}}{\text{Volume}} \\
&= \frac{20.79 \text{ g}}{5.5 \text{ mL}} \\
&= 3.78 \text{ g/mL} \\
&\approx 3.8 \text{ g/mL}
\end{aligned}
$$

Because 5.5 mL has only two significant figures, the answer must be rounded to two significant figures.

Example

Calculate the perimeter [(2 × length) + (2 × width)] and the area (length × width) of a rectangular garden plot that measures 32.8 m by 16 m. Round each answer to the correct number of significant figures.

$$
\begin{aligned}
\text{Perimeter} &= (2 \times 32.8 \text{ m}) + (2 \times 16 \text{ m}) \\
&= 65.6 \text{ m} + 32 \text{ m} \\
&= 97.6 \text{ m} \\
&\approx 98 \text{ m}
\end{aligned}
$$

Area = 32.8 m × 16 m = 524.8 m^2 ≈ 5.2 × 10^2 m^2

Math Skills

Formulas and Equations

An equation is a mathematical sentence that contains one or more variables and one or more mathematical operators (such as $+$, $-$, $\div$, $\times$, and $=$). An equation expresses a relationship between two or more quantities.

A formula is a special kind of equation. A formula such as $V = l \times w \times h$ states the relationship between unknown quantities represented by the variables $V, l, w,$ and h. The formula means that volume (of a rectangular solid) equals length times width times height. Some formulas have numbers that do not vary, such as the formula for the perimeter of a square: $P = 4s$. In this formula, the number 4 is a constant.

To solve an equation or formula for an unknown quantity, first rearrange the equation so that the unknown is on one side of the equation, and all the known quantities are on the other side. Then substitute known values for the variables. Be sure to include units.

Example

An airplane travels in a straight line at a speed of 600 km/h. How far does it fly in 3.5 hours?

Write the formula that relates speed, distance, and time.

$$\text{Speed} = \frac{\text{Distance}}{\text{Time}}$$

$$v = \frac{d}{t}$$

To solve for distance, multiply both sides of the equation by t.

$$v = \frac{d}{t}$$

$$v \times t = \frac{d}{t} \times t$$

$$v \times t = d$$

Substitute in the known values.

$$600 \text{ km/h} \times 3.5 \text{ h} = d$$
$$2100 \text{ km} = d$$

Example

What is the volume of 642 g of gold if the density of gold is 19.3 g/cm³?

Write the formula that relates density, mass, and volume.

$$\text{Density} = \frac{\text{Mass}}{\text{Volume}}$$

$$d = \frac{m}{v}$$

First solve the equation for the unknown quantity, volume (v).

$$d = \frac{m}{v}$$

$$v \times d = m$$

$$v = \frac{m}{d}$$

Then substitute in the known values for m and d.

$$v = \frac{642 \text{ g}}{19.3 \text{ g/cm}^3}$$

$$v = 33.2645 \text{ cm}^3$$

$$v \approx 33.3 \text{ cm}^3$$

Example

A gas has a volume of 5.0 L at a temperature of 200 K. The temperature of the gas is increased under constant pressure until the final volume of the gas is 15 L. What is the final temperature of the gas?

Write the formula that describes how the volume of a gas changes with temperature if the pressure and number of particles are constant.

$$\frac{V_1}{T_1} = \frac{V_2}{T_2}$$

First solve the equation for the unknown quantity, T_2.

$$\frac{V_1}{T_1} = \frac{V_2}{T_2}$$

$$T_2 = \frac{V_2 \times T_1}{V_1}$$

Now substitute the known values for $V_1, V_2,$ and T_1.

$$T_2 = \frac{15 \text{ L} \times 200 \text{ K}}{5 \text{ L}}$$

$$T_2 = 600 \text{ K}$$

Conversion Factors

Many problems involve converting measurements from one unit to another. You can convert units by using an equation that shows how units are related. For example, 1 in. = 2.54 cm relates inches and centimeters.

To write a conversion factor, divide both sides of the equation by 1 in.

$$\frac{1 \text{ in.}}{1 \text{ in.}} = \frac{2.54 \text{ cm}}{1 \text{ in.}}$$

$$1 = 2.54 \text{ cm/in.}$$

Because the conversion factor is equal to 1, you can multiply one side of an equation by it and preserve equality. You can make a second conversion factor by dividing both sides of the equation by 2.54 cm.

$$\frac{1 \text{ in.}}{2.54 \text{ cm}} = \frac{2.54 \text{ cm}}{2.54 \text{ cm}} = 1$$

One conversion factor converts inches to centimeters and the other converts centimeters to inches. Choose the conversion factor that cancels out the unit that you have a measurement for.

Example

Convert 25 inches to centimeters. Use the conversion factor 2.54 cm/in. so that the inches units cancel.

$$25 \text{ in.} \times \frac{2.54 \text{ cm}}{1 \text{ in.}} \approx 64 \text{ cm}$$

Some conversions are more complicated and require multiple steps.

Example

Convert 23°F to a Celsius temperature. The conversion formula is °F = $(\frac{9}{5} \times °C) + 32°F$.

First solve the equation for °C.

$$°F = (\tfrac{9}{5} \times °C) + 32°F$$

$$°F - 32°F = \tfrac{9}{5} \times °C$$

$$\tfrac{5}{9}(°F - 32°F) = °C$$

Now substitute in 23°F.

$$°C = \tfrac{5}{9}(23°F - 32°F) = \tfrac{5}{9}(-9) = -5$$

Thus, 23°F is equivalent to −5°C.

Example

A grocer is selling oranges at a price of 3 for $1.00. How much would 10 oranges cost?

Use the equality 3 oranges = $1.00 to write a conversion factor. The desired conversion factor should have dollars in the numerator so that the oranges units cancel.

$$10 \text{ oranges} \times \frac{\$1.00}{3 \text{ oranges}} = \$3.33$$

Example

Water runs through a hose at a rate of 2.5 gallons per minute. What is the rate of water flow in gallons per day?

To convert gal/min to gal/d, you must use conversion factors based on the following equalities.

60 min = 1 h

24 h = 1 d

$$\frac{2.5 \text{ gal}}{\text{min}} \times \frac{60 \text{ min}}{1 \text{ h}} \times \frac{24 \text{ h}}{1 \text{ d}} = 3600 \text{ gal/d}$$

Example

The density of nitrogen gas is 1.17 g/L. What is the density of nitrogen expressed in micrograms per deciliter (μg/dL)?

Derive the needed conversion factors from the following equalities.

$$10^6 \ \mu g = 1 \text{ g}$$

$$10 \text{ dL} = 1 \text{ L}$$

$$\frac{1.17 \text{ g}}{\text{L}} \times \frac{10^6 \ \mu g}{1 \text{ g}} \times \frac{1 \text{ L}}{10 \text{ dL}} = 1.17 \times 10^5 \ \mu g/dL$$

Math Skills

Data Tables

Data tables help to organize data and make it easier to see patterns in data. If you plan data tables before doing an experiment, they will help you record observations in an orderly fashion.

The data table below shows United States immigration data for the year 2001. Always include units of measurement so people can understand the data.

Immigration to the United States, 2001

Place of Origin	Number of Legal Immigrants
Africa	53,948
Asia	349,776
Europe	175,371
North America	407,888
South America	68,888

Bar Graphs

To make a bar graph, begin by placing category labels along the bottom axis. Add an overall label for the axis *Place of Origin.* Decide on a scale for the vertical axis. An appropriate scale for the data in the table is 0 to 500,000. Label the vertical axis *Number of People.* For each continent, draw a bar whose height corresponds to the number of immigrants. You will need to round off the values. For example, the bar for Africa should correspond to 54,000 people. Add a graph title to make it clear what the graph shows.

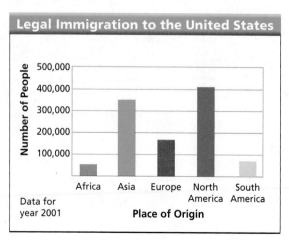

Circle Graphs

Use the total number to calculate percentages. For example, the percentage of immigrants from Africa in 2001 was 53,948 ÷ 1,061,984 = 0.051 ≈ 5%. Multiply each percent by 360° to find the central angle of each wedge. For Africa, the central angle is 18°. Use a protractor to draw each central angle. Color and label the wedges and finish your graph with a title.

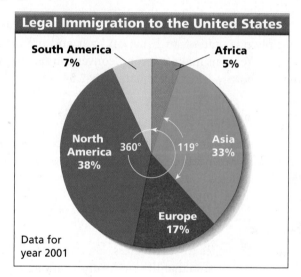

Line Graphs

The slope of a straight-line graph equals the "rise over the run." The rise is the change in the *y* values and the run is the change in the *x* values. Using points A and B on the graph below gives

$$\text{Slope} = \frac{\text{Rise}}{\text{Run}} = \frac{5-3}{9-3} = \frac{2}{6} = 0.33$$

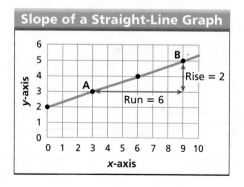

21st Century Skills

The Partnership for 21st Century Skills is the leading advocacy organization focused on infusing skills for the 21st century into education. The organization brings together the business community, education leaders, and policy makers to define a powerful vision for 21st century education to ensure every child's success as citizens and workers by providing tools and resources to help facilitate and drive change.

Today's students will spend their adult lives in a multitasking, multifaceted, technology-driven, diverse, vibrant world—and they must arrive equipped to do so. The goal of 21st Century Learning is to bridge the gap between how students live and how they learn.

21st century student outcomes can be organized into four sections, each describing a particular set of skills, knowledge, and expertise.

Core Subjects and 21st Century Themes

Let's start with Core Subjects and 21st Century Themes. Today's students will still need to master core subjects such as English (reading or language arts), world languages, arts, mathematics, economics, sciences, geography, history, government, and civics. However, they can move beyond basic competence to higher levels of understanding if schools weave into those subjects such themes as global awareness; financial, economic, business, and entrepreneurial literacy; civic literacy; and health literacy.

Learning and Innovation Skills

The next section, Learning and Innovation Skills, prepares students for increasingly complex life and work environments. Skills such as creativity and innovation allow students to implement, analyze, refine, and evaluate new ideas. Critical thinking and problem-solving skills allow students to make their way through the multistep process required to find solutions—be they conventional or innovative—to non-familiar problems. Communication and collaboration skills will be key to success in today's global, interconnected, multicultural world.

Information, Media, and Technology Skills

The 21st century is a technology- and media-suffused environment that requires mastery of the skills in the blue section—Information, Media, and Technology Skills. These skills include information literacy, media literacy, and ICT (information, communications, and technology) literacy. Students must learn to access, evaluate, and use information from a wide variety of sources. They will need to know how to recognize, understand, and create media messages. In order to function in the new knowledge economy, today's students will need to use digital devices, communication and networking tools, and social networks professionally as well as personally.

Life and Career Skills

The ultimate goal is to prepare students for success beyond the classroom with Life and Career Skills. This is a globally competitive information age with complex life and work environments. These environments require such skills as flexibility and adaptability, initiative and self-direction, social and cross-cultural skills, productivity and accountability, and leadership and responsibility.

Adapted from Partnership for 21st Century Skills, 177 N. Church Avenue, Suite 305, Tucson, AZ 85701, 520-623-2466; www.21stcenturyskills.org.

Understanding Globes

A globe is a scale model of Earth. It shows the actual shapes, sizes, and locations of all Earth's landmasses and bodies of water. Features on the surface of Earth are drawn to scale on a globe. This means that a small unit of measure on the globe stands for a large unit of measure on Earth.

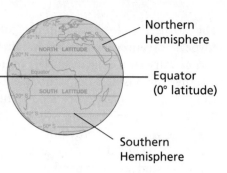

Northern Hemisphere

Equator (0° latitude)

Southern Hemisphere

Parallels of Latitude

Geographers divide the globe along imaginary horizontal lines called parallels of latitude. One of these latitude lines is the equator, located halfway between the North and South poles. Parallels of latitude are measured in degrees (°). One degree of latitude represents a distance of about 69 miles (111 kilometers).

All the latitudes, land, and water north of the equator are in the Northern Hemisphere.

The equator marks 0° latitude and divides Earth into the Southern and Northern Hemispheres.

All the latitudes, land, and water south of the equator are in the Southern Hemisphere.

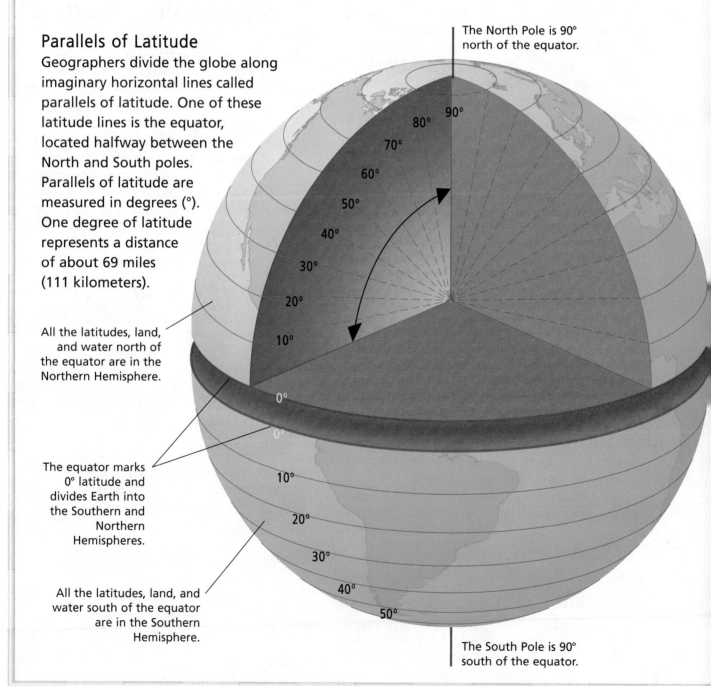

The North Pole is 90° north of the equator.

The South Pole is 90° south of the equator.

Meridians of Longitude

Geographers also divide the globe along imaginary vertical lines called meridians of longitude, which are measured in degrees (°). The longitude line called the Prime Meridian runs from pole to pole through Greenwich, England. All meridians of longitude come together at the North and South Poles.

All the longitudes, land, and water west of the Prime Meridian are in the Western Hemisphere.

Western Hemisphere

WEST LONGITUDE   EAST LONGITUDE
80° W 40° W 20° W   20° E 40° E/60° E

Eastern Hemisphere

Prime Meridian (0° longitude)

120°
110°
100°
90° 80° 70° 60° 50° 40° 30° 20° 10° 0°
20°
10°
0°

All the longitudes, land, and water east of the Prime Meridian are in the Eastern Hemisphere.

The Prime Meridian marks 0° longitude and divides the globe into the Eastern and Western Hemispheres.

The Global Grid

Together, the pattern of parallels of latitude and meridians of longitude is called the global grid. Using the lines of latitude and longitude, you can locate any place on Earth. For example, the location of 30° north latitude and 90° west longitude is usually written as 30° N, 90° W. Only one place on Earth has these coordinates—the city of New Orleans, in the state of Louisiana.

▲ Compass
Wherever you are on Earth, a compass can be used to show direction.

Map Projections

Maps are drawings that show regions on flat surfaces. Maps are easier to use and carry than globes, but they cannot show the correct size and shape of every feature on Earth's curved surface. They must shrink some places and stretch others. To make up for this distortion, mapmakers use different map projections. No one projection can accurately show the correct area, shape, distance, and direction for all of Earth's surface. Mapmakers use the projection that has the least distortion for the information they are presenting.

▲ Global gores
Flattening a globe creates a string of shapes called gores.

Same-Shape Maps

Map projections that accurately show the shapes of landmasses are called same-shape maps. However, these projections often greatly distort, or make less accurate, the size of landmasses as well as the distance between them. In the projection below, the northern and southern areas of the globe appear more stretched than the areas near the equator.

To turn Earth into a same-shape map, mapmakers must stretch the gores into rectangles.

Equator

Stretching the gores makes parts of Earth larger. This enlargement becomes greater toward the North and South Poles.

Mercator projection ▶
One of the most common same-shape maps is the Mercator projection, named for the mapmaker who invented it. The Mercator projection accurately shows shape and direction, but it distorts distance and size. Because the projection shows true directions, ships' navigators use it to chart a straight-line course between two ports.

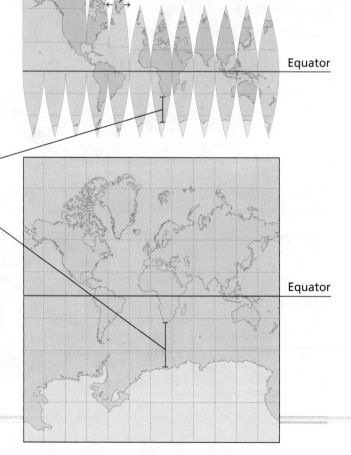

Equator

Equal-Area Maps

Map projections that show the correct size of landmasses are called equal-area maps. In order to show the correct size of landmasses, these maps usually distort shapes. The distortion is usually greater at the edges of the map and less at the center.

To turn Earth's surface into an equal-area map, mapmakers have to squeeze each gore into an oval.

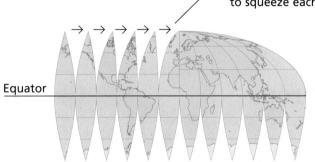

The tips of all the gores are then joined together. The points at which they join form the North and South Poles. The line of the equator stays the same.

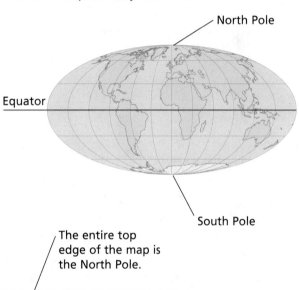

North Pole

Equator

South Pole

Robinson Maps

Many of the maps in this book use the Robinson projection, which is a compromise between the Mercator and equal-area projections. The Robinson projection gives a useful overall picture of the world. It keeps the size and shape relationships of most continents and oceans, but distorts the size of the polar regions.

The entire top edge of the map is the North Pole.

The map is least distorted at the equator.

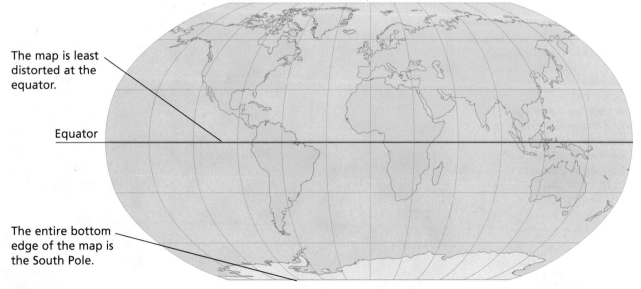

Equator

The entire bottom edge of the map is the South Pole.

How to Use a Map

Mapmakers provide several clues to help you understand the information on a map. Maps provide different clues, depending on their purpose or scale. However, most maps have several clues in common.

Locator globe
Many maps are shown with locator globes. They show where on the globe the area of the map is located.

Title
All maps have a title. The title tells you the subject of the map.

Compass rose
Many maps show direction by displaying a compass rose with the directions north, east, south, and west. The letters N, E, S, and W are placed to indicate these directions.

Key
Often a map has a key, or legend. The key shows the symbols and colors used on the map, and what each one means.

Scale bar
A scale bar helps you find the actual distances between points shown on the map. Most scale bars show distances in both miles and kilometers.

Western Europe

Key	
——	National border
⊛	National capital
•	Other city

SHETLAND ISLANDS (U.K.)

North Sea

Glasgow

Copenhagen

DENMARK

UNITED KINGDOM

Dublin

IRELAND

Hamburg
Berlin

NETHERLANDS
Amsterdam

London

The Hague

GERMANY

Brussels

Prague

BELGIUM

Frankfurt

CZECH REPUBLIC

LUXEMBOURG

Luxembourg

Paris

Munich

Vienna

AUSTRIA

English Channel

FRANCE

Bern

LIECHTENSTEIN

SWITZERLAND

Lyon

Milan

SAN MARINO

Bay of Biscay

Toulouse

MONACO

ITALY

Adriatic Sea

Marseille

ANDORRA

VATICAN CITY

CORSICA (France)

Rome

PORTUGAL

Madrid

Barcelona

SARDINIA (Italy)

Tyrrhenian Sea

Lisbon

SPAIN

BALEARIC ISLANDS (Spain)

Seville

Mediterranean Sea

SICILY (Italy)

0 miles 300
0 kilometers 300
Lambert Azimuthal Equal Area

Maps of Different Scales

Maps are drawn to different scales, depending on their purpose. Here are three maps drawn to very different scales. Keep in mind that maps showing large areas have smaller scales. Maps showing small areas have larger scales.

▲ **Greater London**
Find the gray square on the main map of Western Europe (left). This square represents the area shown on the map above. It shows London's boundaries, the general shape of the city, and the features around the city. This map can help you find your way from the airport to the center of town.

▲ **Central London**
Find the gray square on the map of Greater London. This square represents the area shown on the map above. This map moves you closer into the center of London. Like the zoom on a computer or a camera, this map shows a smaller area but in greater detail. It has the largest scale (1 inch represents about 0.9 mile). You can use this map to explore downtown London.

Key

■ Point of interest

▬ Park

0 miles   0.5   1
0 kilometers   1

▲ **A London Landmark**
The Houses of Parliament lie to the east of St. James's Park and just west of the River Thames.

Physical Maps

Physical maps represent what a region looks like by showing its major physical features, such as hills and plains. Physical maps often show elevation and relief. Elevation, indicated by colors, is the height of the land above sea level. Relief, indicated by shading, shows how sharply the land rises or falls.

Physical Africa Key

ELEVATION

Feet	Meters
More than 13,000	More than 3,960
6,500–13,000	1,980–3,960
1,600–6,500	480–1,980
650–1,600	200–480
0–650	0–200
Below sea level	Below sea level

——— National border

- - - - Disputed border

Strait of Gibraltar
Mediterranean Sea
Atlas Mountains
Canary Islands
Tropic of Cancer
Cape Verde Islands
Senegal R.
Ahaggar Mountains
Tibesti Mountains
Qattara Depression
Libyan Desert
Nile R.
S A H A R A
Niger R.
S A H E L
Lake Chad
White Nile R.
Blue Nile R.
Lake Tana
Gulf of Aden
Fouta Djallon
Volta R.
Benue R.
Adamawa Highlands
Ethiopian Highlands
Sudd
ATLANTIC OCEAN
Gulf of Guinea
Bioko
São Tomé
Equator
Ubangi R.
Congo R.
Congo Basin
Lake Albert
Lake Turkana
Great Rift Valley
Lake Victoria
Kilimanjaro 19,341 ft (5,895 m)
Serengeti Plain
Zanzibar
Lake Tanganyika
INDIAN OCEAN
Lake Nyasa
Comoros
Zambezi R.
Mozambique Channel
Madagascar
Mauritius
Réunion
Namib Desert
Okavango Basin
Kalahari Desert
Limpopo R.
Tropic of Capricorn
Orange R.
Drakensberg
Cape of Good Hope
Cape Agulhas

0 miles 1,000
0 kilometers 1,000
Lambert Azimuthal Equal Area

▲ The Congo Basin
The Congo Basin is a major physical feature of Africa. The key shows that its elevation is within the range of 200–480 meters (650–1,600 feet).

Climate Maps

The boundary lines on a map do not always represent exact divisions. In this climate map of India, the boundaries between color-coded regions show gradual shifts in the local climate. In the northwest, the climate gradually changes from arid to semiarid.

India: Climate Regions Key

- Tropical wet
- Tropical wet and dry
- Semiarid
- Arid
- Humid subtropical
- Highland
- — National border
- • City

PAKISTAN

CHINA

NEPAL

BHUTAN

BANGLADESH

MYANMAR

INDIA

SRI LANKA

• Delhi

Calcutta (Kolkata)

Mumbai (Bombay)

Chennai (Madras)

Tropic of Cancer

0 miles 500
0 kilometers 500
Lambert Conformal Conic

▲ **Rain in Delhi**
Delhi has a humid subtropical climate. During its rainy season, Delhi receives heavy rainfall.

Topographic Maps

Topographic maps provide information on the elevation, relief, and slope of the ground surface. A topographic map uses contour lines to show you the surface features of an area as if you were looking down on them from above. Each contour line on the map connects points of equal elevation. Closely spaced contour lines show steep slopes. Widely spaced contour lines show gentle slopes or flat areas.

Crater Lake Topography Key

▬▬▬	Primary highway
▬▬▬	Secondary highway
▭	Forest
▭	Exposed rock
⬭	Contour line: elevation
⬭	Contour line: depression

Contour line interval: 200 feet

0 miles   3

0 kilometers   3

Contour Lines ▶
In the topographic map of Crater Lake National Park, closely spaced contour lines surrounding the lake represent steep slopes along the lake's perimeter. For this map, the contour interval, or the change in elevation from one contour line to the next, is 200 feet.

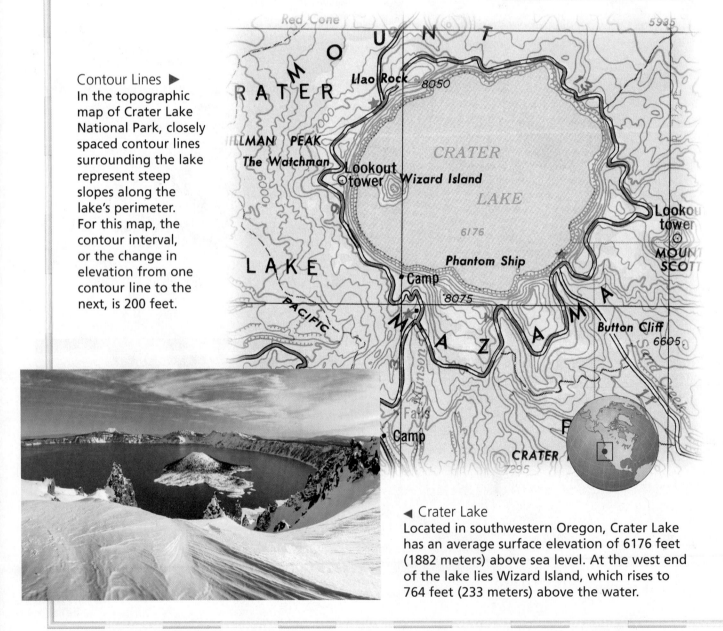

◀ Crater Lake
Located in southwestern Oregon, Crater Lake has an average surface elevation of 6176 feet (1882 meters) above sea level. At the west end of the lake lies Wizard Island, which rises to 764 feet (233 meters) above the water.

SI (*Système International d'Unités*) is a revised version of the metric system, which was originally developed in France in 1791. SI units of measurement are used by scientists throughout the world. The system is based on multiples of ten. Each unit is ten times larger or ten times smaller than the next unit. The most commonly used SI units are given below.

You can use conversion factors to convert between SI and non-SI units. Try the following conversions. How tall are you in meters? What is your weight in newtons? What is your normal body temperature in degrees Celsius?

Metric ruler

10 mm = 1 cm

Commonly Used Metric Units

Length	The distance from one point to another
meter (m)	A meter is slightly longer than a yard. 1 meter = 1000 millimeters (mm) 1 meter = 100 centimeters (cm) 1000 meters = 1 kilometer (km)

Volume	The amount of space an object takes up
liter (L)	A liter is slightly more than a quart. 1 liter = 1000 milliliters (mL)

Mass	The amount of matter in an object
gram (g)	A gram has a mass equal to about one paper clip. 1000 grams = 1 kilogram (kg)

Temperature	The measure of hotness or coldness
degrees Celsius (°C)	0°C = freezing point of water at sea level 100°C = boiling point of water at sea level

Riders   Beams

Triple-Beam Balance

Metric–Customary Equivalents

2.54 centimeters (cm) = 1 inch (in.)
1 meter (m) = 39.37 inches (in.)
1 kilometer (km) = 0.62 miles (mi)
1 liter (L) = 1.06 quarts (qt)
250 milliliters (mL) = 1 cup (c)
9.8 newtons (N) = 2.2 pounds (lb)
°C = 5/9 × (°F − 32)

Boiling point of water at sea level

Human body temperature

Freezing point of water

Thermometer

Graduated cylinder

The laboratory balance is an important tool in scientific investigations. You can use a balance to determine the masses of materials that you study or experiment with in the laboratory.

Different kinds of balances are used in the laboratory. One kind of balance is the triple-beam balance. The balance that you may use in your science class is probably similar to the balance illustrated. To use the balance properly, you should learn the name, location, and function of each part of the balance you are using.

The Triple-Beam Balance

The triple-beam balance is a single-pan balance with three beams The back, or 100-gram, beam is divided into ten units of 10 grams. The middle, or 500-gram, beam is divided into five units of 100 grams. The front, or 10-gram, beam is divided into ten major units, each of which is 1 gram. Each 1-gram unit is further divided into units of 0.1 gram. What is the largest mass you could measure with a triple-beam balance?

The following procedure can be used to find the mass of an object with a triple-beam balance.

1. When no object is on the pan, and the riders are at zero, make sure the pointer is at zero. If it is not, use the adjustment screw to zero the balance.
2. Place the object on the pan.
3. Move the rider on the middle beam notch by notch until the horizontal pointer drops below zero. Move the rider back one notch.
4. Move the rider on the back beam notch by notch until the pointer again drops below zero. Move the rider back one notch.
5. Slowly slide the rider along the front beam until the pointer stops at zero. The mass of the object is the sum of the readings on the three beams.

Pointer (at zero)

Pan

Riders

Beams

Adjustment screw

TRIPLE BEAM BALANCE
700 SERIES   U.S. PAT. NO. 6,176,830   700 SERIES
2610g   Capacity   5 lb 2 oz

Triple-Beam Balance

Element	Symbol	Atomic Number	Atomic Mass†	Element	Symbol	Atomic Number	Atomic Mass†
Actinium	Ac	89	(277)	Neodymium	Nd	60	144.24
Aluminum	Al	13	26.982	Neon	Ne	10	20.179
Americium	Am	95	(243)	Neptunium	Np	93	(237)
Antimony	Sb	51	121.75	Nickel	Ni	28	58.71
Argon	Ar	18	39.948	Niobium	Nb	41	92.906
Arsenic	As	33	74.922	Nitrogen	N	7	14.007
Astatine	At	85	(210)	Nobelium	No	102	(259)
Barium	Ba	56	137.33	Osmium	Os	76	190.2
Berkelium	Bk	97	(247)	Oxygen	O	8	15.999
Beryllium	Be	4	9.0122	Palladium	Pd	46	106.4
Bismuth	Bi	83	208.98	Phosphorus	P	15	30.974
Bohrium	Bh	107	(264)	Platinum	Pt	78	195.09
Boron	B	5	10.81	Plutonium	Pu	94	(244)
Bromine	Br	35	79.904	Polonium	Po	84	(209)
Cadmium	Cd	48	112.41	Potassium	K	19	39.098
Calcium	Ca	20	40.08	Praseodymium	Pr	59	140.91
Californium	Cf	98	(251)	Promethium	Pm	61	(145)
Carbon	C	6	12.011	Protactinium	Pa	91	231.04
Cerium	Ce	58	140.12	Radium	Ra	88	(226)
Cesium	Cs	55	132.91	Radon	Rn	86	(222)
Chlorine	Cl	17	35.453	Rhenium	Re	75	186.21
Chromium	Cr	24	51.996	Rhodium	Rh	45	102.91
Cobalt	Co	27	58.933	Roentgenium	Rg	111	(272)
Copernicium	Cn	112	(277)	Rubidium	Rb	37	85.468
Copper	Cu	29	63.546	Ruthenium	Ru	44	101.07
Curium	Cm	96	(247)	Rutherfordium	Rf	104	(261)
Darmstadtium	Ds	110	(269)	Samarium	Sm	62	150.4
Dubnium	Db	105	(262)	Scandium	Sc	21	44.956
Dysprosium	Dy	66	162.50	Seaborgium	Sg	106	(263)
Einsteinium	Es	99	(252)	Selenium	Se	34	78.96
Erbium	Er	68	167.26	Silicon	Si	14	28.086
Europium	Eu	63	151.96	Silver	Ag	47	107.87
Fermium	Fm	100	(257)	Sodium	Na	11	22.990
Fluorine	F	9	18.998	Strontium	Sr	38	87.62
Francium	Fr	87	(223)	Sulfur	S	16	32.06
Gadolinium	Gd	64	157.25	Tantalum	Ta	73	180.95
Gallium	Ga	31	69.72	Technetium	Tc	43	(98)
Germanium	Ge	32	72.59	Tellurium	Te	52	127.60
Gold	Au	79	196.97	Terbium	Tb	65	158.93
Hafnium	Hf	72	178.49	Thallium	Tl	81	204.37
Hassium	Hs	108	(265)	Thorium	Th	90	232.04
Helium	He	2	4.0026	Thulium	Tm	69	168.93
Holmium	Ho	67	164.93	Tin	Sn	50	118.69
Hydrogen	H	1	1.0079	Titanium	Ti	22	47.90
Indium	In	49	114.82	Tungsten	W	74	183.85
Iodine	I	53	126.90	Uranium	U	92	238.03
Iridium	Ir	77	192.22	Vanadium	V	23	50.941
Iron	Fe	26	55.847	Xenon	Xe	54	131.30
Krypton	Kr	36	83.80	Ytterbium	Yb	70	173.04
Lanthanum	La	57	138.91	Yttrium	Y	39	88.906
Lawrencium	Lr	103	(262)	Zinc	Zn	30	65.38
Lead	Pb	82	207.2	Zirconium	Zr	40	91.22
Lithium	Li	3	6.941				
Lutetium	Lu	71	174.97				
Magnesium	Mg	12	24.305				
Manganese	Mn	25	54.938				
Meitnerium	Mt	109	(268)	† Number in parentheses gives the mass number of the most stable isotope			
Mendelevium	Md	101	(258)				
Mercury	Hg	80	200.59	* Name not officially assigned			
Molybdenum	Mo	42	95.94				

Identifying Common Minerals

Metallic Luster, Mostly Dark-Colored

Mineral	Hardness	Density (g/cm³)	Luster	Streak	Color	Additional Information
Pyrite FeS_2	6–6.5	5.0	Metallic	Greenish black	Light yellow	Harder than chalcopyrite; called "fool's gold," but harder than gold and very brittle
Magnetite Fe_3O_4	6	5.2	Metallic	Black	Iron black	Very magnetic; important iron ore; some varieties known as "lodestone"
Hematite Fe_2O_3	5.5–6.5	4.9–5.3	Metallic or earthy	Red or reddish brown	Reddish brown to black; also steel gray crystals	Most important ore of iron; known as "red ocher;" often used as red pigment in paint
Chalcopyrite $CuFeS_2$	3.5–4	4.1–4.3	Metallic	Greenish black	Golden yellow, often tarnished	Most important copper ore; softer than pyrite and more yellow; more brittle than gold
Copper Cu	2.5–3	8.96	Metallic	Copper red	Copper red to black	Can be pounded into various shapes and drawn into wires; used in making electrical wires, coins, pipes
Gold Au	2.5–3	19.3	Metallic	Yellow	Rich yellow	Can be pounded into various shapes and drawn into wires; does not tarnish; used in jewelry, coins, dental fillings
Silver Ag	2.5–3	10.5	Metallic	Silver to light gray	Silver white, tarnishes to black	Can be pounded into various shapes and drawn into wires; used in jewelry, coins, electrical wire
Galena PbS	2.5	7.4–7.6	Metallic	Lead gray	Lead gray	Main ore of lead; used in shields against radiation
Graphite C	1–2	2.3	Metallic to dull	Black	Black	Feels greasy; very soft; used as pencil "lead" and as a lubricant

Nonmetallic Luster, Mostly Dark-Colored

Mineral	Hardness	Density (g/cm³)	Luster	Streak	Color	Additional Information
Garnet $[Ca,Mg,Fe]_3$ $[Al,Fe,Cr]_2(SiO_4)_3$	7–7.5	3.5–4.3	Glassy to resinous	White, light brown	Red, brown, black, green	A group of minerals used in jewelry, as a birthstone, and as an abrasive
Olivine $[Mg,Fe]_2SiO_4$	6.5–7	3.3–3.4	Glassy	White or gray	Olive green	Found in igneous rocks; sometimes used as a gem
Hornblende $NaCa_2[Mg,Fe,Al]_5$ $[Si,Al]_8O_{22}(OH)_2$	5–6	3.0–3.4	Glassy, silky	White to gray	Dark green to brown, black	Found in igneous and metamorphic rocks
Biotite $K[Mg,Fe]_3$ $AlSiO_{10}(OH)_2$	2.5–3	2.8–3.4	Glassy or pearly	White to gray	Dark green, brown, or black	A type of mica, sometimes used as a lubricant

Nonmetallic Luster, Mostly Light-Colored

Mineral	Hardness	Density (g/cm³)	Luster	Streak	Color	Additional Information
Diamond C	10	3.5	Brilliant	White	Colorless and varied	Hardest known substance; used in jewelry, as an abrasive, in cutting instruments
Topaz $Al_2SiO_4[F,OH]_2$	8	3.5–3.6	Glassy	White	Straw yellow, pink, bluish, greenish	Used in jewelry, as a birthstone
Quartz SiO_2	7	2.6	Glassy, greasy	White	Colorless, white; any color when not pure	The second most abundant mineral; many varieties gems (amethyst, cat's eye, bloodstone, agate, jasper, onyx); used in making glass
Feldspar $[K,Na,Ca]AlSi_3O_8$	6	2.6	Glassy	Colorless, white	Colorless, white, various colors	As a family, the most abundant of all minerals; makes up more than 60 percent of Earth's crust
Fluorite CaF_2	4	3.0–3.3	Glassy	Colorless	Purple, light green, yellow, bluish green, other colors	Some types fluorescent (glow when exposed to UV light); used in making steel
Dolomite $CaMg(CO_3)_2$	3.5–4	2.8	Glassy or pearly	White	Colorless, white, pinkish, or light tints	Used in making concrete and cement; fizzes slowly in dilute hydrochloric acid
Calcite $CaCO_3$	3	2.7	Glassy	White to grayish	Colorless, white, pale tints	Easily scratched; bubbles in dilute hydrochloric acid
Halite $NaCl$	2.5	2.1–2.6	Glassy	White	Colorless or white	Occurs as perfect cubic crystals; has salty taste
Gypsum $CaSO_4 \bullet 2H_2O$	2	2.3	Glassy, pearly, silky	White	Colorless, white, light tints	Very soft; used in manufacture of plaster of Paris; form known as alabaster used for statues
Sulfur S	2	2.0–2.1	Resinous to greasy	White	Yellowish to yellowish brown	Used in making many medicines, in production of sulfuric acid, and in vulcanizing rubber
Talc $Mg_3Si_4O_{10}(OH)_2$	1	2.7–2.8	Pearly to greasy	White	Gray, white, greenish	Very soft; used in talcum powder, found mostly in metamorphic rocks; also used in soapstone "

United States Physical Map **899**

This weather map shows data collected from many weather stations. Below the map is an explanation of what the symbols mean.

Weather Map

Explanation of Fronts

Cold Front
Boundary between a cold air mass and a warm air mass. Brings brief storms and cooler weather.

Warm Front
Boundary between a warm air mass and a cold air mass. Usually accompanied by precipitation.

Stationary Front
Boundary between warm and cold air masses when no movement occurs. Long periods of precipitation.

Occluded Front
Boundary on which a warm front has been overtaken by a cold front. Brings precipitation.

Weather	Symbol
Drizzle	
Fog	
Hail	
Haze	
Rain	
Shower	
Sleet	
Smoke	
Snow	
Thunderstorm	
Hurricane	

Wind Speed (mph)	Symbol
1–2	
3–8	
9–14	
15–20	
21–25	
26–31	
32–37	
38–43	
44–49	
50–54	
55–60	
61–66	
67–71	
72–77	

Cloud Cover (%)	Symbol
0	
10	
20–30	
40	
50	
60	
70–80	
90	
100	

How Symbols Are Used on a Weather Map

Amount of cloud cover (100%)

Atmospheric pressure (millibars)

Temperature (°F)

38   1018

Wind direction (from the southwest)

Wind speed (21–25 mph)

To find the relative humidity, measure the wet-bulb and dry-bulb temperatures with a sling psychrometer. Find the dry-bulb reading in the left column and the difference between readings at the top of the table. The number where these readings intersect is the relative humidity in percent.

Relative Humidity (percent)														
Dry-Bulb Reading (°C)	Difference Between Wet-Bulb and Dry-Bulb Readings (°C)													
	1	2	3	4	5	6	7	8	9	10	11	12	13	14
5	86	72	58	45	33	20	7							
6	86	73	60	48	35	24	11							
7	87	74	62	50	38	26	15							
8	87	75	63	51	40	29	19	8						
9	88	76	64	53	42	32	22	12						
10	88	77	66	55	44	34	24	15	6					
11	89	78	67	56	46	36	27	18	9					
12	89	78	68	58	48	39	29	21	12					
13	89	79	69	59	50	41	32	23	15	7				
14	90	79	70	60	51	42	34	26	18	10				
15	90	80	71	61	53	44	36	27	20	13	6			
16	90	81	71	63	54	46	38	30	23	15	8			
17	90	81	72	64	55	47	40	32	25	18	11			
18	91	82	73	65	57	49	41	34	27	20	14	7		
19	91	82	74	65	58	50	43	36	29	22	16	10		
20	91	83	74	66	59	51	44	37	31	24	18	12	6	
21	91	83	75	67	60	53	46	39	32	26	20	14	9	
22	92	83	76	68	61	54	47	40	34	28	22	17	11	6
23	92	84	76	69	62	55	48	42	36	30	24	19	13	8
24	92	84	77	69	62	56	49	43	37	31	26	20	15	10
25	92	84	77	70	63	57	50	44	39	33	28	22	17	12
26	92	85	78	71	64	58	51	46	40	34	29	24	19	14
27	92	85	78	71	65	58	52	47	41	36	31	26	21	16
28	93	85	78	72	65	59	53	48	42	37	32	27	22	18
29	93	86	79	72	66	60	54	49	43	38	33	28	24	19
30	93	86	79	73	67	61	55	50	44	39	35	30	25	21

Autumn Sky

To use this chart, hold it up in front of you and turn it so the direction you are facing is at the bottom of the chart. The chart works best at 35° N latitude, but it can be used at other latitudes. It works best at the following dates and times: September 1 at 10:00 P.M., October 1 at 8 P.M., and November 1 at 6 P.M.

Winter Sky

To use this chart, hold it up in front of you and turn it so the direction you are facing is at the bottom of the chart. The chart works best at 35° N latitude, but it can be used at other latitudes. It works best at the following dates and times: December 1 at 10:00 P.M., January 1 at 8 P.M., and February 1 at 6 P.M.

Spring Sky

To use this chart, hold it up in front of you and turn it so the direction you are facing is at the bottom of the chart. The chart works best at 35° N latitude, but it can be used at other latitudes. It works best at the following dates and times: March 1 at 10:00 P.M. and April 1 at 8 P.M.

Summer Sky

To use this chart, hold it up in front of you and turn it so the direction you are facing is at the bottom of the chart. The chart works best at 35° N latitude, but it can be used at other latitudes. It works best at the following dates and times: May 15 at 11:00 P.M. and June 15 at 9 P.M.

The following problems provide additional practice for solving equations and word problems. If you need help, look at the Math Skills Boxes on the referenced pages, where you will find solutions to similar problems.

Using Scientific Notation
(See Math Skills, page 15.)

1. The floor of a room measures 7.5 m by 6.0 m.
   a. What area of carpeting (in m^2) would you need to cover the entire floor? Express your answer in scientific notation.
   b. What would the area be in cm^2? (*Hint:* 10^4 $cm^2 = 1$ m^2).
   c. Suppose you want to tile the floor with square tiles that measure 30.5 cm on a side. How many tiles would you need? (*Hint:* Divide the total floor area by the area of a single tile.)

2. A mercury thermometer exchange program collected 1045 mercury thermometers in a month.
   a. If each thermometer contains 0.70 g of mercury, what is the total mass of mercury? Express your answer in scientific notation.
   b. A hazardous waste container holds 100.0 cm^3. Can this container hold all of the mercury? (*Hint:* Find the volume by dividing the mass by the density of mercury, 11.3 g/cm^3.)

The Combined Gas Law
(See Math Skills, page 80.)

1. The air in a bicycle tire is at a temperature of 11.0°C and a pressure of 542 kPa. What is the pressure in the tire if the temperature increases to 29.0°C while you ride the bicycle? Assume the volume of the tire does not change.

2. A helium tank holds 20.0 L of helium at a pressure of 3050 kPa. How many balloons can the tank fill if each balloon holds 2.0 L of gas at a pressure of 105 kPa? The balloons and the tank are both at room temperature. (*Hint:* Find the volume the helium in the tank would expand to if its pressure were reduced to 105 kPa. Then divide by the volume of one balloon.)

Formulas and Names for Compounds
(See Math Skills, page 174.)

1. Write the formulas for the ionic compounds lead(II) sulfide and lithium nitrate.
2. Name the molecular compounds with these formulas: NBr_3, SCl_2, and CCl_4.
3. Write the names for the ionic compounds $FeCl_2$ and $FeCl_3$.

Balancing Chemical Equations
(See Math Skills, page 195.)
Balance the following equations.
1. $H_2 + Cl_2 \rightarrow HCl$
2. $Ca(OH)_2 + HCl \rightarrow CaCl_2 + H_2O$
3. $Fe + O_2 \rightarrow Fe_3O_2$
4. $C_2H_4 + O_2 \rightarrow CO_2 + H_2O$

Balancing Nuclear Equations
(See Math Skills, page 295.)

1. Write a balanced nuclear equation for the beta decay of bismuth-210.
2. Write a balanced nuclear equation for the alpha decay of polonium-214.
3. Determine the product for the alpha decay of uranium-234.
4. What is the product of the beta decay of phosphorus-30?

Measuring Speed
(See Math Skills, page 333.)

1. A runner travels 3.0 kilometers in 24 minutes, then another 2.5 kilometers in 27 minutes, and finally 1.2 kilometers in 15 minutes. What is the runner's average speed?
2. A bus travels 140 km in 3.0 hours and then stops for a 30-minute rest stop. The bus then travels 120 km in 2.0 hours. What is the average speed for the entire trip?
3. A plane's average speed for a 300.0-km trip is 550 km/h. How long did the flight take?

Measuring Acceleration
(See Math Skills, page 346.)

1. During a crash, a bicycle racer moving at 17 m/s comes to a complete stop in 1.5 seconds. Calculate the bicycle's deceleration.
2. A ball is thrown straight up into the air. It comes to a rest at the highest point after 2.0 seconds. How fast was it going when it was thrown upward?

Newton's Second Law
(See Math Skills, page 367.)

1. A truck with a mass of 2200 kg accelerates when the traffic light turns green. If the net force on the truck is 3500 N in the forward direction, what is the truck's acceleration?
2. A bicycle with its rider has a total mass of 95 kg. If the bicycle accelerates at a rate of 2.0 m/s^2, what is the net force acting on the bicycle?
3. What net force is needed to accelerate a 9000-kg truck at the rate of 2.0 m/s^2?

Calculating Power
(See Math Skills, page 415.)

1. While lifting a box 0.75 m straight up, you exert an upward force of 320 N on the box. How much work do you do on the box? What is the power if you take 2.0 s to lift the box?
2. A dog sled is pulled at a constant horizontal speed of 8.0 m/s by a team of dogs. What is the power of the dogs if they are applying a constant horizontal force of 200.0 N to the sled? (*Hint:* Calculate the work done in one second).
3. How much work can a 500-watt engine do in 1.0 hour?

Calculating IMA and AMA
(See Math Skills, page 425.)

1. A crowbar is 0.75 m long and the fulcrum is located 10.0 cm from the end of the bar. What is the ideal mechanical advantage of the crowbar?
2. A person changing a tire exerts a force of 520 N on a car jack to apply a lifting force of 12,000 N. What is the actual mechanical advantage of the car jack?
3. A pair of pliers has an actual mechanical advantage of 3.5. If you were to squeeze the handles together with a force of 3.0 N, how much force would the jaws of the pliers exert?
4. If a machine has an efficiency of 35%, and you do 1500 J of work on the machine, what will be the work output of the machine?

Kinetic Energy
(See Math Skills, page 448.)

1. A 13,000-kg automobile moves at 28 m/s. What is the automobile's kinetic energy?
2. Two birds fly at the same speed, 4.0 m/s. One bird has a mass of 0.25 kg and the other has a mass of 0.75 kg. What is the kinetic energy of each bird?

Conservation of Energy
(See Math Skills, page 458.)

1. An 80.0-kg diver climbs a ladder up to a high-dive platform 10.0 meters above the ground.
a. How much gravitational potential energy does the diver gain?
b. After diving, what is the diver's speed at the water? Assume all of the potential energy has been converted to kinetic energy.
2. A 4.0-kg bowling ball returns to a bowler along a horizontal track at a speed of 5.0 m/s. At the end of the track, the ball must rise up an incline to a height of 1.0 m. Show that the ball has enough energy to make it to the top of the ramp. Assume friction can be ignored.

Specific Heat
(See Math Skills, page 477.)

1. How much heat is needed to raise the temperature of a plastic beaker by 10.0°C? The beaker's mass is 24.4 g and the specific heat of the plastic is 1.90 J/g•°C.
2. Tin has a specific heat of 0.23 J/g•°C. How much heat is needed to raise the temperature of 550 g of tin from 65°C to 125°C?
3. What mass of water will change its temperature by 10.0°C when 500.0 J of heat is added to it?

Speed of Mechanical Waves
(See Math Skills, page 506.)

1. A wave on a rope has a wavelength of 1.5 m and a frequency of 3.0 Hz. What is the speed of the wave?
2. A motorboat in a lake makes a surface wave with a frequency of 13 Hz and a wavelength of 0.15 m. What is the speed of the wave?
3. Seven ocean wave crests pass by a pier in 28.0 s. If the wave speed is 11 m/s, what is the wavelength of the waves?

Calculating Wave Speed
(See Math Skills, page 535.)

1. A cell phone transmits a carrier wave at a frequency 1900 MHz. What is the wavelength of the wave? (Assume the wave moves at the speed of light in a vacuum.)
2. A carrier wave from an FM station has a frequency 94.5 MHz. What is the wavelength?
3. A light-emitting diode (LED) emits light with a wavelength of 630 nanometers. What is the frequency of the light and what color is the LED?

Power, Voltage, and Current
(See Math Skills, page 611.)

1. A flashlight uses a 6.0-W light bulb connected to 3.6-V nickel-cadmium battery. How much current does the bulb use?
2. A hair dryer has a power rating of 1600 W. If it is connected to a 120-volt line, how much current does it draw?

Appendix J | Selected Answers

Answers to even-numbered Math Practice and Section Assessment questions that involve calculations are given below. Use these answers to check your work.

Chapter 1
Math Practice, page 15
2. Distance = 2.6×10^{13} m
Section 1.3 Assessment, page 21
8. 1.5×10^{-4} cm^3

Chapter 3
Math Practice, page 80
2. $T_2 = 580$ K
Section 3.2 Assessment, page 81
10. $P_2 = 281$ kPa

Chapter 6
Math Practice, page 174
2. Cu_2S
4. sodium hydroxide
Section 6.3 Assessment, page 175
8. lithium chloride, barium oxide, sodium nitride, lead sulfate
10. K_2S

Chapter 7
Math Practice, page 195
2 a. $2H_2O_2 \rightarrow 2H_2O + O_2$
  b. $Mg + 2HCl \rightarrow H_2 + MgCl_2$
Section 7.1 Assessment, page 198
10. $2Mg + O_2 \rightarrow 2MgO$

Chapter 10
Math Practice, page 295

2. $^{14}_{6}C \rightarrow {}^{14}_{7}N + {}^{0}_{-1}e$

4. $^{90}_{38}Sr \rightarrow {}^{90}_{39}Y + {}^{0}_{-1}e$
Section 10.1 Assessment, page 297

10. $^{226}_{88}Ra \rightarrow {}^{222}_{86}Rn + {}^{4}_{2}He$

Chapter 11
Math Practice, page 333
2. $v = 62$ km/h
Math Practice, page 346
2. $(v_f - v_i) = 36$ m/s
4. $v_i = -25$ m/s
Section 11.3 Assessment, page 348
8. $a = 0.83$ m/s^2

Chapter 12
Math Practice, page 367
2. $a = 2$ m/s^2
4. $m = 50$ kg
Section 12.2 Assessment, page 369
6. Deceleration = 11 m/s^2

Chapter 14
Math Practice, page 415
2. Power = 7.5 W
Section 14.1 Assessment, page 416
8. Power = 50 W
Math Practice, page 425
2. IMA = 10
Section 14.3 Assessment, page 426
8. Efficiency = 80%

Chapter 15
Math Practice, page 448
2. 440 kJ
Section 15.1 Assessment, page 452
8. PE = 44 kJ
Math Practice, page 458
2. PE = 2100 J; $v = 7.7$ m/s
Section 15.2 Assessment, page 459
10. $h = 0.20$ m

Chapter 16
Math Practice, page 477
2. $Q = 34$ kJ
4. $\Delta T = 10.0°C$
Section 16.1 Assessment, page 478
10. $Q = 7.8$ kJ

Chapter 17
Math Practice, page 506
2. Speed = 0.4 m/s
4. Wavelength = 0.5 km
Section 17.2 Assessment, page 507
10. Period = 0.5 s

Chapter 18
Math Practice, page 535
2. Wavelength = 440 m
Section 18.1 Assessment, page 538
10. Wavelength = 0.190 m

Chapter 20
Math Practice, page 611
2. $I = 0.32$ amps
Section 20.3 Assessment, page 613
8. $I = 0.85$ amps

Glossary

A

abrasion a form of mechanical weathering that occurs when rocks scrape or grind against one another (p. 710)

absolute age the time that has passed since a rock formed (p. 734)

absolute brightness a description of how bright a star really is; a characteristic property of a star that does not depend on the star's distance from Earth (p. 837)

absolute zero a temperature of 0 kelvins (pp. 78, 475)

absorption lines a set of dark lines that show frequencies at which light has been absorbed from a star's bright spectrum (p. 837)

acceleration the rate at which velocity changes (p. 342)

accretion the process of adding mass in the formation of the planets by collisions between planetesimals (p. 819)

accuracy the closeness of a measurement to the true value of what is measured (p. 19)

acid a compound that produces hydronium ions (H_3O^+) when dissolved in water; a proton donor (p. 241)

actual mechanical advantage the ratio of the output force to the input force in a machine (p. 422)

air mass a large body of air that has consistent properties throughout, such as temperature and moisture content, at a given altitude (p. 765)

air pressure the pressure caused by the weight of a column of air in Earth's atmosphere (p. 748)

air resistance fluid friction acting on an object moving through the air (p. 360)

alkali metals the elements in Group 1A of the periodic table, not including hydrogen (p. 140)

alkaline earth metals the elements in Group 2A of the periodic table (p. 141)

alloy a mixture of two or more elements, at least one of which is a metal, that has the characteristic properties of a metal (p. 178)

alluvial fan a fan-shaped deposit of sediment, on land formed as a stream flows out of the mountains and onto a plain (p. 716)

alpha particle a positively charged particle, emitted by certain radioactive nuclei, made up of two protons and two neutrons; a helium nucleus (p. 293)

alternating current (AC) a flow of electric charge that regularly reverses its direction (p. 604)

amino acids compounds that contain both carboxyl and amino functional groups (p. 280)

amplitude the maximum displacement of a medium from the rest position (p. 507)

amplitude modulation (AM) a method of transmitting a radio signal in which the amplitude of the carrier wave varies while its frequency remains the same (p. 541)

analog signal a smoothly varying signal produced by continuously changing the voltage or current in a circuit (p. 619)

angle of incidence the angle an incident ray makes with a line perpendicular to a surface it strikes (p. 570)

angle of reflection the angle a reflected ray makes with a line perpendicular to a surface it strikes (p. 570)

angle of refraction the angle a light ray makes with the normal after it enters a new medium at an angle (p. 575)

anion an ion with a negative charge (p. 160)

anticyclone a weather system with a swirling center of high air pressure (p. 769)

antinode a point of maximum displacement midway between two nodes in a standing wave (p. 512)

apparent brightness the brightness of a star as it appears from Earth (p. 836)

aquifer a permeable rock layer that is saturated with water (p. 707)

Archimedes' principle the equivalence of the buoyant force on an object and the weight of the fluid displaced by the object (p. 401)

aromatic hydrocarbons hydrocarbons that contain a ring structure similar to benzene (p. 266)

asteroid belt region between the orbits of Mars and Jupiter where most asteroids in the solar system are found (p. 809)

asteroids small, rocky solar-system bodies, most of which are found orbiting the sun in a region between Mars and Jupiter (p. 809)

asthenosphere a layer of softer, weaker rock beneath Earth's lithosphere, which can flow slowly (p. 662)

astigmatism an eye condition in which objects at any distance appear blurry because of the distorted shape of the cornea (p. 592)

astronomical unit (AU) a unit of distance that equals the average distance from Earth to the sun; 149,598,000 kilometers (p. 793)

astronomy the study of the universe beyond Earth (p. 4)

atmosphere the layer of gases that surrounds Earth (p. 747)

atom the smallest particle of an element (p. 39)

atomic mass unit (amu) one twelfth the mass of a carbon-12 atom (p. 134)

atomic number a unique number for each element that equals the number of protons in an atom of that element (p. 110)

aurora a colorful display of light in the ionosphere, produced when charged particles from the sun are attracted to Earth's magnetic poles (p. 751)

average speed the total distance traveled divided by the time it takes to travel that distance (p. 333)

Glossary

B

background radiation nuclear radiation that occurs naturally in the environment (p. 296)

barometer an instrument used to measure air pressure (p. 748)

barred-spiral galaxy a spiral galaxy in which spiral arms extend outward from a bar running through the center of the galaxy (p. 848)

base a compound that produces hydroxide ions (OH^-) when dissolved in water; a proton acceptor (p. 242)

batholith the largest type of intrusive igneous rock mass (p. 696)

battery a device that converts chemical energy into electrical energy (p. 606)

beta particle an electron emitted by an unstable nucleus (p. 294)

big bang theory the theory of the beginning of the universe in an instant, billions of years ago, in an enormous explosion (p. 854)

binary star a star system with two stars that revolve around each other (p. 847)

biology the study of life and life processes (p. 4)

biomass energy the chemical energy stored in living things (p. 464)

black hole an object whose surface gravity is so great that not even electromagnetic waves can escape from it (p. 844)

boiling point the temperature at which a substance boils; the temperature at which vapor pressure is equal to atmospheric pressure (p. 47)

Boyle's law the inverse variation of the volume of a gas with its pressure if the temperature and the number of particles are constant (p. 79)

buffer a solution that is resistant to large changes in pH (p. 248)

buoyancy the ability of a fluid to exert an upward force on an object placed in it (p. 400)

buoyant force an upward force acting on an object in a fluid (p. 400)

C

caldera huge depression at the top of a volcano created when the central vent and magma chamber collapse after an eruption (p. 691)

calorimeter instrument used to measure thermal energy released or absorbed during a chemical or physical change (p. 478)

camera an optical instrument that records an image of an object (p. 582)

carbohydrate a compound composed of carbon, hydrogen, and oxygen in which the ratio of hydrogen to oxygen atoms is 2 : 1 (p. 278)

catalyst a substance that affects the rate of a chemical reaction without being used up in the reaction (p. 215)

cation an ion with a positive charge (p. 160)

central heating system a heating system that heats many rooms from one central location (p. 489)

centripetal force a force that continuously changes the direction of an object to make it move in a circle (p. 381)

chain reaction a series of fission reactions triggered by neutrons released during the fission of a nucleus (p. 311)

Charles's law the direct proportion of the volume of a gas to its temperature (in kelvins) if the pressure and the number of particles of the gas are constant (p. 78)

chemical bond the force that holds atoms or ions together as a unit (p. 160)

chemical change change that occurs when a substance reacts and forms one or more new substances (p. 56)

chemical energy the energy stored in chemical bonds (pp. 206, 451)

chemical equation a representation of a chemical reaction in which the reactants and products are expressed as formulas (p. 193)

chemical formula notation that shows what elements a compound contains and the ratio of the atoms or ions of these elements in the compound (p. 161)

chemical property any property that produces a change in the composition of matter (p. 54)

chemical weathering the process in which rock is broken down by chemical reactions (p. 710)

chemistry the study of the composition, structure, properties, and reactions of matter (p. 4)

chromosphere the middle layer of the sun's atmosphere, just outside the photosphere (p. 831)

cinder cone a small, steep-sided volcano formed from a combination of ash and cinders (p. 693)

circuit breaker a switch that opens when the current in a circuit is too high (p. 612)

cirque a large bowl-shaped valley carved out of a mountainside by a glacier (p. 720)

cirrus clouds thin, white, wispy clouds, often with a feathery or veil-like appearance (p. 763)

clastic rocks sedimentary rocks that form from the broken fragments of other rocks (p. 672)

cleavage a mineral's tendency to split along regular, well-defined planes (p. 668)

climate the long-term weather conditions of a place or region (p. 778)

cloud a dense, visible mass of tiny water droplets or ice crystals that are suspended in the atmosphere (p. 761)

coefficients numbers that appear before a formula in a chemical equation to show the relative proportions of each reactant and product (p. 194)

coherent light light waves having the same wavelength, with the crests and troughs lined up (p. 560)

cold front a front that occurs when a cold air mass overtakes a warm air mass (p. 767)

colloid a mixture that contains some particles that are intermediate in size between the small particles in a solution and the larger particles in a suspension (p. 44)

combustion reaction a chemical reaction in which a substance reacts rapidly with oxygen, often producing heat and light (p. 204)

comet a mass of rock, dust, and ice that partially vaporizes when it passes near the sun (p. 815)

complementary colors of light any two colors of light that combine to form white light (p. 552)

complementary colors of pigments any two colors of pigments that combine to make black pigment (p. 553)

composite volcano a volcano that forms from a combination of lava and ash (p. 693)

compound a substance that is made from two or more simpler substances and can be broken down into those simpler substances (p. 40)

compound machine a combination of two or more simple machines that operate together (p. 435)

compression an area of a longitudinal wave where the particles of the medium are close together (p. 502)

computer a programmable device that can store and process information (p. 622)

concave lens a lens that is curved inward at the center and is thickest at the outside edges (p. 576)

concave mirror a mirror that is curved inward (p. 572)

concentration the amount of solute dissolved in a certain amount of solvent (p. 238)

condensation the phase change in which a substance changes from a gas or vapor to a liquid (p. 90)

conduction the transfer of thermal with no overall transfer of matter, within a material or between materials that are touching (p. 479); the transfer of electric charge by direct contact with a conductor (p. 602)

conductivity a material's ability to allow heat or electric charges to flow (p. 46)

cones light-sensitive neurons in the retina that detect color (p. 589)

constant acceleration a steady change in velocity (p. 345)

constellation a group of stars that appears to form a pattern as seen from Earth (p. 846)

constructive interference the interaction among two or more waves in which displacements combine to produce a wave with a larger displacement (p. 511)

continental drift the process in which the continents move slowly across Earth's surface (p. 677)

continental glacier a thick sheet of ice that covers a large area of a continent or large island (p. 719)

continental shelf the gently sloping plain that forms an apron of shallow water along the edges of most continents (p. 726)

controlled experiment an experiment in which only one variable, the manipulated variable, is deliberately changed at a time (p. 8)

convection the transfer of thermal energy when particles of a fluid move from one place to another (p. 480)

convection current circulation of a fluid in a loop as the fluid alternately heats up and cools down (p. 481)

convection zone the region inside the sun where thermal engergy is transferred outward mainly by convection currents (p. 831)

convergent boundary a boundary at which tectonic plates collide (p. 682)

conversion factor a ratio of equivalent measurements that is used to convert a quantity from one unit to another (p. 18)

convex lens a lens that is curved outward at the center and is thinnest at the outside edges (p. 576)

convex mirror a mirror that is curved outward (p. 573)

core the dense sphere at Earth's center, made mostly of iron and nickel (p. 663); the central region of the sun where nuclear fusion occurs (p. 830)

Coriolis effect the change that Earth's rotation causes in the motion of objects (p. 759)

cornea the transparent outer coating of the eye (p. 588)

corona the outermost layer of the sun's atmosphere, extending far above the chromosphere (p. 831)

covalent bond a chemical bond in which two atoms share a pair of valence electrons (p. 166)

crater a bowl-shaped pit at the top of the central vent in a volcano (p. 691); a round depression in the surface of a planet, moon, asteroid, or comet, caused by the impact of a meteoroid (p. 797)

crest the highest point of a transverse wave (p. 501)

critical angle the angle of incidence that produces an angle of refraction equal to 90 degrees (p. 578)

critical mass the smallest possible mass of a fissionable material that can sustain a chain reaction (p. 311)

crust the rocky outer layer of Earth (p. 661)

crystals solids whose particles are arranged in a lattice structure (p. 162)

cumulus clouds puffy white clouds, usually with flat bottoms, that look like piles of cotton balls (p. 763)

cyclone a weather system with a center of low air pressure (p. 769)

Glossary

D

dark matter matter that does not emit radiation that astronomers can detect (p. 855)

decibel a unit that compares the intensities of different sounds (p. 515)

decomposition reaction a chemical reaction in which a compound breaks down into two or more simpler substances (p. 200)

deflation the process that occurs when wind picks up and removes surface material (p. 723)

delta a mass of sediment deposited at the mouth of a river where the river enters a large body of water (p. 716)

density the ratio of a material's mass to its volume (p. 17)

density currents currents caused by differences in the density of ocean water (p. 727)

deposition the phase change in which a gas or vapor changes directly into a solid without first changing into a liquid (p. 91); the placement of sediment that has been transported from another location (p. 713)

desert an extremely dry region (p. 780)

destructive interference the interaction among two or more waves in which displacements combine to produce a wave with a smaller displacement (p. 511)

dew point the temperature at which air becomes saturated with water vapor (p. 761)

diffraction the bending of a wave as it moves around an obstacle or passes through a narrow opening (p. 510)

diffuse reflection reflection that occurs when parallel light waves strike a rough, uneven surface and reflect in many different directions (p. 547)

digital signal a signal that encodes information as a string of 1's and 0's (p. 619)

dike a structure formed when magma hardens in a crack that cuts across rock layers (p. 696)

diode a solid-state component with an n-type semiconductor joined to a p-type semiconductor (p. 621)

direct current (DC) a flow of electric charge in only one direction (p. 604)

direct proportion a relationship between two variables in which their ratio is constant (p. 23)

dispersion the process of dissolving by breaking into smaller pieces (p. 230), the process in which white light separates into colors (p. 551)

dissociation the separation of ions in an ionic compound as the compound dissolves (p. 229)

distance the length of the path between two points (p. 329)

distillation a process that separates the substances in a solution based on their boiling points (p. 50)

divergent boundary a boundary at which tectonic plates move away from each other (p. 682)

Doppler effect a change in sound frequency caused by motion of the sound source, motion of the listener, or both (p. 516)

double-replacement reaction a chemical reaction in which two compounds exchange positive ions and form two new compounds (p. 203)

dunes deposits formed from windblown sand (p. 724)

E

earthquake a movement of Earth's crust that occurs when rocks in the crust suddenly shift, releasing stored energy (p. 684)

eclipse event that occurs when the shadow of one body in space, such as a planet or moon, falls on another (p. 799)

ecliptic plane the plane in space containing Earth's orbit (p. 792)

efficiency the percentage of the work input that becomes work output in a machine (p. 425)

elastic potential energy the potential energy of an object that is stretched or compressed (p. 450)

electric charge a property that causes subatomic particles such as protons and electrons to attract or repel one another (p. 600)

electric circuit a complete path through which electric charge can flow (p. 609)

electric current a continuous flow of electric charge (p. 604)

electric field a field in a region of space that exerts electric forces on charged particles; a field produced by electric charges or by changing magnetic fields (pp. 533, 602)

electric force the attraction or repulsion between electrically charged objects (p. 601)

electric motor a device that uses an electromagnet to turn an axle (p. 639)

electric power the rate at which electrical energy is converted to another form of energy (p. 611)

electrical conductor a material through which electric charge can flow easily (p. 605)

electrical energy the energy associated with electric charges (p. 452)

electrical insulator a material through which charge cannot flow easily (p. 605)

electrolyte a compound that produces ions when it dissolves (p. 249)

electromagnet a solenoid with a ferromagnetic core (p. 637)

electromagnetic energy a form of energy consisting of changing electric and magnetic fields (p. 452)

electromagnetic force a force associated with charged particles, which has two aspects, electric force and magnetic force (pp. 378, 635)

electromagnetic induction the process of generating a current by moving an electrical conductor relative to a magnetic field (p. 642)

electromagnetic radiation the transfer of energy by electromagnetic waves (p. 533)

electromagnetic spectrum the full range of electromagnetic radiation (p. 540)

electromagnetic wave a transverse wave consisting of changing electric and changing magnetic fields (p. 533)

electron a negatively charged subatomic particle that is found in the space outside the nucleus of an atom (p. 108)

electron cloud a visual model of the most likely locations for the electrons in an atom (p. 116)

electron configuration the arrangement of electrons in the orbitals of an atom (p. 118)

electron dot diagram a diagram of an atom, ion or molecule in which each dot represents a valence electron (p. 158)

electronics the science of using electric currents to process or transmit information (p. 618)

electronic signal information sent as patterns in the controlled flow of electrons through a circuit (p. 618)

element a substance that cannot be broken down into simpler substances (p. 39)

elliptical galaxies spherical or oval-shaped galaxies with no trace of spiral arms and very little gas or dust between stars (p. 848)

El Niño the periodic warming of water in the central and eastern Pacific Ocean (p. 781)

endothermic a description of a change in which a system absorbs energy from its surroundings (p. 86)

endothermic reaction a chemical reaction that absorbs energy from its surroundings (p. 209)

energy the ability to do work (p. 447)

energy conservation the practice of finding ways to use less energy or to use energy more efficiently (p. 466)

energy conversion the process of changing energy from one form to another (p. 454)

energy levels the possible energies that electrons in an atom can have (p. 114)

enzyme a protein that acts as a catalyst for reactions in cells (p. 284)

epicenter the point on Earth's surface directly above the focus of an earthquake (p. 686)

equilibrium a state in which the forward and reverse paths of a physical or chemical change take place at the same rate (p. 216)

equinox a day that marks the beginning of spring or autumn; a day on which the length of daylight and darkness are approximately equal (p. 754)

era a major stage in Earth's geologic history (p. 734)

erosion the process that wears down and carries away rock and soil (p. 709)

evaporation the process that changes a substance from a liquid to a gas at temperatures below the substance's boiling point (p. 89)

exothermic a description of a change in which a system releases energy to its surroundings (p. 86)

exothermic reaction a chemical reaction that releases energy to its surroundings (p. 208)

external combustion engine a heat engine in which the fuel burns outside the engine (p. 486)

extinct a description of a type of organism that is no longer found living on Earth (p. 733)

extrusive rock an igneous rock that forms at Earth's surface (p. 671)

F

farsightedness an eye condition that causes nearby objects to be blurry (p. 592)

fault a break in Earth's crust (p. 685)

ferromagnetic material a material that can be magnetized because it contains magnetic domains (p. 632)

filtration a process that separates materials based on the size of their particles (p. 50)

fission a nuclear reaction in which an atomic nucleus is split into two smaller parts (p. 309)

flammability a material's ability to burn in the presence of oxygen (p. 54)

flood plain the flat area along a stream that is covered only during floods (p. 716)

fluid a substance or mixture that flows and has no shape of its own (p. 591)

fluid friction a friction force that opposes the motion of an object through a fluid (p. 360)

fluorescence a process in which phosphorescent material converts radiation into visible light (p. 559)

focal point the point at which light rays parallel to the axis of a mirror or lens meet or appear to meet (p. 572)

focus the location beneath Earth's surface where an earthquake begins (p. 686)

fog a cloud that is touching or is near to the ground (p. 762)

fold a bend in layers of rock (p. 685)

foliated rock a metamorphic rock with crystals arranged in parallel bands (p. 674)

force a push or a pull that acts on an object (p. 356)

fossil the preserved remains or traces of a living organism (p. 732)

Glossary

fossil fuels rich deposits of hydrocarbon mixtures that formed from the remains of organisms (p. 267, p. 462)

fracture the way a mineral breaks, determined by the mineral's crystal structure (p. 668)

frame of reference a system of objects that are not moving with respect to one another (p. 328)

free fall the movement of an object toward Earth because of gravity (p. 343)

frequency the number of complete cycles per unit time for a periodic motion (p. 504)

frequency modulation (FM) a method of transmitting a radio signal in which the frequency of the carrier wave varies while its amplitude remains the same (p. 541)

friction a force that opposes the motion of objects that touch as they move past each other (p. 359)

front a sharply defined boundary that forms when two unlike air masses meet (p. 767)

fulcrum the fixed point a lever rotates around (p. 428)

functional group an atom or group of atoms that determines the properties of an organic compound (p. 272)

fuse a device that prevents overheating due to current overload in a circuit (p. 612)

fusion a nuclear reaction in which the nuclei of two atoms combine to form a larger nucleus (p. 315)

G

galaxy a huge group of stars, star systems, star clusters, dust, and gas bound together by gravity (p. 848)

galvanometer a device that uses an electromagnet to measure small amounts of current (p. 638)

gamma ray a penetrating form of radiation emitted by an unstable nucleus (p. 294)

gas the state of matter in which a material has neither a definite shape nor a definite volume (p. 70)

gas giant a large, massive planet (such as Jupiter, Saturn, Uranus, or Neptune) that is composed mainly of hydrogen and helium (p. 811)

generator a device that converts mechanical energy into electrical energy by the relative motion of a coil of wire with respect to a magnetic field (p. 643)

geocentric a description of a model of the solar system in which all of the planets revolve around Earth (p. 791)

geologists scientists who study Earth and the processes that have shaped Earth over time (p. 660)

geology the study of the origin, history, and structure of Earth (p. 4)

geothermal energy thermal energy beneath Earth's surface (p. 464)

giant a large, massive, bright star that is somewhat smaller and fainter than a supergiant (p. 839)

glacier a large mass of ice and snow moving on land (p. 706)

global warming an increase in the temperature of Earth's lower atmosphere, caused in part by increased levels of carbon dioxide or water vapor (p. 782)

global wind a wind that blows over long distances from a specific direction (p. 758)

globular cluster a large spherical-shaped group of older stars that usually lacks sufficient amounts of gas and dust to form new stars (p. 847)

gravitational force an attractive force that acts between any two objects (p. 380)

gravitational potential energy potential energy that depends upon an object's height above a reference point (p. 449)

gravity the attraction between any two objects because of their masses (p. 361)

greenhouse effect a process in which gases in Earth's atmosphere, such as water vapor and carbon dioxide, allow visible light to pass through but absorb reradiated infrared radiation that warms the lower atmosphere (p. 755)

ground state a state in which all the electrons in an atom have the lowest possible energies (p. 118)

grounding the transfer of excess charge through a conductor to Earth (p. 613)

groundwater the fresh water found beneath Earth's surface within cracks and among particles of rock and soil (p. 704)

group a column of elements in a periodic table (p. 131)

H

half-life the time required for one half of a sample of a radioactive isotope to decay (p. 299)

halogens the elements in Group 7A of the periodic table (p. 144)

hardness the resistance of a mineral to scratching (p. 668)

heat the transfer of thermal energy from one object to another because of a difference in temperature (p. 474)

heat engine any device that converts thermal energy into work (p. 483)

heat of fusion the energy a substance must absorb in order to change from a solid to a liquid (p. 86)

heat of vaporization the energy a substance must absorb in order to change from a liquid to a gas (p. 88)

heat pump a device that uses work to transfer thermal energy from a colder area to a warmer area (p. 490)

heliocentric a description of a model of the solar system in which Earth and other planets revolve around the sun (p. 791)

hertz (Hz) the unit of measure for frequency, equal to one cycle per second (p. 504)

heterogeneous mixture a type of mixture in which the parts of the mixture are noticeably different from one another (p. 41)

homogeneous mixture a type of mixture in which the substances are so evenly distributed that it is difficult to distinguish one substance in the mixture from another (p. 42)

horsepower (hp) a common unit of power, equal to about 746 watts (p. 416)

hot spot a region where a rising column of magma extends from beneath the lithosphere to reach Earth's surface (p. 693)

H-R diagram the Hertzsprung-Russell diagram, a graph of the surface temperature versus absolute brightness of a sample of stars (p. 838)

Hubble's Law the direct variation of the speed at which a galaxy is moving away from Earth with its distance from Earth (p. 853)

humidity the amount of water vapor in a given volume of air (p. 760)

hurricane a large tropical cyclone with winds of at least 119 kilometers per hour (74 miles per hour) (p. 771)

hydraulic action the process by which ocean waves erode rock (p. 728)

hydraulic system a device that uses a pressurized fluid acting on pistons of different sizes to increase force (p. 395)

hydrocarbon an organic compound that contains only the elements hydrogen and carbon (p. 264)

hydroelectric energy energy obtained from flowing water (p. 463)

hydrogen fuel cell a cell that generates electricity from a controlled reaction between hydrogen and oxygen (p. 608)

hypothesis a proposed answer to a question (p. 8)

I

ice ages periods when climates are colder than usual and glaciers cover a large portion of Earth's surface (p. 781)

ideal mechanical advantage (IMA) the mechanical advantage of a machine in the absence of friction (p. 423)

igneous rock rock that forms from magma or lava (p. 671)

image a copy of an object formed by reflected or refracted rays of light (p. 547)

impermeable a description of a material through which water cannot easily pass (p. 707)

incandescent a description of an object hot enough to glow (p. 558)

inclined plane a slanted surface along which a force moves an object to a different elevation (p. 431)

index fossil a fossil of a species that is easily identified, occurred over a large area, and lived for a well-defined period of time (p. 733)

index of refraction the ratio of the speed of light in a vacuum to the speed of light in a medium (p. 575)

indicator a substance that changes color in the presence of an acid or a base (p. 241)

induction the transfer of charge without contact between materials (p. 603)

inertia the tendency of an object to resist a change in its motion (p. 364)

inorganic a description of a material that is not organic (p. 665)

input arm the distance between the fulcrum in a lever and the input force (p. 428)

input distance the distance through which the input force acts in a machine (p. 419)

input force the force exerted on a machine (p. 419)

instantaneous speed the rate at which an object is moving at a given moment in time (p. 334)

integrated circuit a thin slice of silicon that contains many solid-state components; a microchip (p. 622)

intensity the rate at which a wave's energy flows through a given unit of area (pp. 515, 538)

interference the interaction of two or more waves that combine in a region of overlap (p. 510)

internal combustion engine a heat engine in which the fuel burns inside the engine (p. 487)

intrusive rock an igneous rock that forms underground from hardened magma (p. 671)

inverse proportion a relationship in which the product of two variables is a constant when all other variables are held constant (p. 23)

ion an atom or group of atoms that has a positive or negative charge (p. 159)

ionic bond the force that holds cations and anions together (p. 160)

ionization the process by which neutral molecules gain or lose electrons (p. 230)

ionosphere a region of charged particles, or ions, in Earth's atmosphere that overlaps the lower thermosphere (p. 751)

iris the colored part at the front of the eye, which expands and contracts to control the amount of light entering the eye (p. 589)

irregular galaxy a galaxy with a disorganized appearance (p. 848)

isobar a line on a weather map that connects points of equal air pressure (p. 777)

isotherm a line on a weather map that connects points of equal air temperature (p. 777)

isomers organic compounds with the same molecular formula but with different structural formulas (p. 265)

isotopes atoms of a given element that have different numbers of neutrons and different mass numbers (p. 112)

Glossary

J

jet stream a belt of high-speed wind in the upper troposphere (p. 759)

joule (J) the SI unit of work, equal to 1 newton-meter (p. 414)

K

kinetic energy the energy an object has due to its motion (pp. 71, 447)

Kuiper belt a wide belt beyond Pluto's orbit where objects mostly made of ice and rock orbit the sun (p. 815)

L

land breeze a local wind that occurs when cooler air over land moves toward water (p. 757)

laser a device that generates a beam of coherent light (p. 560)

lava magma that flows over Earth's surface (p. 671)

lava plateau a high, level region of hardened lava (p. 696)

law of conservation of charge law stating that the total electric charge in an isolated system is constant; electric charge is never created or destroyed (p. 602)

law of conservation of momentum law stating that the total momentum of a system does not change if no net force acts on the system (p. 376)

law of superposition law stating that in rock layers that are undisturbed, younger rocks lie above older rocks, and the oldest rocks are at the bottom (p. 733)

length the straight-line distance between two points (p. 16)

lens an object made of any thin, transparent material that has one or two curved surfaces that can refract light (p. 576)

lever a rigid bar that is free to move around a fixed point (p. 428)

lift an upward force due to a pressure difference between the top and bottom of a wing (p. 396)

lightning a sudden naturally occurring electrical discharge in the atmosphere (p. 770)

light-year the distance that light travels in a vacuum in a year, about 9.5 trillion kilometers (p. 834)

linear graph a graph in which the displayed data form a straight line (p. 347)

liquid the state of matter in which a material has a definite volume but not a definite shape (p. 69)

lithosphere a layer of relatively cool, rigid rock that includes the uppermost part of the mantle as well as Earth's crust (p. 662)

local wind a wind that blows over a short distance (p. 757)

loess a deposit formed from windblown dust (p. 724)

longitudinal wave a wave in which the vibration of the medium is parallel to the direction the wave travels (p. 502)

longshore drift the process by which ocean waves move sand along a shore (p. 729)

loudness a physical response to the intensity of sound, modified by physical factors (p. 515)

luminous a description of an object that gives off its own light (p. 558)

luster the way a mineral's surface reflects light (p. 667)

M

machine a device that changes a force (p. 417)

magma a mixture of molten rock and gases, including water vapor, which forms underground (p. 671)

magma chamber pocket in which magma collects before a volcanic eruption (p. 691)

magnetic domain a region that has a large number of atoms with aligned magnetic fields (p. 632)

magnetic field a field in a region of space that exerts magnetic forces; a field produced by magnets, by changing electric fields, or by moving charges (pp. 533, 631)

magnetic force the force a magnetic field exerts on a magnet, on a ferromagnetic material, or on a moving electric charge (p. 630)

magnetic pole a region on a magnet where the force produced by the magnet is strongest (p. 630)

magnetosphere the area surrounding Earth that is influenced by Earth's magnetic field (p. 632)

main sequence a diagonal band on the H-R diagram, which represents about 90% of all stars (p. 839)

malleability the ability of a solid to be hammered without shattering (p. 46)

manipulated variable the variable that causes a change in another variable (p. 8)

mantle a thick layer of hot but solid rock beneath Earth's crust (p. 662)

maria the low, flat plains of basalt on the moon formed by ancient lunar lava flows (p. 797)

mass the amount of matter in an object (p. 16); a measure of the inertia of an object, which depends on the amount of matter the object contains (p. 365)

mass extinction a boundary between geologic eras when many different kinds of organisms became extinct within a relatively short time (p. 735)

mass movement the downward movement of rock and soil due to gravity, including landslides, mudflows, creep, and slumping (p. 712)

mass number the sum of the number of protons and neutrons in the nucleus of an atom (p. 110)

meander a looplike bend in a river formed when slow-moving water deposits sediment on the inside curve of the river (p. 716)

mechanical advantage the number of times that a machine increases an input force (p. 421)

mechanical energy the energy associated with the motion and position of everyday objects (p. 450)

mechanical wave a disturbance in matter that carries energy from one place to another (p. 500)

mechanical weathering the process of physically breaking rock into smaller fragments (p. 710)

medium the material through which a wave travels (p. 500)

melting point the temperature at which a substance changes from solid to liquid (p. 47)

mesosphere the lower portion of Earth's mantle (p. 662); the layer of Earth's atmosphere immediately above the stratosphere (p. 750)

metals elements that are good conductors of heat and electric current (p. 135)

metallic bond the attraction between a metal cation and the shared electrons that surround it (p. 176)

metalloids elements with properties that fall between those of metals and nonmetals (p. 136)

metamorphic rock rock that has been changed by temperature, pressure, or reactions with hot water (p. 674)

meteoroid a chunk of rock that moves through the solar system (p. 797)

meteorologist scientist who studies and tries to predict weather (p. 774)

microscope an optical instrument that uses lenses to provide enlarged images of very small, near objects (p. 584)

mid-ocean ridge a chain of underwater mountains (p. 678)

mineral a naturally occurring, inorganic solid with a crystal structure and a definite chemical composition (p. 665)

mirage a false or distorted image (p. 548)

model a representation of an object or event (p. 10)

molarity the number of moles of a dissolved solute per liter of solution (p. 239)

molar mass the mass of one mole of a substance (p. 196)

mole an amount of a substance that contains approximately 6.02×10^{23} particles of the substance (p. 195)

molecule a neutral group of atoms that are joined together by one or more covalent bonds (p. 166)

momentum the product of an object's mass and its velocity (p. 374)

monomer a small organic molecule that joins with other monomers to form a polymer (p. 275)

monsoon a wind system that shows a seasonal reversal of direction (p. 759)

moon a relatively small natural body in space that revolves around a planet (p. 792)

moraines mounds of till formed at the downhill end of a glacier and along its sides (p. 721)

N

neap tide a tide at the first or last quarter moon, when there is the least change between daily high and low tides (p. 801)

nearsightedness an eye condition in which distant objects are blurry (p. 590)

nebula a large cloud of gas and dust spread out over a large volume of space (p. 840)

net force the overall force acting on an object after all the forces are combined (p. 357)

network solid a solid in which all the atoms are linked by covalent bonds (p. 263)

neutralization a chemical reaction between an acid and a base (p. 244)

neutron a neutral subatomic particle that is found in the nucleus of an atom (p. 109)

neutron star the dense core left after a high-mass star has exploded as a supernova (p. 844)

newton (N) the SI unit for force, equal to the force that causes a 1-kilogram mass to accelerate at a rate of 1 meter per second squared ($1 \text{ N} = 1 \text{ kg} \cdot \text{m/s}^2$) (p. 357)

noble gases the elements in Group 8A of the periodic table (p. 145)

node a point on a standing wave that has no displacement from the rest position (p. 512)

nonlinear graph a graph in which the displayed data form a curved line (p. 348)

nonmetals elements that are poor conductors of heat and electric current (p. 136)

nonrenewable energy resource a source of energy that exists in limited quantities and, once used, cannot be replaced except over the course of millions of years (p. 462)

nuclear energy the energy stored in atomic nuclei (p. 452)

nuclear radiation charged particles and electro-magnetic waves that are emitted from the nuclei of radioisotopes (p. 293)

nucleic acid a large, nitrogen-containing polymer, found mainly in the nuclei of cells (p. 279)

nucleus the dense, positively charged mass located in the center of an atom (p. 105)

Glossary

O

observation information obtained through the senses (p. 8)

occluded front a front that occurs when a warm air mass is caught between two cooler air masses (p. 768)

Ohm's law the relationship of voltage, current, and resistance: $V = IR$ (p. 607)

Oort cloud thought to be a very sparse sphere of comets encircling the solar system out to a distance of about 50,000 AU (p. 815)

opaque a description of a material that either absorbs or reflects all of the light that strikes it so nothing can be seen through it (p. 547)

orbital a region of space around the nucleus where an electron is likely to be found (p. 117)

organic compounds compounds that contain carbon and hydrogen, often combined with a few other elements such as oxygen or nitrogen (p. 262)

output arm the distance between the fulcrum in a lever and the output force (p. 428)

output distance the distance an output force acts through in a machine (p. 420)

output force the force exerted by a machine (p. 420)

oxbow lake a lake formed when a river forms a new path by cutting off a meander loop from the rest of the river (p. 716)

oxidation-reduction (redox) reaction a chemical reaction in which electrons are transferred from one reactant to another (p. 204)

ozone layer a region of ozone concentration in the stratosphere (p. 750)

P

Pangaea an ancient supercontinent formed about 300 million years ago, which later gave rise to today's continents (p. 677)

parallax an apparent change in position of an object with respect to a distant background when viewed from different locations (p. 835)

parallel circuit an electric circuit with two or more paths through which charge can flow (p. 610)

pascal (Pa) the SI unit of pressure, equal to 1 newton per square meter (N/m^2) (p. 391)

penumbra a region of the moon's shadow that surrounds the umbra and is less dark than the umbra (p. 800)

period a row in a periodic table of elements (p. 131); the time required for one complete cycle of a periodic motion (p. 504); a unit of geologic time into which geologists divide eras (p. 734)

periodic law the pattern of repeating properties displayed by elements in the periodic table (p. 131)

periodic motion any motion that repeats at regular time intervals (p. 504)

periodic table an arrangement of elements in columns, based on a set of properties that repeat from row to row (p. 127)

permeable a description of a material that water can easily pass through (p. 707)

pH a measure of the hydronium ion concentration of a solution (p. 247)

phase change a reversible physical change that occurs when a substance changes from one state of matter to another (p. 84)

phases the different shapes of the illuminated side of the moon as seen from Earth (p. 798)

phosphor a solid material that emits light by fluorescence (p. 559)

photoelectric effect the emission of electrons from a metal caused by light striking the metal (p. 537)

photon a packet of electromagnetic energy (p. 537)

photosphere the thin innermost layer of the sun's atmosphere, which is the visible surface of the sun (p. 831)

photosynthesis a process in which plants chemically combine carbon dioxide and water into carbohydrates, a process requiring light and chlorophyll (p. 282)

physical change a change that occurs when some properties of a material change, but the substances in the material stay the same (p. 51)

physical property any characteristic of a material that can be observed or measured without changing the composition of the substances in the material (p. 45)

physics the study of matter and energy and the interactions between the two through forces and motion (p. 4)

pigment a material that selectively absorbs certain colors of light and reflects other colors (p. 553)

pipe a narrow vertical channel through which magma rises to Earth's surface (p. 691)

pitch the frequency of a sound as a listener perceives it (p. 515)

plane mirror a mirror with a flat surface (p. 571)

planetary nebula a glowing cloud of gas surrounding a dying low-mass star (p. 842)

planetesimals asteroid-sized bodies in the protoplanetary disk from which the planets formed by accretion (p. 819)

plasma a state of matter in which atoms have been stripped of their electrons (p. 315)

plate tectonics the theory that pieces of Earth's lithosphere, called plates, move about slowly on top of the asthenosphere (p. 676)

plucking a process in which glacial ice widens cracks in bedrock beneath a glacier, which carries away the loosened pieces of rock (p. 720)

polar covalent bond a covalent bond in which electrons are not shared equally (p. 168)

polarized light a type of light including light with waves that vibrate in only one plane (p. 548)

polar zones the regions from latitude 66.5° north to the north pole, and from latitude 66.5° south to the south pole, which are generally cold (p. 753)

polyatomic ion a covalently bonded group of atoms that has a positive or negative charge and acts as a unit (p. 172)

polymer a large molecule formed when many smaller molecules are linked together by covalent bonds (p. 275)

potential difference voltage, or the difference in electrical potential energy between two places in an electric field (p. 606)

potential energy energy that is stored as a result of position or shape (p. 448)

power the rate of doing work (p. 414)

precipitate a solid that forms and separates from a liquid mixture (p. 57)

precision a gauge of how exact a measurement is (p. 19)

pressure the result of a force distributed over an area (pp. 75, 390)

primary colors three specific colors that can be combined in varying intensities to create millions of colors (p. 552)

products new substances formed as a result of a chemical reaction (p. 192)

projectile motion the curved path of an object in free fall after it is given an initial forward velocity (p. 362)

prominences huge loops of gas that erupt from sunspot regions and extend upward from the photosphere into the chromosphere and sometimes into the corona (p. 833)

protein a long polymer that forms when amino acids bond together (p. 280)

proton a positively charged subatomic particle that is found in the nucleus of an atom (p. 108)

protoplanetary disk a large disk-shaped cloud of dust and gas formed as the solar nebula rotated faster and flattened out (p. 819)

protostar a contracting nebula with enough mass to form a star (p. 841)

pulley a simple machine that consists of a rope that fits into a groove in a wheel (p. 432)

pulsar a spinning neutron star that appears to give off strong pulses of radio waves (p. 844)

pupil the opening that allows light to enter the eye (p. 589)

pure substance matter that always has exactly the same composition; an element or compound (p. 39)

P waves primary waves; longitudinal waves caused by earthquakes (p. 686)

Q

quark a subatomic particle theorized to be among the basic units of matter (p. 305)

quasar enormously bright center of a distant young galaxy (p. 849)

R

radiation the transfer of energy by waves moving through space (p. 481)

radiation zone a region of closely-packed plasma outside the core of the sun, where energy is transferred by the absorption and reradiation of light (p. 830)

radioactivity the process in which an unstable atomic nucleus emits charged particles and energy (p. 292)

radioisotope an isotope with an unstable nucleus (p. 292)

rarefaction an area of a longitudinal wave where the particles of the medium are spread out (p. 502)

ray diagram a diagram that shows how light rays change direction when they strike mirrors and pass through lenses (p. 570)

reactant a substance that undergoes change in a chemical reaction (p. 192)

reaction rate the rate at which reactants change into products over time (p. 212)

reactivity the property that describes how readily a substance combines chemically with other substances (p. 55)

real image a copy of an object formed at the point where light rays actually meet (p. 572)

red shift a shift toward the red wavelengths of light from stars or galaxies moving away from Earth (p. 852)

reflecting telescope a telescope that uses mirrors and convex lenses to collect and focus light (p. 581)

reflection the interaction that occurs when a wave bounces off a surface that it cannot pass through (p. 508)

refracting telescope a telescope that uses only lenses to collect and focus light (p. 581)

refraction the bending of a wave as it enters a new medium at an angle (p. 509)

refrigerant a fluid that vaporizes and condenses inside the tubing of a heat pump (p. 490)

regular reflection a reflection that occurs when parallel light waves strike a surface and all reflect in the same direction (p. 547)

relative age the age of a rock compared to the ages of other rocks above or below it in a sequence of rock layers (p. 732)

relative humidity the ratio of the amount of water vapor in the air to the maximum amount of water vapor that air can contain at that temperature (p. 760)

Glossary

relative motion movement in relation to a frame of reference (p. 329)

renewable energy resource a source of energy that can be replaced in a relatively short period of time (p. 463)

resistance the opposition to the flow of electric charges in a material (p. 605)

resonance the response of a standing wave to another wave of the same frequency, with dramatic increase in amplitude of the standing wave (p. 521)

responding variable a variable that changes in response to a change in the manipulated variable (p. 8)

resultant vector the vector sum of two or more vectors (p. 331)

retina the inner surface of the back of the eye, containing light-sensitive nerve endings (p. 589)

reversible reaction a chemical reaction in which the conversion of reactants into products and the conversion of products into reactants happens at the same time (p. 217)

revolution the movement of one body around another (p. 752)

ring a disk made of many small particles of rock and ice in orbit around a planet (p. 811)

rock a solid combination of minerals or other materials (p. 665)

rock cycle a series of processes in which rocks continuously change from one type to another (p. 674)

rods light-sensitive neurons in the retina that detect low-intensity light and distinguish black, white, and gray (p. 589)

rolling friction a friction force that acts on rolling objects, caused by the change in shape at the point of rolling contact (p. 360)

rotation the spinning of a planet or moon on its axis (p. 752)

runoff water that flows over Earth's surface (p. 706)

S

salinity the proportion of dissolved salts in water (p. 725)

salt an ionic compound formed when an acid reacts with a base (p. 244)

saltation movement of particles such as sand carried by water or wind in a series of little leaps (p. 714)

saturated hydrocarbon a hydrocarbon in which all of the bonds are single bonds (p. 264)

saturated solution a solution that contains as much solute as the solvent can normally hold at a given temperature (p. 236)

saturated zone the region beneath Earth's surface where pore spaces are entirely filled with groundwater (p. 707)

scattering a process by which light is redirected as it passes through a medium (p. 549)

science a system of knowledge about the natural world and the methods used to find that knowledge (p. 3)

scientific law a statement that summarizes a pattern found in nature (p. 9)

scientific method an organized plan used for gathering, organizing, and communicating information (p. 7)

scientific notation a way of expressing a value as the product of a number between 1 and 10 and a power of 10 (p. 14)

scientific theory a well-tested explanation for a set of observations or experimental results (p. 9)

screw an inclined plane wrapped around a cylinder (p. 431)

sea breeze a local wind that occurs when cooler air over the water flows toward the land (p. 757)

sea-floor spreading the process by which new oceanic crust is created at mid-ocean ridges, as older crust moves away (p. 678)

secondary color new color that results when any two of the primary colors are combined (p. 552)

sediment small, solid pieces of material that come from rocks or living organisms (p. 672)

sedimentary rock rock that forms over time as sediment is squeezed and cemented together (p. 672)

seismic waves vibrations that carry the energy released during an earthquake (p. 684)

seismograph a device that can detect and record seismic waves (p. 687)

semiconductor a crystalline solid that conducts electric current only under certain conditions (p. 621)

series circuit an electric circuit with only one path through which charge can flow (p. 610)

shield volcano a wide, relatively flat volcano that results from quiet eruptions of low-viscosity lava (p. 693)

significant figures all the digits in a measurement that are directly measured, plus the last digit, which is estimated (p. 19)

silicate a rock made of compounds of silicon and oxygen, generally containing metals such as alluminum, iron, or calcium (p. 661)

sill a structure formed when magma hardens in a crack parallel to existing rock layers (p. 696)

single-replacement reaction a chemical reaction in which one element takes the place of another element in a compound (p. 202)

sinkhole a hole that results when erosion weakens a layer of limestone, causing portions of the ground to suddenly collapse (p. 717)

sliding friction a friction force that opposes the motion of an object as it slides over a surface (p. 359)

slope the steepness of a line, equal to the ratio of a vertical change to the corresponding horizontal change (pp. 23, 334)

solar energy sunlight that is converted into usable energy (p. 464)

solar flare a dramatic eruption on the sun's surface, usually near sunspots, that produces X-rays and sends charged particles into space at speeds of 1000 km/s or more (p. 833)

solar nebula a cloud of dust and gas that can eventually collapse to form one or more stars with a planetary system (p. 818)

solar system the sun, planets, their moons, and a variety of smaller objects that revolve around the sun (p. 792)

solar wind a stream of electrically charged particles that flows from the sun outward through the solar system (p. 831)

solenoid a coil of current-carrying wire that produces a magnetic field (p. 637)

solid the state of matter in which materials have a definite shape and a definite volume (p. 69)

solstice the day that marks the start of summer or winter; the day when the sun is directly overhead at latitude 23.5° north or latitude 23.5° south (p. 753)

solubility the maximum amount of solute that normally dissolves in a given amount of solvent at a certain temperature (p. 235)

solute a substance whose particles are dissolved in a solution (p. 229)

solution a mixture that forms when substances dissolve and form a homogeneous mixture (p. 42)

solvent a substance in which a solute dissolves (p. 229)

sonar a technique for determining the distance to an object under water (p. 516)

sound wave a longitudinal wave consisting of compressions and rarefactions, which travels through a medium (p. 514)

space probe an unpiloted vehicle that carries scientific instruments into space and transmits information back to Earth (p. 794)

specific heat the amount of heat needed to raise the temperature of one gram of a material by one degree Celsius (p. 476)

speed the ratio of the distance an object moves to the amount of time the object moves (p. 332)

spiral galaxy a galaxy like the Milky Way with a bulge of stars at the center and arms extending outward like a pinwheel (p. 848)

spring tide a tide at the new or full moon when the change between daily high and low tides is the greatest (p. 801)

stalactite an icicle-like formation on a cavern ceiling that forms when water drips from the cavern ceiling (p. 717)

stalagmite a pillar of minerals in a cavern formed when water drips down to the cavern floor (p. 717)

standing wave a wave that appears to stay in one place and does not seem to move through a medium (p. 512)

star a large, glowing ball of gas in space that generates energy through nuclear fusion in its core (p. 834)

star system a group of two or more stars held together by gravity (p. 847)

static electricity the study of the behavior of electric charges, including how charge is transferred between objects (p. 602)

static friction a friction force that acts on objects that are not moving (p. 359)

stationary front a front that occurs when two air masses have formed a boundary but neither is moving (p. 768)

stratosphere the layer of Earth's atmosphere above the troposphere (p. 750)

stratus clouds flat layers of clouds that cover much or all of the sky (p. 762)

streak the color of a mineral's powder (p. 666)

stress the forces of deformation acting on the rocks of Earth's crust (p. 685)

strong nuclear force the powerful attractive force that binds protons and neutrons together in the nucleus (pp. 308, 379)

subduction the process by which oceanic crust sinks into the mantle through a trench (p. 679)

sublimation the phase change in which a substance changes from a solid to a gas or vapor without changing to a liquid first (p. 91)

substance matter that always has exactly the same composition; an element or compound (p. 39)

substituted hydrocarbon a hydrocarbon in which one or more hydrogen atoms have been replaced, or substituted (p. 272)

sunspot an area of gas in the sun's photosphere that is cooler than the surrounding gases (p. 832)

superconductor a material that has almost zero resistance when it is cooled to low temperatures (p. 605)

supergiant a very large, massive, bright star ranging in size from 100 to 1000 times the diameter of the sun (p. 839)

supernova an enormous explosion in which the byproducts of a supergiant star's lifetime of fusion are flung into space (p. 843)

supersaturated solution a solution that contains more solute than the solvent can normally hold at a given temperature (p. 236)

Glossary

surface current a large stream of ocean water that moves continuously in about the same path (p. 726)

surface wave a wave that travels along a surface separating two media (p. 503); a transverse wave that develops when a seismic wave reaches Earth's surface (p. 687)

suspension a heterogeneous mixture that separates into layers over time (p. 43)

S waves secondary waves; transverse waves caused by earthquakes (p. 687)

synthesis reaction a chemical reaction in which two or more substances react to form a single substance (p. 200)

T

technology the use of scientific knowledge to solve practical problems (p. 3)

telescope an optical instrument that uses lenses (or lenses and mirrors) to collect and focus light from distant objects (p. 580)

temperate zones the regions between latitude 23.5° north and latitude 66.5° north, and between latitude 23.5° south and 66.5° south, which are generally cooler than the tropics (p. 753)

temperature a measure of how hot or cold an object is compared to a reference point (p. 475)

terminal velocity the constant velocity of a falling object when the force of air resistance equals the force of gravity (p. 361)

terrestrial planets the four planets closest to the sun (Mercury, Venus, Earth, and Mars), which are similar in structure to Earth (p. 803)

thermal conductor a material that conducts thermal energy well (p. 480)

thermal energy the total potential and kinetic energy related to the motion of all the particles in an object (p. 451)

thermal expansion the increase in volume of a material when its temperature increases (p. 476)

thermal insulator a material that conducts thermal energy poorly (p. 480)

thermodynamics the study of conversions between thermal energy and other forms of energy (p. 482)

thermogram a color-coded picture using variations in infrared radiation to show variations in temperature (p. 543)

thermometer an instrument that measures temperature (p. 20)

thermosphere the outermost layer of Earth's atmosphere (p. 751)

thunder the sound produced by rapidly expanding air along the path of a lightning discharge (p. 770)

thunderstorm a small weather system that includes thunder and lightning (p. 770)

tides the regular rise and fall of water in the oceans (p. 801)

till glacial sediment left behind when a glacier melts (p. 721)

tornado a small but intense windstorm that takes the form of a rotating column of air that touches the ground (p. 770)

total internal reflection the complete reflection of a light ray back into its original medium when the angle of incidence is greater than the critical angle of refraction (p. 578)

transform boundary a boundary at which tectonic plates slide past each other, moving in opposite directions (p. 682)

transformer a device that increases or decreases the voltage of two linked AC circuits (p. 644)

transistor a solid-state component with three layers of semiconductor material, used to turn current on or off or to increase the strength of electronic signals (p. 621)

transition metals elements that form a bridge between elements on the left and right sides of the periodic table (p. 136)

translucent a description of a material that scatters light that passes through it (p. 547)

transmutation the conversion of one element to another through a nuclear reaction (p. 303)

transparent a description of a material that allows most of the light that strikes it to pass through (p. 546)

transpiration the loss of water through the leaves of plants (p. 705)

transuranium elements elements with atomic numbers greater than 92 (p. 304)

transverse wave a wave that causes a medium to vibrate at right angles to the direction in which the wave travels (p. 501)

trench a long, deep depression in the ocean floor where old oceanic crust sinks into the mantle (p. 679)

tributary a smaller stream that flows into a major river (p. 706)

tropic zone a warm region between latitude 23.5° south and latitude 23.5° north (p. 753)

troposphere the lowest layer of Earth's atmosphere, where most weather occurs (p. 749)

trough the lowest point of a transverse wave (p. 501)

tsunami a large sea wave generated by an underwater earthquake, volcano, or landslide (p. 685)

turbine a device with fanlike blades that turn when pushed, for example, by water or steam (p. 646)

U

umbra the darkest part of a shadow (p. 800)

uniformitarianism the principle that geologic processes operating today also operated in the past (p. 661)

unsaturated hydrocarbon a hydrocarbon that contains one or more double or triple bonds (p. 265)

unsaturated solution a solution in which more solute can be dissolved at a given temperature (p. 236)

upwelling the movement of water from the deep ocean to the ocean's surface (p. 728)

V

valence electron an electron that is in the highest occupied energy level of an atom (p. 139)

valley glacier a long, narrow mass of moving ice and snow that usually begins near a mountain peak and winds down from the mountains through a valley formed originally by a stream (p. 719)

vaporization the phase change in which a substance changes from a liquid into a gas (p. 88)

vapor pressure the pressure caused by the collisions of particles in a vapor with the walls of a container (p. 89)

vector a quantity that has a direction associated with it (p. 330)

velocity the speed and direction an object is moving, measured relative to a reference point (p. 336)

vent an opening in the ground where magma escapes to Earth's surface (p. 691)

virtual image a copy of an object formed at the point from which light appears to be coming (p. 571)

viscosity the tendency of a liquid to keep from flowing; resistance to flowing (p. 45)

vitamin an organic compound that organisms need in small amounts, but cannot produce (p. 284)

volcanic neck a structure that forms when magma hardens in a volcano's pipe (p. 696)

volcano a mountain that forms when magma reaches the surface (p. 690)

voltage potential difference, the difference in electrical potential energy between two places in an electric field (p. 606)

volume the amount of space taken up by an object (p. 16)

W

warm front a front that occurs when a warm air mass overtakes a cold air mass (p. 768)

waste heat thermal energy discharged into an area at a lower temperature without being converted into useful work (p. 483)

water cycle the continuous movement of water in all its forms among Earth's oceans, atmosphere, and land (p. 705)

watershed the area of land that contributes water to a river system (p. 706)

water table the top surface of the saturated zone (p. 707)

watt (W) the SI unit of power, equal to one joule per second (p. 415)

wavelength the distance between a point on a wave and the same point on the next cycle of the wave (p. 505)

weak nuclear force a powerful attractive force that acts over a short range (p. 380)

weather the condition of the atmosphere at a particular place at a particular time (p. 749)

weathering the process by which rocks are chemically altered or physically broken into fragments (p. 710)

wedge a V-shaped object whose sides are two inclined planes sloped toward each other (p. 431)

weight the force of gravity acting on an object (p. 367)

wheel and axle a simple machine that consists of two rigidly attached disks or cylinders, each one with a different radius (p. 430)

white dwarf the small, dense, but dim remains of a low- or medium-mass star (p. 839)

wind the mainly horizontal movement of air from areas of higher pressure to areas of lower pressure (p. 757)

work the product of distance and the force in the direction an object moves (p. 412)

work input the work done on a machine as the input force acts through the input distance (p. 419)

work output the work done by a machine as the output force acts through the output distance (p. 420)

Spanish Glossary

A

abrasion / abrasión una forma de desgaste mecánico que se produce cuando las rocas se desgastan o muelen unas contra otras. (pág. 710)

absolute age / edad absoluta el tiempo transcurrido desde la formación de una roca (pág. 734)

absolute brightness / brillo absoluto una descripción de lo brillante que es una estrella; una propiedad característica de una estrella que no depende de la distancia entre la estrella y la Tierra (pág. 837)

absolute zero / cero absoluto una temperatura de 0 kelvin (págs. 78, 475)

absorption lines / líneas de absorción un conjunto de líneas oscuras que muestran las frecuencias a las que la luz ha sido absorbida desde el espectro brillante de una estrella (pág. 837)

acceleration / aceleración la tasa a la cual cambia la velocidad (pág. 342)

accretion / acreción el proceso de agregar masa en la formación de los planetas mediante la colisión entre planetesimales (pág. 819)

accuracy / exactitud la cercanía de una medida al valor real de lo que se mide (pág. 19)

acid / ácido un compuesto que produce iones hidronios (H_3O^+) cuando se disuelve en agua; un donante de protones (pág. 241)

actual mechanical advantage / ventaja mecánica real la relación de la fuerza desarrollada con respecto a la fuerza aplicada en una máquina (pág. 422)

air mass / masa de aire un gran volumen de aire que tiene propiedades uniformes en toda su extensión, tales como temperatura y porcentajes de humedad, a una determinada altura (pág. 765)

air pressure / presión atmosférica la presión que produce el peso de una columna de aire en la atmósfera terrestre (pág. 748)

air resistance / resistencia del aire fricción de un fluido que actúa sobre un objeto que se mueve a través del aire (pág. 360)

alkali metals / metales alcalinos los elementos del Grupo 1A de la tabla periódica, sin incluir el hidrógeno (pág. 10)

alkaline earth metals / metales terreo-alcalinos los elementos del Grupo 2A de la tabla periódica (pág. 141)

alloy / aleación una mezcla de dos o más elementos, de los cuales al menos uno es un metal, que tiene las propiedades características de un metal (pág. 178)

alluvial fan / abanico aluvial un depósito de sedimentos con forma de abanico, que se forma sobre tierra firme cuando un arroyo fluye desde las montañas hacia una planicie (pág. 716)

alpha particle / partícula alfa una partícula de carga positiva que es emitida por algunos núcleos radiactivos y está formada por dos protones y dos neutrones; un núcleo de helio (pág. 293)

alternating current (AC) / corriente alterna (CA) un flujo de energía eléctrica que cambia de positiva a negativa a intervalos regulares (pág. 604)

amino acids / aminoácidos compuestos que contienen los grupos funcionales carboxilo y amino (pág. 280)

amplitude / amplitud el máximo desplazamiento de un determinado medio desde su posición de reposo (pág. 507)

amplitude modulation (AM) / amplitud modulada (AM) un método para la transmisión de señales de radio en el que la amplitud de la onda transmisora varía mientras que la frecuencia permanece estable (pág. 541)

analog signal / señal análoga una señal de variación gradual que se produce al cambiar continuamente el voltaje o corriente en un circuito (pág. 619)

angle of incidence / ángulo de incidencia el ángulo que forma un rayo incidente con una línea perpendicular a la superficie sobre la que impacta (pág. 570)

angle of reflection / ángulo de reflexión el ángulo que forma un rayo reflejado con una línea perpendicular a la superficie sobre la que impacta (pág. 570)

angle of refraction / ángulo de refracción el ángulo que forma un rayo de luz con el normal después de ingresar a un nuevo medio a un ángulo determinado (pág. 575)

anion / anión un ión de carga negativa (pág. 160)

anticyclone / anticiclón un sistema climático con un centro turbulento de alta presión atmosférica (pág. 769)

antinode / antinodo un punto de máximo desplazamiento a mitad de camino entre dos nodos y una onda estacionaria (pág. 512)

apparent brightness / magnitud aparente el brillo de una estrella como se aprecia desde la Tierra (pág. 836)

aquifer / acuífero una capa de rocas permeables que está saturada de agua (pág. 707)

Archimedes' principle / principio de Arquímedes la equivalencia de la fuerza de flotación de un objeto y el peso del fluido desplazado por el objeto (pág. 401)

aromatic hydrocarbons / hidrocarburos aromáticos hidrocarburos que contienen una estructura de anillos similar al benceno (pág. 26)

asteroid belt / cinturón de asteroides región entre las órbitas de Marte y Júpiter donde se encuentran la mayoría de los asteroides del sistema solar (pág. 809)

asteroids / asteroides cuerpos rocosos pequeños del sistema solar, la mayor parte de los cuales se encuentra orbitando alrededor del Sol en una región entre Marte y Júpiter (pág. 809)

asthenosphere / astenosfera una capa de roca más suave y débil debajo de la litosfera terrestre, que puede fluir lentamente (pág. 662)

astigmatism / astigmatismo condición de los ojos en la que los objetos situados a cualquier distancia aparecen borrosos debido a la forma distorsionada de la córnea (pág. 592)

astronomical unit (AU) / unidad astronómica (UA) una unidad de distancia que equivale a la distancia promedio de la Tierra al Sol; 149,598,000 kilómetros (pág. 793)

astronomy / astronomía el estudio del Universo más allá de la Tierra (pág. 4)

atmosphere / atmósfera la capa de gases que rodea a la Tierra (pág. 747)

atom / átomo la partícula más pequeña de un elemento (pág. 39)

atomic mass unit (amu) / unidad de masa atómica (uma) una doceava parte de la masa que tiene un átomo de carbono-12 (pág. 134)

atomic number / número atómico un único número por cada elemento que equivale al número de protones en un átomo de ese elemento (pág. 110)

aurora / aurora una muestra colorida de luces en la ionosfera, que se produce cuando las partículas con carga que provienen del Sol son atraídas por los polos magnéticos terrestres (pág. 751)

average speed / rapidez media la distancia total recorrida dividida por el tiempo que se necesita para recorrer esa distancia (pág. 333)

B

background radiation / radiación de fondo radiación nuclear que se produce naturalmente en el ambiente (pág. 296)

barometer / barómetro un instrumento que sirve para medir la presión del aire (pág. 748)

barred-spiral galaxy / galaxias espirales barradas una galaxia espiral en la que los brazos del espiral se extienden hacia fuera desde una barra que corre a través del centro de la galaxia (pág. 848)

base / base un compuesto que produce iones hidróxidos (OH^-) cuando se disuelve en agua; un receptor de protones (pág. 242)

batholith / batolito el tipo más grande de masa de roca ígnea intrusa (pág. 696)

battery / batería un artefacto que convierte la energía química en energía eléctrica (pág. 606)

beta particle / partícula beta un electrón emitido por un núcleo inestable (pág. 294)

big bang theory / teoría del Big Bang la teoría que sostiene que el Universo comenzó en un instante, hace miles de millones de años, con una enorme explosión (pág. 854)

binary star / estrella binaria un sistema de estrellas con dos estrellas que giran cada una alrededor de la otra (pág. 847)

biology / biología el estudio de la vida y los procesos vitales (pág. 4)

biomass energy / energía de la biomasa la energía química que se almacena en las cosas vivas (pág. 464)

black hole / agujero negro un objeto cuya gravedad superficial es tan grande que ni siquiera las ondas electromagnéticas pueden escaparse (pág. 844)

boiling point / punto de ebullición la temperatura a la cual hierve una sustancia; la temperatura a la cual la presión del vapor es igual a la presión atmosférica (pág. 47)

Boyle's law / ley de Boyle la variación inversa del volumen de un gas y su presión si la temperatura y el número de partículas son constantes (pág. 79)

buffer / búfer una solución que es resistente a grandes cambios en su pH (pág. 248)

buoyancy / flotación la capacidad que tiene un fluido de ejercer una fuerza ascendente en los objetos colocados en él (pág. 400)

buoyant force / fuerza de flotación una fuerza ascendente que actúa sobre un objeto colocado en un fluido (pág. 400)

C

caldera / caldera amplia depresión en la parte superior de un volcán que se forma cuando la boca central y la cámara magmática se derrumban después de una erupción (pág. 691)

calorimeter / calorímetro instrumento que sirve para medir la energía térmica que se libera o absorbe durante un cambio químico o físico (pág. 478)

camera / cámara fotográfica un instrumento óptico que registra la imagen de un objeto (pág. 582)

carbohydrate / carbohidrato un compuesto de carbono, hidrógeno y oxígeno en el cual la relación de los átomos de hidrógeno respecto de los átomos de oxígeno es de 2:1 (pág. 278)

catalyst / catalizador una sustancia que afecta la velocidad de una reacción química sin que sea usada en la reacción (pág. 215)

cation / catión un ión con carga positiva (pág. 160)

central heating system / sistema de calefacción central un sistema de calefacción que calienta varias habitaciones desde una ubicación central (pág. 489)

Spanish Glossary

centripetal force / fuerza centrípeta una fuerza que cambia continuamente la dirección de un objeto para hacerlo moverse en un círculo (pág. 381)

chain reaction / reacción en cadena una serie de reacciones de fisión disparadas por neutrones liberados durante la fisión de un núcleo (pág. 311)

Charles's law / ley de Charles la proporción directa del volumen de un gas con respecto a su temperatura (en kelvins), si la presión y el número de partículas del gas son constantes (pág. 78)

chemical bond / enlace químico la fuerza que mantiene los átomos e iones juntos como una unidad (pág. 160)

chemical change / cambio químico cambio que se produce cuando una sustancia reacciona y forma una o más sustancias nuevas (pág. 56)

chemical energy / energía química la energía almacenada en los enlaces químicos (págs. 206, 451)

chemical equation / ecuación química una representación de una reacción química en la cual los reactantes y los productos se expresan como fórmulas (pág. 193)

chemical formula / fórmula química notación que muestra los elementos que contienen un compuesto y la relación de los átomos o iones de estos elementos en el compuesto (pág. 161)

chemical property / propiedad química toda propiedad que produce un cambio en la composición de la materia (pág. 54)

chemical weathering / desgaste químico el proceso en el que una roca es desintegrada por las reacciones químicas (pág. 710)

chemistry / química el estudio de la composición, estructura, propiedades y reacciones de la materia (pág. 4)

chromosphere / cromosfera la capa intermedia de la atmósfera solar, inmediatamente por fuera de la fotosfera (pág. 831)

cinder cone / cono de escoria un volcán pequeño y de laderas empinadas formado por una combinación de ceniza y toba volcánica (pág. 693)

circuit breaker / interruptor de circuito un interruptor que se abre cuando la corriente en un circuito es demasiado alta (pág. 612)

cirque / circo glaciar un amplio valle con forma de tazón creado por un glaciar en la ladera de una montaña (pág. 720)

cirrus clouds / nubes cirros nubes delgadas, blancas y tenues, a menudo con apariencia de velos o plumas (pág. 763)

clastic rocks / rocas clásticas rocas sedimentarias que se forman de fragmentos que se desprenden de otras rocas (pág. 672)

cleavage / exfoliación la tendencia que posee un mineral de dividirse a lo largo de planos regulares y bien definidos (pág. 668)

climate / clima las condiciones a largo plazo del tiempo de un lugar o región (pág. 778)

cloud / nube una masa densa y visible de minúsculas gotas de agua o cristales de hielo que se encuentran suspendidos en la atmósfera (pág. 761)

coefficients / coeficientes los números que aparecen antes de una fórmula en una ecuación química para mostrar las proporciones relativas de cada reactante y producto (pág. 194)

coherent light / luz coherente ondas de luz que tienen la misma longitud de onda, con sus crestas y valles alineados (pág. 560)

cold front / frente frío un frente que se produce cuando una masa de aire frío rebasa a una masa de aire caliente (pág. 767)

colloid / coloide una mezcla que contiene algunas partículas que son de tamaño intermedio entre las partículas pequeñas de una solución y las partículas grandes de una suspensión (pág. 44)

combustion reaction / reacción de combustión una reacción química en la que una sustancia reacciona rápidamente con el oxígeno, produciendo a menudo calor y luz (pág. 204)

comet / cometa una masa de roca, polvo y hielo que se vaporiza parcialmente cuando pasa cerca del Sol (pág. 815)

complementary colors of light / colores complementarios de la luz dos colores cualesquiera de luz que se combinan para formar luz blanca (pág. 552)

complementary colors of pigments / colores complementarios de pigmentos dos colores cualesquiera de pigmentos que se combinan para formar un pigmento negro (pág. 553)

composite volcano / volcán compuesto un volcán que se forma de una combinación de lava y ceniza (pág. 693)

compound / compuesto una sustancia que está formada por dos o más sustancias más simples y que se puede descomponer en esas sustancias más simples (pág. 40)

compound machine / máquina compuesta una combinación de dos o más máquinas simples que operan juntas (pág. 435)

compression / compresión un área en una onda longitudinal en la cual las partículas de ese medio están juntas entre sí (pág. 502)

computer / computadora un artefacto programable que puede almacenar y procesar información (pág. 622)

concave lens / lente cóncava lente curvada hacia dentro en el centro y que tiene mayor grosor en los bordes exteriores (pág. 576)

concave mirror / espejo cóncavo un espejo que se curva hacia dentro (pág. 572)

concentration / concentración la cantidad de soluto disuelto en una determinada cantidad de solvente (pág. 238)

condensation / condensación el cambio de fase en el que una sustancia cambia de gas o vapor a líquido (pág. 90)

conduction / conducción la transferencia de energía térmica sin transferencia significativa de materia, dentro de un material o entre materiales en contacto (pág. 479); la transferencia de carga eléctrica por contacto directo con un conductor (pág. 602)

conductivity / conductividad la capacidad que tiene un material de permitir que fluyan el calor o las cargas eléctricas (pág. 46)

cones / conos las neuronas sensibles a la luz de la retina que detectan el color (pág. 589)

constant acceleration / aceleración constante un cambio continuo en la velocidad (pág. 345)

constellation / constelación un grupo de estrellas que parecen formar un patrón cuando se las observa desde la Tierra (pág. 846)

constructive interference / interferencia constructiva la interacción entre dos o más ondas en las que los desplazamientos se combinan para formar una onda con un desplazamiento más amplio (pág. 511)

continental drift / deriva continental proceso en el que los continentes se mueven lentamente a través de la superficie de la Tierra (pág. 677)

continental glacier / glaciar continental capa espesa de hielo que cubre una zona extensa de un continente o una isla grande (pág. 719)

continental shelf / plataforma continental llanura con leve declive que forma un manto de aguas poco profundas a lo largo de las costas de la mayor parte de los continentes (pág. 726)

controlled experiment / experimento controlado experimento en el que una sola variable, la variable manipulada, se cambia deliberadamente en un momento determinado (pág. 8)

convection / convección transferencia de energía térmica cuando las partículas de un fluido se mueven de un lugar a otro (pág. 480)

convection current / corriente de convección circulación de un fluido en un circuito cuando el fluido se calienta y se enfría alternativamente (pág. 481)

convection zone / zona de convección región dentro del Sol en que la energía térmica se transfiere hacia fuera principalmente por medio de corrientes de convección (pág. 831)

convergent boundary / borde convergente límite en el que colisionan o chocan las placas tectónicas (pág. 682)

conversion factor / factor de conversión una razón de medidas equivalentes que se usan para convertir una determinada cantidad de una unidad a otra (pág. 18)

convex lens / lente convexa lente curvada hacia fuera en el centro y más delgada en los bordes exteriores (pág. 576)

convex mirror / espejo convexo espejo curvado hacia afuera (pág. 573)

core / núcleo esfera densa ubicada en el centro de la Tierra que está formada principalmente por hierro y níquel (pág. 663); región central del Sol donde se produce la fusión nuclear (pág. 830)

Coriolis effect / efecto de Coriolis el cambio que la rotación de la tierra produce en el movimiento de los objetos (pág. 759)

cornea / córnea capa externa y transparente del ojo (pág. 588)

corona / corona la capa más externa de la atmósfera solar que se extiende muy por encima de la cromosfera (pág. 831)

covalent bond / enlace covalente enlace químico en el que dos átomos comparten un par de electrones de valencia (pág. 166)

crater / cráter un orificio curvo en la cima de la boca central de un volcán (pág. 691); depresión circular en la superficie de un planeta, luna, asteroide o cometa provocada por un meteoroide (pág. 797)

crest / cresta el punto más alto de una onda transversal (pág. 501)

critical angle / ángulo crítico el ángulo de incidencia que produce un ángulo de refracción igual a 90 grados (pág. 578)

critical mass / masa crítica la masa más pequeña posible de un material fisionable que puede generar una reacción en cadena (pág. 311)

crust / corteza la capa rocosa más externa de la Tierra (pág. 661)

crystals / cristales sólidos cuyas partículas se encuentran dispuestas en una estructura reticular (pág. 162)

cumulus clouds / nubes cúmulos nubes blancas y esponjosas, generalmente con bases planas, que parecen bolitas de algodón apiladas (pág. 763)

cyclone / ciclón un sistema climático con un centro de baja presión atmosférica (pág. 769)

D

dark matter / materia negra materia que no emite radiación que pueda ser detectada por los astrónomos (pág. 855)

decibel / decibelio una unidad que compara las intensidades de diferentes sonidos (pág. 515)

Spanish Glossary

decomposition reaction / reacción de descomposición una reacción química en la que un compuesto se separa en dos o más sustancias más simples (pág. 200)

deflation / deflación el proceso que ocurre cuando el viento levanta y transporta materiales de la superficie (pág. 723)

delta / delta una masa de sedimento que se deposita en la desembocadura de un río en el lugar en que éste penetra en una gran masa de agua (pág. 716)

density / densidad la relación entre el volumen y la masa de un material (pág. 17)

density currents / corrientes de densidad las corrientes que se producen debido a las diferencias en la densidad del agua del océano (pág. 727)

deposition / deposición cambio de fase en el que un gas o vapor cambia directamente al estado sólido sin pasar primero por el estado líquido (pág. 91); la colocación de sedimento que ha sido transportado de otro sitio (pág. 713)

desert / desierto una región extremadamente seca (pág. 780)

destructive interference / interferencia destructiva la interacción entre dos o más ondas cuyos desplazamientos se combinan para producir una onda con un desplazamiento menor (pág. 511)

dew point / punto de rocío la temperatura a la que el aire se satura de vapor de agua (pág. 761)

diffraction / difracción la curvatura de una onda que se mueve alrededor de un obstáculo o pasa a través de una abertura estrecha (pág. 510)

diffuse reflection / reflexión difusa la reflexión que se produce cuando ondas de luz paralelas chocan contra una superficie áspera y desigual, y se reflejan en muchas direcciones diferentes (pág. 547)

digital signal / señal digital una señal que codifica la información como una secuencia de unos y ceros (pág. 619)

dike / dique una estructura que se forma cuando el magma se endurece dentro de una grieta que atraviesa diferentes capas de rocas (pág. 696)

diode / diodo un componente de estado sólido con un semiconductor de tipo n unido a un semiconductor de tipo p (pág. 621)

direct current (DC) / corriente directa (CD) el flujo de carga eléctrica que corre en una sola dirección (pág. 604)

direct proportion / proporción directa una relación entre dos variables cuya proporción es constante (pág. 23)

dispersion / dispersión el proceso de disolución por rotura en partes pequeñas (pág. 230); proceso en el que la luz blanca se separa en colores (pág. 551)

dissociation / disociación separación de iones en un compuesto iónico a medida que éste se disuelve (pág. 229)

distance / distancia longitud de la trayectoria entre dos puntos (pág. 329)

distillation / destilación el proceso que separa las sustancias en una solución según sus puntos de ebullición (pág. 50)

divergent boundary / borde divergente límite en el que las placas tectónicas se separan unas de otras (pág. 682)

Doppler effect / efecto Doppler un cambio en la frecuencia de sonido provocada por el movimiento de la fuente de sonido, movimiento de la persona que escucha o de ambos (pág. 516)

double-replacement reaction / reacción de sustitución doble una reacción química en la que dos componentes intercambian iones positivos y forman otros dos nuevos compuestos (pág. 203)

dunes / dunas los depósitos de arena que se forman cuando ésta es transportada por el viento (pág. 724)

E

earthquake / terremoto un movimiento de la corteza terrestre que se produce cuando las rocas en la corteza cambian de posición repentinamente y liberan energía que estaba almacenada (pág. 684)

eclipse / eclipse fenómeno que se produce cuando la sombra de un cuerpo del espacio, tales como un planeta o luna, se proyecta sobre otro cuerpo (pág. 799)

ecliptic plane / plano eclíptico el plano del espacio que contiene la órbita de la Tierra (pág. 792)

efficiency / eficiencia porcentaje de trabajo de entrada que se transforma en trabajo de salida en una máquina (pág. 425)

elastic potencial energy / energía elástica potencial energía potencial de un objeto al ser estirado o comprimido (pág. 450)

electric charge / carga eléctrica una propiedad que provoca atracción o rechazo entre partículas subatómicas como los protones y electrones (pág. 600)

electric circuit / circuito eléctrico recorrido completo a través del cual puede fluir la carga eléctrica (pág. 609)

electric current / corriente eléctrica un flujo continuo de carga eléctrica (pág. 604)

electric field / campo eléctrico campo en una región del espacio que ejerce fuerzas eléctricas sobre partículas cargadas; campo generado por cargas eléctricas o por campos magnéticos variables (págs. 533, 602)

electric force / fuerza eléctrica la atracción o rechazo entre objetos con carga eléctrica (pág. 601)

electric motor / motor eléctrico un aparato que utiliza un electroimán para mover o rotar un eje (pág. 639)

electric power / potencia eléctrica la velocidad a la que la energía eléctrica se convierte en otro tipo de energía (pág. 611)

electrical conductor / conductor eléctrico un material a través del cual la carga eléctrica puede fluir fácilmente (pág. 605)

electrical energy / energía eléctrica energía asociada con las cargas eléctricas (pág. 452)

electrical insulator / aislante eléctrico un material a través del cual la carga eléctrica no puede fluir fácilmente (pág. 605)

electrolyte / electrolito un compuesto que produce iones al ser disuelto (pág. 249)

electromagnet / electroimán un solenoide con núcleo ferromagnético (pág. 637)

electromagnetic energy / energía electromagnética una forma de energía que consiste en campos eléctricos y magnéticos variables (pág. 452)

electromagnetic force / fuerza electromagnética una fuerza asociada con las partículas cargadas, la cual tiene dos aspectos, fuerza eléctrica y fuerza magnética (págs. 378, 635)

electromagnetic induction / inducción electromagnética el proceso de generación de corriente en el que un conductor eléctrico se mueve en relación a un campo magnético (pág. 642)

electromagnetic radiation / radiación electromagnética la transferencia de energía por medio de ondas electromagnéticas (pág. 533)

electromagnetic spectrum / espectro electromagnético rango completo de radiación electromagnética (pág. 540)

electromagnetic wave / onda electromagnética onda transversal formada por campos eléctricos y campos magnéticos variables (pág. 533)

electron / electrón una partícula subatómica con carga negativa que se encuentra en el espacio fuera del núcleo de un átomo (pág. 108)

electron cloud / nube de electrones modelo visual de las ubicaciones más probables de los electrones en un átomo (pág. 116)

electron configuration / configuración de electrones la disposición de los electrones en las órbitas de un átomo (pág. 118)

electron dot diagram / diagrama de puntos de electrones diagrama de un átomo, ión o molécula en el que cada punto representa la valencia de un electrón (pág. 158)

electronics / electrónica la ciencia que utiliza corrientes eléctricas para procesar o transmitir información (pág. 618)

electronic signal / señal electrónica información enviada en forma de patrones en el flujo controlado de electrones a través de un circuito (pág. 618)

element / elemento sustancia que no puede ser descompuesta en sustancias más simples (pág. 39)

elliptical galaxies / galaxias elípticas galaxias de formas esféricas u ovaladas sin rastros de brazos en espiral y muy poco gas o polvo entre sus estrellas (pág. 848)

El Niño / El Niño el calentamiento periódico del agua en las regiones central y oriental del Océano Pacífico (pág. 781)

endothermic / endotérmico la descripción de un cambio en el que un sistema absorbe energía de su entorno (pág. 86)

endothermic reaction / reacción endotérmica una reacción química que absorbe energía del entorno (pág. 209)

energy / energía capacidad de realizar un trabajo (pág. 447)

energy conservation / conservación de la energía práctica para encontrar formas de utilizar menos energía o de utilizarla en forma más eficiente (pág. 466)

energy conversion / conversión de la energía el proceso de cambiar energía de una forma a otra (pág. 454)

energy levels / niveles energéticos energías posibles que pueden tener los electrones de un átomo (pág. 114)

enzyme / enzima una proteína que actúa como catalítico para las reacciones en las células (pág. 284)

epicenter / epicentro el punto sobre la superficie de la Tierra que está ubicado directamente por encima del foco de un terremoto (pág. 686)

equilibrium / equilibrio estado en el que las trayectorias hacia delante y hacia atrás de un cambio físico o químico se realizan a la misma velocidad (pág. 216)

equinox / equinoccio día que marca el comienzo de la primavera o del otoño; día en el que la duración de la luz diurna y la oscuridad son aproximadamente iguales (pág. 754)

era / era una de las etapas principales en la historia geológica de la Tierra (pág. 734)

erosion / erosión el proceso que desgasta y transporta la roca y el suelo (pág. 709)

evaporation / evaporación el proceso por el cual una sustancia en estado líquido se transforma en gas a temperaturas por debajo del punto de ebullición de esa sustancia (pág. 89)

exothermic / exotérmico descripción de un cambio en el que el sistema libera energía hacia su entorno (pág. 86)

exothermic reaction / reacción exotérmica una reacción química que libera energía hacia el entorno (pág. 208)

Spanish Glossary

external combustion engine / motor de combustión externa un motor térmico en el que el combustible se quema fuera de él (pág. 486)

extinct / extinto descripción de un tipo de organismo que no se encuentra vivo sobre la Tierra (pág. 733)

extrusive rock / roca extrusiva roca ígnea que se forma sobre la superficie de la Tierra (pág. 671)

F

farsightedness / hipermetropía condición de los ojos que provoca una visión borrosa de los objetos cercanos (pág. 592)

fault / falla una grieta en la corteza terrestre (pág. 685)

ferromagnetic material / material ferromagnético un material que puede ser magnetizado por su contenido de dominios magnéticos (pág. 632)

filtration / filtración proceso que separa los materiales de acuerdo al tamaño de sus partículas (pág. 50)

fission / fisión una reacción nuclear en que el núcleo de un átomo se separa en dos partes pequeñas (pág. 309)

flammability / flamabilidad capacidad que tiene un material de quemarse en presencia de oxígeno (pág. 54)

flood plain / llanura de inundación zona llana a lo largo de un curso de agua que sólo se inunda en las crecidas (pág. 716)

fluid / fluido sustancia o mezcla que fluye y que no tiene forma definida (pág. 391)

fluid friction / fricción de fluido una fuerza de fricción que se opone al movimiento de un objeto dentro de un fluido (pág. 360)

fluorescence / fluorescencia proceso en el que un material fosforescente convierte la radiación en luz visible (pág. 559)

focal point / punto de enfoque punto en el que se encuentran o parecen encontrarse los rayos de luz paralelos al eje de un espejo o lente (pág. 572)

focus / foco lugar por debajo de la superficie de la Tierra donde comienza un terremoto (pág. 686)

fog / niebla una nube que toca o está muy cerca del suelo (pág. 762)

fold / pliegue doblez en capas rocosas (pág. 685)

foliated rock / roca foliada una roca con cristales dispuestos en bandas paralelas (pág. 674)

force / fuerza la atracción o rechazo que actúa sobre un objeto (pág. 356)

fossil / fósil restos o rastros preservados de un organismo viviente (pág. 732)

fossil fuels / combustibles fósiles mezclas de depósitos ricos en hidrocarburos que se formaron a partir de restos de organismos (pág. 267)

fracture / fractura modo en el que se rompe un mineral, determinado por su estructura de cristales (pág. 668)

frame of reference / marco de referencia un sistema de objetos que no se mueve con respecto a otro (pág. 328)

free fall / caída libre movimiento de un objeto hacia la Tierra por causa de la gravedad (pág. 343)

frequency / frecuencia cantidad de ciclos completos en una unidad de tiempo para producir un movimiento periódico (pág. 504)

frequency modulation (FM) / frecuencia modulada (FM) método de transmisión de una señal de radio en el que varía la frecuencia de la onda portadora mientras su amplitud permanece igual (pág. 541)

friction / fricción fuerza que se opone al movimiento de los objetos que se tocan a medida que cada uno de ellos se mueve con respecto al otro (pág. 359)

front / frente línea divisoria muy bien definida que se forma cuando se encuentran dos masas de aire diferentes (pág. 767)

fulcrum / fulcro punto fijo alrededor del cual gira una palanca (pág. 428)

functional group / grupo funcional átomo o grupo de átomos que determina las propiedades de un compuesto orgánico (pág. 272)

fuse / fusible dispositivo que evita el sobrecalentamiento de un circuito por sobrecarga (pág. 612)

fusion / fusión una reacción nuclear en la que se combinan los núcleos de dos átomos para formar un núcleo más grande (pág. 315)

G

galaxy / galaxia un enorme grupo de estrellas, sistemas de estrellas, cúmulos de estrellas, polvo y gas unidos por la gravedad (pág. 848)

galvanometer / galvanómetro un aparato que utiliza un electroimán para medir pequeñas cantidades de corriente (pág. 638)

gamma ray / rayo gamma una forma penetrante de radiación que emite un núcleo inestable (pág. 294)

gas / gas estado de la materia en el que un material no tiene forma ni volumen definidos (pág. 70)

gas giant / gigante de gas planeta grande y de gran masa (como Júpiter, Saturno, Urano o Neptuno) compuesto principalmente por helio e hidrógeno (pág. 811)

generator / generador un aparato que convierte la energía mecánica en energía eléctrica por el movimiento relativo de una bobina de alambre respecto de un campo magnético (pág. 643)

geocentric / geocéntrico descripción de un modelo de sistema solar en el que todos los planetas giran alrededor de la Tierra (pág. 791)

geologists / geólogos científicos que estudian la Tierra y los procesos que la han ido formando a través del tiempo (pág. 660)

geology / geología estudio del origen, historia y estructura de la Tierra (pág. 4)

geothermal energy / energía geotérmica energía térmica existente debajo de la superficie de la Tierra (pág. 464)

giant / gigante estrella grande, brillante y de gran masa pero algo más pequeña y más débil que un supergigante (pág. 839)

glacier / glaciar gran masa de hielo y nieve que se desliza sobre la tierra (pág. 706)

global warming / calentamiento global incremento de la temperatura en la capa inferior de la atmósfera terrestre, provocado en parte por los elevados niveles de dióxido de carbono o vapor de agua (pág. 782)

global wind / viento global viento que sopla sobre grandes extensiones de terreno desde una dirección específica (pág. 758)

globular cluster / cúmulo globular grupo grande de estrellas viejas y de forma esférica que le faltan, por lo general, polvo y gas suficiente para formar nuevas estrellas (pág. 847)

gravitational force / fuerza gravitatoria una fuerza de atracción que actúa entre dos objetos cualesquiera (pág. 380)

gravitational potential energy / energía potencial gravitacional energía potencial que depende de la altura de un objeto por encima de un punto de referencia (pág. 449)

gravity / gravedad atracción entre dos objetos cualesquiera por efecto de sus masas (pág. 361)

greenhouse effect / efecto invernadero proceso en el que los gases de la atmósfera de la Tierra, tales como el vapor de agua y el dióxido de carbono, permiten el paso de la luz visible, pero absorben la radiación infrarroja que calienta la parte inferior de la atmósfera (pág. 755)

ground state / estado basal estado en el que todos los electrones de un átomo tienen la mínima energía posible (pág. 118)

grounding / conexión a tierra la transferencia del exceso de carga a través de un conductor a Tierra (pág. 613)

groundwater / aguas freáticas aguas frescas que se encuentran por debajo de la superficie de la Tierra dentro de grietas y entre partículas de roca y tierra (pág. 704)

group / grupo columna de elementos en una tabla periódica (pág. 131)

H

half-life / vida media tiempo que requiere la mitad de una muestra de un isótopo radiactivo para descomponerse (pág. 299)

halogens / halógenos los elementos del Grupo 7A de la tabla periódica (pág. 144)

hardness / dureza resistencia de un mineral a las raspaduras (pág. 668)

heat / calor transferencia de energía térmica de un objeto a otro debido a la diferencia de temperatura (pág. 474)

heat engine / motor térmico todo artefacto que transforma la energía térmica en trabajo (pág. 483)

heat of fusion / calor de fusión la energía que debe absorber una sustancia para pasar del estado sólido al líquido (pág. 86)

heat of vaporization / calor de vaporización la energía que debe absorber una sustancia para pasar del estado líquido al gaseoso (pág. 88)

heat pump / bomba térmica dispositivo que utiliza el trabajo para transferir energía térmica de un área más fría a un área más cálida (pág. 490)

heliocentric / heliocéntrico descripción de un modelo del sistema solar en el que la Tierra y los planetas giran alrededor del Sol (pág. 791)

hertz (Hz) / hercios (Hz) unidad para medir la frecuencia que equivale a un ciclo por segundo (pág. 504)

heterogeneous mixture / mezcla heterogénea tipo de mezcla en la que sus partes son notoriamente diferentes unas de otras (pág. 41)

homogeneous mixture / mezcla homogénea tipo de mezcla en la que las sustancias están distribuidas en forma tan pareja que es difícil distinguir una de otra (pág. 42)

horsepower (hp) / caballo de potencia (hp) unidad de potencia que equivale aproximadamente a 746 vatios (pág. 416)

hot spot / punto caliente región en la que una columna de magma ascendente se extiende desde la parte inferior de la litosfera hacia la superficie de la Tierra (pág. 693)

H-R (Hertzsprung-Russell) diagram / diagrama Hertzsprung-Russell gráfico de la temperatura de superficie comparada a la magnitud absoluta de una muestra de estrellas (pág. 838)

Hubble's Law / ley de Hubble variación directa de la velocidad a la que una galaxia se aleja de la Tierra con respecto a su distancia de ésta (pág. 853)

humidity / humedad cantidad de vapor de agua en un volumen determinado de aire (pág. 760)

hurricane / huracán ciclón tropical de grandes dimensiones con vientos de al menos 119 km por hora (74 millas por hora) (pág. 771)

hydraulic action / acción hidráulica proceso por el cual las olas del océano erosionan la roca (pág. 728)

hydraulic system / sistema hidráulico dispositivo que utiliza la acción de un fluido presurizado sobre pistones de diferentes tamaños para aumentar la fuerza (pág. 395)

Spanish Glossary

hydrocarbon / hidrocarburo compuesto orgánico que solamente contiene hidrógeno y carbono (pág. 264)

hydroelectric energy / energía hidroeléctrica energía que se obtiene a partir del agua en movimiento (pág. 463)

hydrogen fuel cell / pila de combustible de hidrógeno pila que genera electricidad a partir de una reacción controlada entre hidrógeno y oxígeno (pág. 608)

hypothesis / hipótesis una respuesta propuesta ante una pregunta (pág. 8)

I

ice ages / glaciaciones períodos en los que los climas son más fríos de lo habitual y los glaciares cubren una gran parte de la superficie de la Tierra (pág. 781)

ideal mechanical advantage (IMA) / ventaja mecánica ideal (VMI) ventaja mecánica de una máquina en ausencia de fricción (pág. 423)

igneous rock / roca ígnea roca que se forma a partir del magma o lava (pág. 671)

image / imagen copia de un objeto formada por rayos de luz que se reflejan o refractan (pág. 547)

impermeable / impermeable descripción de un material a través del cual el agua no puede pasar fácilmente (pág. 707)

incandescent / incandescente descripción de un objeto lo suficientemente caliente como para brillar (pág. 558)

inclined plane / plano inclinado superficie inclinada a lo largo de la cual una fuerza mueve un objeto hacia una elevación diferente (pág. 431)

index fossil / fósil indicador fósil de una especie fácilmente identificable, que habitó en una zona extensa y vivió durante un período bien definido (pág. 733)

index of refraction / índice de refracción la relación entre la velocidad de la luz en un vacío y la velocidad de la luz en un medio (pág. 575)

indicator / indicador una sustancia que cambia de color en presencia de un ácido o una base (pág. 241)

induction / inducción transferencia de carga entre materiales, sin entrar en contacto (pág. 603)

inertia / inercia la tendencia de un objeto a resistir un cambio en su movimiento (pág. 364)

inorganic / inorgánico descripción de un material no orgánico (pág. 665)

input arm / brazo de entrada distancia entre el fulcro en una palanca y la fuerza aplicada (pág. 428)

input distance / distancia de entrada distancia a través de la cual la fuerza aplicada actúa en una máquina (pág. 419)

input force / fuerza aplicada fuerza que se ejerce sobre una máquina (pág. 419)

instantaneous speed / rapidez instantánea velocidad a la que se mueve un objeto en un momento dado en el tiempo (pág. 334)

integrated circuit / circuito integrado delgada capa de silicio que contiene muchos componentes; microchip (pág. 622)

intensity / intensidad velocidad a la que fluye la energía de una onda a través de una determinada unidad de espacio (págs. 515, 538)

interference / interferencia la interacción de dos o más ondas que se combinan en una zona en común (pág. 510)

internal combustion engine / motor de combustión interna máquina térmica en la que el combustible se quema dentro de la máquina (pág. 487)

intrusive rock / roca intrusiva roca ígnea que se forma bajo tierra a partir del magma endurecida (pág. 671)

inverse proportion / proporción inversa la relación en la que el producto de dos variables es una constante cuando todas las demás variables permanecen constantes (pág. 23)

ion / ión un átomo o grupo de átomos que tiene carga positiva o negativa (pág. 159)

ionic bond / enlace iónico fuerza que mantiene unidos a cationes y aniones (pág. 160)

ionization / ionización proceso por el cual las moléculas neutrales ganan o pierden electrones (pág. 230)

ionosphere / ionosfera región de partículas cargadas, o iones, de la atmósfera terrestre que se superpone con la parte más baja de la termosfera (pág. 751)

iris / iris parte coloreada del frente del ojo que se expande y contrae para controlar la cantidad de luz que penetra en él (pág. 589)

irregular galaxy / galaxia irregular una galaxia con apariencia desorganizada (pág. 848)

isobar / isobara línea trazada en un mapa del tiempo que une los puntos con igual presión atmosférica (pág. 777)

isotherm / isoterma línea trazada en un mapa del tiempo que une los puntos con igual temperatura del aire (pág. 777)

isomers / isómeros compuestos orgánicos con la misma fórmula molecular pero con diferente fórmula estructural (pág. 265)

isotopes / isótopos átomos de un determinado elemento que posee diferentes cantidades de neutrones y diferentes cantidades de masa (pág. 112)

J

jet stream / corriente de chorro un cinturón de vientos de alta velocidad que se encuentran en las capas superiores de la troposfera (pág. 759)

joule (J) / julio (J) unidad de trabajo de SI que equivale a 1 newton por metro (pág. 414)

K

kinetic energy / energía cinética la energía que tiene un objeto debido a su movimiento (págs. 71, 447)

Kuiper belt / cinturón de Kuiper un cinturón ancho más allá de la órbita de Plutón donde los objetos, compuestos principalmente de hielo y roca, giran en órbitas alrededor del Sol (pág. 815)

L

land breeze / brisa terrestre un viento local que ocurre cuando el aire más fresco se mueve hacia el agua (pág. 757)

laser / láser un dispositivo que genera un haz de luz coherente (pág. 560)

lava / lava magma que fluye hacia la superficie de la Tierra (pág. 671)

lava plateau / meseta de lava región plana elevada formada por lava endurecida (pág. 696)

law of conservation of charge / ley de la conservación de la carga ley que establece que la carga eléctrica total en un sistema aislado se mantiene constante; la carga eléctrica nunca se crea ni se destruye (pág. 602)

law of conservation of momentum / ley de la conservación del momento ley que establece que el momento total de un sistema no cambia si no hay fuerza neta que actúe sobre el sistema (pág. 376)

law of superposition / ley de superposición ley que establece que en las capas de roca no alteradas, las rocas más jóvenes están sobre las rocas más viejas y las rocas más viejas están debajo de todo (pág. 733)

length / longitud la distancia en línea recta entre dos puntos (pág. 16)

lens / lente un objeto hecho con material transparente y delgado que tiene una o dos superficies curvas que pueden refractar luz (pág. 576)

lever / palanca una barra rígida que puede moverse libremente alrededor de un punto fijo (pág. 428)

lift / fuerza de elevación una fuerza hacia arriba creada por la diferencia de presión entre la parte superior y la parte inferior de un ala (pág. 396)

lightning / rayo una descarga eléctrica natural que ocurre en forma repentina en la atmósfera (pág. 770)

light-year / año luz la distancia que viaja la luz en un vacío durante un año, de aproximadamente 9.5 billones de kilómetros (pág. 834)

linear graph / gráfica lineal una gráfica en la que los datos mostrados forman una línea recta (pág. 347)

liquid / líquido el estado de la materia en el que un material tiene un volumen definido pero no una forma definida (pág. 69)

lithosphere / litósfera una capa de roca rígida, relativamente fría, que comprende la parte superior del manto y la corteza terrestre (pág. 662)

local wind / viento local viento que sopla sobre una distancia corta (pág.757)

loess / loes un depósito que forma el polvo transportado por el viento (pág. 724)

longitudinal wave / onda longitudinal una onda en la que la vibración del medio es paralela a la dirección en que viaja la onda (pág. 502)

longshore drift / deriva litoral el proceso en el que las olas del océano mueven arena a lo largo de la costa (pág. 729)

loudness / volumen una respuesta física a la intensidad del sonido, modificada por factores físicos (pág. 515)

luminous / luminoso la descripción de un objeto que emite su propia luz (pág. 558)

luster / brillo la forma en que la superficie de un mineral refleja la luz (pág. 667)

M

machine / máquina un dispositivo que cambia una fuerza (pág. 417)

magma / magma una mezcla de roca fundida, gases y vapor de agua que se forma bajo la superficie (pág. 671)

magma chamber / cámara magmática zona en forma de bolsa en donde se acumula el magma antes de una erupción volcánica (pág. 691)

magnetic domain / dominio magnético una región que tiene muchos átomos con campos magnéticos alineados (pág. 632)

magnetic field / campo magnético un campo en una región del espacio que ejerce fuerzas magnéticas; un campo producido por imanes, por campos eléctricos variables o por cargas en movimiento (págs. 533, 631)

magnetic force / fuerza magnética la fuerza que un campo magnético ejerce sobre un imán, sobre un material ferromagnético o sobre una carga eléctrica en movimiento (pág. 630)

magnetic pole / polo magnético una región de un imán en donde la fuerza es mayor (pág. 630)

magnetosphere / magnetosfera el área que rodea la Tierra y que está bajo la influencia del campo magnético (pág. 632)

main sequence / secuencia principal una banda diagonal en el diagrama H-R, que representa aproximadamente el 90% de todas las estrellas (pág. 839)

malleability / maleabilidad la capacidad que tiene un sólido de ser golpeado sin quebrarse (pág. 46)

Spanish Glossary

manipulated variable / variable manipulada la variable que causa un cambio en otra variable (pág. 8)

mantle / manto capa gruesa de roca caliente pero sólida que se encuentra debajo de la corteza terrestre (pág. 662)

maria / maria llanuras de basalto planas y bajas sobre la Luna formadas por antiguos caudales de lava (pág. 797)

mass / masa la cantidad de materia que tiene un objeto (pág. 16); medida de la inercia de un objeto que depende de la cantidad de materia que contiene el mismo (pág. 365)

mass extinction / extinción masiva el límite entre eras geológicas en el que diversas formas de organismos vivos se extinguieron en un período relativamente corto (pág. 735)

mass movement / movimiento masivo el movimiento hacia abajo de roca y tierra debido a la gravedad, por ejemplo alud, soliflucción, reptación y desprendimiento (pág. 712)

mass number / número de masa la suma del número de protones y neutrones del núcleo de un átomo (pág. 110)

meander / meandro curva en forma de lazo que se forma en un río cuando el agua en movimiento lento deposita sedimento en la curva interior del río (pág. 716)

mechanical advantage / ventaja mecánica la cantidad de veces que una máquina aumenta la fuerza aplicada (pág. 421)

mechanical energy / energía mecánica la energía relacionada con el movimiento y la posición de objetos cotidianos (pág. 450)

mechanical wave / onda mecánica la perturbación en la materia que lleva energía de un lugar a otro (pág. 500)

mechanical weathering / desgaste mecánico proceso de fragmentación físico de las rocas en partes más pequeñas (pág. 710)

medium / medio el material a través del cual viajan las ondas (pág. 500)

melting point / punto de fusión temperatura a la cual una sustancia cambia de sólida a líquida (pág. 47)

mesosphere / mesosfera la porción inferior del manto de la Tierra (pág. 662); la capa de la atmósfera terrestre que está justo encima de la estratosfera (pág. 750)

metals / metales elementos que son buenos conductores de calor y corriente eléctrica (pág. 135)

metallic bond / enlace metálico la atracción existente entre un catión metálico y los electrones compartidos que lo rodean (pág. 176)

metalloids / metaloides elementos con propiedades que están entre las de los metales y los no metales (pág. 136)

metamorphic rock / roca metamórfica roca que ha sido transformada por la temperatura, presión o reacciones con agua caliente (pág. 674)

meteoroid / meteoroide trozo de roca que se mueve a través del sistema solar (pág. 797)

meteorologist / meteorólogo científico que estudia e intenta predecir el tiempo (pág. 774)

microscope / microscopio instrumento óptico que usa lentes para agrandar la imagen de objetos cercanos y muy pequeños (pág. 584)

mid-ocean ridge / dorsal oceánica cadena montañosa que se encuentra sumergida en el agua (pág. 678)

mineral / mineral sólido inorgánico que ocurre de forma natural con estructura cristalina y composición química definida (pág. 665)

mirage / espejismo imagen falsa o distorsionada (pág. 548)

model / modelo representación de un objeto o evento (pág. 10)

molarity / molaridad el número de moles de un soluto disuelto por litro de solución (pág. 239)

molar mass / masa molar masa de un mol de una sustancia (pág. 196)

mole / mol cantidad de una sustancia que contiene aproximadamente 6.02×10^{23} partículas de la sustancia (pág. 195)

molecule / molécula un grupo neutro de átomos, unidos entre sí por uno o más enlaces covalentes (pág. 166)

momentum / momento producto de la masa de un objeto y su velocidad (pág. 374)

monomer / monómero una pequeña molécula orgánica que se une con otros monómeros para formar un polímero (pág. 275)

monsoon / monzón un sistema de vientos que sopla en dirección contraria según la época del año (pág. 759)

moon / luna cuerpo natural relativamente pequeño en el espacio que gira alrededor de un planeta (pág. 792)

moraines / morrenas un montón de sedimentos que se acumula al pie de un glaciar y a lo largo de los lados (pág. 721)

N

neap tide / marea muerta marea que se produce en el primero o último cuarto de luna, cuando la diferencia entre las mareas alta y baja diarias es mínima (pág. 801)

nearsightedness / miopía una condición ocular que hace que los objetos distantes aparezcan borrosos (pág. 590)

nebula / nebulosa una nube grande de gas y polvo que se expande en un gran volumen de espacio (pág. 840)

net force / fuerza neta la fuerza total que actúa sobre un objeto después que todas las fuerzas se combinan (pág. 357)

network solid / sólido reticulado un sólido que tiene todos sus átomos unidos por enlaces covalentes (pág. 263)

neutralization / neutralización la reacción química entre un ácido y una base (pág. 244)

neutron / neutrón una partícula subatómica neutra que se encuentra en el núcleo de un átomo (pág. 109)

neutron star / estrella de neutrones el centro denso que queda cuando una estrella de gran masa ha explotado como una supernova (pág. 844)

newton (N) / newton (N) la unidad de fuerza del SI que equivale a la fuerza que hace que 1 kilogramo de masa se acelere a razón de 1 metro por segundo cuadrado (1 N = 1 kg•m/s^2 (pág. 357)

noble gases / gases nobles elementos en el Grupo 8A de la tabla periódica (pág. 145)

node / nodo un punto de una onda que no presenta desplazamiento con respecto a la posición de reposo (pág. 512)

nonlinear graph / gráfica no lineal una gráfica en que los datos trazados o mostrados forman una línea curva (pág. 348)

nonmetals / no metales elementos que son malos conductores del calor y la corriente eléctrica (pág. 136)

nonrenewable energy resource / recurso energético no renovable una fuente de energía que existe en cantidades limitadas y que una vez utilizada no puede ser reemplazada salvo con el transcurso de millones de años (pág. 462)

nuclear energy / energía nuclear la energía que se encuentra almacenada en los núcleos atómicos (pág. 452)

nuclear radiation / radiación nuclear partículas y ondas electromagnéticas con carga emitidas desde el núcleo de los radioisótopos (pág. 293)

nucleic acid / ácido nucleico un polímero grande con nitrógeno que se encuentra principalmente en el núcleo de las células (pág. 279)

nucleus / núcleo masa densa con carga positiva que se encuentra ubicada en el centro de un átomo (pág. 105)

O

observation / observación información que se obtiene a través de los sentidos (pág. 8)

occluded front / frente ocluido un frente que se produce cuando una masa de aire caliente queda atrapada entre dos masas de aire más frío (pág. 768)

Ohm's law / ley de Ohm la relación entre voltaje, corriente y resistencia V = IR (pág. 607)

Oort cloud / nube de Oort se cree que es una esfera espesa de cometas que rodea al sistema solar por fuera hasta una distancia de aproximadamente 50,000 UA (pág. 815)

opaque / opaco la descripción de un material que absorbe o refleja toda la luz que incide sobre él de modo que no puede verse nada a través del mismo (pág. 547)

orbital / orbital región de espacio alrededor del núcleo en donde es posible encontrar un electrón (pág. 117)

organic compounds / compuestos orgánicos compuestos que contienen carbón e hidrógeno, a menudo se combinan con algunos otros elementos tales como el oxígeno o nitrógeno (pág. 262)

output arm / brazo de salida la distancia entre el fulcro en una palanca y la fuerza desarrollada (pág. 428)

output distance / distancia de salida distancia a través de la cual actúa una fuerza desarrollada de una máquina (pág. 420)

output force / fuerza desarrollada fuerza que ejerce una máquina (pág. 420)

oxbow lake / laguna de brazo muerto laguna que se forma cuando un río forma un nuevo paso y deja un meandro aislado del curso principal del río (pág. 716)

oxidation-reduction (redox) reaction / reacción de oxidación-reducción (redox) una reacción química en la que hay transferencia de electrones entre los reactantes (pág. 204)

ozone layer / capa de ozono una región de concentración de ozono en la estratosfera (pág. 750)

P

Pangaea / Pangea antiguo supercontinente que se formó hace unos 300 millones de años, que luego dio origen a los actuales continentes (pág. 677)

parallax / paralaje el cambio aparente en la posición de un objeto con respecto a un fondo lejano cuando es visto desde diferentes ubicaciones (pág. 835)

parallel circuit / circuito en paralelo un circuito eléctrico con dos o más pasos a través de los que puede fluir carga (pág. 610)

pascal (Pa) / pascal (Pa) unidad de presión del SI que equivale a 1 newton por metro cuadrado (N/m^2) (pág. 391)

penumbra / penumbra región de sombra de la Luna que rodea la umbra y es menos oscura que la umbra (pág. 800)

period / período hilera en una tabla periódica de elementos (pág. 131); el tiempo que se necesita para tener un ciclo completo de movimiento periódico (pág. 504); unidad de tiempo geológico que los geólogos usan para dividir las eras (pág. 734)

periodic law / ley periódica el patrón de repetición de propiedades que muestran los elementos en la tabla periódica (pág. 131)

periodic motion / movimiento periódico todo movimiento que se repite a intervalos regulares (pág. 504)

periodic table / tabla periódica una organización de elementos en columnas basada en una serie de propiedades que se repiten de hilera en hilera (pág. 127)

permeable / permeable la descripción de un material a través del cual el agua puede pasar con facilidad (pág. 707)

pH / pH una medida de la concentración del ión de hidronio que tiene una solución (pág. 247)

phase change / cambio de fase un cambio físico reversible que ocurre cuando una sustancia cambia de un estado de materia a otro (pág. 84)

phases / fases las diversas formas del lado iluminado de la Luna visto desde la Tierra (pág. 798)

phosphor / fósforo material sólido que emite luz por fluorescencia (pág. 559)

photoelectric effect / efecto fotoeléctrico la emisión de electrones de un metal causada por la luz que llega hasta un metal (pág. 537)

photon / fotón paquete de energía electromagnética (pág. 537)

photosphere / fotosfera una delgada capa interna de la atmósfera del Sol, que es la superficie visible del Sol (pág. 831)

photosynthesis / fotosíntesis proceso en que las plantas combinan químicamente dióxido de carbono y agua para formar carbohidratos, proceso que requiere luz y clorofila (pág. 282)

physical change / cambio físico un cambio que ocurre cuando algunas propiedades de un material cambian, pero las sustancias del material permanecen constantes (pág. 51)

physical property / propiedad física toda característica de un material que se puede observar o medir sin cambiar la composición de las sustancias del material (pág. 45)

physics / física el estudio de materia y energía y las interacciones entre las dos a través de fuerzas y movimiento (pág. 4)

pigment / pigmento un material que absorbe selectivamente ciertos colores de luz y refleja otros colores (pág. 553)

pipe / chimenea canal estrecho y vertical por donde el magma sube a la superficie de la Tierra (pág. 691)

pitch / tono frecuencia de un sonido como lo percibe quien lo escucha (pág. 515)

plane mirror / espejo plano espejo con superficie plana (pág. 571)

planetary nebula / nebulosa planetaria una nube brillante de gas que rodea una estrella moribunda de baja masa (pág. 842)

planetesimals / planetesimales cuerpos con tamaño de asteroides en el disco protoplanetario que se combinan para formar planetas (pág. 819)

plasma / plasma el estado de la materia en el que los átomos han sido despojados de sus electrones (pág. 315)

plate tectonics / tectónica de placas teoría que establece que trozos de litosfera de la Tierra, llamados placas, se mueven lentamente sobre la astenosfera (pág. 676)

plucking / arranque glaciar un proceso en el que los hielos glaciales agrandan las grietas en lechos de roca debajo de un glaciar, y arrastra los trozos sueltos de roca (pág. 720)

polar covalent bond / enlace polar covalente enlace covalente en el que los electrones no se comparten por igual (pág. 168)

polarized light / luz polarizada tipo de luz que tiene luz con ondas que vibran en un solo plano (pág. 548)

polar zones / zonas polares regiones que son generalmente frías y se extienden desde latitud norte 66.5° hasta el Polo Norte y desde latitud sur 66.5° hasta el Polo Sur (pág. 753)

polyatomic ion / ión poliatómico un grupo de átomos con enlaces covalentes de átomos que tiene carga positiva o negativa y actúa como unidad (pág. 172)

polymer / polímero una molécula de gran tamaño que se forma cuando muchas moléculas pequeñas están unidas entre sí por enlaces covalentes (pág. 275)

potential difference / diferencia potencial voltaje, es decir, la diferencia de energía eléctrica potencial entre dos puntos de un campo eléctrico (pág. 606)

potential energy / energía potencial energía que se almacena como consecuencia de la posición o forma (pág. 448)

power / potencia tasa de realizar trabajo (pág. 414)

precipitate / precipitado un sólido que se forma y se separa de una mezcla líquida (pág. 57)

precision / precisión medida de cuán exacta es una medición (pág. 19)

pressure / presión resultado de una fuerza distribuida sobre un área (págs. 75, 390)

primary colors / colores primarios tres colores específicos que se pueden combinar en intensidades variadas para crear millones de colores (pág. 552)

products / productos sustancias nuevas que se forman como consecuencia de una reacción química (pág. 192)

projectile motion / movimiento de proyectil la trayectoria curvada de un objeto en caída libre después de haber recibido una velocidad horizontal inicial (pág. 362)

prominences / protuberancias solares lazos grandes de gas que erupcionan desde las regiones de manchas solares y se extienden hacia arriba desde la fotosfera hacia la cromosfera y a veces hasta dentro de la corona (pág. 833)

protein / proteína polímero grande que se forma cuando los aminoácidos se unen entre sí (pág. 280)

proton / protón una partícula subatómica con carga positiva que se encuentra en el núcleo de un átomo (pág. 108)

protoplanetary disk / disco protoplanetario una nube grande de polvo y gas, en forma de disco, que se formó cuando la nebulosa solar rotaba más rápido y luego comenzó a aplanarse (pág. 819)

protostar / protoestrella nebulosa que se contrae con suficiente masa para formar una estrella (pág. 841)

pulley / polea una máquina simple con una cuerda que pasa por el canal de una rueda (pág. 432)

pulsar / púlsar estrella de neutrón que gira y emite fuertes pulsaciones de ondas radio (pág. 844)

pupil / pupila abertura que permite la entrada de luz en el ojo (pág. 589)

pure substance / sustancia pura material que siempre tiene exactamente la misma composición; elemento o compuesto (pág. 39)

P waves / ondas P ondas primarias; ondas longitudinales que producen los terremotos (pág. 686)

Q

quark / quark partícula subatómica que según las teorías se encuentra entre las unidades básicas de la materia (pág. 305)

quasar / quásar el centro de gran tamaño y muy luminoso de las galaxias jóvenes distantes (pág. 849)

R

radiation / radiación transferencia de energía por ondas que se mueven en el espacio (pág. 481)

radiation zone / zona de radiación región de plasma que se encuentra firmemente unida fuera del centro del sol, en donde la energía se transfiere por la absorción y nueva radiación de luz (pág. 830)

radioactivity / radiactividad proceso en el que un núcleo atómico inestable emite partículas con carga y energía (pág. 292)

radioisotope / radioisótopo isótopo con núcleo inestable (pág. 292)

rarefaction / rarefacción área de una onda longitudinal en que las partículas del medio se esparcen (pág. 502)

ray diagram / diagrama de rayo diagrama que muestra cómo los rayos de luz cambian de dirección cuando chocan contra los espejos y pasan a través de los lentes (pág. 570)

reactant / reactante una sustancia que sufre cambios durante una reacción química (pág. 192)

reaction rate / velocidad de reacción velocidad con que los reactantes se transforman en productos en un tiempo determinado (pág. 212)

reactivity / reactividad propiedad que describe con qué facilidad una sustancia se combina químicamente con otras sustancias (pág. 55)

real image / imagen real copia de un objeto que se forma en el punto en que los rayos de luz se encuentran (pág. 572)

red shift / desplazamiento hacia el rojo un desplazamiento hacia las longitudes de onda rojas de la luz proveniente de las estrellas o galaxias que se alejan de la Tierra (pág. 852)

reflecting telescope / telescopio reflector telescopio que utiliza espejos y lentes convexas para reunir y enfocar luz (pág. 581)

reflection / reflexión la interacción que se produce cuando una onda rebota contra una superficie que no puede atravesar (pág. 508)

refracting telescope / telescopio refractor telescopio que usa sólo lentes para reunir y enfocar luz (pág. 581)

refraction / refracción la curva de una onda al entrar en ángulo en un nuevo medio (pág. 508)

refrigerant / refrigerante fluido que se vaporiza y se condensa dentro de la tubería de una bomba de calor (pág. 490)

regular reflection / reflexión regular reflexión que se produce cuando ondas de luz paralelas chocan contra una superficie y todas se reflejan en la misma dirección (pág. 547)

relative age / edad relativa la edad de una roca comparada con las edades de otras rocas, por encima o por debajo de la misma, en una secuencia de capas de roca (pág. 732)

relative humidity / humedad relativa proporción de la cantidad de vapor de agua en el aire con respecto a la cantidad máxima de vapor de agua que el aire puede contener a esa temperatura (pág. 760)

relative motion / movimiento relativo movimiento en relación al marco de referencia (pág. 329)

renewable energy resource / recurso renovable de energía fuente de energía que se puede reemplazar en períodos relativamente cortos (pág. 463)

resistance / resistencia oposición al flujo de cargas eléctricas en un material (pág. 605)

resonance / resonancia la respuesta de una onda estacionaria a otra onda de la misma frecuencia, con gran incremento de amplitud de la onda estacionaria (pág. 521)

responding variable / variable respuesta variable que cambia en respuesta a un cambio en la variable manipulada (pág. 8)

Spanish Glossary

resultant vector / vector resultante la suma vectorial de dos o más vectores (pág. 331)

retina / retina superficie interna de la parte posterior del ojo, que contiene terminales nerviosas sensibles a la luz (pág. 589)

reversible reaction / reacción reversible una reacción química en la que la conversión de reactantes en productos y la conversión de productos en reactantes se produce al mismo tiempo (pág. 217)

revolution / revolución o traslación movimiento o giro de un cuerpo alrededor de otro (pág. 752)

ring / anillo disco que está formado por muchas partículas pequeñas de roca y hielo que giran alrededor de un planeta (pág. 811)

rock / roca una combinación sólida de minerales u otros materiales (pág. 665)

rock cycle / ciclo de roca una serie de procesos en que las rocas cambian continuamente de un tipo al otro (pág. 674)

rods / bastoncillos neuronas sensibles a la luz en la retina que detectan luz de baja intensidad y distinguen blanco, negro y gris (pág. 589)

rolling friction / fricción de rodamiento fuerza de fricción que actúa sobre objetos rodantes y que se produce debido al cambio de forma en el punto de contacto de rodamiento (pág. 360)

rotation / rotación movimiento de un planeta o luna sobre su eje (pág. 752)

runoff / escorrentía agua que fluye sobre la superficie de la Tierra (pág. 706)

S

salinity / salinidad proporción de sales disueltas en agua (pág. 725)

salt / sal compuesto iónico que se forma cuando un ácido reacciona con una base (pág. 244)

saltation / salto movimiento de partículas como la arena que es arrastrada por el agua o viento en una serie de pequeños saltos (pág. 714)

saturated hydrocarbon / hidrocarburo saturado un hidrocarburo que tiene todos sus enlaces simples (pág. 264)

saturated solution / solución saturada una solución que contiene la cantidad de soluto que el solvente puede contener a una cierta temperatura (pág. 236)

saturated zone / zona saturada una región debajo de la superficie de la Tierra en que los espacios de los poros están totalmente llenos de aguas freáticas (pág. 707)

scattering / dispersión proceso en el que la luz cambia de dirección cuando atraviesa un medio (pág. 549)

science / ciencia sistema de conocimientos sobre el mundo natural y los métodos que se usan para encontrar esos conocimientos (pág. 3)

scientific law / ley científica una afirmación que resume un patrón que se encuentra en la naturaleza (pág. 9)

scientific method / método científico un plan organizado que se utiliza para recoger, organizar y transmitir información (pág. 7)

scientific notation / notación científica una forma de expresar un valor como el producto de un número entre 1 y 10 y una potencia de 10 (pág. 14)

scientific theory / teoría científica una explicación bien comprobada que corresponde a un conjunto de observaciones o resultados experimentales (pág. 9)

screw / tornillo plano inclinado envuelto alrededor de un cilindro (pág. 431)

sea breeze / brisa marina viento local que se produce cuando el aire más fresco que se encuentra sobre el agua fluye hacia la tierra (pág. 757)

sea-floor spreading / expansión del suelo marino proceso por el que se crea nueva corteza oceánica en las dorsales oceánicas, a medida que la corteza más vieja desaparece (pág. 678)

secondary color / color secundario color nuevo que resulta cuando se combinan dos colores primarios (pág. 552)

sediment / sedimento piezas sólidas y pequeñas de material que provienen de rocas y organismos vivos (pág. 672)

sedimentary rock / roca sedimentaria roca que se forma a través del tiempo a partir de la compactación y consolidación de los sedimentos (pág. 672)

seismic waves / ondas sísmicas vibraciones que transmiten la energía liberada durante un terremoto (pág. 684)

seismograph / sismógrafo un dispositivo para detectar y registrar ondas sísmicas (pág. 687)

semiconductor / semiconductor un sólido cristalino que conduce corriente eléctrica sólo bajo ciertas condiciones (pág. 621)

series circuit / circuito en serie circuito eléctrico con un sólo trayecto a través del cual puede fluir la carga (pág. 610)

shield volcano / volcán en escudo un volcán ancho, relativamente plano que se origina como consecuencia de erupciones tranquilas con lava de baja viscosidad (pág. 693)

significant figures / cifras significativas todos los dígitos que se miden directamente en una medición, más el último dígito, que es aproximado (pág. 19)

silicate / silicato roca formada por compuestos de silicio y oxígeno, que por lo general contiene metales como aluminio, hierro o calcio (pág. 661)

sill / dique concordante una estructura que se forma cuando el magma se endurece en una grieta paralela a las capas de roca existentes (pág. 696)

single-replacement reaction / reacción de sustitución simple una reacción química en la que un elemento toma el lugar de otro en un compuesto (pág. 202)

sinkhole / socavones agujero que se forma cuando la erosión debilita una capa de piedra caliza, lo que provoca el derrumbe repentino de algunas partes del suelo (pág. 717)

sliding friction / fricción de deslizamiento una fuerza de fricción que se opone al movimiento de un objeto a medida que se desliza sobre una superficie (pág. 359)

slope / pendiente línea inclinada que equivale a la proporción de un cambio vertical con el correspondiente cambio horizontal (págs. 23, 334)

solar energy / energía solar luz solar que se convierte en energía utilizable (pág. 464)

solar flare / fulguración solar erupción repentina en la superficie solar que, por lo general, ocurre cerca de las manchas solares, produce rayos X y envía partículas con carga al espacio a velocidades de 1000 km/s o más (pág. 833)

solar nebula / nebulosa solar nube de polvo y gas que eventualmente puede desaparecer para formar una o más estrellas con un sistema planetario (pág. 818)

solar system / sistema solar el Sol, los planetas, sus lunas y una variedad de objetos pequeños que giran alrededor del Sol (pág. 792)

solar wind / viento solar una corriente de partículas con cargas eléctricas que fluye desde el Sol hacia afuera a través del sistema solar (pág. 831)

solenoid / solenoide una bobina de alambre conductor que produce un campo magnético (pág. 637)

solid / sólido estado de la materia en el que los materiales tienen una forma definida y un volumen definido (pág. 69)

solstice / solsticio día que marca el comienzo del verano o del invierno; día en que el Sol está directamente encima a una latitud norte 23.5° o latitud sur 23.5° (pág. 753)

solubility / solubilidad cantidad máxima de soluto que se disuelve normalmente en una cierta cantidad de solvente a cierta temperatura (pág. 235)

solute / soluto una sustancia cuyas partículas se disuelven en una solución (pág. 229)

solution / solución una mezcla que se forma cuando se disuelven sustancias y forman una mezcla homogénea (pág. 42)

solvent / solvente una sustancia en la que se disuelve un soluto (pág. 229)

sonar / sonar técnica que sirve para determinar la distancia a un objeto bajo el agua (pág. 516)

sound wave / onda sonora onda longitudinal que consiste en compresiones y rarefacciones y que viaja a través de un medio (pág. 514)

space probe / sonda espacial vehículo no pilotado que lleva instrumentos científicos al espacio y envía datos a la Tierra (pág. 794)

specific heat / calor específico cantidad de calor que se necesita para elevar la temperatura de un gramo de material un grado Celsius (pág. 476)

speed / rapidez proporción de la distancia a que se mueve un objeto con respecto a la cantidad de tiempo en que se mueve el objeto (pág. 332)

spiral galaxy / galaxia espiral una galaxia como la Vía Láctea que tiene una gran cantidad de estrellas en su centro con brazos que se extienden hacia fuera como un molinete (pág. 848)

spring tide / marea viva marea de luna nueva o llena cuando el cambio entre las marea alta y baja diarias es más pronunciado (pág. 801)

stalactite / estalactita una formación tipo carámbano en el techo de una caverna que se forma cuando el agua gotea desde el techo de la caverna (pág. 717)

stalagmite / estalagmita un pilar de minerales en una caverna que se forma cuando el agua gotea hacia el piso de la caverna (pág. 717)

standing wave / onda estacionaria onda que parece quedarse en un lugar y no moverse a través de un medio (pág. 512)

star / estrella bola de gas grande y brillante en el espacio que genera energía a través de la fusión nuclear en su centro (pág. 834)

star system / sistema de estrellas grupo de dos o más estrellas que permanecen unidas por la fuerza de gravedad (pág. 847)

static electricity / electricidad estática estudio del comportamiento de las cargas eléctricas y de la manera en que la carga se transfiere entre objetos (pág. 602)

static friction / fricción estática fuerza de fricción que actúa sobre los objetos que no se mueven (pág. 359)

stationary front / frente estacionario un frente que ocurre cuando dos masas de aire han formado un límite pero ninguna se mueve (pág. 768)

stratosphere / estratosfera capa de la atmósfera terrestre que se encuentra sobre la troposfera (pág. 750)

stratus clouds / nubes estratos capas planas de nubes que cubren gran parte o todo el cielo (pág. 762)

streak / veta el color del polvo de un mineral (pág. 666)

stress / esfuerzo las fuerzas de deformación que actúan sobre las rocas de la corteza terrestre (pág. 685)

strong nuclear force / fuerza nuclear fuerte una fuerza potente de atracción que une protones y neutrones en el núcleo (págs. 308, 379)

subduction / subducción proceso en el que la corteza oceánica se hunde en el manto a través de una grieta (pág. 679)

Spanish Glossary

sublimation / sublimación cambio de fase en que una sustancia cambia de estado sólido a gaseoso o vapor sin pasar por el estado líquido primero (pág. 91)

substance / sustancia materia que siempre tiene exactamente la misma composición; elemento o compuesto (pág. 39)

substituted hydrocarbon / hidrocarburo sustituido hidrocarburo en el que uno o más átomos de hidrógeno han sido reemplazados o sustituidos (pág. 272)

sunspot / mancha solar área de gas en la fotosfera del Sol que es más fría que los gases que la circundan (pág. 832)

superconductor / superconductor un material con resistencia casi cero al ser enfriado a temperaturas bajas (pág. 605)

supergiant / supergigante una estrella de gran tamaño, masiva y muy brillante que tiene un diámetro entre 100 y 1000 veces el diámetro del Sol (pág. 839)

supernova / supernova una explosión enorme en la que los restos de la fusión de una estrella supergigante son arrojados al espacio (pág. 843)

supersaturated solution / solución supersaturada una solución que contiene más cantidad de soluto que el solvente puede retener normalmente a una determinada temperatura (pág. 236)

surface current / corriente superficial una corriente de agua oceánica de gran tamaño que se mueve contiuamente en casi el mismo trayecto (pág. 726)

surface wave / onda superficial onda que viaja a lo largo de una superficie y que separa dos medios (pág. 503); onda transversal que se produce cuando una onda sísmica alcanza la superficie de la Tierra (pág. 687)

suspension / suspensión una mezcla heterogénea que se separa con el tiempo en capas (pág. 43)

S waves / ondas S ondas secundarias; ondas transversales que producen los terremotos (pág. 687)

synthesis reaction / reacción de síntesis reacción química en la que dos o más sustancias reaccionan para formar una sola sustancia (pág. 200)

T

technology / tecnología uso del conocimiento científico para resolver problemas prácticos (pág. 3)

telescope / telescopio un instrumento óptico que usa lentes (o lentes y espejos) para recoger y enfocar luz desde objetos lejanos (pág. 580)

temperate zones / áreas templadas regiones que son generalmente más frescas que los trópicos y están situadas entre latitud norte 23.5° y latitud norte 66.5° y entre latitud sur 23.5° y latitud sur 66.5° (pág. 753)

temperature / temperatura es una medición de cuán caliente o frío está un objeto si se lo compara con un punto de referencia (pág. 475)

terminal velocity / velocidad terminal velocidad constante de un objeto en caída cuando la fuerza de resistencia del aire es igual a la fuerza de gravedad (pág. 361)

terrestrial planets / planetas telúricos los cuatro planetas más cercanos al Sol (Mercurio, Venus, Tierra y Marte) que tienen una estructura similar a la Tierra (pág. 803)

thermal conductor / conductor térmico un material que conduce bien la energía térmica (pág. 480)

thermal energy / energía térmica la energía potencial y cinética total relacionada con el movimiento de todas las partículas de un objeto (pág. 451)

thermal expansion / expansión térmica aumento de volumen de un material cuando incrementa su temperatura (pág. 476)

thermal insulator / aislante térmico material que no conduce bien la energía térmica (pág. 480)

thermodynamics / termodinámica estudio de las conversiones entre energía térmica y otras formas de energía (pág. 482)

thermogram / termograma un dibujo o imagen con código de colores que utiliza variaciones en la radiación infrarroja y que sirve para mostrar los cambios en la temperatura (pág. 543)

thermometer / termómetro un instrumento que sirve para medir la temperatura (pág. 20)

thermosphere / termosfera la capa más externa de la atmósfera terrestre (pág. 751)

thunder / trueno el sonido que produce el aire que se expande rápidamente a lo largo del trayecto de una descarga de un relámpago (pág. 770)

thunderstorm / tormenta de truenos un pequeño sistema meteorológico que tiene truenos y relámpagos (pág. 770)

tides / mareas la subida y bajada regular de las aguas del océano (pág. 801)

till / tillita sedimento o arcilla glacial que queda al derretirse el glaciar (pág. 721)

tornado / tornado una tormenta de viento pequeña pero intensa que toma la forma de una columna de aire giratoria que toca el suelo (pág. 770)

total internal reflection / reflexión interna total la reflexión completa de un rayo de luz que regresa a su medio original cuando el ángulo de incidencia es mayor que el ángulo crítico de refracción (pág. 578)

transform boundary / borde de transformación límite en el que las placas tectónicas se deslizan a lo largo de sí mismas, moviéndose en direcciones opuestas (pág. 682)

transformer / transformador un dispositivo que aumenta o disminuye el voltaje de dos circuitos CA conectados (pág. 644)

transistor / transistor un componente en estado sólido que tiene tres capas de material semiconductor y que sirve para encender o apagar corriente o para incrementar la fuerza de señales electrónicas (pág. 621)

transition metals / metales de transición elementos que forman un puente entre los elementos que se encuentran en el lado izquierdo y derecho de la tabla periódica (pág. 136)

translucent / translúcido descripción de un material que dispersa luz que pasa a través del mismo (pág. 547)

transmutation / transmutación la conversión de un elemento en otro por medio de una reacción nuclear (pág. 303)

transparent / transparente descripción de un material que deja pasar la mayor parte de la luz que incide sobre él (pág. 546)

transpiration / transpiración pérdida de agua a través de las hojas de las plantas (pág. 705)

transuranium elements / elementos del grupo transuranio elementos que tienen números atómicos mayores que 92 (pág. 304)

transverse wave / onda transversal onda que hace vibrar a un medio en ángulos rectos en la dirección en que viaja la onda (pág. 50)

trench / fosa una depresión larga y profunda en el suelo oceánico donde la antigua corteza oceánica se hunde en el manto (pág. 679)

tributary / afluente una corriente de agua pequeña que desemboca en un río principal (pág. 706)

tropic zone / zona tropical región cálida entre la latitud sur 23.5° y latitud norte 23.5° (pág. 753)

troposphere / troposfera capa inferior de la atmósfera terrestre en donde ocurre mayormente el clima (pág. 749)

trough / valle punto más bajo de una onda transversal (pág. 501)

tsunami / tsunami gran ola causada por un terremoto en el fondo del mar, volcán, o derrumbe costero (p. 685)

turbine / turbina un dispositivo con paletas en forma de ventilador que giran cuando son impulsadas, por ejemplo, por agua o vapor (pág. 646)

U

umbra / umbra parte más oscura de la sombra (pág. 800)

uniformitarianism / uniformismo el principio que establece que los procesos geológicos que ocurren en la actualidad también ocurrieron en el pasado (pág. 661)

unsaturated hydrocarbon / hidrocarburo no saturado hidrocarburo que contiene uno o más enlaces dobles o triples (pág. 265)

unsaturated solution / solución no saturada una solución en que puede disolverse más soluto a una determinada temperatura (pág. 236)

upwelling / afloramiento el movimiento del agua desde las profundidades hacia la superficie del océano (pág. 728)

V

valence electron / electrón de valencia electrón que se encuentra en el nivel energético más alto ocupado que tiene un átomo (pág. 139)

valley glacier / glaciar de montaña una masa larga y estrecha de hielo y nieve en movimiento que comienza, por lo general, cerca del pico de una montaña y se dirige hacia abajo a través del valle y que ha sido formado en un principio por una corriente de agua (pág. 719)

vaporization / vaporización cambio de fase en que una sustancia cambia de estado líquido a gaseoso (pág. 88)

vapor pressure / presión de vapor presión que producen las colisiones o choques de partículas en un vapor dentro de las paredes de un contenedor (pág. 89)

vector / vector una cantidad que tiene una dirección asociada con la misma (pág. 330)

velocity / velocidad la rapidez y la dirección en la que se mueve un objeto y se mide según un punto de referencia (pág. 336)

vent / boca una abertura en el suelo por donde el magma fluye a la superficie terrestre (pág. 691)

virtual image / imagen virtual una copia de un objeto que se forma en el punto desde donde parece venir la luz (pág. 571)

viscosity / viscosidad la tendencia que tiene un líquido a dejar de fluir; resistencia a fluir (pág. 45)

vitamin / vitamina un compuesto orgánico que no producen los organismos vivos pero lo necesitan en pequeñas cantidades (pág. 284)

volcanic neck / cuello volcánico una estructura que se forma cuando el magma se endurece en una chimenea volcánica (pág. 696)

volcano / volcán una montaña que se forma cuando el magma alcanza la superficie (pág. 690)

voltage / voltaje diferencia potencial, la diferencia de energía eléctrica potencial entre dos puntos en un campo eléctrico (pág. 606)

volume / volumen la cantidad de espacio que ocupa un objeto (pág. 16)

Spanish Glossary

W

warm front / frente cálido un frente que se produce cuando una masa de aire caliente rebasa una masa de aire frío (pág. 768)

waste heat / calor perdido energía térmica descargada en un área a una temperatura más baja que no se convierte en trabajo útil (pág. 483)

water cycle / ciclo del agua movimiento continuo del agua en todas sus formas, entre los océanos, atmósfera y la tierra (pág. 705)

watershed / cuenca hidrográfica un territorio con vertientes que fluyen a un sistema fluvial (pág. 706)

water table / nivel freático es la parte superior de una zona saturada (pág. 707)

watt (W) / vatio (W) unidad de potencia del SI que equivale a un julio por segundo (pág. 415)

wavelength / longitud de onda la distancia entre un punto de la onda y el mismo punto en el siguiente ciclo de la onda (pág. 505)

weak nuclear force / fuerza nuclear débil fuerza de atracción potente que actúa sobre un alcance corto o a corta distancia (pág. 380)

weather / clima la condición de la atmósfera en un lugar determinado en un momento determinado (pág. 749)

weathering / desgaste proceso de fragmentación químico o físico de las rocas (pág. 710)

wedge / cuña objeto en forma de V que tiene lados en forma de dos planos inclinados, el uno hacia el otro (pág. 431)

weight / peso fuerza de gravedad que actúa sobre un objeto (pág. 367)

wheel and axle / rueda y eje una máquina simple que está formada por dos discos o cilindros rígidamente unidos y cada uno tiene un radio diferente (pág. 430)

white dwarf / enana blanca resto pequeño, opaco y denso de una estrella de masa mediana o baja (pág. 839)

wind / viento un movimiento de aire, principalmente horizontal, que proviene de áreas de mayor presión hacia áreas de menor presión (pág. 757)

work / trabajo el producto de la distancia y fuerza en la dirección en que se mueve un objeto (pág. 412)

work input / trabajo de entrada trabajo que realiza una máquina cuando la fuerza aplicada actúa a través de la distancia de entrada (pág. 419)

work output / trabajo de salida trabajo que realiza una máquina cuando la fuerza desarrollada actúa a través de la distancia de salida (pág. 420)

Index

The page on which a term is defined is indicated in **bold-face** type.

Index

biomass energy, **464**
bismuth, 143
bits, and bytes, 614
bitterness, 242
black holes, 846, **848**, 849
Blanchard Springs Caverns, 199
blood, 250–253
   crossmatching, 253
   equilibrium reactions in, 218
blood banks, 252
Bohr, Niels, 113–116
boiler, 271, 489
boiling, 89–90
boiling point, **47**
   atmospheric pressure and, 89–90
   of chlorocarbons, 273
   of hydrocarbons, 268
   of methane, 169
   of naphthalene, 85
   of nitrogen and oxygen, 143
   solutions and, 231
Boltwood, Bertram, 681
bonds, chemical, 156–159, **160**–181
   breaking of, 207, 232, 284
   covalent, 165–169, 172
   double, 167, 266
   energy and, 206–207, 451
   ionic, 158–164
   metallic, 176–177
   triple, 167, 266
boron, 142, 182, 621
boron family (Group 3A), 142
Bose, Satyendra, 70
Bose-Einstein condensate (BEC), 70
Boyle, Robert, 79
Boyle's law, 78, **79**, 80
brain scanning, 545
branched-chain hydrocarbons, 265
brass, 180
breathing, 75, 77
breezes, 757
brightness of stars, 840–841, 843
bromine, 39, 144
   in Mendeleev's periodic table, 128
   molecules of, 166
bronze, 180
Bronze Age, 179
Bryce Canyon, 709
buffers, 248
   in blood, 251
bumper cars, 375
buoyancy, **400**–405
   Archimedes' principle, 401
   calculating, 405
   density and, 401–404
   of submarines, 402–403
buoyant force, **400**–405
burning, 54, 192, 270, 282
butane, 265
   in natural gas, 267
bytes, 24, 614

cacao beans, 242
Cactus Hill site, 288
calcite, 669, 711
calcium, 141
   as essential element, 146
   compounds of, 137, 141, 170, 199, 203, 204, 673
   oxidation of, 204
caldera, **691**
Calorie (kilocalorie), 212
calorimeter, **478**
Caloris Basin (Mercury), 808
camera obscura, 582
cameras, 580, **582**–584
   digital, 583, 620
cancer, radiation therapy for, 545
capacitors, 622
capsaicin, 41
Carothers, Wallace, 276
carbohydrates, **278**, 282, 283
carbon, 39, 142, 192, 193
   as essential element, 146–147
   forms of, 98, 263
   molar mass of, 196
   in steel, 180
carbon-12, as standard for atomic masses, 134
carbon-14, 293, 300–301, 313
carbon capture, 786
carbon chemistry, 260–285
   hydrocarbons, 264–269
   polymers, 275–280
   reactions in cells, 282–284
carbon dioxide, 54, 57, 192, 193, 200, 238, 268, 747
   in blood, 251
   global warming and, 782, 784, 786
   as nonpolar molecule, 168, 169
carbon family (Group 4A), 142
carbonic acid, 203, 269, 711, 717
carbon monoxide, 268
carboxyl group, 273
Carlsbad Caverns, 717
Careers in Science, 34–35, 324–325, 656–657
cars. *See* automobiles.
Cassini space probe, 798, 811, 817
catalysts, 214, **215**
   enzymes as, 284
cathode-ray tube (CRT), 103, 619
cations, **160**, 161, 172
   in metals, 177
caves, 199, 226, 717
Cellarius, Andreas, 795
cell phones, 542, 622
cells, reactions in, 280, 282–284
cellular respiration, 283
cellulose, 264, 278
Celsius scale, 20, 475
Cenozoic Era, 738

central heating systems, **489**
central processing unit (CPU), 614, 615
centrifuge, 252
centripetal force, **381**
Cepheid variable stars, 855
Ceres, 818
cesium, 140
Chadwick, James, 109, 115
chain reactions, **311**, 313, 316–317
charge
   conservation of, 602
   electric, 102, 600–601
charged coupled device (CCD), 620
charging
   by conduction, 602
   by friction, 602
   by induction, 603
Charles, Jacques, 78
Charles's law, **78**, 80
Charon (moon), 818
chemical bonds. *See* bonds, chemical.
chemical change, **56**–58, 191, 192, 216
chemical equations, 192–198
chemical energy, **206**, 282–283, **451**
chemical equilibrium, 217
   factors affecting, 218–219
   manipulating, 220–221
   types of, 216–217
chemical formula, **161**
   in chemical reactions, 193
   subscripts in, 166, 173, 174
   writing, 173, 175
chemical properties of matter, **54**–58
   to identify materials, 60–61
   observing, 54–55
chemical reactions. *See* reaction(s), chemical.
chemical weathering, 269, **710**–711
chemistry, **4**
Chernobyl nuclear accident (1986), 313
chloride ion, 160
chlorine, 138, 144
   electron dot diagram for, 159
   isotopes of, 134
   molecules of, 166
   reactions of, 144, 159, 168
chloromethane, 272
chlorophyll, 141, 282
choroid, 589
chromium, 59
   in stainless steel, 180
chromosphere, **835**
ciliary muscles, 589
cinder cones, **693**, 694
circle graphs, 24
circuit breaker, **612**
circuit diagrams, **609**–610
circuits, electric, 609–613
   integrated, 183, 622
   parallel, 610

power and energy
   calculations, 611–612
   safety issues, 612–613, 623
   series, 610
circulating pump, 489
circulation of blood, 251
cirques, **720**
cirrostratus clouds, 763
cirrus clouds, 762, **763**
citric acid, 247, 248, 273
citrus fruits, 284
clastic rock, **672**
clay, 49
   silicates in, 142
Clean Coal Technology Program, 270
clean energy, 786
cleavage of minerals, **668**
Clermont, 422
Cliffs of Dover, 673
climate, **782**–786
   classifying, 778–779
   El Niño and, 783
   global warming, 784-786
   greenhouse gases and, 784
   ice ages, 783
   ocean circulation and, 783
   plate tectonics and, 782
   precipitation, 780
   solar activity and, 783
   temperature, 779-780
   volcanic activity and, 783
climate maps, 892
clocks, digital vs. analog, 19
clouds, **761**–763, 767
   cirrus, 762, 763
   cumulus, 763
   formation of, 761
   lightning and, 603
   of Neptune, 818
   stratus, 762–763
clusters, star, 851
coal, 267, 462
   electric generation with, 646
   burning, 270–271
coal-fired power stations, 270–271
cobalt, 146
coefficients, of chemical equation, **194**
co-enzyme, 284
coherent light, **560**
cold fronts, 765, **767**
cold packs, 235
colloids, **44**, 52
color(s), 550–557
   complementary, 552, 553
   as indicator of chemical change, 57
   of minerals, 666
   mixing, 552–553, 563
   of objects, 551–552
   pigments, 553, 554–555
   primary, 108, 552, 553
   of rocks, 670
   secondary, 552
   separating white light into, 551
   of stars, 840

Index

Index

UV radiation, 532, 540, 543, 544, 556, 750
vacuum, light in, 574
vacuum tubes, 183, 619
valence electrons, **139**
    reactivity and, 159
    representative groups and, 140–145
valley glacier, **719**
valleys
    U-shaped, 720, 721
    V-shaped, 715
vanadium, 147, 178
vapor pressure, **89**
vaporization, 85, **88**–90
    of petroleum, 268
variables, types of, 8
vector, **330**
    resultant, 331
vector addition, 337
velocity, **336**–337
    change in, 345
    combining, 337
    of falling objects, 343, 349
    rate of change of. *See* acceleration.
    terminal, 361, 370–371
vent, volcanic, **691**
Venus, 808, 809
vernal equinox, 754
vibration, of particles in solids, 74
video surveillance, 579
Viking space probes, 810
vinegar, 57, 273
vinyl records, 519
Virgo Cluster, 854
virtual images, **571,** 573, 576
viscosity, **45**
    of magma, 692
visible light, 452, 540, 543
vision problems, correcting, 590–592
    astigmatism, 592
    farsightedness, 592
    laser surgery, 591
    nearsightedness, 590
vitamin C, in fruit juices, 285
vitamin D, 544
vitamins, **284**
volcanic necks, **696**
volcanic rocks, 695
volcanoes, **690**–696
    eruptions of, 692
    formation of, 691
    igneous features of, 696
    location of, 693
    Martian, 807
    types of, 693–695
    on Venus, 809
voltage, 606–607
    household, 612, 647
    transformers and, 644–645
volume, **16**
    gas pressure and, 77, 78, 79
    percent by, 238
V-shaped valleys, 715

warm fronts, **768**

waste, radioactive, 311, 312–313
waste heat, **483**
water, 40, 704–708, 713–717
    acid-base property of, 245
    in atmosphere, 760–764, 784
    composition of, 40
    compression of, 67
    decomposition of, 40, 200
    formation of, 40, 197
    fresh, 706–708
    heat of fusion of, 86
    heat of vaporization of, 88
    on Mars, 812
    mass vs. volume graph of, 23
    molecules of, 88
    on the moon, 797, 806
    from neutralization reactions, 244
    as nutrient, 146, 147
    percentage of body mass, 147
    phases of, 84
    as polar molecule, 168, 169
    purifying, 52–53
    reactions of, 47, 197, 200, 230, 242
    resources, 708
    synthesis of, 200
    transparency of, 546
water cycle, **705**–706
water deposition, 716
water erosion, 714–716
waterfall, 715
water pressure, 391
watershed (drainage basins), **706**–707
water table, **707**
Watt, James, 416, 422, 486
watt (W), **415,** 611
wave fronts, 509
wavelength, **505,** 506
    of electromagnetic waves, 535
    of gamma rays, 545
    of infrared rays, 543
    of microwaves, 542
    of ultraviolet rays, 544
    of visible light, 543
    of X-rays, 544
waves. *See also* electromagnetic waves; light; mechanical waves; sound.
    deposition from ocean, 729
    erosion from ocean, 728–729
    seismic, 684, 686–687
wave speed, 505–506
wax, properties of, 49, 54
weak nuclear force, **380**
weather, **749,** 765–778
    air masses, 765–767
    fronts, 767–768
    low- and high-pressure systems, 768–769
    predicting, 774–777
    storms, 769–771

weather balloons, 81
weathering, **710**–712
    chemical, 269, 710–711
    mechanical, 710
    rates of, 711
weather map, 776–777, 900
weather stations, 775, 900
weather systems, 768
Web Codes. *See* Go Online.
wedge, 427, **431**
Wegener, Alfred, 677, 681
weight, 357, **367,** 368–369, 398–399
    calculating, 368
weighted averages, 134
welding, 158, 178, 266
whales, noise pollution and, 513
wheel and axle, 427, **430**
white blood cells, 250
white dwarfs, **843,** 844, 846, 847
Whitney, Eli, 422
wildfires, 210–211
Wilson, Robert, 858
WIMPs, 855
wind(s), 356, 723–724, **757**–759
    air pressure and, 757
    currents and, 726–728
    global, 758–759, 780
    local, 757
    solar, 835
wind deposition, 724
wind energy, 464
wind erosion, 723
wind turbines, 465
wings, 396–397
Winter Triangle, 840
Wöhler, Friedrich, 262
wood, arsenic-treated, 59
    carving of, 47
wool, properties of, 38
work, **412**–414
    calculating, 413–414
    conversion of heat to, 483
    direction and, 413
    energy and, 447
    heat and, 474
    heat transfer and, 482
    machines and, 417–420
    motion and, 412–413
    power and, 414–416
    units of, 414
work input, **419**
work output, **420**
Writing in Science, 6, 11, 44, 91, 105, 115, 118, 129, 138, 179, 181, 205, 215, 239, 249, 280, 284, 301, 305, 313, 331, 375, 377, 382, 404, 423, 435, 466, 492, 512, 519, 545, 553, 573, 583, 592, 603, 607, 647, 663, 675, 681, 696, 717, 724, 754, 777, 811, 813, 824, 837, 848

x-axis (horizontal axis), 23

xenon, 145
X-rays, 452, 532, 540, 543, 544, 556–557

y-axis (vertical axis), 23
Yosemite Valley, 721
Young, Thomas, 536

zinc, 241
    in brass, 180
    in Mendeleev's periodic table, 128
    as trace element, 146, 147

Acknowledgments

Staff Credits

The people who made up the Prentice Hall *Physical Science: Concepts in Action* team—representing design services, editorial, editorial services, market research, marketing services, education technology, production services, project office, and publishing processes—are listed below. Bold type denotes the core team members.

Leann Davis Alspaugh, Neil Benjamin, **Barbara Bertell**, Suzanne Biron, Diane Braff, Kristen Cetrulo Braghi, Kenneth Chang, Jonathan D. Cheney, **Todd Christy,** Bob Craton, Kathleen J. Dempsey, **Frederick Fellows,** Jonathan Fisher, Kathryn Fobert, Paul Gagnon, Julia Gecha, Robert Graham, Ellen Welch Granter, Susan Hutchinson, **Judie Jozokos,** Kelly Kelliher, Dotti Marshall, Tim McDonald, Terri Mitchell, **Jen Paley, Caroline M. Power,** Siri Schwartzman, Malti Sharma, Emily Soltanoff, Jennifer Teece.

Additional Credits

Ann Bekebrede, Frances Jenkins, Matt Walker

The DK Designs team who contributed to *Prentice Hall Physical Science: Concepts in Action* were as follows: Samantha Borland, Marian Broderick, Carole Curcie, Richard Czapnik, Nigel Duffield, Cynthia Frazer, James A. Hall, Rose Horridge, Heather Jones, Anthony Limerick, David Lloyd, Marie Osborn, Leyla Ostovar, Ralph Pitchford, Pamela Shiels, Andrew Szudek.

Maps

Maps and globes on pages 880–887 were created by **DK Cartography.** The team consisted of Tony Chambers, Damien Demaj, Julia Lunn, Ed Merritt, David Roberts, Ann Stephenson, Gail Townsley, and Iorwerth Watkins.

Illustration

Leann Davis Alspaugh: 223; DK Picture Library: 487, 517, 581, 584, 621, 662, 668, 677, 680, 682, 691, 693, 705, 706, 715, 727, 736–737, 750, 752ml, 752bl, 754, 758, 767, 768, 779, 796–797, 803, 804tl, 804m, 805, 822–823, 834, 843, 846–847, 853, 888–889; Stephen Durke: 802; Paul Gagnon: 4; Gene Givan: 234, 272, 289; Ellen Welch Granter: 16, 17, 22b, 23, 24b, 92, 134b, 150, 208l, 208r, 215, 221, 469, 470, 542, 543, 558, 559, 563, 564, 566, 567r, 775; Graph/fix: Bruce Cowie: 130b, 358, 361, 396, 413, 418, 431, 480, 481, 482, 491b, 512, 571, 674, 675, 685, 704b, 765b, 804tr; J/B Woolsey Associates: 131, 132–133, 134t, 140, 141, 142, 143, 144, 145, 153, 155, 161t; George Kelvin: 259, 343, 601, 605, 606, 609, 632, 633, 636, 638, 639, 643, 647; George Ladas: 336, 337, 343; Matt Mayerchak: 2, 7, 14, 22t, 100t, 108, 113, 126, 130t, 139, 152, 158, 165, 170, 176, 186, 192, 199, 206, 212, 216, 222, 292, 298, 303, 308t, 318, 356, 363, 372, 378, 384, 390, 394, 400t, 406r, 412t, 417, 421t, 427, 440, 446, 453, 462, 468, 474, 479, 486t, 494, 500, 504t, 508, 514t, 526, 570t, 574, 580, 588, 594, 660, 664, 670, 676, 684, 690, 704t, 709, 713, 719, 725, 732, 752t, 774, 778, 794, 800, 807, 814, 822, 832; Morgan-Cain & Associates: 20, 29, 30, 31, 65, 85b, 88, 97, 123l, 123r, 127, 159t, 159b, 160, 161b, 162, 164, 166t, 166b, 168t, 168b, 169, 171, 172t, 172b, 173, 175, 177, 187, 188l, 188r, 224, 225, 229, 230, 231, 237, 263, 264, 294–295, 296, 299t, 308l, 309, 310, 311, 319, 320, 321, 359, 368, 376, 380, 381, 382, 385, 387, 391, 395b, 397, 400b, 401, 406l, 407, 408, 409, 419, 428, 441, 442, 443l, 471, 475t, 475b, 478, 486b, 489, 490, 492, 496, 497, 501, 502, 503, 504b, 505, 507, 509t, 511, 516, 527, 528, 529, 570l, 572bl, 572br, 573tl, 573tr, 575t, 576l, 576r, 577t, 577m, 577b, 578, 584b, 585, 589, 590, 592, 595, 596l, 596r, 597, 686, 689, 701, 743, 757, 776, 791, 817, 827, 829, 836, 857b, 863, 864, 865, 869, 869, 875bl, 877, 878, 883, 885, 886–887, 891; Jen Paley: 24t, 26, 28, 38, 41, 42, 45, 47, 54, 60, 62, 64, 68, 71, 72t, 75, 78l, 84, 94, 96, 109, 112, 117, 119, 120, 154, 167, 184, 189, 197, 293, 299b, 357, 377, 383, 386, 392, 395t, 405, 421b, 433, 438, 439, 443r, 463, 476, 479b, 491t, 493, 509b, 514b, 515, 532, 539, 546, 550, 567l, 575b, 667, 676, 697b, 699, 700, 720, 734–735b, 742, 746, 747, 755t, 755b, 759, 760, 765t, 766, 769, 787, 790, 808, 815, 828, 833b, 838, 840, 844, 850, 856t, 860, 862, 875ml, 875tr, 875mr, 880tl, 880bl, 880mr, 880br; Precision Graphics: 44, 46, 69, 70, 72, 77, 78r, 89, 95, 100b, 102, 103, 104, 121, 122, 193, 194, 207, 217, 230, 258, 262, 264, 265, 266, 267, 273, 274, 276, 279, 282, 331, 430, 432, 533, 534, 536, 537, 538, 540, 541, 548, 663, 678, 679, 682, 686, 707, 710, 712, 714, 720, 723, 728, 729, 733, 734t,

748, 753, 770, 780–781, 833t, 839, 839, 842, 848, 856b, 857t, 858; www.TrevorJohnston.com: 8, 85t; courtesy of USGS: 785; XNR Productions Inc.: 697t

Cover design Maria Keogh/Kokopelli Design Studio, Inc.;

Cover photo Tom Sanders/Aerial Focus

Photo research Paula Wehde

Dorling Kindersley picture research done in London, England, by Cynthia Frazer and Marie Osborn; Dorling Kindersley illustrations done by Richard Bonson, KJA. Artists.com, and Martin Sanders in London, England.

Photographs

Every effort has been made to secure permission and provide appropriate credit for photographic material. The publisher deeply regrets any omission and pledges to correct errors called to its attention in subsequent editions.

Unless otherwise acknowledged, all photographs are the property of Pearson Education, Inc.

Photo locators denoted as follows: Top (T), Center (C), Bottom (B), Left (L), Right (R), Background (Bkgd)

Front Matter

i, ii, Tom Sanders; **iv** (B) ©Fukuhara Inc./Corbis; **vi** (TL) Photo Researchers, Inc.; **vii** (B) Alain Nogues/Corbis; **viii** (B) Donald Miralle/Staff/Getty Images; **x** (B) ©Palenque/Fotolia; **xi** (TR) Brad Thompson/Fotolia; **xiii** (B) Breck P. Kent Natural History Photography; **xv** (B) Colin Keates/DK Images; **xviii** (C) Rosenfeld Images Ltd./Photo Researchers, Inc.

2 Jeff Gentner/©AP Images, (BC) Photo Researchers, Inc., (TR) Rosenfeld Images Ltd./Photo Researchers, Inc., (BL) Science Photo Library/Photo Researchers, Inc.; **3** (B) ©AP Images, (TL) Courtesy of AT&T Archives and History Center, Warren, NJ, (B) M_G/Shutterstock, (TR, C) Ryan McVay/Getty Images; **4** (T) ©Emi Allen/SuperStock, (BCL) ©Paul Seheult/Corbis, (CL) ©Andrew Lambert Photography/Science Source, (TCR) AGStockUSA, (TR) John W. Bova/Photo Researchers, Inc., (L) Kevin Fleming/Corbis, (BR) Leland Bobbé/Corbis, (C) NASA, NASA/Photo Researchers, Inc.; **5** (B) Richard Berenholtz/Corbis; **6** Dennis MacDonald/PhotoEdit, Inc.; **7** (BR, B) Dennis MacDonald/PhotoEdit, Inc., (TR) Rosenfeld Images Ltd./Photo Researchers, Inc.; **9** (BR) Colin Cuthbert/Newcastle University/Photo Researchers, Inc.; **10** (T) ©The Boeing Company; **11** (TR) Steve Chenn/Corbis; **12** (BL) Jeremy Sutton Hibbert/Rex Features, Limited, (R) Rex Features, Limited; **13** (CR, BR) ©DK Images, (CC) Anna Clopet/Corbis; **14** (BL) Frank Zullo/Photo Researchers, Inc., (TR) Rosenfeld Images Ltd./Photo Researchers, Inc.; **16** (TL) Will Hart/PhotoEdit, Inc.; **17** (TR, T) ©Don Farrall/Getty Images, (B) C Squared Studios/Getty Images; **18** Jonathan Nourok/PhotoEdit, Inc.; **19** (CR) ©DK Images, (B) Tom Pantages; **21** (L) Baloncici/Shutterstock, (TR) Sally and Richard Greenhill Photo Library; **22** (TR) Rosenfeld Images Ltd./Photo Researchers, Inc.; **25** (TR) ©AP Images, (TL) Layne Kennedy/Corbis; **32** ©R. Wallace/Stock Photos/Corbis; **34** (TR) Blend Images/Alamy, (CL) Mark Richards/PhotoEdit, Inc., (BR) Scott Speakes/Corbis, (BR) Jochen Tack/Alamy; **35** (BR) Bill Aron/PhotoEdit, Inc., (TR) Peter Beck/Corbis, (BL) Reuters/Corbis, (TL) The Image Works, Inc.; **36** Peter Menzel/Stock Boston; **38** (T) Peter Menzel/Stock Boston, (BL) Phil Banko/Corbis; **39** (BR) ©Lester V. Bergman/Corbis, (R, L, BC) Charles D. Winters/Photo Researchers, Inc.; **40** (CL) Bill Aron/PhotoEdit, Inc., (TL) Dave King/Courtesy of The Science Museum, London/©DK Images, (BL) Mark A. Schneider/Photo Researchers, Inc.; **41** (BL) Alexey V Smirnov/Shutterstock; **42** (CL) Fukuhara, Inc./Corbis; **43** (TR) Danylchenko Iaroslav/Shutterstock, (TC) Dennis MacDonald/PhotoEdit, Inc., (BL) Grafton Marshall Smith/Corbis; **44** (TL) Rachel Epstein/PhotoEdit, Inc.; **45** (TBR) E. J. Tarbuck, (T) Peter Menzel/Stock Boston, (B) Ross Durant Photography/Getty Images; **46** (B) Araldo de Luca/Corbis; **47** (TR) Jeffrey Greenberg/Photo Researchers, Inc.; **48** (B) Pavel Klimenko/Fotolia; **49** (CR) Bridgeman Art Library, (TR) David Samuel Robbins/Himalayan Odyssey Tours; **50** (T) Eda Rogers; **51** (TR) Nancy Ney/Corbis, (C) Paul A. Souders/Corbis; **54** (BL) Michelle Garrett/Corbis, (T) Peter Menzel/Stock Boston; **55** (B) Chinch Gryniewicz; Ecoscene/Corbis; **57** (TL) Grant Smith/Corbis, (TR) Pat Bruno/Positive Images, (BL) Charles D. Winters/Science Source, (BR) Souders Studios/Getty Images; **58** (T) ©Mike Rex/Alamy Images; **59** ©Richard Schultz/Corbis; **63** (CR) C.C. Lockwood/Photoshot; **64** (TR) ©IndexStock/SuperStock; **66** Charles Mauzy/Corbis; **68** (T) Charles Mauzy/

Corbis; **69** (BR) Charles D. Winters/Photo Researchers, Inc., (TR) Clive Streeter/ DK Images; **71** (BR) Chris Mooney/Getty Images; **72** (TR) Charles Thatcher/Getty Images; **73** (BR) Photo(s) by Jim Whitmer; **74** (TR, TC) Michael Cogliantry/Getty Images; **75** (T) Charles Mauzy/Corbis, (B) Zen Shui/SuperStock; **76** Tony Freeman/PhotoEdit, Inc.; **81** (T) Pat Lanza/Photoshot; **84** (B) ©Mlenny Photograhy/Alexander Hafemann/iStockphoto, (T) Charles Mauzy/Corbis; **86** (BL) AGStockUSA, (TR) JTB MEDIA CREATION, Inc./Alamy; **87** (T) Matthew Stockman/ Getty Images; **89** (BR) Dave King/Courtesy of The Science Museum, London/©DK Images, (TR) Steve & Dave Maslowski/Photo Researchers, Inc.; **90** fotosav/ Shutterstock; **91** Margo Wright/Courtesty Tinker Take-Off; **98** News & Media Relations, Rice University; **100** (T) News & Media Relations, Rice University; **101** (BR) Clive Streeter/©DK Images, (T) Stephen Frisch/Stock Boston; **102** (BL) Clive Streeter/DK Images; **103** (B) Mary Kate Denny/PhotoEdit, Inc.; **105** (TR) Bettmann/Corbis; **108** (BL) Michael Powers/Stock Boston, (T) News & Media Relations, Rice University; **110** (B) ©Joel Arem/Photo Researchers, Inc., (TL) Charles D. Winters/Photo Researchers, Inc., (C) Russell Lappa/Photo Researchers, Inc.; **111** (TR) Science Museum/Science & Society Picture Library; **113** (B) Bohdan Hrynewych/Stock Boston, (T) News & Media Relations, Rice University; **116** Chris Curtis/Shutterstock; **118** (TL) William Sallaz/Duoma/Corbis; **119** (TR) Jerry Mason/Photo Researchers, Inc.; **120** ©Joel Arem/Photo Researchers, Inc.; **124** adisa/Fotolia; **126** (BL) Michael Newman/PhotoEdit, Inc., (TR) adisa/Fotolia; **129** (TR) Alan Schein Photography/Corbis, (C) Kenneth Eward/ Photo Researchers, Inc.; **130** (B) Pedro Sousa/Alamy, (TR) adisa/Fotolia; **135** (BR) David Parker/Photo Researchers, Inc., (BL) Science Photo Library/Photo Researchers, Inc.; **136** (T) Comstock Images/Getty Images, (B) Jonathan Nourok/PhotoEdit, Inc.; **138** (TR) ©David R. Frazier/Photo Researchers, Inc., Andrew Lambert Photography/Science Source, (TL) ©sciencephotos/Alamy Images, (CR, CL) Charles D. Winters/Photo Researchers, Inc., (TC) Dave King/ Courtesy of The Science Museum, London/©DK Images, (CR) Fundamental Photographs, (TRL) Richard Megna/Fundamental Photographs, (TCL) Science Photo Library/Photo Researchers, Inc.; **139** (B) Mike Fiala/Getty Images, (TR) adisa/Fotolia; **140** (TR) Richard Megna/Fundamental Photographs; **141** (L, BL) ©inga spence/Alamy Images, (C) ©Stefano Scata/Getty Images, (R) Gina Sanders/Shutterstock; **142** (TR) ©Michael Ventura/Alamy Images, (BL) Dana White/PhotoEdit, Inc.; **143** (T) David Nunuk/Science Photo Library/Photo Researchers, Inc.; **144** (TL) Andrew Lambert Photography/Science Source, (TR) Elena Rooraid/PhotoEdit, Inc., (B) Pearson Education/Prentice Hall College; **145** (T) Raymond Gendreau/Getty Images; **147** (TR) ©DK Images, (BR) Martin Brigdale/©DK Images, (BL) Philip Dowell/©DK Images, (CC) Roger Phillips/©DK Images, (CL) Stephen Hayward/©DK Images, (CR) Steve Gorton/©DK Images; **156** George D. Lepp/Corbis; **158** (TR) George D. Lepp/Corbis, (BL) Horie Corporation; **161** (BR) Arestov Andrew/Fotolia; **162** (TR) ©M. Claye/Jacana Scientific Control/Photo Researchers, Inc.; **163** (TCR) Colin Keates/©DK Images, (TR) Colin Keates/The Natural History Museum, London/©DK Images; **165** (B) Charles Gupton/Stock Boston, (TR) George D. Lepp/Corbis; **166** (TL) Mark M. Lawrence/Corbis; **170** (T) George D. Lepp/Corbis, (BL) Jennifer Cheung; **171** (TR, TL) Thomas Markusen/Markusen Metal Studios Ltd.; **172** (TL) ©Matthias Kulka/Corbis; **176** (BL) Andrew Syred/Photo Researchers, Inc., (T) George D. Lepp/Corbis; **178** (BC) ©Dave King/Motoring Picture Library. National Motor Museum, Beaulieu/DK Images, (CR) Hulton Archive/Getty Images; **179** (L) Bettmann/Corbis, (CR) George Hall/Corbis, (C) John Carter/Photo Researchers, Inc.; **180** (TL) ©SuperStock/AGE Fotostock, (TR) Paul Conklin/PhotoEdit, Inc.; **181** (T) ©age fotostock/SuperStock; **182** (BL) ©DK Images, (BC) Colin Keates/©DK Images; **183** (TC) ©Clive Streeter/Courtesy of The Science Museum, London/DK Images, (TR) Clive Streeter/©DK Images, (TR) Jan Hinsch/ Science Photo Library/Photo Researchers, Inc., (C) Matthew Ward/©DK Images, (BL) Tony Craddock/Photo Researchers, Inc.; **188** (T) Honda, ho/©AP Images; **190** John Warden/Superstock; **192** John Warden/Superstock; **192** (BL) ©Charles O'Rear/Corbis; **194** (TL) Stock Connection; **197** John E. Kelly/Getty Images; **199** John Warden/Superstock; **199** (BR) David Bartruff/Stock Boston; **200** (TL) Tom Pantages; **201** (TR) Don Johnston/Getty Images; **202** (TR) Clive Steeter/©DK Images, (TC, BL) Clive Streeter/©DK Images; **203** (TR) Richard Megna/Fundamental Photographs; **204** (TL) Charles D. Winter/Photo Researchers, Inc., (B) Richard Megna/Fundamental Photographs; **206** John Warden/Superstock; **206** (BL) Bill Bachmann/PhotoEdit, Inc.; **209** (TR) Richard Megna/Fundamental Photographs; **210** (R) Francis Specker/©AP Images, (BL) Ted Soqui/Getty Images; **211** (BC) Mike Stewart/Corbis, (CR) Paul A. Souders/ Corbis, (T) PAUL CROCK/AFP/Getty Images; **212** John Warden/Superstock; **212** (BL) Will Hart; **213** (BR) Steven Martine/©AP Images; **214** (BL) ©DK Images; **216** John Warden/Superstock; **216** (B) David Sailors Photography, (B) David Sailors/Corbis; **218** (B) Edgar Fahs Smith Collection/Rare Book and Manuscript Library, University of Pennsylvania, (T) Getty Images, (TR) UpperCut Images/Alamy; **219** (TR) Ken Graham/Accent Alaska; **226** Robbie Shone /Photo Researchers, Inc.; **228** (T) Robbie Shone /Photo Researchers, Inc., (B) Sea Images/PhotoLibrary Group, Inc.; **229** (TR) Chris Collins/Corbis; **230** (TL) Eric Kamp/PhotoLibrary Group, Inc.; **231** (TR) Annie Griffiths Belt/Corbis; **233** (TR) Dick Makin Imaging; **235** (T) Robbie Shone/Photo Researchers, Inc.; **236** (R) Fundamental Photographs, (TL) Jules Frazier/Getty Images, (C, BL) Richard Megna/Fundamental Photographs; **237** (BR) Mark Hanauer/Corbis; **238** (BR) Steve Gorton/©DK Images; **239** (TR) Bill Varie/Corbis; **240** (T) Robbie Shone/ Photo Researchers, Inc., (B) Russ Lappa; **241** (BR) Paul Silverman/Fundamental Photographs; **242** Charles Gullung/Corbis; **243** (T) Bob Krist/Corbis, (T) PictureNet/Corbis; **244** (BL) James L. Amos/Corbis; **246** (T) Robbie Shone/Photo Researchers, Inc., (B) The Image Works, Inc.; **249** (TR) Denkou Images/Getty Images; **256** (R) Fundamental Photographs, (L, C) Richard Megna/Fundamental Photographs; **260** Arnulf Husmo/Getty Images; **262** (T) Arnulf Husmo/Getty Images, (B) Mark A. Johnson/Corbis; **264** (TL) Javier Larrea Roa/AGE Fotostock; **266** (BL) C. Marvin Lang/University of Wisconsin at Stevens Point, (T) Dmitry Kosterev/Shutterstock, (C) Jupiterimages/Thinkstock; **267** (B) ©David Lyons/ Alamy Images, (T) AnnaC/Fotolia; **268** (TL) Barry Rowland/AGE Fotostock; **269** (T) Spencer Platt/Getty Images; **272** (T) Arnulf Husmo/Getty Images; **273** (BR) Gucio_55/Fotolia; **274** (TR) Hisham Ibrahim/Getty Images; **275** (T) Arnulf Husmo/Getty Images, (B) Digital Vision/Getty Images; **276** (B) ©David Lyons/ Alamy Images, (TC) Andy Crawford/©DK Images, (TR) Michael Conroy/©AP Images, (TL) Michael Pole/Corbis; **277** (B) ©DK Images, (CR) Simon Belcher/ Alamy, (TR) The Advertising Archive; **278** ©Bichon/photocuisine/Corbis; **279** (BL) Stephen Simpson/Getty Images; **280** (L) Andrew Whittuck/DK Images; **281** Scott Camazine/Photo Researchers, Inc., (TL) Yogi, Inc./Corbis; **282** (B) Aldo Torelli/Getty Images, (T) Arnulf Husmo/Getty Images; **283** (TR) Jane Sapinsky/ SuperStock; **284** (TL) Michael P. Gadomski/Photo Researchers, Inc.; **287** (CR) Shannon Fagan/Corbis; **290** CERN/Photo Researchers, Inc.; **292** (B) ©The Granger Collection, NY, (TR) CERN/Photo Researchers, Inc., (BC) Jean-Loup Charmet/Science Photo Library/Photo Researchers, Inc.; **293** (TR) Francois Gohier/Photo Researchers, Inc.; **296** (TL) Roberto de Gugliemo/Photo Researchers, Inc.; **298** (TR) CERN/Photo Researchers, Inc., (BL) Kenneth Garrett; **301** ©The Trustees of The British Museum; **302** (T) Creatas/©Punchstock; **303** (TR) CERN/Photo Researchers, Inc., (BR) David Lees/Corbis; **304** NASA; **305** (TR) David Parker/Science Photo Library/Photo Researchers, Inc.; **306** (BL) Science Source, (CR) Gustoimages/Science Source; **308** (TR) CERN/Photo Researchers, Inc.; **309** (BR) ©AP Images; **311** (BR) Matthew McVay/Getty Images; **312** (BR) Hulton Archive/Getty Images, (BL) Photo Researchers, Inc., (BC) Physics Today Collection/American Institute of Physics/Photo Researchers, Inc.; **313** (TC, BL) Science Source/Photo Researchers, Inc. (R) Idaho National Laboratory; **314** Patrick Landmann/Photo Researchers, Inc.; **315** (TR) Maximilian Stock Ltd/Science Source; **322** Jon Arnold/Getty Images; **324** (TR) Michael J. Doolittle/The Image Works, Inc., (L) Reuters/Corbis, (BR) Robert Brenner/ PhotoEdit, Inc.; **325** (TR) ©Syracuse Newspapers/Suzanne Dunn/The Image Works, Inc., (BL) Adam Woolfitt/Corbis, (C) urbanlight/Shutterstock, (BR) Lou Jones/Getty Images; **326** ©Duomo/Corbis; **328** (TR) ©Duomo/Corbis, (BL) Tony Freeman/PhotoEdit, Inc.; **329** (T) Pedro Coll/AGE Fotostock; **332** (T) ©Duomo/ Corbis, (B) Dennis O'Clair/Getty Images; **334** (TR) Leonard Lessin/Peter Arnold, Inc., (T) Steve Krongard/Getty Images; **335** (T) Melissa Carroll/iStockphoto; **336** (T) ©Randy Wells/Corbis, (BL) Sharon Green/Corbis; **338** (CR) ©DK Images, (R) Joel W. Rogers/Corbis, (BL) Stephen Oliver/©DK Images; **340** (TR) ESA/CE/EUROCONTROL/Photo Researchers, Inc.; **341** (TL) Cen Lu/AGE Fotostock, (TL) dyoma/Shutterstock, (CR) Niels Poulsen DK/Alamy Images, (TR) Stephen Oliver/©DK Images; **342** (T) ©Duomo/Corbis, (BL) Vico Collective/Alin Dragulin/Getty Images.; **344** (TL) Barnabas Kindersley/©DK Images, (B) Diana Jarvis/DK Images; **345** (TR) Benjamin Rondel/Corbis; **347** (T) Karl Weatherly/ Getty Images, (B) Michael Newman/PhotoEdit, Inc.; **355** Bob Martin/Getty Images; **356** (BL) ©AP Images, (TR) Bob Martin/Getty Images; **357** (R, L) George Doyle/Getty Images; **358** (T) Daniel Koebe/Corbis; **361** (TR) James Steinberg/ Photo Researchers, Inc., (BR) Nicholas Bergkessel, Jr./Photo Researchers, Inc.; **362** (R) Fundamental Photographs, (TC) Peticolas/Megna/Fundamental

Photographs; **363** (C) ©Bettmann/Corbis, (B) ©The Granger Collection, NY, (TR) Bob Martin/Getty Images; **364** (TL) Bettmann/Corbis, (BR, BL) Insurance Institute for Highway Safety, (CL) Sheila Terry/Science Photo Library/Photo Researchers, Inc.; **365** (BR, BL) Insurance Institute for Highway Safety; **366** (C) ©Mercedes Benz/©DK Images; **369** (TR) ©AP Images, (TL) Bettmann/Corbis; **370** (R) Steve Fitchett/Getty Images; **371** (TR, CR, BL) David Wootton Photography; **372** (TR) Bob Martin/Getty Images, (BL) Joe McBride/Getty Images; **373** (R) Duomo/Corbis; **374** (T) ©Doug Martin/Photo Researchers, Inc., (CR) Corbis, (L) Mary Evans Picture Library; **375** (BL) Bettmann/Corbis, (BR) Joyrides/Joe Schwartz, (CC) Macduff Everton/Corbis; **378** (TR) Bob Martin/Getty Images, (BL) Ludek Press/Science Photo Library/Photo Researchers, Inc.; **379** (BR) Michelle D. Bridwell/PhotoEdit, Inc., (TR) Tony Anderson/Getty Images; **388** ©Guy Grenier/Masterfile Corporation; **390** (T) ©Guy Grenier/Masterfile Corporation, (B) Aaron Haupt/Stock Boston, (CL) Jonathan Nourok/PhotoEdit, Inc.; **391** (BR) Charles D. Winter/Photo Researchers, Inc.; **392** ©sciencephotos/Alamy Images; **394** (T) ©Guy Grenier/Masterfile Corporation; **395** (BL) moodboard/SuperStock; **396** (T) Firefly Productions/Corbis; **398** (R) Cameron Heryet/Getty Images; **400** (T) ©Guy Grenier/Masterfile Corporation; **402** (BL) Steve Kaufman/Corbis; **404** (T) Layne Kennedy/Corbis; **406** (TL) ©sciencephotos/Alamy Images; **410** Paul Chesley/Getty Images; **412** (TR) Paul Chesley/Getty Images, (BL) Reuters/Corbis; **414** (B) ©David Grossman/The Image Works, Inc., (TL) Dennis MacDonald/PhotoEdit, Inc.; **416** (T) Kevin Fleming/Corbis, (CL) Tony Freeman/PhotoEdit, Inc.; **417** (R) David Buffington/Corbis, (TR) Paul Chesley/Getty Images; **418** (T) Tony Freeman/PhotoEdit, Inc.; **420** (TL) Kevin Fleming/Corbis; **421** (TR) Paul Chesley/Getty Images; **422** (BL) ©Bettmann/Corbis, (BC) North Wind Picture Archives, (BR) Science & Society Picture Library; **423** (BR) Lambert/Stone/Getty Images, (CL, CC) Science & Society Picture Library; **424** (BL) Wolfgang Deuter/Corbis; **426** (TL) Michael Rosenfeld/Getty Images; **427** (B) ©Rube Goldberg Inc., (TR) Paul Chesley/Getty Images; **428** (C) Richard Hutchings/PhotoEdit, Inc., (TR) Rob Crandall/The Image Works, Inc.; **430** (BL) Neil Beer/Corbis; **431** (TR) Michael Thompson/Animals Animals/Earth Scenes; **432** (TL) H. David Seawell/Corbis; **435** (TR) ©Fukuhara Inc./Corbis; **436** (T) DK Images; **437** (CR) John Kelly/Getty Images; **439** (TR) Getty Images; **444** David A. Northcott/Corbis; **446** (TR) David A. Northcott/Corbis, (BL) Accent Alaska.com/Alamy; **447** (TR) David R. Frazier/Photo Researchers, Inc., (C) Michael Pohuski/Getty Images, (B) Mike Powell/Getty Images; **448** (BL) Adamsmith/Getty Images; **449** ©Flirt/SuperStock; **450** (TR) CSA Images, (TL) Mark Thompson/Getty Images; **451** (R) Dawson Jones/Stock Boston, (B) Tom Stewart/Corbis; **452** (B) ©Myron Jay Dorf/Corbis, (T) ©Warren Faidley/Corbis; **453** (B) American Museum of Natural History, (TR) David A. Northcott/Corbis; **454** (T) Myron Jay Dorf/Corbis; **455** (T) Donald Miralle/Staff/Getty Images; **456** (TL) John W. Bova/Photo Researchers, Inc., (B) Alexander Sakhatovsky/Shutterstock; **457** (TR) Gilbert Iundt/TempSport/Corbis; **459** (T) Topham/The Image Works, Inc.; **460** (R) Alchemy/Alamy; **461** (B) Detroit Publishing Co./Library of Congress, (CL) Premier Rides; **462** (TR) David A. Northcott/Corbis, (B) George Hunter/Getty Images; **463** (TR) David Parker/Science Photo Library/Photo Researchers, Inc.; **464** (B) ©Visions of America/Joe Sohm/Getty Images, (TL) Charles Krebs/Corbis; **465** (TR) Dave King/©DK Images; **466** John Elk/Stock Boston; **472** ©W.A. Sharman; Milepost 92 ?/Corbis; **474** (BL) ©The Granger Collection, NY, (TR) ©W.A. Sharman; Milepost 92 ?/Corbis; **475** (B) Duncan Smith/Corbis, (TR) Jonelle Weaver/Getty Images; **479** (TR) ©W.A. Sharman; Milepost 92 ?/Corbis, (BR) Alfred Pasieka/Photo Researchers, Inc.; **480** (BL) Andreas Lander/Newscom, (T) Penina/Getty Images, (BR) Steve Cohen/Getty Images; **481** Philip Lewis/Alamy Images; **482** Johner Images/Alamy; **483** Geoffrey Wheeler/National Institute of Standards and Technology; **484** (C) BRE Global Limited; **486** (T) ©W.A. Sharman; Milepost 92 ?/Corbis; **491** (B) olivier/Shutterstock; **495** Insadco Photography RF/AGE Fotostock; **498** Peter Sterling/Getty Images; **500** (B) M. Timothy O'Keefe/Photoshot, (T) Peter Sterling/Getty Images; **504** (T) Peter Sterling/Getty Images; **508** JoLin/iStockphoto, (T) Peter Sterling/Getty Images; **509** (BL) Timothy Mulholland/Alamy; **510** (TL) Fundamental Photographs, (TR) Richard Megna/Fundamental Photographs; **512** (TL, CL) Richard Megna/Fundamental Photographs; **513** (TL) ©Stephen Frink; **514** (T) Peter Sterling/Getty Images; **515** (B) C Squared Studios/Getty Images, (T) Martin Fox/PhotoLibrary Group, Inc.; **516** (TL) Darryl Torckler/Getty Images; **518** (BR) Clive Streeter/©DK Images, (BC) Dave King/DK Images, (BL) The Science Museum, London/DK Images; **519** (BL) Bettmann/Corbis, (CC) Corbis, (TC) Paul Fleet/Alamy; **520** (TR) ©DK Images, (CC) DK Images; **521** (TR) Talaske, Inc.; **522** (B) Randy Jolly/Corbis;

523 (BL) Alan Thornton/Getty Images; **530** (Bkgrd,) Andrew Woodley/Alamy Images; **532** (B) Rob Bartee/SuperStock; **536** (TL) Dave King/©DK Images; **539** (B) ©The Print Collector/Alamy Images; **541** (B) Image Source/Corbis, (T) Robert E. Daemmrich/Getty Images; **542** Spencer Grant/PhotoEdit, Inc.; **543** (TR, TL) FLIR Systems, Inc; **544** (BL) David Arky/Corbis; **545** (T) WDCN/Univ. College London/Photo Researchers, Inc.; **546** (B) ©Stephen Frink; **547** (B) Arthur Morris/Corbis, (TL) C Squared Studios/Getty Images, (TR) Stockbyte/Getty Images; **548** (TL) ©Southern Illinois University/Photo Researchers, Inc.; **550** (BR) B Busco/The Image Bank/Getty Images, (BL) Jerome Wexler/Photo Researchers, Inc.; **551** (TL) Dave King/Courtesy of The Science Museum, London/©DK Images; **552** (BL) Leonard Lessin/Photo Researchers, Inc.; **554** (B) ©DK Images; **555** (T) ©DK Images, (BCR) Tate Enterprises, Ltd; **556** (CR, BL) Volker Steger/Photo Researchers, Inc.; **557** (TR) ©1996 Board of Trustees, National Gallery of Art, Washington, D.C. Gift of Mr. and Mrs. Robert Woods Bliss. Photograph by Lorene Emerson./Image ©2003 Board of Trustees, National Gallery of Art, Washington, (CL) ©National Gallery, London, (CC) RAPHAEL/©National Gallery, London; **558** (L, B) ©David R. Frazier/Photo Researchers, Inc., (T) Andrew Woodley/Alamy Images; **559** (TR) Benjamin Simeneta/Alamy; **560** (BC) ©DK Images, (C) Dave King/©DK Images; **562** (TL, CL) Tony Freeman/PhotoEdit, Inc.; **565** PhotoEdit, Inc.; **568** David Frates/Positive Images; **570** (B) Andrey Tarantin/Shutterstock, (TR) David Frates/Positive Images, (R) Kochneva Tetyana/Shutterstock; **571** (TR) Ariel Skelley/Corbis; **574** (TR) David Frates/Positive Images; **576** (BL) Darwin Dale/Photo Researchers, Inc.; **577** (BR) Peter Finger/Corbis; **579** (TL) Stockbyte/Getty Images; **580** (BL) ©Richard Wainscoat/Alamy, (TR) David Frates/Positive Images; **582** (BR) Corbis, (L) Giraudon/Bridgeman Art Library, (CR) Science & Society Picture Library; **583** (CL) ©DK Images, (BC) Corbis, (R) Judith Collins/Alamy; **587** (TR) BSIP, Edwige/Photo Researchers, Inc., (TCR) Dave King/DK Images; **588** (BL) Dave Greenwood/Getty Images, (T) David Frates/Positive Images; **591** (B) ©DK Images, (TR, TCR) Paul Parker/Photo Researchers, Inc.; **598** Kent Wood/Photo Researchers, Inc.; **600** (TR) Kent Wood/Photo Researchers, Inc., (BL) Michael Newman/PhotoEdit, Inc.; **602** (BL) ©DK Images, (CL) Andy Crawford/©DK Images; **607** (R) Fundamental Photographs; **608** (TL) Grantpix/Photo Researchers, Inc.; **609** (B) Dennis MacDonald/PhotoEdit, Inc.; **612** (B) Russ Lappa; **613** (R) Fundamental Photographs, (T) Stockbyte/Getty Images; **614** (BL) bigfishphotoagent/Alamy Images, (C) Daisy Images/Alamy; **616** (TR) Lawrence Migdale/Photo Researchers, Inc., (CL) Matthew Klein, (BL) NASA; **617** (L) Richard Lam/©AP Images; **618** (BL) Ephraim Ben-Shimon/Corbis, (BR) Michael Matisse/Getty Images; **619** (TR) ©DK Images, (CR) DK Images, (B) Science & Society Picture Library; **620** (TR) Franka Bruns/©AP Images; **622** (T) Digital Vision/Getty Images; **626** ©Visions of America, LLC/Alamy, (CR) Getty Images; **628** Photoshot; **630** (TR) Photoshot, (BL) Reprinted by permission of Houghton Mifflin Company. All rights reserved.; **631** (T, C) Richard Megna/Fundamental Photographs, (CR, BR) Spencer Grant/Photo Researchers, Inc.; **634** (TR) Jose Luis Pelaez, Inc./Corbis; **635** (BR) Bettmann/Corbis, (TR) Photoshot; **638** (BR) Harvey Schwartz/PhotoLibrary Group, Inc.; **640** (B) ©DK Images; **641** (BL) Sovereign, ISM/Photo Researchers, Inc.; **642** JTB Photo Communications, Inc./Aflo Foto Agency, (TR) Photoshot; **644** (T) SuperStock; **645** (BR) Lloyd Cluff/Corbis; **646** (BL) A & C Wiley/Wales/PhotoLibrary Group, Inc., (TR) David Papazian/Corbis; **654** (C) David Nunuk/Science Photo Library/Photo Researchers, Inc.; **656** (BC) David Frazier/Photo Researchers, Inc., (TR) Photo Researchers, Inc., (CL) Reuters/Corbis; **657** (CR) Bojan Brecelj/Corbis, (BR) James King-Holmes/Science Photo Library/Photo Researchers, Inc., (TC) Pat Lanza/Photoshot, (TL) Stock Boston, (BL) yuri19/Fotolia.; **658** Pete Turner/Getty Images; **660** (BL) Gary Kazanjan/©AP Images, (TR) Pete Turner/Getty Images; **661** (TR) Martin & Marli Miller; **664** (R) Mark Burnett/Photo Researchers, Inc., (TR) Pete Turner/Getty Images; **665** (BR) Phillip Hayson/Photo Researchers, Inc., (T) pmphoto/Fotolia; **666** (TL, B) Breck P. Kent Natural History Photography, (CL) Roberto De Gugliemo/Science Photo Library/Photo Researchers, Inc.; **667** (L) Breck P. Kent Natural History Photography, (TR) Charles D. Winters/Photo Researchers, Inc., (TC) Marvin Dembinsky Photo Associates/Alamy Images; **668** (T) Colin Keates/DK Images; **669** ©Chip Clark/Smithsonian Institution, (TL) Breck P. Kent Natural History Photography; **670** Tony Duffy/Getty Images, (TR) Pete Turner/Getty Images; **671** (TR) Simon Fraser/Science Photo Library/Photo Researchers, Inc.; **672** (BL) Breck P. Kent Natural History Photography, (TL) Galyna Andrushko/Fotolia; **673** (T) Francois Gohier/Photo Researchers, Inc., (B) Lynn McLaren/Photo Researchers, Inc.; **674** (B) ©Dirk Wiersma/Photo Researchers, Inc., (T) ©Doug Martin/Photo

956 *Acknowledgments*

Researchers, Inc., (TC) Aaron Haupt/Photo Researchers, Inc., (BM) Breck P. Kent Natural History Photography; **675** (TR) Breck P. Kent Natural History Photography, (TL) Jan Butchofsky/Corbis, (CL) Jim Sugar/Corbis, (TC) Galyna Andrushko/ Fotolia; **676** (TR) Pete Turner/Getty Images, (BL) Science Source/Photo Researchers, Inc.; **677** (TL) Martin Land/Science Photo Library/Photo Researchers, Inc.; **678** (T) Science Source/Photo Researchers, Inc.; **680** (BR) Bettmann/Corbis, (BL) Harry Taylor/©DK Images, (C) Pascal Goetgheluck/Photo Researchers, Inc., (CR) Time & Life Pictures/Getty Images; **681** (CC) NASA, (CR) Roger Harris/Photo Researchers, Inc., (BL) Science Museum, London/DK Images; **683** (TR) elxeneize/Shutterstock; **684** (TR) Pete Turner/Getty Images, Suzanne Plunkett/©AP Images; **685** (TR) David Parker/Science Photo Library/ Photo Researchers, Inc., (B) Gunter Marx/Alamy; **688** (TR) Joseph Sohm/Visions of America/Photo Researchers, Inc., (BR) Seismogram ©UC Regents, UC Berkeley Seismological Laboratory; **690** (B) David Weintraub/Photo Researchers, Inc., (TR) Pete Turner/Getty Images; **692** (T) Breck P. Kent Natural History Photography, (B) G. Brad Lewis/Getty Images; **694** (BC) Francesca Yorke/©DK Images, (C) Jim Sugar, (BR) Mike Severns/©DK Images, (BL) Rob Reichenfeld/©DK Images; **695** (TR) Colin Keates/©DK Images, (TC) Dave King/©DK Images, (T) DK Images; **696** (T) ©Thomas Wiewandt; **702** ©Thomas Wiewandt; **704** (T) ©Thomas Wiewandt, (C, B) Planetary Visions Ltd/Photo Researchers, Inc.; **707** (TR) Samuel R. Maglione/Photo Researchers, Inc.; **708** (T) ©Eberhard Hummel/AGE Fotostock; **709** (T) ©Thomas Wiewandt, (B) Breck P. Kent Natural History Photography; **710** (T,) William H. Mullins/Photo Researchers, Inc.; **711** (T) ©Egmont Strigl/PhotoLibrary Group, Inc., (BC) David Lyons/©DK Images, (TR) Egmont Strigl/Photolibrary Group, Inc., (CR) Martin Miller/Photo Researchers, Inc.; **713** (T) ©Thomas Wiewandt, (B) Larry Miller/ Photo Researchers, Inc.; **716** (B) Animals Animals/Earth Scenes, (B) blickwinkel/ Alamy Images, (CL) Martin & Marli Miller, (T) James Steinberg/Science Source; **717** (TR) Bruce Roberts/Photo Researchers, Inc.; **718** (T) ©Melvyn P. Lawes; Papilio/Corbis; **719** (T) ©Thomas Wiewandt, (BR) Bernhard Edmaier/Photo Researchers, Inc.; **720** (B) John Buttenkant/Photo Researchers, Inc.; **721** (T,) ©MERVYN REES/Alamy Images; **722** (TR) BRUCE COLEMAN INC./Alamy Images; **723** (B) ©Radius Images/Alamy; **724** (T) Mark J. Terril/©AP Images; **725** (B) ©Jim Corwin/Photo Researchers, Inc., (T) ©Thomas Wiewandt; **727** (B) ©Joel Arem/Photo Researchers, Inc.; **728** (BL) Christophe Boisvieux/Corbis, (BR) George Gerster/Photo Researchers, Inc., (BC) Jason Hawkes/Corbis; **730** (TR) frantisek hojdysz/Fotolia, (B) Mike Dunning/©DK Images; **731** (TL) Amos Nachoum/Corbis, (CR) Science Source/Photo Researchers, Inc.; **732** (T) ©Thomas Wiewandt, (B) Andy/Fotolia; **735** (R) ©The Natural History Museum, London; **738** (TR) ©The Natural History Museum, London, (TL) John Sibbick; **744** Stocktrek/Corbis; **746** (CL) ©AP Images, (B) Palenque/Fotolia, (TR) Stocktrek/Corbis; **749** (L) ©Paul Seheult/Corbis, (TR) Karl Shone/©DK Images; **751** N. Rosing/Okapia/Photo Researchers, Inc.; **752** (Bkgrd) Liane Cary/AGE Fotostock, (TR) Stocktrek/Corbis; **755** (BR) Corbis, (B) Stocktrek/Corbis; **756** (TR) NASA; **758** (BL) Peter Christopher/Masterfile Corporation; **760** (BL) Karl Shone/©DK Images, (TR) Stocktrek/Corbis; **761** (B) ©Ashway/Alamy Images, (T) ©John Warburton-Lee Photography/Alamy Images; **762** (TL) ©Martin Cameron/Alamy Images, (CL) Adam Jones/Photo Researchers, Inc., (BL) David R. Frazier/Photo Researchers, Inc., (Bkgrd) redbrickstock/Alamy; **763** (TR) ©blickwinkel/Alamy Images, (C, B) ©Chris Cheadle/Alamy Images, (TL) Trevor McDonald/Photo Researchers, Inc.; **764** (TL) Kennan Ward/Corbis; **765** (BR) Carl Roessler/Getty Images, (TR) Stocktrek/Corbis; **769** (TR) Science Source/Photo Researchers, Inc.; **770** (L) Weatherstock® ; **771** Comstock/Thinkstock; **772** (BC) NOAA, (B) NOAA/©AP Images; **773** (BL) ©Matthew Cavanaugh/epa/Corbis;

774 ©Mark A. Schneider/Photo Researchers, Inc., (TR) Stocktrek/Corbis; **775** (TR) Simon Fraser/Photo Researchers, Inc.; **776** (TCL) Weather Graphics Courtesy of AccuWeather, Inc.; **777** David R. Frazier Photolibrary, Inc./Photo Researchers, Inc.; **778** (TR) Stocktrek/Corbis; **780** (TL) Daryl Balfour/Getty Images; **781** (TR) Martin & Marli Miller, Photo Researchers, Inc.; **782** Deborah Davis/Getty Images, weareadventurers/iStockphoto; **785** Pgiam/iStockphoto; **786** Jeff Gentner/©AP Images; **792** Science Photo Library/Photo Researchers, Inc.; **794** (TR) Science Photo Library/Photo Researchers, Inc., (B) cduschinger/ Fotolia; **795** (TR) Bettmann/Corbis, (TL) Stapleton Collection/Corbis; **798** (B) NASA, (TL) NASA Jet Propulsion Laboratory/©AP Images, (BL) Science Source/ Photo Researchers, Inc., (T) Stocktrek Images/Getty Images; **799** (C) ©DK Images, (TR) GRIN/NASA; **800** (B) ©AP Images, (TR) Science Photo Library/ Photo Researchers, Inc.; **801** (B) Corbis, (T) Brad Thompson/Fotolia; **804** (BR) Frank Zullo/Photo Researchers, Inc., (T) Science Photo Library/Photo Researchers, Inc.; **806** (T) NASA; **807** (TR) Science Photo Library/Photo Researchers, Inc., (BR) Victor Habbick Visions/Photo Researchers, Inc.; **808** (BL) U.S. Geological Survey/Science Source; **809** (B) ©Science Source/Photo Researchers, Inc., (T, C) Science Source; **810** (BC) ©Bettmann/Corbis, (CR, BL) NASA, (BL) Ria Novosti/Science Photo Library/Photo Researchers, Inc.; **811** (C) ©DK Images, (BR) Marshall Space Flight Center/NASA Image Exchange, (CR) NASA; **812** (B) European Space Agency/Photo Researchers, Inc., (BL) JPL-Caltech/Cornell/NMMNH/NASA, (TR) Photo Researchers, Inc., (TL) Stocktrek Images, Inc./Alamy (TC) RGB Ventures LLC dba SuperStock/Alamy; **813** (B) Science Source, (T) Agencia el Universal/El Universal de Mexico/Newscom; **814** (BL) Photo Researchers, Inc., (TR) Science Photo Library/Photo Researchers, Inc.; **815** (BR) James Stevenson/©DK Images; **816** (B) D. Ducros/Photo Researchers, Inc., (C) NASA, (TL) NASA/Science Photo Library/Photo Researchers, Inc.; **818** (TL) Bettmann/Corbis, (BL) NASA; **819** (CR) DK Images; **820** (BL) ©DK Images, (T) Raymond Turvey/©DK Images; **821** (BL) ©Charles O'Rear/Corbis, (CR) Alan Keohane/©DK Images, (TCL) Getty Images; **822** (TR) Science Photo Library/Photo Researchers, Inc.; **824** (TL) Corbis; **830** (C) David Malin/Anglo-Australian Observatory; **832** (TR) David Malin/Anglo-Australian Observatory, (B) Reed Kaestner/Corbis; **833** (B) Science Source; **835** (TR) David Nunuk/Science Photo Library/Photo Researchers, Inc.; **836** Science Source/ Photo Researchers, Inc.; **837** (T) ©Roger Ressmeyer/Skylab/NRL/NASA/Corbis, Science Source/Photo Researchers, Inc.; **838** (TR, B) David Malin/Anglo-Australian Observatory; **840** (BL) Eckhard Slawik/Photo Researchers, Inc.; **841** (BR) ©Galaxy Picture Library, (T) Matthew Borkowski/Stock Boston; **844** (TR) David Malin/Anglo-Australian Observatory, (B) Leland Bobbé/Corbis; **845** (TR) David Malin/Anglo-Australian Observatory; **847** (TR) Corbis, (CR) European Southern Observatory/Science Photo Library/Photo Researchers, Inc.; **849** (TR) NASA Image Exchange; **850** (CL) ©Scala/Art Resource, NY, (TR) David Malin/ Anglo-Australian Observatory; **851** (BR) David Malin/Anglo-Australian Observatory, (CR) Stattmayer/Getty Images; **852** (CL, BL) David Malin/Anglo-Australian Observatory, (B) Eckhard Slawik/Photo Researchers, Inc., (CL) Royal Observatory/Science Photo Library/Photo Researchers, Inc.; **854** (BL) Hubble Heritage Team/NASA, (T) NASA Image Exchange; **856** (TR) David Malin/Anglo-Australian Observatory; **858** (B) NASA; **866** Rosenfeld Images Ltd./Photo Researchers, Inc.; **868** (BL) Richard Megna/Fundamental Photographs; **870** Jerry Howard/Positive Images; **871** blickwinkel/Alamy; **885** (BR) Barnabas Kindersley/©DK Images; **889** (BR) Lonely Planet Images; **890** (BL) Hutchison Picture Library; **891** (BR) Rob Elliott/AFP/Getty Images; **892** (B) Mathew Connolly/Shutterstock, (T) U.S. Geological Survey; **902** (T, B) Griffith Observatory; **903** (T, B) Griffith Observatory.

Periodic Table of the Elements

Legend (key):

Atomic number

6
C
Carbon
12.011

Element symbol · Element name · Atomic mass

Classification box:

Nonmetals	Metals	Metalloids
C	Li	B
Br	Hg	
H		Tc

Solid · Liquid · Gas · Not found in nature

Main Table

Group 1A (1)

| 1 **H** Hydrogen 1.0079 |
| 3 **Li** Lithium 6.941 |
| 11 **Na** Sodium 22.990 |
| 19 **K** Potassium 39.098 |
| 37 **Rb** Rubidium 85.468 |
| 55 **Cs** Cesium 132.91 |
| 87 **Fr** Francium (223) |

Group 2A (2)

| 4 **Be** Beryllium 9.0122 |
| 12 **Mg** Magnesium 24.305 |
| 20 **Ca** Calcium 40.08 |
| 38 **Sr** Strontium 87.62 |
| 56 **Ba** Barium 137.33 |
| 88 **Ra** Radium (226) |

Transition metals

3B (3)	4B (4)	5B (5)	6B (6)	7B (7)	8B (8)	8B (9)	8B (10)	1B (11)	2B (12)
21 **Sc** Scandium 44.956	22 **Ti** Titanium 47.90	23 **V** Vanadium 50.941	24 **Cr** Chromium 51.996	25 **Mn** Manganese 54.938	26 **Fe** Iron 55.847	27 **Co** Cobalt 58.933	28 **Ni** Nickel 58.71	29 **Cu** Copper 63.546	30 **Zn** Zinc 65.38
39 **Y** Yttrium 88.906	40 **Zr** Zirconium 91.22	41 **Nb** Niobium 92.906	42 **Mo** Molybdenum 95.94	43 **Tc** Technetium (98)	44 **Ru** Ruthenium 101.07	45 **Rh** Rhodium 102.91	46 **Pd** Palladium 106.4	47 **Ag** Silver 107.87	48 **Cd** Cadmium 112.41
71 **Lu** Lutetium 174.97	72 **Hf** Hafnium 178.49	73 **Ta** Tantalum 180.95	74 **W** Tungsten 183.85	75 **Re** Rhenium 186.21	76 **Os** Osmium 190.2	77 **Ir** Iridium 192.22	78 **Pt** Platinum 195.09	79 **Au** Gold 196.97	80 **Hg** Mercury 200.59
103 **Lr** Lawrencium (262)	104 **Rf** Rutherfordium (261)	105 **Db** Dubnium (262)	106 **Sg** Seaborgium (263)	107 **Bh** Bohrium (264)	108 **Hs** Hassium (265)	109 **Mt** Meitnerium (268)	110 **Ds** Darmstadtium (269)	111 **Rg** Roentgenium (272)	112 **Cn** Copernicium (277)

Groups 3A–8A (13–18)

3A (13)	4A (14)	5A (15)	6A (16)	7A (17)	8A (18)
					2 **He** Helium 4.0026
5 **B** Boron 10.81	6 **C** Carbon 12.011	7 **N** Nitrogen 14.007	8 **O** Oxygen 15.999	9 **F** Fluorine 18.998	10 **Ne** Neon 20.179
13 **Al** Aluminum 26.982	14 **Si** Silicon 28.086	15 **P** Phosphorus 30.974	16 **S** Sulfur 32.06	17 **Cl** Chlorine 35.453	18 **Ar** Argon 39.948
31 **Ga** Gallium 69.72	32 **Ge** Germanium 72.59	33 **As** Arsenic 74.922	34 **Se** Selenium 78.96	35 **Br** Bromine 79.904	36 **Kr** Krypton 83.80
49 **In** Indium 114.82	50 **Sn** Tin 118.69	51 **Sb** Antimony 121.75	52 **Te** Tellurium 127.60	53 **I** Iodine 126.90	54 **Xe** Xenon 131.30
81 **Tl** Thallium 204.37	82 **Pb** Lead 207.2	83 **Bi** Bismuth 208.98	84 **Po** Polonium (209)	85 **At** Astatine (210)	86 **Rn** Radon (222)
113 ***Uut** Ununtrium (284)	114 ***Uuq** Ununquadium (289)	115 ***Uup** Ununpentium (288)	116 ***Uuh** Ununhexium (293)		118 ***Uuo** Ununoctium (299)

*Name not officially assigned

Lanthanide Series

| 57 **La** Lanthanum 138.91 | 58 **Ce** Cerium 140.12 | 59 **Pr** Praseodymium 140.91 | 60 **Nd** Neodymium 144.24 | 61 **Pm** Promethium (145) | 62 **Sm** Samarium 150.4 | 63 **Eu** Europium 151.96 | 64 **Gd** Gadolinium 157.25 | 65 **Tb** Terbium 158.93 | 66 **Dy** Dysprosium 162.50 | 67 **Ho** Holmium 164.93 | 68 **Er** Erbium 167.26 | 69 **Tm** Thulium 168.93 | 70 **Yb** Ytterbium 173.04 |

Actinide Series

| 89 **Ac** Actinium (227) | 90 **Th** Thorium 232.04 | 91 **Pa** Protactinium 231.04 | 92 **U** Uranium 238.03 | 93 **Np** Neptunium (237) | 94 **Pu** Plutonium (244) | 95 **Am** Americium (243) | 96 **Cm** Curium (247) | 97 **Bk** Berkelium (247) | 98 **Cf** Californium (251) | 99 **Es** Einsteinium (252) | 100 **Fm** Fermium (257) | 101 **Md** Mendelevium (258) | 102 **No** Nobelium (259) |